The New College
LATIN & ENGLISH
Dictionary

JOHN C. TRAUPMAN, Ph.D.
St. Joseph's College, Philadelphia

AMSCO SCHOOL PUBLICATIONS, INC.
315 Hudson Street / New York, N.Y. 10013

THE NEW COLLEGE LATIN & ENGLISH DICTIONARY

ISBN 0-87720-560-4

Originally published under the title
The New Collegiate Latin & English Dictionary

Published by Amsco School Publications, Inc., by arrangement with the copyright owners.

Cover photograph from the Bettmann Archive, Inc.

Printed in the United States of America

7 8 9

JOHN C. TRAUPMAN, author of *The New College Latin & English Dictionary,* is Chairman of the Classics Department of St. Joseph's College, Philadelphia. Professor Traupman received his A.B. from Moravian College and his Ph.D. from Princeton University. He has served as President of the Philadelphia Classical Society.

EDWIN B. WILLIAMS (1891–1975), under whose editorship *The New College Latin & English Dictionary* was prepared, was Chairman of the Department of Romance Languages, Dean of the Graduate School, and Provost of the University of Pennsylvania. Among his many works on the Spanish, Portuguese, and French languages are *The Williams Spanish and English Dictionary* and *The New College Spanish & English Dictionary*. He created and coordinated the New College series of original dictionaries—Spanish, French, Italian, Latin, and (forthcoming) German.

The New College Latin & English Dictionary is the first all-new Latin-English–English-Latin dictionary compiled in the United States in the last sixty years, and it is the first ever to be prepared on the basis of modern lexicographical principles. The definitions of more than 40,000 words and phrases are based on the foremost authorities and have been organized to achieve the utmost clarity, precision, and convenience. Obsolete definitions have been eliminated.

Features for maximum clarity and convenience:

1. Mythological references →
2. Geographical and historical references →
3. Biographical references →
4. Principal parts of verbs →
5. Transitive and intransitive meanings differentiated →
6. All Latin entries and subentries in bold face →
7. Long and short vowel markings in vocabulary entries →
8. Definitions in contemporary English →
9. Dot indicates where inflectional elements are added →
10. Latin phrases with full translations →

Cadm·us -ī *m* son of Phoenician king Agenor, brother of Europa, and founder of Thebes

Cann·ae -ārum *f pl* village in Apulia where Hannibal won great victory over Romans in 216 B.C.

Caes·ar -ăris *m* C. Julius Caesar (102?-44 B.C.)

canō canĕre cecinī cantum *vt* to sing; to play; to speak in a singsong tone; to sing the praises of, celebrate; to prophesy, predict, foretell; (mil) to blow, sound; **signa canere** to sound the signal for battle; *vi* to sing; to play; (of birds) to sing; (of roosters) to crow; (of frogs) to croak; **receptui canere** to sound retreat; **tibiā canere** to play the flute

capess·ō -ĕre -īvī or **-iī -ītum** *vt* to try to reach, make for, seize, get hold of, snatch at; to take up, undertake, engage in;

capulār·is -e *adj* with one foot in the grave

carc·er -ĕris *m* prison, jail; prisoner; (term of reproach) jailbird; *m pl* starting gate (*at racetrack*); **ad carceres a calce revocari** to have to start all over again

INTRODUCTION

Both Latin and English entry words, as well as illustrative phrases under entry words, are treated in strictly alphabetical order.

Adverbs on the Latin-English side are inserted as separate entries and translated in that position without cross-reference to the corresponding adjective.

Adverbs on the English-Latin side ending in **-ly** are listed under their adjectives.

Compound words are generally given in their assimilated forms, e.g., **accurrō** rather than **adcurrō**. Cross-references are provided as guides for those using texts which employ the unassimilated forms.

The letter **j** has been used in place of consonantal **i** because some recent texts have begun to use the former again and because students can thus more readily distinguish the consonant from the vowel.

If a feminine substantive, singular or plural, of the first declension, a neuter substantive, singular or plural, of the second declension, or a masculine substantive of the second declension falls alphabetically more than one word before or after the corresponding adjective, it is inserted as a separate entry and translated in that position, and a cross-reference to it is given under the adjective; for example, **nāt•a -ae** *f* occurs fifteen entries before **nāt•us -a -um** *adj* . . . ; *f* see **nata.**

If such a substantive does not fall alphabetically more than one word before or after the corresponding adjective, it is treated under the adjective.

Many of the variations in spelling of Latin words are indicated by means of cross-references, e.g., **sēpiō** see **saepio.**

Only those past participles are listed as separate entries whose difference in form from the first person singular present indicative warrants such listing, provided they fall alphabetically more than one word before or after the first person singular present indicative.

Only the first person singular present indicative and the present infinitive of regular active verbs of the first conjugation are given; in the case of deponent verbs, the perfect is added. For the other three conjugations and for irregular and defective verbs, all principal parts in use are given.

Discriminations between two or more meanings of the entry word are often shown by means of English words in parentheses.

Transitive and intransitive verbs, with their dependent

constructions, are clearly differentiated and are presented in a fixed order of transitive first and intransitive second.

Centered periods within entry words indicate division points at which inflectional elements are to be added.

All source words and phrases are printed in boldface type.

On the English-Latin side a boldface dash represents the vocabulary entry.

On the Latin-English side, the twofold purpose in marking the quantity of vowels is (1) to indicate accentuation of words and (2) to provide the basis for scansion of Classical Latin verse. Thus, all vowels that are long by nature and occur in open syllables are marked, whereas vowels in closed syllables, whether long or short by nature, are not marked, since the syllable in either case is long. However, since a vowel followed by a mute and a liquid can be open or closed, its quantity is marked when it is long. As a further aid to pronunciation, in words of three or more syllables, the short vowel of the penult is marked.

On the English-Latin side, Latin vowels have been marked to distinguish:

(a) words otherwise spelled alike: **lēvis, levis**

(b) the genitive singular and the nominative and accusative plural from the nominative singular of the fourth declension

(c) the ablative singular from the nominative singular of nouns of the first declension whenever the distinction is not clear from the context

(d) the nominative and genitive singular from the accusative plural of *i*-stem words of the third declension

(e) the infinitive of verbs of the second conjugation from the infinitive of verbs of the third conjugation.

On the English-Latin side, the genitive of the nouns of the fourth declension is provided in order to distinguish these nouns from nouns of the second declension ending in **-us.**

John C. Traupman

PRONUNCIATION

Vowels

	CLASSICAL METHOD	ECCLESIASTICAL METHOD
ă	Like *a* in *a*go: **compărō**	(Generally as in the Classical Method. However, in practice the different values of the vowels are frequently not rigidly adhered to.)
ā	Like *a* in f*a*ther: **imāgō**	
ĕ	Like *e* in p*e*t: **propĕrō**	
ē	Like *a* in l*a*te: **lēnis**	
ĭ	Like *i* in h*i*t: **ĭdem**	
ī	Like *ee* in k*ee*n: **amīcus**	
ŏ	Like *o* in *o*ften: **mŏdus**	
ō	Like *o* in h*o*pe: **nōmen**	
ŭ	Like *u* in p*u*t: **ŭt**	
ū	Like *u* in r*u*de: **ūtor**	
y̆	Like *ü* in German H*ü*tte: **my̆rīca**	
ȳ	Like *ü* in German *ü*ber: **Tȳdeus**	

Diphthongs

	CLASSICAL METHOD	ECCLESIASTICAL METHOD
ae	Like *y* in b*y*: **caecus**	Like *a* in l*a*te: **caecus**
au	Like *ow* in n*ow*: **nauta**	As in the Classical Method
ei	Like *ey* in gr*ey*: **deinde**	As in the Classical Method
eu	Like *eu* in f*eu*d: **Orpheus**	Like *eu* in Italian n*eu*tro: **euge**
oe	Like *oi* in *oi*l: **coepit**	Like *a* in l*a*te: **coepit**
ui	Like *uey* in gl*uey*: **cui** After **q**, like *wee* in *wee*k: **qui**	As in the Classical Method

Consonants

	CLASSICAL METHOD	ECCLESIASTICAL METHOD
b	As in English	As in English
c	Always like *c* in *c*an: **cīvis, cantō, actus**	Before **e, i, ae,** or **oe** like *ch* in *ch*erry: **excelsis, cīvis, caelum, coepit,** but before other letters like *c* in *c*an: **cantō, actus**
d	As in English	As in English
f	As in English	As in English
g	Always like *g* in *g*o: **genus, gula, gallīna, grātus**	Before **e** or **i** like *g* in *g*entle: **genus, regīna,** but before other letters except **g** and **n** (see under Consonant Groups) like *g* in *g*o: **gula, gallīna, fugō, grātus**
h	As in English	As in English
j	Like *y* in *y*es: **jungō, jam**	As in the Classical Method
k	As in English	As in English
l	As in English	As in English
m	As in English, but in verse final **m** before an initial vowel in the following word was presumably not pronounced	As in English
n	As in English	As in English
p	As in English	As in English
q	As in English and used only before consonantal **u**	As in English
r	Trilled as in the Romance languages	As in the Classical Method
s	Always like *s* in *s*ing: **miser, mors**	Like *s* in *s*ing: **salūs,** but when standing between two vowels or when final and preceded by a voiced consonant, like *z* in do*z*en: **miser, mors**
t	Like English *t*, but unaspirated	As in the Classical Method

	CLASSICAL METHOD	ECCLESIASTICAL METHOD
u	Like *w* in *w*ine, when unaccented, preceded by **q**, sometimes by **s**, and sometimes by **g**, and followed by a vowel: **qui•a, suā•vis** (but **su•ō•rum**), **dis•tin•guō** (but **ex•i•gŭ•us**)	As in the Classical Method
v	Like *w* in *w*ine: **vīvō**	As in English
x	Like *x* (= ks) in si*x*: **exactus**	Like *x* (=ks) in si*x*: **pax**; but in words beginning with **ex** and followed by a vowel, **h**, or **s**, like *x* (= gz) in e*x*haust: **exaudī, exhālō, exsolvō**
z	*Like dz* in a*dz*e: **zōna**	As in the Classical Method

Consonant Groups

	CLASSICAL METHOD	ECCLESIASTICAL METHOD
bs	Like *ps* in a*ps*e: **obsidĕō, urbs**	Like *bs* in o*bs*ession: **obsidĕō**, but in the final position, like *bs* in o*bs*erve: **urbs**
bt	Like *pt* in ca*pt*ain: **obtinēre**	Like *bt* in o*bt*ain: **obtinēre**
cc	Like *kk* in boo*kk*eeper: **ecce, occīdō, occāsum, occlūdō**	Before **e** or **i** like *tch* in ca*tch*: **ecce, occīdō**; but before other letters, like *kk* in boo*kk*eeper: **occāsum, occlūdō**
ch	Like *ch* in *ch*aotic: **pulcher**	As in the Classical Method
gg	Like *gg* in le*g g*uard: **agger**	Before **e** or **i** like *dj* in a*dj*ourn: **agger**; but before other letters, like *gg* in le*g g*uard: **aggrĕgō**
gn	As in English	Like *ny* in ca*ny*on: **dignus**
gu	See consonant **u**	As in the Classical Method
ph	Like *p-h* in to*p-h*eavy: **phōca**	Like *ph* in *ph*oenix: **phōca**
qu	See consonant *u*	As in the Classical Method
sc	Like *sc* in *sc*ope: **sciō, scūtum**	Before **e** or **i** like *sh* in *sh*in: **ascendō, sciō**; but before other letters, like *sc* in *sc*ope: **scandō, scūtum**
su	See consonant **u**	As in the Classical Method
th	Like *t* in *t*ake: **theātrum**	As in the Classical Method
ti	Like *ti* in English pa*ti*o: **nātĭō**	When preceded by **s**, **t**, or **x** or when followed by a consonant, like *ti* in English pa*ti*o: **hostĭa, admixtĭō, fortĭter**; but when unaccented, followed by a vowel, and preceded by any letter except **s**, **t**, or **x**, like *tzy* in ri*tzy*: **nātĭō, pretĭum**

SYLLABIFICATION

1. Every Latin word has as many syllables as it has vowels or diphthongs: **ae·ger, fī·li·us, Bai·ae**

2. When a word is divided into syllables:

   a) a single consonant between two vowels goes with the following syllable (**h** is regarded as a consonant; **ch, ph, th, qu,** and somtimes **gu** and **su** are regarded as single consonants)*: **a·ger, ni·hil, a·qua, ci·cho·rē·um**

   b) the first consonant of a combination of two or more consonants goes with the preceding vowel: **tor·men·tum, mit·tō, mon·strum**

   c) a consonant group consisting of a mute (**b, d, g, p, t, c**) followed by **l** or **r** is generally left undivided and goes with the following vowel: **pa·trēs, a·cris, du·plex.** In Classical poetry this combination is often treated like any other pair of consonants: **pat·rēs, ac·ris, dup·lex**

   d) prefixes form separate syllables even if the division is contrary to above rules: **ab·est, ob·lā·tus, abs·ti·nĕ·ō, ab·stō**

3. A syllable ending in a vowel or diphthong is called *open*; all others are called *closed*

4. The last syllable of a word is called the *ultima*; the next to last is called the *penult*; the one before the penult is called the *antepenult*

---

* The double consonant **x** goes with the preceding vowel: **dix·it**

QUANTITY OF VOWELS

1. A vowel is *long* (**lēvis**) or *short* (**lĕvis**) according to the length of time required for its pronunciation

2. A vowel is long:

   a) before **ns, nf,** (and perhaps **gn**): **ingēns, īnfāns, (māgnus)**

   b) when resulting from a contraction: **nīl = nĭhĭl, cōgō = cŏăgō, inīquus = inaequus**

3. A vowel is short:

   a) before another vowel or **h: dĕa, trăhō**

   b) generally before **nd** and **nt: amăndus, amănt**

4. Diphthongs are long: **causae**

QUANTITY OF SYLLABLES

1. Syllables are distinguished as *long* or *short* according to the length of time required for their pronunciation

2. A syllable is long:

   a) if it contains a long vowel or a diphthong: **vē·nī, scrī·bō, cau·sae** (such a syllable is said to be *long by nature*)

   b) if it contains a short vowel followed by **x, z,** or any two consonants except a mute (**b, d, g, p, t, c**) followed by **l** or **r: sax·um, gaz·a, mit·tō, cur·sor** (such a syllable is said to be *long by position,* but the vowel is pronounced *short*)

3. A syllable is short:

   a) if it contains a short vowel followed by a vowel or by a single consonant (**h** is regarded as a consonant; **ch, ph, th, qu,** and sometimes **gu** and **su** are regarded as single consonants): **me·us, ni·hil, ge·rit, a·qua**

   b) if it contains a short vowel followed by a mute (**b, d, g, p, t, c**) plus **l** or **r,** but it is sometimes long in verse: **flă·grans, ba·ră·thrum, ce·lĕ·brō** (such a syllable is said to be *common*)

NOTE: In this dictionary, long vowels are marked except before **x, z,** or two or more consonants unless the two consonants are a mute plus a liquid. Only the short penult of words of three or more syllables is marked.

ACCENT

1. Words of two syllables are accented on the first syllable: **om′nēs, tan′gō, ge′rit**

2. Words of more than two syllables are accented on the penult if it is long: **a·mī′cus, re·gun′tur** and on the antepenult if the penult is short: **fa·mi′li·a, ge′rĭ·tur**

3. These rules apply to words with enclitics appended (**-ce, -dum, -met, -ne, -que, -ve**): **vos′met, lau·dat′ne, de′ă·que** (nominative), **de·ā′que** (ablative)

4. In the second declension, the contracted genitive and the contracted vocative of nouns in **-ius** and the contracted genitive of those in **-ium** retain the accent of the nominative: **Vir·gĭ′lī, in·gĕ′nī**

5. Certain words which have lost a final **-e** retain the accent of the complete forms: **il·līc′** for **il·lī′ce, tan·tōn′** for **tan·tō′ne**

6. Certain compounds of **faciō,** in which a feeling for the individuality of the components was preserved, retain the accent of the simple verb: **be·ne·fă′cit**

ABBREVIATIONS

abbr	abbreviation	*interrog*	interrogative
abl	ablative	*loc*	locative
acc	accusative	*m*	masculine noun
adj	adjective	*masc*	masculine
adv	adverb	*math*	mathematics
astr	astronomy	*med*	medicine
bot	botany	*mil*	military
c.	circa, about	*m pl*	masculine plural noun
cent.	century	*mus*	music
coll	colloquial	*n*	neuter noun
com	commercial	*neut*	neuter
comp	comparative	*nom*	nominative
conj	conjunction	*n pl*	neuter plural noun
d.	died	*p*	participle
dat	dative	*phil*	philosophy
defect	defective	*pl*	plural
eccl	ecclesiastical	*pol*	politics
esp.	especially	*pp*	past participle
f	feminine noun	*prep*	preposition
fem	feminine	*pres*	present
fig	figurative	*pron*	pronoun
fl	floruit	*reflex*	reflexive
f pl	feminine plural noun	*rel*	relative
fut	future	*rhet*	rhetoric
genit	genitive	*s*	substantive
gram	grammar	*singl*	singular
impers	impersonal	*subj*	subjunctive
impv	imperative	*superl*	superlative
indecl	indeclinable	*v defect*	defective verb
indef	indefinite	*vi*	intransitive verb
inf	infinitive	*v impers*	impersonal verb
interj	interjection	*vt*	transitive verb

LATIN-ENGLISH

A

ā *interj* ah!
ā or **ab** *prep* (with *abl*) (of agency) by; (of time) since, after, from; (of space) from, away from; at, on, in; **a latere** on the side; **a tergo** in the rear
abactus *pp* of **abigo**
abăc·us -ī *m* cupboard; game board; abacus, counting board; panel; tray
abaliēnātĭ·ō -ōnis *f* transfer of property
abaliēn·ō -āre *vt* to alienate, estrange; to sell; to separate
Abantiăd·ēs -ae *m* descendant of Abas
Ab·ās -antis *m* king of Argos, father of Acrisius and grandfather of Perseus
abāv·us -ī *m* great-great-grandfather
abdicātĭ·ō -ōnis *f* abdication, renunciation, resignation
abdĭc·ō -āre *vt* to abdicate, renounce, resign; to disinherit; **se magistratu abdicare** to resign from office
ab·dīcō -dīcĕre -dixī -dictum *vt* (in augury) to disapprove of, forbid
abdĭtē *adv* secretly, privately
abdĭt·us -a -um *adj* hidden, secret
ab·dō -dĕre -dĭdī -dĭtum *vt* to hide; to remove, withdraw; to plunge (*e.g., a sword*)
abdōm·en -ĭnis *n* abdomen, belly; (fig) gluttony, greed
ab·dūcō -dūcĕre -duxī -ductum *vt* to lead away, take away; to seduce; to alienate
ab·ĕō -īre -iī -ĭtum *vi* to go away, depart; to vanish, disappear; to pass away, die; (of time) to pass, elapse; to change, be changed; to retire
abequĭt·ō -āre *vi* to ride off
aberrātĭ·ō -ōnis *f* wandering, escape, relief
aberr·ō -āre *vi* to wander, go astray; to deviate, differ
abesse *inf* of **absum**
abhinc *adv* ago
abhorr·ĕō -ēre -ŭī *vi* to shrink back; (with **ab** + *abl*) **a** to be averse to; **b** to be inconsistent with, differ from; **c** to be free from
abiegn·us -a -um *adj* fir
abĭ·ēs -ĕtis *f* fir; ship; spear; writing tablet
ab·ĭgō -igĕre -ēgī -actum *vt* to drive away, get rid of; to banish, expel
abĭt·us -ūs *m* departure; outlet; end
abjectē *adv* abjectly, meanly
abject·us -a -um *adj* abject, mean; downhearted
ab·jiciō -jicĕre -jēcī -jectum *vt* to throw away, throw down; to slight; to give up; to humble, debase
abjūdĭc·ō -āre *vt* to take away (*by judicial decree*)
ab·jungō -jungĕre -junxī -junctum *vt* to unyoke; to detach
abjūr·ō -āre *vt* to deny on oath
ablātīv·us -a -um *adj & m* ablative
ablātus *pp* of **aufero**
ablēgātĭ·ō -ōnis *f* sending away, sending off; banishment
ablēg·ō -āre *vt* to send away; to remove, banish; to dismiss
abligurr·ĭō or **abligūr·ĭō -īre -īvī** or **-iī -ītum** *vt* to squander, waste
ablŏc·ō -āre *vt* to lease, rent out
ab·lūdō -lūdĕre -lūsī -lūsum *vi* to be unlike; (with **ab** + *abl*) to differ from
ab·lŭō -luĕre -lŭī -lūtum *vt* to wash away, cleanse, remove
ablūtĭ·ō -ōnis *f* washing, cleansing
abnĕg·ō -āre *vt* to refuse, turn down
abnĕp·ōs -ōtis *m* great-great-grandson
abnept·is -is *f* great-great-granddaughter
abnoct·ō -āre *vi* to stay out all night, sleep out
abnorm·is -e *adj* irregular, unorthodox
ab·nŭō -nuĕre -nŭī -nūtum *vt* to refuse, deny
abol·ĕō -ēre -ēvī -ĭtum *vt* to abolish, destroy, annihilate
abol·escō -escĕre -ēvī *vi* to decay, vanish, die out
abolitĭ·ō -ōnis *f* abolition
abōmĭn·or -ārī -ātus sum *vt* to detest
aborīgĭn·ēs -um *m pl* aborigines, original inhabitants
ab·orĭor -orīrī -ortus sum *vi* to miscarry; to fail; (of stars, etc.) to set
abortĭ·ō -ōnis *f* miscarriage
abortīv·us -a -um *adj* prematurely born
abort·us -ūs *m* miscarriage
ab·rādō -rādĕre -rāsī -rāsum *vt* to scrape off, shave; (fig) to squeeze out, rob
ab·ripĭō -ripĕre -ripŭī -reptum *vt* to take away by force, carry off; to squander
ab·rōdō -rōdĕre -rōsī -rōsum *vt* to gnaw off

abrogātĭ·ō -ōnis *f* repeal
abrŏg·ō -āre *vt* to repeal, annul
abrotŏn·um -ī *n* southernwood (*aromatic, medicinal plant*)
ab·rumpō -rumpĕre -rūpī -ruptum *vt* to break off; to tear, sever
abruptē *adv* abruptly, rashly
abruptĭ·ō -ōnis *f* breaking off; divorce
abrupt·us -a -um *pp* of **abrumpo;** *adj* abrupt, steep; *n* precipice
abs *prep* (with *abl*, confined almost exclusively to the combination **abs te**) by, from
abs·cēdō -cēdĕre -cessī -cessum *vi* to go away, depart; to retire; to desist
abscessĭ·ō -ōnis *f* diminution
abscess·us -ūs *m* departure, absence, remoteness
abs·cīdō -cīdĕre -cīdī -cīsum *vt* to cut off, chop off; to cut short
ab·scindō -scindĕre -scĭdī -scissum *vt* to tear off, break off; to divide
abscīs·us -a -um *pp* of **abscido;** *adj* steep, precipitous; concise; abrupt
absconditē *adv* secretly; obscurely; profoundly
abscondĭt·us -a -um *adj* concealed, secret
abs·condō -condĕre -condī or **-condĭdī -condĭtum** *vt* to hide; to lose sight of, leave behind; to bury (*weapon*)
abs·ens -entis *pres p* of **absum;** *adj* absent
absentĭ·a -ae *f* absence
absil·iō -īre -iī or **-ŭī** *vi* to jump away
absimĭl·is -e *adj* unlike; (with *dat*) unlike
absinth·ium -iī or **-ī** *n* wormwood
abs·is -īdis *f* vault, arch; orbit (*of a star*)
ab·sistō -sistĕre -stĭtī *vi* to withdraw, depart; to cease, lay off
absolūtē *adv* perfectly
absolūtĭ·ō -ōnis *f* acquittal; perfection, completeness
absolūtōrĭ·us -a -um *adj* of acquittal, granting acquittal
absolūt·us -a -um *adj* perfect, complete, unqualified
ab·solvō -solvĕre -solvī -solūtum *vt* to release, set free, detach; to acquit; to finish off; to pay off, discharge
absŏn·us -a -um *adj* discordant, incongruous, incompatible
absorb·ĕō -ēre -ŭī *vt* to swallow, devour; to engross
absque *prep* (with *abl*) without, apart from, but for; **absque me foret** if it had not been for me
abstēmĭ·us -a -um *adj* abstemious, temperate, sober
abs·tergĕō -tergēre -tersī -tersum *vt* to wipe off, wipe dry; to expel, banish
absterr·ĕō -ēre -ŭī -ĭtum *vt* to scare away, deter
abstin·ens -entis *adj* temperate, forbearing; continent, chaste
abstinenter *adv* with restraint
abstinentĭ·a -ae *f* abstinence, self-control
abs·tinĕō -tinēre -tinŭī -tentum *vt* to withhold, keep away; *vi* to abstain, refrain; (with *genit*, *abl*, or with **ab** + *abl*, with *inf*, with **quin** or **quominus**) to refrain from
abst·ō -āre *vi* to stand at a distance, stand aloof
abs·trăhō -trahĕre -traxī -tractum *vt* to pull away, drag away, remove, detach
abs·trūdō -trūdĕre -trūsī -trūsum *vt* to push away; to conceal
abstrūs·us -a -um *adj* hidden, deep, abstruse; reserved
absum abesse afŭī *vi* to be away, be absent, be distant; (with *abl* or **ab** + *abl*) to be removed from, keep aloof from, be disinclined to; (with **ab** + *abl*) **a** to be different from, be inconsistent with; **b** to be free from; **c** to be unsuitable to, be unfit for; (with *dat*) to be of no help to
ab·sūmō -sūmĕre -sumpsī -sumptum *vt* to take away, diminish; to consume, use up, waste; to destroy, ruin
absurdē *adv* out of tune; absurdly
absurd·us -a -um *adj* out of tune; absurd, illogical, senseless, silly
Absyrt·us -ī *m* son of Aeëtes, king of Colchis, killed by his sister Medea when she eloped with Jason
abund·ans -antis *adj* overflowing, abundant; rich, affluent
abundanter *adv* copiously
abundantĭ·a -ae *f* abundance, wealth
abundē *adv* abundantly, amply
abund·ō -āre *vi* to overflow; to abound; to be rich
abūsĭ·ō -ōnis *f* incorrect use (*of figure of speech*)
abusque *prep* (with *abl*) all the way from
ab·ūtor -ūtī -ūsus sum *vi* (with *abl*) **a** to use up; **b** to misuse, abuse
Abȳd·os or **Abȳd·us -ī** *f* town on Hellespont, opposite Sestos
āc *conj* (usually used before consonants) and, and also, and moreover, and in particular; (in comparisons) than, as
Acadēmĭ·a -ae *f* Academy (*where Plato taught*); Platonic philosophy; Cicero's villa near Puteoli
Acadēmĭc·us -a -um *adj* Academic; *m* Academic philosopher; *n pl* Cicero's treatise on Academic philosophy
acalanth·is -ĭdis *f* thistlefinch
acanth·us -ī *m* acanthus
Acarnānĭ·a -ae *f* district of N.W. Greece
Acast·us -ī *m* son of Pelias

ac·cēdō -cēděre -cessī -cessum *vi* to come near, approach; (with *dat* or **ad** + *acc*) **a** to assent to, agree with, approve of; **b** to come near in resemblance, be like, resemble; **c** to be added to; (with **ad** or **in** + *acc*) to enter upon, undertake; **accedit ut** or **quod** there is the additional fact that

accelěr·ō -āre *vt* to speed, quicken; *vi* to hurry

ac·cendō -cenděre -cendī -censum *vt* to light up, set on fire; (fig) to kindle, inflame, excite, awaken

accens·ěō -ēre -ŭī -um *vt* to reckon, regard

accens·us -ī *m* attendant, orderly; *m pl* rear-echelon troops

accent·us -ūs *m* accent

acceptĭ·ō -ōnis *f* accepting, receiving

accept·ō -āre *vt* to accept, receive

accept·or -ōris *m* recipient, approver

acceptr·ix -īcis *f* recipient (*female*)

accept·us -a -um *pp* of **accipio**; *adj* welcome, pleasing; *n* receipt; credit side (*in account books*)

accers·ō -ěre -īvī -ītum *vt* to call, summon; to bring, procure

accessĭ·ō -ōnis *f* approach; passage, entrance; admittance

ac·cīdō -cīděre -cīdī -cīsum *vt* to cut down; to impair, weaken; to eat up

ac·cĭdō -ciděre -cĭdī *vi* to fall; to happen, occur; (with *dat*) to happen to, befall; (with **in** + *acc*) to fall on, fall upon; (with *dat* or **ad** + *acc*) to fall before, fall at (*e.g., someone's feet*); **aures** or **auribus** or **ad aures accidere** to reach or strike the ears

ac·cingō -cingěre -cinxī -cinctum *vt* to gird; to arm, equip, furnish; to make ready; **accingi** or **se accingere** (with *dat* or with **ad** or **in** + *acc*) to prepare oneself for, to enter upon, to undertake

ac·cĭō -cīre -cīvī -cītum *vt* to call, send for, invite

ac·cipĭō -cipěre -cēpī -ceptum *vt* to take, receive, accept; to admit, let in; to welcome, entertain; to hear, learn, understand; to interpret, explain; to undertake, assume, undergo; to approve of, assent to

accipĭt·er -ris *m* hawk, falcon

accīs·us -a -um *pp* of **accīdo**; *adj* impaired, ruined; troubled, disordered

accīt·us -ūs *m* summons, call

Acc·ĭus -ĭī or **ī** *m* Roman tragic poet (170-85? B.C.)

acclāmātĭ·ō -ōnis *f* shout, acclamation

acclām·ō -āre *vt* to hail, acclaim; *vi* to shout, cry out; (with *dat*) to shout at

acclār·ō -āre *vt* to make clear, make known

acclīnāt·us -a -um *adj* prostrate; sloping; (with *dat*) sloping toward

acclīn·is -e *adj* (with *dat*) **a** leaning on or against; **b** inclined toward, disposed to

acclīn·ō -āre *vt* (with *dat* or **in** + *acc*) to lean or rest (*something*) against; **se acclinare** (with **ad** + *acc*) (fig) to be inclined toward

acclīv·is -e *adj* sloping upwards, uphill, steep

acclīvĭt·ās -ātis *f* slope, ascent

accŏl·a -ae *m* neighbor

ac·cŏlō -colěre -colŭī -cultum *vt* to dwell near

accommodātē *adv* suitably, fittingly

accommodātĭ·ō -ōnis *f* adjustment, compliance, accommodation

accommŏdāt·us -a -um *adj* (with *dat* or **ad** + *acc*) fit for, adapted to, suitable to

accommŏd·ō -āre *vt* (with *dat* or **ad** + *acc*) to adjust or adapt or apply (*something*) to; **se accommodare** (with **ad** + *acc*) to apply or devote oneself to

accommŏd·us -a -um *adj* fit, suitable; (with *dat*) fit for, adapted to, suitable to

ac·crēdō -crēděre -crēdĭdī -crēdĭtum *vi* (with *dat*) to believe, give credence to

ac·crescō -crescěre -crēvī -crētum *vi* to grow larger, increase, be added

accrētĭ·ō -ōnis *f* increase

accubitĭ·ō -ōnis *f* reclining at table

accŭb·ō -āre *vi* to lie nearby; to recline at table; (with *dat*) to lie near

accūd·ō -ěre *vt* to coin

ac·cumbō -cumběre -cubŭī -cubĭtum *vi* to take one's place at table

accumulātē *adv* abundantly

accumulāt·or -ōris *m* hoarder

accumŭl·ō -āre *vt* to heap up, amass; to load, overwhelm

accūrātē *adv* carefully, accurately, exactly

accūrātĭ·ō -ōnis *f* carefulness, accuracy

accūrāt·us -a -um *adj* careful, accurate, exact, studied

accūr·ō -āre *vt* to take care of, attend to

ac·currō -curręre -currī -cursum *vi* to run up; (with **ad** or **in** + *acc*) to run to

accurs·us -ūs *m* running, concourse

accūsābĭl·is -e *adj* blameworthy

accūsātĭ·ō -ōnis *f* accusation; indictment, bill of indictment

accūsātīv·us -a -um *adj & m* accusative

accūsāt·or -ōris *m* accuser, prosecutor; informer

accūsātōrĭē *adv* like an accuser or prosecutor

accūsātōrĭ·us -a -um *adj* accuser's, prosecutor's

accūsātr·ix -īcis *f* accuser (*female*)

accūsĭt·ō -āre *vt* to keep on accusing

accūs·ō -āre *vt* to accuse, prosecute; to reproach, blame
ac·er -ĕris *n* maple tree
āc·er -ris -re *adj* sharp, pointed; pungent, stinging, penetrating, piercing, shrill; sagacious, keen, judicious; energetic, enthusiastic, ardent, brave; passionate, fierce, violent; severe, vigorous
acerbē *adv* bitterly, harshly
acerbĭt·ās -ātis *f* bitterness, harshness, sharpness, sourness; distress
acerb·ō -āre *vt* to embitter, aggravate
acerb·us -a -um *adj* bitter, harsh, sour; unripe; severe; morose, rough; untimely, premature; painful, troublesome; sad
acern·us -a -um *adj* maple
acerr·a -ae *f* incense box
acersecŏm·ēs -ae *m* young man, youth
acervātim *adv* in heaps; briefly
acerv·ō -āre *vt* to heap or pile up
acerv·us -ī *m* heap, pile; multitude; (in logic) sorites
acescō acescĕre acŭī *vi* to turn sour
Acest·ēs -ae *m* mythical king of Sicily
acētābŭl·um -ī *n* vinegar bottle
acēt·um -ī *n* sour wine, vinegar; (fig) pungent wit, shrewdness
Achaemĕn·ēs -is *m* first king of Persia, grandfather of Cyrus
Achaemenĭ·us -a -um *adj* Persian
Achae·us -a -um *adj & m* Achaean; Greek
Achai·a or **Achāĭ·a -ae** *f* province in northern part of the Peloponnesus on Gulf of Corinth; Greece
Achāĭc·us -a -um *adj & m* Achaean; Greek
Achāt·ēs -ae *m* companion of Aeneas; river in Sicily
Achelō·üs -ī *m* river in N.W. Greece; river god
Achĕr·ōn -ontis or **Achĕr·os -ī** *m* river in Hades
Achill·ēs -is *m* Greek warrior, son of Peleus and Thetis
Achillē·us -a -um *adj* of Achilles
Achillīd·ēs -ae *m* descendant of Achilles
Achīv·us -a -um *adj* Achaean, Greek
Acīdalĭ·a -ae *f* Venus
acĭd·us -a -um *adj* sour, tart; (of sound) harsh, shrill; sharp, keen, pungent; unpleasant, disagreeable
acĭ·ēs -ēī *f* sharpness, sharp edge; keenness of vision, glance; eyesight, eye, pupil; mental power; battle line, battle array, battlefield, battle; debate
acīnăc·ēs -is *m* scimitar
acĭn·um -ī *n* or **acĭn·us -ī** *m* berry, grape; seed in berry
acipens·er -ĕris or **acipens·is -is** *m* sturgeon
Ac·is -ĭdis *m* son of Faunus, loved by Galatea, changed into a river
acl·ys -ȳdis *f* small javelin
aconīt·um -ī *n* wolf's-bane; strong poison
ac·or -ōris *m* sour taste, sourness
acqui·escō -escĕre -ēvī -ētum *vi* to become quiet; to rest; to die; (with *abl, dat,* or with **in** + *abl*) to find rest in, acquiesce in, be content with, find pleasure in, rejoice in
ac·quīrō -quīrĕre -quīsīvī -quīsītum *vt* to acquire, obtain, gain, win
Acrăg·ās -antis *m* town on S.W. coast of Sicily
acrēdŭl·a -ae *f* bird (*perhaps owl or nightingale*)
ācricŭl·us -a -um *adj* irritable, peevish
ācrimōnĭ·a -ae *f* sharpness, pungency; irritation; energy
Ācrisiōniăd·ēs -ae *m* descendant of Acrisius; Perseus
Ācris·ĭus -ĭī or **-ī** *m* king of Argos, father of Danaë
ācrĭter *adv* sharply, keenly, vehemently, severely
acroām·a -ătis *n* entertainment; entertainer
Ācrocerauni·a -ōrum *n pl* promontory on the Adriatic Sea in Epirus
Ācrocorinth·us -ī *f* citadel of Corinth
act·a -ae *f* seashore, beach
act·a -ōrum *n pl* deeds, actions; public acts; proceedings of the senate; records, minutes; journal
Actae·ōn -ŏnis *m* grandson of Cadmus, changed into a stag
Actae·us -a -um *adj* Attic, Athenian
actĭ·ō -ōnis *f* doing, performance, action, activity; proceedings; (law) suit, process, action, permission for a suit; delivery, gesticulation; plot, action (*of play*)
actĭt·ō -āre *vt* to plead (*cases*) often; to perform (*plays*) often
Act·ĭum -ĭī or **-ī** *n* promontory in Epirus (*where Octavian defeated Antony and Cleopatra in* 31 B.C.)
actīv·us -a -um *adj* (gram) active; practical (*opposite of contemplative*)
act·or -ōris *m* doer, performer; (law) plaintiff, pleader, advocate; agent, manager; player, actor; **actor summarum** cashier, accountant
Act·or -ŏris *m* companion of Aeneas
actuārĭŏl·um -ī *n* small barge
actuārĭ·us -a -um *adj* swift; *m* stenographer; *f* swift ship; *n* swift ship
actuōsē *adv* energetically
actuōs·us -a -um *adj* energetic, very active
actus *pp* of **ago**
act·us -ūs *m* act, performance; driving, motion, impulse; right of way; public business; presentation, delivery, gesture, recital; act (*of play*)
actūtum *adv* instantly, immediately
acŭl·a -ae *f* rivulet

aculeāt•us -a -um *adj* prickly; (fig) stinging, sharp, subtle
acule•us -i *m* barb, sting; point; sarcasm
acūm•en -ĭnis *n* point, sharpness; sting (*of insect*); pungency; shrewdness, ingenuity, cunning
acŭō acuĕre acŭī acūtum *vt* to make sharp or pointed, to whet; to exercise; to stimulate; to give an edge to, enhance; to tease
ac•us -ūs *f* needle, pin; **acu rem tangere** to hit the nail on the head
acūtē *adv* acutely, sharply, keenly
acūtŭl•us -a -um *adj* somewhat sharp, rather subtle
acūt•us -a -um *pp* of **acuo;** *adj* sharp, pointed; shrill; intelligent
ad *prep* (with *acc*) (of space) to, towards, near, at; (of time) toward, about, until, at, on, by; (with numbers) about, almost; for the purpose of, to; according to, in consequence of; with respect to; compared with
adactĭ•ō -ōnis *f* enforcing
adactus *pp* of **adigo**
adact•us -ūs *m* bringing together; snapping (*of jaws*)
adaequē *adv* equally
adaequ•ō -āre *vt* to make level; to equal, match; (fig) to put on the same level; *vi* to be on the same level, be equal; (with *dat*) to be level with
adamantē•us -a -um *adj* made of steel
adamantĭn•us -a -um *adj* hard as steel, adamantine
adăm•ās -antis *m* adamant; steel; diamond
adambŭl•ō -āre *vi* (with **ad** + *acc*) to walk about near
adăm•ō -āre *vt* to fall in love with
ad•aperĭō -aperīre -aperŭī -apertum *vt* to uncover, throw open
adăqu•ō -āre *vt* to water; *vi* to fetch water
adauct•us -ūs *m* growth
ad•augĕō -augēre -auxī -auctum *vt* to increase, aggravate
adaugesc•ō -ĕre *vi* to begin to grow
ad•bĭbō -bibĕre -bĭbī -bibĭtum *vt* to drink in; to listen attentively to
adbīt•ō -ĕre *vi* to come near, approach
adc- = acc-
ad•dĕcet -decēre *v impers* it becomes
addens•ĕō -ēre or **addens•ō -āre** *vt* to close (*ranks*)
ad•dīcō -dīcĕre -dixī -dictum *vt* to assign; to doom; to dedicate, devote; *vi* (in augury) to be favorable
ad•discō -discĕre -didĭcī *vt* to learn in addition
additāment•um -ī *n* addition
ad•dō -dĕre -dĭdī -dĭtum *vt* to add, increase; to impart, bestow
ad•docĕō -docēre -docŭī -doctum *vt* to teach in addition
addubĭt•ō -āre *vt* to call into doubt; *vi* to begin to feel doubt; to hesitate
ad•dūcō -dūcĕre -duxī -ductum *vt* to lead up, bring up; to draw together, wrinkle; to prompt, induce, persuade, move
adduct•us -a -um *adj* drawn tight, strained; narrow, tight (*place*); strict, serious, stern (*character*)
ad•ĕdō -esse -ēdī -ēsum *vt* to nibble at; to eat up, consume; to waste
ademptĭ•ō -ōnis *f* taking away
ad•ĕō -īre -ĭī or **-īvī -ĭtum** *vt* to approach; to attack; to consult, apply to; to visit; to undertake, set about, undergo; *vi* to go up, come up; (with **ad** + *acc*) **a** to go to, approach; **b** to enter upon, undertake, set about, submit to
adĕō *adv* to such a degree, so; (following pronouns and numerals, to give emphasis) precisely, exactly, quite, just, chiefly; (at the beginning of sentence) thus far, to such an extent; even, indeed, truly
ad•eps -ĭpis *m* or *f* fat; corpulence
adeptĭ•ō -ōnis *f* obtaining, attainment
adeptus *pp* of **adipiscor**
adequĭt•ō -āre *vi* to ride up; (with *dat* or **ad** + *acc*) to ride up to, ride towards
adesse *inf* of **adedo** or of **adsum**
adēsur•ĭō -īre -īvī *vi* to be very hungry
adēsus *pp* of **adedo**
ad•haerĕō -haerēre -haesī -haesum *vi* (with *dat* or *abl* or with **in** + *abl*) **a** to cling to, stick to; **b** to keep close to, hang on to
ad•haerescō -haerescĕre -haesī -haesum *vi* to stick; to falter; (with *dat* or *abl*, with **ad** + *acc*, or with **in** + *abl*) **a** to stick to, cling to; **b** to be devoted to; **c** to correspond to, accord with
adhaesĭ•ō -ōnis *f* clinging, adhesion
adhaes•us -ūs *m* adhering, adherence
adhib•ĕō -ēre -ŭī -ĭtum *vt* to bring, put, add; to summon, invite; to apply; to use, employ; to consult; to handle, treat
adhinn•ĭō -īre -ĭī or **īvī -ītum** *vt* to whinny after, lust after; *vi* (with *dat* or with **ad** or **in** + *acc*) **a** to whinny after, lust after, crave; **b** to whinny in delight at
adhortātĭ•ō -ōnis *f* exhortation, encouragement
adhortāt•or -ōris *m* cheerer, supporter
adhort•or -ārī -ātus sum *vt* to cheer on, encourage
adhūc *adv* thus far, hitherto; till now; as yet, still; besides, in addition, moreover
ad•ĭgō -igĕre -ēgī -actum *vt* to drive; to drive home, thrust; to compel; to inflict; to bind (*by oath*)
ad•ĭmō -imĕre -ēmī -emptum *vt* to withdraw, take away; to carry off
adipāt•us -a -um *adj* fatty, greasy; gross, bombastic; *n* pastry (*made in fat*)

ad·ipiscor -ipiscī -eptus sum *vt* to reach, get, obtain, win
aditiāl·is -e *adj* inaugural
aditi·ō -ōnis *f* approach
adit·us -ūs *m* approach, access; entrance; admittance, audience, interview; beginning, commencement; chance, opportunity
adjac·ĕō -ēre -ŭī *vt* to adjoin; *vi* (with *dat* or **ad** + *acc*) **a** to lie near or at; **b** to border on, be contiguous with
adjecti·ō -ōnis *f* addition, annexation
adjectīv·us -a -um *adj* adjectival
ad·jiciō -jicĕre -jēcī -jectum *vt* to add, increase; (with *dat* or **ad** + *acc*) **a** to throw (*weapon*) at; **b** to add (*something*) to; **c** to turn or direct (*eyes, mind, etc.*) to; (with **in** + *acc*) to hurl (*weapon*) at
adjūdic·ō -āre *vt* to adjudge, award; to ascribe, assign
adjūment·um -ī *n* aid, help, support
adjunct·a -ōrum *n pl* accessory circumstances
adjuncti·ō -ōnis *f* joining, union; addition; (rhet) repetition
ad·jungō -jungĕre -junxī -junctum *vt* (with *dat*) to yoke or harness (*animal*) to; (with *dat* or **ad** + *acc*) **a** to add, attach, join (*something*) to; **b** to apply, direct (*mind, attention, etc.*) to
adjūr·ō -āre *vt* to swear to, confirm by oath; *vi* to swear
adjūtābil·is -e *adj* helpful
adjūt·ō -āre *vt* to help, assist; *vi* (with *dat*) to be of assistance to
adjūt·or -ōris *m* helper, assistant, promoter; aide, adjutant, deputy, secretary; supporting actor
adjūtōr·ium -iī or **-ī** *n* help, support
adjūtr·ix -īcis *f* helper, assistant (*female*)
ad·jūvō -juvāre -jūvī -jūtum *vt* to help, encourage, sustain; *vi* to be of use, be profitable
adl- = all-
admātūr·ō -āre *vt* to bring to maturity; to hasten, expedite
ad·mētior -mētīrī -mensus sum *vt* to measure out
Admēt·us -ī *m* king of Pherae in Thessaly, husband of Alcestis
admīgr·ō -āre *vi* (with **ad** + *acc*) **a** to go to; **b** to be added to
adminicŭl·ō -āre or **adminicŭl·or -ārī -ātus sum** *vt* to prop, support
adminicŭl·um -ī *n* prop, support, stake, pole; rudder; aid; assistant
administ·er -rī *m* assistant, attendant
administr·a -ae *f* assistant, attendant (*female*)
administrāti·ō -ōnis *f* help, aid; administration, management, government
administrāt·or -ōris *m* administrator, manager, director
administr·ō -āre *vt* to administer, manage, direct
admīrābil·is -e *adj* admirable, wonderful; strange, surprising, paradoxical
admīrābilit·ās -ātis *f* admiration, wonder, wonderfulness
admīrābiliter *adv* admirably; astonishingly, paradoxically
admīrāti·ō -ōnis *f* admiration, wonder, surprise
admīrāt·or -ōris *m* admirer
admīr·or -ārī -ātus sum *vt* to admire, wonder at, be surprised at
ad·miscĕō -miscēre -miscŭī -mixtum *vt* to mix, add; to involve, implicate; to join, mingle; (with *dat*, with **ad** or **in** + *acc*, or with **cum** + *abl*) to add (*something*) to, to mix or mix up (*something*) with; **se admiscere** to get involved, to meddle
admissār·ius -iī or **-ī** *m* stallion, stud; lecherer
admissi·ō -ōnis *f* interview, audience
admiss·um -ī *n* crime
ad·mittō -mittĕre -mīsī -missum *vt* to let in, admit; to let go, let loose; to put at a gallop; to allow; to commit (*crime*)
admixti·ō -ōnis *f* admixture
admixtus *pp* of **admisceo**
admoderātē *adv* appropriately
admŏdum *adv* to the limit; very, quite, fully; (with numbers) just about; (with negatives) at all; (in answers) quite so, yes
admoen·iō -īre *vt* to besiege, blockade
admōl·ior -īrī -ītus sum *vt* to bring up, move up; **admoliri** (with *inf*) to strive to, struggle to
admon·ĕō -ēre -ŭī -itum *vt* to admonish, remind, suggest; to warn; to urge
admoniti·ō -ōnis *f* admonition, reminder, suggestion
admonit·or -ōris *m* admonisher, reminder
admonitr·ix -īcis *f* admonisher, reminder (*female*)
admonit·um -ī *n* admonition
admonit·us -ūs *m* suggestion; reproof
ad·mordĕō -mordēre -momordī -morsum *vt* to bite at, gnaw at; (fig) to fleece
admōti·ō -ōnis *f* moving, movement
ad·movĕō -movēre -mōvī -mōtum *vt* to move up, bring up, bring near; to lead on, conduct; (with *dat* or **ad** + *acc*) **a** to move or bring (*something*) to; **b** to apply (*something*) to; **c** to direct (*attention, etc.*) to; *vi* to draw near, approach
admūg·iō -īre *vi* (with *dat*) to low to, bellow to
admurmurāti·ō -ōnis *f* murmuring
admurmŭr·ō -āre *vi* to murmur (*in approval or disapproval*)
admutil·ō -āre *vt* to clip close; (fig) to clip, cheat

adn- = **ann-**
ad·olĕō -olēre -olŭī -ultum *vt* to magnify; to honor, worship; to sacrifice, burn; to pile up (*altars*); to sprinkle (*altars*)
adol·ĕō -ēre *vi* to smell
adolesc·ens -entis *m* young man; *f* young woman
adol·escō -escĕre -ēvī *vi* to grow, grow up; to be kindled, burn
Adōn·is -is or **-idis** *m* son of Cinyras, king of Cyprus, loved by Venus
adoper·iō -īre -ŭī -tum *vt* to cover up; to close
adopīn·or -ārī *vi* to suppose, conjecture
adoptātī·ō -ōnis *f* adopting (*of child*)
adoptī·ō -ōnis *f* adoption (*of child*)
adoptīv·us -a -um *adj* adoptive, by adoption
adopt·ō -āre *vt* to adopt; to select; to graft (*plants*)
ad·or -ōris or **-ŏris** *n* spelt
adōrātī·ō -ōnis *f* adoration, worship
adōrĕ·a -ae *f* reward for valor; praise, glory
adōrĕ·us -a -um *adj* of spelt
ad·orior -orīrī -ortus sum *vt* to rise up against, attack, assault; to attempt; to undertake
adorn·ō -āre *vt* to equip, get ready; to adorn
adōr·ō -āre *vt* to implore, entreat; to ask for; to adore, worship
adp- = **app-**
ad·rādō -rādĕre -rāsī -rāsum *vt* to scrape, shave; to lop off
Adrast·us -ī *m* king of Argos, father-in-law of Tydeus and Polynices
adr- = **arr-**
adsc- = **asc-**
adse- = **ass-**
adsi- = **assi-**
adso- = **asso-**
adsp- = **asp-**
adst- = **ast-**
adsu- = **assu-**
ad·sum -esse -fŭī *vi* to be near, be present; to appear; to be at hand; to be of assistance; (with *dat*) to share in, participate in, stand by, assist; **animo** or **animis adesse** to pay attention; to cheer up
adt- = **att-**
adūlātī·ō -ōnis *f* fawning, cringing, servility, flattery
adūlāt·or -ōris *m* flatterer
adūlātōrĭ·us -a -um *adj* flattering
adulesc·ens -entis *adj* young
adulesc·ens -entis *m* young man; *f* young woman
adulescentĭ·a -ae *f* youth, young people
adulescentŭl·a -ae *f* little girl
adulescentŭl·us -ī *m* young man
adūl·ō -āre *vi* to fawn
adūl·or -ārī -ātus sum *vt* to flatter (*in a servile manner*); *vi* (with *dat*) to kowtow to
adult·er -ĕra -ĕrum *adj* adulterous, unchaste; *m* adulterer; *f* adulteress
adulterīn·us -a -um *adj* adulterous; forged, counterfeit
adulter·ĭum -ĭī or **-ī** *n* adultery; adulteration
adultĕr·ō -āre *vt* to defile, corrupt; to falsify; *vi* to commit adultery
adult·us -a -um *adj* grown, mature, adult
adumbrātim *adv* in outline
adumbrātĭ·ō -ōnis *f* sketch, outline
adumbrāt·us -a -um *adj* shadowy, sketchy, unreal, fictitious, dim, imperfect
adumbr·ō -āre *vt* to shade, overshadow; to sketch; to represent
aduncĭt·ās -ātis *f* curvature
adunc·us -a -um *adj* curved, hooked
adurg·ĕō -ēre *vt* to pursue closely
ad·ūrō -ūrĕre -ussī -ustum *vt* to set on fire; to scorch; to nip, freeze; (fig) to inflame
adusque *adv* entirely, throughout
adusque *prep* (with *acc*) all the way to, as far as, right up to
adustĭ·ō -ōnis *f* burning
adust·us -a -um *pp* of **aduro;** *adj* scorched; sunburned
advectīcĭ·us -a -um *adj* imported, foreign
advectĭ·ō -ōnis *f* transportation
advect·ō -āre *vt* to keep on conveying
advect·us -ūs *m* conveyance
ad·vĕhō -vehĕre -vexī -vectum *vt* to carry, convey, transport; **(equo) advehi** (with **ad** or **in** + *acc*) to ride to; **(nave) advehi** (with **ad** + *acc*) to sail to
advēl·ō -āre *vt* to veil; to wreathe
advĕn·a -ae *m* or *f* stranger, foreigner
ad·venĭō -venīre -vēnī -ventum *vi* to arrive; (with **ad** or **in** + *acc* or with *acc* of limit of motion) to arrive at, come to, reach
adventīcĭ·us -a -um *adj* foreign, strange, extraneous; unusual, extraordinary; unearned
advent·ō -āre *vi* to keep coming closer, approach
advent·or -ōris *m* visitor, guest; customer
advent·us -ūs *m* arrival, approach
adversārĭ·us -a -um *adj* (with *dat*) turned towards, opposed to, opposite; *m & f* adversary, enemy, rival; *n pl* journal, notebook, memoranda; assertions (*of opponent*)
adversātr·ix -īcis *f* opponent (*female*)
adversĭ·ō -ōnis *f* directing, direction
advers·ō -āre *vt* to direct (*attention*)
advers·or -ārī -ātus sum *vi* (with *dat*) to oppose, resist
adversum or **adversus** *adv* in the opposite direction; *prep* (with *acc*) facing, opposite, towards; compared with, contrary to
advers·us -a -um *adj* opposite, in front; facing; unfavorable, hostile;

adverso flumine upstream; *n* misfortune; opposite
ad·vertō or **ad·vortō -vertĕre -vertī -versum** *vt* (with *dat* or **in** + *acc*) **a** to turn or direct (*something*) to; **b** to steer (*ship*) to; **animum** or **animos advertere** to pay attention; **animum** or **animos advertere** (with *dat* or **ad** + *acc*) to give attention to, attend to, heed, observe; *vi* to land; (with **in** + *acc*) to punish
advesper·ascit -ascĕre -āvit *v impers* evening approaches
advigĭl·ō -āre *vi* to be vigilant, keep watch; (with *dat*) to keep watch over, bestow attention on; (with **pro** + *abl*) to watch out for
advocātĭ·ō -ōnis *f* legal assistance; legal counsel; the bar; period of time allowed to procure legal assistance; delay, adjournment
advocāt·us -ī *m* witness; advocate, counsel; helper, friend
advŏc·ō -āre *vt* to call, summon; to consult
advŏl·ō -āre *vi* (with *dat* or with **ad** or **in** + *acc*) **a** to fly to; **b** to dash to
ad·volvō -volvĕre -volvī -volūtum *vt* (with *dat* or **ad** + *acc*) to roll (*something*) to or toward; **advolvi** or **se advolvere genua** or **genibus** (*with genit*) to fall prostrate before
advor- = **adver-**
adўt·um -ī *n* sanctuary; tomb
Aeacĭd·ēs -ae *m* descendant of Aeacus
Aeăc·us -ī *m* king of Aegina, father of Peleus, Telamon, and Phocus, and judge of the dead
aed·ēs or **aed·is -is** *f* shrine, temple; building; *f pl* rooms, apartments; house
aedicŭl·a -ae *f* chapel, shrine; small room, closet; small house; *f pl* small house
aedificātĭ·ō -ōnis *f* constructing, building; structure, building
aedificātiuncŭl·a -ae *f* tiny building
aedificāt·or -ōris *m* builder, architect
aedific·ĭum -ĭī or **-ī** *n* building
aedifĭc·ō -āre *vt* to build, construct, establish
aedīlĭcĭ·us -a -um *adj* aedile's; *m* ex-aedile
aedīl·is -is *m* aedile
aedīlĭt·ās -ātis *f* aedileship
aedis see **aedēs**
aeditŭ·us or **aeditĭm·us** or **aeditŭm·us -ī** *m* temple attendant, sacristan
Aeēt·ēs -ae *m* king of Colchis and father of Medea
Aegae·us -a -um *adj* Aegean; *n* Aegean Sea
Aegāt·ēs -um *f pl* three islands W. of Sicily
aeg·er -ra -rum *adj* sick, infirm, unsound; dejected; painful
Aeg·eus -ĕī *m* king of Athens, father of Theseus
Aegīd·ēs -ae *m* Theseus
Aegīn·a -ae *f* island off Attica; mother of Aeacus
aeg·is -ĭdis *f* shield of Minerva and of Jupiter; aegis, protection
Aegisth·us -ī *m* son of Thyestes, seducer of Clytemnestra, and murderer of Agamemnon
aegrē *adv* painfully; with difficulty; reluctantly; hardly, scarcely
aegr·ĕō -ēre *vi* to be sick
aegr·escō -escĕre *vi* to become sick; to be aggravated, get worse; to be troubled
aegrimōnĭ·a -ae *f* sorrow, anxiety, trouble
aegritūd·ō -ĭnis *f* sickness; sorrow
aegr·or -ōris *m* illness
aegrōtātĭ·ō -ōnis *f* sickness, disease
aegrōt·ō -āre *vi* to be sick; to languish
aegrōt·us -a -um *adj* sick
Aegypt·us -ī *f* Egypt; *m* mythical king of Egypt, whose 50 sons married the 50 daughters of his brother Danaüs
aelĭn·os -ī *m* dirge
aemŭl·a -ae *f* rival (*female*)
aemulātĭ·ō -ōnis *f* emulation, rivalry
aemulāt·or -ōris *m* rival, imitator
aemulāt·us -ūs *m* rivalry
aemŭl·or -ārī -ātus sum *vt* to emulate, rival; *vi* (with *dat*) to be envious of, be jealous of
aemŭl·us -a -um *adj* (with *genit* or *dat*) emulous of, envious of, jealous of, striving after; *m* rival
Aeneăd·ēs -ae *m* descendant of Aeneas; Trojan; Roman; Augustus
Aenē·ās -ae *m* son of Venus and Anchises, and hero of Virgil's epic
Aenē·is -ĭdis or **-ĭdos** *f* Aeneid (*Virgil's epic*)
aēnĕ·us or **ahēnĕ·us -a -um** *adj* bronze
aenigm·a -ătis *n* riddle, mystery
aēnĭp·ēs -ĕdis *adj* bronze-footed
aēn·us or **ahēn·us -a -um** *adj* bronze; (fig) firm, invincible; *n* cauldron
Aeolĭ·a -ae *f* realm of Aeolus, king of winds; group of islands near Sicily
Aeolĭ·ī -ōrum or **Aeŏl·ēs -um** *m pl* Aeolians (*inhabitants of N.W. Asia Minor*)
Aeŏl·is -ĭdis *f* Aeolia, N.W. part of Asia Minor
Aeŏl·us -ī *m* god of winds
aequābĭl·is -e *adj* equal, alike; consistent, uniform; fair, impartial
aequābilĭt·ās -ātis *f* equality; uniformity; impartiality
aequābiliter *adv* equally; uniformly
aequaev·us -a -um *adj* of the same age
aequāl·is -e *adj* equal; even, level; of the same age, contemporary

aequāl·is -is *m* or *f* comrade; contemporary
aequālĭt·ās -ātis *f* equality; evenness; smoothness
aequālĭter *adv* equally; evenly
aequanimĭt·ās -ātis *f* calmness, patience; kindness; impartiality
aequātĭ·ō -ōnis *f* equal distribution; **aequatio bonorum** communism
aequē *adv* equally; justly, fairly; **aeque . . . ac** or **atque** or **et** just as, as much as, as; **aeque . . . ac si** just as if; **aeque . . . quam** as . . . as, in the same way as
Aequ·ī -ōrum *m pl* people of central Italy
aequilibrĭt·ās -ātis *f* balance
aequilibr·ĭum -ĭī or **-ī** *n* horizontal position; equilibrium
aequinoctiāl·is -e *adj* equinoctial
aequinoct·ĭum -ĭī or **-ī** *n* equinox
aequiperābĭl·is -e *adj* (with *dat* or **cum** + *abl*) comparable to
aequipĕr·ō or **aequipăr·ō -āre** *vt* to compare; to equal, rival, come up to; (with *dat*, with **ad**+ *acc*, or **cum** + *abl*) to compare (*something*) to; *vi* (with *dat*) **a** to become equal to, be equal to; **b** to attain to
aequĭt·ās -ātis *f* evenness, conformity, symmetry, equity; calmness
aequ·or -ŏris *n* level surface; sea, ocean
aequorĕ·us -a -um *adj* of the sea, marine
aequ·us -a -um *adj* level, even, flat; favorable, friendly; fair, just; calm; *n* level, plain; justice, fairness
ā·ēr -ĕris *m* air, atmosphere, sky; weather; mist
aerāment·um -ī *n* bronze vessel or utensil
aerārĭ·us -a -um *adj* copper, bronze; of mines; financial, fiscal; *m* coppersmith; low-class Roman citizen; *f* mine; smelting furnace; *n* treasury
aerāt·us -a -um *adj* bronze; rich
āĕrĕ·us -a -um *adj* aerial, airy, lofty, high
aerĕ·us -a -um *adj* bronze
aerĭf·er -ĕra -ĕrum *adj* carrying cymbals
aerĭp·ēs -ĕdis *adj* bronze-footed
āĕrĭ·us -a -um *adj* aerial, airy, lofty, high
Āĕrŏp·ē -ēs or **Āĕrŏp·a -ae** *f* wife of Atreus, mother of Agamemnon and Menelaus
aerūgĭnōs·us -a -um *adj* rusty
aerūg·ō -ĭnis *f* copper rust, verdigris; corroding passion, envy, greed
aerumn·a -ae *f* need, want, trouble, hardship, calamity
aerumnābĭl·is -e *adj* full of troubles, calamitous
aerumnōs·us -a -um *adj* full of troubles, wretched, distressed
aes aeris *n* crude metal, copper, bronze; bronze object; armor, statue, utensil, trumpet; money; payment; reward; *n pl* wages, soldier's pay; **aes alienum** debt
Aeschȳl·us -ī *m* Athenian tragic poet (525-456 B.C.)
Aesculāp·ĭus -ĭī or **-ī** *m* god of medicine, son of Apollo and Coronis
aesculēt·um -ī *n* oak forest
aesculĕ·us -a -um *adj* oak
aescŭl·us -ī *f* Italian oak
Aes·ōn -ŏnis *m* Thessalian prince, father of Jason, restored to youth by Medea
aest·ās -ātis *f* summer; summer heat
aestĭf·er -ĕra -ĕrum *adj* heat-bearing, sultry
aestimābĭl·is -e *adj* valuable
aestimātĭ·ō -ōnis *f* appraisal, assessment; esteem
aestimāt·or -ōris *m* appraiser
aestĭm·ō -āre *vt* to appraise, rate, value, estimate; to esteem, judge, hold
aestīv·a -ōrum *n pl* summer camp; campaign season, campaign; summer pastures
aestīv·ō -āre *vi* to pass the summer
aestīv·us -a -um *adj* summer
aestuār·ĭum -ĭī or **ī** *n* tidal waters, lagoon, estuary, marsh; air shaft
aestŭ·ō -āre *vi* to boil, seethe; to burn, glow; to undulate, swell, be tossed, heave; to waver, hesitate; to be excited
aestuōsē *adv* hotly, impetuously
aestuōs·us -a -um *adj* sultry; billowy
aest·us -ūs *m* agitation; glow, heat, sultriness; surge, billows, ebb and flow; tide; raging, seething, passion; uncertainty, irresolution
aet·ās -ātis *f* lifetime, age, generation
aetātŭl·a -ae *f* tender age
aeternĭt·ās -ātis *f* eternity, immortality
aetern·ō -āre *vt* to perpetuate, immortalize
aeternum *adv* forever; constantly, perpetually
aetern·us -a -um *adj* eternal, everlasting, immortal, imperishable
aeth·ēr -ĕris or **-ĕros** *m* upper air, sky, heaven
aetherĭ·us -a -um *adj* ethereal, heavenly, celestial; of the upper world
Aethĭ·ops -ŏpis *m* Ethiopian; Negro; blockhead
aethr·a -ae *f* ether, pure air, serene sky; air, sky, heavens
Aetn·a -ae or **Aetn·ē -ēs** *f* volcano in Sicily
Aetōlĭ·a -ae *f* district in N. Greece
aevĭt·ās -ātis *f* age, lifetime
aev·um -ī *n* or **aev·us -ī** *m* age, lifetime, life; time, period; generation; eternity
Āf·er -ra -rum *adj & m* African
affābĭl·is -e *adj* affable, courteous, kind
affābilĭt·ās -ātis *f* affability, courtesy

affăbrē *adv* in a workmanlike manner, cunningly
affătim *adv* sufficiently, enough, satisfactorily
affāt·us -ūs *m* address, discourse
affectātĭ·ō -ōnis *f* eager desire; affectation, conceit
affectāt·or -ōris *m* affected person
affectāt·us -a -um *adj* choice, select; farfetched, studied
affectĭ·ō -ōnis *f* disposition, state of mind; inclination, partiality; affection, love
affect·ō -āre *vt* to grasp, seize; to pursue, strive after, aim at; to try to win over; to affect, feign
affect·us -a -um *adj* furnished, provided, gifted; weakened, impaired, sick; affected, moved, touched
affect·us -ūs *m* state, disposition, mood; feeling, passion, emotion; affection
affĕrō afferre attŭlī allātum *vt* to bring, carry, convey; to report, announce; to introduce, apply, employ, exert, exercise; to produce, cause, occasion, impart; to allege, assign; to contribute, help; **manus afferre** (with *dat*) to lay hands on, attack, do violence to, rob, plunder
af·ficĭō -ficĕre -fēcī -fectum *vt* to treat, handle, manage; to affect, move, influence, impress; to attack, afflict; to impair, weaken; (*abl* and verb may be rendered by the verb corresponding to the *abl*): **cruce afficere** to crucify; **honoribus afficere** to honor; **supplicio afficere** to punish
af·fīgō -fīgĕre -fixī -fixum *vt* (with *dat* or **ad** + *acc*) to fasten, attach, affix, annex (*something*) to; (with *dat*) to impress (*something*) upon (*mind*)
af·fingō -fingĕre -finxī -fictum *vt* to form, fashion besides; to make up, invent; (with *dat*) to attach, affix, add, join, contribute (*something*) to
affīn·is -e *adj* adjoining, neighboring; related by marriage; (with *dat* or **ad** + *acc*) taking part in, privy to, associated with
affīn·is -is *m* or *f* in-law
affīnĭt·ās -ātis *f* relationship by marriage
affirmātē *adv* with solemn assurance, positively, certainly
affirmātĭ·ō -ōnis *f* affirmation, assertion, declaration
affirm·ō -āre *vt* to strengthen; to confirm, encourage; to aver, assert
afflāt·us -ūs *m* breeze, blast, breath; inspiration
affl·ĕō -ēre *vi* to weep
afflictātĭ·ō -ōnis *f* physical pain, torture
afflictō -āre *vt* to shatter, damage, harass, injure; to trouble, vex, distress, torment
afflict·or -ōris *m* destroyer, subverter
afflict·us -a -um *adj* damaged, shattered; cast down, downhearted; vile
af·flīgō -flīgĕre -flixī -flictum *vt* to knock, strike down; (fig) to crush
affl·ō -āre *vt* (with *dat*) **a** to breathe (*something*) upon; **b** to impart (*something*) to; *vi* (with *dat*) **a** to breathe upon; **b** to be favorable to
afflŭ·ens -entis *adj* flowing; rich, affluent; abounding, numerous
affluenter *adv* lavishly, abundantly
affluentĭ·a -ae *f* abundance
af·flŭō -fluĕre -fluxī -fluxum *vi* (with *dat* or **ad** + *acc*) **a** to flow to, flow towards, glide by; **b** to hasten to, flock to; (with *abl*) to abound in
af·for -fārī -fātus sum *vt* to address, accost, pray to
affŏre = adfuturus esse
affŏrem = adessem
afformīd·ō -āre *vi* to be afraid
af·fulgĕō -fulgēre -fulsī *vi* to shine, beam, dawn, appear; (with *dat*) to shine on
af·fundō -fundĕre -fūdī -fūsum *vt* (with *dat*) **a** to pour, sprinkle, scatter (*something*) on; **b** to send or despatch (*someone*) to; **affundi** or **se affundere** (with *dat*) to throw oneself at, prostrate oneself before
Afrĭc·us -a -um *adj* African; *m* S.W. Wind; *f* originally the district of Carthage, made a Roman province in 146 B.C.; continent of Africa
Agamemn·ōn -ŏnis *m* king of Mycenae, son of Atreus and of Aërope, brother of Menelaus, and commander in chief of Greek forces at Troy
Aganipp·ē -ēs *f* fountain on Mount Helicon, sacred to the Muses
agās·ō -ōnis *m* driver, groom; lackey
agĕdum *interj* come on!; well!
agell·us -ī *m* little field, plot
agēm·a -ătis *n* corps or division (*of soldiers*)
Agēn·or -ŏris *m* son of Belus, king of Phoenicia, father of Cadmus and Europa, and ancestor of Dido
Agēnorĭd·ēs -ae *m* descendant of Agenor; Cadmus; Perseus
ag·er -rī *m* field, ground, arable land, farm, estate; territory, district
agg·er -ĕris *m* fill dirt, rubbish, soil, mound; rampart, dike, dam, pier; fortification; causeway; funeral pile
aggĕr·ō -āre *vt* to pile up, fill up, amass, increase; stimulate
ag·gĕrō -gerĕre -gessī -gestum *vt* to bring forward, utter; (with *dat* or **ad** + *acc*) to bring, convey (*something*) to
aggest·us -ūs *m* accumulation
agglomĕr·ō -āre *vt* to wind up (*as on a ball*); to annex; **se agglomare** (with *dat*) to attach oneself to, join
agglūtĭn·ō -āre *vt* to glue, paste, solder, cement
aggravesc·ō -ĕre *vi* to grow heavy
aggrăv·ō -āre *vt* to make heavier; to make worse, aggravate
ag·gredĭor -grĕdī -gressus sum *vt* to approach; to address; to attack; to undertake, begin

aggrĕg·ō -āre *vt* to assemble, collect; to attach, join, include, implicate

aggressi·ō -ōnis *f* attack, assault; introduction

agĭl·is -e *adj* easily moved, agile, nimble, quick; busy, active

agilĭt·ās -ātis *f* mobility, agility, nimbleness, quickness, activity

agitābĭl·is -e *adj* easily moved, light

agitātĭ·ō -ōnis *f* motion, movement, agitation; activity, pursuit; prosecution

agitāt·or -ōris *m* driver, charioteer

agĭt·ō -āre *vt* to set in motion, drive on, impel; to hunt, chase, pursue; to drive, urge, support, insist on; to practice, exercise; to observe, keep, celebrate; to obey, carry out; to spend, pass (*time*); to shake, toss, disturb; to vex, distress; to stimulate, excite; to deride, insult; to criticize; to consider, deliberate on; to discuss, debate; *vi* to live, dwell, be

Āglaur·ōs -ī *f* daughter of Cecrops, changed by Mercury into a stone

agm·en -ĭnis *n* herd, flock, troop, crowd; body, mass; army (*on march*), procession, train

agn·a -ae *f* ewe, lamb (*female*)

ag·nascor -nascī -nātus sum *vi* to be born (*after the father has made his will*)

agnātĭ·ō -ōnis *f* blood relationship (*on father's side*)

agnāt·us -ī *m* relative (*on father's side*)

agnell·us -ī *m* little lamb

agnīn·a -ae *f* mutton

agnitĭ·ō -ōnis *f* recognition, acknowledgment, admission; knowledge

ag·noscō -noscĕre -nōvī -nĭtum *vt* to recognize, identify, acknowledge

agn·us -ī *m* lamb

agō agĕre ēgī actum *vt* to drive, lead, conduct; to chase, hunt; to drive away, steal; to spend (*time*); to do, act, perform; to manage, administer, carry on; to plead, transact, discuss, propose; to play, act the part of; to accuse, impeach; to exercise, practice, perform, deliver, pronounce; to treat; **agi** to be at stake; **se agere** to behave, deport oneself

ag·ōn -ōnis *m* contest, combat (*in* public games)

agrārĭ·us -a -um *adj* agrarian; *m pl* land-reform party

agrest·is -e *adj* rustic; boorish, wild, savage

agricŏl·a -ae *m* farmer, peasant

Agricŏl·a -ae *m* father-in-law of Tacitus

agricultūr·a -ae *f* agriculture

Agrigent·um -ī *n* city on south coast of Sicily (*sometimes called Acragas*)

agripĕt·a -ae *m* colonist, settler

Agripp·a -ae *m* son-in-law of Augustus, husband of Julia, and father of Agrippina

Agrippīn·a -ae *f* wife of Tiberius; daughter of Agrippa and Julia, and mother of Caligula

āh *interj* ah!, ha!, oh!

aha *interj* aha!

ai *interj* (denoting grief) alas!

āin = aisne (*see* **aio**)

aiō *vt & vi* (used mainly in present and imperfect indicative) I say; I say yes, I say so; I affirm, assert, tell, relate; **ain** (= **aisne**) **tandem?, ain tu?, ain tute?,** or **ain vero?** (colloquial phrase, expressing surprise) do you really mean it?, you don't say!, really?

Āj·ax -ācis *m* son of Telamon, king of Salamis; son of Oileus, king of the Locri

āl·a -ae *f* wing; armpit; squadron (*of cavalry*); flank (*of battle line*)

alăc·er -ris -re *adj* lively, brisk, quick, eager, active, cheerful

alacrĭt·ās -ātis *f* liveliness, briskness, eagerness, cheerfulness

alăp·a -ae *f* slap; emancipation (*of slave*)

ālārĭ·ī -ōrum *m pl* auxiliaries, allies

ālār·is -e *adj* (mil) on the flank, of the flank

ālārĭ·us -a -um *adj* (*mil*) on the flank, of the flank

ālāt·us -a -um *adj* winged

alaud·a -ae *f* lark

alāz·ōn -ŏnis *m* boaster

Alb·a -ae *f* town, also called Alba Longa, mother city of Rome, founded by Ascanius, son of Aeneas

albāt·us -a -um *adj* dressed in white

alb·ĕō -ēre -ŭī *vi* to be white

albesc·ō -ĕre *vi* to become white, whiten; to dawn

albĭc·ō -āre *vt* to make white, whiten *vi* to be white

albĭd·us -a -um *adj* white, whitish

Albĭ·ōn -ōnis *f* Britain

albitūd·ō -ĭnis *f* whiteness

Albŭl·a -ae *f* Tiber River

albŭl·us -a -um *adj* whitish

alb·um -ī *n* white; white tablet, record, list, register

Albunĕ·a or **Albūn·a -ae** *f* fountain at Tibur; nymph of the fountain

alb·us -a -um *adj* dead white, white, bright; favorable

Alcae·us -ī *m* Greek lyric poet of Lesbos, contemporary with Sappho (610 B.C.)

alcēd·ō -ĭnis *f* kingfisher, halcyon

alcēdōnĭ·a -ōrum *n pl* halcyon days; (fig) deep calm, tranquillity

alc·ēs -is *f* elk

Alcibiăd·ēs -is *m* Athenian politician, disciple of Socrates (450?-404 B.C.)

Alcīd·ēs -ae *m* Hercules

Alcimĕd·ē -ēs *f* wife of Aeson and mother of Jason

Alcinŏ·ūs -ī *m* king of the Phaea-

cians, by whom Ulysses was entertained
Alcmēn·a or **Alcumēn·a -ae** or **Alcmēn·ē -ēs** *f* wife of Amphitryon and mother of Hercules by Jupiter
ālĕ·a -ae *f* dice game; chance, risk, venture
āleāt·or -ōris *m* dice player, gambler
āleātōrĭ·us -a -um *adj* of dice, gambling
ālĕ·ō -ōnis *m* gambler
āl·es -ĭtis *adj* winged; swift
āl·es -ĭtis *m* or *f* winged creature, fowl, bird; *m* poet; *f* augury, omen, sign
al·escō -escĕre *vi* to grow up, increase
Alexand·er -rī *m* Paris, son of Priam and Hecuba; Alexander the Great, king of Macedon
Alexandrē·a or **Alexandrī·a -ae** *f* city in Egypt, founded by Alexander the Great
alg·a -ae *f* seaweed
al·gĕō -gēre -sī *vi* to be cold, feel cold
al·gescō -gescĕre -sī *vi* to catch cold; to become cold
algĭd·us -a -um *adj* cold
alg·or -ōris *m* cold, chilliness
alg·us -ūs *m* cold
alĭā *adv* by another way
alĭās *adv* at another time; **alias . . . alias** at one time . . . at another, sometimes . . . sometimes
alĭbī *adv* elsewhere; otherwise, in other respects; **alibi . . . alibi** in one place . . . in another, here . . . there
alicŭbī *adv* at any place, somewhere, anywhere
alicunde *adv* from somewhere, from any place, from someone else
aliēnātĭ·ō -ōnis *f* transfer (*of property*); separation, alienation; aversion, dislike
aliēnigĕn·a -ae *m* foreigner, alien, stranger
aliēn·ō -āre *vt* to make strange, transfer, sell; to alienate, set at variance; to remove, separate; to make insane, drive mad
aliēn·us -a -um *adj* another's; foreign; contrary, hostile; strange, unsuitable, incongruous, inconsistent, inconvenient; *m* stranger, foreigner
ālĭ·ger -gĕra -gĕrum *adj* wearing wings, winged
alimentārĭ·us -a -um *adj* alimentary
aliment·um -ī *n* nourishment, food, provisions; fuel
alimōnĭ·a -ae *f* or **alimōn·ĭum -ĭī** or **-ī** *n* nourishment, food, support
alĭō *adv* to another place, elsewhere
aliōquī or **aliōquīn** *adv* otherwise, in other respects, for the rest; besides; in general; in any case
aliorsum or **aliorsus** *adv* in another direction; in another manner, in a different sense
ālĭp·ēs -ĕdis *adj* wing-footed, swift-footed
alipt·ēs or **alipt·a -ae** *m* wrestling trainer
alĭquā *adv* somehow, in any direction
alĭquam *adv* in some degree
aliquamdĭū *adv* for some time
aliquandō *adv* sometime or other, once; at any time, ever; sometimes, now and then; for once, now; finally, now at last
aliquantisper *adv* for a while, for a time
aliquantō *adv* somewhat, a little, rather
aliquantŭlum *adv* somewhat
aliquantŭl·us -a -um *adj* little, small
aliquantum *adv* somewhat, a little, rather
aliquant·us -a -um *adj* considerable
aliquātĕnus *adv* for some distance, to a certain extent, somewhat; in some respects, partly
alĭ·quī -qua -quod *adj* some, any
alĭquid *adv* to some extent, at all
alĭ·quid -cūjus *pron* something, anything; something important
alĭ·quis -cūjus *pron* someone, somebody, anyone; someone important
alĭquō *adv* to some place, somewhere
alĭquot (indecl) *adj* some, several, a few
aliquotĭens *adv* several times
aliquōvorsum *adv* to some place, one way or another
alĭter *adv* otherwise, else, differently
aliŭbī *adv* elsewhere; **aliubi . . . aliubi** here . . . there
āl·ĭum -ĭī or **-ī** *n* garlic
aliunde *adv* from another source, from elsewhere
alĭ·us -a -ud *adj* another, other, different; *pron* another; **alii . . . alii** some . . . others; **alius . . . alius** one . . . another, the one . . . the other; **alius ex alio** one after another
al·lābor -lābī -lapsus sum *vi* to glide, slide, slip; to flow
allabōr·ō -āre *vi* to work hard
allacrĭmō -āre *vi* to weep, shed tears
allaps·us -ūs *m* stealthy approach
allātr·ō -āre *vt* to revile; (*of sea*) to break against, dash against
allātus *pp* of **affero**
allaud·ō -āre *vt* to praise highly
all·ēc -ēcis *n* fish sauce
Allectō (indecl) *f* one of the three Furies
allect·ō -āre *vt* to allure, entice
allēgātĭ·ō -ōnis *f* sending, despatching
allēg·ō -āre *vt* to commission, deputize, despatch; to allege; to instigate
al·lĕgō -legĕre -lēgī -lectum *vt* to select, elect
allevāment·um -ī *n* alleviation, relief

allevātī·ō -ōnis *f* raising, elevating; easing
allĕv·ō -āre *vt* to lift up, raise; to alleviate; to comfort; to lighten
all·ex -ĭcis *m* (the) big toe; midget
al·lĭciō -licĕre -lexī -lectum *vt* to attract
al·līdō -līdĕre -līsī -līsum *vt* (with *dat* or with **ad** or **in** + *acc*) to dash (*something*) against; **allidi** to be wrecked
allĭg·ō -āre *vt* to bind, fetter; to bandage; to hinder, detain; to impugn, accuse; (with **ad** + *acc*) to bind (*something*) to
al·linō -linĕre -lēvī -lĭtum *vt* to smudge; (with *dat*) to smear (*something*) on
all·ĭum -ĭī or **-ī** *n* garlic
Allobrŏg·ēs -um *m pl* Gallic tribe living between the Rhone and the Isère
allocūtī·ō -ōnis *f* address; consoling, comforting
alloqu·ĭum -ĭī or **-ī** *n* address, conversation; encouragement, consolation
al·lŏquor -lŏquī -locūtus sum *vt* to speak to, address; to exhort, rouse; to console, comfort
allūdī·ō -āre *vi* to play, jest
al·lūdō -lūdĕre -lūsī -lūsum *vi* to play, joke; (of waves) (with *dat*) to play against
al·lŭō -luĕre -lŭī *vt* to wash
alluvī·ēs -ēī *f* inundation, pool (*left by flood waters*); alluvial land
alluvī·ō -ōnis *f* inundation; alluvial land
alm·us -a -um *adj* nourishing; genial, kind, propitious, indulgent, bountiful
aln·us -ī *f* alder tree; ship
al·ō -ĕre -ŭī -tum or **-ĭtum** *vt* to feed, nourish, rear; to support, maintain; to promote; to increase, strengthen
alŏ·ē -ēs *f* aloe; bitterness
alogī·a -ae *f* folly
Alp·ēs -ĭum *f pl* Alps
alpha (indecl) *n* alpha (*first letter of Greek alphabet*)
Alphē·us or **Alphē·os -ī** *m* chief river of the Peloponnesus
Alpĭc·us -a -um *adj* Alpine
Alpīn·us -a -um *adj* Alpine
alsĭ·us or **als·us -a -um** *adj* chilly, cool, cold
altār·ĭa -ĭum *n pl* altar top, altar, high altar
altē *adv* high, on high, highly, deeply, far, remotely; loftily, profoundly
alt·er -ĕra -ĕrum *adj* one (*of two*); a second, the second, the next; *pron* one (*of two*), the one, the other; a second one, the second one, the next one; another (*one's fellow man*); **alter . . . alter** the one . . . the other, the former . . . the latter
altercātī·ō -ōnis *f* debate, dispute, discussion
alterc·ō -āre or **alterc·or -ārī -ātus sum** *vi* to quarrel, wrangle, bicker
alternīs *adv* by turns, alternately
altern·ō -āre *vt* to do by turns; to exchange; *vi* to alternate
altern·us -a -um *adj* one after another, alternate, mutual, every other
alterŭt·er -ra -rum (*f* also: **altĕra utra**; *n* also: **altĕrum utrum**) *adj* one (*of two*), either, one or the other; *pron* one, either one, one or the other
Althae·a -ae *f* daughter of Thestius, wife of Oeneus, king of Calydon, and mother of Meleager
alticinct·us -a -um *adj* active, busy, energetic
altĭl·is -e *adj* fattened, fat, full; rich
altisŏn·us -a -um *adj* high-sounding; sounding from on high
altitŏn·ans -antis *adj* thundering on high
altitūd·ō -ĭnis *f* height; depth; (fig) depth, reserve, secrecy
altivŏl·ans -antis *adj* high-flying
alt·or -ōris *m* foster father
altrinsĕcus *adv* on the other side
altr·ix -īcis *f* nourisher, foster mother
altrōvorsum *adv* on the other side
alt·us -a -um *adj* high; deep, profound; ancient, remote (*lineage*); *n* high seas, the deep; heaven; **ab alto** from on high, from heaven; **ex alto** farfetched
ālūcĭn·or -ārī *vi* to indulge in small talk, ramble
alumn·a -ae *f* foster daughter; pupil
alumn·us -ī *m* foster son; pupil
alūt·a -ae *f* soft leather; shoe; purse
alveār·ĭum -ĭī or **ī** *n* beehive
alveŏl·us -ī *m* tray, basin; bed of a stream; game board
alvĕ·us -ī *m* hollow, cavity; tub; bathtub; riverbed; hull of boat, boat; game board; beehive
alv·us -ī *m* belly, bowels, stomach; womb; boat; beehive
amābĭl·is -e *adj* lovable, lovely, attractive, pleasant
amābilĭt·ās -ātis *f* charm
amābilĭter *adv* lovingly, delightfully
Amalthē·a -ae *f* nymph who fed infant Jupiter with goat's milk; sibyl at Cumae
āmandātī·ō -ōnis *f* sending away
āmand·ō -āre *vt* to send away, remove
am·ans -antis *adj* loving, affectionate; **amans patriae** patriotic; *m* lover
amanter *adv* lovingly, affectionately
amārăc·us -ī *m* or *f* marjoram
amarant·us -ī *m* amaranth
amārē *adv* bitterly
amāritī·ēs -ēī *f* bitterness
amāritūd·ō -ĭnis *f* bitterness; sadness, sorrow, trouble
amār·or -ōris *m* bitterness
amār·us -a -um *adj* bitter; *n pl* disappointments
amās·ĭus -ĭī or **-ī** *m* lover

amāti·ō -ōnis *f* love affair
amāt·or -ōris *m* lover, friend; **amator patriae** patriot
amātorcŭl·us -ī *m* poor little lover
amātōrĭ·us -a -um *adj* erotic, love; *n* love charm
amātr·ix -īcis *f* mistress, girl friend
Amāz·ōn -ŏnis *or* **Amāzŏn·is -ĭdis** *f* Amazon (*member of mythical female warrior tribe dwelling in the Caucasus*)
ambact·us -ī *m* vassal
ambāg·ēs -is *f* winding, labyrinth; double-talk, evasion, digression; ambiguity, obscurity; **per ambages** enigmatically
amb·ĕdō -esse -ēdī -ēsum *vt* to eat up; (of fire) to char; to waste
ambĭg·ō -ĕre *vt* to go around, avoid; *vi* to waver, hesitate, be undecided; to argue, debate, wrangle; **ambigitur** it is uncertain
ambigŭē *adv* doubtfully, indecisively
ambiguĭt·ās -ātis *f* ambiguity, double meaning
ambigŭ·us -a -um *adj* wavering, changeable; uncertain, doubtful; disputed; unreliable, untrustworthy; ambiguous, dark, obscure; *n* doubt, uncertainty, paradox
amb·ĭō -īre *vt* to go around, encircle; (pol) ot canvass; to entreat, solicit, court
ambitĭ·ō -ōnis *f* (pol) campaigning (*by lawful means*); popularity, flattery; ambition (*in good or bad sense*); partiality, favortism; pomp, ostentation
ambitiōsē *adv* ostentatiously; from a desire to please
ambitiōs·us -a -um *adj* winding, entwining; publicity-conscious, eager for popularity, ambitious; ostentatious
ambĭt·us -ūs *m* winding, revolution; circuit, circumference, border, orbit; (pol) illegal campaigning, bribery; pomp, ostentation; circumlocution; (rhet) period
amb·ō -ae -ō *adj* both, two; *pron* both, the two
Ambracĭ·a -ae *f* district of Epirus in N.W. Greece
ambrosĭ·us -a -um *adj* ambrosial, divine, immortal; *f* food of the gods
ambūbāĭ·a -ae *f* Syrian flute player
ambulācr·um -ī *n* walk, avenue
ambulātĭ·ō -ōnis *f* (act) walk; (place) walk
ambulātiuncŭl·a -ae *f* short walk; (place) small promenade
ambulāt·or -ōris *m* peddler; idler
ambŭl·ō -āre *vt* to traverse, travel; *vi* to walk, take a walk; to march, travel; to strut
amb·ūrō -ūrĕre -ussī -ustum *vt* to burn up, scorch, singe; to consume; to numb, nip
amell·us -ī *m* wild aster
ām·ens -entis *adj* out of one's mind, mad; foolish, stupid
āmentĭ·a -ae *f* madness; folly
āment·ō -āre *vt* to fit (*a javelin*) with a strap
āment·um -ī *n* strap
am·es -ĭtis *m* pole for fowler's net
amethystĭn·us -a -um *adj* dressed in purple; *n pl* purple garments
amethyst·us -ī *f* amethyst
amīc·a -ae *f* girl friend, lady friend
amīcē *adv* in a friendly manner
amic·ĭō -īre -ŭī -tum *vt* to wrap around; to cover, clothe, wrap
amīcĭter *adv* in a friendly way
amīcitĭ·a -ae *f* friendship
amict·us -ūs *m* wrap, cloak; style, fashion (*in dress*)
amīcŭl·a -ae *f* girl friend
amīcŭl·um -ī *n* wrap, mantle
amīcŭl·us -ī *m* pal, buddy
amīc·us -a -um *adj* friendly; *m* friend; patron
āmĭgr·ō -āre *vi* to move away, emigrate
āmissĭ·ō -ōnis *f* loss
amĭt·a -ae *f* aunt (*father's sister*)
ā·mittō -mittĕre -mīsī -missum *vt* to lose, let slip; **fidem amittere** to break one's word
amnicŏl·a -ae *m* or *f* riverside plant (*e.g., willow tree*)
amnicŭl·us -ī *m* brook
amn·is -is *m* river; **secundo amni** downstream
am·ō -āre *vt* to love, like, be fond of; to fall in love with; **amabo** or **amabo te** (coll) please
amoenē *adv* charmingly
amoenĭt·ās -ātis *f* charm
amoen·us -a -um *adj* charming, pleasant; *n pl* charming sights
amōl·ĭor -īrī *vt* to remove; to put aside, put away; **se amoliri** to remove oneself, clear out
amōm·um -ī *n* amomum plant (*aromatic shrub*)
am·or or **am·ōs -ōris** *m* love, affection; object of affection, love; Cupid; *m pl* love affair
āmōtĭ·ō -ōnis *f* removal
ā·movĕō -movēre -mōvī -mōtum *vt* to remove, withdraw, put away, put aside; to steal; **se amovere** to retire, withdraw
Amphiarā·üs -ī *m* famous Greek seer
amphibolĭ·a -ae *f* (rhet) ambiguity
Amphī·ōn -ŏnis *m* son of Antiope by Jupiter, twin brother of Zethus, king of Thebes, and husband of Niobe
amphitheātr·um -ī *n* amphitheater
Amphitrȳ·ō or **Amphitrȳ·ōn -ōnis** *m* husband of Alcmena
Amphitryōniăd·ēs -is *m* Hercules
amphŏr·a -ae *f* amphora; liquid measure (*about* 7 *gallons*)
amplē *adv* largely, abundantly, broadly, spaciously; splendidly
am·plector -plectī -plexus sum *vt* to embrace, entwine, enclose, encircle; to grab, get hold of; to understand, comprehend; to embrace, include, comprise; to sum up; to em-

brace affectionately, esteem, cling to; (mil) to occupy, cover
amplex·ō -āre or **amplex·or -ārī -ātus sum** *vt* to embrace; to honor, esteem
amplex·us -ūs *m* circuit; embrace, caress
amplificātī·ō -ōnis *f* extension, enlargement; (rhet) amplification, development
amplificāt·or -ōris *m* enlarger, amplifier
amplificē *adv* splendidly
amplific·ō -āre *vt* to enlarge, extend, widen; to increase; (rhet) to enlarge upon, develop
amplĭ·ō -āre *vt* to widen, enlarge; to enhance; to postpone (*judgment*), adjourn (*court, in order to gather further evidence*); to remand
amplĭter *adv* splendidly
amplitūd·ō -ĭnis *f* width, size, bulk, extent; greatness, dignity, importance, high rank; (rhet) development, amplification
amplĭus *adv* any further, any more, any longer, besides; further, more, longer; **amplius uno die** one day longer; longer than one day; **nec amplius** no longer
amplĭus *adj* (neuter comparative of **amplus**) more, further, else; (with numerals) more than; **hoc amplius** this further point; **nihil amplius** nothing further, no more; **quid amplius** what more, what else; *n* more, a larger amount; **amplius negoti** more trouble
ampl·us -a -um *adj* ample, large, wide, spacious; strong, great, powerful; grand, imposing, splendid; eminent, prominent, illustrious, distinguished
ampull·a -ae *f* bottle, jar, flask; bombast
ampullār·ĭus -ĭī or **-ī** *m* flask maker
ampull·or -ārī -ātus sum *vi* to be bombastic
amputātĭ·ō -ōnis *f* pruning
ampŭt·ō -āre *vt* to lop off, prune; to curtail, shorten; **amputata loqui** to speak disconnectedly
Amūl·ĭus -ĭī or **-ī** *m* king of Alba Longa, brother of Numitor, and granduncle of Romulus and Remus
amurc·a -ae *f* dregs of oil
amygdăl·a -ae *f* almond tree
amygdăl·um -ī *n* almond
amyst·is -ĭdis *f* drinking bottoms up
an *conj* (introducing the latter clause of a disjunctive direct or indirect question) or
anabăthr·a -ōrum *n pl* bleachers
Anăcrĕ·ōn -ōntis *m* famous lyric poet of Teos (*fl* 540 B.C.)
anadēm·a -ătis *n* fillet, headband
anagnost·ēs -ae *m* reader, reciter
analectr·is -ĭdis *f* shoulder pad (*to improve the figure*)
anapaest·us -a -um *adj* anapestic; *m* anapest; *n* poem in anapestic meter
an·as -ătis *f* duck; **anas fluvialis** wild duck
anaticŭl·a -ae *f* duckling
anatīn·us -a -um *adj* duck's
anatocism·us -ī *m* compound interest
Anaxagŏr·ās -ae *m* Greek philosopher of Clazomenae, teacher of Pericles and Euripides (500?-428 B.C.)
Anaximand·er -rī *m* Greek philosopher of Miletus (610-547 B.C.)
Anaximĕn·ēs -is *m* Greek philosopher of Miletus (*fl* 544 B.C.)
an·ceps -cipĭtis *adj* two-headed; two-edged; twin-peaked; amphibious; double, twofold; doubtful, undecided, ambiguous; hazardous, critical; *n* danger, peril
Anchīs·ēs -ae *m* son of Capys and father of Aeneas
Anchīsiăd·ēs -ae *m* son of Anchises, Aeneas
ancīl·e -is *n* oval shield said to have fallen from heaven in reign of Numa, second king of Rome
ancill·a -ae *f* maidservant
ancillār·is -e *adj* maidservant's
ancillŭl·a -ae *f* young slave (*female*)
ancŏr·a -ae *f* anchor
ancorāl·e -is *n* cable
ancorārĭ·us -a -um *adj* of an anchor
Ancȳr·a -ae *f* Ankara, capital of Galatia
andabăt·a -ae *m* blindfold gladiator
And·ēs -ium *f pl* village near Mantua, birthplace of Virgil
androgȳn·us -ī *m* or **androgȳn·ē -ēs** *f* hermaphrodite
Andromăch·a -ae or **Andromăch·ē ēs** *f* Hector's wife
Andromĕd·a -ae *f* daughter of Cepheus and Cassiope, rescued from a sea monster by Perseus
andr·ōn -ōnis *m* corridor
Andronīc·us -ī *m* Lucius Livius Andronicus (*fl* 241 B.C., *first epic and dramatic poet of the Romans*)
Andr·os -ī *f* Aegean island
ānell·us -ī *m* little ring
anēth·um -ī *n* anise, dill
anfract·us -ūs *m* curve, bend (*of road*); orbit; digression, prolixity
angell·us -ī *m* small corner
angĭn·a -ae *f* tonsillitis, inflamation of the throat
angiport·us -ūs *m* or **angiport·um -ī** *n* alley
ang·ō -ĕre *vt* to choke, throttle; to distress, tease, trouble
ang·or -ōris *m* strangling, suffocation; anguish
anguicŏm·us -a -um *adj* snake-haired
anguicŭl·us -ī *m* small snake
anguĭf·er -ĕra -ĕrum *adj* snaky
anguigĕn·a -ae *m* offspring of a dragon; Theban
anguill·a -ae *f* eel
anguinĕ·us -a -um *adj* snaky; serpent-like
anguīn·us -a -um *adj* snaky

anguĭp·ēs -ĕdis *adj* serpent-footed
angu·is -is *m* or *f* snake, serpent
Angu·is -is *m* or *f* Dragon, Hydra (*constellation*)
Anguitĕn·ens -entis *m* Ophiuchus (*constellation*)
angulār·is -e *adj* angular
angulāt·us -a -um *adj* angular
angŭl·us -ī *m* angle, corner; nook, recess; **ad parīs angulos** at right angles
angustē *adv* within narrow limits, closely, hardly, scarcely; briefly, concisely
angustĭ·ae -ārum *f pl* narrow place, defile; narrow passage, strait; (fig) shortness; scarcity, want, deficiency; difficulty, tight spot, perplexity, distress, straits; narrow-mindedness
angusticlāvĭ·us -a -um *adj* wearing a narrow purple stripe
angust·ō -āre *vt* to make narrow
angust·us -a -um *adj* narrow, close, short, brief (*time*); scanty (*means*); difficult, critical; narrow-minded; base, mean; *n* narrowness; critical condition, danger
anhēlĭt·us -ūs *m* panting, difficulty in breathing, puffing; breath, breathing; vapor
anhēl·ō -āre *vt* to breathe out; to pant after; *vi* to pant, puff; to exhale; (of fire) to roar
anhēl·us -a -um *adj* panting, puffing
anicŭl·a -ae *f* little old woman, silly old woman
Aniēns·is -e or **Aniēn·us -a -um** *adj* of the Anio (*tributary of the Tiber*)
anīl·is -e *adj* of an old woman
anīlĭt·ās -ātis *f* old age (*of women*)
anīlĭter *adv* like an old woman
anĭm·a -ae *f* air, wind, breeze; breath; breath of life, life; soul (*as the principle of life, opposed to* **animus** *as the principle of thought and feelings*); spirit, ghost
animadversĭ·ō -ōnis *f* attention, observation; reproach, criticism; punishment
animadvers·or -ōris *m* observer
animad·vertō or **animad·vortō -vertĕre -vertī -versum** *vt* to pay attention to, attend to; to notice, observe, realize; to reproach, criticize; to punish
anĭm·al -ālis *n* animal; living creature
animāl·is -e *adj* consisting of air; animate, living
anim·ans -antis *adj* living, animate; *m & f & n* living being; animal
animātĭ·ō -ōnis *f* living being
animāt·us -a -um *adj* courageous; inclined, disposed; (with **erga** or **in** + *acc*) disposed toward
anĭm·ō -āre *vt* to make alive, to animate; to encourage
animōsē *adv* courageously; eagerly
animōs·us -a -um *adj* full of air, airy; full of life, living, animate; blowing violently; full of courage, bold, spirited, undaunted; proud
animŭl·a -ae *f* little soul, life
animŭl·us -ī *m* darling
anĭm·us -ī *m* soul (*as principle of intellection and sensation, whereas* **anima** *is soul as principle of life*); intellect, understanding, mind, thought, reason; memory; knowledge; sense, consciousness; judgment, opinion; imagination; heart, feelings, passions; spirit, courage, morale; disposition, character; pride, haughtiness; will, purpose, desire, inclination; pleasure, delight; confident hope; **aequo animo** patiently, calmly; **animi causā** for amusement; **bono animo esse** to take heart; **ex animo** from the bottom of the heart, sincerely; **ex animo effluere** to slip one's mind; **in animo habere** (*with inf*) to intend to; **meo animo** in my opinion
Anĭ·ō -ēnis *m* tributary of the Tiber
An·ĭus -ĭī or **-ī** *m* king and priest on Delos who welcomed Aeneas
annāl·is -e *adj* lasting a year, annual; **lex annalis** law fixing minimum age for holding public offices; *m pl* annals, chronicle
annăt·ō -āre *vi* (with *dat* or **ad** + *acc*) to swim to
anne *conj* (pleonastic form of **an**) or
an·nectō -nectĕre -nexŭī -nexum *vt* (with *dat* or **ad** + *acc*) to tie, connect, annex (*something*) to; (with *dat*) to apply (*something*) to
annex·us -ūs *m* connection
annicŭl·us -a -um *adj* one year old, yearling
an·nītor -nītī -nīsus sum or **nixus sum** *vi* (with *dat* or **ad** + *acc*) to press against, lean on; (with **ut** or *inf*) to strive to
anniversārĭ·us -a -um *adj* annual, yearly
ann·ō -āre *vi* (with *dat*, with **ad** + *acc*, or with *acc* of limit of motion) to swim to or towards; (with *dat*) to swim with or along with
annōn *conj* or not
annōn·a -ae *f* year's crop; grain; price of grain; cost of living; high price
annōs·us -a -um *adj* aged, old
annotātĭ·ō -ōnis *f* notation, remark
annōtĭn·us -a -um *adj* last year's
annŏt·ō -āre *vt* to write down, note down; to comment on; to observe, perceive
annumĕr·ō -āre *vt* (with *dat*) to count out (*money*) to; (with *dat* or **in** + *acc*) to add (*something*) to, to include (*someone*) among
annuntĭ·ō -āre *vt* to announce, make known, proclaim
an·nŭō -nuĕre -nŭī -nūtum *vt* to designate by a nod; to indicate, declare; (with *dat*) to promise, grant (*something*) to; *vi* to nod, nod as-

sent; (with *dat*) to nod assent to, to be favorable to, smile on
ann·us -ī *m* year; season; age, time of life; year of office; **ad annum** for the coming year, a year hence; **annum** or **in annum** for a year; **per annos** year to year
annŭ·us -a -um *adj* lasting a year; annual, yearly; *n pl* yearly pay, pension
an·quīrō -quīrĕre -quīsīvī -quīsītum *vt* to search carefully; to examine, inquire into; (with *genit* or *abl* of the charge) to accuse (*someone*) of; *vi* to hold an inquest
ans·a -ae *f* handle; opportunity
ansāt·us -a -um *adj* having handles; **homo ansatus** man with arms akimbo
ans·er -ĕris *m* gander
ante *adv* before, previously; in front, forwards
ante *prep* (with *acc*) before; more than, above
antĕā *adv* before, previously, formerly
ante·capĭō -capĕre -cēpī -ceptum *vt* to receive beforehand; to take possession of beforehand, preoccupy; to anticipate
ante·cēdō -cēdĕre -cessī -cessum *vt* to precede; to excel, surpass; *vi* (with *dat*) **a** to have precedence over; **b** to excel, surpass
antecessĭ·ō -ōnis *f* antecedent cause
antecess·or -ōris *m* (mil) scout; *m pl* advance guard
antecurs·or -ōris *m* (mil) scout; *m pl* advance guard
ante·ĕō -īre -iī *vt* to precede; to excel, surpass; to anticipate, prevent; *vi* to precede; to take the lead; (with *dat*) **a** to go before; **b** to excel, surpass
ante·fĕrō -ferre -tŭlī -lātum *vt* to prefer; to anticipate
antefix·us -a -um *pp* of **antefigo;** *n pl* images, statues, etc., affixed to roofs and gutters of homes or temples
ante·gredĭor -grĕdī -gressus sum *vt* to precede
antehab·ĕō -ēre *vt* to prefer
antĕhāc *adv* before this time, before now, formerly
antelātus *pp* of **antefero**
antelūcān·us -a -um *adj* before dawn
antemerīdiān·us -a -um *adj* before noon
ante·mittō -mittĕre -mīsī -missum *vt* to send out ahead
antenn·a -ae *f* yardarm, sail yard
Antēn·or -ŏris *m* Trojan who after the fall of Troy went to Italy and founded Patavium
antepīlān·ī -ōrum *m pl* front ranks, front line
ante·pōnō -pōnĕre -posŭī -positum *vt* to prefer; to serve (*food*)
antepŏt·ens -entis *adj* very wealthy
antĕquam or **ante . . . quam** *conj* before
Antĕr·ōs -ōtis *m* avenger of unrequited love
ant·ēs -ium *m pl* rows (*e.g., of vines*)
antesignān·us -ī *m* soldier who fought in front of the standards to defend them; leader, commander
ante·stō or **anti·stō -stāre -stĕtī** *vi* to excel, be distinguished; (with *dat*) to be superior to
antest·or -ārī -ātus sum *vt* to call as witness
ante·venĭō -venīre -vēnī -ventum *vt* to anticipate, thwart; to surpass, excel; *vi* to become more distinguished; (with *dat*) **a** to anticipate; **b** to surpass, excel
ante·vertō -vertĕre -vertī -versum *vt* to go or come before, precede; to anticipate; to prefer
antevŏl·ō -āre *vi* to dash out ahead
anticipātĭ·ō -ōnis *f* preconception, foreknowledge
anticĭp·ō -āre *vt* to anticipate
antīc·us -a -um *adj* front, foremost
Antigŏn·ē -ēs *f* daughter of Theban king Oedipus; daughter of Trojan king Laomedon
Antilŏch·us -ī *m* son of Nestor, killed by Hector at Troy
Antiphăt·ēs -ae *m* king of the Laestrygones, who sank the fleet of Greeks returning from Troy with Ulysses
antīquārĭ·us -a -um *adj & m* antiquarian
antīquē *adv* in former times; in the good old style
antīquĭt·ās -ātis *f* antiquity; men of former times, the ancients; the good old days
antīquĭtus *adv* in former times, of old; from ancient times; in the old style
antīqu·ō -āre *vt* to reject (*law, bill*)
antīqu·us -a -um *adj* old, ancient; oldfashioned, venerable; *m pl* ancients, ancient authors; *n* antiquity; old custom
antist·es -ĭtis *m* priest presiding over temple, high priest
antist·es -ĭtis or **antistĭt·a -ae** *f* priestess presiding over temple, high priestess
Antisthĕn·ēs -is or **-ae** *m* pupil of Socrates and founder of Cynic philosophy
antithĕt·on -ī *n* (rhet) antithesis
antr·um -ī *n* cave, cavern
ānulār·ĭus -iī or **-ī** *m* ring maker
ānulāt·us -a -um *adj* wearing a ring
ānŭl·us -ī *m* ring, signet ring
ān·us -ī *m* anus, rectum; ring
an·us -ūs *f* old woman; hag
anxiē *adv* uneasily
anxiĕt·ās -ātis *f* anxiety, trouble
anxĭf·er -ĕra -ĕrum *adj* causing anxiety
anxĭ·us -a -um *adj* worried, troubled; disquieting

apăge *interj* go on!; scram!
apēliōt·ēs -ae *m* east wind
Apell·ēs -is *m* famous Greek painter (*fl 4th cent.* B.C.)
ap·er -rī *m* boar
aper·iō -īre -ŭī -tum *vt* to uncover, open, lay bare, disclose, reveal; to prove, demonstrate; to explain, recount
apertē *adv* openly, frankly, candidly
apert·ō -āre *vt* to keep on laying bare
apert·us -a -um *pp* of **aperio;** *adj* bare, uncovered, exposed; without decks; clear (*style*); frank, candid (*character*); manifest, plain, evident; accessible, unobstructed; *n* open space; **in aperto** in the open; **in aperto esse** to be clear, evident, well known, notorious
ap·ex -ĭcis *m* point, top, summit; hat, cap, crown; crowning glory
aphract·us -ī *f* or **aphract·um -ī** *n* ship without deck
apiār·ĭus -ĭī or **-ī** *m* beekeeper
apicŭl·a -ae *f* little bee
ap·is -is *f* bee
ap·iscor -iscī -tus sum *vt* to pursue; to take, reach, gain, get
ap·ĭum -ĭī or **-ī** *n* celery
aplustr·e -is *n* stern
apoclēt·ī -ōrum *m pl* select committee (*of Aetolian League*)
apodytēr·ĭum -ĭī or **-ī** *n* dressing room (*at a bath*)
apolactiz·ō -āre *vt* to kick aside, scorn
Apoll·ō -ĭnis *m* son of Jupiter and Latona, twin brother of Diana, god of the sun, divination, archery, healing, poetry, and music
Apollodōr·us -ī *m* famous rhetorician, teacher of Augustus; famous Athenian grammarian and author of an extant work on mythology (*fl* 140 B.C.)
apolŏg·us -ī *m* story, fable
apophorēt·a -ōrum *n pl* presents for house guests
aposphrāgism·a -ătis *n* device on signet ring, seal
apothēc·a -ae *f* warehouse, storehouse, magazine
apparātē *adv* with much preparation, sumptuously
apparātĭ·ō -ōnis *f* preparation
apparāt·us -a -um *adj* prepared, well prepared; sumptuous
apparāt·us -ūs *m* getting or making ready, preparing, providing; equipment, apparatus, paraphernalia; pomp, magnificence
appār·ĕō -ēre -ŭī -ĭtum *vi* to appear, become visible; to be seen, show oneself; (with *dat*) to wait on, serve; **apparet** it is evident, clear, certain
appāritĭ·ō -ōnis *f* attendance, service; *f pl* household servants
appārĭt·or -ōris *m* servant; attendant of public official (*e.g., aide, lictor, secretary*)
appăr·ō -āre *vt* to prepare, make ready, provide
appellātĭ·ō -ōnis *f* addressing; appeal; naming, calling by name; name, title; pronunciation
ap·pellō -pellĕre -pŭlī -pulsum *vt* (with *dat* or **ad** + *acc*) to drive (*something*) to, steer (*ship*) to; *vi* (*of ship*) to land
appell·ō -āre *vt* to accost, address; to appeal to; (law) to sue; to name, call; to mention by name; to pronounce
appendicŭl·a -ae *f* small addition
append·ix -ĭcis *f* addition, supplement
ap·pendō -pendĕre -pendī -pensum *vt* to weigh; to pay out; (fig) to weigh, consider
appĕt·ens -entis *adj* greedy, avaricious; (with *genit*) eager for, craving
appetenter *adv* eagerly, greedily
appetentĭ·a -ae *f* craving, desire; (with *genit*) craving for, desire for
appetītĭ·ō -ōnis *f* grasping, craving; (with *genit*) grasping at, craving for
appetīt·us -ūs *m* craving, desire; *m pl* appetites, passions
appĕt·ō -ĕre -īvī -ītum *vt* to try to reach; to lay hold of; to make for, head for; to attack, assail, assault; *vi* to approach, draw near
apping·ō -ĕre *vt* to paint; to write
ap·plaudō -plaudĕre -plausī -plausum *vt* (with *dat*) to strike (*something*) against; *vi* to applaud
applicātĭ·ō -ōnis *f* applying, application
applicāt·us -a -um *adj* (with **ad** + *acc*) inclined to; (with *dat*) lying close to, attached to
applicĭt·us -a -um *adj* (with *dat*) applied or joined to, attached to
applĭc·ō -āre -āvī or **-ŭī -ātum** or **ĭtum** *vt* to bring in close contact; (with *dat* or **ad** + *acc*) **a** to apply, attach, add, join (*something*) to; **b** to steer (*ship*) toward; **c** to devote (*attention, mind*) to
applōr·ō -āre *vt* to deplore, lament
ap·pōnō -pōnĕre -posŭī -posĭtum *vt* to serve (*food*); (with *dat* or **ad** + *acc*) to put or lay (*something*) near, at, or beside; (with *dat*) **a** to set (*food*) before; **b** to appoint or designate (*someone*) to (*a duty, task*); **c** to reckon (*something*) as
apporrect·us -a -um *adj* stretched out
apport·ō -āre *vt* to carry or bring up; to cause; (with *dat*) to carry (*something*) to
apposc·ō -ĕre *vt* to demand in addition
apposĭtē *adv* appropriately, pertinently
apposĭt·us -a -um *pp* of **appono;** *adj* fit, suitable, appropriate; (with *dat*) situated near, continguous with, bordering on; (with **ad** + *acc*) suited to, fit for
appōt·us -a -um *adj* drunk

apprĕc·or -ārī -ātus sum *vt* to pray to, worship
appre·hendō -hendĕre -hendī -hensum *vt* to seize, take hold of; (mil) to occupy
apprīmē *adv* chiefly, especially
ap·prĭmō -primĕre -pressī -pressum *vt* (with *dat*) to press (*something*) close to
approbātĭ·ō -ōnis *f* approbation, approval; proof
approbāt·or -ōris *m* one who seconds or approves
apprŏbē *adv* very well
apprŏb·ō -āre *vt* to approve; to prove
appromitt·ō -ĕre *vt* to promise in addition
appropĕr·ō -āre *vt* to hasten, speed up; *vi* to hurry
appropinquātĭ·ō -ōnis *f* approach
appropinqu·ō -āre *vi* to approach; (with *dat* or **ad** + *acc*) to come near to, approach
appugn·ō -āre *vt* to fight, attack
appuls·us -ūs *m* landing, approach
aprīcātĭ·ō -ōnis *f* basking in the sun
aprīc·or -ārī *vi* to bask, sun oneself
aprīc·us -a -um *adj* sunny; *n* sunny spot
Aprīl·is *adj* of April; **mensis Aprilis** April, month of April
aprugn·us -a -um *adj* of a wild boar
aps- = **abs-**
apsūmēd·ō -ĭnis *f* devouring
aptē *adv* closely; suitably
apt·ō -āre *vt* to fasten, fit, adjust; to make ready, equip
apt·us -a -um *adj* suitable, adapted, appropriate, proper
apud *prep* (with *acc*) at, by, near, among; at the house of; before, in the presence of; in the writings of; over, (with influence) over
Āpūlĭ·a -ae *f* district in S.W. Italy
aqu·a -ae *f* water; *f pl* baths, spa; **aquā et igni interdicere** to outlaw; **aquam praebere** (with *dat*) to entertain (*guests*)
aquaeduct·us -ūs *m* aqueduct
aquālicŭl·us -ī *m* belly, stomach
aquāl·is -e *adj* of water; *m & f* washbasin
aquārĭ·us -a -um *adj* of water; *m* water-conduit inspector
Aquār·ĭus -ĭī or **-ī** *m* Aquarius (*constellation; sign of the Zodiac*)
aquātĭc·us -a -um *adj* growing in water; watery, moist, humid
aquātĭl·is -e *adj* living or growing in water, aquatic
aquātĭ·ō -ōnis *f* fetching water; water hole
aquāt·or -ōris *m* water carrier
aquĭl·a -ae *f* eagle (*bird; Roman legionary standard*); (fig) legion; gable of house
aquĭl·ex -ĕgis *m* water finder, douser; water-conduit inspector
aquilĭf·er -ĕrī *m* standard-bearer
aquilīn·us -a -um *adj* eagle's
aquĭl·ō -ōnis *m* north wind; north
aquilōnĭ·us -a -um *adj* northerly
aquĭl·us -a -um *adj* swarthy
Aquīn·um -ī *n* town of the Volsci, birthplace of Juvenal
Aquītānĭ·a -ae *f* province in S.W. Gaul
aqu·or -ārī -ātus sum *vi* to fetch water
aquōs·us -a -um *adj* rainy, humid, full of water
aquŭl·a -ae *f* small stream, brook
ār·a -ae *f* altar
Ār·a -ae *f* Altar (*constellation*)
arabarch·ēs -ae *m* customs officer in Egypt
Arabĭ·a -ae *f* Arabia
Arabĭc·us or **Arabĭ·us** or **Arăb·us -a -um** *adj* Arabian
Arachn·ē -ēs *f* Lydian girl whom Minerva changed into a spider
arānĕ·a -ae *f* spider; cobweb
arāneŏl·a -ae *f* small spider
arāneŏl·us -ī *m* small spider
arāneōs·us -a -um *adj* full of cobwebs
arānĕ·us -a -um *adj* spider's; *m* spider; *n* spider web
Ar·ar -ăris *m* tributary of the Rhone
arātĭ·ō -ōnis *f* cultivation, tilling, agriculture; arable land
arātiuncŭl·a -ae *f* small plot, small farm
arāt·or -ōris *m* farmer; *m pl* farmers on state-owned land
arātr·um -ī *n* plow
Arāt·us -ī *m* Greek author of poem on astronomy (*fl* 270 B.C.)
arbĭt·er -rī *m* eyewitness; arbiter, judge, umpire; ruler, director, controller
arbĭtr·a -ae *f* eyewitness (*female*)
arbitrārĭō *adv* uncertainly
arbitrārĭ·us -a -um *adj* uncertain
arbitrāt·us -ūs *m* decision; inclination, pleasure; direction, guidance
arbitr·ĭum -ĭī or **-ī** *n* decision, judgment; mastery, power, control, authority
arbĭtr·or -ārī -ātus sum *vt & vi* to decide or judge (*as an arbiter*); to testify; to think, suppose
arb·or or **arb·ōs -ŏris** *f* tree; mast, oar, ship; gallows
arborĕ·us -a -um *adj* of a tree; treelike
arbust·us -a -um *adj* wooded, planted with trees; *n* orchard; vineyard planted with trees; *n pl* trees
arbutĕ·us -a -um *adj* of arbutus
arbŭt·um -ī *n* fruit of arbutus
arbŭt·us -ī *f* arbutus, strawberry tree
arc·a -ae *f* chest, box, safe; coffin; prison cell
Arcadĭ·a -ae *f* district of central Peloponnesus
arcānō *adv* in secret, privately
arcān·us -a -um *adj* secret, concealed, private; *n* secret; sacred mystery
arc·ĕō -ēre -ŭī *vt* to shut up, en-

close; to keep at a distance, keep off; to hinder, prevent; (with *abl* or **ab** + *abl*) to keep (*someone*) off, away from
arcessīt·us -a -um *pp* of **arcesso;** *adj* farfetched
arcessīt·us -ūs *m* summons
arcess·ō -ĕre -īvī -ītum *vt* to send for, fetch, summon; (law) to arraign; to derive
archetўp·us -a -um *adj & n* original
Archilŏch·us -ī Greek iambic poet of Paros (*c.* 714-676 B.C.)
archimagīr·us -ī *m* chief cook
Archimēd·ēs -is *m* scientist and mathematician of Syracuse (287-212 B.C.)
archipīrāt·a -ae *m* pirate captain
architect·ōn -ŏnis *m* architect, master builder; master in cunning
architect·or -ārī -ātus sum *vt* to build, construct
architectūr·a -ae *f* architecture
architect·us -ī *m* architect; deviser, author, inventor, contriver
arch·ōn -ŏntis *m* archon (*chief magistrate in Athens*)
arcitĕn·ens -entis *adj* holding a bow, wearing a bow
Arcitĕn·ens -entis *m* Archer (*constellation*)
Arctophȳl·ax -ăcis *m* Boötes (*constellation*)
Arct·os -ī *m* the Great and Little Bear (*double constellation*)
arct·os -ī *m* North Pole; North; north wind; night
Arctūr·us -ī *m* brightest star in Boötes
arcŭl·a -ae *f* small box, jewelry box; (rhet) ornament
arcŭ·ō -āre *vt* to curve
arc·us -ūs *m* bow; rainbow; curve; arch, triumphal arch
Ardĕ·a -ae *f* town in Latium
ardĕ·a -ae *f* heron
ardelĭ·ō -ōnis *m* busybody
ard·ens -entis *adj* blazing, burning, hot, fiery; gleaming, glittering; smarting, burning; (of emotions) glowing, hot, ardent
ardenter *adv* ardently, eagerly, passionately
ardĕō ardēre arsī *vi* to be on fire, burn, blaze; to flash, glow; to smart, burn
ardesc·ō -ĕre *vi* to catch fire; to gleam, glitter; (of passions) to become more intense, increase in violence
ard·or -ōris *m* heat, flame; flashing, brightness; heat (*of passions*); loved one, flame
ardŭ·us -a -um *adj* steep, high; difficult; *n* difficulty
ārĕ·a -ae *f* open space; park, playground; building site; threshing floor
arēna see **harena**
ār·ĕō -ēre *vi* to be dry; to be thirsty
āreŏl·a *f* small open space
Arēopăg·us -ī *m* criminal court in Athens; hill where criminal court met
Ar·ēs -is *m* Greek god of war
āresc·ō -ĕre *vi* to become dry; to wither
aretālŏg·us -ī *m* braggart
Arethūs·a -ae *f* nymph pursued by river god Alpheus in Peloponnesus and changed by Diana into a fountain; fountain near Syracuse
Argē·ī -ōrum *m pl* consecrated places in Rome ascribed to Numa; figures of men, made of rushes and thrown annually into the Tiber
argentārĭ·us -a -um *adj* silver; financial, pecuniary; *m* banker; *f* banking; bank; silver mine
argentāt·us -a -um *adj* plated or ornamented with silver
argenteŏl·us -a -um *adj* made of pretty silver
argentĕ·us -a -um *adj* silver, silvery
argent·um -ī *n* silver; silver plate; money
Argē·us or **Argīv·us** or **Argolĭc·us -a -um** *adj* Argive; Greek
Arg·ī -ōrum *m pl* Argos, town in N.E. Peloponnesus
Argīlēt·um -ī *n* district in Rome between the Quirinal and Capitoline
argill·a -ae *f* clay
Arg·ō -ūs *f* Jason's ship
Argŏl·is -ĭdis *f* district around Argos
Argonaut·ae -ārum *m pl* argonauts
Argos *n* (only *nom* and *acc*) Argos
argūmentātĭ·ō -ōnis *f* argumentation; proof
argūment·or -ārī -ātus sum *vt* to adduce as proof; (with **de** + *abl*) to conclude from; *vi* to bring evidence
argūment·um -ī *n* evidence, proof, argument; theme, plot; topic; subject, motif (*of artistic representation*)
arg·ŭō -uĕre -ŭī -ūtum *vt* to prove; to reveal, betray; to accuse, charge, impeach (*person*), find fault with (*thing*)
Arg·us -ī *n* many-eyed monster set over Io and killed by Mercury
argūtē *adv* subtly; craftily
argūtĭ·ae -ārum *f pl* subtlety; brightness, genius, cunning, shrewdness
argūtŭl·us -a -um *adj* somewhat subtle
argūt·us -a -um *adj* clearcut, clear, bright, distinct; penetrating, piercing; chatty; acute, subtle; bright, smart, witty; cunning, sly
argyrasp·is -ĭdis *adj* wearing a silver shield
Ariadn·a -ae *f* daughter of Minos, king of Crete, who extricated Theseus from the labyrinth
Arĭcĭ·a -ae *f* town in Latium on the Via Appia
āridŭl·us -a -um *adj* somewhat dry

ārĭd·us -a -um *adj* dry, parched, withered; meager; (of style) dry, dull
arĭ·ēs -ĕtis *m* ram; battering ram; beam (*used as breakwater*)
Arĭ·ēs -ĕtis *m* Aries (*sign of the Zodiac*)
ariĕt·ō -āre *vt & vi* to butt, ram
Ariobarzān·ēs -is *m* king of Cappadocia
Arī·ōn -ŏnis *m* early Greek poet and musician, rescued from drowning by dolphin
arist·a -ae *f* ear of grain
Aristarch·us -ī *m* Alexandrine critic and scholar (*fl* 156 B.C.); stern critic
aristolochĭ·a -ae *f* birthwort
Aristophăn·ēs -is *m* the most famous Greek comic poet (*c.* 444-380 B.C.)
Aristotĕl·ēs -is *m* Aristotle (384-322 B.C.)
arithmētĭc·a -ōrum *n pl* arithmetic
āritūd·ō -ĭnis *f* dryness
arm·a -ōrum *n pl* armor, defensive arms, arms; warfare; camp life; armed men; equipment, tools
armāment·a -ōrum *n pl* ship's gear
armāmentār·ium -iī or **-ī** *n* arsenal, armory
armāriŏl·um -ī *n* little chest, little closet
armār·ium -iī or **-ī** *n* cupboard, chest
armātūr·a -ae *f* outfit, equipment, armor; light-armed troops
armāt·us -a -um *adj* armed, equipped; *m* armed man
Armenĭ·a *f* country in N.E. Asia Minor
armeniăc·um -ī *n* apricot
armeniăc·us -ī *f* apricot tree
armentāl·is -e *adj* of a herd
armentār·ius -iī or **-ī** *m* herdsman
arment·um -ī *n* herd
armĭf·er -ĕra -ĕrum *adj* armed
armĭg·er -ĕra -ĕrum *adj* armed; producing warriors; *m* armed person; armor-bearer
armill·a -ae *f* armlet, bracelet
armillāt·us -a -um *adj* wearing a bracelet
armipŏt·ens -entis *adj* powerful in arms, warlike
armisŏn·us -a -um *adj* reverberating with arms
arm·ō -āre *vt* to furnish with arms, to arm; to rouse to arms
arm·us -ī *m* shoulder, shoulder blade, upper arm; flank (*of animal*)
ar·ō -āre *vt* to plow, till
Arpīn·um -ī *n* town in Latium, birthplace of Marius and Cicero
arquāt·us -a -um *adj* jaundiced
arrect·us -a -um *pp* of **arrigo;** *adj* upright; steep, precipitous
arrēp·ō -ĕre -sī *vi* (with *dat* or **ad** + *acc*) to creep towards, steal up on
arrhăb·ō -ōnis *m* deposit (*of money*)
ar·rīdĕō -rīdēre -rīsī -rīsum *vt* to smile at; *vi* (with *dat*) **a** to smile at or on, laugh with; **b** to be favorable to; **c** to be pleasing to, please
ar·rigō -rigĕre -rexī -rectum *vt* to erect, raise; to rouse, excite
ar·ripiō -ripĕre -ripŭī -reptum *vt* to snatch, seize; (fig) to grasp quickly; (law) to arrest, arraign; to satirize
ar·rōdō -rōdĕre -rōsī -rōsum *vt* to gnaw at
arrŏg·ans -antis *adj* arrogant
arroganter *adv* arrogantly
arrogantĭ·a -ae *f* assumption, presumption; arrogance
arrŏg·ō -āre *vt* to question; to associate; to assume for oneself, claim
ars artis *f* skill; craft, trade; method, way, manner, means; artificial means; work of art; science, theory; manual, textbook; *f pl* cunning; moral qualities, character
artē *adv* closely, tightly; (to love) deeply, dearly; (to sleep) soundly
Artĕm·is -ĭdis *f* Greek counterpart of Diana
artērĭ·a -ae *f* artery; windpipe
arthrītĭc·us -a -um *adj* arthritic
articulātim *adv* piecemeal; (to speak) articulately, distinctly
articŭl·ō -āre *vt* to utter distinctly, articulate
articŭl·us -ī *m* joint, knuckle; finger; limb; (gram) clause; turning point; **in ipso articulo temporis** in the nick of time
artĭf·ex -ĭcis *adj* skillful, ingenious; artistic; broken, trained (*horse*); *m* craftsman, artist, master; originator, contriver, author
artificiōsē *adv* skillfully
artificiōs·us -a -um *adj* skillful, ingenious, accomplished; artificial
artifĭc·ium -iī or **-ī** *n* skill, workmanship; artistic work, work of art; art, profession; cleverness, cunning; theory
art·ō -āre *vt* to pack closely; to compress, contract; to limit
artolagăn·us -ī *m* cake
artopt·a -ae *m* baker; bread pan (*to bake in*)
art·us -a -um *adj* close, tight; confined, restricted; dense, firm; scanty, small, needy; strict, severe; sound, deep (*sleep*); stingy; *n* narrow space; tight spot, difficulty
art·us -ūs *m* joint; *m pl* joints, limbs
ārŭl·a -ae *f* small altar
arund·ō -ĭnis *f* reed; shaft, arrow; pipe, flute; pen; fishing rod; hobbyhorse; (in weaving) comb
arvīn·a -ae *f* grease
arv·us -a -um *adj* arable; *n* arable land, soil, land, plain, region; grain
arx arcis *f* fortress, stronghold, citadel, castle, protection, refuge, mainstay; height, summit; **arcem facere e cloaca** to make a mountain out of a molehill
ās assis *m* pound (*divisible into twelve ounces*); bronze coin; **heres ex asse** sole heir

Ascān·ĭus -ĭī or **-ī** *m* son of Aeneas and Creusa and founder of Alba Longa

ascendō ascendĕre ascendī ascensum *vt* to climb; to mount (*horse*); to board (*ship*); *vi* to climb up, ascend; (of voice) to rise; (with **ad** or **in** + *acc*) to climb, climb up to; (with **super** or **supra** + *acc*) to rise above, surpass

ascensĭ·ō -ōnis *f* climbing up, ascent

ascens·us -ūs *m* climbing up, ascent; means of ascending, approach; step, degree; (fig) climb, rise

ascĭ·a -ae *f* ax; mason's trowel

asc·ĭō -īre *vt* to associate with oneself, admit

asc·iscō -iscĕre -īvī -ītum *vt* to adopt, approve (*bill*); to adopt (*custom*); to assume, claim, arrogate; to receive, admit (*e.g., as ally, citizen, etc.*); (with **in** + *acc*) to admit (*someone*) to

ascīt·us -a -um *adj* acquired (*as opposed to innate*)

Ascr·a -ae *f* birthplace of Hesiod in Boeotia

a·scrībō -scrībĕre -scripsī -scriptum *vt* to add (*by writing*); to impute, ascribe, attribute; to enroll, register; to reckon, number, class

ascriptīcĭ·us -a -um *adj* enrolled, registered

ascriptĭ·ō -ōnis *f* addition (*in writing*)

ascriptīv·us -ī *m* (mil) reserve

ascript·or -ōris *m* supporter

asell·a -ae *f* little ass

asell·us -ī *m* little ass

Āsĭ·a -ae *f* Roman province; Asia Minor; Asia

asīl·us -ī *m* gadfly

asĭn·us -ī *m* ass; fool

Ās·is -ĭdis *f* Asia

asōt·us -ī *m* playboy

asparăg·us -ī *m* asparagus

aspargō see **aspergo**

aspectābĭl·is -e *adj* visible

aspect·ō -āre *vt* to look at, gaze at; to look with respect at; to face, lie in the direction of; to observe

aspect·us -ūs *m* look, sight, glance; sense of sight; manner of appearance, appearance, countenance

aspell·ō -ĕre *vt* to drive away

asp·er -ĕra -ĕrum *adj* rough, uneven; harsh, severe, stormy (*climate*); harsh, grating, hoarse (*sound*); pungent, strong (*smell*); rough, hard, unkind, rude (*character*); austere, rigid (*person*); wild fierce, savage (*animal*); rough, annoying, adverse (*circumstances*) rugged (*style*)

aspĕrē *adv* roughly; (fig) harshly, sternly, severely

a·spergō -spergĕre -spersī -spersum *vt* to sprinkle, scatter, taint; (with *dat*) to sprinkle (*something*) on

asperg·ō -ĭnis *f* sprinkling; spray

asperĭt·ās -ātis *f* uneveness, roughness; severity, fierceness; difficulty, trouble

aspernātĭ·ō -ōnis *f* disdain, contempt

aspern·or -ārī -ātus sum *vt* to disdain, despise, reject

aspĕr·ō -āre *vt* to make rough or uneven, roughen; to make fierce, exasperate; to excite

aspersĭ·ō -ōnis *f* sprinkling; laying on of colors

a·spiciō -spicĕre -spexī -spectum *vt* to catch sight of, spot; to look at; to examine closely, inspect; to observe, consider

aspīrātĭ·ō -ōnis *f* breathing, blowing; evaporation, exhalation; (gram) aspiration

aspīr·ō -āre *vi* to breathe, blow; (with *dat* or with **ad** or **in** + *acc*) to aspire to, desire to reach or obtain, come near to obtaining; (with *dat*) to favor

asp·is -ĭdis *f* asp

asportātĭ·ō -ōnis *f* removal

asport·ō -āre *vt* to carry away

asprēt·a -ōrum *n pl* rough terrain

assĕcl·a -ae *m* hanger-on

assectātĭ·ō -ōnis *f* (respectful) attendance

assectāt·or -ōris *m* attendant, escort; disciple

assect·or -ārī *vt* to follow, tail after

assecŭl·a -ae *m* hanger-on

assensĭ·ō -ōnis *f* assent, approval; *m pl* expressions of approval; (phil) realism

assens·or -ōris *m* backer, supporter

assens·us -ūs *m* assent, approval; *m pl* expressions of approval; (phil) realism; echo

assentātĭ·ō -ōnis *f* assent, agreement; flattery

assentātiuncŭl·a -ae *f* base flattery

assentāt·or -ōris *m* flatterer

assentātōrĭē *adv* flatteringly

assentātr·ix -īcis *f* flatterer (*female*)

as·sentĭō -sentīre -sensī -sensum *vi* to agree; (with *dat*) to assent to, agree with, approve

as·sentĭor -sentīrī -sensus sum *vi* to agree; (with *dat*) to assent to, agree with, approve

assent·or -ārī -ātus sum *vi* to agree always; (with *dat*) to agree with always, to flatter

as·sĕquor -sĕquī -secūtus sum *vt* to pursue, catch up to, reach; to gain, obtain, procure; to come up to, equal, match; to comprehend, understand

ass·er -ĕris *m* pole, stake, post

as·sĕrō -serĕre -sēvī -sĭtum *vt* (with *dat*) to plant (*something*) near

assĕr·ō -ĕre -ŭī -tum *vt* to set free, liberate (*slave*); to protect, defend; to claim, appropriate; **in servitutem asserere** to claim (*someone*) as one's slave

assertĭ·ō -ōnis *f* declaration of civil status
assert·or -ōris *m* defender, champion
asserv·ĭō -īre *vi* (with *dat*) to serve, assist
asserv·ō -āre *vt* to preserve, keep, watch over, guard
assessĭ·ō -ōnis *f* company, companionship
assess·or -ōris *m* companion, assistant; (law) assistant to a judge, counselor
assess·us -ūs *m* company, companionship
assevēranter *adv* emphatically
assevērātĭ·ō -ōnis *f* assertion, protestation; firmness, earnestness
assevēr·ō -āre *vt* to assert strongly, affirm, insist on
as·sidĕō -sidēre -sēdī -sessum *vi* to seat nearby; (with *dat*) **a** to sit near, stand by, attend upon, take care of, keep (*someone*) company; **b** to be busily engaged in; **c** to attend to, mind; **d** to be near (*in some respect*), be like, resemble
as·sīdō -sīdĕre -sēdī *vi* to sit down; (with *acc*) to sit down beside
assidŭē *adv* assiduously, continually, incessantly
assiduĭt·ās -ātis *f* constant presence or attendance; persistence; frequent recurrence
assidŭō *adv* continually
assidŭ·us -a -um *adj* continually present; persistent, tireless, incessant, busy; *m* taxpayer; rich man
assignātĭ·ō -ōnis *f* allotment (*of land*)
assign·ō -āre *vt* to mark out, allot, assign (*land*); to assign, confer; to ascribe, attribute; to consign; to seal
as·silĭō -silīre -silŭī -sultum *vi* to jump; (with *dat*) to jump upon, leap at; (with **ad** + *acc*) **a** to jump to; **b** to have recourse to
assimilĭter *adv* in like manner
assimĭl·is -e *adj* similar; (with *dat*) like
assimulātĭ·ō -ōnis *f* likeness, similarity
assimulāt·us -a -um *adj* similar; counterfeit
assimŭl·ō -āre *vt* to consider as similar, compare; to imitate, counterfeit
as·sistō -sistĕre -stĭtī *vi* to stand nearby; (with **ad** + *acc*) to stand at or by; (with *dat*) to assist, defend
assĭtus *pp* of **assero**
assol·ĕō -ēre *vi* to be usual
assŏn·ō -āre *vi* to echo; (with *dat*) to sound in response to, to echo (*a sound*)
assuē·facĭō -facĕre -fēcī -factum *vt* to train; (with *dat*, with **ad** + *acc*, or with *inf*) to accustom (*someone*) to
assu·escō -escĕre -ēvī -ētum *vt* (with *dat*) to accustom (*someone*) to, make (*someone*) familiar with, familiarize (*someone*) with; *vi* (with *dat*, with **ad** + *acc*, or with *inf*) to become used to
assuētūd·ō -ĭnis *f* habit, custom
assuēt·us -a -um *pp* of **assuesco;** *adj* accustomed, customary, usual; (with *abl*) trained in; (with *dat*, with **ad** or **in** + *acc*, or with *inf*) accustomed to, used to
as·sūgō -ĕre — -suctum *vt* to suck in
assŭl·a -ae *f* splinter, chip, shaving
assulātim *adv* in splinters, in fragments, piecemeal
assult·ō -āre *vt* to assault, attack; *vi* to jump; (with *dat*) to jump to, jump at
assult·us -ūs *m* assault, attack
as·sūmō -ĕre -sumpsī -sumptum *vt* to take up, adopt, accept; to usurp, claim, assume; to receive, obtain, derive
assumptĭ·ō -ōnis *f* taking, receiving, assumption; adoption; (in logic) minor premise
assumptīv·us -a -um *adj* resting on external evidence, extrinsic
assŭ·ō -ĕre *vt* (with *dat*) to sew (*e.g., patch*) on (*e.g., clothes*)
as·surgō -surgĕre -surrexī -surrectum *vi* to rise up, rise, stand up; to mount up, increase, swell; (with *dat*) to yield to, stand up for (*out of respect*)
ass·us -a -um *adj* roasted; *n* roast; *n pl* steam bath, sweat bath
ast *conj* (older form of **at**) but
Astart·ē -ēs *f* Syro-Phoenician goddess, counterpart of Venus
a·射sternō -sternĕre *vt* (with *dat*) to strew (*something*) on; **asterni** (with *dat*) to throw oneself down upon
astipulāt·or -ōris *m* legal assistant; supporter
astipŭl·or -ārī -ātus sum *vi* (with *dat*) to agree with
a·stō -stāre *vi* to stand erect, stand up, stand nearby; (with *dat*) to assist
Astrae·a -ae *f* goddess of justice
astrĕp·ō -ĕre -ŭī -ĭtum *vi* to roar; to make a noise; to applaud; (with *dat*) to assent loudly to, applaud
astrictē *adv* concisely; strictly
astrict·us -a -um *pp* of **astringo;** drawn together, tight; stingy, tight; concise
a·stringō -stringĕre -strinxī -strictum *vt* to tighten, bind fast; to put under obligation, obligate, oblige; (fig) to draw closer; to compress, abridge; to occupy (*attention*); to embarrass
astrologĭ·a -ae *f* astronomy
astrolŏg·us -ī *m* astronomer; astrologer
astr·um -ī *n* star; constellation; *n pl* stars, sky, heaven; immortality
astū (indecl) *n* city
astup·ĕō -ēre *vi* (with *dat*) to be amazed at
ast·us -ūs *m* cunning, cleverness

astutē *adv* slyly
astūti·a -ae *f* skill, dexterity; cunning, astuteness
astūt·us -a -um *adj* clever; sly, cunning
Astyăn·ax -actis *m* son of Hector and Andromache
asȳl·um -ī *n* refuge, sanctuary, asylum
at *conj* but; (in a transition) but, but on the other hand; (in anticipation of an opponent's objection) but, it may be objected; (in an ironical objection) but really, but after all; (after a negative clause, to introduce a qualification) but at least; **at contra** but on the contrary; **at tamen** and yet, but at least
Atābŭl·us -ī *m* sirocco, southeast wind
Atalant·a -ae *f* daughter of King Schoeneus, defeated by Hippomenes in a famous footrace; daughter of Iasius and participant in the Calydonian boar hunt
atat *interj* (expressing surprise, pain, warning) oh!
atăv·us -ī *m* great-great-great-grandfather; ancestor
Ātell·a -ae *f* Oscan town in Campania
Atellān·us -a -um *adj* Atellan; **Atellana** or **fabula Atellana** comic farce which originated in Atella
āt·er -ra -rum *adj* (opposed to **niger** glossy black) dead black, black; dark, gloomy, eerie; black, unlucky; malicious; poisonous
Athăm·ās -antis *m* king of Thessaly, father of Helle and Phrixus by Nephele, and of Learchus and Melecerta by Ino
Athēn·ae -ārum *f pl* Athens
athĕ·os -ī *m* atheist
athlēt·a -ae *m* athlete, wrestler
athlētĭcē *adv* athletically
athlētĭc·us -a -um *adj* athletic
Atl·ās -antis *m* giant supporting the sky, son of Iapetus and Clymene
atŏm·os -ī *f* indivisible particle, atom
atque *conj* (denotes closer internal connection than is implied by **et** and gives prominence to what follows) and, as well as, together with, and even, and . . . too; (after words of comparison) as, than; **atque . . . atque** both . . . and; **atque adeo** and in fact
atquī *conj* but yet, but anyhow, however, rather, and yet
ātrāment·um -ī *n* ink
ātrāt·us -a -um *adj* clothed in black
Atr·eus -eī *m* son of Pelops, brother of Thyestes, father of Agamemnon and Menelaus
Atrīd·ēs -ae *m* descendant of Atreus
ātriens·is -is *m* butler
ātriŏl·um -ī *n* small hall, anteroom
ātrĭt·ās -ātis *f* blackness
ātr·ĭum -iī or **-ī** *n* main room, entrance room (*of Roman house*); hall (*of temples or public buildings*)
atrōcit·ās -ātis *f* hideousness, repulsiveness (*of form, appearance*); fierceness, brutality, cruelty (*of character*); severity, rigidity (*of law*)
atrōcĭter *adv* horribly, fiercely, cruelly, grimly
Ātrŏp·os -ī *f* one of the three Fates
atr·ox -ōcis *adj* horrible, hideous, frightful; savage, cruel, fierce; harsh, stern, unyielding, grim
attactus *pp* of **attingo**
attact·us -ūs *m* touch, contact
attăg·ēn -ēnis *m* woodcock
attagēn·a -ae *f* woodcock
Attalĭc·us -a -um *adj* of Attalus; Pergamean; rich, splendid; *n pl* gold-brocaded garments
Attăl·us -ī *m* king of Pergamum in Asia Minor, who bequeathed his kingdom to Rome
attămen *conj* but still, but yet
attat or **attătae** *interj* (indicating surprise, joy, dismay) oh!
attegĭ·a -ae *f* hut, cottage
attemperātē *adv* on time, in the nick of time
attempt·ō -āre *vt* to try, attempt; to test; to tempt, try to corrupt; to attack
at·tendō -tendĕre -tendī -tentum *vt* to notice, mark; to pay attention to, mind, consider; (with *dat* or **ad** + *acc*) to direct (*mind, attention*) to; *vi* to pay attention, listen
attentē *adv* attentively
attentĭ·ō -ōnis *f* attention, attentiveness
attentō see **attempto**
attent·us -a -um *pp* of **attendo;** *adj* attentive; careful, frugal, industrious
attenuātē *adv* (rhet) without flowery language, simply
attenuāt·us -a -um *adj* weak, weakened; shortened, brief; over-refined, affected; plain, bald (*style*)
attenŭ·ō -āre *vt* to make weak, weaken; to thin, attenuate; to lessen, diminish; to humble
at·tĕrō -terĕre -trīvī -trītum *vt* to rub, wear away, wear out, weaken, exhaust; to waste, destroy
attest·or -ārī -ātus sum *vt* to attest, confirm, corroborate, prove
attex·ō -ĕre -ŭī -tum *vt* to weave; to add
Atth·is -ĭdis *f* Attica
Attĭc·a -ae *f* district of Greece, of which Athens was the capital
attĭcē *adv* in the Attic or Athenian style
atticiss·ō -āre *vi* to speak in the Athenian manner
Attĭc·us -a -um *adj* Attic, Athenian; *m* T. Pomponius Atticus (*friend of Cicero,* 109-32 B.C.)
attĭgō see **attingo**
at·tinĕō -tinēre -tinŭī -tentum *vt* to hold tight, hold on to, hold, de-

tain, hold back; to reach for; *vi* (with **ad** + *acc*) to pertain to, relate to, refer to, concern; **quod ad me attinet** as far as I am concerned

at·tingō -tingĕre -tĭgī -tactum *vt* to touch, come in contact with; to reach, arrive at; to touch (*food*), taste; to touch, lie near, border; to touch upon, mention lightly; to touch, strike, attack; to touch, affect; to undertake, engage in, take in hand, manage; to resemble; to concern, belong to

Att·is -ĭdis *m* priest of Phrygian goddess Cybele

attoll·ō -ĕre *vt* to lift up, raise; to exalt, extol

at·tondĕō -tondēre -tondī -tonsum *vt* to clip, shave, shear; to prune; to crop; to clip, fleece, cheat

attonĭt·us -a -um *adj* thunderstruck, stunned, amazed, dazed, astonished; inspired; frantic

attorqu·ĕō -ēre *vt* to hurl up

at·trăhō -trahĕre -traxī -tractum *vt* to attract, draw, drag by force

attrect·ō -āre *vt* to touch, handle; to appropriate to oneself

attrepĭd·ō -āre *vi* to hobble along

attrib·ŭō -uĕre -ŭī -ūtum *vt* to allot, assign, bestow, give, annex; to impose (*taxes*)

attribūtĭ·ō -ōnis *f* payment of a debt; (gram) predicate

attribūt·us -a -um *pp* of **attribuo;** *n* (gram) predicate

attrīt·us -a -um *pp* of **attero;** *adj* worn away, wasted; shameless

au *interj* ouch!

au·ceps -cŭpis *m* fowler, bird catcher; spy, eavesdropper

auctār·ĭum -ĭī or **-ī** *n* addition

auctifĭc·us -a -um *adj* increasing

auctĭ·ō -ōnis *f* increase; auction

auctiōnārĭ·us -a -um *adj* auction

auctiōn·or -ārī -ātus sum *vi* to hold an auction

auctĭt·ō -āre *vt* to increase greatly

auct·ō -āre *vt* to increase, augment

auct·or -ōris *m* originator, author; writer, historian; reporter, informant (*of news*); authority (*for statement or theory*); proposer, backer, supporter; progenitor (*of race*); founder (*of city*); model, example; adviser, counselor; teacher; guarantor, security; leader, statesman

auctōrāment·um -ī *n* contract; pay, wages

auctōrĭt·ās -ātis *f* origination, source, cause; view, opinion, judgment; advice, counsel, encouragement; might, power, authority, weight, influence, leadership; importance, significance, worth, consequence; example, model, precedent; authority (*for establishing a fact*); document, record; decree (*of senate*); right of possession

auctōr·ō -āre *vt* to bind; **auctorari** or **se auctorare** to hire oneself out

auctus *pp* of **augeo**

auct·us -ūs *m* increase, growth, abundance

aucup·ĭum -ĭī or **-ī** *n* fowling; trap; eavesdropping; **aucupia verborum** quibbling

aucŭp·ō -āre or **aucŭp·or -ārī -ātus sum** *vt* to lie in wait for, watch for, chase, strive after, catch; *vi* to catch birds

audācĭ·a -ae *f* (in good sense) boldness, courage, daring; (in bad sense) recklessness, effrontery, audacity; bold deed; *f pl* adventures

audacter *adv* boldly, audaciously

aud·ax -ācis *adj* (in good sense) bold, daring; (in bad sense) reckless, rash, foolhardy

aud·ens -entis *adj* bold, daring, courageous

audentĭ·a -ae *f* daring, boldness

audĕō audēre ausus sum *vt* to dare, venture, risk; **vix ausim** (*old perf subj*) **credere** I could scarcely dare to believe; *vi* to dare, be bold

audĭ·ens -entis *m* hearer, listener; *m pl* audience

audientĭ·a -ae *f* hearing, attention; **audientiam facere** to command attention, to command silence

aud·ĭō -īre -īvī or **-ĭī ītum** *vt* to hear, listen to, give attention to; to hear, be taught by, learn from; to hear, listen to, grant; to accept, agree with, approve, yield to, grant, allow; to listen to, obey; to be called, be named, be reported, be regarded

audītĭ·ō -ōnis *f* hearsay, rumor, report, news

audītōr·ĭum -ĭī or **-ī** *n* lecture hall; the audience

audīt·us -ūs *m* sense of hearing; a hearing; report, rumor

aufĕrō auferre abstŭlī ablātum *vt* to bear or take away, bear off, remove, withdraw; to snatch away, steal, rob; to sweep away, kill, destroy; to gain, obtain, receive, get; to learn, understand; to mislead, lead into a digression; **auferri e conspectu** to disappear from sight

Aufĭd·us -ī *m* river in Apulia

au·fugĭō -fugĕre -fūgī *vt* to escape, flee from; *vi* to escape, run away

Augē·ās -ae *m* king of Elis whose stables Hercules cleaned by diverting the River Alpheus through them

augĕō augēre auxī auctum *vt* to increase, enlarge, augment, spread; to magnify, extol, exalt; to exaggerate; to enrich; to honor, advance, promote; to feed (*flame*)

augesc·ō -ĕre *vi* to begin to grow; to become larger, increase

aug·ur -ŭris *m* or *f* augur (*priest who foretold the future by observing the flight of birds, lightning, etc.*), prophet, seer

augurāl·is -e *adj* of divination; au-

gur's; *n* area in Roman camp where the general took auspices
augurāti·ō -ōnis *f* prophesying
augurātō *adv* after taking the auguries
augurāt·us -ūs *m* office of augur
augur·ium -iī or **-ī** *n* observation of omens, interpretation of omen, augury; sign, omen; prophesy, prediction, forecast; foreboding
augurĭ·us -a -um *adj* of augurs; **jus augurium** the right to take auguries
augŭr·ō -āre or **augur·or -ārī -ātus sum** *vt* to consult by augury; to consecrate by augury; to conjecture, imagine; to foretell, predict, prophesy; *vi* to act as augur; to take auspices; to play augur
August·a -ae *f* (in imperial period) mother, wife, daughter, or sister of the emperor
Augustāl·is -e *adj* of Augustus; *n pl* games in honor of Augustus; **sodales Augustales** priests of deified Augustus
Augustān·us -a -um *adj* Augustan; imperial
augustē *adv* reverently
august·us -a -um *adj* august, sacred, venerable; majestic, magnificent
August·us -a -um *adj* Augustan, imperial; cognomen of Octavius Caesar and of subsequent emperors; **mensis Augustus** August
aul·a -ae *f* inner court, hall (*of house*); palace; royal court; people of the royal court, the court
aulae·um -ī *n* curtain, canopy; theater curtain; bed cover, sofa cover, tapestry
aulĭc·us -a -um *adj* courtly, princely; *n pl* courtiers
Aul·is -is or **-ĭdis** *f* port in Boeotia from which the Greeks sailed for Troy
auloed·us -ī *m* singer (*accompanied by flute*)
aur·a -ae *f* breeze, breath of air, wind; air, atmosphere; heights, heaven; upper world; odor, exhalation; daylight, publicity; **ad auras ferre** to make known, publicize; **ad auras venire** to come to the upper world; **auram captare** to sniff the air; **aura popularis** popular favor; **auras fugere** to hide; **aura spei** breath of hope
aurārĭ·us -a -um *adj* of gold, golden, gold; *f* gold mine
aurāt·us -a -um *adj* decorated with gold, made of gold, gold-plated, golden; glittering
aureŏl·us -a -um *adj* gold; splendid
aurĕ·us -a -um *adj* of gold, golden; gilded; beautiful, magnificent, splendid; *m* gold coin
auricŏm·us -a -um *adj* golden-haired; with golden foliage
auricŭl·a *f* external ear, ear
aurĭf·er -ĕra -ĕrum *adj* producing or containing gold; (of tree) bearing golden apples
aurĭf·ex -ĭcis *m* goldsmith
aurīg·a -ae *m* or *f* charioteer, driver; (fig) pilot
Aurīg·a -ae *m* Auriga, Wagoner (*constellation*)
aurigĕn·a -ae *m* offspring of gold (*i.e., Perseus*)
aurĭg·er -ĕra -ĕrum *adj* gold-bearing; gilded
aurīg·ō -āre *vi* to drive a chariot, compete in chariot race
aur·is -is *f* ear; *f pl* listeners; critical ears; **aurem admovere** to listen; **auribus servire** to flatter; **auris adhibere** to be attentive, pay attention; **in aurem dextram** or **in aurem utramvis dormire** to sleep soundly, i.e., to be unconcerned
aurītŭl·us -ī *m* ass
aurīt·us -a -um *adj* long-eared; attentive; nosey; **testis auritus** witness by hearsay only; *m* rabbit
aurōr·a -ae *f* morning, dawn, daybreak; the Orient, the East
Aurōr·a -ae *f* goddess of dawn
aur·um -ī *n* gold; color of gold, golden luster; gold cup; gold necklace; gold jewelry; gold plate; golden fleece; gold money; Golden Age
auscultātĭ·ō -ōnis *f* obedience
auscultāt·or -ōris *m* listener
auscult·ō -āre *vt* to hear (*with attention*), listen to; to overhear; *vi* (with *dat*) to obey, listen to
ausim see **audeo**
Ausŏn·ēs -um *m pl* Ausonians (*ancient inhabitants of central Italy*)
Ausonĭd·ae -ārum *m pl* Italians
Ausonĭ·us -a -um *adj* Ausonian, Italian; *m pl* Ausonians, Italians; *f* Ausonia, Italy
ausp·ex -ĭcis *m* augur, soothsayer; author, founder, leader, director, protector; *m pl* witnesses (*at marriage ceremony*)
auspicātō *adv* after taking the auspices; under good omens, at a fortunate moment
auspicāt·us -a -um *adj* consecrated (*by auguries*); auspicious, favorable, lucky
auspic·ium -iī or **-ī** *n* divination (*through observation of flight of birds*), auspices; sign, omen, premonition; command, leadership, guidance, authority; right, power, will, inclination; **auspicium habere** to have the right to take auspices; **auspicium facere** (of birds) to give a sign, to yield an omen
auspĭc·or -ārī -ātus sum *vt* to begin, take up; *vi* to take auspices; to make a start
aust·er -rī *m* south wind; the South
austērē *adv* austerely, severely
austērĭt·ās -ātis *f* austerity
austēr·us -a -um *adj* austere, stern, harsh (*person*); pungent (*smell*); harsh (*taste*); drab, dark (*color*); se-

rious (*talk*); gloomy, sad, hard (*circumstances*)
austrāl·is -e *adj* southern; **cingulus, regio,** or **ora australis** torrid zone
austrīn·us -a -um *adj* from the south, southerly; southern
aus·us -a -um *pp* of **audeo;** *n* daring attempt, enterprise, adventure
aut *conj* or; (correcting what precedes) or, or rather, or else; (adding emphatic alternative) or at least; **aut . . . aut** either . . . or
autem *conj* (regularly follows an emphatic word) but, on the other hand, however; (in a transition) but, and now
autheps·a -ae *f* cooker, boiler (*utensil*)
autogrăph·us -a -um *adj* written with one's own hand, autograph
Autolўc·us -ī *m* father of Anticlea, maternal grandfather of Ulysses, and famous robber
automăt·on -ī *n* automaton
automăt·us -a -um *adj* automatic, spontaneous, voluntary
Automĕd·ōn -ontis *m* charioteer of Achilles
Autonŏ·ē -ēs *f* daughter of Cadmus, wife of Aristaeus, and mother of Actaeon
autumnāl·is -e *adj* autumn, autumnal
autumn·us -a -um *adj* autumn, autumnal; *m* autumn
autŭm·ō -āre *vt* to assert, affirm, say
auxiliār·ēs -ĭum *m pl* auxiliary troops
auxiliār·is -e *adj* auxiliary
auxiliārĭ·us -a -um *adj* auxiliary
auxiliāt·or -ōris *m* helper, assistant
auxiliāt·us -ūs *m* aid
auxilĭ·or -ārī -ātus sum *vi* (with *dat*) **a** to help, aid, assist; **b** to relieve, heal, cure
auxil·ĭum -iī or **-ī** *n* help, aid, assistance; *n pl* auxiliary troops, auxiliaries; military force, military power; **auxilio esse** (with *dat*) to be of assistance to
avārē *adv* greedily
avārĭter *adv* greedily
avāritĭ·a -ae *f* greed, selfishness, avarice; gluttony
avāritĭ·ēs -ēī *f* avarice
avār·us -a -um *adj* greedy, covetous, avaricious; (with *genit*) desirous of, eager for
avē see **aveo**
ā·vĕhō -vehĕre -vexī -vectum *vt* to carry away; **avehi** to ride away, sail away
ā·vellō -vellĕre -vellī (or **-vulsī** or **-volsī**) **-vulsum** (or **-volsum**) *vt* to pull or pluck away; to tear off; to separate, remove; **avelli** or **se avellere** (with **ab** + *abl*) to tear oneself away from, withdraw from
avēn·a -ae *f* oats; reed, stalk, a straw; shepherd's pipe
Aventīn·us -a -um *adj* Aventine; *m & n* Aventine Hill (*one of the seven hills of Rome*)
av·ĕō -ēre *vt* to wish, desire, long for, crave; (with *inf*) to wish to, long to; *vi* to say good-bye; **ave!** or **avete!** hail!, hello!; good morning!; farewell!, good-bye!
Avernāl·is -e *adj* of Lake Avernus
Avern·us -a -um *adj* without birds; of Lake Avernus; *m* Lake Avernus (*near Cumae, said to be an entrance to the lower world*)
āverrunc·ō -āre *vt* to avert
āversābĭl·is -e *adj* abominable
āvers·or -ārī -ātus sum *vt* to repulse, reject, refuse, decline, shun, avoid, send away; *vi* to turn away (*in displeasure, contempt, shame, etc.*)
āvers·or -ōris *m* embezzler
āvers·us -a -um *adj* turned away (*in flight*); rear, in the rear; disinclined, alienated, unfavorable, hostile; (with *dat* or **ab** + *abl*) averse to, hostile to, opposed to, estranged from; *n* the back part, the back; *n pl* the back parts, the back; hinterland; **in adversum** backwards
ā-vertō (or **ā·vortō**) **-vertĕre -vertī -versum** *vt* to turn away, avert; to embezzle, misappropriate; to divert; to alienate; **se avertere** to retire; *vi* to withdraw, retire
avĭ·a -ae *f* grandmother; old wives' tale
āvĭ·a -ōrum *n pl* pathless, lonely places
aviārĭ·us -a -um *adj* of birds, bird; *n* aviary; haunt of wild birds
avĭdē *adv* eagerly, greedily
avidĭt·ās -ātis *f* eagerness, longing, great desire; avarice
avĭd·us -a -um *adj* eager, earnest, greedy; hungry, greedy, voracious, gluttonous, insatiable; (with *genit* or *dat* or with **in** + *acc*) desirous of, eager for
av·is -is *f* bird; sign, omen; **avis alba** rarity
avīt·us -a -um *adj* grandfather's, ancestral; old
āvĭ·us -a -um *adj* out-of-the-way, lonely; trackless, pathless, untrodden; wandering, straying; going astray
āvocāment·um -ī *n* diversion, recreation
āvocātĭ·ō -ōnis *f* distraction, diversion
āvŏc·ō -āre *vt* to call away; to divert, remove, withdraw; to divert, amuse
āvŏl·ō -āre *vi* to fly away; to hasten away, dash off
āvulsus *pp* of **avello**
avuncŭl·us -ī *m* mother's brother, maternal uncle; **avunculus magnus** great-uncle; **avunculus major** great-great-uncle

av·us -ī *m* grandfather; forefather, ancestor
Axĕn·us -ī *m* Black Sea
axicĭ·a -ae *f* scissors
axill·a -ae *f* armpit
ax·is -is *m* axle; chariot, wagon; axis, pole; North Pole; sky; the heavens; region, country; board, plank

B

babae *interj* wonderful!, strange!
Babўl·ōn -ōnis *f* city on Euphrates
Babylōnĭ·a -ae *f* country between Tigris and Euphrates
bāc·a -ae *f* berry; olive; fruit; pearl
bācāt·us -a -um *adj* adorned with pearls
bacc·ar -ăris *n* cyclamen (*plant whose root yields fragrant oil*)
Bacch·a -ae *f* bacchante, maenad
bacchābund·us -a -um *adj* raving, riotous
Bacchān·al -ālis *n* place sacred to Bacchus; *n pl* bacchanalian orgies
bacchātĭ·ō -ōnis *f* orgy; revelry
bacch·or -ārī -ātus sum *vi* to celebrate the festival of Bacchus; to revel, rave, rage
Bacch·us -ī *m* god of wine; (fig) vine; (fig) wine
bācĭf·er -ĕra -ĕrum *adj* bearing berries or olives
bacill·um -ī *n* small staff, wand; lictor's staff
bacŭl·um -ī *n* or **bacŭl·us -ī** *m* stick; staff; scepter
badiss·ō -āre *vi* to go, walk
Baetĭc·us -a -um *adj* of the Baetis; *f* Baetica (*Roman province*)
Baet·is -is *m* river in Spain
Bāĭ·ae -ārum *f pl* resort town at northern extremity of Bay of Naples
bājŭl·ō -āre *vt* to carry, bear
bājŭl·us -ī *m* porter; day laborer
bālaen·a -ae *f* whale
balanāt·us -a -um *adj* anointed with balsam; embalmed
balăn·us -ī *m* or *f* acorn; date; balsam; shell-fish
balătr·ō -ōnis *m* jester, buffoon
bālāt·us -ūs *m* bleating
balb·us -a -um *adj* stammering
balbūt·ĭō -īre *vt & vi* to stammer, stutter
balinĕ·um -ī *n* bath
ballist·a -ae *f* large military device for hurling stones; heavy artillery
ballistār·ĭum -ĭī or **-ī** *n* artillery emplacement
balnĕ·ae -ārum *f pl* baths
balneārĭ·us -a -um *adj* of a bath; *n pl* baths
balneāt·or -ōris *m* bath superintendent
balneŏl·ae -ārum *f pl* baths
balneŏl·um -ī *n* small bath
balnĕ·um -ī *n* bath
bāl·ō -āre *vi* to bleat
balsăm·um -ī *n* balsam; balsam tree
baltĕ·us -ī *m* belt; baldric; girdle
baptister·ĭum -ĭī or **-ī** bath; swimming pool
barāthr·um -ī *n* abyss, chasm, pit; lower world
barb·a -ae *f* beard
barbărē *adv* in a foreign language; barbarously, cruelly
barbarĭ·a -ae or **barbarĭ·ēs -ēī** *f* foreign country, strange land; rudeness, want of culture
barbarĭc·us -a -um *adj* foreign, outlandish
barbarĭēs see **barbaria**
barbăr·us -a -um *adj* foreign; barbarous, savage, uncivilized, rude; *m* foreigner; barbarian
barbātŭl·us -a -um *adj* wearing a small beard
barbāt·us -a -um *adj* bearded; adult; old-time; *m* old-timer; philosopher, longhair; goat
barbĭg·er -ĕra -ĕrum *adj* wearing a beard, bearded
barbĭt·os -ī *m* lyre; lute
barbŭl·a -ae *f* small beard
bard·us -a -um *adj* stupid, dull
bard·us -ī *m* bard
bār·ō -ōnis *m* dunce, blockhead
barr·us -ī *m* elephant
bāsiātĭ·ō -ōnis *f* kissing; kiss
basilĭc·us -a -um *adj* royal; splendid; *f* public building, basilica (*used as law court and exchange*); portico
bāsĭ·ō -āre *vt* to kiss
bas·is -is *f* base, foundation, support; pedestal
bās·ĭum -ĭī or **-ī** kiss
Bassăr·eus -ĕī *m* Bacchus
batill·um -ī *n* brazier
battŭ·ō -ĕre -ī *vt* to beat, pound
beātē *adv* happily
beātĭt·ās -ātis *f* happiness
beātitūd·ō -ĭnis *f* happiness
beāt·us -a -um *adj* happy; prosperous, rich; fertile; abundant; *n* happiness
Bēlĭd·ēs -um *f pl* descendants of Belus, the Danaids, who killed their husbands on their wedding night
bellārĭ·a -ōrum *m pl* dessert
bellāt·or -ōris *adj* warlike; valorous; spirited; *m* warrior
bellātr·ix -īcis *adj* warlike, skilled in war; *f* warrior (*female*)
bellē *adv* prettily, neatly, nicely, well
Bellerŏph·ōn -ontis *m* slayer of Chimaera and rider of Pegasus
bellĭcōs·us -a -um *adj* warlike, martial, valorous

bellĭc·us -a -um *adj* war, military; warlike, fierce; *n* bugle; bugle call
bellĭg·er -ĕra -ĕrum *adj* belligerent, warlike, aggressive; martial; valiant
belligĕr·ō -āre or **belligĕr·or -ārī -ātus sum** *vi* to wage war, fight
bellipŏt·ens -entis *adj* mighty or valiant in war; *m* Mars
bell·ō -āre or **bell·or -ārī -ātus sum** *vi* to wage war, fight
Bellōn·a -ae *f* Roman goddess of war
bellŭl·us -a -um *adj* pretty, lovely, cute, fine
bell·um -ī *n* war; battle
bēlŭ·a -ae *f* beast, monster, brute
bēluōs·us -a -um *adj* full of monsters
Bēl·us -ī *m* Baal; king of Tyre and father of Dido; king of Egypt, father of Danaus and Aegyptus
bene *adv* well; thoroughly; very, quite
bene·dīcō -dīcĕre -dixī -dictum *vt* to speak well of, praise; (eccl) to bless
beneficentĭ·a -ae *f* beneficence, kindness
beneficiārĭ·ī -ōrum *m pl* soldiers exempt from menial tasks
benefĭc·ium -iī or **-ī** *n* kindness, favor, benefit, service; help, support; promotion; right, privilege
benefĭc·us -a -um *adj* generous, liberal, obliging
Benevent·um -ī *n* town in Samnium in S. Italy
benevŏlē *adv* kindly
benevŏl·ens -entis *adj* kindhearted, obliging
benevolentĭ·a -ae *f* benevolence, kindness, goodwill; favor
benevŏl·us -a -um *adj* kind, friendly; devoted, faithful
benignē *adv* in a friendly manner, kindly, courteously; mildly, indulgently; liberally, generously
benignĭt·ās -ātis *f* kindness, friendliness, courtesy; liberality, bounty
benign·us -a -um *adj* kind-hearted; mild, affable; liberal; favorable; bounteous, fruitful
be·ō -āre *vt* to make happy; to bless; to enrich; to refresh
Berecynt·us -ī *m* mountain in Phrygia sacred to Cybele
bēryll·us -ī *m* precious stone, beryl
bēs bessis *m* two thirds
bestĭ·a -ae *f* beast, wild beast
bestiārĭ·us -a -um *adj* of wild beasts; *m* wild-beast fighter
bestiŏl·a -ae *f* little beast
bēt·a -ae *f* beet
bēta (indecl) *n* second letter of Greek alphabet
bibliopōl·a -ae *m* bookseller
bibliothēc·a -ae *f* library
bibliothēcār·ius -iī or **-ī** *m* librarian
bib·ō -ĕre -ī *vt* to drink; to visit, reach, live near (*river*); (fig) to take in, absorb, listen eagerly to
bibŭl·us -a -um *adj* fond of drinking; absorbent; thirsty
bi·ceps -cipĭtis *adj* two-headed; twin-peaked
biclīn·ium -iī or **-ī** *n* table for two
bicŏl·or -ōris *adj* two-colored
bicorn·is -e *adj* two-horned; two-pronged
bid·ens -entis *adj* with two teeth; with two points; two-pronged; *m* hoe, mattock; sacrificial animal; sheep
bident·al -ālis *n* place struck by lightning
bīdŭ·um -ī *n* period of two days; two days
bienn·ium -iī or **-ī** *n* period of two years; two years
bifārĭam *adv* on both sides, twofold, double, in two parts, in two directions
bifārĭ·us -a -um *adj* double, twofold
bif·er -ĕra -ĕrum *adj* bearing fruit twice a year; of twofold form
bifĭd·us -a -um *adj* split in two, forked, cloven
bifŏr·is -e *adj* having two doors; having two holes or openings; double
biformāt·us -a -um *adj* double, having two forms
biform·is -e *adj* double, having two forms
bifr·ons -ontis *adj* two-headed; two-faced
bifurc·us -a -um *adj* two-pronged, forked
bīg·a -ae *f* or **bīg·ae -ārum** *f pl* span of horses, team; two-horse chariot
bijŭg·ī -ōrum *m pl* team of horses; two-horse chariot
bijŭg·is -e *adj* yoked two together; drawn by a pair of horses
bijŭg·us -a -um *adj* yoked two together; two-horse
bilībr·is -e *adj* two-pound
bilingu·is -e *adj* two-tongued; bilingual; hypercritical, deceitful, false
bīl·is -is *f* gall, bile; wrath, anger; **bilis atra** melancholy; madness
bimăr·is -e *adj* situated between two seas
bimarīt·us -ī *m* bigamist
bimāt·er -ris *adj* having two mothers
bimembr·is -e *adj* half man, half beast
bimembr·is -is *m* centaur
bimestr·is -e *adj* two-month-old; lasting two months
bimŭl·us -a -um *adj* two-year-old
bīm·us -a -um *adj* two-year-old; for two years
bīn·ī -ae -a *adj* two by two; two to each, two each; two at a time; a pair of
binoct·ium -iī or **-ī** *n* two nights
binōmĭn·is -e *adj* having two names
bipalm·is -e *adj* two spans long
bipart·iō -īre — -ītum *vt* to divide into two parts; to bisect

bipartītō *adv* in two parts
bipăt·ens -entis *adj* open in two directions
bipedāl·is -e *adj* two feet long, broad, thick, or high
bipennĭf·er -ĕra -ĕrum *adj* wielding a two-edged ax
bipenn·is -e *adj* two-edged; *f* two-edged ax
bip·ēs -ĕdis *adj* two-footed, biped
birēm·is -e *adj* two-oared; with two banks of oars; *f* ship with two banks of oars
bis *adv* twice
Bistŏn·ēs -um *m pl* fierce tribesmen in Thessaly
bisulc·us -a -um *adj* split, cloven; forked
bīt·ō -ĕre *vi* to go
bitūm·en -ĭnis *n* bitumen, asphalt
bivĭ·us -a -um *adj* two-way; *n* crossroads, intersection
blaes·us -a -um *adj* lisping; indistinct
blandē *adv* flatteringly; courteously
blandiloquentĭ·a -ae *f* flattery
blandiloquentŭl·us -a -um *adj* smooth-tongued
blandīment·um -ī *n* flattery, compliment; charm
bland·ior -īrī -ītus sum *vt* to flatter; to coax; to allure; to please
blandĭter *adv* flatteringly
blanditĭ·a -ae *f* caress, flattery, compliment; charm
blandītim *adv* flatteringly
bland·us -a -um *adj* smooth; flattering, fawning; alluring, charming, winsome, pleasant
blatĕr·ō -āre *vi* to talk foolishly, to babble
blatt·a -ae *f* cockroach; moth
blenn·us -ī *m* idiot, blockhead
blitĕ·us -a -um *adj* silly; tasteless
blit·um -ī *n* tasteless vegetable, kind of spinach
boārĭ·us -a -um *adj* cattle
Boeotĭ·a -ae *f* district north of Attica in central Greece, the capital of which was Thebes
bōlēt·us -ī *n* mushroom
bol·us -ī *m* throw (*of the dice*); cast (*of the net*); (fig) haul, piece of good luck, gain; choice morsel
bombax *interj* strange!; indeed!
bomb·us -ī *m* booming; buzzing, humming
bombȳcĭn·us -a -um *adj* silk, silken
bomb·ȳx -ȳcis *m* silkworm; silk; silk garment
Bon·a De·a (*genit:* **Bon·ae De·ae**) *f* goddess of chastity and fertility
bonĭt·ās -ātis *f* goodness, integrity; kindness, benevolence
bon·us -a -um *adj* good; honest, virtuous; faithful, patriotic; fit, suitable; able, clever; brave; noble; auspicious, favorable; useful, advantageous; *n* good; profit, advantage; *n pl* goods, property
bo·ō -āre *vi* to cry aloud; to roar
Boōt·ēs -ae *m* constellation containing the bright star Arcturus
borĕ·as -ae *m* north wind
borĕ·us -a -um *adj* north, northern
bōs bovis *m* or *f* ox, bull; cow
Bospŏr·us -ī *m* strait between Thrace and Asia Minor, connecting Propontis and Black Sea
botŭl·us -ī *m* sausage
bovīl·e -is *n* ox stall
bovill·us -a -um *adj* cattle
brāc·ae -ārum *f pl* pants, trousers
brācāt·us -a -um *adj* wearing trousers; foreign, barbarian; effeminate
bracchiāl·is -ē *adj* of the arm
bracchiŏl·um -ī *n* dainty arm
bracch·ĭum -ĭī or **-ī** *n* arm, lower arm; claw; bough; tendril; arm of the sea; sail yard
bractĕ·a -ae *f* gold leaf; gold foil
bracteŏl·a -ae *f* very thin gold leaf
brassĭc·a -ae *f* cabbage
breviār·ĭum -ĭī or **-ī** *n* summary, abridgement; statistics
brevicŭl·us -a -um *adj* rather short
breviloqu·ens -entis *adj* brief (*in speech*)
breviloquentĭ·a -ae *f* brevity
brevī *adv* briefly, in a few words; shortly, in a short time
brĕv·is -e *adj* short, little, brief; concise; small; shallow; narrow; *n pl* shoals, shallows
brevĭt·ās -ātis *f* brevity; smallness; shortness
brevĭter *adv* shortly, briefly
Britannĭ·a -ae *f* Britain; British Isles
Brom·ĭus -ĭī or **-ī** *m* Bacchus
brūm·a -ae *f* winter solstice; winter; winter's cold
brūmāl·is -e *adj* wintry
Brundis·ĭum -ĭī or **-ī** *n* port in S.E. Italy on Adriatic Sea
Bruttĭ·ī -ōrum *m pl* inhabitants of toe of Italy
Brūt·us -ī *m* Lucius Junius Brutus (*credited with having driven out the last Roman king, Tarquinius Superbus*); Marcus Junius Brutus (*one of the murderers of Julius Caesar*)
brūt·us -a -um *adj* heavy, unwieldy; dull, stupid
būbīl·e -is *n* ox stall
būb·ō -ōnis *m* owl
būbŭl·a -ae *f* beef
bubulcĭt·or -ārī -ātus sum *vi* to be a herdsman; to ride herd
bubulc·us -ī *m* cowherd; plowman
būbŭl·us -a -um *adj* of cows or oxen
būcaed·a -ae *m* flogged slave
bucc·a -ae *f* cheek; loudmouthed person; trumpeter; parasite; mouthful
buccell·a -ae *f* small mouthful; morsel
buccŭl·a -ae *f*. little cheek; visor
buccŭlent·us -a -um *adj* loudmouthed
būcĕr(ĭ)·us -a -um *adj* horned
būcĭn·a -ae *f* (curved) trumpet; war trumpet; shepherd's horn
būcināt·or -ōris *m* trumpeter
būcolĭc·us -a -um *adj* pastoral, bucolic
būcŭl·a -ae *f* heifer

būf·ō -ōnis *m* toad
bulb·us -ī *m* onion
būl·ē -ēs *f* (Greek) council, senate
būleut·a -ae *m* councilor
būleuter·ium -iī *or* **-ī** *n* meeting place of Greek council
bull·a -ae *f* bubble; boss, stud, knob; amulet; badge (*symbol of boyhood*)
bullāt·us -a -um *adj* inflated, bombastic; studded; wearing a bulla, i.e., still a child
būmast·us -ī *f* species of grape with large clusters
būr·is -is *m* curved handle of plow
bustirăp·us -ī *m* ghoul, grave robber
bustuārĭ·us -a -um *adj* of a tomb or pyre
bust·um -ī *n* pyre; tomb, sepulcher
buxĭf·er -ĕra -ĕrum *adj* producing boxwood trees
bux·um -ī *n* boxwood; (spinning) top; comb; writing tablet (*made of boxwood*)
bux·us -ī *f* boxwood tree
Byzant·ĭum -iī or **-ī** *n* city on the Bosporus, later named Constantinople

C

caball·us -ī *m* pack horse, nag, hack
cachinnātĭ·ō -ōnis *f* loud or immoderate laughter
cachinn·ō -āre *vi* to laugh loud; to roar (*with laughter*)
cachinn·ō -ōnis *m* scoffer
cachinn·us -ī *m* loud laugh; jeering; rippling, roaring
cac·ō -āre *vt* to defile; *vi* to defecate
cacoēth·es -is *n* malignant disease; itch
cacūm·en -ĭnis *n* point, tip, top, peak
cacūmĭn·ō -āre *vt* to make pointed; to sharpen
Cāc·us -ī *m* son of Vulcan, a giant who lived on the Aventine Hill, killed by Hercules
cadāv·er -ĕris *n* corpse, carcass
cadāverōs·us -a -um *adj* cadaverous, ghastly
Cadmē·us -a -um *adj* Cadmean; Theban; *f* citadel of Thebes
Cadm·us -ī *m* son of Phoenician king Agenor, brother of Europa, and founder of Thebes
cadō cadĕre cecĭdī cāsum *vi* to fall, sink, drop; to be slain, die, be sacrificed; to happen; to belong, refer, be suitable, apply; to abate, subside, flag, decline, decay, vanish, fail, cease; to end, close
cadūceāt·or -ōris *m* herald
cadūcĕ·us -ī *m* herald's staff, caduceus
cadūcĭf·er -ĕra -ĕrum *adj* with herald's staff
cadūc·us -a -um *adj* falling, fallen; inclined to fall; frail, perishable, transitory; vain, futile, ineffectual; (law) lapsed, without heir
cad·us -ī *m* jar, flask, jug
caecigĕn·us -a -um *adj* born blind
caecĭt·ās -ātis *f* blindness
caec·ō -āre *vt* to make blind; to make obscure
Caecŭb·um -ī *n* famous wine from S. Latium
caec·us -a -um *adj* blind; invisible; vague, random, aimless, uncertain, unknown; making invisible, blinding; dark, gloomy, obscure
caed·ēs -is *f* murder, slaughter, massacre; bloodshed, gore; the slain
caed·ō caedĕre cecīdī caesum *vt* to hack at, chop; to strike, beat; to fell, cut down, cut off, cut to pieces; to kill, murder
caelām·en -ĭnis *n* engraving, basrelief
caelāt·or -ōris *m* engraver
caelātūr·a -ae *f* engraving
cael·ebs -ĭbis *adj* unmarried, single (*whether bachelor or widower*)
cael·es -ĭtis *adj* heavenly, celestial
caelest·ĭa -ĭum *n pl* heavenly bodies
caelest·is -e *adj* heavenly, celestial; divine, supernatural
caelest·is -is *m* deity
caelibāt·us -ūs *m* celibacy
caelicŏl·a -ae *m* god
caelĭf·er -ĕra -ĕrum *adj* supporting the sky
caelipŏt·ens -entis *adj* powerful in heaven
caelĭt·ēs -um *m pl* inhabitants of heaven, gods
Cael·ĭus Mon·s (*genit:* **Cael·iī** or **-ī Mon·tis**) *m* Caelian Hill in Rome
cael·ō -āre *vt* to engrave in relief, to emboss, to carve; to cast; to fashion, compose; to adorn
cael·um -ī *n* sky, heaven, heavens; air, climate, weather; engraver's chisel, burin
caement·um -ī *n* quarry stone; rubble; cement
caenōs·us -a -um *adj* dirty, filthy, muddy
caen·um -ī *n* dirt, filth, mud, mire
caep·a -ae *f* or **caep·e -is** *n* onion
Caere (indecl) *n* city in Etruria
caerimōnĭ·a -ae *f* rite; ritual, religious ceremony; sanctity, sacredness; awe, reverence, veneration
caerŭl·a -ōrum *n pl* sea
caerŭlĕ·us or **caerŭl·us -a -um** adj blue, azure, dark-blue, green, dark-green; dark, gloomy
Caes·ar -ăris *m* C. Julius Caesar (102?-44 B.C.)

caesariāt·us -a -um *adj* long-haired
caesarĭ·ēs -ēī *f* hair
caesīcĭ·us -a -um *adj* bluish, dark blue
caesim *adv* by cutting; in short clauses, in a clipped style
caesĭ·us -a -um *adj* bluish-grey; blue-eyed; gray-eyed; cat-eyed
caesp·es -ĭtis *m* sod, turf, grass; altar of sod
caest·us -ūs *m* boxing glove
caetr·a -ae *f* short Spanish shield
caetrāt·us -a -um *adj* armed with a shield
Caiēt·a -ae *f* nurse of Aeneas; town on coast of Latium
Caius see **Gaius**
Calăb·er -ra -rum *adj* Calabrian
Calabrĭ·a -ae *f* S.W. peninsula of Italy
Cală·is -is *m* son of Boreas and Orithyia, and brother of Zetes
calamist·er -rī *m* hair curler, curling iron; (rhet) flowery language
calamistrāt·us -a -um *adj* curled (*with a hair curler*)
calamistr·um -ī *n* curling iron
calamĭt·ās -ātis *f* loss, injury, damage; misfortune, calamity, disaster; military defeat
calamitōsē *adv* unfortunately
calamitōs·us -a -um *adj* disastrous, ruinous, destructive; exposed to injury, suffering great damage, unfortunate
calăm·us -ī *m* reed, stalk; pen; arrow; fishing rod; pipe
calathisc·us -ī *m* small wicker basket
calăth·us -ī *m* wicker basket; milk pail; wine cup
calāt·or -ōris *m* servant, attendant
calc·ar -āris *n* spur; stimulus
calcārĕ·um -ī *n* heel
calceāment·um -ī *n* shoe
calceāt·us -ūs *m* sandal, shoe
calcĕ·ō -āre *vt* to furnish with shoes, to shoe
calceolār·ĭus -ĭī or **-ī** *m* shoemaker
calceŏl·us -ī *m* small shoe, half-boot
calcĕ·us -ī *m* shoe, half-boot
Calch·ās -antis *m* Greek prophet at Troy
calcĭtr·ō -āre *vi* to kick; to resist; to be stubborn; to kick up one's heels
calcĭtr·ō -ōnis *m* blusterer
calc·ō -āre *vt* to tread, tread under foot; to trample on, oppress; to scorn, abuse
calculāt·or -ōris *m* arithmetic teacher; accountant, bookkeeper
calcŭl·us -ī *m* pebble, stone; kidney stone; counter of an abacus; stone used in games; stone used in voting; vote, sentence, decision
caldārĭ·us -a -um *adj* warm-water; *n* hot bath
caldus see **calidus**
Calēdonĭ·a -ae *f* Highlands of Scotland
cale·facĭō or **cal·facĭō -facĕre -fēcī -factum** *vt* to warm, heat; to rouse up, excite, make angry
calefact·ō -āre *vt* to warm, heat
Calend·ae -ārum *f pl* first day of Roman month, calends
calendār·ĭum -ĭī or **-ī** *n* account book
cal·ĕō -ēre -ŭī *vi* to be warm, hot; to feel warm; to glow; to be hot with passion; to be troubled, be perplexed; to be zealously pursued; to be new or fresh
Cal·ēs -ĭum *f pl* Campanian town famous for its wine
cal·escō -escĕre -ŭī *vi* to get warm or hot; to become excited, be inflamed
calĭd·a or **cald·a -ae** *f* warm water
calĭdē *adv* quickly, promptly
calĭd·us or **cald·us -a -um** *adj* warm, hot; eager, rash, hasty, hotheaded, vehement; quick, ready, prompt; *n* warm drink; *f* see **calida**
caliendr·um -ī *n* wig (*for women*)
calĭg·a -ae *f* shoe, soldier's boot; soldier
caligāt·us -a -um *adj* wearing soldier's boots; (of a peasant) wearing clodhoppers
cālīg·ō -ĭnis *f* mist, vapor, fog; gloom, darkness, obscurity; mental blindness; calamity, affliction
cālīg·ō -āre *vt* to veil in darkness, to obscure; to make dizzy; *vi* to steam, reek; to be wrapped in mist or darkness; to be blind, grope
caligŭl·a -ae *f* small military boot
Caligŭl·a -ae *m* pet name given by the soldiers to Gaius Caesar when he was a small boy
cal·ix -ĭcis *m* cup; pot; (fig) wine
callaĭn·us -a -um *adj* turquoise
call·ĕō -ēre -ŭī *vt* to know by experience or practice, to understand; (with *inf*) to know how to; *vi* to be callous, to be thick-skinned; to be insensible; to be experienced, clever, skillful
callidĭt·ās -ātis *f* skill; shrewdness; cunning, craft
callĭdē *adv* skillfully, expertly, shrewdly; well; cunningly
callĭd·us -a -um *adj* expert, adroit, skillful; ingenious, prudent, dexterous; clever, shrewd; sly, cunning, crafty, calculating
Callimăch·us -ī *m* famous Alexandrine poet and grammarian (*c.* 270 B.C.)
Calliŏp·ē -ēs or **Calliopē·a -ae** *f* Calliope (*muse of epic poetry*)
call·is -is *m* stony, uneven footpath; mountain path; cattle trail; mountain pasture; mountain pass, defile
Callist·ō -ūs *f* daughter of Lycaon, king of Arcadia, who was changed into the constellation Helice or Ursa Major
callōs·us -a -um *adj* hard-skinned; thick-skinned, callous; solid, hard, thick

call·um -ī *m* hard or thick skin; insensibility, stupidity

cal·ō -āre *vt* to call out, proclaim; to convoke

cāl·ō -ōnis *m* soldier's servant; menial servant, drudge

cal·or -ōris *m* warmth, heat, glow; passion, love; fire, zeal, impetuosity, vehemence

calth·a -ae *f* marigold

calthŭl·a -ae *f* yellow robe

calumnĭ·a -ae *f* trickery; pretense, evasion; false statement, misrepresentation, fallacy; false accusation, malicious charge; conviction for malicious prosecution

calumniāt·or -ōris *m* malicious prosecutor, perverter of the law, pettifogger

calumnĭ·or -ārī -ātus sum *vt* to accuse falsely; to misrepresent, calumniate; to blame unjustly; to put in a false light

calv·a -ae *f* scalp, bald head

calvit·ĭum -ĭī or **-ī** *n* baldness

calv·us -a -um *adj* bald

cal·x -cis *f* heel; (fig) foot, kick; **calcibus caedere** to kick

cal·x -cis *f* pebble; limestone, lime; finish line (*marked with lime*), goal; **ad calcem pervenire** to reach the goal; **ad carceres a calce revocari** to be recalled from the finish line to the starting gate; to have to start all over again

Calỹd·ōn -ōnis *f* town in Aetolia, scene of the famous boar hunt led by Meleager

Calyps·ō -ūs *f* nymph, daughter of Atlas, who entertained Ulysses on the island of Ogygia

camell·a -ae *f* drinking cup

camēl·us -ī *m* camel

Camēn·a -ae *f* Muse; poem; poetry

camĕr·a -ae *f* vault, arched roof, arch; houseboat

Camerīn·um -ī *n* town in Umbria

Camill·a -ae *f* Volscian female warrior who assisted Turnus against Aeneas

Camill·us -ī *m* M. Furius Camillus, who freed Rome from the Gauls

camīn·us -ī *m* fireplace; furnace; forge; **oleum addere camino** to pour oil on the fire

cammăr·us -ī *m* lobster

Campānĭ·a -ae *f* district on E. coast of central Italy

campest·er -ris -re *adj* flat, level; overland (*march*); (of city) situated in a plain; (of army) fighting in a plain; (of sports, elections, etc.) held in the Campus Martius; *n* shorts (*worn in sports*); *n pl* flat lands

camp·us -ī *m* flat space, plain; sports field; level surface, surface (*of sea*); **Campus Martius** field near the Tiber used for sports, elections, military exercises, etc.

cam·ur -ūra -ŭrum *adj* crooked, concave

canāl·is -is *m* pipe, conduit, gutter

cancell·ī -ōrum *m pl* railing, grating; barrier (*at sports, public events*); boundaries, limits

canc·er -rī *m* crab; the South; tropical heat; cancer (*disease*)

Canc·er -rī *m* Cancer (*northern zodiacal constellation; sign of the zodiac*)

cande·faciō -facĕre -fēcī -factum *vt* to make dazzling white; to make glow, make red-hot

candēl·a -ae *f* candle, torch, taper; waxed cord; **candelam apponere valvis** to set the house on fire

candelābr·um -ī *n* candlestick, candelabrum, chandelier; lamp stand

cand·ens -entis *adj* shining white, glittering, dazzling, glowing

cand·ĕō -ēre *vi* to be shining white, glitter, shine; to be white-hot

cand·escō -escĕre -ŭī *vi* to become white, begin to glisten; to get redhot

candidātōrĭ·us -a -um *adj* of a candidate, candidate's

candidāt·us -a -um *adj* clothed in white; *m* candidate for office

candĭdē *adv* in dazzling white; clearly, simply, sincerely

candidŭl·us -a -um *adj* pretty white

candĭd·us -a -um *adj* (*cf* **albus**) shiny white, white, bright, dazzling, gleaming, sparkling; fair, radiant (*complexion*); candid, open, sincere, frank (*person*); bright, cheerful (*circumstances*); clear, bright (*day*); (of winds) bringing clear weather; white, silvery (*poplar, hair, etc.*); clear, unaffected (*style*); clothed in white; **candida sententia** vote of acquittal

cand·or -ōris *m* glossy whiteness, brightness, radiance; candor, sincerity; naturalness (*of style*); brilliance (*of discourse*)

cān·ens -entis *adj* grey, white

cān·ĕō -ēre -ŭī *vi* to be grey, be white

cānesc·ō -ĕre *vi* to grow white, become grey; to grow old; (of discourse) to lose force, grow dull

can·ī -ōrum *m pl* grey hair

canĭcŭl·a -ae *f* small dog, pup; (as term of abuse) little bitch

Canīcŭl·a -ae *f* Canicula, Sirius, Dog Star (*brightest star in Canis Major*)

canīn·us -a -um *adj* canine; snarling, spiteful, caustic; **canina littera** letter R

can·is -is *m* or *f* dog, hound; (term of reproach to denote vile person, enraged person, hanger-on, etc.) dog; worst throw (*in dice*)

Can·is -is *m* Canis Major (*constellation, of which the brightest star is Canicula*)

canistr·um -ī *n* wicker basket (*for bread, fruit, flowers, etc.*)

cānitĭ·ēs (*genit* not in use) *f* greyness; grey hair; old age

cann•a -ae *f* reed; reed pipe, flute
cannăb•is -ae *f* or **cannăb•um -ī** *n* hemp
Cann•ae -ārum *f pl* village in Apulia where Hannibal won great victory over Romans in 216 B.C.
canō canĕre cecinī cantum *vt* to sing; to play; to speak in a singsong tone; to sing the praises of, celebrate; to prophesy, predict, foretell; (mil) to blow, sound; **signa canere** to sound the signal for battle; *vi* to sing; to play; (of birds) to sing; (of roosters) to crow; (of frogs) to croak; **receptui canere** to sound retreat; **tibiā canere** to play the flute
can•or -ōris *m* tune, sound, melody, song; tone (*of instruments*)
canōr•us -a -um *adj* melodious, musical; singsong, jingling; *n* melody, charm (*in speaking*)
Cantabrĭ•a -ae *f* district in N.W. Spain
cantām•en -ĭnis *n* incantation, spell
cantāt•or -ōris *m* singer
canthăr•is -ĭdis *f* beetle; Spanish fly
canthăr•us -ī *m* wide-bellied drinking vessel with handles, tankard
canthēr•ĭus or **cantēr•ĭus -iī** or **-ī** *m* gelding; eunuch
canth•us -ī *m* iron tire; wheel
cantĭc•um -ī *n* song; aria in Roman comedy; (in delivery of speech) singsong
cantilēn•a -ae *f* old song, gossip; **cantilenam eandem canere** to sing the same old song, harp on the same theme
cantĭ•ō -ōnis *f* singing; incantation, charm, spell
cantĭt•ō -āre *vt* to keep on singing or playing, to sing or play repeatedly
cantiuncŭl•a -ae *f* catchy tune
cant•ō -āre *vt* to sing; to play; to sing of, celebrate, praise in song; to harp on, keep repeating; to predict; to drawl out; (of actor) to play the part of; *vi* to sing, to play; (of instruments) to sound; to drawl; (of rooster) to crow; **ad surdas aures cantare** to preach to deaf ears
cant•or -ōris *m* singer, poet; eulogist; actor, player; musician
cantr•ix -īcis *f* musician, singer (*female*)
cant•us -ūs *m* tune, melody, song, playing; incantation; prediction; magic spell
cān•us -a -um *adj* white, grey; aged, old venerable
capācĭt•ās -ātis *f* capacity
cap•ax -ācis *adj* capacious, spacious, wide, roomy; (of mind) able to grasp, receptive, capable
capēd•ō -ĭnis *f* cup or bowl used in sacrifices
capēduncŭl•a -ae *f* small cup or bowl used in sacrifices
capell•a -ae *f* she-goat, nanny goat
Capell•a -ae *f* Capella (*star of the first magnitude in Auriga*)
Capēn•a -ae *f* Porta Capena (*a gate in the Servian Wall which marked the start of the Via Appia*)
cap•er -rī *m* he-goat, billy goat
caperr•ō -āre *vt & vi* to wrinkle
capess•ō -ĕre -īvī or **-iī -ītum** *vt* to try to reach, make for, seize, get hold of, snatch at; to take up, undertake, engage in; **capessere rem publicam** to be engaged in politics
capillāt•us -a -um *adj* having hair, hairy; **bene capillatus** having a fine head of hair
capill•us -ī *m* hair
capĭō capĕre cēpī captum *vt* (archaic *fut:* **capso**) to take hold of, grasp, seize; to occupy; to take up, assume (*office*); to catch, capture; to captivate, charm; to cheat, seduce, mislead, delude; to defeat, overcome (*in suite*); to convince (*in a dispute*); to reach, arrive at, land at; to exact, extort, accept as a bribe; to take, obtain, get, enjoy, reap (*profit, advantage*); to acquire, cherish, cultivate, adopt (*habits, etc.*); to form, conceive, come to, reach (*conclusions, plans, thoughts, resolutions, purposes*); to take, derive, draw, obtain (*examples, proofs, instances*); to entertain, conceive, receive, experience (*impressions, feelings*); (of feelings, experiences) to seize, overcome, occupy, take possession of; to suffer, be subjected to (*injury*); to hold, contain, be large enough for; to comprehend, grasp
cap•is -ĭdis *f* bowl (*with one handle, used in sacrifices*)
capistr•ō -āre *vt* to muzzle
capistr•um -ī *n* halter, muzzle
capĭt•al or **capit•āle -ālis** *n* capital offense
capitāl•is -e *adj* relating to the head or life; (law) affecting a man's life or civil status; (of crime) punishable by death, punishable by loss of civil rights, capital; dangerous, deadly, mortal; chief, preeminent, distinguished, of first rank
capĭt•ō -ōnis *m* big-head
Capitōlīn•us -a -um *adj* Capitoline; *m* Capitoline Hill; *m pl* persons in charge of the Capitoline games
Capitōl•ĭum -iī or **-ī** *n* the Capitol (*temple of Jupiter on the summit of Mons Tarpeius*); the Capitoline Hill (*including temple and citadel*); citadel (*of any city*)
capitulātim *adv* briefly, summarily
capitŭl•um -ī *n* small head; (as term of endearment) dear fellow
Cappadocĭ•a -ae *f* country in Asia Minor between the Taurus and Pontus
capr•a -ae *f* she-goat, nanny goat; body odor of armpits
caprĕ•a -ae *f* wild goat, roe
Caprĕ•ae -ārum *f pl* island at S. end of Bay of Naples off Sorrento

capreŏl·us -ī *m* roebuck, chamois; prop, support
Capricorn·us -ī *m* Capricorn (*sign of the zodiac*)
caprific·us -ī *f* wild fig tree
caprigĕn·us -a -um *adj* of goats; **caprigenum pecus** herd of goats
caprimulg·us -ī *m* rustic
caprīn·us -a -um *adj* of goats, goat; **de lana caprina rixari** to argue over nothing
caprīp·ēs -ĕdis *adj* goat-footed
caps·a -ae *f* holder, container, box, case (*esp. for book rolls*)
capsō see **capio**
capsŭl·a -ae *f* small box
capt·a -ae *f* captive, prisoner (*female*)
captātī·ō -ōnis *f* hunt, quest; **captatio verborum** verbalism, sophistry
captāt·or -ōris *m* (fig) hound; **aurae popularis captator** publicity hound
captī·ō -ōnis *f* taking, catching; fraud; loss, disadvantage; sophism
captiōsē *adv* slyly, insidiously, deceptively
captiōs·us -a -um *adj* deceitful; captious, sophistical; dangerous, harmful
captiuncŭl·a -ae *f* quibble, sophism
captīvit·ās -ātis *f* captivity; conquest, capture
captīv·us -a -um *adj* caught, taken captive; prisoner's; captured, conquered; *mf* prisoner of war, captive
capt·ō -āre *vt* to catch at eagerly; to keep reaching for; to try to catch, chase after; to strive after, long for, desire earnestly; to try to hear; to try to trap, entice, allure; to adopt (*plan*); to try to cause (*laughter*); to watch for (*opportunity*); to begin (*conversation*)
captūr·a -ae *f* capture; quarry
capt·us -a -um *pp* of **capio;** *adj* **oculis et auribus captus** blind and deaf; **mente captus** mad, crazy; *m* captive, prisoner
capt·us -ūs *m* mental grasp, mental capacity; notion
Capŭ·a -ae *f* chief city of Campania
capulār·is -e *adj* with one foot in the grave
capŭl·us -ī *m* coffin; hilt, handle
cap·ut -ĭtis *n* head; top, summit, point, extremity; source (*of river*); root (*of plant*); top (*of tree*); head, leader; capital (*of country*); main point (*of discourse*); chapter, principal division, heading; substance, summary; (com) capital; main course; life, civil status; **capitis accusare** to accuse of a capital offense; **capitis damnare** to condemn to death; **capitis res** matter of life and death; **diminutio capitis** loss of civil rights; **diminutio capitis maxima** condemnation to death or slavery; **diminutio capitis media** loss of citizenship; **diminutio capitis minima** change of status (*as by adoption or, in the case of women, by marriage*)
Cap·ys -yŏs *m* son of Assaracus and father of Anchises; companion of Aeneas; eighth king of Alba Longa
carbasĕ·us -a -um *adj* linen, canvas
carbăs·us -ī *f* (*pl:* **carbăs·a -ōrum** *n*) fine Spanish flax; linen garment; sail, canvas; awning
carb·ō -ōnis *m* charcoal
carbōnār·ĭus -ĭī or **-ī** *m* charcoal burner, collier
carbuncŭl·us -ī *m* small piece of coal; grief, sorrow; precious stone, garnet
carc·er -ĕris *m* prison, jail; prisoner; (term of reproach) jailbird; *m pl* starting gate (*at racetrack*); **ad carceres a calce revocari** to have to start all over again
carcerārĭ·us -a -um *adj* prison
carchēs·ĭum -ĭī or **-ī** *n* drinking cup (*slightly contracted in the middle*); upper part of mast (*similarly formed*)
cardiăc·us -ī *m* dyspeptic
card·ō -ĭnis *m* hinge; turning point, crisis; (astr) axis, pole; **cardo rerum** critical juncture, crisis
cardŭ·us -ī *m* thistle
cārē *adv* at a high price, dearly; highly
cārect·um -ī *m* sedge
cār·ĕō -ēre -ŭī *vi* (with *abl* or *genit*) **a** to be without; **b** to miss; **c** to be free from; **d** to keep away from, be absent from; **e** to abstain from
cār·ex -ĭcis *f* sedge
Cārĭ·a -ae *f* province in S.W. Asia Minor
carĭ·ēs (*genit* not in use) *f* decay, rot
carīn·a -ae *f* bottom of ship, keel; ship
Carīn·ae -ārum *f pl* the Keels (*district in Rome Between the Caelian and Esquiline Hills*)
carīnār·ĭus -ĭī or **-ī** *m* dyer of yellow
cariōs·us -a -um *adj* rotten, decayed, crumbled; wrinkled
cār·is -ĭdis *f* crab
cārit·ās -ātis *f* dearness, costliness, high price, high cost of living; affection, love
carm·en -ĭnis *n* song, tune; lyric poetry, poetry; incantation, charm; oracular utterance; ritual formula, legal formula; adage
Carment·a -ae or **Carment·is -is** *f* Roman goddess of prophecy, the mother of Evander, who came with him from Arcadia to Latium
Carmentāl·is -e *adj* of Carmenta; **Porta Carmentalis** gate at Rome near temple of Carmenta (*also called* **Porta Scelerata,** *i.e., ominous gate*)
carnār·ĭum -ĭī or **-ī** *n* meat hook; pantry
Carneăd·ēs -is *m* famous philoso-

pher, born at Cyrene, and founder of the New Academy (215-130 B.C.)
carnĭf·ex -ĭcis *m* hangman, executioner; murderer, butcher; scoundrel
carnificīn·a -ae *f* execution; torture, torment
carnifĭc·ō -āre *vt* to mutilate, cut to pieces, behead
car·ō -nis or **carn·is -is** *f* flesh, meat; **caro ferina** venison; **caro putida** carrion; (fig) rotten egg
car·ō -ĕre *vt* to card (*wool*)
Carpăth·us -ī *f* island between Crete and Rhodes
carpatĭn·us -a -um *adj* of rough leather; *f* crude shoe
carpent·um -ī *n* two-wheeled covered carriage (*esp. used by women on holidays*)
carp·ō -ĕre -sī -tum *vt* to pluck, pick, cull; to carp at, criticize, take apart; to enjoy, make use of; to crop, browse on (*grass*); to pick, gather (*fruit*); to separate into parts, divide; (mil) to harass, weaken (*esp. by repeated attacks*); **auras vitales carpere** to breathe the breath of life; **diem carpere** to make the most of the present; **gyrum carpere** to go in a circle; **iter** or **viam carpere** to make one's way, pick one's way, travel; **vellera carpere** to spin
carptim *adv* piecemeal, separately, in parts; at different times; at different points; gradually
carpt·or -ōris *m* carver (*of food*)
Carrh·ae -ārum *f pl* town in Mesopotamia where Crassus was defeated and killed by the Parthians (53 B.C.)
carrūc·a -ae *f* four-wheeled carriage
carr·us -ī *m* four-wheeled wagon
Carthāginiens·is -e *adj & mf* Carthaginian
Carthāg·ō -ĭnis *f* Carthage (*city in N. Africa, founded as a Phoenician colony in 9th cent.* B.C.)
caruncŭl·a -ae *f* little piece of meat
cār·us -a -um *adj* dear, high-priced, expensive, costly; dear, beloved, esteemed; loving, affectionate
cas·a -ae *f* cottage, cabin, hut
casc·us -a -um *adj* old, primitive
cāseŏl·us -ī *m* small piece of cheese
cāsĕ·us -ī *m* cheese
casĭ·a -ae *f* mezereon (*fragrant plant with purple flowers*)
Cassandr·a -ae *f* daughter of Priam and Hecuba who had the gift of prophecy but was believed by no one
cass·ēs -ium *m pl* hunting net, snare; spider web
cassĭd·a -ae *f* metal helmet
Cassiŏp·ē -ēs or **Cassiopē·a -ae** *f* wife of Cepheus and mother of Andromeda, afterwards made a constellation
Cass·ius -iī or **-ī** *m* C. Cassius Longinus (*one of the murderers of Caesar*)
cass·is -ĭdis *f* metal helmet
cass·ō -āre *vi* to totter, trip
cass·us -a -um *adj* empty, hollow; (fig) empty, groundless, vain, pointless; (with *abl*) deprived of, devoid of, without; **cassus lumine** without life, dead; **in cassum** to no purpose, pointlessly
Castăl·is -ĭdis *adj* Castalian; **sorores Castalides** Muses; *f* Muse
Castalĭ·us -a -um *adj* Castalian; *f* fountain on Mt. Parnassus, sacred to Apollo and the Muses
castanĕ·a -ae *f* chestnut tree; chestnut
castē *adv* purely, chastely, spotlessly; virtuously; devoutly, piously
castellān·us -a -um *adj* of a fort, of a castle; *m* occupant of a castle or fortress; *m pl* garrison (*of a fortress*)
castellātim *adv* one fortress after another; **castellatim dissipati** (troops) stationed in various fortresses
castell·um -ī *n* fort, fortress, stronghold, castle; (fig) defense, shelter, refuge
castērĭ·a -ae *f* rowers' quarters
castīgābĭl·is -e *adj* punishable
castīgātĭ·ō -ōnis *f* correction, punishment; censure, reproof
castīgāt·or -ōris *m* corrector, critic
castīgātōrĭ·us -a -um *adj* reproving
castīgāt·us -a -um *adj* small, contracted, slender
castīg·ō -āre *vt* to correct, make right, blame, reprove, censure, chide, find fault with, punish; to correct, amend; to hold in check, restrain
castimōnĭ·a -ae *f* purity, morality; chastity, abstinence
castĭt·ās -ātis *f* purity, chastity
cast·or -ŏris *m* beaver
Cast·or -ŏris *m* son of Tyndareus, twin brother of Pollux, brother of Helen and Clytemnestra, and patron of sailors
castorĕ·um -ī *m* bitter, strong-smelling secretion of beavers
castrens·is -e *adj* camp, military
castr·ō -āre *vt* to castrate
castr·um -ī *n* fort, fortress, castle; *n pl* military camp; day's march; the service, army life; (pol) party; (phil) school; **bina castra** two camps; **castra facere** or **habere** to encamp; **castra movere** to break camp; **castra munire** to construct a camp; **castra ponere** to pitch camp; **castra una** one camp
cast·us -a -um *adj* (morally) pure, chaste, spotless, guiltless, virtuous; religious, pious, holy, sacred
casŭl·a -ae *f* little hut, little cottage
cās·us -ūs *m* falling; (fig) fall, downfall, overthrow, end; chance, event, happening, occurrence, emergency; occasion, opportunity; misfortune, mishap, accident, calamity; fall,

death; fate; (gram) case; **non consulto sed casu** not on purpose but by chance

catagelasĭm·us -a -um *adj* bantering, jeering; exposed to ridicule

catagrăph·us -a -um *adj* painted, colored

cataphract·ēs -ae *m* coat of mail

cataphract·us -a -um *adj* mail-clad

catăpl·us -ī *m* arrival of ship; arriving ship or fleet

catapult·a -ae *f* catapult; (fig) missile

catapultārĭ·us -a -um *adj* catapulted, shot (*from catapult*)

cataract·a or **catarract·a** or **catarract·ēs -ae** *f* waterfall, cataract (*esp. on the Nile*); floodgate; drawbridge

cataractrĭ·a -ae *f* spice

catast·a -ae *f* stage on which slaves were displayed for sale

catē *adv* skillfully, wisely

catēĭ·a -ae *f* javelin

catell·a -ae *f* puppy (*female*); small chain

catell·us -ī *m* puppy; small chain

catēn·a -ae *f* chain; series; barrier, restraint, bond

catēnāt·us -a -um *adj* chained

caterv·a -ae *f* crowd, throng, band, mob; troop (*of actors*); (mil) troop, horde

catervātim *adv* in companies, by troops; in crowds or flocks (*of plague-stricken people*)

cathĕdr·a -ae *f* armchair, cushioned seat; litter, sedan; professional chair

Catilīn·a -ae *m* L. Sergius Catiline (*Roman patrician whose conspiracy was exposed by Cicero in* 63 B.C.)

catill·ō -āre *vi* to lick the plate

catill·us -ī *m* plate

catīn·us -ī *m* plate, pot, bowl

Cat·ō -ōnis *m* M. Porcius Cato (*model of Roman aristocratic conservatism,* 239-149 B.C.); M. Porcius Cato Uticensis (*grandson of Porcius Cato, inveterate enemy of Caesar,* 95-45 B.C.)

catōn·ĭum -ĭī or **-ī** *n* lower world

Catull·us -ī *m* C. Valerius Catullus (*lyric and elegiac poet of Verona,* 86-54 B.C.)

catŭl·us -ī *m* puppy; whelp, cub

cat·us -a -um *adj* sharp, shrewd, keen; sly, cunning

Caucăs·us -ī *m* Caucasus mountains

caud·a -ae *f* tail (*of animal*); penis; **caudam jactare** (with *dat*) to flatter; **caudam trahere** to be mocked

caudĕ·us -a -um *adj* of wood, wooden

caud·ex or **cōd·ex -ĭcis** *m* trunk (*of tree*); block (*of wood to which one was tied for punishment*); book, ledger; blockhead

caudicāl·is -e *adj* of wood cutting

Caud·ĭum -ĭī *or* **-ī** *n* town in Samnium

caul·ae -ārum *f pl* hole, opening passage; sheepfold, pen

caul·is -is *f* stalk, stem; cabbage stalk, cabbage

caup·ō -ōnis *m* innkeeper

caupōn·a -ae *f* inn, tavern; retail shop

caupōnĭ·us -a -um *adj* of a shop or tavern

caupōn·or -ārī -ātus sum *vt* to trade in or traffic in

caupōnŭl·a -ae *f* small inn or tavern

caus·a or **causs·a -ae** *f* (law) lawsuit, case; grounds, cause, motive, purpose, reason; good reason, just cause; pretext, pretense; inducement, occasion, opportunity; side, party, faction, cause; condition, situation, position; (rhet) matter of discussion, subject matter; matter, business, concern; commission, charge; personal relationship, connexion; **causā** (with *genit*) for the sake of, on account of; **causā cadere** to lose a case; **causam agere, causam dicere,** or **causam orare** to plead a case; **causam cognoscere** to examine a case (*as judge*); **vestrā causā** in your interests; **per causam** (with *genit*) under the pretext of; **sine causa** without good reason

causārĭ·us -a -um *adj* sick; *m* (mil) malingerer, goldbrick

causĭ·a -ae *f* Macedonian hat (*with wide brim*)

causidĭc·us -ī *m* pleader, lawyer; shyster

causifĭc·or -ārī -ātus sum *vi* to make excuses

caus·or -ārī -ātus sum *vt* to pretend, give as a reason

caussa see **causa**

causŭl·a -ae *f* petty lawsuit; minor cause

cautē *adv* cautiously, carefully; with security

cautēl·a -ae *f* precaution

caut·ēs -is *f* rock, crag

cautim *adv* warily, cautiously

cautĭ·ō -ōnis *f* caution, wariness; guarantee, provision; (law) bond, security, bail, warranty; **mea cautio est** I must see to it; **mihi cautio est** I must take care

caut·or -ōris *m* wary person; bondsman, surety

caut·us -a -um *adj* cautious, careful; safe, secure

cavaed·ĭum -ĭī or **-ī** *n* inner court of Roman house

cavĕ·a -ae *f* cavity; enclosure for animals: cage, den, stall, beehive, bird cage; auditorium, theater; **prima cavea** section of auditorium for nobility; **ultima cavea** section for lower classes

cavĕō cavēre cāvī cautum *vt* to guard against, beware of; to keep clear of; to stipulate, decree, order; to guarantee; *vi* to be careful, look out, be on one's guard; (with *abl* or

ab + *abl*) to be on one's guard against; (with **ab** + *abl*) to get a guarantee from; (with *dat*) **a** to guarantee, give a guarantee to; **b** to provide for, take care of; **cave tangere** (= **noli tangere**) do not touch

cavern·a -ae *f* hollow, cavity, cave, cavern; vault; hold (*of ship*)

cavill·a -ae *f* jeering, scoffing

cavillāti·ō -ōnis *f* banter, scoffing, raillery; sophistry, quibbling

cavillāt·or -ōris *m* scoffer; quibbler, sophist

cavill·or -ārī -ātus sum *vt* to scoff at, mock, criticize, satirize; *vi* to scoff, jeer; to quibble

cav·ō -āre *vt* to hollow out, excavate; to pierce, run through

cav·us -a -um *adj* hollow, hollowed; concave, vaulted; deep-channeled (*river*); *m & n* hole, cavity, hollow

-ce demonstrative enclitic appended to pronouns and adverbs (like colloquial English *here, there,* with *this* or *that*); **hice** (for **hicce**) this (*here*); **hujusce** of this (*here*); (when followed by the enclytic **-ne,** the form becomes **-ci: hicine, sicine**)

Cecropid·ae -ārum *m pl* descendants of Cecrops, Athenians

Cecrŏp·is -idis *f* female descendant of Cecrops (*esp. Aglauros*); Procne; Philomela; Athenian woman

Cecr·ops -ŏpis *m* first king of Athens

cēdō cēdĕre cessī cessum *vt* to grant, concede, yield, give up; *vi* to go, move, walk, walk along; to go away, depart, withdraw; (of time) to pass; (of events) to turn out; to pass away, die; (mil) to retreat; (with *dat*) **a** to befall, fall to the lot of, accrue to; **b** to yield to, submit to, give in to; **c** to yield (*in rank*) to, be inferior to; **d** to comply with, conform to, obey; (with **in** + *acc*) to be changed into, become; (with **pro** + *abl*) to pass for, be the equivalent of, be the price of; **bonis** or **possessionibus alicui cedere** to give up or cede one's property to someone; **foro cedere** to go bankrupt

cedo (*pl:* **cette**) (old *impv*) here with, bring here, give here; let's hear, tell, out with; look at; **cedo dum!** all right!; come now!; **cedo ut inspiciam** let me look

cedr·us -ī *f* cedar, juniper; cedar wood; cedar oil

Celaen·ō -ūs *f* daughter of Atlas and one of the Pleiades; one of the Harpies; greedy woman

cēlāt·um -ī *n* secret

celĕb·er -ris -re *adj* crowded, populous, frequented; well-attended; famous; well-known, common, usual; solemn, festive; numerous, repeated, frequent

celebrāti·ō -ōnis *f* large assembly; festival, celebration; *f pl* throngs

celebrāt·us -a -um *adj* much-frequented, much-visited, crowded, populous; celebrated, famous, renowned; customary, usual, frequent; solemn, festive; trite, familiar, often-repeated

celebrit·ās -ātis *f* throng, crowd, multitude, large assembly; publicity; repetition, frequency; fame, renown; celebration

celĕbr·ō -āre *vt* to frequent, crowd, fill, visit in crowds; to repeat, practice, exercise; to publicize, advertise, honor, glorify; to escort, attend; to cause to resound

cel·er -ĕris -ĕre *adj* swift, speedy, quick, rapid, hurried; rash, hasty

celĕrĕ *adv* quickly

Celĕr·ēs -um *m pl* mounted bodyguards of Roman kings

celerip·ēs -ĕdis *adj* swift-footed

celerit·ās -ātis *f* speed, quickness, rapidity

celeriter *adv* quickly, speedily

celĕr·ō -āre *vt* to quicken, speed up, accelerate; *vi* to be quick, rush, speed

cell·a -ae *f* storeroom, storehouse, grain elevator, silo; cheap apartment, garret; sanctuary (*of temple, where the cult image stood*); cell (*of beehive*)

cellāri·us -a -um *adj* of a storeroom; *m* storekeeper, butler

cellŭl·a -ae *f* small storeroom, small apartment

cēl·ō -āre *vt* to hide, conceal; to veil (*feelings*); to keep (*something*) secret, keep quiet about; (with *acc* of thing and *acc* of person from whom one conceals) to keep (*someone*) in the dark about, hide (*something*) from (*someone*); **celari** (with **de** + *abl*) to be kept in ignorance of

cel·ox -ōcis *adj* swift, quick; *f* swift-sailing ship, cutter, speedboat

cels·us -a -um *adj* high, lofty, towering, prominent, erect; lofty, elevated (*thoughts*); high (*rank*); proud, haughty

Celt·ae -ārum *m pl* Celts (*who occupied most of W. Europe*); (in more restricted sense) inhabitants of central Gaul

Celtibēr·ī -ōrum *m pl* Celtiberians (*early people of Central Spain*)

cēn·a -ae *f* principal meal, dinner; dish, course; company at dinner

cēnācŭl·um -ī *n* dining room (*usually on an upper floor*); attic

cēnātic·us -a -um *adj* dinner

cēnāti·ō -ōnis *f* dining room

cēnāt·us -a -um *adj* having dined; spent in feasting

cēnit·ō -āre *vi* to dine habitually, dine often

cēn·ō -āre *vt* to make a meal of, dine on, eat; *vi* to dine, eat dinner

cens·ĕō -ēre -ŭī -um *vt* to assess, rate, estimate, tax; to esteem, appreciate, value; (of senate) to decree, resolve; to propose, move, vote, argue, suggest, advise; to think, believe, hold, suppose, imagine, expect

censi·ō -ōnis *f* rating, assessment, taxation; opinion

cens·or -ōris *m* censor (*one of two Roman magistrates who took the census and exercised general control over morals, etc.*); severe judge of morals, critic

censōri·us -a -um *adj* of the censors; subject to censure; rigid, stern, austere; **homo censorius** ex-censor; **lex censoria** contract (*drawn up by censors*) for leasing buildings

censūr·a -ae *f* office of censor, censorship; criticism

cens·us -ūs *m* census; register of the census; income bracket; wealth, property; rich presents, gifts; **censum agere** or **habere** to hold a census; **censu prohibere** to exclude from citizenship, disenfranchise

centaurē·um -ī *n* centaury (*medical herb*)

Centaur·us -ī *m* centaur (*creature fabled to be half man and half horse*); Centaurus (*southern constellation between the Southern Cross and Hydra*)

centēn·ī -ae -a *adj* one hundred each; **deciens centena milia passum** ten hundred thousand paces, one million paces

centēsim·us -a -um *adj* hundredth; *f* hundredth part, one percent; (com) 1% monthly (12% per annum)

centi·ceps -cipitis *adj* hundred-headed

centiēs or **centiens** *adv* a hundred times; (fig) a great many times

centimān·us -a -um *adj* hundred-handed

cent·ō -ōnis *m* patchwork, quilt

centum (indecl) *adj* hundred

centumgemin·us -a -um *adj* hundredfold

centumpl·ex -icis *adj* hundredfold

centumpond·ium -iī or **-ī** *n* hundred pounds, hundred-pound weight

centumvirāl·is -e *adj* of the centumviri

centumvir·ī -ōrum *m pl* panel of one hundred (*jurors chosen annually to try civil suits under a quaestor, esp. concerning inheritances*)

centuncŭl·us -ī *m* piece of patchwork, cloth of many colors, saddle cloth

centuri·a -ae *f* (mil) company, century (*theoretically composed of one hundred men*); (pol) century (*one of the* 193 *groups into which Servius Tullius divided the Roman people*)

centuriātim *adv* by companies, by centuries

centuriāt·us -a -um *adj* divided into companies or centuries; **comitia centuriata** centuriate assembly (*legislative body which met in the Campus Martius to elect high magistrates, decree war, etc.*)

centuri·ō -ōnis *m* centurion (*commander of an infantry company*)

centuri·ō -āre *vt* to divide into centuries

centuriōnāt·us -ūs *m* election of centurions

centuss·is -is *m* a hundred aces (*bronze coins*)

cēnŭl·a -ae *f* little dinner

Cephăl·us -ī *m* husband of Procris, whom he unintentionally shot

Ceph·eus -ĕī *m* king of Ethiopia, husband of Cassiope and father of Andromeda

Cephīs·us -ī *m* river in Attica; river in Phocis and Boeotia

cēr·a -ae *f* wax; writing tablet (*covered with wax*); wax seal; wax bust of an ancestor; cell (*of beehive*)

Ceramīc·us -ī *m* cemetery of Athens

cērār·ium -iī or **-ī** *n* fee for affixing a seal

cerast·ēs -ae *m* horned serpent

cerăs·us -ī *f* cherry tree; cherry

cērāt·us -a -um *adj* waxed

Cerbĕr·us -ī *m* three-headed dog which guarded the entrance to the lower world

cercopithēc·us -ī *m* long-tailed monkey

cercūr·us -ī *m* swift-sailing ship, cutter

cerd·ō -ōnis *m* workman, laborer

Cereāl·ia -ium *n pl* festival of Ceres (*April* 10*th*)

Cereāl·is -e *adj* of Ceres; of grain; **arma Cerealia** utensils for grinding and baking

cerebrōs·us -a -um *adj* hot-headed

cerĕbr·um -ī *n* brain; head, skull; understanding; hot temper

Cer·ēs -ĕris *f* goddess of agriculture and mother of Proserpine; grain bread, food

cērĕ·us -a -um *adj* of wax, waxen; wax-colored; soft, pliant; *m* candle

cērinth·a -ae *f* wax flower

cērĭn·us -a -um *adj* wax-colored; *n pl* wax-colored clothes

cernō cernĕre crēvī crētum *vt* (of sight) to discern, distinguish, make out, see; (of mind) to discern, see, understand; to decide, decree, determine; **hereditatem cernere** to formally declare oneself heir to an inheritance, accept an inheritance

cernŭ·us -a -um *adj* with face turned toward the earth, stooping forwards

cērōm·a -ătis *n* wrestler's oil

cērōmatĭc·us -a -um *adj* smeared with oil, oily, greasy

cerrīt·us -a -um *adj* crazy, frantic

certām·en -ĭnis *n* contest, match; rivalry; (mil) battle, combat

certātim *adv* with a struggle, in rivalry

certātĭ·ō -ōnis *f* contest; rivalry, discussion, debate

certē *adv* surely, certainly, unquestionably, undoubtedly, of course; (in answers) yes, certainly; (to restrict an assertion) at least, at any rate

certō *adv* for certain, for sure; surely, in fact, really

cert·ō -āre *vi* to fight, contend, struggle, do battle; to compete; (law) to debate; (with *inf*) to strive to

cert·us -a -um *adj* certain, determined, resolved, fixed, settled; specific, particular, certain, precise, definite; faithful, trusty, dependable; sure of aim, unerring; unwavering, inexorable; **certiorem facere** to inform; **certum est mihi** (with *inf*) I am determined to; **certum habere** to regard as certain; **pro certo** for sure; **pro certo habere** to be assured

cērŭl·a -ae *f* piece of wax; **cerula miniata** red pencil (*of a critic*)

cēruss·a -ae *f* ceruse, white paint

cērussāt·us -a -um *adj* painted white

cerv·a -ae *f* hind, deer

cervīc·al -ālis *n* pillow, cushion

cervīcŭl·a -ae *f* slender neck

cervīn·us -a -um *adj* of a stag or deer

cerv·ix -īcis *f* neck; nape of the neck; **in cervicibus nostris esse** to be on our necks., i.e., to have (*something or someone unpleasant*) on our hands; **a cervicibus nostris avertere** to get (*someone*) off our neck, get rid of (*someone*); **cervicibus sustinere** to shoulder (*responsibility*)

cerv·us -ī *m* stag, deer; (mil) palisade

cessātĭ·ō -ōnis *f* letup, delay; inactivity, idleness, cessation

cessāt·or -ōris *m* idler, loafer

cessĭ·ō -ōnis *f* surrendering, relinquishment

cess·ō -āre *vi* to let up, slack off, become remiss, stop; to be inactive, be idle, do nothing; to lie fallow

cestrosphendŏn·ē -ēs *f* artillery piece for hurling stones

cest·us or **cest·os -ī** *m* girdle (*esp. of Venus*)

cētār·ĭum -ĭī or **-ī** *n* fish pond

cētār·ĭus -ĭī or **-ī** *m* fish dealer

cētĕra *adv* otherwise, in all other respects, for the rest

cēterōquī or **cēterōquīn** *adv* otherwise, in all other respects, for the rest

cētĕrum *adv* otherwise, in all other respects, for the rest; but, yet, still, on the other hand

cētĕr·us -a -um *adj* the other, the remaining, the rest of; *pron m pl & f pl* the others, all the rest, everybody; *n* the rest

Cethēg·us -ī *m* C. Cernelius Cethegus (*fellow conspirator of Catiline*)

cette see **cedo**

cēt·us -ī (*pl:* **cēt·ē**) *m* sea monster: whale, shark, seal, dolphin

ceu *conj* (in comparisons) as, just as; (in comparative conditions) as if, just as if; **ceu cum** as when

cēv·ĕō -ēre *vi* (*cf* **criso**) (of a male) to move the haunches

Cē·yx -ȳcis *m* king of Trachis, who was changed into a kingfisher, as was his wife Alcyone

Chaldae·us -a -um *adj* Chaldaean; *m* astrologer, fortune-teller

chalybēĭ·us -a -um *adj* steel

Chalȳb·es -um *m pl* people of Pontus in Asia Minor noted as steelworkers

chal·ybs -ȳbis *m* steel

Chāŏn·es -um *m pl* a tribe in Epirus

Chāonĭ·us -a -um *adj* Chaonian; of Epirus; *f* Chaonia (*district of Epirus*)

Cha·os -ī *n* chaos, the unformed world, empty space, shapeless mass from which the world was formed; **a Chao** from the beginning of the world

char·a -ae *f* wild cabbage

charistĭ·a -ōrum *n pl* Roman family festival

Charĭt·es -um *f pl* the Graces

Char·ōn -ontis *m* ferryman of the lower world

chart·a -ae *f* sheet of papyrus; sheet of paper; writing, letter, poem; book; record

chartŭl·a -ae *f* sheet of paper; letter, note

Charybd·is -is *f* whirlpool between Italy and Sicily, personified as a female monster

Chatt·ī -ōrum *m pl* people of central Germany

Chēl·ae -ārum *f pl* the Claws (*of Scorpio*); Libra (*constellation into which Scorpio extends*)

chelȳdr·us -ī *m* water snake

chely·s (*genit* not in use; *acc:* **chelyn**) *f* tortoise; lyre

cheragr·a -ae *f* arthritis in the hand

chīliarch·ēs -ae or **chīliarch·us -ī** *m* commander of 1000 men; Persian chancellor (*highest office next to the king*)

Chimaer·a -ae *f* fire-breathing monster, with lion's head, goat's body, and dragon's tail

Chi·os -ī *f* island off coast of Asia Minor, famous for its wine

chīrogrăph·um -ī *n* handwriting; autography; document; **falsa chirographa** forgeries

Chīr·ōn -ōnis *m* Chiron (*centaur, tutor of Aesculapius, Hercules, and Achilles, and famous for his knowledge of medicine and prophecy*)

chīronŏm·os -ī or **chīronŏm·ōn -untis** *m* pantomimist

chīrurgĭ·a -ae *f* surgery

Chi·us -a -um *adj & mf* Chian; *n* Chian wine; *n pl* Chian cloth

chlamydāt·us -a -um *adj* wearing a military uniform

chlam·ys -ȳdis *f* military cloak; gold-brocaded mantle
Choerĭl·us -ī *m* incompetent Greek panegyrist of Alexander the Great
chorāg·ĭum -ĭī or **-ī** *n* choreography
chorāg·us -ī *m* choragus (*man who finances the chorus*)
choraul·ēs -ae *m* flute player who accompanied the choral dance
chord·a -ae *f* gut string, string (*of musical instrument*); cord, rope
chorē·a -ae *f* dance
chorē·us -ī *m* trochee
chor·us -ī *m* chorus; choir
Chrem·ēs -ētis or **-is** or **-ī** *m* miserly old man (*in Roman comedy*)
Christiān·us -ī *m* Christian
Christ·us -ī *m* Christ
Chrȳsē·is -ĭdis *f* Agamemnon's slave girl, daughter of Chryses
Chrȳs·ēs -ae *m* priest of Apollo
Chrysipp·us -ī *m* famous Stoic philosopher (290-210 B.C.)
chrȳsolĭth·os -ī *m* chrysolite, topaz
chrȳs·os -ī *m* gold
cibārĭ·us -a -um *adj* of food; common, coarse (*food of slaves*); *n pl* rations, provisions, food allowance
cibāt·us -ūs *m* food
cib·ō -āre *vt* to feed
cibōr·ĭum -ĭī or **-ī** *n* drinking cup
cib·us -ī *m* food; feed; (fig) food, nourishment
cicād·a -ae *f* locust, harvest fly
cicātrīcōs·us -a -um *adj* scarred, covered with scars
cicātr·ix -īcis *f* scar
cicc·us -ī *m* core of pomegranate; something worthless, trifle
cic·er -ĕris *n* chick-pea
Cicĕr·ō -ōnis *m* M. Tullius Cicero (*orator and statesman*, 106-43 B.C.)
cīchorē·um -ī *n* endive
Cicŏn·es -um *m pl* Thracian tribe
cicōnĭ·a -ae *f* stork
cic·ur -ŭris *adj* tame
cicūt·a -ae *f* hemlock tree; hemlock poison; pipe, flute (*carved from hemlock tree*)
ciĕō ciēre cīvī citum *vt* to set in motion, move; to stir, agitate; to call for, send for; to summon for help; to invoke, appeal to; to call on by name, mention by name; to start, bring about; to renew (*combat*)
Cilicĭ·a -ae *f* country in S. Asia Minor
Cilicĭ·us -a -um *adj* Cilician; *n* garment of goat's hair
Cil·ix -ĭcis *adj & m* Cilician
Cimbr·ī -ōrum *m pl* Germanic tribe (*defeated by Marius in* 101 B.C.)
cīm·ex -ĭcis *m* bug
Cimmerĭ·ī -ōrum *m pl* people in the Crimea; mythical people living in perpetual darkness in caves at Cumae
cinaedĭc·us -a -um *adj* lewd
cinaed·us -ī *m* sodomite; lewd dancer
cincinnāt·us -a -um *adj* curly-haired
Cincinnāt·us -ī *m* L. Quinctius Cincinnatus (*famous Roman hero, dictator in* 458 B.C.)
cincinn·us -ī *m* curled hair, artificial curl (*of hair*); (rhet) highly artificial expression
cincticŭl·us -ī *m* small belt or sash
cinctūr·a -ae *f* belt, sash
cinct·us -ūs *m* tucking up; belt, sash; **cinctus Gabinius** Gabinian style of wearing toga (*usually employed at religious festivals*)
cinctūt·us -a -um *adj* wearing a belt or sash; old-fashioned
cinefact·us -a -um *adj* reduced to ashes
cinerār·ĭus -ĭī or **-ī** *m* curling iron, hair curler
cingō cingĕre cinxī cinctum *vt* to surround, encircle; to wreathe (*head*); to tuck up (*garment*); (mil) to beleaguer, invest; to cover, protect; **cingi in proelia** to prepare oneself for battle, get ready for battle; **ferrum cingi** to put on one's sword
cingŭl·a -ae *f* belt; sash (*worn by women*); girth (*worn by horses, etc.*); sword belt; chastity belt
cingŭl·um -ī *m* belt; sword belt; sash (*worn by women*); girdle, chastity belt
cingŭl·us -ī *m* zone (*of the earth*)
cinĭfl·ō -ōnis *m* hair curler
cin·is -ĕris *m* ashes; ruin, death
Cinn·a -ae *m* L. Cornelius Cinna (*consul* 87-84 B.C. *and supporter of Marius, d.* 84 B.C.)
cinnamōm·um or **cinnăm·um -ī** *n* cinnamon; *n pl* cinnamon sticks
Cinȳr·ās -ae *m* father of Myrrha and Adonis
cipp·us -ī *m* stake, post, pillar; gravestone; (mil) palisade
circā *adv* around, round about, all around, in the vicinity; *prep* (with *acc*) (of place) around, surrounding, about, among, through, in the neighborhood of, near; attending, escorting (*persons*); (of time) at about, around, towards; (with numerals) about, nearly, almost; concerning, in respect to
circamoer·ĭum -ĭī or **-ī** *n* area on both sides of a city wall
Circ·ē -ēs or **-ae** *f* daughter of Helios and Perse, famous for her witchcraft
circens·is -e *adj* of the racetrack; *m pl* races
circĭn·ō -āre *vt* to make round; to circle
circĭn·us -ī *m* (geometer's) compass, pair of compasses
circĭter *adv* (of time and number) nearly, about, approximately; *prep* (with *acc*) about, near
circlus see **circulus**
circuĕō see **circumeo**
circuitĭō see **circumitio**
circuĭt·us or **circumĭt·us -ūs** *m* circuit; going round, revolution; de-

tour; circumference; circumlocution; (rhet) period
circulāt·or -ōris *m* peddler, vendor
circŭl·or -ārī -ātus sum *vi* to gather around (*for conversation*); to stroll about
circŭl·us or **circl·us -ī** *m* circle, circuit; ring, hoop; social circle; (astr) orbit
circum *adv* about, all around; *prep* (with *acc*) around, about; in the neighborhood of
circum·ăgō -agĕre -ēgī -actum *vt* to turn around; to sway (*emotionally*); **circumagi** or **se circumagere** to go out of one's way, go in a round about way; (of time) to pass away, roll around
circumăr·ō -āre *vt* to plow around
circumcaesūr·ā -ae *f* contour, outline
circum·cīdo -cīdĕre -cīdī -cīsum *vt* to cut around, trim; to cut short, cut down on; to abridge, shorten; to circumcise
circumcircā *adv* all around
circumcīs·us -a -um *pp* of **circumcido;** *adj* steep; inaccessible; abridged, short
circum·clūdō -clūdĕre -clūsī -clūsum *vt* to shut in, hem in, enclose, surround
circumcŏl·ō -ĕre *vt* to live near
circumcurs·ō -āre *vt & vi* to run around
circum·dō -dare -dĕdī -dătum *vt* to surround, enclose, encircle; (with *dat*) to place or put (*something*) around
circum·dūcō -dūcĕre -duxī -ductum *vt* to lead around, draw around; (with double *acc*) to lead (*someone*) around to; **aliquem omnia praesidia circumducere** to take someone around to all the garrisons
circum·ĕō or **circu·ĕō -īre -īvī** or **iī -ĭtum** *vt* to go around, go around to, visit, make the rounds of; to surround, encircle, enclose, encompass; to get around, circumvent, deceive, cheat; *vi* to go around, make a circuit
circumequĭt·ō -āre *vt* to ride around
circum·fĕrō -ferre -tŭlī -lātum *vt* to carry around, hand around; to publicize, spread abroad; to purify; **circumferri** to revolve; **oculos circumferre** to look around, glance about
circum·flectō -flectĕre -flexī -flexum *vt* to turn around, wheel about
circumfl·ō -āre *vt* to blow around; (fig) to buffet
circum·flŭō -fluĕre -fluxī *vt* to flow around; to surround; to overflow; *vi* to be overflowing, abound
circumflŭ·us -a -um *adj* flowing around; surrounded (*by water*)
circumforānĕ·us -a -um *adj* strolling about from market to market, itinerant; around the forum
circum·fundō -fundĕre -fūdī -fūsum *vt* to pour around; to surround, cover, envelop; **circumfundi** or **se circumfundere** to crowd around; **circumfundi** (with *dat*) to cling to
circumgĕm·ō -ĕre *vt* to growl around (*e.g., a sheepfold*)
circumgest·ō -āre *vt* to carry around
circum·gredĭor -grĕdī -gressus sum *vt* to surround
circumitĭ·ō or **circuitĭ·ō -ōnis** *f* going round; patrolling; circumlocution
circumĭtus see **circuitus**
circumjac·ĕō -ēre *vi* (with *dat*) to lie near, border on, be adjacent to
circum·jicĭō -jicĕre -jēcī -jectum *vt* to throw or place around; to surround; (with *dat*) to throw (*something*) around (*someone or something*); **fossam circumjicere** to dig a trench all around
circumject·us -a -um *adj* surrounding, adjacent; (with *dat*) adjacent to; *n pl* neighborhood
circumject·us -ūs *m* surrounding; embrace
circumlātus *pp* of **circumfero**
circumlĭg·ō -āre *vt* to bind; (with *dat*) to bind or fasten (*something*) to
circum·lĭnō -linĕre — -lītum *vt* to smear all over; to anoint
circumlŭ·ō -ĕre *vt* to flow around
circumluvĭ·ō -ōnis *f* island (*formed by a river flowing in a new channel*)
circum·mittō -mittĕre -mīsī -missum *vt* to send around
circummūn·ĭō or **circummoen·ĭō -īre** *vt* to fortify
circummūnītĭ·ō -ōnis *f* investment (*of town*); circumvallation
circumpadān·us -a -um *adj* situated along the Po River
circumpend·ĕō -ēre *vi* to hang around
circumplaud·ō -ĕre *vt* to applaud from every direction
circum·plector -plectī -plexus sum *vt* to clasp, embrace, surround
circumplĭc·ō -āre *vt* to wind; (with *dat*) to wind (*something*) around
circum·pōnō -pōnĕre -posŭī -posĭtum *vt* (with *dat*) to place or set (*something*) around
circumpōtātĭ·ō -ōnis *f* round of drinks
circumrēt·ĭō -īre -īvī -ītum *vt* to snare
circum·rōdō -rōdĕre -rōsī *vt* to nibble all around; to hesitate to say; to slander, backbite
circumsaep·ĭō or **circumsēp·ĭō -īre -sī -tum** *vt* to fence in, enclose
circumscind·ō -ĕre *vt* to strip off
circum·scrībō -scrībĕre -scripsī -scriptum *vt* to draw a line around, mark the boundary of; to

limit, restrict; to set aside; to defeat the purpose of; to trap, defraud
circumscriptē *adv* comprehensively; (rhet) in periods
circumscriptĭ•ō -ōnis *f* encircling; circle; circuit, limit, boundary; comprehensive statement; cheating, deceiving; (rhet) period
circumscript•or -ōris *m* cheat
circumscript•us -a -um *pp* of **circumscribo;** *adj* restricted, limited; (rhet) periodic
circumsĕc•ō -āre *vt* to cut around
circum•sedĕō -sedēre -sēdī -sessum *vt* to beset, besiege, invest, blockade
circumsēpĭō see **circumsaepio**
circumsessĭ•ō -ōnis *f* besieging, blockading
circumsīd•ō -ĕre *vt* to besiege
circumsil•ĭō -īre *vi* to hop around, dance around
circum•sistō -sistĕre -stĕtī *vt* to stand around, surround
circumsŏn•ō -āre *vt* to make resound, fill with sound; *vi* to resound everywhere; (with *dat*) to resound to
circumsŏn•us -a -um *adj* noisy
circumspectātr•ix -īcis *f* spy (*female*)
circumspectĭ•ō -ōnis *f* looking around; circumspection, caution
circumspect•ō -āre *vt* to search attentively, watch for; *vi* to keep looking around, look around anxiously
circumspect•us -a -um *pp* of **circumspicio;** *adj* well-considered; guarded (*words*); circumspect, cautious (*person*)
circumspect•us -ūs *m* consideration; view
circum•spicĭō -spicĕre -spexī -spectum *vt* to look around for, survey, see; to consider, examine; *vi* to be circumspect, be cautious, be on the watch; **se circumspicere** to think highly of oneself
circumstant•ēs -ĭum *m pl* bystanders
circum•stō -stāre -stĕtī *vt* to surround, envelop; (of terror, etc.) to grip, confront, overwhelm; *vi* to stand around
circumstrĕp•ō -ĕre *vt* to surround with noise or shouts
circumsurg•ō -ĕre *vi* (of mountains) to rise all around
circumtent•us -a -um *adj* tightly covered
circumtĕr•ō -ĕre *vt* to rub shoulders with, crowd around
circumtext•us -a -um *adj* with embroidered border
circumtŏn•ō -āre -ŭī *vt* to crash around (*someone*)
circumtons•us -a -um *adj* clipped
circum•vādō -vādĕre -vāsī *vt* to attack on every side; (of terror, etc.) to grip, confront
circumvăg•us -a -um *adj* flowing around, encircling
circumvall•ō -āre *vt* to blockade, invest
circumvectĭ•ō -ōnis *f* carting around (*of merchandise*); revolution (*of sun*)
circumvect•ō -āre *vt* to carry around
circumvect•or -ārī -ātus sum *vt* to ride or cruise around; to describe; *vi* to ride about, cruise about
circum•vĕhor -vĕhī -vectus sum *vt* to ride or cruise around; to describe, express by circumlocution; *vi* to ride about, cruise about
circumvēl•ō -āre *vt* to veil, envelop, cover
circum•venĭō -venīre -vēnī -ventum *vt* to encircle, surround; to go around to; to surround (*in a hostile manner*), invest; to distress, afflict, oppress; to circumvent, cheat, deceive
circumvert•ō -ĕre *vt* to turn (*something*) around; **circumverti** to turn oneself around, turn around; **circumverti axem** to turn around an axle
circumvest•ĭō -īre *vt* to clothe, wrap
circumvinc•ĭō -īre *vt* to bind, tie up
circumvīs•ō -ĕre *vt* to look around, glare around at
circumvolĭt•ō -āre *vt & vi* to fly around, dash about, rove around; to hover around
circumvŏl•ō -āre *vt* to fly around, hover about, flit about
circum•volvō -volvĕre — -volūtum *vt* to wind, roll around; **circumvolvi** or **se circumvolvere** (with *dat* or *acc*) to revolve around, wind oneself around
circ•us -ī *m* circle; racetrack; (astr) orbit
Circ•us Maxĭm•us (*genit:* **Circ•ī Maxĭm•ī**) *m* oldest racetrack in Rome, between the Palatine and Aventine, alleged to have been built by Tarquinius Priscus
cirrāt•us -a -um *adj* curly-haired
Cirrh•a -ae *f* town near Delphi, sacred to Apollo
cirr•us -ī *m* lock, curl; forelock; fringe
cis *prep* (with *acc*) on this side of; within
Cisalpīn•us -a -um *adj* Cisalpine, on the Roman side of the Alps
cis•ĭum -ĭī or **-ī** *n* light two-wheeled carriage
Cissē•is -ĭdis *f* Hecuba
Ciss•eus -ĕī *m* king of Thrace and father of Hecuba
cist•a -ae *f* box, chest
cistell•a -ae *f* small box
cistellātr•ix -īcis *f* female slave in charge of a money box
cistellŭl•a -ae *f* small box
cistern•a -ae *f* cistern, reservoir
cistophŏr•us -ī *m* Asiatic coin
cistŭl•a -ae *f* small box
citātim *adv* quickly, hastily

citāt·us -a -um *adj* quick, speedy, rapid; **citato equo** at full gallop
citerĭ·or -us *adj* on this side; nearer to earth, more down to earth, more mundane
Cithaer·ōn -ōnis *m* mountain range dividing Attica from Boeotia
cithăr·a -ae *f* zither, lyre, lute; art of playing the zither, lyre, or lute
citharist·a -ae *m* zither player, lute player
citharistrĭ·a -ae *f* zither player, lutist (*female*)
cithariz·ō -āre *vt* to play the zither, lyre, or lute
citharoed·us -ī *m* singer accompanied by zither, lyre, or lute
citĭm·us -a -um *adj* nearest
citĭus *adv* sooner, rather; **dicto citius** no sooner said than done; **serius aut citius** sooner or later
cito *adv* quickly; soon
cit·ō -āre *vt* to excite, rouse; to call, summon, cite; to call to witness, appeal to
citrā *adv* on this side, on the near side; **citra cadere** to fall short; *prep* (with *acc*) on this side of, on the near side of; (of time) since, before; short of, less than
citrĕ·us -a -um *adj* of citrus wood
citrō *adv* to this side, this way; **ultro citro, ultro citroque,** or **ultro et citro** to and fro, up and down; mutually
citr·us -ī *f* citrous tree; citron tree
cit·us -a -um *pp* of **cieo;** *adj* quick, rapid, swift
cīvĭc·us -a -um *adj* civil; civic; **corona civica** oak-leaf crown awarded for saving a fellow soldier's life
cīvīl·is -e *adj* civil; civic; political; civilian; democratic; polite; **jus civile** rights as a citizen, civil rights; civil law; **ratio civilis** political science
cīvīlĭt·ās -ātis *f* politics; courtesy
cīvīlĭter *adv* like a citizen; as an ordinary citizen would; politely
cīv·is -is *m* or *f* citizen; fellow citizen; private citizen
cīvĭt·ās -ātis *f* citizenship; state, commonwealth, community
clād·ēs -is *f* disaster, ruin, damage, loss; (mil) defeat; (fig) scourge
clam *adv* secretly, privately, in secret; stealthily; *prep* (with *abl* or *acc*) without the knowledge of, unknown to; **clam habere aliquem** to keep someone in the dark; **neque clam me est** nor is it unknown to me
clāmāt·or -ōris *m* loudmouth
clāmitātĭ·ō -ōnis *f* bawling, noise, racket
clāmĭt·ō -āre *vt & vi* to cry out, yell
clām·ō -āre *vt* to call out, call upon; to proclaim, declare; to invoke; *vi* to cry out, yell, shout
clām·or -ōris *m* shout, cry, call; acclamation, applause; outcry, complaint; war cry; noise, sound, echo
clāmōs·us -a -um *adj* clamorous, noisy
clancŭlum *adv* secretly, privately; *prep* (with *acc*) unknown to
clandestīnō *adv* secretly
clandestīn·us -a -um *adj* clandestine, secret, hidden
clang·or -ōris *m* clang, din, shrill cry
clārē *adv* distinctly, clearly; brightly; with distinction
clār·ĕō -ēre *vi* to be clear, be bright, be distinct; to be evident; to be famous
clār·escō -escĕre -ŭī *vi* to become clear, become distinct, become bright; to become obvious; to become famous
clārigātĭ·ō -ōnis *f* demand for satisfaction, ultimatum; fine
clārĭg·ō -āre *vi* to give an ultimatum
clārisŏn·us -a -um *adj* clear-sounding, loud
clārĭt·ās -ātis *f* clarity, distinctness; clearness (*of style*); celebrity, distinction
clāritūd·ō -ĭnis *f* brightness; distinction, fame
clār·ō -āre *vt* to make clear, explain, illustrate; to make famous; to illuminate
Clar·os -ī *f* town in Asia Minor near Colophon, famous for a temple and an oracle of Apollo
clār·us -a -um *adj* clear, distinct, bright; plain, manifest; famous, renowned; notorious
classiārĭ·us -a -um *adj* naval; *m pl* marines
classicŭl·a -ae *f* flotilla
classĭc·us -a -um *adj* first-class; naval; *m pl* marines; *n* battle signal; bugle
class·is -is *f* fleet; army; (pol) class
clāthr·ī or **clātr·ī -ōrum** *m pl* bars, cage, lattice
clātrāt·us -a -um *adj* barred
claud·ĕō -ēre or **claud·ō -ĕre** *vi* to limp; to falter, hesitate, waver
claudicātĭ·ō -ōnis *f* limping
claudĭc·ō -āre *vi* to be lame, limp; to waver; to be defective
Claud·ĭus -ĭī or **-ī** *m* Appius Claudius Caecus (*censor in* 312 B.C. *and builder of the Appian aqueduct and the Appian Way*); Roman emperor, 41-54 A.D.
claudō claudĕre clausī clausum *vt* to bolt, bar, shut, close; to bring to a close, conclude; to lock up, imprison; to blockade, hem in; to limit, restrict; to cut off, block; **agmen claudere** to bring up the rear; **numeris** or **pedibus claudere** to put into verse; **transitum claudere** to block traffic
claud·us -a -um *adj* lame, limping; crippled, imperfect, defective; wavering, untrustworthy
claustr·a -ōrum *n pl* lock, bar, bolt; gate, dam, dike; barrier, barricade; cage, den; fortress, defenses

clausŭl·a -ae *f* close, conclusion, end; (rhet) close of a period
claus·us -a -um *pp* of **claudo;** *n* enclosure
clāv·a -ae *f* cudgel, club, knotty branch
clāvār·ĭum -ĭī or **-ī** *n* allowance to soldiers for shoe nails
clāvicŭl·a -ae *f* tendril
clāvĭg·er -ĕra -ĕrum *adj* carrying a club; carrying keys; *m* club bearer (*Hercules*); key bearer (*Janus*)
clāv·is -is *f* key; **clavīs adimere uxori** to take the keys away from a wife, get a divorce
clāv·us -ī *m* nail; rudder, helm; purple stripe (*on a tunic, broad for senators, narrow for knights*); **clavus anni** beginning of the year; **clavus trabalis** spike; **trabali clavo figere** to nail down, clinch
Cleanth·ēs -is *m* Stoic philosopher, pupil of Zeno (300?-220 B.C.)
clēm·ens -entis *adj* gentle, mild, merciful, kind, compassionate; mitigated, qualified, toned down
clēmenter *adv* gently, mildly, mercifully, kindly, compassionately; by degrees, gradually
clēmentĭ·a -ae *f* mildness, mercy, clemency, compassion
Cle·ōn -ōnis *m* Athenian demagogue after death of Pericles in 429 B.C.
Cleopātr·a -ae *f* queen of Egypt (68-31 B.C.)
clep·ō -ĕre -sī -tum *vt* to steal
clepsȳdr·a -ae *f* water clock; (fig) time (*allotted to speakers*); **clepsydram dare** (with *dat*) to give (*someone*) the floor; **clepsydram petere** to ask for the floor
clept·a -ae *m* thief
cli·ens -entis *m* client, dependant (*freeman protected by a patron*); follower, retainer; companion, favorite; vassal
client·a -ae *f* client (*female*)
clientēl·a -ae *f* clientele; patronage, protection; *f pl* allies, dependants; clienteles
clientŭl·us -ī *m* poor client
clīnām·en -ĭnis *n* swerve
clīnāt·us -a -um *adj* bent, inclined
Clī·ō -ūs *f* Muse of history
clipeāt·us -a -um *adj* armed with a shield
clipĕ·um -ī *n* or **clipĕ·us -ī** *m* round bronze Roman shield; medallion; disc (*of sun*)
clītell·a -ae *f* saddlebag; *f pl* packsaddle
clitellārĭ·us -a -um *adj* carrying a packsaddle
clīvōs·us -a -um *adj* hilly, full of hills; steep
clīv·us -ī *m* slope, ascent, hill; slope, pitch; **adversus clivum** uphill; **primi clivi** foothills
Clīv·us Sac·er (*genit:* **Clīv·ī Sac·rī**) *m* part of the Via Sacra ascending the Capitoline Hill, also called Clivus Capitolinus
cloāc·a -ae *f* sewer, drain; **cloaca maxima** main sewer (*draining the valley between the Capitoline, Palatine, and Esquiline*)
Cloācīn·a -ae *f* Venus
Clōdĭ·a -ae *f* sister of Publius Clodius Pulcher and thought to be the person called Lesbia in Catullus' poems
Clōd·ĭus -ĭī or **-ī** *m* Publius Clodius Pulcher (*notorious enemy of Cicero who caused the latter to be exiled in* 58 B.C. *and was himself killed by Milo in* 52 B.C.)
Cloelĭ·a -ae *f* Roman girl who was given as hostage to Porsenna and escaped by swimming the Tiber
Clōth·ō (*genit* not in use; *acc:* **-ō**) *f* one of the three Fates
clu·ĕō -ēre or **clu·ĕor -ērī** *vi* to be named, be spoken of, be reputed, be famous
clūn·is -is *m* or *f* buttock
clūrīn·us -a -um *adj* of apes
Clūs·ĭum -ĭī or **-ī** *n* ancient Etruscan town
Clūs·ĭus -ĭī or **-ī** *m* Janus
Clymĕn·ē -ēs *f* wife of Merops and mother of Phaëthon
Clytaemnestr·a -ae *f* wife of Agamemnon, sister of Helen, Castor, and Pollux, and mother of Electra, Iphigenia, and Orestes, the latter of whom killed her
Cnid·us -ī *f* town in Caria, famous for worship of Venus
coacervātĭ·ō -ōnis *f* piling up, accumulation
coacerv·ō -āre *vt* to pile up, accumulate
coac·escō -escĕre -ŭī *vi* to become sour
coact·ō -āre *vt* to force
coact·or -ōris *m* collector (*of money*); **agminis coactores** rearguard elements
coactus *pp* of **cogo;** *adj* forced, unnatural, hypocritical; *n* felt
coact·us -ūs *m* coercion, compulsion
coaedifĭc·ō -āre *vt* to build up (*an area*), fill with buildings; **loci coaedificati** built-up areas
coaequ·ō -āre *vt* to level off, make level, bring down to the same level
coagmentātĭ·ō -ōnis *f* combination, union
coagment·ō -āre *vt* to join, glue, cement
coagment·um -ī *n* joint
coāgŭl·um -ī *n* rennet
coal·escō -escĕre -ŭī -ĭtum *vi* to grow firm, take root; to increase, become strong, become established, thrive
coangust·ō -āre *vt* to contract, compress; to limit, restrict
coarct- = coart-
coargŭ·ō -ĕre -ī *vt* to prove conclusively, demonstrate; to refute, prove wrong or guilty; (with *genit* of the charge) to prove (*someone*) guilty of

coartātĭ·ō -ōnis *f* crowding together
coart·ō -āre *vt* to crowd together, confine; to shorten, abridge
coccināt·us -a -um *adj* clothed in scarlet
coccinĕ·us or **coccĭn·us -a -um** *adj* scarlet
cocc·um -ī *n* scarlet
coclĕ·a or **cochlĕ·a -ae** *f* snail
cocleār·e -is *n* spoon
cocl·es -ĭtis *m* person blind in one eye
Cocl·es -ĭtis *m* Horatius Cocles (*famous for defending the Pons Sublicius against Porsenna's army*)
coctĭl·is -e *adj* baked; brick
coct·us -a -um *pp* of **coquo;** *adj* well-considered
Cōcȳt·us -ī *m* river of the lower world
cōdex see **caudex**
cōdicill·ī -ōrum *m pl* small trunks of trees, fire logs; note; petition; codicil
Codr·us -ī *m* last king of Athens, who sacrificed his life for an Athenian victory (1160-1132 B.C.)
coel- = **cael-**
co·ĕmō -emĕre -ēmī -emptum *vt* to buy up
coëmptĭ·ō -ōnis *f* marriage (*contracted by fictitious sale of contracting parties*); fictitious sale of an estate (*to relieve it of religious obligations*)
coëmptiōnāl·is -e *adj* of a fictitious marriage; used in a mock sale; worthless
coen- = **caen-**
co·ĕō -īre -īvī or **-ĭī -ĭtum** *vt* **societatem coire** to enter an agreement, form an alliance; *vi* to come or go together; to meet, assemble; to be united, combine; to mate, copulate; to congeal, curdle; to agree; to conspire; to clash (*in combat*); (of wounds) to close, heal up
coep·ĭō -ĕre -ī -tum *vt & vi* to begin
coept·ō -āre *vt* to begin eagerly; to try; (with *inf*) to try to; *vi* to begin, make a beginning
coept·us -a -um *pp* of **coepio;** *n* beginning; undertaking
coept·us -ūs *m* beginning
coëpulōn·us -ī *m* dinner guest
coërc·ĕō -ēre -ŭī -ĭtum *vt* to enclose, confine, hem in; to limit; to restrain, check, control
coërcitĭ·ō -ōnis *f* coercion; right to punish
coët·us -ūs *m* coming together, meeting; crowd, company
Coe·us -ī *m* Titan, father of Latona
cōgitātē *adv* deliberately
cōgitātĭ·ō -ōnis *f* thinking, deliberating; reflection, meditation; thought, plan, design; reasoning power, imagination
cōgĭt·ō -āre *vt* to consider, ponder, reflect on; to imagine; (with *inf*) to intend to; *vi* to think, reflect, meditate
cōgitāt·us -a -um *adj* well-considered, deliberate; *n pl* thoughts, ideas
cognātĭ·ō -ōnis *f* relationship by birth; agreement, resemblance, affinity; relatives, family
cognāt·us -a -um *adj* related by birth; related, similar, connected; *mf* relative
cognitĭ·ō -ōnis *f* learning, acquiring knowledge; notion, idea, knowledge; recognition; (law) inquiry, investigation, trial; (with *genit*) knowledge of, acquaintance with
cognĭt·or -ōris *m* advocate, attorney; defender, protector; witness
cognĭtus *pp* of **cognosco;** *adj* acknowledged
cognōm·en -ĭnis *n* surname, family name (*e.g., Caesar*); name
cognōment·um -ī *n* surname; name
cognōmināt·us -a -um *adj* synonymous
cognōmĭn·is -e *adj* like-named, of the same name
co·gnoscō -gnoscĕre -gnōvī -gnĭtum *vt* to become acquainted with, get to know, learn; to recognize, identify; to inquire into, investigate; to criticize, appreciate; to reconnoiter; **cognovisse** to know
cō·gō -gĕre -ēgī -actum *vt* to gather together, collect, convene; to thicken, condense, curdle; to pressure, bring pressure upon; to compel, force; to coax; to exact, extort; to infer, conclude; **agmen cogere** to bring up the rear
cohaer·ens -entis *adj* adjoining, continuous; consistent; harmonious
cohaerentĭ·a -ae *f* coherence, connection
co·haerĕō -haerēre -haesī -haesum *vi* to stick or cling together, cohere; to be consistent, be in agreement; (with *abl*) to consist of, be composed of; (with **cum** + *abl*) to be closely connected with, be in harmony with, be consistent with; **inter se cohaerere** to be consistent
co·haerescō -haerescĕre -haesī *vi* to cling together, cohere
cohēr·ēs -ēdis *m* or *f* coheir
cohib·ĕō -ēre -ŭī *vt* to hold together, hold close, confine; to hold back, repress, check, stop
cohonest·ō -āre *vt* to do honor to, celebrate
cohorr·escō -escĕre -ŭī *vi* to shiver all over
cohor·s -tis *f* yard (*esp. for cattle or chickens*); train, retinue, escort; (mil) cohort (*comprising 3 maniples or 6 centuries and forming one tenth of a legion*)
cohortātĭ·ō -ōnis *f* encouragement
cohorticŭl·a -ae *f* small cohort
cohort·or -ārī -ātus sum *vt* to encourage, cheer up, urge on
coïtĭ·ō -ōnis *f* conspiracy, coalition; agreement
coït·us -ūs *m* meeting; sexual union
colăph·us -ī *m* slap, blow with a fist

Colch·is -ĭdis *f* country on E. end of the Black Sea; Medea
cōlĕ·us -ī *m* sack, scrotum
cōl·is -is *m* stalk, cabbage
collabasc·ō -ĕre *vi* to waver, totter
collabefact·ō -āre *vt* to shake hard
collabe·fīō -fiĕrī -factus sum *vi* to collapse, be ruined, fall to pieces
col·lābor -lābī -lapsus sum *vi* to collapse, fall to pieces
collacerāt·us -a -um *adj* torn to pieces
collacrimātĭ·ō -ōnis *f* weeping
collacrĭm·ō -āre *vt* to cry bitterly over; *vi* to cry together
collactĕ·a -ae *f* foster sister
collār·e -is *n* collar
Collātĭ·a -ae *f* old town in Latium
Collātīn·us -ī *m* husband of Lucretia
collātĭ·ō -ōnis *f* bringing together; contribution of money, collection; comparison, analogy; **signorum collatio** clash of troops
collāt·or -ōris *m* contributor
collātus *pp* of **confero**
collaudātĭ·ō -ōnis *f* warm praise
collaud·ō -āre *vt* to praise highly
collax·ō -āre *vt* to make loose
collect·a -ae *f* contribution of money
collectīcĭ·us -a -um *adj* hastily-gathered
collectĭ·ō -ōnis *f* gathering; summing up, recapitulation; inference
collectus *pp* of **colligo**
collect·us -ūs *m* collection
collēg·a -ae *m* colleague, partner (*in office*); associate, companion; fellow member (*of a club*)
collēg·ĭum -ĭī or **-ī** *n* association in office; official body, board, college, guild, company, corporation, society
collībert·us -ī *m* fellow freedman
collĭb·et or **collŭb·et -ēre -ŭit -ĭtum** *v impers* it pleases
col·līdō -līdĕre -līsī -līsum *vt* to smash to pieces, shatter, crush; to cause to clash, set at variance
colligātĭ·ō -ōnis *f* binding together, connection
collĭg·ō -āre *vt* to tie together, connect; to unite, combine; to fasten, chain; to stop, hinder
col·lĭgō -ligĕre -lēgī -lectum *vt* to pick up, gather together, collect; to contract, compress, concentrate; to acquire gradually; to infer, conclude, gather; to assemble, bring together; to enumerate; to gather, repair; to check, control (*horse*); **animum colligere, mentem colligere,** or **se colligere** to collect or compose oneself, muster one's courage, rally, come to, come around; **vasa colligere** to pack up (*for the march*)
Collīn·a Port·a (*genit:* **Collīn·ae Port·ae**) *f* Colline Gate (*near the Quirinal Hill*)
collīnĕ·ō -āre *vt* to aim straight; *vi* to hit the mark
col·līnō -linĕre -lēvī -lĭtum *vt* to smear; to defile
colliquefact·us -a -um *adj* dissolved, melted
coll·is -is *m* hill
collocātĭ·ō -ōnis *f* arrangement; giving in marriage
collŏc·ō -āre *vt* to place, put in order, arrange; to station, deploy; to give in marriage; to lodge, quarter; to occupy, employ; **se collocare** to settle, settle down (*in a place*)
collocuplēt·ō -āre *vt* to enrich, make quite rich
collocūtĭ·ō -ōnis *f* conversation, conference
colloqu·ĭum -ĭī or **-ī** *n* conversation, conference
col·lŏquor -lŏquī -locūtus sum *vt* to talk to; *vi* to talk together, converse, hold a conference
collŭbet see **collĭbet**
collūc·ĕō -ēre *vi* to shine brightly, be entirely illuminated; (fig) to be resplendent
col·lūdō -lūdĕre -lūsī -lūsum *vi* to play together; to be in collusion; (with *dat*) to play with
coll·um -ī *n* neck
col·lŭō -luĕre -lŭī -lūtum *vt* to wash out, rinse, moisten; **ora colluere** to wet the mouth, quench the thirst
collūsĭ·ō -ōnis *f* collusion
collūs·or -ōris *m* playmate; fellow-gambler
collustr·ō -āre *vt* to light up; to survey, inspect; (in painting) to represent in bright colors
collutulent·ō -āre *vt* to soil, defile
colluvĭ·ō -ōnis or **colluvĭ·ēs** (*genit* not in use) *f* dregs, impurities, filth; rabble
collȳb·us -ī *m* conversion of currency; rate of exchange
collȳr·a -ae *f* noodles, macaroni
collȳr·ĭum -ĭī or **-ī** *n* eyewash
colō colĕre colŭī cultum *vt* to till, cultivate, work; to live in (*a place*); to guard, protect; to honor, cherish, revere, worship; to adorn, dress; to practice, follow; to experience, live through, spend
colocāsĭ·a -ae *f* lotus, water lily
colōn·a -ae *f* peasant woman
colōnĭ·a -ae *f* colony, settlement; colonists, settlers
colōnĭc·us -a -um *adj* colonial
colōn·us -ī *m* settler; farmer
col·or or **col·ōs -ōris** *m* color, hue, tint; external condition; complexion; tone, style; luster; grace; colorful pretext
colōrāt·us -a -um *adj* colored, tinted; healthily tanned
colōr·ō -āre *vt* to color, tan; (fig) to give a certain tone to
colossē·us -a -um *adj* colossal
coloss·us -ī *m* gigantic statue, colossus
colostr·a -ae *f* or **colostr·um -ī** *n* first milk after delivery, colostrum

colŭb·er -rī *m* snake, adder
colŭbr·a -ae *f* snake, adder (*female*)
colubrĭf·er -ĕra -ĕrum *adj* snaky
colubrīn·us -a -um *adj* snaky; wily, sly
cōl·um -ī *n* strainer
columb·a -ae *f* pigeon, dove (*female*)
columb·ar -āris *n* collar
columbār·ium -iī or **-ī** *n* pigeonhole; (fig) vault with niches for cinerary urns
columbīn·us -a -um *adj* of a dove or pigeon; *m* little dove
columb·us -ī *m* pigeon, dove
columell·a -ae *f* small column
colŭm·en -ĭnis *n* height, summit, peak; gable; pillar; head, leader; support, prop
columna·a -ae *f* column, pillar, post; (fig) pillar, support; waterspout; **ad columnam** (i.e., **Maeniam**) **pervenire** or **ad columnam adhaerescere** to be brought to punishment (*because at the Columna Maenia in the Roman forum criminals and debtors were tried*); *f pl* display columns (*in bookshop*); bookshop
Columna·a Maenĭ·a (*genit:* **Columnae Maenĭ·ae**) *f* column in the Roman forum, possibly of the Basilica Porcia supporting a projecting balcony (**maenianum**), at which thieves and slaves were whipped and to which debtors were summoned for trial; whipping post
columnār·ium -iī or **-ī** *n* tax on house pillars
columnār·ius -iī or **-ī** *m* criminal debtor (*punished at the Columna Maenia*)
colurn·us -a -um *adj* made of hazel wood
col·us -ī *or* **-ūs** *m* or *f* distaff
cōlȳphĭ·a -ōrum *n pl* choice cuts of meat, loin cuts
com·a -ae *f* hair (*of the head*); mane (*of horse or lion*); fleece; foliage; grass; sunbeams
com·ans -antis *adj* hairy, long-haired; plumed (*helmet*); leafy; **comans stella** comet
cōmarch·us -ī *m* chief burgess
comāt·us -a -um *adj* long-haired; leafy
combĭb·ō -ĕre -ī *vt* to drink up; to absorb; to swallow, engulf; to repress, conceal (*tears*); to imbibe, acquire (*knowledge*)
combĭb·ō -ōnis *m* drinking partner
comb·ūrō -ūrĕre -ussī -ustum *vt* to burn up, consume; (fig) to ruin
com·ĕdō -edĕre (or **-esse**) **-ēdī -ēsum** (or **-estum**) *vt* to eat up, consume, devour; to waste, squander, dissipate, spend; **se comedere** to pine away
com·es -ĭtis *m* or *f* companion, fellow traveler; associate, comrade; attendant, retainer, dependant; concomitant, consequence
comēt·ēs -ae *m* comet
cōmĭcē *adv* like a comedy
cōmĭc·us -a -um *adj* of comedy, comic; **comicum aurum** stage money; *m* actor (*of comedy*); playwright (*of comedy*)
cōm·is -e *adj* courteous, polite; kind, friendly; (with *dat* or with **erga** or **in** + *acc*) friendly toward
cōmissābund·us -a -um *adj* parading in a riotous bacchanalian procession; carousing
cōmissātĭ·ō -ōnis *f* riotous bacchanalian procession; wild drinking party
cōmissāt·or -ōris *m* drinking partner, reveler, guzzler
cōmiss·or or **cōmīs·or -ārī -ātus sum** *vi* to join in a bacchanalian procession; to revel, guzzle
cōmĭt·ās -ātis *f* politeness, courteousness; kindness, friendliness
comitāt·us -ūs *m* escort, retinue; imperial retinue, court; company (*traveling together*), caravan
cōmĭter *adv* politely, courteously; kindly
comitĭ·a -ōrum *n pl* comitia, popular assembly; elections; **comitia consularia** or **comitia consulum** election of consuls; **comitia praetoria** election of praetors
comitiāl·is -e *adj* of the assembly; of the elections, election
comitiāt·us -ūs *m* assembly of the people in the comitia
comit·ium -iī or **-ī** *n* comitium, assembly place
comĭt·ō -āre or **comĭt·or -ārī -ātus sum** *vt* to accompany, attend, follow
commacŭl·ō -āre *vt* to spot, stain; to defile
commanipulār·is -is *m* comrade in the same brigade
commarīt·us -ī *m* fellow husband
commeāt·us -ūs *m* passage, thoroughfare; leave of absence, furlough; transport, passage, convoy; (mil) lines of communication; (mil) supplies; **in commeatu esse** to be on a furlough
commedĭt·or -ārī -ātus sum *vt* to practice; to imitate
commemĭn·ī -isse *vt & vi* to remember well
commemorābĭl·is -e *adj* memorable, worth mentioning
commemorātĭ·ō -ōnis *f* recollection, remembrance; mentioning, reminding
commemŏr·ō -āre *vt* to keep in mind, remember; to bring up (*in conversation*), to mention, recount, relate; *vi* (with **de** + *abl*) to be mindful of
commendābĭl·is -e *adj* commendable, praiseworthy
commendātĭcĭ·us -a -um *adj* of recommendation, of introduction; **litterae commendaticiae** letter of introduction or of recommendation

commendātī·ō -ōnis *f* recommendation, recommending; commendation, praise; excellence, worth
commendāt·or -ōris *m* backer, supporter
commendātr·ix -īcis *f* backer, supporter (*female*)
commendāt·us -a -um *adj* commended, recommended, acceptable, approved
commend·ō -āre *vt* to entrust, commit; to recommend; to render acceptable
commentāriŏl·um -ī *n* short treatise
commentār·ĭum -ĭī or **-ī** *n* or **commentār·ĭus -ĭī** or **-ī** *m* notebook, journal, diary, notes, memorandum; (law) brief; *pl* memoirs
commentātī·ō -ōnis *f* careful study, deep reflection; preparation; essay, treatise
commentīcĭ·us -a -um *adj* thought out; invented, fictitious, imaginary; ideal; forged, false; legendary
comment·or -ārī -ātus sum *vt* to think over, consider well, study; to invent, contrive, make up; to prepare, produce (*writings*); to discuss, write about; to imitate, adopt the language of; *vi* to meditate, deliberate, reflect; to experiment in speaking, attempt to speak
comment·or -ōris *m* inventor
comment·us -a -um *pp* of **comminiscor;** *adj* fictitious, feigned, invented, pretended; *n* invention, fiction, fabrication; device, contrivance
commĕ·ō -āre *vi* to come and go; to go back and forth; to travel repeatedly; to make frequent visits
commerc·ĭum -ĭī or **-ī** *n* trade, commerce; right to trade; dealings, business; communication, correspondence; **belli commercia** ransom
commerc·or -ārī *vt* to deal in, purchase
commer·ĕo -ēre -ŭī -ĭtum or **commer·ĕor -ērī -ĭtus sum** *vt* to earn, merit, deserve fully; to be guilty of
com·mētĭor -mētīrī -mensus sum *vt* to measure; (with **cum** + *abl*) to measure (*something*) in terms of
commēt·ō -āre *vi* to go often
commĭgr·ō -āre *vi* to move, migrate
commīlit·ĭum -ĭī *or* **-ī** *n* comradeship, companionship, fellowship
commīlit·ō -ōnis *m* fellow soldier, army buddy
comminātī·ō -ōnis *f* threatening, menacing; *f pl* violent threats
com·mingō -mingĕre -minxī -mictum *vt* to urinate on; to wet (*bed*); to defile, pollute; **commictum caenum** (term of reproach) dirty skunk
com·miniscor -miniscī -mentus sum *vt* to contrive, invent, devise
commĭn·or -ārī -ātus sum *vt* to threaten violently
commin·ŭō -uĕre -ŭī -ūtum *vt* to lessen considerably, diminish; to break up, shatter; to weaken, impair; to humble, crush, humiliate
commĭnus *adv* hand to hand, at close quarters; near at hand, near; **comminus conferre signa** to engage in hand-to-hand fighting
com·miscĕō -miscēre -miscŭī -mixtum *vt* to mix together, mix up, join together; to unite, bring together, mingle
commiserātī·ō -ōnis *f* pitying; (rhet) appeal to compassion
commiseresc·ō -ĕre *vi* (with *genit*) to feel pity for; *v impers* (with *genit*) **me commiserescit ejus** I pity him
commisĕr·or -ārī -ātus sum *vt* to feel sympathy for; *vi* (rhet) to try to evoke sympathy
commissĭ·ō -ōnis *f* beginning (*of fight, game, etc.*)
commissūr·a -ae *f* connection; joint
commiss·us -a -um *pp* of **committo;** *n* offense, crime; secret; undertaking
commītĭg·ō -āre *vt* to soften up
com·mittō -mittĕre -mīsī -missum *vt* to connect, unite; to match (*for a fight, etc.*); to start, commence; to undertake; to commit, perpetrate; to entrust, commit; to engage in (*battle*); to incur (*penalty*); **se committere** (with *dat* or **in** + *acc*) to venture into
commodĭt·ās -ātis *f* proportion, symmetry; aptness of expression; convenience, comfort; right time; pleasantness (*of personality*); courtesy, kindness
commŏd·ō -āre *vt* to adjust, adapt; to bestow, supply, lend, give; *vi* to be obliging; (with *dat*) to adapt oneself to, be obliging to
commodŭlē or **commodŭlum** *adv* nicely, conveniently
commŏdum *adv* at a good time, in the nick of time; **commodum cum** just at the time when
commŏd·us -a -um *adj* adapted, suitable, fit, convenient; opportune (*time*); convenient, comfortable, advantageous; agreeable, obliging, pleasant (*person*); **quod commodum est** just as you please; *n* convenience, opportunity; profit, advantage; privilege, favor; loan; pay, reward; **commodo tuo** at your convenience
commōl·ĭor -īrī -ītus sum *vt* to set in motion
commone·facĭō -facĕre -fēcī -factum *vt* to recall, call to mind; (with *acc* of person and *genit* of thing) to remind (*someone*) of
common·ĕō -ēre -ŭī -ĭtum *vt* to remind, warn; (with *genit* or **de** + *abl*) to remind (*someone*) of
commonstr·ō -āre *vt* to point out clearly
commorātĭ·ō -ōnis *f* delaying, stay-

ing; residence, sojourn; (rhet) dwelling (*on some point*)
com·morior -mŏrī -mortŭus sum *vi* (with *dat* or with **cum** + *abl*) to die with, die at the same time as
commŏr·or -ārī -ātus sum *vt* to stop, detain; *vi* to linger, stay, stop off; (with **apud** + *acc*) to stay at the house of; **in sententia commorari** to stick to an opinion
commōtĭ·ō -ōnis *f* commotion; **animi commotio** excitement
commōtiuncŭl·a -ae *f* minor inconvenience
commōt·us -a -um *adj* excited, angry; deranged, insane; impassioned, lively (*style*)
com·movĕō -movēre -mōvī -mōtum *vt* to stir up, agitate, shake; to disturb, unsettle, disquiet, excite, shake up; to arouse, provoke; to stir up, generate, produce; to start, introduce (*novelties*); to displace, dislodge (*enemy*); to refute
commūn·e -is *n* community, state; **in commune** for general use, for all; in general
commūnicātĭ·ō -ōnis *f* imparting, communicating
commūnĭc·ō -āre or **commūnĭc·or -ārī** *vt* to make common; to communicate, impart, share; to share in, take part in; to unite, connect, join
commūnĭ·ō -ōnis *f* sharing in common
commūn·ĭō -īre -īvī or **-ĭī -ītum** *vt* to fortify, strengthen, barricade
commūn·is -e *adj* common, public, universal, general; familiar; courteous, affable; democratic; **loca communia** public places; **loci communes** commonplaces, general topics; **sensus communis** common sense; *n* see **commune**
commūnĭter *adv* in common, together
commūnītĭ·ō -ōnis *f* road building; (rhet) introduction
commurmŭr·ō -āre or **commurmŭr·or -ārī** *vi* to murmur, grumble
commūtābĭl·is -e *adj* changeable, subject to change; interchangeable
commūtātĭ·ō -ōnis *f* changing, change, alteration
commūtāt·us -ūs *m* change, alteration
commūt·ō -āre *vt* to change, alter; to interchange, exchange; (with *abl* or **cum** + *abl*) to exchange (*something*) for
cōm·ō -ĕre -psī -ptum *vt* to comb, arrange, braid; to adorn, deck out
cōmoedĭ·a -ae *f* comedy
cōmoedĭcē *adv* as in comedy
cōmoed·us -ī *m* comic actor
comōs·us -a -um *adj* with long hair, hairy; leafy
compact·us -a -um *pp* of **compingo;** *adj* compact, well built; *n* agreement
compāg·ēs -is *f* joining together, joint, structure, framework
compāg·ō -ĭnis *f* connection
comp·ar -ăris *adj* equal, on an equal level; (with *dat*) matching
comp·ar -ăris *m* or *f* comrade; playmate; perfect match; spouse
comparābĭl·is -e *adj* comparable
comparātĭ·ō -ōnis *f* comparison; arrangement; acquisition, preparation, provision; relative position (*of planets*)
comparātīv·us -a -um *adj* comparative
compār·ĕō -ēre -ŭī *vi* to be visible, be plain, be evident, appear; to be at hand, be present
compăr·ō -āre *vt* to put together, get together, provide; to prepare, arrange; to match; to compare; to procure, get, obtain, collect; to appoint, establish, constitute; **se comparare** (with **ad** or **in** + *acc*) to prepare oneself for, get ready for
comp·ascō -ascĕre — -astum *vt & vi* to feed together
compascŭ·us -a -um *adj* of public grazing
compec·iscor -iscī -tus sum *vi* to come to an agreement
compect·us -a -um *adj* in agreement, agreed; *n* agreement; **compecto** by agreement, according to the agreement
comped·ĭō -īre — -ītum *vt* to shackle
compellātĭ·ō -ōnis *f* rebuke, reprimand
compell·ō -āre *vt* to summon, call; to call to account, bring to book; to reproach; (law) to arraign
com·pellō -pellĕre -pŭlī -pulsum *vt* to drive together; to crowd, concentrate; to compel, force, urge, drive on
compendiārĭ·us -a -um *adj* short, abridged; **via compendiaria** shortcut
compend·ĭum -ĭī or **-ī** *n* careful weighing; saving (*of money*); profit; shortening, abridging; shortcut; **compendi facere** to save; **compendi fieri** to be brief; **suo privato compendio servire** to serve one's own private interests
compensātĭ·ō -ōnis *f* compensation, recompense
compens·ō -āre *vt* to compensate, make up for
com·percō -percĕre -persī *vt* to save, hoard up
comperendinātĭ·ō -ōnis *f* or **comperendināt·us -ūs** *m* (law) two-day adjournment
comperendĭn·ō -āre *vt* to adjourn (*court*) for two days; to put off (*defendant*) for two days
comper·ĭō -īre -ī -tum or **comper·ĭor -īrī -tus sum** *vt* to find out, ascertain, learn; **compertum habeo** or **compertum mihi est**

I have ascertained, I know for certain

compert·us -a -um *adj* discovered, well authenticated; (with *genit*) convicted of

comp·ēs -ĕdis *f* shackle (*for the feet*); (fig) bond

compesc·ō -ĕre -ŭī *vt* to confine, restrain, suppress, check, chain down

competīt·or -ōris *m* competitor, rival

competītr·ix -īcis *f* competitor, rival (*female*)

compĕt·ō -ĕre -īvī or **-iī -ītum** *vi* to coincide, come together, meet; to be adequate, be suitable; (with **ad** + *acc*) to be capable of

compīlāti·ō -ōnis *f* pillaging, plundering; (contemptuously said of a collection of documents) compilation

compīl·ō -āre *vt* to pillage, plunder

com·pingō -pingĕre -pēgī -pactum *vt* to put together, frame, compose; to confine, lock up, put (*in jail*)

compitāl·ia -ium or **-iōrum** *n pl* festival celebrated annually at the crossroads in honor of the Lares of the crossroads on a day appointed by the praetor

compitālici·us -a -um *adj* of the crossroads

compitāl·is -e *adj* of the crossroads

compit·um -ī *n* crossroads, intersection

complac·ĕō -ēre -ŭī or **-itus sum** *vi* (with *dat*) to be quite pleasing to, suit just fine

complān·ō -āre *vt* to make even or level; to raze to the ground, pull down

com·plector -plectī -plexus sum *vt* to embrace, clasp; to comprise; (of writings) to include; to grasp, understand; to display affection for, display esteem for; to enclose (*an area*); to seize, take possession of

complēment·um -ī *n* complement

compl·ĕō -ēre -ēvī -ētum *vt* to fill, fill up; (mil) to bring (*legion, etc.*) to full strength; (mil) to man; to complete; to impregnate; to fill with sound, make resound; to supply fully, furnish

complēt·us -a -um *adj* complete; perfect

complexi·ō -ōnis *f* combination, connection; conclusion in a syllogism; dilemma; (rhet) period

complex·us -ūs *m* embrace; (fig) love, affection; close combat; **in complexum alicujus venire** to come to close grips with someone

complicāt·us -a -um *adj* complicated, involved

complic·ō -āre *vt* to fold up

complōrāti·ō -ōnis *f* or **complōrāt·us -ūs** *m* groaning, lamentation, wailing

complōr·ō -āre *vt* to mourn for

complūr·ēs -ium *adj* several; a good many

complūriens or **complūriēs** *adv* several times, a good many times

compluscŭl·ī -ae -a *adj* a fair number of

compluv·ium -iī or **-ī** *n* rain trap (*quadrangular open space in middle of Roman house towards which the roof sloped so as to direct the rain into a basin, called impluviun, built into the floor*)

com·pōnō -pōnĕre -posŭī -positum *vt* to put together, join; to construct, build; to compose, write; to arrange, settle, agree upon, fix, set; to match, pair, couple; to compare, contrast; to put away; take down, lay aside; to lay out, bury (*the dead*); to compose, pacify, allay, calm, appease, quiet, reconcile; to feign, invent, concoct, contrive

comport·ō -āre *vt* to carry together, bring in, collect, gather, accumulate

comp·os -ŏtis *adj* (with *genit* or *abl*) in possession of, master of, having control over; having a share in, participating in; **compos animi** or **compos mentis** sane; **compos sui** self-controlled; **compos voti** having one's prayer answered

composītē *adv* in an orderly manner, orderly, regularly; **composite dicere** to speak logically

compositi·ō -ōnis *f* putting together, connecting, arranging, composition; matching (*of gladiators, etc.*); reconciliation (*of friends*); orderly arrangement (*of words*)

composit·or -ōris *m* composer, author

compositūr·a -ae *f* connection

composit·us -a -um *pp* of **compono;** *adj* compound (*words, etc.*); prepared, well arranged, orderly; made-up, feigned, false; adapted; composed, calm, settled; *n* agreement, compact; **composito** or **ex composito** by agreement, as agreed, as had been arranged

compotāti·ō -ōnis *f* drinking party

compot·iō -īre -īvī -ītum *vt* (with *acc* of person and *abl* of thing) to make (*someone*) master of, put (*someone*) in possession of

compōt·or -ōris *m* drinking partner

compōtr·ix -īcis *f* drinking partner (*female*)

comprans·or -ōris *m* dinner companion, fellow guest

comprecāti·ō -ōnis *f* public supplication

comprĕc·or -ārī -ātus sum *vt* to pray earnestly to, implore, supplicate

compre·hendō -hendĕre -hendī -hensum or **compren·dō -dĕre -dī -sum** *vt* to bind together, unite; to take hold of, grasp, seize, catch, apprehend; to attack, seize, arrest, capture, apprehend; to detect, discover; to occupy (*places*); to grasp, perceive, comprehend, take in; to express, describe, narrate, recount; **ignem comprehendere** to catch fire; **memoriā comprehendere** to remember; **numero comprehendere** to enumerate, count

comprehensibil·is -e *adj* comprehensible, conceivable, intelligible

comprehensi·ō -ōnis *f* seizing, laying hold of; arrest; comprehension, perception; combining; (rhet) period

comprendō see **comprehendo**

compressi·ō -ōnis *f* pressing closely; embrace; (rhet) compression

compress·us -ūs *m* compression; embrace

com·prīmō -primĕre -pressī -pressum *vt* to press together, bring together, compress, close; to embrace; to check, curb, restrain; to keep back, suppress, withhold, conceal; **animam comprimere** to hold the breath; **compressis manibus sedere** to sit on folded hands, to not lift a hand; **ordines comprimere** to close ranks

comprobāti·ō -ōnis *f* approbation, approval

comprobāt·or -ōris *m* enthusiastic backer

comprŏb·ō -āre *vt* to approve, sanction, acknowledge; to prove, establish, make good, confirm, verify

comprōmiss·um -ī *n* mutual agreement to abide by arbiter's decision

comprō-mittō -mittĕre -mīsī -missum *vi* to agree to abide by an arbiter's decision

compt·us -a -um *pp* of **como;** *adj* neat, elegant

compt·us -ūs *m* hairdo

com·pungō -pungĕre -punxī -punctum *vt* to puncture, prick; to tattoo; to prod

compŭt·ō -āre *vt* to compute, count

computresc·ō -ĕre *vi* to become putrid, rot

Cōm·um -ī *n* Como (*town N. of the Po and birthplace of Pliny the Younger*)

cōnām·en -ĭnis *n* effort, struggle; support, prop; **conamen mortis** attempt at suicide

cōnāt·um -ī *n* effort, exertion; attempt, undertaking, venture

cōnāt·us -ūs *m* effort; endeavor; impulse, inclination, tendency; undertaking

concăc·ō -āre *vt* to defile with excrement

concaed·ēs -ĭum *f pl* log barricade

concale·faciō -facĕre -fēcī -factum *vt* to warm up

concall·escō -escĕre -ŭī *vi* to grow hard; to become insensible; to become shrewd

concastīg·ō -āre *vt* to punish severely

concăv·ō -āre *vt* to curve, bend

concăv·us -a -um *adj* concave, hollow; curved, arched, bent, vaulted; deep (*valley*)

con·cēdō -cēdĕre -cessī -cessum *vt* to give up, relinquish, cede; to pardon, overlook; to allow, grant; *vi* to go away, give way, depart, withdraw, retire; (with *dat*) **a** to yield to, submit to, give way to, succumb to; **b** to submit to, comply with; **c** to make allowance for, pardon; **d** to be inferior to; (with **in** + *acc*) to pass over to, be merged in; **fato concedere, naturae concedere,** or **vitā concedere** to die

concelĕbr·ō -āre *vt* to frequent, fill; to pursue (*studies*); to fill with life, enliven; to celebrate; to make widely known, proclaim, publish

concēnāti·ō -ōnis *f* dining together

concenti·ō -ōnis *f* singing together, harmony

concenturi·ō -āre *vt* to marshal by the hundreds; (with *dat*) to bring (*fear*) to

concent·us -ūs *m* concert, symphony; harmony; choir; concord, agreement, harmony

concepti·ō -ōnis *f* conception (*becoming pregnant*); (law) composing legal formulas

conceptīv·us -a -um *adj* movable (*holidays*)

concept·us -ūs *m* conception (*becoming pregnant*), pregnancy

concerp·ō -ĕre -sī -tum *vt* to tear up, tear to shreds; (fig) to cut up, abuse, revile

concertāti·ō -ōnis *f* controversy, dispute

concertāt·or -ōris *m* rival

concertātōri·us -a -um *adj* controversial

concert·ō -āre *vi* to fight it out; to quarrel, debate

concessi·ō -ōnis *f* concession; admission (*of guilt with plea for mercy*)

concess·ō -āre *vt* (with *inf*) to stop (*doing something*)

concess·us -a -um *pp* of **concedo;** *n* concession (*thing allowed*)

concess·us -ūs *m* permission, leave

conch·a -ae *f* clam, oyster, mussel, murex; clam shell, oyster shell, mussel shell; pearl; purple dye; trumpet (*of Triton*); vessel (*containing ointments, etc.*); vulva

conch·is -is *f* bean

conchīt·a -ae *m* clam digger, conch digger

conchȳliāt·us -a -um *adj* purple

conchȳl·ium -iī or **-ī** *n* shellfish, clam, oyster; murex; purple dye, purple; purple garments

concĭd·ō -ĕre -ī *vi* to collapse; to fall (*in battle*); (fig) to decline, fail, fall, decay, perish, go to ruin; (of winds) to subside

con·cīdō -cīdĕre -cīdī -cīsum *vt* to cut up, cut to pieces, kill; to beat severely; (fig) to crush (*with arguments*); (rhet) to chop up (*sentences*)

con·ciĕō -ciēre -cīvī -cītum or **-cĭō**

-cīre -cīvī -cītum *vt* to assemble; to shake, stir up; (fig) to rouse, stir up, provoke
conciliābŭl·um -ī *n* public meeting place
conciliātĭ·ō -ōnis *f* union, bond; conciliating, winning over; inclination, bent, desire
conciliāt·or -ōris *m* mediator, promoter
conciliātrīcŭl·a -ae *f* procuress, madame
conciliātr·ix -īcis *f* mediator, promoter, match maker (*female*)
conciliāt·us -a -um *adj* (with **ad** + *acc*) endeared to, favorable to
conciliāt·us -ūs *m* union, connection, combination
concilĭ·ō -āre *vt* to bring together, unite, connect; to unite (*in feeling*), make friendly, win over; to bring about (*by mediation*); to acquire, win
concil·ĭum -ĭī or **-ī** *n* gathering, meeting, assembly; council; combination, union
concinnē *adv* nicely, elegantly
concinnĭt·ās -ātis or **concinnitūd·ō -ĭnis** *f* finish, elegance, symmetry (*of style*)
concinn·ō -āre *vt* to make symmetrical, get right, adjust; to bring about, produce, cause; to make (*e.g., insane*)
concinn·us -a -um *adj* symmetrical; neat, elegant; courteous, agreeable, nice; polished (*style*)
concĭn·ō -ĕre -ŭī *vt* to sing, celebrate; to prophesy; *vi* to sing or play together, harmonize; (fig) to agree, harmonize
concĭō see **concieo**
concĭō see **contio**
concipĭl·ō -āre *vt* to carry off
con·cipĭō -cipĕre -cēpī -ceptum *vt* to take hold of, take up, take, receive; to take in, absorb; to imagine, conceive, think; to understand, comprehend, perceive; to catch (*fire*); to entertain (*hope*); to draw up in formal language; to announce in formal language
concīsē *adv* concisely
concīsĭ·ō -ōnis *f* (rhet) dividing a sentence into short phrases
concīs·us -a -um *pp* of **concido;** *adj* cut up, short, concise
concitātē *adv* vigorously, vividly
concitātĭ·ō -ōnis *f* rapid movement; excitement; sedition, agitation
concitāt·or -ōris *m* instigator, ringleader; rabble-rouser
concitāt·us -a -um *adj* rapid, swift; excited
concĭt·ō -āre *vt* to stir up, rouse, urge; to cause, occasion
concĭt·or -ōris *m* instigator, ringleader; rabble-rouser
conclāmātĭ·ō -ōnis *f* loud shouting, yell; acclamation
conclāmĭt·ō -āre *vi* to keep on shouting, keep on yelling
conclām·ō -āre *vt* to shout, yell; to call to (*for help*); to call repeatedly by name, bewail (*the dead*); to exclaim; **jam conclamatum est** all's lost; **vasa conclamare** to give the signal to pack up (*for the march*); *vi* to shout, yell, cry out; **ad arma conclamare** to sound the alarm (*for an attack*)
conclāv·e -is *n* room; bedroom; dining room; cage, stall, coop
con·clūdō -clūdĕre -clūsī -clūsum *vt* to shut up, enclose; to include, comprise; to round off, conclude (*letter, speech*); to end rhythmically; to deduce, infer, conclude
conclūsē *adv* (rhet) in rhythmical cadence
conclūsĭ·ō -ōnis *f* blockade; end, conclusion; conclusion (*of a speech*), peroration; conclusion (*of syllogism*); (rhet) period
conclūsiuncŭl·a -ae *f* false conclusion
conclūs·us -a -um *pp* of **concludo;** *adj* confined; *n* logical conclusion
concŏl·or -ōris *adj* of the same color
concomitāt·us -a -um *adj* escorted
con·cŏquō -coquĕre -coxī -coctum *vt* to cook thoroughly; to boil down; to digest; to stomach, put up with; to cook up, concoct (*plans*); to weigh seriously, reflect upon, consider well; to prepare, ripen
concordĭ·a -ae *f* concord, harmony, good rapport; union
concordĭter *adv* harmoniously
concord·ō -āre *vi* to be of one mind, be in harmony, agree
concor·s -dis *adj* of the same mind, concordant, agreeing, harmonious
concrēbr·escō -escĕre -ŭī *vi* to grow strong
concrēd·ō -ĕre -ĭdī -ĭtum *vi* to entrust, commit, consign
concrĕm·ō -āre *vt* to burn to ashes, burn up
concrĕp·ō -āre -ŭī -ĭtum *vi* to rattle, creak, grate, clash, sound, make noise; **digitis concrepare** to snap the fingers
con·crescō -crescĕre -crēvī -crētum *vi* to grow together; to congeal, curdle, clot; to stiffen; to take shape, grow, increase
concrētĭ·ō -ōnis *f* condensing, congealing; matter, substance
concrēt·us -a -um *pp* of **concresco;** *adj* grown together, compounded; condensed, congealed, curdled, thick, stiff, hard; frozen; inveterate; dim (*light*); *n* hardness, solid matter
concrīmĭn·or -ārī *vi* to make bitter charges
concrucĭ·ō -āre *vt* to torture
concubīn·a -ae *f* concubine
concubīnāt·us -ūs *m* concubinage, free love
concubīn·us -ī *m* adulterer
concubĭt·us -ūs *m* reclining together (*at table*); sexual intercourse
concubĭ·us -a -um *adj* used only in

the expression **concubiā nocte** early in the night, at bedtime; *n* bedtime

conculc·ō -āre *vt* to trample under foot, despise, treat with contempt

con·cumbō -cumbĕre -cubŭī -cubĭtum *vi* to lie together; (with **cum** + *abl*) to sleep with, have intercourse with

concup·iscō -iscĕre -īvī -ītum *vt* to long for, covet; to aspire to, strive after

concūr·ō -āre *vt* to take good care of

con·currō -currĕre -currī or **-cucurrī -cursum** *vi* to run together, flock together; to unite; to strike one another, crash; (mil) to clash, engage in combat; to happen at the same time, coincide; (with **ad** + *acc*) to have recourse to, run for help to; **concurritur** the armies meet, there is a clash

concursāti·ō -ōnis *f* running together; rushing about; (mil) skirmishing

concursāt·or -ōris *m* (mil) skirmisher

concursi·ō -ōnis *f* meeting, concurrence; (rhet) repetition for emphasis

concurs·ō -āre *vt* to run around to; **domos concursare** to run from house to house; *vi* to rush about excitedly, dash up and down; (mil) to skirmish

concurs·us -ūs *m* running together, concourse, assembly; union, combination; collision; (mil) rush, charge, clash

concuss·us -ūs *m* shaking, concussion

con·cutiō -cutĕre -cussī -cussum *vt* to strike together, bang together; to convulse; to strike, shake, shatter; to shock; to wave (*the hand*); to brandish (*weapon*); to shake out, ransack, examine; to shake, alarm, trouble, terrify

condal·ium -iī or **-ī** *n* slave's ring

condĕc·et -ēre *v impers* it befits, it becomes

condecŏr·ō -āre *vt* to grace, honor, adorn

condemnāt·or -ōris *m* accuser, prosecutor

condemn·ō -āre *vt* to condemn, convict, find guilty, sentence, doom; to blame, condemn; to prosecute successfully, bring a conviction against

condens·ō -āre *vt* to press close together, condense

condens·us -a -um *adj* close together, thick, crowded

condici·ō -ōnis *f* arrangement, settlement, agreement; stipulation, terms, condition; state, situation; circumstances, rank, place; marriage contract, marriage; **ea condicione ut** on condition that; **sub condicione** conditionally; **vitae condicio** way of life, living conditions

con·dīcō -dīcĕre -dixī -dictum *vt* to talk over, arrange together; to promise; **cenam condicere** (with *dat*) or **ad cenam condicere** (with *dat*) to make a dinner engagement with (*someone*)

condignē *adv* very worthily

condign·us -a -um *adj* fully deserving; (with *abl*) fully worthy of

condiment·um -ī *n* seasoning, spice

cond·iō -īre -īvī or **-iī -ītum** *vt* to preserve, pickle (*fruits, vegetables*); to season; to embalm (*the dead*); (fig) to spice, give spice to

condiscipulāt·us -ūs *m* companionship at school

condiscipŭl·us -ī *m* schoolmate, school companion, fellow student

con·discō -discĕre -didicī *vt* to learn by heart

conditiō see **condicio**

conditi·ō -ōnis *f* preserving (*of fruits, etc.*); seasoning, spicing

condĭt·or -ōris *m* founder, builder; author, composer

conditōr·ium -iī or **-ī** *n* coffin, cinerary urn; tomb

condĭt·us -a -um *pp* of **condio;** *adj* seasoned, spicy; polished (*style*)

con·dō -dĕre -didī -ditum *vt* to build, found; to write, compose (*poetry*); to establish (*an institution*); to store, treasure, hoard; to preserve, pickle; to bury; to conceal, hide, suppress; to shut (*eyes*); to sheathe (*sword*); to place (*soldiers*) in ambush; to plunge, bury (*sword*); to imprison; to memorize; to store up

condoce·faciō -facĕre -fēcī -factum *vt* to train well

condoc·ĕō -ēre -ŭī -tum *vt* to teach, instruct thoroughly

condol·escō -escĕre -ŭī *vi* to begin to ache, get very sore

condōnāti·ō -ōnis *f* donating, donation

condōn·ō -āre *vt* to give, present, deliver, abandon, surrender; to adjudge; (with double *acc*) to make (*someone*) a present of; (with *acc* of thing and *dat* of person) to forgive, pardon (*someone an offense*); **condonare alicui pecunias creditas** to remit someone's debt

condorm·iō -īre *vi* to sleep soundly

condorm·iscō -iscĕre -īvī *vi* to fall sound asleep

condūcibĭl·is -e *adj* advantageous, profitable; (with **ad** + *acc*) just right for

con·dūcō -dūcĕre -duxī -ductum *vt* to draw together, collect, assemble; to connect, unite; to hire, rent, borrow; to bribe; to employ; to induce; to contract for; *vi* to be of use; (with *dat*) to be useful to, profitable to; (with **ad** or **in** + *acc*) to be conducive to

conducticĭ·us -a -um *adj* hired, mercenary

conducti·ō -ōnis *f* bringing together; recapitulation; hiring, renting

conduct·or -ōris *m* contractor; lessee, tenant

conduct·us -a -um *pp* of **conduco;** *m pl* hired men; (mil) mercenaries; *n* rented apartment, rented house

conduplicātĭ·ō -ōnis *f* doubling; (humorously) embrace

conduplĭc·ō -āre *vt* to double; **corpora conduplicare** (humorously) to embrace

condūr·ō -āre *vt* to harden, make very hard

cond·us -ī *m* storeroom manager

cō·nectō -nectĕre -nexŭī -nexum *vt* to tie; to connect, join, link; to state as a conclusion; (with *dat*) to implicate (*someone or something*) in; (with *dat* or **cum** + *abl*) to join (*something*) to, connect (*something*) with

cōnexĭ·ō -ōnis *f* logical conclusion

cōnex·us -a -um *pp* of **conecto;** *adj* connected, joined; **per affinitatem conexus** (with *dat*) related by marriage to; *n* necessary inference, logical connection, necessary consequence

cōnex·us -ūs *m* combination

confābŭl·or -ārī -ātus sum *vt* to discuss; *vi* to converse, have a talk

confarreātĭ·ō -ōnis *f* solemn marriage ceremony in the presence of the Pontifex Maximus and ten witnesses

confarrĕ·ō -āre *vt* to marry with solemn rites

confātāl·is -e *adj* bound by the same fate

confectĭ·ō -ōnis *f* completion, successful completion; chewing, mastication

confect·or -ōris *m* finisher, executor; destroyer, consumer

con·fercĭō -fercīre — -fertum *vt* to stuff, cram, pack together; to stuff full

con·fĕrō -ferre -tŭlī -lātum *vt* to bring together; to contribute (*money, etc.*); to condense, compress; to bring together (*plans, ideas, etc.*), discuss, talk over; to bear, convey, direct; to devote, apply, confer, bestow, give, lend, grant; to ascribe, attribute, impute, assign; to put off, defer, postpone; (with **in** + *acc*) to change or transform (*someone or something*) into; to compare, contrast; **capita conferre** to put heads together, confer; **gradum conferre** (with **cum** + *abl*) to walk together with; **lites conferre** to quarrel; **pedem cum pede conferre** to fight toe to toe; **se conferre** (with **in** + *acc*) **a** to go to, head for; **b** to have recourse to; **c** to join (*a group, etc.*); **sermones conferre** (with **cum** + *abl*) to engage in conversation with, to engage (*someone*) in conversation; **signa conferre** to engage in combat, begin fighting

confertim *adv* (mil) shoulder to shoulder

confert·us -a -um *pp* of **confercio;** *adj* crowded, packed, thick, dense; (mil) shoulder to shoulder

confervēfac·ĭō -ĕre *vt* to make glow, make melt

con·fervescō -fervescĕre -ferbŭī *vi* to begin to boil, grow hot

confessĭ·ō -ōnis *f* confession, acknowledgment

confess·us -a -um *pp* of **confiteor;** *adj* acknowledged, incontrovertible, certain; *m* self-acknowledged criminal; *n* admission; **ex confesso** admittedly, beyond doubt; **in confessum venire** to be generally admitted

confestim *adv* immediately, without delay, suddenly

conficĭ·ens -entis *adj* productive, efficient; (with *genit*) productive of; efficient in; *n pl* (with *genit*) sources of

con·ficĭō -ficĕre -fēcī -fectum *vt* to make, manufacture, construct; to make ready, prepare, bring about, complete, accomplish, execute, fulfill; to bring about, cause; to bring together, collect; to get together, secure, obtain; to use up, wear out, exhaust; to finish off, weaken, sweep away, destroy, kill; to run through (*money, inheritance*); to chew (*food*); to complete, finish, spend, pass (*time*)

confictĭ·ō -ōnis *f* fabrication, invention (*of an accusation*)

confīd·ens -entis *adj* trustful; self-confident; presumptuous, smug

confīdenter *adv* confidently; smugly

confīdentĭ·a -ae *f* confidence; self-confidence, smugness

confīdentilŏqu·us -a -um *adj* speaking confidently

con·fīdō -fīdĕre -fīsus sum *vi* to have confidence, be confident, be sure; (with *dat*) to confide in, rely on, trust, believe; **sibi confidere** to rely on oneself, have self-confidence

con·fīgō -fīgĕre -fixī -fixum *vt* to fasten, join together; to pierce, transfix; (fig) to paralyze

con·fingō -fingĕre -finxī -fictum *vt* to make up, invent, fabricate

confīn·is -e *adj* having common boundaries, adjoining; (fig) closely related, akin

confīn·ium -ĭī or **-ī** *n* common boundary, frontier; (fig) borderline; *n pl* neighbors; confines

confirmātĭ·ō -ōnis *f* confirmation, encouragement; affirmation, verification, corroboration; (rhet) presentation of evidence

confirmāt·or -ōris *m* guarantor, surety

confirmāt·us -a -um *adj* resolute, confident, courageous; established, certain

confirmĭt·ās -ātis *f* firmness; stubbornness

confirm·ō -āre *vt* to strengthen, reinforce; to confirm, sanction, ratify; to encourage; to corroborate; to assert positively; **se confirmare** to recover, get back one's strength
confisc·ō -āre *vt* to deposit in a bank; to confiscate
confīsĭ·ō -ōnis *f* confidence, assurance
con·fitĕor -fitērī -fessus sum *vt* to confess, acknowledge, admit; to reveal; *vi* to confess
conflăgr·ō -āre *vi* to burn, be on fire; (fig) to burn
conflictĭ·ō -ōnis *f* conflict
conflict·ō -āre *vt* to beat down, strike down; to ruin; **conflictari** to be afflicted, be tormented; *vi* to contend, struggle, fight
conflict·or -ārī -ātus sum *vi* to struggle, wrestle
conflict·us -ūs *m* striking together; wrestling, struggle
con·flīgō -flīgĕre -flixī -flictum *vt* to throw or knock together; (with **cum** + *abl*) to contrast (*something*) with, compare (*something*) with; *vi* to come into conflict, clash, fight, battle; (with **cum** + *abl*) to come into conflict with, clash with; (with **adversus** + *acc* or **contra** + *acc*) to fight against; **inter se confligere** to collide, collide with one another
confl·ō -āre *vt* to kindle, ignite; to inflame (*passions*); to melt down (*metals*); to bring together, get up, raise (*army, money, etc.*); to forge, invent (*accusation*); to bring about, cause, occasion, produce
conflŭ·ens -entis *m* confluence, junction (*of rivers*); *m pl* confluence
con·flŭō -fluĕre -fluxī *vi* to flow or run together; (fig) to pour in together, come together in crowds
con·fodĭō -fodĕre -fōdī -fossum *vt* to dig up (*soil*); to stab; (fig) to stab
conformātĭ·ō -ōnis *f* shape, form, fashion; idea, notion; arrangement (*of words*); expression (*in the voice*); (rhet) figure of speech
conform·ō -āre *vt* to shape, fashion, put together; to modify, educate
confoss·us -a -um *pp* of **confodio;** *adj* full of holes
confractus *pp* of **confringo**
confragōs·us -a -um *adj* rough, rugged (*terrain*); *n pl* rough terrain
confrĕm·ō -ĕre -ŭī *vi* to grumble
confrĭc·ō -āre *vt* to rub vigorously, rub in; **genua confricare** to nag, pester
con·fringō -fringĕre -frēgī -fractum *vt* to smash, crush; to break down, destroy
con·fugĭō -fugĕre -fūgī *vi* to flee, take refuge, run for help; (with **ad** + *acc*) (fig) **a** to resort to, have recourse to; **b** to appeal to
confug·ĭum -ĭī or **-ī** *n* place of refuge, shelter
confulg·ĕō -ēre *vi* to glitter, sparkle
con·fundō -fundĕre -fūdī -fūsum *vt* to pour together, blend, mingle; to mix up, jumble together, confuse, bewilder, perplex; to spread, diffuse
confūsē *adv* in disorder, in confusion
confūsĭ·ō -ōnis *f* mixing, blending; confusion, mixup, trouble; **confusio oris** blush
confūs·us -a -um *pp* of **confundo;** *adj* confused, perplexed; troubled, confused (*look*)
confūt·ō -āre *vt* to prevent (*water, etc.*) from boiling over; to repress, stop; to silence, confute
congĕl·ō -āre *vt* to cause to freeze up, freeze, harden; **in lapidem congelare** to petrify; *vi* to freeze, freeze up
congemĭnātĭ·ō -ōnis *f* doubling
congemĭn·ō -āre *vt* to double
congĕm·ō -ĕre -ŭī *vt* to deplore deeply; *vi* to gasp, sigh, or groan deeply
cong·er -rī *m* eel
congerĭ·ēs -ēī *f* heap, pile, mass; funeral pile; accumulation
con·gĕrō -gerĕre -gessī -gestum *vt* to bring together; to heap up, build up; to keep up, multiply, repeat (*arguments*); (with **in** + *acc*) **a** to shower (*weapons*) upon, send a barrage of (*weapons*) upon; **b** to heap (*curses, favors, etc.*) upon
congĕr·ō -ōnis *m* thief
congerr·ō -ōnis *m* playmate
congestīcĭ·us -a -um *adj* piled up
congest·us -ūs *m* heap, mass, accumulation
congiāl·is -e *adj* holding a gallon
congiārĭ·us -a -um *adj* holding a gallon; *n* gift of one gallon (*e. g., of oil*) apiece to the people; bonus to the army; gift of money to the Roman people; gift of money among private friends
cong·ĭus -ĭī or **-ī** *m* Roman liquid measure equaling six sextarii, i.e., about six pints
conglacĭ·ō -āre *vi* to freeze up
conglisc·ō -ĕre *vi* to blaze up
conglobātĭ·ō -ōnis *f* massing together
conglŏb·ō -āre *vt* to make round, form into a ball, roll up
conglomĕr·ō -āre *vt* to roll up, group together, crowd together; **se in forum conglomerare** to crowd into the forum
conglūtinātĭ·ō -ōnis *f* gluing together; (fig) combining (*of words*)
conglūtĭn·ō -āre *vt* to glue, cement; (fig) to weld together, cement
congraec·ō -āre *vt* to squander like the Greeks
congrātŭl·or -ārī -ātus sum *vi* to offer congratulations
con·gredĭor -grĕdī -gressus sum *vt* to meet, accost, address, associate with; to fight; *vi* to come together, meet; to fight; (with **cum** + *abl*) **a**

to meet with; **b** to associate with; **c** to fight against

congregābĭl·is -e *adj* gregarious

congregātĭ·ō -ōnis *f* flocking together, congregation, union, association

congrĕg·ō -āre *vt* to herd together; to unite, associate

congressĭ·ō -ōnis *f* meeting, conference

congressus *pp* of **congredior**

congress·us -ūs *m* meeting, association, society, union; hostile encounter, contest, fight

congrŭ·ens -entis *adj* coinciding, corresponding; suitable, consistent; self-consistent, uniform, harmonious

congruenter *adv* consistently; (with *dat* or **ad** + *acc*) in conformity with; **congruenter naturae vivere** to live in conformity with nature

congruentĭ·a -ae *f* consistency, symmetry

congrŭ·ō -ĕre -ŭī *vi* to coincide; to correspond, agree, be consistent; (with **ad** + *acc* or with **cum** + *abl*) to coincide with; (with *dat* or **cum** + *abl*) to correspond to, agree with, be consistent with; (with *dat* or **in** + *acc*) to agree (*in feeling, opinion*) with

congrŭ·us -a -um *adj* agreeing, agreeable

cōnicĭō or **cōicĭō** see **conjicio**

cōnĭf·er -ĕra -ĕrum *adj* coniferous

cōnĭg·er -ĕra -ĕrum *adj* coniferous

cō·nītor -nītī -nixus sum or **-nīsus sum** *vi* to make a great effort, struggle, exert oneself; (with **in** + *acc*) to struggle toward, press on toward, try to reach

cōnīv·ĕō -ēre -ī *vi* to close the eyes (*in sleep, from light, from fear, etc.*), to blink; (of sun or moon) to be darkened, be eclipsed; (fig) to be drowsy; (with **in** + *abl*) to connive at, wink at, overlook

conjectĭ·ō -ōnis *f* throwing, barrage (*of missiles*); conjecture, interpretation

conject·ō -āre *vt* to conjecture, infer, conclude, guess

conject·or -ōris *m* interpreter of dreams, seer

conjectr·ix -īcis *f* interpreter of dreams, seer (*female*)

conjectūr·a -ae *f* conjecture, guess, inference; interpretation

conjectūrāl·is -e *adj* conjectural

conject·us -ūs *m* throwing together; crowding together; connecting; heap, crowd, pile; throwing, casting, hurling; turning, directing (*eyes*); casting (*a glance*); barrage (*of stones, weapons*); **ad** or **intra teli conjectum venire** to come within range of a weapon

con·jicĭō -jicĕre -jēcī -jectum *vt* to pile together (*e.g., baggage*); to conclude, infer, conjecture; to interpret (*omen*); to throw, fling, cast; to throw in (*e.g., words in a letter or speech*); **se in fugam** or **se in pedes conjicere** to take to one's heels

conjugāl·is -e *adj* conjugal

conjugātĭ·ō -ōnis *f* etymological relationship (*of words*)

conjugāt·or -ōris *m* uniter (*said of Hymen, god of marriage*)

conjugiāl·is -e *adj* marriage

conjug·ĭum -ĭī or **-ī** *n* union (*e.g., of body and soul*); marriage, wedlock; mating (*of animals*); (fig) husband, wife, spouse

conjŭg·ō -āre *vt* to form (*friendship*); **verba conjugata** cognates

conjunctē *adv* conjointly; at the same time; (in logic) conditionally, hypothetically; **conjuncte vivere** to live intimately together

conjunctim *adv* jointly

conjunctĭ·ō -ōnis *f* combination, union; association, connection; friendship; intimacy; marriage; relationship (*by blood or by marriage*); sympathy, affinity; (gram) conjunction

conjunct·us -a -um *adj* (with *dat* or *abl*) bordering upon, near; (with *dat* or *abl*, or with **cum** + *abl*) **a** connected with; **b** agreeing with, conforming with; *n* connection

con·jungō -jungĕre -junxī -junctum *vt* to join together, connect, unite; to unite in making (*war*); to unite or join in marriage; to unite (*by bonds of friendship*); (with *dat*) to add (*e.g., words*) to (*e.g., a letter*)

con·junx or **con·jux -jŭgis** *m* married person, spouse, husband; *m pl* married couple; *f* married person, spouse, wife; fiancee; bride; the female (*of animals*)

conjūrātĭ·ō -ōnis *f* conspiracy, plot; alliance

conjūrāt·us -a -um *adj* bound together by an oath, allied, associate; (mil) sworn in; *m pl* conspirators

conjūr·ō -āre *vi* to take an oath together; to plot, conspire

conjux see **conjunx**

conl- = **coll-**

comm- = **comm-**

Con·ōn -ōnis *m* famous Athenian admiral (*fl* 400 B.C.); famous mathematician and astronomer of Samos (283-222 B.C.)

cōnōpē·um or **cōnōpĕ·um -ī** *n* mosquito net

cōn·or -ārī -ātus sum *vt* to try, endeavor, venture, attempt

conquassātĭ·ō -ōnis *f* severe shaking; disturbance

conquass·ō -āre *vt* to shake hard; (fig) to shatter, upset, disturb

con·quĕror -quĕrī -questus sum *vt* to complain bitterly about, deplore; *vi* to complain, complain bitterly

conquestĭ·ō -ōnis *f* complaining, complaint; (rhet) appeal for sympathy; (with *genit*, with **de** + *abl*, or with **adversus** + *acc*) complaint about

conquest·us -ūs *m* loud complaint

conqui·escō -escĕre -ēvī -ētum *vi* to rest, take a rest; to find rest, find recreation; to keep quiet, remain inactive; to slacken, flag; to lie dormant; to take a nap; to stop, pause

conquinisc·ō -ĕre *vi* to squat, stoop down

con·quīrō -quīrĕre -quīsīvī -quīsītum *vt* to search for, look for; to procure, bring together, collect; (fig) to search for, go after (*pleasures, etc.*)

conquīsītĭ·ō -ōnis *f* search; procuring, collection; (mil) conscription, draft, recruitment

conquīsīt·or -ōris *m* recruiting officer

conquīsīt·us -a -um *pp* of **conquiro;** *adj* chosen, select

conr- = **corr-**

consaep·ĭō or **consēp·ĭō -īre -sī -tum** *vt* to fence in, hedge in, enclose

consaept·um -ī *n* enclosure

consalūtātĭ·ō -ōnis *f* exchange of greetings

consalūt·ō -āre *vt* to greet (*as a group*), greet cordially; *vi* **inter se consalūtāre** to greet one another, exchange greetings

consān·escō -escĕre -ŭī *vi* to heal up; to recover

consanguinĕ·us -a -um *adj* related by blood; *m* brother; *m pl* relatives; *f* sister

consanguinĭt·ās -ātis *f* blood relationship; **consanguinitate propinquus** closely related

consaucĭ·ō -āre *vt* to wound severely

consccelerāt·us -a -um *adj* wicked, depraved, criminal; (fig) rotten to the core

conscelĕr·ō -āre *vt* to stain with guilt, dishonor, disgrace

con·scendō -scendĕre -scendī -scensum *vt* to climb up, mount, ascend; to board (*ship*); **aequor navibus conscendere** to go to sea; *vi* to climb; to go aboard, board; (with **in** + *acc*) to go aboard (*ship*)

conscensĭ·ō -ōnis *f* embarkation; **in navīs conscensio** boarding the ships

conscientĭ·a -ae *f* joint knowledge; consciousness, knowledge; moral sense, conscience; good conscience; bad conscience; scruple; sense of guilt, remorse

con·scindō -scindĕre -scĭdī -scissum *vt* to tear up, tear to pieces; (fig) to tear to pieces, abuse

consc·ĭō -īre *vt* to become conscious of (*wrong*)

consc·iscō -iscĕre -īvī or **-ĭī -ītum** *vt* to approve or decide upon; **(sibi) mortem consciscere** to decide upon death for oneself, commit suicide

conscĭ·us -a -um *adj* sharing knowledge with another; cognizant, conscious, aware; (with *genit* or *dat*) having knowledge of, aware of, privy to; *mf* partner, accomplice, confidant(e), confederate

conscrĕ·or -ārī -ātus sum *vi* to clear the throat

con·scrībō -scrībĕre -scripsī -scriptum *vt* to enlist, enroll; to write, write up, compose; to prescribe

conscriptĭ·ō -ōnis *f* document, draft; record, report

conscript·us -a -um *pp* of **conscribo;** *m* senator; **patres conscripti** members of the senate

consĕc·ō -āre -ŭī -tum *vt* to cut up into small pieces, dismember

consecrātĭ·ō -ōnis *f* consecration; deification (*of emperors*)

consĕcr·ō -āre *vt* to make holy, consecrate, dedicate to a god; to dedicate to the gods below, doom to destruction, execrate; to immortalize, deify

consectārĭ·us -a -um *adj* logic; *n pl* conclusions, inferences

consectātĭ·ō -ōnis *f* eager pursuit

consectātr·ix -īcis *f* pursuer (*female*)

consectĭ·ō -ōnis *f* cutting up

consect·or -ārī -ātus sum *vt* to follow eagerly, go after; to follow up, pursue, chase, hunt; to overtake; to imitate, follow

consecūtĭ·ō -ōnis *f* effect, consequences; (rhet) order, sequence

consen·escō -escĕre -ŭī *vi* to grow old, grow old together; to become gray; to become obsolete; to waste away, fade, decline; to degenerate, sink

consensĭ·ō -ōnis *f* agreement, unanimity; harmony; plot, conspiracy

consens·us -ūs *m* agreement, unanimity; agreement, harmony; plot, conspiracy; **consensū** with one accord; **in consensum vertere** to become a general custom; **omnium vestrum consensu** with the agreement of all of you, as you all agree

consentānĕ·us -a -um *adj* (with *dat* or **cum** + *abl*) agreeing with, according to, in accord with, proper for; **consentaneum est** it is reasonable; *n pl* concurrent circumstances

consentĭ·ens -entis *adj* unanimous

con·sentĭō -sentīre -sensī -sensum *vt* **bellum consentire** to agree to war, vote for war; *vi* to agree; (with *inf*) to agree, plot, conspire to; (with **cum** + *abl*) to harmonize with, fit in with, be consistent with

consēp- = **consaep-**

consĕqu·ens -entis *adj* reasonable;

corresponding, logical, fit, suitable; *n* consequence, conclusion

consequentĭ·a -ae *f* consequence, natural sequence

con·sĕquor -sĕquī -secūtus sum *vt* to follow, follow up, pursue, go after; to catch up with, catch, reach, attain to, arrive at; (fig) to follow, copy, imitate; to obtain, get, acquire; to understand, perceive, learn; (of speech) to be equal to, do justice to; (of time) to come after, follow; to result from, be the consequence of, arise from

con·sĕrō -serĕre -serŭī -sertum *vt* to entwine, tie, join, string together; **manum** or **manūs conserere** to fight hand to hand, engage in close combat; **proelium conserere** to begin fighting

con·sĕrō -serĕre -sēvī -sĭtum *vt* to sow, plant

consertē *adv* in close connection, connectedly

conserv·a -ae *f* fellow slave (*female*)

conservātĭ·ō -ōnis *f* keeping, preserving

conservāt·or -ōris *m* preserver, defender

conservit·ĭum -ĭī or **-ī** *n* servitude

conserv·ō -āre *vt* to keep safe, preserve, maintain; (fig) to keep intact

conserv·us -ī *m* fellow slave

consess·or -ōris *m* table companion; fellow spectator; (law) assessor

consess·us -ūs *m* assembly, court

consīderātē *adv* with caution, deliberately

consīderātĭ·ō -ōnis *f* contemplation, consideration

consīderāt·us -a -um *adj* circumspect, cautious; well considered, deliberate

consīdĕr·ō -āre *vt* to look at closely, inspect, examine, survey; to consider, contemplate; reflect upon

con·sīdō -sīdĕre -sēdī -sessum *vi* to sit down, be seated, settle; (of assemblies) to hold sessions, be in session; (mil) to encamp, take up a position; to settle, stay (*in residence*); to settle, sink down, subside; (fig) to settle, sink, be buried; to diminish, subside, abate, die out

consign·ō -āre *vt* to seal, sign; to certify, attest, vouch for; to note, register, record

consil·escō -escĕre -ŭī *vi* to become still, calm down

consiliārĭ·us -a -um *adj* counseling; *m* counselor, adviser; interpreter, spokesman

consiliāt·or -ōris *m* counselor

consiliō *adv* intentionally, purposely

consilĭ·or -ārī -ātus sum *vi* to take counsel, consult; (with *dat*) to give counsel to, advise

consil·ĭum -ĭī or **-ī** *n* consultation, deliberation; deliberative body, council; council of war; plan, measure, stratagem; decision; purpose, intention, design, policy; judgment, wisdom, prudence, discretion, sense; cabinet; advice, counsel; **consilium capere** or **consilium inire** or **consilium suscipere** to form a plan, come to a decision, decide, determine; **consilium est mihi** (with *inf*) I intend to; **non est consilium mihi** (with *inf*) I don't mean to; **privato consilio** for one's own purposes

consimĭl·is -e *adj* quite similar; (with *genit* or *dat*) completely similar to, just like

consip·ĭō -ĕre *vi* to be sane

con-sistō -sistĕre -stĭtī -stĭtum *vi* to come to a stop, come to rest, stop, pause, halt, take a stand, stand still; to grow hard, become solid, set; (mil) to take up a position, be posted, make a stand; (of ships) to come to anchorage, to ground; (of travelers) to halt on a journey; to be firm, be steadfast, continue, endure; to be, exist, occur, take place; (with *abl* or with **in** + *abl*) to consist of, depend on

consitĭ·ō -ōnis *f* sowing, planting

consĭt·or -ōris *m* sower, planter

consitūr·a -ae *f* sowing, planting

consōbrīn·a -ae *f* first cousin (*daughter of a mother's sister*)

consōbrīn·us -ī *m* first cousin (*son of mother's sister*)

consociātĭ·ō -ōnis *f* association, society

consociāt·us -a -um *adj* held in common, shared

consocĭ·ō -āre *vt* to associate, join, unite, connect, share

consōlābĭl·is -e *adj* consolable

consōlātĭ·ō -ōnis *f* consolation, comfort; encouragement; alleviation

consōlāt·or -ōris *m* comforter

consōlātōrĭ·us -a -um *adj* comforting; **litterae consolatoriae** letter of condolence

consōl·or -ārī -ātus sum *vt* to console, comfort, reassure, soothe, encourage, cheer up; to relieve, alleviate, mitigate

consomnĭ·ō -āre *vt* to dream about

consŏn·ō -āre -ŭī *vi* to sound together, ring, resound, reecho; (with *dat* or with **cum** + *abl*) to harmonize with, agree with; **inter se consonare** to agree, harmonize

consŏn·us -a -um *adj* harmonious; (fig) fit, suitable

consōp·ĭō -īre *vt* to put to sleep

consor·s -tis *adj* having a common lot, of the same fortune; common; shared in common; *mf* partner, associate; *m* brother; *f* wife; sister

consortĭ·ō -ōnis *f* partnership, association, fellowship

consort·ĭum -ĭī or **-ī** *n* partnership; participation; (with *genit*) partnership in

conspect·us -a -um *pp* of **conspicio**; *adj* visible; in full sight; conspicuous, striking

conspect·us -ūs *m* look, sight, view; sight (*power of seeing*); mental view;

being seen, appearance on the scene; **conspectu in medio** before all eyes

con·spergō -spergĕre -spersī -spersum *vt* to sprinkle, splatter

conspiciend·us -a -um *adj* worth seeing; distinguished

conspicill·um -ī *n* (with *genit*) keeping an eye on

con·spiciō -spicĕre -spexī -spectum *vt* to look at attentively, observe, fix the eyes upon; to catch sight of, spot; to look at with admiration; to face (*e.g., the forum*); to perceive, see, discern; **conspici** to be conspicuous, be noticed, be admired, attract attention

conspĭc·or -ārī -ātus sum *vt* to catch sight of, spot, see

conspicŭ·us -a -um *adj* visible, in sight; conspicuous, striking, remarkable, distinguished

conspīrātĭ·ō -ōnis *f* agreement, unanimity, harmony, concord; plot, conspiracy

conspīrāt·us -a -um *adj* conspiring, in conspiracy

conspīr·ō -āre *vi* to breathe together, blow together, sound together; to act in unison, to agree; to plot together, conspire

conspons·or -ōris *m* coguarantor

con·spŭō -spuĕre — -spūtum *vt* to spit on; **nive conspuere** to sprinkle with snow

conspurc·ō -āre *vt* to defile, mess up

conspūt·ō -āre *vt* to spit on in contempt

constabil·iō -īre -īvī -ītum *vt* to establish, confirm

const·ans -antis *adj* constant, uniform, steady, fixed, stable, regular, invariable, persistent; consistent, harmonious; (fig) faithful, constant, trustworthy

constanter *adv* constantly, steadily, uniformly, invariably; consistently; calmly

constantĭ·a -ae *f* steadiness, firmness, constancy, perseverance; harmony, symmetry, consistency; steadfastness; self-possession

consternātĭ·ō -ōnis *f* consternation, dismay, alarm; disorder, disturbance; mutiny; wild rush, stampede

con·sternō -sternĕre -strāvī -strātum *vt* to spread, cover; to pave; to thatch; **constrata navis** ship with deck

constīp·ō -āre *vt* to crowd together

constit·ŭō -uĕre -ŭī -ūtum *vt* to set up, erect, establish; to settle (*e.g., a people in a place*); to set up, establish (*authority*); to settle, determine, fix (*date, price, penalty*); to arrange, set in order, organize; to construct, erect; to designate, select, assign, appoint; to decide, arbitrate, decree, judge; (mil) to station, post, deploy

constitūtĭ·ō -ōnis *f* constitution, nature; disposition; regulation, ordinance, order; definition; (rhet) issue, point of discussion

constitūt·us -a -um *pp* of **constituo;** *adj* ordered, arranged; **bene constitutum corpus** good constitution; *n* agreement, arrangement

con·stō -stāre -stĭtī -stātum *vi* to stand together; to agree, correspond; to stand firm, remain unchanged, be constant; to stand still, stand firm; to be in existence; (of facts) to be established, be undisputed, be well known; (com) to tally, be correct; (with *abl* of price) to cost; **non mihi satis constat** I have not quite made up my mind; **ratio constat** the account tallies, is correct

constrāt·us -a -um *pp* of **consterno;** *n* flooring

con·stringō -stringĕre -strinxī -strictum *vt* to tie up; to shackle, chain; (fig) to bind, restrain; (rhet) to condense, compress

constructĭ·ō -ōnis *f* building, construction; arrangement (*of words*)

con·strŭō -struere -struxī -structum *vt* to heap up, pile up; to construct, build up; (gram) to construct

constuprāt·or -ōris *m* rapist

constŭpr·ō -āre *vt* to rape

consuād·ĕō -ēre *vi* (with *dat*) to advise strongly

Consuāl·ĭa -ĭum *n pl* feast of Consus, ancient Italian god of fertility, celebrated on August 21st

consuās·or -ōris *m* adviser

consūcĭd·us -a -um *adj* very juicy

consūd·ō -āre *vi* to sweat profusely

consuē·faciō -facĕre -fēcī -factum *vt* to accustom, inure

consu·escō -escĕre -ēvī -ētum *vt* to accustom, inure; *vi* to become accustomed; (with *inf*) to become accustomed to; (with **cum** + *abl*) to cohabit with

consuētĭ·ō -ōnis *f* sexual intercourse

consuētūd·ō -ĭnis *f* custom, habit; usage, idiom; social intercourse, social ties; sexual intercourse; **ad consuetudinem** (with *genit*) according to the custom of; **consuetudine** or **ex consuetudine** according to custom, from habit; **pro consuetudine mea** according to my habit, as is my habit; **ut fert consuetudo** as is usual

consuēt·us -a -um *pp* of **consuesco;** *adj* usual, regular, customary

con·sul -sŭlis *m* consul (*one of the two highest magistrates of the Roman republic*); **consul designatus** consul-elect; **consulem creare, dicere,** or **facere** to elect a consul; **consul ordinarius** consul who entered office on the first of January; **consul suffectus** consul chosen in the course of the year to fill a vacancy in the consulship

consulār·is -e *adj* consular; **aetas**

consularis minimum legal age for election to consular office; **comitia consularia** consular elections; *m* ex-consul
consulāriter *adv* like a consul, in a manner worthy of a consul
consulāt·us -ūs *m* consulship; **consulatum petere** to run for the consulship; **se consulatu abdicare** to resign from the consulship
consŭl·ō -ĕre -ŭī -tum *vt* to consult, ask advice of; to consider; to advise (*something*), offer as advice; **boni consulere** to regard favorably; *vi* to deliberate, reflect; (with **ad** or **in** + *acc*) to reflect on, take into consideration; (with *dat*) to look after; (with **in** + *acc*) to take measures against; (with **de** + *abl*) to pass sentence on
consultātĭ·ō -ōnis *f* mature deliberation, consideration; consulting, inquiry; subject of consultation, case
consultē *adv* deliberately, after due consideration
consultō *adv* deliberately, on purpose
consult·ō -āre *vt* to reflect on, consider maturely; to ask (*someone*) for advice, consult; *vi* to deliberate, reflect; (with *dat*) to take into consideration, look after, care for; **in medium consultare** to look after the common good
consult·or -ōris *m* counselor, adviser; advisee, client
consultr·ix -īcis *f* protectress
consult·us -a -um *pp* of **consulo;** *adj* skilled, experienced; *m* expert; **juris consultus** legal expert, lawyer; *n* deliberation, consideration; decree, decision, resolution; response (*from an oracle*)
consummāt·us -a -um *adj* consummate, perfect
consumm·ō -āre *vt* to sum up; to finish, complete, accomplish, perfect
con·sūmō -sūmĕre -sumpsī -sumptum *vt* to use up, consume, exhaust; to devour; to squander; to wear out, destroy; to spend, waste (*money, time, effort*)
consumptĭ·ō -ōnis *f* consumption, wasting
consumpt·or -ōris *m* destroyer
con·sŭō -suĕre -sŭī -sūtum *vt* to stitch together, sew up
con·surgō -surgĕre -surrexī -surrectum *vi* to stand up; to rise in a body; (with **ad** or **in** + *acc*) to aspire to
consurrectĭ·ō -ōnis *f* rising up, standing up in a body
Cons·us -ī *m* ancient Italian deity of agriculture and fertility
consusurr·ō -āre *vi* to whisper together
contābēfac·iō -ĕre *vt* to wear out completely, consume, waste
contāb·escō -escĕre -ŭī *vi* to waste away
contabulātĭ·ō -ōnis *f* flooring; story
contabŭl·ō -āre *vt* to cover with boards; to build with (*several*) stories
contact·us -ūs *m* touch, contact; contagion; (fig) contagion, infection
contāg·ēs -is *f* touch, contact
contāgĭ·ō -ōnis *f* touching; touch; contact; contagion, infection; moral contagion, bad example
contāg·ium -iī or **-ī** *n* touch, contact; contagion; moral contamination
contāmināt·us -a -um *adj* polluted, contaminated, impure, vile, degraded; *m pl* perverted youths
contāmin·ō -āre *vt* to bring into contact, mingle, blend; to corrupt, defile; (fig) to corrupt, stain, taint, spoil
contechn·or -ārī -ātus sum *vi* to devise plots, think up tricks
con·tĕgō -tegĕre -texī -tectum *vt* to cover up; to hide; to protect
contemĕr·ō -āre *vt* to defile
con·temnō -temnĕre -tempsī -temptum *vt* to think little of, depreciate, slight, belittle, disregard; to despise, defy
contemplātĭ·ō -ōnis *f* viewing, surveying, contemplation
contemplāt·or -ōris *m* contemplator, observer
contemplāt·us -ūs *m* contemplation
contempl·ō -āre or **contempl·or -ārī -ātus sum** *vt* to observe, survey, gaze upon, contemplate
contemptim *adv* contemptuously
contemptĭ·ō -ōnis *f* belittling, despising; **in contemptionem venire** (with *dat*) to become an object of contempt to
contempt·or -ōris *m* or **contemptr·ix -īcis** *f* scorner, despiser
contempt·us -a -um *pp* of **contemno;** *adj* contemptible, despicable
contempt·us -ūs *m* belittling, despising, scorn; **contemptui esse** to be an object of contempt
con·tendō -tendĕre -tendī -tentum *vt* to stretch, draw tight; to tune (*instrument*); to aim, shoot, hurl; (fig) to strain, stretch, exert; to hold, assert, maintain; to compare, contrast; to direct (*course*); *vi* to exert oneself; to compete, contend, fight; to travel, march; (with *inf*) to be in a hurry to; (with **in** + *acc*) to rush to, head for; (with **ad** + *acc*) to strive for, aspire to
contentē *adv* with great effort, earnestly; closely, scantily, sparingly
contentĭ·ō -ōnis *f* competition, struggle, dispute; straining, exertion, effort; contrast, comparison, antithesis
content·us -a -um *pp* of **contendo;** *adj* tense, tight, taut, strained; eager, intense
content·us -a -um *pp* of **contineo;** *adj* content, satisfied

contermĭn·us -a -um *adj* (with *dat*) bordering upon
con·tĕrō -terĕre -trīvī -trītum *vt* to grind to powder, pulverize, crumble; (fig) to wear away, wear out, use up; to consume, waste (*time*)
conterr·ĕō -ēre -ŭī -ĭtum *vt* to frighten, scare the life out of
contest·or -ārī -ātus sum *vt* to call to witness; (fig) to prove, attest; **litem contestari** to open a lawsuit by calling witnesses
contex·ō -ĕre -ŭī -tum *vt* to weave together; to brace together; to connect; to devise, build; to compose (*writings*); to dream up (*a charge*)
contextē *adv* in a coherent manner
context·us -a -um *pp* of **contexo;** *adj* connected
context·us -ūs *m* connection, coherence
contic·escō or **contic·iscō -escĕre -ŭī** *vi* to become quite still, fall completely silent, hush; to keep silence; (fig) to cease, abate
conticinnō *adv* in the evening
contignātĭ·ō -ōnis *f* floor, story
contign·ō -āre *vt* to lay a floor on
contigŭ·us -a -um *adj* touching, adjoining; within reach; (with *dat*) bordering on, near
contĭn·ens -entis *adj* contiguous, adjacent; unbroken, uninterrupted; self-controlled, continent; (with *dat*) bordering on, contiguous with, adjacent to
contĭn·ens -entis *f* continent, mainland
contĭn·ens -entis *n* chief point, main point (*of a speech*)
continenter *adv* in unbroken succession; without interruption; (sitting) close together; moderately, temperately
continentĭ·a -ae *f* self-control; continence
con·tinĕō -tinēre -tinŭī -tentum *vt* to hold or keep together; to keep within bounds, confine; to contain, comprise, include; to control, repress
con·tingō -tingĕre -tĭgī -tactum *vt* to come into contact with; (fig) to touch, affect; to touch, border on; to reach, reach to; to contaminate; *vi* to happen, turn out, come to pass; (with *dat*) **a** to touch, border on; **b** to happen to, befall
continuātĭ·ō -ōnis *f* unbroken series, succession; (rhet) period
continŭ·ō -āre *vt* to make continuous, join together, connect; to extend; to continue, carry on, draw out, prolong; to pass, occupy (*time*); **continuari** (with *dat*) **a** to be contiguous with, adjacent to; **b** to follow closely upon
continŭō *adv* immediately, without delay; as a necessary consequence, necessarily
continŭ·us -a -um *adj* continuous, unbroken; successive; **dies continuos quinque** for five successive days
contĭ·ō -ōnis *f* meeting, rally; public meeting (*of the people or of soldiers*); speech, pep talk, harangue
contiōnābund·us -a -um *adj* haranguing
contiōnāl·is -e *adj* typical of a public assembly; demagogic
contiōnārĭ·us -a -um *adj* mob-like
contiōnāt·or -ōris *m* demagogue, public agitator, rabble-rouser
contiōn·or -ārī -ātus sum *vi* to hold forth at a rally, to harangue; to come to a rally; to make a statement at a rally
contiuncŭl·a -ae *f* short harangue, trifling speech
contoll·ō -ĕre *vt* to bring together
contŏn·at -āre *v impers* it is thundering hard
contor·quĕō -quēre -sī -tum *vt* to whirl, twist; to throw hard; to twist (*words*) around
contortē *adv* intricately
contortiōn·ēs -um *f pl* intricacies (*of language*)
contort·or -ōris *m* perverter; **contortor legum** pettifogger
contortŭl·us -a -um *adj* rather complicated
contortuplicāt·us -a -um *adj* all twisted up
contort·us -a -um *pp* of **contorqueo;** *adj* involved, intricate; vehement (*speech*)
contrā *adv* in opposition, opposite, in front, face to face; in turn, in return, on the other hand, on the other side; reversely, in the opposite way, the other way; on the contrary, conversely; **contra atque** or **ac** contrary to, otherwise than; **contra dicere** to reply, say in reply; to raise objections; **contra dicitur** the objection is raised; **contra ferire** to make a counterattack; **contra qua fas est** contrary to divine law; **contra quam senatus consuluisset** contrary to what the senate would have decided, contrary to the senate resolution; **quin contra** nay on the contrary, in fact it's just the opposite
contrā *prep* (with *acc*) opposite, opposite to, facing, towards, against; in answer to, in reply to; (in hostile sense) against, with, in opposition to, as the opponent of; against, injurious to, unfavorable to; contrary to, the reverse of; in violation of; against, in defiance of; **contra ea putare** to think otherwise; **quod contra** whereas, while; **valere contra** to counterbalance
contractĭ·ō -ōnis *f* drawing together, contraction; shortening (*of syllable*); despondency
contractiuncŭl·a -ae *f* slight mental depression
contract·us -a -um *pp* of **contraho;** *adj* contracted; narrow, lim-

ited (*place*); brief; pinching (*poverty*); in seclusion; **res contracta** contract

contract•us -ūs *m* shrinking

contrā•dīcō -dīcĕre -dixī -dictum *vi* (with *dat*) to contradict, speak against

contrādictĭ•ō -ōnis *f* objection, refutation

con•trăhō -trahĕre -traxī -tractum *vt* to draw together, collect, assemble; to contract, shorten, narrow, abridge, lessen, diminish; to wrinkle; (fig) to bring about, accomplish, cause, produce, incur; to conclude (*bargain*); to transact (*business*); to settle (*an account*); to complete (*business arrangements*)

contrārĭē *adv* in opposite ways, in a different way

contrārĭ•us -a -um *adj* opposite; contrary, conflicting; hostile, antagonistic; from the opposite direction; (with *dat*) opposed to, contrary to; *n* the opposite, the contrary, the reverse; antithesis; **ex contrario** on the contrary, on the other hand; **in contraria** in opposite directions; **in contraria versus** changed into its opposite

contrectābilĭter *adv* appreciably, tangibly

contrectātĭ•ō -ōnis *f* handling, touching

contrect•ō -āre *vt* to touch, handle; (fig) to defile; (fig) to dwell upon, consider

contrem•iscō -iscĕre -ŭī *vt* to shudder at; *vi* to tremble all over; to waver

contrĕm•ō -ĕre -ŭī *vi* to tremble all over; to quake

contrib•ŭō -uĕre -ŭī -ūtum *vt* to bring together, enroll together, associate, unite, incorporate; to contribute, add

contrist•ō -āre *vt* to sadden, cover with gloom; (fig) to darken, cloud

contrīt•us -a -um *pp* of **contero;** *adj* worn out, common, trite

contrōversĭ•a -ae *f* controversy, quarrel, dispute, debate; civil lawsuit, litigation; subject of litigation; contradiction; question; **sine controversia** indisputably

contrōversiōs•us -a -um *adj* much disputed, controversial

contrōvers•us -a -um *adj* disputed, controversial, questionable, undecided

contrucīd•ō -āre *vt* to cut down, cut to pieces, massacre; (fig) to wreck, make a mess of

con•trūdō -trūdĕre -trūsī -trūsum *vt* to crowd together

contrunc•ō -āre *vt* to hack to pieces

contubernāl•is -is *m* army comrade, army buddy; junior staff officer; (coll) husband (*of slave*); personal attendant; comrade, companion, associate; colleague; *f* (coll) wife (*of slave*)

contubern•ĭum -ĭī or **-ī** *n* military companionship; common war tent; concubinage; marriage (*of slaves*); hovel (*of slaves*)

con•tuĕor -tuērī -tuĭtus sum *vt* to look at attentively, regard, survey

contuĭt•us or **contūt•us -ūs** *m* sight, observation

contumācĭ•a -ae *f* stubbornness, defiance, willfulness; constancy, firmness

contumācĭter *adv* stubbornly, defiantly

contŭm•ax -ācis *adj* stubborn, defiant

contumēlĭ•a -ae *f* mistreatment, rough treatment; outrage, insult, abuse, affront

contumēlĭōsē *adv* abusively

contumēlĭōs•us -a -um *adj* bringing dishonor; insulting, abusive; reproachful, insolent

contumŭl•ō -āre *vt* to bury

con•tundō -tundĕre -tŭdī -tūsum *vt* to crush, grind, pound, bruise; (fig) to crush, destroy, break, subdue; to baffle

conturbātĭ•ō -ōnis *f* confusion, consternation

conturbāt•us -a -um *adj* confused, distracted, disordered, in confusion

conturb•ō -āre *vt* to confuse, throw into confusion; to disquiet, disturb; to upset (*plans*); **rationes** or **rationem conturbare** to be bankrupt; *vi* to be bankrupt

cont•us -ī *m* pole

cōnūbiāl•is -e *adj* marriage, connubial

cōnūb•ĭum -ĭī or **-ī** *n* intermarriage; right to intermarry according to Roman law; marriage; sexual intercourse; **jus conubi** right to intermarry

cōn•us -ī *m* cone; apex (*of helmet*)

convăd•or -ārī -ātus sum *vt* to subpoena

conval•escō -escĕre -ŭī *vi* to grow strong; to regain strength, convalesce; (fig) to improve

convall•is -is *f* valley

convās•ō -āre *vt* to pack up, pack

convect•ō -āre *vt* to heap together; to bring home

convect•or -ōris *m* fellow passenger

con•vĕhō -vehĕre -vexī -vectum *vt* to collect, bring in (*esp. the harvest*)

con•vellō -vellĕre -vellī -vulsum *vt* to tear away, pull off, pluck, wrest; to tear to pieces, dismember; to break, shatter; (fig) to turn upside down, subvert, overthrow; **convellere signa** to break camp

convĕn•ae -ārum *m pl* or *f pl* strangers; refugees, vagabonds

convenī•ens -entis *adj* agreeing, harmonious, consistent; appropriate; (with *dat* or with **cum** + *abl*) consistent with, appropriate to; (with **ad** + *acc*) appropriate for, suitable for

convenienter *adv* consistently; suitably; (with **cum** + *abl* or with **ad** + *acc*) in conformity with
convenienti·a -ae *f* agreement, accord, harmony; conformity
con·veniō -venīre -vēnī -ventum *vt* to meet, go to meet; to interview; *vi* to come together, meet, gather, come in a body; to coincide; to unite, combine; to come to an agreement, agree; (with **ad** + *acc*) to fit (*as a shoe fits the foot*); (with *dat*, with **ad** or **in** + *acc*, or with **cum** + *abl*) to be applicable to, appropriate to, fit; **convenit** it is fitting, proper; **convenit inter se** (with *dat*) there is harmony among
conventīcī·us -a -um *adj* coming together, gathering together; *n* fee for attending the assembly
conventicŭl·um -ī *n* small gathering; meeting place
conventī·ō -ōnis *f* agreement, contract
convent·us -a -um *pp* of **convenio;** *n* agreement, contract
convent·us -ūs *m* gathering, assembly; congress; district court; company, corporation; agreement; **ex conventu** by agreement; of one accord; **conventum agere** to hold court
con·verrō or **con·vorrō -verrĕre -verrī -versum** *vt* to sweep together, sweep up; to brush thoroughly; (fig) to scoop up (*e.g., an inheritance*)
conversātī·ō -ōnis *f* social intercourse; conversation
conversī·ō -ōnis *f* revolving, revolution; (fig) alteration, change; (rhet) repetition of word at end of clause; (rhet) balancing of phrases
convers·ō -āre *vt* to turn around; **se conversare** to revolve
con·vertō or **con·vortō -vertĕre -vertī -versum** *vt* to cause to turn, turn back, reverse; (fig) to turn, direct (*laughter, attention*); to convert, transform; to translate; to attract (*attention*); (mil) **sese convertere** to retreat; *vi* to return; to change, be changed, turn; (with **in** + *acc*) to be changed into, turn into
convest·iō -īre *vt* to clothe, cover
convex·us -a -um *pp* of **conveho;** *adj* rounded off; arched, convex; concave; sloping down; *n* vault, arch
convīciāt·or -ōris *m* reviler
convīci·or -ārī -ātus sum *vt* to revile
convīc·ium -iī or **-ī** *n* noise, chatter; wrangling; jeers, invective, abuse; cry of protest; reprimand; **conviciis consectari aliquem** to keep after someone with abuses
convictī·ō -ōnis *f* companionship; companions
convict·or -ōris *m* bosom friend
convict·us -ūs *m* association, socializing; close friends; feast, banquet
con·vincō -vincĕre -vīcī -victum *vt* to refute, prove wrong; to convict, prove guilty; to prove true, demonstrate clearly
convīs·ō -ĕre *vt* to examine, search; to shine on
convīv·a -ae *m* guest, table companion
convīvāl·is -e *adj* convivial, festive
convīvāt·or -ōris *m* master of ceremonies; host
convīv·ium -iī or **-ī** *n* banquet, dinner; dinner party; *n pl* dinner guests; **convivium agitare** to throw a party
con·vīvō -vīvĕre -vixī *vi* to live together; (with **cum** + *abl*) to feast with
convīv·or -ārī -ātus sum *vi* to feast together, have a party
convocātī·ō -ōnis *f* calling together
convŏc·ō -āre *vt* to call together, assemble
convŏl·ō -āre *vi* to flock together; (fig) to flock together, gather hastily
con·volvō -volvĕre -volvī -volūtum *vt* to roll together; to roll up (*a scroll*); to fasten together, interweave; to wrap; **se convolvere** to roll along; to go in a circle
convŏm·ō -ĕre *vt* to vomit on, vomit all over
convortō see **converto**
convulnĕr·ō -āre *vt* to wound seriously
convulsus *pp* of **convello**
coōper·iō -īre -ŭī -tum *vt* to cover; to overwhelm
coōptātī·ō -ōnis *f* cooption, election of a colleague by vote of incumbent members
coōpt·ō -āre *vt* to coopt
coōr·ior -īrī -tus sum *vi* to rise, rise suddenly; (fig) (of war) to break out; (of wind) to arise
coōrt·us -ūs *m* rising, originating
cōp·a -ae *f* barmaid
cophĭn·us -ī *m* basket
cōpi·a -ae *f* abundance, supply, store, plenty; multitude, large number; wealth, prosperity; opportunity, means; command of language, fluency, richness of expression; (with *genit*) power over; (with *dat*) access to; **pro copia** according to opportunity, according to ability; *f pl* troops, armed forces; provisions, supplies
cōpiŏl·ae -ārum *f pl* small contingent of troops
cōpiōsē *adv* abundantly, plentifully; (rhet) fully, at length
cōpiōs·us -a -um *adj* plentiful; well supplied, rich, wealthy; eloquent, fluent (*speech*); (with *abl*) abounding in, rich in
cōp·is -e *adj* rich, well supplied
cōpŭl·a -ae *f* cord, string, rope, leash; (fig) tie, bond

cōpŭlātĭ·ō -ōnis *f* coupling, joining, union; combining (*of words*)
cōpŭl·ō -āre *vt* to couple, join; (fig) to unite; (with *dat* or with **cum** + *abl*) to couple with, join to, combine with
cōpŭl·or -ārī -ātus sum *vt* to join, clasp; **dexteras copulari** to shake hands
coqu·a -ae *f* cook (*female*)
coquīn·ō -āre *vi* to be a cook
co·quō -quĕre -xī -ctum *vt* to cook; to fry, roast, bake, boil; to prepare (*a meal*); to burn, parch; to ripen, mature; to digest; to disturb, worry, disquiet; to plan, concoct, dream up
coqu·us or **coc·us -ī** *m* cook
cor cordis *n* heart; mind, judgment; (as seat of feelings) heart, soul; dear friend; *n pl* persons, souls; **cordi esse** (with *dat*) to please, be dear to, be agreeable to
cōram *adv* in person, personally; publically, openly; in someone's presence, face to face; *prep* (coming before or after *abl*) before, in the presence of, face to face with
corb·is -is *m* or *f* wicker basket
corbīt·a -ae *f* slow-sailing merchant ship
corbŭl·a -ae *f* small basket
corcŭl·um -ī *n* little heart; sweetheart; poor fellow
Corcȳr·a -ae *f* island off the coast of Epirus, identified with Scheria, the island of Alcinous
cordātē *adv* wisely, prudently
cordol·ĭum -ĭī or **-ī** *n* heartache
Corfīn·ĭum -ĭī or **-ī** *n* town in Central Italy which served as headquarters of Italian allies during the Social War against Rome in 90-89 B.C.
coriandr·um -ī *n* coriander
Corinthĭ·us -a -um *adj* Corinthian; **aes Corinthium** alloy of gold, silver, and copper, used in making expensive jewelry, etc.; *m pl* Corinthians; *n pl* costly Corinthian products
Corinth·us -ī *f* Corinth
Coriŏl·ī -ōrum *m pl* town in Latium, capital of the Volsci, from the capture of which, in 493 B.C., C. Marcius received the surname of Coriolanus
cor·ĭum -ĭī or **-ī** *n* or **cor·ĭus -ĭī** or **-ī** *m* skin, hide; bark; leather
Cornēlĭ·us -a -um *adj* Cornelian; **gens Cornelia** Cornelian tribe (*famous Roman tribe, especially for the Scipios, the Gracchi, and Sulla*); *f* Cornelia (*daughter of Scipio Africanus Major and mother of the Gracchi*)
corneŏl·us -a -um *adj* horny
cornĕ·us -a -um *adj* horny; of the cornel tree; of cornel wood
cornĭc·en -ĭnis *m* horn blower
cornīc·or -ārī -ātus sum *vi* to caw
cornīcŭl·a -ae *f* poor little crow
corniculār·ĭus -ĭī or **-ī** *m* soldier decorated with a horn-shaped medal for bravery; adjutant to a centurion
cornicŭl·um -ī *n* little horn; horn-shaped decoration, awarded for bravery
cornĭg·er -ĕra -ĕrum *adj* horn-bearing, horned
cornĭp·ēs -ĕdis *adj* hoofed
corn·ix -īcis *f* crow (*whose appearance on one's left side was considered a favorable omen and whose cries were regarded as a sign of rain*)
corn·ū -ūs or **corn·um -ī** *n* horn; horn, trumpet; lantern; funnel; oil cruet; hoof; bill (*of bird*); horn (*of moon*); branch (*of river*); arm (*of bay*); tongue (*of land*); crest socket (*of helmet*); roller end (*of book*); (mil) wing, flank; **cornua addere** (with *dat*) to give courage to, add strength to; **cornua sumere** to gain strength
corn·um -ī *n* cornel cherry
corn·us -ī *f* cornel cherry tree; dogwood tree; spear, shaft, javelin
coroll·a -ae *f* small garland
corollar·ĭum -ĭī or **-ī** *n* garland; gilt wreath given as reward to actors; gift, gratuity
corōn·a -ae *f* crown, garland; circle of bystanders; (mil) cordon of besiegers; ring of defense; **corona civica** decoration for saving a life; **corona muralis** decoration for being the first to scale an enemy wall; **corona navalis** decoration for naval victory; **sub corona vendere** to sell (*captives*) as slaves; **sub corona venire** (of captives) to be sold at public auction
Corōn·a -ae *f* Ariadne's crown, Corona Borealis (*constellation*)
corōnārĭ·us -a -um *adj* for a crown; **aurum coronarium** gold collected in the provinces for a victorious general
Corōnē·ā -ae *f* town in Boeotia
Corōn·eus -ĕī *m* king of Phocis whose daughter was changed into a crow
Corōnīd·ēs -ae *m* Aesculapius, the son of Coronis
Corōn·is -ĭdis *f* daughter of Phlegyas and mother of Aesculapius
corōn·ō -āre *vt* to crown, wreathe; to enclose, encircle, shut in
corporĕ·us -a -um *adj* physical, of the body; corporeal, substantial; of flesh
corpulent·us -a -um *adj* corpulent
corp·us -ŏris *n* body; matter, substance; flesh; trunk; corpse; person, individual; body, frame, structure; framework; community; corporation; particle, grain
corpuscŭl·um -ī *n* puny body; particle, atom; (as term of endearment) little fellow
cor·rādō -rādĕre -rāsī -rāsum *vt* to scrape together, rake up; (fig) to scrape (*e.g., money*) together

correctĭ·ō -ōnis *f* correction, improvement, amendment; rhetorical restatement
correct·or -ōris *m* reformer; censor, critic
correctus *pp* of **corrigo**
cor·rēpō -rēpĕre -repsī *vi* to creep, slink; **in dumeta correpere** (fig) to beat around the bush, indulge in jargon
correptĭus *adv* more briefly; **correptius exire** to end in a short vowel, have a short vowel
correptus *pp* of **corripio**
corrīd·ĕō -ēre *vi* to laugh out loud
corrigĭ·a -ae *f* shoelace
cor·rigō -rigĕre -rexī -rectum *vt* to make straight, straighten out; to smooth out; to correct, improve, reform; to make up for (*delay*); to make the best of
cor·ripĭō -ripĕre -ripŭī -reptum *vt* to seize, snatch up, carry off; to speed up, rush; to steal, carry off; to attack; to shorten, contract; to reprove, accuse, reproach; to cut (*a period of time*) short
corrōbŏr·ō -āre *vt* to strengthen, invigorate, corroborate; (fig) to fortify, encourage
cor·rōdo -rōdĕre -rōsī -rōsum *vt* to gnaw, chew up
corrŏg·ō -āre *vt* to go asking for, collect, drum up, solicit
corrōsus *pp* of **corrodo**
corrūg·ō -āre *vt* to wrinkle, corrugate; **nares corrugare** (with *dat*) to cause (*someone*) disgust
cor·rumpō -rumpĕre -rūpī -ruptum *vt* to burst; to break to pieces, smash; to destroy completely, ruin, waste; to mar, corrupt, adulterate; to falsify, tamper with (*documents*); to bribe; to seduce, corrupt
corrŭ·ō -ĕre -ī *vt* to shatter, wreck, ruin; *vi* to fall down, tumble, sink; (fig) to fall, fail, sink, go down
corruptē *adv* corruptly, perversely; in a lax manner
corruptēl·a -ae *f* corruption, seduction; bribery; seducer, misleader
corruptĭ·ō -ōnis *f* corrupting, ruining, breaking up; corrupt condition
corrupt·or -ōris *m* or **corruptr·ix -īcis** *f* corrupter, seducer, briber
corrupt·us -a -um *pp* of **corrumpo;** *adj* corrupt, spoiled, bad, ruined
cort·ex -ĭcis *m* or *f* bark, shell, hull, rind; cork; **nare sine cortice** to swim without a cork life preserver; to be on one's own
cortīn·a -ae *f* kettle, caldron; tripod; (fig) vault of heaven
corŭlus see **corylus**
corusc·ō -āre *vt* to shake, brandish; *vi* to flit, flutter, to oscillate; to tremble; to flash. gleam
corusc·us -a -um *adj* oscillating, vibrating, tremulous; flashing, gleaming, glittering
corv·us -ī *m* raven; (mil) grapnel
Corybant·ēs -ĭum *m pl* Corybantes (*priests of Cybele*)
Corybantĭ·us -a -um *adj* of the Corybantes
cōrўc·us -ī *m* punching bag
corylēt·um -ī *n* cluster of hazel trees
corўl·us or **corŭl·us -ī** *f* hazel tree
corymbĭf·er -ĕra -ĕrum *adj* wearing or bearing clusters of ivy berries; *m* Bacchus
corymb·us -ī *m* cluster (*esp. of ivy berries*)
coryphae·us -ī *m* leader, head
cōrўt·os or **cōrўt·us -ī** *m* quiver (*for arrows*)
cōs cōtis *f* flint; grindstone, whetstone
Cō·s or **Co·ūs -ī** *f* small island in the Aegean Sea, famous for its wine and fine linen
cosmēt·a -ae *m* slave in charge of the wardrobe
cost·a -ae *f* rib; (fig) side, wall
cost·um -ī *n* perfume
cothurnāt·us -a -um *adj* wearing the tragic buskin; suitable to tragedy; tragic, of tragedy
cothurn·us -ī *m* high boot; hunting boot; buskin (*worn by tragic actors*); subject of tragedy; tragedy; lofty style of Greek tragedy
cōtīd- = cottid-
cottăb·us -ī *m* game which consisted in flicking drops of wine on a bronze vessel
cottăn·a or **cottŏn·a -ōrum** *n pl* Syrian figs
cottīdiānō *adv* daily
cottīdiān·us or **cotīdiān·us -a -um** *adj* daily; everyday, ordinary
cottīdiē or **cōtīdiē** *adv* daily, every day
coturn·ix -īcis *f* quail
Cotyttĭ·a -ōrum *n pl* festival of Cotytto
Cotytt·o -ūs *f* Thracian goddess of lewdness
Coūs see **Cos**
Cō·us -a -um *adj* Coan; *n* Coan wine; *n pl* Coan garments
covinnārĭ·us -ĭī or **-ī** *m* soldier who fought from a chariot
covinn·us -ī *m* war chariot of the Britons and the Belgae; coach
cox·a -ae *f* hipbone
coxend·ix -īcis *f* hip
crābr·ō -ōnis *m* hornet; **irritare crabrones** (fig) to stir up a hornet's nest
cramb·ē -ēs *f* cabbage; **crambe repetita** warmed-over cabbage; same old story
Crant·or -ōris *m* Greek Academic philosopher of Soli in Cilicia (*fl* 300 B.C.)
crāpŭl·a -ae *f* drunkenness; hangover
crāpulārĭ·us -a -um *adj* for (*i.e., to prevent*) a hangover
crās *adv* tomorrow; (fig) in the future

crassē *adv* thickly; rudely; confusedly; dimly
crassitūd·ō -inis *f* thickness, density; dregs
crass·us -a -um *adj* thick, dense; dense, dull, stupid
Crass·us -ī *m* L. Licinius Crassus (*famous orator, d* 90 B.C.); M. Licinius Crassus (*triumvir, together with Caesar and Pompey,* 112?-53 B.C.)
crastin·us -a -um *adj* tomorrow's; (old *abl* form) **die crastini** tomorrow; *n* tomorrow; **in crastinum differre** to put off till tomorrow
crāt·ēr -ēris *m* or **crātēr·a -ae** *f* mixing bowl; bowl; crater
Crāt·ēr -ēris *m* Bowl (*constellation*)
crāt·is -is *f* wickerwork; harrow; ribs of shield; (mil) faggots (*for filling trenches*); joint, rib (*of body*); honeycomb
creātī·ō -ōnis *f* election
creāt·or -ōris *m* creator; procreator, father; founder
creātr·ix -īcis *f* creatress; mother
crēb·er -ra -rum *adj* luxuriant, prolific (*growth*); numerous, crowded; repeated; frequent
crēbr·escō *or* **crēb·escō -escĕre -ŭī** *vi* to increase, become frequent; to gain strength
crēbrĭt·ās -ātis *f* frequency
crēbrō *adv* repeatedly, frequently, again and again
crēdibĭl·is -e *adj* credible, trustworthy
crēdibilĭter *adv* credibly
crēdĭt·or -ōris *m* creditor, lender
crēd·ō -ĕre -idī -ĭtum *vt* to lend, loan; to entrust, consign; to believe; to think, believe, suppose, imagine; *vi* (with *dat*) to believe, put faith in, have trust or confidence in; **credas** one would image; **satis creditum est** it is believed on good evidence
crēdulĭt·ās -ātis *f* credulity, trustfulness
crēdŭl·us -a -um *adj* credulous, trustful; gullible; (with *dat* or **in** with *acc*) trusting in
crem·ō -āre *vt* to burn to ashes; to cremate
Cremōn·a -ae *f* town in N. Italy, which became a Roman colony in 209 B.C.
crem·or -ōris *m* juice obtained from animal or vegetable substances; broth
cre·ō -āre *vt* to create, produce; to elect to office; to cause, occasion; to beget, bear
Cre·ō or **Cre·ōn -ontis** *m* brother of Jocaste and brother-in-law of Oedipus; king of Corinth who gave his daughter in marriage to Jason
crep·er -ĕra -ĕrum *adj* dark; (fig) uncertain, doubtful
crepĭd·a -ae *f* slipper, sandal
crepidāt·us -a -um *adj* sandal-wearing
crepīd·ō -ĭnis *f* base, pedestal; quay, pier; dam, dike, causeway
crepidŭl·a -ae *f* small sandal
crepĭt·ō -āre *vi* to make noise, rattle, crackle, creak, chatter, rumble, rustle
crepĭt·us -ūs *m* noise, rattle, creak, chatter, rumble, rustle
crep·ō -āre -ŭī -ĭtum *vt* to make rattle; to talk noisily about, chatter about; *vi* to make noise, rattle, crackle, creak, chatter, rumble, rustle
crepundi·a -ōrum *n pl* rattle; toys
crepuscŭl·um -ī *n* dusk, twilight; dimness, obscurity; *n pl* darkness
crescō crescĕre crēvī crētum *vi* to come into being, arise; to grow, grow up; to increase, swell; to prosper, thrive; to become great, attain honor
crēt·a -ae *f* chalk; white clay; cosmetic
Crēt·a -ae *f* Crete
crētāt·us -a -um *adj* chalked; dressed in white (*as candidate for office*)
crētĕ·us -a -um *adj* of chalk, of clay
crētī·ō -ōnis *f* (law) formal acceptance of an inheritance
crētōs·us -a -um *adj* abounding in chalk or clay
crētŭl·a -ae *f* white clay (*used for seals*)
crētus *pp* of **cerno;** *pp* of **cresco**
Creūs·a -ae *f* daughter of Priam and wife of Aeneas; daughter of Creon, king of Corinth and wife of Jason
crībr·um -ī *n* sieve; **imbrem in cribrum gerere** to carry coals to Newcastle
crīm·en -ĭnis *n* charge, accusation; reproach; guilt, crime; **esse in crimine** to be accused
crīminātī·ō -ōnis *f* accusation; slander, false charge
crīmināt·or -ōris *m* accuser
crīmĭn·ō -āre or **crīmĭn·or -ārī -ātus sum** *vt* to accuse; to slander; to complain of, denounce
crīminōsē *adv* by way of accusation, accusingly, reproachfully
crīminōs·us -a -um *adj* accusing, reproachful, slanderous
crīnāl·is -e *adj* for the hair; *n* hairpin
crīn·is -is *m* hair; (fig) tail of a comet
crīnīt·us -a -um *adj* long-haired; **stella crinita** comet
crīs·ō -āre *vi* (of women) to wiggle the buttocks
crisp·ans -antis *adj* curled, wrinkled
crisp·ō -āre *vt* to curl, wave (*hair*); to swing, wave, brandish (*a weapon*)
crisp·us -a -um *adj* curled, waved (*hair*); curly-headed; curled, wrinkled; tremulous, quivering
crist·a -ae *f* cock's comb; crest, plume

cristāt·us -a -um *adj* crested, plumed
critĭc·us -ī *m* critic
crocĕ·us -a -um *adj* of saffron; saffron-colored, yellow, golden
crocĭn·um -ī *n* saffron
crōc·iō -īre *vi* to croak
crocodīl·us -ī *m* crocodile
crocōtāri·us -a -um *adj* of saffron-colored clothes
crocōtŭl·a -ae *f* saffron-colored dress
croc·us -ī *m* or **croc·um -ī** *n* crocus; saffron; saffron color
Croes·us -ī *m* king of Lydia, famous for his wealth (590?-546 B.C.)
crotalistri·a -ae *f* castanet dancer
crotăl·um -ī *n* castanet
cruciābilitāt·ēs -um *f pl* torments
cruciābilĭter *adv* with torture
cruciāment·um -ī *n* torture
cruciāt·us -ūs *m* torture; mental torment; instrument of torture; (humorously) calamity
crucĭ·ō -āre *vt* to put to wrack, torture, torment; (fig) to grieve, torment
crūdēl·is -e *adj* cruel, hardhearted; (with **in** + *acc*) cruel toward
crūdēlĭt·ās -ātis *f* cruelty
crūdēlĭter *adv* cruelly
crūd·escō -escĕre -ŭī *vi* to grow violent, grow worse
crūdĭt·ās -ātis *f* indigestion
crūd·us -a -um *adj* bloody, bleeding; uncooked, raw; unripe, green; undressed (*hide*); undigested; suffering from indigestion; hoarse; fresh, vigorous (*old age*); cruel, merciless
cruent·ō -āre *vt* to bloody, stain with blood; (fig) to wound
cruent·us -a -um *adj* gory, bloodstained; bloodthirsty, cruel; blood-red
crumēn·a or **crumīn·a -ae** *f* purse, pouch; (fig) money
crumill·a -ae *f* purse
cru·or -ōris *m* gore, blood; *m pl* bloodshed, murder
cruppellāri·ī -ōrum *m pl* mail-clad combatants
crūrifrag·ius -iī or **-ī** *m* slave with broken shins
crūs crūris *n* leg, shin
crust·a -ae *f* crust, shell, rind, bark; inlaid work, mosaic; stucco
crustŭl·um -ī *n* cooky
crust·um -ī *n* pastry
crux crucis *f* cross, gallows; trouble, misery; gallows bird; tormentor; **i in malam crucem** (coll) go hang yourself
crypt·a -ae *f* underground passage, covered gallery
cryptoportĭc·us -ūs *f* covered walk
crystallĭn·us -a -um *adj* made of crystal; *n pl* crystal vases
crystall·us -ī *f* or **crystall·um -ī** *n* crystal
cubiculār·is -e *adj* bedroom
cubiculāri·us -a -um *adj* bedroom; *m* chamberlain
cubicŭl·um -ī *n* bedroom; emperor's box in the theater
cubīl·e -is *n* bed, couch; marriage bed; lair, nest, hole; kennel; **avaritiae cubilia** (fig) den of greediness
cubĭt·al -ālis *n* elbow cushion
cubitāl·is -e *adj* of the elbow; one cubit long
cubĭt·ō -āre *vi* to be in the habit of lying down; (with **cum** + *abl*) to go to bed with, have intercourse with
cubĭt·um -ī *n* elbow; cubit
cubĭt·us -ūs *m* lying down; intercourse
cub·ō -āre -ŭī or **-āvī -ĭtum** *vi* to lie, lie down; to recline at table; to lie in bed; to lie sick; (of roof) to slope; (of towns, etc.) to lie on a slope
cucull·us -ī *m* cowl, hood
cucūl·us -ī *m* cuckoo; lazy farmer
cucŭm·is -ĕris *m* cucumber
cucurbĭt·a -ae *f* gourd; (med) cupping glass
cūd·ō -ĕre *vt* to strike, beat, pound; thresh; to forge; to coin, stamp
cuicuimŏdī or **quoiquoimŏdī** *adj* any kind of
cuj·ās -ātis *pron* from what country
culcĭt·a -ae *f* mattress, feather tick; cushion, pillow
culcitell·a -ae *f* little cushion
cūlĕus see **culleus**
cul·ex -ĭcis *m* or *f* gnat
culīn·a -ae *f* kitchen; cuisine
cullĕ·us or **cūlĕ·us -ī** *m* leather bag (*for holding liquids*); scrotum
culm·en -ĭnis *n* stalk; top, summit; roof; (fig) height, pinnacle, zenith
culm·us -ī *m* stalk, stem; straw, thatch
culp·a -ae *f* fault, blame; immorality; **in culpa esse** or **in culpa versari** to be at fault
culpĭt·ō -āre *vt* to blame, find fault with
culp·ō -āre *vt* to blame, reproach, censure, find fault with, complain of
cult·a -ōrum *n pl* plantation; grain fields
cultē *adv* elegantly, sophisticatedly, with refinement
cultell·us -ī *m* small knife
cult·er -rī *m* knife; razor; plowshare
cultĭ·ō -ōnis *f* cultivation; tilling of the ground, agriculture
cult·or -ōris *m* tiller, planter, cultivator, farmer; inhabitant; supporter; worshiper
cultr·ix -īcis *f* cultivator (*female*); inhabitant (*female*); (fig) nurse
cultūr·a -ae *f* tilling, cultivating; agriculture; care, cultivation (*of the mind*); (with *genit*) playing up to (*e.g., influential friends*)
cult·us -a -um *pp* of **colo;** *adj* tilled, cultivated; neat, well dressed, prim; cultivated, refined, civilized (*person*); cultured, refined (*mind*)
cult·us -ūs *m* tilling, cultivation (*of land*); care, tending, keeping (*of flocks, etc.*); care (*of body*); training, education; culture, refinement, civilization; high style of living; luxury;

style of dress, fancy clothes; fancy outfit; worship, reverence, veneration
culull·us -ī *m* drinking cup
cūl·us -ī *m* buttock
cum *prep* (with *abl*) (accompaniment) with, together with, in company with; (time) at the same time with, at the time of, at, with; (circumstance, manner, etc.) with, under, in, in the midst of, among, in connection with; **cum eo quod** or **cum eo ut** on condition that; **cum pace** peacefully; **cum prima luce** at dawn; **cum primis** especially, particularly; **mecum** at my house
cum, quum, or **quom** *conj* when, at the time when; whenever; when, while, as; since, now that, because; although; **cum maxime** just when; especially when, just while; just then, just now; **cum primum** as soon as; **cum . . . tum** both . . . and, not only . . . but also, while . . . so too; **praesertim cum** or **cum praesertim** especially since, especially as; **quippe cum** since of course; **utpote cum** seeing that
Cūm·ae -ārum *f pl* town on coast of Campania and oldest Greek colony in Italy, famous as the residence of its Sibyl
Cūmān·us -a -um *adj* Cumaean; *n* Cicero's estate near Cumae
cumb·a or **cymb·a -ae** *f* boat, skiff
cumĕr·a -ae *f* bin
cumīn·um -ī *n* cumin (*medicinal plant, said to produce paleness*)
cumque, cunque, or **quomque** *adv* at any time
cumulātē *adv* fully, completely, abundantly, copiously
cumulāt·us -a -um *adj* increased, augmented; filled, full, perfect, complete
cumŭl·ō -āre *vt* to heap up, pile up; to amass, accumulate; to overload; to make complete, make perfect, crown
cumŭl·us -ī *m* heap, pile; increase, addition
cūnābŭl·a -ōrum *n pl* cradle
cūn·ae -ārum *f pl* cradle; nest
cunctābund·us -a -um *adj* hesitant, loitering, delaying
cunct·ans -antis *adj* hesitant, reluctant, dilatory
cunctanter *adv* hesitantly, slowly
cunctātĭ·ō -ōnis *f* hesitation, reluctance, delay
cunctāt·or -ōris *m* dawdler, slowpoke
cunct·or -ārī -ātus sum *vi* to hesitate, delay, linger, be in doubt; **cunctatus brevi** after a moment's hesitation
cunct·us -a -um *adj* all together, the whole, all, entire
cuneātim *adv* in the form of a wedge
cuneāt·us -a -um *adj* wedge-shaped
cunĕ·ō -āre *vt* to fasten with a wedge; (fig) to wedge in, squeeze in
cunĕ·us -ī *m* wedge; wedge-form sections of seats in the theater; (mil) troops formed up in the shape of a wedge
cunīcŭl·us -ī *m* rabbit; burrowing underground; (mil) mine
cunque see **cumque**
cūp·a -ae *f* vat
cuped- = cupped-
cupĭdē *adv* eagerly
cupidĭt·ās -ātis *f* eagerness, enthusiasm, desire; passion, lust; ambition; greed, avarice; partisanship
cupīd·ō -ĭnis *m* eagerness, desire, longing; passion, lust; greed, avarice
Cupīd·ō -ĭnis *m* Cupid (*son of Venus*)
Cupīdinĕ·us -a -um *adj* Cupid's
cupĭd·us -a -um *adj* eager, enthusiastic, desirous, longing; ambitious; (with *genit*) desirous of, longing for, fond of, attached to
cupĭ·ens -entis *adj* eager, enthusiastic; (with *genit*) desirous of, longing for, fond of, enthusiastic about
cupienter *adv* eagerly, enthusiastically
cup·iō -ĕre -īvī or **iī -ītum** *vt* to wish, be eager for, long for, desire
cupīt·or -ōris *m* daydreamer
cuppēdĭ·a -ōrum *n pl* or **cupēdĭ·a -ae** *f* delicacies; sweet tooth
cuppēdinār·ĭus or **cupēdinār·ĭus -ĭī** or **-ī** *m* confectioner
cuppēd·ō -ĭnis *f* desire, longing
cupp·ēs -ĕdis *adj* fond of delicacies
cupressēt·um -ī *n* cypress grove
cupressĕ·us -a -um *adj* cypress
cupressĭf·er -ĕra -ĕrum *adj* cypress-bearing
cupress·us -ī or **-ūs** *f* cypress tree; box of cypress
cūr or **quor** *adv* why
cūr·a -ae *f* care, concern, worry; care, pains, attention; heartache; object of concern; sweetheart; administration, management, charge; trusteeship, guardianship; means of healing, cure, treatment; guardian, keeper; study, reflection; literary effort, literary work; **curae esse** (with *dat*) to be of concern to
cūrābĭl·is -e *adj* troublesome
cūral·ĭum -ĭī or **-ī** *n* coral
cūrātĭ·ō -ōnis *f* management, administration; office; treatment, cure
cūrātĭus *adv* more carefully
cūrāt·or -ōris *m* superintendent, manager; (law) guardian, keeper
cūrātūr·a -ae *f* care, attention; dieting
cūrāt·us -a -um *adj* cared-for, attended-to; anxious, earnest
curculĭ·ō -ōnis *m* weevil
curculiuncŭl·us -ī *m* little weevil; (fig) trifle
Cur·ēs -ĭum *m pl* ancient Sabine town
Cūrēt·ēs -um *m pl* mythical people of Crete who attended Jupiter at his birth

cūri·a -ae *f* curia, ward (*one of the thirty parts into which Romulus divided the Roman people*); meeting place of a curia; senate building
cūriāl·is -is *m* member of a curia or ward
cūriātim *adv* by curiae, by wards
cūriāt·us -a -um *adj* composed of curiae or wards; passed by the assembly of curiae; **comitia curiata** assembly of the curiae
cūri·ō -ōnis *m* ward boss; **curio maximus** chief ward boss
cūri·ō -ōnis *adj* lean, emaciated
cūriōsē *adv* carefully; curiously; (of style) affectedly
cūriōsit·ās -ātis *f* curiosity
cūriōs·us -a -um *adj* careful, diligent; curious, prying, inquisitive; careworn
cur·is or **quir·is -ītis** *f* spear
cūr·ō -āre *vt* to take care of, look after, attend to, trouble oneself about; to take charge of, see to; to provide for the payment of, settle up; to attend to (*the body with food, washing, etc.*); to cure; to worry about; **cura ut** see to it that; (at the end of a letter) **cura ut valeas** take care of yourself
curriculō *adv* at full speed, quickly
curricul·um -ī *n* race; lap (*of race*); racetrack; racing chariot; (fig) career
currō currĕre cucurrī cursum *vt* to run over, skim over, traverse; *vi* to run, dash, hurry; to sail; to move quickly, flow along; to fly; (of a speech) to move along; (of night, day) to pass away
curr·us -ūs *m* chariot, car; war chariot; triumphal car; triumph; racing chariot; plow wheel; ship
cursim *adv* on the double
cursit·ō -āre *vi* to keep running around, run up and down; to vibrate
curs·ō -āre *vi* to run around, run up and down
curs·or -ōris *m* runner, racer; courier; errand boy
cursūr·a -ae *f* running; haste, speed
curs·us -ūs *m* running, speeding, speed; trip; course, direction; suitable time or weather for travel; rapid movement, speed, flow; flow, progress; **magno cursu** at top speed; **cursus honorum** political career
curt·ō -āre *vt* to shorten; to circumcise
curt·us -a -um *adj* shortened; gelded, castrated; circumcised; broken; defective
curūl·is -e *adj* official, curule; **aedilis curulis** patrician aedile; **sella curulis** curule chair, official chair (*used by consuls, praetors, and patrician aediles*)
curvām·en -inis *n* curve, bend
curvātūr·a -ae *f* curvature; **curvatura rotae** rim of a wheel
curv·ō -āre *vt* to curve, bend, arch; (fig) to affect, move, stir
curv·us -a -um *adj* curved, bent; crooked; concave, arched, hollow; winding (*stream, shore*); (fig) crooked; *n* wrong, crookedness
cusp·is -idis *f* point, pointed end; bayonet; spearhead; spear, javelin; trident; scepter; sting (*of scorpion*)
custōdēl·a -ae *f* watch, guard, care
custōdi·a -ae *f* watch, guard, care; sentry, guard; sentry post; custody, prison; **custodiam agitare** to keep guard, be on guard; **in libera custodia** under surveillance, under house arrest
custōd·iō -īre -īvī or **-iī -ītum** *vt* to guard, watch over, protect, defend; to hold in custody; to keep an eye on; to keep carefully, preserve; **memoriā custodire** to keep in mind, remember well
cust·ōs -ōdis *m* guard, guardian, watchman; protector, bodyguard; jailer, warden; (mil) sentinel; spy; *m pl* garrison; *f* guardian; protectress; box, container
cuticul·a -ae *f* skin, cuticle
cut·is -is *f* skin; **cutem curare** (fig) to look after one's own skin
Cyan·ē -ēs *f* nymph who was changed into a fountain
cyathiss·ō -āre *vi* to serve wine
cyăth·us -ī *m* ladle; liquid measure (*one-twelfth of a sextarius, i.e., a half pint*)
cybae·a -ae *f* merchant ship
Cybĕl·ē or **Cybēl·ē -ēs** *f* originally a Phrygian goddess of fertility later worshiped in Rome as Ops or Mater Magna
Cyclăd·es -um *f pl* Cyclades (*group of islands in Aegean Sea*)
cycl·as -ădis *f* woman's formal gown
cyclic·us -a -um *adj* cyclic; **poeta cyclicus** cyclic poet (*one of a group of poets treating the epic sagas revolving around the Trojan War*)
Cycl·ops -ōpis *m* mythical one-eyed giant of Sicily, esp. Polyphemus
cycnē·us -a -um *adj* swan's
cycn·us or **cygn·us -ī** *m* swan; (fig) poet
Cycn·us *or* **Cygn·us -ī** *m* king of the Ligurians, son of Sthenelus, changed into a swan, and placed among the stars; son of Neptune, changed into a swan
Cydōni·us -a -um *adj* Cretan; *n* quince
cygnus see **cycnus**
cylindr·us -ī *m* cylinder; roller (*for rolling ground*)
Cyllēn·ē -ēs or **-ae** *f* mountain in Arcadia where Mercury was born
Cyllēni·us -a -um *adj* of Mt. Cyllene; *m* Mercury
cymb·a -ae *f* boat, skiff
cymbăl·um -ī *n* cymbal
cymb·ium -iī or **-ī** *n* small cup

Cynicē *adv* like the Cynics
Cynic·us -a -um *adj* Cynic, relating to the Cynic philosophy; *m* Cynic philosopher, esp. Diogenes, its founder (412-323 B.C.)
cynocephăl·us -ī *m* dog-headed ape
Cynosūr·a -ae *f* Cynosure (*the northern constellation Ursa Minor*)
Cynthĭ·us -a -um *adj* of Mt. Cynthus; Cynthian; *m* Apollo; *f* Diana
Cynth·us -ī *m* mountain of Delos, famous as the birthplace of Apollo and Diana
cypariss·us -ī *f* cypress tree
Cyprĭ·us -a -um *adj* Cypriote; *f* Venus
Cypr·us or **Cypr·os -ī** *f* Cyprus (*island off the coast of Asia Minor*)
Cypsĕl·us -ī *m* despot of Corinth (655-625 B.C.)
Cyrēn·ē -ēs *f* or **Cyrēn·ae -ārum** *f pl* chief city of Greek settlement in N.E. Africa
Cyr·us -ī *m* founder of the Persian monarchy in 559 B.C. (*d.* 529 B.C.); Cyrus the Younger (*under whom Xenophon served, d.* 401 B.C.)
Cyt·ae -ārum *f pl* town in Colchis, birthplace of Medea
Cytae·is -ĭdis *f* Medea
Cythēr·a -ōrum *n pl* island off the S. coast of the Peloponnesus, famous for worship of Venus
Cytherē·is -ĭdis *f* Venus
Cytherēĭ·us -a -um *adj* Cytherean; **heros Cythereius** Aeneas; *f* Venus
Cytherē·us -a -um *adj* Cytherean; *f* Venus
cytĭs·us -ī *m* or *f* clover
Cytōriăc·us -a -um *adj* of Cytorus, Cytorian; **pecten Cytoriacus** comb made of boxwood
Cytōr·us or **Cytōr·os -ī** *m* mountain of Paphlagonia, famous for its boxwood
Cyzĭc·um -ī *n* or **Cyzĭc·us** or **Cyzĭc·os -ī** *f* town on Sea of Marmora

D

Dāc·ī -ōrum *m pl* Dacians (*people of the lower Danube*)
dactylĭc·us -a -um *adj* dactylic
dactȳl·us -ī *m* dactyl
daedăl·us -a -um *adj* skillful, artistic, artfully constructed
Daedăl·us -ī *m* mythical builder of the labyrinth in Crete and the first to build wings and fly
Damascēn·us -a -um *adj* of Damascus
Damasc·us -ī *f* Damascus (*capital of Coele-Syria*)
damm·a or **dām·a -ae** *f* deer; venison
damnātĭ·ō -ōnis *f* condemnation
damnātōrĭ·us -a -um *adj* guilty (*verdict*)
damnāt·us -a -um *adj* criminal; hateful
damnifĭc·us -a -um *adj* harmful, injurious, pernicious
damnigerŭl·us -a -um *adj* harmful, injurious
damn·ō -āre *vt* to find guilty, sentence, condemn; to disapprove of, reject, blame; to consecrate, offer as a sacrifice, doom to the gods below; (with *genit* or *abl* of charge or punishment) to find (*someone*) guilty of; **capite** or **capitis damnare** to condemn to death; **de majestate damnare** to find guilty of treason; **voti damnare** to oblige (*someone*) to fulfill a vow
damnōsē *adv* destructively, so as to bring ruin
damnōs·us -a -um *adj* damaging, injurious, destructive, pernicious; prodigal; **canes damnosi** crap (*worst throw of the dice*); *m* spendthrift
damn·um -ī *n* loss, damage, harm, injury; misfortune; fine, penalty; fault; defect
Dană·ē -ēs *f* daughter of Acrisius and mother of Perseus
Danaĭd·ēs -um *f pl* daughters of Danaus who killed their husbands on their wedding night, with the exception of Hypermnestra, and as punishment were made to carry water in the lower world
Dană·us -ī *m* king of Argos and father of fifty daughters; *m pl* Greeks
danist·a -ae *m* money lender, banker
danistĭc·us -a -um *adj* money-lending, banking, of bankers
danō see **dō**
Dānuv·ius -iī or **-ī** *m* Danube
Daphn·ē -ēs *f* nymph pursued by Apollo and changed into a laurel tree
Daphn·is -ĭdis *m* handsome young Sicilian shepherd, the inventor of pastoral song
dapĭn·ō -āre *vt* to serve (*food*)
dap·s -is *f* ceremonial feast; sumptuous meal, banquet; simple food, poor meal
dapsĭl·is -e *adj* sumptuous, costly
Dardăn·us -a -um *adj* Dardanian, Trojan; Roman (*descendant of Aeneas*); *m* son of Jupiter and Electra and ancestor of the Trojan race; *m pl* people of Upper Moesia (*on Danube*)
Darē·us -ī *m* Darius (*king of Persia,* 521-485 B.C.); Darius Ochus or

Nothus (*king of Persia,* 424-405 B.C.); Darius Codomanus (*last king of Persia,* 336-331 B.C.)
datārī·us -a -um *adj* to be handed out, to give away
datātim *adv* giving in turn, passing from one to another
datī·ō -ōnis *f* giving, alloting; (law) right of alienation
datīv·us -a -um *adj* & *m* dative
dat·ō -āre *vt* to keep giving away, be in the habit of giving
dat·or -ōris *m* giver
dat·us -ūs *m* giving
Daul·is -idis *f* town in Phocis, famous for the fable of Procne and Philomela
Daun·us -ī *m* king of Apulia and ancestor of Turnus, the opponent of Aeneas
dē *prep* (with *abl*) (of space) down from, from, away from, out of; (of origin) from, of, descended from, derived from; (of separation) from among, out of; (of time) immediately after; about, concerning, of, in respect to; for, on account of, because of; according to, in imitation of; **de improviso** unexpectedly; **de industria** on purpose; **de integro** afresh, all over again; **de novo** anew
de·a -ae *f* goddess
dealb·ō -āre *vt* to whiten, whitewash, plaster
deambulātī·ō -ōnis *f* strolling, walking about, stroll, walk
deambŭl·ō -āre *vi* to go for a walk, take a stroll
deăm·ō -āre *vt* to be in love with; to be much obliged to
dearm·ō -āre *vt* to disarm
deartŭ·ō -āre *vt* to tear limb from limb, dismember; (fig) to waste, wreck
deascī·ō -āre *vt* to smooth with an ax; (coll) to cheat, con
dēbacch·or -ārī -ātus sum *vi* to rant and rave
dēbellāt·or -ōris *m* conqueror
dēbell·ō -āre *vt* to fight it out with, wear down, subdue; *vi* to fight it out to the end; to bring a war to an end
dēb·ĕō -ēre -ŭī -ĭtum *vt* to owe; to be responsible for; (with *inf*) **a** to have to, be bound to, be obliged to; **b** to be destined to, be fated to; (with *dat*) to owe (*e.g., a favor*) to, be indebted to (*someone*) for; **deberi** (with *dat*) to be due to
dēbĭl·is -e *adj* lame, crippled, frail, feeble, paralyzed
dēbilĭt·ās -ātis *f* lameness, debility, weakness, helplessness
dēbilitātī·ō -ōnis *f* disabling, paralyzing
dēbilĭt·ō -āre *vt* to lame; to disable, debilitate, weaken; to unnerve; to paralyze
dēbitī·ō -ōnis *f* debt
dēbĭt·or -ōris *m* debtor; person under obligation
dēbĭt·um -ī *n* debt; obligation
dēblatĕr·ō -āre *vt* to blurt out
dēcant·ō -āre *vt* to repeat monotonously; *vi* to sing on to the end; to stop singing
dē·cēdō -cēdĕre -cessī -cessum *vi* to withdraw, clear out, depart; to retire, retreat, fall back, abandon a position; to give place, make way, make room, yield; to depart, disappear, die; to abate, subside, cease; to go wrong, go awry; (with *dat*) to yield to, give in to; (with **de** + *abl*) to give up, relinquish, abandon
decem (indecl) *adj* ten; (fig) large number of
Decemb·er -ris *adj* & *m* December
decemjŭg·is -is *m* ten-horse chariot
decempĕd·a -ae *f* ten-foot measuring rod, ten-foot rule
decempedāt·or -ōris *m* surveyor
decempl·ex -icis *adj* tenfold
decemprīm·ī or **decem prīm·ī -ōrum** *m pl* board of ten (*governing Italian towns*)
decemscalm·us -a -um *adj* ten-oared
decemvirāl·is -e *adj* decemviral; **leges decemvirales** laws passed by the decemviri
decemvirāt·us -ūs *m* decemvirate
decemvĭr·ī -ōrum *m pl* decemviri, ten-man commission (*appointed in Rome at different times and for various purposes*); **decemviri legibus scribundis** commission to codify the laws (451 B.C.); **decemviri sacris faciundis** commission for attending to religious matters
decenn·is -e *adj* ten-year, lasting ten years
dec·ens -entis *adj* proper, becoming; handsome, pretty; decent, proper
decenter *adv* becomingly, decently, properly, with propriety
decentĭ·a -ae *f* propriety, decency
dē·cernō -cernĕre -crēvī -crētum *vt* to sift, separate; to decide, settle, determine, decree, resolve, vote; to decide by combat, fight out; to fight, combat; *vi* to contend, compete, struggle; to put forward a proposal; (with **de** or **pro** + *abl*) to fight over, fight for (*in court*)
dēcerp·ō -ĕre -sī -tum *vt* to pluck off, tear away, break off, gather, crop; to derive, enjoy (*e.g., benefits, satisfaction*); **aliquid de gravitate decerpere** to detract somewhat from the dignity
dēcertātī·ō -ōnis *f* decision, decisive struggle
dēcert·ō -āre *vi* to fight it out, decide the issue
dēcessĭ·ō -ōnis *f* withdrawing; retirement, departure (*from a province*); decrease; disappearance
dēcess·or -ōris *m* retiring official, predecessor in office
dēcess·us -ūs *m* withdrawal; retirement (*of official from a province*); decease, death

dec·et -ēre -ŭit (used only in 3d *sing* & *pl*) *vt* to befit, be becoming to; (with *inf*) it is fitting to (*someone*) to, it is proper for (*someone*) to; *vi* to be fitting, be proper; (with *dat* & *inf*) it is fitting to (*someone*) to, it is proper for (*someone*) to
dēcĭd·ō -ĕre -ī *vi* to fall down; to fall dead, die; to fall, drop, sink, fail, perish
dē·cīdō -cīdĕre -cīsī -cīsum *vt* to cut off, cut away; to cut short, terminate, put an end to, decide, settle; **pennas decidere** (fig) to clip (*someone's*) wings
deciens or **deciēs** *adv* ten times; **deciens centena milia** or **deciens** million
decimānus see **decumanus**
decĭm·us or **decŭm·us -a -um** *adj* the tenth; **cum decimo** tenfold; **cum decimo effecit ager** the field produced a tenfold return; **decimum** for the tenth time
dē·cipĭō -cipĕre -cēpī -ceptum *vt* to deceive, cheat; to snare, mislead, beguile; to escape the notice of; **aliquem laborum decipere** to make one forget his troubles; **laborum decipi** to be freed of troubles, forget one's troubles
dēcisĭ·ō -ōnis *f* decision, settlement
decīsum *pp* of **decīdo**
Dec·ĭus -ĭī or **-ī** *m* P. Decius Mus (*Roman hero who voluntarily gave his life in battle during the Latin War in* 340 B.C. *to bring victory to the Roman army; his son who likewise gave his life in Samnite War in* 295 B.C.)
dēclāmātĭ·ō -ōnis *f* practice in public speaking; theme or subject matter in rhetorical exercise; loud talking, shouting, hubbub
dēclāmāt·or -ōris *m* elocutionist, declaimer; ranter
dēclāmātōrĭ·us -a -um *adj* rhetorical
dēclāmĭt·ō -āre *vt* to plead (*cases*); *vi* to practice public speaking; to bluster
dēclām·ō -āre *vt* to recite; *vi* to practice public speaking
dēclārātĭ·ō -ōnis *f* disclosure, declaration
dēclār·ō -āre *vt* to make clear, make evident, disclose; to proclaim, announce officially; to show, prove, demonstrate; to mean, express, signify; to declare (*as chosen for office*)
dēclīnātĭ·ō -ōnis *f* leaning away, bending aside, swerving; shunning, avoiding; digression; (gram) declension
dēclīn·ō -āre *vt* to deflect; to parry, avoid; to decline, conjugate; *vi* to deviate; to digress
dēclīv·e -is *n* declivity, slope
dēclīv·is -e *adj* sloping, steep, downhill
dēclīvĭt·ās -ātis *f* sloping terrain
dēcoct·a -ae *f* cold drink
dēcoct·or -ōris *m* bankrupt; (coll) old rake
dēcoct·us -a -um *pp* of **decoquo;** *adj* boiled down; mellow (*style*)
dēcoll·ō -āre *vt* to behead
dēcōl·ō -āre *vi* to trickle away, come to naught, fail
dēcŏl·or -ōris *adj* off-color, faded; dark, tanned; degenerate
dēcolōrātĭ·ō -ōnis *f* discoloring
dēcolōr·ō -āre *vt* to discolor, stain, deface
dē·cŏquō -coquĕre -coxī -coctum *vt* to boil down, boil thoroughly; to bring to ruin; *vi* to go bankrupt
dec·or -ōris *m* beauty, grace, elegance, charm; ornament
decōrē *adv* beautifully, gracefully; suitably, properly
decŏr·ō -āre *vt* to beautify, adorn, embellish; to decorate, honor
decōr·us -a -um *adj* beautiful, graceful, adorned; decorous, proper, suitable; fine, handsome; noble; *n* grace, propriety
dēcrepĭt·us -a -um *adj* decrepit, broken down, worn out
dē·crescō -crescĕre -crēvī -crētum *vi* to grow less, become fewer, diminish, subside, wane
dēcrēt·us -a -um *pp* of **decerno;** *n* decision, decree; principle, doctrine
decŭm·a or **decĭm·a -ae** *f* tenth part, tithe, land tax; largess to the people
decumān·us or **decimān·us -a -um** *adj* paying tithes; of the tenth cohort, of the tenth legion; *m* tax collector; *m pl* men of the tenth legion; *f* tax collector's wife; **porta decumana** main gate of a Roman camp on the side turned away from the enemy
decumāt·ēs -ĭum *adj* subject to tithes
dē·cumbō -cumbĕre -cubŭī *vi* to lie down; to recline at table; to fall (*in battle*)
decŭm·ō or **decĭmō -āre** *vt* to decimate
decurĭ·a -ae *f* decuria, group of ten; tenth part (*of a curia*); division, class (*without reference to number*); panel (*of judges*); social club
decuriātĭ·ō -ōnis *f* dividing into decuries
decuriāt·us -ūs *m* dividing into decuries
decurĭ·ō -āre *vt* (pol) to divide into groups of ten; (fig) to divide into groups
decurĭ·ō -ōnis *m* decurion (*head of a decuria*); (mil) cavalry officer (*in charge of ten men*); senator of a municipality or colony
dē·currō -currĕre -cucurrī or **-currī -cursum** *vt* to pass over, run over, traverse; to pass through (*life*); to get over (*troubles*); to discuss, treat; *vi* to run down; (mil) to parade, maneuver; (of river, ship) to run down to the sea; to run for

help; to sail; to land; **eo decursum est ut** it got to the point where
dēcursĭ·ō -ōnis *f* (mil) dress parade; maneuvers; raid, descent
dēcurs·us -ūs *m* running down; downward course; (mil) dress parade; (mil) maneuvers; (mil) raid; end of course, completion; **decursus honorum** completion of political career
dēcurtāt·us -a -um *adj* cut down, cut off short, mutilated; clipped (*style*)
dec·us -ŏris *n* beauty, glory, honor, dignity; virtue, worth; source of glory; *n pl* great deeds, distinctions
dēcuss·ō -āre *vt* to divide crosswise (*in the form of an* X)
dē·cutĭō -cutĕre -cussī -cussum *vt* to shake off, beat off, strike down; to chop off (*head*); to break down (*wall with battering ram*)
dē·dĕcet -decēre -decŭit (used only in 3d *sing* & *pl*) *vt* it ill becomes, ill befits; (with *inf*) it is a disgrace to
dēdecŏr·ō -āre *vt* to disgrace, dishonor, bring shame to; to make a sham of
dēdecōr·us -a -um *adj* disgraceful, dishonorable, unbecoming
dēdĕc·us -ŏris *n* disgrace, dishonor, shame; vice, crime, outrage; (mil) disgraceful defeat; **dedecori esse** (with *dat*) to be a source of disgrace to; **dedecus admittere** to incur disgrace; **per dedecus** disgracefully
dēdicātĭ·ō -ōnis *f* dedication, consecration
dēdĭc·ō -āre *vt* to dedicate, consecrate, set aside; to declare (*property in a census return*)
dēdign·or -ārī -ātus sum *vt* to scorn, disdain, look down on; (with double *acc*) to scorn (*someone*) as; **aliquem maritum dedignari** to regard someone as an unworthy husband
dē·discō -discĕre -didĭcī *vt* to forget
dēditīc·ĭus -ĭī or **-ī** *m* captive; *m pl* prisoners of war
dēditĭ·ō -ōnis *f* surrender, capitulation
dēdĭt·us -a -um *pp* of **dedo;** *adj* (with *dat*) given to, devoted to, addicted to; (with **in** + *abl*) absorbed in; *m pl* prisoners of war, captives
dē·dō -dĕre -dĭdī -dĭtum *vt* to give up, surrender; to devote; to apply; to abandon; **aliquem hostibus in cruciatum dedere** to hand someone over to the enemy to be tortured; **deditā operā** on purpose, intentionally; **neci** or **ad necem dedere** to put to death
dēdoc·ĕō -ēre -ŭī -tum *vt* to cause to forget; (with *inf*) to teach (*someone*) not to
dēdol·ĕō -ēre -ŭī *vi* to grieve no more
dēdŏl·ō -āre *vt* to chop away; to chop smooth
dē·dūcō -dūcĕre -duxī -ductum *vt* to lead or draw down; to launch (*ship*); to accompany, escort; to lead out (*colonists to new colony*); to conduct (*bride to her husband*), give away (*bride*); to evict; to subtract, deduct, diminish; to summon (*as witness*); to divert, mislead; to derive (*name*); to compose (*poetry*); to dissuade; to spin out (*thread*); to comb out (*hair*)
dēductĭ·ō -ōnis *f* leading or drawing off; settling (*of colonists*); (law) eviction; reduction; inference; **rationis deductio** train of reasoning
dēduct·us -a -um *pp* of **deduco;** *adj* drawn down; bent inwards, concave; lowered, modest; subtle, well wrought (*poem*)
deerr·ō -āre *vi* to go astray, wander away; **a vero deerrare** (fig) to stray from the truth
dēfaec·ō -āre *vt* to cleanse of dregs; to wash; (fig) to clear up, make clear
dēfatīgātĭ·ō -ōnis *f* exhaustion
dēfatīg·ō -āre *vt* to wear out, exhaust
dēfatiscor see **defetiscor**
dēfectĭ·ō -ōnis *f* failure; defection, desertion; weakening, exhaustion; eclipse; **defectio animi** mental breakdown; **in defectione esse** to be up in revolt
dēfect·or -ōris *m* defector, deserter; rebel
dēfect·us -a -um *pp* of **deficio;** *adj* weak, worn out
dēfect·us -ūs *m* failing, failure; desertion; revolt; eclipse
dē·fendō -fendĕre -fendī -fensum *vt* to repel, beat off, avert; to defend, protect, guard; to keep off (*the cold*); to answer (*a charge*); to champion (*a cause*); to support, uphold, maintain (*an argument*); to play the part of (*a character*); (law) to defend
dēfensĭ·ō -ōnis *f* defense
dēfensĭt·ō -āre *vt* to defend often; **causas defensitare** to be a lawyer
dēfens·ō -āre *vt* to defend, protect
dēfens·or -ōris *m* defender, protector; (law) defense lawyer; (law) guardian; champion (*of people*); *m pl* garrison
dēfensus *pp* of **defendo**
dē·fĕrō -ferre -tŭlī -lātum *vt* to bring or carry down; to bear off, carry away; to throw (*ship*) off course; to offer, confer, grant; to inform against, indict; to give an account of, announce, report; to recommend; to register; **ad aerarium deferre** to recommend (*someone*) for a monetary reward (*because of outstanding service to the State*); **ad consilium deferre** to take into consideration
dē·fervescō -fervescĕre -fervī or **-ferbŭī** *vt* & *vi* to cool off, calm down; (of a speech) to lose momentum; (of passions) to die out

dēfess·us -a -um *adj* weary, worn out, exhausted
dē·fetiscor or **dē·fatiscor -fetiscī -fessus sum** *vi* to become weary, tired
dē·ficiō -ficĕre -fēcī -fectum *vt* to fail, disappoint; to desert, abandon; *vi* to fail, be a failure; to defect, desert; to secede; (of arms, food, etc.) to run short, run out; (of strength, morale, etc.) to fail, grow weak, droop, sink; (of sun, moon) to be eclipsed; (of fire) to die out; (com) to be bankrupt
dē·fīgō -fīgĕre -fixī -fixum *vt* to fix, fasten down; to drive down; to fix, concentrate (*eyes, attention*); to root to the spot, astound, stupefy; to bewitch, enchant; **in terra defigere** to stick, plant, set up (*something*) in the ground
dē·fingō -fingĕre -finxī *vt* to form, mold; to portray; to disfigure, deface
dēfīn·iō -īre -īvī -ītum *vt* to set bounds to, limit; (fig) to limit, define, explain; to fix, determine, appoint; to delimit, bring to a finish, end; to assign, prescribe
dēfīnītē *adv* precisely
dēfīnītī·ō -ōnis *f* boundary; (fig) marking out, prescribing; definition
dēfīnītīv·us -a -um *adj* explanatory
dēfīnīt·us -a -um *adj* definite, precise
dē·fīō -fĭerī *vi* to fail, be lacking
dēflagrātī·ō -ōnis *f* conflagration
dēflăgr·ō -āre *vt* to burn down; *vi* to burn down, go up in flames; to perish, be destroyed; (of passions) to cool off, be allayed, subside
dē·flectō -flectĕre -flexī -flexum *vt* to deflect, bend aside, turn away, divert; (fig) to turn away, lead astray; *vi* to turn away, digress, deviate
defl·ĕō -ēre -ēvī -ētum *vt* to cry bitterly for; to mourn as lost; *vi* to cry bitterly
defloccāt·us -a -um *adj* stripped of wool, shorn; bald (*head*)
deflōr·escō -escĕre -ŭī *vi* to shed blossoms; (fig) to fade, droop
deflŭ·ō -ĕre -xī *vi* to flow or float down; to glide down, slide, fall; to flow out, run dry; to vanish, pass away, disappear, cease; to go out of style, become obsolete
dē·fodiō -fodĕre -fōdī -fossum *vt* to dig down; to hollow out; to bury, hide, conceal
dēfŏre = dēfutūrum esse
dēformātī·ō -ōnis *f* disfiguring, defacing
dēform·is -e *adj* shapeless, amorphous; misshapen, disfigured, ugly; degrading; degraded; unbecoming, humiliating
dēformĭt·ās -ātis *f* deformity, ugliness, hideousness; vileness, turpitude
dēformĭter *adv* without grace, without beauty
dēform·ō -āre *vt* to form from a pattern; to sketch, delineate; to deform, disfigure, mar
dēfossus *pp* of **defodio**
defraud·ō or **defrūd·ō -āre** *vt* to defraud, rob; to cheat; **genium suum defraudare** to deny oneself some pleasure
defrēnāt·us -a -um *adj* unbridled, uncontrolled
defrĭc·ō -āre -ŭī -ātum *vt* to rub down; to brush (*teeth*); (fig) to satirize
de·fringō -fringĕre -frēgī -fractum *vt* to break off, break to pieces
defrūdo see **defraudo**
defrŭt·um -ī *n* new wine
dē·fugĭō -fugĕre -fūgī *vt* to run away from, avoid, shirk; to evade (*e.g., authority, law*); *vi* to run off, escape
dēfunct·us -a -um *pp* of **defungor;** *adj* finished; dead
dē·fundō -fundĕre -fūdī -fūsum *vt* to pour out; to empty (*e.g., bucket*)
dē·fungor -fungī -functus sum *vi* (with *abl*) **a** to perform, finish, be done with; **b** to have done with, get rid of; **defunctus jam sum** I'm safe now; **defungi vitā** or **defungi** to die; **parvo victu defungi** to do with or be content with little food
dēfūsus *pp* of **defundo**
dēgĕn·er -ĕris *adj* degenerate; unworthy; ignoble
dēgenĕr·ō -āre *vt* to disgrace, dishonor, fall short of; *vi* to be inferior to one's ancestors, be degenerate; (fig) to fall off, degenerate, decline
dēgĕr·ō -ĕre *vt* to carry off, carry away
dēg·ō -ĕre -ī *vt* to spend, pass (*time, life*); **aetatem degere** to live; *vi* to live
dēgrandĭnat *v impers* it is hailing hard
dēgrăv·ō -āre *vt* to weigh down; (fig) to burden, distress, inconvenience, overpower
dē·gredĭor -grĕdī -gressus sum *vi* to march down, go down, walk down, descend; **ad pedes degredi** to dismount
dēgrunn·iō -īre *vi* to grunt hard, grunt out loud
dēgust·ō -āre *vt* to taste; (fig) to taste, sample, try, experience; (of weapon) to graze
dehinc *adv* from here; from now on; then, next; hereafter
dehisc·ō -ĕre *vi* to part, divide, gape, yawn
dehonestāment·um -ī *n* blemish, disfigurement, dishonor, disgrace
dehonest·ō -āre *vt* to dishonor, disgrace
dehort·or -ārī -ātus sum *vt* to advise to the contrary, dissuade
Dēianīr·a -ae *f* daughter of Oeneus and wife of Hercules

dein see **deinde**
deinceps *adv* one after another, in succession, in order; in regular order, without interruption
deinde or **dein** *adv* (of place) from that place, from there; (of time) then, thereafter, thereupon, afterwards; (in enumerating facts, presenting arguments) secondly, next in order, in the next place
Dēiotăr·us -ī *m* king of Galatia (*defended by Cicero before Caesar in the latter's house*)
Dēiphŏb·us -ī *m* son of Priam and Hecuba, and husband of Helen after Paris' death
dējectĭ·ō -ōnis *f* (law) eviction
dēject·us -a -um *pp* of **dejicio;** *adj* low, depressed, sunken (*place*); discouraged, downhearted, despondent
dēject·us -ūs *m* felling (*of trees*); steep slope
dējĕr·ō or **dējūrō -āre** *vi* to swear solemnly
dē·jicĭō -jicĕre -jēcī -jectum *vt* to throw down, fling down; to fell, bring low, kill; to depose (*from office*); to lower (*eyes*); to drive off course; (law) to evict; (mil) to dislodge, drive out; to deprive; (with *abl* or **de** + *abl*) to deprive (*someone*) of, prevent (*someone*) from obtaining, rob (*someone*) of; **oculos dejicere** (with **ab** + *abl*) to divert the eyes from; to turn away from
dējung·ō -ĕre *vt* to unyoke; to sever
dējūrō see **dejero**
dējŭv·ō -āre *vt* to fail to help
dē·lābor -lābī -lapsus sum *vi* to slip down, fall down, sink down; to glide down, float down; (fig) to come down, sink; (fig) to stoop, condescend; (with **ad** + *acc*) to be inclined toward, be partial to, tend toward; (with **in** + *acc*) to sneak in among
dēlacĕr·ō -āre *vt* to tear to pieces
dēlāment·or -ārī -ātus sum *vt* to grieve deeply for
delass·ō -āre *vt* to tire out, weary
dēlātĭ·ō -ōnis *f* reporting; informing, denouncing; **nominis delatio** indicting of a person
dēlāt·or -ōris *m* reporter; informer, denouncer
dēlātus *pp* of **defero**
dēlectābĭl·is -e *adj* delightful, enjoyable
dēlectāment·um -ī *n* delight, amusement, pastime
dēlectātĭ·ō -ōnis *f* delight, pleasure, charm, amusement, satisfaction
dēlect·ō -āre *vt* to delight, amuse, charm; to attract, allure; **delectari** (with *abl*) to be delighted by, delight in; *v impers* **me ire delectat** I like to go, I enjoy going
dēlect·us -a -um *pp* of **deligo;** *adj* picked, choice, select
dēlect·us -ūs *m* choosing, choice
dēlēgātĭ·ō -ōnis *f* substitution, delegation (*of one person for another*); payment (*of debt*)
dēlēg·ō -āre *vt* to assign, transfer; to attribute, impute, ascribe
dēlēnifĭc·us -a -um *adj* soothing, seductive
dēlēnīment·um -ī *n* palliative, solace, comfort; allurement, bait
dēlēn·ĭō or **dēlīn·ĭō -īre -īvī -ītum** *vt* to soothe, calm down, console, appease; to allure, seduce, win over
dēlēnīt·or -ōris *m* charmer, cajoler
dēl·ĕō -ēre -ēvī -ētum *vt* to destroy, annihilate, overthrow, extinguish, raze; to blot out, erase, obliterate (*writing*); to annul, put an end to, abolish, finish
dēlētr·ix -īcis *f* destroyer
Dēliăc·us -a -um *adj* Delian, of or from Delos
dēlīberābund·us -a -um *adj* deliberating maturely
dēlīberātĭ·ō -ōnis *f* considering, weighing; deliberation, consultation; **habet res deliberationem** the matter requires thought, needs consideration
dēlīberātīv·us -a -um *adj* deliberative; requiring deliberation
dēlīberāt·or -ōris *m* thoughtful person
dēlīberāt·us -a -um *adj* resolved upon, determined
dēlībĕr·ō -āre *vt* to weigh well, ponder; to resolve, determine; to consult (*oracle*); *vi* to reflect, deliberate; (with **de** + *abl*) to think seriously about, think over well
dēlīb·ō -āre *vt* to sip, take a sip of; to taste, take a taste of, nibble at; to take away, detract, subtract, remove
dēlĭbr·ō -āre *vt* to strip the bark off (*trees*); to peel
dēlibūt·us -a -um *adj* anointed; defiled, stained, smeared; steeped
dēlicātē *adv* delicately, softly, luxuriously
dēlicāt·us -a -um *adj* delicate, dainty, tender, soft; pampered, spoiled; dainty, fastidious
dēlicĭ·ae -ārum *f pl* allurements, enticements, delights; whims, pet ideas, fanciful ideas; voluptuousness; favorite, sweetheart, darling; **delicias facere** to play tricks; **delicias facere** (with *dat*) to play around with (*a girl*); **esse in deliciis** (with *dat*) to be the pet or favorite of; **habere in deliciis** to have as a pet or favorite
dēliciŏl·ae -ārum *f pl* darling
delic·ĭum -ĭī or **-ī** *n* sweetheart; favorite
dēlĭc·ō -āre *vt* to make clear, explain
dēlict·um -ī *n* fault, offense, wrong, transgression, defect
dēlicŭ·us -a -um *adj* lacking, wanting
dēlĭg·ō -āre *vt* to tie up, bind together, bind fast
dē·lĭgō -ligĕre -lēgī -lectum *vt* to

choose, select, pick out, single out, elect; to gather, gather in
dē·lingō -lingĕre -linxī *vt* to lick off; to have a lick of
dēlīni- = deleni-
dē·linquō -linquĕre -līquī -lictum *vi* to fail, be wanting, fall short; to do wrong, commit a fault or crime
dē·liquescō -liquescĕre -licŭī *vi* to melt, melt away, dissolve; to pine away
dēliquĭ·ō -ōnis *f* failure; (with *genit*) failure to get
dēliqu·ĭum -ĭī or **-ī** *n* failure
dēlĭqu·ō or **dēlĭc·ō -āre** *vt* to clear up, explain
dēlīrāment·um -ī *n* nonsense, absurdity
dēlīrātĭ·ō -ōnis *f* silliness, folly, madness; infatuation; dotage
dēlīr·ō -āre *vi* to be off the beam, be crazy, be mad; to drivel
dēlīr·us -a -um *adj* crazy, demented, silly; in dotage
dēlit·escō -escĕre -ŭī *vi* to conceal oneself, lie hidden, lurk
dēlītĭg·ō -āre *vi* to rant
Dēlĭ·us -a -um *adj* Delian, of Delos
Dēl·os -ī *f* sacred island in the Cyclades, where Apollo was born
Delph·ī -ōrum *m pl* town in Phocis, in Central Greece, famous for the shrine and oracle of Apollo; inhabitants of Delphi
delphīn·us -ī or **delph·īn -īnis** *m* dolphin
Delphīn·us -ī m Dolphin (*constellation*)
Deltōt·on -ī *n* Triangulum (*constellation*)
dēlūbr·um -ī *n* shrine, temple, sanctuary
dēluct·ō -āre or **dēluct·or -ārī -ātus sum** *vi* to wrestle
dēlūdifĭc·ō -āre *vt* to make fun of
dē·lūdō -lūdĕre -lūsī -lūsum *vt* to dupe, mock, deceive, delude
dēlumb·is -e *adj* enervated, enfeebled, weakened
dēmad·escō -escĕre -ŭī *vi* to become drenched; to be moistened
dēmand·ō -āre *vt* to hand over, entrust
dēmarch·us -ī *m* demarch (*chief of a village in Attica*); (fig) tribune of the people
dēm·ens -entis *adj* out of one's mind, demented, distracted, mad; senseless, wild, reckless
dēmensus *pp* of **demetior;** *n* ration, allowance
dēmenter *adv* insanely
dēmentĭ·a -ae *f* insanity, madness; *f pl* follies
dement·ĭō -īre *vi* to be mad
dēmer·ĕō -ēre -ŭī -ĭtum or **dēmer·ĕor -ērī -ĭtus sum** *vt* to earn, merit, deserve; to serve well, do a service to
dē·mergō -mergĕre -mersī -mersum *vt* to sink, plunge, submerge; (fig) to plunge, cast down, overwhelm
dēmessus *pp* of **dēmeto**
dē·mētĭor -mētīrī -mensus sum *vt* to measure off, measure out
dē·mĕtō -metĕre -messŭī -messum *vt* to mow, reap, cut off, cut down, harvest
dēmigrātĭ·ō -ōnis *f* emigration
dēmĭgr·ō -āre *vi* to migrate, emigrate, move, depart; (fig) to depart, die
dēmin·ŭō -uĕre -ŭī -ūtum *vt* to make smaller, lessen, diminish; (fig) to remit, reduce, lessen; **capite deminuere** to deprive of citizenship
dēminūtĭ·ō -ōnis *f* lessening, diminution, abridging; (law) right of disposing of property; **capitis diminutio** loss of civil rights; **provinciae diminutio** shortening of term of office
dēmīr·or -ārī -ātus sum *vt* to be surprised at, be amazed at
dēmissē *adv* low; humbly, modestly; abjectly, meanly
dēmissīcĭ·us -a -um *adj* allowed to hang down, flowing
dēmissĭ·ō -ōnis *f* letting down, sinking, lowering; **demissio animi** low morale
demiss·us -a -um *pp* of **demitto;** *adj* low, low-lying (*place*); drooping (*lips, etc.*); bent (*head*); allowed to hang down, flowing, loose (*hair*); downhearted, dejected; shy, unassuming, retiring, humble; poor, humble
dēmītĭg·ō -āre *vt* to make mild; **demitigari** to grow more lenient
dē·mittō -mittĕre -mīsī -missum *vt* to drop, let drop, let sink, lower; to bring downstream; to land (*ship*); to grow (*beard*); to move down (*troops from higher place*); **se demittere** to descend; to stoop, bend down
dēmiurg·us or **dāmiurg·us -ī** *m* chief magistrate in a Greek state
dēm·ō -ĕre -psī -ptum *vt* to take away, remove, withdraw, subtract; (with *dat* or with **de** + *abl*) to take away from, subtract from, withhold from
Dēmocrĭt·us -ī *m* famous philosopher of Abdera, in Thrace, founder of the atomic theory (460-361 B.C.)
dēmōl·ĭor -īrī -ītus sum *vt* to demolish, pull down
dēmōlītĭ·ō -ōnis *f* pulling down (*of statues*)
dēmonstrātĭ·ō -ōnis *f* pointing out; explanation
dēmonstrātīv·us -a -um *adj* showy
dēmonstrāt·or -ōris *m* indicator
dēmonstr·ō -āre *vt* to point out clearly; to state precisely, explain, describe; to mention, speak of; to demonstrate, prove, establish
dē·morĭor -mŏrī -mortŭus sum *vi* to die, die off
dēmŏr·or -ārī -ātus sum *vt* to delay, detain; to hinder, block; *vi* to wait

Dēmosthĕn·ēs -is *m* greatest Greek orator (384-322 B.C.)
dē·movĕō -movēre -mōvī -mōtum *vt* to remove, move away, dispossess, expel; to remove, discharge (*from office*); (fig) to divert, turn away
demptus *pp* of **demo**
dēmūgīt·us -a -um *adj* bellowing, lowing
dē·mulcĕō -mulcēre -mulsī *vt* to stroke lovingly, to caress
dēmum *adv* at last, finally; not till then; (to give emphasis) precisely, exactly, just; (to give assurance) in fact, certainly, to be sure, as a matter of fact; **decimo demum anno** not till the tenth year; **modo demum** only now, not till now; **nunc demum** now at last, not till now; **post demum** not till after; **sic demum** thus finally; **tum demum** then at length, not till then
dēmurmŭr·ō -āre *vt* to grumble right through (*e.g., a performance*)
dēmūtātĭ·ō -ōnis *f* changing, perversion, degeneracy
dēmūt·ō -āre *vt* to change, alter; to make worse; *vi* to change one's mind
dēnār·ĭus -ĭī or **-ī** *m* Roman silver coin, originally containing ten aces, later eighteen, approximately equivalent to twenty-five cents; money
dēnarr·ō -āre *vt* to recount in detail
dēnās·ō -āre *vt* to bite the nose off (*the face*)
dēnăt·ō -āre *vi* to swim downstream
dēnĕg·ō -āre *vt* to deny, refuse, turn down; *vi* to say no, give a flat refusal
dēn·ī -ae -a *adj* in sets of ten, ten each, in tens; ten; tenth
dēnicāl·is -e *adj* purifying from death; **feriae denicales** purification service (*after death in the household*)
dēnĭque *adv* finally, at last; in short, in a word, briefly; (for emphasis) just, precisely; (ironical) of course; **octavo denique mense** not till after the eighth month; **tum denique** then at last, only then, not till then
dēnōmĭn·ō -āre *vt* to name, designate
dēnorm·ō -āre *vt* to make crooked or irregular; to disfigure, spoil
dēnŏt·ō -āre *vt* to mark down, specify; to take careful note of. observe closely
den·s -tis *m* tooth; ivory; point, prong, fluke; (fig) tooth (*of envy, hatred, time, etc.*); **albis dentibus deridere aliquem** to laugh heartily at someone; **dens Indus** elephant's tusk
densē *adv* closely, thickly; in quick succession, repeatedly
densĭt·ās -ātis *f* closeness, thickness
dens·ō -āre or **dens·ĕō -ēre — -ētum** *vt* to make thick, thicken; to press close together; to close (*ranks*); to condense (*a speech*)
dens·us -a -um *adj* dense, close, crowded, thick; frequent, continuous; intense (*love, cold*); concise (*style*)
dentāl·ĭa -ĭum *n pl* plow beam
dentāt·us -a -um *adj* toothed, having teeth; serrated; polished (*paper*)
dentifrangibŭl·us -a -um *adj* tooth-breaking; *m* thug; *n* fist
dentilĕg·us -ī *m* toothpicker (*one who picks up teeth after they have been knocked out*)
dent·ĭō -īre *vi* to teethe, cut one's teeth
dē·nūbō -nūbĕre -nupsī -nuptum *vi* (of a woman) to marry beneath one's rank
dēnūd·ō -āre *vt* to denude, strip naked, strip bare; (fig) to lay bare (*facts*)
dēnuntiātĭ·ō -ōnis *f* intimation, warning, threat; announcement, proclamation; **senatūs denuntiatio** senate ordinance; **testimoni denuntiatio** summons to testify
dēnuntĭ·ō -āre *vt* to intimate; to give notice of; to announce officially; to give official warning to; (mil) to report to, give an official report to; to warn, threaten; **denuntiare testimonium** (with *dat*) to give (*someone*) a summons to testify
dēnŭō *adv* anew, afresh, once more, all over again
deonĕr·ō -āre *vt* to unload
deorsum or **deorsus** *adv* downwards, down; (of position) down, below
deoscŭl·or -ārī -ātus sum *vt* to kiss warmly, kiss up and down
dēpaciscor see **depeciscor**
dēpact·us -a -um *adj* lashed down; driven tight
dēparc·us -a -um *adj* very stingy
dē·pascō -pascĕre -pāvī -pastum or **dē·pascor -pascī -pastus sum** *vt* to feed off, graze on; to consume; to destroy, waste; (fig) to prune off (*excesses of style*)
dēpec·iscor or **dēpac·iscor -iscī -tus sum** *vt* to agree upon, bargain for, settle by bargaining
dē·pectō -pectĕre — -pexum *vt* to comb, curry; to curry (*one's hide*), flog
dēpeculāt·or -ōris *m* embezzler, plunderer
dēpecŭl·or -ārī -ātus sum *vt* to embezzle, plunder
dē·pellō -pellĕre -pŭlī -pulsum *vt* to drive off, drive away, drive out, expel; to avert; (mil) to dislodge; (with **quin** or with **de** or **ab** + *abl*) to avert, deter, dissuade, wean from; (with *abl*) to dislodge from; *vi* to deviate
dēpend·ĕō -ēre *vi* to hang down; (with *abl*) to be derived from; (with **de** + *abl*) to depend upon; (with **ex** + *abl*) to hang down from
dē·pendō -pendĕre -pendī -pen-

sum *vt* to pay up; **poenam dependere** (with *dat*) to pay the penalty to

dēper·dō -dĕre -dĭdī -dĭtum *vt* to lose completely; to ruin, destroy

dēper·ĕō -īre -iī *vt* to be hopelessly in love with; *vi* to go to ruin, perish; to be lost, finished

dē·pingō -pingĕre -pinxī -pictum *vt* to paint, portray; to embroider; to portray, describe, represent (*in words or thoughts*)

dē·plangō -plangĕre -planxī *vt* to grieve over, cry one's heart out over

deplex·us -a -um *adj* gripping firmly, grasping

deplōrābund·us -a -um *adj* weeping bitterly, sobbing

deplōr·ō -āre *vt* to cry over, mourn; to despair of; *vi* to take it hard, cry bitterly

deplŭ·it -ĕre -it *v impers* it is raining hard, pouring down

dē·pōnō -pōnĕre -posŭī -posĭtum *vt* to lay down; to put down, put aside, get rid of; to bet, wager; to deposit; (with **apud** + *acc*) to entrust to, commit to the care of; **bellum deponere** to give up war; **imperium deponere** to relinquish power, renounce power

dēpopulātĭ·ō -ōnis *f* ravaging, pillaging

dēpopulāt·or -ōris *m* pillager, marauder

dēpopŭl·ō -āre or **depopŭl·or -ārī -ātus sum** *vt* to ravage, pillage, lay waste; to depopulate; (fig) to waste, destroy, wreck

dēport·ō -āre *vt* to carry down; to carry away; to bring home (*victory*); to transport; to banish; (fig) to win

dē·poscō -poscĕre -poposcī *vt* to demand, require; to request earnestly; to challenge; **sibi deposcere** to claim (*something*) for oneself

dēposĭt·us -a -um *pp* of **depono;** *adj* despaired of; *n* deposit (*of money as first payment*); deposit (*for safe keeping*)

dēprāvātē *adv* perversely

dēprāvātĭ·ō -ōnis *f* distorting; (fig) distortion

dēprāv·ō -āre *vt* to make crooked, distort; to pervert, corrupt, seduce; to misrepresent

dēprecābund·us -a -um *adj* imploring

dēprecātĭ·ō -ōnis *f* supplication· deprecation, averting by prayer; invocation, earnest entreaty; (with *genit*) intercession against (*danger, etc.*)

dēprecāt·or -ōris *m* intercessor (*generally against rather than for*)

dēprĕc·or -ārī -ātus sum *vt* to pray against, avert by prayer; to pray for, beg for; to intercede in behalf of; to plead in excuse

dēpre·hendō -hendĕre -hendī -hensum or **dēpren·dō -dĕre -dī -sum** *vt* to get hold of; to arrest, intercept; to surprise, catch in the act; to detect, discover, find out; to perceive, understand; to embarrass

dēprehensĭ·ō -ōnis *f* detection

dēpress·us -a -um *pp* of **deprimo;** *adj* low, suppressed (*voice*); low (*land*)

dē·prĭmō -prĭmĕre -pressī -pressum *vt* to depress, press down, weigh down; to plant deep; to dig (*e.g., a trench*) deep; to sink (*a ship*)

dēproelĭ·or -ārī -ātus sum *vi* to fight it out, battle fiercely

dē·prōmō -prōmĕre -prompsī -promptum *vt* to take down; to bring out, produce

dēpropĕr·ō -āre *vt* to make in a hurry; *vi* to hurry

deps·ō -ĕre -ŭī -tum *vt* to knead

dēpŭd·et -ēre -ŭit *v impers* **eum depudet** he has no sense of shame

dēpūg·is or **dēpȳg·is -is** *adj* without buttocks, with thin buttocks

dēpugn·ō -āre *vi* to fight hard; to fight it out; (with **cum** + *abl*) to be in a death struggle with

dēpulsĭ·ō -ōnis *f* averting; (rhet) defense

dēpuls·ō -āre *vt* to push aside; **de via depulsare** to push out of the way

dēpuls·or -ōris *m* averter

dēpulsus *pp* of **depello**

dēpung·ō -ĕre *vt* to mark off, designate

dēpurg·ō -āre *vt* to clean

dēpŭt·ō -āre *vt* to prune; to reckon, consider

dēpȳgis see **depugis**

dēque *adv* down, downwards

dērect·us -a -um *pp* of **derigo;** *adj* straight, direct, level, upright, perpendicular; (fig) straightforward, direct, simple, right

dērelictĭ·ō -ōnis *f* dereliction, disregarding, neglecting

dēre·linquō -linquĕre -līquī -lictum *vt* to leave behind, forsake, abandon

dērepente *adv* suddenly

dērēp·ō -ĕre -sī *vi* to creep down

dēreptus *pp* of **deripio**

dē·rīdĕō -rīdēre -rīsī -rīsum *vt* to deride

dērīdicŭl·us -a -um *adj* quite ridiculous; *n* derision, mockery; absurdity; **deridiculo esse** to be the object of derision, be the butt of ridicule

dērig·escō -escĕre -ŭī *vi* to grow stiff, grow rigid; to curdle

dē·rigō -rigĕre -rexī -rectum *vt* to direct, aim; to steer (*ship*); to draw up in battle line; (fig) to direct, guide, regulate; (with *dat* or with **ad** or **in** + *acc*) to direct or aim at, guide to; (with **ad** + *acc*) to regulate (*e.g., life*) according to

dē·ripĭō -ripĕre -ripŭī -reptum *vt* to tear down, tear off, pull down

dērīs·or -ōris *m* scoffer, cynic

dērīs·us -ūs *m* derision
dērīvātī·ō -ōnis *f* diversion, diverting (*of river from its course*)
dērīv·ō -āre *vt* to draw off, divert; to derive
dērŏg·ō -āre *vt* to propose to repeal in part; to restrict, modify; to take away, diminish, impair
dērōs·us -a -um *adj* gnawed away, nibbled
dēruncĭn·ō -āre *vt* to plane off; to cheat
dērŭ·ō -ĕre -ŭī *vt* to throw down, overthrow, demolish; to detract
dērupt·us -a -um *adj* rough, steep, broken; *n pl* crevasses
dēsaev·iō -īre -iī *vi* to rage furiously; to run wild
dēsalt·ō -āre *vi* to dance
de·scendō -scendĕre -scendī -scensum *vi* to climb down, descend, come or go down; to dismount; to fall, sink, sink down, penetrate; (fig) to go down, sink, sink down, penetrate; (fig) to lower oneself, stoop, yield; (mil) to march down
descensĭ·ō -ōnis *f* going down; **descensio Tiberina** sailing down the Tiber
descens·us -ūs *m* climbing down, descent; slope, descent
desc·iscō -iscĕre -īvī or **-iī -ītum** *vi* to revolt, desert; (fig) to depart, deviate, fall off; (with **ab** + *abl*) **a** to revolt from, break allegiance with; **b** to deviate from, fall away from
de·scrībō -scrībĕre -scripsī -scriptum *vt* to write out, transcribe, copy; to describe, represent, portray, draw, design, sketch
descriptē see **discripte**
descriptĭ·ō -ōnis *f* copy; representation, diagram, sketch, map; description
descriptus *pp* of **describo**
dēsĕc·ō -āre -ŭī -tum *vt* to cut off
dēsĕr·ō -ĕre -ŭī -tum *vt* to desert, abandon, forsake; (law) to forfeit
dēsert·or -ōris *m* deserter
dēsert·us -a -um *pp* of **desero;** *adj* deserted; unpopulated, uninhabited; *n pl* wilderness, desert
dēserv·iō -īre *vi* (with *dat*) to be a slave to, serve devotedly
dēs·es -ĭdis *adj* sitting down, sitting at ease; lazy; apathetic, lifeless, idle
dēsicc·ō -āre *vt* to dry up; to drain
dē·sidĕō -sidēre -sēdī *vi* to sit idle, remain inactive
dēsīderābĭl·is -e *adj* desirable
dēsīderātĭ·ō -ōnis *f* missing, feeling the absence; **desideratio voluptatum** the missing of pleasures, yearning for pleasures
dēsīder·ium -iī or **-ī** *n* longing, missing, feeling of loss; want, need, necessity; request, petition; **ex desiderio laborare** to be homesick; **me desiderium tenet** (with *genit*) I miss, am homesick for
dēsīdĕr·ō -āre *vt* to miss, long for, feel the want of; (mil) to lose (*men*) as casualties; **desiderari** (mil) to be missing, be lost, be a casualty
dēsidĭ·a -ae *f* idleness, inactivity; laziness; apathy
dēsidiābŭl·um -ī *n* place to lounge, hangout
dēsidiōsē *adv* idly
dēsidōs·us -a -um *adj* idle, indolent, lazy; causing idleness or laziness; spent in idleness
dē·sīdō -sidĕre -sēdī *vi* to sink, settle down; (fig) to sink, deteriorate
dēsignātĭ·ō -ōnis *f* specification; designation, election to office
dēsignātor see **dissignator**
dēsign·ō -āre *vt* to mark out, point out, designate, define, trace; to denote, describe, represent; to appoint, choose, elect; **consul designatus** consul-elect
dē·siliō -silīre -silŭī -sultum *vi* to jump down, alight; **ab equo desilire** to dismount; **de nave desilire** to jump overboard; (fig) to venture forth
dē·sinō -sinĕre -siī -sĭtum *vt* to give up, abandon; **furere desinere** to stop raging; *vi* to stop, come to a stop, end; (with **in** + *acc*) to end in; **similiter desinere** to have similar endings
dēsipĭ·ens -entis *adj* foolish, silly
dēsipientĭ·a -ae *f* folly, foolishness
dēsip·iō -ĕre *vi* to be silly, act foolishly
dē·sistō -sistĕre -stĭtī -stĭtum *vi* to stop, desist; to get stuck, stick; (with *abl* or with **ab** or **de** + *abl*) to desist from, abandon, give up (*an action begun*); **desistere a defensione** to give up the defense
dēsĭtus *pp* of **desino**
dēsōl·ō -āre *vt* to leave desolate, leave alone, forsake, abandon; **desolatus** (with *abl*) deprived of
despect·ō -āre *vt* to look down on, overlook, command a view of; to look down on, despise
despect·us -a -um *pp* of **despicio;** *adj* contemptible
despect·us -ūs *m* commanding view, view
despēranter *adv* hopelessly
despērātĭ·ō -ōnis *f* desperation, despair
despērāt·us -a -um *adj* despaired of; hopeless; desperate, hopeless
despēr·ō -āre *vt* to despair of; *vi* to despair, give up hope; (with **de** + *abl*) to despair of
despicātĭ·ō -ōnis *f* contempt; *f pl* feelings of contempt
despicāt·us -a -um *adj* despicable; **aliquem despicatum habere** to hold someone in contempt
despicĭ·ens -entis *adj* contemptuous; (with *genit*) contemptuous of
despicientĭ·a -ae *f* despising, contempt

de·spiciō -spicĕre -spexī -spectum *vt* to despise, look down on, express contempt for; *vi* to look down; (with **in** + *acc*) to look down on, have a view of
despĭc·or -ārī -ātus sum *vt* to despise, disdain
despoliāt·or -ōris *m* robber, plunderer, marauder
despolĭ·ō -āre *vt* to strip, rob, plunder
de·spondĕō -spondēre -spondī -sponsum *vt* to pledge, promise solemnly; to promise in marriage; to give up, lose; **animum despondere** or **animos despondere** to lose heart
despūm·ō -āre *vt* to skim off, skim; *vi* to stop foaming
despŭ·ō -ĕre *vt* to spit upon, show contempt for; *vi* to spit (*on the ground*)
desquām·ō -āre *vt* to take the scales off, to scale (*fish*); (fig) to peel off
destill·ō -āre *vt* to drip, distil; *vi* to trickle down, drip
destimŭl·ō -āre *vt* to goad on, stimulate
destinātĭ·ō -ōnis *f* establishing; resolution, determination, purpose, design
destināt·us -a -um *adj* fixed, determined; **destinatum est mihi** (with *inf*) I have made up my mind to; *n pl* designs, intentions
destĭn·ō -āre *vt* to lash down, secure; (fig) to fix, determine, resolve; to design, destine; to appoint, designate; to take aim at
destit·ŭō -uĕre -ŭī -ūtum *vt* to set apart; to set down, place; to forsake, abandon; to leave in the lurch, leave high and dry, betray, desert; (with **ab** + *abl*) to rob of, leave destitute of
destitūtĭ·ō -ōnis *f* forsaking, abandonment; disappointment
destrict·us -a -um *adj* severe, rigid
de·stringō -stringĕre -strinxī -strictum *vt* to strip; to unsheathe; to give (*someone*) a rubdown; to brush gently against, skim; (of weapon) to graze; (fig) to criticize, satirize
destructĭ·ō -ōnis *f* pulling down (*e.g., of walls*); destruction, demolition; refutation
de·strŭō -struĕre -struxī -structum *vt* to pull down, demolish, destroy; (fig) to ruin
dēsubĭtō or **dē subĭtō** *adv* suddenly
dēsūdasc·ō -ĕre *vi* to begin to sweat all over
dēsūd·ō -āre *vi* to sweat; (with *dat*) (fig) to sweat over, work hard at
dēsuē·fīō -fĭĕrī -factus sum *vi* to become unused or unaccustomed
dēsu·escō -escĕre -ēvī -ētum *vi* to become unaccustomed
dēsuētūd·ō -ĭnis *f* disuse, lack of use
dēsuēt·us -a -um *pp* of **desuesco;** *adj* unused, out of use, obsolete; out of practice; (with *dat*) unused to, unfamiliar with
dēsult·or -ōris *m* circus rider who leaps from one horse to another; **amoris desultor** (fig) fickle lover
dēsultōrĭ·us -a -um *adj* of a circus rider; **equus desultorius** show horse
dēsultūr·a -ae *f* leaping down (*from horse*), dismounting
dē·sum -esse -fŭī -futūrus *vi* to fall short, fail; to fail in one's duty; to be absent, be missing; (with *dat*) to be absent from, be missing from, be lacking from; **sibi deesse** to cheat oneself, sell oneself short; **tempori deesse** or **occasioni temporis deesse** to pass up the opportunity, pass up the chance
dē·sūmō -sūmĕre -sumpsī -sumptum *vt* to pick out, choose; to assume, undertake; **sibi hostem desumere** to take on an enemy
dēsŭper *adv* from above, from overhead
dēsurg·ō -ĕre *vi* to rise; **cenā desurgere** to get up from the table
dē·tĕgō -tegĕre -texī -tectum *vt* to detect, uncover, expose, lay bare; to reveal, disclose, betray; **formidine detegi** to be betrayed by fear
dē·tendō -tendĕre — -tensum *vt* to unstretch; to take down (*tent*)
dētentus *pp* of **detineo**
dē·tergĕō -tergēre -tersī -tersum *vt* to wipe off, wipe away, wipe clean; (fig) to wipe clean; **mensam detergere** to eat up everything on the table
dēterĭ·or -us *adj* inferior, worse, poorer, meaner; less favorable, worse (*time*); degenerate (*person*); (mil) weaker (*e.g., in cavalry*)
dēterĭus *adv* worse
dēterminātĭ·ō -ōnis *f* boundary; conclusion, end; end (*of speech*)
dētermĭn·ō -āre *vt* to bound, limit, prescribe; to determine, settle
dē·tĕrō -terĕre -trīvī -trītum *vt* to rub away, wear away; to wear out; to lessen, weaken, detract from; **calces alicujus deterere** to tread on someone's heels
dēterr·ĕō -ēre -ŭī -ĭtum *vt* to deter, frighten away, discourage; (with *abl*, or with **ab** or **de** + *abl*, or with **ne, quin,** or **quominus**) to deter or discourage from; **deterruit quominus hostes persequerentur** he discouraged them from pursuing the enemy
dētersus *pp* of **detergeo**
dētestābĭl·is -e *adj* detestable, abominable
dētestātĭ·ō -ōnis *f* execration, curse; averting (*by sacrifices or prayers*)
dētest·or -ārī -ātus sum *vt* to curse, execrate; to invoke (*the gods*); to avert; to plead against; to detest, loathe, abhor; (with **in** + *acc*) to

call down (*e.g., vengeance*) upon; **invidiam detestari** to avert envy, avoid unpopularity

dētex·ō -ĕre -ŭī -tum *vt* to weave, finish weaving; (fig) to finish, finish off

dē·tinĕō -tinēre -tinŭī -tentum *vt* to hold back, keep back; to hold up, detain; to occupy, keep occupied; (with **ab** or **de** + *abl*) to keep back from; (with *abl* or with **in** + *abl*) to occupy (*e.g., day, mind*) with, keep (*someone*) busied with

dē·tondĕō -tondēre -totondī or **-tondī -tonsum** *vt* to cut off, clip off, shear off (*hair, wool*); (fig) to strip

dētŏn·ō -āre -ŭī *vi* to stop thundering; (of Jupiter) to thunder down

dētonsus *pp* of **detondeo**

dē·torquĕō -torquēre -torsī -tortum *vt* to twist or bend aside; to twist out of shape; to turn aside; to turn, direct; to avert (*eyes*); to divert, pervert; to distort, misrepresent (*words*)

dētractĭ·ō -ōnis *f* taking away, wresting; removal; (rhet) ellipsis

detractō see **detrecto**

detract·or -ōris *m* detractor

dē·trăhō -trahĕre -traxī -tractum *vt* to drag down, drag away, pull down, pull away; to remove, withdraw; to take away, deprive, rob, strip; to induce to come down, draw down (*e.g., an enemy from a strong position*); to disparage, detract, slander; (with *dat* or **de** + *abl*) to take away from (*someone*), rob (*someone*) of

dētrectātĭ·ō -ōnis *f* drawing back, avoidance; **militiae detrectatio** draft dodging

dētrectāt·or -ōris *m* detractor, disparager

dētrect·ō or **detract·ō -āre** *vt* to draw back from, shirk, decline, reject, refuse; to disparage, depreciate; to demean; **militiam detrectare** to dodge the draft

dētrīmentōs·us -a -um *adj* detrimental, harmful

dētrīment·um -ī *n* detriment, loss, damage; **detrimentum accipere** or **detrimentum capere** to incur or suffer harm; **detrimentum inferre** or **detrimentum afferre** to cause harm

dētrītus *pp* of **detero**

dē·trūdō -trūdĕre -trūsī -trūsum *vt* to push down, push away, push off; (mil) to dislodge; (law) to evict; to postpone, put off; **aliquem de sua sententia detrudere** to force someone to change his mind

detrunc·ō -āre *vt* to cut off, chop off; (fig) to mutilate, behead

dēturb·ō -āre *vt* to beat down, expel, tear down, strike down; (mil) to dislodge, force to come down; to eject, dispossess; **aliquem de sanitate deturbare** to drive a person mad

Deucalĭ·ōn -ōnis *m* son of Prometheus, who, together with his wife Pyrrha, was the sole survivor of the Deluge

de·unx -uncis *m* eleven twelfths; **heres ex deunce** heir to eleven twelfths

de·ūrō -ūrĕre -ussī -ustum *vt* to burn up, destroy; (of frost) to nip

de·us -ī (*nom pl:* **deī** or **dī;** *genit pl:* **deōrum** or **deum**) *m* god, deity; (of a person) god, divine being; *m pl* (of persons in high places) the powers that be; **di boni!** good heavens!; **di hominesque** all the world; **di meliora!** Heaven forbid!; **dis volentibus** with the help of the gods; **di te ament!** bless your little heart!

deustus *pp* of **deuro**

de·ūtor -ūtī -ūsus sum *vi* (with *abl*) to mistreat

dēvast·ō -āre *vt* to devastate, lay waste

dē·vĕhō -vehĕre -vexī -vectum *vt* to carry down, carry away, carry off; **devehi** to ride down, sail down

dē·vellō -vellĕre -vellī or **-volsī -vulsum** *vt* to pluck off

dēvēl·ō -āre *vt* to unveil

dēvenĕr·or -ārī -ātus sum *vt* to reverence, worship; to avert by prayer

dē·venĭō -venīre -vēnī -ventum *vi* to come down, arrive; (with *acc* of extent of motion or with **ad** or **in** + *acc*) to arrive at, reach; (with **ad** + *acc*) to happen to, befall

dēverbĕr·ō -āre *vt* to thrash soundly

dēvers·or -ārī -ātus sum *vi* to stay as a guest; (with **apud** + *acc*) to stay at the house of

dēvers·or -ōris *m* guest

dēversōriŏl·um -ī *n* small inn, motel

dēversōrĭ·us or **dēvorsorĭ·us -a -um** *adj* of an inn; fit to stay at; **taberna deversoria** inn; *n* inn, hotel

dēverticŭl·um or **dēvorticŭl·um -ī** *n* side road, detour; digression; inn, hotel, tavern; low haunt, dive; refuge

dē·vertō (or **dē·vortō**) **-vertĕre -vertī -versum** or **dē·vertor -vertī -versus sum** *vi* to turn aside, turn away; to stay as guest, spend the night; (with **ad** or **apud** + *acc*) to stay with or at the house of; (with **ad** + *acc*) to have recourse to, resort to

dēvex·us -a -um *adj* inclining, sloping, steep; (with **ad** + *acc*) prone to, inclined to

dē·vincĭō -vincīre -vinxī -vinctum *vt* to tie up, clamp; (fig) to bind fast, obligate, unite closely; **se vino devincire** (coll) to get tight

dē·vincō -vincĕre -vīcī -victum *vt* to conquer, subdue

dēvinct·us -a -um *pp* of **devincio;** *adj* (with *dat*) strongly attached to
dēvītāti·ō -ōnis *f* avoidance
dēvīt·ō -āre *vt* to avoid
dēvi·us -a -um *adj* out of the way, off the beaten track; devious; living apart, solitary, sequestered; inconsistent
dēvŏc·ō -āre *vt* to call down; to call off, recall, call away; to allure, seduce; **deos ad auxilium devocare** to invoke the gods for help
dēvŏl·ō -āre *vi* to fly down; to fly away; to hasten down, hasten away
dē·volvō -volvĕre -volvī -volūtum *vt* to roll down; **ad spem inanem pacis devolvi** to fall back on false hopes of peace; **devolvi** to roll down, go tumbling down, sink down
dēvŏr·ō -āre *vt* to devour, gulp down; to consume, waste, squander (*money, etc.*); (of the sea) to engulf, swallow up; to swallow, mumble (*words*); to repress (*tears*); to bear with patience
dēvor- = dever-
dēvorti·a -ōrum *n pl* side roads, detour
dēvōti·ō -ōnis *f* self-sacrifice; cursing, outlawing; incantation, spell; **capitis devotio** or **vitae devotio** sacrifice of one's life
dēvōt·ō -āre *vt* to lay a spell on, bewitch, jinx
dēvōt·us -a -um *pp* of **devoveo;** *adj* devoted, faithful; accursed; (with *dat*) **a** devoted to, faithful to; **b** addicted to, given to (*wine, drinking*)
dē·vovĕō -vovēre -vōvī -vōtum *vt* to devote, vow, sacrifice, dedicate; to mark out, doom, destine; to curse, execrate; to bewitch; **se devovere dis** to devote oneself to death
dēvulsus *pp* of **devello**
dext·ans -antis *m* five sixths
dextell·a -ae *f* little right hand; right-hand man
dext·er -ĕra -ĕrum or **-ra -rum** *adj* right, on the right side; handy, dexterous; lucky, propitious, favorable; opportune, right; *f* right hand; right side, the right; **a dextra laevaque** to the right and left, right and left, everywhere; **dextrā** with the right hand; (fig) with valor; **dextrā** (with *acc*) to the right of; **dextram dare** or **dextram tendere** to give a pledge of friendship; **dextram renovare** to renew a solemn pledge
dextĕrē or **dextrē** *adv* dexterously, skillfully; **dextre fortunā uti** (fig) to play the cards right
dexterit·ās -ātis *f* dexterity, adroitness; readiness
dextrorsum or **dextrorsus** or **dextrōvorsum** *adv* to the right, towards the right side
dī see **deus**
Dī·a -ae *f* ancient name of the island of Naxos; mother of Mercury
diabathrār·ius -iī or **-ī** *m* shoemaker
diadēm·a -ătis *n* diadem
diaet·a -ae *f* diet; living room
dialecticē *adv* logically
dialectic·us -a -um *adj* dialectical; *m* dialectician; *f* dialectics, logic; *n pl* dialectics, logical discussions
dialect·os -ī *f* dialect
Diāl·is -e *adj* of Jupiter; of Jupiter's high priest; **apex Dialis** high priest's miter; **conjux Dialis** high priest's wife; **flamen Dialis** high priest of Jupiter
dialŏg·us -ī *m* dialogue, conversation
Diān·a or **Dīān·a -ae** *f* Diana (*goddess of hunting, patroness of virginity, of the moon as Luna, of childbirth as Lucina, and of incantations and magic as Hecate*); (fig) Diana's temple; (fig) moon; **iracunda Diana** lunacy
diāri·a -ōrum *n pl* daily ration
dibăph·us -ī *f* crimson robe; official robe of magistrate
dic·a -ae *f* lawsuit, case, judicial process, judicial proceedings; **dicam scribere** (with *dat*) to sue (*someone*); **sortiri dicas** to select a jury
dicācit·ās -ātis *f* wittiness, sarcasm
dicācŭl·us -a -um *adj* quick-witted, sharp
dicāti·ō -ōnis *f* declaration of intent of becoming a citizen
dic·ax -ācis *adj* witty, sharp, sarcastic, caustic; pert
dichorē·us -ī *m* double trochee
dici·ō -ōnis *f* jurisdiction, sway, authority, control, rule, dominion, sovereignty; **in dicione esse** (with *genit*) or **sub dicione esse** (with *genit*) to be under the control of, be subject to, be under the jurisdiction of; **in dicionem redigere** (with *genit*) or **dicioni subjicere** (with *genit*) to bring (*someone*) under the control of
dicis causā or **grātiā** *adv* for show, for the sake of appearances
dic·ō -āre *vt* to dedicate, consecrate; to deify; to inaugurate; to set apart, devote; (with *dat*) to devote (*e.g., time, energy*) to; **se dicare** (with *dat* or **in** + *acc*) to dedicate oneself to
dīcō dīcĕre dixī dictum *vt* to say, tell; to indicate, mention, specify, point out; to nominate, appoint; to fix, set, appoint (*day or date*); to speak, deliver, recite; to pronounce, utter, articulate; to call, name; to assert, affirm; to describe, relate, celebrate; to tell, predict; (with double *acc*) to appoint (*someone*) as; **causam dicere** to plead or defend a case; **diem dicere** (with *dat*) to set a date for; **facete dictum!** well put!; **sententiam dicere** to

express an opinion; **testimonium dicere** to give evidence

dicrŏt·um -ī *n* bireme

dictamn·us -ī *f* dittany (*wild marjoram, growing in abundance on Mt. Dicte in Crete*)

dictāt·a -ōrum *n pl* lessons, rules; dictation

dictāt·or -ōris *m* dictator (*emergency magistrate in Rome with absolute authority, legally appointed for a maximum six-month term*); **chief** magistrate (*of Italic town*)

dictātōrĭ·us -a -um *adj* dictatorial

dictātr·ix -īcis *f* mistress of ceremonies

dictātūr·a -ae *f* dictatorship

Dict·ē -ēs *f* mountain in Crete where Jupiter was hidden in a cave from his father Saturn

dictĭ·ō -ōnis *f* saying, speaking, uttering; diction, style; conversation; oracular response, prediction; **dictio causae** defense of a case; **dictio testimoni** right to give testimony; **juris dictio** administration of justice; jurisdiction

dictĭt·ō -āre *vt* to keep saying, to state emphatically; **causas dictitare** to practice law; **ut dictitabat** as he used to say, as he continually alleged

dict·ō -āre *vt* to say repeatedly, reiterate; to dictate; to compose; to suggest, remind

dict·us -a -um *pp* of **dīco;** *n* saying word, statement; witticism; maxim, proverb; prediction, prophecy; order, command, instruction; promise, assurance

Dictynn·a -ae *f* Diana

dī·dō or **dis·dō -dĕre -dīdī -dĭtum** *vt* to publicize, broadcast, disseminate; to distribute, hand out

Dīd·ō -ūs (*acc:* **Dīdō**) *f* daughter of Tyrian king Belus, sister of Pygmalion, foundress and queen of Carthage, also called Elissa

dī·dūcō -dūcĕre -duxī -ductum *vt* to draw apart, part, sever, separate, split; to undo, untie; to divide, distribute; to scatter, disperse; (in mathematics) to divide; **animus diductus** (with *abl*) the mind torn between (*alternatives*)

diēcŭl·a -ae *f* little while

diērect·us -a -um *adj* (coll) finished, done for; **i dierectus** or **abi dierectus!** go to the devil!

di·ēs -ēī *m* or *f* day; time, period, space of time, interval; daylight, light of day; anniversary; daybreak; season; **dicere diem** (with *dat*) to impeach, bring an accusation against; **diem ex die** from day to day, day after day; **diem noctemque** day and night, uninterruptedly; **dies meus** my birthday; **in diem** for the moment; for a future day; **in dies** (more and more) every day; **multo denique die** not till late in the day; **postridie ejus diei** the day after that; **post tertium ejus diei** two days after that

Diespĭt·er -ris *m* Jupiter

diffām·ō -āre *vt* to divulge (*something*); to defame (*someone*)

differentĭ·a -ae *f* difference, diversity; specific difference, species

differĭt·ās -ātis *f* difference

diffĕrō differre distŭlī dīlātum *vt* to carry in different directions; to scatter, disperse; to publicize, spread around, divulge; to defer, postpone, delay; to humor; to get rid of, put off; to distract, disquiet; *vi* to differ, be different, be distinguished; (with **ab** + *abl*) to differ from

differt·us -a -um *adj* stuffed, crowded, overcrowded

diffĭcĭl·is -e *adj* difficult, hard; surly, cantankerous; hard to manage, hard to please

difficilĭter *adv* with difficulty, barely

difficult·ās -ātis *f* difficulty, hardship, trouble, distress; surliness; poverty, financial embarrassment

difficulter *adv* with difficulty, barely

diffīd·ens -entis *adj* diffident, anxious, nervous

diffīdenter *adv* without confidence, distrustfully

diffīdentĭ·a -ae *f* diffidence, mistrust, distrust

dif·fīdō -fīdĕre -fīsus sum *vi* (with *dat*) to distrust, despair of

dif·findō -findĕre -fĭdī -fissum *vt* to split, split apart, divide; (law) **diem diffindere** to cut short the business day; (fig) to detract

dif·fingō -ĕre *vt* to form differently, remodel; to alter

diffissus *pp* of **diffindo**

diffĭt·ĕor -ērī *vt* to disavow, disown

diffl·ō -āre *vi* to blow away; to disperse

difflŭ·ō -ĕre *vi* to flow in different directions, flow away; to dissolve, melt away, disappear; (with *abl*) to wallow in (*luxury, vice*)

dif·fringō -fringĕre — -fractum *vt* to shatter, break apart, smash

dif·fugĭō -fugĕre -fūgī *vi* to flee in different directions; to disperse; to disappear

diffug·ĭum -ĭī or **-ī** *n* dispersion

diffundĭt·ō -āre *vt* to pour out, scatter; to waste

dif·fundō -fundĕre -fūdī -fūsum *vt* to pour, pour out; to scatter, diffuse, spread, extend; to give vent to; to cheer up, gladden

diffūsē *adv* diffusely; fully, at length, in detail

diffūsĭl·is -e *adj* diffusive, expanding

diffūs·us -a -um *pp* of **diffundo;** *adj* spread out, spread abroad; wide; prolix; protracted

diffutūt·us -a -um *adj* exhausted by excessive sexual indulgence

Dīgentĭ·a -ae *f* small stream on Horace's Sabine farm
dī·gĕrō -gerĕre -gessī -gestum *vt* to spread about, distribute, divide; to arrange, assort, catalogue; to interpret; to digest
dīgestĭ·ō -ōnis *f* arrangement; (rhet) enumeration
dīgestus *pp* of **digero**
digitŭl·us -ī *m* little finger
digĭt·us -ī *m* finger; inch (*one sixteenth of a Roman foot*); toe; **caelum digito attingere** to reach the heights of happiness, be thrilled; **digitis concrepare** to snap the fingers; **digito uno attingere** to touch lightly, touch tenderly; **digitum intendere** (with **ad** + *acc*) to point the finger at; **digitus pollex** thumb; **in digitos arrectus** on tiptoe; **minimus digitus** little finger
digladĭ·or -ārī -ātus sum *vi* to fight hard
dignātĭ·ō -ōnis *f* esteem, respect; dignity, honor
dignē *adv* worthily, fitly
dignĭt·ās -ātis *f* worth, worthiness; dignity; authority, rank, reputation, distinction, majesty; self-respect; dignitary; political office; dignity (*of style*)
dign·ō -āre or **dign·or -ārī -ātus sum** *vt* to think worthy; (with *abl*) to think worthy of; (with double *acc*) to think (*someone*) worthy of being (*e.g., a son*)
dignosc·ō or **dīnosc·ō -ĕre** *vt* to distinguish; (with *abl*) to distinguish (*someone*) from; **dominum ac servum dignoscere** to know the difference between master and slave
dign·us -a -um *adj* worthy, deserving (*person*); fit, adequate, suitable, deserved, proper; (with *abl*) worthy of
dī·gredĭor -grĕdī -gressus sum *vi* to move apart, separate; to deviate; to digress
digressĭ·ō -ōnis *f* parting, separation; deviation; digression
digressus *pp* of **digredior**
digress·us -ūs *m* departure; digression
dījūdicātĭ·ō -ōnis *f* decision
dījūdĭc·ō -āre *vt* to decide, settle; **vera et falsa dijudicare** or **vera a falsis dijudicare** to distinguish between truth and falsehood
dījun = disjun
dī·lābor -lābī -lapsus sum *vi* to fall apart, break up; (of ice, etc.) to break up, dissolve; to disperse; to break up, decay; (of time) to slip away; (of water) to flow in different directions
dīlacĕr·ō -āre *vt* to tear to pieces
dīlāmĭn·ō -āre *vt* to split in two; **nuces dilaminare** to crack nuts
dīlanĭ·ō -āre *vt* to tear to pieces
dīlapĭd·ō -āre *vt* to demolish (*a structure of stone*); to squander
dīlapsus *pp* of **dilabor**
dīlarg·ĭor -īrī -ītus sum *vt* to hand out generously, lavish
dīlātĭ·ō -ōnis *f* postponement, delay
dīlāt·ō -āre *vt* to dilate, stretch, broaden, extend, enlarge; (fig) to amplify, spread, extend; to drawl out
dīlāt·or -ōris *m* procrastinator, slowpoke
dīlātus *pp* of **differo**
dīlaud·ō -āre *vt* to praise enthusiastically
dīlect·us -a -um *pp* of **diligo;** *adj* beloved
dīlect·us -ūs *m* selection; (mil) selective service, draft; draftees; recruitment; **dilectum habere** to conduct a draft; **legiones ex novo dilectu conficere** to bring the legions to full strength with new draftees
dīlĭg·ens -entis *adj* careful, conscientious, accurate; exacting, strict; thrifty, industrious; (with *genit*) observant of; (with **ad** + *acc* or with **in** + *abl*) careful in, careful to, conscientious about
dīligenter *adv* carefully, diligently, industriously
dīligentĭ·a -ae *f* diligence, care, industry, attentiveness, faithfulness; economy, frugality; (with *genit*) regard for
dī·ligō -ligĕre -lexī -lectum *vt* to single out; to esteem, love, value, prize; to approve, be content with, appreciate
dīlōrĭc·ō -āre *vt* to tear open
dīlūc·ĕō -ēre *vi* to be clear, be evident; (with *dat*) to be obvious to
dī·lūcescō -lūcescĕre -luxī *vi* to grow light, dawn
dīlūcĭdē *adv* clearly, distinctly, plainly
dīlūcĭd·us -a -um *adj* clear, distinct, plain, evident
dīlūcŭl·um -ī *n* daybreak, dawn
dīlūd·ĭum -ĭī or **-ī** *n* intermission
dīl·ŭō -uĕre -ŭī -ūtum *vt* to wash away, break up, separate; to dilute; to get rid of (*worries, annoyances*); to atone for; to explain, solve
dīluvĭ·ēs -ēī *f* inundation, flood, deluge
dīluvĭ·ō -āre *vt* to inundate, flood, deluge
dīluv·ĭum -ĭī or **-ī** *n* flood, deluge; (fig) destruction
dīmān·ō -āre *vi* to flow in different directions; (fig) to spread around
dīmensĭ·ō -ōnis *f* measurement
dī·mētĭor -mētīrī -mensus sum *vt* to measure out, measure off; to count off
dīmēt·ō -āre or **dīmēt·or -ārī -ātus sum** *vt* to measure out, mark out (*area*)
dīmicātĭ·ō -ōnis *f* fight, combat, struggle; contest, rivalry

dīmic·ō -āre *vi* to fight, struggle; to be in conflict, run a risk, be in peril; (with **cum** + *abl*) to fight against; **de capite dimicare** or **de vita dimicare** to fight for one's life
dīmidiāt·us -a -um *adj* half, in half
dīmidĭ·us -a -um *adj* half; broken in two, broken; **dimidius patrum, dimidius plebis** half patrician, half plebeian; *n* half; **dimidium militum quam** half as many soldiers as
dīmissĭ·ō -ōnis *f* dismissal, discharging, sending out
dī·mittō -mittĕre -mīsī -missum *vt* to send away, send around, send out, scatter, distribute; to break up, dismiss, disband; (mil) to discharge; to let loose; to divorce (*wife*); to leave, desert, abandon, give up, relinquish; to let go, let slip, forgo, forsake, renounce; to remit
dimminŭ·ō or **dīminŭ·ō -ĕre** *vt* to break to pieces, smash, shatter
dī·movĕō -movēre -mōvī -mōtum *vt* to move apart, part, separate; to disperse, dismiss, scatter; to lure away
Dindymēn·ē -ēs *f* Cybele (*also called Magna Mater by the Romans*)
Dindўm·us -ī *m* or **Dindўm·a -ōrum** *n pl* mountain in Asia Minor, sacred to Cybele
dīnoscō see **dignosco**
dīnumerātĭ·ō -ōnis *f* enumeration, counting up
dīnumĕr·ō -āre *vt* to enumerate, count up, compute; to count out, pay
diōbolār·is -e *adj* costing two obols
Diodŏt·us -ī *m* Stoic philosopher and tutor of Cicero (*d.* 59 B.C.)
dioecēs·is -is *f* district, governor's jurisdiction
dioecēt·ēs -ae *m* treasurer; secretary of revenue
Diogĕn·ēs -is *m* famous Ionic philosopher and pupil of Anaximenes (*5th cent.* B.C.); Cynic philosopher, born at Sinope, in Pontus (412?-323 B.C.)
Diomēd·ēs -is *m* son of Tydeus and king of Argos; hero at Troy
Diōn·ē -ēs or **Diōn·a -ae** *f* mother of Venus
Dionўsĭ·a -ōrum *n pl* Greek festival of Bacchus
Dionўsĭ·us -ī *m* tyrant of Syracuse (430-367 B.C.); Dionysus the Younger (397-330?)
Dionўs·us or **Dionўs·os -ī** *m* Bacchus
diōt·a -ae *f* two-handled wine jar
diplōm·a -ătis *n* official letter of recommendation
Dipўl·on -ī *n* N.W. gate at Athens
Dir·a -ae *f* a Fury; *f pl* the Furies (*goddesses of revenge and remorse*)
dir·ae -ārum *f pl* curse, execration
Dircae·us -a -um *adj* Dircean, Boeotian; **cycnus Dircaeus** Dircean or Boeotian swan (*i.e., Pindar, famous lyric poet from Boeotia,* 522?-442 B.C.)
Dirc·ē -ēs *f* famous fountain in Boeotia
dīrect·us -a -um *pp* of **dirigo;** *adj* straight, direct; straightforward
diremptus *pp* of **dirimo**
diremp̄t·us -ūs *m* separation
dīreptĭ·ō -ōnis *f* plundering, pillaging; *f pl* acts of pillage
dīrept·or -ōris *m* plunderer
dīreptus *pp* of **diripio**
dirib·ĕō -ēre — -ĭtum *vt* to sort (*votes taken out of the ballot box*)
diribitĭ·ō -ōnis *f* sorting
diribĭt·or -ōris *m* sorter (*of ballots*)
diribitōr·ium -ĭī or **-ī** *n* sorting room
dī·rĭgō -rigĕre -rexī -rectum *vt* to put in order, arrange, line up, deploy
dir·ĭmō -imĕre -ēmī -emptum *vt* to take apart, part, separate, divide; to break off, disturb, interrupt; to separate, dissolve; to put off, delay; to break off, end, bring to an end; to nullify, bring to naught
dī·ripĭō -ripĕre -ripŭī -reptum *vt* to tear apart, tear to pieces; to lay waste, pillage, plunder, ravage; to snatch away, tear away; to whip out (*sword*); to steal
dīrĭt·ās -ātis *f* mischief; misfortune; cruelty
dī·rumpō or **dis·rumpō -rumpĕre -rūpī -ruptum** *vt* to break to pieces, smash, shatter; to break off (*friendship*); to sever (*ties*); **dirumpi** to burst (*with laughter, envy, indignation, etc.*)
dīrŭ·ō -ĕre -ī -tum *vt* to pull apart, demolish, destroy, overthrow; to scatter, disperse; (mil) to break up (*enemy formation*); to bankrupt
dīr·us -a -um *adj* fearful, awful; ominous, ill-omened; dreadful, awful, abominable; cruel, relentless, fierce; **temporibus diris** in the reign of terror; **venena dira** deadly poisons
dī·s -tis *adj* rich, wealthy; rich, fertile (*land*); rich, generous, expensive (*offerings*); (with *abl*) abounding in
Dī·s -tis *m* Pluto (*king of the lower world*)
dis·cēdō -cēdĕre -cessī -cessum *vi* to go away, depart; to separate, be severed; to disperse, scatter, be dissipated, disappear; (mil) to march off, break camp; to come off (*victorious, etc.*); to deviate; to swerve; to pass away, vanish, cease; (with **ab** + *abl*) **a** to forsake (*e.g., friends*); **b** to deviate from, swerve from; **c** to abandon, give up; (with **ex** or **de** + *abl*) to go away from, depart from; (with **ad** + *acc*) to depart for; (with **in** + *acc*) to vote for; **discedere in Catonis sen-**

tentiam to vote for Cato's proposal
disceptātĭ·ō -ōnis *f* dispute, difference of opinion; discussion, debate
disceptāt·or -ōris *m* or **disceptātr·ix -īcis** *f* arbitrator
discept·ō -āre *vt* to debate, dispute, discuss, treat; to decide, settle (*controversies, wars*); *vi* to act as umpire; to be at stake
dis·cernō -cernĕre -crēvī -crētum *vt* to separate, mark off, divide; to keep apart; to distinguish between; to discern, make out, distinguish
dis·cerpō -cerpĕre -cerpsī -cerptum *vt* to tear to pieces, mangle, mutilate; (fig) to tear apart (*with words, arguments*)
discessĭ·ō -ōnis *f* separation, division; separation, divorce; (in the senate) division, formal vote; **discessio sine ulla varietate** unanimous vote
discess·us -ūs *m* separation, parting; going away, departure; banishment; marching away, marching off
discid·ĭum -ĭī or **-ī** *n* parting, separation; discord, dissension, disagreement; divorce
discīd·ō -ĕre *vt* to cut to pieces, cut up
discinct·us -a -um *pp* of **discingo;** *adj* without a girdle; dissolute, loose; effeminate, voluptuous
di·scindō -scindĕre -scĭdī -scissum *vt* to tear apart, tear open, rend, tear; **amicitias discindere** to break off ties of friendship
dis·cingō -cingĕre -cinxī -cinctum *vt* to take off, ungird; to loose; (fig) to relax
disciplīn·a -ae *f* instruction, training, teaching, education; learning, knowledge, science; discipline; custom, habit; system; **militaris disciplina** basic training; **rei publicae disciplina** statesmanship
discipŭl·us -ī *m* or **discipŭl·a -ae** *f* pupil, student; disciple, follower
discissus *pp* of **discindo**
dis·clūdō -clūdĕre -clūsī -clūsum *vt* to keep apart, divide, shut off; **iram et cupiditatem locis discludere** to assign anger and passion to their proper places
discō discĕre didĭcī *vt* to learn, learn to know, become acquainted with; to be told (*e.g., the truth*); (with *inf*) to learn how to
discobŏl·us -ī *m* discus thrower
discŏl·or -ōris *adj* of a different color; different; (with *dat*) different from
discondūc·ō -ĕre *vi* to be unprofitable
disconven·ĭō -īre *vi* to disagree; to be inconsistent
discordābil·is -e *adj* discordant, disagreeing
discordĭ·a -ae *f* discord, dissension, disagreement; mutiny
discordiōs·us -a -um *adj* prone to discord, seditious
discord·ō -āre *vi* to quarrel, disagree; (with *dat* or **ab** + *abl*) to be out of harmony with, be opposed to
discor·s -dis *adj* discordant, inharmonious; disagreeing, at variance; contradictory, inconsistent; warring (*winds, etc.*); (with *abl*) inconsistent with, at variance with, different from
discrepantĭ·a -ae *f* discrepancy, dissimilarity, difference
discrepātĭ·ō -ōnis *f* disagreement, dispute
discrepĭt·ō -āre *vi* to be completely different
discrĕp·ō -āre -ŭī *vi* to be different in sound, sound different; to be out of tune; to disagree, be different, be inconsistent, vary, differ; to be disputed; (with *dat* or *abl* or with **ab** or **cum** + *abl*) to disagree with, be different from, be inconsistent with; *v impers* there is a difference of opinion, it is undecided, it is a matter of dispute; **discrepat inter scriptores rerum** there is a difference of opinion among historians
di·scrībō -scrībĕre -scripsī -scriptum *vt* to distribute, classify, divide; to assign, apportion; (with **in** + *acc*) to distribute among, divide among
discrīm·en -ĭnis *n* dividing line; interval, intervening space, division, distance, separation; discrimination, difference, distinction; critical moment, turning point; decision, determination; crisis, jeopardy, peril, danger, risk; decisive battle
discrīmĭn·ō -āre *vt* to divide, separate; to apportion
discriptē *adv* orderly, lucidly, distinctly
discriptĭ·ō -ōnis *f* distribution, classification
discript·us -a -um *pp* of **discribo;** *adj* well arranged; secluded
discrucĭ·ō -āre *vt* to torture; to distress, torment
dis·cumbō -cumbĕre -cubŭī -cubĭtum *vi* to take their places at the table; (of several) to go to bed
discup·ĭō -ĕre *vt* (coll) to want badly; (with *inf*) (coll) to be dying to
dis·currō -currĕre -cucurrī or **-currī -cursum** *vi* to run in different directions, scamper about, run up and down, dash around
discurs·us -ūs *m* running up and down, running about; (mil) pincer movement
disc·us -ī *m* discus
dis·cutĭō -cutĕre -cussī -cussum *vt* to knock apart; to smash to pieces, shatter; to break up, disperse, scatter, dispel; to frustrate, bring to naught; to suppress, destroy
disertē or **disertim** *adv* eloquently
disert·us -a -um *adj* fluent, well-spoken; clear, articulate

disject·ō -āre *vt* to toss about
disject·us -a -um *pp* of **disjicio;** *adj* scattered; dilapidated
disject·us -ūs *m* scattering
dis·jiciō -jicĕre -jēcī -jectum vt to drive apart, scatter, break up; to tear to pieces; to ruin, destroy; to thwart, frustrate, wreck; (mil) to break up (*enemy formation*)
disjuncti·ō or **dījuncti·ō -ōnis** *f* separation, alienation; diviation, variation; dilemma; asyndeton (*succession of clauses without conjunctions*)
disjunct·us -a -um *adj* separate, distinct; distant, remote; disjointed, disconnected, incoherent (*speech*); logically opposed; *n pl* opposites
dis·jungō or **dī·jungo -jungĕre -junxī -junctum** *vt* to unyoke; to sever, divide, part, remove; to separate, part, estrange, disunite, alienate
dispālesc·ō -ĕre *vi* to be divulged, spread
dispāl·or -ārī -ātus sum *vi* to wander about, straggle
dis·pandō (or **dis·pendō**) **-pandĕre — -pansum** (or **dis·pennō -pennĕre — -pessum**) *vt* to stretch out, extend; to spread out, expand
dis·pār -păris *adj* different, unlike; unequal, ill-matched; unequal, of different lengths
disparĭl·is -e *adj* different, dissimilar
disparilĭter *adv* differently
dispăr·ō -āre *vt* to separate, segregate
dispartĭō or **dispartĭor** see **dispertio**
dispectus *pp* of **dispicio**
dis·pellō -pellĕre -pŭlī -pulsum *vt* to disperse, scatter; to drive away, dispel
dispend·ĭum -ĭī or **-ī** *n* expense, cost; loss
dispendō see **dispando**
dispennō see **dispando**
dispensātĭ·ō -ōnis *f* weighing out, doling out; management, superintendence, direction, administration; position of superintendent or treasurer
dispensāt·or -ōris *m* household manager, chief butler; cashier, treasurer
dispens·ō -āre *vt* to weigh out, pay out; to distribute, manage (*household stores*); to regulate, manage, superintend
dispercut·iō -ĕre *vt* to knock out; **cerebrum dispercutere** (with *dat*) (coll) to knock out (*someone's*) brains
disper·dō -dĕre -dĭdī -dĭtum *vt* to spoil, ruin; to squander
disper·ĕō -īre -ĭī *vi* to go to ruin; to go to waste; to be undone, perish; **disperii!** (coll) I'm finished; **dispeream si** (coll) I'll be darned if
di·spergō -spergĕre -spersī -spersum *vt* to scatter about, disperse; to splatter; to distribute, scatter (*e.g., men*) without organization; to spread, extend (*war, rumor, etc.*)
dispersē *adv* here and there; occasionally
dispersus *pp* of **dispergo**
dispert·ĭō -īre -īvī or **-ĭī -ītum** or **dispert·ĭor** or **dispart·ĭor -īrī -ītus sum** *vt* to distribute, divide; to assign (*e.g., gates, areas*) as posts to be guarded
dispessus *pp* of **dispando**
di·spiciō -spicĕre -spexī -spectum *vt* to see clearly, make out, distinguish, detect; to consider carefully, perceive, detect, discern, discover, reflect on
displic·ĕō -ēre -ŭī -ĭtum *vi* to be unpleasant, be displeasing; (with *dat*) to displease; **sibi displicere** to be dissatisfied with oneself; to be in a bad humor
dis·plōdō -plōdĕre — -plōsum *vi* to explode
dis·pōnō -pōnĕre -posŭī -posĭtum *vt* to place here and there; to distribute, arrange, set in order; to station, post, assign; to adjust, order, dispose; **diem disponere** to arrange the day's schedule
disposĭtē *adv* orderly, methodically
dispositĭ·ō -ōnis *f* orderly arrangement, development (*of theme, essay*)
dispositūr·a -ae *f* orderly arrangement
disposĭt·us -a -um *pp* of **dispono;** *adj* well arranged; methodical, orderly
disposĭt·us -ūs *m* orderly arrangement
dispŭd·et -ēre -ŭit *v impers* (with *inf*) it is a great shame to
dispulsus *pp* of **dispello**
dis·pungō -pungĕre -punxī -punctum *vt* to check, balance, audit (*an account*)
disputātĭ·ō -ōnis *f* arguing; argument, debate
disputāt·or -ōris *m* disputant, debater
dispŭt·ō -āre *vt* to dispute, discuss; (com) to estimate, compute; to examine, treat, explain
disquīr·ō -ĕre *vt* to examine in detail
disquīsītĭ·ō -ōnis *f* inquiry, investigation
disrumpō see **dirumpo**
dissaep·ĭō -ĕre -sī -tum *vt* to separate, wall off, fence off
dissaept·um -ī *n* partition, barrier
dissāvĭ·or or **dissuāvĭ·or -ārī -ātus sum** *vt* to kiss passionately
dissĕc·ō -āre -ŭī -tum *vt* to cut apart, dissect
dissēmĭn·ō -āre *vt* to disseminate
dissensĭ·ō -ōnis *f* difference of opinion, disagreement; dissension; conflict, incompatibility
dissens·us -ūs *m* dissension, discord

dissentānĕ·us -a -um *adj* disagreeing, contrary

dis·sentĭō -sentīre -sensī -sensum *vi* to differ in opinion, disagree, dissent; to differ, be in conflict, be inconsistent; (with *dat* or with **ab** or **cum** + *abl*) to differ with, disagree with; (with **ab** + *abl*) to differ from, be opposed to

disserēn·at -āre *v impers* it is clearing up

dis·sĕrō -serĕre -sēvī -sĭtum *vt* to scatter; to sow here and there; to stick in the ground at intervals

dissĕr·ō -ĕre -ŭī -tum *vt* to arrange; to examine; to discuss, argue, treat

disserp·ō -ĕre *vi* to creep about; to spread gradually

dissertĭ·ō -ōnis *f* gradual abolition, severance

dissert·ō -āre *vt* to discuss, treat

dissertus *pp* of **dissero** (to arrange)

dis·sidĕō -sidēre -sēdī -sessum *vi* to be located far apart, be distant, be remote; to disagree, be at variance; to differ, be unlike; (of a garment) to be on crooked; (with **ab** or **cum** + *abl*) to disagree with

dissignātĭ·ō -ōnis *f* arrangement

dissignāt·or -ōris *m* master of ceremonies; usher (*at the theater*); undertaker

dissign·ō -āre *vt* to regulate, arrange; to contrive

dissil·ĭō -īre -ŭī *vi* to fly apart, split, break up, burst; to be dissolved

dissimĭl·is -e *adj* dissimilar, unlike, different; (with *genit* or *dat* or with **atque** or **ac**) to be dissimilar to, different from

dissimilĭter *adv* differently

dissimilitūd·ō -ĭnis *f* difference

dissimulanter *adv* secretly, slyly

dissimulantĭ·a -ae *f* faking, hiding, dissembling

dissimulātĭ·ō -ōnis *f* concealing, disguising; Socratic irony

dissimulāt·or -ōris *m* dissembler, faker

dissimŭl·ō -āre *vt* to dissemble, conceal, disguise; to keep secret; to pretend not to see, ignore

dissipābĭl·is -e *adj* diffusible, dispersible

dissipātĭ·ō -ōnis *f* scattering, dispersal, dissipation; destruction

dissĭp·ō or **dissŭp·ō -āre** to scatter, disperse; to break up (*enemy formation*); to demolish, overthrow; to squander, dissipate; to circulate, spread; to drive away (*worries*)

dissĭt·us *pp* of **dissero** (to scatter)

dissociābĭl·is -e *adj* separating, estranging; incompatible

dissociātĭ·ō -ōnis *f* separation

dissocĭ·ō -āre *vt* to dissociate, separate; to ostracize; to set at variance, estrange; to divide into factions; to detach

dissolūbĭl·is -e *adj* dissoluble, separable

dissolūtē *adv* disconnectedly, loosely; carelessly

dissolūtĭ·ō -ōnis *f* dissolution, dissolving, breaking up; abolishing, destruction; refutation; looseness, dissoluteness; asyndeton (*succession of clauses without conjunctions*)

dissolūt·us -a -um *adj* disconnected, loose; careless, negligent, remiss; loose, licentious, dissolute; *n* asyndeton (*succession of clauses without conjunctions*)

dis·solvō -solvĕre -solvī -solūtum *vt* to dissolve, break up, loosen; to free, release; (fig) to break up; to pay; to refute; to unite; **animam dissolvere** to die; **legem dissolvere** to abrogate or annul a law; **poenam dissolvere** to pay the penalty

dissŏn·us -a -um *adj* dissonant, discordant, jarring, confused (*sounds, voices*); different; (with *abl*) differing from, different from

dissor·s -tis *adj* having a different fate; unshared

dis·suādĕō -suādēre -suāsī -suāsum *vt* to advise against, dissuade, object to, oppose

dissuāsĭ·ō -ōnis *f* dissuasion; (with *genit*) opposition to, objection to

dissuās·or -ōris *m* objector, opponent

dissuāvĭor see **dissavior**

dissult·ō -āre *vi* to fly apart, burst

dis·sŭō -suĕre — -sūtum *vt* to unstitch; to untie, undo, unfasten

dissŭpō see **dissipo**

distaed·et -ēre *v impers* it makes (*one*) tired; (with *genit*) it makes (*one*) tired of; **me distaedet loqui** I'm sick and tired of speaking

distantĭ·a -ae *f* distance, remoteness; difference, diversity

dis·tendō (or **dis·tennō**) **-tendĕre -tendī -tentum** *vt* to stretch apart, stretch out; to distend, swell; to distract, perplex

distent·us -a -um *pp* of **distendo;** *adj* distended; *pp* of **distineo;** *adj* busy, occupied, distracted

distermĭn·ō -āre *vt* to separate by a boundary, divide, limit

distĭch·on -ī *n* couplet

distinctē *adv* distinctly, clearly, with precision

distinctĭ·ō -ōnis *f* distinction, differentiation, discrimination; difference; (gram) punctuation

distinct·us -a -um *pp* of **distinguo;** *adj* distinct, separate; studded, adorned; varied, diversified; lucid (*speaker*); eminent

distinct·us -ūs *m* difference, distinction

dis·tinĕō -tinēre -tinŭī -tentum *vt* to keep apart, separate; to detain, hold back, hinder; to employ, engage, divert; to put off, delay; (mil) to keep (*troops*) from meet-

ing; to keep divided; to stand in the way of (*peace, victory, etc.*); to distract
di·stinguō -stinguĕre -stinxī -stinctum *vt* to mark off; to separate, part; to set off (*with colors, gold, etc.*); to distinguish, specify; to punctuate
dist·ō -āre *vi* to stand apart, be separate, be distant; to differ, be different; (with *dat* or **ab** + *abl*) to differ from; *v impers* there is a difference, it is important, makes a difference
dis·torquĕō -torquēre -torsī -tortum *vt* to twist, distort; to curl (*lips*); to roll (*eyes*)
distortĭ·ō -ōnis *f* twisting; contortion
distort·us -a -um *pp* of **distorqueo;** *adj* distorted, misshapen, deformed; perverse
distractĭ·ō -ōnis *f* pulling apart; dividing; discord, dissension
distract·us -a -um *adj* severed, separate
dis·trăhō -trahĕre -traxī -tractum *vt* to pull or drag apart, separate forcibly; to tear away, drag away, remove; to distract; to sever, break up; to estrange, alienate; to prevent, frustrate; to end, settle (*e.g., disputes*); to sell at retail, sell (*e.g., land*) in lots
distrib·ŭō -uĕre -ŭī -ūtum *vt* to distribute
distribūtē *adv* methodically
distribūtĭ·ō -ōnis *f* distribution, apportionment, division
district·us -a -um *adj* drawn in opposite directions; distracted, busied, engaged
di·stringō -stringĕre -strinxī -strictum *vt* to draw apart; to distract, draw the attention of
distrunc·ō -āre *vt* to cut in two, hack apart
disturbātĭ·ō -ōnis *f* destruction
disturb·ō -āre *vt* to throw into confusion; to smash up, demolish; to break up (*a marriage*); to frustrate
dītesc·ō -ĕre *vi* to grow rich
dīthyrambĭc·us -a -um *adj* dithyrambic; *m* dithyramb (*song in honor of Bacchus*)
dīthyramb·us -ī *m* dithyramb
dītĭ·ae -ārum *f pl* wealth
dīt·ō -āre *vt* to make rich, enrich; **ditari** to get rich
diū *adv* by day, in the daytime; long, for a long time; in a long time; **diu noctuque** by day and by night, continually; **iam diu** this long; **satis diu** long enough
diurn·us -a -um *adj* of the day, by day, day, daytime; daily, of each day; day's, of one day; **acta diurna** daily newspaper; **merum diurnum** daytime drinking; *n* account book; *n pl* record, journal, diary
dī·us -a -um *adj* godlike, divine, noble
diūtīnē *adv* for a long time
diūtīn·us -a -um *adj* long, lasting
diūtissimē *adv* for a very long time; longest; **iam diutissime** long, long ago
diūtius *adv* longer, still longer; **paulum diutius** a little too long
diūturnĭt·ās -ātis *f* length of time, long duration; durability
diūturn·us -a -um *adj* long, long-lasting
dīv·a -ae *f* goddess
dīvārĭc·ō -āre *vt* to stretch out, spread
dī·vellō -vellĕre -vellī -vulsum *vt* to tear apart, tear to pieces; to tear away; to untie; to wrest, remove, separate; to estrange
dī·vendō -vendĕre — -vendĭtum *vt* to sell piecemeal, retail
dīverbĕr·ō -āre *vt* to zip through, fly through
diverb·ĭum -ĭī *or* **-ī** *n* dialogue, verbal exchange
dīversē or **dīvorsē** *adv* in different directions; differently
dīversĭt·ās -ātis *f* diversity, difference; contradiction, direct opposite
dīvers·us or **dīvors·us -a -um** *pp* of **diverto;** *adj* in different directions; apart, separate; different; remote, opposite, diametrically opposed; hostile; unsettled, irresolute; dissimilar, distinct; *m pl* individuals; *n* opposite direction, different quarter, opposite side, opposite view
dī·vertō or **dī·vortō -vertĕre -vertī -versum** *vi* to go different ways; to turn off; to stop off, stay
dīv·es -ĭtis *adj* rich, wealthy; costly, precious, sumptuous; plentiful, abundant; (with *genit* or *abl*) rich in, abounding in
dīvex·ō -āre *vt* to plunder; to violate
dīvidĭ·a -ae *f* worry, trouble, nuisance; dissension, antagonism
dī·vĭdō -vidĕre -vīsī -vīsum *vt* to divide, force apart; to divide, distribute, share; to break up, destroy; to arrange, apportion; to separate, distinguish; to separate, segregate, keep apart; to accompany (*songs with music*); **sententiam dividere** to break down a proposal (*so as to vote on each part separately*)
dīvidŭ·us -a -um *adj* divisible; divided, separated
dīvīnātĭ·ō -ōnis *f* clairvoyance; forecasting, predicting, divination; (law) selection of the most suitable prosecutor
dīvīnē *adv* through divine power; prophetically, by divine inspiration; divinely, gorgeously
dīvīnĭt·ās -ātis *f* divinity, godhead; prophetic power, clairvoyance; excellence
dīvīnĭtus *adv* from heaven, from god; providentially; prophetically; divinely, in a godlike manner; excellently

dīvīn·ō -āre *vt* to divine, predict, prophesy, foresee, dread

dīvīn·us -a -um *adj* divine, heavenly; divinely inspired, prophetic; godlike, superhuman, excellent, gorgeous; **divinum jus** natural law; **divinum jus et humanum** natural and positive law; **divinum scelus** sacrilege; **rerum divinarum et humanarum scientia** physics and ethics; **rem divinam facere** to worship; to sacrifice; **res divina** worship; sacrifice; **res divinae** religious affairs, religion; *m* prophet; *n* offering; *n pl* divine matters; religious duties; **agere divina humanaque** to perform religious and secular duties; **divina humanaque** things divine and human, the whole world

dīvīsĭ·ō -ōnis *f* division, distribution

dīvīs·or -ōris *m* distributer; person hired by a candidate to distribute bribes

dīvīs·us -a -um *pp* of **divido;** *adj* separate, distinct

dīvīs·us -ūs *m* distribution; **divisui facilis** easily divided, easy to divide

dīvitĭ·ae -ārum *f pl* riches, wealth; richness (*of soil*); costly things

dīvolg- = divulg-

dīvor- = diver-

dīvortĭum -ĭī or **-ī** *n* separation; divorce; fork (*of road or river*); **divortium facere cum aliqua** to divorce some woman

dīvulgāt·us -a -um *adj* common, widespread

dīvulg·ō -āre *vt* to divulge, spread among the people; to publish (*a book*); to spread, publicize, advertise

dīvulsus *pp* of **divello**

dīv·us -a -um *adj* divine; deified; *m* god, deity; *n* sky; the open; **sub divo** out in the open, under the open sky; **sub divum rapere** to bring out in the open

dō dare dedī datum (danit = dat; danunt = dant; dane = dasne; duim = dem) *vt* to give; to offer; to offer, dedicate; to give out, pay (*money*); to bestow, confer; to permit, grant, concede, allow; to give up, hand over; to communicate, tell; to ascribe, impute, assign; to cause, produce, make; to furnish, afford, present; to grant, admit; to administer (*medicine*); to utter, give expression to, announce; **legem dare** to enact a law; **locum dare** (with *dat*) to make way for; **nomen dare** to enlist; **operam dare** to pay attention; **operam dare** (with *dat*) to pay attention to, give or devote attention to, look out for; **poenam** or **poenas dare** to pay the penalty; **se dare** to present oneself; to plunge, rush; **velum dare** to set sail; **veniam dare** to grant pardon

doc·ĕō -ēre -ŭī -tum *vt* to teach, instruct; to instruct, give instructions to; (with double *acc*) to teach (*someone something*); **fabulam docere** to teach a play (*to the actors*), produce a play, put on a play

dochm·ĭus -ĭī or **-ī** *m* dochmaic foot (*consisting of a trochee and a cretic*)

docĭl·is -e *adj* docile, easily taught, teachable; docile, tractable

docilĭt·ās -ātis *f* docility, aptitude for learning

doctē *adv* learnedly, skillfully; shrewdly, cleverly

doct·or -ōris *m* teacher

doctrīn·a -ae *f* teaching, instruction, education, training; lesson; erudition, learning; science

doct·us -a -um *pp* of **doceo;** *adj* learned, skilled, experienced, clever, trained; cunning, shrewd; (with *abl*, with **ad** + *acc*, or **in** + *abl*) skilled in, experienced in, clever at

document·um -ī or **docŭm·en -ĭnis** *n* example, model, pattern; object lesson, warning; evidence, proof

Dōdōn·a -ae *f* town in Epirus, famous for the oracular oak tree sacred to Jupiter

Dōdōnae·us -a -um *adj* of Dodona

dodr·ans -antis *m* three fourths; **heres ex dodrante** heir entitled to three fourths of the estate

dogm·a -ătis *n* doctrine, tenet

dolābr·a -ae *f* pickax, mattock

dol·ens -entis *adj* painful, smarting; distressing

dolenter *adv* painfully; with sorrow

dol·ĕō -ēre -ŭī -ĭtum *vt* to give pain to, hurt; *vi* to feel pain, be sore, ache, smart; to grieve, be sorry, be hurt; take offense; (with *dat*) to give pain to, afflict, hurt; **caput mihi dolet** I have a headache

dōlĭār·is -e *adj* fat, tubby

dōlĭŏl·um -ī *n* small barrel

dōl·ĭum -ĭī or **-ī** *n* large wine jar

dol·ō -āre *vt* to chop; to beat, beat up, drub; (fig) to hack out (*e.g., a poem*)

dol·ō or **dol·ōn -ōnis** *m* pike; string; fore topsail

Dol·ō -ōnis *m* Dolon (*Trojan spy*)

Dolŏp·es -um *m pl* a people of Thessaly

dol·or -ōris *m* pain, ache, smart; pain, grief, distress, anguish; indignation, resentment, chagrin; pathos; object of grief; **capitis dolor** headache; **dentis dolor** toothache; **esse dolori** (with *dat*) to be a cause of grief or resentment to

dolōsē *adv* shrewdly, slyly

dolōs·us -a -um *adj* wily, cunning, deceitful

dol·us -ī *m* trick, device; deceit, cunning, trickery; **dolus malus** (law) intentional deceit, willful wrong, fraud, malice

domābĭl·is -e *adj* tameable

domesticātim *adv* at home

domestĭc·us -a -um *adj* of the house or home; domestic, household;

familiar, private, personal; domestic, native, of one's own country; **bellum domesticum** civil war; *m pl* members of the household or family
domī *adv* at home
domicil·ium -iī or **-ī** *n* residence, home
domin·a or **domn·a -ae** *f* lady of the house; mistress, owner; lady; sweetheart; wife
domin·ans -antis *adj* ruling, holding sway; **nomen dominans** word in its literal sense; *m* ruler
dominātĭ·ō -ōnis *f* mastery; tyranny, despotism, absolute power; *f pl* control, supremacy; rulers
dominat·or -ōris *m* ruler, lord
dominātr·ix -īcis *f* ruler, mistress
dominat·us -ūs *m* absolute rule, sovereignty, tyranny; control, mastery
dominic·us -a -um *adj* of a lord, lord's, master's
Dominic·us -a -um *adj* (eccl) the Lord's
domin·ium -iī or **-ī** *n* absolute ownership; banquet, feast
domin·or -ārī -ātus sum *vi* to be master, be lord, have dominion; to play the master, domineer; (with **in** + *acc* or **in** + *abl*) to lord it over, tyrannize
domin·us -ī *m* owner, proprietor, possessor, master, ruler, lord; ruler, despot, tyrant; commander, chief; entertainer, host
Domin·us -ī *m* (eccl) Lord, Master
domiport·a -ae *f* snail
Domitiān·us -ī *m* T. Flavius Domitianus (*son of Vespasian, brother of Titus, and Roman emperor,* 81-96 A.D.)
domit·ō -āre *vt* to train, break in
domit·or -ōris *m* or **domitr·ix -īcis** *f* tamer
domit·us -ūs *m* taming
dom·ō -āre -uī -itum *vt* to tame, break in; to domesticate; to master, subdue, vanquish, conquer
dom·us -ūs or **-ī** (*dat*: **domuī** or **domō**; *abl*: **domō** or **domū**; *locat*: **domī** rarely **domō** or **domuī**; *genit pl:* **domuum** or **domōrum**) *f* house, building, mansion, palace; home, residence, family; native country; philosophical sect; **domi** at home; **domi militiaeque** at home and in the field, in peace and in war; **domum** homewards, home
dōnābil·is -e *adj* worthy of a gift
dōnār·ium -iī or **-ī** *n* gift repository of a temple; sanctuary; altar; votive offering
dōnātĭ·ō -ōnis *f* donation
dōnātīv·um -ī *n* (mil) bonus
dōnec *conj* while; as long as; until
dōn·ō -āre *vt* to present, bestow, grant, confer; to forgive, pardon; to give up, sacrifice; **aliquem civitate donare** to present someone with citizenship; **civitatem alicui donare** to bestow citizenship on someone
dōn·um -ī *n* gift, present; votive offering, sacrifice; **ultima dona** funeral rites, obsequies
dorc·as -ădis *f* gazelle
Dōr·ēs -um *m pl* Dorians (*one of the four Hellenic tribes*)
Dōric·us or **Dōrici·us -a -um** *adj* Dorian; Greek
Dōr·is -idis *f* daughter of Oceanus, wife of Nereus, and mother of fifty sea nymphs
dorm·iō -īre -īvī or **-iī -ītum** *vi* to sleep; to be inactive, be idle, be lazy
dormītāt·or -ōris *m* dreamer
dormit·ō -āre *vi* to be sleepy, be drowsy; to nod, fall asleep
dormītōri·us -a -um *adj* for sleeping; **cubiculum dormitorium** bedroom
dors·um -ī *n* back; ridge; reef
dōs dōtis *f* dowry
Dossenn·us -ī *m* hunchback, clown (*well-known character in early Italic comedy*)
dōtāl·is -ē *adj* of a dowry, given as a dowry, dotal
dōt·ō -āre *vt* to endow
drachm·a or **drachum·a -ae** *f* drachma (*Greek coin approximately the value of a denarius*)
drac·ō -ōnis *m* dragon; huge serpent
Drac·ō -ōnis *m* Dragon (*constellation*); Draco (*Athenian lawgiver, notorious for his severity, c.* 621 B.C.)
dracōnigen·us -a -um *adj* sprung from a dragon; **urbs draconigena** Thebes
drāpet·a -ae *m* runaway slave
drom·as -ădis *m* dromedary, camel
drom·os -ī *m* Spartan racetrack
Druid·ēs -um or **Druid·ae -ārum** *m pl* Druids (*priests and sages of the Gauls and Britons*)
Drūsill·a -ae *f* Livia Drusilla (*second wife of Augustus and mother of Tiberius,* 63 B.C.-29 A.D.)
Drūs·us -ī *m* Livius Drusus (*tribune of the people with C. Gracchus in* 122 B.C.); M. Livius Drusus (*former's son, famous orator and tribune of the people in* 91 B.C.); Nero Claudius Drusus (*son of Livia, brother of Tiberius,* 38-9 B.C.)
Dry·ad -ădis *f* dryad (*wood nymph*)
Dryŏp·es -um *m pl* people of Epirus
dubiē *adv* doubtfully; **haud dubie** undoubtedly, indubitably
dubitābil·is -e *adj* doubtful
dubitanter *adv* doubtingly, hesitantly
dubitātĭ·ō -ōnis *f* doubt, uncertainty; wavering, hesitancy, irresolution; hesitation, delay; (rhet) pretended embarrassment (*to win over the sympathy of the audience*)
dubit·ō -āre *vt* to doubt; to consider, ponder; *vi* to be doubtful, be in doubt, be uncertain, be perplexed;

to deliberate; to waver, hesitate, delay

dubĭ·us -a -um *adj* wavering, doubtful, dubious, uncertain, irresolute; dubious, undermined; precarious, critical, adverse, difficult; dim (*light*); overcast (*sky*); indecisive (*battle*); *n* doubt, question; **haud pro dubio habere** to regard as beyond doubt; **in dubium venire** to come in question; **in dubium vocare** to call in question; **procul dubio** beyond doubt, undoubtedly

ducēnārĭ·us -a -um *adj* receiving a salary of 200,000 sesterces

ducēn·ī -ae -a *adj* two hundred each

ducentēsĭm·a -ae *f* half percent

ducent·ī -ae -a *adj* two hundred

ducentĭens or **ducentĭēs** *adv* two hundred times

dūcō dūcĕre duxī ductum *vt* to lead, guide, direct, conduct; to lead, command; to lead, march; to draw, pull, haul; to draw out, protract, prolong; to put off, stall (*someone*); to pass, spend (*time*); to pull at (*oars*); to mislead, take in, fool, trick; to draw, attract; to draw (*lots*); to draw in, breathe in, inhale; to suck in, drink; to draw, trace; to construct, form, fashion, shape; to run (*a wall from one point to another*); to assume, get (*name*); to lead home, marry (*a woman*); to calculate, compute; to regard, consider, hold, account; to derive, trace (*lineage*); to spin (*wool*); (of a road) to lead, take (*someone*)

ductim *adv* in a continuous stream

ductĭt·ō -āre *vt* to take home, marry (*a woman*); to lead on, trick, deceive, cheat

duct·ō -āre *vt* to lead; to draw; to accompany, escort

duct·or -ōris *m* leader, commander, general; guide, pilot

duct·us -ūs *m* drawing, conducting; line, row; leadership, command; **oris ductus** facial expression

dūdum *adv* a short time ago, a little while ago; just now; once, formerly; **cum dudum** just as; **haud dudum** not long ago, just now; **jam dudum** for some time; **jam dudum eum exspecto** I have been expecting him; **quam dudum** how long; **ut dudum** just as

Duill·ĭus or **Duīl·ĭus -ĭī** or **-ī** *m* Roman consul who won Rome's first naval engagement against the Carthaginians off Sicily in 260 B.C.

duim see **do**

dulcēd·ō -ĭnis *f* sweetness; pleasantness, charm, delightfulness

dulc·escō -escĕre -ŭī *vi* to become sweet

dulcicŭl·us -a -um *adj* rather sweet

dulcĭf·er -ĕra -ĕrum *adj* full of sweetness, sweet

dulc·is -e *adj* pleasant, charming, delightful; dear, friendly, kind; sweet

dulcĭter *adv* agreeably, pleasantly, sweetly

dulcitūd·ō -ĭnis *f* sweetness

dūlĭcē *adv* like a slave

Dūlich·ĭum -ĭī or **-ī** *n* or **Dūlichĭ·a -ae** *f* island in the Ionian Sea, belonging to the realm of Ulysses

dum *adv* up to now, yet, as yet; now; **age dum!** or **agite dum!** come now!; all right!; **nemo dum** no one yet, no one as yet; **non dum** not yet, not as yet

dum *conj* while, during the time in which; as long as; until; provided that, if only; **dum modo** or **dummodo** provided that, if only; **exspectabam dum rediret** I was waiting for him to return

dūmēt·um -ī *n* thicket, underbrush

dummŏdo *conj* provided that, if only

dūmōs·us -a -um *adj* overgrown with bushes, bushy

dumtaxat *adv* strictly speaking, at least; only, simply, merely

dūm·us -ī *m* bush, bramble

du·o -ae -o *adj* two

duodecĭens or **duodecĭēs** *adv* twelve times

duodĕcim (indecl) *adj* twelve

duodecĭm·us -a -um *adj* twelfth

duodēn·ī -ae -a *adj* twelve each, twelve apiece, twelve; a dozen; **duodenis assibus** at twelve percent

duodēquadrāgēsĭm·us -a -um *adj* thirty-eighth

duodēquadrāgintā (indecl) *adj* thirty-eight

duodēquinquāgēsĭm·us -a -um *adj* forty-eighth

duodētrīcĭens or **duodētrīcĭēs** *adv* twenty-eight times

duodētrīgintā (indecl) *adj* twenty-eight

duodēvīcēn·ī -ae -a *adj* eighteen each

duodēvīgintī (indecl) *adj* eighteen

duoetvīcēsimān·ī -ōrum *n pl* soldiers of the twenty-second legion

duoetvīcēsĭm·us -a -um *adj* twenty-second

duovĭrī see **duumviri**

dupl·a -ae *f* double the price

dupl·ex -ĭcis *adj* twofold, double; divided into two; in double rows; double, twice as big, twice as long; complex, compound; two-faced, double-dealing, false

duplicār·ius -ĭī or **-ī** *m* soldier receiving double pay

duplicĭter *adv* doubly, on two accounts

duplĭc·ō -āre *vt* to double; to bend double; to enlarge, lengthen, increase

dupl·us -a -um *adj* double, twice as much, twice as large; *n* double price; **in duplum** twice the amount, double; **in duplum ire** to pay twice as much, pay double

dupond·ius -iī or **-ī** *m* or **dupond·ium -iī** or **-ī** *n* two-ace coin, worth about five cents
dūrābil·is -e *adj* durable, lasting
dūrām·en -inis *n* hardness
dūratē·us -a -um *adj* wooden
dūrē or **dūriter** *adv* hard, sternly, rigorously, roughly; stiffly, awkwardly
dūr·escō -escĕre -ŭī *vi* to grow hard, harden
dūrit·ās -ātis *f* hardness, toughness, harshness
dūriter see **dure**
dūriti·a -ae or **dūriti·ēs -ēī** *f* hardness; austerity; strictness, harshness, rigor; oppressiveness; insensibility, callousness
dūriuscŭl·us -a -um *adj* somewhat hard, rather harsh
dūr·ō -āre *vt* to make hard, harden, solidify; (fig) to harden, inure, toughen up; to make insensible, to dull, blunt; to bear, endure; *vi* to be inured, be tough; to endure, last, remain, continue, hold out; (of hills) to continue unbroken, extend
dūr·us -a -um *adj* hard; lasting; rough (*to the senses*); tough, hardy, hale; rough, rude, uncouth; shameless, brazen; harsh, cruel, callous, insensible; severe, oppressive; parsimonious, miserly
duum·vir -virī *m* member of a commission or board of two
duumvirāt·us -ūs *m* duumvirate, office of a duumvir
duumvir·ī -ōrum or **duovir·ī -ōrum** *m pl* two-man commission; **duumviri ad aedem faciendam** two-man commission for the construction of a temple; **duumviri juri dicundo** two-man board of colonial magistrates; pair of judges; **duumviri navales** two-man commission to equip the navy; **duumviri perduellionis** criminal court; **duumviri sacrorum** two-man commission in charge of the Sibylline books
dux ducis *m* or *f* conductor, guide; leader, head, author, ringleader; general
Dym·ās -antis *m* father of Hecuba, the queen of Troy
dynăm·is -is *f* store, plenty
dynast·ēs -ae *m* ruler, prince, petty monarch
Dyrrach·ium -iī or **-ī** *n* Adriatic port in Illyria which served as landing place for those who sailed from Italy

E

ē see **ex**
eā *adv* there, that way
ea ejus *f pron* she
eādem *adv* by the same way, the same way; at the same time; likewise, by the same token
eāpropter *adv* therefore
eapse see **ipse**
eātĕnus *adv* to such a degree, so far
ebĕnus see **hebenus**
ēbĭb·ō -ĕre -ī *vt* to drink up, drain; to absorb; to spend in drinks, squander
ēbland·ior -īrī -ītus sum *vt* to coax out, obtain by flattery
Eborăc·um or **Eburāc·um -ī** *n* town of the Brigantes in Britain, York
ēbriĕt·ās -ātis *f* drunkenness
ēbriŏl·us -a -um *adj* tipsy
ēbriōsit·ās -ātis *f* habitual drunkenness, heavy drinking
ēbriōs·us -a -um *adj* & *m* drunk
ēbri·us -a -um *adj* drunk; drunken (*acts, words*), of a drunk; (fig) intoxicated (*e.g., with love, power*)
ēbull·iō -īre *vt* to brag about; *vi* to bubble up, boil over
ebŭl·um -ī *n* or **ebŭl·us -ī** *m* danewort, dwarf elder
eb·ur -ŏris *n* ivory; ivory objects; statue, flute, scabbard; elephant
eburāt·us -a -um *adj* inlaid with ivory
eburneŏl·us -a -um *adj* ivory
eburnĕ·us or **eburn·us -a -um** *adj* ivory; white as ivory; **ensis eburneus** sword with ivory hilt; **dentes eburnei** tusks (*of elephant*)
ēcastor *interj* by Castor!
ecca see **ecce**
eccam see **ecce**
ecce *interj* see!, look!, look here!, here!; **ecce me** here I am; (colloquially combined with the pronouns **is, ille,** and **iste**): **ecca** (i.e., **ecce** + **ea**) or **eccam** (i.e., **ecce** + **eam**) here she is; **eccilla** or **eccistam** there she is; **eccillum** or **eccum** here he is; **eccos** here they are
eccĕrē *interj* there!
eccheum·a -ătis *n* pouring out
ecclēsi·a -ae *f* Greek assembly of people; (eccl) church, congregation
ecdĭc·us -ī *m* legal representative of a community
ecf- = **eff-**
echidn·a -ae *f* viper
Echidn·a -ae *f* hydra; **Echidna Lernaea** Lernaean hydra; monstrous mother of Cerberus, half woman and half serpent
Echīnăd·es -um *f pl* cluster of small islands off Acarnania
echīn·us -ī *m* sea urchin; dishpan
Echī·ōn -ŏnis *m* hero who sprang from the dragon's teeth sown by

Cadmus, married Agave, and became father of Pentheus

Ēch·ō -ūs *f* nymph who was changed by Hera into an echo

eclŏg·a -ae *f* literary selection; eclogue

eclogāri·ī -ōrum *m pl* excerpted literary passages

ecquandō *adv* ever, at any time; (in indirect questions) whether ever

ecquī *conj* whether

ecqu·ī -ae or **-od** *adj* any

ec·quid -cūjus *pron* anything; (in indirect questions) whether, if at all

ec·quis -cūjus *pron* any, anyone; (in indirect questions) whether anyone

ecquō *adv* anywhere

eculē·us -ī *m* foal, colt; small equestrian statue; wooden torture rack

edācit·ās -ātis *f* gluttony

ed·ax -ācis *adj* gluttonous; (fig) devouring, destructive

ēdent·ō -āre *vt* to knock the teeth out of

ēdentŭl·us -a -um *adj* toothless, old

edĕpol *interj* by Pollux!, gad!

edĕra see **hedera**

ē·dīcō -dīcĕre -dixī -dictum *vt* to proclaim, announce, decree, ordain, appoint

ēdictī·ō -ōnis *f* edict, order

ēdict·ō -āre *vt* to proclaim, publish

ēdict·um -ī *n* decree, edict, proclamation; edict of a praetor listing rules he would follow in his capacity as judge; order, command

ē·discō -discĕre -didĭcī *vt* to learn by heart, learn thoroughly

ēdissĕr·ō -ĕre -ŭī -tum *vt* to explain in detail, analyze fully

ēdissert·ō -āre *vt* to explain fully, explain in all details

ēditīcī·us -a -um *adj* set forth, proposed; **judices editicii** panel of jurors (*subject to challenge by the defendant*)

ēditī·ō -ōnis *f* statement, account, published statement; publishing, publication; edition (*of a book*); (law) declaration (*of the form of judicial procedure to be followed*)

ēdĭt·us -a -um *adj* high; (with *abl*) descended from; *n* height; command, order

e·dō -dĕre -dĭdī -dĭtum *vt* to give out, put forth, bring forth, emit; to give birth to, bear; to publish; to tell, announce, declare, disclose; to show, display, produce, perform; to bring about, cause; to promulgate

edō edĕre (or **esse**) **ēdī ēsum** *vt* to eat; (fig) to devour, consume, destroy; **pugnos edere** to eat fists, to get a good beating

ēdoc·ĕō -ēre -ŭī -tum *vt* to teach thoroughly; to instruct clearly; to inform; to show clearly; (with double *acc*) to teach (*someone something*) well

ēdŏl·ō -āre *vt* to chop out, hack out; to finish, prepare

ēdŏm·ō -āre -ŭī -ĭtum *vt* to conquer, subdue

Ēdōn·ī -ōrum *m pl* Thracian tribe noted for its heavy drinking

Ēdōn·is -ĭdis *adj* Edonian; *f* bacchante

ēdorm·iō -īre -īvī or **iī** *vt* to sleep off; **crapulam edormire** to sleep off a hangover; *vi* to sleep soundly

ēdormisc·ō -ĕre *vt* to sleep off; **crapulam edormiscere** to sleep off a hangover

ēducātī·ō -ōnis *f* rearing; education

ēducāt·or -ōris *m* foster father; tutor, instructor

ēducātr·ix -īcis *f* nurse

ēdŭc·ō -āre *vt* to bring up; to train, educate, develop; to produce

ē·dūcō -dūcĕre -duxī -ductum *vt* to draw out; to take away; to draw (*sword*); to draw out, spend (*time*); to lead out, march out (*army*); to summon (*to court*); to hatch; to rear, bring up, educate, train; to raise, erect

edūl·is -e *adj* edible

ēdūr·ō -āre *vi* to last, continue

ēdūr·us -a -um *adj* hard, tough; (fig) tough

Ēētī·ōn -ōnis *m* father of Andromache and king of Thebe in Cilicia

effarcīō see **effercio**

effāt·us -a -um *pp* of **effor;** *adj* solemnly pronounced; solemnly dedicated; *n* axiom; prediction

effectī·ō -ōnis *f* accomplishment, performing; efficient cause

effectīv·us -a -um *adj* producing, practical

effect·or -ōris *m* or **effectr·ix -īcis** *f* producer, author

effect·us -a -um *pp* of **efficio**; *adj* finished, complete; *n* effect

effect·us -ūs *m* effecting, completion; operation; effect, result, consequence

effēminātē *adv* effeminately, like a woman

effēmināt·us -a -um *adj* effeminate

effēmĭn·ō -āre *vt* to make a woman of; to represent as a woman; to effeminate, enervate

efferāt·us -a -um *adj* wild, brutal, savage

ef·fercīō or **ec·fercīō** or **ef·farcīō -fercīre — -fertum** *vt* to stuff; to fill in (*e.g., a ditch*)

efferit·ās -ātis *f* wildness, barbarism

effĕr·ō -āre *vt* to make wild, brutalize; to exasperate

effĕrō or **ecfĕrō efferre extŭlī ēlātum** *vt* to carry out, bring out, bring forth; to utter, express; to publish, spread (*news*); to carry out for burial, bury; to produce, bear; to name, designate; to lift up, raise; to promote, advance; to bring out, expose; to praise, extol; to sweep off one's feet; **efferri** (fig) to be

carried away; **se efferre** to be haughty, be proud, be conceited
effert·us -a -um *pp* of **effercio;** *adj* full, crammed, bulging
effĕr·us -a -um *adj* wild, fierce, savage
ef·fervescō -fervescĕre -fervī *vi* to boil, boil over; to burst forth
efferv·ō -ĕre *vi* to boil over; (of bees) to swarm out; (of volcano) to erupt
effēt·us -a -um *adj* effete, spent; vain, delusive; (with *genit*) incapable of
efficācĭt·ās -ātis *f* efficiency
efficācĭter *adv* efficiently, effectively
effĭc·ax -ācis *adj* efficient, effective, efficacious
efficĭ·ens -entis *adj* efficient, effective; **res efficientes** causes
efficienter *adv* efficiently
efficientĭ·a -ae *f* efficiency, efficacy, influence
ef·ficĭō -ficĕre -fēcī -fectum *vt* to bring about, bring to pass, effect, cause, produce; to make, form; to finish, complete, accomplish; (of a field) to yield, produce; (of numbers) to amount to; to prove, show; **ita efficitur ut** thus it follows that
effictus *pp* of **effingo**
effigĭ·ēs -ēī or **effigĭ·a -ae** *f* effigy, likeness, semblance; opposite number; copy, imitation; image; statue, figure, portrait; ghost, phantom
ef·fingō -fingĕre -finxī -fictum *vt* to mold, form, fashion; to imitate; to wipe out, wipe clean; to represent, portray; to imagine
effīō passive of **efficio**
efflāgitātĭ·ō -ōnis *f* urgent demand
efflāgitāt·us -ūs *m* urgent request; **efflagitatu meo** at my insistence
efflāgĭt·ō -āre *vt* to demand, insist upon
efflictim *adv* (to love, desire) desperately
efflict·ō -āre *vt* to strike dead
ef·flīgō or **ecf·flīgō -flīgĕre -flixī -flictum** *vt* to strike dead, exterminate
effl·ō or **ecfl·ō -āre** *vt* to breathe out; **animam efflare** to expire
efflōr·esco -escĕre -ŭī *vi* to bloom, blossom, flourish
efflŭ·ō or **ecflŭ·ō -ĕre -xī** *vi* to flow out, flow forth, run out; to slip away, drop out, disappear; (of a rumor) to get out, circulate; **ex pectore effluere** to be forgotten
effluv·ĭum -ĭī or **-ī** *n* outlet; **effluvium lacūs** outlet of a lake
ef·fodĭō or **ecf·fodĭō -fodĕre -fōdī -fossum** *vt* to dig up; to gouge out (*eyes*); to root out, gut; to excavate
ef·for or **ec·for -fārī -fātus sum** *vt* to speak out, say out loud, tell; (in augury) to mark off, consecrate (*area*); *vi* to state a proposition
effossus *pp* of **effodio**
effrēnātē *adv* without restraint, out of control
effrēnātĭ·ō -ōnis *f* impetuosity
effrēnāt·us -a -um *adj* unbridled; (fig) unbridled, unrestrained
ef·fringō or **ec·fringō -fringĕre -frēgī -fractum** *vt* to break open, smash, break off; to break in (*door*)
ef·fugĭō -fugĕre -fūgī *vt* to escape; to escape the notice of; *vi* to escape; (with *abl* or with **ab** or **ex** + *abl*) to escape from
effug·ĭum -ĭī or **-ī** *n* escape, flight; means of escape; avoidance
ef·fulgĕō -fulgēre -fulsī *vi* to shine forth, gleam, glitter
effult·us -a -um *adj* propped up, supported
ef·fundō or **ec·fundō -fundĕre -fūdī -fūsum** *vt* to pour out, pour forth; to fling (*weapon*); to give up, let go, abandon, resign; to throw down; to produce in abundance; to lavish, waste, squander, run through; to empty out (*bags, etc.*); to given vent to, pour out; **effundi** or **se effundere** to pour out, rush out; to yield, indulge
effūsē *adv* far and wide; at random, in disorder; lavishly; immoderately
effūsĭ·ō -ōnis *f* outpouring, rushing out; shedding; effusion; profusion, lavishness, extravagance; *f pl* excesses
effūs·us -a -um *pp* of **effundo;** *adj* spread out, extensive, broad, wide; relaxed, loose; disheveled; lavish; straggly, disorderly; lavish; loose, dissolute
effūt·ĭō -īre — -ītum *vt & vi* to blab, babble, chatter
ef·futŭō or **ec·futŭō -futuĕre -futŭī -futūtum** *vt* to exhaust through excesses
ēgelĭd·us -a -um *adj* chilly, cool; lukewarm
eg·ens -entis *adj* needy, poor; (with *genit*) in need of
egēn·us -a -um *adj* needy, destitute; (with *genit* or *abl*) in need of
eg·ĕō -ēre -ŭī *vi* to be needy, suffer want; (with *genit* or *abl*) **a** to be in need of; **b** to lack, be without; **c** to want, desire, miss
Ēgerĭ·a -ae *f* nymph whom King Numa visited at night for advice
ē·gĕrō -gerĕre -gessī -gestum *vt* to carry out, take away, remove; to discharge, vomit, emit
egest·ās -ātis *f* need, want, poverty; (with *genit*) lack of
ēgestĭ·ō -ōnis *f* squandering
ēgestus *pp* of **egero**
ego *pron* I
egŏmet *pron* I personally, I and nobody else
ē·gredĭor -grĕdī -gressus sum *vt* to go beyond, pass; to quit; (fig) to go beyond, surpass; *vi* to go out, come out; to march out; to set sail, put out to sea; to disembark, land; to go up, climb; to digress
ēgregĭē *adv* exceptionally, singularly, uncommonly, splendidly

ēgregĭ·us -a -um *adj* exceptional, singular, uncommon; distinguished, illustrious; *n* honor, distinction
ēgressus *pp* of **egredior**
ēgress·us -ūs *m* departure; way out, exit; disembarking, landing; mouth (*of river*); digression; *m pl* comings and goings
ēgurgĭt·ō -āre *vt* to pour out, lavish
ehem *interj* (expressing pleasant surprise) ha!, aha!
eheu *interj* (expressing pain) oh!
eho *interj* (expressing rebuke) look here!, see here!; **eho dum!** look here now!
ei *interj* (expressing fear or dismay) golly!
ēĭa or **hēĭa** *interj* (expressing joy or surpise) ah!, ah ha!; good!; (expressing haste) quick!, come on!
ējacŭl·or -ārī -ātus sum *vt* to squirt (*e.g., water*); **se ejaculari** to squirt
ējectāment·a -ōrum *n pl* refuse; jetsam
ējectĭ·ō -ōnis *f* ejection; banishment, exile
ēject·ō -āre *vt* to spout forth; to keep throwing up (*e.g., blood*)
eject·us -ūs *m* emission
ējĕr·ō or **ējūr·ō -āre** *vt* to refuse upon oath, abjure, forswear; to deny on oath; to resign, abdicate; to disown, abandon
ē·jicĭō -jicĕre -jēcī -jectum *vt* to throw out, drive out, put out, eject, expel; to banish, drive into exile; to utter; to run aground; to reject, disapprove; to boo (*someone*) off the stage; **ejici** to be stranded; **se ejicere** (of passions) to break out, come to the fore
ējulātĭ·ō -ōnis *f* wailing, lamenting
ējŭl·ō -āre *vi* to wail, lament
ējūrō see **ejero**
ē·lābor -lābī -lapsus sum *vi* to glide off; to slip away, escape; to pass away, disappear; (with *abl* or with **super** + *acc*) to glance off
ēlabōrāt·us -a -um *adj* studied, overdone; elaborate, finished
ēlabōr·ō -āre *vt* to work out, elaborate; to produce; *vi* to make a great effort, take great pains; (with *inf*) to strive to
ēlāmentābĭl·is -e *adj* pathetic
ēlangu·escō -escĕre -ī *vi* to slow down, slacken, let up
ēlapsus *pp* of **elabor**
ēlātē *adv* proudly
ēlātĭ·ō -ōnis *f* elation, ecstasy
ēlātr·ō -āre *vt* to bark out
ēlāt·us -a -um *pp* of **effero;** *adj* high, elevated; exalted; haughty, proud
ē·lăvō -lavāre -lāvī -lautum or **-lōtum** *vt* to wash out; (coll) to clean out, rob
Elĕ·a -ae *f* town in Lucania in S. Italy, birthplace of Eleatic philosophy
Eleātĭc·ī -ōrum *m pl* Eleatics, Eleatic philosophers
ēlecĕbr·a -ae *f* snare; seductress
ēlectē *adv* tastefully
ēlectĭl·is -e *adj* choice, dainty
ēlectĭ·ō -ōnis *f* choice; *f pl* selection
ēlect·ō -āre *vt* to select, choose; to wheedle out, coax out (*a secret*)
Ēlectr·a -ae *f* Pleiad, daughter of Atlas and Pleione and the mother of Dardanus by Jupiter; daughter of Agamemnon and Clytemnestra
ēlectr·um -ī *n* amber; electrum (*alloy of gold and silver*); *f pl* amber beads
ēlect·us -a -um *pp* of **eligo;** *adj* select, picked, choice; (mil) elite
ēlect·us -ūs *m* choice
ēlĕg·ans -antis *adj* fine, elegant, refined; choosy; fine, choice, select
ēleganter *adv* tastefully, neatly, elegantly
ēlegantĭ·a -ae *f* elegance, refinement, taste, propriety
elĕg·ī -ōrum *m pl* elegiac verses
elegī·a or **elegē·a -ae** *f* elegy
Elĕl·ĕus -ĕī *m* (epithet of) Bacchus
elementārĭ·us -a -um *adj* elementary; **senex elementarius** old schoolteacher
element·um -ī *n* first principle, element; *n pl* elements, rudiments; beginnings; ABC's
elench·us -ī *m* pearl
elephantomăch·a -ae *m* fighter mounted on an elephant
elephant·us -ī or **elĕph·ās -antis** *m* elephant; (fig) ivory
Eleus·īn -īnis *f* Eleusis (*sacred city in Attica, famous for its cult of Demeter*)
Eleusīn·us -a -um *adj* Eleusinian; **Eleusina mater** Ceres
ēlĕv·ō -āre *vt* to lift up, raise; to alleviate; to lessen, diminish; to make light of, disparage
ē·licĭō -licĕre -licŭī -licĭtum *vt* to elicit, draw out; to lure out, entice; to conjure up
Ēlic·ĭus -ĭī or **-ī** *m* (epithet of) Jupiter
ē·līdō -līdĕre -līsī -līsum *vt* to knock out, strike out, tear out, force out; to shatter, smash to pieces, crush; to force out, stamp out; (fig) to stamp out
ē·lĭgō -ligĕre -lēgī -lectum *vt* to pluck out; to pick out, choose
ēlīmĭn·ō -āre *vt* to carry outside; to spread abroad
ēlīm·ō -āre *vt* to file; to finish off, perfect
ēlingu·is -e *adj* without tongue, speechless; (fig) inarticulate
ēlingu·ō -āre *vt* (coll) to tear out the tongue of
Ēl·is or **Āl·is -ĭdis** *f* district and town on the W. coast of the Peloponnesus in which Olympia is located
Eliss·a or **Elīs·a -ae** *f* Dido
ēlīsus *pp* of **elido**

ēlix·us -a -um *adj* wet through and through, soaked
ellam = ecce + illam
elleborōs·us -a -um *adj* crazy
ellebŏr·us or **hellebŏr·us -ī** *m* or **ellebŏr·um -ī** *n* hellebore (*plant used for mental illness*)
ellips·is -is *f* ellipsis
ellum = ecce + illum
ēlŏc·ō -āre *vt* to lease out, rent out
ēlocūtĭ·ō -ōnis *f* style of speaking, delivery
ēlog·ĭum -ĭī or **-ī** *n* saying, maxim; inscription, epitaph; clause (*in a will*)
ēlŏqu·ens -entis *adj* eloquent
ēloquenter *adv* eloquently
ēloquentĭ·a -ae *f* eloquence
ēloqu·ĭum -ĭī or **-ī** *n* eloquence
ē·lŏquor -lŏquī -locūtus sum *vt* to speak out, declare; *vi* to give a speech
ēlōtus *pp* of **elavo**
ē·lūcĕō -lūcēre -luxī *vi* to shine forth; to glitter
ēluct·or -ārī -ātus sum *vt* to struggle out of, struggle through (*e.g., deep snow*); to surmount; *vi* to force a way out
ēlūcŭbr·ō -āre or **ēlūcŭbr·or -ārī -ātus sum** *vt* to compose by lamp light
ē·lūdō -lūdĕre -lūsī -lūsum *vt* to elude, parry, avoid; to escape, shun; to delude, deceive; to make fun of; to get the better of, outmaneuver; *vi* to end the game
ē·lūgĕō -lūgēre -luxī *vt* to mourn for; to cease to mourn
ēlumb·is -e *adj* loinless; bland (*style*)
ē·lŭō -luĕre -lŭī -lūtum *vt* to wash off, wash clean; to wash away; (fig) to wash away, remove, get rid of
ēlūsus *pp* of **eludo**
ēlūt·us -a -um *pp* of **eluo;** *adj* washed out, watery, insipid
ēluvĭ·ēs -ēī *f* inundation, overflow; sewage
ēluvĭ·ō -ōnis *f* deluge
Ēlys·ĭum -ĭī or **-ī** *n* realm of the blessed in the lower world
em *interj* (expressing wonder or emphasis) there!
emācĭt·ās -ātis *f* fondness for shopping
ēmancipātĭ·ō or **ēmancupātĭ·ō -ōnis** *f* emancipation; transfer of property
ēmancipāt·us -a -um *adj* made over, sold
ēmancĭp·ō or **ēmancŭp·ō -āre** *vt* to transfer; to declare (*a son*) free and independent, emancipate; to surrender, abandon
ēmān·ō -āre *vi* to flow out; to trickle out, leak out; to become known
Ēmathĭ·a -ae *f* Macedonia
Ēmăth·is -ĭdis *adj* Macedonian; *f pl* the Pierides (*daughters of the Macedonian king Pierus*)
ēmātūr·escō -escĕre -ŭī *vi* to begin to ripen; to soften; (fig) to soften
em·ax -ācis *adj* fond of shopping
emblēm·a -ătis *n* mosaic, inlaid wood
embol·ĭum -ĭī or **-ī** *n* interlude
ēmendābĭl·is -e *adj* capable of correction
ēmendātē *adv* faultlessly
ēmendātĭ·ō -ōnis *f* emendation, correction
ēmendāt·or -ōris *m* or **ēmendātr·ix -īcis** *f* corrector
ēmendāt·us -a -um *adj* faultless
ēmendīc·ō -āre *vt* to obtain by begging
ēmend·ō -āre *vt* to emend, correct; to reform, improve, revise; to atone for
ēmensus *pp* of **emetior**
ēment·ĭor -īrī -ītus sum *vt* to falsify, fabricate, feign; *vi* to tell a lie
ēmerc·or -ārī -ātus sum *vt* to buy up; to bribe
ēmer·ĕō -ēre or **ēmer·ĕor -ērī -ĭtus sum** *vt* to merit fully; to lay under obligation; (mil) to serve out (*term of service*); **aliquem emerere** to do someone a favor or favors
ē·mergō -mergĕre -mersī -mersum *vt* to raise (*from the water*); **emergi** or **se emergere** to raise oneself up, rise; *vi* to emerge; to rise (*in power*); to extricate oneself; (with **ex** + *abl*) to get clear of
ēmerĭt·us -a -um *pp* of **emereor;** *adj* worn out, unfit for service; *m* veteran
ēmersus *pp* of **emergo**
emetĭc·a -ae *f* emetic
ē·mētĭor -mētīrī -mensus sum *vt* to measure out; to traverse, travel over; to live through; to impart, bestow
ēmĕt·ō -ĕre *vt* to mow down
ēmĭc·ō -āre -ŭī -ātum *vi* to dart out, shoot out, dash out; to flash out; (fig) to shine, be prominent
ēmĭgr·ō -āre *vi* to move out, depart; **e vita migrare** to pass on, die
ēmĭn·ens -entis *adj* projecting out, prominent, high; eminent
ēminentĭ·a -ae *f* projection, prominence; (in painting) highlights
ēmin·ĕō -ēre -ŭī *vi* to stand out, project; to be conspicuous, stand out; (in painting) to be highlighted
ēmĭn·or -ārī -ātus sum *vt* to threaten
ēmĭnus *adv* out of range, at a distance; from afar
ēmīr·or -ārī -ātus sum *vt* to be greatly surprised at, stand aghast at
ēmissār·ĭum -ĭī or **-ī** *n* drain, outlet
ēmissār·ĭus -ĭī or **-ī** *m* scout, spy
ēmissīcĭ·us -a -um *adj* prying, spying
ēmissĭ·ō -ōnis *f* discharge, hurling, shooting; releasing, letting off
ēmĭssus *pp* of **emitto**
ēmiss·us -ūs *m* emission
ē·mittō -mittĕre -mīsī -missum *vt* to sound out; to hurl, discharge,

shoot; to let go, let slip, let loose, drop, release, let out; to send out, publish; to allow to escape; to emancipate, set at liberty; to utter; to pass up (*an opportunity*); **animam emittere** to give up the ghost; **emitti** or **se emittere** (with **ex** + *abl*) to break out of (*e.g., jail*)

emō emĕre ēmī emptum *vt* to buy; to pay for; to gain, obtain, acquire; to bribe; **bene emere** to buy cheap; **in diem emere** to buy on credit; **male emere** to pay dearly for

ēmodĕr·or -ārī -ātus sum *vt* to moderate

ēmodŭl·or -ārī -ātus sum *vt* to sing the praises of, celebrate in song

ēmōl·ior -īrī -ītus sum *vt* to accomplish

ēmoll·iō -īre -īvī or **-iī -ītum** *vt* to soften; to make mild; to enervate

ēmŏl·ō -ĕre — -ĭtum *vt* to grind up; to consume

ēmolument·um -ī *n* profit, gain, advantage

ēmon·ĕō -ēre *vt* to advise, admonish

ē·morior -mŏrī -mortŭus sum *vi* to die, die off; (fig) to die out

ēmortuāl·is -e *adj* of death; **dies emortualis** day of one's death

ēmortŭus *pp* of **emorior**

ē·movĕō -movēre -mōvī -mōtum *vt* to move out, remove, expel; to dislodge; to shake (*e.g., foundations of wall*)

Empedŏcl·ēs -is *m* philosopher of Sicily who is said to have jumped into the crater of Mt. Aetna (*fl* 444 B.C.)

emphăs·is -is *f* emphasis, stress

empīrĭc·us -ī *m* self-trained physician

empor·ĭum -iī or **-ī** *n* market town, market, mart

emptĭ·ō -ōnis *f* buying, purchase; thing purchased, purchase

emptĭt·ō -āre *vt* to be in the habit of buying

empt·or -ōris *m* buyer, purchaser

emptus *pp* of **emo**

ēmūg·iō -īre *vt* to bellow out

ē·mulgĕō -mulgēre — -mulsum *vt* to drain out; to exhaust

ēmunct·us -a -um *adj* discriminating; **naris emunctae esse** to have discriminating tastes

ē·mungō -mungĕre -munxī -munctum *vt* to blow the nose of; to swindle; (with *abl*) to cheat (*someone*) of; **emungi** to blow one's nose

ēmūn·iō -īre -īvī or **-iī -ītum** *vt* to build up; to fortify; to make a road through (*woods*)

ēn *interj* (in questions) really?; (in commands) come on!; (to call attention) look!, see!

ēnarrābĭl·is -e *adj* describable, intelligible

ēnarrātĭ·ō -ōnis *f* description; analysis

ēnarr·ō -āre *vt* to explain in detail, describe; to interpret

ē·nascor -nascī -nātus sum *vi* to grow out, sprout, arise

ēnăt·ō -āre *vi* to swim away, escape by swimming; (fig) to get away with it

ēnātus *pp* of **enascor**

ēnāvĭg·ō -āre *vt* to sail over, traverse; *vi* to sail away; (fig) to escape

Encelăd·us -ī *m* one of the giants whom Jupiter buried under Aetna

endrŏm·is -ĭdis *f* athlete's bathrobe

Endymĭ·ōn -ōnis *m* handsome young man with whom Luna fell in love and who was doomed to everlasting sleep on Mt. Patmos in Caria

ē·nĕcō (or **ē·nīcō**) **-necāre -necŭī** (or **-nicāvī**) **-nectum** (or **-necātum**) *vt* to kill, kill off; to exhaust, wear out; (coll) to kill, pester to death

ēnervāt·us -a -um *adj* without sinews; without energy or force

ēnerv·is -e *adj* weak, feeble

ēnerv·ō -āre *vt* to weaken, enervate, render impotent

ēnīcō see **eneco**

enim *conj* namely, for instance; yes, indeed, certainly; in fact, to be sure; (in replies) of course, no doubt; for, because

enimvērō *adv* yes indeed, to be sure, certainly; (ironical) of course

Enīp·eus -ĕī *m* tributary of the Peneus in Thessaly

ēnīsus *pp* of **enitor**

ēnit·ĕō -ēre -ŭī *vi* to shine out, sparkle; to be distinguished or conspicuous

ēnitesc·ō -ĕre *vi* to begin to shine, begin to brighten, become conspicuous

ē·nītor -nītī -nīsus or **nixus sum** *vt* to work one's way up, climb; to give birth to; *vi* to exert oneself, make an effort; (with *inf*) to struggle to, strive to

ēnixē *adv* strenuously, earnestly

ēnix·us -a -um *pp* of **enitor;** *adj* strenuous, earnest

Ennĭ·us -ī *m* father of Latin literature, writer of tragedy, comedy, epic, and satire, born at Rudiae in Calabria (239-169 B.C.)

Ennosigae·us -ī *m* (epithet of Neptune) Earthshaker

ēn·ō -āre *vi* to swim out, swim away, escape by swimming

ēnōdātē *adv* without knots; plainly, clearly

ēnōdātĭ·ō -ōnis *f* solution, explanation

ēnōd·is -e *adj* without knots; plain, clear

ēnōd·ō -āre *vt* to explain, clarify

ēnorm·is -e *adj* irregular; enormous

ēnormĭt·ās -ātis *f* irregular shape

ēnōt·escō -escĕre -ŭī *vi* to become known

ēnŏt·ō -āre *vt* to take notes of, note down

ensicŭl·us -ī *m* small sword
ensĭf·er -ĕra -ĕrum *adj* with a sword, wearing a sword
ensĭg·er -ĕra -ĕrum *adj* with a sword, wearing a sword
ens·is -is *m* sword
enthȳmēm·a -ătis *n* thought, reflection; condensed syllogism
ē·nūbō -nūbĕre -nupsī *vi* (said of a woman) to marry out of one's rank
ēnucleātē *adv* plainly
ēnucleāt·us -a -um *adj* pure, clean; straightforward; simple, clear (*style*)
ēnuclĕ·ō -āre *vt* (fig) to give in a nutshell, explain to the point
ēnumerātĭ·ō -ōnis *f* enumeration
ēnumĕr·ō -āre *vt* to count up; to pay; to recount, relate, detail, describe
ēnuntiātĭ·ō -ōnis *f* (in logic) proposition
ēnuntĭ·ō -āre *vt* to disclose, reveal, betray; to say, assert, express
ēnuptĭ·ō -ōnis *f* right to marry outside the clan
ēnutr·ĭō -īre -īvī or **-ĭī -ītum** *vt* to nourish, raise, bring up (*children*)
eō īre īvī or **ĭī ĭtum** *vi* to go; to go, walk, sail, ride; (mil) to march; (of time) to pass; (of events) to go on, happen, turn out; **in sententiam ire** to vote for a bill
eō *adv* there, to that place; to that end, to that purpose; so far, to such an extent, to such a pitch; on that account, for that reason, with that in view; **eo ero brevior** I will be all the briefer; **eo magis** all the more; **eo maxime quod** especially because; **eo quo** to the place to which; **eo . . . quo** the . . . the . . .; **eo quod** because; **eo . . . ut** to such an extent . . . that
eōdem *adv* to the same place, purpose, or person
Ēōs (*nom* only) *f* Dawn
Ēō·us -ī *m* morning star; inhabitant of the East, Oriental; one of the horses of the sun
Epamīnond·ās -ae *m* famous Theban general who fought against the Spartans (*d.* 362 B.C.)
Epăph·us -ī *m* son of Jupiter and Io
ēpast·us -a -um *adj* eaten up
Epē·us or **Epī·us -ī** *m* builder of the Trojan horse
ephēb·us -ī *m* young man (18 *to* 20 *years of age*)
ephēmĕr·is -ĭdis *f* diary, journal
Ephĕs·us -ī *f* city in Asia Minor with famous temple of Diana
ephippiāt·us -a -um *adj* riding a saddled horse
ephipp·ĭum -ĭī or **-ī** *n* saddle
ephŏr·us -ī *m* ephor (*Spartan magistrate*)
Ephȳr·a -ae or **Ephȳr·ē -ēs** *f* ancient name of Corinth
Epicharm·us -ī *m* Greek philosopher and writer of early comedy (540-450 B.C.)
epichȳs·is -is *f* jug
epicrŏc·us -a -um *adj* transparent, thin
Epicūr·us -ī *m* Greek philosopher, born on Samos (342-270 B.C.)
epĭc·us -a -um *adj* epic
epidictĭc·us -a -um *adj* for display
epidipn·is -ĭdis *f* dessert
epigramm·a -ătis *n* inscription; short poem, epigram
epilŏg·us -ī *m* epilogue, peroration
epimēnĭ·a -ōrum *n pl* month's rations
Epimēth·eus -ĕī *m* son of Iapetus and brother of Prometheus
epirēd·ĭum -ĭī or **-ī** *n* trace
epistol·ĭum -ĭī or **-ī** *n* note
epistŭl·a -ae *f* letter
epitaph·ĭum -ĭī or **-ī** *n* eulogy
epithalam·ĭum -ĭī or **-ī** *n* wedding song
epithēc·a -ae *f* addition, increase
epitŏm·a -ae or **epitŏm·ē -ēs** *f* epitome, abridgment
epitȳr·um -ī *n* olive salad
epŏd·es -um *m pl* seafish
ep·ops -ŏpis *m* hoopoe
epos (*nom* & *acc* only) *n* epic
ēpōt·us or **expōt·us -a -um** *adj* drained to the dregs; drunk dry
epŭl·ae -ārum *f pl* courses, dishes; sumptuous meal, banquet; **epulae regum** dinner fit for a king
epulār·is -e *adj* at dinner, of a dinner; **sermo epularis** talk at dinner
epŭl·ō -ōnis *m* dinner guest, guest at a banquet; **Tresviri** or **Septemviri Epulones** college of priests who superintended the state dinner to the gods
epŭl·or -ārī -ātus sum *vt* to feast on; *vi* to attend a dinner; (with *abl*) to feast on
epŭl·um -ī *n* banquet, feast
equ·a -ae *f* mare
equ·es -ĭtis *m* rider; (mil) trooper, cavalryman; cavalry; *m pl* cavalry
Equ·es -ĭtis *m* knight; capitalist (*member of Roman middle class*); equestrian order, bourgeoisie
equest·er -ris -re *adj* cavalry; equestrian; middle class, bourgeois, capitalist
equĭdem *adv* truly, indeed, in any event; (with first person) for my part, as far as I am concerned; of course, to be sure
equīn·us -a -um *adj* horse's
equīrĭ·a -ōrum *n pl* horse race
equitāt·us -ūs *m* cavalry
equĭt·ō -āre *vi* to ride, ride a horse
equulĕ·us -ī *m* foal, colt; small equestrian statue; torture rack
equ·us -ī *m* horse; **equis virisque** or **equis viris** (fig) with might and main; **equo merere** to serve in the cavalry; **equo vehi** to ride, to ride a horse; **equus bipes** sea

horse; **in equo** mounted; *m pl* (fig) chariot
er·a -ae *f* mistress of the house
ērādīc·ō or **exrādīc·ō -āre** *vt* to root out, uproot, destroy
ē·rādō -rādĕre -rāsī -rāsum *vt* to scratch out, erase, obliterate
erăn·us -ī *m* mutual insurance society
Erătō (*nom* only) *f* Muse of erotic poetry; Muse
Eratosthĕn·ēs -is *m* famous Alexandrine geographer, poet, and philosopher (276-196 B.C.)
erc- see **herc-**
Erĕb·us -ī *m* god of darkness, son of Chaos and brother of Night; lower world
Erechth·eus -ĕī *m* mythical king of Athens, son of Hephaestus
ērect·us -a -um *pp* of **erigo;** *adj* erect, upright; noble, elevated, lofty; haughty; attentive, alert, tense; resolute, courageous
ē·rēpō -rēpĕre -repsī *vt* to crawl through (*field*); to crawl up (*mountain*); *vi* to crawl out
ēreptĭ·ō -ōnis *f* robbery
ērept·or -ōris *m* robber
ēreptus *pp* of **eripio**
ergā *prep* (with *acc*) to, towards; against
ergastŭl·um -ī n prison; *n pl* inmates
ergō *adv* therefore, consequently; (resumptive) well then, I say, as I was saying; (with imperatives) then, now; **quid ergo?** why then?; *prep* (with preceding *genit*) for the sake of; **illius ergo** for his sake
Erichthon·ĭus -ĭī or **-ī** *m* mythical king of Athens; son of Dardanus, father of Tros, and king of Troy
ēric·ĭus -ĭī or **-ī** *m* hedgehog; (mil) beam with iron spikes
Ēridăn·us -ī *m* Po river (*so called by the Greeks*)
erifŭg·a -ae *m* runaway slave
ē·rīgō -rigĕre -rexī -rectum *vt* to set up straight, straighten out (*e.g., tree*); to set up, erect; to cheer up, encourage; to arouse, excite; (mil) to deploy troops on a slope; **erigi** or **se erigere** to raise oneself, arise
Ērigŏn·ē -ēs *f* Virgo (*constellation*)
erīl·is -e *adj* master's, mistress's
Erīn·ys -ўos *f* Fury; (fig) frenzy
Eriphўl·a -ae or **Eriphўl·ē -ēs** *f* wife of the seer Amphiaraus and the mother of Alcmaeon, who killed her for betraying Amphiaraus
ē·ripĭō -ripĕre -ripŭī -reptum *vt* to snatch away, pull out, tear out; to deliver, rescue; to rob; (with *dat* or with **ab** or **ex** + *abl*) to take away from, wrest from, rescue from; **se eripere** to escape
ērogātĭ·ō -ōnis *f* paying out, payment
ērogĭt·ō -āre *vt* to try to find out
ērŏg·ō -āre *vt* to allocate, expend; to bequeath; (with **in** + *acc*) **a** to allocate to, expend on; **b** to bequeath to
Er·ōs -ōtis *m* Cupid
errābund·us -a -um *adj* wandering, straggling
errātĭc·us -a -um *adj* erratic, roving, wandering
errātĭ·ō -ōnis *f* wandering
errāt·um -ī *n* error, mistake
errāt·us -ūs *m* roving, wandering about
err·ō -āre *vi* to wander, lose one's way, stray, roam; to waver; to err, make a mistake, be mistaken; (with **in** + *abl*) to be mistaken about
err·ō -ōnis *m* vagrant, vagabond
err·or -ōris *m* wandering, wavering, uncertainty; error; cause of error, deception; maze, winding, intricacy
ērub·escō -escĕre -ŭī *vt* to blush at; to be ashamed of; to respect; *vi* to grow red, redden; to blush
ērūc·a -ae *f* colewort
ēruct·ō -āre *vt* to belch, vomit, throw up; (fig) to belch
ērud·ĭō -īre -ĭī -ītum *vt* to educate, teach, instruct
ērudītē *adv* learnedly
ērudītĭ·ō -ōnis *f* instructing, instruction; erudition
ērudītŭl·us -a -um *adj* somewhat experienced, somewhat skilled
ērudīt·us -a -um *adj* educated, learned, accomplished
ē·rumpō -rumpĕre -rūpī -ruptum *vt* to cause to break out; to give vent to; **iram in hostes erumpere** to vent one's wrath on the enemy; *vi* to burst out, break out
ē·rŭō -ruĕre -rŭī -rŭtum *vt* to root up, uproot, dig out; to undermine, demolish, destroy; to draw out, elicit; to rescue; to plow up
ēruptĭ·ō -ōnis *f* eruption; (mil) sortie, sally
ēruptus *pp* of **erumpo**
er·us -ī *m* master of the house, head of the family; lord, owner, proprietor
ērŭtus *pp* of **eruo**
erv·um -ī *n* pulse, vetch
Erycīn·us -a -um *adj* of Mt. Eryx (*in Sicily*); of Venus; Sicilian; *f* Venus
Erymanth·is -ĭdis *f* Callisto (*changed into a bear and made a constellation*)
Erymanth·us -ī *m* mountain range in Arcadia, where Hercules killed a boar
Erysichth·ōn -ōnis *m* son of Thessalian king Triopas, punished with insatiable hunger for having cut down a grove sacred to Ceres
erythīn·us -ī *m* red mullet
Er·yx -ўcis or **Erўc·us -ī** *m* mountain on W. coast of Sicily, famous for its temple to Venus
esc·a -ae *f* dish; food; bait

escārī·us -a -um *adj* of food; of bait; *n pl* dishes, courses
e·scendō -scendĕre -scendī -scensum *vt* & *vi* to climb, climb up
escensī·ō or **exscensī·ō -ōnis** *f* climb, climbing
esculent·us -a -um *adj* edible; *n pl* edibles
esculētum see **aesculetum**
escŭlus see **aesculus**
ēsĭt·ō -āre *vt* to be accustomed to eating
Esquilī·ae -ārum *f pl* Esquiline Hill in Rome
Esquilīn·us -a -um *adj* Esquiline; *f* Esquiline gate
essedār·ius -iī or **-ī** *m* soldier fighting from a chariot
esse *inf* of **sum;** *inf* of **edo**
essĕd·um -ī *n* combat chariot (*used by Gauls and Britons*)
essentĭ·a -ae *f* essence
estr·ix -īcis *f* glutton (*female*)
essĭt·ō -āre *vt* to be accustomed to eating
ēsuriāl·is -e *adj* of hunger
ēsur·iō -īre — -ītum *vt* to be hungry for; *vi* to be hungry
ēsurītĭ·ō -ōnis *f* hunger
ēsus *pp* of **edo**
et *adv* besides, also; even, I mean
et *conj* and; (for emphasis) and even, yes and; (antithetical) however, but; **et . . . et** both . . . and, not only . . . but also
etĕnim *conj* for, and as a matter of fact
etēsĭ·ae -ārum *m pl* periodic winds (*on the Aegean Sea*)
ēthĭc·ē -ēs *f* ethics
ēthologĭ·a -ae *f* portrayal of character
ētholŏg·us -ī *m* impersonator
etĭam *conj* also, and also, besides, likewise; (of time) yet, as yet, still, even now; (in affirmation) yes, yes indeed, certainly, by all means; (emphatic) even, rather; (with emphatic imperatives) but just; **etiam atque etiam** again and again, repeatedly
etiamnunc or **etiamnum** *adv* even now, even at the present time, still
etiamsī *conj* even if, although
etiamtum or **etiamnunc** *adv* even then, till then, still
Etrūrĭ·a -ae *f* district N. of Rome
Etrusc·us -a -um *adj* & *mf* Etruscan
etsī *conj* even if, although
etymologĭ·a -ae *f* etymology
eu *interj* well done!, bravo!
Euan or **Euhan** *m* Bacchus
Euand·er or **Euandr·us -rī** *m* Evander (*Arcadian who founded Pallanteum at the foot of the Palatine hill*)
eu·ans or **euh·ans -antis** *adj* crying Euan or Euhan (*Bacchic cry*)
euax *interj* hurray!
Euboe·a -ae *f* island off the E. coast of Attica and Boeotia
Euēn·us -ī *m* river in Aetolia
euge or **eugĕpae** *interj* well done!, terrific!
euh·ans -antis *adj* shouting Euan (*Bacchic cry*)
Euhēmĕr·us -ī *m* Greek writer who attempted to prove that all the ancient myths were actually historical events (*fl* 316 B.C.)
Euh·ĭus -ĭī or **-ī** *m* Bacchus
Euhoe or **Euoe** *interj* ecstatic cry of revelers at festival of Bacchus
Eu·ĭus -ĭī or **-ī** *m* Bacchus
Eumenĭd·es -um *f pl* Erinyes or Furies (*goddesses of vengeance*)
eunŭch·us -ī *m* eunuch
Euoe see **Euhoe**
Euphorb·us -ī *m* brave Trojan warrior whose soul Pythagoras asserted had transmigrated to himself
Euphrāt·ēs -is *m* Euphrates River
Eupŏl·is -ĭdis *m* famous Athenian comic poet (446?-411 B.C.)
Eurīpĭd·ēs -is *m* Athenian tragic poet (485-405 B.C.)
Eurīp·us -ī *m* strait between Boeotia and Euboea; channel, canal
Eurōp·a -ae or **Eurōp·ē -ēs** *f* daughter of Agenor and mother of Sarpedon and Minos by Jupiter; he, in the shape of a bull, carried her off to Crete
Eurōt·as -ae *m* chief river in Laconia
Eur·us -ī *m* S.E. wind; east wind; wind
Eurydĭc·ē -ēs *f* wife of Orpheus
Eurypӯl·us -ī *m* Greek warrior who fought at Troy
Eurysth·eus -ĕī *m* son of Sthenelus, grandson of Perseus, and king of Nycenae, who imposed the twelve labors of Hercules
Eurӯt·is -ĭdis *f* Iole (*with whom Hercules fell in love*)
Eurӯt·us -ī *m* king of Oechalia and father of Iole
euschēmē *adv* gracefully
Euterp·ē -ēs *f* Muse of lyric poetry
Euxīn·us Pont·us or **Euxīn·us -ī** *m* or **Pont·us -ī** *m* Black Sea
ē·vādō -vādĕre -vāsī -vāsum *vt* to pass, pass by; to pass through, escape; *vi* to go out; to turn out, become, prove to be, turn out to be; to get away, escape; to rise, climb
ēvăg·or -ārī -ātus sum *vt* to stray beyond, transgress; *vi* (mil) to maneuver; (fig) to spread
ēval·escō -escĕre -ŭī *vi* to grow strong; to increase; (of a word or expression) to gain currency; (with *inf*) to be able to; (with **in** + *acc*) to develop into
ēvān·escō -escĕre -ŭī *vi* to vanish, pass away, die away; (of wine) to become vapid; to be forgotten, perish
ēvānĭd·us -a -um *adj* vanishing
ēvast·ō -āre *vt* to devastate, wreck completely
evasus *pp* of **evado**

ē·vĕhō -vehĕre -vexī -vectum *vt* to carry out, convey out; to carry abroad, spread abroad; to lift up, raise; **evehi** to ride, sail, drift

ē·vellō -vellĕre -vellī or **-vulsī -vulsum** *vt* to tear or pluck out: to eradicate

ē·venĭō -venīre -vēnī -ventum *vi* to come out, come forth; to come to pass, happen; to follow, result, turn out, end; *v impers* it happens

ēvent·um -ī *n* event, occurrence; result, effect, consequence; fortune, experience

ēvent·us -ūs *m* event, accident, fortune, lot, fate; good fortune, success; issue, consequence, result

ēverbĕr·ō -āre *vt* to strike hard; to beat violently

ēverricŭl·um -ī *n* broom; dragnet

ē·verrō -verrĕre -verrī -versum *vt* to sweep out; (fig) to clean out, strip

ēversĭ·ō -ōnis *f* overthrow, subversion, destruction

ēvers·or -ōris *m* subverter, destroyer

ēversus *pp* of **everro;** *pp* of **everto**

ē·vertō or **ē·vortō -vertĕre -vertī -versum** *vt* to overturn, turn upside down; to overthrow, upset; to turn out, expel, eject; to subvert, destroy, ruin

ēvestīgāt·us -a -um *adj* tracked down

ēvictus *pp* of **evinco**

ēvĭd·ens -entis *adj* evident, visible, plain

ēvidenter *adv* evidently, plainly, clearly

ēvidentĭ·a -ae *f* distinctness, clearness (*in speech*)

ēvigĭl·ō -āre *vt* to watch through (*the night*); to work through the night writing (*e.g., books*); *vi* to be wide-awake; (fig) to be on one's toes

ēvīl·escō -escĕre -ŭī *vi* to depreciate, become worthless

ē·vincĭō -vincīre -vinxī -vinctum *vt* to tie up; to crown, wreathe

e·vincō -vincĕre -vīcī -victum *vt* to conquer completely, trounce; to prevail over

ēvinctus *pp* of **evincio**

ēvĭr·ō -āre *vt* to unman, castrate

ēviscĕr·ō -āre *vt* to disembowel; to mangle

ēvitābĭl·is -e *adj* avoidable

ēvītātĭ·ō -ōnis *f* avoidance

ēvīt·ō -āre *vt* to avoid, escape

ēvocāt·ī -ōrum *m pl* veterans called up again; reenlisted veterans

ēvocāt·or -ōris *m* recruiter

ēvŏc·ō -āre *vt* to call out, summon; to challenge; (mil) to call up (*for service*); to evoke, excite, stir

ēvolgō see **evulgo**

ēvŏl·ō -āre *vi* to fly out, fly away; to rush out, dash out; (fig) to soar

ēvolūtĭ·ō -ōnis *f* unrolling a book; (fig) reading

ē·volvō -volvĕre -volvī -volūtum *vt* to roll out, unroll, unfold; to spread; to unroll, read, study; to unfold, disclose; to free, extricate; to repel; to evolve, develop

ē·vŏmō -vomĕre -vomŭī -vomĭtum *vt* to vomit, spew out, disgorge

ēvulg·ō or **ēvolg·ō -āre** *vt* to divulge, make public

ēvulsĭ·ō -ōnis *f* pulling out, extraction (*of a tooth*)

ēvulsus *pp* of **evello**

ex or **ē** *prep* (with *abl*) (of space) out of, from; down from; up from, above; (of time) from, from . . . onward, immediately after, following, since; (cause or origin) from, through, by, on account of, by reason of; (transition) from, out of; from being; (conformity) after, according to, in conformity with; (means) with, by means of; (partitive) out of, from among, among; made of, out of

exacerb·ō -āre *vt* to exasperate, provoke

exactĭ·ō -ōnis *f* driving out, expulsion; supervision; exaction, collection; tax, tribute

exact·or -ōris *m* expeller; supervisor; tax collector

exact·us -a -um *pp* of **exigo;** *adj* exact, precise

exac·ŭō -uĕre -ŭī -ūtum *vt* to sharpen; to sharpen, stimulate, excite, inflame

exadversum or **exadvorsum** or **exadversus** *adv* on the opposite side; *prep* (with *dat* or *acc*) across from, right opposite

exaedificātĭ·ō -ōnis *f* construction

exaedifĭc·ō -āre *vt* to finish building, build, construct; (fig) to complete

exaequātĭ·ō -ōnis *f* leveling; uniformity

exaequ·ō -āre *vt* to level, make level; (fig) to equal, regard as equal; **exaequari** (with *dat*) to be put on the same level with

exaestŭ·ō -āre *vi* to seethe, boil; to ferment

exaggerātĭ·ō -ōnis *f* (fig) elevation, enlargement; **animi exaggeratio** broadening of the mind

exaggĕr·ō -āre *vt* to pile up; to enlarge; to enhance

exagitāt·or -ōris *m* critic

exagĭt·ō -āre *vt* to stir up, keep on the move; to scare away; to criticize, satirize; to irritate; to excite, stir up (*feelings*)

exagōg·a -ae *f* exportation

exalb·escō -escĕre -ŭī *vi* to turn pale

exām·en -ĭnis *n* swarm; crowd; tongue of scale; weighing, consideration; examination

exāmĭn·ō -āre *vt* to weigh; to consider; to try, test, examine

examussim *adv* exactly

exancl•ō -āre *vt* to draw off, drain; to drain to the dregs
exanimāl•is -ē *adj* dead, lifeless; deadly
exanimātĭ•ō -ōnis *f* breathlessness; terror, panic
exanĭm•is -e or **exanĭm•us -a -um** *adj* breathless, terrified; dead, lifeless; fainting (*e.g., from fear*)
exanĭm•ō -āre *vt* to knock the breath out of; to wind, tire, weaken; to deprive of life, kill; to scare out of one's wits; to dishearten; to agitate
exanĭmus see **exanimis**
ex•ardescō -ardescĕre -arsī -arsum *vi* to catch fire; to flare up; (fig) to flare up, be provoked, be exasperated
exār•escō -escĕre -ŭī *vi* to become quite dry, dry up
exarm•ō -āre *vt* to disarm
exăr•ō -āre *vt* to plow up; to raise, produce; to write (*on wax with a stylus*), write down, note; to furrow, wrinkle; **frontem rugis exarare** to knit one's brow
exasciāt•us -a -um *adj* hewn out; properly planned, properly worked out
exaspĕr•ō -āre *vt* to make rough, roughen; to exasperate
exauctōr•ō -āre *vt* (mil) to discharge, cashier
exaud•ĭō -īre -īvī -ītum *vt* to hear clearly; to discern; to perceive, understand; to listen to; to grant
exaug•ĕō -ēre *vt* to increase; to confirm
exaugurātĭ•ō -ōnis *f* desecration, profaning
exaugŭr•ō -āre *vt* to desecrate, profane
exauspĭc•ō -āre *vi* to find the omens good
exballist•ō -āre *vt* to put an end to, finish off
exbĭbō see **ebibo**
excaec•ō -āre *vt* to blind; to stop up (*a river, pipe, etc.*); to darken
excandescentĭ•a -ae *f* mounting anger, outburst of anger
excand•escō -escĕre -ŭī *vi* to grow white hot; to reach a pitch (*of emotion*)
excant•ō -āre *vt* to charm away
excarnifĭc•ō -āre *vt* to tear to pieces, torture to death
excăv•ō -āre *vt* to hollow out
ex•cēdō -cēdĕre -cessī -cessum *vt* to exceed, pass, surpass; *vi* to go out, go away, withdraw, depart, disappear; to die; **e medio excedere** or **e vita excedere** to depart from life, die
excell•ens -entis *adj* excellent, outstanding, distinguished, superior
excellenter *adv* excellently
excellentĭ•a -ae *f* excellence, superiority
ex•cellō -cellĕre *vi* to excel, be superior
excelsē *adv* high, loftily
excelsĭt•ās -ātis *f* loftiness
excels•us -a -um *adj* high, lofty; eminent; *n* height; high social status; **in excelso aetatem** or **vitam agere** to be in the limelight
exceptĭ•ō -ōnis *f* exception, restriction, limitation; (law) objection raised by a defendant against an accuser's statement
except•ō -āre *vt* to catch, catch up to
exceptus *pp* of **excipio**
ex•cernō -cernĕre -crēvī -crētum *vt* to sift out, separate
ex•cerpō -cerpĕre -cerpsī -cerptum *vt* to pick out, extract; to pick out, choose, gather; to leave out, omit, except
excerpt•um -ī *n* excerpt
excess•us -ūs *m* departure; death; digression
excĕtr•a -ae *f* snake
excidĭ•ō -ōnis *f* destruction
excid•ĭum -ĭī or **-ī** *n* overthrow, destruction; cause of destruction
ex•cĭdō -cidĕre -cĭdī *vi* to fall out; (of an utterance) to slip out, escape; to pass away, perish; to degenerate; to disappear; to be forgotten; (with **in** + *acc*) to degenerate into; (with *abl* or **ex** + *abl*) **a** to be deprived of, lose; **b** to forget, miss; (with *dat* or **de** + *abl*) **a** to fall from; **b** to escape from (*lips*); **e memoria excidere** to slip the memory
ex•cīdō -cīdĕre -cīdī -cīsum *vt* to cut out, cut off, cut down; to raze, demolish; (fig) to banish, eliminate
exciĕō see **excio**
exc•ĭō -īre -īvī or **-ĭī -ītum** or **exci•ĕō -ēre** *vt* to call (*someone*) out, summon; to awaken (*from sleep*); to disturb; to frighten; to stir up, excite; to produce, occasion
ex•cipĭō -cipĕre -cēpī -ceptum *vt* to take out, remove; to rescue; to exempt; to take, receive, catch, capture; to follow, succeed; to catch, intercept; to be exposed to; to incur; to receive, welcome; to take up eagerly; to listen to, overhear; to except, make an exception of; to reach (*a place*); to mention in particular; to take on, withstand
excīsĭ•ō -ōnis *f* destruction
excīsus *pp* of **excīdo**
excitāt•us -a -um *adj* excited, lively, vigorous; loud
excĭt•ō -āre *vt* to wake, rouse; to raise, stir up; to erect, construct, produce; to cause, occasion; (fig) to arouse, awaken, incite, inspire, stimulate, enliven, encourage; to startle
excītus *pp* of **excio**
exclāmātĭ•ō -ōnis *f* exclamation
exclām•ō -āre *vt* to exclaim; *vi* to shout, yell
ex•clūdō -clūdĕre -clūsī -clūsum *vt* to exclude, shut out, shut off; to

remove, separate; to hatch; (coll) to knock out (*an eye*); to prevent
exclūsĭ•ō -ōnis *f* exclusion
exclūsus *pp* of **excludo**
excoctus *pp* of **excoquo**
excōgitātĭ•ō -ōnis *f* thinking out, inventing, contriving
excōgitāt•us -a -um *adj* choice
excōgĭt•ō -āre *vt* to think out, devise, contrive
ex•cŏlō -colĕre -colŭī -cultum *vt* to tend, cultivate, work carefully; to refine, ennoble, perfect, improve; to worship
ex•cŏquō -coquĕre -coxī -coctum *vt* to cook out, boil away; to dry up, bake thoroughly; to harden, temper (*steel*)
excor•s -dis *adj* senseless, silly, stupid
excrēment•um -ī *n* excretion
excrĕō see **exscreo**
ex•crescō -crescĕre -crēvī -crētum *vi* to grow out; to grow up, rise up
excruciābĭl•is -e *adj* deserving torture
excrucĭ•ō -āre *vt* to torture, torment; to trouble, harass, distress
excubĭ•ae -ārum *f pl* standing guard; sentry; watchfire
excubĭt•or -ōris *m* sentry
excŭb•ō -āre -ŭī -ĭtum *vi* to sleep out of doors; to stand guard; to be attentive, be on the alert
ex•cūdō -cūdĕre -cūdī -cūsum *vt* to beat or strike out; to hammer out; to forge; (fig) to hatch (*eggs*); (fig) to hammer out, write up, hammer into shape
exculc•ō -āre *vt* to kick out; to tread down on; to stomp
excultus *pp* of **excolo**
excūrāt•us -a -um *adj* carefully attended to
ex•currō -currĕre -cucurrī or **-currī -cursum** *vi* to run or dash out; (mil) to sally forth, make an incursion; to project, extend; (fig) to fan out, expand
excursĭ•ō -ōnis *f* sally, sortie; inroad, invasion; outset, opening (*of a speech*)
excurs•or -ōris *m* skirmisher, scout
excurs•us -ūs *m* reconnoitering, running out ahead; raid, charge, attack, invasion; digression
excūsābĭl•is -e *adj* excusable
excūsātē *adv* excusably, without blame
excūsātĭ•ō -ōnis *f* excuse
excūsāt•us -a -um *adj* free from blame, exempt
excūs•ō -āre *vt* to free from blame, excuse; to exempt; to make excuses for, apologize for; to allege in excuse, plead as an excuse
excussus *pp* of **excutio**
excūsus *pp* of **excudo**
ex•cutĭō -cutĕre -cussī -cussum *vt* to shake out, shake off shake loose; to knock out (*e.g., teeth*); (of horse) to throw, throw off; to shake out (*garment*); to jilt, give a cold shoulder to; to toss, throw; to shake out, search; to examine, investigate; (fig) to shake off, discard, banish
exdorsŭ•ō -āre *vt* to fillet
exec- see **exsec-**
ex•ĕdō -esse -ēdī -ēsum *vt* to eat up, consume; to destroy; to prey on; to hollow; to wear away, corrode
exĕdr•a -ae *f* sitting room; lecture room; hall
exedr•ĭum -ĭī or **-ī** *n* sitting room, parlor, living room
exempl•ar or **exempl•āre -āris** *n* copy; likeness; pattern, model, ideal
exemplār•is -e *adj* following a model
exempl•um -ī *n* sample, example, typical instance; precedent; pattern, make, character; model, pattern (*of conduct*); object lesson; warning; copy, transcript; portrait
exemptus *pp* of **eximo**
exentĕr•ō -āre *vt* to disembowel; to empty, exhaust; to torture, torment
ex•ĕō -īre -ĭī -ĭtum *vt* to pass beyond, cross; to parry, ward off, avoid; (fig) to exceed; *vi* to go out, go forth; to go away, withdraw, depart, retire; to march out; to disembark; to pour out, gush out, flow out; to escape, be freed; to pass away, perish; (of time) to run out, expire; to get out, become public; to burgeon forth; (of hills) to rise; **ex urna exire** to come out of, fall out of the urn (*said of lots*)
exeq- = **exseq-**
exerc•ĕō -ēre -ŭī -ĭtum *vt* to exercise, train; (mil) to drill, exercise, train; to keep (*someone*) busy, keep (*someone*) going; to supervise; to cultivate, work (*the soil*); to engage, occupy (*the mind*); to practice, follow (*a trade, occupation*); to carry into effect; to disturb, worry
exercitātĭ•ō -ōnis *f* exercise, practice, experience, training; (with *genit*) practice in
exercitāt•us -a -um *adj* experienced, trained, disciplined; troubled, worried, disturbed
exercit•ĭum -ĭī or **-ī** exercise, training
exercĭt•ō -āre *vt* to keep in training, exercise
exercĭt•or -ōris *m* trainer
exercĭt•us -a -um *pp* of **excerceo;** *adj* disciplined; experienced; trying, tough, harassing; harassed, vexed
exercĭt•us -ūs *m* army; infantry; (pol) assembly of the people; army of followers; swarm, flock, multitude
exĕrō see **exsero**
exēs•or -ōris *m* corrosive factor, underminer
exēsus *pp* of **exedo**
exhālātĭ•ō -ōnis *f* exhalation, vapor
exhāl•ō -āre *vt* to exhale, breathe out; *vi* to steam; to breathe one's last, expire

ex·hauriō -haurīre -hausī -haustum *vt* to draw out, empty, exhaust; to take away, remove; to drain dry; to bring to an end; to undergo, endure (*troubles*); to discuss fully
exhērēd·ō -āre *vt* to disinherit
exhēr·ēs -ēdis *adj* disinherited
exhib·ĕō -ēre -ŭī -ĭtum *vt* to hold out; to present, produce; to display, exhibit; to cause, occasion; to render, make
exhilăr·ō -āre *vt* to cheer up
exhorr·escō -escĕre -ŭī *vt* to shudder at; *vi* to be terrified
exhortātĭ·ō -ōnis *f* encouragement; *f pl* words of encouragement
exhort·or -ārī -ātus sum *vt* to encourage
ex·ĭgō -igĕre -ēgī -actum *vt* to drive out, push out, thrust out, expel; to demand, exact, collect, require; to pass, spend, complete, close (*life, time*); to finish, complete, conclude; to ascertain, determine; to weigh, consider, estimate, examine, try, test; to dispose of
exigŭē *adv* briefly, slightly, sparingly, barely
exiguĭt·ās -ātis *f* shortness, smallness, meagerness, scantiness, scarcity
exigŭ·us -a -um *adj* short, small, meager, scanty, poor, paltry, inadequate; a little, a bit of
exiliō see **exsilio**
exīl·is -e *adj* thin, small, meager, feeble, poor; cheerless, dreary; depleted (*ranks*); worthless, insincere; dry, flat (*style*)
exīlĭt·ās -ātis *f* thinness; meagerness, dreariness
exīlĭter *adv* drily, drearily, jejunely
exilĭum see **exsilium**
exim see **exinde**
eximĭē *adv* exceptionally
eximĭ·us -a -um *adj* taken out, exempted; exempt; select, special, exceptional
ex·ĭmō -imĕre -ēmī -emptum *vt* to take out, take away, remove; to exempt; to free, release, let off; to make an exception of; to waste, lose (*time*); to banish (*e.g., worries*)
exin see **exinde**
exinān·ĭō -īre -īī -ītum *vt* to empty completely; to plunder; (fig) to clean out, fleece
exinde or **exim** or **exin** *adv* from that place, from that point; (in enumerating) after that, next, then; (of time) from that point, after that, then, furthermore, next; accordingly
existimātĭ·ō -ōnis *f* appraisal, judgment, estimate, opinion, decision, verdict; reputation, good name, character; (com) credit; **vulgi existimatio** public opinion
existimāt·or -ōris *m* critic, judge
existĭm·ō or **existŭm·ō -āre** *vt* to appraise, evaluate, value, estimate; to think, judge, consider, regard; **in hostium numero existimare** to regard as an enemy
existō see **exsisto**
exitiābĭl·is -e *adj* deadly, fatal, destructive; (with *dat*) fatal to
exitiāl·is -e *adj* deadly, fatal
exitĭ·ō -ōnis *f* going out, exit
exitiōs·us -a -um *adj* deadly, destructive
exit·ĭum -ĭī or **-ī** *n* destruction, ruin; cause of destruction
exĭt·us -ūs *m* going out, exit, departure; way out, outlet, exit; end, close, conclusion; **ad exitum adducere** to bring to a close
exlecĕbra see **elecebra**
ex·lex -lēgis *adj* without law, bound by no law; lawless, heedless of laws
exobsĕcr·ō or **exopsĕcr·ō -āre** *vi* to make an earnest entreaty
exocŭl·ō -āre *vt* to knock the eyes out of
exod·ĭum -ĭī or **-ī** *n* farce (*presented after the main feature*)
exol·escō -escĕre -ēvī -ētum *vi* to decay, fade; to become obsolete
exolēt·us -a -um *adj* full-grown; *m* (fig) old rake
exonĕr·ō -āre *vt* to unload; (fig) to relieve, free, exonerate
exoptābĭl·is -e *adj* highly desirable, long-awaited
exoptāt·us -a -um *adj* longed-for, welcome, desired
exopt·ō -āre *vt* to long for, wish earnestly, desire greatly
exōrābĭl·is -e *adj* accessible, sympathetic, placable
exōrābŭl·a -ōrum *n pl* enticements, bait, arguments
exōrāt·or -ōris *m* lucky petitioner
ex·ordĭor -ordīrī -orsus sum *vt & vi* to begin, start, commence
exord·ĭum -ĭī or **-ī** *n* beginning, start, commencement, origin; introduction
ex·orĭor -orīrī -ortus sum *vi* to come out, come forth, rise, appear; to begin, arise, be caused, be produced
exornātĭ·ō -ōnis *f* embellishment
exorn·ō -āre *vt* to fit out, furnish, equip, provide, supply; to adorn, embellish, decorate, set off, give luster to
exōr·ō -āre *vt* to prevail upon, win over; to gain or obtain by entreaty; to appease
exorsus *pp* of **exordior;** *n pl* beginning, commencement; introduction, preamble
exors·us -ūs *m* beginning, commencement; introduction
exortus *pp* of **exorior**
exort·us -ūs *m* rising; the East, the Orient
ex·os -ossis *adj* boneless
exoscŭl·or -ārī -ātus sum *vt* to kiss lovingly, kiss tenderly
exoss·ō -āre *vt* to bone, take the bones out of

exostr·a -ae *f* movable stage; **in exostra** in public
exōs·us -a -um *adj* hating, detesting; hated, detested
exōtic·us -a -um *adj* foreign, exotic
expall·escō -escĕre -ŭī *vt* to turn pale at, dread; *vi* to turn pale
expalliāt·us -a -um *adj* robbed of one's cloak
expalp·ō -āre *vt* to coax out
ex·pandō -pandĕre -pandī -pansum *vt* to spread out, unfold, expand
expătr·ō -āre *vt* to waste, squander
expav·escō -escĕre -ŭī *vt* to panic at; *vi* to panic
expect- = exspect-
expecūliāt·us -a -um *adj* stripped of property
exped·iō -īre -iī or **-īvī -ītum** *vt* to unfetter, extricate, disentangle; to get out, get ready; to clear for action; to clear (*roads of obstacles*); to free, extricate (*from troubles*); to put in order, arrange, settle, adjust, set right; to explain, unfold, clear up, disclose, recount, relate; **expedit** *v impers* it is expedient, useful, advantageous
expedītē *adv* without obstacles, without difficulty, quickly, promptly
expedīti·ō -ōnis *f* expedition, campaign, special mission
expedīt·us -a -um *adj* unencumbered, unhampered, unobstructed; (mil) lightly equipped; ready, prompt; ready at hand, convenient; **in expedito habere** to have at hand
ex·pellō -pellĕre -pŭlī -pulsum *vt* to drive out, eject, expel; to disown
ex·pendō -pendĕre -pendī -pensum *vt* to weigh out; to pay out, pay down, lay out, expend; to rate, estimate; to ponder, consider; to pay (*penalty*)
expens·us -a -um *adj* paid out, spent; *n* payment, expenditure
expergē·faciō -facĕre -fēcī -factum *vt* to awaken, wake up; to arouse, excite
exper·giscor -giscī -rectus sum *vi* to wake up; to be alert
experg·ō -ĕre -ī -ĭtum *vt* to awaken, wake up
experi·ens -entis *adj* enterprising, active; (with *genit*) ready to undergo
experienti·a -ae *f* test, trial, experiment; experience, practice; effort
experīment·um -ī *n* test, experiment, proof; experience
exper·ior -īrī -tus sum *vt* to test, try, prove; to experience, endure, find out; to try to do, attempt; to measure strength with; *vi* to go to court
experrectus *pp* of **expergiscor**
exper·s -tis *adj* (with *genit*) having no share in, devoid of, free from, without
expert·us -a -um *pp* of **experior**; *adj* tried, proved, tested; (with *genit*) experienced in
expetess·ō -ĕre *vt* to desire, long for
expĕt·ō -ĕre -īvī or **-iī -ītum** *vt* to ask for, demand; to aim at, head for; to desire, long for, wish; *vi* (with **in** + *acc*) to befall; to fall upon, assail
expiāti·ō -ōnis *f* expiation, atonement; satisfaction
expictus *pp* of **expingo**
expīlāti·ō -ōnis *f* pillaging, plundering, ransacking
expīlāt·or -ōris *m* plunderer, robber
expīl·ō -āre *vt* to pillage, plunder, rob, ransack; to plagiarize
ex·pingō -pingĕre -pinxī -pictum *vt* to paint up; to depict; to paint true to life
expi·ō -āre *vt* to purify, cleanse ritually; to atone for, expiate; to avert (*curse, bad omen*)
expīrō see **exspiro**
expisc·or -ārī -ātus sum *vt* to fish for (*information*), ferret out, try to find out
explānātē *adv* plainly, clearly, distinctly
explānāti·ō -ōnis *f* explanation; clear pronunciation
explānāt·or -ōris *m* explainer; interpreter
explānāt·us -a -um *adj* plain, distinct
explān·ō -āre *vt* to explain, make clear; to pronounce clearly
ex·plaudō -plaudĕre -plausī -plausum *vt* to boo at, hiss at; to reject
explēment·um -ī *n* filling, stuffing
ex·plĕō -ēre -ēvī -ētum *vt* to fill out, fill up; to complete; to satisfy (*desires*); to make good, repair (*losses*); to fulfill, perform, accomplish, discharge
explēti·ō -ōnis *f* satisfying
explēt·us -a -um *adj* full, complete, perfect
explicātē *adv* clearly, plainly
explicāti·ō -ōnis *f* unfolding, uncoiling; analysis; interpretation
explicāt·or -ōris *m* or **explicātr·ix -īcis** *f* explainer
explicāt·us -a -um *adj* plain, clearcut
explicāt·us -ūs *m* unfolding; explanation, interpretation
explicit·us -a -um *adj* disentangled; simple, easy
explic·ō -āre -āvī or **-ŭī -ātum** or **-ĭtum** *vt* to unfold, unroll; to spread out; to loosen, undo; (mil) to exceed, deploy; to set free, release; to set in order, arrange, adjust, settle; to set forth, exhibit, explain
ex·plōdō or **ex·plaudō -plōdĕre -lōsī -plōsum** *vt* to drive off by clapping; to boo (*off the stage*); to disapprove, discredit
explōrātē *adv* after careful examination; for sure, for certain

explōrātĭ•ō -ōnis *f* exploration, examination
explōrāt•or -ōris *m* scout, spy
explōrāt•us -a -um *adj* sure, certain
explōr•ō -āre *vt* to explore, investigate; (mil) to reconnoiter; to probe, search; to test, try, try out
explōsĭ•ō -ōnis *f* booing (*of an actor*)
expol•iō -īre -īvī or **-iī -ītum** *vt* to polish; (fig) to polish, refine, adorn
expolītĭ•ō -ōnis *f* polishing, finishing off, embellishing
expolīt•us -a -um *adj* polished, lustrous; refined
ex•pōnō -pōnĕre -posŭī -posĭtum or **-postum** *vt* to put out; to expose, abandon; to expose, lay open; to reveal, publish; to exhibit, relate, explain; to offer, tender; to set on shore, disembark, land
expor•rĭgō -rigĕre -rexī -rectum *vt* to stretch out, spread, spread out; **exporge frontem** (coll) smooth out your brow, quit frowning
exportātĭ•ō -ōnis *f* exportation
export•ō -āre *vt* to carry out; to export
ex•poscō -poscĕre -poposcī *vt* to demand, beg, insist upon; to demand the surrender of
expositīcĭ•us -a -um *adj* foundling
expositĭ•ō -ōnis *f* exposing; (rhet) narration, explanation (*of details of a case*)
exposĭt•us -a -um *pp* of **expono;** *adj* accessible; accessible, affable
expostulātĭ•ō -ōnis *f* insistent demand; complaint
expostŭl•ō -āre *vt* to demand, insist on; to complain of; (with **cum** + *abl* of person) to complain of (*something*) to (*someone*); *vi* to lodge a complaint; (with **cum** + *abl*) to lodge a complaint with
expostus *pp* of **expono**
expōtus see **epotus**
express•us -a -um *adj* distinct, clear, express; distinct, real
ex•prīmō -primĕre -pressī -pressum *vt* to press out, squeeze out; (fig) to squeeze out, wring, extort; to model, form, portray; to represent, imitate, copy, describe, express; to translate; to pronounce, articulate
exprobrātĭ•ō -ōnis *f* reproach
exprŏbr•ō -āre *vt* to reproach, find fault with; (with *dat*) to cast (*something*) up to, put the blame for (*something*) on; *vi* (with *dat*) to complain to
ex•prōmō -prōmĕre -prompsī -promptum *vt* to bring out, fetch out; to give vent to; to disclose, display, exhibit; to give utterance to, utter, express, state
expugnābĭl•is -e *adj* vulnerable to attack, pregnable
expugnācĭ•or -us *adj* more potent
expugnātĭ•ō -ōnis *f* assault; (with *genit*) assault on
expugnāt•or -ōris *m* attacker; **expugnator pudicitiae** assailant
expugn•ō -āre *vt* to assault, storm; to conquer (*persons*) in war; (fig) to conquer, overcome; (fig) to achieve, accomplish; (fig) to wrest, extort
expulsĭ•ō -ōnis *f* expulsion
expuls•ō -āre *vt* to drive out, expel
expuls•or -ōris *m* expeller
expulsus *pp* of **expello**
expultr•ix -īcis *f* expeller (*female*)
ex•pungō -pungĕre -punxī -punctum *vt* to expunge; to cancel; to remove
expurgātĭ•ō -ōnis *f* justification, excuse
expurg•ō -āre *vt* to cleanse, purify; to cure; to vindicate, excuse, justify
expūtesc•ō -ĕre *vi* to rot away
expŭt•ō -āre *vt* to prune, lop off; to consider; to comprehend
ex•quīrō -quīrĕre -quīsīvī -quīsītum *vt* to investigate, scrutinize; to search for, look for; to ransack; to devise
exquīsītē *adv* carefully, accurately; exquisitely
exquīsīt•us -a -um *pp* of **exquiro;** *adj* carefully considered, choice, exquisite
exrādīcĭtus *adv* from the very roots
exsaev•iō -īre *vi* to cease raging, calm down
exsangu•is -e *adj* bloodless; pale; feeble; causing paleness
ex•sarcĭō or **ex•sercĭō -sarcīre — -sartum** *vt* to patch up; (fig) to repair
exsatĭ•ō -āre *vt* to satiate, satisfy fully, glut
exsaturābĭl•is -e *adj* appeasable
exsatŭr•ō -āre *vt* to satiate, satisfy completely
exsce- = **esce**
ex•scindō -scindĕre -scĭdī -scissum *vt* to annihilate, destroy
exscrĕ•ō -āre *vt* to cough up, spit out
ex•scrībō -scrībĕre -scripsī -scriptum *vt* to write down; to write out in full; to copy; (fig) to copy, take after, resemble
exsculp•ō -ĕre -sī -tum *vt* to carve out; to scratch out, erase; (fig) to extort
exsĕc•ō or **exsĭc•ō -āre -ŭī -tum** *vt* to cut out, cut away, cut off; to castrate; to deduct
exsecrābĭl•is -e *adj* accursed; bitter, merciless, deadly; execrating, cursing
exsecrātĭ•ō -ōnis *f* curse, execration; solemn oath
exsecrāt•us -a -um *adj* accursed, detestable
exsĕcr•or -ārī -ātus sum *vt* to curse, execrate; *vi* to take a solemn oath
exsectĭ•ō -ōnis *f* cutting out

exsecūtĭ•ō -ōnis *f* execution, performance; discussion
exsecūtus *pp* of **exsequor**
exsequĭ•ae -ārum *f pl* funeral procession, funeral rites
exsequiāl•is -e *adj* funeral; **carmina exsequialia** dirges
ex•sĕquor -sĕquī -secūtus sum *vt* to follow out; to accompany to the grave; to perform, execute, accomplish, carry out; to follow up, investigate: to pursue, go after; to avenge, punish; to say, tell, describe, relate
exsĕr•ō -ĕre -ŭī -tum *vt* to untie, disconnect; to stretch out (*one's arms*); to stick out (*the tongue in disdain*); to bare, uncover
exsert•ō -āre *vt* to keep on stretching or sticking out
exsertus *pp* of **exsero;** *adj* uncovered, bare; protruding
exsībĭl•ō -āre *vt* to hiss off the stage
exsiccāt•us -a -um *adj* dry, uninteresting
exsicc•ō -āre *vt* to dry up; to drain dry
exsĭcō see **exseco**
exsign•ō -āre *vt* to mark down exactly, write down in detail
ex•siliō -silīre -silŭī *vi* to jump out, leap up; to start; **exsilire gaudio** to jump for joy
exsil•ĭum -iī or **-ī** *n* exile, banishment (*voluntary or involuntary*); place of exile
ex•sistō -sistĕre -stĭtī -stĭtum *vi* to come out, come forth; to appear, emerge; to exist, be; to arise, proceed; to turn into, become; to be visible
ex•solvō -solvĕre -solvī -solūtum *vt* to loosen, untie; to release, free, set free; to discharge, pay; to keep, fulfill; to satisfy (*hunger*); to break open, wound; to solve, explain; to throw off, get rid of; to repay, requite; to give out (*awards, punishment*)
exsomn•is -e *adj* sleepless
exsorb•ĕō -ēre -ŭī *vt* to suck up, drain; to drain, exhaust; to grasp at eagerly, welcome
exsor•s -tis *adj* without lots; chosen specially; (with *genit*) having no share in, free from
exspatĭ•or -ārī -ātus sum *vi* to go off course; to digress
exspectābĭl•is -e *adj* expected, anticipated
exspectātĭ•ō -ōnis *f* expectation, suspense; **exspectationem facere** to cause suspense
exspectāt•us -a -um *adj* expected, awaited, desired
exspect•ō -āre *vt* to await, wait for, look out for; to hope for, long for, anticipate
ex•spergō -spergĕre — -spersum *vt* to sprinkle, scatter
exspēs *adj* hopeless, forlorn; (with *genit*) without hope of
exspīrātĭ•ō -ōnis *f* breathing out, exhalation
exspīr•ō -āre or **expīr•ō -āre** *vt* to breathe out, exhale, emit; *vi* to expire, breathe one's last; (fig) to come to an end, cease
exsplend•escō -escĕre -ŭī *vi* to glitter, shine
exspolĭ•ō -āre *vt* to strip; to pillage
es•spŭō -spuĕre -spŭī -spūtum *vt* to spit out; (fig) to banish (*e.g., worries*)
exstern•ō -āre *vt* to startle, scare; to terrify; to stampede (*horses*)
exstill•ō -āre *vi* to drop, trickle out; to melt
exstimulāt•or -ōris *m* instigator
exstimŭl•ō -āre *vt* to instigate, goad on
exstinctĭ•ō -ōnis *f* extinction
exstinct•or -ōris *m* extinguisher; suppressor; destroyer
ex•stinguō -stinguĕre -stinxī -stinctum *vt* to extinguish, put out; to destroy, kill; to abolish, annul; **extingui** to die, die out; to be forgotten
exstirp•ō -āre *vt* to extirpate, root out, eradicate
exst•ō -āre *vi* to stand out, protrude, project; to stand out, be prominent, be conspicuous; to be visible; to appear; to exist, be extant
exstructĭ•ō -ōnis *f* erection
ex•strŭō -struĕre -struxī -structum *vt* to pile up, heap up; to build, erect
exsuct•us -a -um *pp* of **exsugo;** *adj* dried up
exsūd•ō -āre *vt* to sweat; (fig) to sweat out, sweat over; *vi* to pour out
ex•sūgō -sūgĕre -suxī -suctum *vt* to suck out
exs•ul or **ex•ul -ŭlis** *m* or *f* exile, refugee
exsŭl•ō -āre *vi* to be an exile, be a refugee
exsultātĭ•ō -ōnis *f* exultation, jumping for joy
exsultim *adv* friskily
exsult•ō or **exult•ō -āre** *vi* to jump up; to frisk about; (of horses) to rear, prance; to exult, rejoice, jump for joy; to revel, run riot; to boast; (of speech) to range freely
exsuperābĭl•is -e *adj* climbable; superable
exsuperantĭ•a -ae *f* superiority
exsupĕr•ō -āre *vt* to surmount; to exceed, surpass; to overpower; *vi* to rise; (of flames) to shoot up; to be superior, excel, be conspicuous, prevail
exsurd•ō -āre *vt* to deafen; (fig) to dull
ex•surgō -surgĕre -surrexī *vi* to get up, rise, stand up; (fig) to rise, recover strength; **foras exsurgere** to get up and go out
exsuscĭt•ō -āre *vt* to rouse from sleep; to fan (*fire*); to excite, stir up

ext·a -ōrum *n pl* vital organs (*of sacrificial animals*)
extāb·escō -escĕre -ŭī *vi* to waste away, pine away; to disappear
extār·is -e *adj* used for cooking the sacrificial victim; sacrificial
extemplō or **extempŭlō** *adv* immediately, right away; on the spur of the moment
ex·tendō -tendĕre -tendī -tentum or **-tensum** *vt* to stretch out, spread out, extend; to enlarge, increase; to widen, broaden; to prolong, continue; to pass, spend; to exert, strain; **extendi** to stretch out, extend; **labellum extendere** to pout
extent·ō -āre *vt* to exert, strain
extent·us -a -um *pp* of **extendo;** *adj* extensive, wide; **extentis itineribus** by forced marches
extenuātī·ō -ōnis *f* extenuation; thinning out
extenuāt·us -a -um *adj* thinned, reduced; trifling; weak, faint
extenŭ·ō -āre *vt* to thin out; to lessen, diminish, extenuate, detract from
exter or **extĕr·us -a -um** *adj* external, outward; foreign, strange
exterĕbr·ō -āre *vt* to bore out; to extort
ex·tergĕō -tergēre -tersī -tersum *vt* to wipe out, wipe clean; (fig) to wipe out, plunder
exterĭ·or -us *adj* outer, exterior
exterĭus *adv* on the outside
extermĭn·ō -āre *vt* to drive out, banish; to put aside, put away, remove
extern·us -a -um *adj* external, outward; foreign, strange; *m* foreigner, stranger, foreign enemy; *n pl* foreign goods
ex·tĕrō -terĕre -trīvī -trītum *vt* to rub out, wear away; (fig) to crush
exterr·ĕō -ēre -ŭī -ĭtum *vt* to frighten, terrify
extersus *pp* of **extergeo**
extĕrus see **exter**
extex·ō -ĕre *vt* to unweave; (fig) to cheat
extim·escō -escĕre -ŭī *vt* to become terribly afraid of, dread; *vi* to become afraid
extĭm·us -a -um *adj* outermost, farthest, most remote
extisp·ex -ĭcis *m* soothsayer, diviner (*who makes predictions by inspecting the entrails of animals*)
extoll·ō -ĕre *vt* to lift up; to erect; to postpone; to extol, praise; to raise, exalt; to beautify; **animos extollere** to raise the morale
ex·torquĕō -torquēre -torsī -tortum *vt* to wrench, wrest; to dislocate; to extort
extorr·is -e *adj* driven out of one's country, banished, exiled
extort·or -ōris *m* extorter
extortus *pp* of **extorqueo;** *adj* deformed
extrā *adv* outside, on the outside; **extra quam** except in the case that; **extra quam si** unless; *prep* (with *acc*) outside, outside of, beyond; apart from, aside from; contrary to; except, besides; without; **extra jocum** all joking aside
ex·trăhō -trahĕre -traxī -tractum *vt* to pull out, drag out; to drag out, prolong; to waste (*time*); to extricate, release, rescue; to remove
extrānĕ·us -a -um *adj* extraneous, external, irrevelant, strange; *m* stranger
extrāordinārĭ·us -a -um *adj* extraordinary
extrārĭ·us -a -um *adj* outward, external; unrelated (*by family ties*)
extrēm·a -ōrum *n pl* end (*e.g., of a marching column, of strip of land, of life*)
extrēmĭt·ās -ātis *f* extremity, end
extrēmō *adv* finally, at last
extrēmum *adv* finally, at last; for the last time
extrēm·us -a -um *adj* extreme, outermost, on the end; latest, last; (of degree) utmost, extreme; lowest, meanest; **extrema aetas** advanced old age; **extrema cauda** tip of the tail; **extremā lineā amare** to love at a distance; **extrema manus** final touches; **extremis digitis attingere** to touch lightly; to touch lightly on; to hold tenderly; **extremus ignis** flickering flame; **in extremo libro secundo** at the end of the second book; *n* end; extremity; **ad extremum** at last; at the end; utterly; **in extremo** in mortal danger, in a crisis
extrīc·ō -āre or **extrīc·or -ārī -ātus sum** *vt* to extricate; to clear up; to obtain with difficulty
extrinsĕcus *adv* from outside, from abroad; on the outside, outside
extrītus *pp* of **extero**
ex·trūdō -trūdĕre -trūsī -trūsum *vt* to thrust out, drive out; to get rid of
extum·ĕō -ēre *vi* to swell up
ex·tundō -tundĕre -tūdī -tūsum *vt* to beat out, hammer out; to fashion; to devise; to extort
exturb·ō -āre *vt* to drive out, chase out, drive away; to divorce; to knock out
exūbĕr·ō -āre *vi* to grow luxuriantly; to abound
exulcĕr·ō -āre *vt* to make sore, aggravate; to exasperate
exulŭl·ō -āre *vt* to invoke with cries; *vi* to howl
exunctus *pp* of **exungo**
exund·ō -āre *vi* to overflow; **in litora exundare** to wash up on the shores
ex·ungō -ungĕre — -unctum *vt* to oil down, rub with oil

ex·ŭō -uĕre -ŭī -ūtum *vt* to take off, pull off; to shake off; to unclothe; to strip, deprive; to cast aside, cast off; to bare
exurg·ĕō -ēre *vt* to squeeze out
ex·ūrō -ūrĕre -ussī -ustum *vt* to burn out, burn up; to dry up; to consume, destroy; (fig) to inflame
exustĭ·ō -ōnis *f* conflagration
exustus *pp* of **exuro**
exūtus *pp* of **exuo**
exuvĭ·ae -ārum *f pl* clothing; equipment; arms; hide; slough; booty, spoils

F

fab·a -ae *f* bean
fabāl·is -e *adj* bean; **stipulae fabales** bean stalks
fābell·a -ae *f* short story; fable, tale; short play
fab·er -ra -rum *adj* skilled; *m* craftsman; smith; carpenter; (mil) engineer; **faber ferrarius** blacksmith; **faber tignarius** carpenter
Fab·ĭus -ĭī or **-ī** *m* Quintus Fabius Maximus Cunctator, elected consul five times and appointed dictator in 217 B.C. to conduct the war against Hannibal (*d.* 203 B.C.); Quintus Fabius Pictor, first Roman historian to use prose (*fl* 225 B.C.)
fabrē *adv* skillfully
fabrē·facĭō -facĕre -fēcī -factum *vt* to build, make; to forge
fabrĭc·a -ae *f* trade, industry; workshop, factory; piece of work, structure, production; **fabricam fingere** (with **ad** + *acc*) (coll) to pull a trick on
fabricātĭ·ō -ōnis *f* structure, construction
fabricāt·or -ōris *m* builder, architect, producer, creator
fabrĭc·or -ārī -ātus sum or **fabrĭc·ō -āre** *vt* to build, construct, produce, forge; to prepare, form; to coin (*words*)
fabrīl·is -e *adj* craftman's, carpenter's, sculptor's; *n pl* tools
fābŭl·a -ae *f* story, tale; talk, conversation, conversation piece; small talk; affair, matter, concern; myth, legend; drama, play; dramatic poem; **fabulae!** (coll) baloney!; **lupus in fabula!** (coll) speak of the devil!
fābulār·is -e *adj* legendary
fābŭl·or -ārī -ātus sum *vt* to say, invent; *vi* to talk, chat, gossip
fābulōs·us -a -um *adj* legendary
fabŭl·us -ī *m* small bean
facess·ō -ĕre -īvī -ītum *vt* to do eagerly, perform, accomplish; to bring on, cause, create; **negotium alicui facessere** to cause someone trouble; *vi* to go away, depart
facētē *adv* facetiously, humorously, wittily, brilliantly
facētĭ·ae -ārum *f pl* clever thing, clever talk, witticism, humor
facēt·us -a -um *adj* witty, humorous; fine, polite; elegant; brilliant
facĭ·ēs -ēī *f* make, form, shape; face, look; look, appearance; nature, character; external appearance, pretense, pretext
facĭl·is -e *adj* easy; nimble; suitable, convenient; ready, quick; easy, easygoing, good-natured; favorable, prosperous; gentle (*breeze*); easily-borne, slight (*loss*); **ex** or **e facili** easily; **in facili esse** to be easy; **facilis victu** prosperous, well-off, well-to-do
facĭle *adv* easily, without trouble; unquestionably, by far, far; quite, fully; promptly, readily, willingly; pleasantly, well; **non facile** hardly
facilĭt·ās -ātis *f* facility, easiness, ease; readiness; fluency; suitability; good nature, affability, courteousness; levity
facinorōs·us or **facinerōs·us -a -um** *adj & m* criminal
facĭn·us -ŏris *n* deed, action; crime, villany
facĭō facĕre fēcī factum (faxim = fēcĕrim; faxō = fēcĕrō) *vt* to make, fashion, frame, create, build, erect; to do, perform; to make, produce, compose; to bring about, cause, occasion; to acquire, gain, get, accumulate; to incur, suffer; to render, grant, give, confer; to grant, admit; to assume, suppose; to assert, say, represent, depict; to choose, appoint; to follow, practice; to regard, prize, value; **certiorem facere** to inform; **copiam facere** to afford the opportunity; **fac ita esse** suppose it were so, granted that it is so; **fidem facere** to give one's word; **pecuniam facere** or **stipendium facere** to make money, earn money; **promissum facere** to fulfill a promise; **sacra facere** to sacrifice; **verbum facere** to speak; **viam facere** (with *dat*) to make way for; *vi* to do, act; to take part, take sides; (with *dat* or with **ad** + *acc*) to be satisfactory for, be fit for, do for
factĕon = faciendum
factĭ·ō -ōnis *f* doing; making; party, faction; partisanship; company, social set, association, class; oligarchy; (with *genit*) right to make (*e.g., a will*)
factiōs·us -a -um *adj* busy; parti-

san; oligarchical; factious, revolutionary, seditious
factĭt·ō -āre *vt* to keep doing or making; to practice (*e.g., trade*); (with double *acc*) to declare (*someone*) to be (*e.g., heir*)
fact·or -ōris *m* (in playing ball) batter
fact·us -a -um *pp* of **facio;** *n* deed, act; accomplishment, exploit
facŭl·a -ae *f* little torch
facult·ās -ātis *f* opportunity, means; feasibility; ability, capacity, mental resources; material resources, means, supplies, abundance
fācundē *adv* eloquently
fācundĭ·a -ae *f* eloquence
fācundĭt·ās -ātis *f* eloquence
fācund·us -a -um *adj* eloquent, fluent
faecĕ·us -a -um *adj* morally impure, morally rotten
faecŭl·a -ae *f* wine lees
faenĕbr·is -e *adj* of interest, regarding interest; **res faenebris** indebtedness
faenerātĭ·ō -ōnis *f* lending at interest, investment
faenerātō *adv* with interest
faenerāt·or -ōris *m* money lender, investor, capitalist
faenĕr·or -ārī -ātus sum or **faenĕr·ō -āre** *vt* to lend at interest; to invest; to ruin through high interest rates; *vi* to bring interest, bring profit; **faeneratum beneficium** (fig) a favor richly repaid
faenĕ·us -a -um *adj* made of hay
faenīl·ĭa -ĭum *n pl* hayloft
faenisĕc·a -ae *m* peasant
faen·um or **fēn·um -ī** *n* hay; **faenum habet in cornu** (fig) he's crazy
faen·us or **fēn·us -ŏris** *n* interest; debt (*as result of heavy interest*); capital; (fig) profit, gain, advantage
faenuscŭl·um or **fēnuscŭl·um -ī** *n* a little interest
fae·x -cis *f* dregs, sediments, grounds, lees; (fig) dregs
fāginĕ·us or **fāgĭn·us** or **fāgĕ·us -a -um** *adj* beech
fāg·us -ī *f* beech tree
fal·a *or* **phal·a -ae** *f* movable wooden siege tower; scaffold
falārĭc·a or **phalārĭc·a -ae** *f* incendiary missile
falcār·ĭus -ĭī or **-ī** *m* sickle maker
falcāt·us -a -um *adj* fitted with scythes, scythed; sickle-shaped, curved
falcĭf·er -ĕra -ĕrum *adj* scythe-bearing
Falern·us -a -um *adj* Falernian; **ager Falernus** district in N. Campania, famous for its wine; *n* Falernian wine
Falisc·ī -ōrum *m pl* a people of S.E. Etruria
fallācĭ·a -ae *f* deception, deceit, trick
fallācĭter *adv* deceptively, deceitfully, fallaciously
fall·ax -ācis *adj* deceptive, deceitful, fallacious
fallō fallĕre fefellī falsum *vt* to cause to fall, trip; to lead into error; to deceive, trick, dupe, cheat; to fail to live up to, disappoint; to wile away; to escape the notice of, slip by; **fidem fallere** to break one's word; **me fallit** I do not know; **nisi** or **ni fallor** unless I'm mistaken; **opinionem fallere** (with *genit*) to fail to live up to the expectations of
falsē *adv* falsely
falsidĭc·us -a -um *adj* speaking falsely, lying
falsifĭc·us -a -um *adj* acting dishonestly
falsijūrĭ·us -a -um *adj* swearing falsely
falsilŏqu·us -a -um *adj* lying
falsimōnĭ·a -ae *f* trick
falsipăr·ens -entis *adj* bastard
falsō *adv* mistakenly, wrongly, erroneously; falsely, deceitfully, untruly
fals·us -a -um *pp* of **fallo;** *adj* mistaken, wrong, erroneous; false, untrue; lying, deceitful; vain, groundless, empty; spurious, sham, fictitious; *n* error; lying, perjury; lie, untruth, falsehood
fal·x -cis *f* sickle; pruning hook, pruning knife; (mil) hook for pulling down walls
fām·a -ae *f* talk, rumor, report; saying, tradition; reputation; fame, renown, glory, name; infamy, notoriety; public opinion
famēlĭc·us -a -um *adj* famished, starved
fam·ēs -is *f* hunger, starvation; poverty; famine; greed; (rhet) bald style, poverty of expression
fāmigerātĭ·ō -ōnis *f* rumor
fāmigerāt·or -ōris *m* gossip, rumormonger
famĭlĭ·a -ae or **-ās** *f* household slaves, domestics; household; house, family; family estate; fraternity; sect, school; **familiam ducere** to be the head of a sect; **pater familias** head of the household
familiār·is -e *adj* domestic, family, household; familiar, intimate; (in augury) one's own (*part of the sacrificial animal*); *m* servant, slave; acquaintance, friend, companion
familiārĭt·ās -ātis *f* familiarity, intimacy; association, friendship
familiārĭter *adv* on friendly terms
fāmōs·us -a -um *adj* much talked of; famous, renowned; infamous, notorious; slanderous, libelous; **carmen famosum** lampoon
famŭl·a -ae *f* slave, maid, maidservant
famulār·is -e *adj* of slaves, of servants
famulāt·us -ūs *m* servitude, slavery

famŭl·or -ārī -ātus sum *vi* to be a slave; (with *dat*) to serve

famŭl·us -a -um *adj* serviceable; *m* servant, attendant

fānātic·us -a -um *adj* fanatic, enthusiastic, inspired; wild, frantic

fān·um -ī *n* shrine, sanctuary, temple

fār farris *n* spelt; coarse meal, grits; sacrificial meal; bread; dog biscuit; *n pl* grain

far·ciō -cīre -sī -tum *vt* to stuff, cram

farfăr·us or **farfĕr·us -ī** *m* coltsfoot (*plant*)

farīn·a -ae *f* flour; powder; character, quality

farrāg·ō -inis *f* mash (*for cattle*); medley, hodgepodge

farrāt·us -a -um *adj* filled with grain; made with grain

fart·is -is *f* stuffing, filling, mincemeat; **fartim facere ex hostibus** to make mincemeat of the enemy

fart·or -ōris *m* fattener of fowls

fartus *pp* of **farcio**

fās (indecl) *n* divine law; sacred duty; divine will, fate; right; **fas est** it is right, it is lawful, it is permitted

fascĭ·a -ae *f* bandage, swathe; girth; fillet; wisp of cloud

fasciātim *adv* in bundles

fascicŭl·us -ī *m* small bundle

fascĭn·ō -āre *vt* to cast an evil eye on, bewitch, jinx; to envy

fascĭn·um -ī *n* or **fascĭn·us -ī** *m* evil eye; jinx; witchcraft; charm, amulet; penis

fasciŏl·a -ae *f* small bandage

fasc·is -is *m* bundle, pack, parcel, fagot; load, burden; baggage; *m pl* fasces (*bundle of rods and ax, carried before high magistrates by lictors as symbols of authority*); high office, supreme power, consulship

fassus *pp* of **fateor**

fast·ī -ōrum *m pl* calendar, almanac; annals; register of higher magistrates

fastīd·iō -īre -īvī or **-iī -ītum** *vt* to disdain, despise, snub, turn up the nose at; *vi* to feel disgust, feel squeamish; to be snobbish, be haughty

fastīdiōsē *adv* fastidiously, squeamishly; disdainfully, snobbishly

fastīdiōs·us -a -um *adj* fastidious, squeamish; disdainful, snobbish; refined, delicate

fastīd·ium -iī or **-ī** *n* fastidiousness, squeamishness, distaste, disgust, loathing; snobbishness, haughtiness, contempt

fastīgātē *adv* sloped (*like a gable*), sloping up, sloping down

fastīgāt·us -a -um *adj* rising to a point; sloping down

fastīg·ium -iī or **-ī** *n* gable; pediment; roof, ceiling; slope; height, elevation, top, edge; depth, depression; finish, completion; rank, dignity; main point, heading, highlight (*of story, etc.*)

fast·us -a -um *adj* legal (*day*); **dies fastus** court day

fast·us -ūs *m* disdain, contempt, arrogance; *m pl* brash deeds; calendar

fātāl·is -e *adj* fateful, destined, preordained; fatal, deadly; **deae fatales** the Fates

fātālĭter *adv* according to fate, by fate

fatĕor fatērī fassus sum *vt* to admit, acknowledge; to disclose, reveal

fāticăn·us or **fāticĭn·us -a -um** *adj* prophetic

fātidĭc·us -a -um *adj* prophetic

fātĭf·er -ĕra -ĕrum *adj* fatal, deadly

fatīgātĭ·ō -ōnis *f* fatigue, weariness

fatīg·ō -āre *vt* to fatigue, weary, tire; to worry, torment, harass, wear down; to importune, pray to constantly

fātilŏqu·a -ae *f* prophetess

fatisc·ō -ĕre or **fatisc·or -ī** *vi* to split, crack, give way; (fig) to crack, break down, collapse from exhaustion

fatuĭt·ās -ātis *f* silliness

fāt·um -ī *n* divine utterance, oracle; fate, destiny, doom; calamity, mishap, ruin; death; **ad fata novissima** to the last; **fato obire** to meet death, die; **fatum proferre** to prolong life

fātus *pp* of **for**

fatŭ·us -a -um *adj* silly, foolish; clumsy; *m* fool

fauc·ēs -ium *f pl* upper part of the throat, throat, gullet; strait, channel; pass, defile, gorge; (fig) jaws; **fauces premere** (with *genit*) to choke, throttle

Faun·us -ī *m* mythical king of Latium, father of Latinus, and worshiped as the Italian Pan; *m pl* Fauns, woodland spirits

faustē *adv* favorably, auspiciously

faustĭt·ās -ātis *f* fertility; good fortune, happiness

Faustŭl·us -ī *m* shepherd who raised Romulus and Remus

faust·us -a -um *adj* auspicious, favorable, fortunate, lucky

faut·or or **favĭt·or -ōris** *m* promoter, patron, supporter, fan

fautr·ix -īcis *f* patroness, protectress

favĕ·a -ae *f* favorite girl, pet slave girl

favĕō favēre fāvī fautum *vi* (with *dat*) to be favorable to, favor, support, side with; (with *inf*) to be eager to; **favere linguis** or **favere ore** to observe a reverent silence

favill·a -ae *f* ashes, embers; (fig) spark, beginning

favĭtor see **fautor**

Favōn·ius -iī or **-ī** *m* west wind (*also called Zephyrus*)

fav·or -ōris *m* favor, support; applause; appreciation (*shown by applause*)
favōrābĭl·is -e *adj* popular
fav·us -ī *m* honeycomb
fa·x -cis *f* torch; wedding torch; wedding; funeral torch; funeral; meteor, shooting star, comet; firebrand; fire, flame; guiding light; instigator; flame of love; stimulus, incitement; cause of ruin, destruction; **dicendi faces** fiery eloquence; **dolorum faces** pangs of grief
faxim see **facio**
febrīcŭl·a -ae *f* slight fever
febr·is -is *f* fever
Febrŭ·a -ōrum *n pl* Roman festival of purification and expiation, celebrated on February 15th
Februārĭ·us -a -um *adj* & *m* February
febrŭ·um -ī *n* purgation, purification
fēcundĭt·ās -ātis *f* fertility, fruitfulness; (rhet) overstatement
fēcund·ō -āre *vt* to fertilize
fēcund·us -a -um *adj* fertile, fruitful; abundant, rich; fertilizing; (with *genit* or *abl*) rich in, abounding in
fe·l -llis *n* gallbladder; gall, bile; bitterness, animosity; poison
fēl·ēs -is *f* cat
fēlīcĭt·ās -ātis *f* fertility; luck, good fortune, piece of luck; felicity, happiness
fēlīcĭter *adv* fruitfully, abundantly; favorably, auspiciously; luckily; happily; successfully
fēl·ix -īcis *adj* fruit-bearing; fruitful, fertile; favorable, auspicious; lucky; happy; successful
fēmell·a -ae *f* girl
fēmĭn·a -ae *f* female; woman
fēmināt·us -a -um *adj* effeminate
fēminĕ·us -a -um *adj* woman's; effeminate, unmanly
fēminīn·us -a -um *adj* (gram) feminine
fem·ur -ŏris or **-ĭnis** *n* thigh
fēn- = faen-
fenestr·a -ae *f* window; hole (*for earrings*); (fig) opening, opportunity; (mil) breach (*in a wall*)
fer·a -ae *f* wild beast, wild animal
ferācĭus *adv* more fruitfully
Fērāl·ĭa -ĭum *n pl* festival of the dead, celebrated on February 17th or 21st
fērāl·is -e *adj* funeral; deadly, fatal; gloomy, dismal
fer·ax -ācis *adj* fertile, fruitful; (with *genit*) productive of
fercŭl·um -ī *n* food tray; dish, course; litter for carrying spoils in a victory parade or cult images in religious processions
fercŭl·us -ī *m* litter bearer
ferē or **fermē** *adv* approximately, nearly, almost, about, just about; generally, as a rule, usually; (with negatives) practically; **nemo fere** practically no one
ferentār·ĭus -ĭī or **-ī** *m* light-armed soldier; eager helper
Feretr·ĭus -ĭī or **-ī** *m* epithet of Jupiter
ferĕtr·um -ī *n* litter, bier
fērĭ·ae -ārum *f pl* holidays, vacation; (fig) leisure
fēriāt·us -a -um *adj* vacationing, taking it easy, relaxing, taking time off
ferīn·us -a -um *adj* of wild animals; **caro ferina** venison; *f* game, venison
fer·ĭō -īre *vt* to strike, hit, shoot, knock; to kill; to slaughter, sacrifice (*an animal*); to coin; (fig) to strike, reach, affect; (fig) to cheat, trick; **cornu ferire** to butt; **foedus ferire** to make a treaty; **securi ferire** to behead; **verba ferire** to coin words
ferĭt·ās -ātis *f* wildness, fierceness
fermē see **fere**
ferment·um -ī *n* yeast; beer; (fig) ferment, provocation, vexation, anger, passion
ferō ferre tulī or **tetŭlī lātum** *vt* to bear, carry; to bear, produce, bring forth; to bear, endure; to lead, drive, conduct, direct; to bring, offer; to receive, acquire, obtain, win; to take by force, carry off, plunder, ravage; to manifest, display, make known, report, relate, say, tell; to propose, bring forward; to allow, permit; to cause, create; to set in motion; to call, name; (in accounting) to enter; **aegre ferre** to be annoyed at; **caelo supinas manus ferre** to raise the hands heavenward in prayer; **ferri** to move, rush; to sail; to fly; to flow along; (fig) to be carried away (*e.g., with ambition, greed*); **ferri** or **se ferre** to rush, flee; **iter ferre** to pursue a course; **laudibus ferre** to extol; **legem ferre** to propose a bill; **moleste ferre** to be annoyed at; **pedem ferre** to come, go, move, get going; **prae se ferre** to display, manifest; **se ferre obviam** (with *dat*) to rush to meet; **repulsam ferre** to experience defeat (*at the polls*); **sententiam ferre** to pass judgment; to cast a vote; **signa ferre** (mil) to begin marching; **ventrem ferre** to be pregnant; *vi* to say, e.g., **ut ferunt** as people say, as they say; to allow, permit, e.g., **si occasio tulerit** if occasion permit; to lead, e.g., **iter ad oppidum ferebat** the road led to the town
ferōcĭ·a -ae *f* courage, bravery, spirit; ferocity, barbarity; presumption
ferōcĭt·ās -ātis *f* courage, spirit, fierceness, aggressiveness; ferocity, barbarity; pride, presumption

ferōcĭter *adv* bravely, courageously, aggressively; defiantly; haughtily
Fērōnĭ·a -ae *f* early Italic goddess of groves and fountains, and patroness of ex-slaves
fer·ox -ōcis *adj* brave, intrepid, warlike; defiant; overbearing, haughty, insolent
ferrāment·um -ī *n* tool, implement
ferrārĭ·us -a -um *adj* iron; **faber ferrarius** blacksmith; *m* blacksmith; *f pl* iron mines, iron works
ferrātĭl·is -e *adj* fit to be chained
ferrāt·us -a -um *adj* iron-plated; iron-tipped; in chains; in armor; **calx ferrata** spur; *m pl* soldiers in armor
ferrĕ·us -a -um *adj* iron, made of iron; hardhearted, cruel; firm, unyielding
ferricrepĭn·us -a -um *adj* (coll) clanking chains
ferriter·ĭum -ĭī or **-ī** *n* (coll) brig, jug
ferritĕr·us -ī *m* (coll) glutton for punishment
ferritrīb·ax -ācis *adj* (coll) chainsore (*sore from dragging chains*)
ferrūginĕ·us or **ferrūgĭn·us -a -um** *adj* rust-colored, dark, dusky
ferrūg·ō -ĭnis *f* rust; verdigris; dark red; dark color; gloom
ferr·um -ī *n* iron; tool, implement; iron object: sword, dart, arrowhead, ax, plowshare, crowbar, spade, scissors, curling iron; **ferro atque igni** with fire and sword; **ferro decernere** to decide by force of arms
fertĭl·is -e *adj* fertile, fruitful, productive; fertilizing; (with *genit*) productive of
fertilĭt·ās -ātis *f* fertility, fruitfulness
ferŭl·a -ae *f* reed, stalk; rod, whip
fer·us -a -um *adj* wild; uncultivated, untamed; savage, uncivilized; rude, cruel, fierce; wild, desert (*place*); *m* wild beast, wild horse, lion, stag; *f* wild beast
fervē·facĭō -facĕre -fēcī -factum *vt* to heat, boil
ferv·ens -entis *adj* seething, burning, hot; (fig) hot, heated, violent, impetuous
ferventer *adv* (fig) heatedly, impetuously
ferv·ĕō -ēre or **ferv·ō -ĕre -ī** *vi* to boil, seethe, steam; to foam; to swarm; to be busy, bustle about; (fig) to burn, glow, rage, rave
fervesc·ō -ĕre *vi* to become boiling hot, begin to boil, grow hot
fervĭd·us -a -um *adj* boiling, seething, hot; fermenting (*grapes*); hot, highly spiced; (fig) hot, fiery, violent, impetuous, hot-blooded
fervō see **ferveo**
ferv·or -ōris *m* heat, boiling heat; boiling; fermenting; fever; raging (*of the sea*); (fig) heat, vehemence, ardor, passion
Fescennĭ·a -ae *f* town in Etruria
Fescennīn·us -a -um *adj* Fescennine, of Fescennia; *m pl* Fescennine verses (*rude form of dramatic dialogue*)
fess·us -a -um *adj* tired, exhausted, worn out
festīnanter *adv* quickly
festīnātĭ·ō -ōnis *f* hurrying, haste, hurry
festīnātō *adv* hurriedly
festīn·ō -āre *vt & vi* to rush, hurry, accelerate; **jussa festinare** to carry out orders promptly
festīn·us -a -um *adj* hasty, quick, speedy
festīvē *adv* gaily; humorously
festīvĭt·ās -ātis *f* gaiety, fun; humor
festīv·us -a -um *adj* holiday, festal; gay, merry; agreeable, pleasing, pretty; humorous
festūc·a -ae *f* stalk; rod with which slaves were tapped when freed
fest·us -a -um *adj* joyous, festive, in holiday mood; *n* holiday; feast; **festum agere** to observe a holiday
fētĭāl·is -is *m* member of a college of priests who performed the ritual in connection with declaring war and making peace
fetiāl·is -e *adj* negotiating, diplomatic; fetial, of the fetial priests
fetĭd·us -a -um *adj* fetid, stinking
fētūr·a -ae *f* breeding, bearing; offspring, young
fēt·us -a -um *adj* pregnant, breeding; fruitful, teeming, productive
fēt·us -ūs *m* breeding; (of plants) producing, bearing; offspring, young, brood; fruit, produce; (fig) growth, production
fi *interj* (expressing disgust at a bad smell) phew!
fib·er -rī *m* beaver
fibr·a -ae *f* fiber, filament; *f pl* entrails
fībŭl·a -ae *f* clasp, pin, brooch, buckle; brace, clamp
fīcedŭl·a or **fīcēdŭl·a -ae** *f* beccafico (*small bird*)
fictē *adv* falsely, fictitiously
fictĭl·is -e *adj* clay, earthen; *n* jar; clay statue; *n pl* earthenware
fictĭ·ō -ōnis *f* forming, formation; disguising; supposition; fiction
fict·or -ōris *m* sculptor, molder, shaper
fictr·ix -īcis *f* maker, creator (*female*)
fict·um -ī *n* falsehood, fiction, pretense
fictūr·a -ae *f* shaping, fashioning
fict·us -a -um *pp* of **fingo;** *adj* false, fictitious; **vox ficta** falsehood
fīcŭl·us -ī *m* little fig
fīculn·us or **fīculnĕ·us -a -um** *adj* of a fig tree
fīc·us -ī or **-ūs** *f* fig; fig tree
fidēcommiss·um or **fideīcommiss·um -ī** *n* trust fund
fidēlĭ·a -ae *f* earthen pot, pail,

bucket; **duo parietes de eadem fidelia dealbare** to whitewash two walls with one pail, to kill two birds with one stone

fidēl·is -e *adj* faithful, loyal; trusty, trustworthy, true, sure, safe (*ship, port, advice, etc.*); (with *dat* or **in** + *acc*) faithful to; *m* confidant

fidēlĭt·ās -ātis *f* faithfulness, loyalty, fidelity

fidēlĭter *adv* faithfully, loyally; securely, certainly

Fīdēn·ae -ārum *f pl* ancient town in Latium

fīd·ens -entis *adj* confident; resolute; bold

fīdenter *adv* confidently; resolutely; boldly

fīdentĭ·a -ae *f* self-confidence, boldness

fid·ēs -ēī *f* trust, faith, reliance, confidence; credence, belief; trustworthiness, conscientiousness, honesty; promise, assurance, word, word of honor; protection, guarantee; promise of protection, safe conduct; (com) credit; confirmation, proof, fulfilment; **de fide mala** in bad faith, dishonestly; **Di vostram fidem!** for heaven's sake!; **ex fide bona** in good faith, honestly; **fidem dare** to give one's word, offer a guarantee; **fidem facere** to inspire confidence; **fidem fallere** to break one's word; **fidem habere** (with *dat*) to have confidence in; to convince; **fidem servare** to keep one's word; **pro fidem deum!** for heaven's sake!; **res fidesque** capital and credit

fid·ēs -is *f* string (*of a musical instrument*); *f pl* stringed instrument: lyre, lute, zither

fidĭc·en -ĭnis *m* lutist, lyre player; lyric poet

fidicĭn·us -a -um *adj* stringed-instrument; *f* lutist, lyre player (*female*)

fidicŭl·a -ae *f* or **fidicŭl·ae -ārum** *f pl* small lute

fīdissĭmē *adv* most faithfully

Fīd·ius -ĭī or **-ī** *m* epithet of Jupiter; **medius fidius!** honest to goodness!

fīdō fīdĕre fīsus sum *vi* (with *dat* or *abl*) to trust, put confidence in

fīdūcĭ·a -ae *f* trust, confidence, reliance; self-confidence; trustworthiness; (law) deposit, pledge, security, mortgage

fīdūciārĭ·us -a -um *adj* held in trust

fīd·us -a -um *adj* trusty, dependable; certain, sure, safe

figlīn·us or **figulīn·us -a -um** *adj* potter's

fīgō fīgĕre fīxī fīxum *vt* to fix, fasten, affix, attach, nail; to drive in; to pierce; to erect, set up; to build; to post up, hang up

figulār·is -e *adj* potter's

figŭl·us -ī *m* potter; bricklayer

figūr·a -ae *f* figure, shape, form; phantom, ghost; nature, kind; figure of speech

figūrāt·us -a -um *adj* figurative

figūr·ō -āre *vt* to shape, form, mold, fashion; to train, educate

fīlātim *adv* thread by thread

fīlĭ·a -ae *f* daughter

filicāt·us -a -um *adj* engraved with fern patterns

fīliŏl·a -ae *f* little daughter

fīliŏl·us -ī *m* little son

fīl·ius -ĭī or **-ī** *m* son; **terrae filius** a nobody

fil·ix -ĭcis *f* fern

fīl·um -ī *n* thread; fillet; string, cord; wick; figure, shape (*of a woman*); texture, quality, style (*of speech*)

fimbrĭ·ae -ārum *f pl* fringe, border, end

fim·us -ī *m* dung, manure; mire

findō findĕre fidī fissum *vt* to split, split in half

fingō fingĕre finxī fictum *vt* to shape, form; to mold, model (*in clay, stone, etc.*); to arrange, dress, trim; to imagine, suppose, think, conceive; to contrive, invent, pretend, feign; to compose (*poetry*); to disguise (*looks*); to trump up (*charges*); (with double *acc*) to represent as, depict as; **ars fingendi** sculpture; **linguā fingere** to lick; **se fingere** (with **ad** + *acc*) to adapt oneself to; to be subservient to

fīnient·ēs -ĭum *m pl* horizon

fīn·iō -īre -īvī or **-ĭī -ītum** *vt* to limit; (fig) to set bounds to, limit, restrain; to mark out, fix, determine; to put an end to, finish complete; **finiri** to come to an end, end; *vi* to come to an end; to die

fīn·is -is *m* or *f* boundary, border, limit; end; purpose, aim; extreme limit, summit, highest degree; starting point; goal; death; **fine** (with *genit*) up to, as far as; **finem facere** (with *genit* or *dat*) to put an end to; **quem ad finem** how long, to what extent; *m pl* boundaries, country, territory, land

fīnītē *adv* to a limited degree

fīnitĭm·us or **fīnitŭm·us -a -um** *adj* neighboring, bordering; (with *dat*) **a** bordering upon; **b** (fig) bordering upon, akin to; *m pl* neighbors

fīnīt·or -ōris *m* surveyor

fīnīt·us -a -um *adj* limited; (rhet) rhythmical

fīō fĭĕrī factus sum *vi* to come into being, arise; to be made, become, get; to happen; **fieri non potest quin** it is inevitable that; **fieri potest ut** it is possible that; **ita fit ut** or **quo fit ut** thus it happens that

firmām·en -ĭnis *n* prop, support

firmāment·um -ī *n* prop, support; support, mainstay; main point

firmāt·or -ōris *m* establisher, promoter

firmē *adv* firmly, steadily
firmĭt·ās -ātis *f* firmness, strength; steadfastness, stamina, endurance
firmĭter *adv* firmly, steadily
firmitūd·ō -ĭnis *f* firmness, strength, durability; (fig) stability, constancy
firm·ō -āre *vt* to strengthen, fortify, support; to encourage, strengthen, fortify, assure, reinforce; to establish, prove, confirm; to declare, aver
firm·us -a -um *adj* firm, strong, hardy, stable; (fig) firm, steadfast, trusty, true, faithful, lasting; **firmus ad bellum** toughened for combat
fiscāl·is -e *adj* fiscal
fiscell·a -ae *f* small basket
fiscĭn·a -ae *f* small basket
fisc·us -ī *m* basket; money box; state treasury; imperial treasury, emperor's privy purse, imperial revenues
fissĭl·is -e *adj* easy to split; split
fissĭ·ō -ōnis *f* dividing, splitting
fiss·us -a -um *pp* of **findo;** *adj* cloven; *n* slit, fissure
fistūc·a -ae *f* mallet
fistŭl·a -ae *f* pipe, tube; water pipe; hollow stalk or reed; flute; fistula, ulcer
fīsus *pp* of **fido**
fix·us -a -um *pp* of **figo;** *adj* fixed, immovable; permanent
flābellifĕr·a -ae *f* female slave who waved a fan
flābell·um -ī *n* fan
flābĭl·is -e *adj* of air
flābr·a -ōrum *n pl* gusts of wind; breezes, winds
flacc·ĕō -ēre *vi* to be flabby; to lose heart; (of a speech) to get dull
flacc·escō -escĕre -ŭī *vi* to become flabby; to wither, droop
flaccĭd·us -a -um *adj* flabby; languid, feeble
flacc·us -a -um *adj* flabby
flagell·ō -āre *vt* to whip
flagell·um -ī *n* whip; scourge; riding crop; young shoot, sucker; arm (*of a polypus*); sting (*e.g., of conscience*)
flāgitātĭ·ō -ōnis *f* demand
flāgitāt·or -ōris *m* persistent demander
flāgitiōsē *adv* shamefully, disgracefully
flāgitiōs·us -a -um *adj* shameful, disgraceful, profligate
flāgit·ĭum -ĭī or **-ī** *n* shame, disgrace, scandalous conduct, scandal; rascal, good-for-nothing
flāgĭt·ō -āre *vt* to demand; (with double *acc* or with *acc* of thing or **ab** + *abl* of person) to demand (*something*) from (*someone*)
flagr·ans -antis *adj* blazing, flaming, hot; shining, glowing, glittering; ardent, hot, vehement, eager
flagranter *adv* vehemently, ardently
flagrantĭ·a -ae *f* blazing, glow; **flagiti flagrantia** utter disgrace
flagritrĭb·a -ae *m* (coll) (said of a slave) victim of constant whipping
flagr·ō -āre *vi* to blaze, be on fire; (with *abl*) **a** to glow with, flare up in; **b** to be the victim of (*e.g., envy*)
flagr·um -ī *n* whip
flām·en -ĭnis *m* flamen (*priest of a specific deity*); **flamen Dialis** priest of Jupiter
flām·en -ĭnis *n* gust, gale; breeze
flāminĭc·a -ae *f* wife of a flamen
Flāminīn·us -ī *m* T. Quintus Flamininus (*consul of* 198 B.C., *and conqueror of Philip of Macedon at Cynoscephalae, in Thessaly, in* 197 B.C.)
flāmin·ĭum -ĭī or **-ī** *n* office of flamen, priesthood
Flāminĭ·us -a -um *adj* Flaminian; **via Flaminia** road leading from Rome to Ariminum; *m* Gaius Flaminius (*conqueror of Insubrian Gauls in* 223 B.C., *builder of the Circus Flaminius and the Flaminian highway in* 220 B.C., *and casualty in the battle at Lake Trasimenus in* 217 B.C.)
flamm·a -ae *f* flame, fire, blaze; star; torch; flame of passion, fire of love, glow, passion; sweetheart; danger, destruction; **flamma fumo est proxima** where there's smoke there's fire; **flammam concipere** to catch fire
flammār·ĭus -ĭī or **-ī** *m* maker of bridal veils
flammeŏl·um -ī *n* bridal veil
flammesc·ō -ĕre *vi* to become inflamed, become fiery
flammĕ·us -a -um *adj* flaming, fiery; flashing (*eyes*); flame-covered; *n* bridal veil
flammĭf·er -ĕra -ĕrum *adj* fiery
flamm·ō -āre *vt* to set on fire; (fig) to inflame, incense; *vi* to burn, glow, blaze
flammŭl·a -ae *f* little flame
flāt·us -ūs *m* blowing, breathing, breath; breeze, wind; snorting; arrogance
flāv·ens -entis *adj* yellow, golden
flāvesc·ō -ĕre *vi* to become yellow, become golden-yellow
Flāvĭ·us -a -um *adj* Flavian; **gens Flavia** Flavian clan (*to which the emperors Vespasian, Titus, and Domitian belonged*)
flāv·us -a -um *adj* yellow, blond, reddish-yellow, golden
flēbĭl·is -e *adj* pitiful, pathetic, deplorable; crying, tearful
flēbilĭter *adv* tearfully, mournfully
flectō flectĕre flexī flexum *vt* to bend, curve; to turn, wheel about, turn around; to wind, twist, curl; to direct, avert, turn away (*eyes, mind, etc.*); to double, sail around (*a cape*); to modulate (*voice*); to change (*the mind*); to persuade, move, appease; **viam** or **iter flectere** (with **ad** + *acc*) to make one's way toward, head toward; *vi* to turn, go, march

flēmĭn·a -um *n pl* swollen, bloody ankles
fl·ĕō -ēre -ēvī -ētum *vt* to cry for, mourn for; *vi* to cry
flēt·us -ūs *m* crying; *m pl* tears
flexanĭm·us -a -um *adj* moving, touching
flexibĭl·is -e *adj* flexible; shifty, fickle
flexĭl·is -e *adj* flexible, pliant
flexilŏqu·us -a -um *adj* ambiguous
flexĭ·ō -ōnis *f* bending, turning; modulation (*of the voice*)
flexĭp·ēs -ĕdis *adj* creeping (*ivy*)
flexuōs·us -a -um *adj* winding (*road*)
flexūr·a -ae *f* bending, winding
flexus *pp* of **flecto**
flex·us -ūs *m* bending, turning, winding; shift, change, transition, crisis
flict·us -ūs *m* clashing, banging together
fl·ō -āre *vt* to blow, breathe; to coin (*money*); *vi* to blow
flocc·us -ī *m* lock (*of hair, wool*); down; **flocci facere** to think little of, disregard, not give a hoot about
Flōr·a -ae *f* goddess of flowers, whose festival was celebrated on April 28th
flōr·ens -entis *adj* blooming; prosperous; flourishing, in the prime; (with *abl*) in the prime of, at the height of
flōr·ĕō -ēre -ŭī *vi* to bloom, blossom; to be in one's prime; (of wine) to foam, ferment; to be prosperous, be eminent; (with *abl*) **a** to abound in; **b** to swarm with, be filled with
flōr·escō -escĕre -ŭī *vi* to begin to bloom, begin to blossom
flōrĕ·us -a -um *adj* flowery; made of flowers
flōrĭd·us -a -um *adj* flowery; fresh, pretty; florid (*style*)
flōrĭf·er -ĕra -ĕrum *adj* flowery
flōrilĕg·us -a -um *adj* (of bees) going from flower to flower
flōr·us -a -um *adj* luxuriant
fl·ōs -ōris *m* flower; bud, blossom; best (*of anything*); prime (*of life*); youthful beauty, innocence; crown, glory; nectar; literary ornament
floscŭl·us -ī *m* little flower, floweret; flower, pride, glory
fluctifrăg·us -a -um *adj* wave-breaking (*shore*), surging
fluctuātĭ·ō -ōnis *f* wavering, vacillating
fluctŭ·ō -āre or **fluctŭ·or -ārī -ātus sum** *vi* to fluctuate, undulate, wave; to be restless; to waver, vacillate, fluctuate
fluctuōs·us -a -um *adj* running (*sea*)
fluct·us -ūs *m* wave, billow; flowing, undulating; turbulence, commotion; disorder, unrest; **fluctus in simpulo** tempest in a tea cup
flu·ens -entis *adj* loose, flowing; (morally) loose; effeminate; fluent
fluent·a -ōrum *n pl* flow, stream, river
fluenter *adv* like a wave
fluĭd·us or **flūvĭd·us -a -um** *adj* flowing, fluid; soft; relaxing
fluĭt·ō or **flūt·ō -āre** *vi* to float, swim; to sail; to toss about; to hang loose, flap; to be uncertain, waver; to stagger
flūm·en -ĭnis *n* flowing, stream, river, flood; fluency; (fig) flood (*e.g., of tears, words, etc.*); **flumine adverso** upstream; **secundo flumine** downstream
flūminĕ·us -a -um *adj* river
flu·ō -ĕre -xī -xum *vi* to flow; to run down, drip; to overflow; (of branches) to spread; to sink, drop, droop; to pass away, vanish, perish; to be fluent; to be monotonous; to spring, arise, proceed
flūtō see **fluito**
fluviāl·is -e *adj* river, of a river
fluviātĭl·is -e *adj* river, of a river
flūvĭdus see **fluidus**
fluv·ius -ĭī or **-ī** *m* river; running water, stream
flux·us -a -um *adj* flowing, loose; careless; loose, dissolute; frail, weak; transient, perishable
fōcāl·e -is *n* scarf
fōcill·ō -āre *vt* to warm, revive
focŭl·um -ī *n* stove
focŭl·us -ī *m* brazier; (fig) fire
foc·us -ī *m* hearth, fireplace; brazier; funeral pile; altar; home, family
fodĭc·ō -āre *vt* to poke, nudge
fodĭō fodĕre fōdī fossum *vt* to dig, dig out; (fig) to prod, goad, prick
foecund- = fecund-
foedē *adv* foully, cruelly, shamefully
foederāt·us -a -um *adj* confederated, allied
foedifrăg·us -a -um *adj* treacherous, perfidious
foedĭt·ās -ātis *f* foulness, hideousness
foed·ō -āre *vt* to make hideous, disfigure; to pollute, defile, disgrace
foed·us -a -um *adj* foul, filthy, horrible, ugly, disgusting, repulsive; disgraceful, vile
foed·us -ĕris *n* treaty, charter, league; compact, agreement; law; **aequo foedere** on equal terms, mutually; **foedere certo** by fixed law; **foedere pacto** by fixed agreement
foen- = faen-
foet·ĕō -ēre *vi* to stink
foetĭd·us -a -um *adj* stinking
foet·or -ōris *m* stink, stench
foetu- = fētu-
foliāt·us -a -um *adj* leafy; *n* nard oil
fol·ium -ĭī or **-ī** *n* leaf; **folium recitare Sibyllae** to tell the gospel truth
follicŭl·us -ī *m* small bag, sack; shell, skin; eggshell
foll·is -is *m* bag; punching bag; bellows; money bag; puffed-out cheeks

fōment·um -ī *n* bandage; mitigation, alleviation
fōm·es -ĭtis *m* tinder
fon·s -tis *m* spring, fountain; spring water, water; stream; lake; source, origin, fountainhead
fontān·us -a -um *adj* spring
fonticŭl·us -ī *m* little spring, little fountain
for fārī fātus sum *vt & vi* to say, speak, utter
forābĭl·is -e *adj* vulnerable
forām·en -ĭnis *n* hole, opening
forās *adv* out, outside; **foras dare** to publish (*writings*)
forc·eps -ĭpis *m* or *f* forceps, tongs
ford·a -ae *f* pregnant cow
fore = futur·us -a -um esse to be about to be
forem = essem
forens·is -e *adj* of the forum, in the forum; public, forensic
forf·ex -ĭcis *f* scissors
for·is -is *f* door, gate; *f pl* double doors; opening, entrance; (fig) door
forīs *adv* outside, out of doors; abroad, in foreign countries; from outside, from abroad
form·a -ae *f* form, shape, figure; beauty; shape, image; mold, stamp; shoemaker's last; vision, apparition, phantom; species, form, nature, sort, kind; outline, design, sketch, plan
formāment·um -ī *n* shape
formāt·or -ōris *m* fashioner
formātūr·a -ae *f* fashioning, shaping
Formĭ·ae -ārum *f pl* town in S. Latium
formīc·a -ae *f* ant
formīcīn·us -a -um *adj* ant-like
formīdābĭl·is -e *adj* terrifying
formīd·ō -āre *vt* to fear, dread; *vi* to be frightened
formīd·ō -ĭnis *f* fear, dread, awe, terror; scarecrow; threats
formīdolōsē *adv* dreadfully, terribly
formīdolōs·us -a -um *adj* dreadful, terrifying, terrible; afraid, terrified
form·ō -āre *vt* to form, shape, mold, build; to make, produce, invent; to imagine; to regulate, direct
formōsē *adv* beautifully, gracefully
formōsĭt·ās -ātis *f* beauty
formōs·us -a -um *adj* shapely, beautiful, handsome
formŭl·a -ae *f* nice shape, beauty; form, formula, draft; contract, agreement; rule, regulation; (law) regular method, formula, rule; (phil) principle
fornācāl·is -e *adj* of an oven
fornācŭl·a -ae *f* small oven
forn·ax -ācis *f* oven, furnace, kiln; forge
fornicāt·us -a -um *adj* arched
forn·ix -ĭcis *m* arch, vault; arcade; brothel
fornus see **furnus**
for·ō -āre *vt* to bore, pierce
fors *adv* perhaps, chances are, there is a chance, possibly
for·s -tis *f* chance, luck, fortune, accident; **forte** by chance, accidentally, by accident; as it happens, as it happened; perhaps
forsan, forsit, or **forsĭtan** *adv* perhaps
fortasse or **fortassis** *adv* perhaps
forte see **fors**
forticŭl·us -a -um *adj* quite bold, rather brave
fort·is -e *adj* strong, mighty, powerful; brave, courageous, valiant, resolute, steadfast, firm
fortĭter *adv* strongly, vigorously, firmly, bravely, boldly
fortitūd·ō -ĭnis *f* strength; bravery, courage, resolution
fortuītō *adv* by chance, accidentally, casually
fortuīt·us -a -um *adj* accidental, fortuitous, casual
fortūn·a -ae *f* chance, luck, fate, fortune; good luck, prosperity; bad luck, misfortune; lot, circumstances, state, rank, position; property, goods, fortune
fortūnātē *adv* fortunately, prosperously
fortūnāt·us -a -um *adj* fortunate, lucky, prosperous, happy; rich, well-off
fortūn·ō -āre *vt* to make happy, make prosperous, bless
forŭl·ī -ōrum *m pl* bookcase
for·um -ī *n* shopping center, market, marketplace; market town; trade, commerce; forum, civic center; court; public life, public affairs; jurisdiction; **cedere foro** to go bankrupt; **extra suum forum** beyond his jurisdiction; **forum agere** to hold court; **forum attingere** to enter public life; **in foro versari** to be engaged in commerce
For·um Appĭī (*genit*: **For·ī Appĭī**) *n* town in Latium on the Via Appia
For·um Aurēlĭī (*genit*: **For·ī Aurēlĭī**) *n* town N. of Rome on the Via Aurelia
For·um Julĭī (*genit*: **For·ī Julĭī**) *n* town in S. Gaul, colony of the eighth legion
for·us -ī *m* gangway; tier of seats; tier of a beehive
foss·a -ae *f* ditch, trench; **fossam deprimere** to dig a deep trench
fossĭ·ō -ōnis *f* digging
foss·or -ōris *m* digger; lout, clown
fossūr·a -ae *f* digging
fossus *pp* of **fodio**
fōtus *pp* of **foveo**
fovĕ·a -ae *f* small pit; (fig) pitfall
fovĕō fovēre fōvī fōtum *vt* to warm, keep warm; to fondle, caress; to love, cherish; to support, encourage; to pamper
fract·us -a -um *pp* of **frango;** *adj* interrupted, irregular; weak, feeble
frāg·a -ōrum *n pl* strawberries
fragĭl·is -e *adj* fragile, brittle;

crackling; weak, frail; unstable, fickle

fragilit·ās -ātis *f* weakness, frailty

fraglō see **fragro**

fragm·en -inis *n* fragment; *n pl* debris, ruins, wreckage

fragment·um -ī *n* fragment, remnant

frag·or -ōris *m* crash, noise, uproar, din; applause; clap of thunder

fragōs·us -a -um *adj* broken, uneven, rough; crashing, roaring

fragr·ō or **fragl·ō -āre** *vi* to smell sweet, be fragrant; to reek

framĕ·a -ae *f* German spear

frangō frangĕre frēgī fractum *vt* to break in pieces, smash to pieces, shatter; to grind, crush; (fig) to break down, overcome, crush, dishearten, humble, weaken, soften, move, touch; **diem mero frangere** to break up the day with wine

frāt·er -ris *m* brother; cousin; friend, comrade

frātercŭl·us -ī *m* little brother

frāternē *adv* like a brother

frāternĭt·ās -ātis *f* brotherhood

frātern·us -a -um *adj* brotherly; brother's; fraternal

frātricīd·a -ae *m* murderer of a brother, a fratricide

fraudātĭ·ō -ōnis *f* swindling

fraudāt·or -ōris *m* swindler

fraud·ō -āre *vt* to swindle, cheat, defraud; to embezzle; (with *abl*) to defraud (*someone*) of, cheat (*someone*) of

fraudulentĭ·a -ae *f* tendency to swindle, deceitfulness

fraudulent·us -a -um *adj* fraudulent; deceitful, treacherous

frau·s -dis *f* fraud, deception, trickery; error, delusion; crime, offense; harm, damage; deceiver, fraud, cheat; **sine fraude** without harm

fraxinĕ·us or **fraxĭn·us -a -um** *adj* of ash wood, ashen

fraxĭn·us -ī *f* ash tree; spear (*made of ash wood*)

Fregell·ae -ārum *f pl* ancient Volscan city on the Liris River, in Latium, made a Roman colony in 328 B.C.

fremebund·us -a -um *adj* roaring

fremĭt·us -ūs *m* roaring, growling, snorting; din, noise

frem·ō -ĕre -ŭī -ĭtum *vt* to grumble at, complain loudly of; to demand angrily; *vi* to roar, growl, snort, howl, grumble, murmur; to resound

frem·or -ōris *m* roaring, grumbling, murmuring

frend·ō -ĕre -ŭī *vi* to gnash the teeth; **dentibus frendere** to gnash the teeth

frēnī see **frenum**

frēn·ō -āre *vt* to bridle, curb; (fig) to curb, control

frēn·um -ī *n* or **frēn·a -ōrum** *n pl* or **frēn·ī -ōrum** *m pl* bridle, bit; (fig) curb, control, restraint

frequ·ens -entis *adj* crowded, in crowds, numerous, filled; frequent, repeated, usual, common; (may be rendered adverbially) often, repeatedly

frequentātĭ·ō -ōnis *f* piling up

frequenter *adv* frequently, often; in great numbers

frequentĭ·a -ae *f* crowd, throng; crowded assembly, large attendance

frequent·ō -āre *vt* to visit often, frequent, resort to; to do often, repeat; to crowd, people, stock; to attend (*e.g., games*) in large numbers

fretens·is -e *adj* **fretense mare** Strait of Messina

fret·um -ī *n* strait, channel; sea, waters; (fig) seething flood

frēt·us -a -um *adj* confident; (with *dat* or *abl*) supported by, relying on, depending on

fret·us -ūs *m* strait

fric·ō -āre -ŭī -tum *vt* to rub, rub down

frictus *pp* of **frigo**

frīgefact·ō -āre *vt* to make cold or cool

frīg·ĕō -ēre *vi* to be cold, be chilly; to freeze; (fig) to be numbed, be lifeless, be dull; (fig) to get a cool reception, be snubbed, get a cold shoulder; (fig) to fall flat

frīgesc·ō -ĕre *vi* to become cold, become chilled; to become lifeless

frīgidārĭ·us -a -um *adj* cooling

frīgĭdē *adv* feebly

frīgidŭl·us -a -um *adj* rather cold; rather faint

frīgĭd·us -a -um *adj* cold, cool; numbed, dull, lifeless, indifferent, unimpassioned, feeble; flat, insipid, trivial; *f* cold water

frīgō frīgĕre frixī frictum *vt* to fry, roast

frīg·us -ŏris *n* cold, coldness, chill, coolness; frost; cold of winter, winter; coldness of death, death; chill, fever; cold shudder, chill; cold region; cold reception; coolness, indifference; slowness, inactivity; *n pl* cold spell, cold season

frigutt·ĭō -īre *vi* to stutter

fri·ō -āre *vt* to crumble

fritill·us -ī *m* dice box

frīvŏl·us -a -um *adj* frivolous, trifling, worthless, sorry, pitiful; *n pl* trifles

frondāt·or -ōris *m* pruner

frond·ĕō -ēre *vi* to have leaves; to become green

frondesc·ō -ĕre *vi* to get leaves

frondĕ·us -a -um *adj* leafy, covered with leaves

frondĭf·er -ĕra -ĕrum *adj* leafy

frondōs·us -a -um *adj* full of leaves, leafy

fron·s -dis *f* foliage; leafy bough, green bough; chaplet, garland

fron·s -tis *f* forehead, brow; front end, front; countenance, face, look; face, façade; van, vanguard; exterior, appearance; outer end of a scroll; sense of shame; **a fronte** in front; **frontem contrahere** to knit the brow, frown; **frontem ferire** to hit oneself on the head (*in self-annoyance*); **frontem remittere** to smooth the brow, to cheer up; **in fronte** (in measuring land) in breadth, frontage; **salvā fronte** without shame; **tenuis frons** low forehead

frontāl·ĭa -ĭum *n pl* frontlet (*ornament for forehead of a horse*)

front·ō -ōnis *m* one with a large forehead

fructuārĭ·us -a -um *adj* productive; subject to land tax

fructuōs·us -a -um *adj* fruitful, productive

fructus *pp* of **fruor**

fruct·us -ūs *m* produce, fruit; proceeds, profit, income, return, revenue; enjoyment, satisfaction; benefit, reward, results, consequence

frūgāl·is -e *adj* frugal; honest; worthy

frūgālĭt·ās -ātis *f* frugality, economy; temperance; honesty; worth

frūgālĭter *adv* frugally, economically; temperately

frūgēs see **frux**

frūgī (indecl) *adj* frugal; temperate; honest, worthy; useful, proper

frūgĭf·er -ĕra -ĕrum *adj* fruitful, productive, fertile; profitable

frūgifĕr·ens -entis *adj* fruitful

frūgilĕg·us -a -um *adj* (of ants) food-gathering

frūgipăr·us -a -um *adj* fruitful

fruĭtus *pp* of **fruor**

frūmentārĭ·us -a -um *adj* of grain, grain; grain-producing; of provisions; **res frumentaria** (mil) supplies, quartermaster corps; *m* grain dealer

frūmentātĭ·ō -ōnis *f* (mil) foraging

frūmentāt·or -ōris *m* grain merchant; (mil) forager

frūment·or -ārī -ātus sum *vi* (mil) to forage

frūment·um -ī *n* grain; wheat; *n pl* grain fields, crops

frūn·iscor -iscī -ītus sum *vt* to enjoy

fruor fruī fructus sum or **fruĭtus sum** *vt* to enjoy; *vi* (with *abl*) **a** to enjoy, delight in; **b** to enjoy the company of; **c** (law) to have the use and enjoyment of

frustillātim *adv* in bits

frustrā *adv* in vain, uselessly, for nothing; without reason, groundlessly; **frustra discedere** to go away disappointed; **frustra esse** to be mistaken; **frustra habere** to have (*someone*) confused or baffled

frustrām·en -ĭnis *n* deception

frustrātĭ·ō -ōnis *f* deception; frustration

frustrāt·us -ūs *m* deception; **frustratui habere** (coll) to take for a sucker

frustr·or -ārī -ātus sum or **frustr·ō -āre** *vt* to deceive, trick; to disappoint; to frustrate

frustulent·us -a -um *adj* crumby, full of crumbs

frust·um -ī *n* crumb, bit, scrap; **frustum pueri** (coll) whippersnapper

frut·ex -ĭcis *m* shrub, bush; (coll) blockhead

fruticēt·um -ī *n* thicket, shrubbery

frutĭc·ō -āre or **frutĭc·or -ārī -ātus sum** *vi* to sprout; to become bushy; (fig) (of the hair) to become bushy

fruticōs·us -a -um *adj* bushy, overgrown with bushes

frux frūgis *f* or **frūg·ēs -um** *f pl* fruit, produce, grain, vegetables; barley meal (*for sacrifice*); fruits, benefit, result; **se ad frugem bonam recipere** to turn over a new leaf; **expers frugis** worthless

fūcāt·us -a -um *adj* dyed, colored, painted; artificial, spurious

fūc·ō -āre *vt* to dye red, redden, paint red; to disguise, falsify

fūcōs·us -a. -um *adj* painted, colored; spurious, phoney

fūc·us -ī *m* red paint; rouge; drone; bee glue; disguise, pretense, deceit

fue or **fu** *interj* phui!

fug·a -ae *f* flight, escape; avoidance; exile; speed, swift passage; disappearance; (with *genit*) avoidance of, escape from; **fugae sese mandare, fugam capere, fugam capessere, fugam facere, se in fugam conferre, se in fugam conjicere,** or **sese in fugam dare** to flee, take flight; **in fugam conferre, in fugam conjicere, in fugam dare,** or **in fugam impellere** to put to flight

fugācĭus *adv* more cautiously, with one eye on flight

fug·ax -ācis *adj* apt to flee, fleeing; shy, timid; swift; passing, transitory; (with *genit*) shy of, shunning, avoiding, steering clear of, averse to

fugĭ·ens -entis *adj* fleeing, retreating; (with *genit*) avoiding, averse to

fugĭō fugĕre fūgī fugĭtum *vt* to escape, escape from, run away from, shun, avoid; to leave (*esp. one's country*); to be averse to, dislike; to escape the notice of, escape, be unknown to; **fuge** (with *inf*) do not; **fugit me scribere** I forgot to write; *vi* to flee, escape, run away; to go into exile; to speed, hasten; to vanish, disappear; to pass away, perish

fugĭt·ans -antis *adj* fleeing; (with *genit*) averse to

fugitīv·us -a -um *adj* & *m* runaway, fugitive

fugĭt·ō -āre *vt* to run away from

fugĭt·or -ōris *m* deserter

fug·ō -āre *vt* to put to flight, drive away, chase away; to exile, banish; to avert

fulcīm·en -ĭnis *n* support, prop, pillar

fulcīō fulcīre fulsī fultum *vt* to prop up, support; to secure, sustain
fulcr•um -ī *n* bed post; couch, bed
fulgĕō fulgēre fulsī or **fulg•ō -ĕre** *vi* to gleam, flash, blaze, shine, glare; to shine, be conspicuous, be illustrious
fulgĭd•us -a -um *adj* flashing, shining
fulgō see **fulgeo**
fulg•or -ōris *m* flash of lightning, lightning; brightness; thing struck by lightning
fulgurāl•is -e *adj* of lightning; **libri fulgurales** books on lightning
fulgurāt•or -ōris *m* interpreter of lightning
fulgurīt•us -a -um *adj* struck by lightning
fulgŭr•ō -āre *vi* to lighten, send lightning; *v impers* it is lightning
fulĭc•a -ae or **ful•ix -ĭcis** *f* coot (*waterfowl*)
fūlĭg•ō -ĭnis *f* soot; black paint
fulix see **fulica**
full•ō -ōnis *m* fuller
fullōnĭc•a -ae *f* fuller's craft, fulling
fullōnĭ•us -a -um *adj* fuller's
fulm•en -ĭnis *n* thunderbolt, lightning bolt; (fig) bolt, bolt out of the blue
fulment•a -ae *f* heel
fulminĕ•us -a -um *adj* of lightning, lightning; shine, sparkling, flashing
fulmĭn•ō -āre *vi* to lighten; (fig) to flash
fultūr•a -ae *f* support, prop
fultus *pp* of **fulcio**
fulv•us -a -um *adj* yellow, yellowish brown, reddish yellow, tawny; blond
fūmĕ•us -a -um *adj* smoky
fūmĭd•us -a -um *adj* smoking, smoky
fūmĭf•er -ĕra -ĕrum *adj* smoking
fūmifĭc•ō -āre *vi* to smoke; to burn incense
fūmifĭc•us -a -um *adj* smoking, steaming
fūm•ō -āre *vi* to smoke, fume, steam, reek
fūmōs•us -a -um *adj* smoked, smoky
fūm•us -ī *m* smoke, steam, fume
fūnāl•e -is *n* rope; torch; chandelier, candelabrum
fūnambŭl•us -ī *m* tightrope walker
functĭ•ō -ōnis *f* performance
functus *pp* of **fungor**
fund•a -ae *f* sling; sling stone; dragnet
fundām•en -ĭnis *n* foundation
fundāment•um -ī *n* foundation; (fig) basis, ground, beginning; **a fundamentis** utterly, completely; **fundamenta agere, jacere,** or **locare** to lay the foundations
fundāt•or -ōris *m* founder
fundāt•us -a -um *adj* well-founded, established
fundĭt•ō -āre *vt* to sling, shoot with a sling; (fig) to sling (*e.g.,* *words*) around
fundĭt•or -ōris *m* slinger
fundĭtus *adv* from the bottom, utterly, entirely
fund•ō -āre *vt* to found, build, establish; to secure to the ground, make fast
fundō fundĕre fūdī fūsum *vt* to pour, pour out; to melt (*metals*); to cast (*in metal*); to pour in streams, shower, hurl; (mil) to pour in (*troops*); (mil) to rout; to pour out, empty; to spread, extend, diffuse; to bring forth, bear, yield in abundance; to throw to the ground, bring down; to give up, lose, waste; to utter, pour out (*words*)
fund•us -ī *m* bottom; farm, estate; (law) sanctioner, authority
fūnĕbr•is -e *adj* funeral; deadly, murderous
fūnerāt•us -a -um *adj* done in, killed
fūnerĕ•us -a -um *adj* funeral; deadly, fatal
fūnĕr•ō -āre *vt* to bury; **prope funeratus** almost sent to my (*his, etc.*) grave
fūnest•ō -āre *vt* to defile with murder, desecrate
fūnest•us -a -um *adj* deadly, fatal, calamitous; sad, dismal, mournful; **annales funesti** obituary column
fungĭn•us -a -um *adj* of a mushroom
fungor fungī functus sum *vi* (with *abl*) **a** to perform, execute, discharge, do; **b** to busy oneself with, be engaged in; **c** to finish, complete; **morte fungi** to suffer death, die
fung•us -ī *m* mushroom, fungus; candle snuff; (fig) clown
fūnicŭl•us -ī *m* cord
fūn•is -is *m* rope, cable, cord; rigging; **funem ducere** (fig) to command; **funem reducere** (fig) to change one's mind; **funem sequi** (fig) to serve, follow
fūn•us -ĕris *n* funeral rites, funeral, burial; corpse; death, murder; havoc; ruin, destruction; **sub funus** on the brink of the grave; *n pl* shades of the dead
fūr fūris *m* or *f* thief; (fig) rogue, rascal
fūrācissĭmē *adv* quite like a thief
fūr•ax -ācis *adj* thievish
furc•a -ae *f* fork; fork-shaped prop (*for supporting vines, bleachers, etc.*); wooden yoke (*put around slave's neck as punishment*)
furcĭf•er -ĕrī *m* rogue, rascal
furcill•a -ae *f* little fork
furcill•ō -āre *vt* to support, prop up
furcŭl•a -ae *f* fork-shaped prop; *f pl* narrow pass, defile
Furcŭl•ae Caudīn•ae (*genit*: **Furcŭl•ārum Caudīn•ārum**) *f pl* Caudine Forks (*mountain pass near Caudium, in Samnium, where the Roman army was trapped in* 321 B.C. *by the Samnites and made to pass under the yoke*)

furenter *adv* furiously
furf·ur -ŭris *m* chaff; bran
Furĭ·a -ae *f* Fury (*one of the three goddesses of frenzy and vengeance, who were named Megaera, Tisiphone, and Alecto*)
furĭ·a -ae *f* frenzy, madness, rage; remorse; madman
furiāl·is -e *adj* of the Furies; frenzied, frantic, furious; infuriated
furiālĭter *adv* frantically
furibund·us -a -um *adj* frenzied, frantic, mad; inspired
fūrīn·us -a -um *adj* of thieves
furĭ·ō -āre *vt* to drive mad, infuriate
furiōsē *adv* in a rage, in a frenzy
furiōs·us -a -um *adj* frenzied, frantic, mad, furious; maddening
furn·us or **forn·us -ī** *m* oven; bakery
fur·ō -ĕre *vi* to be crazy, be out of one's mind, rage, rave
fūr·or -ārī -ātus sum *vt* to steal, pilfer; to pillage; to plagiarize; to obtain by fraud; to withdraw in secret; to impersonate
fur·or -ōris *m* madness, rage, fury, passion; furor, excitement; prophetic frenzy, inspiration; passionate love
furtifĭc·us -a -um *adj* thievish
furtim *adv* secretly, by stealth, clandestinely
furtīvē *adv* secretly, stealthily
furtīv·us -a -um *adj* stolen; secret, hidden, furtive
furt·um -ī *n* theft, robbery; trick, stratagem; secret action, intrigue; secret love; *n pl* intrigues; secret love affair; stolen goods
fūruncŭl·us -ī *m* petty thief
furv·us -a -um *adj* black, dark, gloomy, eerie
fuscĭn·a -ae *f* trident
fusc·ō -āre *vt* to blacken
fusc·us -a -um *adj* dark, swarthy; low, muffled, indistinct (*sound*)
fūsē *adv* widely; in great detail
fūsĭl·is -e *adj* molten, liquid
fūsĭ·ō -ōnis *f* outpouring, effusion
fust·is -is *m* club, stick, cudgel; beating to death (*as a military punishment*)
fustitudĭn·us -a -um *adj* (coll) whip-happy (*jail*)
fustuār·ĭum -ĭī or **-ī** *n* beating to death (*as a military punishment*)
fūs·us -a -um *pp* of **fundo;** *adj* spread out; broad, wide; diffuse (*style*)
fūs·us -ī *m* spindle
futtĭl·is or **fūtĭl·is -e** *adj* brittle; futile, worthless, untrustworthy
futtilĭt·ās or **fūtilĭt·ās -ātis** *f* futility, worthlessness
fut·ŭō -uĕre -ŭī -ūtum *vt* to have sexual intercourse with (*a woman*)
futūr·us -a -um *fut p* of **sum;** *adj* & *n* future

G

Gabĭ·ī -ōrum *m pl* ancient town in Latium
Gad·ēs -ĭum *f pl* Cadiz (*town in S. Spain*)
gaes·um -ī *n* Gallic spear
Gaetūl·ī -ōrum *m pl* a people in N.W. Africa along the Sahara Desert
Gā·ĭus -ī *m* Roman praenomen (*the names of Gaius and Gaia were formally given to the bridegroom and bride at the wedding ceremony*)
Galăt·ae -ārum *m pl* Galatians (*a people of central Asia Minor*)
Galatĭ·a -ae *f* Galatia (*country in central Asia Minor*)
Galb·a -ae *m* Servius Sulpicius Galba, the Roman emperor from June, 68 A.D., to January, 69 A.D. (5 B.C.-69 A.D.)
galbanĕ·us -a -um *adj* of galbanum
galban·um -ī *n* galbanum (*resinous sap of a Syrian plant*)
galbĭn·us -a -um *adj* chartreuse; (fig) effeminate; *n pl* pale green clothes
galĕ·a -ae *f* helmet
galeāt·us -a -um *adj* helmeted
galērĭcŭl·um -ī *n* cap
galērīt·us -a -um *adj* wearing a farmer's cap, countryish
galēr·um -ī *n* or **galēr·us -ī** *m* cap; (fig) wig
gall·a -ae *f* gallnut
Gall·ī -ōrum *m pl* Gauls (*inhabitants of modern France and N. Italy*)
Gallĭ·a -ae *f* Gaul
Gallĭc·us -a -um *adj* Gallic
gallīn·a -ae *f* chicken, hen; (as term of endearment) chick
gallīnācĕ·us or **gallīnācĭ·us -a -um** *adj* poultry
gallīnār·ĭus -ĭī or **-ī** *m* poultry farmer
Gallograec·ī -ōrum *m pl* Galatians (*Celts who migrated from Gaul to Asia Minor in the 3rd cent.* B.C.)
Gall·us -a -um *adj* Gallic; *m* Gaul; priest of Cybele; C. Cornelius Gallus, lyric poet and friend of Virgil (69-27 B.C.)
gall·us -ī *m* rooster, cock
gānĕ·a -ae *f* or **gānĕ·um -ī** *n* brothel, dive; cheap restaurant
gānĕ·ō -ōnis *m* glutton
gānĕum see **ganea**
Gangarĭd·ae -ārum *m pl* an Indian people on the Ganges
Gang·es -is *m* Ganges River

gann·iō -īre *vi* to snarl, growl
gannīt·us -ūs *m* snarling, growling
Ganymēd·ēs -is *m* Ganymede (*handsome youth carried off to Olympus by the eagle of Jupiter to become the cupbearer of the gods*)
Garamant·es -um *m pl* tribe in N. Africa
Gargaphī·ē -ēs *f* valley in Boeotia sacred to Diana
Gargān·us -ī *m* mountain in S.E. Italy
garr·iō -īre *vt* to chatter, prattle, talk; **nugas garrire** to talk nonsense; *vi* to chatter, chat; (of frogs) to croak
garrulit·ās -ātis *f* talkativeness; chattering
garrŭl·us -a -um *adj* talkative, babbling, garrulous
gar·um -ī *n* fish sauce
gaud·ens -entis *adj* cheerful
gauděō gaudēre gāvīsus sum *vt* to rejoice at; **gaudium gaudere** to feel joy; *vi* to rejoice, be glad, feel pleased; (with *abl*) to delight in; **in se gaudere** or **in sinu gaudere** to be secretly glad
gaud·ium -iī or **-ī** *n* joy, gladness, delight; sensual pleasure, enjoyment; joy, cause of joy; **mala mentis gaudia** gloating
gaul·us -ī *m* bucket
gausăp·e -is or **gausăp·um -ī** *n* felt; (fig) shaggy beard
gāvīsus *pp* of **gaudeo**
gaz·a -ae *f* royal treasure; treasure, riches
gelĭdē *adv* coldly, indifferently
gelĭd·us -a -um *adj* cold, icy, frosty; icy cold, stiff, numbed; *f* cold water
gel·ō -āre *vt* & *vi* to freeze
Gelōn·ī -ōrum *m pl* Scythian tribe
gel·u -ūs *n* or **gel·um -ī** *n* or **gel·us -ūs** *m* coldness, cold, frost, ice; chill, coldness (*of death, old age, fear*)
gemebund·us -a -um *adj* sighing, groaning
gemellipăr·a -ae *f* mother of twins
gemell·us -a -um *adj* & *m* twin
gemĭnātĭ·ō -ōnis *f* doubling; compounding
gemĭn·ō -āre *vt* to double; to join, unite, pair; to repeat, reproduce
gemĭn·us -a -um *adj* twin; double, twofold, two, both; similar; *m pl* twins
gemĭt·us -ūs *m* sigh, groan
gemm·a -ae *f* bud; gem, jewel; jeweled goblet; signet ring, signet; eye of a peacock's tail; literary gem
gemmāt·us -a -um *adj* set with jewels, jeweled
gemmĕ·us -a -um *adj* set with jewels, jeweled; brilliant, glittering, sparkling
gemmĭf·er -ĕra -ĕrum *adj* gem-producing
gemm·ō -āre *vi* to sprout, bud; to sparkle
gem·ō -ĕre -ŭī -ĭtum *vt* to sigh over, lament; *vi* to sigh, groan, moan; to creak
Gemōnĭ·ae -ārum *f pl* steps on the Capitoline slope from which criminals were thrown
gen·a -ae *f* or **gen·ae -ārum** *f pl* cheek; cheekbone; eye socket; eye
geneālŏg·us -ī *m* genealogist
gen·er -ĕrī *m* son-in-law; daughter's boyfriend or fiancé
generāl·is -e *adj* of a species, generic; general, universal
generālĭter *adv* in general, generally
generasc·ō -ĕre *vi* to be generated
generātim *adv* by species, by classes; in general, generally
generāt·or -ōris *m* producer, breeder
genĕr·ō -āre *vt* to beget, procreate, produce, engender
generōsĭus *adv* more nobly
generōs·us -a -um *adj* of good stock, highborn, noble; noble, noble-minded
genĕs·is -is *f* birth, creation; horoscope
genesta see **genista**
genetīv·us -a -um *adj* inborn, innate; (gram) genitive; *m* genitive case
genĕtr·ix -īcis *f* mother, ancestress
geniāl·is -e *adj* nuptial, bridal; genial; joyous, festive, merry
geniālĭter *adv* merrily
geniculāt·us -a -um *adj* knotted, having knots, jointed
genist·a or **genest·a -ae** *f* broom plant; broom
genitābĭl·is -e *adj* productive
genitāl·is -e *adj* generative, productive; of birth; **dies genitalis** birthday
genitālĭter *adv* fruitfully
genitīvus see **genetivus**
genĭt·or -ōris *m* father, creator
genĭtrix see **genetrix**
genĭtus *pp* of **gigno**
gen·ĭus -iī or **-ī** *m* guardian spirit; taste, appetite, natural inclination; talent, genius
gen·s -tis *f* clan; stock; tribe; folk, nation, people; species, breed; descendant, offspring; *f pl* foreign nations; **longe gentium abire** to be far, far away; **minime gentium** by no means; **ubi gentium** where in the world, where on earth
gentĭc·us -a -um *adj* tribal; national
gentīlicĭ·us -a -um *adj* family
gentīl·is -e *adj* family, hereditary; tribal; national; *m* clansman, kinsman
gentīlĭt·ās -ātis *f* clan relationship
gen·ū -ūs *n* knee; **genibus minor** kneeling; **genibus nixus** on one's knees; **genuum junctura** knee joint
genuāl·ĭa -ĭum *n pl* garters
genuīn·us -a -um *adj* innate, natural; of the cheek; jaw, of the jaw; *m pl* back teeth

gen·us -ĕris *n* race, descent, lineage, breed, stock, family; noble birth; tribe; nation, people; descendant, offspring, posterity; kind, sort, species, class; rank, order, division; fashion, way, style; matter, respect; genus; sex; gender; **aliquid id genus** (*acc* of description instead of *genit* of quality) something of that sort; **in omni genere** in every respect

geōgraphĭ·a -ae *f* geography

geōmĕtr·ēs -ae *m* geometer, mathematician

geōmetrĭ·a -ae *f* geometry

geōmetrĭc·us -a -um *adj* geometrical; *n pl* geometry

georgĭc·us -a -um *adj* agricultural; *n pl* Georgics (*poems on farming by Virgil*)

ger·ens -entis *adj* (with *genit*) managing (*e.g., a business*)

germān·a -ae *f* full sister, real sister

germānē *adv* sincerely

Germān·ī -ōrum *m pl* Germans

Germānĭ·a -ae *f* Germany

Germānĭc·us -a -um *adj* Germanic; *m* cognomen of Tiberius' nephew and adoptive son (15 B.C.-19 A.D.)

germānĭt·ās -ātis *f* brotherhood, sisterhood (*relationship between brothers and sisters of the same parents*); relationship between colonies of the same mother-city

germān·us -a -um *adj* having the same parents; brotherly; sisterly; genuine, real, true; *m* full brother, own brother; *f* see **germana**

germ·en -ĭnis *n* sprout, bud, shoot, offspring; embryo

germĭn·ō -āre *vt* to put forth, grow (*hair, wings, etc.*); *vi* to sprout

gerō gerĕre gessī gestum *vt* to bear, carry, wear, have, hold; to bring; to display; exhibit, assume; to bear, produce; to carry on, manage, govern, regulate, administer; to carry out, transact, do, accomplish; **bellum gerere** to fight, carry on war; **dum ea geruntur** while that was going on; **gerere morem** (with *dat*) to gratify, please, humor; **personam gerere** (with *genit*) to play the part of; **rem gerere** to run a business, conduct an affair; **se gerere** to behave; **se gerere** (with **pro** + *abl*) to claim to be for; **se medium gerere** to remain neutral

ger·ō -ōnis *m* porter

gerr·ae -ārum *f pl* trifles, nonsense

gerr·ō -ōnis *m* (coll) loafer

gerulifigŭl·us -ī *m* accomplice; (with *genit*) accomplice in

gerŭl·us -ī *m* porter

Gērȳ·ŏn -ōnis or **Gēryŏn·ēs -ae** *m* mythical three-headed king of Spain who was slain by Hercules

gestām·en -ĭnis *n* that which is worn or carried, load; vehicle, litter; *n pl* ornaments; accouterments; arms

gestātĭ·ō -ōnis *f* drive (*place where one drives*)

gestāt·or -ōris *m* bearer, carrier

gestĭ·ō -ōnis *f* performance

gest·ĭō -īre -īvī or **-ĭī -ītum** *vi* to be delighted, be thrilled, be excited; to be eager; (with *inf*) to be itching to, long to

gestĭt·ō -āre *vt* to be in the habit of carrying or wearing

gest·ō -āre *vt* to bear, wear, carry; to carry about, blab, tell; to cherish; **gestari** to ride, drive, sail (*esp. for pleasure*)

gest·or -ōris *m* tattler

gestus *pp* of **gero;** *adj* **res gestae** accomplishments, exploits

gest·us -ūs *m* gesture; gesticulation; posture, bearing, attitude

Get·ae -ārum *m pl* Thracian tribe of the lower Danube

gibb·us -ī *m* hump

Gigant·es -um *m pl* Giants (*race of gigantic size, sprung from Earth as the blood of Uranus fell upon her. They tried to storm heaven but were repelled by the gods with the aid of Hercules and placed under various volcanoes*)

gignō gignĕre genŭī genĭtum *vt* to beget, bear, produce; to cause, occasion, create, begin

gilv·us -a -um *adj* pale-yellow; **equus gilvus** palomino

gingīv·a -ae *f* gum (*of the mouth*)

glab·er -ra -rum *adj* hairless, bald, smooth; *m* young slave, favorite slave

glaciāl·is -e *adj* icy, frozen

glacĭ·ēs -ēī *f* ice; *f pl* ice fields

glacĭ·ō -āre *vt* to turn into ice, freeze

gladiāt·or -ōris *m* gladiator; *m pl* gladiatorial combat, gladiatorial show; **gladiatores dare** or **gladiatores edere** to stage a gladiatorial show

gladiātōrĭ·us -a -um *adj* gladiatorial; *n* gladiator's pay

gladiātūr·a -ae *f* gladiatorial profession

glad·ĭus -ĭī or **-ī** *m* sword; murder, death; **gladium educere** or **gladium stringere** to draw the sword; **gladium recondere** to sheathe the sword

glaeb·a -ae *f* lump of earth, clod; soil, land; lump, piece

glaebŭl·a -ae *f* small lump; bit of land, small farm

glaesum see **glesum**

glandĭf·er -ĕra -ĕrum *adj* acorn-producing

glandiōnĭd·a -ae *f* choice morsel

gland·ĭum -ĭī or **-ī** *n* choice cut (*of meat*)

glan·s -dis *f* mast; nut; acorn; chestnut; bullet

glārĕ·a -ae *f* gravel

glāreōs·us -a -um *adj* full of gravel, gravelly
glaucōm·a -ătis *n* cataract; **glaucomam ob oculos objicere** (with *dat*) to throw dust into the eyes of
glauc·us -a -um *adj* grey-green, greyish; bright, sparkling
Glauc·us -ī *m* leader of the Lycians in the Trojan War; fisherman of Anthedon, in Euboea, who was changed into a sea deity
glēba see **glaeba**
glēs·um or **glaes·um -ī** *n* amber
glī·s -ris *m* dormouse
glisc·ō -ĕre *vi* to grow, swell up, spread, blaze up; to grow, increase
globōs·us -a -um *adj* spherical
glob·us -ī *m* ball, sphere, globe; crowd, throng, gathering; clique
glomerām·en -ĭnis *n* ball, globe
glomĕr·ō -āre *vt* to form into a ball, gather up, roll up; to collect, gather together, assemble
glom·us -ĕris *n* ball of yarn
glōrĭ·a -ae *f* glory, fame; glorious deed; thirst for glory, ambition; pride, boasting, bragging
glōriātĭ·ō -ōnis *f* boasting, bragging
glōriŏl·a -ae *f* bit of glory
glōrĭ·or -ārī -ātus sum *vt* (only with *neut pron* as object) to boast about, e.g., **haec gloriari** to boast about this; **idem gloriari** to make the same boast; *vi* to boast, brag; (with *abl* or with **de** or **in** + *abl*) to take pride in, boast about; (with **adversus** + *acc*) to boast or brag to (*someone*)
glōriōsē *adv* gloriously; boastfully, pompously
glōriōs·us -a -um *adj* glorious, famous; boastful
glossēm·a -ătis *n* word to be glossed
glūt·en -ĭnis *n* glue
glūtinăt·or -ōris *m* bookbinder
glūtĭn·ō -āre *vt* to glue together
glutt·iō or **glūt·iō -īre** *vt* to gulp down
glutt·ō -ōnis *m* glutton
Gnae·us or **Gnē·us -ī** *m* Roman praenomen
gnār·us -a -um or **gnārŭr·is -e** *adj* skillful, expert; known; (with *genit*) familiar with, versed in, expert in
gnātus see **natus**
gnāv- = **nav-**
gnōbĭlis see **nobilis**
Gnōsĭ·a -ae or **Gnōsĭ·as -ădis** or **Gnōs·is -ĭdis** *f* Ariadne (*daughter of King Minos*)
gnoscō see **nosco**
Gnoss·us or **Gnōs·us -ī** *f* Cnossos (*ancient capital of Crete and residence of Minos*)
gnōtus see **nosco**
gōb·ius or **cōb·ius -iī** or **-ī** or **gōbi·ō -ōnis** *m* goby (*small fish*)
Gorgĭ·as -ae *m* famous orator and sophist of Leontini, in Sicily (*c.* 480-390 B.C.)
Gorg·ō -ōnis *f* Gorgon (*a daughter of Phorcys and Ceto*); *f pl* Gorgons (*Stheno, Medusa, and Euryale*)
Gorgōnĕ·us -a -um *adj* Gorgonian; **Gorgoneus equus** Pegasus; **Gorgoneus lacus** fountain Hippocrene on Mount Helicon
grabāt·us -ī *m* cot
Gracch·us -ī *m* Tiberius Sempronius Gracchus (*social reformer and tribune in* 133 B.C.); Gaius Sempronius Gracchus (*younger brother of Tiberius and tribune in* 123 B.C.)
gracĭl·is -e or **gracĭl·us -a -um** *adj* slim, slender; thin, skinny; poor; slight, insignificant; plain, simple (*style*)
gracilĭt·ās -ātis *f* slenderness; thinness, leanness, meagerness
grācŭl·us or **graccŭl·us -ī** *m* jackdaw
gradātim *adv* step by step, gradually, little by little
gradātĭ·ō -ōnis *f* climax
gradior gradī gressus sum *vi* to go, walk, step
Grādīv·us or **Grădīv·us -ī** *m* epithet of Mars
grad·us -ūs *m* step, pace, walk, gait; step, degree, grade, stage; approach, advance, progress; status, rank; station, position; step, rung, stair; footing; **concito gradu** on the double; **de gradu dejicere** (fig) to throw off balance; **gradum celerare** or **gradum corripere** to pick up the pace, speed up the pace; **gradum conferre** (mil) to come to close quarters; **gradūs ferre** (mil) to charge; **pleno gradu** on the double; **suspenso gradu** on tiptoe
Graecē *adv* Greek, in Greek; **Graece loqui** to speak Greek; **Graece scire** to know Greek
Graecĭ·a -ae *f* Greece; **Magna Graecia** southern Italy
graeciss·ō -āre *vi* to ape the Greeks
graec·or -ārī -ātus sum *vi* to go Greek, act like a Greek
Graecŭl·us -a -um *adj* (in contemptuous sense) Greek through and through, hundred-percent Greek; *mf* Greekling, dirty little Greek
Graec·us -a -um *adj & mf* Greek; *n* Greek, Greek language
Grā·iī or **Grā·ī -ōrum** *m pl* Greeks
Grāiugĕn·a -ae *m* Greek, Greek by birth
grall·ae -ārum *f pl* stilts
grallăt·or -ōris *m* stilt walker
grām·en -ĭnis *n* grass; meadow, pasture; plant, herb
grāminĕ·us -a -um *adj* grassy, of grass; of bamboo
grammatĭc·us -a -um *adj* grammatical, of grammar; *m* teacher of literature and language; philologist; *f & n pl* grammar; philology
grānārĭ·a -ōrum *n pl* granary
grandaev·us -a -um *adj* old, aged
grandesc·ō -ĕre *vi* to grow, grow big

grandicŭl·us -a -um *adj* rather large; pretty tall
grandĭf·er -ĕra -ĕrum *adj* productive
grandilŏqu·us -ī *m* braggart
grandĭn·at -āre *v impers* it is hailing
grand·ĭō -īre *vt* to enlarge, increase
grand·is -e *adj* full-grown, grown up, tall; large, great; aged; important, powerful, strong; grand, lofty, dignified (*style*); loud, strong (*voice*); heavy (*debt*); dignified (*speaker*)
grandĭt·ās -ātis *f* grandeur
grand·ō -ĭnis *f* hail
grānĭf·er -ĕra -ĕrum *adj* (of ants) grain-carrying
grān·um -ī *n* grain, seed
graphĭcē *adv* masterfully
graphĭc·us -a -um *adj* masterful
graph·ium -iī or **-ī** *n* stilus
grassāt·or -ōris *m* vagabond, tramp; bully; prowler
grass·or -ārī -ātus sum *vi* to walk about, prowl around; to hang around, loiter; to go, move, proceed; (with **adversus** or **in** + *acc*) to attack, waylay
grātē *adv* willingly, with pleasure; gratefully
grātēs (*genit* not in use) *f pl* thanks, gratitude; **grates agere** (with *dat*) to thank, give thanks to; **grates habere** (with *dat*) to feel grateful to
grātĭ·a -ae *f* grace, charm, pleasantness, loveliness; influence, prestige; love, friendship; service, favor, kindness; thanks, gratitude, acknowledgment; cause, reason, motive; **cum gratia** (with *genit*) to the satisfaction of; with the approval of; **eā gratiā ut** for the reason that; **exempli gratiā** for example; **gratiā** (with *genit*) for the sake of, on account of; **gratiam facere** (with *dat* of person and *genit* of thing) to pardon (*someone*) for (*a fault*); **gratias agere** (with *dat*) to thank, give thanks to; **gratias habere** (with *dat*) to feel grateful to; **in gratiam** (with *genit*) in order to win the favor of, in order to please; **in gratiam habere** to regard (*something*) as a favor; **meā gratiā** for my sake; **quā gratiā** why
Grātĭ·ae -ārum *f pl* Graces (*Aglaia, Euphrosyne, and Thalia, daughters of Jupiter by Eurynome*)
grātificātĭ·ō -ōnis *f* kindness
grātific·or -ārī -ātus sum *vt* to give up, surrender, sacrifice; *vi* (with *dat*) **a** to do (*someone*) a favor; **b** to gratify, please
grātiīs *adv* gratis, free, for nothing, gratuitously
grātiōs·us -a -um *adj* popular, influential; obliging
grātīs *adv* gratis, free, for nothing, gratuitously
grāt·or -ārī -ātus sum *vi* to rejoice; to express gratitude; (with *dat*) to congratulate; **invicem inter se gratari** to congratulate one another
grātuītō *adv* gratuitously, gratis, for nothing; for no particular reason
grātuīt·us -a -um *adj* gratuitous, free, spontaneous; voluntary; unprovoked
grātulābund·us -a -um *adj* congratulating
grātulātĭ·ō -ōnis *f* congratulation; rejoicing, joy; public thanksgiving
grātulāt·or -ōris *m* congratulator, well-wisher
grātŭl·or -ārī -ātus sum *vi* to be glad, rejoice, manifest joy; (with *dat*) **a** to congratulate; **b** to render thanks to
grāt·us -a -um *adj* pleasing, pleasant, agreeable, welcome; thankful, grateful; deserving thanks, earning gratitude; *n* favor; **gratum facere** (with *dat*) to do (*someone*) a favor
gravanter *adv* reluctantly
gravātē *adv* with difficulty; unwillingly, grudgingly
gravātim *adv* with difficulty; unwillingly
gravēdinōs·us -a -um *adj* prone to catch colds
gravēd·ō -ĭnis *f* cold, head cold
gravesc·ō -ĕre *vi* to grow heavy; (fig) to become worse
gravidĭt·ās -ātis *f* pregnancy
gravĭd·ō -āre *vt* to impregnate
gravĭd·us -a -um *adj* loaded, filled, full; pregnant; (with *abl*) teeming with
grav·is -e *adj* heavy, weighty; burdensome; troublesome, oppressive, painful, harsh, hard, severe, unpleasant; unwholesome, indigestible; important, influential, venerable, grave, serious; pregnant; hostile; low, deep, bass; flat (*note*); harsh, bitter, offensive (*smell or taste*); impressive (*speech*); stormy (*weather*); oppressive (*heat*)
gravĭt·ās -ātis *f* weight; severity, harshness, seriousness; importance; dignity, influence; pregnancy; violence, vehemence
gravĭter *adv* heavily, ponderously; hard, violently, vehemently; severely, harshly, unpleasantly, disagreeably; sadly, sorrowfully; with dignity, with propriety, with authority; (to feel) deeply; (to smell) offensive, strong; (to speak) impressively; **graviter ferre** to take (*something*) hard
grav·ō -āre *vt* to weigh down, load, load down; to burden, be oppressive to; to aggravate; to increase
grav·or -ārī -ātus sum *vt* to feel annoyed at, object to, refuse, decline; to bear with reluctance, regard as a burden; *vi* to feel annoyed, be vexed
gregāl·is -e *adj* of the herd or flock; common; **sagulum gregale** uni-

form of a private; *m pl* comrades, companions

gregārĭ·us -a -um *adj* common; (mil) of the same rank; **miles gregarius** private

gregātim *adv* in flocks, in herds, in crowds

grem·ĭum -ĭī or **-ī** *n* lap, bosom; womb

gressus *pp* of **gradior**

gress·us -ūs *m* step; course, way

gre·x -gis *m* flock, herd; swarm; company, group, crowd, troop, set, clique, gang; theatrical cast

gruis see **grus**

grunn·ĭō or **grund·ĭō -īre -īvī** or **-ĭī -ītum** *vi* to grunt

grunnīt·us -ūs *m* grunt, grunting

grū·s or **gru·is -is** *m* or *f* crane

grȳ (indecl) *n* scrap, crumb

gryps grȳpis *m* griffin

gubernācŭl·um or **gubernācl·um -ī** *n* rudder, tiller, helm; *n pl* (fig) helm

gubernātĭ·ō -ōnis *f* navigation

gubernāt·or -ōris *m* navigator, pilot; governor

gubernātr·ix -īcis *f* directress

gubern·ō -āre *vt* to navigate, pilot; to direct, govern

gul·a -ae *f* gullet, throat; palate, appetite, gluttony

gulōs·us -a -um *adj* appetizing, dainty

gurg·es -ĭtis *m* abyss, gulf, whirlpool; waters, flood, depths, sea; spendthrift

gurgulĭ·ō -ōnis *m* gullet, windpipe

gurgust·ĭum -ĭī or **-ī** *n* dark hovel; (fig) hole in the wall

gustātōr·ĭum -ĭī or **-ī** *n* appetizer

gustāt·us -ūs *m* sense of taste; flavor, taste

gust·ō -āre *vt* to taste; (fig) to enjoy; to overhear; *vi* to have a snack

gust·us -ūs *m* tasting; appetizer

gutt·a -ae *f* drop; spot, speck

guttātim *adv* drop by drop

guttŭl·a -ae *f* tiny drop

gutt·ur -ŭris *n* gullet, throat, neck; *n pl* throat, neck

gūt·us or **gutt·us -ī** *m* cruet, flask

Gy·ās -ae *m* hundred-armed giant

Gȳg·ēs -is or **-ae** *m* king of Lydia (716-678 B.C.)

gymnasiarch·us -ī *m* manager of a gymnasium

gymnas·ĭum -ĭī or **-ī** *n* gymnasium

gymnastĭc·us -a -um *adj* gymnastic

gymnĭc·us -a -um *adj* gymnastic

gymnosophist·ae -ārum *m pl* Hindu Stoics

gynaecē·um or **gynaecī·um -ī** *n* women's apartments

gypsāt·us -a -um *adj* covered with plaster

gyps·um -ī *n* gypsum, plaster

gȳr·us -ī *m* circle, cycle, ring, orbit, course

H

ha, hahae, hahahae *interj* expression of joy, satisfaction, or laughter

habēn·a -ae *f* strap; *f pl* reins; (fig) reins, control; **habenae rerum** reins of the state; **habenas adducere, dare, effundere,** or **immittere** (with *dat*) to give free rein to

hab·ĕō -ēre -ŭī -ĭtum *vt* to have, hold, keep; to retain, detain; to contain; to possess, own; to wear; to treat, handle, use; to hold, conduct (*meeting*); to deliver (*speech*); to occupy, inhabit; to pronounce, utter (*words*); to hold, manage, govern, wield; to hold, think, consider, believe; to occupy, engage, busy; to occasion, produce, render; to know, be informed of, be acquainted with; to take, accept, endure, bear; **in animo habere** to have on one's mind; **in animo habere** (with *inf*) to intend to; **pro certo habere** to regard as certain; **secum** or **sibi habere** to keep (*something*) to oneself, keep secret; **se habere** (with *adv*) to be,feel (*well, etc.*); *vi* **bene habet** it is well, all is well; **sic habet** that's how it is

habĭl·is -e *adj* handy; suitable, convenient; active, nimble; skillful

habilĭt·ās -ātis *f* aptitude

habitābĭl·is -e *adj* habitable, fit to live in

habitātĭ·ō -ōnis *f* dwelling, house

habitāt·or -ōris *m* inhabitant, tenant

habĭt·ō -āre *vt* to inhabit; *vi* to dwell, live, stay, reside; (with **in** + *abl*) **a** to live in, reside at; **b** to be always in (*a certain place*); **c** (fig) to dwell upon

habitūd·ō -ĭnis *f* condition, appearance

habĭt·us -a -um *adj* well-kept, fat, stout

habĭt·us -ūs *m* condition (*of the body*); character, quality; style, style of dress, attire; disposition, state of feeling; habit

hāc *adv* this way, in this way

hactĕnus *adv* to this place, thus far; up till now, hitherto, so far; to this extent, so far, so much

Hadrĭ·a -ae *f* city in Picenum, the birthplace of Hadrian; city in the country of the Veneti, on the coast of the sea named after it; *m* Adriatic Sea

Hadriān·us -ī *m* Hadrian (*Roman emperor*, 117-138 A.D.)
haec hōrum (*neut pl* of **hoc**) *adj & pron* these
haec hūjus (older form; **haece;** *genit*: **hujusce**) (*fem* of **hic**) *adj* this; the present, the actual; the latter; (occasionally) the former; **haec . . . haec** one . . . another; *pron* this one, she; the latter; (occasionally) the former; **haec . . . haec** one . . . another one; **haecine** (**haec** with *interrog* enclitic **-ne**) is this . . .?
haece see **haec**
haecĭne see **haec**
Haed·ī -ōrum *m pl* pair of stars in the constellation Auriga
haedilĭ·a -ae *f* little kid
haedill·us -ī *m* (term of endearment) little kid or goat
haedīn·us -a -um *adj* kid's, goat's
haedŭl·us -ī *m* little kid, little goat
haed·us -ī *m* young goat, kid
Haemonĭ·a -ae *f* Thessaly
Haem·us or **Haem·os -ī** *m* mountain range in Thrace
haerĕō haerēre haesī haesum *vi* to cling, stick; to hang around, linger, stay, remain fixed, remain in place; to be rooted to the spot, come to a standstill, stop; to be embarrassed, be at a loss, hesitate, be in doubt; (with *dat* or *abl* or with **in** + *abl*) **a** to cling to, stick to, adhere to, be attached to; **b** to loiter in, hang around in, waste time in (*a place*) or at (*an activity*); **c** to adhere to, stick by (*an opinion, purpose*); **d** to gaze upon; **e** to keep close to; **in terga, in tergis,** or **tergis hostium haerere** to pursue the enemy closely
haeresc·ō -ĕre *vi* to adhere
haerĕs·is -is *f* sect, school of thought
haesitābund·us -a -um *adj* hesitating, faltering
haesitantĭ·a -ae *f* stammering
haesitātĭ·ō -ōnis *f* hesitation, indecision; stammering
haesitāt·or -ōris *m* hesitator
haesĭt·ō -āre *vi* to get stuck; to stammer; to hesitate, be undecided, be at a loss
hahae hahahae *interj* expression of joy, satisfaction, or laughter
halagŏra -ae *f* salt market
hāl·ans -antis *adj* fragrant
hāl·ēc -ēcis *n* fish sauce
haliaeĕt·os -ī *m* sea eagle, osprey
hālĭt·us -ūs *m* breath; steam, vapor
hall·ex -ĭcis *m* big toe
hallūcĭn·or or **hālūcĭn·or -ārī -ātus sum** *vi* to daydream, have hallucinations, talk wildly
hāl·ō -āre *vt* to exhale; *vi* to exhale; to be fragrant
halophant·a -ae *m* scoundrel
hālūcinor see **hallucinor**
ham·a or **am·a -ae** *f* bucket, pail
Hamādrȳ·as -ădis *f* wood nymph
hāmātĭl·is -e *adj* with hooks
hāmāt·us -a -um *adj* hooked, hook-shaped
Hamĭlc·ar -ăris *m* famous Carthaginian general in the First Punic War, surnamed Barca, and father of Hannibal (*d.* 228 B.C.)
hāmiōt·a -ae *m* angler
hāmŭl·us -ī *m* small hook
hām·us -ī *m* hook, fishhook
Hannĭb·al -ălis *m* son of Hamilcar Barca and famous general in the Second Punic War (246-172 B.C.)
har·a -ae *f* pen, coop, stye
harēn·a -ae *f* sand; seashore, beach; arena; *f pl* desert
harēnōs·us -a -um *adj* sandy
hariŏl·or -ārī -ātus sum *vi* to foretell the future; to talk gibberish
hariŏl·us -ī *m* or **hariŏl·a -ae** *f* soothsayer
harmonĭ·a -ae *f* harmony
harpăg·ō -āre *vt* to steal
harpăg·ō -ōnis *m* hook, harpoon, grappling hook; greedy person
Harpalȳc·ē -ēs *f* daughter of a Thracian king, brought up as a warrior
harp·ē -ēs *f* scimitar
Harpȳī·ae -ārum *f pl* Harpies (*mythical monsters, half woman, half bird*)
harundĭf·er -ĕra -ĕrum *adj* reed-bearing
harundinĕ·us -a -um *adj* made of reed
harundinōs·us -a -um *adj* overgrown with reeds
harund·ō -ĭnis *f* reed, cane; fishing rod; pen; shepherd's pipe; arrow shaft, arrow; fowler's rod; weaver's comb; hobbyhorse (*toy*)
harusp·ex -ĭcis *m* soothsayer who foretold the future from the inspection of the vital organs of animals; prophet
haruspĭc·a -ae *f* soothsayer (*female*)
haruspicīn·us -a -um *adj* of divination; *f* art of divination
haruspic·ĭum -ĭī or **-ī** *n* divination
Hasdrŭb·al or **Asdrŭb·al -ălis** *m* brother of Hannibal (*d.* 207 B.C.); son-in-law of Hamilcar Barca (*d.* 221 B.C.)
hast·a -ae *f* spear; **sub hasta vendere** to sell at auction, auction off
hastāt·us -a -um *adj* armed with a spear; *m pl* soldiers in first line of a Roman battle formation
hastīl·e -is *n* shaft; spear, javelin
hau or **au** *interj* cry of pain or grief
haud or **haut** or **hau** *adv* not, hardly, not at all, by no means
hauddum *adv* not yet
haudquāquam *adv* not at all, by no means
haurĭō haurīre hausī haustum *vt* to draw, draw up, draw out; to drain, drink up; to spill, shed; to swallow, devour, consume, exhaust; to derive; (fig) to drink in, seize upon, imbibe
haustr·um -ī *n* scoop, bucket

haustus *pp* of **haurio**
haust•us -ūs *m* drawing (*of water*); drinking, swallowing; drink, draught; handful; stream (*of blood*)
haut see **haud**
havĕō see **aveo**
hebdŏm•as -ădis *f* week
Hēb•ē -ēs *f* goddess of youth, daughter of Juno, and cupbearer of the gods
hebĕn•us -ī *f* ebony
heb•ĕō -ēre *vi* to be blunt, be dull; (fig) to be inactive, be sluggish
heb•es -ĕtis *adj* blunt, dull; faint, dim; dull, obtuse, stupid
hebesc•ō -ĕre *vi* to grow blunt, grow dull; to become faint or dim; to lose vigor
hebĕt•ō -āre *vt* to blunt, dull, dim
Hebr•us -ī *m* principal river in Thrace
Hecăt•ē -ēs *f* goddess of magic and witchcraft and often identified with Diana
hecatomb•ē -ēs *f* hecatomb
Hect•or -ŏris *m* son of Priam and Hecuba, husband of Andromache, and bravest Trojan warrior in fighting the Greeks
Hecŭb•a -ae or **Hecŭb•ē -ēs** *f* wife of Priam who, after the destruction of Troy, became a captive of the Greeks and was eventually changed into a dog
hedĕr•a -ae *f* ivy
hederĭg•er -ĕra -ĕrum *adj* wearing ivy
hederōs•us -a -um *adj* overgrown with ivy
hēdȳchr•um -ī *n* perfume
hei hēia see **ei, ēia**
Helĕn•a -ae or **Helĕn•ē -ēs** *f* Helen (*wife of Menelaus, sister of Clytemnestra, Castor, and Pollux, who was abducted by Paris*)
Helĕn•us -ī *m* prophetic son of Priam and Hecuba
Hēliăd•es -um *f pl* daughters of Helios and sisters of Phaëthon, who were changed into poplars and whose tears were changed to amber
Helĭc•ē -ēs *f* Big Bear (*constellation*)
Helĭc•ōn -ōnis *m* mountain in Boeotia sacred to the Muses and to Apollo
Helicōniăd•es or **Helicōnĭd•es -um** *f pl* Muses
Hell•as -ădis *f* Greece
Hell•ē -ēs *f* daughter of Athamas and Nephele who, while riding the golden-fleeced ram, fell into the Hellespont and drowned
hellĕbor- = **ellebor-**
Hellespont•us -ī *m* Dardanelles
hellŭ•ō -ōnis *m* glutton, squanderer
hellŭ•or -ārī -ātus sum *vi* to be a glutton
hel•ops or **el•ops** or **ell•ops -ŏpis** *m* highly-prized fish (*perhaps the sturgeon*)
helvell•a -ae *f* delicious herb
Helvētĭ•ī -ōrum *m pl* people of Gallia Lugdunensis (*modern Switzerland*)
helv•us -a -um *adj* light-bay
hem *interj* (expression of surprise) well!
hēmerodrŏm•us -ī *m* courier
hēmicill•us -ī *m* mule
hēmicycl•ĭum -ĭī or **-ī** *n* semicircle of seats
hēmīn•a -ae *f* half of a sextarius (*half a pint*)
hendecasyllăb•ī -ōrum *m pl* hendecasyllabics (*verses with eleven syllables*)
hēpatārĭ•us -a -um *adj* of the liver
heptēr•is -is *f* galley with seven banks of oars
hera see **era**
Hēr•a -ae *f* Greek goddess identified with Juno
Hēraclīt•us -ī *m* early Greek philosopher of Ephesus who believed that fire was the primary element of all matter (*fl* 513 B.C.)
herb•a -ae *f* blade, stalk; herb, plant; grass, lawn; weed
herbesc•ō -ĕre *vi* to sprout
herbĕ•us -a -um *adj* grass-green
herbĭd•us -a -um *adj* grassy
herbĭf•er -ĕra -ĕrum *adj* grassy, grass-producing; made of herbs
herbōs•us -a -um *adj* grassy; made with herbs
herbŭl•a -ae *f* little herb
hercisc•ō -ĕre *vi* to divide an inheritance
herct•um or **erct•um -ī** *n* inheritance
Herculānĕ•um -ī *n* town on the seacoast of Campania which was destroyed with Pompeii in an eruption of Vesuvius in 79 A.D.
Hercŭl•ēs -is or **-ī** *m* son of Jupiter and Alcmena, husband of Deianira, and after his death and deification, husband of Hebe
hercŭlēs or **hercŭle** or **hercle** *interj* by Hercules!
here *adv* yesterday
hērēditārĭ•us -a -um *adj* of or about an inheritance; inherited, hereditary
hērēdĭt•ās -ātis *f* inheritance
hērēd•ĭum -ĭī or **-ī** *n* inherited estate
hēr•ēs -ēdis *m* heir; (fig) heir, successor; *f* heiress
herī or **here** *adv* yesterday
herif- herīl- = **erif- eril-**
Hermāphrodīt•us -ī *m* son of Hermes and Aphrodite who combined with the nymph Salmacis to become one person
Herm•ēs or **Herm•a -ae** *m* Greek god identified with Mercury
Hermiŏn•ē -ēs or **Hermiŏn•a -ae** *f* daughter of Helen and Menelaus and wife of Orestes
Hērodŏt•us -ī *m* father of Greek history, born at Halicarnassus on coast of Asia Minor (484-425 B.C.)

hērōĭc·us -a -um *adj* heroic, epic
hērōīn·a -ae *f* demigoddess
hērō·is -ĭdis *f* demigoddess
hēr·ōs -ōis *m* demigod, hero (*rarely used of men born of human parents*)
hērō·us -a -um *adj* heroic, epic
herus see **erus**
Hēsiŏd·us -ī *m* Hesiod (*early Greek poet, born in Boeotia, 8th cent.* B.C.)
Hēsiŏn·ē -ēs or **Hēsiŏn·a -ae** *f* daughter of Laomedon, king of Troy, whom Hercules rescued from a sea monster
Hespĕr·us or **Hespĕr·os -ī** *m* evening star
hestern·us -a -um *adj* yesterday's
hetairī·a -ae *f* secret society
hetairĭc·ē -ēs *f* Macedonian mounted guard
heu! *interj* (expression of pain or dismay) oh!, ah!
heus! *interj* (to draw attention) say there!, hey!
hexamĕt·er -rī *m* hexameter verse
hexēr·is -is *f* ship with six banks of oars
hiāt·us -ūs *m* opening; open or gaping mouth; mouthing, bluster; basin (*of fountain*); chasm; (gram) hiatus
Hibēr·es -um *m pl* Spaniards
hibern·a -ōrum *n pl* winter quarters
hībernācŭl·a -ōrum *n pl* winter bivouac; winter residence
hībern·ō -āre *vi* to spend the winter; to stay in winter quarters; (fig) to hibernate
hībern·us -a -um *adj* winter, in winter, wintry
hibisc·um -ī *n* hibiscus
hibrĭd·a or **hybrĭd·a -ae** *m* or *f* hybrid, mongrel, half-breed
hīc (or **hic**) **hūjus** (older form: **hīce hūjusce**) *adj* this; the present, the actual; the latter; (occasionally) the former; **hic . . . hic** one . . . another; *pron* this one, he; this man, myself, your's truly (*i.e., the speaker or writer*); the latter; (occasionally) the former; (in court) the defendant, my defendant; **hic . . . hic** one . . . another; **hicine** (**hic** with *interrog* enclitic **-ne**) is this . . . ?
hīc *adv* here, in this place; at this point; in this affair, in this particular, herein
hīce see **hic**
hīcĭne see **hic**
hiemāl·is -e *adj* winter, wintry; stormy
hiĕm·ō -āre *vi* to spend the winter, pass the winter; to be wintry, be cold, be stormy
hiem·s or **hiem·ps -is** *f* winter; cold; storm
Hiĕr·ō -ōnis *m* ruler of Syracuse and patron of philosophers and poets (?-466 B.C.); friend of the Romans in the First Punic War (306?-215 B.C.)
Hierosolȳm·a ōrum *m pl* Jerusalem
hiŏt·ō -āre *vi* to keep yawing
hilăre *adv* cheerfully, merrily, gaily
hilăr·is -e or **hilăr·us -a -um** *adj* cheerful, merry, gay
hilarĭt·ās -ātis *f* cheerfulness, gaiety
hilaritūd·ō -ĭnis *f* cheerfulness
hilăr·ō -āre *vt* to cheer up
hilarŭl·us -a -um *adj* merry little
hilărus see **hilaris**
hill·ae -ārum *f pl* smoked sausage
Hīlōt·ae or **Īlōt·ae -ārum** *m pl* Helots (*slaves of the Spartans*)
hīl·um -ī *n* something, trifle
hinc *adv* from here, from this place; on this side, here; for this reason; from this source; after this, henceforth, from now on
hinn·iō -īre *vi* to whinny, neigh
hinnīt·us -ūs *m* neighing
hinnulĕ·us -ī *m* fawn
hĭ·ō -āre *vt* to sing; *vi* to open, be open; to gape; to yawn; to make eyes (*in surprise or greedy longing*)
hippagōg·ī -ōrum *f pl* ships for transporting horses and cavalry
Hipparch·us -ī *m* son of Pisistratus, the tyrant of Athens, who was slain by Harmodius and Aristogiton in 514 B.C.
Hippī·ās -ae *m* son of Pisistratus, the tyrant of Athens, and tyrant of Athens himself, 527-510 B.C.
hippocentaur·us -ī *m* centaur
Hippocrăt·ēs -is *m* famous physician, founder of scientific medicine (*c.* 460-380 B.C.)
Hippocrēn·ē -ēs *f* spring on Mt. Helicon, sacred to the Muses and produced when the hoof of Pegasus hit the spot
Hippodăm·ē -ēs or **Hippodamē·a** or **Hippodamī·a -ae** *f* daughter of Oenamaus, the king of Elis, and wife of Pelops; daughter of Adrastus and wife of Pirithous
hippodrŏm·os -ī *m* racetrack
Hippolȳt·ē -ēs or **Hippolȳt·a -ae** *f* Amazonian wife of Theseus; wife of Acastus, king of Magnesia
Hippolȳt·us -ī *m* son of Theseus and Hippolyte
hippomăn·es -is *n* membrane of the head of a new-born foal; discharge of a mare in heat
Hippomĕn·ēs -ae *m* son of Megareus who competed with Atalanta in a race and won her as his bride
Hippōn·ax -actis *m* Greek satirist (*fl* 540 B.C.)
hippotoxŏt·ae -ārum *m pl* mounted archers
hippūr·us -ī *m* goldfish
hīr·a -ae *f* empty gut
hircīn·us or **hirquīn·us -a -um** *adj* goat, of a goat
hircōs·us -a -um *adj* smelling like a goat
hirc·us -ī *m* goat

hirnĕ·a -ae *f* jug
hirsūt·us -a -um *adj* hairy, shaggy, bristly; prickly; rude
Hirt·ĭus -ĭī or **-ī** *m* Aulus Hirtius (*consul in* 43 B.C. *and author of the eighth book of Caesar's Memoirs on the Gallic War*)
hirt·us -a -um *adj* hairy, shaggy; uncouth
hirūd·ō -ĭnis *f* bloodsucker, leech
hirundinīn·us -a -um *adj* swallow's
hirund·ō -ĭnis *f* swallow
hisc·ō -ĕre *vt* to murmur, utter; *vi* to open, gape, yawn; to open the mouth
Hispān·ī -ōrum *m pl* Spaniards
Hispānĭ·a -ae *f* Spain
Hispāniens·is -e *adj* Spanish
hispĭd·us -a -um *adj* hairy, shaggy, rough
Hist·er or **Ist·er -rī** *m* lower Danube
historĭ·a -ae *f* history; account, story; theme (*of a story*)
historĭc·us -a -um *adj* historical; *m* historian
histrĭc·us -a -um *adj* theatrical
histrĭ·ō -ōnis *m* actor
histriōnāl·is -e *adj* theatrical; histrionic
histriōnĭ·a -ae *f* dramatics, art of acting
hiulcē *adv* with frequent hiatus
hiulc·ō -āre *vt* to split open
hiulc·us -a -um *adj* split, split open; open, gaping; with hiatus
hōc hūjus (older form: **hōce;** *genit:* **hūjusce)** (*neut* of **hic**); *adj* this; the present, the actual; the latter; (occasionally) the former; *pron* this one, it; the latter; (occasionally) the former; (with *genit*) this amount of, this degree of, so much; **hoc erat quod** this was the reason why; **hoc est** that is, I mean, namely; **hocine (hoc** with *interrog* enclitic **-ne)** is this . . . ?; **hoc facilius** all the more easily
hōce see **hoc**
hōcĭne see **hoc**
hodĭē *adv* today; now, nowadays; still, to the present; at once, immediately; **hodie mane** this morning; **numquam hodie** (coll) never at all, never in the world
hodiern·us -a -um *adj* today's; **hodiernus dies** this day, today
holĭt·or -ōris *m* grocer
holitōrĭ·us -a -um *adj* vegetable
hol·us -ĕris *n* vegetables
Homēr·us -ī *m* Homer
homicīd·a -ae *m* or *f* murderer, killer
homicīd·ĭum -ĭī or **-ī** *n* murder, manslaughter
hom·ō -ĭnis *m* or *f* human being, man, person, mortal; mankind, human race; fellow; fellow creature; (coll) this one; *m pl* persons, people; infantry; bodies, corpses; members (*of the senate*); **inter homines esse** to be alive; to see the world
homull·us -ī or **homucĭ·ō -ōnis** or **homuncŭl·us -ī** *m* poor man, poor creature
honest·a -ae *f* lady
honestāment·um -ī *n* ornament
honest·ās -ātis *f* good reputation, respectability; sense of honor, respect; beauty, grace; honesty, integrity, uprightness; decency; *f pl* respectable persons, decent people
honestē *adv* honorably, respectably, decently, virtuously
honest·ō -āre *vt* to honor, dignify, embellish, grace
honest·us -a -um *adj* honored, respected; honorable, decent, respectable, virtuous; handsome; *m* gentleman; *n* virtue, good
hon·or or **hon·ōs -ōris** *m* honor, esteem; position, office, post; mark of honor, reward, acknowledgment; offering, rites (*to the gods or the dead*); beauty, grace, charm; glory, fame, reputation; **honoris causā** out of respect, with all respect
honōrābĭl·is -e *adj* honorable
honōrārĭ·us -a -um *adj* honored, respected, highly esteemed; honorary, conferring honor
honōrātē *adv* with honor, honorably
honōrāt·us -a -um *adj* honored, respected; in high office; honorable, respectable; **honoratum habere** to hold in honor
honōrifĭcē *adv* honorably, respectfully
honōrifĭc·us -a -um *adj* honorable, complimentary
honōr·ō -āre *vt* to honor, respect; to embellish, decorate
honōr·us -a -um *adj* honorable, complimentary
honōs see **honor**
hoplomăch·us -ī *m* gladiator
hōr·a -ae *f* hour; time; season; **in diem et horam** continually; **in horam vivere** to live from hand to mouth; **quota hora est?** what time is it?; *f pl* clock; **in horas** from hour to hour, every hour
Hor·a -ae *f* wife of Quirinus (*i.e., of deified Romulus*), called Hersilia before her death
Hōr·ae -ārum *f pl* Hours (*daughters of Jupiter and Themis and goddesses who kept watch at the gates of heaven*)
hōrae·us -a -um *adj* pickled
Horāt·ĭus -ĭī *or* **-ī** *m* Quintus Horatius Flaccus (65-8 B.C.); Horatius Cocles (*defender of the bridge across the Tiber in the war with Porsenna*)
hordĕ·um -ī *n* barley
horĭ·a -ae *f* fishing boat
horiŏl·a -ae *f* small fishing boat
hornō *adv* this year, during this year
hornōtĭn·us -a -um *adj* this year's
horn·us -a -um *adj* this year's

hōrolog·ĭum -ĭī or **-ī** *n* clock; water clock; sundial
horrend·us -a -um *adj* horrendous, horrible, terrible; awesome
horr·ens -entis *adj* bristling, bristly, shaggy
horr·ĕō -ēre -ŭī *vt* to dread; to shudder at, shrink from; to be amazed at; *vi* to stand on end, stand up straight; to get gooseflesh; to shiver, tremble, quake, shake; to look frightful, be rough
horr·escō -escĕre -ŭī *vt* to dread, become terrified at; *vi* to stand on end; (of the sea) to become rough; to begin to shake or shiver; to start (*in fear*)
horrĕ·um -ī *n* barn, shed; silo, granary; wine cellar; beehive
horribĭl·is -e *adj* horrible, terrifying; amazing
horrĭdē *adv* roughly, rudely, sternly
horridŭl·us -a -um *adj* rather shaggy; somewhat shabby; somewhat unsophisticated (*style*)
horrĭd·us -a -um *adj* bristling, bristly, shaggy, prickly; rude, uncouth, rough, rugged, wild; disheveled; blunt, unpolished, course (*manner*); frightful, frightened, awful
horrĭf·er -ĕra -ĕrum *adj* causing shudders; freezing, chilling; terrifying
horrificē *adv* awfully
horrifĭc·ō -āre *vt* to make rough, ruffle; to terrify, appall
horrifĭc·us -a -um *adj* frightful, terrifying
horrisŏn·us -a -um *adj* frightening (*sound*), frightening to hear
horr·or -ōris *m* bristling; shivering, shuddering, quaking; dread, horror; awe, reverence; chill; thrill
horsum *adv* this way, here
hortām·en -ĭnis *n* injunction; encouragement
hortāment·um -ī *n* encouragement
hortātĭ·ō -ōnis *f* exhortation, encouragement
hortāt·or -ōris *m* backer, supporter, rooter, instigator
hortāt·us -ūs *m* encouragement, cheering, cheer
Hortens·ĭus -ĭī or **-ī** *m* Quintus Hortensius (*famous orator and friendly competitor of Cicero,* 114-50 B.C.)
hort·or -ārī -ātus sum *vt* to encourage, cheer, incite, instigate; to give a pep talk to (*soldiers*)
hortŭl·us -ī *m* little garden, garden plot
hort·us -ī *m* garden; *m pl* park
hosp·es -ĭtis *m* host, entertainer; guest, visitor; friend; stranger, foreigner
hospĭt·a -ae *f* hostess; guest, visitor; friend; stranger, foreigner
hospitāl·is -e *adj* host's; guest's; hospitable
hospitālĭt·ās -ātis *f* hospitality
hospitālĭter *adv* hospitably, as a guest
hospit·ĭum -ĭī or **-ī** *n* hospitality, friendship; welcome; guest room; lodging; inn
hostĭ·a -ae *f* victim, sacrifice
hostiāt·us -a -um *adj* bringing offerings
hostĭc·us -a -um *adj* hostile; foreign, strange; *n* enemy territory
hostīl·is -e *adj* enemy's, enemy, hostile
hostīlĭter *adv* hostilely, like an enemy
Hostīl·ĭus -ĭī or **-ī** *m* Tullus Hostilius (*third king of Rome*)
hostīment·um -ī *n* compensation, recompense
host·ĭō -īre *vi* to return like for like
host·is -is *m* or *f* enemy
hūc *adv* here, to this place; to this, to this point, so far; to such a pitch; for this purpose; **huc atque illuc** here and there, in different directions; **hucine? (huc** + *interrog* enclitic) so far?
hui! *interj* (expressing surprise or admiration) wow!
hūjusmŏdī or **hūjuscemŏdī** *adj* of this sort, such
humānē or **hūmānĭter** *adv* like a man; politely, gently, with compassion
hūmānĭt·ās -ātis *f* human nature; mankind; kindness, compassion; courtesy; culture, refinement, civilization
hūmānĭtus *adv* humanly; humanely, kindly, compassionately
hūmān·us -a -um *adj* of man, human; humane, kind, compassionate; courteous; cultured, refined, civilized, well educated
humātĭ·ō -ōnis *f* burial
hūme- = ume-
humī *adv* on or in the ground
hūmid- = umid-
humĭl·is -e *adj* low, low-lying, low-growing; shallow; stunted; low, common, colloquial; lowly, humble, poor, obscure, insignificant; base, mean, small-minded, cheap
humilĭt·ās -ātis *f* lowness; lowliness, insignificance; smallness of mind, meanness, cheapness
humilĭter *adv* low, deeply; meanly, abjectly
hum·ō -āre *vt* to bury
hum·us -ī *f* ground, earth; land, region, country
hyacinthĭn·us -a -um *adj* of the hyacinth; crimson
hyacinth·us or **hyacinth·os -ī** *m* hyacinth
Hyacinth·us or **Hyacinth·os -ī** *m* Spartan youth, who was accidently killed by his friend Apollo and from whose blood flowers of the same name sprang
Hyăd·es -um *f* Hyads (*group of sev-*

en stars in the head of the constellation Taurus whose rising with the sun was accompanied by rainy weather)
hyaen·a -ae *f* hyena
hyăl·us -ī *m* glass
Hybl·a -ae or **Hybl·ē -ēs** *f* Sicilian mountain, famous for its honey
hybrĭd·a -ae *m* or *f* hybrid, mongrel, half-breed
Hydasp·ēs -is *m* tributary of the Indus River
Hȳdr·a -ae *f* Hydra (*seven-headed dragon killed by Hercules*); Hydra or Anguis (*constellation*); fifty-headed monster at the gates of the lower world
hydraulĭc·us -a -um *adj* hydraulic
hydraul·us -ī water organ
hydrĭ·a -ae *f* jug, urn
Hydrochŏ·us -ī *m* Aquarius (*constellation*)
hydrōpĭc·us -a -um *adj* dropsical
hydr·ops -ōpis *m* dropsy
hydr·us or **hydr·os -ī** *m* serpent
Hyl·ās -ae *m* youthful companion of Hercules who was carried off by the nymphs as he was drawing water
Hyll·us or **Hūl·us -ī** *m* son of Hercules and husband of Iole
Hym·ēn -ĕnis or **Hymenae·us** or **Hymenae·os -ī** *m* Hymen (*god of marriage*); wedding ceremony; wedding; wedding song
Hymett·us or **Hymett·os -ī** *m* mountain in E. Attica, famous for its honey
Hypăn·is -is *m* river in Sarmatia (*modern Bug*)
hyperbăt·on -ī *n* (rhet) transposition of words
hyperbŏl·ē -ēs *f* hyperbole
Hyperborĕ·ī -ōrum *m pl* legendary people in the land of the midnight sun
Hyperī·ōn -ŏnis *m* son of Titan and Earth, father of the Sun
Hypermestr·a -ae or **Hypermestr·ē -ēs** *f* the only one of the fifty daughters of Danaus who did not kill her husband on her wedding night
hypocaust·um or **hypocaust·on -ī** *n* sweat bath
hypodidascăl·us -ī *m* instructor
hypomnēm·a -ătis *n* memorandum, note
Hypsipȳl·ē -ēs *f* queen of Lemnos at the time of the Argonauts
Hyrcān·ī -ōrum *m pl* a people on the Caspian Sea

I

ia- = ja-
Iacch·us -ī *m* Bacchus; wine
iambē·us -a -um *adj* iambic
iamb·us -ī *m* iamb; iambic poem, iambic poetry
ianthĭn·a -ōrum *n pl* violet-colored garments
Iapĕt·us -ī *m* Titan, father of Prometheus, Epimetheus, and Atlas
Iāpȳd·es -um *m pl* Illyrian tribe
Iāp·yx -ȳgis *m* son of Daedalus who ruled in S. Italy; wind that blew from Apulia to Greece
Ias·ĭus -ĭī or **-ī** *m* son of Jupiter and Electra and brother of Dardanus
Iās·ōn -ŏnis *m* Jason (*son of Aeson, leader of the Argonauts, and husband of Medea and afterwards of Creusa*)
iasp·is -ĭdis *f* jasper
Ībēr- = Hiber-
ibi or **ibī** *adv* there, in that place; then, on that occasion; therein
ibīdem *adv* in the same place, just there; at that very moment; at the same time; in the same matter
īb·is -is or **-ĭdis** *f* ibis (*bird sacred to the Egyptians*)
Īcăr·us -ī *m* son of Daedalus, who, on his flight from Crete with his father, fell into the sea; father of Penelope
ichneum·ōn -ŏnis *m* ichneumon (*Egyptian rat that eats crocodile eggs*)
īcō īcĕre īcī ictum *vt* to hit, strike, shoot
īc·ōn -ŏnis *f* image
icterĭc·us -a -um *adj* jaundiced
ict·is -ĭdis *f* weasel
ictus *pp* of **īcō**
ict·us -ūs *m* stroke, blow, hit; cut, sting, bite, wound; range; stress, beat; **sub ictum** within range
id *adv* for that reason, therefore
id ejus (*neut* of **is**) *adj* this, that, the said, the aforesaid; *pron* it; a thing, the thing; **ad id** for that purpose; **aliquid id genus** something of that sort, something like that; **cum eo . . . ut** on condition that, with the stipulation that; **eo plus** the more; **ex eo** from that time on; as a result of that, consequently; **id consili** some sort of plan, some plan; **id quod** a thing which, the thing which; **id temporis** at that time; of that age; **in id** to that end; **in eo esse** to depend on it; **in eo esse . . . ut** to be so far gone that, to get to the point where
Īd·a -ae or **Īd·ē -ēs** *f* mountain near Troy; mountain in Crete where Jupiter was brought up
Īdal·ĭum -ĭī or **-ī** *n* city in Cyprus dear to Venus

idcircō *adv* on that account, for that reason, therefore
īdem eădem idem *adj* the same, the very same, exactly this; (often equivalent to a mere connective) also, likewise; *pron* the same one
identĭdem *adv* again and again, continually, habitually; now and then, at intervals
idĕō *adv* therefore
idiōt·a -ae *m* uneducated person, ignorant person, layman
īdōl·on -ī *n* apparition, ghost
idōnĕē *adv* suitably
idōnĕ·us -a -um *adj* suitable, fit, proper; (with *dat* or with **ad** or **in** + *acc*) fit for, capable of, suited for, convenient for, sufficient for
Īd·ūs -ŭum *f pl* Ides (*fifteenth day of March, May, July, and October, and thirteenth of the other months; interest, debts, and tuition were often paid on the Ides*)
ie- = **je-**
iens euntis *pres p* of **eo**
igĭtur *adv* then, therefore, accordingly; (resumptive after parenthetical matter) as I was saying; (in summing up) so then, in short
ignār·us -a -um *adj* ignorant, unaware, inexperienced; unsuspecting; senseless; unknown, strange, unfamiliar; (with *genit*) unaware of, unfamiliar with
ignāvē *adv* listlessly, lazily
ignāvĭ·a -ae *f* listlessness, laziness; cowardice
ignāvĭter *adv* listlessly
ignāv·us -a -um *adj* listless, lazy, idle, inactive; relaxing; cowardly, bastardly; unproductive (*field, etc.*)
ignesc·ō -ĕre *vi* to catch fire, become inflamed, burn; (fig) to flare up
ignĕ·us -a -um *adj* of fire, on fire, fiery; red-hot, fiery
ignicŭl·us -ī *m* small fire, little flame, spark
ignĭf·er -ĕra -ĕrum *adj* fiery
ignigĕn·a -ae *m* son of fire (*epithet of Bacchus*)
ignĭp·ēs -ĕdis *adj* fiery-footed
ignipŏt·ens -entis *adj* lord of fire (*epithet of Vulcan*)
ign·is -is *m* fire; conflagration; watch fire, signal fire; torch; lightning, bolt of lightning; funeral pyre; star; brightness, glow, brilliancy, splendor; (fig) fire, rage, fury, love, passion; flame, sweetheart; agent of destruction, fanatic; *m pl* love poems
ignōbĭl·is -e *adj* insignificant, obscure, unknown, undistinguished; low-born, ignoble
ignōbilĭt·ās -ātis *f* obscurity; humble birth
ignōminĭ·a -ea *f* ignominy, dishonor, disgrace; **ignominiā afficere** to dishonor, disgrace; **ignominia senatūs** public censure imposed by the senate
ignōminiōs·us -a -um *adj* disgraced, degraded; disgraceful, shameful, ignominious; *m* infamous person
ignōrābĭl·is -e *adj* unknown
ignōrantĭ·a -ae *f* ignorance
ignōrātĭ·ō -ōnis *f* ignorance
ignōr·ō -āre *vt* to not know, be ignorant of, be unfamiliar with; to mistake, misunderstand; to ignore, disregard, take no notice of
ignosc·ens -entis *adj* forgiving
ig·noscō -noscĕre -nōvī -nōtum *vt* (with *dat* of person and *acc* of the offense) to pardon, forgive, excuse (*someone a fault*); *vi* (with *dat*) to pardon, forgive, excuse
ignōt·us -a -um *adj* unknown, unfamiliar, strange; inglorious; unnoticed; low-born, ignoble; vulgar; ignorant
īl·ex -ĭcis *f* holm oak
Īlĭ·a -ae *f* Rhea Silvia (*mother of Romulus and Remus*)
īl·ĭa -ĭum *n pl* guts, intestines; groin, belly
Īliăc·us -a -um *adj* Trojan
Īlĭ·as -ădis *f* Iliad; Trojan woman
īlĭcet *adv* (ancient form for adjourning an assembly) let us go; all is lost, kaput; at once, immediately, instantly
īlĭcō *adv* on the spot, right then and there; immediately
īlign·us or **īlignĕ·us -a -um** *adj* of holm oak, oak
Īl·ĭos -ĭī or **-ī** *f* Troy
Īlīthȳĭ·a -ae *f* goddess who aided women in childbirth
Īl·ĭum -ĭī or **-ī** or **Īlĭ·on -ī** *n* Troy
Īlĭ·us -a -um *adj* Trojan
illa *adv* that way
ill·a -īus *adj fem* that; that famous; *pron* that one; she
illabefact·us -a -um *adj* unbroken, uninterrupted
il·lābor -lābī -lapsus sum *vi* to flow; to sink, fall; fall in, cave in; to slip; (with *dat* or with **ad** or **in** + *acc*) to flow into, enter into, penetrate
illabōr·ō -āre *vi* (with *dat*) to work at, work on
illāc *adv* that way
illacessīt·us -a -um *adj* unprovoked
illacrimābĭl·is -e *adj* unlamented, unwept; inexorable
illacrĭm·ō -āre or **illacrĭm·or -ārī -ātus sum** *vi* (with *dat*) to cry over
ill·aec (*acc:* **-anc;** *abl:* **-āc**) *adj fem* that; *pron* she
illaes·us -a -um *adj* unhurt, unharmed
illaetābĭl·is -e *adj* sad, melancholy
illapsus *pp* of **illabor**
illaquĕ·ō -āre *vt* to trap
illātus *pp* of **infero**
illaudāt·us -a -um *adj* without fame, obscure; detestable
ill·e -īus *adj masc* that; that famous; the former; **ille aut ille** this or

that, such and such; *pron* that one; he; the former one
illecĕbr·a -ae *f* attraction, allurement
illecebrōs·us -a -um *adj* alluring, seductive
illect·us -a -um *adj* unread
illect·us -ūs *m* allurement
illepĭdē *adv* inelegantly, rudely, impolitely
illepĭd·us -a -um *adj* inelegant, impolite, churlish
ill·ex -ĭcis *m* or *f* lure, decoy
ill·ex -ēgis *adj* lawless
illībāt·us -a -um *adj* undiminished, unimpaired
illīberāl·is -e *adj* ungenerous, stingy
illīberālĭt·ās -ātis *f* stinginess
ill·ic (*acc:* **-unc;** *abl:* **-ōc**) *adj masc* that; *pron* he
illic *adv* there, yonder, in that place; in that matter, therein
il·licĭō -licĕre -lexī -lectum *vt* to allure, attract, seduce, mislead, lead astray
illicitāt·or -ōris *m* fake bidder (*one who bids at an auction to make others bid higher*)
illicĭt·us -a -um *adj* unlawful
il·līdō -līdĕre -līsī -līsum *vt* to smash to pieces, crush; (with *dat* or with **ad** or **in** + *acc*) to smash (*something*) against
illĭg·ō -āre *vt* to attach, connect; to tie, bind; to oblige; to impede, hamper
illim *adv* from there
illīm·is -e *adj* unmuddied, clear
illinc *adv* from there; on that side; **hinc illinc** from one side to another
il·lĭnō -linĕre -lēvī -lĭtum *vt* to cover; to smear; (with *dat*) to smear or spread (*something*) on
illiquefact·us -a -um *adj* melted
illīsus *pp* of **illido**
illiterāt·us -a -um *adj* uneducated, illiterate
illĭtus *pp* of **illino**
illō or **illōc** *adv* there, to that place; to that point
illōt·us -a -um *adj* unwashed, dirty
illūc *adv* to that place, in that direction; to that person, to him, to her; to that matter; to that point
ill·ūc (*acc:* **-ūc;** *abl:* **-ōc**) *adj neut* that; *pron* it
illuc·ĕō -ēre *vt* to shine on; *vi* to blaze
il·lucescō -lucescĕre -luxī *vi* to grow light, dawn, to begin to shine
ill·ud -īus *adj neut* that; the former; *pron* it
il·lūdō -lūdĕre -lūsī -lūsum *vt* to make fun of, ridicule; to waste, abuse; *vi* (with *dat*) to play around with, do mischief to
illūminātē *adv* clearly
illūmĭn·ō -āre *vt* to light up, make bright, illuminate; to illustrate
illūsĭ·ō -ōnis *f* irony
illustr·is -e *adj* bright, clear, brilliant; plain, distinct, evident; distinguished, famous, illustrious, noble
illustr·ō -āre *vt* to light up, illuminate; to make clear, clear up, explain, illustrate; to adorn, embellish; to make famous
illūsus *pp* of **illudo**
illuvĭ·ēs -ēī *f* inundation; offscouring, filth, dirt
Illyrĭc·us -a -um *adj* Illyrian; *n* Illyria
Illyrĭ·us -a -um *adj & m* Illyrian; *f* Illyria (*country on the E. coast of the Adriatic Sea*)
Īl·us -ī *m* son of Tros, father of Laomedon, and founder of Ilium; Ascanius
imāginārĭ·us -a -um *adj* imaginary
imāginātĭōn·ēs -um *f pl* imaginings
imāgĭn·or -ārī -ātus sum *vt* to imagine
imāg·ō -ĭnis *f* image, likeness, picture, bust; bust of ancestor; ghost, vision; echo; appearance, semblance, shadow; mental picture, image, conception, thought, idea; figure of speech, simile, metaphor
imbēcillĭt·ās -ātis *f* weakness, feebleness; helplessness
imbēcillius *adv* more weakly, more faintly
imbēcill·us -a -um *adj* weak, feeble; helpless
imbell·is -e *adj* anti-war, pacifistic; peaceful; unfit for war, soft, cowardly; peaceful, quiet
imb·er -ris *m* rain, shower, rain storm; rain cloud; water; stream of tears; shower (*of gold, spears, etc.*)
imberb·is -e or **imberb·us -a -um** *adj* beardless
im·bĭbō -bibĕre -bĭbī *vt* to imbibe, drink in; to resolve on; **animo imbibere** to conceive, form (*e.g., an opinion*)
imbr·ex -ĭcis *f* tile
imbrĭc·us -a -um *adj* rainy
imbrĭf·er -ĕra -ĕrum *adj* rainy
im·bŭō -buĕre -bŭī -būtum *vt* to wet, soak, saturate; to stain, taint, infect, imbue, fill, steep; to instruct, train, educate
imitābĭl·is -e *adj* imitable
imitām·en -ĭnis *n* imitation; *n pl* likeness, image
imitāment·a -ōrum *n pl* pretense
imitātĭ·ō -ōnis *f* imitation; pretense
imitāt·or -ōris *m* or **imitātr·ix -īcis** *f* imitator
imitāt·us -a -um *adj* fictitious, copied
imĭt·or -ārī -ātus sum *vt* to imitate, copy, portray; to ape
immad·escō -escĕre -ŭī *vi* to become wet
immānē *adv* savagely
immān·is -e *adj* huge, enormous, monstrous; inhuman, savage, monstrous
immānĭt·ās -ātis *f* vastness, enor-

mity; savageness, cruelty, monstrousness, barbarity

immansuēt·us -a -um *adj* wild, savage

immātūrĭt·ās -ātis *f* overanxiousness

immātūr·us -a -um *adj* immature, unripe, premature

immedicābĭl·is -e *adj* incurable

immĕm·or -ŏris *adj* forgetful, forgetting; negligent

immemorābĭl·is -e *adj* not worth mentioning; untold

immemorāt·a -ōrum *n pl* novelties

immensĭt·ās -ātis *f* immensity; *f pl* immense stretches

immens·us -a -um *adj* immense, unending; *n* infinite space, infinity

immĕr·ens -entis *adj* undeserving, innocent

im·mergō -mergĕre -mersī -mersum *vt* to immerse, dip, plunge; (with **in** + *acc*) to dip (*something*) into; **se immergere** (with **in** + *acc*) **a** to plunge into; **b** to insinuate oneself into

immerĭtō *adv* undeservedly, innocently

immerĭt·us -a -um *adj* undeserving, innocent; undeserved, unmerited; **immerito meo** through no fault of mine

immersābĭl·is -e *adj* unsinkable

immersus *pp* of **immergo**

immētāt·us -a -um *adj* unmeasured

immĭgr·ō -āre *vi* to immigrate; (with **in** + *acc*) **a** to move into; **b** (fig) to invade

immin·ĕō -ēre *vi* to project, stick out; to be near, be imminent, be near at hand; to threaten, menace; (with *dat*) **a** to jut out over; **b** to look out over, overlook (*a view*); **c** to hover over, loom over, threaten; (with *dat* or **in** + *acc*) to be intent on, be eager for

immin·ŭō -uĕre -ŭī -ūtum *vt* to lessen, curtail; to weaken, impair; to infringe upon, encroach upon, violate, subvert, destroy

imminūtĭ·ō -ōnis *f* lessening; mutilation; understatement

im·miscĕō -miscēre -miscŭī -mixtum *vt* to mix in, intermix, blend; (fig) to mix up, confound; **immisceri** or **se immiscere** (with *dat*) **a** to join, join in with, mingle with, get lost in (*e.g., a crowd*); **b** to blend with, disappear in (*e.g., night, cloud, etc.*); **manūs manibus immiscere** (of boxers) to mix it up

immiserābĭl·is -e *adj* unpitied

immisericordĭter *adv* unmercifully

immisericor·s -dis *adj* merciless, pitiless

immissĭ·ō -ōnis *f* letting grow, letting alone

immissus *pp* of **immitto**

immīt·is -e *adj* unripe, sour, green; rude, harsh, stern, severe; pitiless, inexorable

im·mittō -mittĕre -mīsī -missum *vt* to insert; to let in, let go in, admit; let go of, let drop; to let go, let fly, launch; to set on, incite, egg on; **immitti** or **se immittere** (with *dat* or **in** + *acc*) **a** to plunge or dive into; **b** to rush against, attack; **in terram immittere** to ground

immixtus *pp* of **immisceo**

immo or **immō** *adv* (in contradiction or correction of preceding words) no, on the contrary, or rather; (in confirmation of preceding words) quite so, yes indeed; **immo vero** yes and in fact

immōbĭl·is -e *adj* motionless, unshaken; immovable; clumsy

immoderātē *adv* without limit; immoderately, extravagantly

immoderātĭ·ō -ōnis *f* lack of moderation, excess

immoderāt·us -a -um *adj* unmeasured, limitless; immoderate, uncontrolled, excessive

immodestē *adv* immoderately, shamelessly

immodestĭ·a -ae *f* excesses; insubordination

immodest·us -a -um *adj* immoderate, uncontrolled

immodĭcē *adv* excessively

immodĭc·us -a -um *adj* huge, enormous; immoderate, excessive; (with *genit* or *abl*) given to, excessive in

immodulāt·us -a -um *adj* unrhythmical

immolātĭ·ō -ōnis *f* sacrifice

immolāt·or -ōris *m* sacrificer

immōlīt·us -a -um *adj* constructed, erected; *n pl* buildings

immŏl·ō or **inmŏl·ō -āre** *vt* to immolate, sacrifice, offer

im·morĭor -mŏrī -mortŭus sum *vi* (with *dat*) to die in, die upon; (fig) to get sick over

immŏr·or -ārī -ātus sum *vi* (with *dat*) to dwell upon

immors·us -a -um *adj* bitten into; excited

immortāl·is -e *adj* immortal

immortālĭt·ās -ātis *f* immortality

immortālĭter *adv* infinitely

immortŭus *pp* of **immorior**

immōt·us -a -um *adj* unmoved, immovable; unshaken, undisturbed, steadfast

immūg·iō -īre -īvī or **-ĭī -ītum** *vi* to bellow, roar

immulg·ĕō -ēre *vt* to milk

immunditĭ·a -ae *f* dirtiness, filth

immund·us -a -um *adj* dirty, filthy, foul

immūn·ĭō -īre -īvī *vt* to reinforce, fortify

immūn·is -e *adj* without duty or office; tax-exempt, free, exempt; pure, innocent; (with *abl* or **ab** + *abl*) free from, exempt from; (with *genit*) free of, free from, devoid of, without

immūnĭt·ās -ātis *f* immunity, exemption, exemption from taxes
immūnīt·us -a -um *adj* unfortified, undefended; unpaved (*street*)
immurmŭr·ō -āre *vi* to grumble; (with *dat*) (of the wind) to whisper among
immūtābĭl·is -e *adj* immutable, unchangeable
immūtābilĭt·ās -ātis *f* immutability
immūtātĭ·ō -ōnis *f* exchange, substitution; metonymy
immūtāt·us -a -um *adj* unchanged
immūt·ō -āre *vt* to change, alter; to substitute
impācāt·us -a -um *adj* restless; aggressive
impactus *pp* of **impingo**
impall·escō -escĕre -ŭī *vi* (with *abl*) to turn pale at
im·pār -ăris *adj* uneven, odd (*numbers*); uneven (*in size or length*); not matching, unlike (*in color or appearance*); unequal; unfair; ill-matched; uneven, crooked; (with *dat*) not a match for, inferior to, unable to cope with
imparāt·us -a -um *adj* unprepared
impariter *adv* unequally
impast·us -a -um *adj* unfed, hungry
impatĭ·ens -entis *adj* impatient; (with *genit*) unable to stand, endure, tolerate
impatienter *adv* impatiently; intolerably
impatientĭ·a -ae *f* impatience; (with *genit*) inability to stand or endure
impavĭdē *adv* fearlessly
impavĭd·us -a -um *adj* fearless, dauntless
impedīment·um -ī *n* impediment, hindrance; difficulty; *n pl* baggage, luggage; mule train
imped·iō -īre -īvī or **-ĭī -ītum** *vt* to entangle; to hamper, hinder; to entwine, encircle; to clasp, embrace; to block up (*road*); to hinder, prevent; to embarrass; **impedire** (with **ne, quin,** or **quominus**) to prevent (*someone*) from
impedītĭ·ō -ōnis *f* obstacle, obstruction
impedīt·us -a -um *adj* hampered; obstructed, blocked; difficult, intricate; impassable; busy, occupied
im·pellō -pellĕre -pŭlī -pulsum *vt* to strike against, strike, reach; to push, drive, drive forward, impel, propel; to urge, persuade, stimulate, induce; to force, compel; to put to rout; to swell (*sails*)
impend·ĕō -ēre *vi* to be near, be at hand, be imminent, threaten; (with *dat*) to hang over; (with *dat* or **in** + *acc*) to hover or loom over, threaten
impendiōs·us -a -um *adj* extravagant
impend·ĭum -ĭī or **-ī** *n* expense, cost, outlay; interest (*paid out*); loss
im·pendō -pendĕre -pendī -pensum *vt* to weigh out, pay out; to expend, devote, apply, employ; (with **in** + *acc*) **a** to spend (*money*) on; **b** to expend (*effort*) on, pay (*attention*) to
impenetrābĭl·is -e *adj* impenetrable
impens·a -ae *f* expense, cost, outlay; waste; contribution; **meis impensis** at my expense
impensē *adv* at a high cost, expensively; with great effort
impens·us -a -um *pp* of **impendo;** *adj* high, costly, expensive; strong, vehement, earnest; *n* high price
impĕr·ans -antis *m* master, ruler, conqueror
imperāt·or -ōris *m* commander, general; commander in chief; emperor; director, master, ruler, leader
imperātōrĭ·us -a -um *adj* of a general, general's; imperial
imperātr·ix -īcis *f* controller, mistress
imperāt·um -ī *n* command, order
impercept·us -a -um *adj* unperceived, unknown
impercuss·us -a -um *adj* noiseless
imperdĭt·us -a -um *adj* unscathed
imperfect·us -a -um *adj* unfinished, imperfect
imperfoss·us -a -um *adj* unpierced, not stabbed
imperiōs·us -a -um *adj* imperial; magisterial; tyrannical, overbearing, domineering, imperious
imperītē *adv* unskillfully, clumsily, ignorantly
imperītĭ·a -ae *f* inexperience, awkwardness, ignorance
imperĭt·ō -āre *vt & vi* to command, rule, govern
imperīt·us -a -um *adj* inexperienced, unfamiliar, ignorant, unskilled; (with *genit*) inexperienced in, unacquainted with, ignorant of
imper·ĭum -ĭī or **-ī** *n* command, order; right to command; exercise of authority; military commission, supreme command; mastery, sovereignty; realm, empire, dominion, supremacy, authority; public office, magistracy; term of office
imperjūrāt·us -a -um *adj* sacrosanct, inviolable
impermiss·us -a -um *adj* forbidden, unlawful
impĕr·ō -āre *vt* to requisition, give orders for, order, demand; (with *acc* of thing demanded and *dat* of source demanded from) to demand (*e.g., hostages*) from; *vi* to be in command, rule, be master; (with *dat*) to give orders to, order, command, govern, master
imperterrĭt·us -a -um *adj* undaunted, unterrified
impert·iō -īre *vt* (with *dat*) to impart, communicate, bestow, assign, direct (*something*) to, share (*something*) with; (with *acc* of person and *abl* of thing) to present (*someone*) with

imperturbāt·us -a -um *adj* unperturbed, unruffled
impervi·us -a -um *adj* impassable; (with *dat*) impervious to
impetibil·is -e *adj* intolerable
impĕt·ō -ĕre *vt* to make for; to attack
impetrābil·is -e *adj* obtainable; successful
impetrāti·ō -ōnis *f* obtaining, procurement
impetr·iō -īre *vt* to try to obtain through favorable omens
impĕtr·ō -āre *vt* to obtain, procure (*by asking*); to achieve, accomplish, bring to pass
impĕt·us -ūs *m* attack, assault; rush; impetus, impetuosity, vehemence, vigor, violence, fury, force; impulse, passion
impex·us -a -um *adj* uncombed; unpolished
impiē *adv* wickedly
impiĕt·ās -ātis *f* impiety, irreverence; disloyalty; treason
impĭg·er -ra -rum *adj* diligent, active, energetic
impĭgrē *adv* energetically, actively, quickly
impigrĭt·ās -ātis *f* energy, activity
im·pingō -pingĕre -pēgī -pactum *vt* (with *dat* or **in** + *acc*) **a** to fasten to; **b** to pin against, force against, dash against; **c** to press or force (*something*) on; **d** to fling at
impĭ·ō -āre *vt* to make irreverent
impĭ·us -a -um *adj* impious, irreverent; disobedient, undutiful; disloyal, unpatriotic; wicked, unscrupulous, shameless
implăcābĭl·is -e *adj* implacable, unappeasable
implăcāt·us -a -um *adj* unappeased, unsatisfied
implăcĭd·us -a -um *adj* fierce, savage
impl·ĕō -ēre -ēvī -ētum *vt* to fill up; to satisfy; to fatten; to impregnate, make pregnant; to enrich; to cover with writing, fill up (*a book*); to discharge, fulfill, execute, implement; to complete, finish, end; to spend (*time*)
implex·us -a -um *adj* enfolded, entwined; involved
implicāti·ō -ōnis *f* entanglement; incorporation; embarrassment
implicāt·us -a -um *adj* entangled, involved, complicated, confused
implicisc·or -ī *vi* to become confused
implicĭtē *adv* intricately
implicĭtus *pp* of **implico;** *adj* confused, confounded; **implicitus morbo** disabled by sickness, sick
implĭc·ō -āre -āvī -ātum or **-āre -ŭī -ĭtum** *vt* to entangle, involve, enfold, envelop; to embrace, clasp, grasp; to connect, unite, join; to involve, implicate, engage; to embarrass; **se dextrae implicare** to embrace, shake hands
implōrāti·ō -ōnis *f* begging, imploring
implōr·ō -āre *vt* to implore, appeal to, call upon for aid; (with double *acc*) to beg (*someone*) for; (with **ab** + *abl*) to ask for (*something*) from
implūm·is -e *adj* without feathers, unfledged
impl·ŭō -uĕre -ŭī -ūtum *vi* (with *dat*) to rain on
impluviāt·us -a -um *adj* shaped like an impluvium, square
impluv·ium -iī or **-ī** *n* skylight, impluvium (*opening in the roof of the atrium of the Roman house to get rid of smoke and let in light*); built-in basin in the atrium to catch the rain water; uncovered space in the atrium
impolītē *adv* simply, without fancy words
impolīt·us -a -um *adj* unpolished, rough; unrefined, inelegant; unfinished
impollūt·us -a -um *adj* unsullied
im·pōnō -pōnĕre -posŭī -posĭtum or **-postum** *vt* to impose; to establish, introduce; to place, set; to inflict, impose, dictate; to assign; to apply, give; to impose, assess, exact; to put (*someone*) in charge; (with *dat*, with **in** + *acc*, **in** + *abl*, or **supra** + *acc*) to place, put, set, lay (*someone or something*) on or in; (with *dat*) **a** to impose (*taxes, etc.*) upon; **b** to put (*someone*) in charge of; *vi* (with *dat*) to impose upon, trick, cheat
import·ō -āre *vt* to bring in, import; to introduce
importūnĭt·ās -ātis *f* importunity, rudeness, insolence; unfitness
importūn·us -a -um *adj* inconvenient, unsuitable; troublesome, annoying; lacking consideration for others, rude, ruthless, churlish; stormy; ill-omened
importuōs·us -a -um *adj* without a harbor
imp·os -ŏtis *adj* without control; (with *genit*) without control of
imposĭtus *pp* of **impono**
impossibĭl·is -e *adj* impossible
impostus *pp* of **impono**
impŏt·ens -entis *adj* impotent, powerless; having no control of oneself, wild, uncontrollable, impetuous, violent
impotenter *adv* impotently, weakly
impotentĭ·a -ae *f* weakness, helplessness; lack of self-control, violence, fury, passion
impraesentiārum *adv* for the present, under present circumstances
imprans·us -a -um *adj* without breakfast, fasting
imprecāti·ō -ōnis *f* imprecation, curse
imprĕc·or -ārī -ātus sum *vt* to call down (*a curse*); to invoke
impressi·ō -ōnis *f* pressure; assault, attack, charge; rhythmical beat;

emphasis; impression (*on the mind*)
impressus *pp* of **imprimo**
imprīmīs or **in prīmīs** *adv* in the first place, chiefly, especially
im·prĭmō -priměre -pressī -pressum *vt* to press down; to impress, imprint, stamp; (fig) to impress, engrave, mark
improbātĭ·ō -ōnis *f* disapprobation, blame
imprŏbē *adv* badly, wickedly, wrongfully; recklessly; persistently
improbĭt·ās -ātis *f* wickedness, depravity; roguishness
imprŏb·ō -āre *vt* disapprove, condemn, blame, reject
improbŭl·us -a -um *adj* naughty
imprŏb·us -a -um *adj* below standard, poor, inferior, bad, shameless; rebellious, unruly; restless, indomitable, self-willed; cruel, merciless; persistent
imprōcēr·us -a -um *adj* undersized
imprōdict·us -a -um *adj* not postponed
imprompt·us -a -um *adj* slow
improperāt·us -a -um *adj* slow, deliberate
impropri·us -a -um *adj* unsuitable
improsp·er -ěra -ěrum *adj* unfortunate
improspěrē *adv* unfortunately
imprōvidē *adv* without foresight, thoughtlessly
imprōvĭd·us -a -um *adj* not foreseeing, not anticipating; (with *genit*) indifferent to
imprōvīs·us -a -um *adj* unexpected; **de improviso, ex improviso** or **improviso** unexpectedly; *n pl* emergencies
imprūd·ens -entis *adj* not foreseeing, not anticipating, unsuspecting, off one's guard; inconsiderate; (with *genit*) unaware of, ignorant of, heedless of, not experienced in
imprūdenter *adv* without foresight, thoughtlessly, inconsiderately, imprudently
imprūdentĭ·a -ae *f* thoughtlessness; ignorance, imprudence
impūb·ēs -ěris or **-is** *adj* youthful, young; innocent, chaste, celibate, virgin
impŭd·ens -entis *adj* shameless
impudenter *adv* shamelessly
impudentĭ·a -ae *f* shamelessness
impudīcitĭ·a -ae *f* immodesty, lewdness, shamelessness
impudīc·us -a -um *adj* immodest, lewd, shameless
impugnātĭ·ō -ōnis *f* assault, attack
impugn·ō -āre *vt* to assault, attack; (fig) to impugn
impulsĭ·ō -ōnis *f* pressure; impulse
impuls·or -ōris *m* instigator
impulsus *pp* of **impello**
impuls·us -ūs *m* push, pressure, impulse, shock; instigation, incitement
impūne or **inpūne** *adv* with impunity, unpunished, scot-free; safely, unscathed
impūnĭt·ās -ātis *f* impunity
impūnītē *adv* with impunity
impūnĭt·us -a -um *adj* unpunished; unrestrained
impūrē *adv* impurely
impūrĭt·ās -ātis *f* impurity
impūr·us -a -um *adj* impure, unclean, filthy; (morally) impure, filthy, vile
imputāt·us -a -um *adj* unpruned, untrimmed
impŭt·ō -āre *vt* to charge to someone's account, enter in an account; (with *dat*) to charge to, ascribe to, give credit for (*something*) to, put the blame for (*something*) on
īmŭl·us -a -um *adj* cute little
īm·us -a -um *adj* deepest, lowest; last; the bottom of, the foot of, the tip of; *n* bottom, depth; **ab imo** utterly; **ab imo ad summum** from top to bottom; **ex imo** utterly, completely; *n pl* lower world
in *prep* (with *abl*) in, on, upon, among, at; before; under; during, within, in, at, in the course of, on the point of, in case of, in relation to; subject to, affected by, engaged in, involved in; (with *acc*) into, up to, towards; till, to, for; in relation to, about, respecting, against; for, with a view to, according to, after
inaccess·us -a -um *adj* inaccessible
inac·escō -escěre -ŭī *vi* to turn sour
Īnachĭd·ēs -ae *m* descendant of Inachus; Perseus; Epaphus
Īnăch·is -ĭdis *f* female descendant of Inachus (*esp. Io*)
Īnăch·us or **Īnăch·os -ī** *m* first king or Argos and father of Io
inadsc- = **inasc-**
inadt- = **inatt-**
inadust·us -a -um *adj* unburned
inaedifĭc·ō -āre *vt* to build on, build as an addition, erect, construct; to wall up, barricade; (with **in** + *abl*) to build (*something*) on top of
inaequābĭl·is -e *adj* uneven
inaequābilĭter *adv* unevenly, unequally
inaequāl·is -e *adj* uneven, unequal; unlike, changeable, inconstant
inaequālĭt·ās -ātis *f* unevenness
inaequālĭter *adv* unevenly
inaequāt·us -a -um *adj* unequal
inaequ·ō -āre *vt* to level off
inaestimābĭl·is -e *adj* inestimable; invaluable; valueless
inaestŭ·ō -āre *vi* **bilis inaestuat** anger flares up
inaffectāt·us -a -um *adj* unaffected, natural
inamābĭl·is -e *adj* hateful, revolting
inamāresc·ō -ěre *vi* to become bitter
inambitiōs·us -um *adj* unambitious
inambulātĭ·ō -ōnis *f* walking about, strutting about

inambŭl·ō -āre *vi* to walk up and down
inamoen·us -a -um *adj* unpleasant
inānĭ·ae -ārum *f pl* emptiness
inānilogist·a -ae *m* chatterbox
inānīment·um -ī *n* empty space
inanĭm·us -a -um *adj* inanimate
inān·e -is *n* empty space, vacuum; emptiness; worthlessness
inān·is -e *adj* empty, void; deserted, abandoned, unoccupied; hollow; worthless, idle; lifeless, unsubstantial; penniless, poor; unprofitable; groundless, unfounded
inānĭt·ās -ātis *f* empty space, emptiness; uselessness, worthlessness
inānĭter *adv* uselessly, vainly
inarāt·us -a -um *adj* untilled, fallow
in·ardescō -ardescĕre -arsī *vi* to catch fire, burn, glow
ināresc·ō -ĕre *vi* to become dry, dry up
inascens·us -a -um *adj* not climbed
inassuēt·us -a -um *adj* unaccustomed
inattenuāt·us -a -um *adj* undiminished; unappeased
inaud·ax -ācis *adj* timid, cowed
inaud·ĭō -īre -īvī or **-ĭī -ītum** *vt* to hear, learn
inaudīt·us -a -um *adj* unheard-of, unusual; without a hearing in court
inaugurātō *adv* after taking the auspices
inaugŭr·ō -āre *vt* to inaugurate, consecrate, install; *vi* to take the auspices
inaurāt·us -a -um *adj* gilded, gilt
inaur·ēs -ĭum *f pl* earrings
inaur·ō -āre *vt* to goldplate, gild; to line the pockets of (*someone*) with gold, to make rich
inauspicātō *adv* without consulting the auspices
inauspicāt·us -a -um *adj* undertaken without auspices; unlucky
inaus·us -a -um *adj* unattempted
inb- = imb-
inbīt·ō -ĕre *vt* enter
incaedŭ·us -a -um *adj* uncut
incal·escō -escĕre -ŭī *vi* to grow warm or hot; to get excited
incalfac·ĭō -ĕre *vt* to warm, heat
incallĭdē *adv* unskillfully
incallĭd·us -a -um *adj* unskillful; stupid, simple, clumsy
incand·escō -escĕre -ŭī *vi* to become white; to get white-hot
incān·escō -escĕre -ŭī *vi* to get grey
incantāt·us -a -um *adj* enchanted
incān·us -a -um *adj* grown grey
incassum *adv* in vain
incastīgāt·us -a -um *adj* unscolded, unpunished
incautē *adv* incautiously, recklessly
incaut·us -a -um *adj* incautious, inconsiderate, thoughtless, reckless; unforeseen, unexpected; unguarded
in·cēdō -cēdĕre -cessī -cessum *vi* to go, step, move, walk, stalk; to proceed, go forward; to come along, happen, occur, appear, arrive; to advance, go on
incelebrāt·us -a -um *adj* unheralded
incēnāt·us -a -um *adj* supperless
incendiār·ĭus -ĭī or **-ī** *m* agitator
incend·ĭum -ĭī or **-ī** fire; heat
in·cendō -cendĕre -cendī -censum *vt* to light, set on fire, burn; to light up, make bright; (fig) to inflame, fire, excite, enrage
incēn·is -e *adj* dinnerless, without dinner
incensĭ·ō -ōnis *f* burning
incensus *pp* of **incendo**
incens·us -a -um *adj* not registered (*with the censor*)
inceptĭ·ō -ōnis *f* beginning; undertaking
incept·ō -āre *vt* to begin; to undertake
incept·or -ōris *m* beginner, originator
incept·us -a -um *pp* of **incipio;** *n* beginning; undertaking, attempt, enterprise; subject, theme
in·cernō -cernĕre -crēvī -crētum *vt* to sift
incēr·ō -āre *vt* to wax, cover with wax
incertō *adv* not for certain
incert·ō -āre *vt* to render doubtful, make uncertain
incert·us -a -um *adj* uncertain, vague, obscure; doubtful, dubious; unsure, hesitant; *n* uncertainty, insecurity; contingency; **in incertum** for an indefinite time
incess·ō -ĕre -īvī *vt* to fall upon, assault, reproach, accuse, attack; (fig) to attack
incess·us -ūs *m* walk, gait, pace; tread, trampling; invasion, attack
incestē *adv* impurely, sinfully; indecently
incest·ō -āre *vt* to pollute, defile; to violate (*a girl*)
incest·us -a -um *adj* polluted, defiled, unclean, impure, sinful; lewd, unchaste, incestuous
incest·us -ūs *m* indecency, incest
in·cĭdō -cidĕre -cĭdī -cāsum *vi* to happen, occur; (with **in** or **ad** + *acc*) to fall into, fall upon; (with **in** + *acc*) **a** to come upon unexpectedly, fall in with; **b** to attack; (with *dat* or **in** + *acc*) **a** to occur to (*mentally*); **b** to fall on (*a certain day*); **c** to befall; **d** to agree with
in·cīdō -cīdĕre -cīdī -cīsum *vt* to carve, engrave, inscribe; to cut, sever; (fig) to cut into, cut short, put an end to, break off, interrupt
incīl·e -is *n* ditch, trench
in·cingō -cingĕre -cinxī -cinctum *vt* to drape; to wreathe; to invest, surround
incĭn·ō -ĕre *vt* to sing; to play
incipessō see **incipisso**
in·cipĭō -cipĕre -cēpī -ceptum *vt & vi* to begin, start

incipiss·ō -ĕre *vt* to begin
incīsē or **incīsim** *adv* in short phrases
incīsĭ·ō -ōnis *f* or **incīs·um -ī** *n* clause
incīsus *pp* of **incido**
incitāment·um -ī *n* incitement, incentive
incitātĭ·ō -ōnis *f* inciting, rousing; speed
incitātĭus *adv* rather impetuously
incitāt·us -a -um *adj* rapid, speedy; **equo incitato** at full gallop
incĭt·ō -āre *vt* to incite, urge on, spur on, drive on; to stimulate; to inspire; to stir up, arouse; to increase, augment; **currentem incitare** (fig) to spur a willing horse; **se incitare** to rush
incĭt·us -a -um *adj* rapid, swift; immovable; **ad incita redigere** to bring to a standstill
inclāmĭt·ō -āre *vt* to cry out against, abuse
inclām·ō -āre *vt* to shout at, scold, chide; *vi* to yell
inclār·escō -escĕre -ŭī *vi* to become famous
inclēm·ens -entis *adj* inclement, harsh, unmerciful
inclēmenter *adv* harshly, severely
inclēmentĭ·a -ae *f* harshness, severity, rigor
inclīnātĭ·ō -ōnis *f* leaning; inclination, tendency, bias; change; inflection
inclīnāt·us -a -um *adj* inclined, prone; sinking; low, deep
inclīn·ō -āre *vt* to bend, turn, to turn back, drive back, repulse; (fig) to divert, shift (*e.g., blame*); to change, alter; **inclinari** (mil) to fall back, give way; **inclinari** or **se inclinare** to lean, bend, turn; to change (*esp. for the worse*); *vi* to bend, turn, lean, dip, sink, (mil) to fall back, give way; (fig) to change, deteriorate; (fig) to change for the better
inclĭt·us -a -um *adj* famous
in·clūdō -clūdĕre -clūsī -clūsum *vt* to shut in, confine, lock up; to include, insert; to block, obstruct, shut off, stop up; (fig) to include, embrace, comprehend; to restrain, control; to close, end (*e.g., day*)
inclūsĭ·ō -ōnis *f* locking up, confinement
inclŭt·us or **inclĭt·us -a -um** *adj* famous
incoct·us -a -um *pp* of **incoquo**; *adj* uncooked, raw
incōgitābĭl·is -e *adj* thoughtless, inconsiderate
incōgĭt·ans -antis *adj* unthinking, thoughtless
incōgitantĭ·a -ae *f* thoughtlessness
incōgitāt·us -a -um *adj* thoughtless, inconsiderate
incōgĭt·ō -āre *vt* to think up
incognĭt·us -a -um *adj* not investigated; unknown, unrecognized, unidentified; unparalleled
incohāt·us -a -um *adj* unfinished
incŏh·ō -āre *vt* to begin, start
incŏl·a -ae *m & f* inhabitant, resident
incŏl·ō -ĕre -ŭī *vt* to live in, inhabit, occupy; *vi* to live, reside
incolŭm·is -e *adj* unharmed, safe and sound, unscathed, alive; (with *abl*) safe from
incolumĭt·ās -ātis *f* safety
incomitāt·us -a -um *adj* unaccompanied
incommendāt·us -a -um *adj* unprotected
incommŏdē *adv* at the wrong time; inconveniently; unfortunately
incommodestĭc·us -a -um *adj* (coll) ill-timed, inconvenient
incommodĭt·ās -ātis *f* inconvenience; unsuitableness; disadvantage
incommŏd·ō -āre *vi* (with *dat*) to be inconvenient to, to be annoying to, to inconvenience
incommŏd·us -a -um *adj* inconvenient, annoying; *n* inconvenience; trouble, setback, disaster
incommūtābĭl·is -e *adj* unchangeable
incomparābĭl·is -e *adj* unequaled, incomparable
incompert·us -a -um *adj* unknown, forgotten
incompositē *adv* in disorder
incomposĭt·us -a -um *adj* disordered, confused, unstudied, uncouth; irregular
incomprehensibĭl·is -e *adj* incomprehensible
incompt·us -a -um *adj* unkempt, messy; primitive, rude (*discourse*)
inconcess·us -a -um *adj* forbidden, unlawful
inconcilĭ·ō -āre *vt* to deceive, trick, to rob, fleece
inconcinn·us -a -um *adj* clumsy, awkward; absurd
inconcuss·us -a -um *adj* unshaken
incondĭtē *adv* confusedly
incondĭt·us -a -um *adj* unorganized, disorderly, confused, irregular; rough, undeveloped (*style*); raw (*jokes*)
inconsīderātē *adv* thoughtlessly
inconsīderāt·us -a -um *adj* thoughtless
inconsōlābĭl·is -e *adj* incurable
inconst·ans -antis *adj* inconsistent, fickle, shifty
inconstanter *adv* inconsistently
inconstantĭ·a -ae *f* inconsistency, fickleness
inconsultē *adv* indiscreetly
inconsult·us -a -um *adj* indiscreet, ill-advised, imprudent; not consulted
inconsult·us -ūs *m* **inconsultu meo** without consulting me
inconsumpt·us -a -um *adj* unconsumed
incontāmĭnāt·us -a -um *adj* untainted

incontent·us -a -um *adj* loose, untuned (*string*)
incontin·ens -entis *adj* incontinent
incontinenter *adv* without self-control, incontinently
incontinenti·a -ae *f* lack of self-control
inconveni·ens -entis *adj* unsuitable, dissimilar
in·cŏquō -coquĕre -coxī -coctum *vt* to boil, cook; to dye
incorrect·us -a -um *adj* uncorrected, unrevised
incorruptē *adv* justly, fairly
incorrupt·us -a -um *adj* untainted; uncorrupted, unspoiled; genuine, pure
incrēbr·escō or **incrēb·escō -escĕre -ŭī** *vi* to grow, rise, increase, spread
incrēdibĭl·is -e *adj* incredible
incrēdibilĭter *adv* incredibly
incrēdŭl·us -a -um *adj* incredulous
incrēment·um -ī *n* growth, increase; increment, addition; addition to the family, offspring
increpĭt·ō -āre *vt* to scold, rebuke
incrĕp·ō -āre -ŭī (or **-āvī**) **-ĭtum** (or **-ātum**) *vt* to cause to make noise; to rattle; (*of Jupiter*) to thunder at; to scold, rebuke; *vi* to make a noise, to rustle, rattle, clatter, clash; to speak angrily
incr·escō -escĕre -ēvī *vi* to grow, increase; (with *dat* or *abl*) to grow in or upon
incrētus *pp* of **incerno**
incruentāt·us -a -um *adj* unbloodied
incruent·us -a -um *adj* bloodless, without bloodshed
incrust·ō -āre *vt* to cover with a coat, encrust
incŭb·ō -āre -ŭī -ĭtum *vi* (with *dat*) **a** to lie in or upon; **b** to lean on; **c** to brood over; **d** to watch jealously over
inculc·ō -āre *vt* to impress, inculcate; (with *dat*) to force (*something*) upon
inculpāt·us -a -um *adj* blameless
incultē *adv* uncouthly, roughly
incult·us -a -um *adj* untilled, uncultivated; neglected, slovenly; rough, uneducated, uncivilized; *n pl* desert, wilderness
incult·us -ūs *m* neglect; dirt, squalor
in·cumbō -cumbĕre -cubŭī -cubĭtum *vi* (with *dat* or **in** + *acc*) **a** to lean on or against; **b** to lie down on (*a couch, bed*); **c** to bend to (*the oars*); **d** to light on, fall on; **e** (fig) to press upon, burden, oppress, weigh down; **f** to apply onself to, take pains with, pay attention to; (with **ad** or **in** + *acc*) to be inclined towards, lean towards
incūnābŭl·a -ōrum *n pl* baby clothes, swaddling clothes; (fig) cradle, infancy, birthplace, source, origin
incūrāt·us -a -um *adj* neglected; uncured
incūri·a -ae *f* carelessness, negligence
incūriōsē *adv* carelessly
incūriōs·us -a -um *adj* careless, unconcerned, indifferent; neglected
in·currō -currĕre -currī or **-cucurrī -cursum** *vt* to attack; *vi* (with *dat* or **in** + *acc*) **a** to run into, rush at, charge, attack, invade; **b** to extend to; **c** to meet, run into; **d** to fall on, coincide with
incursi·ō -ōnis *f* incursion, invasion, raid; assault, attack, collision
incurs·ō -āre *vt* to assault, attack; to invade; *vi* (with *dat* or **in** + *acc*) **a** to assault, attack; **b** to run into, bump against; **c** to strike, meet (*e.g., the eyes*); **d** to affect, touch, move
incurs·us -ūs *m* assault, attack; invasion; impulse
incurv·ō -āre *vt* to bend, curve
incurv·us -a -um *adj* bent, crooked
inc·ūs -ūdis *f* anvil
incūsāti·ō -ōnis *f* accusation
incūs·ō -āre *vt* to blame, find fault with, accuse
incuss·us -ūs *m* shock
incussus *pp* of **incutio**
incustōdīt·us -a -um *adj* unguarded; unconcealed; imprudent
incūs·us -a -um *adj* forged; **lapis incusus** indented millstone
in·cutiō -cutĕre -cussī -cussum *vt* to throw; to produce; (with *dat* or **in** + *acc*) to strike (*something*) on or against; (with *dat*) **a** to strike into, instill in; **b** to throw at, to fling upon; **metum incutere** (with *dat*) to inspire fear in, strike fear in; **scipionem in caput alicujus incutere** to beat someone over the head with a stick
indāgāti·ō -ōnis *f* investigation, search
indāgāt·or -ōris *m* or **indāgātr·ix -īcis** *f* investigator
indāg·ō -āre *vt* to track down, hunt; (fig) to track down, investigate, explore
indāg·ō -ĭnis *f* dragnet; **indagine agere** to ferret out
indaudiō see **inaudio**
inde *adv* from there; from that source, therefrom; from that time on, after that, thereafter; then; from that cause
indēbĭt·us -a -um *adj* not owed, not due
indĕc·ens -entis *adj* unbecoming, improper, indecent
indecenter *adv* improperly, indecently
indec·ĕō -ēre *vt* to be improper for
indeclīnāt·us -a -um *adj* unchanged, constant
indĕc·or -ŏris or **indecŏr·is -e** *adj* disgraceful, dishonorable, cowardly

indecōrē *adv* indecently, improperly
indecŏr·ō -āre *vt* to disgrace
indecōr·us -a -um *adj* unsightly, improper, disgraceful
indēfens·us -a -um *adj* undefended
indēfess·us -a -um *adj* tireless; not tired
indēflēt·us -a -um *adj* unwept
indēject·us -a -um *adj* undemolished
indēlēbĭl·is -e *adj* indestructible, indelible
indēlībāt·us -a -um *adj* undiminished
indemnāt·us -a -um *adj* unconvicted
indeplōrāt·us -a -um *adj* unwept
indeprens·us -a -um *adj* undetected
indeptus *pp* of **indipiscor**
indēsert·us -a -um *adj* unforsaken
indespect·us -a -um *adj* unfathomable
indestrict·us -a -um *adj* unscathed
indētons·us -a -um *adj* unshorn
indēvītāt·us -a -um *adj* unerring (*e.g., arrow*)
ind·ex -ĭcis *m* index, sign, mark, indication, proof; title (*of book*); informer, spy; index finger
Indĭ·a -ae *f* India
indicātĭ·ō -ōnis *f* value; price
indīc·ens -entis *adj* not speaking; **me indicente** without a word from me
indic·ĭum -ĭī or **-ī** *n* information, disclosure, evidence; indication, proof, permission to give evidence; reward for giving evidence
indĭc·ō -āre *vt* to point out; to reveal, disclose, make known; to betray, inform against, accuse; to put a price on; *vi* to give evidence
in·dīcō -dīcĕre -dixī -dictum *vt* to proclaim, announce, publish; to summon, convoke; to impose (*a fine*); **bellum indicere** to declare war; **diem indicere** to set a date
indict·us -a -um *adj* unsaid; **causā indictā** without a hearing
Indĭc·us -a -um *adj* Indian; *m* Indian; *n* indigo
indĭdem *adv* from the same place; from the same source, from the same thing
indiffĕr·ens -entis *adj* (morally) indifferent; unconcerned, indifferent
indigĕn·a -ae *adj masc & fem* native
indĭg·ens -entis *adj* indigent; (with *genit*) in need of
indigentĭ·a -ae *f* indigence, want, need; craving
indig·ĕō -ēre -ŭī *vi* (with *genit* or *abl*) to need, be in need of, require; (with *genit*) to crave, desire
indĭg·es -ĕtis *adj* indigenous, native; *m* native god; national hero
indīgest·us -a -um *adj* unarranged, confused
indignābund·us -a -um *adj* indignant, highly indignant
indign·ans -antis *adj* indignant; impatient, reluctant
indignātĭ·ō -ōnis *f* indignation, displeasure; provocation, occasion for indignation; *f pl* expressions of indignation
indignē *adv* unworthily, undeservedly; indignantly
indignĭt·ās -ātis *f* unworthiness; indignation; indignity, shameful treatment; enormity, shamefulness
indign·or -ārī -ātus sum *vt* to be indignant at, displeased at, angry at, offended at
indign·us -a -um *adj* unworthy, undeserving; undeserved; (with *abl*) **a** unworthy of; **b** not deserving; **c** not worth; (with *genit*) unworthy of, undeserving of; **indignum!** shame!
indĭg·us -a -um *adj* (with *genit* or *abl*) in need of, needing
indīlĭg·ens -entis *adj* careless
indīligenter *adv* carelessly
indīligentĭ·a -ae *f* carelessness
ind·ipiscor -ipiscī -eptus sum or **indipisc·ō -ĕre** *vt* to obtain, get; to attain, reach
indīrept·us -a -um *adj* unplundered
indiscrēt·us -a -um *adj* closely connected; indiscriminate, undistinguishable; confused
indisertē *adv* without eloquence
indisert·us -a -um *adj* not eloquent; at a loss for words
indisposĭt·us -a -um *adj* confused, disorderly
indissolūbĭl·is -e *adj* imperishable, indestructible
indistinct·us -a -um *adj* indistinct, obscure; confused
indĭtus *pp* of **indo**
indīvidŭ·us -a -um *adj* indivisible; inseparable; *n* atom, indivisible particle
in·dō -dĕre -dĭdī -dĭtum *vt* to put, place; to introduce; to impart, give; (with **in** + *acc*) to put or place (*something*) into or on, insert in
indocĭl·is -e *adj* difficult to teach, slow to learn; hard to learn; untaught
indoctē *adv* unskillfully
indoct·us -a -um *adj* untaught, untrained, unschooled; illiterate, ignorant
indolentĭ·a -ae *f* freedom from pain, insensibility
indŏl·ēs -is *f* inborn quality, natural quality; nature, character, disposition; natural ability, talent, genius
indol·escō -escĕre -ŭī *vi* to feel sorry; to feel resentment
indomābĭl·is -e *adj* untameable
indomĭt·us -a -um *adj* untamed, wild; (fig) wild, unmanageable
indorm·ĭo -īre -īvī or **-ĭī -ītum** *vi* to fall asleep; to grow careless; (with *dat* or *abl* or with **in** + *abl*) **a** to fall asleep at or on; **b** to fall asleep over; **c** to become careless about
indōtāt·us -a -um *adj* without dowry; poor; without funeral rites

or funeral honors; **ars indotata** unadorned style; **corpora indotata** bodies that have not been accorded the usual honors paid to the dead

indubitābĭl·is -e *adj* indubitable

indubitāt·us -a -um *adj* undoubted

indubĭt·ō -āre *vi* (with *dat*) to begin to distrust, begin to doubt

indubĭ·us -a -um *adj* undoubted, certain

indūcĭ·ae -ārum *f pl* armistice, truce

in·dūcō -dūcĕre -duxī -ductum *vt* to lead or bring in; to bring in, introduce; to induce, persuade, seduce, move; to overlay, drape, wrap, cover, put on, clothe; to strike out, erase; to repeal, cancel; to present, exhibit; to mislead, delude; (with **in** + *acc*) **a** to lead to, lead into, lead against; **b** to bring into, introduce into; **c** (fig) to introduce (*e.g., a new custom*) into; **d** to enter into (*account books*), charge to (*someone's account*); (with *dat* or **super** + *acc*) to put (*item of apparel*) on, spread over, wrap around, draw over; **animum inducere** or **in animum inducere** to make up one's mind, convince oneself, be convinced, conclude, suppose, imagine

inductĭ·ō -ōnis *f* bringing in, introduction, admission; resolution, determination; intention; induction, generalization; **animi inductio** inclination; **erroris inductio** deception

induct·or -ōris *m* (referring to a whip) persuader

induct·us -ūs *m* persuasion, inducement

indūcŭl·a -ae *f* skirt, petticoat

indulg·ens -entis *adj* indulgent, lenient; (with *dat* or **in** + *acc*) lenient toward, kind toward

indulgenter *adv* indulgently, leniently, kindly

indulgentĭ·a -ae *f* indulgence, leniency, kindness

in·dulgĕō -dulgēre -dulsī *vt* (with *dat*) to grant, concede (*something*) to; **veniam indulgere** (with *dat*) to make allowances for; *vi* (with *dat*) **a** to be lenient toward, be kind to, be tender to; **b** to yield to, give way to; **c** to indulge in, be addicted to; **sibi indulgere** to be self-indulgent, take liberties

ind·ŭō -uĕre -ŭī -ūtum *vt* to put on (*e.g., a tunic*); to cover, wrap, clothe, array, envelop; to engage in; to assume, put on; to assume the part of; to involve, entangle; (with *dat*) to put (*e.g., a tunic*) on (*someone*)

indup- = **imp-**

indūr·escō -escĕre -ŭī *vi* to become hard, harden

indūr·ō -āre *vt* to harden

Ind·us -a -um *adj* Indian; *m* Indian; Ethiopian; mahout

industrĭ·a -ae *f* industry, diligence; **industriā** or **de** or **ex industria** or **ob industriam** on purpose

industrĭē *adv* industriously, diligently

industrĭ·us -a -um *adj* industrious, diligent, painstaking

indūtĭ·ae or **indūcĭ·ae -ārum** *f pl* armistice, truce

indūtus *pp* of **induo;** *adj* (with *acc* or *abl*) dressed in, wearing

indūt·us -ūs *m* wearing; clothing

induvĭ·ae -ārum *f pl* clothes

inebrĭ·ō -āre *vt* to make drunk; (fig) to fill (*e.g., ear with gossip*)

inedĭ·a -ae *f* fasting; starvation

inēdĭt·us -a -um *adj* not made known, unknown, unpublished

inēlĕg·ans -antis *adj* inelegant, undistinguished

inēleganter *adv* without distinction

inēluctābĭl·is -e *adj* inescapable

inēmor·ior -ī *vi* (with *dat*) to die in or at

inempt·us -a -um *adj* unpurchased; without ransom

inēnarrābĭl·is -e *adj* indescribable

inēnarrābilĭter *adv* indescribably

inēnōdābĭl·is -e *adj* inexplicable

in·ĕō -īre -iī -ĭtum *vt* to enter; to enter upon, undertake, form; to begin, engage in; **consilium inire** to form a plan; **consilium inire ut, qua,** or **quemadmodum** to plan how to (*do something*); **inire numerum** (with *genit*) to go into an enumeration of, enumerate; **inire rationem** (with *genit*) to form an estimate of; **inire rationem ut, qua,** or **quemadmodum** to consider, find out, or figure out how to (*do something*); **viam inire** to begin a trip; to find a way, devise a means

ineptē *adv* foolishly, absurdly, inappropriately, pointlessly

ineptĭ·a -ae *f* foolishness; *f pl* nonsense; trifles

inept·iō -īre *vi* to be absurd, make a fool of oneself

inept·us -a -um *adj* foolish, silly; inept, awkward, absurd; unsuitable, out of place; tactless, tasteless

inerm·is -e or **inerm·us -a -um** *adj* unarmed, defenseless; undefended; toothless (*gums*); harmless

inerr·ans -antis *adj* not wandering, fixed

inerr·ō -āre *vi* to wander about

iner·s -tis *adj* unskillful, incompetent; inactive, sluggish; weak, soft, helpless; stagnant, motionless; ineffective, dull, insipid; numbing (*cold*); expressionless (*eyes*); uneventful, leisurely (*time*)

inertĭ·a -ae *f* lack of skill, ignorance, rudeness; inactivity, laziness

inērudīt·us -a -um *adj* uneducated; crude, inconsiderate

inesc·ō -āre *vt* to bait; (fig) to bait, trap, deceive

inēvect·us -a -um *adj* mounted

inēvītābĭl·is -e *adj* inevitable, inescapable
inexcĭt·us -a -um *adj* unexcited, calm
inexcūsābĭl·is -e *adj* without excuse; admitting no excuse
inexercitāt·us -a -um *adj* untrained
inexhaust·us -a -um *adj* unexhausted, not wasted; inexhaustible
inexōrābĭl·is -e *adj* inexorable, relentless; unswerving, strict
inexperrect·us -a -um *adj* unawakened
inexpert·us -a -um *adj* untried, untested; novel; (with *abl*, or with **in** or **adversus** + *acc*) inexperienced in, unaccustomed to
inexpiābĭl·is -e *adj* inexpiable, not to be atoned for; irreconcilable, implacable
inexplēbĭl·is -e *adj* insatiable
inexplēt·us -a -um *adj* unsatisfied, unfilled
inexplicābĭl·is -e *adj* inextricable; inexplicable; impassable (*road*); involved, unending (*war*)
inexplōrātō *adv* without reconnoitering
inexplorāt·us -a -um *adj* unexplored; unfamiliar
inexpugnābĭl·is -e *adj* impregnable, unassailable; invincible
inexspectāt·us -a -um *adj* unexpected
inexstinct·us -a -um *adj* unextinguished; insatiable
inexsuperābĭl·is -e *adj* insuperable, insurmountable
inextrīcābĭl·is -e *adj* inextricable
infăbrē *adv* unskillfully
infabricāt·us -a -um *adj* unshaped, untrimmed
infacētē *adv* witlessly
infacētĭ·ae -ārum *f pl* coarse jokes
infacēt·us -a -um *adj* not witty, not funny, dull, stupid
infācund·us -a -um *adj* ineloquent
infāmĭ·a -ae *f* bad reputation, bad name; disrepute, disgrace, scandal; embarrassment
infām·is -e *adj* infamous, notorious, disreputable, disgraceful
infām·ō -āre *vt* to defame, dishonor, disgrace
infand·us -a -um *adj* unspeakable, shocking
inf·ans -antis *adj* speechless, unable to speak; baby, infant, young; childish, silly; (fig) incapable of speaking, tongue-tied; *m* or *f* infant
infantĭ·a -ae *f* infancy; childishness; inability to speak; lack of eloquence
infar- = infer-
infatŭ·ō -āre *vt* to make a fool of
infaust·us -a -um *adj* ill-omened, unpropitious; unfortunate
infect·or -ōris *m* dyer
infect·us -a -um *pp* of **inficio;** *adj* not made, not done, undone, unfinished, unachieved; unfeasible; impossible
infēcundĭt·ās -ātis *f* unfruitfulness
infēcund·us -a -um *adj* unfruitful
infēlīcĭt·ās -ātis *f* bad luck, misfortune
infēlīcĭter *adv* unhappily; unluckily, unsuccessfully
infēlīc·ō -āre *vt* to make unhappy
infēl·ix -īcis *adj* unfruitful; unhappy, unfortunate; causing misfortune, ruinous; ill-omened; pessimistic
infensē *adv* hostilely, aggressively
infens·ō -āre *vt* to antagonize; to make dangerous; *vi* to be hostile
infens·us -a -um *adj* hostile, antagonistic; dangerous; (with *dat* or **in** + *acc*) **a** hostile to, antagonistic toward; **b** dangerous to
in·fercĭō or **infarcĭō -fercīre -fersī -fersum** or **-fertum** *vt* to stuff, cram
infĕr·a -ōrum *n pl* lower world
infĕr·ī -ōrum *m pl* the dead; the world below
inferĭ·ae -ārum *f pl* rites and offerings to the dead
inferĭ·or -us *adj* lower, farther down; (fig) inferior, lower; subsequent, later
inferĭus *adv* lower, too low
infernē *adv* below, beneath
infern·us -a -um *adj* lower; infernal, of the lower world
infĕrō inferre intŭlī illātum *vt* to bring in, introduce, carry in; to import; to bring forward, adduce, produce, make, occasion, incite, cause; to offer, render, sacrifice; to bury, inter; **arma, bellum, gradum, pedem,** or **signa inferre** to make an attack, make an advance, begin hostilities; **arma, bellum, pedem** or **signa inferre** (with *dat* or with **in** or **contra** + *acc*) to attack, advance against, invade; **conversa signa inferre** (with *dat*) to turn around and attack; **ignem inferre** (with *dat*) to set fire to; **se inferre** to go, march, rush, charge, plunge; **se in periculum inferre** to expose oneself to danger; *vi* to infer, conclude
infĕr·us -a -um *adj* lower; southern
in·fervescō -fervescĕre -ferbŭī *vi* to simmer, boil
infestē *adv* hostilely, violently, outrageously
infest·ō -āre *vt* to annoy; to infest; to attack
infest·us -a -um *adj* infested, molested, disturbed, unsafe; hostile, aggressive; dangerous; threatening
inficēt- = infacēt-
in·ficĭō -ficĕre -fēcī -fectum *vt* to dip, dye, tint; to infect; to stain; to corrupt, spoil; to imbue, instruct; (fig) to poison, infect
infidēl·is -e *adj* unfaithful, untrue, disloyal
infidēlĭt·ās -ātis *f* infidelity, unfaithfulness, disloyalty
infidēlĭter *adv* disloyally

infīd·us -a -um *adj* untrustworthy, treacherous

in·fīgō -fīgĕre -fixī -fixum *vt* to drive in, nail, thrust; to imprint, fix, impress; (with *dat*) **a** to drive into, thrust into; **b** to impale on; **c** to imprint on or in

infimātis see **infumatis**

infīm·us or **infŭm·us -a -um** (*superl* of **inferus**) *adj* lowest, last; lowest, worst, humblest; **ab infimo colle** at the foot of the hill; **infimum mare** the botton of the sea; *n* bottom

in·findō -findĕre -fĭdī -fissum *vt* (with *dat*) to cut (*e.g., furrows*) into

infīnĭt·ās -ātis *f* endlessness, infinity

infīnītē *adv* without bounds, without end, infinitely; without exception

infīnītĭ·ō -ōnis *f* boundlessness, infinity

infīnīt·us -a -um *adj* unlimited, boundless; without end, endless, infinite; countless; indefinite

infirmātĭ·ō -ōnis *f* invalidation; refutation

infirmē *adv* weakly, faintly, feebly

infirmĭt·ās -ātis *f* weakness, feebleness; infirmity, sickness; inconstancy

infirm·ō -āre *vt* to weaken, enfeeble; to refute, disprove; to annul

infirm·us -a -um *adj* weak, faint, feeble; infirm, sick; trivial; inconstant

infissus *pp* of **infindo**

infit *v defect* he, she, it begins

infitĭ·ae -ārum *f pl* denial; **infitias ire** (with *acc*) to deny

infitiāl·is -e *adj* negative

infitiātĭ·ō -ōnis *f* denial

infitiāt·or -ōris *m* repudiator

infitĭ·or -ārī -ātus sum *vt* to deny, repudiate, contradict, disown

infixus *pp* of **infigo**

inflammātĭ·ō -ōnis *f* setting on fire; **inflammationem inferre** (with *dat*) to set on fire

inflamm·ō -āre *vt* to set on fire, kindle, light up; (fig) to inflame, excite

inflātĭ·ō -ōnis *f* swelling up; **habet inflationem faba** beans cause gas

inflātĭus *adv* too pompously

inflāt·us -a -um *adj* blown up, swollen, inflated; haughty; turgid (*style*)

inflāt·us -ūs *m* puff, blast; inspiration

in·flectō -flectĕre -flexī -flexum *vt* to bend, curve, bow, turn aside; to change; to influence; to inflect

inflēt·us -a -um *adj* unwept

inflexibĭl·is -e *adj* inflexible

inflexĭ·ō -ōnis *f* bending

inflexus *pp* of **inflecto**

inflex·us -ūs *m* curve

in·flīgō -flīgĕre -flixī -flictum *vt* to strike, smash, dash, swing; to inflict (*wound*); to bring (*e.g., disgrace*)

infl·ō -āre *vt* to blow (*horn*), play (*flute*); to inspire; to inflate, puff up, fill

in·flŭō -fluĕre -fluxī *vi* (with **in** + *acc*) **a** to flow into; **b** (fig) to spill over into, stream into, pour into

in·fodĭō -fodĕre -fōdī -fossum *vt* to dig; to bury

informātĭ·ō -ōnis *f* sketch; idea

inform·is -e *adj* unformed, shapeless; ugly, hideous

inform·ō -āre *vt* to form, shape

infŏr·ō -āre *vt* to bring into court

infortūnāt·us -a -um *adj* unfortunate

infortūn·ĭum -ĭī or **-ī** *n* misfortune, calamity; punishment

infossus *pp* of **infodio**

infrā *adv* below, underneath; down south, down the coast; *prep* (with *acc*) below, beneath, under; later than

infractĭ·ō -ōnis *f* weakening; **animi infractio** discouragement

infract·us -a -um *pp* of **infringo;** *adj* broken, weakened, exhausted; **infractos animos gerere** to feel down and out

infragĭl·is -e *adj* unbreakable, strong

infrĕm·ō -ĕre -ŭī *vi* to growl, bellow, roar; to rage

infrēnāt·us -a -um *adj* unbridled

infrend·ĕō -ēre or **infrend·ō -ĕre** *vi* **dentibus infrendere** to gnash the teeth

infrēn·is -e or **infrēn·us -a -um** *adj* unbridled

infrēn·ō -āre *vt* to put a bridle on; to harness; (fig) to curb

infrēnus see **infrenis**

infrĕqu·ens -entis *adj* uncrowded, not numerous; poorly attended; thinly populated; inconstant, irregular

infrequentĭ·a -ae *f* small number, scantiness; poor attendance; emptiness

in·fringō -fringĕre -frēgī -fractum *vt* to break, break in; to impair, affect, subdue, weaken, break down

infr·ons -ondis *adj* leafless

infructuōs·us -a -um *adj* unfruitful; pointless

infūcāt·us -a -um *adj* painted over, varnished; hidden

infŭl·a -ae *f* bandage; fillet; mark of distinction, badge of honor

infumāt·is or **infimāt·is -is** *m* one of the lowest (*in rank*)

infŭmus see **infimus**

in·fundō -fundĕre -fūdī -fūsum *vt* to pour in, pour on, pour out; (with *dat* or **in** + *acc*) **a** to pour into, pour upon; **b** to administer to; **infundi** or **se infundere** (with *dat*) to lay on, spread out on

infusc·ō -āre *vt* to darken, obscure; to stain, corrupt, sully

infūsus *pp* of **infundo;** *adj* diffused, permeating; fallen (*snow*); crowded

ingemĭn·ō -āre *vt* to redouble; to repeat, reiterate; *vi* to redouble
ingem·iscō or **ingem·escō -iscĕre -ŭī** *vi* to groan, heave a sigh; (with *dat* or **in** + *abl*) to groan over, sigh over
ingĕm·ō -ĕre -ŭī *vt* to groan over, sigh over; *vi* (with *dat*) to sigh over
ingenĕr·ō -āre *vt* to engender, generate, produce, create
ingeniāt·us -a -um *adj* naturally endowed, talented
ingeniōsē *adv* ingeniously
ingeniōs·us -a -um *adj* ingenious, clever, talented; (with *dat* or **ad** + *acc*) naturally suited to
ingenĭt·us -a -um *adj* inborn, natural
ingen·ĭum -ĭī or **-ī** *n* innate or natural quality; nature, temperament, character, bent, inclination; natural ability, talent, genius; clever person, genius
ing·ens -entis *adj* huge, vast; great, mighty, powerful
ingenŭē *adv* liberally; frankly
ingenuĭt·ās -ātis *f* noble birth; noble character; frankness
ingenŭ·us -a -um *adj* native, indigenous; natural; free-born; like a freeman, noble; frank
in·gĕrō -gerĕre -gessī -gestum *vt* to carry in, throw in, heap; to hurl, shoot (*weapon*); to pour out (*angry words*), heap (*abuse*)
inglōrĭ·us -a -um *adj* inglorious, without glory, inconspicuous
ingluvĭ·ēs -ēī *f* crop, maw; gluttony
ingrātē *adv* unpleasantly; unwillingly; ungratefully
ingrātificʹ·us -a -um *adj* ungrateful
ingrātĭīs or **ingrātīs** *adv* without thanks; unwillingly
ingrāt·us -a -um *adj* unpleasant, unwelcome; ungrateful; receiving no thanks, unappreciated; thankless
ingravesc·ō -ĕre *vi* to grow heavier; to become pregnant; to grow worse; to become more serious; to become weary; to become dearer (*in price*); to become more important
in·gredĭor -grĕdī -gressus sum *vt* to enter; to undertake; to begin; to walk in, follow (*footsteps*); *vi* to go in, enter; to go, walk, walk along; to begin, commence; to begin to speak; (with **in** + *acc*) **a** to go in, enter; **b** to enter upon, begin, take up, undertake; **in rem publicam ingredi** to enter politics, enter public life
ingressĭ·ō -ōnis *f* entering; walking; gait, pace; beginning
ingress·us -ūs *m* entering; (mil) inroad; walking; gait; beginning
ingrŭ·ō -ĕre -ī *vi* to come, come on, rush on; (of war) to break out; (of rain) to pour down; (with *dat* or **in** + *acc*) to fall upon, attack
ingu·en -ĭnis *n* groin; swelling, tumor; *n pl* private parts
ingurgĭt·ō -āre *vt* to gorge, stuff; **se ingurgitare** to stuff oneself; **se ingurgitare** (with **in** + *acc*) to steep oneself in, devote oneself to
ingustāt·us -a -um *adj* untasted
inhabĭl·is -e *adj* clumsy, unhandy; (with *dat* or **ad** + *acc*) unfit for
inhabitābĭl·is -e *adj* uninhabitable
inhabĭt·ō -āre *vt* inhabit
in·haerĕō -haerēre -haesī -haesum *vi* to stick, cling; (fig) to cling, adhere; to be inherent; (with *dat*, with **ad** + *acc*, or with **in** + *abl*) **a** to cling to; **b** to be closely connected with; **c** to gaze upon
in·haerescō -haerescĕre -haesī *vi* to stick fast, take hold
inhăl·ō -āre *vt* (with *dat*) to breathe (*e.g., bad breath*) on (*someone*)
inhib·ĕō -ēre -ŭī -ĭtum *vt* to hold back, curb, check, control; to use, practice, perform; to apply, inflict; **retro navem inhibere** to back up the ship; *vi* to row backwards, backwater
inhibitĭ·ō -ōnis *f* backing up
inhĭ·ō -āre *vt* to gape at; to covet; *vi* to stand open-mouthed, be amazed
inhonestē *adv* dishonorably, disgracefully; dishonestly
inhonest·ō -āre *vt* to dishonor, disgrace
inhonest·us -a -um *adj* dishonorable, disgraceful, shameful, inglorious; indecent; ugly, degrading
inhonōrāt·us -a -um *adj* unhonored, disregarded, unrewarded
inhonōr·us -a -um *adj* defaced
inhorr·ĕō -ēre -ŭī *vi* to stand on end, bristle
inhorr·escō -escĕre -ŭī *vi* to stand on end, bristle; to vibrate; to shiver, tremble, shudder
inhospitāl·is -e *adj* inhospitable, unfriendly
inhospitālĭt·ās -ātis *f* inhospitality
inhospĭt·us -a -um *adj* inhospitable
inhūmānē *adv* inhumanly, savagely
inhūmānĭt·ās -ātis *f* inhumanity, barbarity; churlishness; extreme stinginess
inhūmānĭter *adv* impolitely
inhūmān·us -a -um *adj* inhuman, savage; brutal; crude, impolite
inhumāt·us -a -um *adj* unburied
inĭbi or **inĭbī** *adv* there, in that place; near at hand
inimīc·a -ae *f* (personal) enemy (*female*)
inimīcē *adv* hostilely, in an unfriendly way
inimīcitĭ·a -ae *f* unfriendliness, enmity; *f pl* feuds
inimīc·ō -āre *vt* to make into enemies, set at odds
inimīc·us -a -um *adj* unfriendly, hostile; harmful; *m* (personal) enemy; **inimicissimus suus** his bitterest enemy
inīquē *adv* unequally, unevenly; unfairly
inīquĭt·ās -ātis *f* unevenness; in-

equality; disadvantage; unfairness
inīqu·us -a -um *adj* uneven, unequal; not level, sloping; unfair; adverse, harmful; dangerous, unfavorable; prejudiced; excessive; impatient, discontented; **iniquo animo** impatiently, unwillingly; *m* enemy, foe
initĭ·ō -āre *vt* to initiate, begin; to initiate (*into mysteries*)
init·ĭum -ĭī or **-ī** *n* entrance; beginning; *n pl* elements; first principles; sacred rites, sacred mysteries
inĭtus *pp* of **ineo**
inĭt·us -ūs *m* entrance; beginning
in·jiciō -jicĕre -jēcī -jectum *vt* to throw, inject; to impose, apply; to inspire, infuse; to cause, occasion; to furnish (*a cause*); to bring up, mention (*a name*); (with *dat* or **in** + *acc*) to throw or fling into, on or over; (with *dat* or **in** + *acc*) **a** to throw oneself into, rush into, expose oneself to; **b** to fling oneself down on; **c** (of the mind) to turn itself to, concentrate on, reflect on; **manum injicere** (with *dat*) to lay hands on, take possession of
injūcundĭt·ās -ātis *f* unpleasantness
injūcundĭus *adv* rather unpleasantly
injūcund·us -a -um *adj* unpleasant
injūdicāt·us -a -um *adj* undecided
in·jungō -jungĕre -junxī -junctum *vt* to join, attach, fasten; to inflict, impose; (with *dat*) **a** to join, attach, fasten to; **b** to inflict on, impose (*e.g., taxes, obligations*) on
injūrāt·us -a -um *adj* not under oath
injūrĭ·a -ae *f* injury, wrong, outrage, injustice; insult, affront; harshness, severity; revenge; damage, harm; ill-gotten goods; **injuriā** unjustly, undeservedly, innocently; **per injuriam** unjustly, outrageously
injūriōsē *adv* unjustly, wrongfully
injūriōs·us -a -um *adj* unjust, wrongful; harmful
injūrĭ·us -a -um *adj* unjust, wrong
injūr·us -a -um *adj* wrongful
injussū (*abl* only) *m* without orders; **injussu meo** without my orders
injuss·us -a -um *adj* unasked, unbidden, voluntary
injustē *adv* unjustly
injustitĭ·a -ae *f* injustice
injust·us -a -um *adj* unjust
inl- = **ill-**
inm- = **imm-**
innābĭl·is -e *adj* unswimmable
in·nascor -nascī -nātus sum *vi* (with *dat*) to be born in, grow in or on; (with **in** + *abl*) (fig) to originate in
innăt·ō -āre *vt* to swim; *vi* (with *dat*) to swim around in, float on; (with **in** + *acc*) to swim into
innāt·us -a -um *pp* of **innascor;** *adj* inborn, natural
innāvigābĭl·is -e *adj* unnavigable
in·nectō -nectĕre -nexŭī -nexum *vt* to entwine; to tie, fasten together; to join, attach, connect; (fig) to devise, invent, plan
in·nītor -nītī -nixus sum or **-nīsus sum** *vi* (with *abl*) to lean on, rest on, be supported by
inn·ō -āre *vt* to swim; to sail, sail over; *vi* (with *abl*) **a** to swim in, float on; **b** to sail on; **c** (of the sea) to wash against (*a shore*)
innŏc·ens -entis *adj* harmless; guiltless, innocent; upright; unselfish; (with *genit*) innocent of
innocenter *adv* blamelessly
innocentĭ·a -ae *f* innocence; integrity; unselfishness
innocŭē *adv* harmlessly; innocently
innocŭ·us -a -um *adj* harmless, innocuous; innocent; unharmed
innōt·escō -escĕre -ŭī *vi* to become known; to become notorious
innŏv·ō -āre *vt* to renew, restore; **se innovare** (with **ad** + *acc*) to return to
innoxĭ·us -a -um *adj* harmless; safe; innocent; unhurt; (with *genit*) innocent of
innūbĭl·us -a -um *adj* cloudless
innŭb·a -ae (*fem* only) *adj* unmarried
in·nūbō -nūbĕre -nupsī *vi* (with *dat*) to marry into
innumerābĭl·is -e *adj* innumerable
innumerābilĭt·ās -ātis *f* countless number
innumerābilĭter *adv* innumerably
innumerāl·is -e *adj* innumerable
innumĕr·us -a -um *adj* countless
in·nŭō -nuĕre -nŭī -nūtum *vi* to give a nod; (with *dat*) to nod to
innupt·a -ae (*fem* only) *adj* unmarried; *f* unmarried girl, maiden
innutr·ĭō -īre -īvī or **-ĭī -ītum** *vt* (with *dat*) to bring up in
Īn·ō -ūs *f* daughter of Cadmus and Harmonia, wife of Athamas, mother of Learchus and Melicerta, and stepmother of Phrixus and Helle; pursued by mad Athamas, she and Melicerta hurled themselves into the sea, whereupon they were changed into sea deities
inoblīt·us -a -um *adj* unforgetful
inobrŭt·us -a -um *adj* not overwhelmed
inobservābĭl·is -e *adj* unnoticed
inobservantĭ·a -ae *f* inattention
inobservāt·us -a -um *adj* unobserved
inoccidŭ·us -a -um *adj* never setting
inodōr·us -a -um *adj* odorless
inoffens·us -a -um *adj* unobstructed, uninterrupted, unhindered
inofficiōs·us -a -um *adj* irresponsible; not obliging
inŏl·ens -entis *adj* odorless
inol·escō -escĕre -ēvī *vi* to become inveterate; (with *dat*) to grow on or in

inōminăt·us -a -um *adj* ill-omened, inauspicious
inopĭ·a -ae *f* lack, want, need, poverty; scarcity; barrenness (*of style*); helplessness
inopīn·ans -antis *adj* unsuspecting, taken by surprise
inopīnanter *adv* unexpectedly
inopīnātō *adv* unexpectedly, by surprise
inopīnāt·us -a -um *adj* not expected, unexpected, unsuspected, surprising; *n* surprise; **ex inopinato** by surprise
inopīn·us -a -um *adj* unexpected
inopiōs·us -a -um *adj* (with *genit*) in need of
in·ops -ŏpis *adj* without means or resources; poor, needy, destitute; helpless, weak, forlorn; bald (*style*); poor (*expression*); pitiful, wretched, contemptible; (with *genit*) destitute of, stripped of, without; (with *abl*) lacking in, deficient in, poor in
inōrāt·us -a -um *adj* not presented; **re inoratā** without presenting one's case
inordināt·us -a -um *adj* disordered
inornāt·us -a -um *adj* unadorned; plain (*style*); unheralded
inp- = imp-
inpendiōs·us -a -um *adj* extravagant
inperc·ō -ĕre *vi* (with *dat*) to spare
inpluviāt·us -a -um *adj* square, shaped like an impluvium
inpūrāt·us -a -um *adj* (morally) defiled
inpūritĭ·ae -ārum *f pl* (moral) impurity
inquam *v defect* say; after one or more words of direct quotation, e.g., **Desilite, inquit, milites et . . .** "Jump down, fellow soldiers", he says, "and . . ."; in emphatic repetition, e.g., **tuas, tuas inquam suspiciones . . .** your suspicions, yes I say yours . . . ; **inquit** it is said, one says
inquĭ·ēs -ētis *adj* restless
inquiēt·ō -āre *vt* to disquiet, disturb
inquiēt·us -a -um *adj* restless, unsettled
inquilīn·us -ī *m* tenant, inhabitant
inquināté *adv* filthily
inquināt·us -a -um *adj* filthy, foul
inquĭn·ō -āre *vt* to mess up, defile, contaminate
in·quīrō -quīrĕre quīsīvī -quīsītum *vt* to search for, inquire into, examine, pry into; *vi* to hold an investigation; to hold a preliminary hearing
inquīsītĭ·ō -ōnis *f* search, inquiry, investigation; preliminary hearing; (with *genit*) search for, inquiry into, investigation of
inquīsīt·or -ōris *m* inspector, examiner; spy; (law) investigator
inquīsīt·us -a -um *pp* of **inquiro;** *adj* not investigated
inquit see **inquam**
inr- = irr-
insalūbr·is -e *adj* unhealthy
insalūtāt·us -a -um *adj* ungreeted
insānābĭl·is -e *adj* incurable
insānē *adv* crazily, madly
insānĭ·a -ae *f* insanity, madness, frenzy; rapture; mania; excess; inspiration
insān·ĭō -īre -īvī or **-ĭī -ītum** *vi* to be crazy, be mad, be insane; to be absurd, be wild
insānĭt·ās -ātis *f* unsoundness, disease
insān·us -a -um *adj* insane, mad, crazy; absurd, foolish; excessive, extravagant; monstrous, outrageous; inspired; maddening
insatiābĭl·is -e *adj* insatiable; that cannot cloy, uncloying
insatiābiliter *adv* insatiably
insatiĕt·ās -ātis *f* insatiety
insaturābĭl·is -e *adj* insatiable
insaturābiliter *adv* insatiably
in·scendō -scendĕre -scendī -scensum *vt & vi* to climb up, mount
inscensĭ·ō -ōnis *f* mounting; **in navem inscensio** boarding a ship
inscensus *pp* of **inscendo**
inscĭ·ens -entis *adj* unaware; silly, stupid
inscienter *adv* ignorantly, inadvertently
inscientĭ·a -ae *f* ignorance; inexperience; foolishness; awkwardness
inscīt·us -a -um *adj* ignorant, clumsy, stupid
inscĭ·us -a -um *adj* ignorant, unaware
in·scrībō -scrībĕre -scripsī -scriptum *vt* to inscribe; to ascribe; to title (*a book*); to assign, attribute, appropriate; to advertise; to address (*a letter*); (with *dat* or **in** + *abl*) to write (*something*) on or in
inscriptĭ·ō -ōnis *f* inscribing
inscript·us -a -um *pp* of **inscribo;** *adj* unwritten
in·sculpō -sculpĕre -sculpsī -sculptum *vt* to cut, carve, engrave; (with *abl* or **in** + *abl*) to cut, carve, or engrave upon
insectātĭ·ō -ōnis *f* hot pursuit
insectāt·or -ōris *m* persecutor
insect·or -ārī -ātus sum or **insect·ō -āre** *vt* to pursue, attack; to attack with words, criticize
insect·us -a -um *adj* indented, notched
insecūtus *pp* of **insequor**
insēdābiliter *adv* incessantly
insen·escō -escĕre -ŭī *vi* (with *dat*) to grow old amidst, grow old over
insensĭl·is -e *adj* imperceptible
insepult·us -a -um *adj* unburied
insĕqu·ens -entis *adj* next, following, succeeding
in·sĕquor -sĕquī -secūtus sum *vt* to follow, follow after; to succeed, to follow up; to attack; to prosecute; to pass, overtake; to reproach;

to strive after; *vi* to follow, come next

in·sĕrō -serĕre -sēvī -sĭtum *vt* to graft; (fig) to implant

in·sĕrō -serĕre -serŭī -sertum *vt* to insert; to introduce; to involve; to join, enroll, associate; to mingle, blend; to let in

insert·ō -āre *vt* to insert

inserv·ĭō -īre -īvī or **-ĭī -ītum** *vt* to serve, obey; *vi* to be a slave, be a subject; (with *dat*) to serve, be subservient to, be devoted to

insessus *pp* of **insido**

insībĭl·ō -āre *vi* (of the wind) to whistle, hiss

in·sidĕō -sidēre -sēdī -sessum *vt* to hold, occupy; *vi* to sit down; to settle down; to be deep-seated; (with *abl* or *in* + *abl*) **a** to sit on; **b** to settle down on or in; **c** (fig) to be fixed in, stamped in

insidĭ·ae -ārum *f pl* ambush; plot, trap; **insidias dare, comparare, collocare, parare,** or **struere** (with *dat*) to lay a trap for

insidiāt·or -ōris *m* soldier in ambush; (fig) plotter, subversive

insidĭ·or -ārī -ātus sum *vi* to lie in wait; (with *dat*) **a** to lie in wait for; **b** (fig) to plot against; **c** (fig) to watch for (*an opportunity*)

insidiōsē *adv* insidiously, by underhand means

insidiōs·us -a -um *adj* insidious, treacherous, tricky

in·sīdō -sīdĕre -sēdī -sessum *vt* to occupy, keep possession of, possess; *vi* (with *dat*) to settle in or on; (with **in** + *abl*) (fig) to become fixed in

insign·e -is *n* insignia, mark, token; (mil) decoration, medal; standard; coat of arms; signal; honor, distinction; brilliant passage, gem; *n pl* insignia, regalia, uniform, attire, accouterments

insign·ĭō -īre -īvī or **-ĭī -ītum** *vt* to make conspicuous, distinguish

insign·is -e *adj* conspicuous, distinguished; prominent, eminent, extraordinary, singular

insignītē *adv* extraordinarily, notably

insignīter *adv* remarkably

insignīt·us -a -um *adj* marked, conspicuous, clear, glaring; distinguished, striking, notable

insilĭ·a -ĭum *n pl* treadle (*of a loom*)

insil·ĭō -īre -ŭī or **-īvī** *vt* to jump up on, mount; *vi* (with *dat*) to jump on; (with **in** + *acc*) **a** to jump into or on; **b** to jump on, mount, climb aboard

insimulātĭ·ō -ōnis *f* charge, accusation

insimŭl·ō -āre *vt* to accuse, accuse falsely, allege

insincēr·us -a -um *adj* mixed, spoiled, not pure

insinuātĭ·ō -ōnis *f* winning sympathy

insinŭ·ō -āre *vt* to bring in secretly, sneak in; **se insinuare** (with **inter** + *acc*) to wriggle in between, work one's way between or among; **se insinuare in familiaritatem** (with *genit*) to ingratiate oneself with

insipĭ·ens -entis *adj* foolish

insipienter *adv* foolishly

insipientĭ·a -ae *f* foolishness

in·sistō -sistĕre -stĭtī *vt* to stand on, trample on; to set about, keep at (*a task, etc.*); to follow, chase after, pursue; **iter insistere** or **viam insistere** to enter upon a course, pursue a course; *vi* to stand, stop, come to a standstill; to pause; (with *dat*) **a** to tread on the heels of, pursue closely; **b** to press on with; **c** (fig) to dwell upon; (with *dat* or **in** + acc) to set foot on or in, step on, tread on, stand on; (with *dat* or **in** + *abl*) to persist in; (with **ad** or **in** + *acc*) to keep at, keep after, keep the pressure on, pursue vigorously

insitĭ·ō -ōnis *f* grafting; grafting time

insitīv·us -a -um *adj* grafted; (fig) spurious

insĭt·or -ōris *m* grafter

insĭt·us -a -um *pp* of **insero;** *adj* inborn, innate; incorporated

insociābĭl·is -e *adj* incompatible

insōlābilĭter *adv* unconsolably

insŏl·ens -entis *adj* unaccustomed, unusual; immoderate, excessive; extravagant; insolent; (with *genit* or **in** + *abl*) unaccustomed to, inexperienced in; **in aliena re insolens** free with someone else's money

insolenter *adv* unusually; excessively; insolently

insolentĭ·a -ae *f* unusualness, strangeness, novelty; inexperience; affectation; insolence, arrogance

insolesc·ō -ĕre *vi* to become strange; to become insolent; to become elated

insolĭd·us -a -um *adj* soft

insolĭt·us -a -um *adj* unaccustomed, inexperienced; unusual, strange, uncommon; *n* the unusual

insomnĭ·a -ae *f* insomnia, sleeplessness

insomn·is -e *adj* sleepless

insomn·ium -ĭī or **-ī** *n* nightmare; dream

insŏn·ō -āre -ŭī *vi* to make noise; to sound, resound, roar; **calamis insonare** to make music with a reed pipe; **flagello insonare** to crack the whip; **pennis insonare** to flap the wings

ins·ons -ontis *adj* innocent; harmless

insōpīt·us -a -um *adj* sleepless

insŏp·or -ōris *adj* sleepless

inspect·ō -āre *vt* to look at, view, observe

inspectus *pp* of **inspicio**

inspēr·ans -antis *adj* not expecting

inspērāt·us -a -um *adj* unhoped for, unexpected, unforeseen; unwelcome; **ex insperato** unexpectedly
in·spergō -spergĕre -spersī -spersum *vt* to sprinkle
in·spiciō -spicĕre -spexī -spectum *vt* to inspect, look into, examine, consider; to inspect, review; to look at, consult (*books*)
inspīc·ō -āre *vt* to make pointed; to sharpen
inspīr·ō -āre *vt* to inspire, infuse, enkindle; *vi* (with *dat*) to blow on, breathe on
inspoliāt·us -a -um *adj* undespoiled
inspūt·ō -āre *vt* to spit on
instābĭl·is -e *adj* unstable, unsteady; (fig) unsteady, changeable
inst·ans -antis *adj* present; immediate, threatening, urgent
instanter *adv* vehemently
instantĭ·a -ae *f* presence; vehemence
instar (indecl) *n* image, likeness, appearance, resemblance; (with *genit*) like, equal to, as large as, worth, as good as
instaurātĭ·ō -ōnis *f* renewal, repetition
instaurātīv·us -a -um *adj* begun anew, repeated
instaur·ō -āre *vt* to set up; to renew, repeat, start all over again (*esp. games and celebrations*); to repay, requite
in·sternō -sternĕre -strāvī -strātum *vt* to cover
instīgāt·or -ōris *m* or **instīgātr·ix -īcis** *f* instigator, ringleader
instīg·ō -āre *vt* to instigate, goad on, stimulate, incite
instill·ō -āre *vt* (with *dat*) to pour (*something*) on, instill (*something*) in
instimulāt·or -ōris *m* instigator
instimŭl·ō -āre *vt* to stimulate, urge on
instinct·or -ōris *m* instigator
instinct·us -a -um *adj* incited, inspired
instinct·us -ūs *m* inspiration, impulse
instipŭl·or -ārī -ātus sum *vi* to bargain
instĭt·a -ae *f* border, flounce; (fig) lady
institĭ·ō -ōnis *f* standing still
instĭt·or -ōris *m* salesman, huckster, hawker
instit·ŭō -uĕre -ŭī -ūtum *vt* to set, fix, plant; to set up, erect, establish; to arrange; to build, make, construct; to prepare, make ready; to provide, furnish; to institute, organize, set up; to appoint, designate; to undertake, begin; to decide, determine; to control, direct, govern; to teach, train, instruct, educate
institūtĭ·ō -ōnis *f* arrangement; custom; instruction, education; *f pl* principles of education
institūt·um -ī *n* practice, custom, usage; precedent; principle; decree, regulation, stipulation, terms; purpose, intention; **ex instituto** according to custom
in·stō -stāre -stĭtī *vt* to follow, pursue; to work hard at; to menace, threaten; *vi* to be at hand, approach, be impending; to insist; (with *dat* or **in** + *abl*) to stand on or in; (with *dat*) **a** to be close to; **b** to be on the heels of, pursue closely; **c** to harass
instrātus *pp* of **insterno**
instrēnŭ·us -a -um *adj* lethargic
instrĕp·ō -āre -ŭī -ĭtum *vi* to creak, rattle
instructĭ·ō -ōnis *f* construction; array
instructĭus *adv* with better preparation
instruct·or -ōris *m* supervisor
instruct·us -a -um *pp* of **instruo;** *adj* provided, equipped, furnished; prepared, arranged; instructed, versed
instruct·us -ūs *m* equipment; stock-in-trade (*of an orator*)
instrūment·um -ī *n* instrument, tool, utensil; equipment; dress, outfit; repertory, stock-in-trade; means, supply, provisions; document
in·strŭō -struĕre -struxī -structum *vt* to build up, construct; to furnish, prepare, provide, fit out; to instruct; (mil) to deploy
insuās·um -ī *n* dark-orange color
insuāv·is -e *adj* unpleasant, disagreeable
insūd·ō -āre *vi* (with *dat*) to sweat on, drip sweat on
insuēfact·us -a -um *adj* accustomed
in·suescō -suescĕre -suēvī -suētum *vt* to accustom, familiarize; *vi* (with *dat*, with **ad** + *acc*, or with *inf*) to get used to
insuēt·us -a -um *adj* unusual; (with *genit* or *dat*, with **ad** + *acc*, or with *inf*) unused to
insŭl·a -ae *f* island; apartment building
insulān·us -ī *m* islander
insulsē *adv* in poor taste; insipidly, absurdly
insulsĭt·ās -ātis *f* lack of taste; silliness, absurdity
insuls·us -a -um *adj* unsalted, without taste; coarse, tasteless, insipid; silly, absurd; bungling; *f pl* silly creatures (*i.e., women*)
insult·ō -āre *vt* to insult, scoff at, taunt; (of votaries) to dance about in; *vi* to jump, gambol, prance; to gloat; (with *abl*) **a** to jump in, cavort in, gambol on, jump upon; **b** to gloat over; (with *dat* or **in** + *acc*) to scoff at, gloat over
insultūr·a -ae *f* jumping in
insum inesse infŭī *vi* to be there; (with *dat* or **in** + *abl*) **a** to be in, be on; **b** to be implied in, be contained in, be in, belong to

in·sūmō -sūmĕre -sumpsī -sumptum *vt* to spend, devote, waste; (with *dat* or **in** + *acc*) to devote to, apply to; (with *abl* or **in** + *abl*) to expend on; **operam insumere** (with *dat*) to devote effort to, waste effort on

in·sŭō -suĕre -sŭī -sūtum *vt* to sew up; (wth *dat*) **a** to sew up in; **b** to embroider (*something*) on

insŭper *adv* above, overhead, on the top; from above; moreover, besides, in addition; *prep* (with *acc*) above, over, over and above; (with *abl*) in addition to, besides

insuperābĭl·is -e *adj* insurmountable; unconquerable

in·surgō -surgĕre -surrexī -surrectum *vi* to rise, stand up; to rise, stand high, tower; to rise, increase, grow, grow intense; to rise to power; (with *dat*) **a** to rise up against; **b** to strain at (*e.g., oars*)

insusurr·ō -āre *vt* (with *dat*) to whisper (*something*) to; **insusurrare in aurem** (with *genit*) to whisper into the ear of; **sibi cantilenam insusurrare** to hum a tune to oneself; *vi* to whisper; (of wind) to blow gently

intāb·escō -escĕre -ŭī *vi* to melt away gradually, dissolve gradually; (fig) to waste away, pine away

intactĭl·is -e *adj* intangible

intact·us -a -um *adj* untouched; uninjured, intact; unpolluted; untried; unmarried; virgin, chaste

intact·us -ūs *m* intangibility

intāmināt·us -a -um *adj* unsullied

intect·us -a -um *pp* of **intego;** *adj* uncovered; naked; open, frank

integell·us -a -um *adj* fairly pure or chaste; in fair condition

intĕg·er -ra -rum *adj* whole, complete, intact, unimpaired; unhurt, unwounded; healthy, sound, fresh; new, fresh; pure, chaste; untouched, unaffected; unbiased, unprejudiced; unattempted; unsubdued, unconquered; unbroken (*horse*); not worn, unused; inexperienced, ignorant; virtuous, honest, blameless, irreproachable; healthy, sane; **ab integro** or **de integro** anew, all over again; **in integrum restituere** to restore to a former condition; to pardon; **integrum alicui esse** (with *inf*) to be in someone's power to

in·tĕgō -tegĕre -texī -tectum *vt* to cover up; to protect

integrasc·ō -ĕre *vi* to break out fresh, start all over again

integrātĭ·ō -ōnis *f* renewal, new beginning

intĕgrē *adv* wholly, entirely; honestly; correctly

integrĭt·ās -ātis *f* soundness; integrity; innocence; purity, chastity; correctness

intĕgr·ō -āre *vt* to make whole; to heal, repair; to renew, begin again; to refresh

integument·um -ī *n* covering; lid; protection

intellectus *pp* of **intellego**

intellect·us -ūs *m* perception; comprehension, understanding; intellect

intellĕg·ens -entis *adj* intelligent; (with *genit*) appreciative of; (with **in** + *abl*) versed in

intellegenter *adv* intelligently

intellegentĭ·a -ae *f* intelligence; understanding, knowledge; perception, judgment, discrimination, taste, skill; concept, notion; (with *genit*) knowledge or understanding of; (with **in** + *abl*) judgment in

intel·lĕgō -legĕre -lexī -lectum *vt* to understand, perceive, discern, comprehend, gather; to realize, recognize; to have an accurate knowledge of, be an expert in; *vi* **intellego** (in answers) I understand, I get it

intemerāt·us -a -um *adj* undefiled, pure; pure, undiluted

intempĕr·ans -antis *adj* intemperate, without restraint; profligate; excessive

intemperanter *adv* intemperately

intemperantĭ·a -ae *f* intemperance, lack of self-control; extravagance, excess

intemperātē *adv* intemperately

intemperāt·us -a -um *adj* excessive

intemperārĭ·ae -ārum *f pl* wild outbursts, wildness

intemperĭ·ēs -ēī *f* wildness, excess; outrageous conduct, excesses; **intemperies aquarum** heavy rain; **intemperies caeli** stormy weather

intempestīvē *adv* at a bad time, inopportunely

intempestīv·us -a -um *adj* untimely, unseasonable; poorly timed

intempest·us -a -um *adj* unseasonable; dark, dismal; unhealthy; **nox intempesta** dead of night

intemptāt·us or **intentāt·us -a -um** *adj* unattempted

in·tendō -tendĕre -tendī -tentum or **-tensum** *vt* to stretch, stretch out, extend, spread out; to stretch, bend (*e.g., bow*); to aim, direct, shoot (*weapon*); to increase, magnify, intensify; to intend; to urge, incite; to aim at, intend; to assert, maintain; to aim, turn, direct; to raise (*voice*); to stretch (*truth*); to direct, turn, focus (*mind, attention*); to pitch (*tent*)

intentātus see **intemptatus**

intentē *adv* intently, attentively

intentĭ·ō -ōnis *f* stretching, straining, tension; attention; effort, exertion; accusation

intent·ō -āre *vt* to stretch out; to aim, direct; to threaten

intent·us -a -um *pp* of **intendo;** *adj* taut, tense; intent, attentive; eager, waiting, tense; strict (*discipline*); vigorous, tense, nervous (*speech*)

intent·us -ūs *m* stretching out, extending (*of the palms*)
intep·ĕō -ēre -ŭī *vi* to be lukewarm
intep·escō -pescĕre -ŭī *vi* to grow warm, be warmed
inter *prep* (with *acc*) between, among, amidst; during, within, in the course of; in spite of; (in classifying) among, in, with; **inter se** each other, one another, mutual, mutually
interaestŭ·ō -āre *vi* to retch
interāment·a -ōrum *n pl* framework of a ship
Interamn·a -ae *f* town in Latium, on the Liris; town in Umbria, birthplace of Tacitus
interapt·us -a -um *adj* joined together
interāresc·ō -ĕre *vi* to dry up
interātim *adv* meanwhile
interbĭb·ō -ĕre *vt* to drink up
interbīt·ō -ĕre *vi* to come to nothing
intercalār·is -e *adj* intercalary, inserted
intercalārĭ·us -a -um *adj* intercalary, inserted
intercăl·ō -āre *vt* to intercalate, insert
intercapēd·ō -ĭnis *f* interruption, break, pause
inter·cēdō -cēdĕre -cessī -cessum *vi* to come or go in between; (of time) to intervene, pass, occur; to act as an intermediary; to intercede; (of tribunes) to exercise the veto; (with *dat*) **a** to veto, protest against; **b** to interfere with, obstruct, hinder
interceptĭ·ō -ōnis *f* interception
intercept·or -ōris *m* embezzler
interceptus *pp* of **intercipio**
intercessĭ·ō -ōnis *f* intercession, mediation; (tribune's) veto
intercess·or -ōris *m* intercessor, mediator; interferer, obstructor; tribune exercising the veto
inter·cĭdō -cidĕre -cĭdī *vi* to fall short, miss the mark; to happen in the meantime; to drop out, be lost
inter·cīdō -cīdĕre -cīdī -cīsum *vt* to cut through, sever, cut down
intercĭn·ō -ĕre *vt* to interrupt with song or music
inter·cipĭō -cipĕre -cēpī -ceptum *vt* to intercept; to cut off (*the enemy*); to interrupt, cut off, preclude; to appropriate; to misappropriate; to receive by mistake (*e.g., poison*)
intercīsē *adv* piecemeal
intercīsus *pp* of **intercido**
inter·clūdō -clūdĕre -clūsī -clūsum *vt* to shut off, shut out, cut off; to stop, block up; to hinder, prevent; to blockade, shut in; to cut off, intercept, separate, divide
interclūsĭ·ō -ōnis *f* stopping; parenthesis; **animae interclusio** shortwindedness
interclūsus *pp* of **intercludo**
intercolumn·ĭum -ĭī or **-ī** *n* space between columns, intercolumniation
inter·currō -currĕre -cucurrī -cursum *vi* to intervene, mediate; to mingle; to rush in
intercurs·ō -āre *vi* to crisscross; to infiltrate; **inter se intercursare** to crisscross each other
intercurs·us -ūs *m* intervention
interc·us -ŭtis *adj* between the skin and flesh; **aqua intercus** dropsy
inter·dīcō -dīcĕre -dixī -dictum *vt* to forbid, prohibit; *vi* to make a provisional decree; **aquā et igni interdicere** (with *dat*) to outlaw, banish
interdictĭ·ō -ōnis *f* prohibiting; **aquae et igni interdictio** banishment
interdict·um -ī *n* prohibition; contraband; provisional decree (*of a praetor*)
interdictus *pp* of **interdico**
interdĭū or **interdĭūs** *adv* by day, in the daytime
interd·ō -āre *vt* to give intermittently; to distribute
interduct·us -ūs *m* punctuation
interdum *adv* sometimes, now and then, occasionally; meanwhile
interdŭ·ō -āre *vt* **floccum interduo** or **nihil interduo** I don't give a hoot
interĕā *adv* meanwhile, in the interim; meanwhile, anyhow, nevertheless
interemptus *pp* of **interimo**
inter·ĕō -īre -ĭī -ĭtum *vi* to be done for, be finished, perish, be lost; to become extinct
ride in between
interequĭt·ō -āre *vt* to ride between (*e.g., the ranks or columns*); *vi* to
interfātĭ·ō -ōnis *f* interruption
interfectĭ·ō -ōnis *f* killing
interfect·or -ōris *m* or **interfectr·ix -īcis** *f* killer
inter·ficĭō -ficĕre -fēcī -fectum *vt* to destroy; to kill
inter·fīō -fĭĕrī *vi* to pass away, be destroyed
inter·flŭō -fluĕre -fluxī *vt* to flow between; *vi* to flow in between
inter·fodĭō -fodĕre -fōdī -fossum *vi* to pierce
interf·or -ārī -ātus sum *vt & vi* to interrupt
interfug·ĭō -ĕre *vi* to scatter
interfulg·ĕō -ēre *vi* (with *abl*) to shine amidst or among
interfūs·us -a -um *adj* spread here and there; (with *acc*) flowing between
interĭbi *adv* in the meantime
intĕrim *adv* meanwhile; for the moment; sometimes; however, anyhow
inter·ĭmō -imĕre -ēmī -emptum *vt* to do away with, abolish; to kill
inter·ĭor -ĭus *adj* inner, interior; inner side of; secret, private; deeper, more profound; more intimate, more personal, more confidential
interitĭ·ō -ōnis *f* ruin, destruction
interĭt·us -ūs *m* ruin; death

interĭus *adv* on the inside, in the middle; too short; (to listen) closely
interjac·ĕō -ēre *vi* (with *dat*) to lie between
interjacĭō see **interjicio**
interjectĭ·ō -ōnis *f* interjection; parenthesis
interject·us -a -um *pp* of **interjicio;** *adj* (with *dat* or **inter** + *acc*) set or lying between
interject·us -ūs *m* interposition; interval
inter·jicĭō -jicĕre -jēcī -jectum *vt* to interpose; (with *dat* or **inter** + *acc*) **a** to throw or set (*something*) between; **b** to intermingle (*something*) with, intermix (*something*) with
inter·jungō -jungĕre -junxī -junctum *vt* to join together; to clasp
inter·lābor -lābī -lapsus *vi* to glide or flow in between
inter·lĕgō -legĕre -lēgī -lectum *vt* to pick or pluck here and there
inter·lĭnō -linĕre -lēvī -lĭtum *vt* to smear; to alter by erasing
inter·lŏquor -lŏquī -locūtus sum *vi* to interrupt; (with *dat*) to interrupt (*someone*)
inter·lūcĕō -lūcēre -luxī *vi* to shine through; to lighten now and then; to be transparent; to be plainly visible
interlūnĭ·a -ōrum *n pl* new moon
interlŭ·ō -ĕre *vt* to flow between, wash
intermenstrŭ·us -a -um *adj* of the new moon; *n* new moon
intermināt·us -a -um *adj* endless
intermĭn·or -ārī -ātus sum *vt* (with *dat*) to threaten (*someone*) with (*something*); *vi* to threaten
inter·miscĕō -miscēre -miscŭī -mixtum *vt* to intermingle
intermissĭ·ō -ōnis *f* interruption
inter·mittō -mittĕre -mīsī -missum *vt* to interrupt, break off, suspend, omit, neglect; to leave gaps in, leave unoccupied, leave undefended; to allow (*time*) to pass; *vi* to pause, stop
intermixtus *pp* of **intermisceo**
inter·morĭor -mŏrī -mortŭus sum *vi* to die suddenly; to faint
intermortŭ·us -a -um *adj* dead; unconscious; (fig) half-dead, moribund
intermundĭ·a -ōrum *n pl* outer space
intermūrāl·is -e *adj* intermural, between two walls
internāt·us -a -um *adj* (with *dat*) growing among or between
internecīn·us -a -um *adj* internecine, exterminating, of extermination
internecĭ·ō -ōnis *f* massacre, extermination
internecīv·us -a -um *adj* exterminating; **bellum internecivum** war of extermination
internĕc·ō -āre *vt* to kill off, exterminate
internect·ō -ĕre *vt* to intertwine
internit·ĕō -ēre *vi* to shine out
internōd·ĭum -ĭī or **-ī** *n* space between two joints
inter·noscō -noscĕre -nōvī -nōtum *vt* to distinguish, recognize; (with **ab** + *abl*) to distinguish (*one thing*) from (*another*)
internuntĭ·ō -āre *vi* to exchange messages
internunt·ĭus -ĭī or **-ī** *m* or **internuntĭ·a -ae** *f* messenger, courier, mediator, go-between
intern·us -a -um *adj* internal; civil, domestic
in·tĕrō -terĕre -trīvī -trītum *vt* to rub in, mash together
interpellātĭ·ō -ōnis *f* interruption
interpellāt·or -ōris *m* interrupter, disturber
interpell·ō -āre *vt* to interrupt, break in on; to disturb, obstruct, hinder; to raise as an objection
interpŏl·is -e *adj* patched up
interpŏl·ō -āre *vt* to polish, dress up; to interpolate, falsify
inter·pōnō -pōnĕre -posŭī -posĭtum *vt* to insert, interpose, intersperse; to introduce, insert; to introduce, admit (*a person*); to let (*time*) pass or elapse; to alter, falsify (*writings*); to allege, use as pretext; **operam** or **studium interponere** to apply effort; **se interponere** (with *dat* or **in** + *acc*) to interfere with, meddle with, get mixed up with
interpositĭ·ō -ōnis *f* insertion; introduction; parenthesis
interposĭtus *pp* of **interpono**
interposĭt·us -ūs *m* interposition
interpr·es -ĕtis *m & f* mediator, negotiator; middleman, broker; interpreter; expounder; translator
interpretātĭ·ō -ōnis *f* interpretation, explanation; meaning; translation
interprĕt·or -ārī -ātus sum *vt* to interpret, put a construction on, construe; to understand, infer, conclude; to decide, determine; to translate
inter·prĭmō -primĕre -pressī -pressum *vt* to squeeze
interpunct·a -ōrum *n pl* pauses, punctuation
interpunctĭ·ō -ōnis *f* punctuation
interpunct·us -a -um *adj* well-divided
inter·quiescō -quiescĕre -quiēvī *vi* to rest awhile; to pause awhile
interregn·um -ī *n* interregnum (*time between death of one king and election of another or similar interval between consuls*)
inter·rex -rēgis *m* interrex, regent
interrĭt·us -a -um *adj* undaunted
interrogātĭ·ō -ōnis *f* question; interrogation, cross-examination; syllogism

interrogāt·um -ī *n* question
interrŏg·ō -āre *vt* to ask, question; to interrogate, cross-examine; to indict, sue
inter·rumpō -rumpĕre -rūpī -ruptum *vt* to break apart, break in half, break up, smash; to divide, scatter; to interrupt, break off
interruptē *adv* with interruptions
interruptus *pp* of **interrumpo**
inter·saepĭō -saepīre -saepsī -saeptum *vt* to fence off, enclose; to stop up, close, cut off
inter·scindō -scindĕre -scĭdī -scissum *vt* to tear apart, tear down; to cut off, separate
inter·scrībō -scrībĕre -scripsī -scriptum *vt* to write (*something*) in between
inter·sĕrō -serĕre -serŭī *vt* to interpose; to allege as an excuse
interspīrātĭ·ō -ōnis *f* breathing pause, correct breathing (*in delivering a speech*)
interstinct·us -a -um *adj* blotchy
inter·stinguō -stinguĕre — -stinctum *vt* to spot, blotch; to extinguish
interstring·ō -ĕre *vt* to strangle
inter·sum -esse -fŭī *vi* to be present, assist, take part; to differ; to be of interest; (with *dat*) to be present at, attend, take part in; (with **in** + *abl*) to be present at; *v impers* there is a difference; it makes a difference; it is of importance; it is of interest; (with **inter** + *acc*) there is a difference between; (with **in** + *abl*) there is a difference among; (with *genit* or with *fem* of possessive pronouns **meā, tuā, nostrā,** *etc.*) it make a difference to, it is of importance to, it concerns (*me, you, us, etc.*); (with *genit* of value, e.g., **magni, permagni, tanti,** or with *adv* **multum, plurimum, maxime**) it makes a (*great, very great, such a great*) difference, it is of (*great, very great, such great*) importance, it is of (*great, very great, such great*) concern; **ne minimum quidem interest** there is not the slightest difference; **nihil omnino interest** there is no difference whatever
intertext·us -a -um *adj* interwoven
inter·trăhō -trahĕre -traxī *vt* (with *dat*) to take (*something*) away from
intertrīment·um -ī *n* wear and tear; loss, wastage
interturbātĭ·ō -ōnis *f* confusion, turmoil
interturb·ō -āre *vt* to confuse
intervall·um -ī *n* interval, space, distance; interval of time, spell, pause, intermission; contrast, difference
inter·vellō -vellĕre -vulsī -vulsum *vt* to pluck here and there
inter·venĭō -venīre -vēnī -ventum *vt* to interfere with; *vi* to happen along; to intervene, intrude; to happen, occur; (with *dat*) to interfere with, interrupt, put a stop to, come in the way of, oppose, prevent
intervent·or -ōris *m* intruder, untimely visitor
intervent·us -ūs *m* intervention, intrusion; mediation
inter·vertō or **inter·vortō -vertĕre -vertī -versum** *vt* to divert, embezzle; (with *acc* of person and *abl* of thing) to rob or cheat (*someone*) of
inter·vīsō -vīsĕre -vīsī -vīsum *vt* to visit from time to time; to look after
intervolĭt·ō -āre *vi* to flit about
intervŏm·ō -ĕre -ŭī -ĭtum *vt* (with **inter** + *acc*) to throw up amongst
intervulsus *pp* of **intervello**
intestābĭl·is -e *adj* infamous, notorious; wicked
intestātō *adv* intestate
intestāt·us -a -um *adj* intestate; unconvicted by witnesses
intestāt·us -a -um *adj* castrated
intestīn·us -a -um *adj* internal; *n* & *n pl* intestines
in·texō -texĕre -texŭī -textum *vt* to interweave, interlace; to weave; to embroider; to surround, envelop
intĭb·um -ī *n* endive
intĭmē *adv* intimately, cordially
intĭm·us or **intŭm·us -a -um** *adj* innermost; deepest, most profound; most secret, most intimate; *m* intimate friend
in·tingō or **in·tinguō -tingĕre -tinxī -tinctum** *vt* to dip, soak
intolerābĭl·is -e *adj* intolerable; irresistible
intolerand·us -a -um *adj* intolerable
intolĕr·ans -antis *adj* intolerable, insufferable; (with *genit*) unable to stand, unable to put up with
intoleranter *adv* intolerably, immoderately, excessively
intolerantĭ·a -ae *f* unbearableness, insolence
intŏn·ō -āre -ŭī -ātus *vt* to thunder out; *vi* to thunder
intons·us -a -um *adj* unshorn, untrimmed; long-haired; rude
in·torquĕō -torquēre -torsī -tortum *vt* to twist, turn, roll; (with **circum** + *acc*) to wrap (*something*) around; (with *dat* or **in** + *acc*) to aim, cast, throw (*a weapon*) at
intort·us -a -um *adj* twisted; tangled; (fig) crooked
intrā *adv* on the inside, inside, within; inward; *prep* (with *acc*) inside, within; during, within, in the course of, in less than; less than, fewer than, within the limits of
intrābĭl·is -e *adj* inaccessible
intractābĭl·is -e *adj* intractable, unmanageable; formidable, dangerous
intractāt·us -a -um *adj* untamed, wild; unbroken (*horse*); unattempted

intrem·iscō -iscĕre -ŭī *vi* to begin to shake or tremble
intrĕm·ō -ĕre -ŭī *vi* to shake, tremble, shiver
intrepĭdē *adv* calmly, intrepidly
intrepĭd·us -a -um *adj* calm, intrepid, not nervous
intrīc·ō -āre *vt* to entangle, involve
intrinsĕcus *adv* on the inside
intrīt·us -a -um *adj* not worn away; (fig) not worn out
intrō *adv* inwards, inside, in
intr·ō -āre *vt & vi* to enter; to penetrate
intrō·dūcō -dūcĕre -duxī -ductum *vt* to introduce
intrōducti·ō -ōnis *f* introduction
intro·ĕō -īre -iī -ĭtum *vt & vi* to enter
intrō·fĕrō -ferre -tŭlī -lātum *vt* to carry in
intrō·gredĭor -grĕdī -gressus sum *vi* to step inside
introĭt·us -ūs *m* entrance; beginning, prelude
intrōlātus *pp* of **introfero**
intrō·mittō -mittĕre -mīsī -missum *vt* to let in, admit
introrsum or **introrsus** *adv* inwards, towards the inside; (fig) inwardly, inside
intrō·rumpō -rumpĕre -rūpī -ruptum *vi* to break in, enter by force
introspect·ō -āre *vt* to look in on
intrō·spiciō -spicĕre -spexī -spectum *vt* to look into, look at; (fig) to inspect, examine, observe; *vi* (with **in** + *acc*) to look into; (fig) to look into, inspect, examine
intŭb·um -ī *n* endive
in·tuĕor -tuērī -tuĭtus sum *vt* to look at, gaze upon; to contemplate, consider; to look up to, have regard for, admire; to keep an eye on
intum·escō -escĕre -ŭī *vi* to swell up, rise; (of voice) to grow louder; (of river) to rise; to become angry; to get a big head, swell with pride
intumulāt·us -a -um *adj* unburied
in·tŭor -tŭī *vt* to look at, gaze at; to consider
inturbĭd·us -a -um *adj* undisturbed, quiet
intus *adv* inside, within; at home, in; to the inside; from within
intūt·us -a -um *adj* unguarded; unsafe
inŭl·a -ae *f* elecampane (*plant*)
inult·us -a -um *adj* unavenged; unpunished, without being punished
inumbr·ō -āre *vt* to shade; to cover
inundātĭ·ō -ōnis *f* inundation
inund·ō -āre *vt* to flood, inundate; *vi* to overflow; **sanguine inundare** to run red with blood
in·ungō -ungĕre -unxī -unctum *vt* to anoint
inurbānē *adv* impolitely, rudely; without wit
inurbān·us -a -um *adj* impolite, rude, rustic
in·urgĕō -urgēre -ursī *vi* to butt
in·ūrō -ūrĕre -ussī -ustum *vt* to burn in, brand, imprint; (with *dat*) **a** to brand upon, imprint upon, affix to; **b** to inflict upon
inūsitātē *adv* unusually, strangely
inūsitāt·us -a -um *adj* unusual, strange, uncommon, extraordinary
inustus *pp* of **inuro**
inūtĭl·is -e *adj* useless, unprofitable; impractical; injurious, harmful
inūtilĭt·ās -ātis *f* uselessness; harmfulness
inūtilĭter *adv* uselessly, unprofitably
in·vādō -vādĕre -vāsī -vāsum *vt* to come or go into, enter; to enter upon, undertake, attempt; to invade, attack, assault, rush upon; (fig) to seize, take possession of; *vi* to come or go in; to invade; (with **in** + *acc*) **a** to assail, attack, invade; **b** to seize, get possession of, usurp
inval·escō -escĕre -ŭī *vi* to grow stronger
invalĭd·us -a -um *adj* weak, feeble, impotent; inadequate, unsuitable
invāsus *pp* of **invado**
invectĭ·ō -ōnis *f* importing, importation; arrival by boat
in·vĕhō -vehĕre -vexī -vectum *vt* to carry in, bring in (*by cart, horse, boat, etc.*); (with *dat*) to bring (*e.g., evils*) upon; **invehi** (with *acc* or **in** + *acc*) **a** to ride into, sail into; **b** to attack; **c** to inveigh against, attack (*with words*); **invehi equo** to ride a horse; **invehi nave** to sail; **se invehere** (with *acc* or **in** + *acc*) to rush against, attack
invendibĭl·is -e *adj* unsalable
in·venĭō -venīre -vēnī -ventum *vt* to come upon, find, come across, discover; to find out, invent, devise; to learn, ascertain; to acquire, get, reach, earn
inventĭ·ō -ōnis *f* inventiveness; inventing, invention
invent·or -ōris *m* or **inventr·ix -īcis** *f* inventor, author, discoverer
invent·us -a -um *pp* of **invenio;** *n* invention, discovery
invenust·us -a -um *adj* having no sex appeal; homely, unattractive; unlucky in love
inverēcund·us -a -um *adj* disrespectful, immodest, shameless
inverg·ō -ĕre *vt* to pour upon
inversĭ·ō -ōnis *f* inversion (*of words*); irony; allegory
invers·us -a -um *adj* turned upside down; turned inside out
in·vertō -vertĕre -vertī -versum *vt* to invert, turn upside down, upset, reverse, turn inside out; to transpose, reverse; to pervert, abuse, misrepresent; to use ironically
invesperasc·it -ĕre *v impers* evening is approaching, twilight is falling
investīgātĭ·ō -ōnis *f* investigation

investīgāt·or -ōris *m* investigator, researcher
investīg·ō -āre *vt* to track, trace, search after; to investigate, search into, search after
inveter·ascō -ascĕre -āvī *vi* to begin to grow old, grow old; to become fixed, become established; to become rooted, grow inveterate; to become obsolete
inveterātī·ō -ōnis *f* chronic illness
inveterāt·us -a -um *adj* inveterate, long-standing
invĭcem or **in vicem** *adv* in turn, taking turns, one after another, alternately; mutually, each other
invict·us -a -um *adj* unconquered; invincible
invĭd·ens -entis *adj* envious, jealous
invidentĭ·a -ae *f* enviousness, jealousy
in·vidĕō -vidēre -vīdī -vīsum *vt* to cast an evil eye on; to envy, begrudge; *vi* (with *dat*) to envy, begrudge; (with *dat* of person and *abl* of cause or **in** + *abl*) to begrudge (*someone something*), envy (*someone because of something*)
invidĭ·a -ae *f* envy, jealousy; unpopularity; **invidiae esse** (with *dat*) to be a cause of envy to; **invidiam habere** to be unpopular, be hated
invidiōsē *adv* spitefully
invidiōs·us -a -um *adj* envious, spiteful; envied; causing envy
invĭd·us -a -um *adj* envious, jealous; (with *dat*) hostile to, unfavorable to
invigĭl·ō -āre *vi* to be alert, be on one's toes; (with *dat*) to be on the lookout for, keep an eye on, pay attention to, watch over; (with **pro** + *abl*) to watch over
inviolābĭl·is -e *adj* inviolable; invulnerable, indestructible
inviolātē *adv* inviolately
inviolāt·us -a -um *adj* inviolate, unhurt; inviolable
invīsitāt·us -a -um *adj* rarely seen; not seen before, unknown, strange
in·vīsō -vīsĕre -vīsī -vīsum *vt* to visit, get to see; to look into, inspect; to look after; to get sight of
invīs·us -a -um *pp* of **invideo;** *adj* unseen; hateful, detested; hostile
invītāment·um -ī *n* attraction, allurement, inducement
invītātĭ·ō -ōnis *f* invitation; challenge
invītāt·us -ūs *m* invitation
invītē *adv* unwillingly, against one's wish
invīt·ō -āre *vt* to invite; to entertain; to summon, challenge; to ask, request; to allure, attract; to encourage, court
invīt·us -a -um *adj* reluctant, unwilling, against one's will; **invitā Minervā** against one's better judgment, against the grain
invĭ·us -a -um *adj* without a road, trackless, impassable; *n pl* rough terrain
invocātĭ·ō -ōnis *f* invocation
invocāt·us -a -um *adj* unbidden
invŏc·ō -āre *vt* to invoke, call upon, appeal to
involāt·us -ūs *m* flight
involgō see **invulgo**
involĭt·ō -āre *vi* (with *dat*) (of long hair) to float over, trail over
invŏl·ō -āre *vt* to swoop down upon, pounce upon; *vi* to swoop down; (with **in** + *acc*) to swoop down upon, pounce upon
involŭcr·e -is *n* smock
involŭcr·um -ī *n* wrapper, cover, case, envelope; (fig) cover-up, front
involūt·us -a -um *adj* complicated
in·volvō -volvĕre -volvī -volūtum *vt* to wrap up, involve, envelop; to cover completely, overwhelm; (with *dat* or **in** + *acc*) to pile (*something*) on; **se involvere** (with *dat*) (fig) to get all wrapped up in
involvŏl·us -ī *m* caterpillar
invulg·ō -āre *vi* to give evidence
invulnerāt·us -a -um *adj* unwounded
iō *interj* ho!
io- = jo-
Ī·ō -ūs or **Ī·ōn -ōnis** *f* Io (*daughter of Argive King Inachus, changed by Jupiter into a heifer, and driven by Juno in this form over the world under the surveillance of hundred-eyed Argus*)
Ĭocast·a -ae or **Ĭocast·ē -ēs** *f* wife of Laius and mother as well as wife of Oedipus
Ĭolā·us -ī *m* son of Iphicles and companion of Hercules
Ĭŏl·ē -ēs *f* daughter of Eurytus, the king of Oechalia, who fell in love with Hercules
Īōn see **Io**
Ĭōn·es -um *m pl* Ionians (*Greek inhabitants of the W. coast of Asia Minor*)
Ĭōnĭ·cus -a -um *adj* Ionic; *m* Ionic dancer; *n pl* Ionic dance
Ĭōnĭ·us -a -um *adj* Ionian; *f* Ionia (*coastal district of Asia Minor*); *n* Ionian Sea (*off the W. Coast of Greece*)
iōta (*indecl*) *n* iota (*ninth letter of the Greek alphabet*)
Īphianass·a -ae *f* Iphigenia
Īphigenī·a -ae *f* daughter of Agamemnon and Clytemnestra, who was to have been sacrificed at Aulis but was saved by Diana and conveyed to the Tauric Chersonese, where she became priestess of Diana
Īphĭt·us -ī *m* Argonaut, son of Eurytus and Antiope
ips·a -īus or **-ĭus** *adj* self, very, just, mere, precisely; in person; by herself, alone; of herself, of her

own accord; *pron* she herself; mistress of the house
ips·e (or **ips·us**) **-īus** (or **-ĭus**) *adj* self, very, just, mere, precisely; in person; by himself, alone; of himself, of his own accord; *pron* he himself; master; host
ips·um -īus or **-ĭus** *adj* self, very, just, mere, precisely; by itself, alone; of itself, spontaneously; **nunc ipsum** just now; **tunc ipsum** just then; *pron* it itself, that itself; **ipsum quod . . .** the very fact that . . .
ipsus see **ipse**
īr·a -ae *f* ire, wrath, resentment
īrācundē *adv* angrily; passionately
īrācundĭ·a -ae *f* quick temper; anger, wrath, violence, passion; resentment
īrācund·us -a -um *adj* hot-tempered, quick-tempered, irritable; angry; resentful
īrasc·or -ī *vi* to get angry, fly into a rage; (with *dat*) to get angry at
īrātē *adv* angrily
īrāt·us -a -um *adj* angry, irate, enraged; (with *dat*) angry at
Īr·is -ĭdis *f* goddess of the rainbow and messenger of the gods
īrōnī·a -ae *f* irony
irrās·us -a -um *adj* unshaven
irratiōnāl·is -e *adj* irrational
ir·raucescō -raucescĕre -rausī *vi* to become hoarse
irredivīv·us -a -um *adj* irreparable
irrĕd·ux -ŭcis *adj* one-way (*road*)
irreligāt·us -a -um *adj* not tied
irreligiōsē *adv* impiously
irreligiōs·us -a -um *adj* impious, irreligious
irremeābĭl·is -e *adj* not to be traversed; one-way
irreparābĭl·is -e *adj* irretrievable
irrepert·us -a -um *adj* undiscovered, not found
ir·rēpō -rēpĕre -repsī -reptum *vi* to creep in; (fig) to sneak in; (with **ad** or **in** + *acc*) to creep toward or into; (fig) to sneak up on
irreprehens·us -a -um *adj* blameless
irrequiēt·us -a -um *adj* restless
irresect·us -a -um *adj* untrimmed
irresolūt·us -a -um *adj* not loosened, still tied
irrēt·ĭō -īre -īvī or **-ĭī -ītum** *vt* to trap
irretort·us -a -um *adj* not turned back
irrevĕr·ens -entis *adj* irreverent, disrespectful
irreverenter *adv* irreverently, disrespectfully
irreverentĭ·a -ae *f* irreverence, disrespect
irrevocābĭl·is -e *adj* irrevocable; implacable, relentless
irrevocāt·us -a -um *adj* not called back, not asked back
ir·rīdĕō -rīdēre -rīsī -rīsum *vt* to ridicule, laugh at, mock; *vi* to laugh, joke; (with *dat*) to laugh at
irrīdicŭlē *adv* with no sense of humor
irrigātĭ·ō -ōnis *f* irrigation
irrĭg·ō -āre *vt* to irrigate, water; to inundate; (fig) to diffuse; (fig) to flood, steep, soak
irrigŭ·us -a -um *adj* wet, soaked, well-watered; refreshing
irrīsĭ·ō -ōnis *f* ridicule, mockery
irrīs·or -ōris *m* reviler, mocker
irrīsus *pp* of **irrideo**
irrīs·us -ūs *m* mockery, derision; laughing stock, object of derision
irrītābĭl·is -e *adj* easily excited, easily enraged, irritable, sensitive
irrītām·en -ĭnis *n* incentive; provocation
irrītāment·um -ī *n* incentive; provocation
irrītātĭ·ō -ōnis *f* incitement; irritation, provocation; stimulant
irrīt·ō -āre *vt* to incite, excite, provoke, enrage
irrĭt·us -a -um *adj* invalid, null and void; futile, pointless, useless; unsuccessful (*person*)
irrogātĭ·ō -ōnis *f* imposing (*e.g., of a fine*)
irrŏg·ō -āre *vt* to impose, inflict; to object to (*proposals*)
irrōr·ō -āre *vt* to wet, moisten, sprinkle
irruct·ō -āre *vi* to belch
ir·rumpō -rumpĕre -rūpī -ruptum *vt* to rush into, break down; *vi* to rush in; (with *dat* or **in** + *acc*) **a** to rush into, rush through; **b** (fig) to intrude upon
ir·rŭō -ruĕre -rŭī *vi* to rush in, force one's way in; to make a slip (*in speaking*); (with **in** + *acc*) to rush into, rush on, invade, attack; **inruere in odium** (with *genit*) to incur the anger of
irruptĭ·ō -ōnis *f* invasion
irrupt·us -a -um *pp* of **irrumpo;** *adj* unbroken
Īr·us -ī *m* beggar in the palace of Ulysses in Ithaca
is ejus *adj* this, that, the said, the aforesaid; *pron* he; **is qui** he who, the person who, the one who
Īs·is -is or **-ĭdis** *f* Egyptian goddess
Ismarĭ·us -a -um *adj* of Mt. Ismarus in Thrace; Thracian
Īsocrăt·ēs -is *m* famous orator and teacher of rhetoric at Athens (436-338 B.C.)
ista see **iste**
istāc *adv* that way
istactĕnus *adv* thus far
istaec see **istic**
ist·e -a -ud *adj* that of yours; this, that, the very, that particular; such, of such a kind; that terrible, that despicable; *pron* that one; (in court) your client
Isthm·us or **Isthm·os -ī** *m* Isthmus of Corinth

ist·ic -aec -oc or **-uc** *adj* that, that of yours; *pron* the one, that one
istīc *adv* there, in that place; herein; on this occasion
istinc *adv* from there, from where you are
istīusmŏdī or **istīmŏdī** or **istīus modī** or **istī modī** *adj* that kind of, such
istō *adv* where you are; therefore; in that matter
istōc *adv* there, to where you are, yonder
istorsum *adv* in that direction
istūc *adv* there, to that place, to where you are, that way; **istuc veniam** I'll come to that matter
istūcĭne see **istic**
istud see **iste**
ita *adv* thus, so, in this manner, in this way; (of natural consequence) thus, accordingly, therefore, under these circumstances; (in affirmation) yes, true, exactly; (in questions) really?, truly?; **ita . . . ut** (in comparisons) just as, although . . . nevertheless; (as correlatives) both . . . and, both . . . as well as; (in restriction) on condition that, in sofar as, on the assumption that; (of degree) to such a degree . . . that, so much . . . that, so . . . that; **non ita** not very, not especially; **quid ita?** how so?, what do you mean?
Ītalĭ·a -ae *f* Italy
Ītalĭc·us -a -um *adj* Italian
Ītăl·is -ĭdis *adj* Italian; *f pl* Italian women
Ītalĭ·us -a -um *adj* Italian; *f* see **Italia**
Ītăl·us -a -um *adj* Italian
ităque *conj* and so, and thus, accordingly, therefore, consequently
item *adv* likewise, besides, moreover, also
it·er -inĕris *n* journey, trip, march, walk; day's march, day's journey; route; right of way; passage (*of voice, etc.*); method, course, way, road; **ex itinere** or **in itinere** en route; **iter flectere** to change course; **iter terrestre** overland route; **maximis itineribus** by marching at top speed
iterātĭ·ō -ōnis *f* repetition
itĕr·ō -āre *vt* to repeat, renew; to plow again
itĕrum *adv* again, a second time; **iterum atque iterum** repeatedly, again and again
Ithăc·a -ae or **Ithăc·ē -ēs** *f* island off the W. coast of Greece in the Ionian Sea and home of Odysseus
itĭdem *adv* in the same way
itĭ·ō -ōnis *f* going, walking
it·ō -āre *vi* to go
it·us -ūs *m* going; going away, departure
It·ys -ўos *m* son of Tereus and Procne, who was killed by Procne and served up as food to Tereus
iu- = **ju-**
Ixī·ōn -ŏnis *m* son of Antion or of Jupiter, king of the Laipthae in Thessaly, and father of Pirithous; he was allowed into heaven by Jupiter after killing his father-in-law, but for trying to seduce Juno, was tied to a wheel and sent flying into Tartarus

J

jac·ĕō -ēre -ŭī *vi* to lie, lie down; to lie ill, be sick; to lie dead, to have fallen; to lie in ruins; to hang loose; to lie idle, rest; to lie, be situated; to lie flat, lie low; to feel low, be despondent; to lie prostrate, be powerless; to fall, fail, be refuted; to be low in someone's opinion; to linger, stay
jacĭō jacĕre jēcī jactum *vt* to lay, build, establish, set, found, construct; to throw, cast, fling; to emit, produce; to sow, scatter; to throw away; to mention, utter, declare, intimate
jact·ans -antis *adj* boasting, bragging, showing off
jactanter *adv* boastfully
jactantĭ·a -ae *f* boasting, showing off
jactātĭ·ō -ōnis *f* tossing to and fro; swaying; shaking; writhing; boasting, bragging, showing off; gesticulation; **jactatio animi** agitation; **jactatio maritima** seasickness
jactāt·us -ūs *m* tossing, waving
jactĭt·ō -āre *vt* to display, show off
jact·ō -āre *vt* to throw, hurl; to toss about, shake; to throw away, throw out, throw overboard; to disturb, disquiet, stir up; to consider, discuss; to throw out, mention; to brag about, show off; **jactari** to toss, rock; (of money) to fluctuate in value; **se jactare** to boast, show off, throw one's weight around
jactūr·a -ae *f* throwing away, throwing overboard; loss, sacrifice
jactus *pp* of **jacio**
jact·us -ūs *m* toss, throw, cast
jaculābĭl·is -e *adj* missile
jaculāt·or -ōris *m* thrower, shooter; light-armed soldier; spearman
jaculātr·ix -īcis *f* huntress
jacŭl·or -ārī -ātus sum *vt* to throw; to shoot at; (fig) to aim at, strive after
jacŭl·us -a -um *adj* throwing, casting; *n* dart, javelin; casting net
jājūn- = **jejun-**

jam *adv* (present) now, already; (past) already, by then; (future) very soon, right away; (in transition) now, next, moreover; (for emphasis) actually, precisely, quite; (in a conclusion) then surely; **jam dudum** long ago, long since; **jam inde** immediately; **jam jam** even now, at every moment; **jam . . . jam** at one time . . . at another; **jam nunc** even now; **jam pridem** long since; **jam tum** even then, even at that time

Jānicŭl·um -ī *n* Roman hill on the right bank of the Tiber

jānit·or -ōris *m* doorman

jānĭtr·ix -īcis *f* portress

jānŭ·a -ae *f* door, house door; entrance; (fig) entrance, approach

Jānuārĭ·us -a -um *adj & m* January

jān·us -ī *m* covered passage, arcade

Jān·us -ī *m* Janus (*old Italian deity, represented as having two faces*); temple of Janus (*at the bottom of the Argiletum in the Forum*)

jec·ur -ŏris *n* liver; (as the seat of emotions) anger, lust

jecuscŭl·um -ī *n* little liver

jējūnē *adv* (fig) drily

jējūniōs·ĭor or **jājūniōs·ĭor -ĭus** *adj* fasting, hungry

jējūnĭt·ās or **jājūnĭt·ās -ātis** *f* fasting; dryness (*of style*)

jējūn·ĭum -ĭī or **-ī** *n* fasting, fast; hunger: leanness

jējūn·us or **jājūn·us -a -um** *adj* fasting; hungry; poor (*land*); thin; insignificant, paltry, contemptible, low; dry (*style*)

jentācŭl·um -ī *n* breakfast

joc·or -ārī -ātus sum or **joc·ō -āre** *vt* to say in jest; *vi* to joke, crack a joke, be joking

jocōsē *adv* humorously, as a joke, jokingly

jocōs·us -a -um *adj* humorous, funny, clowning

joculār·is -e *adj* humorous, funny

joculārĭ·us -a -um *adj* ludicrous

joculāt·or -ōris *m* joker

jocul·or -ārī -ātus sum *vi* to joke

jocŭl·us -ī *m* joke

joc·us -ī (*pl:* **joc·ī -ōrum** *m* or **joc·a -ōrum** *n*) *m* joke; laughingstock; child's play; **joco remoto** all joking aside; **per jocum** as a joke, jokingly

jub·a -ae *f* mane; crest

jub·ar -ăris *n* radiance, brightness; sunshine

jubāt·us -a -um *adj* crested

jubĕō jubēre jussī jussum *vt* to order; (pol) to order, decree, enact, ratify; to designate, appoint, assign; (med) to prescribe; **jube fratrem tuum salvere** (in letters) best regards to your brother

jūcundē *adv* pleasantly, delightfully, agreeably

jūcundĭt·ās -ātis *f* pleasantness, delight, enjoyment, agreeableness; *f pl* favors

jūcund·us -a -um *adj* pleasant, delightful, agreeable

Jūdae·us -a -um *adj* Jewish; *m* Jew; *f* Jewess; Judaea, Palestine

jūd·ex -ĭcis *m* judge; juror; arbitrator; umpire; critic, scholar; **judex morum** censor; **me judice** in my judgment

jūdicātĭ·ō -ōnis *f* judicial investigation; (fig) judgment, opinion

jūdicāt·us -a -um *adj* decided, determined; *m* condemned person; *n* decision, precedent; fine; **judicatum facere** to carry out a decision; **judicatum solvere** to pay a fine

jūdicāt·us -ūs *m* judgeship

jūdiciāl·is -e *adj* judicial, forensic

jūdiciārĭ·us -a -um *adj* judiciary

jūdic·ĭum -ĭī or **-ī** *n* trial, court, court of justice; sentence; jurisdiction; opinion, decision; faculty of judging, judgment, good judgment, taste, tact, discretion

jūdĭc·ō -āre *vt* to judge; to examine; to sentence, condemn; to form an opinion of; to conclude; to declare, proclaim; (with *dat* of person and *acc* of the offense) to convict (*someone*) of; (with *genit*) to find (*someone*) guilty of; (with *dat* of person and *genit* of the offense) to convict (*someone*) of

jugāl·is -e *adj* yoked together; nuptial

jugātĭ·ō -ōnis *f* tying up

jūgĕr·um -ī *n* jugerum (*land measure: about two thirds of an acre*)

jūg·is -e *adj* continual, perennial, inexhaustible

jugl·ans -andis *f* walnut tree

jugōs·us -a -um *adj* hilly

Jugŭl·ae -ārum *f pl* Orion's belt (*three stars in the constellation Orion*)

jugŭl·ō -āre *vt* to cut the throat of, kill, murder; to destroy; to silence

jugŭl·um -ī *n* or **jugŭl·us -ī** *m* throat

jug·um -ī *n* yoke, collar; pair, team; (mil) yoke (*consisting of a spear laid crosswise on two upright spears, under which the conquered had to pass*); crossbar (*of a loom*); thwart (*of a boat*); common bond, union; wedlock; pair, couple; mountain ridge; *n pl* heights

Jugurth·a -ae *m* king of Numidia (160-104 B.C.)

Jūlĭ·a -ae *f* aunt of Julius Caesar and wife of Marius; daughter of Julius Caesar and wife of Pompey (*d.* 54 B.C.); daughter of Augustus by Scribonia (39 B.C.-14 A.D.)

Jūlĭ·us -a -um *adj* Julian; of July; *m* Roman praenomen; July

jūment·um -ī *n* beast of burden, horse, mule

juncĕ·us -a -um *adj* of reeds; slim, slender

juncōs·us -a -um *adj* overgrown with reeds

junctĭ·ō -ōnis *f* joining

junctūr·a -ae *f* joining, uniting, joint, juncture; connection, relationship; combination
junct·us -a -um *pp* of **jungo;** *adj* connected, associated, united, attached
junc·us -ī *m* reed
jungō jungĕre junxī junctum *vt* to join, join together, unite, connect; to yoke, harness; to couple, pair, mate; to bridge (*a river*); to bring together, unite, associate, ally; to add; to compose (*poems*); to combine (*words*)
jūni·or -ōris *adj* younger
jūnipĕr·us -ī *f* juniper
Jūni·us -a -um *adj* June, of June; *m* Roman praenomen; June
jūn·ix -īcis *f* heifer
Jūn·ō -ōnis *f* daughter of Saturn and wife and sister of Jupiter
Juppĭter (or **Jupĭter** or **Diespĭter**) **Jovis** *m* son of Saturn, brother and husband of Juno, and chief god of the Romans
jūrāt·or -ōris *m* judge; assistant censor
jūreconsult·us -ī *m* legal expert, lawyer
jūrejūr·ō -āre *vi* to swear
jūreperītus see **jurisperitus**
jurg·ium -iī or **-ī** *n* quarrel; *n pl* reproaches
jurg·ō -āre *vi* to quarrel
jūridiciāl·is -e *adj* juridical
jūrisconsult·us or **jūreconsult·us -ī** *m* legal expert, lawyer
jūrisdicti·ō -ōnis *f* administration of justice; jurisdiction
jūrisperīt·us or **jūreperīt·us -ī** *m* legal expert, lawyer
jūr·ō -āre *vt* to swear; to swear by, attest, call to witness; to swear to, attest; *vi* to swear, take an oath; to conspire; (with **in** + *acc*) to swear allegiance to, swear to observe, vow obedience to; **in haec verba jurare** to swear according to the prescribed form; to conspire against; **jurare calumniam** to swear that the accusation is not false
jū·s -ris *n* juice, broth, gravy, soup; law (*as established by society and custom rather than statute law*); right, justice; law court, court of justice; legal right, authority, permission, prerogative; jurisdiction; **in jus ire** to go to court; **jure** by right, rightfully, in justice; **jus dicere** to sit as judge, hold court; **jus gentium** international law; **jus publicum** common right; **summum jus** strict letter of the law
jūs jūrand·um (*genit*: **jūr·is jūrand·ī**) *n* oath
jussū (*abl* only) *m* by order; **meo jussu** by my order
juss·us -a -um *pp* of **jubeo;** *n* order, command, bidding
justē *adv* justly, rightly
justifĭc·us -a -um *adj* just-dealing
justitĭ·a -ae *f* justice, fairness
justit·ium -iī or **-ī** *n* suspension of legal business; (fig) standstill
just·us -a -um *adj* just, fair; justified, well-founded; formal; in due order, according to protocol, regular; *n* justice; due measure; **plus quam justo** more than due measure, too much; *n pl* rights; formalities; ceremonies, due ceremony; funeral rites, obsequies
Jūturn·a -ae *f* nymph, sister of Turnus, the king of the Rutuli
jūtus *pp* of **juvo**
juvenāl·is -e *adj* youthful; juvenile
Juvenāl·is -is *m* Juvenal (*D. Junius Juvenalis, Roman satirist in the time of Domitian and Trajan, c. 62-142 A.D.*)
juvenc·us -a -um *adj* young; *m* bullock; young man; *f* heifer; girl
juven·escō -escĕre -ŭī *vi* to grow up; to get young again
juvenīl·is -e *adj* youthful; juvenile; cheerful
juvenīlĭter *adv* youthfully, boyishly
juvĕn·is -e *adj* young; *m* young man (*between the ages of twenty and forty-five*); warrior; *f* young lady
juvĕn·or -ārī -ātus sum *vi* to act like a kid
juvent·a -ae *f* youth
juvent·ās -ātis *f* youth, prime of life, manhood; (collectively) young people, youth
juvent·ūs -ūtis *f* youth, prime of life, manhood; (collectively) young people, youth
juvō juvāre jūvī jūtum *vt* to help; to please, delight; **juvat** (with *inf*) it helps to; **juvat me** it delights me, I am glad
juxtā *adv* nearby, in close proximity; alike, in like manner, equally; (with **ac, atque, et, quam,** or **cum**) as well as, just the same as; *prep* (with *acc*) close to, near to, next to; next to, immediately after; near, bordering upon; next door to
juxtim *adv* near; equally

K

Kalend·ae or **Calend·ae -ārum** *f pl* Kalends (*first day of the Roman month*); **tristes Kalendae** gloomy Kalends (*because interest was due on the Kalends*)
Kalendār·ium -iī or **-ī** *n* account book
Karthāginiens·is -e *adj* Carthaginian
Karthāg·ō -inis *f* Carthage (*city of N. Africa*)

L

labasc·ō -ĕre *vi* to waver; to give in, yield
lābēcŭl·a -ae *f* blemish, spot, stain (*e.g., on someone's reputation*)
labe·faciō -facĕre -fēcī -factum *vt* to cause to totter, to shake, to weaken; (fig) to weaken, ruin, destroy
labefact·ō -āre *vt* to shake; (fig) to weaken, ruin, destroy
labell·um -ī *n* lip
lābell·um -ī *n* small basin
lāb·ēs -is *f* fall, falling down; stroke, blow, ruin, destruction; blemish, spot, defect; disgrace, discredit
labĭ·a -ae *f* lip
Labiēn·us -ī *m* Caesar's officer who defected to Pompey
labiōs·us -a -um *adj* thick-lipped
lab·ĭum -ĭī or **-ī** *n* lip
lab·ō -āre *vi* to totter, wobble; to waver, hesitate, be undecided; to fall to pieces, go to ruin
lābor lābī lapsus sum *vi* to glide, slide, slip; to slip, fall, sink; to slip away, disappear, escape; (of time) to slip by, pass, elapse; (fig) to fade
lab·or or **lab·ōs -ōris** *m* effort; trouble, distress, suffering; work, task
labōrĭf·er -ĕra -ĕrum *adj* struggling
labōriōs·us -a -um *adj* full of troubles, troublesome; energetic, industrious
labōr·ō -āre *vt* to work out, make, produce; *vi* to work; to suffer, be troubled; to be in danger; (with *inf*) to try to
labōs see **labor**
labr·um -ī *n* lip, edge
lābr·um -ī *n* basin, tub, bathtub
labrusc·a -ae *f* wild vine
labrusc·um -ī *n* wild grape
labyrinthē·us -a -um *adj* labyrinthine
labyrinth·us -ī *m* labyrinth
lac lactis *n* milk; milk of plants
Lacaen·a -ae *f* Spartan woman
Lacedaem·ōn -ŏnis *f* Sparta
Lacedaemonĭ·us -a -um *adj* Spartan
lac·er -ĕra -ĕrum *adj* mangled, torn, lacerated, mutilated; lacerating, tearing
lacerātĭ·ō -ōnis *f* tearing, laceration, mangling
lacern·a -ae *f* coat, topcoat, overcoat
lacernāt·us -a -um *adj* wearing an overcoat
lacĕr·ō -āre *vt* to lacerate, tear, mangle; to slander, abuse; to waste, squander, destroy; to wreck (*ship*)
lacert·us -a -um *adj* muscular, brawny; *m* lizard; upper arm, muscle; *m pl* muscles, strength, brawn; *f* lizard
lacess·ō -ĕre -īvī or **-ĭī -ītum** *vt* to provoke, exasperate; to challenge; to move, arouse
Lachĕs·is -is *f* one of the three Fates
lacinĭ·a -ae *f* flap (*of a garment*)
Lacīn·ĭum -ĭī or **-ī** *n* promontory in Bruttium with a temple to Juno
Lac·ō or **Lac·ōn -ōnis** *m* Spartan; Spartan dog
Lacōnĭ·a -ae *f* district of the Peloponnesus of which Sparta was the chief city
Lacōnĭc·us -a -um *adj* Spartan; *n* sweat bath
lacrĭm·a or **lacrŭm·a -ae** *f* tear; gumdrop (*plant*)
lacrimābĭl·is -e *adj* worthy of tears, deplorable
lacrimābund·us -a -um *adj* tearful, about to break into tears
lacrĭm·ō or **lacrŭm·ō -āre** *vt* to cry for, shed tears over; (of trees) to drip; *vi* to cry, shed tears
lacrimōs·us -a -um *adj* crying, tearful; causing tears, bringing tears to the eyes
lacrimŭl·a -ae *f* teardrop, little tear; (fig) crocodile tear
lacrum- = lacrim-
lact·ans -antis *adj* milk-giving
lactārĭ·us -a -um *adj* milky
lactātĭ·ō -ōnis *f* allurement
lact·ens -entis *adj* suckling; milky, juicy, tender; full of milk; *m* suckling
lacteŏl·us -a -um *adj* milk-white
lact·ēs -ĭum *f pl* intestines; **laxae lactes** empty stomach
lactesc·ō -ĕre *vi* to turn to milk
lactĕ·us -a -um *adj* milky, full of milk, milk-colored, milk-white
lact·ō -āre *vt* to cajole, wheedle
lactūc·a -ae *f* lettuce
lacūn·a -ae *f* ditch, hole, pit; pond, pool; (fig) hole, gap
lacūn·ar -āris *n* paneled ceiling
lacūn·ō -āre *vt* to panel
lacūnōs·us -a -um *adj* sunken
lac·us -ūs *m* vat; tank, pool, reservoir, cistern; lake
laedō laedĕre laesī laesum *vt* to knock, strike; to hurt, rub open; to wound; to break (*promise, pledge*); to offend, outrage, violate; (with **ad** + *acc*) to smash (*something*) against
laen·a -ae *f* lined coat
Lāërt·ēs -ae *m* father of Ulysses
Lāërtiăd·ēs -ae *m* Ulysses
laesĭ·ō -ōnis *f* attack, provocation
Laestrȳg·ōn -ŏnis *m* Laestrygonian (*one of the mythical race of cannibals in Italy, founders of Formiae*)
laes·us *pp* of **laedo**
laetābĭl·is -e *adj* cheerful, glad
laet·ans -antis *adj* joyful, glad
laetātĭ·ō -ōnis *f* rejoicing, joy
laetē *adv* joyfully, gladly

laetific·ans -antis *adj* joyous
laetific·ō -āre *vt* to gladden, cheer up; **laetificari** to rejoice
laetific·us -a -um *adj* joyful, cheerful
laetiti·a -ae *f* joyfulness, gladness, exuberance
laet·or -ārī -ātus sum *vi* to rejoice, be glad
laet·us -a -um *adj* rejoicing, glad, cheerful; happy, fortunate, auspicious; fertile, rich, smiling (*grain*); sleek, fat (*cattle*); bright, cheerful (*appearance*); cheering, welcome (*news*)
laevē *adv* awkwardly
laev·us -a -um *adj* left, on the left side; awkward, stupid; ill-omened; lucky, propitious; *f* left hand, left side; *n* the left; *n pl* the area on the left
lagăn·um -ī *n* pancake
lagē·os -ī *f* Greek vine
lagoen·a or **lagōn·a -ae** *f* jug
lagō·is -idis *f* grouse
lagunculˇ·a -ae *f* flask
Lāïăd·ēs -ae *m* son of Laius (*Oedipus*)
Lāï·us -ī *m* Laius (*father of Oedipus*)
lall·ō -āre *vi* to sing a lullaby
lām·a -ae *f* swamp, bog
lambĕr·ō -āre *vt* to tear to pieces
lamb·ō -ĕre -ī *vt* to lick, lap; (of a river) to wash, flow by; (of ivy) to cling to
lāment·a -ōrum *n pl* wailing, moaning, lamentation
lāmentābil·is -e *adj* pitiable; doleful; mournful, sorrowful
lāmentāri·us -a -um *adj* sorrowful, pitiful
lāmentāti·ō -ōnis *f* lamentation
lāment·or -ārī -ātus sum *vt* to cry over, lament; *vi* to wail, cry
lami·a -ae *f* witch, sorceress
lāmin·a or **lammin·a** or **lamn·a -ae** *f* plate, leaf (*of metal or wood*); blade; coin; peel, shell
lamp·as -ădis *f* torch; brightness; day; meteor; lamp
Lam·us -ī *m* mythical king of the Laestrygonians; son of Hercules and Omphale
lān·a -ae *f* wool; working in wool, spinning, **lana aurea** golden fleece; **lanam trahere** to card wool; **lanas ducere** to spin wool; **rixari de lana caprina** to argue over nothing
lānār·ius -iī or **-ī** *m* wool worker
lānāt·us -a -um *adj* woolly; *f pl* sheep
lancĕ·a -ae *f* lance, spear
lancin·ō -āre *vt* to squander, waste
lānĕ·us -a -um *adj* woolen; soft
langue·faciō -facĕre -fēcī -factum *vt* to make tired
langu·ens -entis *adj* languid, drooping, listless
langu·ĕō -ēre *vi* to be tired, be weary; to be weak, feeble (*from disease*); (fig) to be dull, languid, listless; to be without energy
langu·escō -escĕre -uī *vi* to become weak, grow faint; (fig) to become listless; to decline, decrease; to relax
languidē *adv* weakly, faintly, without energy
languidŭl·us -a -um *adj* languid; withered, faded
languid·us -a -um *adj* weak, faint, languid, sluggish; listless; enervating
langu·or -ōris *m* weakness, faintness, languor; dullness, listlessness, sluggishness
laniāt·us -ūs *m* mangling; *f pl* mental anguish
laniēn·a -ae *f* butcher shop
lānific·ium -iī or **-ī** *n* weaving
lānific·us -a -um *adj* spinning, weaving, of spinning, of weaving
lānig·er -ĕra -ĕrum *adj* fleecy; *m* sheep (*ram*); *f* sheep (*ewe*)
lani·ō -āre *vt* to tear to pieces, mangle
lanist·a -ae *m* gladiator trainer, fencing master; (*in derision*) ringleader
lānit·ium -iī or **-ī** *n* wool
lan·ius -iī or **-ī** *m* butcher; (*in derision*) executioner, butcher
lantern·a -ae *f* lantern
lanternār·ius -iī or **-ī** *m* guide
lānūg·ō -inis *f* down (*of plants, cheeks, etc.*)
Lānuv·ium -iī or **-ī** *n* town in Latium on the Appian Way
lan·x -cis *f* dish, platter; scale
Lāocŏ·ōn -ontis *m* son of Priam and priest of Apollo, who, with his two sons, was killed by two serpents from the sea
Lāomĕd·ōn -ontis *m* king of Troy and father of Priam and Ganymede
Lāomedontē·us or **Lāomedonti·us -a -um** *adj* Trojan
Lāomedontiăd·ēs -ae *m* son of Laomedon; Priam; *m pl* Trojans
lapăth·um -ī *n* or **lapăth·us -i** *f* sorrel (*plant*)
lapicīd·a -ae *m* stonecutter, quarry worker
lapicīdin·ae -ārum *f pl* stone quarry
lapidāri·us -a -um *adj* stone; **latomiae lapidariae** stone quarries
lapidāti·ō -ōnis *f* throwing stones
lapidāt·or -ōris *m* stone thrower
lapidĕ·us -a -um *adj* of stones, stone, stony; **lapideus sum** (fig) I am petrified
lapid·ō -āre *vt* to throw stones at; *v impers* it is raining stones, it is hailing stones
lapidōs·us -a -um *adj* full of stones, stony; hard as stone; gritty (*bread*)
lapill·us -ī *m* pebble; precious stone, gem, jewel; *m pl* small stones (*esp. for mosaics*)
lap·is -idis *m* stone; milestone; platform; boundary stone, landmark; tombstone; precious stone, gem, pearl, jewel, stone statue; marble

table; **lapides loqui** to speak harsh words
Lapĭth·ae -ārum *m pl* mountain tribe in Thessaly that fought the centaurs at the marriage of their king Pirithous
lapp·a -ae *f* burr
lapsĭ·ō -ōnis *f* sliding, slipping; (fig) tendency
laps·ō -āre *vi* to keep slipping, stumble
laps·us -a -um *pp* of **labor;** *adj* fallen
laps·us -ūs *m* falling, fall, sliding, slipping, gliding, flow, flight; blunder, error, fault, slip
laqueār·ĭa -ĭum *n pl* paneled ceiling
laqueāt·us -a -um *adj* paneled, having a paneled ceiling
laquĕ·us -ī *m* noose; snare; (fig) snare, trap; *m pl* (fig) subtleties
Lār Laris *m* tutelary deity, household god; hearth, home; *m pl* hearth, home, house, household, family
lard·um -ī *n* lard, fat
Larentĭ·a -ae *f* wife of Faustulus who reared Romulus and Remus
largē *adv* liberally, generously
largifĭc·us -a -um *adj* bountiful
largiflŭ·us -a -um *adj* gushing
largilŏqu·us -a -um *adj* talkative
larg·ĭor -īrī -ītus sum *vt* to give generously, bestow freely; to lavish; to bestow, confer; to grant, concede; *vi* to give bribes, bribe
largĭt·ās -ātis *f* generosity, bounty
largītĭ·ō -ōnis *f* generosity; bribery
largīt·or -ōris *m* generous donor; spendthrift; briber
larg·us -a -um *adj* abundant, plentiful, large, much; generous, liberal, bountiful, profuse
lārĭd·um -ī *n* lard, bacon fat
Lāriss·a -ae *f* town in Thessaly on the Peneus River
Lār·ĭus -ĭī or **-ī** *m* Lake Como
lar·ix -ĭcis *f* larch tree
larv·a -ae *f* mask; ghost
larvāt·us -a -um *adj* bewitched
lasăn·um -ī *n* chamber pot
lasarpīcĭf·er -ĕra -ĕrum *adj* producing asafetida (*used as an antispasmodic*)
lascīvĭ·a -ae *f* playfulness; petulence; lewdness
lascīvĭbund·us -a -um *adj* petulant, roguish
lascīv·ĭō -īre -ĭī -ītum *vi* to frolic, be frisky; to run riot, run wild
lascīv·us -a -um *adj* playful, frisky; brash, impudent, petulant; licentious, lustful; luxuriant (*growth*)
lāserpīc·ĭum -ĭī or **-ī** *n* silphium (*plant which yielded asafetida*)
lassitūd·ō -ĭnis *f* physical weariness, lassitude
lass·ō -āre *vt* to fatigue, exhaust
lassŭl·us -a -um *adj* somewhat tired
lass·us -a -um *adj* tired, weary, fatigued, exhausted
lātē *adv* widely, extensively; profusely; **late longeque** far and wide
latĕbr·a -ae *f* hiding place, hideaway, hideout; (fig) loophole
latebricŏl·a -ae *m* or *f* person who hangs around dives or brothels
latebrōsē *adv* secretly
latebrōs·us -a -um *adj* full of holes; hidden, secret; porous
lat·ens -entis *adj* hidden, secret
latenter *adv* in secret
lat·ĕō -ēre -ŭī *vi* to lie hidden, lie concealed, lurk; to keep out of sight, sulk; to live a retired life, remain in obscurity, remain unknown, escape notice; to be in safety; to avoid a summons, lie low; to be obscure
lat·er -ĕris *m* brick, tile; **laterem lavare** to waste effort
laterām·en -ĭnis *n* earthenware
latercŭl·us -ī *m* small brick; tile; biscuit
latericĭ·us -a -um *adj* brick, made of brick; *n* brickwork
lātern·a -ae *f* lantern
latesc·ō -ĕre *vi* to hide
lat·ex -ĭcis *m* liquid, fluid; water; spring; wine; oil
latibŭl·um -ī *n* hiding place, hideout, lair, den; (fig) refuge
lātīclāvĭ·us -a -um *adj* having a broad crimson stripe (*distinctive mark of senators, military tribunes of the equestrian order, and of sons of distinguished families*)
Latīnē *adv* Latin, in Latin; in proper Latin; in plain Latin; **Latine loqui** to speak Latin; to speak correct Latin; **Latine reddere** to translate into Latin; **Latine scire** to understand Latin
Latīnĭt·ās -ātis *f* pure Latin, Latinity; Latin rights and privileges
Latīn·us -a -um *adj* Latin; possessing Latin rights and privileges; *m* Latinus (*king of the Laurentians, who gave his daughter Lavinia in marriage to Aeneas*); *n* Latin language; **in Latinum convertere** to translate into Latin
lātĭ·ō -ōnis *f* bringing, rendering; proposing
latĭt·ō -āre *vi* to keep hiding oneself; to be concealed, hide, lurk; to lie low (*in order to avoid a summons*)
lātitūd·ō -ĭnis *f* breadth, width; size, extent; broad pronunciation; richness of expression
lātĭus *adv* of late
Latĭ·us -a -um *adj* of Latium, Latin, Roman; *n* Latium (*district in W. central Italy, in which Rome was situated*); **jus Lati** or **Latium** Latin political rights and privileges
Lātō·is -ĭdis *f* Diana
lātom- = lautom-
Lātōn·a -ae *f* daughter of the Titan Coeus and Phoebe, and mother of Apollo and Diana
Lātōnigĕn·a -ae *m* or *f* child of Latona; *m pl* children of Latona, i.e., Apollo and Diana

Lātōnī·us -a -um *adj* of Latona; *f* Diana
lāt·or -ōris *m* bringer, bearer; proposer (*of a law*)
Lātō·us -ī *m* Apollo
lātrāt·or -ōris *m* barker; dog
lātrāt·us -ūs *m* barking
lātrīn·a -ae *f* wash room, toilet
lātr·ō -āre *vt* to bark at, snarl at; to clamor for; *vi* to bark; (fig) to rant
latr·ō -ōnis *m* mercenary; freebooter; brigand, bandit; (in chess) pawn
latrōcin·ium -iī or **-ī** *n* military service (*as a mercenary*); freebooting; brigandage, banditry, vandalism, piracy, robbery, highway robbery; villany, outrage; band of robbers
latrōcin·or -ārī -ātus sum *vi* to serve as a mercenary, be a mercenary soldier; to be a bandit, be a highwayman, be a pirate
latruncŭl·us -ī *m* small-time bandit
lātumi·ae -ārum *f pl* stone quarry; prison
lātus *pp* of **fero**
lāt·us -a -um *adj* wide, broad; extensive; widespread; broad (*pronunciation*); diffuse (*style*)
lat·us -ĕris *n* side, flank; body, person; lungs; lateral surface; coast; (mil) flank, wing; **a latere** (mil) on the flank; **a latere** (with *genit*) **a** at the side of, in the company of; **b** from among the friends of; **aperto latere** (mil) on the exposed flank; **latere tecto** scot free; **latus dare** to expose oneself; **latus tegere** (with *genit*) to walk by the side of, to escort (*someone*)
latuscŭl·um -ī *n* small side
laudābil·is -e *adj* laudable, praiseworthy
laudābiliter *adv* laudably
laudāti·ō -ōnis *f* commendation; eulogy, panegyric, funeral oration; (in court) testimony by a character witness
laudāt·or -ōris *m* praiser; eulogist, panegyrist; (law) character witness
laudāt·us -a -um *adj* praiseworthy, commendable, excellent
laud·ō -āre *vt* to praise, commend; to name, quote, cite; to pronounce a funeral oration over
laurĕ·a -ae *f* laurel tree; laurel, laurel branch, laurel crown, bay wreath; triumph
laureāt·us -a -um *adj* laureate, laureled, crowned with laurel; **litterae laureatae** communiqué announcing victory
Laurent·ēs -um *m pl* Laurentians (*people of Lanuvium*)
Laurentīn·us or **Laurenti·us -a -um** *adj* Laurentian
laureŏl·a -ae *f* little laurel crown; triumph
laurĕ·us -a -um *adj* laurel, of laurel; *f* see **laurea**
lauricŏm·us -a -um *adj* laurel-covered (*mountain*)
laurif·er -ĕra -ĕrum *adj* crowned with laurel
laurig·er -ĕra -ĕrum *adj* wearing laurel
laur·us -ī *f* laurel tree, bay tree; triumph, victory
laus laudis *f* praise, commendation; fame, glory; approval, praiseworthy deed; merit, worth
Laus·us -ī *m* son of Numitor and brother of Rhea Silvia; son of Mezentius, killed by Aeneas
lautē *adv* sumptuously, splendidly; excellently
lauti·a -ōrum *n pl* state banquet (*given to foreign ambassadors and official guests*)
lautiti·a -ae *f* luxury, high living
lautumi·ae or **lātomi·ae** or **lātumi·ae -ārum** *f pl* stone quarry; prison
laut·us -a -um *adj* expensive, elegant, fine; well-heeled; refined, fashionable
lavābr·um -ī *n* bath
lavāti·o -ōnis *f* washing, bathing, bath; bathing kit
Lāvīni·us -a -um *adj* Lavinian, of Lavinium; *n* town in Latium founded by Aeneas; *f* wife of Aeneas
lavō lavāre (or **lavĕre**) **lāvī lautum** (or **lavātum** or **lōtum**) *vt* to wash, bathe; to wet, drench; to wash away; **lavi** to wash, wash oneself, bathe; *vi* to wash, wash oneself, bathe
laxāment·um -ī *n* relaxation, respite, letup, mitigation
laxāt·us -a -um *adj* loose, extended (*e.g., ranks*)
laxē *adv* loosely, widely; freely
laxit·ās -ātis *f* roominess, extent
lax·ō -āre *vt* to extend, widen, expand, open; to open, undo, release; to relax, slacken; to mitigate; (fig) to release, relieve; *vi* (of price) to go down
lax·us -a -um *adj* roomy, wide; loose, slack; prolonged, extended (*time*); (fig) relaxed, easygoing, free; low (*price*)
le·a -ae *f* lioness
leaen·a -ae *f* lioness
Lēand·er -rī *m* youth of Abydos who swam across the Hellespont every night to his lover Hero of Sestos
Learch·us -ī *m* son of Athamas and Ino, killed by his mad father
leb·ēs -ētis *m* pan, cauldron, basin
lectīc·a -ae *f* litter; sofa, couch
lectīcār·ius -iī or **-ī** *m* litter bearer
lectīcŭl·a -ae *f* small litter; small bier
lecti·ō -ōnis *f* selection; reading, reading aloud; perusal; **lectio senatūs** revision of the senate roll (*by the censor*)
lectisterniāt·or -ōris *m* slave who arranged the seating at table
lestistern·ium -iī or **-ī** *n* ritual feast (*at which images of the gods were placed on couches at the table*)

lectĭt•ō -āre *vt* to read and reread; to like to read
lectiuncŭl•a -ae *f* light reading
lect•or -ōris *m* reader (*esp. slave who read aloud to his master*)
lectŭl•us -ī *m* cot; small couch, settee; humble bier
lect•us -ī or **-ūs** *m* bed, couch; bier
lect•us -a -um *pp* of **lego;** *adj* select, choice, special, elite
Lēd•a -ae or **Lēd•ē -ēs** *f* Tyndarus's wife, whom Jupiter visited in the form of a swan and who bore Helen, Clytemnestra, Castor, and Pollux
lēgātĭ•ō -ōnis *f* embassy, mission, legation; members of an embassy; work or report of work of a mission; nominal staff appointment; command of a legion; **legatio libera** junket (*all-expenses-paid trip, a privilege granted to senators, nominally in an official capacity, to visit the provinces to transact private business*)
lēgāt•um -ī *n* bequest, legacy
lēgāt•us -ī *m* deputy, representative; ambassador, envoy; adjutant (*of a consul, proconsul, or praetor*); commander of a legion
lēgĭf•er -ĕra -ĕrum *adj* law-giving
legĭ•ō -ōnis *f* legion (*divided into* 10 *cohorts and numbering between* 4,200 *and* 6,000 *men*); army
legiōnārĭ•us -a -um *adj* legionary
lēgirŭp•a -ae or **lēgirup•ĭō -ōnis** *m* lawbreaker
lēgitĭmē *adv* legitimately, lawfully; properly
lēgitĭm•us -a -um *adj* legitimate, lawful; regular, right, just, proper; *n pl* legal formalities
legiuncŭl•a -ae *f* under-manned legion
lēg•ō -āre *vt* to commission; to send on a public mission, despatch; to delegate, deputize; to bequeath, will; (fig) to entrust
legō legĕre lēgī lectum *vt* to gather, collect, pick; to pick out, choose; to pick one's way through, cross; to sail by, coast along; to read, peruse; to recite, read out loud; to pick up, steal; to pick up (*news, rumor*); **fila legere** to wind up the thread of life; **senatum legere** to read off the senate roll
lēgulē•ĭus -ĭī or **-ī** pettifogger
legūm•en -ĭnis *n* leguminous plant; vegetable; pulse; bean
lemb•us -ī *m* cutter, yacht (*built for speed*), speedboat
lemm•a -ătis *n* theme, subject matter; epigram
Lemnicŏl•a -ae *m* inhabitant of Lemnos, i.e., Vulcan
lemniscāt•us -a -um *adj* heavily decorated (*with combat ribbons*)
lemnisc•us -ī *m* ribbon which hung down from a victor's wreath
Lemnĭ•us -a -um *adj* Lemnian; *m* Lemnian; Vulcan
Lemn•os or **Lemn•us -ī** *f* large island in the Aegean
Lemŭr•ēs -um *m pl* ghosts
Lemūrĭ•a -ōrum *n pl* night festival to drive ghosts from the house
lēn•a -ae *f* procuress, madame; seductress
Lēnae•us -a -um *adj* Lenaean, Bacchic; *m* Bacchus
lēnē *adv* gently
lēnīm•en -ĭnis *n* consolation, comfort, compensation, reward
lēnīment•um -ī *n* alleviation
lēn•ĭō -īre -īvī *or* **-ĭī -ītum** *vt* to soften, alleviate, soothe, calm; *vi* to calm down
lēn•is -e *adj* soft, gentle, mild, smooth, calm; gradual (*slope*); (fig) gentle, mild, kind
lēnĭt•ās -ātis *f* softness, gentleness, mildness, smoothness; (fig) gentleness, mildness, tenderness, clemency
lēnĭter *adv* softly, gently, mildly; (fig) mildly, quietly, calmly; (of style) smoothly; halfheartedly
lēnĭtūd•ō -ĭnis *f* softness, mildness, gentleness, smoothness
lēn•ō -ōnis *m* pander, procurer, pimp; seducer
lēnōcin•ĭum -ĭī or **-ī** *n* pandering, pimping; allurement, attraction; bawdy or gaudy clothes; flattery
lēnōcĭn•or -ārī -ātus sum *vi* to be a pimp; (with *dat*) **a** to play up to, humor, pander to; **b** to stimulate, promote
lēnōnĭ•us -a -um *adj* pimp's
len•s -tis *f* lentil
lentē *adv* slowly; indifferently, halfheartedly; calmly, leisurely, deliberately
lent•esc•ō -ĕre *vi* to get sticky, soften; (fig) to soften, weaken; (with **ad** + *acc*) to stick to
lentiscĭf•er -ĕra -ĕrum *adj* (of a region) producing mastic trees
lentisc•us -ī *f* mastic tree; toothpick (*made of mastic wood*)
lentitūd•ō -ĭnis *f* slowness; insensibility, apathy, dullness
lent•ō -āre *vt* to bend
lentŭl•us -a -um *adj* somewhat slow
lent•us -a -um *adj* sticky, clinging; pliant, limber; slow, sluggish; lingering; irresponsive, reluctant, indifferent, backward; slow-moving; tedious; drawling; at rest, at leisure, lazy; calm, unconcerned
lēnŭl•us -ī *m* little pimp
lēnuncŭl•us -ī *m* little pimp; small sailboat, skiff
le•ō -ōnis *m* lion
Le•ō -ōnis *m* Lion (*constellation*)
Leōnĭd•ās -ae *m* king of Sparta (487-480 B.C.), who fell at Thermopylae in 480 B.C. after a gallant stand
leōnīn•us -a -um *adj* lion's, of a lion
Leontīn•ī -ōrum *m pl* town in E. Sicily
lep•as -ădis *f* limpet
lepĭdē *adv* pleasantly, charmingly,

neatly; (as affirmative answer) yes, indeed; (of approval) bravo!
lepĭd·us -a -um *adj* pleasant, charming, neat; effeminate
lep·ōs or **lep·or -ōris** *m* pleasantness, charm, attractiveness
lep·us -ŏris *m* hare
Lep·us -ŏris *m* Hare (*constellation*)
lepuscŭl·us -ī *m* little hare
Lern·a -ae or **Lern·ē -ēs** *f* marsh near Argos, where Hercules slew the Hydra
Lernae·us -a -um *adj* Lernaean
Lesbĭ·us -a -um *adj* Lesbian; *f* pseudonym for the girl friend of the poet Catullus; *n* Lesbian wine
Lesb·os or **Lesb·us -ī** *f* large island in the N. Aegean, the birthplace of the lyric poets Alcaeus and Sappho
less·us (only *acc*: **lessum** in use) *m* wailing
lētāl·is -e *adj* lethal, fatal, mortal
Lēthae·us -a -um *adj* of Lethe; infernal; causing drowsiness
lēthargĭc·us -ī *m* lazy fellow
lētharg·us -ī *m* lethargy
Lēth·ē -ēs *f* Lethe (*river of oblivion in the lower world*); forgetfulness
lētĭf·er -ĕra -ĕrum *adj* deadly, fatal; **locus letifer** mortal spot
lēt·ō -āre *vt* to kill
lēt·um -ī *n* death; ruin, destruction; **leto dare** to put to death
Leuc·as -ădis *f* island off W. Greece
leucasp·is -ĭdis *adj* armed with a white shield
Leucipp·us -ī *m* philosopher, teacher of Democritus, and one of the founders of Atomism (*5th cent.* B.C.)
Leucothĕ·a -ae or **Leucothĕ·ē -ēs** *f* name of Ino, daughter of Cadmus, after she was changed into a sea deity
Leuctr·a -ōrum *n pl* small town in Boeotia where Epaminondas defeated the Spartans in 371 B.C.
levām·en -ĭnis *n* alleviation, comfort, consolation
levāment·um -ī *n* alleviation, comfort, consolation
levātĭ·ō -ōnis *f* lightening; relief, comfort; lessening
levicŭl·us -a -um *adj* somewhat vain
levidens·is -e *adj* poor, inferior
levifĭd·us -a -um *adj* untrustworthy
lĕv·is -e *adj* light, not heavy; light-armed; lightly dressed; light, easily digested; thin, poor (*soil*); light, nimble; flitting; slight, small; unimportant, trivial; unfounded (*rumor*); easy, simple; mild; gentle, easygoing; capricious, unreliable, fickle
lēv·is -e *adj* smooth; slippery; smooth, hairless, beardless; delicate, tender; effeminate; smooth (*style*)
levisomn·us -a -um *adj* light-sleeping
levĭt·ās -ātis *f* lightness; mobility, nimbleness; levity, frivolity; (fig) shallowness
lēvĭt·as -ātis *f* smoothness; (fig) smoothness, fluency
levĭter *adv* lightly; slightly, a little, somewhat; easily, without difficulty; nimbly
lĕv·ō -āre *vt* to lift up, raise; to lighten, relieve, ease; to console, comfort; to lessen, weaken; to release, free; to take away; to avert
lēv·ō -āre *vt* to make smooth, polish; to soothe
lēv·or -ōris *m* smoothness
lex lēgis *f* motion, bill; law, statute; rule, regulation, principle, precept; condition, stipulation; **eā lege ut** with the stipulation that, on condition that; **lege** or **legibus** legally; **lege agere** to proceed legally; **legem abrogare** to repeal a law; **legem ferre** to propose a bill; **legem derogare** to amend a bill or law; **legem jubere** to sanction a law; **legem perferre** to pass a law; **sine legibus** without restraint, without control
lībām·en -ĭnis *n* libation; firstfruits
lībāment·um -ī *n* libation; firstfruits
lībātĭ·ō -ōnis *f* libation
lībell·a -ae *f* small silver coin, ace; small sum; level (*instrument*); **ad libellam** to a tee, exactly; **heres ex libella** sole heir
libell·us -ī *m* small book, pamphlet; notebook; journal, diary; program; handbill, advertisement; petition; answer to a petition; letter; written accusation, indictment, libel; satirical verse
lib·ens or **lub·ens -entis** *adj* willing, ready, glad; merry, cheerful
libenter or **lubenter** *adv* willingly, gladly, with pleasure
lib·er -rī *m* bark of a tree; book; work, treatise; catalog, list, register; letter, rescript
līb·er -ĕra -ĕrum *adj* free; open, unoccupied; unrestricted; unprejudiced; outspoken, frank; uncontrolled, unrestricted; (not slave) free; (of states or municipalities) independent, autonomous; exempt; free of charge; (with *abl* or **ab** + *abl*) free from, exempt from; (with *genit*) free of; *m pl* see **liberi**
Līb·er -ĕrī *m* Italian fertility god, later identified with Bacchus; wine
Lībĕr·a -ae *f* Proserpina; Ariadne, the wife of Bacchus
Līberāl·ĭa -ĭum *n pl* festival of Liber, held on March 17th, at which young men received the toga virilis
līberāl·is -e *adj* relating to freedom, relating to civil status, of free citizens; worthy of a freeman, honorable, gentleman's; courteous; liberal, generous; handsome
līberālĭt·ās -ātis *f* courtesy, politeness; liberality, generosity; grant, gift
līberālĭter *adv* like a freeman, nobly; liberally (*e.g., educated*); courteously; liberally, generously

līberātĭ·ō -ōnis *f* liberation, delivery, freeing, release; acquittal
līberāt·or -ōris *m* liberator
līběrē *adv* freely; frankly, outspokenly; ungrudgingly; like a freeman, liberally
līběr·ī -ōrum *m pl* children
līběr·ō -āre *vt* to set free, free, release; to acquit, discharge; to cancel, get rid of (*e.g., debts*); to exempt; to manumit, set free; (with *abl* or with **ab** or **ex** + *abl*) to free or release from, acquit of; **fidem liberare** to keep one's promise; **nomina liberare** to cancel debts; **se aere alieno liberare** to pay up a debt
lībert·a -ae *f* freedwoman, ex-slave
lībert·ās -ātis *f* liberty, freedom; status of a freeman; political freedom; freedom of speech, freedom of thought; frankness
lībertīn·us -a -um *adj & mf* ex-slave; *m* freedman; *f* freedwoman
lībert·us -ī *m* freedman, ex-slave
lib·et (or **lub·et**) **-ēre -ŭit** (or **libĭtum est**) *v impers* (with *dat*) it pleases, is pleasant, is agreeable to, is nice for (*someone*); (with *inf*) it is nice, pleasant to (*do something*); **si lubet** if you please; **ut lubet** as you please
libīdĭn·or -ārī -ātus sum *vi* to gratify lust
libīdinōsē *adv* willfully; arbitrarily
libīdinōs·us -a -um *adj* willful; arbitrary; lustful, sensual
libīd·ō or **lubīd·ō -ĭnis** *f* desire, longing, inclination, pleasure; will, willfulness, arbitrariness, caprice, fancy; lust; rut, heat; **ex libidine** arbitrarily
libĭt·a -ōrum *n pl* will, pleasure, liking
Libitīn·a -ae *f* burial goddess; implements for burial; grave, death
līb·ō -āre *vt* to taste, sip; to pour as a libation, offer, consecrate; to touch lightly, barely touch, graze; to spill, waste; to extract, collect, compile
lībr·a -ae *f* balance, scales; plummet, level; pound (*of twelve ounces*)
lībrāment·um -ī *n* weight; balance, ballast; plane surface; gravity
lībrārĭ·a -ae *f* forelady (*who weighed out wool for slaves to spin*)
librārĭŏl·us -ī *m* copyist, scribe
librārĭ·us -a -um *adj* book, of books; **taberna libraria** bookstore; *m* copyist, scribe; *n* bookcase
lībrāt·us -a -um *adj* poised; hurled; powerful
lībrīl·is -e *adj* one-pound, weighing a pound
lībrĭt·or -ōris *m* artilleryman
lībr·ō -āre *vt* to balance; to poise, level, hurl, launch; to sway
līb·um -ī *n* cake; birthday cake
Liburnĭ·a -ae *f* district of Illyria between Istria and Dalmatia
Liburn·us -a -um *adj & mf* Liburnian; *f* Liburnian galley
Libў·a -ae or **Libў·ē -ēs** *f* Libya (*Africa*)
Libў·es -um *m pl* Libyans
Libўc·us or **Libyss·us** or **Libystīn·us** or **Libў·us -a -um** or **Libyst·is -ĭdis** *adj* Libyan; (in general) African
lic·ens -entis *adj* free, bold
licenter *adv* freely, boldly, without restraint, licentiously
licentĭ·a -ae *f* license, liberty, freedom; lawlessness, licentiousness
lic·ĕō -ēre *vi* to cost; to be for sale
lic·ĕor -ērī -ĭtus sum *vt* to bid on, bid for, make an offer for; *vi* to bid, make a bid
lic·et -ēre -ŭit or **-ĭtum est** *v impers* it is permitted or lawful; (with *dat & inf*) it is all right for (*someone*) to; **licet** (to express assent) yes, all right
licet *conj* granted that, even if, although
Lich·ās -ae *m* companion of Hercules
līch·ēn -ēnis *m* ringworm
licitātĭ·ō -ōnis *f* bidding (*at auction*); haggling
licĭt·or -ārī -ātus sum *vt* to bid for
licĭt·us -a -um *adj* permissible, lawful
līc·ĭum -ĭī or **-ī** *n* thread
lict·or -ōris *m* lictor (*attendant and bodyguard of a magistrate, of whom twenty-four attended a dictator, twelve a consul, and six a praetor*)
li·ēn -ēnis *m* spleen
liēnōs·us -a -um *adj* splenetic
ligām·en -ĭnis *n* bandage
ligāment·um -ī *n* bandage
lignār·ĭus -ĭī or **-ī** *m* carpenter
lignātĭ·ō -ōnis *f* gathering of lumber
lignāt·or -ōris *m* woodcutter, lumberjack
ligneŏl·us -a -um *adj* wooden
lignĕ·us -a -um *adj* wooden
lign·or -ārī -ātus sum *vi* to gather wood
lign·um -ī *n* wood; timber, firewood, log, plank; writing tablet; tree; **in silvam ligna ferre** to carry coals to Newcastle
lig·ō -āre *vt* to tie, tie up, bandage; to close (*a deal*)
lig·ō -ōnis *m* mattock, hoe; farming
ligŭl·a -ae *f* shoe strap
Lig·ur or **Lig·us -ŭris** *m* or *f* Ligurian
Ligurĭ·a -ae *f* Liguria (*district along the N.W. coast of Italy*)
ligūr·ĭō or **ligurr·ĭō -īre -īvī** or **-ĭī -ītum** *vt* to lick, pick at; to eat daintily; (fig) to prey on; (fig) to be dying for
ligūrītĭ·ō -ōnis *f* daintiness
Ligus see **Ligur**
Liguscĭ·us or **Ligustĭc·us** or **Ligustīn·us -a -um** *adj* Ligurian
ligustr·um -ī *n* privet

lil·ium -iī or **-ī** *n* lily; (mil) trench lined with sharp stakes
līm·a -ae *f* file; (fig) polishing, revision
līmātius *adv* in a more polished manner
līmātŭl·us -a -um *adj* (fig) rather sharp (*judgment*)
līmāt·us -a -um *adj* (fig) polished, refined
līm·ax -ācis *m* or *f* snail
limbolārī·us -a -um *adj* **textores limbolarii** tassel makers, hemmers
limb·us -ī *m* fringe, hem, tassel
līm·en -ĭnis *n* lintel, threshold; doorway, entrance; threshold, outset, beginning; starting gate (*at racetrack*); house, home
līm·es -ĭtis *m* country trail; path; road along a boundary; boundary, frontier; channel, course, way; zodiac
līm·ō -āre *vt* to file; (fig) to polish, refine; to file down, take away from, lessen; to get down to (*the truth*)
līmōs·us -a -um *adj* muddy; mud, growing in mud
limpĭd·us -a -um *adj* limpid, clear
līmŭl·us -a -um *adj* squinting
līm·us -a -um *adj* squinting; sidelong, askance; *m* mud; dirt, grime; ceremonial apron (*worn by priests at sacrifice*)
līnĕ·a -ae *f* line, string, thread; fishing line; plumb line; outline; boundary line, limit; **ad lineam** or **rectā lineā** in a straight line, vertically; horizontally; **extremā lineā amare** to love at a distance; **lineas transire** to go out of bounds
līneāment·um -ī *n* line; characteristic, feature; outline
līnĕ·ō -āre *vt* to make straight, make perpendicular
līnĕ·us -a -um *adj* flaxen, linen
lingō lingĕre linxī linctum *vt* to lick up, lap up
lingu·a -ae *f* tongue; speech, language, dialect; (of animals) note, song, bark; tongue of land; eloquence; **linguā promptus** insolent; **utraque lingua** Greek and Latin
lingŭl·a -ae *f* tongue of land
linguläc·a -ae *m* or *f* gossip, chatterbox
līnĭg·er -ĕra -ĕrum *adj* wearing linen
linō linĕre lēvī or **līvī litum** *vt* to smear; to erase; to cover, overlay; (fig) to mess up
linquō linquĕre līquī *vt* to leave, forsake, depart from; to leave or let alone; to leave in a pinch; **linqui animo** or **linqui** to faint; **linquitur** (with **ut**) it remains to (*do something*)
linteāt·us -a -um *adj* canvas
lintĕ·ō -ōnis *m* linen weaver
linteŏl·um -ī *n* small linen cloth
lint·er -ris *f* skiff; tub, vat
lintĕ·us -a -um *adj* linen; *n* linen, linen cloth; canvas, sail; kerchief
lintricŭl·us -ī *m* small boat
līn·um -ī *n* flax; linen; thread, rope, line; fishing line; net
Lin·us -ī *m* son of Apollo and instructor of Orpheus and Hercules
Lipăr·a -ae or **Lipăr·ē -ēs** *f* island off the N. coast of Sicily; *f pl* the Aeolian islands
Liparae·us -a -um or **Liparens·is -e** *adj* of Lipara
lipp·iō -īre -īvī *or* **-iī -ītum** *vi* to have sore eyes; (of eyes) to burn, ache
lippitūd·ō -ĭnis *f* running eyes, inflammation of the eyes
lipp·us -a -um *adj* with sore eyes, sore-eyed; burning (*eyes*); (fig) blind
lique·faciō -facĕre -fēcī -factum (*passive*: **lique·fīō -fĭerī -factus sum**) *vt* to melt, dissolve; to decompose; to waste, weaken
liqu·ens -entis *adj* clear, limpid; flowing, gliding; liquid, fluid
liquĕō liquēre licŭī *vi* to be liquid; *v impers* it is clear, is apparent, is evident; **liquet mihi** (with *inf*) I am free to; **non liquet** (law) it is not clear (*legal formula used by a hung jury*)
liquescō liquescĕre licŭī *vi* to melt; to decompose; to grow soft, grow effeminate; (fig) to melt away; to become clear
liquĭdē *adv* clearly; (fig) clearly, plainly
liquidiuscŭl·us -a -um *adj* somewhat softer
liquĭdō *adv* clearly, plainly, certainly
liquĭd·us -a -um *adj* liquid, fluid, flowing; clear, transparent; pure (*pleasure*); clear (*voice*); calm (*mind*); clear, evident, certain; *n* liquid, water; clearness, certainty
liqu·ō -āre *vt* to melt, dissolve; to strain, filter
līqu·or -ī *vi* to flow; to melt, dissolve; (fig) to melt away, waste away
liqu·or -ōris *m* fluidity; liquid, fluid; sea
Līr·is -is *m* river between Campania and Latium
līs lītis *f* lawsuit, litigation; matter of dispute; quarrel, wrangling; charge, accusation; **litem intendere** or **litem inferre** (with *dat*) to sue (*someone*); **litem aestimare** to assess damages; **lis capitis** criminal charge
litātĭ·ō -ōnis *f* success in sacrificing, efficacious sacrifice
litātō *adv* with favorable omens
lītĕra see **littera**
litĭc·en -ĭnis *m* clarion player
lītigāt·or -ōris *m* litigant
lītigiōs·us -a -um *adj* quarrelsome, litigious; contested, disputed
lītig·ium -iī or **-ī** *n* quarrel, dispute
lītĭg·ō -āre *vi* to quarrel, squabble; to go to court
lit·ō -āre *vt* to offer duly or accept-

ably; *vi* to offer acceptable sacrifice; to receive a good omen; (with *dat*) to propitiate, satisfy, appease
lītorāl·is -e *adj* shore, of the shore
lītorĕ·us -a -um *adj* seashore, at or along the seashore
littĕr·a or **lītĕr·a -ae** *f* letter (*of the alphabet*); handwriting; *f pl* epistle, letter, dispatch; edict, ordinance; literature, books, literary works; learning, liberal education, scholarship; records, accounts; **littera salutaris** (*i.e.*, **A = absolvo**) vote of acquittal; **littera tristis** (*i.e.*, **C = condemno**) vote of guilty; **litteras discere** to learn to read and write; **litteras scire** to know how to read and write
litterārĭ·us -a -um *adj* of reading and writing; **ludus litterarius** elementary school
litterātē *adv* legibly, in a clear handwriting; literally; learnedly
litterāt·or -ōris *m* elementary-school teacher; grammarian, philologist
litterātūr·a -ae *f* alphabet
litterāt·us -a -um *adj* marked with letters, engraved; learned, scholarly; liberally educated; devoted to literature
litterŭl·a -ae *f* small letter; *f pl* short letter, note; slight literary endeavors
litūr·a -ae *f* erasure; erased passage; correction, emendation; blot, smear; wrinkle
litus *pp* of **lino**
līt·us -ŏris *n* seashore, beach, coast; river bank; **in litus harenas fundere** to carry coals to Newcastle; **litus arare** to waste effort
litŭ·us -ī *m* cavalry trumpet, clarion; (fig) signal; augur's wand (*crooked staff carried by an augur*); **lituus meae profectionis** signal for my departure
līv·ens -entis *adj* black-and-blue, livid
līv·ĕō -ēre *vi* to be black and blue, be livid; to be envious; (with *dat*) to be jealous of
līvesc·ō -ĕre *vi* to turn black and blue
Līvĭ·a -ae *f* second wife of Augustus (58 B.C.-29 A.D.)
līvidŭl·us -a -um *adj* inclined to be jealous, somewhat envious
līvĭd·us -a -um *adj* leaden (*in color*); blue; black and blue; jealous, envious, spiteful
Līv·ĭus -ĭī or **-ī** *m* T. Livius Patavinus or Livy (*famous historian*, 59 B.C.-17 A.D.)
līv·or -ōris *m* leaden color; bluish color; black-and-blue mark; jealousy, envy, spite
lix·a -ae *m* camp follower
locātĭ·ō -ōnis *f* arrangement, placement; renting out, contract, lease
locāt·um -ī *n* lease, contract
locĭt·ō -āre *vt* to lease out
loc·ō -āre *vt* to place, put, set, lay; to establish, constitute, lay, set; to give in marriage, marry off; to let, rent out; to contract for; to invest
locŭl·us -ī *m* little place, spot; pocket
locŭpl·ēs -ētis *adj* rich; reliable, responsible
locuplēt·ō -āre *vt* to make rich, enrich
loc·us -ī (*pl*: **loc·ī -ōrum** *m*; **loc·a -ōrum** *n*) *m* place, site, spot, locality, district; place, seat; period, period of time; opportunity, room, occasion; situation, position, category; rank, degree, birth; passage in a book; topic, subject, point, division; (mil) position, post, station; **adhuc locorum** till now; **ad id locorum** till then; **ex aequo loco dicere** to speak in the senate; to hold a conversation; **ex** or **de loco superiore dicere** to speak from the rostrum; **ex loco inferiore dicere** to speak before a judge, speak in court; **inde loci** since then; **in eo loci** in such a condition; **interea loci** meanwhile; **loci communes** general topics; public places, parks; **loco** (with *genit*) instead of; **loco** or **in loco** at the right time; **loco cedere** to give way, yield; **postea loci** afterwards; **post id locorum** afterwards; **ubicumque loci** whenever
lōcust·a -ae *f* locust
Lōcust·a -ae *f* woman notorious as poisoner in the time of Claudius and Nero
locūtĭ·ō -ōnis *f* speech; way of speaking, pronunciation
locūtus *pp* of **loquor**
lōd·ix -īcis *f* blanket
logĭc·us -a -um *adj* logical; *n pl* logic
log·os or **log·us -ī** *m* word; witticism; *m pl* mere words, empty talk
lōlīgō see **lolligo**
lol·ĭum - ĭī or **-ī** *n* darnel
lollīg·ō or **lōlīg·ō -ĭnis** *f* cuttlefish
lollīguncŭl·a -ae *f* small cuttlefish
lōment·um -ī *n* face cream
Londīn·ĭum -ĭī or **-ī** *n* London
longaev·us -a -um *adj* aged
longē *adv* far, far off, long way off; away, distant; out of reach, of no avail; long, for a long period; (to speak) at greater length; (with comparatives) far, by far, much; **longe lateque** far and wide, everywhere
longinquĭt·ās -ātis *f* length, extent; remoteness, distance; length, duration
longinqu·us -a -um *adj* long, extensive; far off, distant, remote; from afar, foreign; long, prolonged, continued, tedious; **ex** or **e longinquo** from far away
longĭter *adv* far
longitūd·ō -ĭnis *f* length; **in longitudinem** lengthwise

longiuscŭl·us -a -um *adj* pretty long
longur·ĭus -ĭī or **-ī** *m* long pole
long·us -a -um *adj* long; spacious; long, protracted, drawn-out; tedious; **longa navis** battleship; **longum esse** (with *inf*) to be tedious to; *n* length; **in longum** for a long while; **ne longum faciam** in short
loquācĭt·ās -ātis *f* talkativeness
loquācĭter *adv* long-windedly; at length, in detail
loquācŭl·us -a -um *adj* rather talkative
loqu·ax -ācis *adj* talkative, loquacious
loquell·a -ae *f* speech, language
loquĭt·or -ārī -ātus *vi* to chatter away
loquor loquī locūtus sum *vt* to say; to talk of, speak about; to tell, tell of, mention; (fig) to declare, show, indicate; *vi* to speak; to rustle, murmur
lōrār·ĭus -ĭī or **-ī** *m* flogger, slave driver
lōrāt·us -a -um *adj* tied with thongs
lōrĕ·us -a -um *adj* striped
lōrīc·a -ae *f* breastplate; parapet; **libros mutare loricis** to exchange books for arms
lōrīcāt·us -a -um *adj* wearing a breastplate
lōrĭp·ēs -ĕdis *adj* bowlegged
lōr·um -ī *n* strip of leather, thong, strap; whip, scourge; leather badge; *n pl* reins
lōt·os or **lōt·us -ī** *f* lotus; flute (*of lotus wood*)
lōtus *pp* of **lavo**
lub- = lib-
lubentĭ·a -ae *f* pleasure
lūbrĭc·ō -āre *vt* to oil, grease, make smooth
lūbrĭc·us -a -um *adj* slippery; smooth; slimy; gliding; deceitful, tricky; precarious; *n* precarious situation, critical period
Lūc·a bōs (*genit:* **Lūc·ae bovis**) *f* elephant
Lūcānĭ·a -ae *f* district in S.W. Italy
Lūcānĭc·us -a -um *adj* Lucanian; *f* Lucanian sausage
Lūcān·us -a -um *adj* Lucanian; *m* Lucanian; Lucan (*M. Annaeus Lucanus, epic poet,* 39-65 A.D.)
lūc·ar -āris *n* forest tax
lucell·um -ī *n* slight profit
lūcĕō lūcēre luxī *vi* to shine, be light, glow, glitter, be clear; (fig) to be clear, be apparent, be conspicuous; *v impers* it is light, day is dawning
Lūcĕr·ēs -um *m pl* one of the three original Roman tribes
lucern·ae -ae *f* lamp; (fig) midnight oil
lūcescō or **lūciscō lūcescĕre luxī** *vi* to begin to shine; *v impers* it is getting light
lūcĭdē *adv* clearly, distinctly
lūcĭd·us -a -um *adj* shining, bright, clear; lucid, clear
lūcĭf·er -ĕra -ĕrum *adj* shiny
Lūcĭf·er -ĕrī *m* morning star; planet Venus; son of Aurora and Cephalus; day
lūcifŭg·us -a -um *adj* light-shunning
Lūcīl·ĭus -ĭī or **-ī** *m* C. Lucilius (*first Roman satiric poet, c.* 180-102 B.C.)
Lucīn·a -ae *f* goddess of childbirth; childbirth
lūciscō see **lucesco**
Lucrētĭ·a -ae *f* daughter of Spurius Lucretius and wife of Collatinus, who, having been raped by Sextus Tarquinius, committed suicide in 509 B.C.
Lucrēt·ĭus -ĭī or **-ī** *m* Spurius Lucretius (*father of Lucretia and consul in* 509 B.C.); Titus Lucretius Carus (*philosophical poet,* 94?-55? B.C.)
lucrificābĭl·is -e or **lucrifĭc·us -a -um** *adj* profitable
lucrifŭg·a -ae *m* or *f* person not out for gain, disinterested person
Lucrīn·us -a -um *adj* Lucrine; *m* Lake Lucrine (*small lake near Baiae, famous for its oysters*)
lucripĕt·a -ae *m* profiteer
lucr·or -ārī -ātus sum *vt* to gain, win, get
lucrōs·us -a -um *adj* profitable
lucr·um -ī *n* profit, gain; wealth; greed, love of gain; **lucri facere** to gain; **lucri fieri** to be gained; **lucro esse** (with *dat*) to be advantageous for (*someone*); **ponere in lucro** or **in lucris** to regard as gain
luctām·en -ĭnis *n* wrestling; struggle, effort
luct·ans -antis *adj* reluctant
luctātĭ·ō -ōnis *f* wrestling; struggle, contest
luctāt·or -ōris *m* wrestler
luctifĭc·us -a -um *adj* causing sorrow, doleful, woeful
luctisŏn·us -a -um *adj* sad-sounding
luct·or -ārī -ātus sum or **luct·ō -āre** *vi* to wrestle; (with *inf*) to struggle to
luctuōsius *adv* more pitifully
luctuōs·us -a -um *adj* causing sorrow, sorrowful; sad, feeling sad
luct·us -ūs *m* sorrow, mourning, grief, distress; signs of sorrow, mourning clothes; source of grief, affliction
lūcubrātĭ·ō -ōnis *f* moonlighting, working by lamp light; evening gossip; nighttime writing
lūcŭbr·ō -āre *vt* to compose at night; *vi* to moonlight, burn the midnight oil
lūculentē *adv* splendidly, well; (to beat) soundly
lūculenter *adv* brilliantly, smartly, very well

lūculent·us -a -um *adj* bright, brilliant; (fig) brilliant, smart, excellent; considerable (*wealth*); sound (*beating*); trustworthy (*sources*)

Lūcull·us -ī *m* Lucius Licinius Lucullus (*Roman general and politician*, 117-56 B.C.)

Lucŭm·ō or **Lucm·ō -ōnis** *m* Etruscan prince, Etruscan priest

lūc·us -ī *m* sacred grove; woods

lūdĭ·a -ae *f* actress; gladiator (*female*)

lūdibr·ĭum -ĭī or **-ī** *n* derision; subject of derision, butt of ridicule; (fig) plaything, sucker; **ludibrio esse** (with *dat*) to be made a fool of by (*someone*), be taken in by (*someone*); **ludibrio habere** to take for a sucker, make fun of

lūdibund·us -a -um *adj* playful, playing around; without effort, without danger

lūdĭc·er -ra -rum *adj* for sport, in sport; **ludicra exercitatio** sports; athletics; **ludicrum praemium** sports award; **ludicra res** drama; *n* sport, game; toy; show, public game; stage play

lūdificābĭl·is -e *adj* used in mockery

lūdificātĭ·ō -ōnis *f* ridiculing, mocking; fooling, tricking

lūdificāt·or -ōris *m* mocker

lūdificāt·us -ūs *m* mockery

lūdifĭc·ō -āre or **lūdifĭc·or -ārī -ātus sum** *vt* to make a fool of, fool, take for a sucker; to fool, trick, baffle

lūdĭ·ō -ōnis or **lūd·ĭus -ĭī** or **-ī** *m* actor

lūdō lūdĕre lūsī lūsum *vt* to play; to spend in play; to amuse oneself with, do for amusement, practice as a pastime; to imitate, mimic, mock, do a takeoff on, ridicule; to deceive, delude; *vi* to play; to frisk, frolic; to play around, make love; **aleā ludere** to shoot craps; **pilā ludere** to play ball, play tennis

lūd·us -ī *m* play, game, sport, pastime, diversion; school; mere child's play; joke, fun; playing around, fooling around, lovemaking; public show, public game; **amoto ludo** all joking aside; **in ludum ire** to go to school; **per ludum** as a joke, for fun; *m pl* public games, public exhibition; games, tricks; **ludos facere** or **ludos reddere** (with *dat*) to play tricks on, make fun of

luell·a -ae *f* expiation, atonement

lu·ēs -is *f* infection, contagion, plague, pestilence; calamity

Lugdūnens·is -e *adj* of Lyons

Lugdūn·um -ī *n* Lyons (*town in E. Gaul*)

lūgĕō lugēre luxī *vt* to mourn, lament, deplore; *vi* to mourn, be in mourning; to be in mourning clothes

lūgubr·ĭa -ĭum *n pl* mourning clothes

lūgŭbr·is -e *adj* mourning; doleful; disastrous

lumbifrag·ĭum -ĭī or **-ī** *n* physical wreck

lumbrīc·us -ī *m* worm; (as term of reproach) worm

lumb·us -ī *m* loin; *m pl* loins; genital organs

lūm·en -ĭnis *n* light; lamp, torch; brightness, sheen, gleam; daylight; light of the eye, eye; light of life, life; window, window light; distinguished person, luminary, celebrity; glory, pride

lūminăr·e -is *n* window

lūminōs·us -a -um *adj* luminous; (fig) bright, conspicuous

lūn·a -ae *f* moon; month; night; crescent (*worn as ornament by senators on their shoes*); **luna laborans** moon in eclipse, eclipse of the moon; **luna minor** waning moon

lūnār·is -e *adj* lunar, of the moon

lūnāt·us -a -um *adj* crescent-shaped

lūn·ō -āre *vt* to make crescent-shaped, to shape like a crescent

lūnŭl·a -ae *f* little crescent (*ornament worn by women*)

lu·ō -ĕre -ī *vt* to wash; to cleanse, purge; to set free, let go; to pay (*debt of penalty*); to suffer, undergo; to atone for, expiate; to satisfy, appease; to avert by expiation or punishment

lup·a -ae *f* she-wolf; flirt, prostitute

lupān·ar -āris *n* brothel

lupāt·us -a -um *adj* jagged (*like wolf's teeth*); *m pl* or *n pl* jagged bit

Luperc·al -ālis *n* shrine on the Palatine hill sacred to Pan

Lupercāl·ĭa -ĭum *n pl* festival of Lycaean Pan, celebrated in February

Luperc·us -ī *m* Pan

lupill·us -ī *m* small lupine (*plant*)

lupīn·us -a -um *adj* lupine. wolf's; *m* & *n* lupine, wolf's-bane (*plant*); stage money

lup·us -ī *m* wolf; (fish) pike; jagged bit; grapnel

lurc·ō -ōnis *m* glutton

lūrĭd·us -a -um *adj* pale-yellow, wan, ghastly, lurid; making pale

lūr·or -ōris *m* sallowness

luscinĭ·a -ae *f* nightingale

lusciniŏl·a -ae *f* little nightingale

luscin·ĭus -ĭī or **-ī** *m* nightingale

lusciōs·us or **luscitiōs·us -a -um** *adj* purblind, partly blind

lusc·us -a -um *adj* one-eyed

lūsĭ·ō -ōnis *f* play, game

Lūsitān·ī -ōrum *m pl* Lusitanians

Lūsitānĭ·a -ae *f* Lusitania (*modern Portugal and W. part of Spain*)

lūsĭt·ō -āre *vi* to like to play

lūs·or -ōris *m* player, gambler; humorous writer; joker

lustrāl·is -e *adj* lustral, propitiatory; quinquennial

lustrātĭ·ō -ōnis *f* purification, lustration; wandering

lustr·ō -āre *vt* to purify; to travel

over, traverse; to check, examine; to go around, encircle; to survey; (mil) to review (*troops*); to light up, make bright, illuminate; to scan (*with the eyes*); to consider, review

lustr·or -ārī -ātus sum *vi* to frequent brothels

lustr·um -ī *n* haunt, den, lair; wilderness; brothel; sensuality; purificatory sacrifice, lustration; lustrum, period of five years; period of years; **ingens lustrum** one hundred years, century

lūsus *pp* of **ludo**

lūs·us -ūs *m* play, game, sport, amusement; playing around (*amorously*)

lūteŏl·us -a -um *adj* yellowish

lūtĕ·us -a -um *adj* of mud, of clay; muddy; dirty, grimy; (fig) dirty; mud-colored; golden-yellow, yellow, orange

lutĭt·ō -āre *vt* to splatter with mud; (fig) to throw mud at

lut·ō -āre *vt* to make dirty

lutulent·us -a -um *adj* muddy, filthy; (fig) filthy; turbid (*style*)

lut·um -ī *n* mud, mire; clay; yellow

lux lūcis *f* light; light of day, daylight; light of day, life; public view, publicity; the public, the world; light of hope, encouragement; glory; elucidation; **luce** or **luci** by daylight, in the daytime; **lux aestiva** summer; **lux brumalis** winter

lux·ō -āre *vt* to put out of joint, dislocate

lux·or -ārī -ātus sum *vi* to live riotously, have a ball

luxurĭ·a -ae or **luxurĭ·ēs -ēī** *f* luxurience; luxury, extravagance, excess

luxurĭ·ō -āre or **luxurĭ·or -ārī -ātus sum** *vi* to grow luxuriantly; to luxuriate; (of the body) to swell up; (of animals) to be frisky; to run riot, lead a wild life

luxuriōsē *adv* luxuriously, voluptuously

luxuriōs·us -a -um *adj* luxuriant; exuberant; extravagant, voluptuous

lux·us -ūs *m* extravagance, excess, luxury; splendor, pomp, magnificence

Lyae·us -a -um *adj* Bacchic; *m* Bacchus; wine

Lycae·us -a -um *adj* Lycaean (*esp. applied to Pan*); *m* mountain in Arcadia where Jupiter and Pan were worshiped

Lycā·ōn -ŏnis *m* king of Arcadia, the father of Callisto, who was changed into a wolf

Lycāŏn·is -ĭdis *f* Callisto, who was changed into the Great Bear

Lycē·um *or* **Lycī·um -ī** *n* Aristotle's school at Athens

Lyci·us -a -um *adj & m* Lycian; *f* country in S.W. Asia Minor

lychnūch·us -ī *m* lamp stand; chandelier

lychn·us -ī *m* lamp

Lyctĭ·us -a -um *adj* Cretan

Lycurg·us -ī *m* Thracian king who prohibited the worship of Bacchus and was punished with madness and death; Spartan lawgiver (*date unknown*); Athenian orator and friend of Demosthenes (390-324 B.C.)

Lyc·us or **Lyc·os -ī** *m* husband of Antiope, who divorced her to marry Dirce

Lȳdĭ·us -a -um *adj & m* Lydian; Etruscan; *f* country of Asia Minor, whose capital was Sardis

Lȳd·us -a -um *adj & m* Lydian; Etruscan

lymph·a -ae *f* water, spring water; water nymph

lymphātĭc·us -a -um *adj* crazy, frantic; *n* craziness

lymphāt·us -a -um *adj* crazy, mad

Lyncĕ·us -a -um *adj* sharp-eyed; *m* Argonaut, famous for keen vision; son of Egyptus and Hyperraestra

lyn·x -cis *m* or *f* lynx

lyr·a -ae *f* lyre; lyric poetry, lyric

Lyr·a -ae *f* Lyra (*constellation*)

lyrĭc·us -a -um *adj* lyric; of the lyre; *m pl* lyric poets; *n pl* lyric poems

lyrist·ēs -ae *m* lyrist

Lyrnēs·is or **Lyrness·is -ĭdis** *f* Briseis

Lyrnēs·us -ī *f* town in the Troad, the birthplace of Briseis

Lysĭ·ās -ae *m* Athenian orator in the time of Socrates (*c.* 450-370 B.C.)

M

Macăr·eus -ĕī or **-ĕos** *m* son of Aeolus, who lived in incest with his sister Canace

Macĕd·ō -ŏnis *m* Macedonian

Macedonĭc·us -a -um *adj* Macedonian

Macedonĭ·us -a -um *adj* Macedonian; *f* Macedonia (*country lying between Thessaly and Thrace*)

macell·um -ī *n* butcher shop, meat market

mac·ĕō -ēre *vi* to be lean, be skinny

mac·er -ĕra -ĕrum *adj* lean; skinny; thin, poor (*soil*)

Mac·er -rī *m* C. Licinius Macer (*Roman historian and orator who was impeached by Cicero and committed suicide in* 66 B.C.); C. Licinius Macer Calvus (*son of the former, and distinguished orator and poet,* 82-46 B.C.)

mācerĭ·a -ae *f* brick or stone wall; garden wall

mācĕr·ō -āre *vt* to knead, soften, make tender; to weaken, waste; to distress, vex, torment

macesc·ō -ĕre *vi* to grow thin

machaer·a -ae *f* sword

machaerophŏr·us -ī *m* soldier armed with sword

Machā·ōn -ŏnis *m* famous physician of the Greeks in the Trojan War and son of Aesculapius

Machāonĭ·us -a -um *adj* surgical

māchĭn·a -ae *f* machine, engine; crane; pulley, windlass, winch; (fig) scheme, stratagem

māchināment·um -ī *n* machine, engine, contrivance

māchinātĭ·ō -ōnis *f* mechanism; machine; trick

māchināt·or -ōris *m* engineer, machinist; (fig) contriver

māchĭn·or -ārī -ātus sum *vt* to engineer, design, contrive; to scheme, plot

macĭ·ēs -ēī *f* leanness, thinness; barrenness; poverty (*of style*)

macilent·us -a -um *adj* skinny

macresc·ō -ĕre *vi* to grow thin, get skinny

macritūd·ō -ĭnis *f* leanness, skinniness

macrocoll·um -ī *n* large-size sheet of paper

mactābĭl·is -e *adj* deadly

mactāt·us -ūs *m* sacrifice

mactē *interj* well done!; good luck!

mact·ō -āre *vt* to magnify, glorify, honor; to sacrifice; to slaughter, put to death; to destroy, ruin, overthrow; to trouble, afflict

mact·us -a -um *adj* glorified, honored, adored; **macte virtute (esto)** (congratulatory exclamation) good luck!; well done!

macŭl·a -ae *f* spot, stain, blemish; mesh (*of a net*); (fig) stigma, blemish, disgrace, defect

macŭl·ō -āre *vt* to spot; to stain; to defile, pollute; to dishonor

maculōs·us -a -um *adj* spotted; stained

made·faciō -facĕre -fēcī -factus (*passive*: **made·fīō -fĭerī -factus sum**) *vt* to wet, moisten, drench, soak, steep

mad·ens -entis *adj* wet, moist; flowing (*hair*); melting (*snow*); reeking (*with blood*)

mad·ĕō -ēre -ŭī *vi* to be wet, be moist, be soaked, be drenched; to drip; to flow; to be soused; to be full, overflow

mad·escō -escĕre -ŭī *vi* to become wet, become moist

madĭdē *adv* drunkenly

madĭd·us -a -um *adj* wet, moist, drenched; dyed, steeped; drunk

mad·or -ōris *m* moisture

maduls·a -ae *m* souse, drunkard

Maeand·er or **Maeandr·os** or **Maeandr·us -ī** *m* river in Asia Minor, famous for its winding course; winding; winding border; devious course

Maecēn·ās -ātis *m* C. Cilnius Maecenas (*adviser to Augustus and friend of Virgil and Horace, d.* 8 B.C.)

maen·a -ae *f* sprat (*fish*)

Maenăl·is -ĭdis *adj* **Maenalis ursa** Callisto (*who was changed into the Great Bear*)

Maenăl·us or **Maenăl·os -ī** *m* or **Maenăl·a -ōrum** *n pl* Mt. Maenalus (*mountain range in Arcadia, sacred to Pan*)

Maen·as -ădis *f* Bacchante

Maenĭ·us -a -um *adj* Maenian; **Maenia Columna** pillar in the forum at which thieves, slaves, and debtors were tried and flogged

Maeŏn·es -um *m pl* Maeonians (*ancient name of the Lydians*)

Maeonĭd·ēs -ae *m* native of Maeonia; Homer; Etrurian

Maeŏn·is -ĭdis *f* Maeonian woman (*esp. Arachne or Omphale*)

Maeonĭ·us -a -um *adj* Lydians; Homeric; Etruscan; *f* Maeonia, Lydia; Etruria

Maeōt·ae -ārum *m pl* Scythian tribe on Lake Maeotis on the N.E. coast of the Black Sea

Maeōt·is -ĭdis *adj* Maetoic; Scythian; **Maeotis lacus** Sea of Azov

maer·ĕō -ēre *vi* to mourn

maer·or -ōris *m* mourning, sadness

maestĭter *adv* like a mourner

maestitĭ·a -ae *f* sadness, gloom, melancholy

maestitūd·ō -ĭnis *f* sadness

maest·us -a -um *adj* mourning, sad, gloomy

Maev·ĭus -ĭī or **-ī** *m* poetaster often ridiculed by Virgil and Horace

māgāl·ĭa -ĭum *n pl* huts

mage see **magis**

magĭc·us -a -um *adj* magic; **artes magicae** magic

magis or **mage** *adv* more, in a higher degree, rather; **eo magis** all the more, the more; **magis magisque** more and more; **magis . . . quam** or **magis . . . atque** rather . . . than; **non magis . . . quam** not so much . . . as

magist·er -rī *m* chief, master, director; teacher; adviser, guardian; ringleader, author; captain, pilot; (in apposition with another noun) expert; **magister morum** censor; **magister sacrorum** chief priest

magister·ĭum -ĭī or **-ī** *n* directorship, presidency; **magisterium morum** censorship

magistr·a -ae *f* directress, mistress, instructress

magistrāt·us -ūs *m* magisterial office, magistracy; magistrate, official; body of magistrates; military command

magnanimĭt·ās -ātis *f* magnanimity; bravery

magnanĭm·us -a -um *adj* magnanimous; brave

Magn·ēs -ētis *adj & m* Magnesian; *f* city in Caria, near the Meander; city in Lydia near Mt. Sipylus; district in Thessaly on the Aegean Sea

magnidĭc·us -a -um *adj* talking big

magnificē *adv* magnificently, splendidly; pompously

magnificentĭ·a -ae *f* magnificence, grandeur, splendor; pompousness

magnifĭc·ō -āre *vt* to think much of

magnifĭc·us -a -um *adj* grand, great, splendid, august; rich, costly, magnificent; pompous

magniloquentĭ·a -ae *f* lofty style; pompous language

magnilŏqu·us -a -um *adj* sublime; bragging

magnitūd·ō -ĭnis *f* greatness, magnitude, size; large quantity, large number; vastness, extent

magnopĕre or **magnō opĕre** *adv* greatly, very much, particularly; strongly, earnestly, heartily, urgently

magn·us -a -um (*comp*: **major;** *superl*: **maximus**) *adj* big, large, great; long (*time*); high (*price*); important, momentous; significant; impressive; high, powerful (*in rank*); loud (*voice*); heavy (*rain*); advanced (*age*); noble (*character*); proud, boastful; *n* great thing; great value; **magni (pretii) aestimare** or **magni habere** to value highly, have a high regard for; **magno emere** to buy at a high price; **magno vendere** to sell at a high price; **vir magno jam natu** aged man, man advanced in years

mag·us -a -um *adj* magic; **artes magae** magic; *m* learned man (*among the Persians*); magician

Māi·us -a -um *adj & m* May; *f* daughter of Atlas and Pleione, and mother of Mercury by Jupiter

mājāl·is -is *m* castrated hog; (as term of abuse) swine

mājest·ās -ātis *f* majesty, dignity, grandeur; high treason; sovereign power, sovereignty; authority

māj·or -us (*comp* of **magnus**) *adj* bigger, larger, greater; **annos natu major quadraginta** forty years older; **in majus ferre** to exaggerate; **majoris (pretii)** at a higher price; more highly; **major natu** elder, older

mājōr·ēs -um *m pl* ancestors, forefathers

mājuscŭl·us -a -um *adj* somewhat greater; a little older

māl·a -ae *f* cheekbone, upper jaw; *f pl* cheek; (fig) jaws (*e.g., of death*)

malacĭ·a -ae *f* calm at sea, dead calm

malaciss·ō -āre *vt* to soften, soften up

malăc·us -a -um *adj* soft; luxurious

male *adv* badly, wrongly; wickedly, cruelly, maliciously; unfortunately, unsuccessfully, awkwardly; excessively, extremely, very much; (with adjectives having a good sense) not, scarcely, not at all; (with adjectives having a bad sense) very much; terribly; **male audire** to be ill spoken of; **male dicere** (with *dat*) to say nasty things to, abuse; **male emere** to buy at a high price; **male facere** (with *dat*) to treat badly or cruelly; **male habere** to harass; **male metuere** to be terribly afraid of; **male vendere** to sell at a loss; **male vivere** to be a failure in life

maledĭc·ax -ācis *adj* abusive, foul-mouthed

maledĭcē *adv* abusively, slanderously

maledĭc·ens -entis *adj* abusive, foul-mouthed

male·dīcō -dīcĕre -dixī -dictum *vi* (with *dat*) **a** to speak ill of, abuse, slander; **b** to say nasty things to

maledictĭ·ō -ōnis *f* abusive language, abuse

maledictĭt·ō -āre *vi* (with *dat*) to keep saying nasty things to

maledict·um -ī *n* curse; abuse

maledĭc·us -a -um *adj* abusive, scurrilous, foul-mouthed

malefact·or -ōris *m* malefactor

malefact·um or **malfact·um -ī** *n* wrong, injury

malefĭcē *adv* mischievously

maleficentĭ·a -ae *f* harm, wrong, mischief

malefic·ium -ĭī or **-ī** *n* evil deed, crime, offense; harm, injury, wrong, mischief; **maleficium admittere** or **committere** to commit an offense or crime

malefĭc·us -a -um *adj* wicked, vicious, criminal; *m* mischief-maker

malesuād·us -a -um *adj* seductive, tempting

malevŏl·ens -entis *adj* spiteful

malevolentĭ·a -ae *f* spitefulness, malice, meanness

malevŏl·us -a -um *adj* spiteful, malicious, mean; *mf* enemy; jealous person

malĭf·er -ĕra -ĕrum *adj* apple-growing

malignē *adv* spitefully, jealously, meanly; stingily, grudgingly

malignĭt·ās -ātis *f* spite, malice, jealousy, meanness; stinginess

malign·us -a -um *adj* spiteful, malicious, jealous, mean; stingy; (fig) stingy, unproductive (*soil*); scanty (*light*)

malitĭ·a -ae *f* malice, ill-will, bad behavior; *f pl* devilish tricks

malitiōsē *adv* craftily, wickedly

malitiōs·us -a -um *adj* crafty, wicked, malicious, devilish

malleŏl·us -ī *m* small hammer, small mallet; fiery arrow

mallĕ·us -ī *m* hammer, mallet; pole-ax (*for slaughtering animals*)
mālō or **māvŏlō malle mālŭī** *vt* to prefer; *vi* (with *dat*) to incline toward, be more favorably disposed to
malobăthr·um -ī *n* malobathrum oil, betel juice
māl·um -ī *n* apple; **aureum malum** quince; **felix malum** lemon; **malum Punicum** or **malum granatum** pomegranate
mal·um -ī *n* evil, ill; harm; punishment; disaster; hardship
māl·us -ī *m* mast (*of ship*); pole; *f* apple tree
mal·us -a -um *adj* bad; ill, evil; ugly; unpatriotic; adverse, unsuccessful; unlucky; **i in malam rem** go to hell!; *n* see **malum**
malv·a -ae *f* mallow
Măm·ers -ertis *m* Mars
Māmertīn·ī -ōrum *m pl* (*mercenaries of Agathocles who after his death seized Messana, c.* 282 B.C., *and precipitated the First Punic War*)
mamill·a -ae *f* breast, teat
mamm·a -ae *f* breast (*of a woman*); dug
mammeāt·us -a -um *adj* large-breasted, full-bosomed
mānābĭl·is -e *adj* penetrating (*cold*)
manc·eps -ĭpis *m* purchaser; contractor
mancip·ĭum or **mancup·ĭum -ĭī** or **-ī** *n* formal purchase; possession, right of ownership; slave; **mancipio accipere** to take possession of; **mancipio dare** to turn over possession of; **res mancipi** possessions basic to running a farm (*e.g., land, slaves, livestock, farm implements*); **res nec mancipi** possessions other than those needed to run a farm
mancĭp·ō or **mancŭp·ō -āre** *vt* to sell, transfer
manc·us -a -um *adj* crippled, maimed; (fig) defective, imperfect
mandāt·um -ī *n* command, order, commission; *n pl* instructions
mandāt·us -ūs *m* command, order
mand·ō -āre *vt* to commit, entrust; to command, order, enjoin, commission
mandō mandĕre mandī mansum *vt* to chew; to champ; to eat, devour; **humum mandere** to bite the dust (*said of those who fall in battle*)
mandr·a -ae *f* stable, stall; drove of cattle; checkerboard
mandūc·us -ī *m* mask representing a glutton
māne (indecl) *n* morning; *adv* early in the morning; **bene mane** very early; **cras mane** tomorrow morning; **heri mane** yesterday morning; **hodie mane** this morning; **postridie ejus diei mane** the following morning
manĕō manēre mansī mansum *vt* to wait for, await; *vi* to stay, remain; to stop off, pass the night; to last, endure, continue, persist; **in condicione manere** to stick by an agreement; **in sententia manere** to stick to an opinion
mān·ēs -ĭum *m pl* souls of the dead; ghosts; lower world; last remains (*of the body*), ashes
mang·ō -ōnis *m* pushy salesman; slave dealer
manĭc·ae -ārum *f pl* handcuffs; grappling hook; long sleeves; gloves
manicāt·us -a -um *adj* long-sleeved
manicŭl·a -ae *f* little hand
manifestē *adv* plainly, distinctly
manifestō *adv* manifestly, evidently, plainly
manifest·ō -āre *vt* to reveal, betray
manifest·us -a -um *adj* manifest, plain, clear, distinct; exposed, brought to light, detected, caught; (with *genit*) convicted of, caught in; (with *inf*) known to
manipl- = manipul-
manipulār·is -e *adj* of a maniple or company; **miles manipularis** private
manipulār·is -is *m* private; soldier of the same company; comrade
manipulātim *adv* by companies
manipŭl·us or **manipl·us -ī** *m* handful (*esp. of hay*); (coll) gang; (mil) maniple, company (*three of which constituted a cohort*)
Manl·ĭus -ĭī or **-ī** *m* M. Manlius Capitolinus (*consul in* 392 B.C., *who, in* 389 B.C., *saved the Capitoline from the invading Gauls*); T. Manlius Torquatus (*consul in* 340 B.C., *famous for his military discipline*)
mannŭl·us -ī *m* pony
mann·us -ī *m* small Gallic horse
mān·ō -āre *vi* to drip, trickle, flow; to stream; (fig) to spread, emanate
mansĭ·ō -ōnis *f* stopover
mansĭt·ō -āre *vi* to stay on
mansuē·faciō -facĕre -fēcī -factum (*passive*: **mansuē·fīō -fiĕrī -factus sum**) *vt* to tame; (fig) to tame, pacify, civilize
mansu·ēs -is or **-ētis** *adj* tame, mild
mansu·escō -escĕre -ēvī -ētum *vt* to tame; *vi* to grow tame, become tame; (fig) to grow gentle, grow mild
mansuētē *adv* gently, mildly
mansuētūd·ō -ĭnis *f* mildness, gentleness
mansuēt·us -a -um *adj* tame; mild, gentle
mansus *pp* of **mando** and **maneo**
mantēl·e -is *n* napkin, towel
mantell·um or **mantēl·um -ī** *n* mantle
mantĭc·a -ae *f* knapsack
manticĭn·or -ārī -ātus sum *vi* to predict, prophesy
mant·ō -āre *vt* to wait for; *vi* to stay, remain, wait
Mant·ō -ūs *f* prophetic daughter of Tiresias

Mantŭ·a -ae *f* birthplace of Virgil, in N. Italy

manuāl·is -e *adj* that can be held in hand, hand-sized (*e.g., rocks*)

manubĭ·ae -ārum *f pl* money derived from the sale of booty

manubiārĭ·us -a -um *adj* (coll) bringing in the loot

manūbr·ĭum -ĭī or **-ī** *n* handle; hilt

manufestārĭ·us -a -um *adj* plain, obvious

manulĕ·a -ae *f* long sleeve

manuleār·ĭus -ĭī or **-ī** *m* sleeve maker

manuleāt·us -a -um *adj* long-sleeved

manūmissĭ·ō -ōnis *f* manumission, freeing of a slave

manŭ·mittō or **manū·mittō -mittĕre -mīsī -missum** *vt* to manumit, emancipate, set free (*a slave*)

manupret·ĭum -ĭī or **-ī** *n* workman's pay, wages; (fig) pay, reward

man·us -ūs *f* hand; band, company; gang; force, violence, close combat; finishing touch; handwriting; work; workmanship; elephant's trunk; grappling irons; power; (law) power of the husband over his wife; **ad manum habere** to have at hand, have in readiness; **ad manum venire** to come within reach; **e manu** at a distance, from a distance; **in manibus esse** to be in everyone's hands, be well known; to be near, be at hand; to be present; **in manu esse** (with *genit*) to be in the power of, be under the jurisdiction of; **in manu esse** (with *dat*) to be obvious to; **inter manus** under one's hands, with one's care; in one's hands, in one's arms; **manibus pedibusque** (fig) with might and main; **manu** by hand, artificially; (mil) by force of arms; **manu tenere** to know for sure; **manum committere, conserere,** or **conferre** to begin to fight; **manum dare** to lend a hand; **manum injicere** (with *dat*) to lay hands on, arrest; **manus dare** or **manus dedere** to give oneself up, surrender; **per manus** by hand; by force, by main force; from hand to hand, from mouth to mouth, from father to son; **plenā manu** generously; **prae manibus** or **prae manu** at hand, in readiness; **sub manu** or **sub manum** at hand, near; immediately

mapāl·ĭa -ĭum *n pl* African huts; African village, kraal

mapp·a -ae *f* napkin; flag (*used in starting races at the racetrack*)

Marăth·ōn -ōnis *f* site, in E. Attica, of victory by Miltiades over the Persians (490 B.C.)

Marcell·us -ī *m* Roman cognomen in the gens Claudia; M. Claudius Marcellus (*nephew of Augustus, whose premature death is referred to in the Aeneid,* 43-23 B.C.)

marc·ĕō -ēre *vi* to wither, droop, shrivel; to be weak, be feeble, be decrepit, be run-down; to slack off

marcesc·ō -ĕre *vi* to begin to wither, begin to droop; to become weak, become run-down; to become lazy

marcĭd·us -a -um *adj* withered, drooping; groggy

Marc·ĭus -ĭī or **-ī** *m* Ancus Marcius (*fourth king of Rome*)

marcŭl·us -ī *m* small hammer

mar·e -is *n* sea; seawater, saltwater; **mare inferum** Tyrrhenian Sea; **mare nostrum** Mediterranean Sea; **mare superum** Adriatic Sea

Mareōt·a -ae *f* town and lake near Alexandria in Egypt

Mareōtĭc·us -a -um *adj* Mareotic; Egyptian

margarīt·a -ae *f* or **margarīt·um -ī** *n* pearl

margĭn·ō -āre *vt* to furnish with a border; to curb (*a street*)

marg·ō -ĭnis *f* margin, edge, border; frontier

Mariān·ī -ōrum *m pl* partisans of Marius

Marīc·a -ae *f* nymph of Minturnae, mother of Latinus

marīn·us -a -um *adj* sea, of the sea, marine

marisc·a -ae *f* fig; **tumidae mariscae** the piles

marīt·a -ae *f* wife, married woman

marītāl·is -e *adj* marital, nuptial, matrimonial

maritĭmus or **maritŭm·us -a -um** *adj* sea, of the sea; seafaring, maritime; (fig) changeable (*like the sea*); **ora maritima** seacoast; *n pl* seacoast

marīt·ō -āre *vt* to marry; to train (*a vine to a tree*)

marīt·us -a -um *adj* matrimonial nuptial; *m* husband, married man; lover; *f* see **marita**

Mar·ĭus -ĭī or **-ī** *m* C. Marius (*conqueror of Jugurtha and of the Cimbri and Teutons, and seven times consul,* 157-86 B.C.)

marm·or -ŏris *n* marble; marble statue, marble monument; smooth surface of the sea

marmorĕ·us -a -um *adj* marble, made of marble; marble-like

Mar·ō -ōnis *m* cognomen of Virgil

marr·a -ae *f* hoe, weeding hook

Mar·s -tis *m* god of war and father of Romulus and Remus; battle, war; engagement; planet; **aequo Marte** on an equal footing; **suo Marte** by one's own exertions, independently

Mars·ī -ōrum *m pl* Marsians (*a people of S. central Italy, regarded as tough warriors*)

marsupp·ĭum -ĭī or **-ī** *n* pouch, purse

Marsȳ·ās or **Marsȳ·a -ae** *m* satyr who challenged Apollo with the flute and was flayed alive upon his defeat; statue in the Roman forum of Marsyas

Martiāl·is -is *m* M. Valerius Martialis (*commonly called Martial and famous for his epigrams, c.* 40-120 A.D.)
Marticŏl·a -ae *m* worshiper of Mars
Martĭ·us -a -um *adj* Martian, of Mars; sacred to Mars; descended from Mars; March; *m* March, month of March
mās maris *adj* male, masculine; manly, masculine, brave; *m* male
masculīn·us -a -um *adj* male, masculine
mascŭl·us -a -um *adj* male, masculine; manly, vigorous; *m* male
mass·a -ae *f* mass, lump; (coll) chunk of money
Massĭc·us -a -um *adj* Massic; *m* Mt. Massicus (*between Latium and Campania, famous for its wine*); *n* Massic (*wine*)
Massilĭ·a -ae *f* Greek colony on S. coast of Gaul (*modern Marseilles*)
Massȳl·ī -ōrum *m pl* tribe of E. Numidia
mastigĭ·a ae *m* rascal
mastrūc·a -ae *f* sheepskin; (as term of abuse) ninny
mastrūcāt·us -a -um *adj* clothed in sheepskin
matăr·a -ae or **matăr·is -is** *f* Celtic javelin
matell·a -ae *f* chamber pot
matellĭ·ō -ōnis *m* pot
māt·er -ris *f* mother; matron; **mater familias** lady of the house; (of animals) dam; cause, origin, source
mātercŭl·a -ae *f* a little mother, poor mother
māt·erfamiliās -risfamiliās *f* lady of the house, mistress of the household
māterĭ·a -ae or **māterĭ·ēs -ēī** f matter, stuff, material; lumber, wood, timber; fuel; subject, subject matter, theme, topic; cause, source, occasion, opportunity; capacity, natural ability, disposition
māteriār·ĭus -ĭī or **-ī** *m* timber merchant
māteriāt·us -a -um *adj* built with lumber; **male materiatus** built with poor lumber
māterĭēs see **materia**
māterĭ·or -ārī -ātus sum *vi* to fetch or gather wood
mātern·us -a -um *adj* maternal, mother's, of a mother
mātertĕr·a -ae *f* aunt, mother's sister
mathēmatĭc·us -ī *m* mathematician; astrologer
Matīn·us -ī *m* mountain in Apulia, near Horace's birthplace
mātricīd·a -ae *m* matricide, mother's murderer
mātricīd·ĭum -ĭī or **-ī** *n* matricide, murder of one's mother
mātrimōn·ĭum -ĭī or **-ī** *n* matrimony, marriage; **in matrimonium ire** to enter matrimony, get married; **in matrimonium aliquam ducere** to marry some girl
mātrīm·us -a -um *adj* having a mother still living
mātrōn·a -ae *f* married woman, matron, wife; woman of quality, lady
Mātrōnāl·ĭa -ĭum *n pl* festival celebrated by matrons on March 1 in honor of Mars
mātrōnāl·is -e *adj* matronly, womanly, wifely
matt·a -ae *f* straw mat
matŭl·a -ae *f* pot; chamber pot
mātūrātē *adv* in good time
mātūrē *adv* at the right time; in time; betimes, in good time, promptly, quickly; prematurely
mātūr·escō -escĕre -ŭī *vi* to get ripe, ripen, mature
mātūrĭt·ās -ātis *f* ripeness, maturity; (fig) maturity, height, perfection
mātūr·ō -āre *vt* to ripen, bring to maturity; to accelerate, speed up; (with *inf*) to be too quick in doing; *vi* to hasten
mātūr·us -a -um *adj* ripe, mature, full-grown; opportune, at the right time; early, coming early (*e.g., winter*); advanced in years; marriageable; mellow (*with age*)
Mātūt·a -ae *f* goddess of the dawn
mātūtīn·us -a -um *adj* morning, early; **tempora matutina** morning hours
Mauritānĭ·a -ae *f* country of N.W. Africa
Maur·us -a -um *adj* Moorish; African
Maurūsĭ·us -a -um *adj* Moorish, Mauretanian
Māvor·s -tis *m* Mars
Māvortĭ·us -a -um *adj* Martian, of Mars
maxill·a -ae *f* jaw
maximē *or* **maxŭmē** *adv* very, most, especially, particularly; just, precisely, exactly; (in sequences) in the first place, first of all; (in affirmations) by all means, certainly, yes; **immo maxime** certainly not; **nuper maxime** just recently; **quam maxime** as much as possible; **tum cum maxime** at the precise moment when; **tum maxime** just then, precisely at that time; **ut maxime . . . ita maxime** the more . . . so much the more
maximĭt·ās -ātis *f* magnitude
maxĭmus or **maxŭmus** (*superl* of **magnus**) see **magnus**
mazonŏm·us -ī *m* large dish
meāmet = **meā,** *abl fem sing* of **meus,** strengthened by **-met**
meapte = **mea,** *nom fem sing* of **meus,** strengthened by **-pte**
meāt·us -ūs *m* motion, movement; course, channel
mecastor *interj* by Castor!
mēd = **me**
mēcum = **cum me**
medd·ix or **med·ix -ĭcis** *m* magis-

trate (*among the Oscans*); **meddix tuticus** senior magistrate (*among the Oscans*)
Mēdē·a -ae *f* daughter of Aeetes, the king of Colchis, and wife of Jason, famous for her magic
Mēdē·is -ĭdis *adj* magic
med·ens -entis *m* physician
med·ĕor -ērī *vt* to heal; *vi* (with *dat*) to heal, cure, be good for, remedy
Mēd·ī -ōrum *m pl* Medes; Persians; Parthians
Mēdĭ·a -ae *f* Asian country between Armenia, Parthia, Hyrcania, and Assyria
mediastīn·us -ī *m* servant, drudge
mēdic·a -ae *f* alfalfa
medicābĭl·is -e *adj* curable
medicām·en -ĭnis *n* medicine, remedy, drug, antidote; tincture; cosmetic; (fig) cure, remedy
medicāment·um -ī *n* medication, medicine; potion; (fig) relief, antidote; (rhet) embellishment
medicāt·us -ūs *m* magic charm
medicīn·a -ae *f* medicine, medical science; medicine, remedy; doctor's office; (with *genit*) (fig) cure for, remedy for
medĭc·ō -āre *vt* to medicate, cure; to dye
medĭc·or -ārī -ātus sum *vt* to cure; *vi* (with *dat*) to heal, cure
medĭc·us -a -um *adj* medical; healing; *m* doctor, surgeon
Mēdĭc·us -a -um *adj* Median, of the Medes
medĭē *adv* moderately
medĭĕt·ās -ātis *f* mean
medimn·um -ī *n* or **medimn·us -ī** *m* bushel, medimnus (*containing six modii*)
mediŏcr·is -e *adj* medium, average, ordinary; mediocre; narrow, small
mediocrĭt·ās -ātis *f* mean; moderation; mediocrity; *f pl* moderate passions
mediocrĭter *adv* moderately, fairly; not particularly, not very, not much; calmly
Mediolān·um -ī *n* Milan
medioxŭm·us -a -um *adj* (coll) in the middle
meditāment·um -ī *n* practice, drill
meditātē *adv* purposely
meditātĭ·ō -ōnis *f* reflection, contemplation; practice; rehearsal; (with *genit*) reflection on, contemplation of
meditāt·us -a -um *adj* premeditated
mediterrānĕ·us -a -um *adj* inland
medĭt·or -ārī -ātus sum *vt* to think over, reflect on; to practice; to plan, design
medĭ·us -a -um *adj* middle, central, the middle of, in the middle; intervening (*time*); middling, ordinary, common; undecided, neutral, ambiguous; meddling; **in mediā insulā** in the middle of the island; **media pārs** half, one half; *m* mediator; *n* middle, center; community, common good; public, publicity; **e medio abire** to disappear; **in medio relinquere** to leave undecided, leave hanging in the air; **in medium** into the center; on behalf of the public; for the common good; **in medium proferre** to publish
medius fidĭus *interj* by Heaven!
med·ix -icis *m* magistrate (*among the Oscans*); **medix tuticus** senior magistrate
medull·a -ae *f* marrow; middle, center
medullĭtus *adv* (fig) with all one's heart
Medūs·a -ae *f* one of the three Gorgons, the daughter of Phorcys, whose eyes turned everything they looked upon into stone
Medūsae·us -a -um *adj* Medusan; **equus Medusaeus** Pegasus
Megaer·a -ae *f* one of the three Furies
Megalens·ĭa or **Megalēs·ĭa -ĭum** *n pl* festival of Cybele, celebrated on the 4th of April
Megăr·a -ae *f* or **Megăr·a -ōrum** *n pl* town near Athens
Megarē·us or **Megarĭc·us -a -um** *adj* Megarean
megistān·es -um *m pl* grandees
mehercle or **mehercŭle** or **mehercŭles** *interj* by Hercules!
mēi·ō -ĕre *vi* to urinate
mel mellis *n* honey; **meum mel** (as term of endearment) my honey!; *n pl* drops of honey
melancholĭc·us -a -um *adj* melancholy
melandrȳ·um -ī *n* piece of salted tuna
Melanth·ĭus -ĭī or **-ī** *m* goatherd of Ulysses
melcŭl·um -ī *n* (*term of endearment*) little honey
Meleăg·er or **Meleăg·ros -rī** *m* son of King Oeneus of Calydon and participant in the famous Calydonian boar hunt
Meleagrĭd·es -um *f pl* sisters of Meleager, who were changed into birds
Melicert·a or **Melicert·ēs -ae** *m* son of Ino and Athamas, who was changed into a sea god, called by the Greeks Palaemon and by the Romans Portunus
melĭc·us -a -um *adj* musical; lyric
melilōt·os -ī *m* clover
melimēl·a -ōrum *n pl* honey apples
melīn·a -ae *f* mead
mēlīn·a -ae *f* leather wallet
Mēlīn·um -ī *n* pigment; Melian white
melĭ·or -us (*comp* of **bonus**) *adj* better
melisphyll·um -ī *n* balm
Melĭt·a or **Melĭt·ē -ēs** *f* Malta
Melitens·is -e *adj* Maltese
melĭus (*comp* of **bene**) *adv* better
meliuscŭlē *adv* pretty well

meliuscŭl·us -a -um *adj* a little better
mell·a -ae *f* mead
mellicŭl·us -a -um *adj* sweet as honey
mellĭf·er -ĕra -ĕrum *adj* honey-producing
mellifĭc·ō -āre *vi* to make honey
mellill·a -ae *f* (term of endearment) little honey
mellīn·a -ae *f* sweetness, delight
mellīn·a -ae *f* leather wallet
mellīt·us -a -um *adj* honeyed, sweetened with honey; sweet as honey
mel·os -ī (Greek *pl*: **mel·e**) *n* tune, melody, song
Melpomĕn·ē -ēs *f* Muse of tragic poetry
membrān·a -ae *f* membrane, skin; slough; parchment; film
membrānŭl·a -ae *f* small piece of parchment
membrātim *adv* limb by limb; piecemeal, singly; in short sentences
membr·um -ī *n* limb, member; part, division; clause
mēmet *pron* (emphatic form of **me**) me
memĭn·ī -isse *vt* to remember; *vi* (with *genit*) to be mindful of, remember
Memn·ōn -ŏnis *m* son of Tithonus and Aurora, king of the Ethiopians, and ally of the Trojans, who was killed by Achilles
Memnŏnĭd·es -um *f pl* birds that rose from the pyre of Memnon
Memnŏni·us -a -um *adj* Memnonian; Oriental, Moorish, black
mem·or -ŏris *adj* mindful, remembering; having a good memory; reminding; (with *genit*) mindful of, remembering
memorābĭl·is -e *adj* memorable, remarkable
memorand·us -a -um *adj* worth mentioning, notable
memorāt·us -ūs *m* mention
memorĭ·a -ae *f* memory; remembrance; period of recollection, recollection, time, lifetime; a memory, past event, history; historical account; **memoriae prodere** to hand down to posterity; **paulo supra hanc memoriam** not long ago; **post hominum memoriam** within the memory of man; **superiore memoriā** in earlier times
memoriŏl·a -ae *f* weak memory
memorĭter *adv* from memory, by heart; accurately, correctly
memŏr·ō -āre *vt* to mention, bring up, relate; to name, call; *vi* (with **de** + *abl*) to speak of
Memph·is or **-ĭdos** *f* city in central Egypt
Memphitĭc·us -a -um *adj* Egyptian
Menand·er or **Menand·ros -rī** *m* Greek comic playwright, the most important representative of the Attic New Comedy (342-291 B.C.)
Menandrē·us -a -um *adj* of Menander
mend·a -ae *f* fault, blemish
mendāciloquĭ·or -us *adj* more false, more mendacious
mendāc·ium -iī or **-ī** *n* lie
mendāciuncŭl·um *n* white lie, fib
mend·ax -ācis *adj* mendacious, given to lying, false; *m* liar
mendicābŭl·um -ī *n* beggar
mendicĭt·ās -ātis *f* beggary
mendĭc·ō -āre or **mendĭc·or -ārī -ātus sum** *vt* to beg, beg for; *vi* to beg, go begging
mendicŭl·us -a -um *adj* beggarly
mendĭc·us -a -um *adj* needy, poor, poverty-stricken; (fig) poor, sorry, paltry; *m* beggar
mendōsē *adv* faultily, carelessly
mendōs·us -a -um *adj* full of physical defects; full of faults, faulty, incorrect, erroneous; blundering
mend·um -ī *n* defect, fault; blunder
Menelā·us -ī *m* son of Atreus, brother of Agamemnon, and husband of Helen
Menen·ius -iī or **ī** *m* Menenius Agrippa (*patriotic Roman who told the plebs the fable of the belly and the limbs during the secession of the plebs in* 494 B.C.)
Menoec·eus -ĕī or **-ĕos** *m* son of Theban king Creon, who hurled himself off the city walls to save the city
Menoetiăd·ēs -ae *m* Patroclus
Menoet·ius -iī or **-ī** *m* father of Patroclus
men·s -tis *f* mind, intellect; understanding, reason; thought, opinion, intention, plan; courage, boldness; passion, impulse; idea; feeling, heart, soul; purpose; **addere mentem** to give courage; **captus mente** crazy; **demittere mentem** to lose heart; **in mentem venire** to come to mind; **mentis suae esse** to be in one's right mind
mens·a -ae *f* table; meal, course, dinner; guests at table; counter; bank; sacrificial table, altar; **mensa secunda** dessert
mensār·ius -iī or **-ī** *m* banker; treasurer, treasury-board member
mensĭ·ō -ōnis *f* measure, measuring; quantity (*of a syllable*)
mens·is -is *m* month; **primo mense** at the beginning of the month
mens·or -ōris *m* surveyor
menstruāl·is -e *adj* for a month
menstrŭ·us -a -um *adj* monthly; lasting for a month; *n* rations for a month; month's term of office
mensŭl·a -ae *f* little table
mensūr·a -ae *f* measuring, measurement; standard of measure; amount, size, proportion, capacity, extent, limit, degree
mensus *pp* of **metior**
ment·a or **menth·a -ae** *f* mint
mentĭ·ens -entis *m* sophism, fallacy
mentĭ·ō -ōnis *f* mention; **mentio-**

nem facere (with *genit* or **de** + *abl*) to make mention of; **mentiones serere** (with **ad** + *acc*) to throw hints to

ment·ior -īrī -ītus sum *vt* to invent, fabricate; to feign, imitate, fake; *vi* to lie; to act deceitfully

Ment·or -ōris *m* friend of Ulysses; famous artist in metalwork; ornamental cup

ment·um -ī *n* chin

mĕ·ō -āre *vi* to go, pass

mephīt·is -is *f* malaria

mepte *pron* (emphatic form of **mē**) me, me myself

merācŭl·us or **merācl·us -a -um** *adj* pretty pure, rather pure

merāc·us -a -um *adj* pure, unmixed, undiluted, straight

mercābĭl·is -e *adj* buyable

mercāt·or -ōris *m* merchant, trader, dealer, wholesale dealer

mercātōrĭ·us -a -um *adj* merchant, trading; **navis mercatoria** merchant ship

mercātūr·a -ae *f* trading, trade, commerce; purchase; *f pl* goods

mercāt·us -ūs *m* trade, traffic; market, marketplace; fair

mercēdŭl·a -ae *f* poor pay; low rent, low income

mercēnārĭ·us -a -um *adj* hired, paid, mercenary; *m* common laborer, servant

merc·ēs -ēdis *f* pay, wages, salary; bribe; reward, recompense; cost; injury, detriment; stipulation, condition, retribution, punishment; rent, income, interest

mercimōn·ĭum -ĭī or **-ī** *n* merchandise

mer·cor -ārī -ātus sum *vt* to deal in, trade in, purchase

Mercuriāl·is -e *adj* of Mercury; *m pl* corporation of merchants in Rome

Mercur·ĭus -ĭī or **-ī** *m* Mercury (*son of Jupiter and Maia, messenger of the gods, patron of commerce, diplomacy, lying, gambling, and conductor of departed souls to the world below*); Mercury (*planet*)

merd·a -ae *f* droppings, excrement

merend·a -ae *f* lunch, snack

mer·ĕo -ēre -ŭī -ĭtum or **mer·ĕor -ērī -ĭtus sum** *vt* to deserve, merit, be entitled to; to win, earn, acquire, merit; *vi* to serve; to serve in the army; (with **de** + *abl*) to serve, render service to, do a favor for; **bene de re publica merere** or **mereri** to serve one's country well; **de te merui** I have done you a favor, I have treated you well; **equo merere** to serve in the cavalry

meretrīcĭ·us -a -um *adj* prostitute's

meretrīcŭl·a -ae *f* cute little wench

merĕtr·ix -īcis *f* prostitute, harlot, wench, strumpet

merg·ae -ārum *f pl* pitchfork

merg·es -ĭtis *f* sheaf

mergō mergĕre mersī mersum *vt* to dip, plunge, sink; to engulf, swallow up; to swamp, overwhelm, bury, drown; **mergi** to sink, drown; to go bankrupt

merg·us -ī *m* diver (*bird*)

merīdiān·us -a -um *adj* midday, noon; southern, southerly

merīdiātĭ·ō -ōnis *f* siesta

merīdĭ·ēs -ēī *m* midday, noon; south; **spectare ad meridiem** to face south

merīdĭ·ō -āre *vi* to take a siesta

Mērĭŏn·ēs -ae *m* charioteer of Idomeneus

merĭtō *adv* deservedly, rightly

merĭt·ō -āre *vt* to earn regularly

meritōr·ĭus -a -um *adj* rented, hired; *n pl* rented apartment

merĭt·us -a -um *adj* deserved, just, right, proper, deserving; guilty; *n* service, favor, kindness; blame, fault, offense; merit, worth

merobĭb·us -a -um *adj* drinking unmixed wine

Merŏp·ē -ēs *f* one of the Pleiades, the daughter of Atlas and Pleione

Mer·ops -ŏpis *m* king of Ethiopia, husband of Clymene, and reputed father of Phaethon

mer·ops -ŏpis *f* bee eater (*bird*)

mers·ō -āre *vt* to keep dipping or plunging, to immerse; (fig) to engulf; **mersari** (with *dat*) to plunge into

mersus *pp* of **mergo**

merŭl·a -ae *f* blackbird

mer·us -a -um *adj* pure, unmixed, undiluted, unadulterated; (fig) undiluted; (fig) nothing but, mere; *n* wine

mer·x -cis *f* merchandise, wares; **mala merx** (fig) bad lot

Messallīn·a -ae *f* wife of the Emperor Claudius; wife of Nero

Messān·a -ae *f* town in N.E. Sicily

Messāpĭ·us -a -um *adj* Apulian; *f* town and district in S.E. Italy, named after the mythical founder Messapus

mess·is -is *f* harvest; harvest time; **adhuc tua messis in herba est** (fig) don't count your chickens before they are hatched

mess·or -ōris *m* reaper, mower

messōr·ĭus -a -um *adj* reaper's

messus *pp* of **meto**

mēt·a -ae *f* marker for measuring the distance at a racetrack; (fig) goal, end; (fig) turning point, critical moment

metall·um -ī *n* metal; *n pl* mine

metamorphōs·is -is *f* transformation

metaphŏr·a -ae *f* metaphor

mētāt·or -ōris *m* planner; **metator urbis** city planner

Metaur·us -ī *m* small river in Umbria, at the banks of which Hasdrubal was defeated in 207 B.C.

Metell·us -ī *m* Roman surname; Q. Caecilius Metellus Numidicus (*commander of the Roman forces against Jugurtha from* 109 B.C. *until replaced by Marius in* 107 B.C.)
Methymn·a -ae *f* town on the island of Lesbos
mētior mētīrī mensus sum *vt* to measure; to traverse, travel; to judge, estimate; (with *dat*) to measure (*something*) out to, distribute (*something*) among; (with *abl*) to judge (*someone*) by the standard of
metō metĕre messŭī messum *vt* to reap, mow, gather, collect, harvest; (fig) to mow down (*e.g., with the sword*)
mēt·or -ārī -ātus sum *vt* to measure off; to lay out (*e.g., a camp*)
metrēt·a -ae *f* liquid measure (*about nine gallons*)
metuculōs·us -a -um *adj* fearful; scary
metŭ·ens -entis *adj* afraid, apprehensive, anxious
metŭ·ō -ĕre -ī *vt* to fear, be afraid of; *vi* to be afraid, be apprehensive
met·us -ūs *m* fear, anxiety, apprehension
me·us -a -um *adj* my; *pron* mine; **meā interest** it is of importance to me; **meum est** (with *inf*) it is my duty to; **meus est** (coll) I've got him
Mezent·ius -iī or **-ī** *m* Etruscan tyrant of Caere, slain by Aeneas
mī = mihi
mīc·a -ae *f* crumb, morsel
Micips·a -ae *m* son of Masinissa and king of Numidia (148-118 B.C.); *m pl* (fig) Numidians, Africans
mic·ō -āre *vi* to vibrate, quiver, twinkle, sparkle, flash
mictur·iō -īre *vi* to have to urinate
Mid·ās -ae *m* king of Phrygia, at whose touch everything turned to gold (*8th cent.* B.C.)
migrāti·ō -ōnis *f* moving, changing residence; metaphorical use
migrāt·us -ūs *m* transporting
migr·ō -āre *vt* to transport; (fig) to transgress, violate; *vi* to move, change residence, depart, migrate; (fig) to go away, change, turn
mīl·es -itis *m* soldier; infantryman; private; army
Mīlēsi·us -a -um *adj* Milesian, of Miletus
Mīlēt·us -ī *f* Miletus (*town on the W. coast of Asia Minor*)
mīl·ia -ium *n pl* thousands; see **mille**
mīliār·ium -iī or **-ī** *n* milestone
mīlitār·is -e *adj* military
mīlitārĭter *adv* in a military manner, like a soldier
mīlitāri·us -a -um *adj* soldierly, military
mīliti·a -ae *f* army; war; the military; military discipline; **militiae** in war, on the battlefield, in the army; **militiae domique** abroad and at home, on the war front and on the home front
mīlit·ō -āre *vt* to carry on (*war*); *vi* to serve as a soldier, be in the service
mil·ium -iī or **-ī** *n* millet
mille (indecl) *adj* thousand; *n* thousand; **mille homines** a thousand men; **milia** *n pl* thousands; **duo milia passuum** two miles
millēsim·us or **millensim·us -a -um** *adj* thousandth
milliār·ium -iī or **-ī** *n* milestone
milliens or **milliēs** *adv* a thousand times; innumerable times
Mil·ō -ōnis *m* T. Annius Milo (*friend of Cicero and enemy of Clodius, defended by Cicero on a charge of having murdered Clodius in* 52 B.C.)
Miltiăd·ēs -is *m* Athenian general victorious at Marathon (490 B.C.)
mīluīn·us -a -um *adj* rapacious
mīlŭ·us or **milŭ·os -ī** *m* kite (*bird of prey*); gurnard (*fish*)
Mīlŭ·us -ī *m* Kite (*constellation*)
mīm·a -ae *f* actress
Mimallŏn·is -idis *f* Bacchante
Mim·ās -antis *m* one of the giants
mīmĭcē *adv* like a mime actor
mīmic·us -a -um *adj* suitable for the mime, farcical
Mimnerm·us -ī *m* Greek elegiac poet of Colophon (*fl.* 560 B.C.)
mīmŭl·a -ae *f* miserable little actress
mīm·us -ī *m* mime, farce; actor of a mime; (fig) farce
min·a -ae *f* Greek coin (*about* 100 *denarii*)
minăci·ae -ārum *f pl* menaces, threats
minācĭter *adv* threateningly
min·ae -ārum *f pl* menaces, threats; projecting points of a wall
minanter *adv* threateningly
mināti·ō -ōnis *f* threatening
min·ax -ācis *adj* threatening, menacing; projecting, jutting out
min·ĕō -ēre *vi* to project, jut out
Minerv·a -ae *f* goddess of wisdom and of the arts and sciences, identified with Pallas Athene; (fig) skill, genius; spinning and weaving; **invitā Minervā** against one's better judgment
mingō mingĕre minxī mictum *vi* to urinate
miniān·us -a -um *adj* vermilion
miniātŭl·us -a -um *adj* reddish
minĭmē or **minŭmē** *adv* least of all, least, very little; by no means, certainly not, not in the least; **minume gentium** (coll) by no means
minĭm·us or **minŭm·us -a -um** (*superl* of **parvus**) *adj* smallest, least, very small; slightest, very insignificant; youngest; shortest (*time*); **minimus natu** youngest; *n* the least, minimum; lowest price; **minimo emere** to buy at a very low price; **minimo provocare** to

provoke for the least thing or on the flimsiest pretext
minī·ō -āre *vt* to color red, paint red
minist·er -rī *m* servant, attendant, helper; agent, tool, instrument
ministerĭum -ĭī or **-ī** *n* office, ministry, service, occupation, work, employment; retinue
ministr·a -ae *f* servant, attendant, helper; waitress; handmaid
ministrāt·or -ōris *m or* **ministrātr·ix -īcis** *f* assistant, helper
ministr·ō -āre *vt* to serve, wait on; to tend; to execute, carry out (*orders*); (with *dat*) to hand out (*something*) to; (with *abl*) to supply (*someone or something*) with
minitābund·us -a -um *adj* threatening
minĭt·ō -āre or **minĭt·or -ārī -ātus sum** *vt* to make threats of (*e.g., war*); (with *acc* of thing and *dat* of person) to threaten to bring (*e.g., evil, death*) upon, hold (*something*) threateningly over (*someone*); *vi* to make threats; (with *dat* of person threatened and *abl* of means) to threaten (*somone*) with
min·ĭum -ĭī or **-ī** *n* vermilion; red lead
Mīnō·is -ĭdis *f* Ariadne
Mīnōĭ·us or **Mīnō·us -a -um** *adj* of Minos, Cretan
min·or -ārī -ātus sum *vt* to threaten; to promise boastfully; (with *dat* of person and *acc* of thing) to threaten (*someone*) with (*something*), to hold (*something*) over (*someone*) as a threat; *vi* to jut out, project; to be menacing, make threats; (with *dat*) to threaten, make threats to
min·or -us (*comp* of **parvus**) *adj* smaller, less; less, shorter (*time*); younger; inferior, less important; (with *abl*) **a** (of time) too short for; **b** inferior to; **c** unworthy of; (with *inf*) unfit to, incapable of; **dimidio minor quam** half as small as; **minores facere filios quam** to think less of the sons than of; **minor natu** younger; *m pl* descendants, posterity; *n* less, smaller amount; **minoris emere** to buy at a lower price; **minus praedae** less booty
Mīn·ōs -ōis or **-ōnis** *m* son of Zeus and Europa, king of Crete, and, after his death, judge in the lower world; grandson of the former, likewise king of Crete, husband of Pasiphaë, and father of Ariadne and Phaedra
Mīnōtaur·us -ī *m* monstrous offspring of Pasiphaë, half man and half bull, and kept in the labyrinth
minŭmē see **minime**
minŭmus see **minimus**
min·ŭō -uĕre -ŭī -ūtum *vt* to diminish, lessen, reduce; to weaken, lower; to modify (*plans*); to settle (*controversies*); to limit, restrict (*authority*); to offend against, try to cheapen (*e.g., the majesty of the Roman people*); *vi* to diminish, abate, ebb; **minuente aestu** at ebbtide
minus *adv* less; not; by no means, not at all
minuscŭl·us -a -um *adj* rather small, smallish
minūt·al -ālis *n* hamburger, hash
minūtātim *adv* piecemeal; bit by bit
minūtē *adv* in a small-minded way
minūtŭl·us -a -um *adj* tiny
minūt·us -a -um *adj* small, minute; petty, narrow-minded
Minȳ·ae -ārum *m pl* Argonauts, the companions of Jason
Minȳ·ās -ae *m* mythical king of Thessaly
mīrābĭl·is -e *adj* wonderful, marvelous, amazing, extraordinary
mīrābilĭter *adv* wonderfully, amazingly
mīrābund·us -a -um *adj* full of amazement, astonished
mīrācŭl·um -ī *n* wonder, marvel; surprise, amazement
mīrand·us -a -um *adj* fantastic
mīrātĭ·ō -ōnis *f* admiration, wonder
mīrāt·or -ōris *m* admirer
mīrātr·ix -īcis *adj fem* admiring
mīrē *adv* wonderfully, uncommonly, strangely; **mire quam** it is strange how, strangely
mīrificē *adv* wonderfully
mīrific·us -a -um *adj* causing wonder, wonderful
mīrimŏdīs *adv* in a strange way
mirmill·ō -ōnis *m* gladiator (*who fought with Gallic arms*)
mīr·or -ārī -ātus sum *vt* to be amazed at, be surprised at; to look at with wonder, admire
mīr·us -a -um *adj* amazing, surprising, astonishing; wonderful; **mirum est** (with *acc & inf*) it is surprising that; **mirum quam** or **mirum quantum** it is amazing how, it is amazing to what extent
miscellānĕ·a -ōrum *n pl* hash
miscĕō miscēre miscŭī mixtum *vt* to mix, blend, mingle; to combine, associate, share; to mix up, confuse, turn upside down; to mix, prepare, brew
misell·us -a -um *adj* poor little
Mīsēn·um -ī *n* promontory and town near the bay of Naples
mis·er -ĕra -ĕrum *adj* poor; wretched, miserable, unhappy; sorry, worthless
miserābĭl·is -e *adj* miserable, pitiable; piteous
miserābilĭter *adv* pitiably; piteously
miserand·us -a -um *adj* pitiful, deplorable
miserātĭ·ō -ōnis *f* pity, compassion, sympathy; appeal for sympathy
misĕrē *adv* wretchedly, miserably, unhappily; pitifully; desperately
miser·ĕō -ēre -ŭī -ĭtum or **miser·ĕor -ērī -ĭtus sum** *vi* (with *genit*) to pity, feel sorry for, sympathize with; *v impers* (with *acc* of

person who feels pity and *genit* of object of pity), e.g., **miseret** or **miseretur me aliorum** I feel sorry for the others

miseresc·ō -ĕre *vi* to feel pity, feel sympathetic; (with *genit*) to pity, feel sorry for; *v impers* (with *acc* of person who feels pity and *genit* of object of pity), e.g., **me miserescit tui** I feel sorry for you, I pity you

miserĭ·a -ae *f* poverty; misery, unhappiness, distress, trouble

misericordĭ·a -ae *f* pity, sympathy, compassion; mercy

misericor·s -dis *adj* sympathetic, merciful

miserĭter *adv* sadly

misĕr·or -ārī -ātus sum *vt* to deplore; to pity; *vi* to feel pity

missicŭl·ō -āre *vt* to keep sending

missĭl·is -e *adj* missile, flying; *n pl* missiles

missĭ·ō -ōnis *f* release, liberation; sending off, despatching; military discharge; dismissal from office; cessation, end; **sine missione** without letup, to the death

missĭt·ō -āre *vt* to keep sending

missus *pp* of **mitto**

miss·us -ūs *m* letting go, throwing, hurling; sending

mītesc·ō -ĕre *vi* to grow mild, grow mellow, become ripe; (fig) to get soft; (fig) to become gentle, become tame

Mithr·ās -ae *m* Mithra (*sun-god of the Persians*)

Mithridāt·ēs -is *m* Mithridates the Great (*king of Pontus from* 120 B.C. *to* 63 B.C.)

Mithridātē·us or **Mithridātĭc·us -a -um** *adj* Mithridatic

mītigātĭ·ō -ōnis *f* mitigation, soothing

mītĭg·ō -āre *vt* to mellow, ripen; to soften; to calm down, appease, pacify

mīt·is -e *adj* mellow, ripe, soft; calm, placid; mild, gentle

mitr·a -ae *f* miter, turban

mittō mittĕre mīsī missum *vt* to send; let fly, throw, fling, launch; to emit, shed; to let out, utter; to let go of, drop; to free, release, discharge, dismiss; to pass over in silence, omit; to send for, invite; to pass up, forego; to dedicate (*a book*); to yield, produce, export; to dismiss, forget; **sanguinem mittere** to bleed; **sanguinem provinciae mittere** (fig) to bleed a province dry

mītŭl·us -ī *m* limpet

mixtim *adv* promiscuously

mixtūr·a -ae *f* mixing, blending

Mnēmosȳn·ē -ēs *f* mother of the Muses

mnēmosȳn·on -ī *n* souvenir

mōbĭl·is -e *adj* mobile, moveable, portable; nimble, active; shifty, changing; impressionable, excitable

mōbilĭt·ās -ātis *f* mobility; agility, quickness; shiftiness

mōbilĭter *adv* quickly, rapidly

mōbilĭt·ō -āre *vt* to impart motion to, endow with motion

moderābĭl·is -e *adj* moderate

moderām·en -ĭnis *n* control

moderanter *adv* under control

moderātē *adv* with moderation

moderātim *adv* gradually

moderātĭ·ō -ōnis *f* controlling, control, regulation, guidance; moderation, self-control; rules, regulation

moderāt·or -ōris *m* or **moderātr·ix -īcis** *f* controller, director, guide

moderāt·us -a -um *adj* controlled, well regulated, orderly, restrained

modĕr·ō -āre or **modĕr·or -ārī -ātus sum** *vt* to control, direct, guide; *vi* (with *dat*) **a** to moderate, restrain, put restraint upon; **b** to allay, mitigate

modestē *adv* with moderation, discreetly; modestly

modestĭ·a -ae *f* moderation, restraint; discretion; modesty, sense of shame, sense of honor, dignity; propriety; mildness (*of weather*)

modest·us -a -um *adj* moderate, restrained; modest, discreet; orderly, obedient

modiāl·is -e *adj* containing a modius or peck

modĭcē *adv* moderately, with restraint; in an orderly manner; only slightly

modĭc·us -a -um *adj* moderate; small; modest, unassuming; ordinary, puny, trifling

modificāt·us -a -um *adj* regulated (*in length*)

mod·ĭus -ĭī or **-ī** *m* modius, peck (*one sixth of a medimnus*); measure; **pleno modio** in full measure

modo *adv* only, merely, simply, solely; (of time) just now, just recently, lately; presently, in a moment; **modo . . . deinde** (or **tum** or **postea** or **interdum**) first . . . then, at one time . . . next time; **modo . . . modo** now . . . now, sometimes . . . sometimes, at one moment . . . at another; **non modo . . . sed etiam** or **verum etiam** not only . . . but also; *conj* if only, provided that

modulātē *adv* according to measure, in time; melodiously

modulāt·or -ōris *m* director, musician

modŭl·or -ārī -ātus sum *vt* to regulate the time of, measure rhythmically; to modulate; to sing; to play

modŭl·us -ī *m* small measure, small stature

mod·us -ī *m* standard of measurement, measure; time, rhythm; size; limit, boundary; rule, regulation; way, manner, mode; **ad modum** (with *genit*) or **in modum** (with *genit*) or **modo** (with *genit*) in the

manner of, according to the style of, like; **ejus modi homo** that kind of man; **hujus modi homo** this kind of man
moech·a -ae *f* adultress
moechiss·ō -āre *vt* to ravish, rape
moech·or -ārī -ātus sum *vi* to have an affair, commit adultery
moech·us -ī *m* adulterer
moen·ĭa -ĭum *n pl* town walls, ramparts, fortifications; fortified town; castle, stronghold; defenses
moenĭō see **munio**
moerus see **murus**
Moes·ī -ōrum *m pl* a people on the lower Danube
mol·a -ae *f* millstone; mill; flour; *f pl* mill
molār·is -is *m* millstone; molar (*tooth*)
mōl·ēs -is *f* mass, bulk, pile; massive structure, dam, mole, pier; mass (*of people, etc.*); burden, effort, trouble; calamity; might, greatness
molestē *adv* with annoyance; with difficulty, with trouble; **moleste ferre** to be annoyed at, be disgruntled at, just about stand
molestĭ·a -ae *f* annoyance, trouble; worry; affectation (*in style*)
molest·us -a -um *adj* annoying, troublesome, distressing; labored, affected (*style*)
mōlīm·en -ĭnis *n* great exertion, great effort; attempt, undertaking
mōlīment·um -ī *n* great exertion, great effort
mōl·ĭor -īrī -ītus sum *vt* to do with great effort, strain at, exert oneself over; to wield, heave, hurl; to work hard at; to build, erect; to rouse; to displace; to undertake, attempt; to perform; to cause, occasion; *vi* to exert oneself, struggle, take great pains
mōlītĭ·ō -ōnis *f* building, erection; demolition
mōlīt·or -ōris *m* builder
molĭtus *pp* of **molo**
molītus *pp* of **molior**
mollesc·ō -ĕre *vi* to become soft; to become gentle; to become effeminate
mollicŭl·us -a -um *adj* tender, dainty
moll·ĭō -īre -īvī or **-ĭī -ītum** *vt* to make soft, soften; (fig) to soften, mitigate; to demoralize
mollĭp·ēs -ĕdis *adj* soft-footed
moll·is -e *adj* soft; springy; flexible; flabby; mild, calm; easy; gentle (*slope*); sensitive, impressionable; tender, touching; weak, effeminate; amatory (*verses*); complaint; changeable, untrustworthy
mollĭter *adv* softly; gently, smoothly; effeminately; voluptuously; patiently, with fortitude
mollitĭ·a -ae or **mollitĭ·ēs -ēī** *f* softness; flexibility; tenderness; sensitivity; weakness, irresolution; effeminacy, voluptuousness
mollitūd·ō -ĭnis *f* softness; flexibility; susceptibility
mol·ō -ĕre -ŭī -ĭtum *vt* to grind
Moloss·us -a -um *adj* Molossian; *m* Molossian hound; *m pl* Molassians (*a people of Epirus*)
mōl·y -ȳos *n* magic herb
mōm·en -ĭnis *n* movement, motion; momentum
mōment·um -ī *n* movement, motion; alteration; turn, critical time; moment; impulse; momentum; influence, importance; motive
Mon·a -ae *f* Isle of Man
monēdŭl·a -ae *f* jackdaw
mon·ĕō -ēre -ŭī -ĭtum *vt* to call to mind, remind, advise, point out; to warn; to foretell; to teach, instruct, inform
monēr·is -is *f* galley
Monēt·a -ae *f* Juno Moneta, in whose temple on the Capitoline Hill money was kept; coin, money; stamp or die (*for money*)
monētāl·is -e *adj* of the mint; *m* (coll) money man
monīl·e -is *n* necklace
monim- = **monum-**
monĭt·a -ōrum *n pl* warnings; prophecies
monitĭ·ō -ōnis *f* reminder
monĭt·or -ōris *m* reminder, counselor; teacher
monĭt·us -ūs *m* reminder, warning
monogramm·us -a -um *adj* sketchy, shadowy
monopod·ium -ĭī or **-ī** *n* table with a single central leg
monotrŏp·us -a -um *adj* single, alone
mon·s -tis *m* mountain, mountain range; mass, heap; hill; **montis auri polliceri** to make wild promises; **summus mons** mountain top
monstrātĭ·ō -ōnis *f* pointing out
monstrāt·or -ōris *m* displayer; inventor
monstr·ō -āre *vt* to show, to point out, exhibit, make known, advise, teach; to appoint, institute, ordain; to advise, urge
monstr·um -ī *n* sign, portent, wonder; warning; monster, monstrosity; miracle, marvel
monstruōsē *adv* unnaturally
monstruōs·us -a -um *adj* unnatural, strange, monstrous
montān·us -a -um *adj* mountain, of a mountain; mountainous; *m pl* mountaineers; *n pl* mountainous regions
monticŏl·a -ae *m* mountaineer, highlander
montivăg·us -a -um *adj* wandering over the mountains
montōs·us or **montuōs·us -a -um** *adj* mountainous
monument·um -ī *n* reminder; monument, memorial; record (*written or oral*); token of identification
Mopsopĭ·us -a -um *adj* Athenian; *f* Attica, Athens

mor·a -ae *f* delay; pause; spell, period of time; stop-off; division of the Spartan army consisting of from three to seven hundred men
mōrāl·is -e *adj* moral
morāt·or -ōris *m* obstructionist; (in court) lawyer who spoke only to gain time
mōrāt·us -a -um *adj* -mannered; -natured; in character; **bene moratus** well-mannered; **male moratus** ill-mannered, rude
morbid·us -a -um *adj* sickly; causing sickness, unwholesome
morbōs·us -a -um *adj* debauched
morb·us -ī *m* sickness, disease; fault, vice; distress; **in morbum cadere** or **in morbum incidere** to fall sick
mordācius *adv* more bitingly; (fig) more radically
mord·ax -ācis *adj* biting, snapping; (fig) sharp, stinging, caustic, snarling; pungent (*taste*)
mordĕō mordēre momordī morsum *vt* to bite; to eat, devour; to bite, grip, (of cold) to nip; (of words) to cut, hurt; (of a river) to bite its way through
mordic·ēs -um *m pl* bites
mordicus *adv* by biting, with the teeth; (fig) tightly, doggedly
mōrē *adv* foolishly
morēt·um -ī *n* salad
moribund·us -a -um *adj* dying, at the point of death; mortal; deadly
mōrigĕr·ō -āre or **mōrigĕr·or -ārī -ātus sum** *vi* (with *dat*) to humor, pamper, yield to, comply with
mōrigĕr·us -a -um *adj* obedient, obsequious
morior morī mortŭus sum *vi* to die; (fig) to die out, wither, decay, pass away
morm·yr -ȳris *f* Pontic fish
mōrolŏg·us -a -um *adj* speaking nonsense, foolish
mor·or -ārī -ātus sum *vt* to delay, detain; to entertain, hold the attention of; to hinder, prevent; **nihil morari** (with *acc*) **a** to disregard, care nothing for, not value; **b** to have nothing against, have nothing to say against; *vi* to delay, linger, tarry, loiter; to stay, remain, wait; **quid moror?** or **quid multis morer?** why should I drag out the point?, to make a long story short
mōrōsē *adv* morosely, crabbily
mōrōsĭt·ās -ātis *f* moroseness, peevishness, crabbiness
mōrōs·us -a -um *adj* morose, peevish, crabby; fastidious, particular; (fig) stubborn (*disease*)
Morph·eus -ĕos *m* god of dreams
mors mortis *f* death; destruction; corpse; **mortem obire** to meet death; **mortis poena** death penalty; **sibi mortem consciscere** to commit suicide
mors·a -ōrum *n pl* bits, little pieces
morsiuncŭl·a -ae *f* peck, kiss
morsus *pp* of **mordeo**
mors·us -ūs *m* bite; pungency; grip; corrosion; gnawing pain; sting, vicious attack
mortāl·is -e *adj* mortal, subject to death; human, mortal; transient; man-made; *m* mortal, human being
mortālĭt·ās -ātis *f* mortality; mortals, mankind
morticīn·us -a -um *adj* dead; corpse-like, rotting
mortĭf·er or **mortif·ĕrus -ĕra -ĕrum** *adj* lethal, deadly
mortifĕrē *adv* mortally
mortuāl·ia -ium *n pl* dirges
mortŭ·us -a -um *pp* of **morior;** *adj* dead, deceased; withered, decayed; scared to death; *m* corpse
mōrŭl·us -a -um *adj* dark, black
mōr·um -ī *n* blackberry, mulberry
mōr·us -ī *f* mulberry tree
mōr·us -a -um *adj* foolish; *mf* fool
mōs mōris *m* caprice, mood; nature, manner; custom, usage, practice; fashion, style; rule, regulation, law; **de more** or **ex more** according to custom; **morem gerere** (with *dat*) to humor (*someone*); *m pl* morals, character, behavior; customs; laws
Mōs·ēs or **Moys·ēs -is** *m* Moses
mōtĭ·ō -ōnis *f* motion
mōt·ō -āre *vt* to keep moving, keep shifting
mōtus *pp* of **moveo**
mōt·us -ūs *m* motion, movement; gesture; dancing; change (*e.g., of fortune*); impulse, inspiration; emotion, passion; rebellion, riot; **motus animi** emotion; **motus terrae** earthquake
mov·ens -entis *adj* movable; **res moventes** personal property; *n pl* motives
movĕō movēre mōvī mōtum *vt* to move; to stir, shake, disturb; to dislodge (*the enemy*); to eject, expel; to degrade; to remove, take away; to plow; to cause, occasion, promote; to begin; to undertake; to trouble, torment; to move, influence, affect; to dissuade; to exert, exercise; to turn over in the mind, ponder; **se ex loco movere** to budge from the spot; **se movere** to dance; *vi* to move
mox *adv* soon, presently; hereafter; next, then, later on
Moys·ēs -is *m* Moses
mūcid·us -a -um *adj* sniveling, driveling; moldy, musty
Mūc·ius -iī or **-ī** *m* Roman family name
mūcr·ō -ōnis *m* sharp point, sharp edge; sword; edge, boundary; keenness
mūc·us -ī *m* nasal mucus
mūgient·ēs -ium *m pl* oxen
mūgil or **mūgĭl·is -is** *m* mullet
mugin·or -ārī -ātus sum *vi* to dillydally

mūg·iō -īre -īvī or **-iī -ītum** *vi* to bellow, low; to rumble, roar
mūgīt·us -ūs *m* bellowing, lowing; rumbling, roaring
mūl·a -ae *f* mule
mulcĕō mulcēre mulsī mulsum *vt* to stroke, pet; to stir gently; to soothe, alleviate; to appease; to flatter, delight
Mulcĭb·er -ĕrī or **-ĕris** *m* Vulcan; fire
mulc·ō -āre *vt* to beat, cudgel; to mistreat, injure
mulctr·a -ae *f* milk pail
muctrār·ĭum -iī or **-ī** or **muctr·um -ī** *n* milk pail
mulgĕō mulgēre mulsī mulsum or **mulctum** *vt* to milk
muliĕbr·is -e *adj* woman's, womanly, feminine; womanish, effeminate
muliebrĭter *adv* like a woman; effeminately
mulĭ·er -ĕris *f* woman; wife
mulierārĭ·us -a -um *adj* woman's; *m* woman chaser, wolf
muliercŭl·a -ae *f* little woman; little hussy
mulierōsĭt·ās -ātis *f* weakness for women
mulierōs·us -a -um *adj* woman-crazy
mūlīn·us -a -um *adj* mulish
mūlĭ·ō -ōnis *m* mule driver
mūliōnĭ·us -a -um *adj* mule driver's
mullŭl·us -ī *m* little mullet
mull·us -ī *m* mullet
muls·us -a -um *pp* of **mulceo;** *adj* honeyed, sweet as honey; *f* (term of endearment) honey; *n* mead (*wine mixed with honey*)
mult·a -ae *f* fine; penalty; loss of money; **multam certare** to contest a fine; **multam committere** to incur a fine; **multam dicere** (with *dat* of person and *acc* of the fine) to fine (*someone a certain amount*); **multam subire** to incur a fine, be fined
multa *adv* much, very, greatly, earnestly
mult·a -ōrum *n pl* many things; much; **ne multa** in short, to be brief
multangŭl·us -a -um *adj* many-angled
multātīcĭ·us -a -um *adj* fine, of a fine; **multaticia pecunia** fine
multātĭ·ō -ōnis *f* fine, penalty
multēsĭm·us -a -um *adj* trifling, negligible
mult·ī -ōrum *m pl* many men, many; multitude, mass, common people
multibĭb·us -a -um *adj* heavy-drinking
multicăv·us -a -um *adj* porous
multīcĭ·a -ōrum *n pl* diaphanous garments
multifārĭam *adv* in many places
multifĭd·us -a -um *adj* divided into many parts; (of a river) having many tributaries; **dens multifida** comb
multiform·is -e *adj* multiform, manifold
multifŏr·us -a -um *adj* many-holed; (flute) having many stops
multigenĕr·is -e or **multigĕn·us -a -um** *adj* of many kinds, various, complex
multijŭg·is -e or **multijŭg·us -a -um** *adj* yoked together; (fig) various, complex
multilŏqu·ax -ācis *adj* talkative
multiloqu·ium -iī or **-ī** *n* talkativeness
multilŏqu·us -a -um *adj* talkative
multimŏdīs *adv* in many ways
multĭpl·ex -ĭcis *adj* with many folds; winding, labyrinthine, serpentine; manifold; many; (in implied comparisons) many times as great, far greater; varied, complicated; changeable, versatile, many-sided; sly,, cunning; *n* manifold return
multiplicābĭl·is -e *adj* manifold, many
multiplicĭter *adv* in various ways
multiplĭc·ō -āre *vt* to multiply, increase, enlarge
multipŏt·ens -entis *adj* mighty, powerful
multitūd·ō -ĭnis *f* great number, multitude, crowd, throng; rabble, common people
multivŏl·us -a -um *adj* passionate
multō *adv* (with comparatives) much, far, by far, a great deal; **multo aliter ac** far otherwise than, much different from; **multo ante** long before; **multo post** long after; **non multo secus fieri** to turn out just about the same
mult·ō -āre *vt* to punish, fine
mult·us -a -um (*comp:* **plures;** *superl:* **plurimus**) *adj* many a, much, great; abundant, considerable, extensive; tedious, long-winded; full, numerous, thick, loud, heavy, constant; **ad multum diem** till late in the day; **multā nocte** late at night; **multo die** late in the day; (with plural nouns) many; *m pl* see **multi;** *n* much; **multi** of great value, highly; **multi facere** to think highly of, make much of, think much of; **multum est** it is of great importance; **multum temporis** a great deal of time, much time; *n pl* see **multa**
multum *adv* much, greatly, very, often, frequently, far; (with comparatives) much, far; **multum valere** to have considerable influence
mūl·us -ī *m* mule
Mulvĭ·us -a -um *adj* Mulvian; **Mulvius pons** Mulvian bridge (*across the Tiber, above Rome, on the Via Flaminia*)
Mumm·ius -iī or **-ī** *m* L. Mummius Achaicus (*conqueror of Corinth,* 146 B.C.)
mundān·us -ī *m* world citizen

mundē or **munditer** *adv* neatly, cleanly

munditi·a -ae or **munditi·ēs -ēī** *f* neatness, cleanness; elegance; politeness

mundŭl·us -a -um *adj* trim, neat, sharp

mund·us -a -um *adj* neat, clean, nice; fine, smart, sharp, elegant; choice (*words*); *m* neat person; world, universe, heavens; earth, mankind; beauty aids

mūnerigerŭl·us -ī *m* bearer of presents

mūnĕr·ō -āre or **munĕr·or -ārī -ātus sum** *vt* to reward, honor, present; (with *acc* of thing and *dat* of person) to present to

mūnĭ·a -ōrum *n pl* official duties or functions

mūnĭc·eps -ĭpis *m* or *f* citizen of a municipality; fellow citizen, fellow countryman

mūnicipāl·is -e *adj* municipal; (as term of contempt) provincial, country

mūnicip·ĭum -ĭī or **-ī** *n* municipality, town (*whose people were Roman citizens, but otherwise autonomous*)

mūnifĭcē *adv* generously

mūnificentĭ·a -ae *f* generosity

mūnifĭc·ō -āre *vt* to treat generously

mūnifĭc·us -a -um *adj* generous; splendid

mūnīm·en -ĭnis *f* defense

mūnīment·um -ī *n* defense, protection, fortification, rampart; (fig) shelter, defense

mūn·ĭō or **moen·ĭō -īre -īvī** or **-ĭī -ītum** *vt* to wall, defend with a wall, fortify, strengthen, defend, protect, guard, secure; to build (*road*); (fig) to guard, shelter, protect, support

mūn·is -e *adj* obliging

mūnītĭ·ō -ōnis *f* building, fortifying, defending; fortification, rampart, trenches, lines; **munitio fluminum** bridging of rivers; **munitio viae** road construction

mūnīt·ō -āre *vt* to open up (*a road*)

mūnīt·or -ōris *m* builder, engineer

mūnīt·us -a -um *adj* fortified; (fig) protected, safe

mūn·us or **moen·us -ĕris** *n* service, function, duty; gift; service, favor, kindness; duty, tribute; public entertainment, gladiatorial show, extravaganza; tribute (*to the dead*), rite, sacrifice; public office

mūnuscŭl·um -ī *n* small present

mūraen·a -ae *f* moray (*eel-like fish*)

mūrāl·is -e *adj* wall; wall-destroying; wall-defending; **corona muralis** mural crown (*award for being the first to scale the enemy walls*)

mūr·ex -ĭcis *m* murex, mollusk (*yielding purple dye*); purple dye, purple; jagged rock; spiked trap (*as defense against cavalry attack*)

murĭ·a -ae *f* brine

muriātĭc·um -ī *n* pickled fish

mūricīd·us -ī *m* mouse killer; (fig) coward

murmill·ō -ōnis *m* gladiator with Gallic arms, who fought against a retarius

murm·ur -ŭris *n* murmur, murmuring; buzz, hum; roar, crash; growling, grumbling; rumbling; hubbub

murmurill·um -ī *n* low murmur

murmŭr·ō -āre *vi* to murmur; to mutter, grumble; to rumble, roar

murr·a or **murrh·a** or **myrrh·a -ae** *f* myrrh tree; myrrh

murrĕ·us or **myrrhĕ·us -a -um** *adj* made of myrrh; perfumed with myrrh; myrrh-colored, yellowish

murrĭn·us or **myrrhĭn·us -a -um** *adj* of myrrh; *f* drink flavored with myrrh; *n pl* vases

murt- = myrt-

mūr·us -ī *m* wall, city wall; dam, dike; rim (*of dish or pot*); (fig) wall, protection

mūs mūris *m* or *f* mouse, rat

Mūs·a -ae *f* Muse (*patron goddess of poetry, song, dance, literature, astronomy, etc.*); poem, song; talent, genius, taste; *f pl* studies

Mūsae·us -ī *m* mythical pre-Homeric bard and musician in the time of Orpheus

musc·a -ae *f* fly

muscār·ĭum -ĭī or **-ī** *n* fly swatter

muscipŭl·a -ae *f* or **muscipŭl·um -ī** *n* mousetrap

muscōs·us -a -um *adj* mossy

muscŭl·us -ī *m* little mouse; muscle; (mil) mantelet

musc·us -ī *m* moss

Mūsē·us or **Mūsae·us -a -um** *adj* of the Muses, musical, poetic

mūsĭc·a -ae or **mūsĭc·ē -ēs** *f* or **mūsĭc·ā -ōrum** *n pl* music, art of music (*including poetry*)

mūsĭcē *adv* pleasantly

mūsĭc·us -a -um *adj* musical; poetic; cultural; *m* musician

mussĭt·ō -āre *vt* to bear in silence; *vi* to be silent; to mutter, grumble

muss·ō -āre *vt* to bear in silence, bear silently; to brood over; *vi* to mutter, murmur; (of bees) to hum; to hesitate

mustācĕ·us -ī *m* or **mustācĕ·um -ī** *n* cake, wedding cake

mustell·a or **mustēl·a -ae** *f* weasel

mustellīn·us or **mustēlīn·us -a -um** *adj* of a weasel

must·um -ī *n* fresh grape juice, unfermented wine, must; vintage

mūtābĭl·is -e *adj* changeable; fickle

mūtābilĭt·ās -ātis *f* mutability; fickleness

mūtātĭ·ō -ōnis *f* mutation, change, alteration; exchange, interchange

mutĭl·ō -āre *vt* to cut off, lop off, crop; to mutilate; to reduce, shorten, lessen; to rob

mutĭl·us -a -um *adj* maimed, mutilated; defective

Mutīn·a -ae *f* town of N. central Italy, S. of the Po, which played a role in the civil war after the death of Julius Caesar
mūtiō see **muttio**
mūtītiō see **muttitio**
mūt·ō -āre *vt* to move, shift, change, alter; to exchange, interchange, barter, sell; to modify, transform, vary; to change for the better; to change for the worse; (with *abl* or **pro** + *abl*) to exchange or substitute (*something or someone*) for; *vi* to change
mūt·ō -ōnis *m* penis
mutt·iō or **mūt·iō -īre -īvī -ītum** *vi* to mutter, mumble
muttīti·ō or **mūtīti·ō -ōnis** *f* muttering, mumbling
mūtuāti·ō -ōnis *f* borrowing
mūtŭē *adv* mutually; in return
mūtuĭt·ō -āre *vt* to wish to borrow
mūtŭō *adv* mutually, in return
mūtŭ·or -ārī -ātus sum *vt* to borrow; to derive, obtain, get
mūt·us -a -um *adj* mute, speechless; silent, still; *n pl* brutes
mūtŭ·us -a -um *adj* mutual, reciprocal, interchangeable; borrowed, lent; *n* reciprocity; loan; **mutuum dare** (with **cum** + *abl*) to lend to (*someone*); **mutuas pecunias sumere** (with **ab** + *abl*) to borrow money from (*someone*); **mutuum argentum rogare** to ask for a loan of cash
Mycēn·ae -ārum *f pl* or **Mycēn·ē -ēs** *f* Mycene (*city of Agamemnon in Argolis*)
Mycēnae·us -a -um or **Mycēnens·is -e** *adj* Mycenean
Mycēn·is -ĭdis *f* Mycenaean girl (*Iphigenia*)
Mygdŏn·es -um *m pl* a people of Thrace, some of whom later migrated to Phrygia
Mygdonĭ·us -a -um *adj* Phrygian
myopăr·ō -ōnis *m* pirate ship
myrīc·a -ae or **myrīc·ē -ēs** *f* tamarisk
Myrmidŏn·es -um *m pl* Myrmidons (*people of Thessaly whom Achilles led in battle*)
Myr·ōn -ōnis *m* famous Greek sculptor, whose most famous work is the Discus Thrower, 5th cent. B.C.
myropōl·a -ae *m* perfumer
myropōl·ium -iī or **-ī** *n* perfume shop
myrrh- = **murr-**
myrtēt·um or **murtēt·um -ī** *n* myrtle grove
myrtĕ·us or **murtĕ·us -a -um** *adj* myrtle; crowned with myrtle
Myrtō·um mar·e (*genit:* **Myrtō·ī mar·is**) *n* sea between the Peloponnesus and the Cyclades
myrt·um -ī *n* myrtle berry
myrt·us -ūs or **-ī** *f* myrtle
Mȳsi·us -a -um *adj* Mysian; *f* Mysia (*country in N.W. Asia Minor*)
myst·a or **myst·ēs -ae** *m* priest of the mysteries of Ceres; an initiate
mystagōg·us -ī *m* initiator
mystēr·ium -iī or **-ī** *n* secret religion, secret service, secret rite or worship, divine mystery; secret; **mysteria facere** to hold service; **mysteria Romana** festival of Bona Dea
myst·ēs -ae *m* priest of the mysteries of Ceres
mystĭc·us -a -um *adj* mystic
Mytilēn·ae -ārum *f pl* or **Mytilēn·ē -ēs** *f* capital of the island of Lesbos

N

Nabatae·us -a -um *adj* Nabataean; Arabian, Eastern, Oriental; *m pl* Nabataeans; *f* Nabataea (*ancient Arab kingdom S.E. of Palestine*)
nabl·ium -iī or **-ī** *n* Phoenician harp (*an instrument of ten or twelve strings, played with both hands*)
nactus *pp* of **nanciscor**
Naeviān·us -a -um *adj* of Naevius
Naev·ius -iī or **-ī** *m* Cn. Naevius (*early Roman dramatic and epic poet,* c. 270-200 B.C.)
naev·us -ī *m* body mole
Nāi·as -ădis or **Nā·is -ĭdis** or **-ĭdos** *f* Naiad, water nymph
nam *conj* for; for instance; (transitional) now, but now, on the other hand
namque *conj* for, for in fact, for no doubt, for surely
nanciscor nanciscī nanctus sum or **nactus sum** *vt* to get by accident (*esp. by good luck*), obtain, chance upon, find
nān·us -ī *m* dwarf, midget
Napae·ae -ārum *f pl* dell nymphs
nāp·us -ī *m* turnip
Narb·ō -ōnis *m* town in S. Gaul, from which the province of Narbonese Gaul took its name
Narbōnens·is -e *adj* Narbonese
narciss·us -ī *m* narcissus
Narciss·us -ī *m* son of Cephisus and the nymph Liriope, who was changed into a flower of the same name; powerful freedman of Claudius
nard·um -ī *n* or **nard·us -ī** *f* nard, spikenard (*fragrant ointment*)
nār·is -is *f* nostril; *f pl* nostrils, nose; **acutae nares** keen perception; **homo naris obesae** dimwit;

naribus ducere to smell; **naribus uti** (with **ad** + *acc*) to turn up the nose at
narrābĭl·is -e *adj* to be told
narrātĭ·ō -ōnis *f* narration, narrative
narrātiuncŭl·a -ae *f* short story
narrāt·or -ōris *m* narrator, historian
narrāt·um -ī *n* account, statement, narrative
narrāt·us -ūs *m* narration, narrative
narr·ō -āre *vt* to tell, relate, narrate, recount; to describe; *vi* to speak, tell; **bene narrare** (with **de** + *abl*) to tell good news about (*someone*); **male narrare** (with **de** + *abl*) to tell bad news about (*someone*); **tibi narro** I'm telling you, I assure you
narthēc·ĭum -ĭī or **-ī** *n* medicine chest
narus see **gnarus**
Nārycĭ·us -a -um *adj* of Naryx (*city of the Opuntian Locrians and birthplace of Ajax Oileus*)
nascor nascī nātus sum or **gnātus sum** *vi* to be born; to rise, begin, originate, be produced, spring forth, proceed, grow, be found; **post homines natos** since the beginning of the world
Nās·ō -ōnis *m* Publius Ovidius Naso (*Roman poet, born in Sulmo, in central Italy,* 43 B.C.-*c.* 17 A.D.)
nass·a -ae *f* wicker trap (*for catching fish*); (fig) trap
nassitern·a -ae *f* large water jug
nasturc·ĭum -ĭī or **-ī** *n* garden cress
nās·us -ī *m* or **nās·um -ī** *n* nose; sense of smell; sagacity; anger; scorn; nozzle, spout
nāsūtē *adv* sarcastically
nāsūt·us -a -um *adj* big-nosed; satirical, sarcastic
nāt·a or **gnāt·a -ae** *f* daughter
nātālicĭ·us -a -um *adj* birthday, natal; *n pl* birthday party
nātāl·is -e *adj* of birth, natal; *m* birthday; *m pl* birth, origin, lineage
nat·ans -antis *m* or *f* fish
natātĭ·ō -ōnis *f* swimming
natāt·or -ōris *m* swimmer
nat·ēs -ĭum *f pl* buttocks, rear, rear end
nātĭ·ō -ōnis *f* race, stock; tribe, nation, people; (in contemptuous sense) breed, set
nat·is -is *f* buttock, rump; *f pl* see **nates**
nātīv·us -a -um *adj* born; inborn, innate, original; produced by nature, natural; primitive (*words*)
nat·ō -āre *vi* to swim, float; to flow; to swim, overflow, be flooded; (of the eyes) to be glassy; (of birds) to fly, glide; to waver, fluctuate, be uncertain; to hover, move to and fro
nātr·ix -īcis *f* water snake
nātūr·a -ae *f* blood relationship, natural affinity, birth; nature, natural constitution, quality, property; nature, natural disposition, character; physical nature, world, universe; order of the world, course of things; element, substance; reproductive organs
nātūrāl·is -e *adj* natural; by birth, one's own (*e.g., father, son*); produced by nature; according to nature
nātūrālĭter *adv* naturally, by nature
nāt·us or **gnāt·us -a -um** *pp* of **nascor;** *adj* born, made, destined, fit; (with *dat* or with **ad** or **in** or **propter** + *acc*) born for, made for, naturally suited to; (with **annos**) at the age of . . . , . . . years old, e.g., **annos viginti natus** at the age of twenty, twenty years old; **non amplius novem annos natus** no more than nine years old; **pro** or **e re nata** under the existing circumstances, as matters stand; *m* son; *m pl* children; *f* see **nata**
nauarch·us -ī *m* captain of a ship, skipper
nauclērĭc·us -a -um *adj* ship owner's, skipper's
nauclēr·us -ī *m* ship owner, skipper
nauc·um -ī *n* trifle; (mostly in genitive of value with a negative) **non nauci esse** to be of no value, be good for nothing; **non nauci facere** or **non nauci habere** to regard as worthless, regard as good for nothing
naufrag·ĭum -ĭī or **-ī** *n* shipwreck; wreck, ruin, destruction; wreckage; **naufragium facere** to be shipwrecked
naufrăg·us -a -um *adj* shipwrecked, wrecked, of the shipwrecked; causing shipwreck, dangerous to shipping; (fig) ruined; *m* shipwrecked person
naul·um -ī *n* fare
naumachĭ·a -ae *f* simulated sea engagement (*staged as an exercise or for amusement*)
nausĕ·a -ae *f* seasickness; vomiting, nausea
nausĕ·ō -āre *vt* to make (*someone*) throw up; (fig) to belch forth, throw up, utter; *vi* to be seasick; to vomit; to feel squeamish, feel disgust; to cause disgust
nauseŏl·a -ae *f* slight squeamishness
Nausică·a -ae *f* daughter of Alcinous, king of the Phaeacians
naut·a or **nāvĭt·a -ae** *m* sailor, seaman, mariner; captain
nautĕ·a -ae *f* nausea; stinking liquid
nautĭc·us -a -um *adj* nautical, sailors'; *m pl* sailors, seamen
nāvāl·is -e *adj* naval, of ships, of a ship; **castra navalia** camp for the protection of ships; **forma navalis** shape of a ship; *n* tackle, rigging; *n pl* dock, dockyard, shipyard; rigging

nāvicŭl·a -ae *f* small ship
nāviculārĭ·us -a -um *adj* of a small ship; *m* skipper; ship owner; *f* shipping business
nāvifrăg·us -a -um *adj* dangerous, treacherous, causing shipwreck
nāvigābĭl·is -e *adj* navigable
nāvigātĭ·ō -ōnis *f* sailing, navigation, voyage
nāvĭg·er -ĕra -ĕrum *adj* navigable
nāvig·ĭum -ĭī or **-ī** *n* ship
nāvĭg·ō -āre *vt* to sail across, navigate; *vi* to sail, put to sea; (fig) to swim
nāv·is -is *f* ship; **navem appellere** or **navem terrae applicare** to land a ship; **navem deducere** to launch a ship; **navem solvere** to set sail; **navem subducere** to beach a ship; **navis aperta** ship without a deck; **navis longa** battleship; **navis mercatoria** merchant vessel; **navis oneraria** transport, cargo ship; **navis praetoria** flagship; **navis tecta** ship with a deck
nāvĭt·a -ae *m* sailor, seaman; captain
nāvĭt·ās -ātis *f* energy, zeal
nāvĭter *adv* energetically, zealously, actively, busily; utterly, completely
nāv·ō -āre *vt* to do or perform energetically, conduct or prosecute with vigor; **operam navare** to act energetically; **operam navare** (with *dat*) to render assistance to
nāv·us or **gnāv·us -a -um** *adj* energetic, busy
Nax·os -ī *f* largest island of the Cyclades, famous for its wine and as the place where Theseus abandoned Ariadne
nē *interj* (always with a personal or demonstrative pronoun) indeed, certainly, surely; *adv* not; **ne . . . quidem** (to negate emphatically the words placed between) not even; (in negative commands) not; **ne timete** do not fear; *conj* that not, lest; (after verbs and nouns denoting fear) lest, that
-ne enclitic (introducing a question and added to the first important word of a clause)
nebŭl·a -ae *f* mist, fog, vapor; cloud; smoke; darkness, obscurity
nebŭl·ō -ōnis *m* loafer, good-for-nothing
nebulōs·us -a -um *adj* foggy
nec or **neque** *adv* not; *conj* nor, and not; **nec . . . et** not only not . . . but also; **nec . . . nec** or **neque . . . neque** neither . . . nor; **nec non** (introducing an emphatic affirmative) and certainly, and besides
necdum or **neque dum** *conj* and not yet, nor yet
necessārĭē or **necessārĭō** *adv* necessarily, of necessity
necessārĭ·us -a -um *adj* necessary, indispensable, needful, requisite; necessary, inevitable; pressing, urgent; connected by blood or friendship, related, closely connected; *mf* relative, kinsman; friend; *n pl* necessities
necesse (indecl) *adj* necessary; unavoidable, inevitable; requisite; **necesse esse** to be necessary; **necesse habere** to regard as necessary, regard as inevitable
necessĭt·ās -ātis *f* necessity, inevitableness, compulsion, urgency; requirement; privation, want; relationship, friendship, connection
necessitūd·ō -ĭnis *f* necessity, need, want, distress; relationship, bond, connection, relationship, friendship; *f pl* ties of friendship; relatives, friends, personal connections
necessum (indecl) *adj* necessary, requisite; inevitable
necne *adv* or not
necnōn *adv* also, besides, moreover
nec·ō -āre *vt* to kill, murder, slay, destroy
necopīn·ans -antis *adj* unaware
necopīnātō *adv* unexpectedly, by surprise
necopīnāt·us -a -um *adj* unexpected
necopīn·us -a -um *adj* unexpected; unsuspecting, careless, off guard
nect·ar -ăris *n* nectar (*drink of the gods*); nectar (*as term for honey, milk, wine, poetry, sweetness, etc.*)
nectarĕ·us -a -um *adj* of nectar, sweet or delicious as nectar
nectō nectĕre nexŭī or **nexī nexum** *vt* to tie, connect, fasten together, join; to weave; to clasp; to imprison, fetter; to devise, contrive; (fig) to attach, affix
nēcŭbi *conj* lest anywhere, so that nowhere
nēcunde *conj* lest from anywhere
nēdum *adv* (after an expressed or implied negative) much less, still less; (after an affirmative) not to say, much more
nefand·us -a -um *adj* unspeakable, impious, abominable
nefārĭē *adv* impiously, abominably
nefārĭ·us -a -um *adj* impious, abominable, criminal; *n* crime, criminal act
nefās (indecl) *n* crime, wrong, wickedness, act contrary to divine law, sin; criminal, monster; **per omne fas ac nefas** by hook or by crook
nefast·us -a -um *adj* forbidden, unlawful; impious, irreligious; criminal; unlucky, inauspicious; *n* crime, outrage
negātĭ·ō -ōnis *f* denial
negĭt·ō -āre *vt* to deny, refuse, turn down
neglectĭ·ō -ōnis *f* neglect
neglectus *pp* of **neglego**
neglect·us -ūs *m* neglect
neglĕg·ens -entis *adj* negligent, careless, indifferent
neglegenter *adv* carelessly
neglegentĭ·a -ae *f* negligence, carelessness, neglect
neg·lĕgō -legĕre -lexī -lectum *vt*

to be unconcerned about; to neglect, disregard, overlook; to slight, despise
neg·ō -āre *vt* to deny, refuse, decline; *vi* to say no; to refuse
negōtiāl·is -e *adj* business
negōti·ans -antis *m* business man
negōtiāti·ō -ōnis *f* banking, banking business
negōtiāt·or -ōris *m* business man; banker; salesman, dealer
negōtiŏl·um -ī *n* minor matter
negōti·or -ārī -ātus sum *vi* to do business, do banking; to trade
negōtiōs·us -a -um *adj* business; busy
negōt·ium -iī or **-ī** *n* business, occupation, employment; matter, thing, affair; situation; trouble; banking, money lending; trade, commerce; **negotium suum** private affairs; **quid negoti est?** what's the matter?; **quid negoti tibi est?** what business is it of yours?
Nēl·eus -ĕī or **-ĕos** *m* son of Neptune and the nymph Tyro, king of Pylos, and father of Nestor
Nemae·us -a -um *adj* Nemean
Nemĕ·a -ae or **Nemĕ·ē -ēs** *f* town in Argolis, where Hercules slew the Nemean lion and founded the Nemean games
Nemĕ·a -ōrum *n pl* Nemean games (*held every two years at Nemea*)
Nemĕs·is -is or **-ios** *f* goddess of vengeance
nēm·ō -inis *m* or *f* no one, nobody; **nemo quisquam** nobody at all; **nemo unus** no single person, no one by himself; **non nemo** someone, many a one
nemorāl·is -e *adj* sylvan
nemorens·is -e *adj* of a grove; of Diana's grove
nemoricultr·ix -īcis *f* denizen of the forest
nemorivăg·us -a -um *adj* roaming the woods
nemorōs·us -a -um *adj* wooded; covered with foliage
nempe *adv* (in confirmation or in sarcasm) certainly, to be sure, of course, naturally; (in questions) do you mean?
nem·us -ŏris *n* grove; sacred grove; plantation
nēnĭ·a or **naenĭ·a -ae** *f* funeral dirge; doleful song; incantation; ditty
neō nēre nēvī nētum *vt* to spin; to weave
Neoptolĕm·us -ī *m* Pyrrhus, the son of Achilles
nep·a -ae *f* scorpion; crab
Nephelē·is -ĭdos *f* Helle (*daughter of Nephele and Athamas*)
nep·ōs -ōtis *m* grandson; nephew; descendant; spendthrift
Nep·ōs -ōtis *m* Cornelius Nepos (*Roman biographer and friend of Cicero,* c. 100- c. 25 B.C.)
nepōtŭl·us -ī *m* little grandson
nept·is -is *f* granddaughter
Neptūnĭ·us -a -um *adj* of Neptune
Neptūn·us -ī *m* Neptune (*god of the sea and brother of Jupiter*)
nēquam (indecl) *adj* worthless, bad, good for nothing
nēquāquam *adv* by no means, not at all
neque see **nec**
nequĕdum see **necdum**
nequ·ĕō -īre -īvī or **-iī -ītum** *vi* to be unable; (with *inf*) to be unable to, not to be able to, be incapable of; **nequit** (with **quin**) it is impossible to
nēquĭ·or -us *adj* (*comp* of **nequam**) worse, more worthless
nēquīquam or **nēquicquam** *adv* pointlessly, for nothing, to no purpose; without good reason; with impunity
nēquissĭm·us -a -um *adj* (*superl* of **nequam**) worst, most worthless
nēquĭter *adv* worthlessly, wretchedly, miserably, vilely, wrongly
nēquitĭ·a -ae or **nēquitĭ·ēs -ēī** *f* worthlessness, vileness, wickedness
Nērē·is -ĭdis *f* sea nymph, Nereid (*daughter of Nereus, of whom there were* 50)
Nēr·eus -ĕī or **-ĕos** *m* son of Oceanus and Tethys, husband of Doris and father of the Nereids; sea
Nērīn·ē -ēs *f* daughter of Nereus
Nērĭtĭ·us -a -um *adj* of Neritos; **Neritius dux** Ulysses
Nērĭt·os or **Nērĭt·us -ī** *m* island near Ithaca
Nēr·ō -ōnis *m* Nero Claudius Caesar (*Roman emperor* 38-68 A.D.; *reigned* 54-68 A.D.)
Nērōniān·us -a -um *adj* Nero's, Neronian
Nerv·a -ae *m* M. Cocceius Nerva (*Roman emperor* 30-98 A.D., *reigned* 96-98 A.D.)
nervōsē *adv* strongly, vigorously
nervōs·us -a -um *adj* sinewy, brawny, strong
nervŭl·us -ī *m* a little vigor
nerv·us -ī *m* sinew, tendon, muscle; string, wire; bowstring; thong, strap; penis; leather covering of a shield; prison; power, vigor, strength, nerve, force, energy
nesc·iō -īre -īvī or **-iī -ītum** *vt* not to know, be ignorant of, be unacquainted with; (with *inf*) **a** not to know how to; **b** to be unable to; **nescio modo** somehow or other; **nescio quando** sometime or other; **nescio quid** something or other; **nescio quis** someone or other
nescĭ·us -a -um *adj* unaware, not knowing, ignorant; unknown; (with *genit* or **de** + *abl*) ignorant of, unaware of; (with *inf*) not knowing how to, unable to, incapable of; (with *acc & inf*) unaware that, not knowing that
Ness·us -ī *m* centaur who was slain by Hercules with a poisoned arrow for trying to molest his wife
Nest·or -ŏris *m* son of Neleus, king

of Pylos, and wise counselor of the Greeks at Troy

neu see **neve**

neut·er -ra -rum *adj* neither (*of two*); neuter; of neither sex; *pron* neither one (*of two*)

neutĭquam or **ne utĭquam** *adv* on no account, in no way

neutrō *adv* to neither side

neutrŭbi *adv* in neither the one place nor the other

nēve or **neu** *conj* or not, and not; **neve . . . neve** or **neu . . . neu** neither . . . nor

nex necis *f* death, murder, slaughter

nexĭl·is -e *adj* tied up, bound together

nex·um -ī *n* slavery for debt; voluntary servitude for debt

nex·us -a -um *pp* of **necto;** *m* free person who has pledged his person as security for a debt

nex·us -ūs *m* grip; bond; enslavement for debt

nī *adv* not; **quid ni?** why not?; *conj* (in prohibition or negative purpose) that not; (in negative condition) if not, unless

nīcētēr·ĭum -ĭī or **-ī** *n* prize

nic·ō -ĕre -ī *vi* to beckon

nict·ō -āre *vi* to wink; (with *dat*) to wink at

nīdāment·um -ī *n* material for a nest

nīd·or -ōris *m* steam, vapor, smell

nīdŭl·us -ī *m* little nest

nīd·us -ī *m* nest; (fig) home; *m pl* nestlings, brood

nig·er -ra -rum *adj* black; swarthy, dark; dismal; unlucky, ill-omened; black, bad (*character*); malicious

nigr·ans -antis *adj* black, dusky

nigr·escō -escĕre -ŭī *vi* to grow black, grow dark

nigr·ō -āre *vi* to be black

nigr·or -ōris *m* blackness, darkness

nihil or **nīl** (indecl) *n* nothing; (with *genit*) no, not a bit of; **nihil boni** no good, not a bit of good; **nil est** it is pointless, it's no good

nihil or **nīl** *adv* not, not at all, in no respect

nihilōmĭnus *adv* nonetheless, nevertheless, just the same; no less

nihĭl·um or **nīl·um -ī** *n* nothing; **de nihilo** for nothing, for no reason; **nihil est quod, cur,** or **quam ob rem** there is no reason why; **nihili esse** to be worthless, be of no value; **nihili facere** or **nihili pandere** to consider as worthless; **nihilo minus** nonetheless, nevertheless; **nihil quicquam** nothing whatever, nothing at all; **pro nihilo putare** to regard as worthless

nīl see **n'hil**

Nīliăc·us -a -um *adj* Nile, of the Nile, Egyptian

Nīligĕn·a -ae *masc & fem adj* born on the Nile, Egyptian

nīlum see **nihilum**

Nīl·us -ī *m* Nile River; god of the Nile

nimbāt·us -a -um *adj* light, frivolous

nimbĭf·er -ĕra -ĕrum *adj* stormy

nimbōs·us -a -um *adj* stormy, rainy

nimb·us -ī *m* cloud; storm cloud, black rain cloud; rainstorm, heavy shower, pouring rain; (fig) storm

nimĭō *adv* far, much; **nimio plus** far more, much more

nīmīrum *adv* no doubt, certainly, surely; (ironically) doubtless, of course

nimis *adv* very, very much, too much; **non nimis** not particularly

nimĭum *adv* too, too much; very, very much; **nimium quam** or **nimium quantum** very much indeed, ever so much, very; **nimium quam es barbarus** you are as barbarous as can be; **non nimium** not particularly, not very much

nimĭ·us -a -um *adj* very much, very great; too great, excessive; *n* excess, abundance

ningit (or **ninguit**) **ningĕre ninguit** (or **ninxit**) *v impers* it is snowing

ningu·ēs -ĭum *f pl* snowflakes, snow

Nin·us -ī *m* son of Belus, the first king of Assyria, husband of Semiramis, and builder of Nineveh; Nineveh

Niŏb·a -ae or **Niŏb·ē -ēs** *f* daughter of Tantalus and wife of Amphion, who was turned into a weeping mountain after Apollo and Diana had slain her seven sons and seven daughters

Nīr·eus -ĕī or **-ĕos** *m* handsomest Greek at Troy

Nīsē·is -ĭdis *f* Scylla (*daughter of Nisus*)

nisi *conj* unless, if not; except, but

nīsus *pp* of **nitor**

nīs·us or **nix·us -ūs** *m* pressure, effort; labor pain (*of childbirth*); soaring, flight; posture; **nisu immotus eodem** immobile in the same posture

Nīs·us -ī *m* king of Megara, father of Scylla, who betrayed her country by cutting off his purple lock of hair; friend of Euryalus in the Aeneid

nītēdŭl·a -ae *f* dormouse

nit·ens -entis *adj* shining, bright; brilliant; beautiful, glowing with beauty, glamorous; sleek (*cattle*); greasy

nit·ĕō -ēre -ŭī *vi* to shine, gleam, glisten; to be glamorous; to glow with health; (of animals) to be sleek; to be greasy; to be flashy

nit·escō -escĕre -ŭī *vi* to become shiny, become bright; to begin to glow (*with health or beauty*); to grow sleek

nitĭdē *adv* brightly

nitidiuscŭlē *adv* somewhat more sprucely

nitidiuscŭl·us -a -um *adj* a little more shiny

nitĭd·us -a -um *adj* shining, bright; glowing (*with health or beauty*); shiny, greasy; glamorous, flashy; smart, spruce, handsome; cultivated, refined; sleek (*cattle*)
nit·or -ōris *m* brightness, sheen; luster; glamour, beauty, healthy glow; elegance (*of style*); dignity (*of character*)
nītor nītī nixus sum (usually in the literal sense) or **nīsus sum** (usually in the figurative sense) *vi* to make an effort, struggle, strain, strive; to be in labor; to push forward, advance, climb, fly; to contend, insist; (with *abl* or **in** + *acc*) to lean on, support oneself on; (with *abl* or **in** + *abl*) (fig) to depend on, rely on, trust to; (with **ad** + *acc*) to aspire to; (with *inf*) to try to, endeavor to, struggle to
nitr·um -ī *n* soda; soap, cleanser
nivāl·is -e *adj* snowy; covered with snow; cold, wintry; (fig) cold, chilly
nivĕ·us -a -um *adj* of snow, snowy, snow; covered with snow; snow-white
nivōs·us -a -um *adj* snowy
nix nivis *f* snow; *f pl* (fig) grey hair
nix·or -ārī -ātus sum *vi* to struggle hard; (with *abl*) to lean upon, rest on
nixus *pp* of **nitor**
nix·us -ūs see **nisus**
nō nāre *vi* to swim, float; to sail; to fly; (of eyes) to be glazed
nōbĭl·is -e *adj* known; noted; notable, famous; notorious; noble; thorough-bred (*horse*); fine, excellent; *m pl* notables, nobles
nōbilĭt·ās -ātis *f* fame, renown; noble birth; the nobility; excellence
nōbilĭt·ō -āre *vt* to make famous; to make notorious
noc·ens -entis *adj* harmful; guilty criminal
noc·ĕō -ēre -ŭī -ĭtum *vi* (with *dat*) to harm, injure
nocīv·us -a -um *adj* harmful, injurious
noctĭf·er -ĕrī *m* evening star
noctilūc·a -ae *f* moon
noctivăg·us -a -um *adj* night-wandering
noctū *adv* by night, at night
noctŭ·a -ae *f* owl
noctuābund·us -a -um *adj* traveling by night
noctuīn·us -a -um *adj* of owls
nocturn·us -a -um *adj* nocturnal, of night, at night, by night, night
noctuvigĭl·us -a -um *adj* awake at night
nocŭ·us -a -um *adj* harmful, injurious
nōd·ō -āre *vt* to tie in a knot, knot, tie
nōdōs·us -a -um *adj* knotty
nōd·us -ī *m* knot; knob, knot (*in wood*); girdle; bond, tie; obligation; knotty point, difficulty, crisis
nōlō nolle nōlŭī *vt* (with *inf*) to be unwilling to, wish not to, refuse to; *vi* to be unwilling
nom·as -ădis *m* or *f* nomad; Numidian
nōm·en -ĭnis *n* name; gentile name (*e.g., Julius, as distinct from the praenomen*); race, stock; title; noun; bond, claim, debt; debtor; name, fame, reputation; title, pretext, pretense, excuse, account, reason, responsibility, authority, sake, behalf; mere name (*as opposed to reality*); **aetatis nomine** on the pretext of age, on account of age; **eo nomine** on that account; **nomen dare** or **nomen profiteri** to enlist (*in the army*); **nomen deferre** (with *genit*) to bring an accusation against, accuse (*someone*); **nomen dissolvere** or **nomen expedire** or **nomen solvere** to liquidate an account, pay a debt; **nomina sua exigere** to collect one's debt
nōmenclāt·or -ōris *m* name caller (*slave who accompanied his master and identified those whom they met, esp. during a political campaign*)
nōminātim *adv* by name, expressly
nōminātĭ·ō -ōnis *f* nomination for office
nōminātīv·us -a -um *adj & m* nominative
nōmināt·us -a -um *adj* renowned
nōminĭt·ō -āre *vt* to usually call
nōmĭn·ō -āre *vt* to name, call by name; to mention by name; to make famous; to nominate for an office; to denounce, arraign
nomism·a -ătis *n* coin
nōn *adv* not; no; by no means
Nōn·ae -ārum *f pl* Nones (*fifth day in all months, except March, May, July, and October, in which they occurred on the seventh*)
nōnāgensĭm·us or **nōnāgēsĭm·us -a -um** *adj* ninetieth
nōnāgĭens or **nōnāgĭēs** *adv* ninety times
nōnāgintā (indecl) *adj* ninety
nōnān·us -a -um *adj* of the ninth legion; *m* soldier of the ninth legion
nōnārĭ·a -ae *f* prostitute
nondum *adv* not yet
nongent·ī -ae -a *adj* nine hundred
nonne *adv* is it not?; (in indirect questions) whether not; **nonne vides?** don't you see?, you see, don't you?; **quaeritur nonne ire statim velis** the question is whether you do not wish to go at once
nonnull·us -a -um *adj* some, many a; **nonnulli** some, some people
nonnunquam *adv* sometimes
nonnusquam *adv* in some places
nōn·us -a -um *adj* ninth; *f* ninth hour
nōn·us decĭm·us -a -um *adj* nineteenth
Noric·us -a -um *adj* of Noricum; *n* region between the Danube and the Alps
norm·a -ae *f* square (*carpenter's tool*); (fig) rule, standard
nōs *pron* we; us

noscĭt·ō -āre *vt* to examine closely, observe; to recognize, know

noscō noscĕre nōvī nōtum or **gnoscō — gnōvī gnōtum** *vt* to get to know, become acquainted with, recognize, learn; to examine, inquire into; to approve of; **novisse** to have become acquainted with, (*and therefore*) to know

nosmet *pron* (emphatic form of **nōs**) we ourselves; us

nost·er -ra -rum *adj* our, our own; *pron* ours; **noster** our friend; **nostri** our men, our soldiers, our side

nostr·ās -ātis *adj* native, of our country

not·a -ae *f* note, mark, sign; letter, character; note, short letter; punctuation mark; brand (*of wine*); marginal note, critical mark; tattoo marks, brand; distinctive mark, distinctive quality; stamp (*on coin*); brand, stigma; nickname; black mark (*against one's name*); reproach, disgrace; nod, sign, beck; *f pl* letters of the alphabet; shorthand notes; memoranda

notābĭl·is -e *adj* notable, noteworthy, memorable; notorious

notābilĭter *adv* notably, remarkably; perceptibly

notār·ĭus -ĭī or **-ī** *m* stenographer; secretary

notātĭ·ō -ōnis *f* notation, mark; black mark (*of a censor*); choice; observation; etymology

notāt·us -a -um *adj* noted, distinguished

nōt·escō -escĕre -ŭī *vi* to become known

noth·us -a -um *adj* bastard, illegitimate; mongrel; not genuine, phoney

nōtĭ·ō -ōnis *f* acquaintance; (law) investigation; (fig) notion, idea

nōtitĭ·a -ae or **nōtitĭ·ēs -ēī** *f* acquaintance; fame; notion, conception

not·ō -āre *vt* to mark; to mark out; to note, mark, observe; to write down; to record; to take down in shorthand; to mark critically; to brand; to indicate, denote; to brand, reproach

not·us or **not·os -ī** *m* south wind; wind

nōt·us -a -um *pp* of **nosco;** *adj* known, well known; notorious; familiar, customary; *m pl* acquaintances

novācŭl·a -ae *f* razor

novāl·is -is *f* or **novāl·e -is** *n* field plowed for the first time, reclaimed land; cultivated field; fallow land; crops

novātr·ix -īcis *f* renovator, renewer (*female*)

novē *adv* newly, in an unusual manner

novell·us -a -um *adj* new, fresh, young, newly acquired

novem (indecl) *adj* nine

Novemb·er or **Novemb·ris -re** *adj* & *m* November

novendĕcim or **novemdĕcim** (indecl) *adj* nineteen

novendiāl·is or **novemdiāl·is -e** *adj* nine-day; occurring on the ninth day

novensĭl·ēs -ĭum *m pl* new gods (*introduced from abroad*)

novēn·ī -ae -a *adj* in groups of nine, nine each, nine

noverc·a -ae *f* stepmother

novercāl·is -e *adj* stepmother's, of a stepmother, like a stepmother

novīcĭ·us -a -um *adj* new, brand new

novĭens or **novĭēs** *adv* nine times

novissĭmē *adv* very recently, of late

novissĭm·us -a -um *adj* latest, last, most recent; **novissimum agmen** (mil) the rear; **novissima verba** parting words; *m pl* (mil) rear guard

novĭt·ās -ātis *f* newness, novelty; rareness, strangeness, unusualness; novelty of high rank, recently acquired rank

nov·ō -āre *vt* to make new, renovate, renew; to repair, fix; to refresh; to change, alter; to invent, coin (*words*); **res novare** to bring about a revolution

nov·us -a -um *adj* new, young, fresh, novel; strange, unusual, unheard-of; recent, modern; new, unused; inexperienced; renewed, revived; **homo novus** self-made man (*first man of a family to reach a curule office*); **res novae** political innovations, revolution; *n* news

nox noctis *f* night; night activity; sleep; death; darkness, blindness; mental darkness, ignorance; gloom; **ad multam noctem** till late at night; **nocte** or **de nocte** at night, by night; **noctem et dies** night and day; **sub noctem** at nightfall

nox·a -ae *f* harm, injury; offense, fault, guilt, responsibility; punishment

noxĭ·us -a -um *adj* harmful, noxious; guilty; (with *genit* or *abl*) guilty of; *f* harm, damage, injury; blame, guilt; fault, offense; **in noxia esse** to be at fault

nūbēcŭl·a -ae *f* little cloud; gloomy expression

nūb·ēs -is *f* or **nūb·is -is** *m* cloud; gloom; veil

nūbĭf·er -ĕra -ĕrum *adj* cloudy; cloud-capped (*mountain*); cloud-bringing (*wind*)

nūbigĕn·a -ae *adj masc* or *fem* born of clouds

nūbĭl·is -e *adj* marriageable

nūbĭl·us -a -um *adj* cloudy; cloud-bringing (*wind*); troubled; dark, gloomy, melancholy

nūbō nūbĕre nupsi nuptum *vi* (of women) to marry; (with *dat*) to marry (*a man*), be married to (*a man*)

nucifrangibŭl·um -ī *n* (colloquially of teeth) nutcracker

nuclĕ·us -ī *m* nut; kernel, stone (*of fruit*)

nudius *adv* it is now the . . . day since, e.g., **nudius tertius dedi ad te epistolam** it is now the third day since I mailed you a letter; ago, e.g., **nudius tertius decimus** twelve days ago

nūd·ō -āre *vt* to strip, bare; to lay bare, uncover; (mil) to leave undefended; (with *abl*) to divest of

nūd·us -a -um *adj* nude, naked; lightly clothed; bare, empty; defenseless; poor, needy; bare, mere, simple, sole, only; (with *genit* or *abl* or with **ab** + *abl*) bare of, without, stripped of, destitute of, deprived of

nūg·ae -ārum *f pl* trifles, nonsense; good-for-nothing, a nobody

nūgāt·or -ōris *m* joker; fibber, babbler, braggart

nūgātōrĭ·us -a -um *adj* worthless, useless, nonsensical

nūg·ax -ācis *adj* nonsensical

nūgivend·us -ī *m* dealer in women's apparel

nūg·or -ārī -ātus sum *vi* to talk nonsense; (with *dat*) to trick, cheat

null·us -a -um *adj* no; (coll) not, not at all; non-existent, of no account; *pron* none

num *adv* (of time, used only with **etiam**) now, e.g., **etiam num** now, even now, still; *interrog particle* (expecting negative answer) surely not, really, actually, e.g., **num ista est nostra culpa?** is that really our fault?, that isn't our fault, is it?; *conj* (in indirect questions) whether

Num·a -ae *m* Numa Pompilius (*second king of Rome*)

numcŭbi *adv* ever?, at any time?

numell·a -ae *f* shackle

nūm·en -ĭnis *n* nod; will, consent; divine will; divine power, divinity; deity, godhead

numerābĭl·is -e *adj* easily counted, few in number

numerāt·um -ī *n* ready cash

numĕrō *adv* at the right time, just now; too soon

numĕr·ō -āre *vt* to number, count; to pay out (*money*); to consider; to enumerate, mention; to relate, recount; to reckon as one's own, possess, own

numerōsē *adv* rhythmically

numerōs·us -a -um *adj* numerous; rhythmical

numĕr·us -ī *m* member; (mil) division, troop; mere cipher; class, category; rank, position; estimation, regard; rhythm, meter, verse; quantity, measure; portion (*of work*), part, function; **aliquo numero esse** to be of some account; **in numero haberi** (with *genit*) to be regarded as, be ranked among; **nullo numero esse** to be of no account; *m pl* mathematics, astronomy

Numĭd·a -ae *m* Numidian

Numidĭ·a -ae *f* Numidia (*a country of N. Africa*)

Numidĭc·us -a -um *adj* Numidian

Numĭt·or -ōris *m* king of Alba, brother of Amulius, father of Ilia, and grandfather of Romulus and Remus

nummārĭ·us -a -um *adj* financial; mercenary

nummāt·us -a -um *adj* rich; **bene nummatus** well-off, well-to-do

nummulār·ĭus -ĭī or **-ī** *m* banker

nummŭl·ī -ōrum *m pl* petty cash

numm·us -ī *m* coin, cash, money; sesterce (*small silver coin, worth about a nickel*); small sum, trifle, mere nothing; **in nummis habere** to have in ready cash

numquam or **nunquam** *adv* never; **non numquam** sometimes

numquid *adv* (to introduce direct question): **numquid meministi?** do you remember?; (to introduce indirect question): whether

nunc *adv* now; nowadays, today; now, in view of this, but as matters now stand; **nunc . . . nunc** at one time . . . at another, once . . . once

nuncupātĭ·ō -ōnis *f* name, appellation; public pronouncing (*of vows*)

nuncŭp·ō -āre *vt* to name, call; to take or make (*a vow*) publicly; to proclaim publicly

nundĭn·ae -ārum *f pl* market day; marketplace, market town; trade, sale

nundināl·is -e *adj* market

nundinātĭ·ō -ōnis *f* trading, bargaining, buying and selling

nundĭn·or -ārī -ātus sum *vt* to buy; *vi* to hold a market, attend a market; to trade; to gather in large numbers

nundĭn·um -ī *n* market time; **trinum nundinum** period of three market times, i.e., seventeen days

nunq- = **numq-**

nuntiātĭ·ō -ōnis *f* announcement (*by an augur*)

nuntĭ·ō -āre *vt* to announce, declare, report, relate

nuntĭ·us -a -um *adj* bringing news; *m* messenger, courier; news, message; order, injunction; **nuntium remittere** (with *dat*) to send a letter of divorce to, to divorce (*a wife*); *n pl* message, news

nūper *adv* recently

nūpĕr·us -a -um *adj* recent

nupt·a -ae *f* bride, wife

nuptĭ·ae -ārum *f pl* marriage, wedding

nuptiāl·is -e *adj* nuptial, wedding

nur·us -ūs *f* daughter-in-law; young lady, young married woman

nusquam *adv* nowhere; on no occasion; for nothing, to nothing; **nus-**

quam alibi nowhere else; **nusquam esse** to not exist; **nusquam gentium** nowhere in the world
nūt·ō -āre *vi* to keep nodding; to sway to and fro, totter; to hesitate, waver
nūtrīcāt·us -ūs *m* nursing (*of babies*)
nūtrīc·ĭus -ĭī or **-ī** *m* tutor
nūtrīc·ō -āre or **nūtrīc·or -ārī -ātus sum** *vt* to nurse, suckle; to rear, bring up
nūtrīcŭl·a -ae *f* nurse
nūtrīm·en -ĭnis *n* nourishment
nūtrīment·um -ī *n* nutriment, nourishment, support; fuel (*for fire*)
nūtr·ĭō -īre -īvī or **-ĭī -ītum** *vt* to nurse, suckle, nourish, feed; to rear, bring up, support, maintain, foster; to take care of, attend to; to cherish, cultivate
nūtr·ix -īcis *f* nurse; *f pl* breasts
nūt·us -ūs *m* nod; hint, intimation; will, pleasure, command; gravity
nux nucis *f* nut; nut tree, almond tree; **nuces relinquere** (fig) to put away childish things
Nyctē·is -ĭdis *f* Antiope (*wife of Lycus, the king of Thebes, and mother of Amphion and Zethus*)
Nyct·eus -ĕī or **-ĕos** *m* father of Antiope
nymph·a -ae or **nymph·ē -ēs** *f* bride; nymph (*demi-goddesses who inhabit fountains, rivers, sea, woods, and mountains*); water
Nȳs·a -ae *f* mythical birthplace of Bacchus
Nȳsae·us or **Nȳsĭ·us -a -um** *adj* of Nysa, Nysaean
Nȳs·eus -ĕī or **-ĕos** *m* Bacchus
Nȳsigĕn·a -ae *m* native of Nysa

O

ō *interj* oh!
Oax·ēs or **Oax·is -is** *m* river in Crete
ob *prep* (with *acc*) before, in front of; on account of, because of; for the sake of, in the interest of; in return for, instead of; in proportion to, balanced against; **ob rem** to the purpose, usefully, profitably; **quam ob rem** wherefore, accordingly
obaerāt·us -a -um *adj* deeply in debt; *m* debtor
obambŭl·ō -āre *vt* to prowl all over, prowl about (*e.g., the city*); *vi* to walk about, wander, prowl about; (with *dat*) to prowl about near; (with **ante** + *acc*) to wander around in front of
obarm·ō -āre *vt* to arm
obăr·ō -āre *vt* to plow up, plow over
obbrūtesc·ō -ĕre *vi* to grow dull
obc- = occ-
ob·dō -dĕre -dĭdī -dĭtum *vt* to close, lock; to expose
obdorm·ĭō -īre -īvī or **-ĭī -ītum** *vi* to fall asleep
obdorm·iscō -iscĕre -īvī — *vi* to fall asleep
ob·dūcō -dūcĕre -duxī -ductum *vt* to put on (*clothes*); to cover, veil, surround, envelop; to hide; to swallow; to pass (*time*); to bring forward as a candidate; to run or dig (*ditch*); (with *dat* of thing protected) to draw or place (*something*) over; (with *dat* or **ad** + *acc*) to pit (*someone or something*) against
obductĭ·ō -ōnis *f* veiling
obduct·ō -āre *vt* to introduce as a rival
obdūr·escō -escĕre -ŭī *vi* to grow hard, harden; to become insensitive
obdūr·ō -āre *vi* to persist, stick it out
ob·ĕō -īre -īvī or **-ĭī -ĭtum** *vt* to go to meet; to travel, travel to, travel over, wander through, traverse, encircle, visit; to run over, review, enumerate (*in a speech*); to undertake, engage in; **diem edicti obire** to meet one's death; *vi* to go; to pass away, die; to fade, disappear; (of heavenly bodies) to go down, set
obequĭt·ō -āre *vi* to ride up; (with *dat*) to ride up to
oberr·ō -āre *vi* to ramble about, wander around; (with *abl*) **a** to wander about, wander among; **b** to make a mistake on or at
obēs·us -a -um *adj* fat, plump; swollen; crude, coarse
ŏb·ex -ĭcis *m* or *f* bar, bolt; barrier; obstacle, hindrance
obf- = off-
obg- = ogg-
ob·haerescō -haerescĕre -haesī *vi* to get stuck
obīr·ascor -ascī -ātus sum *vi* (with *dat*) to get angry at
obĭter *adv* on the way, as one goes along; (fig) in passing, incidentally
obĭtus *pp* of **obeo**
obĭt·us -ūs *m* approach, visit; death, passing, ruin, downfall; setting (*of heavenly bodies*)
objac·ĕō -ēre -ŭī *vi* (with *dat*) to lie before, lie at
objectātĭ·ō -ōnis *f* reproach
object·ō -āre *vt* to oppose; to expose, endanger; to throw in the way; to cause (*delay*); (with *dat*) **a** to expose to, abandon to; **b** to impute to, throw up (*faults*) to, bring a charge of (*e.g., madness*) against, fling (*charges, abuse*) at; (with *dat & acc & inf*) to throw a hint to (*someone*) that
object·us -a -um *adj* lying in the

way, lying in front; (with *dat*) **a** opposite; **b** exposed to; *n pl* charges, accusations

object·us -ūs *m* interposition; obstacle, hindrance; protection; (with *genit*) protection afforded by

ob·jiciō -jicĕre -jēcī -jectum *vt* to cast, hurl; to present, offer, expose; to hold up as an example; to set up as a defense, use as a defense; (with *dat*) **a** to cast before, throw to, offer to, expose to, set up as a defense against; **b** to throw up (*faults, weaknesses, etc.*) to; **c** to bring upon, inflict on, inspire in; **objici** (with *dat*) to happen to, befall, occur to; **se objicere** (with *dat*) to expose oneself to

objurgāti·ō -ōnis *f* scolding, rebuke

objurgāt·or -ōris *m* critic

objurgātōri·us -a -um *adj* scolding, reproachful

objurgit·ō -āre *vt* to keep on scolding

objurg·ō -āre *vt* to scold, rebuke, blame, reprimand; to chastise, correct; to deter

oblangu·escō -escĕre -ŭī *vi* to taper off

oblātrātr·ix -īcis *f* nagging woman, nag

oblātus *pp* of **offero**

oblectām·en -ĭnis *n* delight

oblectāment·um -ī *n* delight, amusement, pastime

oblectāti·ō -ōnis *f* delight, amusement; attraction; (with *genit*) diversion from

oblect·ō -āre *vt* to attract, delight, amuse, divert; to spend (*time*) pleasantly; **se oblectare** to amuse oneself, enjoy oneself

ob·līdō -līdĕre -līsī -līsum *vt* to crush; to squeeze together, strangle

obligāti·ō -ōnis *f* binding, pledging, obligation

obligāt·us -a -um *adj* obliged, under obligation; (with *dat*) (vow) made to

oblĭg·ō -āre *vt* to tie up, bandage; to bind, oblige, put under obligation, make liable; to hamper, tie down; to embarrass; to mortgage; **fidem obligare** to pledge one's word; **obligari** (with *abl*) **a** to be guilty of; **b** to be obliged to, compelled to

oblīm·ō -āre *vt* to cover with mud; to dissipate, squander

ob·lĭnō -linĕre -lēvī -lĭtum *vt* to smear; (fig) to smear, defile; (fig) to overload

oblīquē *adv* sideways; (fig) indirectly

oblīqu·ō -āre *vt* to turn aside, twist, shift, slant

oblīqu·us -a -um *adj* slanting, crosswise; from the side; indirect; sly; envious; downhill (*road*); **obliquus oculus** disapproving look, envious look; *n* side; **ab obliquo** from the side; **per obliquum** across

oblīsus *pp* of **oblido**

oblit·escō -escĕre -ŭī *vi* to hide

oblittĕr·ō -āre *vt* to erase; to cancel; (fig) to blot out; **nomina oblitterare** to cancel debts

oblĭtus *pp* of **oblino**

oblītus *pp* of **obliviscor**

oblīvi·ō -ōnis *f* oblivion; forgetting; forgetfulness

oblīviōs·us -a -um *adj* forgetful, oblivious; (wine) causing forgetfulness

ob·līviscor -līviscī -lītus sum *vt* to forget; *vi* to forget; (with *genit*) to forget, neglect, disregard, be indifferent to

oblīv·ium -iī or **-ī** *n* forgetfulness, oblivion

oblocūt·or -ōris *m* contradictor

oblong·us -a -um *adj* oblong

ob·lŏquor -lŏquī -locūtus sum *vt* (with *dat*) **a** to interrupt; **b** to answer (*in argument*), contradict; **c** to speak against, abuse, rail at; **d** to accompany (*in music*), sing to

obluct·or -ārī -ātus sum *vi* (with *dat*) to struggle with, fight against, struggle against

oblūd·ō -ĕre *vt* to play jokes on

obmōl·ior -īrī -ītus sum *vt* to make a barricade of

obmurmŭr·ō -āre *vi* (with *dat*) to roar in answer to

obmūt·escō -escĕre -ŭī *vi* to become silent, hush up; to cease

obnāt·us -a -um *adj* growing on (*e.g., the bank of a river*)

ob·nītor -nītī -nixus sum *vi* to strain, struggle, put on the pressure; (with *dat*) **a** to press against, lean against; **b** to resist, oppose

obnīxē *adv* with all one's might, obstinately

obnix·us -a -um *pp* of **obnitor;** *adj* steadfast, firm, resolute

obnoxiē *adv* guiltily; timidly

obnoxiōsius *adv* more slavishly

obnoxiōs·us -a -um *adj* submissive

obnoxi·us -a -um *adj* liable, addicted, guilty; submissive, servile, obedient; weak, timid; obliged, under obligation, indebted; answerable, responsible; liable, subject, exposed; **obnoxium est** (with *inf*) it is dangerous to

ob·nūbō -nūbĕre -nupsī -nuptum *vt* to veil, cover

obnuntiāti·ō -ōnis *f* announcement (of omens)

obnunti·ō -āre *vi* to make an announcement; to make an announcement that the omens are adverse; to announce bad news

oboedi·ens -entis *adj* obedient; (with *dat* or **ad** + *acc*) obedient to

oboedienter *adv* obediently

oboedienti·a -ae *f* obedience

oboed·iō -īre -īvī or **-iī -ītum** *vi* (with *dat*) to give ear to, listen to, obey

obol·ĕō -ēre -ŭī *vt* to smell of; *vi* to smell

ob·orior -orīrī -ortus sum *vi* to rise, appear
obp- = opp-
ob·rēpō -rēpĕre -repsī -reptum *vt* to creep up on, sneak up on; *vi* to creep up; (with *dat*) **a** to creep up on, sneak up on, take by surprise; **b** to trick, cheat; (with **in** + *acc*) to steal over; **obrepere ad honores** to worm one's way into high positions
obrept·ō -āre *vi* to sneak up
obrēt·iō -īre -īvī or **-iī -ītum** *vt* to entangle
obrig·escō -escĕre -ŭī *vi* to stiffen; to freeze
obrōd·ō -ĕre *vt* to gnaw at
obrŏg·ō -āre *vi* (with *dat*) to supersede (*a law*)
ob·rŭō -ruĕre -rŭī -rŭtum *vt* to cover up, cover, hide, bury; to overwhelm, overthrow; to sink, cover with water, swamp, overflow; to overpower, surpass, obscure, eclipse; *vi* to fall to ruin
obruss·a -ae *f* test, proof
obsaep·iō -īre -sī -tum *vt* to fence in; to block (*road*); (fig) to close, block
obsatŭr·ō -āre *vt* to sate, cloy; **istius obsaturari** to have enough of him
obscaen- = obscen-
obscaev·ō -āre *vi* to give a bad omen
obscēnē *adv* obscenely
obscēnit·ās -ātis *f* obscenity
obscēn·us -a -um *adj* dirty, filthy; indecent, obscene; ominous
obscūrātī·ō -ōnis *f* obscuring, darkening; disappearance
obscūrē *adv* indistinctly; secretly, imperceptibly
obscūrit·ās -ātis *f* obscurity
obscūr·ō -āre *vt* to obscure, darken; to cover, hide; to veil (*words*); (of love) to blind; to hide, suppress
obscūr·us -a -um *adj* obscure, dark, shady; obscure, lowly, mean; dim, indistinct, unintelligible; secret; reserved; vague, uncertain; gloomy; *n* the dark, darkness; obscurity
obsecrātī·ō -ōnis *f* entreaty; public appeal to the gods
obsĕcr·ō -āre *vt* to entreat, appeal to, implore
obsecund·ō -āre *vi* (with *dat*) to comply with, humor
obsecūtus *pp* of **obsequor**
obsēp- = obsaep-
obsĕqu·ens -entis *adj* compliant, obedient; indulgent, gracious (*gods*); (with *dat*) obedient to
obsequenter *adv* compliantly, obsequiously
obsequentī·a -ae *f* obsequiousness
obsequiōs·us -a -um *adj* obsequious
obsequ·ium -iī or **-ī** *n* compliance, indulgence; obedience, allegiance
ob·sĕquor -sĕquī -secūtus sum *vi* (with *dat*) to comply with, yield to, give into, gratify, humor
obsĕr·ō -āre *vt* to bolt, bar, lock up
ob·sĕrō -serĕre -sēvī -situm *vt* to sow or plant thickly; to fill, cover
observ·ans -antis *adj* attentive, respectful; (with *genit*) respectful of, attentive to, careful about
observantī·a -ae *f* regard, respect; (with *genit* or **in** + *acc*) regard for, respect for
observātī·ō -ōnis *f* observation; caution, care
observāt·or -ōris *m* observer
observit·ō -āre *vt* to watch carefully, note carefully
observ·ō -āre *vt* to watch, watch out for, take careful note of; to guard; to observe, keep, obey, comply with; to pay attention to, pay respect to
obs·es -idis *m* or *f* hostage; guarantee
obsessī·ō -ōnis *f* blockade
obsess·or -ōris *m* frequenter, regular visitor; blockader
ob·sidĕō -sidēre -sēdī -sessum *vt* to sit near or at, remain by or near; to frequent; (mil) to besiege, invest, blockade; to block, choke; to occupy, fill; to look out for, watch closely; to keep guard over
obsidiāl·is -e *adj* for breaking a blockade; **corona obsidialis** decoration for breaking a blockade
obsidī·ō -ōnis *f* blockade, siege; imminent danger
obsid·ium -iī or **-ī** *n* blockade, siege; imminent danger, great peril; status of hostage
ob·sīdō -sīdĕre -sēdī -sessum *vt* to besiege, invest, beset, blockade; to take possession of, occupy
obsignāt·or -ōris *m* sealer; witness; **obsignator testamenti** witness to a will
obsign·ō -āre *vt* to seal, seal up; to sign and seal; (fig) to stamp, impress
ob·sistō -sistĕre -stitī -stitum *vi* (with *dat*) to stand in the way of, block, resist, oppose, disapprove of, forbid
obsitus *pp* of **obsero** (to sow)
obsole·fīō -fiĕrī -factus sum *vi* to wear out, become spoiled; to become worthless
obsol·escō -escĕre -ēvī -ētum *vi* to wear out, go out of style, become obsolete, get shabby, lose value
obsolētius *adv* rather shabbily
obsolēt·us -a -um *adj* out of date, old, obsolete, worn out; shabby, threadbare; low, mean, poor
obsōnāt·or -ōris *m* shopper
obsōnāt·us -ūs *m* shopping
obsōn·ium -iī or **-ī** *n* shopping items, food
obsōn·ō -āre or **obsōn·or -ārī -ātus sum** *vt* to shop for; **famem obsonare** to work up an appetite; *vi* to go shopping; to provide food; (with **de** + *abl*) to provide a feast for
obsŏn·ō -āre *vi* (with *dat*) to drown out
obsorb·ĕō -ēre -ŭī *vt* to gulp down

obstant·ĭa -ĭum *n pl* obstacles, obstructions
obstētr·ix -īcis *f* midwife
obstinātē *adv* resolutely, with determination; obstinately, stubbornly
obstinātĭ·ō -ōnis *f* resolution, determination; obstinacy, stubbornness
obstināt·us -a -um *adj* resolute, determined, fixed; obstinate, stubborn
obstĭn·ō -āre *vt* to be resolved on, resolve, determine; (with *inf*) to resolve to, determine to; *vi* to be determined, be resolved; (with **ad** + *acc*) to be set on
obstipescō see **obstupesco**
obstĭp·us -a -um *adj* bent, bent to one side; bent forwards, bowed; **capite obstipo stare** to stand with head bowed
ob·stō -stāre -stĕtī *vi* to stand in the way, be in the way, raise opposition; (with *dat*) to stand in the way of, oppose, object to, resist, hinder, obstruct; (with **ne, quin, quominus,** or **cur non**) to prevent (*someone*) from
obstrĕp·ō -ĕre -ŭī -ĭtum *vt* to fill with noise, drown out; *vi* to make a racket, make noise; **a** (with *dat*) to shout at, drown out with shouts, interrupt with shouts; **b** (*of the sea*) to resound against
ob·stringō -stringĕre -strinxī -strictum *vt* to shut in, confine, tie up; (fig) to tie up, involve, put under obligation, oblige; **fidem obstringere** (with *dat*) to pledge one's word to; **obstringi** or **se obstringere** (with *abl*) to get involved in, be guilty of
obstructĭ·ō -ōnis *f* obstruction
obstructus *pp* of **obstruo**
obs·trūdō or **ob·trūdō -trūdĕre -trūsī -trūsum** *vt* to gulp down; (with *dat*) to force (*something*) upon, thrust (*something*) upon
ob·strŭō -struĕre -struxī -structum *vt* to pile up, block up, stop up; (with *dat*) to block or close (*e.g., the road*) against
obstrūsus *pp* of **obstrudo**
obstupe·faciō -facĕre -fēcī -factum *vt* to astound, astonish, paralyze, stupefy
obstup·escō or **obstip·escō -escĕre -ŭī** *vi* to be astounded, be struck dumb, be paralyzed
obstupĭd·us -a -um *adj* stupefied
ob·sum -esse -fŭī *vi* (with *dat*) to be opposed to, be against; to be prejudicial to, harm; **nihil obest dicere** there is no harm in saying
ob·sŭō -suĕre -sŭī -sūtum *vt* to sew on; to sew up
obsurd·escō -escĕre -ŭī *vi* to become deaf; (fig) to turn a deaf ear
ob·tĕgō -tegĕre -texī -tectum *vt* to cover up; to protect; (fig) to conceal, keep secret; **animus sui obtegens** secretive mind
obtemperātĭ·ō -ōnis *f* compliance, obedience
obtempĕr·ō -āre *vi* (with *dat*) to comply with, submit to, obey
ob·tendō -tendĕre -tendī -tentum *vt* to spread, stretch out; to offer as an excuse; to envelop, conceal; **obtendi** (with *dat*) to lie opposite; **obtentā nocte** under cover of darkness
obtentus *pp* of **obtineo**
obtent·us -ūs *m* screen, cover; pretext, pretense
ob·tĕrō -terĕre -trīvī -trītum *vt* to trample on, trample down, crush; (fig) to trample on, crush, degrade, destroy
obtestātĭ·ō -ōnis *f* adjuring, adjuration; solemn entreaty, supplication
obtest·or -ārī -ātum sum *vt* to call as witness; to make an appeal to, implore, entreat
obtex·ō -ĕre -ŭī *vt* to cover, veil
obtic·ĕō -ēre *vi* to be silent
obtic·escō -escĕre -ŭī *vi* to fall silent, be dumbstruck
ob·tinĕō -tinēre -tinŭī -tentum *vt* to get hold of; to hold on to, keep, maintain, preserve, uphold; to assert, maintain; to obtain, gain, acquire; *vi* to continue
ob·tingō -tingĕre -tĭgī *vi* to happen, occur; (with *dat*) to happen to, befall, occur to
obtorp·escō -escĕre -ŭī *vi* to become numb, become stiff, become insensible
ob·torquĕō -torquēre -torsī -tortum *vt* to twist
obtrectātĭ·ō -ōnis *f* detraction, disparagement
obtrectāt·or -ōris *m* detractor, disparager
obtrect·ō -āre *vt* to treat spitefully, mistreat, disparage; to carp at; *vi* (with *dat*) to detract from, disparage, belittle
obtrītus *pp* of **obtero**
obtrūdō see **obstrudo**
obtrunc·ō -āre *vt* to cut off, cut down; (in battle) to cut down, kill
ob·tuĕor -tuērī -tuĭtus sum *vt* to gaze at, gaze upon; to see clearly
ob·tundo -tundĕre -tŭdī -tūsum or **-tunsum** *vt* to beat, beat on, thump on; to blunt; (fig) to pound away at, stun, deafen, annoy, molest, importune
obturb·ō -āre *vt* to throw into disorder; (fig) to disturb, confuse, distract
obturgesc·ō -ĕre *vi* to begin to swell up
obtūr·ō -āre *vt* to block up, stop up, plug up; **aures obturare** to refuse to listen
obtūsus or **obtunsus** *pp* of **obtundo;** *adj* blunt, dull; (fig) dulled, blurred
obtūt·us -ūs *m* stare, gaze
obumbr·ō -āre *vt* to overshadow, shade; to darken, obscure; to cover, screen
obunc·us -a -um *adj* hooked

obust·us -a -um *adj* singed; hardened in the fire; nipped (*by cold*)
obvāg·iō -īre *vi* to whimper
obvall·ō -āre *vt* to fortify
ob·veniō -venīre -vēnī -ventum *vi* to come up, happen, occur; (with *dat*) to fall to the lot of, be alloted to
obvers·or -ārī -ātus sum *vi* to make an appearance, show oneself; (fig) hover
obvers·us -a -um *adj* (with **ad** + *acc*) **a** turned toward, facing; **b** inclined to; (with *dat*) engaged in; *m pl* opponents
ob·vertō or **ob·vortō -vertĕre -vertī -versum** *vt* (with *dat* or **ad** + *acc*) to turn (*something*) towards or in the direction of; (with **in** + *acc*) to turn (*e.g., the soldiers*) to face (*e.g., the enemy*); **obverti** (with **ad** + *acc*) to turn toward
obviam or **ob viam** *adv* (with *dat*) **a** to meet, in order to meet, in the way of; **b** (fig) opposed to; **effundi obviam** (with *dat*) to pour out to meet, go out in great numbers to meet; **obviam esse** (with *dat*) **a** to meet; **b** to oppose, resist; **obviam ire** (with *dat*) or **obviam procedere** (with *dat*) to go to meet; **obviam obsistere** (with *dat*) to stand in the way of (*someone*); **obviam prodire** or **obviam proficisci** or **obviam progredi** (with *dat*) to go out to meet; **obviam venire** (with *dat*) to go to meet, come to meet
obvigilāt·um -ī *n* vigilance
obvi·us -a -um *adj* in the way; exposed, open; accessible (*person*); ready, at hand; (with *dat*) **a** to meet, so as to meet; **b** opposed to; **c** exposed or open to; **obvius esse** (with *dat*) to meet, encounter; **obvius venire** (with *dat*) to come to meet
ob·volvō -volvĕre -volvī -volūtum *vt* to wrap up, cover up
occaec·ō -āre *vt* to blind, make blind; to darken, obscure; to hide; to numb
occall·escō -escĕre -ŭī *vi* to become thick-skinned; (fig) to become callous
occăn·ō -ĕre -ŭī *vi* to sound the charge
occāsi·ō -ōnis *f* occasion, opportunity, good time, chance; pretext; (mil) surprise, raid; **occasionem amittere** to lose the opportunity; **occasionem arripere** to seize the opportunity; **per occasionem** at the right time
occāsiuncŭl·a -ae *f* nice little opportunity
occās·us -ūs *m* setting; sunset, west; (fig) downfall, ruin, death
occāti·ō -ōnis *f* harrowing
occāt·or -ōris *m* harrower
oc·cēdō -cēdĕre -cessī -cessum *vi* to go up; **obviam occedere** (with *dat*) to go to meet
occent·ō -āre *vt* to serenade; to satirize in verse
occept·ō -āre *vt* to begin
occĭd·ens -entis *m* the setting sun; west
occīdĭ·ō -ōnis *f* massacre, annihilation; **occidione occidere** to massacre, annihilate, wipe out
oc·cīdō -cīdĕre -cīdī -cīsum *vt* to knock down; to cut down, slay, kill; to murder; to ruin; to pester to death; **se occidere** to commit suicide
oc·cĭdō -cidĕre -cĭdī -cāsum *vi* to fall, fall down; (of the sun) to go down, set; to fall, be slain, perish; (of hope, etc.) to fade, die; (fig) to be ruined, be lost; **occidi!** I'm finished!
occidŭ·us -a -um *adj* setting; western; (fig) sinking, fading, dying
occill·ō -āre *vt* to smash
oc·cĭnō -cinĕre -cecĭnī or **-cinŭī** *vi* to sound ominous
oc·cipiō -cipĕre -cēpī -ceptum *vt & vi* to begin
occipit·ium -iī or **-ī** or **occĭp·ut -itis** *n* back of the head
occīsĭ·ō -ōnis *f* massacre; **occisionem facere** to cause a massacre
occīs·or -ōris *m* killer, murderer
occīsus *pp* of **occīdo**
occlāmĭt·ō -āre *vt* to shout at; *vi* to cry out, bawl
oc·clūdō -clūdĕre -clūsī -clūsum *vt* to close up, shut up, lock up; to check, control
occ·ō -āre *vt* to harrow
occŭb·ō -āre *vi* to lie; to rest
occulc·ō -āre *vt* to trample down
occŭl·ō -ĕre -ŭī -tum *vt* to cover; to cover up, hide
occultāti·ō -ōnis *f* concealment, hiding
occultāt·or -ōris *m* hideout
occultē *adv* secretly, in concealment
occult·ō -āre *vt* to hide
occult·us -a -um *adj* hidden, secret; reserved (*person*); *n* concealment; secret; **ex occulto** from a place of concealment; secretly
oc·cumbō -cumbĕre -cubŭī -cubĭtum *vt* to fall to, meet; **mortem occumbere** to meet death; *vi* to sink down in death, fall dying; **certae morti occumbere** to meet certain death; **morti occumbere** to fall prey to death; **occumbere** (with **per** + *acc*) to die at the hands of
occupāti·ō -ōnis *f* occupation (*e.g., of a town*); occupation, employment, business; business engagement, task; job; involvement, concern
occupāt·us -a -um *adj* occupied, busied, engaged, involved
occŭp·ō -āre *vt* to occupy, seize; to win, gain; to attack, strike down; to outstrip, overtake; to fill, take up; to invest, loan, lend; (with *inf*) to be the first to
oc·currō -currĕre -currī or **-cu-**

currī -cursum *vi* to run up; (with *dat*) **a** to run up to, run to meet, meet; **b** to rush against, attack; **c** to resist, oppose, counteract; **d** to meet, answer, reply to, object to; **e** to relieve, remedy; **f** to occur to, suggest itself to, present itself to; **g** (fig) to run into, run up against, get involved in

occursātī·ō -ōnis *f* hustle and bustle; excited welcome; officiousness

occurs·ō -āre *vt* to run to meet; *vi* (with *dat*) **a** to run to meet, go or come to meet, meet; **b** to go to meet (*the enemy*), attack, charge, oppose; **c** (of thoughts) to occur to

occurs·us -ūs *m* meeting; (with *genit*) running into (*someone or something*)

Ōceanīt·is -idis *f* ocean nymph

Ōceăn·us -ī *m* ocean; Oceanus (*son of Caelus and Terra, husband of Tethys, and father of rivers and of ocean nymphs*)

ocell·us -ī *m* eye; gem; darling

ōcim·um -ī *n* basil

ōcī·or -us *adj* swifter, quicker

ōcius *adv* more swiftly, more quickly; sooner; more easily; immediately, on the spot; (with *abl*) rather than; **ocius serius** sooner or later; **quam ocissime** as quickly as possible

ocrĕ·a -ae *f* greave, shin guard

ocreāt·us -a -um *adj* wearing shin guards

Octāvī·a -ae *f* sister of Augustus, wife of C. Marcellus, and later of M. Antony (64-11 B.C.); daughter of Claudius and wife of Nero (*murdered in* 62 A.D.)

Octāv·ius -iī or **-ī** *m* C. Octavius (*Emperor Augustus, who, upon adoption by Julius Caesar, became C. Julius Caesar Octavianus,* 63 B.C.-14 A.D.)

octāvum *adv* for the eighth time

octāv·us -a -um *adj* eighth; **octava pars** one eighth; *f* eighth hour of the day (*i.e.,* 2 *p.m.*); *n* **cum octavo efficere** to produce eightfold

octāv·us decim·us -a -um *adj* eighteenth

octiens or **octiēs** *adv* eight times

octingentēsim·us or **octingentensim·us -a -um** *adj* eight hundredth

octingent·ī -ae -a *adj* eight hundred

octip·ēs -ĕdis *adj* eight-footed

octō (indecl) *adj* eight

Octōb·er -ris *adj & m* October

octōdĕcim (indecl) *adj* eighteen

octōgēnārī·us -a -um *adj & m* octogenarian

octōgēn·ī -ae -a *adj* eighty each

octōgēsim·us or **octōgensim·us -a -um** *adj* eightieth

octōgiēs or **octōgiens** *adv* eighty times

octōgintā (indecl) *adj* eighty

octōjŭg·is -e *adj* eight-team

octōn·ī -ae -a *adj* eight at a time, eight each

octōphŏr·os -on *adj* carried by eight carriers; *n* eight-man litter

octuplicāt·us -a -um *adj* eightfold

octŭpl·us -a -um *adj* eightfold; *n* eightfold fine

octuss·is *m* sum of eight aces

oculāt·us -a -um *adj* having eyes; exposed to view, conspicuous; **oculatus testis** eyewitness

oculĕ·us -a -um *adj* many-eyed

oculissim·us -a -um *adj* dearest

oculitus *adv* like one's own eyes, dearly

ocŭl·us -ī *m* eye; eye, bud (*in plants*); sight, vision; mind's eye; apple of the eye; **aequis oculis** contentedly; **altero oculo captus** blind in one eye; **ante oculos** in full view; (fig) obvious; **ante oculos ponere** to imagine; **ex oculis abire** to go out of sight, disappear; **in oculis** in view, in public, in the limelight; **in oculis ferre** or **gestare** to hold dear, value; **oculos adjicere** (with **ad** + *acc*) to eye; to covet; **oculos dejicere** (with **ab** + *abl*) to take one's eyes off; (fig) to lose sight of; **oculos pascere** (with *abl*) to feast one's eyes on; **sub oculis** (with *genit*) in the presence of, under the very nose of

ōd·ī -isse *vt* to have taken a dislike to, dislike, hate, be disgusted at

ōdiōsē *adv* hatefully; unpleasantly

ōdiōsic·us -a -um *adj* odious, unpleasant, annoying

ōdiōs·us -a -um *adj* odious, unpleasant, annoying

ōd·ium -iī or **-ī** *n* dislike, hatred, aversion; object of hatred, nuisance; dissatisfaction, disgust; offensive conduct, insolence; **odio esse** (with *dat*) to be hateful to, be disliked by, be hated by; *n pl* feelings of hatred

od·or or **od·ōs -ōris** *m* odor, smell, scent; stench, stink; pleasant smell, fragrance, perfume; inkling, suggestion, hint; *m pl* perfume

odōrātī·ō -ōnis *f* smell, smelling

odōrāt·us -a -um *adj* fragrant, scented

odōrāt·us -ūs *m* smell, smelling; sense of smell

odōrĭf·er -ĕra -ĕrum *adj* fragrant

odōr·ō -āre *vt* to make fragrant

odōr·or -ārī -ātus sum *vt* to sniff at, scent; to aspire to, aim at; to be sniffing after, search for, investigate; to get a smattering of

odōr·us -a -um *adj* smelly, fragrant; keen-scented

odōs see **odor**

Odrysi·us -a -um *adj & m* Thracian

Odyssē·a or **Odyssī·a -ae** *f* the Odyssey

Oeăg·er -rī *m* king of Thrace and father of Orpheus

Oeagrī·us -a -um *adj* Thracian

Oebalid·ēs -ae *m* male descendant of Oebalus; *m pl* Castor and Pollux

Oebalĭ·us -a -um *adj* Spartan; Tarentine; Sabine; *f* Tarentum (*Spartan colony in S. Italy*)
Oebăl·us -ī *m* king of Sparta, father of Tyndareus, and grandfather of Helen and Clytemnestra
Oedĭp·ūs -ŏdis or **-ī** *m* Oedipus
Oen·eus -ĕī or **-ĕos** *m* king of Calydon, husband of Althaea, and father of Meleager and Deianira
Oenīd·ēs -ae *m* descendant of Oeneus; Meleager; Diomedes (*son of Tydeus*)
Oenomă·us -ī *m* king of Pisa in the Peloponnesus and father of Hippodamia
oenophŏr·um -ī *n* wine-bottle basket
Oenopĭ·a -ae *f* ancient name of Aegina (*island between Attica and Argolis*)
oenopōl·ĭum -ĭī or **-ī** *n* wine shop, tavern
Oenōtrĭ·us -a -um *adj* Oenotrian, Italian; *f* ancient name of S.E. Italy; Italy
oestr·us -ī *m* horsefly, gadfly; fancy, inspiration
oesўp·um -ī *n* lanolin
Oet·a -ae or **Oet·ē -ēs** *f* Mt. Oete (*mountain in S. Thessaly, on which Hercules died*)
Oetae·us -a -um *adj* Oetean; *m* Hercules
ofell·a -ae *f* bit, morsel
off·a -ae *f* pellet, lump, dumpling; swelling; shapeless mass
offātim *adv* in bits, in little lumps
offectus *pp* of **officio**
of·fendō -fendĕre -fendī -fensum *vt* to bump, bump against, stub, strike, hit; to hit upon, come upon, meet with, bump into, stumble upon, find; to offend, shock, vex, disgust; to hurt (*feelings*); to injure (*reputation*); **nihil offendere** to suffer no damage, receive no injury; *vi* to make a blunder, make a mistake, blunder; to give offense, be offensive; to fail, take a loss, be defeated, come to grief; to run aground; (with *dat* or **in** + *abl*) to hit against, bump against; (with *dat*) to give offense to; (with **in** + *acc*) to take offense at; **terrae offendere** to run aground
offens·a -ae *f* offense, affront, injury; displeasure, resentment, hatred; crime; **offensā** (with *genit*) out of hatred for
offensĭ·ō -ōnis *f* stubbing; tripping, stumbling; dislike, displeasure, hatred, digust, aversion; discredit, bad reputation, mishap, failure, disaster, accident, defeat; *f pl* offensive acts; feelings of displeasure
offensiuncŭl·a -ae *f* slight displeasure; minor setback; disappointment
offens·ō -āre *vt & vi* to bump
offens·us -a -um *pp* of **offendo;** *adj* offensive, odious; offended, displeased, annoyed
offens·us -ūs *m* bump; shock; offense
offĕrō offerre obtŭlī oblātum *vt* to offer, bring forward, present, show; to cause, occasion; to confer, bestow, inflict; **se offerre** (with *dat*) **a** to meet, encounter; **b** to expose oneself to
offerūment·a -ae *f* (*said humorously of a blow or welt*) present
officīn·a or **opificīn·a -ae** *f* shop, workshop, factory, office
of·ficĭō -ficĕre -fēcī -fectum *vi* (with *dat*) to get in the way of, interfere with, oppose, obstruct, be detrimental to, hinder
officiōsē *adv* obligingly, courteously
officiōs·us -a -um *adj* ready to serve, obliging; dutiful, obligatory
offic·ĭum -ĭī or **-ī** *n* service, favor, kindness, courtesy; obligation, duty, function, office, part; social obligation, social call, social visit; ceremony, ceremonial observance, attendance; official duty; employment, business, job; sense of duty, conscience; allegiance
of·fīgō -fīgĕre -fixī -fixum *vt* to fasten down, nail down, drive in
offirmāt·us -a -um *adj* determined, resolute
offirm·ō -āre *vt* **se offirmare** to steel oneself, be determined; *vi* to be determined
offlect·ō -ĕre *vt* to turn (*something*) around
offrēnāt·us -a -um *adj* curbed
offūcĭ·a -ae *f* cosmetic; (fig) trick
of·fulgĕō -fulgēre -fulsī -fulsum *vi* (with *dat*) to shine on
of·fundō -fundĕre -fūdī -fūsum *vt* to pour out; to cover, fill; to eclipse; **offundi** (with *dat*) to pour out over, spread over
oggan·ĭō -īre -īvī or **-ĭī -ītum** *vt & vi* to growl
og·gĕrō -gerĕre *vt* to bring, offer, give
Ōgўg·ēs -is or **Ōgўg·us -ī** *m* mythical king of Thebes, in whose reign the Deluge occurred
Ōgygĭ·us -a -um *adj* Theban
oh *interj* oh!
ōhē or **ōhĕ** *interj* whoa!
oi *interj* (*express complaint*) oh no!
Oīl·eus -ĕī or **-ĕos** *m* king of Locris and father of Ajax the archer
olĕ·a -ae *f* olive; olive tree
oleāgĭn·us -a -um *adj* olive, of an olive tree
oleārĭ·us -a -um *adj* oil, of oil; *m* oil merchant
oleast·er -rī *m* oleaster, wild olive tree
Ōlenĭ·us -a -um *adj* of Olenus (*town in Achaia and Aetolia*); Achaian, Aetolian
ol·ens -entis *adj* smelling; fragrant; smelly, stinking; musty
ol·ĕō -ēre -ŭī *vt* to smell of, smell like; (fig) to betray; *vi* to smell; (with *abl*) to smell of
olĕ·um -ī *n* olive oil, oil; (fig) palaestra; **oleum addere camino** (fig) to pour oil on the fire; **oleum**

et operam perdere to waste time and effort

ol·faciō -facĕre -fēcī -factum *vt* to smell

olfact·ō -āre *vt* to sniff at

olid·us -a -um *adj* smelly

ōlim *adv* once, once upon a time; at the time; for a good while; someday, in the future, hereafter; now and then, at times; ever, at any time

olit- = **holit-**

olīv·a -ae *f* olive; olive tree; olive wreath; olive branch; olive staff

olīvēt·um -ī *n* olive grove

olīvĭf·er -ĕra -ĕrum *adj* olive-producing, olive-growing

olīv·um -ī *n* oil; ointment; (fig) palaestra

oll·a -ae *f* pot, jar

olle or **ollus** = **ille**

ol·or -ōris *m* swan

olōrīn·us -a -um *adj* swan, of a swan

olus see **holus**

Olympĭ·a -ae *f* Olympia (*region in Elis, in the Peloponnesus, where the Olympian games were held*)

Olympĭ·a -ōrum *n pl* Olympian games

Olympiăc·us -a -um *adj* Olympian

Olympĭ·as -ădis *f* Olympiad (*period of four years between Olympian games, starting in the year* 776 B.C., *according to which the Greeks reckoned time*); wife of Philip V of Macedon and mother of Alexander the Great

Olympĭc·us or **Olympĭ·us -a -um** *adj* Olympian

Olympionīc·ēs -ae *m* Olympic victor

Olymp·us -ī *m* Mt. Olympus (*mountain on the boundary of Macedonia and Thessaly, regarded as the home of the gods or heaven*)

omās·um -ī *n* tripe; (fig) paunch, belly

ōm·en -ĭnis *n* omen, sign, token, foreboding; solemn assurance

ōment·um -ī *n* fat; bowels

ōmināt·or -ōris *m* diviner

ōmĭn·or -ārī -ātus sum *vt* to forebode, predict, prophesy

ōminōs·us -a -um *adj* ominous

omiss·us -a -um *adj* remiss, negligent

omitto omittĕre omīsī omissum *vt* to let go, let fall, let go of; to give up, abandon; to omit, pass over, say nothing of; to overlook, disregard

omnĭf·er -ĕra -ĕrum *adj* all-sustaining

omnigĕn·us -a -um *adj* of every kind

omnimŏdīs or **omnimŏdo** *adv* by all means, wholly

omnīnō *adv* altogether, entirely, wholly; (with numerals) in all; (in generalizations) in general; (in concessions) no doubt, to be sure, yes, by all means, certainly; **haud omnino** or **non omnino** not quite, not entirely; absolutely not, not at all; not expressly; **omnino nemo** no one at all

omnipăr·ens -entis *adj* all-producing (*earth*)

omnipŏt·ens -entis *adj* almighty

omn·is -e *adj* all, every; every kind of, every sort of; the whole; *m pl* all, all men, everybody; *n* the universe; *n pl* all things, everything, all nature, all the world

omnitŭ·ens -entis *adj* all-seeing

omnivăg·us -a -um *adj* roving everywhere

omnivŏl·us -a -um *adj* all-craving

Omphăl·ē -ēs *f* Lydian queen whom Hercules had to serve

onăg·er or **onagr·us -ī** *m* wild ass

onăg·os -ī *m* ass driver

Onchesmīt·ēs -ae *m* wind blowing from Onchesmus (*harbor in Epirus*)

onerārĭ·us -a -um *adj* carrying freight; **jumenta oneraria** beasts of burden; **oneraria** or **navis oneraria** freighter, transport

onĕr·ō -āre *vt* to load, load down, burden; (fig) to overload, oppress; (fig) to pile on, aggravate

onerōs·us -a -um *adj* onerous, burdensome, oppressive, heavy

on·us -ĕris *n* load, burden; freight, cargo; burden, difficulty; trouble; tax expense; foetus, embryo; **oneri esse** (with *dat*) to be a burden to

onust·us -a -um *adj* loaded, burdened; filled, full

on·yx -ȳchis *m* or *f* onyx; onyx box

opācĭt·ās -ātis *f* shade, darkness

opāc·ō -āre *vt* to shade

opāc·us -a -um *adj* shady; dark, obscure; *n pl* **per opaca locorum** through shady places

opell·a -ae *f* light work

opĕr·a -ae *f* effort, pains, exertion, work, labor; care, attention; service, assistance; leisure, spare time; laborer, workman, artisan; **operae esse** or **operae pretium esse** to be worthwhile; **operam dare** to take pains, exert oneself, be busied, pay attention, give attention; **operam funeri dare** to attend a funeral; **operam sermoni dare** to listen to a conversation; **operam tonsori dare** to see a barber, get a haircut; **operā meā (tuā,** etc.) through my (*your, etc.*) agency, thanks to me (*you, etc.*)

operārĭ·us -a -um *adj* working; *m* working man, workman, laborer; *f* working woman

opercŭl·um -ī *n* lid, cover

operīment·um -ī *n* lid, cover

oper·iō -īre -ŭī -tum *vt* to cover, cover up; to shut, close; to hide; to overwhelm

opĕr·or -ārī -ātus sum *vi* to work, work hard, take pains; (with *dat*) **a** to work hard at, be busied with, be engaged in; **b** to perform (*religious services*); **c** to attend; **d** to worship

operōsē *adv* with great effort, at great pains
operōs·us -a -um *adj* active, busy, painstaking; troublesome, difficult, elaborate; efficacious, powerful (*drugs*)
opert·us -a -um *pp* of **operio;** *adj* closed; hidden; secret; *n* secret; secret place; **in operto** inside, in secret; *n pl* depths; veiled oracles
opēs see **ops**
ophīt·ēs -ae *m* serpentine (*type of marble*)
Ophiūsi·us -a -um *adj* Cyprian; *f* old name of Cyprus
ophthalmi·ās -ae *m* a fish
opic·us -a -um *adj* boorish
opif·er -ĕra -ĕrum *adj* helpful
opif·ex -icis *m* maker, framer, creator; craftsman, mechanic
opificīn·a -ae *f* workshop
ōpili·ō -ōnis *m* shepherd
opīmē *adv* richly, splendidly
opīmit·ās -ātis *f* abundance
opīm·us -a -um *adj* fat, plump; fertile, fruitful; rich, enriched; abundant, copious, plentiful; sumptuous, splendid; lucrative; noble; **spolia opima** armor stripped from one general by another on the field of battle
opīnābil·is -e *adj* conjectural, imaginary
opīnāti·ō -ōnis *f* mere opinion, conjecture, supposition, hunch
opīnāt·or -ōris *m* guesser
opīnāt·us -a -um *adj* supposed, imagined
opīnāt·us -ūs *m* supposition
opīni·ō -ōnis *f* opinion, conjecture, supposition, guess, belief, expectation; general impression, estimation; rumor; reputation, bad reputation; **amplius opinione** beyond expectation, beyond all hopes; **celerius opinione** sooner than expected; **hac opinione ut** under the impression that; **in opinione esse** (with *acc* & *inf*) to be of the opinion that; **praebere opinionem timoris** to convey the impression of fear; **praeter opinionem** contrary to expectation, sooner than expected; **ut opinio mea est** as I suppose
opīniōs·us -a -um *adj* opinionated
opīn·ō -āre or **opīn·or -ārī -ātus sum** *vt* to suppose, imagine, conjecture; *vi* (parenthetical) to suppose, imagine
opipărē *adv* splendidly, sumptuously
opipăr·us -a -um *adj* splendid, sumptuous, ritzy
opisthogrăph·us -a -um *adj* written on the back
opitŭl·or -ārī -ātus sum *vi* (with *dat*) to bring help to, assist
oport·et -ēre -ŭit *v impers* it is right, it is proper; **me ire oportet** I ought to go, should go
op·pangō -pangĕre -pēgī -pactum *vt* to affix, imprint
oppect·ō -ĕre *vt* to comb off; (coll) to pluck, pick, eat
oppēd·ō -ĕre *vi* (with *dat*) **a** to break wind at; **b** (fig) to deride, mock
opper·ior -īrī -tus sum *vt* to wait for, await; (with **num**) to wait and see whether; *vi* to wait
oppĕt·ō -ĕre -īvī or **-iī -ītum** *vt* to go to meet; **mortem oppetere** to go to meet death, perish, die; *vi* to perish, die
oppidān·us -a -um *adj* of a town, in a town; (disparagingly) provincial; *m pl* townsfolk, townspeople
oppidō *adv* absolutely, quite, completely; (as affirmative answer) exactly
oppidŭl·um -ī *n* small town
oppid·um -ī *n* town
oppignĕr·ō -āre *vt* to pledge
oppīl·ō -āre *vt* to shut up, shut off
op·plĕō -plēre -plēvī -plētum *vt* to fill up, choke up
op·pōnō -pōnĕre -posŭī -positum *vt* to put, place, station; to oppose; to expose, lay bare, open; to wager, mortgage; to bring forward, present, adduce, allege; to reply, respond, object; to compare
opportūnē *adv* opportunely, at the right time
opportūnit·ās -ātis *f* suitableness, fitness, convenience; opportunity, right time; advantage
opportūn·us -a -um *adj* suitable, fit, convenient; advantageous, useful; exposed; **tempore opportunissimo** in the nick of time; *n pl* exposed parts
oppositi·ō -ōnis *f* opposition
opposit·us -a -um *pp* of **oppono;** *adj* opposite; (with *dat*) opposite, across from
opposit·us -ūs *m* opposing, opposition
oppressi·ō -ōnis *f* force, violence; violent seizure; suppression, overthrow
oppressiuncŭl·a -ae *f* slight pressure
oppressus *pp* of **opprimo**
oppress·us -ūs *m* pressure
op·primō -primĕre -pressī -pressum *vt* to press down, weigh down; to pressure, put pressure on; to close, shut; to overwhelm; to put down, suppress, quell; to sink (*a ship*); to subvert, overthrow, crush, subdue, overpower; to conceal, suppress; to seize, catch, surprise
opprobrāment·um -ī *n* disgrace, scandal
opprobr·ium -iī or **-ī** *n* disgrace, scandal, reproach; cause of disgrace; taunt, abuse, abusive word
opprŏbr·ō -āre *vt* to taunt
oppugnāti·ō -ōnis *f* assault; (fig) attack, assault, accusation
oppugnāt·or -ōris *m* assailant, attacker
oppugn·ō -āre *vt* to assault, assail, attack, storm; (fig) to attack, assail

ops opis *f* power, might; help, aid; influence, weight; **opem ferre** (with *dat*) to bring help to, help; *f pl* wealth, resources, means; military or political resources

Ops Opis *f* goddess of abundance, sister and wife of Saturn, and identified with Earth

ops- = **obs-**

optābĭl·is -e *adj* desirable

optātĭ·ō -ōnis *f* wishing, wish

optātō *adv* according to one's wish

optāt·us -a -um *adj* longed-for, desired, welcome; *n* wish, desire

optĭgō see **obtego**

optĭm·ās -ātis *m* aristocrat; *m pl* aristocracy, aristocratic party

optĭmē or **optŭmē** (*superl* of **bene**) *adv* very well, thoroughly, best; most opportunely, just in time

optĭm·us or **optŭm·us -a -um** (*superl* of **bonus**) *adj* very good, best; excellent

optĭ·ō -ōnis *m* helper, assistant; (mil) adjutant

optīv·us -a -um *adj* chosen

opt·ō -āre *vt* to choose, select; to wish for, desire

optum- = **optim-**

opŭl·ens -entis *adj* opulent, rich

opulentē or **opulenter** *adv* richly, splendidly

opulentĭ·a -ae *f* opulence, wealth; resources; power

opulentĭt·ās -ātis *f* opulence; power

opulent·ō -āre *vt* to make rich, enrich

opulent·us -a -um *adj* opulent, rich, wealthy; powerful; sumptuous

op·us -ĕris *n* work; product of work, structure, building; literary work, composition, book; work of art, workmanship; deed, achievement; (mil) offensive works, siege works; (mil) defensive works, fortifications; **magno opere** greatly; **quanto opere** how much, how greatly; **tanto opere** so much, so greatly; **opus est** (with *inf*) it is useful or beneficial to; **opus est** (with *dat* of person in need and *abl* of person or thing needed) to need, e.g., **vobis duce opus est** you need a leader

opuscŭl·um -ī *n* little work, minor work

ōr·a -ae *f* boundary, border, edge; coastline, coast; region, district; cable, hawser; (fig) people of the coast, people of the region; **ora maritima** seacoast

ōrācŭl·um or **ōrācl·um -ī** *n* oracle; prophesy

ōrārĭ·us -a -um *adj* coasting; **navis oraria** coaster, coasting vessel

ōrāt·a -ōrum *n pl* prayers, requests

ōrātĭ·ō -ōnis *f* faculty of speech; speech, language; style of speech, manner of speaking, style, expression; oration, speech; theme, subject; prose; eloquence; imperial rescript; **orationem habere** to give a speech

ōrātiuncŭl·a -ae *f* short speech, insignificant speech

ōrāt·or -ōris *m* orator, speaker; spokesman; suppliant

ōrātōrĭē *adv* oratorically

ōrātōrĭ·us -a -um *adj* orator's, oratorical

ōrātr·ix -īcis *f* suppliant (*female*)

ōrāt·us -ūs *m* request

orb·a -ae *f* orphan; widow

orbāt·or -ōris *m* murderer (*of someone's children or parents*)

Orbil·ius -iī or **-ī** *m* Horace's teacher in Venusia

orb·is -is *m* circle; disk, ring, orbit; quoit; hoop; wheel; round shield; eye socket, eye; globe, earth, world, universe; region, territory, country; circuit, round; rotation; cycle, period; (rhet) balance; zodiac; **orbis lacteus** Milky Way; **orbis terrae** or **terrarum** earth, world, universe

orbĭt·a -ae *f* rut, wheel track; (fig) rut, routine

orbĭt·ās -ātis *f* childlessness, widowhood, orphanhood

orbitōs·us -a -um *adj* full of ruts

orb·ō -āre *vt* to bereave of parents, father, mother, children, husband, or wife; to strip, rob, deprive, make destitute

orb·us -a -um *adj* bereaved, bereft; destitute; orphaned, fatherless; childless; widowed; (with *genit* or *abl* or with **ab** + *abl*) bereft of, deprived of, without; *m* orphan; *f* see **orba**

orc·a -ae *f* vat, barrel

Orcăd·es -um *f pl* islands N. of Scotland (*modern Orkneys*)

orch·as -ădis *f* olive

orchestr·a -ae *f* senatorial seats (*in the theater*); (fig) senate

Orc·us -ī *m* lower world; Pluto (*king of the lower world*); death

orde- = **horde-**

ordinārĭ·us -a -um *adj* ordinary, usual, regular

ordinātim *adv* in order, in good order, in succession; regularly, properly

ordinātĭ·ō -ōnis *f* orderly arrangement; orderly government

ordināt·us -a -um *adj* regular; appointed

ordĭn·ō -āre *vt* to set in order, arrange, regulate; to govern, rule; to record chronologically

ordĭor ordīrī orsus sum *vt* to begin, undertake; to describe; *vi* to begin, begin to speak

ord·ō -ĭnis *m* line, row, series; row of seats (*in a theater*); order, methodical arrangement; (pol) rank, order, class; (mil) line, file (*of soldiers*), company, century, command of a company or century; *m pl* officers of a company; promotions; **amplissimus ordo** senatorial order; **ex ordine** in succession, with-

out a break; **extra ordinem** extraordinarily, especially, uncommonly; **ordine, in ordine,** or **per ordinem** in order, in sequence, in detail, with regularity, regularly
Orē·as -ădis *f* Oread, mountain nymph
Orest·ēs -is or **-ae** *m* son of Agamemnon and Clytemnestra who avenged his father's death by killing his mother
orex·is -is *f* longing, appetite
organĭc·us -ī *m* organist
orgăn·um -ī *n* instrument, implement; musical instrument, organ
orgĭ·a -ōrum *n pl* Bacchic revels; orgies
orichalc·um -ī *n* copper ore; brass
ōricill·a -ae *f* lobe
orĭ·ens -entis *m* rising sun, morning sun; morning; day; land of the rising sun, Orient, the East
orīg·ō -ĭnis *f* origin, source, beginning, start; birth, lineage, descent; race, stock, family; founder, progenitor
Ōrī·ōn or **Orī·ōn -ŏnis** or **-ōnis** *m* mythical hunter, turned into a constellation
orĭor orīrī ortus sum *vi* to rise, get up; to become visible, appear; to be born, originate, be descended; to proceed, begin, start
Ōrīthўī·a -ae *f* daughter of Erechtheus and mother of Calais and Zetes by Boreas
oriund·us -a -um *adj* descended, sprung, born
ornāment·um -ī *n* equipment, trappings, apparatus; ornament, adornment, decoration; trinket, jewel; (fig) distinction; rhetorical ornament; pride and joy
ornātē *adv* ornately, elegantly
ornātr·ix -īcis *f* hairdresser (*female*)
ornātŭl·us -a -um *adj* fancy
ornāt·us -a -um *adj* equipped, fitted out, furnished, dressed, harnessed; adorned, decorated, embellished; handsome; illustrious, excellent
ornāt·us -ūs *m* equipment; attire, apparel, outfit; furniture; decoration, ornament; world, universe
orn·ō -āre *vt* to equip, fit out, furnish, dress; to set off, decorate, adorn; to honor, praise, commend
orn·us -ī *f* mountain ash
ōr·ō -āre *vt* to beg, entreat, implore, plead with; to ask for; to plead (*a case*); (with double *acc*) to ask (*someone*) for; *vi* to plead, beg, pray; (with **cum** + *abl*) to plead or argue with
Oront·ēs -is or **-ae** *m* chief river of Syria; companion of Aeneas
Orontē·us -a -um *adj* Syrian
Orph·eus -ĕī or **-ĕos** *m* son of Oeagrus and Calliope, husband of Eurydice, and famous musician and poet
Orphē·us or **Orphĭc·us -a -um** *adj* Orphic
ors·us -a -um *pp* of **ordior;** *n pl* beginnings; utterance, words; attempt
ors·us -ūs *m* beginning; attempt, undertaking
ortus *pp* of **orior**
ort·us -ūs *m* rising; the East; birth, origin; source
Ortygĭ·a -ae or **Ortygĭ·ē -ēs** *f* Delos; island in the port of Syracuse
or·yx -ўgis *m* gazelle
oryz·a -ae *f* rice
os ossis *n* bone; marrow, innermost parts; *n pl* skeleton
ōs ōris *n* mouth; beak; voice, speech, expression; lip, face, countenance, look; sight, presence (*of a person*); impudence; mask, mouth, opening, orifice, front; **habere aliquid in ore** to be talking about something continually; **in ore omnium esse** to be on the lips of everyone, be talked about
osc·en -ĭnis *m* bird of augury (*e.g., crow, raven, owl*)
oscill·um -ī *n* small mask
oscĭt·ans -antis *adj* yawning; (fig) indifferent, bored
oscĭt·ō -āre or **oscĭt·or -ārī -ātus sum** *vi* to gape; to yawn
osculātĭ·ō -ōnis *f* kissing
oscŭl·or -ārī -ātus sum *vt* to kiss; (fig) to make a fuss over
oscŭl·um -ī *n* little mouth; kiss; **breve osculum** peck
Osc·us -a -um *adj* Oscan; *m pl* Oscans (*ancient people of Campania and Samnium*)
Osīr·is -is or **-ĭdis** *m* Egyptian god, the husband of Isis
ōs·or -ōris *m* hater
Oss·a -ae *f* mountain in N.E. Thessaly
ossĕ·us -a -um *adj* bony
ossifrăg·a -ae *f* osprey
ostendō ostendĕre ostendī ostentum *vt* to stretch out, stretch forth; to expose; to show, exhibit, display, present; to reveal, disclose; to declare, make known
ostentātĭ·ō -ōnis *f* display; ostentation, showing off; mere show, pretense
ostentāt·or -ōris *m* show-off
ostent·ō -āre *vt* to show, exhibit; to show off, display, parade, boast of; to declare, point out, set forth
ostent·um -ī *n* portent, prodigy
ostent·us -ūs *m* display, show; **ostentui** for appearances, in pretense
Ostĭ·a -ae *f* or **Ostĭ·a -ōrum** *n pl* Ostia (*port and town at the mouth of the Tiber*)
ostiār·ĭum -ĭī or **-ī** *n* tax on doors
ostiātim *adv* from door to door
ost·ĭum -ĭī or **-ī** *n* door; entrance, mouth
ostrĕ·a -ae *f* or **ostrĕ·um -ī** *n* oyster
ostreāt·us -a -um *adj* covered with oyster shells; (fig) black and blue

ostreōs·us -a -um *adj* abounding in oysters
ostrĭf·er -ĕra -ĕrum *adj* oyster-growing
ostrīn·us -a -um *adj* purple
ostr·um -ī *n* purple; purple dress, purple covering
ōsus *pp* of **odi**
Oth·ō -ōnis *m* L. Roscius Otho (*author of the law in* 67 B.C. *reserving fourteen rows in the theaters for the equestrian order*); M. Salvius Otho (*Roman emperor in* 69 A.D.)
Othr·ys -ўos *m* mountain in S. Thessaly
ōtiŏl·um -ī *n* bit of leisure
ōtĭ·or -ārī -ātus sum *vi* to take it easy
ōtiōsē *adv* at leisure; leisurely, without haste; calmly, fearlessly
ōtiōs·us -a -um *adj* at leisure, relaxing; free from official obligations; quiet, calm; unconcerned, indifferent, neutral; passionless; *m* private person (*not holding public office*); *m pl* civilians, non-combatants
ōt·ĭum -ĭī or **-ī** *n* leisure, free time, relaxation; freedom from public affairs, retirement; peace, quiet; ease, idleness, inactivity
Ovid·ĭus -ĭī or **-ī** *m* P. Ovidius Naso or Ovid (*Latin poet, born at Sulmo,* 43 B.C.-17 A.D.)
ovīl·e -is *n* sheepfold; voting enclosures in the Campus Martius
ovīl·is -e *adj* sheep, of sheep
ovill·us -a -um *adj* sheep, of sheep
ov·is -is *f* sheep; wool; simpleton
ov·ō -āre *vi* to rejoice; to hold a celebration; to celebrate a minor triumph
ōv·um -ī *n* egg; *n pl* wooden balls used to mark the laps at the racetrack

P

pābulātĭ·ō -ōnis *f* foraging
pābulāt·or -ōris *m* forager
pābŭl·or -ārī -ātus sum *vi* to forage; (coll) to make a living
pābŭl·um -ī *n* food, fodder; pasturage, grass; (fig) nourishment
pācāl·is -e *adj* of peace
pācāt·us -a -um *adj* peaceful, quiet, calm; *n* friendly country
Pachȳn·um -ī *n* S.E. point of Sicily
pācĭf·er -ĕra -ĕrum *adj* peace-bringing, peaceful
pācificātĭ·ō -ōnis *f* pacification
pācificāt·or -ōris *m* peacemaker
pācificātōrĭ·us -a -um *adj* peacemaking
pācifĭc·ō -āre *vt* to pacify, appease; *vi* to make peace, conclude peace
pācifĭc·us -a -um *adj* peace-making; peaceable
paciscor pasciscī pactus sum *vt* to bargain for, agree upon; to stipulate; to barter; to betroth; *vi* to come to an agreement, agree, make a bargain, make a contract; (with *inf*) to agree to, pledge oneself to
pac·ō -āre *vt* to pacify, soothe, subdue
pact·a -ae *f* fiancee; bride
pactĭ·ō -ōnis *f* pact, contract, agreement, treaty; condition, stipulation; collusion
Pactŏl·us -ī *m* river in Lydia famous for its gold
pact·or -ōris *m* contractor, negotiator, party (*in a contract*)
pact·us -a -um *pp* of **paciscor** and of **pango;** *n* pact, contract, agreement; way, manner; **aliquo pacto** somehow; **hoc pacto** in this way; **in pacto manere** to stick to the agreement; **quo pacto** how, in what way
Pācuv·ĭus -ĭī or **-ī** *m* Roman tragic poet, native of Brundisium, and nephew of Ennius (*c.* 220-130 B.C.)
Pad·us -ī *m* Po River (*in N. Italy*)
pae·ān -ānis *m* epithet of Apollo as the god of healing; paean, hymn of praise, victory song
paedagōg·ĭum -ĭī or **-ī** *n* training school for pages
paedagōg·us -ī *m* slave in charge of school children; (fig) guide, leader
paedĭc·ō -āre *vt* to have abnormal relations with (*young boys*)
paed·or -ōris *m* filth
pael·ex -ĭcis *f* concubine, mistress
paelicāt·us -ūs *m* concubinage
Paelign·ī -ōrum *m pl* a people of central Italy
paenē *adv* almost, nearly
paeninsŭl·a -ae *f* peninsula
paenitend·us -a -um *adj* regrettable
paenitentĭ·a -ae *f* repentance, regret
paenit·ĕō -ēre -ŭī *vt* to cause to regret; to displease; *vi* (with *genit*) to regret; *v impers* (with *acc* of person), e.g., **me paenitet** I am sorry; (with *acc* of person and *genit* of thing), e.g., **me paenitet consili** I regret the plan, I am dissatisfied with the plan; (with *acc* of person and *inf* or **quod**), e.g., **eos paenitet animum tuum offendisse** or **eos paenitet quod animum tuum offenderint** they regret having offended your feelings
paenŭl·a -ae *f* traveling coat; raincoat
paenulāt·us -a -um *adj* wearing a traveling coat
pae·ōn -ōnis *m* metrical foot con-

taining one long and three short syllables

paeōnī·us -a -um *adj* healing, medicinal

Paest·um -ī *n* town in Lucania in S. Italy

paetŭl·us -a -um *adj* slightly squint-eyed

paet·us -a -um *adj* squinting, squint-eyed; leering

pāgān·us -a -um *adj* of a village, rustic; ignorant, untaught; *m* villager, peasant; (as term of contempt) yokel

Pagăs·a -ae *f* or **Pagăs·ae -ārum** *f pl* town on the coast of Thessaly, from which the Argonauts sailed

Pagasae·us -a -um *adj* Pagasaean; *m* Jason

pāgātim *adv* by villages, in every village

pāgell·a -ae *f* small page

pāgĭn·a -ae *f* page (*of book*)

pāginŭl·a -ae *f* small page

pāg·us -ī *m* village; canton, province; country people, villagers

pāl·a -ae *f* spade

palaestr·a -ae *f* palaestra, wrestling school, gymnasium; school of rhetoric; rhetorical training; school; wrestling; exercise; brothel

palaestrĭcē *adv* as at the palaestra

palaestrĭc·us -a -um *adj* of the palaestra, gymnastic; *f* gymnastics

palaestrīt·a -ae *m* professional wrestler; director of a palaestra

palam *adv* openly, publicly, plainly; **palam esse** to be public, be well known; **palam facere** to make public, disclose; *prep* (with *abl*) before, in the presence of, face to face with

Palātīn·us -a -um *adj* Palatine; imperial

Palāt·ium -iī or **-ī** *n* Palatine Hill (*residential area of distinguished Romans and several Roman emperors*); palace

palāt·um -ī *n* or **palāt·us -ī** *m* palate; taste; literary taste

palĕ·a -ae *f* chaff

paleār·ia -ium *n pl* dewlap

Pal·ēs -is *f* Italic goddess of shepherds and flocks

Palīc·ī -ōrum *m pl* twin sons of Jupiter and the nymph Thalia

Palīl·is -e *adj* of Pales; *n pl* festival of Pales celebrated on April 21st

palimpsest·us -ī *m* palimpsest

Palinūr·us -ī *m* pilot of Aeneas who fell overboard and drowned; promontory named after him

paliūr·us -ī *m* Christ's thorn (*plant*)

pall·a -ae *f* ladies' long robe; outer garment, mantle; tragic actor's costume

Palladi·us -a -um *adj* of Pallas; *n* statue of Pallas, Palladium

Pall·as -ădis or **-ădos** *f* Athene; olive oil, oil; olive tree; Palladium (*Trojan statue of Pallas*)

pall·ens -entis *adj* pale, sallow; grey-green, yellow-green, chartreuse, yellowish, sickly-looking

pall·ĕō -ēre -ŭī *vi* to be pale, look pale; to be yellow, look yellow; to change color, fade; (with *dat*) to grow pale over, worry about

pall·escō -escĕre -ŭī *vt* to turn pale at; *vi* to turn pale; to turn yellow; to fade

palliāt·us -a -um *adj* wearing a Greek cloak; **fabula palliata** Latin play with Greek setting and characters

pallidŭl·us -a -um *adj* somewhat pale

pallĭd·us -a -um *adj* pale, sallow; grey-green, yellow-green, chartreuse

palliolātim *adv* in a mantle

palliolāt·us -a -um *adj* wearing a short mantle, wearing a hood

palliŏl·um -ī *n* short cloak; cape, hood

pall·ium -iī or **-ī** *n* coverlet, cover; Greek cloak

pall·or -ōris *m* paleness, pallor; **pallorem ducere** to turn pale

pallŭl·a -ae *f* short cloak

palm·a -ae *f* palm of the hand, hand; palm tree, date; palm branch, palm wreath; palm of victory, prize, victory, honor, distinction; blade of an oar

palmār·is -e *adj* excellent, deserving the palm or prize

palmārī·us -a -um *adj* prize-winning, excellent; *n* masterpiece

palmāt·us -a -um *adj* embroidered with palm branches; **tunica palmata** palm-embroidered tunic (*worn by a general*)

palm·es -ĭtis *m* vine sprout, vine branch; branch, bough

palmēt·um -ī *n* palm grove

palmĭf·er -ĕra -ĕrum *adj* palm-growing, full of palm trees

palmōs·us -a -um *adj* full of palm trees

palmŭl·a -ae *f* oar blade

pāl·or -ārī -ātus sum *vi* to roam about, wander aimlessly

palpāti·ō -ōnis *f* stroking; *f pl* flattering

palpāt·or -ōris *m* flatterer

palpĕbr·a -ae *f* eyelid

palpĭt·ō -āre *vi* to throb, palpitate, quiver

palp·ō -āre or **palp·or -ārī -ātus sum** *vt* to stroke, pat; to wheedle, coax; to flatter; *vi* (with *dat*) **a** to coax; **b** to flatter

palp·us -ī *m* palm of the hand; coaxing

palūdāment·um -ī *n* military coat; general's coat

palūdāt·us -a -um *adj* wearing a general's coat

palūdōs·us -a -um *adj* swampy, marshy

palumb·ēs -is *m* or *f* pigeon, dove

pāl·us -ī *m* stake, post; wooden post used in sword practice

pal·ūs -ūdis *f* swamp, marsh; sedge
palust·er -ris -re *adj* swampy, marshy, in the swamps
pampinē·us -a -um *adj* of vine tendrils, made of vine leaves; **odor pampineus** bouquet of wines
pampin·us -ī *m* vine shoot, tendril; vine leaf; tendril (*of any plant*)
Pān Pānos *m* Pan (*Greek god of flocks, shepherds, and woods, often identified with Faunus*)
panacē·a -ae *f* or **panăc·es -is** *n* panacea
Panaetōlic·us -a -um *adj* Pan-Aetolian
pānār·ium -iī or **-ī** *n* bread basket
Panchāi·a -ae *f* region in Arabia famous for its frankincense
panchrest·us or **panchrist·us -a -um** *adj* good for everything, universally useful
pancraticē *adv* (coll) fine, splendidly; **pancratice valere** to get along splendidly
pancrat·ium or **pancrat·ion -iī** or **-ī** *n* contest which included both boxing and wrestling
Pandăr·us -ī *m* famous Lycian archer in the Trojan army; companion of Aeneas, killed by Turnus
pandicŭl·or -ārī -ātus sum *vi* to stretch oneself
Pandī·ōn -ŏnis *m* king of Athens and father of Procne and Philomela
Pandīonī·us -a -um *adj* of Pandion
pandō pandĕre pandī pansum or **passum** *vt* to spread out, extend, expand, unfold; to open, lay open, throw open; to reveal, make known, publish
pand·us -a -um *adj* crooked, bent, curved
pangō pangĕre panxī or **pepĕgī -pactum** *vt* to fasten, fix, drive in; to fix, settle, agree upon, determine; to write, compose, celebrate, record; to promise in marriage; **indutias pangere** (with **cum** + *abl*) to conclude an armistice with
pānicē·us -a -um *adj* made of bread; **milites panicei** (coll) Breadville brigade
pānicŭl·a -ae *f* tuft
pānic·um -ī *n* millet
pān·is -is *m* bread, loaf; **panis cibarius** coarse bread; **panis secundus** stale bread
Pānisc·us -ī *m* little Pan
pannicŭl·us -ī *m* rag
Pannonĭ·us -a -um *adj* Pannonian; *f* Pannonia (*country on the Danube*)
pannōs·us -a -um *adj* tattered, ragged; shriveled, wrinkled, sad-looking
pannūcē·us or **pannūcĭ·us -a -um** *adj* ragged; shriveled, wrinkled
pann·us -ī *m* patch; rag
Panŏp·ē -ēs or **Panopē·a -ae** *f* a sea nymph
pans·a -ae *masc & fem adj* flat-footed, splayfooted
pansus *pp* of **pando**
panthēr·a -ae *f* panther
Panthoid·ēs -ae *m* Euphorbus (*Trojan warrior*)
Panth·us -ī *m* priest of Apollo at Troy and father of Euphorbus
pantic·ēs -um *m pl* bowels; sausages
papae *interj* great!, wonderful!
pāp·as -ae or **-ătis** *m* tutor
papāv·er -ĕris *n* poppy
papāverē·us -a -um *adj* of poppies
Paphī·ē -ēs *f* Venus
Paphī·us -a -um *adj* Paphian, of Paphos
Paph·os -ī *f* town in Cyprus sacred to Venus
pāpilĭ·ō -ōnis *m* butterfly
papill·a -ae *f* nipple, teat; breast
papp·ō -āre *vi* to eat baby food, eat pap
papp·us -ī *m* hairy seed (*of certain plants*)
papŭl·a -ae *f* pimple
papȳrif·er -ĕra -ĕrum *adj* papyrus-producing
papȳr·us -ī *m & f* or **papȳr·um -ī** *n* papyrus; paper; garment (*made of papyrus*)
pār paris *adj* equal, like, on a par, equally matched, well matched; suitable, adequate; of equal size; (with *dat* or **cum** + *abl*) equal to, comparable to, similar to, as large as; (with limiting *abl*, **ad** + *acc*, or **in** + *abl*) equal, similar, alike in; **par est** it is right, it is proper; **par proelium** indecisive battle; **ut par est** (used parenthetically) as is only right; *m* companion, comrade; equal; mate, spouse; **pares cum paribus facillime congregantur** birds of a feather flock together; *n* pair, couple; the like; **par pari** like for like, tit for tat
parābil·is -e *adj* available
parasīt·a -ae *f* parasite (*female*)
parasītast·er -rī *m* poor parasite
parasītātĭ·ō -ōnis *f* sponging
parasītic·us -a -um *adj* parasitical
parasīt·or -ārī -ātus sum *vi* to sponge, freeload, be a parasite
parasīt·us -ī *m* parasite, sponger, freeloader
parātē *adv* with preparation; carefully; readily, promptly
parātĭ·ō -ōnis *f* preparing, procuring, acquisition
paratragoed·ō -āre *vi* to talk in a tragic style, be melodramatic
parāt·us -a -um *adj* prepared, ready; well prepared, furnished, equipped; learned, well versed, skilled; (with *dat* or **ad** + *acc*) **a** ready for; **b** equipped to; (with *inf*) prepared to, ready to; (with *abl* or **in** + *abl*) versed in, experienced in
parāt·us -ūs *m* preparation, provision, equipment, outfit; clothing, apparel
Parc·a -ae *f* goddess of Fate, Fate
parcē *adv* sparingly, thriftily; moderately, with restraint; stingily; rarely, seldom

parceprōm·us -ī *m* stingy person

parcō parcĕre pepercī parsum *vt* to spare, use sparingly; *vi* to be sparing, economize; (with *dat*) **a** to spare, use carefully; **b** to show mercy to; **c** to abstain from, refrain from; **d** to refuse (*help*); (with *inf*) to cease, stop (*e.g., doing, talking*)

parc·us -a -um *adj* thrifty, economical, frugal; niggardly, stingy; moderate, conservative; slight, little, scanty, paltry (*thing given*)

pard·us -ī *m* panther

par·ens -entis *adj* obedient; *m* parent, father; ancestor, grandparent; founder, inventor; *m pl* subjects; ancestors; *f* parent, mother

parentāl·is -e *adj* parental; **dies parentalis** memorial day; *n pl* festival in honor of dead ancestors and relatives

parent·ō -āre *vi* to hold memorial service in honor of dead parents or relatives; (with *dat*) **a** to offer sacrifice to (*the dead*); **b** to avenge (*a dead person*) with the death of another person; **c** to appease, satisfy

pār·ĕō -ēre -ŭī *vi* to appear, be visible, be evident, be at hand; (with *dat*) **a** to obey, be obedient to, comply with, be subject to, be subservient to; **b** to yield to, gratify, satisfy (*pleasures, etc.*); **c** to fulfill (*promises*)

parĭ·ēs -ĕtis *m* wall (*esp. partition in a house or building*)

parietīn·ae -ārum *f pl* tumbled-down walls; ruins; (fig) ruins

Parīl·ĭa -ĭum *n pl* festival of Pales (*celebrated on April 21st*)

parĭl·is -e *adj* equal, like; **aetas parilis** same age, like age

parĭō parĕre pepĕrī partum *vt* to bear, bring forth, give birth to; (of animals) to lay, spawn, produce; (fig) to produce, create, devise, cause, effect, accomplish, acquire, obtain

Par·is -ĭdis *m* son of Priam and Hecuba, also called Alexandros; famous pantomime actor in the reign of Nero; famous pantomime actor in the reign of Domitian, the freedman of Domitia

parĭter *adv* equally, in like manner, as well, alike; at the same time, simultaneously, together, at once; **pariter ac** (or **atque**), **pariter ut** as well as; **pariter ac si** just as if; **pariter** (with **cum** + *abl*) together with, at the same time as

parĭt·ō -āre *vt* (with *inf*) to get ready to

Parĭ·us -a -um *adj & mf* Parian

parm·a -ae *f* small round shield; shield

parmāt·us -a -um *adj* armed with a shield, light-armed

parmŭl·a -ae *f* small shield

Parnās·is -ĭdis or **Parnāsĭ·us -a -um** *adj* of Parnassus, Parnassian

Parnās·us or **Parnās·os -ī** *m* mountain in Phocis, in central Greece, sacred to Apollo and the Muses, on whose slopes Delphi was located

par·ō -āre *vt* to prepare, make ready, provide, furnish; to get, procure, acquire, gather, purchase; **se parare** to prepare oneself, get ready; *vi* to get ready, make preparations, make arrangements; (with *dat* or **ad** + *acc*) to get ready for

parŏch·a -ae *f* room and board (*required of provincials for traveling Roman officials*)

parŏch·us -ī *m* official host (*local official who provided accommodations for traveling Roman dignitaries*); host

parops·is -ĭdis *f* dish, dessert dish

Par·os or **Par·us -ī** *f* island of the Cyclades, famous for its white marble

parr·a -ae *f* owl

Parrhăs·is -ĭdis *f* Arcadian woman; Callisto

Parrhasĭ·us -a -um *adj* Arcadian; **Parrhasia virgo** Callisto; *f* district in Arcadia

parricīd·a -ae *m* or *f* parricide (*murder of a parent or close relative*); assassin of a high magistrate; murderer, assassin; traitor, outlaw, criminal

parricīd·ĭum -ĭī or **-ī** *n* parricide (*murderer of a parent or close relative*); murder, assassination; treason, high treason

par·s -tis *f* part, portion, share, section, fraction; side, direction, region; part, function, duty; part of body, member (*esp. genital organs*); *f pl* part, role, character; political party; **ab omni parte** in all respects; **ex altera parte** on the other hand; **ex magna parte** to a great extent; **ex parte** partly; **in eam partem** in that direction; in that sense; in such a manner; **in perjorem partem rapere** to put a worse construction on; **in utramque partem** in both directions; **major pars populi** the majority; **maximam partem** for the most part; **minor pars populi** the minority; **omnibus partibus** in all respects; **pars . . . pars, pars . . . alii** some . . . others; **parte** in part, partly; **pro mea parte** to the best of my abilities; **tres partes** three fourths

parsimōnĭ·a -ae *f* parsimony

parsus *pp* of **parco**

parthenĭc·ē -ēs *f* parthenium (*plant*)

Parthenopae·us -ī *m* son of Meleager and Atalanta and one of the Seven who fought against Thebes

Parthenŏp·ē -ēs *f* one of the Sirens, after whom Naples was originally named

Parthĭ·a -ae *f* Parthia (*country located S.E. of the Caspian*)

Parthĭc·us -a -um *adj* Parthian

Parth·us -a -um *adj & m* Parthian

partĭc·eps -ĭpis *adj* (with *genit*) sharing in, taking part in; *m* partner, confederate
particĭp·ō -āre *vt* to make (*someone*) a partner; to share (*something*)
particŭl·a -ae *f* bit, particle, grain
partim *adv* partly, in part, to some extent; for the most part, mostly; (with *genit* or **ex** + *abl*) some of; **partim . . . partim** some . . . others
partĭ·ō -ōnis *f* bringing forth, producing
part·iō -īre -īvī or **-iī -ītum** or **part·ior -īrī -ītus sum** *vt* to share, distribute, apportion, divide
partītē *adv* with proper divisions, methodically
partītĭ·ō -ōnis *f* division, distribution, sharing; division of a speech
partitūd·ō -ĭnis *f* bearing (*of young*)
partur·iō -īre -īvī or **-iī** *vt* to teem with; to be ready to produce; to bring forth, yield; (fig) to brood over; *vi* to be in labor
partus *pp* of **pario;** *adj* acquired; *n* acquisition, gain, store
part·us -ūs *m* birth; young, offspring; (fig) beginnings
parum *adv* a little, too little, insufficiently; **parum est** it is not enough, it does not suffice; **parum habere** to regard as unsatisfactory; **satis eloquentiae sapientiae parum** enough eloquence but too little wisdom
parumper *adv* for a little while, a moment; **operire parumper** wait a moment
parvĭt·ās -ātis *f* smallness
parvŭl·us or **parvŏl·us -a -um** *adj* tiny; slight, petty; young; *n* childhood, infancy; **ab parvulis** from childhood, from infancy
parv·us -a -um (*comp* **minor;** *superl* **minĭmus**) *adj* small, little, puny; short; young; brief, short (*time*); small, insignificant, unimportant; low, cheap (*price*); *n* a little, trifle; childhood, infancy; **a parvis** or **a parvo** from childhood, from infancy; **parvi esse** to be of little importance; **parvi facere, aestimare, habere,** or **ducere** to think little of, care little for; **parvi refert** it makes little difference, it matters little
pasceŏl·us -ī *m* money bag
pascō pascĕre pāvī pastum *vt* to feed, pasture, keep, raise (*animals*); to cultivate, cherish; to feed (*flames, passions*); to pile up (*debts*); to grow (*beard*); to lay waste, ravage (*fields*); to feast, gratify (*the eyes*); to cherish (*hope*)
pascor pascī pastus sum *vi* to graze, browse, be fed; (with *abl*) **a** to graze on; **b** (fig) to feed on, feast on, thrive on
pascŭ·us -a -um *adj* grazing, pasture; *n* pasture
Pāsiphă·ē -ēs or **Pāsiphă·a -ae** *f* daughter of Helios, sister of Circe, husband of Minos, and mother of Androgeos, Ariadne, Phaedra, and the Minotaur
pass·er -ĕris *m* sparrow; plaice, flounder; **passer marinus** ostrich
passercŭl·us -ī *m* little sparrow
passim *adv* here and there, all over, at random; without order, indiscriminately, promiscuously
passus *pp* of **pando** and of **patior;** *adj* spread out, extended, open; disheveled; dried, dry; *n* wine made from dried grapes, raisin wine
pass·us -ūs *m* step, pace; footstep, track; **mille passūs** mile; **tria milia passuum** three miles
pastill·us -ī *m* lozenge
pastĭ·ō -ōnis *f* pasture, grazing
past·or -ōris *m* shepherd
pastorāl·is -e *adj* shepherd's, pastoral
pastōricĭ·us or **pastōrĭ·us -a -um** *adj* shepherd's, pastoral
pastus *pp* of **pasco**
past·us -ūs *m* pasture, fodder, food; (fig) food
patagiār·ius -iī or **-ī** *m* fringe maker
patagiāt·us -a -um *adj* (tunic) with fringes
Patăr·a -ae *f* town in Lycia with an oracle of Apollo
Patăr·eus -ĕī or **-ĕos** *m* Apollo
Patavīn·us -a -um *adj* of Patavium
Patav·ium -iī or **-ī** *n* city in N. Italy, the birthplace of Livy (*modern Padua*)
pate-faciō -facĕre -fēcī -factus (passive; **pate·fīō -fiĕrī**) *vt* to throw open; to open up, make accessible; to bring to light
patefactĭ·ō -ōnis *f* disclosure
patell·a -ae *f* pan, dish, plate
pat·ens -entis *adj* open, accessible; extensive; exposed; evident
patentius *adv* more openly, more clearly
pat·ĕō -ēre -ŭī *vi* to stand open, be open; to be accessible; to be exposed; to open, stretch out, extend; to be clear, be plain, be well known; to be accessible, be attainable, be free; (of the mind) to be open, be receptive
pat·er -ris *m* father; **pater cenae** host; **pater familias** head of the household, head of the family; *m pl* forefathers; senators
patĕr·a -ae *f* flat dish (*used esp. in making libations*)
pat·erfamiliās -risfamiliās *m* head of the household, head of the family
patern·us -a -um *adj* father's, paternal; ancestral; of a native country, native
pat·escō -escĕre -ŭī *vi* to be opened, be open; to stretch out, extend; to be disclosed, be divulged, become evident
pathic·us -a -um *adj* lustful
patibĭl·is -e *adj* tolerable, endurable; sensitive

patibulāt·us -a -um *adj* gibbeted; wearing a yoke
patibŭl·um -ī *m* fork-shaped yoke (*tied around the neck of a criminal*); fork-shaped gibbet
patī·ens -entis *adj* hardy, tough; hard; stubborn, unyielding, patient, tolerant; (with *genit* or **ad** + *acc*) able to endure, inured to, able to take; **amnis patiens navium** navigable river
patienter *adv* patiently
patienti·a -ae *f* patience, endurance; resignation, forbearance; submissiveness; sexual submission
patĭn·a -ae *f* dish, pan
patinārī·us -a -um *adj* of pans; in a pan; **strues patinaria** pile of dishes
patior pātī passus sum *vt* to experience, undergo, suffer; to put up with, allow; to submit to sexually; **aequo animo pati** to suffer patiently; **aegre pati** to resent, be displeased with
patrāt·or -ōris *m* perpetrator
patrāt·us *adj masc* **pater patratus** plenipotentiary
patrī·a -ae *f* native land, native city, home
patrīcē *adv* paternally
patricī·us -a -um *adj* of patrician status, patrician; *m pl* patricians, patrician class
patrīmōn·ium -iī or **-ī** *n* patrimony, inheritance
patrīm·us -a -um *adj* having a father living
patriss·ō -āre *vi* to take after one's father
patrīt·us -a -um *adj* father's, inherited from one's father
patrī·us -a -um *adj* father's, of a father, fatherly, paternal; ancestral, traditional, heriditary; native; *f* see **patria**
patr·ō -āre *vt* to bring about, effect, achieve, accomplish, perform, finish, conclude; **bellum patrare** to bring the war to an end; **jus jurandum patrare** to take an oath (*confirming a treaty*); **pacem patrare** to conclude a peace
patrōcin·ium -iī or **-ī** *n* patronage, protection, legal defense, legal representation
patrōcĭn·or -ārī -ātus sum *vi* to be a patron, afford protection; (with *dat*) to serve (*someone*) as patron, protect, defend
Patrŏcl·us -ī *m* son of Menoetius and friend of Achilles, who wearing the armor of Achilles, was killed by Hector
patrōn·a -ae *f* legal protectress, patroness; advocate; defender, safeguard
patrōn·us -ī *m* legal protector, patron; advocate (*in court*); defender
patruēl·is -e *adj* of or descended from a father's brother, cousin's; *m* cousin
patrŭ·us -a -um *adj* uncle's; *m* (paternal) uncle
patŭl·us -a -um *adj* open, standing open; spreading, spread out, broad
pauciloqu·ium -iī or **-ī** *n* reticence
paucĭt·ās -ātis *f* paucity, scarcity, small number
paucŭl·ī -ae -a *adj* just a few, very few; *n pl* few words
pauc·us -a -um *adj* few, little; *pron masc pl* few, a few; the select few, elite; **inter paucos (paucas)** or **in paucis** especially; *pron neut pl* a few things, a few words; **paucis** in a few words, briefly
paulātim *adv* little by little, gradually, by degrees; a few at a time
paulisper *adv* for a little while
paulō *adv* (as *abl* of degree of difference in expressions of comparison) by a little, a little, somewhat; **paulo antea** a little before; **paulo post** a little later
paulŭlō *adv* somewhat, a little; cheaply, at a low price
paulŭlum *adv* somewhat, a little
paulŭl·us -a -um *adj* very little; *n* a bit; **paululum pecuniae** a bit of money
paulum *adv* a little, to some extent, to some degree
paul·us -a -um *adj* small, little; *n* bit, trifle; **post paulum** after a bit, after a while
Paul·us -ī *m* L. Aemilius Paulus (*conqueror of Macedonia through the victory at Pydna in* 168 B.C.)
paup·er -ĕris *adj* poor; scanty, meager; (with *genit*) poor in; *m* poor man, pauper
paupercŭl·us -a -um *adj* poor
pauperī·ēs -ēī *f* poverty
paupĕr·ō -āre *vt* to impoverish; (with *abl*) to rob (*someone*) of
paupert·ās -ātis *f* poverty
paus·a -ae *f* pause, stop, end
pausī·a -ae *f* plump olive
pauxillātim *adv* bit by bit, little by little
pauxillisper *adv* by degrees
pauxillŭlum *adv* a little, a bit
pauxillŭl·us -a -um *adj* very little, tiny; *n* bit
pauxillum *adv* a little, a bit
pauxill·us -a -um *adj* very little, tiny; *n* small amount
pavefact·us -a -um *adj* frightened, scared
pavĕō pavēre pāvī *vt* to be scared of; *vi* to be terrified, tremble, or shiver with fear
pavesc·ō -ĕre *vt* to get scared of; *vi* to begin to be alarmed
pavĭdē *adv* in panic
pavĭd·us -a -um *adj* panicky, alarmed, shivering or trembling with fear, startled; with beating heart, nervous; causing alarm
pavīment·ō -āre *vt* to pave
pavīment·um -ī *n* pavement; floor
pav·iō -īre -īvī or **-iī -ītum** *vt* to strike, beat

pavit·ō -āre *vt* to be panicky over; *vi* to quake with fear, be scared to death; to shiver (*with fever*)
pāv·ō -ōnis *m* peacock
pav·or -ōris *m* panic, terror, dismay, quaking, shivering; **pavorem injicere** (with *dat*) to throw the fear of the Lord into, to terrify
pax pācis *f* peace; peace treaty, reconciliation, compact, agreement; harmony, tranquility; favor, pardon (*from the gods*); **pace tua** with your permission, with your leave
pecc·ans -antis *m* offender, sinner
peccāt·um -ī *n* fault, mistake, slip, transgression, sin
pecc·ō -āre *vi* to make a mistake, commit a fault, sin
pecorōs·us -a -um *adj* rich in cattle
pect·en -inis *m* comb; plectrum (*for strumming a lyre*); scallop (*sea food*)
pectō pectĕre pexī pexum *vt* to comb; to card (*wool*); (coll) to clobber (*with stick or fist*)
pect·us -ŏris *n* breast; heart, feeling; soul, conscience, mind, understanding; character, person
pecū (*genit* not in use) *n* flock; *n pl* cattle; pastures
pecuārĭ·us -a -um *adj* of sheep, of cattle; **res pecuaria** livestock; *m* cattle man, cattle breeder, rancher; *f* livestock; *n pl* herds of cattle, herds of sheep
pecūlāt·or -ōris *m* embezzler
pecūlāt·us -ūs *m* embezzlement
pecūliār·is -e *adj* one's own, as one's own private property; special
pecūliāt·us -a -um *adj* rich, well off
pecūlĭ·ō -āre *vt* to give away for good
pecūliōs·us -a -um *adj* owning private property
pecūl·ium -ĭī or **-ī** *n* small savings (*esp. accumulated by slaves*); private property
pecūnĭ·a -ae *f* money; **pecunia praesens** ready cash
pecūniārĭ·us -a -um *adj* pecuniary, financial, money
pecūniōs·us -a -um *adj* rich, wealthy, loaded with money; profitable, bringing in money
pec·us -ŏris *n* cattle, herd, flock; sheep; head of cattle; **pecus equinum** stud; (as term of scorn) cattle
pec·us -ŭdis *f* head of cattle; beast; sheep; domestic animal; land animal (*as opposed to birds*); (as term of abuse) brute, beast, swine
pedāl·is -e *adj* one-foot-long
pedār·ius -ĭī or **-ī** *m* inferior senator (*who let others step all over him*)
ped·es -ĭtis *m* infantryman; pedestrian; infantry
pedest·er -ris -re *adj* infantry; pedestrian; on land, by land; written in prose; prosaic, plain
pedetemptim *adv* by feeling one's way, step by step, slowly, cautiously
pedĭc·a -ae *f* foot chain; trap, snare
pedīculōs·us -a -um *adj* lousy
ped·is -is *m* or *f* louse
pedisĕqu·a -ae *f* attendant, handmaid
pedisĕqu·us -ī *m* footman, page, lackey
peditastell·us -ī *m* poor infantryman
peditāt·us -ūs *m* infantry
pēdīt·um -ī *n* wind, gas
pēdō pēdĕre pepēdī *vi* to break wind
ped·um -ī *n* shepherd's hook
Pēgasē·us or **Pēgasei·us -a -um** *adj* of Pegasus, Pegasean
Pēgasĭd·es -um *f pl* Muses
Pēgăs·us -ī *m* winged horse which sprang from the blood of Medusa and whose hoof, as it hit Mt. Helicon, caused Hippocrene, a fountain dear to the Muses, to flow
pegm·a -ătis *n* bookcase; scaffolding
pējerātiuncŭl·a -ae *f* petty oath
pējerāt·us or **pējurāt·us -a -um** *adj* offended by false oaths; **jus pejeratum** false oath
pējĕr·ō or **perjūr·ō -āre** *vt* to swear falsely by; *vi* to swear a false oath; (coll) to lie
pējerōs·us -a -um *adj* perjured
pēj·or -us (*comp* of **malus**) *adj* worse
pējus (*comp* of **male**) *adv* worse
pelagĭ·us -a -um *adj* of the sea
pelăg·us -ī *n* sea, open sea
pēlăm·is -ĭdis or **pēlăm·ys -ȳdis** *f* young tuna fish
Pelasg·ī -ōrum *m pl* aborigines of Greece
Pēl·eus -ĕī or **-ĕos** *m* king of Thessaly, son of Aeacus, husband of Thetis, and father of Achilles
Pelĭ·ās -ae *m* king of Iolcos in Thessaly and uncle of Jason
Pēlīd·ēs -ae *m* descendant of Peleus; Achilles; Neoptolemus
Pēlĭ·on -ī *n* mountain in E. Thessaly
Pēlĭ·us or **Pēliăc·us -a -um** *adj* of Mt. Pelion
Pell·a -ae or **Pell·ē -ēs** *f* city of Macedonia and birthplace of Alexander the Great
pellăcĭ·a -ae *f* charm, allurement
Pellae·us -a -um *adj* of or from Apella; **Pellaeus juvenis** Alexander
pell·ax -ācis *adj* seductive, alluring
pellectĭ·ō -ōnis *f* perusal
pel·liciō -licĕre -lexī -lectum *vt* to allure, entice, coax, wheedle
pellicŭl·a -ae *f* small hide, skin, fleece
pellĭ·ō -ōnis *m* furrier
pell·is -is *f* skin, hide; leather; felt; tent; shield cover; **detrahere pellem** to expose one's true character
pellīt·us -a -um *adj* clothed in skins, wearing leather coat
pellō pellĕre pepŭlī pulsum *vt* to push, beat, strike, knock, hurl; to

drive out or away, expel, banish; to repel, drive back, rout; to play or strum (*lyre, etc.*); to affect, impress, move, strike; to stamp (*the earth*)

pelluc- = **perl-**

Pelopei·as -ădis or **Pelopē·is -ĭdis** *adj* Peloponnesian

Pelopei·us or **Pelopē·us -a -um** *adj* Pelopian; Mycenaean; Phrygian

Pelopĭd·ae -ārum *m pl* descendants of Pelops

Peloponnens·is -e *adj* Peloponnesian

Peloponnēsiăc·us or **Peloponnēsĭ·us -a -um** *adj* Peloponnesian

Peloponnēs·us -ī *f* the Peloponnesus (*modern Morea*)

Pel·ops -ŏpis *m* son of Tantalus, father of Atreus and Thyestes, and grandfather of Agamemnon and Menelaus

pelōr·is -ĭdis *f* large shellfish

Pelōr·us or **Pelōr·os -ī** *m* N.E. promontory of Sicily

pelt·a -ae *f* small leather shield

peltast·ēs or **peltast·a -ae** *m* soldier armed with a small leather shield

peltāt·us -a -um *adj* armed with a small leather shield

Pēlūs·ĭum -ĭī or **-ī** *n* city on the E. mouth of the Nile

pelv·is -is *f* bucket, basin

penārĭ·us -a -um *adj* food, supply, storage

Penāt·ēs -ĭum *m pl* Penates, household gods; hearth, home, house; cells (*of bees*)

penātĭg·er -ĕra -ĕrum *adj* carrying the household gods

pendĕō pendēre pependī *vi* to hang, hang down, be suspended; to hang loose; to hang down, be flabby, be weak; to depend, be dependent; to be in suspense, be uncertain, hesitate; to hang around, loiter; to hang in the air, be suspended, hover, float, overhang; (with *abl* or with **ab, de** or **ex** + *abl*) **a** to hang down from, hang by; **b** to depend on, be dependent upon; **c** to hang on to, be devoted to; (with **in** + *abl*) to be poised on, hover in, hover over

pendō pendĕre pependī pensum *vt* to weigh, weigh out; to pay, pay out; to weigh, ponder, consider, value, esteem; to pay (*penalty*); **flocci pendere** to think little of; **magni pendere** to think much of, value highly; *vi* to weigh, have weight

pendŭl·us -a -um *adj* hanging, hanging down; doubtful, uncertain

Pēnē·is -ĭdis or **Pēnēĭ·us -a -um** *adj* of Peneus

Pēnelŏp·a -ae or **Pēnelŏp·ē -ēs** *f* daughter of Icarius and Periboea and wife of Ulysses

penes *prep* (with *acc* of person only) in the possession of, in the power of, belonging to, resting with; at the house of, with; **penes se esse** to be in one's senses

penetrābĭl·is -e *adj* penetrating, piercing; penetrable

penetrāl·is -e *adj* penetrating, piercing; inner, internal, interior; *n pl* the interior, center; inner chambers; sanctuary; the interior, hinterlands

penĕtr·ō -āre *vt & vi* to penetrate, enter

Pēnē·us -a -um *adj* of Peneus, of the Peneus River; *m* Peneus River (*largest river in Thessaly*); river god, the father of Cyrene and Daphne

pēnicill·us -ī *m* paint brush, pencil

pēnicŭl·us -ī *m* brush; sponge

pēn·is -is *m* tail; penis; lechery

penĭtē *adv* inwardly

penĭtus *adv* internally, inside, deep within, deeply; from within; thoroughly, completely, through and through; heartily

penĭt·us -a -um *adj* inner, inward

penn·a -ae *f* feather; wing; flight

pennāt·us -a -um *adj* feathered

pennĭg·er -ĕra -ĕrum *adj* winged, feathered

pennipŏt·ens -entis *adj* winged, able to fly

pennŭl·a -ae *f* little wing

pensĭl·is -e *adj* hanging; **uva pensilis** grape hung out to dry

pensĭ·ō -ōnis *f* payment, instalment

pensĭt·ō -āre *vt* to pay; to weigh, ponder, consider; *vi* to be taxable

pens·ō -āre *vt* to weigh out; to weigh, ponder, consider, examine; to compare, contrast; to pay, atone for; to repay, compensate, requite

pens·um -ī *n* work quota; duty, task; consideration, scruple; **pensi esse** to be of value, be of importance; **pensi habere** to value, consider of importance

pensus *pp* of **pendo**

pentēr·is -is *f* galley, quinquereme

Penthesilē·a -ae *f* Amazon, warrior queen who was killed by Achilles at Troy

Penth·eus -ĕī or **-ĕos** *m* king of Thebes, son of Echion and Agave, grandson of Cadmus, and opponent of the Bacchic cult

pen·um -ī *n* supplies, provisions, food

pēnūrĭ·a -ae *f* want, need, dearth

pen·us -ūs or **-ī** *m* or **pen·us -ŏris** *n* supplies, provisions, food

pepl·um -ī *n* or **pepl·us -ī** *m* robe for the statue of Athena

per *prep* (with *acc*) (of space) through, throughout, all over, along; (of time) through, during, for, in the course of, at, at the time of; (of agency) through, by, by means of, at the hands of; (of means or manner) through, by, under pretense of; for the sake of, with a view to; (in oath) by

pēr·a -ae *f* wallet

perabsurd·us -a -um *adj* completely absurd

peraccommodāt·us -a -um *adj* very convenient
perāc·er -ris -re *adj* very sharp
peracerb·us -a -um *adj* very harsh, very sour
perac·escō -escĕre -ŭī *vi* to become completely sour
peractĭ·ō -ōnis *f* conclusion, last act (*of a play*)
peractus *pp* of **perago**
peracūtē *adv* very acutely
peracūt·us -a -um *adj* very sharp; very clear (*voice, intellect*)
peradulesc·ens -entis *adj* very young
peradulescentŭl·us -ī *m* very young man
peraequē *adv* quite evenly, uniformly
peragĭt·ō -āre *vt* to harass
per·ăgō -agĕre -ēgī -actum *vt* to carry through to the end, complete, accomplish; to pierce; to travel through; to harass, disturb, trouble; to describe, relate, go over; to work over, till, cultivate; to deliver (*speech*); (law) to prosecute to a conviction
peragrātĭ·ō -ōnis *f* traveling
perăgr·ō -āre *vt* to travel through, travel, traverse; *vi* (fig) to spread, penetrate
peralt·us -a -um *adj* very high
perăm·ans -antis *adj* (with *genit*) very fond of
peramanter *adv* very lovingly
perambŭl·ō -āre *vt* to travel, traverse, walk through
peramoen·us -a -um *adj* very pleasant, very charming
perampl·us -a -um *adj* very large, very spacious
perangustē *adv* very narrowly
perangust·us -a -um *adj* very narrow
perantīqu·us -a -um *adj* very ancient, very old
perapposĭt·us -a -um *adj* very suitable
perardŭ·us -a -um *adj* very difficult
perargūt·us -a -um *adj* very clear; very sharp, very witty
perarmāt·us -a -um *adj* heavily armed
per·ărō -āre *vt* to plow through; to furrow; to write on (*a wax tablet*); to write
pērātim *adv* bag by bag
perattentē *adv* very attentively
perattent·us -a -um *adj* very attentive
peraudiend·us -a -um *adj* that must be heard to the end
perbacch·or -ārī -ātus sum *vt* to carouse through (*e.g., many days*)
perbeāt·us -a -um *adj* very happy
perbellē *adv* very prettily
perbĕne *adv* very well
perbenevŏl·us -a -um *adj* very friendly
perbenignē *adv* very kindly
perbĭb·ō -ĕre -ī *vt* to drink up, drink in, imbibe
perbīt·ō -ĕre *vi* to go to ruin
perbland·us -a -um *adj* very attractive, very charming
perbŏn·us -a -um *adj* very good, excellent
perbrĕv·is -e *adj* very short, very brief; **perbrevi** or **perbrevi tempore** in a very short time
perbrevĭter *adv* very briefly
perc·a -ae *f* perch
percalefact·us -a -um *adj* warmed through and through
percal·escō -escĕre -ŭī *vi* to become quite hot
percall·escō -escĕre -ŭī *vt* to become thoroughly versed in; *vi* to become very hardened
percār·us -a -um *adj* very dear, very costly; very dear, much loved
percaut·us -a -um *adj* very cautious
percelĕbr·or -ārī -ātus sum *vi* to be quite famous
percĕl·er -ĕris *adj* very quick
percelerĭter *adv* very quickly
per·cellō -cellĕre -cŭlī -culsum *vt* to knock down, beat down, overthrow; to scare to death; to overthrow, ruin; to send scurrying; to hit hard
percens·ĕō -ēre -ŭī *vt* to count up; to review, survey; to travel through, traverse
perceptĭ·ō -ōnis *f* harvesting; comprehension; *f pl* concepts
percept·us -a -um *pp* of **percipio;** *n* precept, rule, doctrine
per·cīdō -cīdĕre -cīdī -cīsum *vt* to smash to pieces
perci·ĕō -ēre or **perc·ĭō -īre -īvī** or **-ĭī -ītum** *vt* to stir up, excite
per·cipĭō -cipĕre -cēpī -ceptum *vt* to get a good hold of; to catch; to occupy, seize; to gather in, harvest, reap; (of the senses) to take in, perceive, feel; (of feelings) to get hold of, get the better of; to learn, know, comprehend, understand, perceive
percĭt·us -a -um *pp* of **percieo;** *adj* aroused, provoked; impetuous, excitable
percoctus *pp* of **percoquo**
percŏl·ō -āre *vt* to strain, filter
per·cŏlō -colĕre -colŭī -cultum *vt* to reverence, revere, worship; to beautify; to crown, complete
percōm·is -e *adj* very courteous
percommŏdē *adv* very conveniently, very well, very suitably
percommŏd·us -a -um *adj* very convenient, very suitable
percontātĭ·ō -ōnis *f* thorough investigation
percontāt·or -ōris *m* inquisitive fellow
percont·or -ārī -ātus sum *vt* to question, investigate, interrogate; (with double *acc*) to ask (*someone something*)
percontŭm·ax -ācis *adj* very stubborn

per·cŏquō -coquĕre -coxī -coctum *vt* to cook through and through, cook thoroughly; to heat thoroughly; to ripen; to scorch, blacken

percrēb·escō or **percrēbr·escō -escĕre -ŭī** *vi* to become prevalent, be spread abroad

percrĕp·ō -āre -ŭī -ĭtum *vi* to resound, ring

percruci·or -ārī -ātus sum *vi* to torment oneself

perculsus *pp* of **percello**

percult·us -a -um *pp* of **percolo;** *adj* decked out; (coll) dolled up (*woman*)

percupĭd·us -a -um *adj* (with *genit*) very fond of

percup·iō -ĕre *vt* (with *inf*) to be eager to, desire very much to, be dying to

percūriōs·us -a -um *adj* very curious

percūr·ō -āre *vt* to heal completely

per·currō -currĕre -cucurrī or **currī -cursum** *vt* to run through, run along, run over, pass over, speed over; (fig) to scan briefly, look over; (in a speech) to treat in succession, go over, run over; (of feelings) to run through, penetrate, pierce; *vi* to run fast, hurry along; (with **ad** + *acc*) to dash to (*e.g., the Forum*); (with **per** + *acc*) **a** to run through or across, travel through; **b** (fig) to run through, mention quickly, treat in succession

percursātĭ·ō -ōnis *f* traveling; **percursatio Italiae** traveling through Italy

percursĭ·ō -ōnis *f* quick survey

percurs·ō -āre *vi* to roam about, range about

percussĭ·ō -ōnis *f* hitting, striking; snapping (*of fingers*); (mus) beat, time

percuss·or -ōris *m* assailant; assassin

percussus *pp* of **percutio**

percuss·us -ūs *m* beating, striking

per·cutiō -cutĕre -cussī -cussum *vt* to beat or hit hard; to pierce, transfix, run through; to shoot, kill; to shock, impress, move, astound; to cut through; to dig (*ditch*); to coin, stamp (*money*); to cheat, trick

perdecōr·us -a -um *adj* very pretty

perdēlīr·us -a -um *adj* very silly, quite mad

perdeps·ō -ĕre -ŭī *vt* to knead thoroughly; (fig) to seduce

perdifficĭl·is -e *adj* very difficult

perdifficilĭter *adv* with great difficulty

perdign·us -a -um *adj* (with *abl*) quite worthy of

perdīlig·ens -entis *adj* very diligent, very conscientious

perdīligenter *adv* very diligently, very conscientiously

per·discō -discĕre -didĭcī *vt* to learn thoroughly, learn by heart

perdisertē *adv* very eloquently

perdĭtē *adv* recklessly, desperately

perdĭt·or -ōris *m* destroyer

perdĭt·us -a -um *adj* ruined, lost; profligate, degenerate, infamous, reckless, incorrigible, hopeless

perdĭū *adv* for a very long time

perdiūturn·us -a -um *adj* long-lasting, protracted

perdīv·es -ĭtis *adj* very rich

perd·ix -īcis *m* partridge

per·dō -dĕre -dĭdī -dĭtum *vt* to wreck, ruin, destroy; to waste, squander; to lose

perdoc·ĕō -ēre -ŭī -tum *vt* to teach thoroughly

perdoctē *adv* very skillfully

perdoct·us -a -um *pp* of **perdoceo;** *adj* very learned, very skillful

perdol·escō -escĕre -ŭī *vi* to become resentful

perdŏm·ō -āre -ŭī -ĭtum *vt* to tame completely, subdue, subjugate

perdormisc·ō -ĕre *vi* to sleep on, keep on sleeping

per·dūcō -dūcĕre -duxī -ductum *vt* to lead, guide; to cover, spread; to prolong, drag out; to induce; to seduce; (with **ad** + *acc*) **a** to lead, bring, guide, escort to; **b** to build, run (*wall, ditch, road, etc.*) to; **c** to prolong, protract, drag out, continue (*something*) to or till; **d** to win over to, convince of

perduct·ō -āre *vt* to lead, conduct

perduct·or -ōris *m* guide; pimp

perdūdum *adv* long long ago

perduellĭ·ō -ōnis *f* treason, high treason

perduell·is -is *m* enemy

perdūr·ō -āre *vi* to hold out, last, endure

per·ĕdō -esse -ēdī -ēsum *vt* to eat up, devour

perĕgrē *adv* abroad, away from home; from abroad; **peregre abire** or **peregre exire** to go abroad

peregrīnābund·us -a -um *adj* traveling around

peregrīnātĭ·ō -ōnis *f* living abroad, travel, touring; roaming, ranging (*said of animals*)

peregrīnāt·or -ōris *m* traveler, wanderer

peregrīnĭt·ās -ātis *f* foreign manners, strange ways

peregrīn·or -ārī -ātus sum *vi* to live abroad, travel abroad, travel around; (fig) to be a stranger

peregrīn·us -a -um *adj* foreign, strange, alien, exotic; (fig) strange, inexperienced; **amores peregrini** love affairs with foreign women; **praetor peregrinus** praetor who tried cases involving foreigners and Roman citizens; **terror peregrinus** fear of a foreign enemy; *mf* foreigner, alien

perēlĕg·ans -antis *adj* very elegant

perēleganter *adv* very elegantly

perēlŏqu·ens -entis *adv* very eloquent

peremn·ĭa -ĭum *n pl* auspices taken before crossing a river
peremptus *pp* of **perimo**
perendiē *adv* the day after tomorrow
perendīn·us -a -um *adj* **dies perendinus** the day after tomorrow; *m* the day after tomorrow
perenn·is -e *adj* perennial, continual, everlasting
perenniserv·os -ī *m* slave for life
perennĭt·ās -ātis *f* continuance, perpetuity
perenn·ō -āre *vi* to last
pērenticīd·a -ae *m* (coll) crook
per·ĕō -īre -ĭī -ĭtum *vi* to pass away, pass on, die; to go to waste, perish, be destroyed; to be lost, be ruined, be undone; to be desperately in love, pine away; (of snow) to melt away; (of iron) to rust away; **perii!** I'm ruined!, I'm finished!, I'm washed up!
perequĭt·ō -āre *vt* to ride up through; *vi* to ride around
pererr·ō -āre *vt* to roam around, wander through; to survey, look (*someone*) over
perērudīt·us -a -um *adj* very learned
perēsus *pp* of **peredo**
perexcels·us -a -um *adj* very high, exalted
perexigŭē *adv* very sparingly
perexigŭ·us -a -um *adj* tiny; insignificant; very short (*day*)
perfacētē *adv* very wittily
perfacēt·us -a -um *adj* very witty, very sharp
perfacĭle *adv* very easily, very readily
perfacĭl·is -ē *adj* very easy; very courteous
perfamiliār·is -e *adj* very close, intimate; *m* very close friend
perfectē *adv* completely, perfectly
perfectĭ·ō -ōnis *f* completion; perfection
perfect·or -ōris *m* perfecter; **dicendi perfector** stylist
perfect·us -a -um *pp* of **perficio;** *adj* complete, finished, perfect, excellent
per·fĕrō -ferre -tŭlī -lātum *vt* to carry through; to endure to the end, bear with patience, put up with; to pass (*a law*); to bring, announce, report (*news*)
per·fĭcĭō -ficĕre -fēcī -fectum *vt* to complete, finish, accomplish, carry out, perform, execute, bring to an end; to bring to completion, finish, perfect; to bring about, cause
perfĭc·us -a -um *adj* perfecting; **natura perfica** nature which perfects
perfidēl·is -e *adj* very faithful, very trusty
perfidĭ·a -ae *f* perfidy, treachery
perfidiōsē *adv* treacherously
perfidiōs·us -a -um *adj* treacherous, faithless
perfĭd·us -a -um *adj* treacherous, untrustworthy, dishonest, sneaky; *m* sneak
per·fīgō -fīgĕre -fixī -fixum *vt* to pierce
perflābĭl·is -e *adj* airy; invisible (*gods*)
perflāgitiōs·us -a -um *adj* utterly disgraceful
perfl·ō -āre *vt* to blow through, blow across
perfluctŭ·ō -āre *vt* to surge through
per·fodĭō -fodĕre -fōdī -fossum *vt* to dig through; to pierce
perfŏr·ō -āre *vt* to bore through, pierce; to make by boring
perfortĭter *adv* very bravely
perfoss·or -ōris *m* **perfossor parietum** burglar
perfossus *pp* of **perfodio**
perfractus *pp* of **perfringo**
perfrĕm·ō -ĕre -ŭī *vi* to snort loud
perfrĕqu·ens -entis *adj* very crowded, over-crowded
perfrĭc·ō -āre -ŭī -ātum or **-tum** *vt* to rub well, rub all over; **os perfricare** to rub away blushes, put on a bold front
perfrīgefac·ĭō -ĕre *vt* (fig) to send a chill over, make shudder
per·frīgescō -frīgescĕre -frixī *vi* to catch a bad cold
perfrīgĭd·us -a -um *adj* very cold, ice-cold
per·fringō -fringĕre -frēgī -fractum *vt* to break through; to break to pieces, batter in, smash; (fig) to break (*laws, etc.*), break up (*conspiracy*)
per·frŭor -frŭī -fructus sum *vi* (with *abl*) to experience to the full, fully enjoy, be delighted by, perform gladly
perfŭg·a -ae *m* military deserter; political turncoat
per·fugĭō -fugĕre -fūgī *vi* (with **ad** or **in** + *acc*) **a** to flee to for refuge; **b** to desert to; **c** (fig) to have recourse to, find comfort in
perfunctĭ·ō -ōnis *f* performance, performing, discharge
perfunctus *pp* of **perfungor**
per·fundō -fundĕre -fūdī -fūsum *vt* to drench, bathe; to sprinkle; to dye; (fig) to fill, flood, steep, inspire
per·fungor -fungī -functus sum *vt* to enjoy; *vi* (with *abl*) **a** to perform, discharge, fulfill; **b** to go through, endure, undergo; **c** to get rid of; **d** to be finished with, be done with; **e** to enjoy
perfŭr·ō -ĕre *vi* to rage wildly, rage on
perfūsus *pp* of **perfundo**
Pergăm·a -ōrum *n pl* or **Pergăm·us -ī** *f* citadel of Troy, Troy
Pergamĕ·us -a -um *adj* Trojan; *m pl* Trojans
Pergăm·um -ī *n* Troy; Pergamum (*city in Mysia, the capital of the Attalid kingdom, famous for its library*)

pergaud·ĕō -ēre *vi* to be very glad

per·gō -gĕre -rexī -rectum *vt* to go on uninterruptedly with, continue; (with *inf*) to continue to; *vi* to go straight on, continue, proceed; (with **ad** + *acc*) to pass on to, proceed to (*esp. in speaking*)

pergraec·or -ārī -ātus sum *vi* to go completely Greek, have a ball

pergrand·is -e *adj* very large, huge; **pergrandis natu** very old

pergraphic·us -a -um *adj* very cunning

pergrāt·us -a -um *adj* very pleasant; *n* distinct pleasure

pergrăv·is -e *adj* very heavy; very important; very impressive

pergraviter *adv* very seriously

pergŭl·a -ae *f* veranda, balcony; school; brothel

Perg·us -ī *m* lake in Sicily, near Henna, where Pluto carried off Proserpina

perhib·ĕō -ēre -ŭī -ĭtum *vt* to hold, assert, maintain; to call, name; to adduce, cite

perhīlum *adv* very little

perhonōrificē *adv* very respectfully, with all due respect

perhonōrific·us -a -um *adj* very honorable, very complimentary; very respectful

perhorr·escō -escĕre -ŭī *vt* to begin to shudder at; to develop a terror of; *vi* to begin to quake, begin to tremble violently

perhorrĭd·us -a -um *adj* horrible, dreadful

perhūmaniter *adv* very kindly

perhūmān·us -a -um *adj* very courteous

Pericl·ēs -is or **-ī** *m* Athenian statesman, son of Xanthippus and political leader of Athens during the city's most flourishing period (c. 495-429 B.C.)

perīclitāti·ō -ōnis *f* test, experiment

periclĭt·or -ārī -ātus sum *vt* to test, put to the test, try; to jeopardize; to risk; *vi* to be in danger, be in jeopardy; to run a risk; (with *abl*) to be in danger of losing (*e.g., life, reputation*); **capite periclitari** to be in danger of losing one's life, risk one's life

perīculōsē *adv* dangerously

perīculōs·us -a -um *adj* dangerous, perilous, risky

perīcŭl·um or **perīcl·um -ī** *n* danger, peril, risk; trial, attempt, experiment, test; literary venture; (law) trial, case, lawsuit, legal record, writ, sentence

peridōnĕ·us -a -um *adj* very suitable; (with *dat* or **ad** + *acc*) well adapted to, well suited to

perillustr·is -e *adj* very clear; very illustrious, very distinguished

perimbēcill·us -a -um *adj* very weak, very feeble

per·ĭmō -imĕre -ēmī -emptum *vt* to take away completely; to destroy; to slay, kill

perimpedīt·us -a -um *adj* rough (*terrain*), full of obstacles

perincommŏdē *adv* very inconveniently

perincommŏd·us -a -um *adj* very inconvenient

perinde *adv* in the same manner, equally, just as, quite as; (with **atque, ac, ut,** or **quam**) just as, exactly as; (with **ac si, quasi, tamquam,** or **quam si**) just as if

perindulg·ens -entis *adj* very tender; (with **ad** + *acc*) very tender toward

perinfirm·us -a -um *adj* very weak

peringeniōs·us -a -um *adj* very clever

perinīqu·us -a -um *adj* very unfair; very upset, very annoyed, very impatient, very reluctant; **periniquo animo pati** or **ferre** to be quite upset at, be quite annoyed at, be very reluctant about

perinsign·is -e *adj* very remarkable

perinvīt·us -a -um *adj* very unwilling

periŏd·us -ī *f* sentence, rhetorical period

peripatētic·us -a -um *adj* peripatetic, Aristotelian; *m pl* peripatetics, Aristotelians

peripetasmăt·a -um *n pl* curtains, drapes

perīrāt·us -a -um *adv* very angry; (with *dat*) very angry with

periscĕl·is -ĭdis *f* anklet

peristrōm·a -ătis *n* carpet

peristyl·ĭum -iī or **-ī** *n* peristyle (*open court surrounded by a colonnade*)

peristȳl·um -ī *n* colonnade around a building, peristyle

perītē *adv* skillfully, expertly

perīti·a -ae *f* experience, practical knowledge, skill; (with *genit*) experience in, familiarity with, knowledge of

perīt·us -a -um *adj* experienced, skillful, expert, familiar; (with *genit* or *abl*, with **in** + *abl*, or with **ad** + *acc*) experienced in, skillful in, expert in or at, familiar with; (with *inf*) skilled in, expert at, e.g., **peritus cantare** skilled in singing, expert at singing

perjūcundē *adv* very pleasantly

perjūcund·us -a -um *adj* very pleasant

perjūr·ium -iī or **-ī** *n* perjury, false oath

perjūrō see **pejero**

perjūr·us or **pejĕr·us -a -um** *adj* perjured, oath-breaking; lying, dishonest

per·lābor -lābī -lapsus sum *vi* to glide along, skim across or over; (with **per** + *acc*) to slip through; (with **ad** + *acc*) to come, move, glide, or slip toward; (with **in** + *acc*) to glide into, slip into

perlaet·us -a -um *adv* very glad, most joyful
perlapsus *pp* of **perlabor**
perlātē *adv* very extensively
perlat·ĕō -ēre -ŭī *vi* to be completely hidden
perlātus *pp* of **perfero**
perlectĭ·ō -ōnis *f* thorough perusal
per·lĕgō -legĕre -lēgī -lectum *vt* to scan, survey thoroughly; to read through
perlepĭdē *adv* very nicely
perlĕv·is -e *adj* very light, very slight
perlevĭter *adv* very lightly, very slightly
perlĭb·ens or **perlŭb·ens -entis** *adj* very willing
perlibenter or **perlubenter** *adv* very gladly
perlīberāl·is -e *adj* very genteel
perlĭb·et or **perlŭb·et -ēre** *v impers* (with *inf*) I should very much like to
perlicĭō see **pellicio**
perlĭt·ō -āre *vi* to sacrifice with favorable omens
perlongē *adv* a long way off, very far
perlonginqu·us -a -um *adj* very long; very tedious
perlub- = **perlib-**
per·lūcĕō or **pel·lūcĕō -lūcēre -luxī** *vi* to shine clearly, be bright; to be clearly visible; to be transparent; to be clear, be intelligible
perlūcidŭl·us -a -um *adj* somewhat transparent
perlŭcĭd·us or **pellūcĭd·us -a -um** *adj* very bright; transparent
perluctuōs·us -a -um *adj* very sad
per·lŭō -luĕre -lŭī -lūtum *vt* to wash thoroughly, wash off, bathe
perlustr·ō -āre *vt* to traverse; to scan, survey, review
permadefac·ĭō -ĕre *vt* to soak through and through, drench
permagn·us -a -um *adj* very great; very important; *n* great thing; **permagno** at a very high price, very dearly; **permagnum aestimare** (with *inf*) to think it quite something to
permānanter *adv* by flowing through
permānasc·ō -ĕre *vi* (*of a report*) to begin to spread
per·manĕō -manēre -mansī -mansum *vi* to last, continue, hold out, remain, persist, endure
permān·ō -āre *vt* to seep through, penetrate; *vi* to penetrate; (with **ad** or **in** + *acc*) **a** to seep through to, seep into, penetrate; **b** (fig) to reach, extend to, penetrate
permansĭ·ō -ōnis *f* persistence, continuance
permarīn·us -a -um *adj* sea-going
permātūr·escō -escĕre -ŭī *vi* to become fully ripe
permediŏcr·is -e *adj* completely normal
permeditāt·us -a -um *adj* well rehearsed, well trained
permensus *pp* of **permetior**
permĕ·ō -āre *vt* to go through, cross over, cross; *vi* (with **in** + *acc*) to penetrate; (with **per** + *acc*) to penetrate, permeate
Permess·us -ī *m* river in Boeotia sacred to Apollo and the Muses
per·mētĭor -mētīrī -mensus sum *vt* to measure out, measure; to traverse, travel, travel over
per·mingō -mingĕre -minxī *vt* to soak with urine; to pollute
permīr·us -a -um *adj* very surprising, truly amazing
per·miscĕō -miscēre -miscŭī -mixtum *vt* to mix together, intermingle; (fig) to mix together, mix up, confuse
permissĭ·ō -ōnis *f* unconditional surrender; permission
permiss·us -a -um *pp* of **permitto;** *n* permission
permiss·us -ūs *m* permission, leave
permitiāl·is -e *adj* destructive, deadly
permitĭ·ēs -ēī *f* wasting away; ruin, decay
per·mittō -mittĕre -mīsī -missum *vt* to let through, let go through; to throw, hurl; to give up, surrender; to concede, relinquish; to let loose, let go; to let, permit, allow, grant; (with *dat*) to give up to, surrender (*something*) to, entrust (*something*) to, grant (*something*) to; (with **in** + *acc*) to send flying at, hurl or throw at
permixtē or **permixtim** *adv* confusedly, promiscuously
permixtĭ·ō -ōnis *f* mixture; confusion, bedlam
permixt·us -a -um *pp* of **permisceo;** *adj* confused, promiscuous
permodest·us -a -um *adj* very modest, very moderate
permolestē *adv* with much trouble; **permoleste ferre** to be quite annoyed at
permolest·us -a -um *adj* very troublesome, very annoying
permŏl·ō -ĕre *vt* to grind up; **alienas uxores permolere** (fig) to seduce other men's wives
permōtĭ·ō -ōnis *f* excitement; **animi permotio** or **mentis permotio** excitement, deep emotion
per·movĕō -movēre -mōvī -mōtum *vt* to stir up, churn up (*the sea);* to move deeply, make a deep impression upon; to excite, agitate, rouse; to influence, induce, prevail on
per·mulcĕō -mulcēre -mulsī -mulsum *vt* to stroke, pet, caress; to soothe, charm; to delight, flatter; to appease, tame, mitigate, allay
permultō *adv* (with comparatives) by far, far, much
permultum *adv* very much; **permultum ante** very often before; **permultum interest** it makes a world of difference

permult·us -a -um *adj* very much, very many; *n* a lot, much
permūn·iō -īre -īvī or **-iī -ītum** *vt* to fortify thoroughly; to finish fortifying
permūtāti·ō -ōnis *f* permutation, complete change; change, alteration; crisis, revolution; exchange, barter; substitution
permūt·ō -āre *vt* to change completely, alter completely; to exchange, interchange
pern·a -ae *f* ham
pernecessāri·us -a -um *adj* very necessary; very closely related; *m* close friend; close relative
pernecesse (indecl) *adj* very necessary, indispensable
pernĕg·ō -āre *vt* to deny flatly; to turn down flat
per·nĕō -nēre -nēvī -nētum *vt* (of the Fates) to spin out
perniciābil·is -e *adj* ruinous
pernici·ēs -ēī *f* ruin, destruction, disaster, calamity; pest, curse
perniciōsē *adj* perniciously, ruinously
perniciōs·us -a -um *adj* pernicious, ruinous
pernīcit·ās -ātis *f* agility, nimbleness, swiftness
pernīciter *adv* nimbly, swiftly
pernig·er -ra -rum *adj* jet black
pernimi·us -a -um *adj* much too much
pern·ix -īcis *adj* agile, nimble, active, swift
pernōbil·is -e *adj* famous, illustrious
pernoct·ō -āre *vi* to spend the night
per·noscō -noscĕre -nōvī -nōtum *vt* to examine thoroughly; to become fully acquainted with, get an accurate knowledge of
pernōt·escō -escĕre -ŭī *vi* to become generally known
pern·ox -octis *adj* all-night; **luna pernox** full moon
pernumĕr·ō -āre *vt* to count up
pēr·ō -ōnis *m* clodhopper, brogue (*worn by peasants and soldiers*)
perobscūr·us -a -um *adj* very obscure
perodiōs·us -a -um *adj* very annoying
perofficiōsē *adv* with devotion, with attention
perol·ĕō -ēre *vi* to have a strong odor
pērōnāt·us -a -um *adj* wearing clodhoppers
peropportūnē *adv* very opportunely, very conveniently
peropportūn·us -a -um *adj* very opportune, very convenient, well timed
peroptātō *adv* very much to one's wish
perŏpus (indecl) *n* great need; **peropus est** it is absolutely essential
perōrāti·ō -ōnis *f* peroration, conclusion of a speech
perōrnāt·us -a -um *adj* very flowery (*style*)
perorn·ō -āre *vt* to enhance the prestige of (*e.g., the senate*)
perōr·ō -āre *vt* to plead (*a case*) all by oneself; to wind up, conclude (*a speech, case*), rest (*a case*); *vi* to give the summation
perōs·us -a -um *adj* hating, detesting
perpāc·ō -āre *vt* to silence completely; to pacify thoroughly
perparcē *adv* very stingily
perparvŭl·us -a -um *adj* tiny
perparv·us -a -um *adj* very small
perpast·us -a -um *adj* well fed
perpauc·ī -ae -a *adj* very few; *n pl* very few words; **perpauca dicere** to speak very briefly
perpaucŭl·ī -ae -a *adj* very few
perpaulum *adv* somewhat, slightly
perpaul·um -ī *n* small bit
perpaup·er -ĕris *adj* very poor
perpauxill·um -ī *n* little bit
perpavefac·iō -ĕre *vt* to frighten the daylight out of
per·pellō -pellĕre -pulsī -pulsum *vt* to push hard; to urge strongly, force
perpendicŭl·um -ī *n* plumb line, plummet; **ad perpendiculum** perpendicularly
per·pendō -pendĕre -pendī -pensum *vt* to weigh carefully, consider; to value, judge
perpĕram *adv* incorrectly, falsely
perp·es -ĕtis *adj* continuous, uninterrupted
perpessi·ō -ōnis *f* suffering, endurance
per·petior -pĕtī -pessus sum *vt* to endure, put up with, stand; to allow, permit
perpĕtr·ō -āre *vt* to accomplish, go through with, carry out, achieve, perform; to perpetrate, commit
perpetuit·ās -ātis *f* perpetuity
perpetŭō *adv* constantly, without interruption, forever
perpetŭ·ō -āre *vt* to perpetuate
perpetŭ·us -a -um *adj* perpetual, continuous, uninterrupted; general, universal; whole, entire; **quaestiones perpetuae** standing courts; permanent committee; *n* **in perpetuum** without a break, continuously; for all time, forever
perplac·ĕō -ēre -ŭī *vi* (with *dat*) to please immensely
perplexābil·is -e *adj* obscure, perplexing
perplexābiliter *adv* perplexingly
perplexē or **perplexim** *adv* confusedly, unintelligibly
perplex·or -ārī -ātus sum *vi* to cause confusion
perplex·us -a -um *adj* intricate, confused; ambiguous, obscure; *n* ambiguity, confusion
perplicāt·us -a -um *adj* entangled
perplŭ·ō -ĕre *vt* (fig) to rain, pour; *vi* (of roof, etc.) to leak, let the rain in

perpol·iō -īre -īvī or **-iī -ītum** *vt* to polish well, bring to a high polish; (fig) to polish up, perfect
perpolīt·us -a -um *adj* polished, refined
perpopŭl·or -ārī -ātus sum *vt* to ravage, devastate
perpōtāti·ō -ōnis *f* heavy drinking; drinking party
perpōt·ō -āre *vt* to drink off; *vi* to drink heavily, drink constantly
per·prĭmō -primĕre -pressī *vt* to press hard, squeeze hard; to lie on
perpropinqu·us -a -um *adj* very near
perprūrisc·ō -ĕre *vi* to begin to itch all over
perpugn·ax -ācis *adj* very belligerent
perpulch·er -ra -rum *adj* very beautiful, very handsome
perpulsus *pp* of **perpello**
perpurg·ō -āre *vt* to cleanse thoroughly, clean up; (fig) to clear up, explain
perpusill·us -a -um *adj* puny
perpŭt·ō -āre *vt* to prune back hard; to clear up, explain in detail
perquam *adv* very, extremely
per·quīrō -quīrĕre -quīsīvī -quīsītum *vt* to search carefully for; to examine carefully
perquīsītius *adv* more accurately, more critically
perquīsīt·or -ōris *m* enthusiast; **auctionum perquisitor** auction enthusiast
perrārō *adv* very rarely, very seldom
perrār·us -a -um *adj* very rare, quite uncommon
perrecondĭt·us -a -um *adj* recondite, abstruse
perrectus *pp* of **pergo**
per·rēpō -rēpĕre -repsī -reptum *vt* to crawl over, crawl along
perrept·ō -āre *vt* to creep through, sneak through; *vi* to creep around
perrīdicŭlē *adv* most absurdly
perrīdicŭl·us -a -um *adj* utterly absurd
perrogāti·ō -ōnis *f* passage (*of a law*)
perrŏg·ō -āre *vt* to ask in succession; to poll (*opinions*); **sententias perrogare** to have roll call (*in the senate*)
per·rumpō -rumpĕre -rūpī -ruptum *vt* to break through, force one's way through; to break in two, shatter, smash; to offend against, violate; *vi* to break through, make a breakthrough
Pers·a or **Pers·ēs -ae** *m* Persian
persaepe *adv* very often
persalsē *adv* very wittily
persals·us -a -um *adj* very witty
persalūtāti·ō -ōnis *f* round of greetings, greeting all in turn
persalūt·ō -āre *vt* to salute one after another
persanctē *adv* very solemnly
persapi·ens -entis *adj* very wise
persapienter *adv* very wisely
perscienter *adv* very wisely, very discreetly
per·scindō -scindĕre -scidī -scissum *vt* to tear to pieces; to scatter (*e.g., clouds*)
perscīt·us -a -um *adj* very clever, very smart
per·scrībō -scrībĕre -scripsī -scriptum *vt* to write out; to describe fully, give in detail; to record, register; to enter (*into an account book*); to make over by writing; to pay by check
perscripti·ō -ōnis *f* entry, official record; check, payment by check
perscript·or -ōris *m* bookkeeper, accountant
perscriptus *pp* of **perscribo**
perscrūt·ō -āre or **perscrūt·or -ārī -ātus sum** *vt* to search or examine thoroughly, scrutinize
per·sĕcō -secāre -secŭī -sectum *vt* to dissect, cut into pieces; (fig) to cut through, cut out, eliminate
persect·or -ārī -ātus sum *vt* to follow eagerly, investigate
persecūti·ō -ōnis *f* prosecution, suing, lawsuit
persecūtus *pp* of **persequor**
per·sedĕō or **per·sidĕō -sedēre -sēdī -sessum** *vi* to remain seated
persegn·is -e *adj* very slow-moving, dull, tedious
per·sentiō -sentīre -sensī -sensum *vt* to perceive clearly; to feel deeply
persentisc·ō -ĕre *vt* to detect; to feel deeply
Persephŏn·ē -ēs *f* daughter of Demeter and queen of the lower world, called Proserpina by the Romans
persĕqu·ens -entis *adj* pursuing; (with *genit*) given to the practice of
per·sĕquor -sĕquī -secūtus sum *vt* to follow persistently, follow up; to be in hot pursuit of, be on the heels of; to chase after, catch up to; to follow verbatim; to imitate, copy; to prosecute; to take vengeance on; to follow out, execute, perform; to describe, explain
Pers·ēs -āe or **Pers·eus -ĕī** *m* last king of Macedonia, conquered by Aemilius Paulus at Pydna (169 B.C.)
Pers·eus -ĕī or **-ĕos** *m* son of Jupiter and Danae, who killed Medusa and slew the sea monster who was about to devour Andromeda
Persē·us or **Persēi·us -a -um** *adj* of Perseus
persevēr·ans -antis *adj* persevering, persistent, relentless
persevēranter *adv* persistently, relentlessly
persevēranti·a -ae *f* perseverance, persistence
persevēr·ō -āre *vt* to persist in; *vi* to persist
persevēr·us -a -um *adj* very strict

Persĭ·a -ae or **Pers·is -ĭdis** *f* Persia
Persĭc·us -a -um *adj* Persian; (fig) luxurious, soft; of Perses (*king of Macedonia*); *m pl* Persians; *f* peach tree; *n* peach; *n pl* Persian history
per·sīdō -sīdĕre -sēdī -sessum *vi* to sink down, penetrate
persign·ō -āre *vt* to record in detail
persimĭl·is -e *adj* very similar; (with *genit* or *dat*) very similar to, very much like
persimpl·ex -ĭcis *adj* very plain, very simple
Pers·is -ĭdis *adj* Persian; *f* Persia; Persian woman
Pers·ĭus -ĭī or **-ī** *m* A. Persius Flaccus (*famous satirist in the reign of Nero,* 34-62 A.D.)
persoll·a -ae *f* little mask; (as term of abuse) you ugly little thing!
persōl·us -a -um *adj* completely alone
per·solvō -solvĕre -solvī -solūtum *vt* to solve, explain; to pay up; to pay (*a penalty*); to fulfill (*a vow*); to render (*thanks*); to offer (*sacrifice*); **poenas persolvere** (with *dat*) to suffer at the hands of
persōn·a -ae *f* mask; part, character; mask, pretense; personality, person, character
personāt·us -a -um *adj* wearing a mask, masked; under false pretenses; **pater personatus** father on the stage
persŏn·ō -āre *vt* to make resound, make ring; to shout; **aurem personare** to make the ear ring; *vi* to resound, reecho; **citharā personare** to play the zither loudly
perspectē *adv* intelligently
perspect·ō -āre *vt* to look all around
perspect·us -a -um *pp* of **perspicio**; *adj* well known, clear, evident
perspecŭl·or -ārī -ātus sum *vt* to examine thoroughly, explore thoroughly
persperg·ō -ĕre *vt* to sprinkle
perspĭc·ax -ācis *adj* sharp-sighted; keen, penetrating, perspicacious
perspicientĭ·a -ae *f* clear perception
per·spicĭō -spicĕre -spexī -spectum *vt* to see through; to look closely at, examine, inspect, observe
perspicŭē *adv* clearly
perspicuĭt·ās -ātis *f* clarity
perspicŭ·us -a -um *adj* clear, transparent; clear, evident, perspicuous
per·sternō -sternĕre -strāvī -strātum *vt* to pave
perstimŭl·ō -āre *vt* to stimulate violently
per·stō -stāre -stĭtī -stātum *vi* to stand firm, hold one's ground; to keep standing; to remain unchanged, last; to be firm, persevere, persist, hold out
perstrātus *pp* of **persterno**
perstrĕp·ō -ĕre -ŭī -ĭtum *vi* to make a loud noise, make a lot of noise
per·stringō -stringĕre -strinxī -strictum *vt* to tie, tie up; to blunt, deaden (*the senses*), dazzle (*the eyes*), deafen (*the ears*); to touch lightly, graze, graze against; to glance over, touch lightly on; to belittle, slight
perstudiōsē *adv* enthusiastically
perstudiōs·us -a -um *adj* very eager, enthusiastic; (with *genit*) very fond of, enthusiastic about
per·suādĕō -suādēre -suāsī -suāsum *vi* (with *dat*) to persuade, convince; **sibi persuasum habere** to convince oneself, be convinced
persuāsĭ·ō -ōnis *f* convincing
persuastr·ix -īcis *f* seductress
persuāsus *pp* of **persuadeo**
persuās·us -ūs *m* persuasion
persubtīl·is -e *adj* very subtle, very ingenious
persult·ō -āre *vt* to gambol about, prance about; to scour (*woods*); *vi* to gambol, prance, run around
per·taedet -taedēre -taesum est *v impers* (with *acc* of person = subject in English and *genit* of thing = object in English) to be weary of, be sick and tired of, be bored with, e.g., **me negotii pertaedet** I am sick and tired of this business
per·tĕgō -tegĕre -texī -tectum *vt* to cover, cover up
pertempt·ō -āre *vt* to test thoroughly; to sound (*someone*) out; to consider well; (fig) to pervade, fill, overwhelm; **gaudia pertemptant pectus** joy fills (*their*) hearts
per·tendō -tendĕre -tendī -tensum or **-tentum** *vt* to press on with, continue, carry out; *vi* to press on, continue, persevere, persist, keep going
pertenŭ·is -e *adj* very thin, very slight, very small, very fine
perterĕbr·ō -āre *vt* to bore through
per·tergĕō -tergēre -tersī -tersum *vt* to wipe off; (of air) to brush lightly against
perterre·facĭō -facĕre -fēcī -factum *vt* to scare the life out of
perterr·ĕō -ēre -ŭī -ĭtum *vt* to frighten, terrify; (with **ab** + abl) to frighten (*someone*) away from
perterricrĕp·us -a -um *adj* terrible-sounding, rattling frightfully
per·texō -texĕre -texŭī -textum *vt* to bring to an end, go through with, accomplish
pertĭc·a -ae *f* pole, rod, staff; measuring pole; (fig) measure
pertim·escō -escĕre -ŭī *vt* to be alarmed at, become afraid of; *vi* to become very frightened, become alarmed
pertinācĭ·ā -ae *f* stubbornness; perseverance, determination
pertinācĭter *adv* stubbornly, tenaciously; perseveringly, constantly
pertĭn·ax -ācis *adj* very tenacious; persevering, steadfast; unyielding, stubborn, obstinate

pertin·ĕō -ēre -ŭī *vi* to reach, extend; (with **per** + acc) to pervade, reach; (with **ad** + *acc*) **a** to extend to, reach; **b** to pertain to, relate to, concern; **c** to apply to, be applicable to, suit, be suitable to; **d** to tend toward, be conducive to; **e** to belong to; **quod pertinet** (with **ad** + *acc*) as regards, as far as concerns
perting·ō -ĕre *vi* to extend
pertolĕr·ō -āre *vt* to put up with, endure to the end
pertorqu·ĕō -ēre *vt* to twist, distort
pertractātē *adv* systematically
pertractātĭ·ō -ōnis *f* handling, treatment
pertract·ō -āre *vt* to handle, fondle; (fig) to handle carefully, treat systematically; to influence
per·trăhō -trahĕre -traxī -tractum *vt* to drag; to allure, lead on, decoy
pertrect- = **pertract-**
pertrist·is -e *adj* very sad, very gloomy
pertumultuōsē *adv* very excitedly, hysterically
per·tundō -tundĕre -tŭdī -tūsum *vt* to punch a hole through, perforate
perturbātē *adv* confusedly, in confusion
perturbātĭ·ō -ōnis *f* confusion, disorder; political disturbance, revolution; mental disturbance; disturbing emotion
perturbātr·ix -īcis *f* disturbing element
perturbāt·us -a -um *adj* disturbed, troubled; excited, alarmed; embarrassed
perturb·is -e *adj* downright shameful
perturb·ō -āre *vt* to throw into confusion, confuse, disturb; to embarrass; to upset, alarm
pertūs·us -a -um *pp* of **pertundo;** *adj* perforated; tattered (*clothes*)
per·ungō -ungĕre -unxī -unctum *vt* to oil well, anoint thoroughly
perurbān·us -a -um *adj* very urbane, very sophisticated; *m* sophisticate
per·ūrō -ūrĕre -ussī -ustum *vt* to burn up; to consume; to inflame, rub sore; to scorch; (of cold) to nip, bite; (fig) to fire, inflame
Perusĭ·a -ae *f* town in Etruria
perustus *pp* of **peruro**
perūtĭl·is -e *adj* very useful, very practical
per·vādō -vādĕre -vāsī -vāsum *vt* to pass through, go through; to spread throughout, pervade; to penetrate, reach; *vi* to spread, penetrate; (with **ad** or **in** + *acc*) to go as far as, spread to, reach, arrive at, penetrate; (with **per** + *acc*) to spread through or over
pervagāt·us -a -um *adj* widespread, prevalent, well known; general, common
pervăg·or -ārī -ātus sum *vt* to spread through or over, pervade; *vi* to wander all over, range about; (with **ad** + *acc*) to spread to, extend to, be known as far as
pervăg·us -a -um *adj* wandering about
pervarĭē *adv* in various versions
pervast·ō -āre *vt* to devastate
pervāsus *pp* of **pervado**
per·vĕhō -vehĕre -vexī -vectum *vt* to bring, carry, convey; to bring (*e.g., supplies*) through; **pervehi** to ride, drive, sail; to reach; **in portum pervehi** to sail into port, reach port
per·vellō -vellĕre -vellī *vt* to pull hard; to pinch hard; to excite, arouse; (fig) to tear apart (*with words*), disparage
per·venĭō -venīre -vēnī -ventum *vt* to come to, reach; *vi* to come up, arrive; (with **ad** or **in** + *acc*) **a** to arrive at, reach; **b** (fig) to attain to
pervēn·or -ārī -ātus sum *vt* to search through (*e.g., all the city*)
perversē or **pervorsē** *adv* wrongly, perversely
perversĭt·ās -ātis *f* perversity, distortion
pervers·us or **pervors·us -a -um** *adj* turned the wrong way, awry, crooked; cross-eyed; (fig) crooked, wrong, perverse; spiteful, malicious
per·vertō or **per·vortō -vertĕre -vertī -versum** *vt* to overturn, upset, knock down; (fig) to abuse, misuse, undo, destroy, pervert
pervespĕrī *adv* late in the evening
pervestīgātĭ·ō -ōnis *f* thorough search, examining, investigation
pervestīg·ō -āre *vt* to track down, hunt down; (fig) to trace, detect
pervĕt·us -ĕris *adj* very old, ancient
pervetust·us -a -um *adj* outdated, antiquated
pervĭam *adv* **perviam facere** to make accessible
pervicācĭ·a -ae *f* persistence; stubbornness
pervicācĭus *adv* more obstinately, more stubbornly
pervĭc·ax -ācis *adj* persistent, determined; headstrong, stubborn, obstinate
pervictus *pp* of **pervinco**
per·vidĕō -vidēre -vīdī -vīsum *vt* to look over, overlook, survey; to see through; to examine, investigate; to realize
pervig·ĕō -ēre -ŭī *vi* to continue to thrive
pervĭg·il (*genit:* **-ĭlis**) *adj* wide awake, ever watchful
pervigilātĭ·ō -ōnis *f* religious vigil
pervigil·ĭum -ĭī or **-ī** *n* all-night vigil
pervigĭl·ō -āre *vt* to spend or pass (*nights, days*) without sleep; *vi* to

stay awake all night, keep an all-night vigil
pervīl·is -e *adj* very cheap
per·vincō -vincĕre -vīcī -victum *vt* to defeat completely, completely overcome, completely get the better of; to outdo, surpass, exceed; to outbid; to convince; to prove; *vi* to win, succeed; to carry a point; (with **ut**) to succeed in, bring it about that; **non pervicit ut referrent consules** he did not succeed in having the consuls make a formal proposal
pervīsus *pp* of **pervideo**
pervĭ·us -a -um *adj* crossable, passable, accessible; *n* passage, thoroughfare
per·vīvō -vīvĕre -vixī *vi* to live on; **pervivere usque ad summam aetatem** to live on to a ripe old age
pervolgō see **pervulgo**
pervolĭt·ō -āre *vt & vi* to fly about, flit about
pervŏl·ō -āre *vt* to fly through or about, flit about; to dart through, pass quickly over; *vi* to fly about, flit about; (with **in** + *acc*) to fly through to, arrive at, reach
per·vŏlō -velle -volŭī *vt* to want badly, wish very much; (with *inf*) to wish very much to; (with *acc & inf*) to eagerly wish (*someone*) to
pervolūt·ō -āre *vt* to turn over often, read through (*books*)
per·volvō -volvĕre -volvī -volūtum *vt* to roll (*someone*) over; to keep reading, read through (*books*); **pervolvi** to be busy, be engaged
pervor- see **perver-**
pervulgāt·us or **pervolgāt·us -a -um** *adj* widely known, very common
pervulg·ō or **pervolg·ō -āre** *vt* to make known, make public, publicize; to frequent; **se pervulgare** to prostitute oneself, become a prostitute
pēs pedis *m* foot; foot (*measure*); foot, meter (*in verse*); leg (*of table, couch, etc.*); sail rope, sheet; **ad pedes descendere** to dismount (*in order to fight on foot*); **aequis pedibus labi** to sail on an even keel; **ante pedes** in plain view; **pede dextro, felice,** or **secundo** auspiciously; **pedem conferre** to come to close quarters; **pedem ferre** to come; to go; **pedem ponere** (with **in** + *abl*) to set foot on; **pedem referre** to go back, retreat; **pedibus** on foot; **pedibus claudere** to set to verse, put in meter; **pedibus ire in sententiam** (with *genit*) to vote in favor of the proposal of; **pedibus itur in sententiam** the proposal is put to a vote, a vote is taken on the proposal; **pedibus merere** or **pedibus mereri** to serve in the infantry; **pedibus vincere** to win a footrace; **pugna ad pedes** infantry battle; **se in pedes conjicere** to take to one's heels; **servus a pedibus** footman; **sub pedibus** under one's sway
pessĭmē (*superl* of **male**) *adv* very badly, most wretchedly
pessĭm·us -a -um (*superl* of **malus**) *adj* worst; *m* scoundrel
pessŭl·us -ī *m* bolt (*of a door*)
pessum *adv* down, to the ground, to the bottom; **pessum dare** to send to the bottom, sink, drown, ruin, destroy; **pessum ire** to go down, sink, go to ruin
pestĭf·er -ĕra -ĕrum *adj* pestilential; destructive, pernicious; *m* trouble maker
pestifĕrē *adv* balefully
pestĭl·ens -entis *adj* pestilential, unhealthful; (fig) destructive, pernicious
pestilentĭ·a -ae *f* unhealthful atmosphere, unhealthful climate; pestilence, plague; destruction, death
pestilĭt·ās -ātis *f* pestilence, plague
pest·is -is *f* contagious disease, plague; destruction, death; trouble maker, anarchist, subversive
petasāt·us -a -um *adj* wearing a hat; (fig) ready to travel
petasĭ·ō or **petăs·ō -ōnis** *m* ham
petasuncŭl·us -ī *m* little ham
petăs·us -ī *m* hat
petaur·um -ī *n* springboard
petess·ō or **petiss·ō -ĕre** *vt* to be eager for, pursue; **pugnam petessere** to be spoiling for a fight
petītĭ·ō -ōnis *f* attack, blow, thrust, aim; petition, request, application; candidacy, political campaign; claim, suit, suing; right to sue; **petitioni se dare** to become a candidate
petīt·or -ōris *m* applicant; political candidate; plaintiff
petītur·ĭō -īre *vi* to be eager for office
petīt·us -a -um *pp* of **peto;** *n* request, desire
petīt·us -ūs *m* (with *genit*) heading for
pet·ō -ĕre -īvī *or* **-ĭī -ītum** *vt* to make for, head for; to attack; to strive for, aim at; to demand, require, exact; to claim, sue for; to beg, desire, entreat; to look for, go in search of, search for; to run after, chase, court (*girls*); to fetch, bring, obtain, draw; to run for (*office*); to refer to, relate to
petorrīt·um -ī *n* open four-wheeled carriage
petr·a -ae *f* rock, crag
petr·ō -ōnis *m* yokel
Petrōn·ĭus -ĭī or **-ī** *m* Petronius Arbiter (*author and master of ceremonies at the court of Nero*)
petŭl·ans -antis *adj* pert, impudent, smart-alecky, petulant, forward
petulanter *adv* pertly, impudently, petulantly

petulanti·a -ae *f* pertness, impudence, forwardness; carelessness
petulc·us -a -um *adj* butting, apt to butt
pex·us -a -um *pp* of **pecto;** *adj* combed; new, still having the nap on
Phaeāc·es -um *m pl* Phaeacians (*people described in the Odyssey as living on a utopian island*)
Phaeācĭ·us -a -um *adj* Phaeacian; *f* Phaeacia
Phaeāc·us -a -um *adj* Phaeacian
Phaedr·a -ae *f* daughter of Minos and Pasiphae and wife of Theseus
Phaedr·us -ī *m* pupil of Socrates; freedman of Augustus and famous writer of Latin fables
Phaest·um -ī *n* town in Crete
Phaëth·ōn -ontis *m* son of Helios and Clymene who was killed trying to drive his father's chariot
Phaëthontē·us -a -um *adj* of Phaethon
Phaëthontiăd·es -um *f pl* sisters of Phaethon
phalang·ae -ārum *f pl* wooden rollers
phalangīt·ae -ārum *m pl* soldiers belonging to a Macedonian phalanx
phal·anx -angis *f* phalanx, battalion (*compact body of heavy-armed men in battle array first developed by the Macedonians*)
phalārĭc·a or **falārĭc·a -ae** *f* firebrand, fiery missile (*shot by a catapult or thrown by hand*)
phalĕr·ae -ārum *f pl* military medals; medallions (*worn by horses on forehead and chest*)
phalerāt·us -a -um *adj* wearing medals, decorated; ornamental
Phalērĭc·us -a -um *adj* of Phaleron
Phalēr·um -ī *n* Athenian harbor
pharĕtr·a -ae *f* quiver
pharetrāt·us -a -um *adj* wearing a quiver
pharmaceutrĭ·a -ae *f* witch, sorceress
pharmacopōl·a -ae *m* druggist; quack
Pharsālĭc·us -a -um *adj* of Pharsalus
Pharsālĭ·us -a -um *adj* Pharsalian; *f* district of Pharsalia
Pharsāl·os or **Pharsāl·us -ī** *f* town in Thessaly near which Caesar defeated Pompey (48 B.C.)
Phar·os or **Phar·us -ī** *m* or *f* island in the harbor at Alexandria famous for its lighthouse; lighthouse
phasēl·us -ī *m* or *f* kidney bean; pinnace (*light boat*); yacht
Phāsiăc·us -a -um *adj* Colchian
Phāsiān·a -ae *f* pheasant (*female*)
Phāsiān·us -ī *m* pheasant
Phāsĭ·as -ădis *adj* Colchian
Phās·is -ĭdis or **-ĭdos** *m* river in Colchis
phasm·a -ătis *n* ghost
Pher·ae -ārum *f pl* city in Thessaly, the home of Admetus
Pherae·us -a -um *adj* of Pherae
phiăl·a -ae *f* saucer
Phīdĭ·ās -ae *m* famous Greek sculptor and friend of Pericles (*fl* 440 B.C.)
philēm·a -ătis *n* kiss
Philēm·ōn -ŏnis *m* pious rustic who was changed into an oak tree while his wife Baucis was changed into a linden tree
Philipp·ī -ōrum *m pl* city in Macedonia where Octavian and Antony defeated Brutus and Cassius (42 B.C.)
Philippĭc·ae -ārum *f pl* series of vitriolic speeches directed at Antony by Cicero
Philipp·us -ī *m* name of several kings of Macedon (*esp. Philip II, son of Amyntas, and father of Alexander the Great, c.* 382-336 B.C.)
philitĭ·a or **phiditĭ·a -ōrum** *n pl* communal meals at Sparta
Phil·ō or **Phil·ōn -ōnis** *m* Academic philosopher and teacher of Cicero
Philoctēt·ēs -ae *m* Greek warrior and famous archer who was abandoned by the Greek army on the island of Lemnos
philologĭ·a -ae *f* love of study, study of literature
philolŏg·us -a -um *adj* learned, scholarly
Philomēl·a -ae *f* daughter of Pandion and sister of Procne, who was changed into a nightingale
philosŏphē *adv* philosophically
philosophĭ·a -ae *f* philosophy
philosŏph·or -ārī *vi* to pursue philosophy
philosŏph·us -a -um *adj* philosophical; *mf* philosopher
phitr·um -ī *n* love potion
philȳr·a -ae *f* inner bark of the lime tree; linden tree
phīm·us -ī *m* dice box
Phīn·eus -ĕī or **-ĕos** *m* king of Salmydessus in Thrace, whom the Argonauts rescued from the torments which the Harpies visited upon him
Phlegĕth·ōn -ontis *m* river of fire in the lower world
Phlegethont·is -ĭdis *adj* of Phlegethon
Phlegȳ·ās -ae *m* king of the Lapiths and father of Ixion
Phlī·ūs -untis *f* city in N.E. Peloponnesus
phōc·a -ae or **phōc·ē -ēs** *f* seal
Phōcaĭc·us or **Phōcē·us** or **Phōcĭ·us -a -um** *adj & mf* Phocian
Phōc·is -ĭdis *f* a country of Greece W. of Boeotia
Phoeb·as -ădis *f* prophetess, priestess of Apollo
Phoeb·ē -ēs *f* moon goddess, the sister of Phoebus; night
Phoebigĕn·a -ae *m* son of Phoebus (*i.e., Asculapius*)
Phoeb·us -ī *m* Apollo as sun god; sun
Phoenīc·ē -ēs *f* Phoenicia

Phoenīc·es -um *m pl* Phoenicians
phoenīcoptĕr·us -ī *m* flamingo
Phoeniss·a -ae *f* Phoenician woman (*esp. Dido*)
phoen·ix -īcis *m* phoenix (*famous Arabian bird which was said to live* 500 *years and from whose ashes a young phoenix would be born*)
Phoen·ix -īcis *m* son of Amyntor and companion of Achilles
Phorc·is -ĭdos *f* female descendant of Phorcus; Medusa
Phorc·us -ī *m* son of Neptune and father of Medusa and the other Gorgons
Phorcȳn·is -ĭdis or **-ĭdos** *f* Medusa
Phraāt·ēs or **Phrahāt·ēs -ae** *m* king of Parthia
phrenēs·is -is *f* frenzy, delirium
phrenētĭc·us -a -um *adj* frenetic, frantic, delirious
Phrix·us -ī *m* son of Athamas and Nephele and brother of Helle, with whom he fled to Colchis mounted on the ram with the golden fleece
Phryg·es -um *m pl* Phrygians (*a people of Asia Minor*)
phrygĭ·ō -ōnis *m* embroiderer
Phrygĭ·us -a -um *adj & mf* Phrygian; Trojan; *f* Phrygia (*a country of Asia Minor*)
Phthī·a -ae *f* home of Achilles in Thessaly
Phthīōt·a or **Phthīōt·ēs -ae** *m* native of Phthia
phthis·is -is *f* consumption, tuberculosis
phy *interj* bah!
phylăc·a -ae *f* jail
phylacist·a -ae *m* jailer; overanxious creditor
phylarch·us -ī *m* tribal chief
physĭc·a -ae or **physĭc·ē -ēs** *f* physics
physĭc·us -a -um *adj* natural, physical, belonging to natural philosophy or physics; *m* natural philosopher, physicist, scientist; *n pl* physics
physiognōm·ōn -ŏnis *m* physiognomist
physiologĭ·a -ae *f* natural philosophy, natural science
piābĭl·is -e *adj* expiable
piāculār·is -e *adj* expiatory, atoning; *n pl* expiatory sacrifices
piācŭl·um -ī *n* propitiatory sacrifice; victim; atonement, expiation; remedy; crime, sacrilege; punishment
piām·en -ĭnis *n* atonement
pīc·a -ae *f* magpie
picārĭ·a -ae *f* place where pitch is made
picĕ·a -ae *f* pine tree
Pīc·ens -entis *adj* Picene, of Picenum
Pīcēn·us -a -um *adj & m* Picene; *n* district of Central Italy on the Adriatic coast
picĕ·us -a -um *adj* made of pitch; pitch-black
pict·or -ōris *m* painter
Pict·or -ōris *m* Q. Fabius Pictor (*earliest Roman historian, who wrote a history of Rome in Greek, fl* 225 B.C.)
pictūr·a -ae *f* painting, art of painting; a painting, picture; embroidery
pictūrāt·us -a -um *adj* painted; embroidered
pict·us -a -um *pp* of **pingo;** *adj* decorated, colored; tattooed; ornate (*style*); false, unreal
pīc·us -ī *m* woodpecker; griffin (*fabulous bird*)
Pīc·us -ī *m* son of Saturn and grandfather of Latinus, who was changed by Circe into a woodpecker
piē *adv* dutifully, affectionately
Pierĭ·a -ae *f* district in Macedonia
Piĕr·is -ĭdis or **-ĭdos** *f* daughter of Pieros; Muse; *f pl* the nine Muses
Pierĭ·us -a -um *adj* Pierian; poetic; musical; *f* see **Pieria;** *f pl* Muses
Piĕr·os or **Piĕr·us -ī** *m* father of the nine Muses
piĕt·ās -ātis *f* responsibility, sense of responsibility, sense of duty; devotion, piety; kindness, tenderness; loyalty, patriotism
pig·er -ra -rum *adj* reluctant, unwilling; apathetic, slow, lazy; numbing (*cold*); slow-moving, tedious, dull (*war, etc.*); backward, slow, dull (*person*)
pig·et -ēre -ŭit or **-ĭtum est** *v impers* it irks, pains, annoys, makes regretful; (with *genit* of cause of feeling), e.g., **piget stultitiae meae** I am irked by my foolishness; (with *inf*), e.g., **illa me composuisse piget** I repent having written those verses
pigmentār·ĭus -ĭī *or* **-ī** *m* paint dealer
pigment·um -ī *n* pigment, paint, color; coloring, color (*of style*)
pignerāt·or -ōris *m* mortgagee
pignĕr·ō -āre *vt* to pledge, mortgage, pawn; (fig) to pledge
pignĕr·or -ārī -ātus sum *vt* to take as pledge, accept in good faith; to claim to
pign·us -ĕris or **-ŏris** *n* pledge, security, guarantee; hostage; mortgage; income from mortgages; wager, stake; (fig) pledge, assurance, proof; *n pl* children
pigrē *adv* slowly, sluggishly
pigritĭ·a -ae or **pigritĭ·ēs -ēī** *f* sluggishness, laziness
pigr·ō -āre or **pigr·or -ārī -ātus sum** *vi* to be slow, be sluggish, be lazy
pīl·a -ae *f* a mortar; pillar; pier
pĭl·a -ae *f* ball; ball game; ballot (*used by jury*); **mea pila est** the ball is mine, I've won; **pilā ludere** to play ball
pīlān·us -ī *m* soldier in the third rank in battle
pīlāt·us -a -um *adj* armed with javelin
pīlent·um -ī *n* ladies' carriage

pilleāt·us -a -um *adj* wearing a felt skullcap (*as a symbol of free status*)
pilleŏl·us -ī *m* skullcap
pillĕ·um -ī *n* or **pillĕ·us -ī** *m* felt cap or hat (*worn by Romans at festivals, esp. at the Saturnalia, and given to a slave when freed as a symbol of his freedom*); freedom, liberty
pilōs·us -a -um *adj* hairy
pīl·um -ī *n* javelin
pīl·us -ī *m* maniple or company of the triarii, company of veteran reserves; **primi pili centurio** chief centurion of a legion (*centurion of the first century of the triarii*); **primus pilus** chief centurion of the triarii and therefore of the legion
pĭl·us -ī *m* hair; (fig) whit; **non pili facere** to care not a whit for
Pimpl·a -ae *f* town in Pieria sacred to the Muses
Pimplē·a -ae or **Pimplē·is -ĭdis** *f* Muse
Pindarĭc·us -a -um *adj* Pindaric
Pindăr·us -ī *m* Pindar (*famous lyric poet from Thebes in Boeotia,* 518-438 B.C.)
Pind·us -ī *m* mountain range separating Thessaly from Epirus
pīnēt·um -ī *n* pine forest
pīnĕ·us -a -um *adj* pine, of pine
pingō pingĕre pinxī pictum *vt* to draw, paint; to embroider; to depict, represent, portray; to stain, color; to decorate; to color, embellish (*style*)
pingu·e -is *n* fat, grease
pinguesc·ō -ĕre *vi* to get fat; to become fertile
pingu·is -e *adj* fat; oily, greasy; juicy; rich, fertile; thick, dense; stupid, dull; quiet, comfortable
pīnĭf·er -ĕra -ĕrum *adj* pine-producing, pine-covered
pīnĭg·er -ĕra -ĕrum *adj* pine-producing, pine-covered
pinn·a -ae *f* feather; wing; flight; fin; feathered arrow; pinnacle, battlement
pinnāt·us -a -um *adj* feathered, winged
pinnĭg·er -ĕra -ĕrum *adj* winged; having fins, finny
pinnĭp·ēs -ĕdis *adj* wing-footed
pinnirăp·us -ī *m* crest-snatcher (*gladiator who tried to get his opponent's helmet crest*)
pinnŭl·a -ae *f* little wing
pīnotēr·ēs -ae *m* hermit crab
pins·ō -ĕre -ī (or **-ŭī**) **-um** (or **-ĭtum**) *vt* to pound
pīn·us -ūs or **-ī** *f* pine tree, fir tree; pine forest; ship; torch; wreath of pine
pi·ō -āre *vt* to appease by sacrifice, propitiate; to honor with religious rites, worship; to purify with religious rites; to atone for, expiate; to avert
pip·er -ĕris *n* pepper
pīpĭl·ō -āre *vi* to chirp
pīpŭl·um -ī *n* or **pīpĭl·us -ī** *m* shrieking, yelling
Pīrae·eus or **Pīrae·us -ī** *m* or **Pīrae·a -ōrum** *n pl* principal harbor of Athens
pīrāt·a -ae *m* pirate
pīrātĭc·us -a -um *adj* pirate; *f* piracy; **piraticam facere** to practice piracy
Pīrēn·ē -ēs *f* fountain on the citadel of Corinth near which Bellerophon caught Pegasus
Pīrithŏ·us -ī *m* son of Ixion and king of the Lapiths
pir·um -ī *n* pear
pir·us -ī *f* pear tree
Pīs·a -ae *f* of **Pīs·ae -ārum** *f pl* Pisa (*city in Elis on the Alpheus River near which the Olympic games were held*)
Pīs·ae -ārum *f pl* Pisa (*ancient city of N. Etruria*)
Pīsae·us -a -um *adj* of Pisa; *f* Hippodamia
piscārĭ·us -a -um *adj* fish, of fishing or fish; **forum piscarium** fish market
piscāt·or -ōris *m* fisherman; fishmonger
piscātōrĭ·us -a -um *adj* fishing; fish
piscāt·us -ūs *m* fishing; fish; (fig) good haul
piscicŭl·us -ī *m* little fish
piscīn·a -ae *f* fish pond; swimming pool
piscīnār·ĭus -ĭī or **-ī** *m* person fond of swimming pools or fish ponds
pisc·is -is *m* fish
Pisc·is -is *m* Piscis (*constellation*)
pisc·or -ārī -ātus sum *vi* to fish
piscōs·us -a -um *adj* full of fish
pisculent·us -a -um *adj* well stocked with fish
Pīsistratĭd·ae -ārum *m pl* sons of Pisistratus (*i.e., Hippias and Hipparchus*)
Pīsistrăt·us -ī *m* enlightened tyrant of Athens (560-527 B.C.)
pistill·um -ī *n* pestle
pist·or -ōris *m* miller; baker
pistrill·a -ae *f* little mill
pistrīn·um -ī *n* flour mill; bakery; drudgery
pistr·is -is or **pistr·ix -īcis** *f* sea monster (*of any kind*); whale, shark; swift ship
pithēc·ĭum -ĭī or **-ī** *n* little ape
Pitth·eus -ĕī or **-ĕos** *m* king of Troezen and father of Aethra, the mother of Theseus
pītuīt·a -ae *f* phlegm; rheum; head cold
pītuītōs·us -a -um *adj* full of phlegm, phlegmatic
pi·us -a -um *adj* conscientious; godfearing, godly, holy; fatherly, motherly, brotherly, sisterly; affectionate; patriotic; good; sacred, holy (*objects connected with religion*)
pix picis *f* pitch; *f pl* chunks of pitch
plācābĭl·is -e *adj* easily appeased; pacifying, appeasing
plācābilĭt·ās -ātis *f* readiness to forgive, conciliatory disposition

plācām·en -ĭnis *n* means of appeasing, peace offering
plācāment·um -ī *n* means of appeasing, peace offering
plācātē *adv* calmly, quietly
plācātĭ·ō -ōnis *f* pacifying, propitiating
plācāt·us -a -um *adj* calm, quiet; appeased, reconciled
plac·ens -entis *adj* pleasing
placent·a -ae *f* cake
plac·ĕō -ēre -ŭī -ĭtum *vi* (with *dat*) to please, satisfy, give pleasure to, be acceptable to; **sibi placere** to be satisfied with oneself, pride oneself; *v impers* it seems right, seems proper; it is settled, is agreed; it is resolved, is decided; **eis placitum est ut considerent** they decided to consider; **senatui placuit** the senate decreed
placĭdē *adv* calmly, placidly, gently, quietly
placĭd·us -a -um *adj* calm, placid, gentle, quiet
placĭt·ō -āre *vi* to be very pleasing
placĭt·us -a -um *adj* pleasing, acceptable; agreed upon; *n* principle, belief, tenet; **ultra placitum laudare** to praise excessively
plāc·ō -āre *vt* to calm, quiet; to appease; to reconcile
plāg·a -ae *f* blow; wound; (fig) blow
plăg·a -ae *f* region, tract, zone; hunting net; mesh of a net; curtain; (fig) trap
plagiār·ĭus -ĭī or **-ī** *n* plunderer; kidnapper; plagiarist
plāgĭg·er -ĕra -ĕrum *adj* covered with welts
plāgigerŭl·us -a -um *adj* covered with welts
plāgipatĭd·a -ae *m* whipping boy
plāgōs·us -a -um *adj* quick to use the rod
plagŭl·a -ae *f* curtain
plagūsĭ·a -ae *f* a fish
planctus *pp* of **plango**
planct·us -ūs *m* beating
plānē *adv* clearly, distinctly; legibly; completely, entirely, quite; certainly, to be sure
plangō plangĕre planxī planctum *vt* to strike, beat; to beat (*breast, head as sigh of grief*); to lament, bewail; *vi* to wail, lament; (fig) to wring the hands
plang·or -ōris *m* striking, beating; beating of the breast; wailing
plānilŏqu·os -a -om *adj* speaking clearly
plānĭp·ēs -ĕdis *m* ballet dancer
plānĭt·ās -ātis *f* distinctness
plānitĭ·ēs -ēī or **plānitĭ·a -ae** *f* flat surface, level ground, plain
plant·a -ae *f* sprout, shoot; young plant, slip; sole (*of the foot*)
plantār·ĭa -ĭum *n pl* slips; young trees; hair
plān·us -a -um *adj* flat, level, even; plain, clear; *n* level ground, plain
plan·us -ī *m* tramp; imposter, cheat
plasm·a -ătis *n* phoney accent
Plataeae·ae -ārum *f pl* Plataea (*town in Boeotia near which the Greeks defeated the Persians in* 479 B.C.)
platalĕ·a -ae *f* waterfowl, spoonbill
platăn·us -ī or **-ūs** *f* plane tree
platē·a or **platĕ·a -ae** *f* street
Plat·ō or **Plat·ōn -ōnis** *m* Plato (*famous Greek philosopher*, 429-348 B.C.)
Platōnic·us -a -um *adj* Platonic; *m pl* Platonists
plaudō plaudĕre plausī plausum *vt* to slap, clap, beat; *vi* to flap, beat, clap; (with *dat*) to applaud, approve of; **alis plaudere** to flap the wings; **manibus plaudere** to clap the hands
plausibĭl·is -e *adj* deserving applause
plaus·or -ōris *m* applauder
plaustr·um -ī *n* wagon, cart
Plaustr·um -ī *n* the Great Bear (*constellation*)
plausus *pp* of **plaudo**
plaus·us -ūs *m* clapping, flapping; clapping of the hands; applause
Plaut·us -ī *m* T. Maccius Plautus (*famous Roman writer of comedies, born at Sarsina in Umbria, c.* 254-184 B.C.)
plēbēcŭl·a -ae *f* rabble
plēbēĭ·us or **plēbēj·us -a -um** *adj* plebeian, of the common people; common, low, vulgar
plēbicŏl·a -ae *m* democrat; demagogue
plēbiscĭt·um -ī *n* decree of the commons
pleb·s -is or **plēb·ēs -ēī** or **-ī** *f* plebeians, common people; the masses, proletariat
plectĭl·is -e *adj* plaited
plectō plectĕre plexī or **plexŭī plexum** *vt* to plait, braid
plect·ō -ĕre *vt* to punish
Plēĭ·as -ădis *f* Pleiad; *f pl* Pleiades (*seven daughters of Atlas and Pleione, who were placed among the stars*)
Plēĭŏn·ē -ēs *f* daughter of Oceanus and Tethys, wife of Atlas, and mother of the Pleiades
plēnē *adv* fully, completely
plēn·us -a -um *adj* full; stout, plump; pregnant; filled, satisfied; full, packed; full, strong, loud (*voice*); full-length, unabridged, uncontracted; abundant, plentiful; advanced, mature (*years*); complete, finished
plērumque *adv* generally, mostly; often, frequently
plēr·usque -ăque -umque *adj* a very great part of, the greater part of, most; very many, a good many; *n* the greatest part
plex·us -a -um *pp* of **plecto;** *adj* plaited
plicātr·ix -īcis *f* woman who folds clothes, folder

plic·ō -āre -āvī or **-ŭī -ātum** or **-ĭtum** *vt* to fold, wind, coil up
Plīn·ĭus -ĭī or **-ī** *m* C. Plinius Secundus (*author of a work on natural history, who perished in the eruption of Vesuvius in* 79 A.D.); C. Plinius Caecilius (*his nephew, author of Letters and a Panegyric to Trajan,* 62 A.D.-*c.* 114 A.D.)
plōrābĭl·is -e *adj* deplorable
plōrāt·or -ōris *m* mourner
plōrāt·us -ūs *m* wailing, wail
plōr·ō -āre *vt* to cry over; *vi* to cry aloud, wail
plostell·um -ī *n* cart
ploxĕm·um -ī *n* wagon frame
pluit pluĕre pluit *vt* it is raining (*stones, blood, etc.*); *vi* it is raining; (with *abl*) it is raining (*stones, etc.*)
plūm·a -ae *f* down, soft feather; (collectively) feathers, down
plūmātĭl·e -is *n* dress embroidered with feathers
plūmāt·us -a -um *adj* covered with feathers
plumbĕ·us -a -um *adj* lead, of lead; leaden, oppressive (*weather*); dull, stupid
plumb·um -ī *n* lead; bullet; pipe; ruler (*for drawing lines*); **plumbum album** tin
plūmĕ·us -a -um *adj* downy, filled with down; like feathers
plūmĭp·ēs -ĕdis *adj* with feathered feet
plūmōs·us -a -um *adj* downy, feathered
plūrĭmum *adv* very much, especially, commonly, generally, most
plūrĭm·us -a -um (*superl* of **multus**) *adj* many a; most; very much; very many; very great, very intense; **plurimam salutem dare** to send warmest greetings; *n* a great deal; **plurimi facere** to think very highly of, think a great deal of; **quam plurimum** as much as possible
plūs *adv* more; **multo plus** much more; **paulo plus** a little more
plūs plūris (*comp* of **multus**) *adj* more; *n* more; too much; **et, quod plus est, Romani estis** and what is more, you are Romans; **plus animi** more courage; **plus nimio** much too much; **plus plusque** more and more; **uno viro plus habere** to have one man too much; **pluris esse** (*genit* of value) to be of more value, of a higher price, worth more, be higher, be dearer; *n pl* more words; **quid plura?** why should I say more?, in short
pluscŭl·us -a -um *adj* a little more, somewhat more; *n* a little more; **plusculum negoti** a little more business
plutĕ·us -ī *m* or **plutĕ·um -ī** *n* (mil) movable mantlet or shed used to protect soldiers in siege work; parapet; couch, dining couch; book shelf; book case; board, slab
Plūt·ō or **Plūt·ōn -ōnis** *m* king of the lower world, husband of Proserpina, and brother of Jupiter and Neptune
pluvĭ·a -ae *f* rain
pluviāl·is -e *adj* rain, of rain, rainy; **fungi pluviales** mushrooms brought out by the rain
pluvĭ·us -a -um *adj* rain, of rain, rainy; **pluvia aqua** rain water; **pluvius arcus** rainbow; *f* see **pluvia**
pōcill·um -ī *n* small drinking cup
pōcŭl·um -ī *n* drinking cup; drink, draught; **poculum ducere** or **exhaurire** to drain a cup
podăgr·a -ae *f* arthritis
podagrōs·us -a -um *adj* arthritic
pōd·ex -ĭcis *m* anus, rectum
pod·ĭum -ĭī or **-ī** balcony; box seat (*for the emperor*)
Poeantiăd·ēs -ae *m* Philoctetes
Poe·ās -antis *m* father of Philoctetes
poēm·a -ătis *n* poem
poēmat·ĭum -ĭī or **-ī** *n* short poem
poen·a -ae *f* compensation, recompense, retribution, satisfaction, penalty, fine, punishment; hardship, loss, pain; (in games) penalty; **poenam** or **poenas dare, dependere, pendere, persolvere, reddere, solvere, suscipere,** or **sufferre** to pay the penalty, make restitution, give satisfaction; **poenam** or **poenas capere, persequi, petere, repetere,** or **reposcere** to exact a penalty, demand satisfaction; **poena mortis** capital punishment, death penalty
poenĭō see **punio**
Poen·us -a -um *adj & m* Carthaginian
poēs·is -is *f* art of poetry; poetry, poems
poēt·a -ae *m* maker, contriver; poet
poētĭc·a -ae or **poētĭc·ē -ēs** *f* art of poetry; poetics
poētĭcē *adv* poetically
poētĭc·us -a -um *adj* poetic, poetical; *f* see **poetica**
poētrĭ·a -ae *f* poetess
poētr·is -ĭdis or **-ĭdos** *f* poetess
pol *interj* by Pollux!; Lord!
polent·a -ae *f* pearl barley
polentārĭ·us -a -um *adj* caused by eating barley
pol·ĭō -īre -īvī or **-ĭī -ītum** *vt* to polish, smooth; (fig) to polish, improve, perfect
polītē *adv* in a polished manner, with taste, smoothly, elegantly
polītĭc·us -a -um *adj* political
polīt·us -a -um *adj* polished, smooth; (fig) polished, smooth, smooth-spoken, smooth-mannered, refined, cultivated
poll·en -ĭnis *n* or **poll·is -ĭnis** *m* or *f* flour
poll·ens -entis *adj* strong, powerful, thriving, able
pollentĭ·a -ae *f* might, power

poll·ĕō -ēre *vi* to be strong, be powerful; to be capable, be able; (of medicines) to be powerful, be efficacious; to have influence; **in re publica plurimum pollere** to have tremendous influence in politics
poll·ex -ĭcis *m* thumb; big toe
pollic·ĕor -ērī -ĭtus sum *vt* to promise
pollicitātĭ·ō -ōnis *f* promise
pollicĭt·or -ārī -ātus sum *vt* to keep promising
pollicĭt·us -a -um *pp* of **polliceor;** *n* promise
pollinārĭ·us -a -um *adj* flour, for flour
pollinct·or -ōris *m* embalmer
pol·lingō -lingĕre -linxī -linctum *vt* to lay out, embalm
Pollĭ·ō -ōnis *m* C. Asinius Pollio (*distinguished orator, poet, historian, patron of literature, and statesman,* 76 B.C.-4 A.D.)
poll·is -ĭnis *m* or *f* flour
pol·lūcĕō -lūcēre -luxī -luctum *vt* to offer, offer up as sacrifice; to serve (*meal*); to entertain
pollūcibilĭter *adv* sumptuously, in grand style
polluctūr·a -ae *f* sumptuous dinner
polluct·us -a -um *pp* of **polluceo;** *n* offering, sacrificial meal
pol·lŭō -luĕre -lŭī -lūtum *vt* to pollute, defile, soil, mess up; to defile, violate
Poll·ux or **Poll·ūcēs -ūcis** *m* son of Tyndareus and Leda, twin brother of Castor, and famous boxer
pol·us -ī *m* end of an axis, pole; North Pole; **polus australis** South Pole
Polyb·ĭus -ĭī or **-ī** *m* Greek historian and friend of Scipio Aemilianus (*c.* 203-120 B.C.)
Polydăm·ās -antis *m* son of Panthus and friend of Hector
Polydōr·us -ī *m* son of Priam and Hecuba, murdered by Polymestor the king of Thrace
Polyhymnĭ·a -ae *f* one of the nine Muses
Polymest·ōr -ŏris *m* king of the Thracian Chersonese, husband of Ilione the daughter of Priam
Polynīc·ēs -is *m* son of Oedipus and Jocasta and brother of Eteocles
Polyphēm·us -ī *m* son of Neptune and one of the Cyclops of Sicily
pōlўp·us -ī *m* polyp (*sea animal; tumor*)
Polyxĕn·a -ae *f* daughter of Priam whom Pyrrhus, the son of Achilles, sacrificed at his father's tomb
pōmārĭ·us -a -um *adj* fruit, of fruit trees; *m* fruit vendor; *n* orchard
pōmerīdiān·us -a -um *adj* afternoon
pōmĕr·ĭum or **pōmoer·ĭum -ĭī** or **-ī** *n* space kept free of buildings inside and outside a city wall
pōmĭf·er -ĕra -ĕrum *adj* fruit-bearing
pōmōs·us -a -um *adj* loaded with fruit
pomp·a -ae *f* solemn or religious procession; retinue; pomp, ostentation
Pompēĭ·us or **Pompēj·us -ī** *m* Pompey the Great (*Roman general and statesman,* 106-48 B.C.)
Pompējān·us -a -um *adj* Pompeian; *m pl* inhabitants of Pompeii; soldiers or followers of Pompey
Pompēj·ī -ōrum *m pl* city south of Naples, destroyed by the eruption of Vesuvius in 79 A.D.
Pompil·ĭus -ĭī or **-ī** *m* Numa Pompilius (*second king of Rome and traditional founder of Roman state religion*)
Pomptīn·us -a -um *adj* Pomptine; **Pomptinae paludes** Pomptine Marshes in Latium
pōm·um -ī *n* fruit; fruit tree
pōm·us -ī *f* fruit tree
pondĕr·ō -āre *vt* to weigh; to consider, ponder
ponderōs·us -a -um *adj* weighty, heavy; full of meaning
pondō *adv* in weight
pondō (*indecl*) *n* pound, pounds; **auri quinque pondo** five pounds of gold
pond·us -ĕris *n* weight; mass; burden; importance; stability of character; *n pl* balance, equilibrium
pōne *adv* behind, after, back; *prep* (with *acc*) behind
pōnō pōnĕre posŭī posĭtum or **postum** *vt* to put, place, put down, set down, set, fix, deposit; to lay aside, lay down; to lay out, spend; to stake; to place, station, post; to set up, erect, build, found; to regard, consider; to cite, assert; to suppose, assume; to lay out for burial; to smooth, calm; to arrange, smooth (*hair*); *vi* to abate, calm down
pons pontis *m* bridge; gangway; drawbridge; deck
pontĭcŭl·us -ī *m* small bridge
pontĭf·ex -ĭcis *m* pontiff, pontifex, priest (*one of a board of fifteen*); **pontifex maximus** chief pontiff
pontificāl·is -e *adj* pontifical
pontificāt·us -ūs *m* pontificate
pontifĭc·us -a -um *adj* pontifical
pont·ō -ōnis *m* ferry
pont·us -ī *m* sea; sea water
Pont·us -ī *m* Euxine or Black Sea; region around the Black Sea; kingdom of Mithridates between Bithynia and Armenia, subsequently a Roman province
pop·a -ae *m* priest's assistant (*attendant who slew the victim*)
popăn·um -ī *n* sacrificial cake
popell·us -ī *m* rabble, mob
popīn·a -ae *f* restaurant; food sold at a restaurant
popīn·ō -ōnis *m* diner at a restaurant
popl·es -ĭtis *m* hollow of the knee;

knee; **duplicato poplite** on bended knee; **contento poplite** with a stiff knee

Pōplicŏla see **Publicola**

poppysm·a -ătis *n* clicking with the tongue (*as sign of approval*)

populābĭl·is -e *adj* destructible

populābund·us -a -um *adj* ravaging, laying waste

populār·ēs -ĭum *m pl* people's party, democrats

populār·ĭa -ĭum *n pl* general-admission seats

populār·is -e *adj* of the people, by the people, for the people, people's, popular; approved by the people, popular; favoring the people, democratic; demagogic; of the same country, native; common, coarse

populār·is -is *m* or *f* fellow countryman; party member; fellow member, associate; (with *genit*) partner or associate in

populārĭt·ās -ātis *f* fellow citizenship; popularity

populārĭter *adv* like the people; like a demagogue; **populariter loqui** to use slang

populātĭ·ō -ōnis *f* ravaging, devastation

populāt·or -ōris *m* ravager, destroyer

populāt·us -ūs *m* devastation

pōpulĕ·us -a -um *adj* of poplars, poplar

pōpulĭf·er -ĕra -ĕrum *adj* filled with poplar trees

pōpuln·us -a -um *adj* of poplars, poplar

popŭl·ō -āre or **popŭl·or -ārī -ātus sum** *vt* to ravage, devastate, lay waste; (fig) to pillage, ruin, destroy, spoil

popŭl·us -ī *m* people (*as a political community*), nation; people, crowd, public; citizens (*as opposed to soldiers*), civilians; region, district

pōpŭl·us -ī *f* poplar tree

porc·a -ae *f* sow

porcell·a -ae *f* little sow

porcell·us -ī *m* little hog

porcīnār·ĭus -ĭī or **-ī** *m* pork seller

porcīn·us -a -um *adj* hog's, pig's; *f* pork

Porc·ĭus -ĭī or **-ī** *m* M. Porcius Cato the Censor (235-149 B.C.); M. Porcius Cato Uticensis (95-46 B.C.)

porcŭl·a or **porculēn·a -ae** *f* little sow

porcŭl·us -ī *m* little pig

porc·us -ī *m* pig, hog

porgō see **porrigo**

Porphyrĭ·ōn -ōnis *m* a Giant

porrect·a -ōrum *n pl* offering; **inter caesa et porrecta** (fig) at the eleventh hour

porrectĭ·ō -ōnis *f* extending, stretching out

porrect·us -a -um *pp* of **porrigo;** *adj* stretched out, extended, extensive, long; protracted (*delay*); laid out, dead; (fig) wide-spread

porric·ĭō -ĕre *vt* to offer up, make an offering of

por·rĭgō or **porg·ō -rigĕre -rexī -rectum** *vt* to reach out, stretch out, extend; to offer, present, hand; to lengthen (*a syllable*); **se porrigere** to extend

porrīg·ō -ĭnis *f* dandruff

porrō *adv* forwards, farther on, on; far off, at a distance; long ago; in the future, hereafter; again, in turn; next, furthermore, moreover, on the other hand

porr·um -ī *n* leek; chive

Porsenn·a or **Porsēn·a** or **Porsinn·a -ae** *m* king of Clusium in Etruria who sided with Tarquin in a war against Rome

port·a -ae *f* city gate; gate; entrance; outlet; camp gate (*of which there were always four*)

portātĭ·ō -ōnis *f* carrying, conveyance

por·tendō -tendĕre -tendī -tentum *vt* to indicate, foretell, portend, predict

portentifĭc·us -a -um *adj* monstrous, abnormal

portentōs·us -a -um *adj* monstrous, abnormal, unnatural, portentous

portent·um -ī *n* portent, omen, sign; monstrosity, monster; fantasy, far-fetched fiction; (as term of contempt) monster, demon

portentus *pp* of **portendo**

porthm·eus -ĕī or **-ĕos** *m* ferryman (*i.e., Charon, who piloted the ferry across the Styx*)

porticŭl·a -ae *f* small portico

portĭc·us -ūs *f* colonnade, portico; (mil) gallery (*formed by placing vineae end to end*); Stoicism

portĭ·ō -ōnis *f* portion, share; ratio, portion; instalment, payment; **pro portione** proportionally, relatively

portiscŭl·us -ī *m* gavel

portĭt·or -ōris *m* customs officer; ferryman, boatman

port·ō -āre *vt* to carry; to bring

portōr·ĭum -ĭī or **-ī** *n* port duty, customs duty; tax (*on peddlers*)

portŭl·a -ae *f* small gate

Portūn·us -ī *m* tutelary deity of harbors

portuōs·us -a -um *adj* having good harbors

port·us -ūs *m* port, harbor; haven, refuge; mouth of a river

posc·a -ae *f* sour drink

poscō poscĕre poposcī *vt* to ask, request, beg, demand; (of things) to require, demand, need, call for, make necessary; (with **ab** + *abl*) to ask for (*something*) from, demand (*something*) of; (with double *acc*) to demand (*something*) of, ask (*someone*) for

Posīdōn·ĭus -ĭī or **-ī** *m* Stoic philosopher at Rhodes, teacher of Cicero

positĭ·ō -ōnis *f* putting, placing, setting; position, posture; situation

posĭt·or -ōris *m* builder
positūr·a -ae *f* posture; formation
posĭt·us -a -um *pp* of **pono;** *adj* situated, located
posĭt·us -ūs *m* position; arrangement
possessĭ·ō -ōnis *f* possession; getting possession, occupation; possession, estate
possessiuncŭl·a -ae *f* small estate
possess·or -ōris *m* possessor, occupant; (law) defendant
possibĭl·is -e *adj* possible
pos·sidĕō -sidēre -sēdī -sessum *vt* to possess, occupy; to have, own; to dwell in, live in; (fig) to take hold of
pos·sīdo -sīdĕre -sēdī -sessum *vt* to take possession of, occupy, seize
possum posse potŭī *vi* to be able; **multum (plus, plurimum) posse** to have much (*more, very great*) influence; **non possum quin exclamem** I can't help exclaiming; **quantum** or **ut fieri potest** as far as is possible
post *adv* (of place) behind, back, backwards; (of time) later, afterwards; (of order) next; **aliquanto post** somewhat later; **multis post annis** many years later; *prep* (with *acc*) (of place) behind; (of time) after, since
postĕā *adv* afterwards, after this, after that, hereafter, thereafter
posteāquam *conj* after
posterĭ·or -us *adj* later, next, following; latter, posterior; inferior, worse; hind
posterĭt·ās -ātis *f* the future, afterages, posterity, later generations; offspring (*of animals*); **in posteritatem** in the future
posterĭus *adv* later, at a later date
postĕr·us -a -um *adj* following, ensuing, next, subsequent, future; *m pl* future generations, posterity, descendants; *n* future time; next day; consequence; **in posterum** till the next day; for the future
post·fĕrō -ferre *vt* to put after; to esteem less; to sacrifice
postgenĭt·us -a -um *adj* born later; *m pl* later generations
posthab·ĕō -ēre -ŭī -ĭtum *vt* to consider of secondary importance; to slight, neglect; (with *dat*) to think (*something*) less important than
posthāc *adv* hereafter, in the future
posthinc or **post hinc** *adv* from here, from this place, next
posthōc or **post hōc** *adv* after this, afterwards
postĭbī *adv* afterwards, then
postīcŭl·um -ī *n* small building in the rear
postīc·us -a -um *adj* hind, back, rear; *n* back door
postidĕā *adv* afterwards, after that
postilēn·a -ae *f* crupper; buttocks
postillā *adv* afterwards

post·is -is *m* door post; door; *m pl* double doors
postlīmin·ĭum -ĭī or **-ī** *n* right to return home and resume one's former rank and privileges, right of recovery; **postliminio** by the right of recovery
postmerīdiān·us -a -um *adj* afternoon
postmŏdo or **postmŏdum** *adv* after a bit, a little later, afterwards
postpart·or -ōris *m* successor, heir
post·pōnō -pōnĕre -posŭī -posĭtum or **-postum** *vt* to consider of secondary importance; to neglect, disregard; (with *dat*) to consider (*something*) of less importance than, set (*something*) aside in favor of
postprincipĭ·a -ōrum *n pl* sequel
postpŭt·ō -āre *vt* to consider of secondary importance; (with **prae** + *abl*) to consider (*something*) less important than
postquam *conj* after, when
postrēmō *adv* at last, finally; **primo . . . deinde . . . postremo** first . . . then . . . finally
postrēmum *adv* for the last time, last of all
postrēm·us -a -um (*superl* of **posterus**) *adj* last, last in line, rear; lowest, worst
postrīdiē *adv* on the day after, on the following day; **postridie mane** the next morning; *prep* (with *genit*), e.g., **postridie ejus diei** on the day after that; (with *acc*), e.g., **postridie ludos** on the day after the games
postrīdŭō *adv* on the day after
postscaen·ĭum -ĭī or **-ī** *n* backstage
post·scrībō -scrībĕre -scripsī scriptum *vt* (with *dat*) to add (*e.g., a name*) to; **Tiberi nomen suo postscribere** to add the name of Tiberius to his own name
postulāt·a -ōrum *n pl* demands, claims, requests
postulātĭ·ō -ōnis *f* demand, request, desire; complaint; (law) application for permission to present a claim
postulāt·us -ūs *m* claim, suit
postŭl·ō -āre *vt* to demand, claim; to arraign, prosecute; to apply for (*a writ from the praetor to prosecute*)
postŭm·us -a -um *adj* last, latestborn
postus *pp* of **pono**
pōtātĭ·ō -ōnis *f* drinking, drinking party
pōtāt·or -ōris *m* drinker
pot·ens -entis *adj* capable; mighty, powerful, strong; efficacious, potent; fit, capable, equal; influential; (with *genit*) **a** capable of, equal to, fit for; **b** having power over; **c** presiding over; **d** having obtained (*one's wish*); **e** having carried out (*an order*)

potentāt·us -ūs *m* political power, rule, dominion
potenter *adv* powerfully, mightily, effectually, vigorously; according to one's ability
potentĭ·a -ae *f* force, power; political power (*esp. unconstitutional power*)
potēr·ĭum -ĭī or **-ī** *n* goblet
potest·ās -ātis *f* power, ability, capacity; efficacy, force; public authority, rule, power, sway, dominion, sovereignty, empire, rule; magisterial power, magistracy, office; possibility, opportunity, permission; person in office, magistrate, ruler; property, quality
potin or **potin'** = **potisne** can you?, are you able?
pōtĭ·ō -ōnis *f* drinking; drink, draught; magic potion
pot·ĭor -īrī -ītus sum *vt* to acquire, get possession of; *vi* (with *genit* or *abl*) to acquire, get possession of, become master of, get hold of, get
potĭ·or -us (*comp* of **potis**) *adj* better, preferable, superior; more important
potis or **pote** (indecl) *adj* able, capable; possible
potissĭmum *adv* chiefly, especially, eminently
potissĭm·us -a -um *adj* chief, principal, most important
potĭus *adv* rather, more, by preference; **potius quam** more than, rather than
pōt·ō -āre *vt* to drink; to absorb
pōt·or -ōris *m* drinker
pōtr·ix -īcis *f* drinker (*female*)
pōtulent·us -a -um *adj* drinkable; *n pl* drinks
pōt·us -a -um *adj* drunk
pōt·us -ūs *m* drink
prae *adv* before, in front; in preference; *prep* (with *abl*) before, in front of; compared with, in comparison with; in view of; because of; by reason of, on account of, through; **prae manu** at hand; **prae se** publicly, openly, plainly; **prae se ferre** to display, manifest, exhibit, profess
praeacŭ·ō -ĕre *vt* to sharpen to a point
praeacūt·us -a -um *adj* pointed
praealt·us -a -um *adj* very high; very deep
praeb·ĕō -ēre -ŭī -ĭtum *vt* to hold out, offer, present; to supply, give; to exhibit, represent, show; to give up, yield, surrender; to cause, occasion; to permit, allow; **se praebere** to show oneself, behave
praebĭb·ō -ĕre -ī *vt* (with *dat*) to drink (*e.g., a toast*) to
praebĭt·or -ōris *m* supplier
praecalĭd·us -a -um *adj* very warm, hot
praecantr·ix -īcis *f* witch, enchantress
praecān·us -a -um *adj* prematurely grey
prae·cavĕō -cavēre -cāvī -cautum *vt* to guard against, try to avoid; *vi* to take precautions, be on one's guard; (with *dat*) to look out for, look after; (with *abl*) to guard against, be on one's guard against
prae·cēdō -cēdĕre -cessī -cessum *vt* to precede, go out before, lead; to surpass, excel; *vi* to excel, be superior; (with *dat*) to excel, be superior to
praecell·ens -entis *adj* superior, excellent, preeminent
praecell·ō -ĕre *vt* to surpass, outdo; *vi* to distinguish oneself, excel; (with *dat*) to rule over
praecels·us -a -um *adj* towering
praecentĭ·ō -ōnis *f* musical prelude (*before a sacrifice*)
praecent·ō -āre *vi* (with *dat*) to sing to
praecentus *pp* of **praecino**
praec·eps -ipĭtis *adj* headfirst; downhill, steep, precipitous; sinking (*sun*); swift, rushing, violent; hasty, rash, inconsiderate; dangerous; *n* edge of a cliff, cliff, precipice; danger, critical situation
praeceps *adv* headfirst
praeceptĭ·ō -ōnis *f* preconception; precept, rule; priority
praecept·or -ōris *m* or **praeceptr·ix -īcis** *f* teacher, preceptor
praecept·um -ī *n* rule, maxim; order, command, direction
prae·cerpō -cerpĕre -cerpsī -cerptum *vt* to pick or gather before time; (with *dat*) (fig) to snatch away from
prae·cīdō -cīdĕre -cīdī -cīsum *vt* to lop off, cut short; to cut, cut through; to damage, mutilate; to break off, finish abruptly, end suddenly (*a speech, etc.*); to end, destroy (*hopes, etc.*); to refuse, decline
prae·cingō -cingĕre -cinxī -cinctum *vt* to gird; to surround, ring; to dress; **ense cingi** to wear a sword; **male cinctus** improperly dressed; **recte cinctus** properly dressed
prae·cĭnō -cinĕre -cinŭī -centum *vt* to predict; (with *dat*) to predict (*something*) to; *vi* to make predictions; (with *dat*) to sing or play before or at (*e.g., dinner, sacrifice*)
prae·cipĭō -cipĕre -cēpī -ceptum *vt* to take or receive in advance; to grasp beforehand, anticipate; to teach, instruct, direct, warn; to prescribe; **animo praecipere** or **cogitatione praecipere** to imagine beforehand, reckon on, anticipate, expect; **oculis praecipere** to see beforehand, get a preview of; **opinione praecipere** to suspect in advance; **pecuniam mutuam praecipere** to get an advance loan
praecipitanter *adv* at a high speed
praecipĭt·ō -āre *vt* to throw down

head first; to hasten, hurry, precipitate; **se praecipitare** to throw oneself down, throw oneself down headfirst, jump down, dive; to sink; *vi* to rush headfirst, rush at top speed, rush thoughtlessly; to fall, sink; to be ruined

praecipŭē *adv* especially, chiefly

praecipŭ·us -a -um *adj* special, peculiar, particular; chief, principal; distinguished, excellent, extraordinary; *n* excellence, superiority; *n pl* outstanding or important elements; **praecipua rerum** highlights

praecīsē *adv* briefly, concisely; absolutely

praecīs·us -a -um *pp* of **praecido;** *adj* abrupt, precipitous ; rugged, rough; brief, abrupt (*speech*)

praeclārē *adv* very clearly; excellently; (to express agreement) very good, splendid

praeclār·us -a -um *adj* very clear; very nice; splendid, noble, distinguished, excellent; famous, distinguished; notorious

prae·clūdō -clūdĕre -clūsī -clūsum *vt* to shut, shut off, obstruct; to hinder, stop, impede; **portas consuli praecludere** to shut the gates on the consul, shut the gates in the consul's face; **vocem praecludere alicui** to shut someone up, to hush someone up

praec·ō -ōnis *m* crier, herald; auctioneer; (fig) pangyrist

precōgĭt·ō -āre *vt* to premeditate

praecognĭt·us -a -um *adj* known beforehand, foreseen

prae-cŏlō -colĕre — -cultum *vt* to cultivate prematurely; (fig) to embrace prematurely

praecomposĭt·us -a -um *adj* arranged beforehand; studied, self-conscious

praecōnĭ·us -a -um *adj* of a public crier, of an auctioneer; *n* crier's office; proclamation, announcement; praising, praise

praecon·sūmō -sumĕre -sumpsī -sumptum *vt* to spend or use up beforehand

praecontrect·ō -āre *vt* to consider in advance

praecordĭ·a -ōrum *n pl* diaphragm, midriff; insides, stomach; breast, heart

praecor·rumpō -rumpĕre -rūpī -ruptum *vt* to bribe in advance

praec·ox -ŏcis *adj* premature, hasty, rash

praecurrent·ĭa -ĭum *n pl* antecedents

prae·currō -currĕre -cucurrī or **-currī -cursum** *vt* to precede, anticipate; to outdo, surpass; *vi* to run out ahead, take the lead; (with **ante** + *acc*) to run out ahead of; (with *dat*) to outdo

praecursĭ·ō -ōnis *f* previous occurrence; (mil) skirmish; (rhet) warm-up (*of the audience*)

praecurs·or -ōris *m* forerunner; spy; (mil) scout; advance guard

praecursōrĭ·us -a -um *adj* sent in advance

prae·cutĭō -cutĕre -cussī -cussum *vt* to wave, brandish in front

praed·a -ae *f* booty, spoils, plunder; prey; **praedae esse** (with *dat*) to fall prey to

praedābund·us -a -um *adj* pillaging, plundering

praedamn·ō -āre *vt* to condemn beforehand; **spem praedamnare** to give up hope too soon

praedātĭ·ō -ōnis *f* pillaging, plunder

praedāt·or -ōris *m* marauder, looter, vandal; hunter; greedy man

praedātōrĭ·us -a -um *adj* marauding, looting; graspy, greedy

praedēlass·ō -āre *vt* to tire out, weaken beforehand

praedestĭn·ō -āre *vt* to predetermine

praediāt·or -ōris *m* real-estate agent

praediātōrĭ·us -a -um *adj* real-estate; **jus praediatorium** mortgage law

praedicābĭl·is -e *adj* praiseworthy, laudable

praedicātĭ·ō -ōnis *f* announcement, publication; praising

praedicāt·or -ōris *m* appreciator; eulogist

praedĭc·ō -āre *vt* to announce, proclaim; to report; to assert; to praise

prae·dīcō -dīcĕre -dixī -dictum *vt* to mention beforehand or earlier; to prearrange; to predict; to order, command beforehand

praedictĭ·ō -ōnis *f* prediction

praedict·um -ī *n* prediction, prophecy; command, order; **velut ex praedicto** as if by prearrangement

praediŏl·um -ī *n* small estate, small farm

praedisc·ō -ĕre *vt* to learn beforehand, find out in advance

praedisposĭt·us -a -um *adj* previously arranged

praedĭt·us -a -um *adj* endowed, gifted, provided, furnished; (with *abl*) endowed with, provided with, furnished with

praed·ĭum -ĭī or **-ī** *n* estate, farm; **praedia urbana** city lots

praedīv·es -ĭtis *adj* very rich

praedīvīn·ō -āre *vt* to know in advance, have a presentiment of

praed·ō -ōnis *m* marauder, looter, robber, pirate

praedoct·us -a -um *adj* instructed beforehand

praed·or -ārī -ātus sum *vt* to raid, plunder, loot, rob; (fig) to rob, ravish; **amores alicujus praedari** to steal away someone's sweetheart; *vi* to plunder, loot, make a raid; (with **ex** + *abl*) to prey on, profit by, take advantage of, e.g., **ex al-**

terius inscientiā praedari to prey on someone else's ignorance

prae-dūcō -dūcĕre -duxī -ductum *vt* to run or construct (*trench, wall*) out in front (*for defensive purposes*)

praedulc·is -e *adj* very sweet; (fig) very satisfying (*honor, reward*)

praedūr·us -a -um *adj* very tough (*skin*); tough, brawny

praeēmin·ĕō -ēre *vt* to surpass, excel; *vi* to project forward, stick out

prae·ĕō -īre -īvī or **-iī -ĭtum** *vt* to lead, precede; to read out, dictate, lead (*prayers*); *vi* to go out ahead, take the lead; (with *dat*) to walk in front of

praefātī·ō -ōnis *f* preface, introduction; formula

praefātus *pp* of **praefor**

praefectūr·a -ae *f* supervision, superintendence; prefectship, office of prefect, superintendency; government of a district; prefecture (*Italian city governed by a Roman prefect*); territory of a prefecture, district

praefect·us -ī *m* prefect, supervisor, superintendent; commander; governor; (with *genit* or *dat*) supervisor of, commander of, prefect or governor of

prae-fĕrō -ferre -tŭlī -lātum *vt* to hold out, carry in front; to prefer; to anticipate; to display, reveal, betray; to offer, present; to offer as a model; **praeferri** to ride past, ride by, march past, outflank; **praeferri** or **se praeferri** (with *dat*) to surpass

praefĕr·ox -ōcis *adj* very belligerent, very defiant

praeferrāt·us -a -um *adj* iron-tipped; (coll) chained (*slave*)

praefervĭd·us -a -um *adj* boiling; (fig) boiling; **ira praefervida** boiling anger

praefestīn·ō -āre *vt* to hurry past; (with *inf*) to be in a hurry to

praefĭc·a -ae *f* hired mourner (*female*)

prae·ficiō -ficĕre -fēcī -fectum *vt* to put (*someone*) in charge; (with double *acc*) to appoint (*someone*) as; (with *dat*) to put (*someone*) in charge of, set (*someone*) over, appoint (*someone*) to command

praefīd·ens -entis *adj* too trustful, overconfident; (with *dat*) too trustful of; **homines sibi praefidentes** overconfident men

prae·fīgō -fīgĕre -fixī -fixum *vt* to fix, fasten, set up in front, fasten on the end; to tip, point; to transfix; **capistris praefigere** to muzzle; **cuspidibus praefixus** pointed; **ferro praefixus** iron-tipped

praefīn·iō -īre -īvī or **-iī -ītum** *vt* to determine in advance; to prescribe, appoint; to limit

praefīnītō *adv* in the prescribed manner

praefiscĭnē or **praefiscĭnī** *adv* meaning no offense

praeflōr·ō -āre *vt* to deflower, deprive of its bloom; (fig) to tarnish, spoil

praeflŭ·ō -ĕre *vt & vi* to flow by

praefōc·ō -āre *vt* to choke, choke up, strangle

prae·fodiō -fodĕre -fōdī *vt* to bury beforehand; to dig in front of; **portas praefodire** to dig trenches in front of the gates

prae·for -fārī -fātus sum *vt* to say beforehand, utter in advance, preface; to address in prayer beforehand; to foretell; to invoke; *vi* to pray beforehand; (with *dat*) to pray before

praefractē *adv* obstinately

praefract·us -a -um *pp* of **praefringo;** resolute, determined; abrupt

praefrīgĭd·us -a -um *adj* very cold, freezing

prae·fringō -fringĕre -frēgī -fractum *vt* to break off at the tip or end, break to pieces, smash

prae·fulciō -fulcīre -fulsī -fultum *vt* to prop up, support in front; (with *dat*) to use (*someone*) as a prop or support for; **illud praefulci ut** make sure that

prae·fulgĕō -fulgēre -fulsī *vi* to shine forth, glitter, sparkle

praegelĭd·us -a -um *adj* very cold

praegest·iō -īre *vi* to be very eager

praegn·ans -antis or **praegn·ās -ātis** *adj* pregnant; (with *abl*) full of, swollen with

praegracĭl·is -e *adj* very lean or slender

praegrand·is -e *adj* huge, very great; very powerful

praegrăv·is -e *adj* very heavy; very fat; oppressive; very tiresome

praegrăv·ō -āre *vt* to weigh down; to outweigh; (fig) to burden

prae·gredior -grĕdī -gressus sum *vt* to go in advance of, go ahead of; to go by, go past; *vi* to walk out in front; (with *dat*) to precede, lead

praegressī·ō -ōnis *f* procession; (fig) precedence

praegustāt·or -ōris *m* taster, sampler

praegust·ō -āre *vt* to taste beforehand, get a sample of

praehib·ĕō -ēre *vt* to offer, furnish, supply; to utter, speak (*words*); **praehibere operam** (with *dat*) to offer to help

praejac·ĕō -ēre *vt* to lie before, be located in front of; *vi* (with *dat*) to lie before

praejūdicāt·us -a -um *adj* decided beforehand; prejudiced; *n* prejudged matter; prejudice; **id pro praejudicato ferre** to take it as a foregone conclusion

praejūdic·ium -iī or **-ī** *n* preliminary hearing; prejudgment; precedent, example

praejūdĭc·ō -āre *vt* to decide beforehand, prejudge
prae·jŭvō -juvāre -jūvī *vt* to help in advance
prae·lābor -lābī -lapsus sum *vt & vi* to glide along, glide by, float by
praelamb·ō -ĕre *vt* to pretaste
praelarg·us -a -um *adj* very ample
praelātus *pp* of **praefero**
prae·lĕgō -legĕre -lēgī -lectum *vt* to sail past
praelĭg·ō -āre *vt* to tie up; (with *dat*) to tie (*something*) to
praelong·us -a -um *adj* very long
prae·lŏquor -lŏquī -locūtus sum *vt* to make (*a speech*) before someone else; to present (*a case*) first; to say by way of preface; *vi* to speak first
prae·lūcĕō -lūcēre -luxī *vi* (with *dat*) **a** to throw light on; **b** to outshine, outdo, surpass
praelūsĭ·ō -ōnis *f* prelude
praelustr·is -e *adj* magnificent
praemandāt·a -ōrum *n pl* warrant for arrest
praemand·ō -āre *vt* to order in advance
praemātūrē *adv* too soon, prematurely
praemātūr·us -a -um *adj* premature
praemedicāt·us -a -um *adj* protected by charms
praemeditātĭ·ō -ōnis *f* premeditation, prior consideration
praemedĭt·or -ārī -ātus sum *vt* to think over beforehand; to practice, practice on (*a musical instrument*)
praemerc·or -ārī -ātus sum *vt* to buy in advance
praemetŭ·ens -entis *adj* apprehensive
praemetuenter *adv* anxiously
praemetŭ·ō -ĕre *vt* to fear beforehand; *vi* (with *dat*) to be apprehensive about
prae·mittō -mittĕre -mīsī -missum *vt* to send out ahead, send in advance; *vi* to send word
praem·ĭum -ĭī or **-ī** *n* prize, reward, recompense; exploit (*worthy of reward*); gift, bribe
praemolestĭ·a -ae *f* apprehension, presentiment of trouble
praemōl·ĭor -īrī *vt* to prepare beforehand
praemon·ĕō -ēre -ŭī -ĭtum *vt* to forewarn; to warn of; to foreshadow, presage, predict
praemonĭt·us -ūs *m* forewarning, premonition
praemonstrāt·or -ōris *m* director, guide
praemonstr·ō -āre *vt* to point out the way to, guide, direct; to predict
prae·mordĕō -mordēre -mordī or **morsī -morsum** *vt* to bite the tip off of; (fig) to crib, pilfer
prae·morĭor -mŏrī -mortŭus sum *vi* to die too soon, die prematurely
praemūn·ĭō -īre -īvī -ītum *vt* to fortify, protect, secure
praemūnītĭ·ō -ōnis *f* (rhet) preparation, conditioning (*of the minds of the hearers*)
praenarr·ō -āre *vt* to relate beforehand
praenăt·ō -āre *vt* to float past, flow by
Praenest·e -is *n* or *f* ancient town in Latium (*modern Palestrina*)
Praenestīn·us -a -um *adj & m* Praenestine
praenit·ĕō -ēre -ŭī *vi* (with *dat*) **a** to outshine; **b** to appear more attractive to
praenōm·en -ĭnis *n* first name
praenosc·ō -ĕre *vt* to find out beforehand, foreknow
praenōtĭ·ō -ōnis *f* innate idea, preconception
praenūbĭl·us -a -um *adj* heavily clouded; dark, gloomy
praenuntĭ·a -ae *f* harbinger, foreteller, omen
praenuntĭ·ō -āre *vt* to foretell
praenuntĭ·us -a -um *adj* foreboding; *m* forecaster, harbinger, omen
praeoccupātĭ·ō -ōnis *f* seizing beforehand, advance occupation
praeoccŭp·ō -āre *vt* to occupy before another; to preoccupy; to anticipate, prevent
praeŏl·it -ĕre *v impers* a smell is emitted, there is a strong smell; **praeolit mihi quod tu velis** I scent your wishes before you express them
praeopt·ō -āre *vt* to prefer
praepand·ō -ĕre *vt* to spread, extend
praeparātĭ·ō -ōnis *f* preparation
praeparāt·us -a -um *adj* prepared, supplied, furnished, ready; *n* stores; **ex ante preparato** from the stores; (fig) by previous arrangement
praepăr·ō -āre *vt* to get ready, prepare, prepare for; to gather together
praepedīment·um -ī *n* impediment, hindrance
praeped·ĭō -īre -īvī or **-ĭī -ītum** *vt* to shackle, chain; to hinder, obstruct, hamper; to embarrass
praepend·ĕō -ēre *vi* to hang down in front
praep·es -ĕtis *adj* nimble, fast; winged; of good omen, favorable; *m* or *f* bird of good omen; bird, large bird
praepilāt·us -a -um *adj* tipped with a ball; **missile prapilatum** blunted missile
praepingu·is -e *adj* very fat; very fertile
praepoll·ĕō -ēre *vi* to be powerful; to be superior; (with *dat*) to surpass in power
praeponděr·ō -āre *vt* to outweigh; to regard as superior
prae·pōnō -pōnĕre -posŭī -posĭ-

tum *vt* (with *dat*) **a** to place, set, put (*something*) in front of or before; **b** to entrust (*someone*) with, put (*someone*) in command of, in charge of; **c** to prefer (*someone or something*) to
praeport·ō -āre *vt* to carry before oneself
praepositi·ō -ōnis *f* preference; prefixing
praeposit·us -a -um *pp* of **praepono;** *adj* preferred, preferable; *m* prefect, commander; *n* that which is desirable, a desirable good
prae·possum -posse -potŭī *vi* to get the upper hand, have the better of it
praepostĕrē *adv* in reversed order, out of order
praepostĕr·us -a -um *adj* inverted, in reverse order; absurd, preposterous
praepŏt·ens -entis *adj* very powerful; (with *genit*) in full control of, fully controlling
praeproperanter or **praeproperē** *adv* very quickly
praeproper·us -a -um *adj* very quick; overhasty, sudden
praepūt·ium -iī or **-ī** *n* foreskin
praequam *conj* in comparison to; **nihil hoc est, praequam alios sumptus facit** this is nothing in comparison to the other expenses that he runs up
praequest·us -a -um *adj* complaining beforehand; **multa praequestus** having first raised many complaints
praeradi·ō -āre *vt* to outshine
praerapid·us -a -um *adj* very swift
praereptus *pp* of **praeripio**
praerig·escō -escĕre -uī *vi* to become very stiff
prae·ripiō -ripĕre -ripuī -reptum *vt* to snatch away, carry off; to anticipate, forestall; to count on too soon, presume upon; (with *dat*) to snatch from, steal from
prae·rōdō -rōdĕre -rōsī -rōsum *vt* to bite the ends of, nibble at; **digitos praerodere** to bite the fingernails
praerogātīv·us -a -um *adj* asked before others; voting first, privileged; *f* first tribe or century to vote; vote of the first tribe or century; previous election; sure sign, omen
praerōsus *pp* of **praerodo**
prae·rumpō -rumpĕre -rūpī -ruptum *vt* to break off, tear away (*something*) in front
praerupt·us -a -um *adj* broken off, broken up; broken up, rough (*terrain*); steep; hasty, impetuous
praes praedis *m* bondsman, surety; collateral
praesaep- = praesep-
praesāg·iō -īre -īvī or **praesāg·ior -īrī** *vt* to have forebodings of, feel beforehand; to cause
praesāgīti·ō -ōnis *f* presentiment, strange feeling, foreboding, prophetic power
praesāg·ium -iī or **-ī** *n* presentiment, presage, prediction
praesāg·us -a -um *adj* divining, prophetic
praesc·iō -īre -īvī *vt* to know beforehand
praescisc·ō -ĕre *vt* to find out or learn beforehand
praesci·us -a -um *adj* prescient; (with *genit*) foreseeing; **praescius venturi** foreseeing the future
prae·scrībō -scrībĕre -scripsī -scriptum *vt* to prefix in writing; to describe beforehand; to determine in advance, prescribe, ordain; to dictate; to outline, map out; to put forward as an excuse
praescripti·ō -ōnis *f* heading, title; preface; pretext; rule, law; limit, restriction
praescript·um -ī *n* regulation, rule, proviso
praesĕc·ō -āre -uī -tum *vt* to cut off, cut out, cut short
praesegmin·a -um *n pl* clippings
praes·ens -entis *adj* present, in person, at hand; existing, contemporary; prompt, immediate, impending; efficacious, powerful, effective; influential; resolute; propitious; **sermo praesens** a face-to-face talk; *n* present time; **ad praesens** or **in praesens** for the present
praesensi·ō -ōnis *f* presentiment; preconception
praesensus *pp* of **praesentio**
praesentāri·us -a -um *adj* ready, at hand
praesenti·a -ae *f* presence; efficacy, effect; **animi praesentia** presence of mind; **in praesentia** at the present time, just now, for the present
praesent·ia -ium *n pl* present circumstances, present state of affairs
prae·sentiō -sentīre -sensī -sensum *vt* to feel beforehand, to realize in advance, have strange feelings about, divine
praesēp·e or **praesaep·e -is** *n* or **praesēp·is** or **praesēp·es -is** *f* stall, stable; crib, manger; room, lodgings; tavern; hovel; beehive
praesēp·iō or **praesaep·iō -īre -sī -tum** *vt* to fence in, barricade
praesertim *adv* especially, particularly, principally; **praesertim cum** especially because
praeserv·iō -īre *vi* (with *dat*) to serve as a slave to
praes·es -idis *m* guard, guardian, protector, defender; president, superintendent; captain, pilot; *f* guardian, protectress
praesid·ens -entis *m* president, ruler
prae·sideō -sidēre -sēdī *vt* to guard, protect, defend; to command, be in comand of; *vi* to be in charge,

be in command; (with *dat*) **a** to watch over, guard, protect; **b** to preside over, direct, manage, command

praesidiārĭ·us -a -um *adj* on garrison duty

praesid·ĭum -ĭī or **-ī** *n* protection, defense; help, assistance; guard, garrison; convoy, escort; garrison post, defensive position

praesignifĭc·ō -āre *vt* to indicate in advance, foretoken

praesign·is -e *adj* outstanding

praesŏn·ō -āre -ŭī *vi* to sound beforehand

praesparg·ō -ĕre *vt* to strew, scatter

praestābĭl·is -e *adj* excellent, outstanding

praest·ans -antis *adj* outstanding, eminent, exceptional

praestantĭ·a -ae *f* excellence, superiority, preeminence

praestern·ō -ĕre *vt* to strew

praest·es -ĭtis *adj* guardian, protecting, presiding

praestīgĭ·ae -ārum *f pl* sleight of hand, juggling, tricks, illusion, deception

praestīgiāt·or -ōris *m* or **praestīgiātr·ix -īcis** *f* juggler, magician; imposter

praestĭn·ō -āre *vt* to buy, shop for

prae·stitŭō -stituĕre -stitŭī -stitūtum *vt* to fix or set up beforehand, prescribe

praestĭtus *pp* of **praesto**

praestō *adv* at hand, ready, present; **praesto esse** (with *dat*) **a** to be on hand for, attend, serve, be helpful to, aid; **b** to be in the way of, resist, oppose

prae·stō -stāre -stĭtī -stĭtum *vt* to excel, be superior to; to show, exhibit, give evidence of, display; to answer for, be responsible for, take upon oneself; to perform, discharge, fulfill; to keep, maintain, retain; **fidem praestare** to keep one's word; **impetūs populi praestare** to be responsible for popular outbreaks; **nihil praestare** to be answerable for nothing; **officia praestare** to perform duties; **se praestare** to show oneself, behave; **socios salvos praestare** to keep the allies safe; **terga hosti praestare** to show one's back to the enemy, retreat; **virtutem praestare** to display courage; *vi* to stand out, be outstanding, be preeminent, be superior; *v impers* it is preferable, it is better

praestōl·or -ārī -ātus sum *vt* to wait for, expect; *vi* (with *dat*) to wait for

prae·stringō -stringĕre -strinxī -strictum *vt* to draw together, squeeze; to blunt (*an edge*); to blind, dazzle (*the eyes*); to dazzle, baffle, confuse

prae·strŭō -struĕre -struxī -structum *vt* to build up, block up, block, stop up; to build up (*e.g., confidence*) beforehand

praes·ul -ŭlis *m* or *f* public dancer

praesult·ō -āre *vi* (with *dat*) to jump around in front of

prae·sum -esse -fŭī *vi* to preside, be in charge, be in command; (with *dat*) **a** to preside over, be in charge of, be in command of; **b** to protect; (with **in** + *abl*) to be governor in

prae·sūmō -sūmĕre -sumpsī -sumptum *vt* to take in advance; to anticipate, take for granted, presume

praesumptĭ·ō -ōnis *f* anticipation

praesūt·us -a -um *adj* sewed up; covered

praetĕg·ō -ĕre *vt* to protect

praetempt·ō -āre *vt* to try out in advance, test in advance; to grope for

prae·tendō -tendĕre -tendī -tentum *vt* to hold or stretch in front of oneself; to present; to offer as an excuse, give as pretext, allege, pretend; (with *dat*) to hold or draw (*e.g., a toga*) in front of (*e.g., the eyes*); **praetendi** (of places) to lie to the front or opposite; **praetendi** (with *dat*) to lie or be situated opposite or over against

praetentō see **praetempto**

praetentus *pp* of **praetendo**

praetep·escō -escĕre -ŭī *vi* (of love) to glow

praeter *conj* besides, other than; *prep* (with *acc*) (of place) past, by, along, before, in front of; (in comparison) above, beyond, more than; against, contrary to, aside from; besides, apart from, except; besides, in addition to

praeterăg·ō -ĕre *vt* (with double *acc*) to drive (*e.g., a horse*) past (*a place*)

praeterbīt·ō -ĕre *vt & vi* to go by or past

praeterĕā *adv* besides, moreover; hereafter, thereafter

praeter·ĕō -īre -īvī or **-ĭī -ĭtum** *vt* to go past, pass by; to skip, pass over in silence, neglect; to escape the notice of; to go beyond; to surpass

praeterequĭt·ans -antis *adj* riding by

praeter·fĕrō -ferre -tŭlī -lātum *vt* (with double *acc*) to carry or take (*someone*) past (*something*); **praeterferri** to move or sweep by (*a place*)

praeterflŭ·ō -ĕre *vt & vi* to flow by

praeter·gredĭor -grĕdī -gressus sum *vt* to march by, go past; to surpass

praeterhāc *adv* in addition

praeterĭt·us -a -um *pp* of **praetereo;** *adj* past, past and gone, bygone; *n pl* bygone events, the past

praeter·lābor -lābī -lapsus sum *vt* to glide by; *vi* to glide by, slip away

praeterlātus *pp* of **praeterfero**

praetermĕ·ō -āre *vt & vi* to go past or by

praetermissĭ·ō -ōnis *f* leaving out, omission; passing over, neglecting; (with *genit*) omission of, neglecting of

praeter·mittō -mittĕre -mīsī -missum *vt* to let pass, let go by; to leave undone; to pass over, omit, disregard, overlook, neglect

praetĕr·ō -ĕre *vt* to wear down in front

praeterquam *adv* besides, other than; **praeterquam quod** apart from the fact that

praetervectĭ·ō -ōnis *f* passing by

praeter·vĕhor -vĕhī -vectus sum *vt & vi* to ride by; to sail by; to march or go by

praetervŏl·ō -āre *vt & vi* to fly by; (of opportunity) to slip by; to escape

praetex·ō -ĕre -ŭī -tum *vt* to border, edge, fringe; to adorn in front; (fig) to cloak, conceal, disguise; to allege as a pretext

praetextāt·us -a -um *adj* wearing the toga praetexta (*crimson-bordered toga*); underage, juvenile, **mores praetextati** loose morals

praetext·us -a -um *pp* of **praetexo;** *adj* bordered; wearing the crimson-bordered toga; **fabula praetexta** Roman tragic drama; *f* toga praetexta (*crimson-bordered toga which was worn by higher magistrates and by freeborn boys*); tragedy; **praetextas docere** to put on tragedies; *n* pretext, pretense, excuse

praetext·us -ūs *m* outward show, splendor; pretense, pretext

praetim·ĕō -ēre *vi* to be apprehensive

praetinct·us -a -um *adj* previously dipped

praet·or -ōris *m* praetor (*judicial magistrate, accompanied by six lictors*); commander; (during the early years of the republic) chief magistrate, chief executive; (in Italian municipalities) chief magistrate; **praetor peregrinus** praetor who had jurisdiction over cases involving foreigners; **praetor urbanus** or **praetor urbis** praetor who had jurisdiction over cases involving Roman citizens

praetōriān·us -a -um *adj* praetorian, belonging to the emperor's bodyguard; *m pl* praetorian guard, soldiers of the praetorian guard

praetōricĭ·us -a -um *adj* received from the praetor (*at public games*)

praetōrĭ·us -a -um *adj* of the commander in chief, of the commander or general; praetor's, of the praetor; propraetor's; **cohors praetoria** general's bodyguard; **comitia praetoria** praetorian elections; **navis praetoria** flagship; **porta praetoria** camp gate nearest the general's tent; **turba praetoria** crowd around the praetor; *n* general's quarters, headquarters; official residence of the governor in a province; council of war; emperor's bodyguard; palace, mansion

praetorqu·ĕō -ēre *vt* to twist beforehand; to strangle first

praetrepĭd·ans -antis *adj* very nervous

praetrepĭd·us -a -um *adj* very nervous, trembling

praetrunc·ō -āre *vt* to cut off, cut short

praetūr·a -ae *f* praetorship; **praeturā se abdicare** to resign the praetorship

praeumbr·ans -antis *adj* casting a shadow; (fig) overshadowing

praeust·us -a -um *adj* burnt at the tip; hardened by fire at the point; frost-bitten

praeut *conj* as compared with, when compared with

praeval·ĕō -ēre -ŭī *vi* to be stronger, have more power; to have greater influence; to have the upper hand

praevalĭd·us -a -um *adj* of superior strength, unusually strong, unusually powerful, imposing; too strong

praevāricātĭ·ō -ōnis *f* collusion

praevāricāt·or -ōris *m* phoney accuser, prosecutor in collusion, prevaricator

praevāric·or -ārī -ātus sum *vi* to make a sham defense or prosecution; (with *dat*) to favor because of collusion

prae·vĕhor -vĕhī -vectus sum *vt* (of a river) to flow past; *vi* to ride in front, ride by; to sail by

prae·venĭo -venīre -vēnī -ventum *vt* to come before, precede, get the jump on, anticipate; to prevent; *vi* to come before, precede

praeverr·ō -ĕre *vt* to sweep before

praevert·ō -ĕre -ī or **prae·vertor -vertī** *vt* to go before, precede, outrun, outstrip; to turn to first, attend to first; to prefer; to come before, anticipate, prevent; to preoccupy; (with *dat* or **prae** + *abl*) to prefer (*someone or something*) to; *vi* (with *dat* or **ad** + *acc*) to go to first, turn to first, attend to first

prae·vidĕō -vidēre -vīdī -vīsum *vt* to foresee

praevitĭ·ō -āre *vt* to taint or pollute beforehand

praevĭ·us -a -um *adj* going before, leading the way

praevŏl·ō -āre *vi* to fly out in front

pragmatĭc·us -a -um *adj* experienced; *m* lawyer, attorney

prandĕō prandēre prandī pransum *vt* to eat for breakfast, eat for lunch; *vi* to have breakfast, have lunch

prand·ĭum -ĭī or **-ī** *n* breakfast, lunch

pransĭt·ō -āre *vt* to usually eat for lunch

prans·or -ōris *m* guest at lunch

prans·us -a -um *pp* of **prandeo;** *adj* having had breakfast, after eating; well fed; **pransus potus** having been wined and dined

prasin·us -a -um *adj* green; **factio prasina** the Greens (*one of the stables of horses at the racetrack in Rome*)

prātens·is -e *adj* meadow, growing in the meadow

prātŭl·um -ī *n* small meadow

prāt·um -ī *n* meadow; (fig) plain (*of the sea*); *n pl* meadow grass

prāvē *adv* crookedly; improperly, wrongly, badly, poorly; **prave facti versūs** poorly written verses

prāvit·ās -ātis *f* crookedness, distortion; impropriety, irregularity; perverseness, depravity

prāv·us -a -um *adj* crooked, distorted, deformed; irregular, improper, wrong, bad; perverse, vicious

Praxitĕl·ēs -is *m* famous Greek Athenian sculptor (*4th cent.* B.C.)

precāriō *adv* upon request

precāri·us -a -um *adj* obtained by prayer; dependent on another's will, uncertain, precarious

precāti·ō -ōnis *f* prayer; **precationes facere** to say prayers

precāt·or -ōris *m* intercessor, suppliant

precēs = *pl* of **prex**

preci·ae -ārum *f pl* grapevine

prec·or -ārī -ātus sum *vt* to entreat, supplicate, pray to; to pray for; to wish for; (with double *acc*) to pray to (*someone*) for; (with *acc* of thing and *abl* of person) to request (*something*) from; (with **pro** + *abl*) to entreat (*e.g., the gods*) on behalf of; (with **ut** or **ne**) to pray that, pray that not; **longum Augusto diem precari** to wish Augustus long life; *vi* to pray; (with **ad** + *acc*) to pray to, e.g., **di ad quos precantur** the gods to whom they pray; **male precari** to curse, utter curses

pre·hendō -hendĕre -hendī -hensum or **prendō prendĕre prendī prensum** *vt* to take hold of, grasp, seize; to detain; to arrest; to occupy; to catch, surprise; to reach, arrive at; to grasp, understand

prēl·um -ī *n* wine press, oil press; clothes press

premō premĕre pressī pressum *vt* to press, squeeze; to lie down on; to hug (*shore*); to suppress, hide; to cover, crown; to press hard, bear down on; to chase, attack; to weigh down, load; to press together, close; to curb, stop; to depress, lower; to mark, impress; to prune; to pressure, urge, importune; to degrade, humble, disparage; to abridge; to subjugate

prensāti·ō -ōnis *f* campaigning (*for office*)

prens·ō or **prehens·ō -āre** *vt* to take hold of, clutch at, grab; to stop, detain; *vi* to campaign, be a candidate

prensus *pp* of **prendo**

pressē *adv* distinctly, with articulation; concisely; accurately; simply

pressi·ō -ōnis *f* fulcrum; leverage

press·ō -āre *vt* to press

press·us -a -um *pp* of **premo;** *adj* closed, shut tight; suppressed; slow; lowered, low, subdued; concise, precise, accurate; articulate

press·us -ūs *m* pressing, pressure; expression (*of the face*)

prest·ēr -ēris *m* waterspout

pretiōsē *adv* at great cost, expensively

pretiōs·us -a -um *adj* previous, valuable; expensive; extravagant

pret·ium -iī or **-ī** *n* price; value, worth; reward, return, recompense; bribe; pay, wages; **in pretio esse** to be prized; to be held in high esteem; **in pretio habere** to prize, hold in high esteem; **pretium curae esse** to be worth the trouble; **pretium habere** to have value, be worth something; **pretium facere** to set a price; **pretium operae esse** to be worth the effort, be worthwhile

prex precis *f* prayer, request; curse, imprecation; intercession

Priamē·is -ïdis *f* daughter of Priam

Priamēi·us -a -um *adj* Priam's, of Priam

Priamid·ēs -ae *m* son of Priam

Priăm·us -ī *m* Priam (*son of Laomedon, husband of Hecuba, father of Hector, Paris, etc., king of Troy at the time of its fall*)

prīdem *adv* long ago, long, since; **haud ita pridem** not so long ago; not long before; **quam pridem** how long ago

prīdiē *adv* the day before, the previous day

prīm·a -ōrum *n pl* first part, beginning; first principles or elements; **cum primus** among the first, especially; **in primis** above all, chiefly, particularly, especially, principally

prīm·ae -ārum *f pl* lead, first rank, highest place, highest importance; **primas dare** (with *dat*) to attach supreme importance to

prīmaev·us -a -um *adj* young, youthful

prīmān·ī -ōrum *m pl* soldiers of the first legion

prīmāri·us -a -um *adj* first in rank; first-rate

prīmigĕn·us -a -um *adj* original

prīmipīl·us -ī *m* first-ranking centurion of a legion

prīmiti·ae -ārum *f pl* firstfruits

prīmitus *adv* originally, at first; for the first time

prīmō *adv* first, in the first place; at first, at the beginning

prīmord·ium -iī or **-ī** *n* origin, beginning; commencement; beginning of a new reign

prīmōr·ēs -um *m pl* chiefs, nobles, leaders; (mil) front line
prīmōr·is -e *adj* first, foremost, extreme, tip of; first, principal; **digituli primores** fingertips; **primori in acie** all the way up front
prīmŭlum *adv* first of all, at first
prīmŭl·us -a -um *adj* very first
prīmum *adv* first, in the first place, before all else; at first; for the first time; **cum primum, ubi primum, ut primum** as soon as; **primum dum** in the first place; **quam primum** as soon as possible
prīm·us -a -um *adj* first, foremost; principal; eminent, distinguished; earliest; **primas partes agere** to play the lead role; **primis digitis** with or at the fingertips; **primo anno** at the beginning of the year or season; **primus in provinciam introiit** he was the first to enter the province; **primus quisque** the very first, the first possible; *f pl* see **primae;** *n* beginning, front; **a primo** from the first, from the beginning; **in primo** in the beginning; (mil) at the head of the column; *n pl* see **prima**
princ·eps -ĭpis *adj* first, in front; foremost, chief; *m* leader, chief; emperor; (mil) maniple, company; captain, company commander, centurion; captaincy, centurionship; *m pl* soldiers of the second line (*between the hastati and triarii*), second line
principāl·is -e *adj* first, foremost; original, primitive; chief, principal; of the emperor; **via principalis** (mil) main street of a camp; **porta principalis** (mil) main gate of a camp
principāt·us -ūs *m* first place; post of commander in chief; principate, rule, sovereignty; origin, beginning
principĭ·a -ōrum *n pl* first principles; foundations; front line, front-line troops; headquarters
principiāl·is -e *adj* initial
princip·ĭum -ĭī or **-ī** *n* start, commencement, origin; beginner, originator; first to vote; right to vote first; **a principio** or **principio** at the beginning, at first
pri·or -us *adj* previous, preceding, prior, former; first; better, superior, preferable
priōr·ēs -um *m pl* forefathers, ancestors, ancients; *f pl* (only *acc*) lead, preference
priscē *adv* in the old-fashioned style
prisc·us -a -um *adj* old, ancient; old-time, old-fashioned; former, previous
pristīn·us -a -um *adj* former, earlier; pristine, primitive, original; preceding, previous, yesterday's; *n* former condition; **in pristinum restituere** to restore to its former condition
pristis see **pistrix**
prius *adv* earlier, before, previously, sooner, first; sooner, rather
priusquam *conj* before
prīvātim *adv* privately, in private, in a private capacity, as a private citizen; at home
prīvātĭ·ō -ōnis *f* removal
prīvātō *adv* at home
prīvāt·us -a -um *adj* private; personal, individual, peculiar; isolated, withdrawn; ordinary (*language*); *m* private citizen, civilian; *n* privacy, retirement; private property, private land; **ex privato** out of one's own pocket; **in privato** in private; **in privatum** for private use
prīvign·a -ae *f* stepdaughter
prīvign·us -ī *m* stepson; *m pl* stepchildren
prīvilēg·ĭum -ĭī or **-ī** *n* special bill directed against an individual; special bill in favor of an individual
prīv·ō -āre *vt* to deprive, rob, strip; to free, release
prīv·us -a -um *adj* every, each single; own, private; (with *genit*) deprived of
prō *adv* (with **quam** or **ut**) just as, according as; *prep* (with *abl*) before, in front of, in, on, in the presence of; for, in behalf of, in favor of, in the service of, on the side of; instead of, in place of, for; in return for, in exchange for, for; just as, as, the same as, for; in proportion to, according to, in comparison with, by virtue of; **pro eo** just the same; **pro eo atque** or **ac** just as, the same as; **pro eo quod** in view of the fact that; **pro se quisque** each one for himself, individually; **pro ut** or **pro eo quantum** as, in proportion as; *interj* oh!; **pro di immortales!** Oh, heavens above!
proāgŏr·us -ī *m* chief magistrate in some provincial towns
proavĭ·a -ae *f* great-grandmother
proavīt·us -a -um *adj* great-grandfather's, ancestral
proăv·us -ī *m* great-grandfather; ancestor, forefather
probābĭl·is -e *adj* worthy of approval, commendable, acceptable, pleasing, agreeable; probable, plausible, credible, likely
probābilit·ās -ātis *f* probability, plausibility
probābilĭter *adv* probably
probātĭ·ō -ōnis *f* approval, approbation, assent; test, trial; proof
probāt·or -ōris *m* approver, supporter, backer
probāt·us -a -um *adj* approved, acceptable; tried, tested, good; esteemed
probē *adv* well, properly, correctly; well, thoroughly, very, very much
probĭt·ās -ātis *f* probity, honesty, worth, goodness
prob·ō -āre *vt* to approve, commend, esteem; to make good, represent as good, make acceptable; to pronounce judgment on; to pro-

nounce approval of; to make credible, prove, show, demonstrate; to test, try, inspect; **probare pro** (with *abl*) to pass (*someone*) off for; **probari pro** (with *abl*) to pass for, be taken for

probriperlecĕbr·ae -ārum *f pl* temptations

probrōs·us -a -um *adj* scandalous, shameful, abusive

probr·um -ī *n* abuse, invective, reproach; shameful act, vile deed; lewdness, indecency; shame, disgrace; charge of disgraceful conduct

prob·us -a -um *adj* good, honest, upright, virtuous, decent; (coll) real, proper, downright

Proc·a or **Proc·ās -ae** *m* king of Alba and father of Numitor and Amulius

procācit·ās -ātis *f* brashness

procāciter *adv* brashly

proc·ax -ācis *adj* brash

prō·cēdō -cēdĕre -cessī -cessum *vi* to proceed, go forward, advance; to make progress, advance; to come out (*in public*), show oneself, appear; to come forth, arise; (of time) to pass, elapse; to turn out, result, succeed; to continue

procell·a -ae *f* violent wind, squall, hurricane, storm; (fig) violence, commotion, storm; (mil) charge, sudden attack

prōcell·ō -ĕre *vt* to throw down; **se procellere in mensam** to lie down at the table

procellōs·us -a -um *adj* gusty

proc·er -ĕris *m* chief, noble, prince, leader

prōcērit·ās -ātis *f* height, tallness; length; *f pl* the different heights

prōcērius *adv* farther, to a greater extent, more

prōcēr·us -a -um *adj* tall; long; **palmae procerae** upraised palms

prōcessi·ō -ōnis *f* advance

prōcessus *pp* of **procedo**

prōcess·us -ūs *m* advance, progress

Prochȳt·a -ae or **Prochȳt·ē -ēs** *f* small island off the Campanian coast

prō·cīdō -cidĕre -cīdī *vi* to fall forwards, fall over, fall down, fall prostrate

prōcinctū (*abl* only) *m* **in procinctu** under arms, ready for combat

prōclāmāt·or -ōris *m* loudmouth

prōclām·ō -āre *vi* to yell

prōclīn·ō -āre *vt* to bend forward, bend; **res proclinata** critical situation, crisis

prōclīv·e -is *n* slope, descent; **in proclivi esse** to be easy

prōclīve *adv* downward, downhill; rapidly

prōclīv·is -e or **prōclīv·us -a -um** *adj* sloping forward; downhill; easy; inclined, disposed, subject, ready, willing

prōclīvit·ās -ātis *f* proclivity, tendency, predisposition

prōclīvus see **proclivis**

Procn·ē or **Progn·ē -ēs** *f* daughter of Pandion, sister of Philomela, wife of Tereus, and mother of Itys, who was changed into a swallow; swallow

proc·ō -āre *vt* to require, demand

prōcons·ul -ŭlis *m* vice-consul, proconsul; governor of a province; military commander

prōconsulār·is -e *adj* proconsular

prōconsulāt·us -ūs *m* proconsulship, proconsulate

prōcrastinātĭ·ō -onis *f* procrastination

prōcrastĭn·ō -āre *vt* to postpone, put off from day to day

prōcreātĭ·ō -ōnis *f* procreation, breeding

prōcreāt·or -ōris *m* procreator, sire, parent, father

prōcreātr·ix -īcis *f* mother

prōcrĕ·ō -āre *vt* to procreate, beget, produce

prōcresc·ō -ĕre *vi* to spring forth, be produced; to continue to grow, grow up

Procr·is -is or **-ĭdis** *f* wife of Cephalus who mistook her for a wild beast and shot her

Procrust·ēs -ae *m* notorious robber in Attica who stretched his victims to the length of his bed or mutilated them if they were too tall

prōcŭb·ō -āre *vi* to lie stretched out

prō·cūdō -cūdĕre -cūdī -cūsum *vt* to forge, fashion; to bring forth, produce

procul *adv* at a distance, in the distance, far; from a distance, from far; **haud procul afuit quin legatos violarent** they came close to outraging the ambassadors

prōculc·ō -āre *vt* to trample upon, trample down

prō·cumbō -cumbĕre -cubŭī -cubitum *vi* to fall down, sink down; to lean forward, bend over, be broken down; to extend, spread; (fig) to go to ruin

prōcūrātĭ·ō -ōnis *f* management, administration, superintendence; expiation, expiatory sacrifice

prōcūrāt·or -ōris *m* procurator, manager, administrator, superintendent, agent, deputy; governor of a province

prōcūrātr·ix -īcis *f* governess, protectress

prōcūr·ō -āre *vt* to manage, administer; to take care of, attend to; to avert by sacrifice; to expiate; *vi* to serve as procurator

prō·currō -currĕre -cucurrī or **-currī -cursum** *vi* to run out ahead, dash forward; to jut out, project

prōcursātĭ·ō -ōnis *f* sally, charge

prōcursātōr·ēs -um *m pl* skirmishers

prōcurs·ō -āre *vi* to keep charging out, continue to skirmish
prōcurs·us -ūs *m* sally, charge, onset
prōcurv·us -a -um *adj* curving forwards; curving, winding (*shore*)
proc·us -ī *m* noble; gigolo; **impudentes proci** shameless candidates
Procȳ·ōn -ōnis *m* Lesser Dog Star, Sirius
prōdactus *pp* of **prodigo**
prōdeambŭl·ō -āre *vi* to go out for a walk
prōd·ĕō -īre -iī -ītum *vi* to go out, come out, go forth, come forth; (of a cliff) to project; (of plants) to come out, appear; to appear in public; to go ahead, advance, proceed
prō·dīcō -dīcĕre -dixī -dictum *vt* to put off, defer, postpone; **diem prodicere** to adjourn a case to a later date
prōdictāt·or -ōris *m* vice-dictator
prōdĭgē *adv* lavishly
prōdigentĭ·a -ae *f* profusion, extravagance; openhandedness
prōdigiālĭter *adv* to a fantastic degree
prōdigiōs·us -a -um *adj* prodigious; freakish
prōdig·ĭum -iī or **-ī** *n* portent; unnatural crime, monstrous crime; monster, freak
prōd·ĭgō -igĕre -ēgī -actum *vt* to squander, waste
prōdĭg·us -a -um *adj* wasteful; lavish, openhanded; (with *genit*) free with; **animae prodigus** free with or careless with one's life; **herbae prodigus locus** spot with luxuriant growth of grass
prōditĭ·ō -ōnis *f* betrayal, treason; **proditionem agere** (with *dat*) to commit treason against, betray
prōdĭt·or -ōris *m* betrayer, traitor
prō·dō -dĕre -dĭdī -dĭtum *vt* to bring out, bring forth, produce; to reveal, disclose; to record, relate, report, hand down, transmit; to proclaim, appoint, elect; to give up, surrender; to forsake, betray; to prolong, protract; (fig) to display, exhibit
prōdoc·ĕō -ēre *vt* to preach publicly
prodrŏm·us -ī *m* forerunner, advance messenger
prō·dūcō -dūcĕre -duxī -ductum *vt* to bring out, bring forth; to produce; to promote, advance; to bring to light, reveal; to bring into the world, produce, raise, bring up; to educate; to drag out, protract, stretch out, lengthen; to lead on, induce; to put off, adjourn; to put (*a slave*) up for sale; to produce (*on the stage*), perform; to bring to court
prōductē *adv* long; **producte litteram dicere** to lengthen the letter or vowel
prōductĭ·ō -ōnis *f* lengthening
prōduct·ō -āre *vt* to drag out, delay
prōduct·us -a -um *pp* of **produco;** *adj* lengthened, prolonged, long
proēgmĕn·on -ī *n* preference
proeliār·is -e *adj* battle, of battle
proeliāt·or -ōris *m* combatant
proelĭ·or -ārī -ātus sum *vi* to battle, fight
proel·ĭum -iī or **-ī** *n* battle, combat, fight; *n pl* fighting men, warriors
Proet·us -ī *m* king of Tiryns
prōfān·ō -āre *vt* to profane, desecrate
profān·us -a -um *adj* unconsecrated, ordinary, common; impious, wicked; ill-omened
profātus *pp* of **profor**
profectĭ·ō -ōnis *f* setting out, departure; source (*of money*)
profectō *adv* really, actually
profectus *pp* of **proficiscor**
prōfectus *pp* of **proficio**
prōfect·us -ūs *m* progress, advance, success; increase, profit
prō·fĕrō -ferre -tŭlī -lātum *vt* to bring forward, advance, bring out; to extend, enlarge; to put off, postpone, defer; to produce, discover, invent; to make known, reveal, publish; to mention, cite, quote; **pedem proferre** to advance; **signa proferre** to march forward
profess·ae -ārum *f pl* professional prostitutes, professionals
professĭ·ō -ōnis *f* public acknowledgment, profession, declaration; registration (*at which property, etc., was declared*); profession, business
profess·or -ōris *m* professor, teacher
professōrĭ·us -a -um *adj* professorial; professional, expert
professus *pp* of **profiteor**
profest·us -a -um *adj* non-holiday, ordinary; **dies profestus** working day
prō·ficiō -ficĕre -fēcī -fectum *vi* to make progress, make headway, advance, have success, succeed; to be useful, do good, help, be conducive; **nihil proficere** to do no good
pro·ficiscor -ficiscī -fectus sum *vi* to set out, start, go, depart; to originate, proceed, arise
pro·fitĕor -fitērī -fessus sum *vt* to declare publicly, acknowledge, confess, profess; to offer freely, promise, volunteer; to follow as a profession, practice (*e.g., law*); to make a declaration of, register (*property, etc.*) before a public official; **indicium profiteri** to volunteer evidence, testify freely; **nomen profiteri** to put one's name in as a candidate, announce oneself a candidate; **se adjutorem profiteri** (with **ad** + *acc*) to volunteer to help (*someone*); **se amicum profiteri** to avow oneself a friend, profess to be a friend; *vi* to make a confession, make an admission; to be a professor, be a teacher

prōflīgāt·or -ōris *m* big spender
prōflīgāt·us -a -um *adj* profligate, dissolute
prōflīg·ō -āre *vt* to knock to the ground, knock down; to defeat, conquer; to bring to an end, do away with, finish off; to ruin, crush; to debase, degrade
prōfl·ō -āre *vt* to breathe out
prōflŭ·ens -entis *adj* flowing along; fluent (*speech*); *f* running water
prōfluenter *adv* easily, effortlessly
prōfluentĭ·a -ae *f* fluency
prō·flŭō -fluĕre -fluxi *vi* to flow out; to flow along; (fig) to proceed
prōfluv·ĭum -ĭī or **-ī** *n* flow
prof·or -ārī -ātus sum *vt* to say, declare; *vi* to speak out
pro·fugĭō -fugĕre -fūgī *vt* to run away from, escape from; *vi* to run away, escape; (with **ad** + *acc*) to take refuge with, take refuge at the house of
profŭg·us -a -um *adj* fugitive; banished, exile; nomadic; *m* fugitive, refugee
pro·fundō -fundĕre -fūdī -fūsum *vt* to pour, pour out; to shed; to utter; to give vent to; to spend freely, waste, squander; **se profundere** (of things) to come pouring out; (of persons) to come pouring out, come charging out, break out
profund·us -a -um *adj* deep; boundless, vast; dense (*forest, cloud*); high (*heaven*); infernal; (fig) bottomless, boundless; *n* depth; the deep, deep sea; (fig) abyss
profūsē *adv* in disorder, helter-skelter, haphazardly; extravagantly
profūsĭ·ō -ōnis *f* profusion
profūs·us -a -um *pp* of **profundo;** *adj* extravagant, lavish, profuse; excessive, expensive
prōgĕn·er -ĕrī *m* granddaughter's husband
prōgenĕr·ō -āre *vt* to beget, produce
prōgenĭ·ēs -ēī *f* line, lineage; progeny, descendants, offspring, posterity
prōgenĭt·or -ōris *m* progenitor, founder, ancestor
prō·gignō -gignĕre -genŭī -genĭtum *vt* to beget, produce
prognārĭter *adv* precisely, exactly
prognāt·us -a -um *adj* born, descended; (with *abl* or with **ab** or **ex** + *abl*) born of, descended from; *m* child; grandson
Prognē see **Procne**
prognostĭc·on or **prognostĭc·um -ī** *n* sign of the future, prognostic
prō·gredĭor -grĕdī -gressus sum *vi* to go forward, march forward, proceed, advance; to go on, make headway, make progress; to go forth, go out
prōgressĭ·ō -ōnis *f* progress, advancement; increase, growth; (rhet) climax
prōgressus *pp* of **progredior**
prōgress·us -ūs *m* progress, advance; march (*of time or events*)
prōh *interj* oh!, O!
prohib·ĕō -ēre -ŭī -ĭtum *vt* to hold back, check, hinder, prevent, avert, keep off; to prohibit, forbid; to keep away; to defend, protect
prohibitĭ·ō -ōnis *f* prohibition
proïnde or **proïn** *adv* consequently, accordingly; **proinde atque** (or **ac), proinde ut,** or **proinde quam** just as, exactly as; **proinde atque si** (or **ac si), proinde quasi** just as if
prōjectĭcĭ·us -a -um *adj* exposed (*child*)
prōjectĭ·ō -ōnis *f* stretching out; **projectio bracchii** stretching out of the arm
prōject·ō -āre *vt* to accuse, blame
prōject·us -a -um *pp* of **projicio;** *adj* jutting out, projecting; prostrate, stretched out; inclined; prone; abject, contemptible; downcast
prōject·us -ūs *m* projection, extension
prō·jicĭō -jicĕre -jēcī -jectum *vt* to throw down, throw out, throw; to throw away, abandon, forsake; to hold out, extend; to throw out, banish, exile; to neglect, desert; to blurt out; to throw away, give up, sacrifice; to put off, delay; to throw overboard; **se projicere ad pedes** (with *genit*) to throw oneself at the feet of, fall prostrate before; **se projicere ex nave** to jump overboard; **se projicere in forum** to rush into the forum
prō·lābor -lābī -lapsus sum *vi* to glide forward, slip or move forward; to fall forwards, fall on one's face; to slip out; (of words) to slip out, escape; to be led on, led astray (*by greed, fear, etc.*); (fig) to fail, go to ruin, collapse
prōlapsĭ·ō -ōnis *f* falling, collapse
prōlapsus *pp* of **prolabor**
prōlātĭ·ō -ōnis *f* expansion, extension (*of territory*); adducing, mentioning (*of precedents*); delay, postponement
prōlāt·ō -āre *vt* to extend; to put off, delay
prōlātus *pp* of **profero**
prōl·ēs -is *f* offspring, progeny, children, descendants; race, stock; child; young man
prōlētār·ĭus -ĭī or **-ī** *m* proletarian; *m pl* proletariat
prō·licĭō -licĕre -lixī *vt* to entice, bring out, incite
prōlixē *adv* freely, wildly; readily, cheerfully, freely
prōlix·us -a -um *adj* long, freely growing, wild (*beard, hair, etc.*); obliging, ready and unwilling; favorable (*circumstances*)
prōlocūtus *pp* of **proloquor**
prōlŏg·us -ī *m* prologue (*of a play*); actor who gives the prologue

prō·lŏquor -lŏquī -locūtus sum *vt & vi* to speak out

prōlub·ium -iī or **-ī** *n* desire, inclination, yen

prō·lūdō -lūdĕre -lūsī -lūsum *vi* to practice; (of boxers) to spar, shadowbox

prō·lŭō -luĕre -lŭī -lūtum *vt* to wash out, flush, wash off, wash away; to wet, drench

prōlūsĭ·ō -ōnis *f* sparring, shadowboxing

prōlūtus *pp* of **proluo**

prōluvĭ·ēs -ēī *f* flood; refuse, sewage

prōmer·ĕō -ēre -ŭī -ĭtum or **prōmer·ĕor -ērī -ĭtus sum** *vt* to deserve, merit, earn; *vi* to be deserving; (with **de** + *abl*) to deserve the gratitude of; **bene de multis promerere** or **promereri** to deserve the full gratitude of many people

prōmerĭt·um -ī *n* reward, due; merit; guilt

Promēth·eus -ĕī or **-ĕos** *m* son of Iapetus and Clymene, brother of Epimetheus, and father of Deucalion, who by teaching men the use of fire, incurred the wrath of Jupiter

Promēthē·us -a -um *adj* Promethean, of Prometheus

Promēthĭd·ēs -ae *m* son of Prometheus, Deucalion (*who, with his wife Pyrrha, was the sole survivor of the Deluge*)

prōmĭn·ens -entis *adj* projecting, prominent; *n* headland

prōmin·ĕō -ēre -ŭī *vi* to jut out, hang forward, bend forward, extend; (with **in** + *acc*) to reach down to

prōmiscam or **prōmiscē** *adv* in common, without distinction, indiscriminately

prōmiscŭē *adv* indiscriminately, promiscuously

prōmiscŭ·us or **prōmisc·us -a -um** *adj* promiscuous, haphazard, indiscriminate, in common, open to all; common, ordinary

prōmissĭ·ō -ōnis *f* promise

prōmiss·or -ōris *m* promiser, four-flusher

prōmiss·us -a -um *adj* allowed to grow, long, hanging down; *n* promise

prō·mittō -mittĕre -mīsī -missum *vt* to let (*e.g., the hair*) grow; to promise; to give promise of, give hope of; *vi* to promise to go; **ad cenam promittere** to promise to go to dinner, make a dinner engagement

prōmō prōmĕre prompsī promptum *vt* to bring out, draw out; to produce (*arguments*); to bring to light, reveal; to bring out, express (*feelings, ideas, emotions*)

prōmontŏr·ium -iī or **-ī** *n* promontory

prōmōt·a -ōrum *n pl* second choice (*things preferred next after absolute good*)

prō·movĕō -movēre -mōvī -mōtum *vt* to move (*something*) forward, cause to advance; to enlarge, extend; to effect, accomplish; to promote (*to higher office*); to bring to light, reveal; to put off, postpone; **nihil promovere** to accomplish nothing, do no good, make no progress

promptē *adv* readily, quickly; easily; frankly

prompt·ō -āre *vt* to give out, distribute

promptū (only *abl*) *m* **in promptu** in readiness, ready, at hand; public, visible, manifest; **in promptu gerere, habere,** or **ponere** to display

promptuārĭ·us -a -um *adj* of a storehouse, storage; **cella promptuaria** (coll) jail

prompt·us -a -um *pp* of **promo**; *adj* prompt, ready; easy; brought to light, evident; bold, enterprising; (with *dat* or with **ad** or **in** + *acc*) **a** ready or prepared for, set for; **b** inclined to, disposed to; (with **in** + *abl*) quick at, prompt at; (with **adversus** + *acc*) ready for, prepared against; (with *inf*) ready to, quick to

prōmulgātĭ·ō -ōnis *f* promulgation, publication

prōmulg·ō -āre *vt* to promulgate, publish

prōmuls·is -ĭdis *f* hors d'oeuvres

prōmuntūr·ium -iī or **-ī** *n* promontory

prōm·us -ī *m* butler

prōmūtŭ·us -a -um *adj* on credit, advanced, given in advance

prōnē *adv* downwards

pronĕp·ōs -ōtis *m* great-grandson

pronept·is -is *f* great-granddaughter

pronoe·a -ae *f* providence

prōnŭb·a -ae *f* patroness of marriage

prōnuntiātĭ·ō -ōnis *f* proclamation, declaration; announcement (*of the jury's verdict*); delivery (*of a speech*); proposition (*in logic*)

prōnuntiāt·or -ōris *m* narrator

prōnuntiāt·um -ī *n* proposition (*in logic*)

prōnuntĭ·ō -āre *vt* to proclaim, announce; to utter, pronounce, express (*opinion, judgment*); to hold out, promise, offer; to recite, deliver, narrate, relate; (in the senate) to formulate, announce, put to a vote

prōnŭr·us -ūs *f* grandson's wife

prōn·us -a -um *adj* leaning, inclined, bending, stooping, bent over, bent forwards; swift, rushing, dashing, moving swiftly along; sloping, steep (*hill, road*); sinking, setting (*sun, etc.*); downhill; easy; inclined, disposed, prone; *n* downward tendency, gravity; *n pl* slopes

prooemĭ·or -ārī *vi* to make an introduction or preface
prooem·ĭum -ĭī or **-ī** *n* preface; prelude; (fig) prelude (*e.g., to a fight*)
propāgātĭ·ō -ōnis *f* propagation; extension, prolongation; **nominis propagatio** perpetuation of the name
propāg·ō -āre *vt* to propagate (*race*); to extend (*territory*); to prolong (*life*)
prōpălam *adv* openly, publicly
prōpatŭl·us -a -um *adj* open; *n* open space; **in propatulo habere** to display
prope *adv* near, nearby; (of time) near, at hand; (of degree) nearly, almost, practically, just about; (with **ab** + *abl*) close by, near to; **prope est cum** the time has come when; *prep* (with *acc*) near, near to; **prope diem** very soon, presently
prō·pellō -pellĕre -pŭlī -pulsum *vt* to drive forward, push forward; to drive away, drive out
propemŏdo or **propemŏdum** *adv* nearly, practically, almost
prō·pendĕō -pendēre -pendī -pensum *vi* to hang down; to preponderate; (with **in** + *acc*) to be inclined to, be favorably disposed to
prōpensē *adv* readily, willingly
prōpensĭ·ō -ōnis *f* propensity, inclination, tendency
prōpens·us -a -um *pp* of **propendeo;** *adj* important; coming near, approaching; inclined, disposed, ready, willing; **propenso animo** with a ready mind, willingly; **propensus in alteram partem** inclined toward the other point of view
properanter *adv* quickly, hastily
properantĭ·a -ae *f* haste
properātĭ·ō -ōnis *f* haste
properātō *adv* quickly, speedily
properāt·us -a -um *adj* hurried, quick, speedy; *n* haste, speed; **properato opus est** speed is required
propĕrē *adv* quickly, in haste, hastily
properĭp·ēs -ĕdis *adj* quick-moving
propĕr·ō -āre *vt* to speed up, accelerate; to prepare hastily, do in haste; *vi* to be quick; to go or move quickly
Propert·ĭus -ĭī or **-ī** *m* Sextus Propertius (*Latin elegiac poet, c. 50-15 B.C.*)
propĕr·us -a -um *adj* quick, speedy
prōpex·us -a -um *adj* combed forward
prōpīnātĭ·ō -ōnis *f* toast
propīn·ō or **prōpīn·ō -āre** *vt* to drink (*e.g., a cup of wine*) as a toast; to drink a toast to, toast; (with *dat*) **a** to drink (*e.g., a cup of wine*) as a toast to; **b** to pass on (*a cup*) to
propinqu·a -ae *f* relative (*female*)
propinquē *adv* near at hand
propinquĭt·ās -ātis *f* proximity, nearness, vicinity; (fig) relationship, affinity; friendship
propinqu·ō -āre *vt* to bring on; to accelerate, hasten; *vi* to draw near, approach; (with *dat*) to draw near to, approach
propinqu·us -a -um *adj* near, neighboring; (of time) near, at hand; related; *m* relative; *f* see **propinqua;** *n* neighborhood, vicinity
propĭ·or -us *adj* nearer, closer; later, more recent; more closely related, more like, more nearly resembling; more intimate, closer; of more concern, of greater import; (with *dat*) **a** nearer to, closer to; **b** closer to in resemblance, more like; (with *acc* or with **ab** + *abl*) closer to
propĭōr·a -um *n pl* closer side (*e.g., of a river*); more recent events
propitĭ·ō -āre *vt* to propitiate, appease
propitĭ·us -a -um *adj* propitious, well-disposed, favorable
propnigē·um -ī *n* room where the bath was heated
propōl·a -ae *m* retailer
prōpollŭ·ō -ĕre *vt* to pollute further
prō·pōnō -pōnĕre -posŭī -posĭtum *vt* to put or place forward, expose to view, display; to propose; to imagine; to offer, propose; to say, report, relate, publish; to threaten; to denounce; to design, determine, intend
Propont·is -ĭdis or **-ĭdos** *f* Sea of Marmora
prōporrō *adv* furthermore; wholly, completely
prōportĭ·ō -ōnis *f* proportion, symmetry; analogy
prōpositĭ·ō -ōnis *f* proposition; intention, purpose; theme; basic assumption (*in logic*)
prōposĭt·us -a -um *pp* of **propono;** *adj* exposed, open; accessible; impending, at hand; *n* intention, design, purpose, resolution; main point, theme; first premise (*in logic*)
prōpraet·or -ōris *m* propraetor (*ex-praetor who was made governor of a province*)
proprĭē *adv* in the strict sense; strictly for oneself, personally; peculiarly, especially
propriĕt·ās -ātis *f* property, peculiarity, quality
proprĭtim *adv* specifically, properly
proprĭ·us -a -um *adj* own; very own; special, peculiar, individual, particular, personal; lasting, permanent
propter *adv* near, near at hand
propter *prep* (with *acc*) near, close to, next to; on account of, because of, for the sake of; through, by means of
proptereă *adv* for that reason, therefore, on that account; **propterea quod** for the very reason that
prōpudiōs·us -a -um *adj* shameful, disgraceful

prōpud·ĭum -ĭī or **-ī** *n* shameful act; (said of a person) disgrace
prōpugnācŭl·um -ī *n* rampart, battlement; defense; (fig) safeguard
prōpugnātĭ·ō -ōnis *f* defense, vindication
prōpugnāt·or -ōris *m* defender, champion
prōpugn·ō -āre *vt* to defend; *vi* to come out and fight; to fight a defensive action, repel an assault; (fig) to put up a defense
prōpulsātĭ·ō -ōnis *f* repulse
prōpuls·ō -āre *vt* to drive back, repel, repulse; (fig) to ward off, repel
prōpulsus *pp* of **propello**
Propylae·a -ōrum *n pl* entrance to the Athenian Acropolis
prōquam *conj* according as
prōr·a -ae *f* prow; (fig) ship; **mihi prora et puppis est** my intention from first to last is
prō·rēpō -rēpĕre -repsī *vi* to creep ahead, crawl out
prōrēt·a -ae *m* look-out at the prow
prōrĕ·us -ī *m* look-out at the prow
prō·ripĭō -ripĕre -ripŭī -reptum *vt* to drag forth, drag out; to rush; **se proripere** to rush, dash
prōrogātĭ·ō -ōnis *f* extension, prolongation (*of a term of office*); postponement
prōrŏg·ō -āre *vt* to prolong, extend; to put off, postpone
prorsum *adv* forwards; (with a negative) absolutely, at all, e.g., **prorsum nihil** absolutely nothing, nothing at all
prorsus *adv* forward; by all means, certainly; in short, in a word; (with a negative) absolutely, at all, e.g., **nullo prorsus modo assentior** I don't agree in any way at all
prō·rumpō -rumpĕre -rūpī -ruptum *vt* to make (*something*) break forth, fling forth; **prorumpi** to burst forth; *vi* to break out, rush out, make an attack
prō·rŭō -ruĕre -rŭī -rŭtum *vt* to overthrow, demolish; *vi* to rush forth; to tumble
prōrupt·us -a -um *pp* of **prorumpo;** *adj* unrestrained
prōsāpĭ·a -ae *f* stock, race, line
proscaen·ĭum -ĭī or **-ī** *n* front part of a stage; *n pl* stage; theater
pro·scindō -scindĕre -scĭdī -scissum *vt* to plow up, break up; (fig) to criticize harshly, satirize, cut to pieces
pro·scrībō -scrībĕre -scripsī -scriptum *vt* to publish in writing; to proclaim, announce; to advertise (*for sale, etc.*); to confiscate (*property*); to punish with confiscation of property, deprive of property; to proscribe, outlaw
proscriptĭ·ō -ōnis *f* advertisement; proscription, notice of confiscation, notice of outlawry
proscriptur·ĭō -īre *vi* to be anxious to hold a proscription
proscript·us -a -um *pp* of **proscribo;** *m* proscribed person, outlaw
prōsĕc·ō -āre -ŭī -tum *vt* to cut off (*esp. parts of a sacrificial victim*)
prōsecūtus *pp* of **prosequor**
prōsĕd·a -ae *f* prostitute
prōsēmĭn·ō -āre *vt* to sow, scatter about, plant; to propagate, raise (*family*)
prō·sentĭō -sentīre -sensī *vt* to sense or realize beforehand
prō·sĕquor -sĕquī -secūtus sum *vt* to escort, attend; to pursue (*enemy*); to chase, follow; to pursue, go on with, continue (*a topic*); to describe in detail; to follow, imitate; to attend, honor
Proserpĭn·a -ae *f* daughter of Ceres and wife of Pluto
prōserp·ō -ĕre *vi* to creep or crawl forwards, creep along
proseuch·a -ae *f* synagogue
prōsil·ĭō -īre -ŭī *vi* to jump forward, jump up; to jump to one's feet; (of blood) to spurt; (of sparks) to shoot out; to rush, dash
prōsŏc·er -ĕrī *m* wife's grandfather
prospect·ō -āre *vt* to view, look out at, gaze upon; (of places) to look towards, command a view of; to look for, hope for, expect, await
prospectus *pp* of **prospicio**
prospect·us -ūs *m* distant view; sight, view; faculty of sight; sight (*thing seen*)
prospecŭl·or -ārī -ātus sum *vt* to look out for, watch for; *vi* to look around, reconnoiter
prosp·er see **prosperus**
prospĕrē *adv* favorably, luckily, as desired, successfully
prosperĭt·ās -ātis *f* success, good fortune, prosperity; **prosperitas valetudinis** good health
prospĕr·ō -āre *vt* to cause to succeed, make happy, make fortunate
prosp·ĕrus or **prosp·er -ĕra -ĕrum** *adj* successful, fortunate, lucky, favorable, prosperous
prospicientĭ·a -ae *f* foresight, precaution
pro·spicĭō -spicĕre -spexī -spectum *vt* to see far off, see in the distance; to spot; to command a view of; to watch for; to look out for, provide for; to foresee; *vi* to look forward; to look into the distance, have a distant view, have a view; to be on the lookout, exercise foresight; (with **in** + *acc*) to command a view of, overlook; **ex superioribus in urbem prospicere** to have a view of the city from a vantage point; **parum prospiciunt oculi** the eyes are nearsighted
pro·sternō -sternĕre -strāvī -strātum *vt* to throw to the ground, throw down, knock down; to wreck, ruin, overthrow, subvert; to debase; **se prosternere** to debase oneself; **se prosternere ad**

pedes (with *genit*) to throw oneself at the feet of, fall down before
prostibĭl·is -is *f* prostitute
prostibŭl·um -ī *n* prostitute
prostit·ŭō -uĕre -ŭī -ūtum *vt* to expose for sale; to prostitute
pro·stō -stāre -stĭtī *vi* to project; (of wares) to be set out for sale; to prostitute oneself, be a prostitute
prostrātus *pp* of **prosterno**
prōsubĭg·ō -ĕre *vt* to dig up, root up
prō·sum -desse -fŭī *vi* to be useful, be of use, do good, be profitable; **multum prodesse** to do a lot of good
Prōtagŏr·ās -ae *m* Greek sophist, contemporary of Socrates, born at Abdera (*c.* 485-415 B.C.)
prō·tĕgō -tegĕre -texī -tectum *vt* to cover in front, cover, cover up; to cover with a roof; to shelter, protect; (fig) to cover, defend, protect
prōtēl·ō -āre *vt* to chase away, drive off
prōtēl·um -ī *n* team of oxen; (fig) row, series
prō·tendō -tendĕre -tendī -tentum *vt* to stretch forth, stretch out, extend
prōtent·us -a -um *adj* extended
prōtĕnus see **protinus**
prō·tĕrō -terĕre -trīvī -trītum *vt* to wear down, rub out; to trample down, trample under foot; (fig) to trample upon, rub out, crush
prōterr·ĕō -ēre -ŭī -ĭtum *vt* to scare away
protervē *adv* boldly, brashly, impudently, brazenly
protervĭt·ās -ātis *f* brashness, brazenness
proterv·us -a -um *adj* bold, brash, brazen, impudent
Prōtesilā·us -ī *m* first Greek casualty in the Trojan War
Prōt·eus -ĕī or **-ĕos** *m* god of the sea with power to assume various forms
prothȳmē *adv* willingly, readily
prothymĭ·a -ae *f* willingness, readiness
prōtĭnam *adv* immediately
prōtĭnus or **prōtĕnus** *adv* straight on, forward, farther on; continuously, right on, without pause; immediately, at once, on the spot
prōtoll·ō -ĕre *vt* to stretch out (*hand*); to put off, postpone
prōtopraxĭ·a -ae *f* priority (*among creditors in receiving payment*)
prō·trăhō -trahĕre -traxī -tractum *vt* to drag forward, drag out; to produce; to reveal, expose, disclose, bring to light
prōtrītus *pp* of **protero**
prō·trūdō -trūdĕre -trūsī -trūsum *vt* to push forwards, push out; to push off, postpone
prōturb·ō -āre *vt* to drive ahead, drive on, drive away, repel; to knock down
proüt *conj* as, just as

prōvect·us -a -um *adj* advanced; **aetate provectus** advanced in years; **nox provecta erat** the night had been far advanced
prō·vĕhō -vehĕre -vexī -vectum *vt* to carry forwards; to transport, convey; to lead, lead on; to promote, advance, raise; **provehi** to ride, drive, move, or sail ahead
prō·veniō -venīre -vēnī -ventum *vi* to go on, proceed; to succeed; to come out, appear; to come out, grow, be produced; to come about, happen
prōvent·us -ūs *m* result, outcome; success; yield, produce; harvest
prōverb·ium -iī or **-ī** *n* proverb
prōvĭd·ens -entis *adj* prudent
prōvidenter *adv* prudently, with foresight
prōvidentĭ·a -ae *f* foresight, foreknowledge; precaution; **providentia deorum** providence
prō·vidĕō -vidēre -vīdī -vīsum *vt* to see in the distance; to see coming; to foresee; to provide for; to provide against, guard against, avert, avoid; to look after, look out for, care for; to prepare, make ready
prōvĭd·us -a -um *adj* foreseeing; prudent, cautious; provident; (with *genit*) providing
prōvincĭ·a -ae *f* sphere of administration; sphere of jurisdiction; office, duty, charge; public office, commission, command, administration; sphere of action; province
prōvinciāl·is -e *adj* provincial, of a province, in a province; **bellum provinciale** war in a province; **molestia provincialis** annoyance of administering a province; *m* provincial
prōvīsĭ·ō -ōnis *f* foresight; precaution; (with *genit*) precaution against
prōvīsō *adv* with forethought
prōvīs·ō -ĕre *vt* to go out to see; to be on the lookout for
prōvīs·or -ōris *m* lookout (*person*); provider
prōvīsū (only *abl*) *m* by looking forward; (with objective *genit*) **a** by foreseeing (*e.g., danger*); **b** by providing, providing for
prōvīsus *pp* of **provideo**
prō·vīvō -vivĕre -vixī *vi* to live on
prōvocātĭ·ō -ōnis *f* appeal (*to a higher court*); challenge
prōvocāt·or -ōris *m* challenger; type of gladiator
prōvŏc·ō -āre *vt* to challenge; to provoke; to exasperate; to stir, stimulate; **bellum provocare** to provoke a war; **beneficio provocatus** touched or stirred by an act of kindness; **in aleam provocare** to challenge to a game of dice; **provocare maledictis** to provoke or exasperate with nasty remarks
prōvŏl·ō -āre *vi* to fly out, rush out, dash out

prō·volvō -volvĕre -volvī -volūtum *vt* to roll forward, roll along; to roll over, overturn; to humble, ruin; **se provolvere** to prostrate oneself, fall down, grovel, humble oneself

prōvŏm·ō -ĕre *vt* to vomit, throw up

proximē or **proxŭmē** *adv* (of place) nearest, next; (of time) most recently, just recently; (with *acc*) close to, next to, at the side of, very much like, closely resembling; (with *dat*) (of place) next to; **proxime atque** almost as much as, nearly the same as; **proxime Pompeium sedebam** I was sitting next to Pompey; **quam proxime** (with *dat* or *acc*) as close as possible to

proximĭt·ās -ātis *f* proximity, vicinity; resemblance, similarity; close relationship

proximō *adv* very recently, just recently

proxĭm·us or **proxŭm·us -a -um** *adj* nearest, next; next, following, ensuing; previous, most recent, latest, last; closely related; adjoining; most direct (*route*); *m* close relative, next of kin; *n* neighborhood; next door, next-door neighbor

prūd·ens -entis *adj* foreseeing, foreknowing; conscious, aware; skilled, skillful, experienced, versed; prudent, discreet, sensible, intelligent; (with *genit* or *abl* or with **in** + *abl*) aware of, conscious of, familiar with, skilled in, experienced in

prūdenter *adv* prudently, cautiously; skillfully

prūdentĭ·a -ae *f* foreseeing; prudence, discretion, good sense; **prudentia juris publici** knowledge of or experience in public law

pruīn·a -ae *f* frost; winter

pruīnōs·us -a -um *adj* frosty

prūn·a -ae *f* live coal

prūnitĭ·us -a -um *adj* of plum-tree wood

prūn·um -ī *n* plum

prūn·us -ī *f* plum tree

prūrīg·ō -ĭnis *f* itching, itch; yen

prūr·ĭō -īre *vi* to itch; to have an itch; (with **in** + *acc*) to be itching for

prytanē·um -ī *n* state dining hall (*where the Prytanes dined*)

prytăn·is -is *m* prytane (*member of the executive body in some Greek states*)

psall·ō -ĕre -ī *vi* to play the lyre or lute

psaltēr·ĭum -ĭī or **-ī** *n* stringed instrument, lute

psaltrĭ·a -ae *f* lutist, musician (*female*)

psec·as -ădis *f* female slave who perfumed her lady's hair

psēphism·a -ătis *n* plebiscite of the Greek assembly

pseudocăt·ō -ōnis *m* a make-believe Cato

pseudomĕn·os or **pseudomĕn·us -ī** *m* fallacious syllogism

pseudothy̆r·um -ī *n* back door

psittăc·us -ī *m* parrot

Psych·ē -ēs *f* maiden loved by Cupid and made immortal by Jupiter

psychomantī·um or **psychomantē·um -ī** *n* place where people attempted to communicate with the dead

-pte *enclitic* (added to pronouns) self, own

ptisanār·ĭum -ĭī or **-ī** *n* gruel

Ptolemae·us -ī *m* Ptolemy (*name of a series of Egyptian kings descended from Lagus, a general of Alexander the Great*)

pūb·ens -entis *adj* mature; juicy (*plant*)

pūber see **pubes**

pūbert·ās -ātis *f* puberty; manhood, virility; sign of maturity, beard

pūb·ēs or **pūb·er -ĕris** *adj* grown up, adult; downy, covered with down; *m pl* grown-ups, adults, men; **pūb·ēs -is** *f* pubic hair; groin; youth, young men, grown-up males; throng, people; bullocks

pūb·escō -escĕre -ŭī *vi* to reach the age of puberty, arrive at maturity; (of plants) to grow up, ripen; (of meadows, etc.) to be clothed, covered (*e.g., with flowers*)

pūblicān·us -a -um *adj* of public revenues; *m* revenue agent

pūblicātĭ·ō -ōnis *f* confiscation

pūblĭcē *adv* publicly, officially, in behalf of the state, for the state; at public expense; generally, universally; **publice dicere** to speak officially

pūblicĭtus *adv* at public expense, at the expense of the state; publicly

pūblĭc·ō -āre *vt* to confiscate; to throw open to the general public; to prostitute

Pūblicŏl·a or **Pōplicŏl·a -ae** *m* Publius Valerius Publicola (*fl* 509 B.C.)

pūblĭc·us -a -um *adj* of the people, public, common; of the state, state, federal, national; common, ordinary, vulgar; common, general, public; **causa publica** affair of national importance; (law) federal case (*i.e., criminal case*); **res publica** state, government, politics, public life, country; *m* public official; *n* public, publicity; public property, national treasury, federal revenue; **de publico** at public expense; **in publico** in public, publicly; **in publicum prodire** to go out in public; **in publicum redigere** to hand over to the national treasury

pudend·us -a -um *adj* shameful, scandalous

pud·ens -entis *adj* modest, bashful

pudenter *adv* modestly, bashfully

pud·ĕō -ēre -ŭī or **pudĭtum est** *vt* to make ashamed; *v impers* (with *acc* of person and *genit* or *abl* of

cause of feeling), e.g., **me tui pudet** I am ashamed of you
pudibund·us -a -um *adj* modest, bashful
pudīcē *adv* chastely, modestly, virtuously
pudīciti·a -ae *f* chastity, modesty, purity
pudīc·us -a -um *adj* chaste, modest, virtuous, pure
pud·or -ōris *m* shame, decency, modesty, sense of shame; sense of honor, propriety; cause for shame, shame, disgrace; blush
puell·a -ae *f* girl; girl friend, sweetheart; young wife
puellār·is -e *adj* young girl's, girlish, youthful
puellāriter *adv* girlishly
puellŭl·a -ae *f* little girl; little sweetheart
puell·us -ī *m* little boy, lad
pu·er -ĕrī *m* boy, lad, young man; servant, slave, page; bachelor; **a pueris** or **a puero** from boyhood, from childhood; **ex pueris excedere** to outgrow childhood
puerīl·is -e *adj* boyish, childish, youthful, puerile
puerīliter *adv* like a child, childishly
pueriti·a or **puerti·a -ae** *f* childhood, boyhood
puerper·ium -iī or **-ī** *n* childbirth, lying-in, giving birth
puerpĕr·us -a -um *adj* helping childbirth, easing labor pains; *f* woman in labor
puertia see **pueritia**
puerŭl·us -ī *m* little boy, little slave
pūg·a or **pȳg·a -ae** *f* rump, rear, buttocks
pug·il -ilis *m* boxer
pugilāti·ō -ōnis *f* boxing
pugilāt·us -ūs *m* boxing
pugilicē *adv* like a boxer
pugillār·is -e *adj* hand-size; *m pl & n pl* notebook
pugillātōri·us -a -um *adj* boxing, punching; **follis pugillatorius** punching bag
pugi·ō -ōnis *m* dagger
pugiuncŭl·us -ī *m* small dagger
pugn·a -ae *f* fist fight, brawl; fight, combat, battle
pugnācit·ās -ātis *f* pugnacity, aggressiveness
pugnāciter *adv* pugnaciously, doggedly
pugnācŭl·um -ī *n* fortress
pugnant·ēs -ium *m pl* fighters, warriors
pugnant·ia -ium *n pl* contradictions, inconsistencies
pugnāt·or -ōris *m* fighter, combatant
pugn·ax -ācis *adj* pugnacious, scrappy, aggressive; quarrelsome; dogged, obstinate
pugnĕ·us -a -um *adj* of the fist; **mergae pugneae** punches
pugn·ō -āre *vt* to fight; *vi* to fight; to contend, dispute; (with *dat* or **cum** + *abl*) **a** to fight, fight against, struggle with, oppose; **b** to contradict
pugn·us -ī *m* fist
pulchell·us -a -um *adj* cute little
pulch·er -ra -rum *adj* beautiful, fair, handsome
pulchrē *adv* beautifully; (as exclamation of applause) fine!; **pulchre mihi est** I am fine
pulchritūd·ō -inis *f* beauty; excellence, attractiveness
pūlē·ium or **pūleg·ium -iī** or **-ī** *n* pennyroyal, mint; (fig) fragrance, pleasantness
pūl·ex -icis *m* flea
pullār·ius -iī or **-ī** *m* keeper of the sacred chickens
pullāt·us -a -um *adj* wearing black, in black, in mourning
pullŭl·ō -āre *vi* to sprout; (of animals) to produce young
pull·us -a -um *adj* dark-grey, dark, blackish; mourning; **toga pulla** mourning toga; *n* dark-grey garment
pull·us -ī *m* young (*of animals*), foal, offspring, chick, chicken
pulmentār·ium -iī or **-ī** *n* relish, appetizer
pulment·um -ī *n* relish; food, rations
pulm·ō -ōnis *f* lung
pulmōnĕ·us -a -um *adj* of the lungs, pulmonary
pulp·a -ae *f* meat, flesh
pulpāment·um -ī *n* meat; game
pulpĭt·um -ī *n* platform; stage
puls pultis *f* pulse, porridge, mush
pulsāti·ō -ōnis *f* knock
puls·ō -āre *vt* to batter, keep hitting; to knock at; to strum (*lyre*); to beat on, strike against; (fig) to jolt, disquiet; *vi* to throb
pulsus *pp* of **pello**
puls·us -ūs *m* push, pushing; beat, beating, striking, stamping, blow, stroke; trample; (fig) impression, influence
pultāti·ō -ōnis *f* knocking (*at the door*)
pultiphagōnid·ēs -ae *m* porridge eater
pultiphăg·us -ī *m* porridge eater
pult·ō -āre *vt* to knock at
pulverĕ·us -a -um *adj* dust, of dust; dusty; fine as dust; raising dust
pulverulent·us -a -um *adj* dusty; raising dust; covered with dust
pulvill·us -ī *m* small cushion
pulvīn·ar -āris *n* cushioned couch, couch; sacred couch for the images of the gods; seat of honor; shrine, temple
pulvīnār·ium -iī or **-ī** *n* cushioned seat of a god; dry dock
pulvīn·us -ī *m* pillow, cushion; seat of honor
pulv·is -ĕris *m* dust, powder; scene of action, arena, field; effort, work
pulviscŭl·us -ī *m* fine dust, fine powder

pūm·ex -ĭcis *m* pumice stone; porous stone, lava
pūmicĕ·us -a -um *adj* pumice, lava
pūmĭc·ō -āre *vt* to smooth or polish with pumice stone
pūmilĭ·ō -ōnis *m* or *f* midget, dwarf, pygmy
punctim *adv* with the point, with the pointed end
punct·um -ī *n* prick, puncture; point, mathematical point; point, spot; vote, ballot; clause, phrase; moment; **puncto temporis eodem** at the same instant; **punctum temporis** moment, instant, point of time
pungō pungĕre pupŭgī punctum *vt* to prick, puncture, dent; to sting, bite; to cause (*a wound*); to stab; (fig) to sting, annoy, trouble, disturb
Pūnicān·us -a -um *adj* Punic, Carthaginian, in the Carthaginian style
Pūnĭcē *adv* Punic, in the Punic language
pūnicĕ·us -a -um *adj* reddish, red, crimson, pink
Pūnĭc·us -a -um *adj* Punic, Carthagianian; red, crimson, reddish, pink; *n* pomegranate
pūn·iō -īre -īvī or **-iī -ītum** or **pūn·ĭor -īrī -ītus sum** *vt* to punish, chastise; to avenge, revenge
pūnīt·or -ōris *m* avenger
pūp·a -ae *f* doll, puppet; girl, lass
pūpill·a -ae *f* orphan girl, ward; minor; pupil (*of the eye*)
pūpillār·is -e *adj* of an orphan, belonging to an orphan
pūpill·us -ī *m* orphan boy, orphan, ward
pupp·is -is *f* stern; ship; (coll) back; **a puppi** astern
pūpŭl·a -ae *f* pupil; eye
pūpŭl·us -ī *m* little boy
pūrē *adv* clearly, brightly; plainly, simply; purely, chastely
purgām·en -ĭnis *n* dirt, filth; means of expiation, purification
purgāment·a -ōrum *n pl* offscourings, refuse, dirt, filth, garbage; (term of abuse) trash, dregs, garbage
purgātĭ·ō -ōnis *f* cleansing, cleaning, cleanup; apology, justification
purgāt·us -a -um *adj* cleansed, clean, pure
purg·ō -āre *vt* to clean, cleanse, clear, clear away, remove; to clear of a charge, exculpate, excuse, justify; to refute; to cleanse, purify ritually; to purge (*the body*)
pūrifĭc·ō -āre *vt* to purify
pūrĭter *adv* purely, cleanly; **vitam puriter agere** to lead a clean life
purpŭr·a -ae *f* purple, deep-red, dark-red; purple or deep-red cloth or garment; royal-purple robe; royalty; consular dignity, imperial dignity
purpurāt·us -a -um *adj* wearing royal purple; *m* courtier
purpurĕ·us -a -um *adj* deep-red, crimson, pink, violet, royal-purple (*and various shades, as applied to roses, poppies, lips, flesh, blood, wine, dawn, hair*)
purpurissāt·us -a -um *adj* rouged
purpuriss·um -ī *m* rouge; red dye
pūr·us -a -um *adj* pure, clear, clean; cleared, cleansed; cleansing, purifying; pure, chaste; plain, naked, unadorned, natural; plain (*toga*), without crimson border; pure, accurate, faultless (*style*); (law) unconditional, absolute; subject to no religious claims; *n* clear sky
pūs pūris *n* pus; (fig) venom, malice
pusill·us -a -um *adj* petty, puny; *n* bit, trifle
pūsĭ·ō -ōnis *m* little boy
pustŭl·a -ae *f* pimple; blister
pustulāt·us or **pusulāt·us -a -um** *adj* refined, purified
putām·en -ĭnis *n* clipping, peeling, shell, husk
putātĭ·ō -ōnis *f* pruning
putāt·or -ōris *m* pruner
putĕ·al -ālis *n* low wall (*around a well or sacred spot*), stone enclosure; **puteal Libonis** stone enclosure in the Roman Forum near which much business was transacted
puteāl·is -e *adj* well, of a well
pūt·ĕō -ēre *vi* to stink; to be rotten, be putrid
Puteolān·us -a -um *adj* of Puteoli
Puteŏl·ī -ōrum *m pl* commercial city on the coast of Campania (*modern Pozzuolo*)
put·er or **put·ris -e** *adj* putrid, rotting; crumbling; flabby
pūt·escō -escĕre -ŭī *vi* to become rotten
putĕ·us -ī *m* well; pit; dungeon
pūtĭdē *adv* disgustingly, disagreeably
pūtidiuscŭl·us -a -um *adj* rather tedious
pūtĭd·us -a -um *adj* stinking, rotten; affected, unnatural (*style*)
putill·us -a -um *adj* tiny
put·ō -āre *vt* to trim, prune; to think, ponder, consider, judge, suppose, imagine; to reckon, estimate, value; to believe in, recognize (*gods*); to clear up, settle (*accounts*); **magni putare** to think highly of; **pro certo putare** to regard as certain; *vi* to think, imagine, suppose
pūt·or -ōris *m* stench
putre·faciō -facĕre -fēcī -factum *vt* to make rotten, rot; to cause to crumble, soften
putresc·ō -ĕre *vi* to become rotten, get moldy
putrĭd·us -a -um *adj* rotten; flabby
putris see **puter**
put·us -a -um *adj* pure, bright, perfectly pure; splendid; unmixed; unmitigated; *m* boy
pyct·a or **pyct·ēs -ae** *m* boxer
Pydn·a -ae *f* city in Macedonia near which Aemilius Paulus defeated

Perseus, the Macedonian king (169 B.C.)

pȳg·a -ae *f* rump, rear, buttocks

Pygmalĭ·ōn -ōnis *m* son of Belus the king of Cyprus and brother of Dido; king of Cyprus who fell in love with a statue

Pylăd·ēs -ae *m* son of Strophius and friend of Orestes

Pyl·ae -ārum *f pl* Thermopylae (*narrow pass in E. Thessaly*)

Pylĭ·us -a -um *adj* of Pylos

Pyl·os -ī *f* Pylos (*home of Nestor in S.E. Peloponnesus*)

pyr·a -ae *f* pyre

pȳrăm·is -ĭdis *f* pyramid; cone

Pȳrăm·us -ī *m* neighbor and boy friend of Thisbe

Pȳrēnae·us -a -um *adj* of the Pyrenees

Pȳrēn·ē -ēs *f* the Pyrenees Mountains

pyrĕthr·on or **pyrĕthr·um -ī** *n* Spanish camomile (*plant*)

pyrōp·us -ī *m* bronze

Pyrrh·a -ae or **Pyrrh·ē -ēs** *f* daughter of Epimetheus, wife of Deucalion, and survivor of the Deluge

Pyrrh·ō -ōnis *m* philosopher of Elis, contemporary of Aristotle, and founder of the philosophical school of Skepticism (*c.* 360-270 B.C.)

Pyrrh·us -ī *m* son of Achilles and founder of Epirus (*also called Neoptolemus*); king of Epirus who invaded Italy to assist the Tarentines against the Romans in 280 B.C. (319-272 B.C.)

Pȳthagŏr·ās -ae *m* Greek philosopher and mathematician (*6th cent.* B.C.)

Pȳthagorē·us or **Pythagorĭc·us -a -um** *adj* Pythagorean

Pȳthĭ·us -a -um *adj* Pythian, Delphic; *m* Apollo; *f* Pythia (*priestess of Apollo at Delphi*); *n pl* Pythian games (*held in honor of Apollo every four years*)

Pȳth·ō -ūs *f* Delphi

Pȳth·ōn -ōnis *m* dragon slain by Apollo near Delphi

pȳtism·a -ătis *n* spit, squirt of wine

pȳtiss·ō -āre *vt* to spit, spit out (*wine*)

pyx·is -ĭdis *f* powder box, cosmetic box

Q

quā *adv* where, in what direction, by what way; to what extent, as far as; whereby, how, by what means; in any way, to any degree; **qua . . . qua** partly . . . partly, both . . . and

quācumque *adv* wherever, by whatever way, in whatever way; by whatever means, howsoever

quādam tenus *adv* to a certain point, only so far and no farther

quadr·a -ae *f* square table, dining table; square crust; square morsel, square bit (*of cheese, etc.*)

quadrāgēn·ī -ae -a *adj* forty each

quadrāgēsim·us or **quadrāgensim·us -a -um** *adj* fortieth; *f* one fortieth; 2½ percent tax

quadrāgiēs or **quadrāgiens** *adv* forty times

quadrāgintā (indecl) *adj* forty

quadr·ans -antis *m* fourth part, a fourth, a quarter; cent (*smallest coin, worth one sixth of an ace*); quarter of a pound; quarter pint (*quarter of a sextarius*); **quadrante lavatum ire** take a bath for one cent (*usual price of a bath*)

quadrant·al -ālis *n* five-gallon jar

quadrantārĭ·us -a -um *adj* quarter; **mulier quadrantaria** two-bit wench (*woman who sold herself for a pittance*); **tabulae quadrantariae** record of debts reduced to a fourth

quadrāt·us -a -um *adj* squared, square; *n* square

quadrīdŭ·um -ī *n* four-day period, four days

quadrienn·ĭum -ĭī or **-ī** *n* four-year period, four years

quadrifārĭam *adv* in four parts

quadrifĭd·us -a -um *adj* split into four parts

quadrīg·ae -ārum *f pl* four-horse team; four-horse chariot

quadrīgār·ĭus -ĭī or **-ī** *m* chariot racer

quadrīgāt·us -a -um *adj* stamped with a four-horse chariot

quadrīgŭl·ae -ārum *f pl* little four-horse team

quadrijŭg·is -e *adj* four-horse-team

quadrijŭg·us -a -um *adj* four-horse-team; *m pl* four-horse team

quadrilībr·is -e *adj* four-pound

quadrīmŭl·us -a -um *adj* only four years old

quadrīm·us -a -um *adj* four-year-old

quadringēnārĭ·us -a -um *adj* consisting of four hundred men each

quadringēn·ī -ae -a *adj* four hundred each

quadringentēsĭm·us -a -um *adj* four-hundredth

quadringentiēs *adv* four hundred times

quadripertīt·us -a -um *adj* fourfold

quadrirēm·is -e *adj* having four banks of oars; *f* quadrireme

quadriv·ĭum -ĭī or **-ī** *n* crossroads

quadr·ō -āre *vt* to make square; to complete; to round out, give rhythmic finish to (*a speech*); *vi* to make a square; to be exact; (of accounts) to agree, come out right, tally; (with *dat* or **in** + *acc*) to suit, fit, seem proper to

quadr·um -ī *n* square; **in quadrum redigere sententias** to balance sentences

quadrupĕd·ans -antis *adj* galloping; *m pl* horses

quadrŭp·ēs -ĕdis *adj* four-footed; on all fours; *mf* quadruped

quadruplāt·or -ōris *m* informer (*who received one fourth of the forfeiture*); corrupt judge

quadrŭpl·ex -icis *adj* quadruple, fourfold

quadruplĭc·ō -āre *vt* to quadruple, increase fourfold

quadrŭpl·or -ārī -ātus sum *vi* to be an informer

quadrŭpl·us -a -um *adj* quadruple, fourfold; *n* four times the amount

quaerit·ō -āre *vt* to keep looking for; to keep asking

quaerō quaerĕre quaesīvī quaesītum *vt* to look for, search for; to try to get; to get, obtain; to try to gain, earn, acquire; to miss, lack; to require, demand, call for; to ask, interrogate; to examine, investigate; to plan, devise, aim at; (with *inf*) to try to, wish to; (with **ab** or **de** or **ex** + *abl*) to ask (*something*) of or from (*someone*); *vi* to hold an examination; (with **de** + *abl*) to ask about, inquire about; **si quaeris** or **si quaerimus** (coll) to tell the truth

quaesīti·ō -ōnis *f* questioning under torture

quaesīt·or -ōris *m* judge (*praetor or other official who presided over a criminal trial*)

quaesīt·us -a -um *pp* of **quaero;** *adj* select, special; far-fetched, artificial, affected; *n* question; *n pl* gains, earnings, acquisitions, store

quaes·ō -ĕre *vt* to beg, ask; **quaeso** (usually parenthetical) please

quaesticŭl·us -ī *m* slight profit

quaesti·ō -ōnis *f* inquiry, investigation, questioning, examination; judicial investigation, criminal trial; court of inquiry, court; questioning under torture, third degree; question, subject of investigation, case; court record; (with **de** + *abl* of the nature of the charge) court investigating a charge of (*e.g., forgery, etc.*); **in quaestione versare** to be under investigation; **quaestio extraordinaria** investigation by a special board; **quaestio inter sicarios** murder trial, court investigating a murder; **quaestio perpetua** standing court; **quaestioni praeesse** to preside over a case, be judge at a trial; **servos in quaestionem dare** or **ferre** to hand over slaves for questioning under torture

quaestiuncŭl·a -ae *f* minor or trifling question

quaest·or -ōris *m* quaestor; financial officer; treasury official; public prosecutor of criminal offenses

quaestōri·us -a -um *adj* quaestor's, of a quaestor; *m* ex-quaestor; *n* quaestor's tent in a camp; quaestor's residence in a province

quaestuōs·us -a -um *adj* profitable, lucrative, productive; acquiring wealth; eager to make a profit, acquisitive; enriched, wealthy

quaestūr·a -ae *f* quaestorship; quaestor's safe, public funds

quaest·us -ūs *m* gain, profit; acquisition; way of making money, job, occupation, business, trade; (fig) profit, gain, benefit, advantage; **ad quaestum** for profit, to make a profit; **quaestui rem publicam habere** to use public office for personal profit; **quaestum facere** to make money

quālĭbet or **quālŭbet** *adv* anywhere, everywhere; in any way, as you please

quāl·is -e *adj* what sort of, what kind of; of such a kind, such as, as; (with quotations and citations) as, as for example; **in hoc bello, quale** in this war, the likes of which; **qualis erat!** what a man he was!

quāl·iscumque -ecumque *adj* of whatever kind; of any kind whatever, any at all; **homines, qualescumque sunt** men, no matter what kind they are

quāl·islĭbet -elĭbet *adj* of whatever kind, of whatever sort

quālĭt·ās -ātis *f* quality, nature, property

quālĭter *adv* as, just as

quāl·us -ī *m* wicker basket, straw basket

quam *adv* (in questions and exclamations) to what extent, how, how much; (in comparisons) as, than; (with superlatives) as . . . as possible, e.g., **quam celerrime** as fast as possible; **quam plurimo vendere** to sell at the highest price possible; **quam primum** as soon as possible; (*after verbs implying preference*) rather than

quamdiū or **quam diū** *adv* how long; *conj* as long as, until

quamlĭbet or **quamlŭbet** *adv* as much as you please

quamŏbrem or **quam ob rem** *adv* for what reason, why; for which reason, wherefore, why

quamquam *conj* though, although

quamvīs *adv* (with *adj* or *adv*) however; ever so; *conj* although

quānam *adv* by what route, by what way

quandō *adv* (in questions) when, at what time; (indefinite, after **si, ne,**

num) ever, at any time; *conj* when; because, since
quandōcumque or **quandōcunque** *adv* at some time or other, some day; *conj* whenever; as often as, no matter when
quandōque *adv* at some time, at one time or other, some day; *conj* whenever; as often as; since
quandōquĭdem *conj* in as much as, whereas, seeing that
quantill·us -a -um *adj* how much, how little
quantĭt·ās -ātis *f* quantity
quantō *adv* by how much, how much; **quanto ante** how much earlier; **quanto . . . tanto** the . . . the
quantopĕre *adv* how much, how greatly; with how great effort, how carefully
quantŭlum *adv* how little; **quantulum interest utrum** how little difference it makes whether
quantŭl·us -a -um *adj* how great, how much, how little, how small, how insignificant
quantul·uscumque -acumque -umcumque *adj* however small, however unimportant
quantum *adv* as much as, so much as, as great an extent; how much, how far, to what extent; (with comparatives) the more, the greater; **quantum in me fuit** as much as I could, to the best of my ability; **quantum maximā voce potuit** at the the top of his voice; **quantum potest** as much (*or fast, quickly, soon, long, etc.*) as possible
quantumcumque *adv* as much as
quantumlĭbet *adv* however much
quantumvīs *adv* however; **quantumvis rusticus** however unsophisticated, although unsophisticated
quant·us -a -um *adj* how great, how much; **quantus quantus** however great, however much; *pron neut* what amount; (with *genit*) how much; **in quantum** to whatever extent, as far as; **quanti** (*genit* of price) at what price, how much, how dearly, how high; **quanto** (*abl* of price) at what price, for how much; **quantum frumenti** how much grain
quant·uscumque -acumque -umcumque *adj* however great; of whatever size; however small, however trifling, however unimportant
quant·uslĭbet -alĭbet -umlĭbet *adj* however great; ever so great
quant·usvīs -ăvīs -umvīs *adj* however great
quāpropter *adv* wherefore, why
quāquā *adv* by whatever route, whatever way
quāquam *adv* by any way
quārē or **quā rē** *adv* by what means, how; from what cause, why; whereby; wherefore
quartadecumān·ī -ōrum *m pl* soldiers of the fourteenth legion
quartān·us -a -um *adj* occurring every fourth day; *f* quartan fever; *m pl* soldiers of the fourteenth legion
quartār·ĭus -ĭī or **-ī** *m* quarter pint
quartō *adv* for the fourth time
quartum *adv* for the fourth time
quart·us -a -um *adj* fourth
quart·us decĭm·us -a -um *adj* fourteenth
quasi *conj* as if, just as if, as though
quasi *adv* as it were, so to speak; about, nearly, almost
quasill·um -ī *n* or **quasill·us -ī** *m* small basket
quassātĭ·ō -ōnis *f* shaking
quass·ō -āre *vt* to keep shaking, keep tossing, keep waving; to batter, shatter, smash to pieces; (fig) to shake, weaken
quass·us -a -um *pp* of **quatio;** *adj* shattered, broken; **vox quassa** weak voice
quate·faciō -facĕre -fēcī -factum *vt* to shake; (fig) to weaken
quātĕnus *adv* how far, to what point; as far as; till when, how long; to what extent; **est quatenus** there is an extent to which; *conj* as far as; insofar as, inasmuch as, seeing that, since, as
quater *adv* four times
quater deciens or **quater deciēs** *adv* fourteen times
quatern·ī -ae -a *adj* four together, four in a group, four each
quatĭō quatĕre — -quassum *vt* to shake, cause to tremble, cause to vibrate; to brandish, wave about; to beat, strike, drive; to batter, crush; (fig) to touch, move, affect; (fig) to plague, harass
quattŭor (indecl) *adj* four
quattuordĕcim (indecl) *adj* fourteen
quattuorvirāt·us -ūs *m* membership on the board of four
quattuorvĭr·ī -ōrum *m pl* board of four officials (*executive board of municipalities and colonies*)
-que *conj* and
quemadmŏdum or **quem ad modum** *adv* in what way, how; *conj* just as, as
qu·ĕō -īre -īvī or **-ĭī -ĭtum** *vi* to be able; (with *inf*) to be able to
quercēt·um -ī *n* oak forest
quercĕ·us -a -um *adj* oak, of oak
querc·us -ūs *f* oak tree; oak-leaf crown (*awarded to a soldier who saved citizen in battle*); acorns
querell·a or **querēl·a -ae** *f* complaint
queribund·us -a -um *adj* complaining; **vox queribunda** whining voice
querimōnĭ·a -ae *f* complaint, grievance; elegy
querĭt·or -ārī -ātus sum *vi* to keep complaining
quern·us -a -um *adj* oak, of oak
queror querī questus sum *vt* to

complain of, complain about; to lament; *vi* to complain; (of birds) to sing, warble, sing sadly, coo mournfully

querquētulān·us -a -um *adj* oak, covered with oak trees

querŭl·us -a -um *adj* complaining, full of complaints, querulous; plaintive; warbling, cooing

questus *pp* of **queror**

quest·us -ūs *m* complaint; plaintive note (*of the nightingale*)

quī quae quod *adj* (interrog) which, what, what kind of; (indefinite) any; *pron* (rel) who, that; (indef, after **si, nisi, num, ne**) anyone

quī *adv* how; why; at what price; whereby; in some way, somehow

quia *conj* because

quiănam *adv* why

quicquam cūjusquam *pron* anything

quicque cūjusque *pron* each, each one

quidquid (*genit* not in use) *pron* whatever

quīcum (old *abl* + **cum**) *pron* with whom, with which

quīcumque quaecumque quodcumque or **quīcunque quaecunque quodcunque** *pron* (rel) whoever, whosoever, everyone who, whatever, whatsoever, everything that, all that; (indef) any whatsoever, any possible, every possible

quid *adv* why

quid cūjus *pron* (interrog) what; (indef, after **si, nisi, num,** or **ne**) anything

quīdam quaedam quiddam *pron* a certain one, a certain person, a certain thing

quīdam quaedam quoddam *adj* a certain; (to soften an expression) a kind of, what one might call

quidem *adv* (emphasizing the word that is placed before it) indeed, in fact; (qualifying or limiting) at least, at any rate; (concessive) it is true; of course; all right; (exemplifying) for example; **ne . . . quidem** (emphasizing the intervening word) not even, e.g., **ne tu quidem** not even you

quidnam cūjusnam *pron* (interrog) what

quidnam *adv* why, why in the world

quidnī *adv* why not

quidpĭam cūjuspĭam *pron* anything, something

quidquid (*genit* not in use; *abl:* **quoquo**) *pron* whatever, whatsoever, everything which; **per quiquid deorum** by all the gods

quidquid *adv* to whatever extent, the further

qui·ēs -ētis *f* quiet, peace, rest; calm, lull; neutrality; sleep; dream; sleep of death, death

qui·escō -escĕre -ēvī -ētum *vt* to stand by and watch, quietly allow; *vi* to rest, keep quiet, be inactive; to rest, sleep, be asleep; to lie still, be still, be undisturbed; to pause, make a pause; to be calm, be unruffled; to be neutral, keep neutral; (with *inf*) to cease to, stop; (with **ab** + *abl*) to be free from

quiētē *adv* quietly, calmly

quiēt·us -a -um *adj* at rest, resting, free from exertion, inactive; quiet, peaceful, undisturbed; neutral; calm, quiet; still, silent; idle; *n pl* period of peace

quīlĭbet quaelĭbet quidlĭbet *pron* anyone, any you wish, no matter who, anything, anything you wish, not matter what, everything

quīlĭbet quaelĭbet quodlĭbet *adj* any, any at all, any you wish

quīn *adv* (interrog) why not; (corroborative) in fact, as a matter of fact; *conj* so that not, without; **facere non possum, quin ad te mittam librum** I can't help sending you the book; **nullo modo introire possem, quin viderent me** I just couldn't walk in without their seeing me; (after verbs of preventing, opposing) from: **milites aegre sunt retenti quin oppidum oppugnarent** the soldiers could barely be kept from assaulting the town; (after verbs of hesitation, doubt, suspicion): **non dubito quin** I do not doubt that; (esp. representing a nominative of a relative pronoun with a negative) that . . . not, without: **nemo aspicere potest quin dicat** no one can look on without saying; **nemo est quin velit** there is no one who does not prefer

quīnam quaenam quodnam *adj* which, what, just which, just what

Quinct- = Quint-

quinc·unx -uncis *m* five twelfths; five percent (*interest*); the figure five (*as arranged on dice or cards*)

quindecĭens or **quindecĭēs** *adv* fifteen times

quindĕcim (indecl) *adj* fifteen

quindecimprīm·ī -ōrum *m pl* executive board of fifteen (*magistrates of a municipality*)

quindecimvirāl·is -e *adj* of the board of fifteen

quindecimvĭr·ī -ōrum *m pl* board of fifteen; **quindecimviri Sibyllini** board of fifteen in charge of the Sibylline Books

quingēnārĭ·us -a -um *adj* of five hundred each, consisting of five hundred men

quingēn·ī -ae -a *adj* five hundred each

quingentēsĭm·us -a -um *adj* five-hundredth

quingent·ī -ae -a *adj* five hundred

quingentĭens or **quingentĭēs** *adv* five hundred times

quīn·ī -ae -a *adj* five each; **quini deni** fifteen each; **quini viceni** twenty-five each

quinquāgēn·ī -ae -a *adj* fifty each

quinquāgēsim·us -a -um *adj* fiftieth; *f* two-percent tax
quinquāginta (indecl) *adj* fifty
Quinquātr·ūs -ŭum *f pl* or **Quinquātr·ia -ium** *n pl* festival in honor of Minerva (*celebrated from March* 19*th to* 23*rd*)
quinque (indecl) *adj* five
quinquennāl·is -e *adj* quinquennial, occurring every five years; five-year, lasting five years
quinquenn·is -e *adj* five years old, of five years
quinquenn·ium -iī or **-ī** *n* five-year period, five years
quinquepartīt·us -a -um *adj* five-fold, divided into five parts
quinqueprīm·ī -ōrum *m pl* five-man board of magistrates
quinquerēm·is -e *adj* having five banks of oars; *f* quinquereme
quinquĕ·vir -virī *m* member of a five-man board
quinquevirāt·us -ūs *m* membership on a board of five
quinquevir·ī -ōrum *m pl* five-man board (*created at various times to serve various purposes*)
quinquiens or **quinquiēs** *adv* five times
quinquiplic·ō -āre *vt* to multiply by five
quintadecimān·ī -ōrum *m pl* soldiers of the fifteenth legion
quintān·us -a -um *adj* of the fifth; *m pl* members of the fifth legion; *f* camp street running between the fifth and sixth maniple (*used as the market street of the camp*)
Quintiliān·us or **Quinctiliān·us -ī** *m* M. Fabius Quintilianus (*Quintilian, famous orator and rhetoric teacher, c.* 35-*c.* 95 A.D.)
Quintīl·is or **Quinctīl·is -e** *adj* & *m* July
quintō or **quintum** *adv* for the fifth time
quint·us -a -um *adj* fifth
Quint·us -ī *m* Roman first name
quint·us decim·us -a -um *adj* fifteenth
quippe *adv* of course, naturally, obviously, by all means; *conj* since, for; **quippe qui** since he (*is, was, will be one who*), inasmuch as he; **multa Caesar questus est quippe qui vidisset** Caesar complained a lot since he had seen
quippiam = quidpiam
quippinī *adv* why not?; of course, to be sure
Quirīnāl·ia -ium *n pl* festival in honor of Romulus (*celebrated on the* 17*th of February*)
Quirīnāl·is -e *adj* of Quirinus; **collis Quirinalis** Quirinal Hill (*one of the seven hills of Rome*)
Quirīn·us -a -um *adj* of Quirinus; *m* Quirinus (*epithet applied to Romulus after his deification, to Janus, to Augustus, and to Antony*)
Quir·is -ītis *m* Roman citizen; inhabitant of Cures (*Sabine town*)
quirītāti·ō -ōnis *f* shrieking, shriek
quirītāt·us -ūs *m* scream, shriek
Quirītēs = *pl* of **Quiris**
quirīt·ō -āre *vi* to scream, shriek
quis cūjus *pron* (interrog) who, which one; (indef) anyone
quīs = quibus
quisnam quaenam (see **quidnam**) *pron* (interrog) who
quispiam cūjuspiam *pron* someone
quispiam quaepiam quodpiam *adj* any
quisquam cūjusquam *pron* anyone, anybody, any person
quisque cūjusque *pron* each, each one, everybody, every one; **doctissimus quisque** every one of great learning, all the most learned; **optimus quisque** all the best ones
quisque quaeque quodque *adj* each
quisquili·ae -ārum *f pl* refuse, trash, junk, rubbish, odds and ends
quisquis (*genit* not in use; *abl:* **quoquo**) *pron* whoever, whosoever, every one who; every one, each
quīvīs quaevīs quidvīs *pron* anyone, anyone you please, anyone at all; **quivis unus** any one person
quīvīs quaevīs quodvīs *adj* any, any you please, any at all
quō *adv* (interrog) where, to what place; what for, to what purpose; (after **si, nisi,** or **ne**) to any place, anywhere; **quo . . . eo** the . . . the; **quo magis . . . eo magis** the more . . . the more; *conj* where, to which place; whereby, wherefore; (replacing **ut** when the clause contains a comparative) in order that, so that
quoad *adv* how far; how long; *conj* as long as; as far as; until
quōcircā *adv* for which reason, wherefore, therefore, that's the reason why
quōcumque *adv* to whatever place, wherever
quod *conj* because; as for the fact that; for the fact that; insofar as; as far as; **quod si** or **quodsi** but if
quōdammŏdo or **quōdam modo** *adv* in a way
quoi = cui
quōjus = cujus
quōlibet *adv* anywhere you please
quom see **cum**
quōminus *conj* that not; (after verbs of hindering) from, e.g., **deterrere aliquem quominus habeat** to keep someone from having
quōmŏdo *adv* (interrog) in what way, how; (rel) just as, as
quōmodocumque *adv* in whatever way, however
quōmodŏnam *adv* in just what way, how then
quōnam *adv* where, where to; to what purpose, to what end
quondam *adv* once, at one time, formerly; at times, sometimes, once in a while; some day, one day (*in the future*)

quōniam *conj* because, seeing that, now that
quōpiam *adv* to any place, anywhere
quoque *adv* too, also
quōquō *adv* to whatever place, wherever
quōquōmŏdo *adv* in whatever way, however
quōquōversum or **quōquōversus** *adv* in every direction, every way
quorsum or **quorsus** *adv* in what direction, where to; to what end, why
quot (indecl) *adj* (interrog) how many; (correlative) as many; **quot Kalendis** every first of the month; **quot mensibus** every month
quotannīs *adv* every year
quotcumque (indecl) *adj* however many
quotēn·ī -ae -a *adj* how many each
quotīdīē *adv* daily
quotiens or **quotiēs** *adv* (interrog) how many times; (correlative) as often as
quotienscumque or **quotienscunque** *adv* however often, as often as
quotquot (indecl) *adj* however many, no matter how many
quotŭm·us -a -um *adj* which in number, which in order
quot·us -a -um *adj* which, what; what a small, what a trifling; **quota hora est?** what time is it?; **quota pars** what part; **quot erit iste liber qui . . .** which will be the book which . . .; **quotus quisque philosophorum invenitur** how rarely is one of the philosophers found, how few philosophers are found
quot·uscumque -acumque -umcumque *adj* just what, just which; **quotacumque pars** just what part
quōusque *adv* how far, how long
quōvīs *adv* to any place whatsoever, anywhere; **quovis gentium** anywhere in the world
quum see **cum** *conj*

R

rabĭdē *adv* rabidly, madly, furiously
rabĭd·us -a -um *adj* rabid, mad, furious, raving, uncontrolled
rabĭ·ēs (*genit* not in use) *f* rage, madness; (fig) rage, anger, fury, wild passion, eagerness
rabĭōsē *adv* furiously, ravingly
rabiōsŭl·us -a -um *adj* half-crazy
rabiōs·us -a -um *adj* rabid, mad, raving, crazy
rabŭl·a -ae *m* ranting lawyer
racēmĭf·er -ĕra -ĕrum *adj* clustered; covered with grape clusters
racēm·us -ī *m* cluster, bunch (*esp. of grapes*); (fig) wine
radĭ·ans -antis *adj* shining, beaming, radiant
radiāt·us -a -um *adj* spoked; having rays, radiant
rādīcĭtus *adv* by the roots, root and all; completely
rādīcŭl·a -ae *f* small root
radĭ·ō -āre or **radĭ·or -ārī -ātus sum** *vt* to radiate; *vi* to radiate, shine, gleam
radiōs·us -a -um *adj* radiant
rad·ĭus -ĭī or **-ī** *m* stake, stick; spoke; ray, beam; shuttle; radius; measuring rod; elongated olive
rād·ix -īcis *f* root; radish; foot (*of hill or mountain*); base, foundation; basis, origin
rādō rādĕre rāsī rāsum *vt* to scrape, scratch; to shave; to scratch out, erase; to graze, touch in passing; to strip off; (of the wind) to lash
raed·a -ae *f* four-wheeled carriage, coach
raedār·ĭus -ĭī or **-ī** *m* coach driver
Raetĭ·us -a -um *adj* Raetian; *f* Raetia (*Alpine country between Germany and Italy*)
Raet·us -a -um *adj* & *m* Raetian
rall·us -a -um *adj* thin, threadbare
rāmāl·ĭa -ĭum *n pl* brushwood, undergrowth
rāment·um -ī *n* or **rament·a -ae** *f* chip, shaving
rāmĕ·us -a -um *adj* of branches, of boughs
rām·ex -ĭcis *m* hernia, rupture; blood vessel of the lung
Ramn·ēs or **Ramnens·ēs -ĭum** *m pl* one of the three original Roman tribes; (fig) blue bloods
rāmōs·us -a -um *adj* branchy, branching; branch-like
rāmŭl·us -ī *m* twig
rām·us -ī *m* branch, bough; branch (*of an antler*); stick, club
rān·a -ae *f* frog; **rana marina** frog fish
ranc·ens -entis *adj* putrid, stinking
rancidŭl·us -a -um *adj* rank, stinking; disgusting
rancĭd·us -a -um *adj* rancid, rank, stinking; disgusting
rānuncŭl·us -ī *m* little frog, tadpole
rapācĭd·a -ae *m* son of a thief
rapācĭt·ās -ātis *f* rapacity, greediness
rap·ax -ācis *adj* rapacious, grasping, grabby, greedy for plunder; insatiable
raphăn·us -ī *m* radish
rapĭdē *adv* rapidly; (to burn) fiercely
rapidĭt·ās -ātis *f* rapidity, velocity, swiftness, rush
rapĭd·us -a -um *adj* tearing away,

seizing; fierce, consuming, white-hot (*fire*); rapid, swift, rushing, hurrying, impetuous

rapīn·a -ae *f* rapine, pillage; prey, booty

rapiō rapĕre rapŭī raptum *vt* to seize and carry off, to snatch, tear, pluck; to drag off; to hurry, drive, cause to rush; to carry off by force, rob, ravish, ravage, lay waste; to lead on hurriedly; **flammam rapere** to catch fire; **in jus rapere** to drag off to court, hale before a court; **se rapere** to hurry, dash, take off

raptim *adv* hurriedly, speedily, suddenly

raptĭ·ō -ōnis *f* abduction, ravishing, rape

rapt·ō -āre *vt* to seize and carry off, drag away; to drag along; to plunder; to hale, arraign

rapt·or -ōris *m* plunderer, robber; rapist

rapt·us -a -um *pp* of **rapio;** *n* plunder, loot

rapt·us -ūs *m* snatching away; looting, robbery; rape, abduction

rāpŭl·um -ī *n* little turnip

rāp·um -ī *n* turnip

rārē *adv* rarely, seldom

rārē·faciō -facĕre -fēcī -factum *vt* to rarefy, thin out

rāresc·ō -ĕre *vi* to grow thin, lose density, become rarefied; to grow wider, widen out, open up; to become fewer; to disappear, die away

rārĭt·ās -ātis *f* looseness of texture; thinness; small number

rārō *adv* rarely, seldom

rār·us -a -um *adj* wide apart, of loose texture, thin; far apart, scattered far apart; scarce, sparse; few; (mil) in open rank; uncommon, rare, unusual

rāsĭl·is -e *adj* shaved smooth, scraped, polished

rastr·um -ī *n* rake; mattock

rāsus *pp* of **rado**

ratĭ·ō -ōnis *f* calculation, computation, reckoning, account; matter, affair, business, transaction; consideration, respect, regard; grounds; scheme, system, method, procedure; theory, doctrine; science; relation, connection, reference; fashion, way, style; reasoning, reason, judgment, understanding; reasonableness, order, law, rule; view, opinion; **propter rationem** (with *genit*) out of regard for; **ratio aeraria** rate of exchange; **ratio atque usus** theory and practice; **ratio constat** the accounts tally; **rationem conferre, referre,** or **deferre** (with *genit*) to render or give an account of, account for; **rationem ducere** to make a calculation, reckon; **rationem habere** (with **cum** + *abl*) to have to do with; **rationem inire** to calculate, make a calculation

ratiōcinātĭ·ō -ōnis *f* (rhet) exercise of the reasoning powers, reasoning; syllogism

ratiōcinātīv·us -a -um *adj* syllogistic

ratiōcināt·or -ōris *m* accountant

ratiōcĭn·or -ārī -ātus sum *vt & vi* to calculate, reckon; to reason, argue, conclude, infer

rat·is -is *f* raft; boat; *f pl* pontoons

ratiuncŭl·a -ae *f* small account; trifling reason; petty syllogism

rat·us -a -um *pp* of **reor;** *adj* reckoned, calculated; fixed, established, settled, certain, sure, approved; **pro rata parte** or **pro rata** in proportion, proportionately; **ratum facere** or **ratum efficere** to confirm, ratify, approve; **ratum habere** or **ducere** to consider valid, regard as certain or sure

raucisŏn·us -a -um *adj* hoarse

rauc·us -a -um *adj* raucous, hoarse; screaming, strident; scraping; deep, deep-voiced

raud·us or **rūd·us -ĕris** *n* copper coin

rauduscŭl·um or **rūduscŭl·um -ī** *n* bit of money

rāv·ĭō -īre *vi* to talk oneself hoarse

rāv·is -is *f* hoarseness

rāv·us -a -um *adj* greyish

re·a -ae *f* defendant, guilty woman

reapse *adv* in fact, actually, really

Reāt·e -is *n* Sabine town

Reātīn·us -a -um *adj & m* Reatine

rebellātĭ·ō -ōnis *f* rebellion

rebellātr·ix -īcis *f* rebel; **Germania rebellatrix** rebel Germany

rebellĭ·ō -ōnis *f* rebellion

rebell·is -e *adj* rebellious; *m pl* rebels

rebell·ĭum -ĭī or **-ī** *n* rebellion

rebell·ō -āre *vi* to rebel

rebīt·ō -ĕre *vi* to go back

rebŏ·ō -āre *vt* to make reecho; *vi* to reecho, bellow back

recalcĭtr·ō -āre *vi* to kick back

recal·ĕō -ēre *vi* to be warmed; (of a river) to run warm (*e.g., with blood*)

recal·escō -escĕre -ŭī *vi* to grow warm again

recal·faciō -facĕre -fēcī *vt* to make warm again, warm up again

recalv·us -a -um *adj* bald in front, with receding hairline

recand·escō -escĕre -ŭī *vi* to grow white; to grow hot, glow; (with *dat*) to grow white, grow hot, glow in response to

recant·ō -āre *vt* to recant; to charm back, charm away; *vi* to reecho

re·cēdō -cēdĕre -cessī -cessum *vi* to go back, go away, withdraw, recede, give ground, fall back; to depart; to vanish, disappear; to stand back, be distant

recell·ō -ĕre *vi* to spring back, recoil

rec·ens -entis *adj* recent, fresh, young; newly arrived, just arrived; modern; fresh, rested; *n pl* recent events

recens *adv* just, recently, lately, newly
recens·ĕō -ēre -ŭī -um *vt* to count, enumerate, number, survey; to review, hold a review of (*the army*); (of a censor) to revise the roll of, review, enroll; to recount, go over again, retell
recensī·ō -ōnis *f* revision
recensus *pp* of **recenseo**
recens·us -ūs *m* review
receptācŭl·um -ī *n* receptacle, container; reservoir; place of refuge, shelter; hiding place
receptī·ō -ōnis *f* reception
recept·ō -āre *vt* to take back; to welcome frequently into the home, entertain; to tug at; **se receptare** to beat a hasty retreat
recept·or -ōris *m* or **receptr·ix -īcis** *f* shelterer; concealer
recept·us -a -um *pp* of **recipio;** *n* obligation
recept·us -ūs *m* taking back, recantation; (mil) retreat; way of escape; refuge, place of retreat; return; **(signum) receptui canere** to sound retreat
recessim *adv* backwards
recess·us -ūs *m* retreat, withdrawal; departure; secluded spot, retreat; inner room, central chamber; recess; background
recharmĭd·ō -āre *vi* to stop being a Charmides (*character in Roman comedy*)
recidīv·us -a -um *adj* recurring, returning; rebuilt
re·cīdo -cīdĕre -cīdī -cīsum *vt* to cut back, cut away, cut off, cut down; to abridge, cut short
re·cĭdō -cidĕre -cĭdī -cāsum or **rec·cĭdō -cidĕre** *vi* to fall back; to jump back, recoil; to suffer a relapse; (fig) to fall back, fall, sink, relapse; to turn out, result; (with **ad** or **in** + *acc*) to pass to, be handed over to
re·cingō -cingĕre — -cinctum *vt* to loosen, undo, take off
recĭn·ō -ĕre *vt* to repeat, reecho; *vi* to sound a warning
reciper- = **recuper-**
re·cipĭō -cipĕre -cēpī -ceptum *vt* to keep back, keep in reserve; to take back, withdraw, bring back, carry back, retake, recover, regain; to take in, accept, receive, welcome; to gain, collect, take in, make (*money*); to take up, assume, undertake; to guarantee, pledge; (mil) to retake, reoccupy, recapture, seize, take, occupy; **ad se** or **in se recipere** to take upon oneself, take responsibility for, promise, guarantee; **se recipere** to get hold of oneself again, regain self-composure, recover, come to again; to retreat, escape; **se recipere** (with **ad** or **in** + *acc*) to retreat to, escape to, find refuge in
reciprŏc·ō -āre *vt* to move back and forth; to turn back; to back (*e.g., a ship*) about, reverse the direction of; to reverse, convert (*a proposition*); *vi* (of the tide) to ebb and flow, rise and fall
reciprŏc·us -a -um *adj* ebbing and flowing, going backwards and forwards
recīsus *pp* of **recīdo**
recitātĭ·ō -ōnis *f* reading aloud, recitation
recitāt·or -ōris *m* reader, reciter
recĭt·ō -āre *vt* to read out, read aloud, recite; to name in writing, appoint, constitute; **senatum recitare** to have roll call in the senate
reclāmātĭ·ō -ōnis *f* cry of disapproval
reclāmĭt·ō -āre *vi* to voice disapproval
reclām·ō -āre *vt* to protest; *vi* to raise a protest, voice disapproval, shout objections; to reverberate; (with *dat*) to express disapproval to, contradict
reclīn·is -e *adj* reclining, leaning back
reclīn·ō -āre *vt* to bend back, lean back, rest; (with **ab** + *abl*) to distract (*someone*) from; **se reclinare** to lean
re·clūdō -clūdĕre -clūsī -clūsum *vt* to open; to lay open, disclose; to draw (*sword*); to break up (*the soil*)
recoctus *pp* of **recoquo**
recōgĭt·ō -āre *vi* (with **de** + *abl*) to think again about, reconsider, reflect on
recognitĭ·ō -ōnis *f* reinvestigation
reco·gnoscō -gnoscĕre -gnōvī -gnitum *vt* to call to mind again, review; to recognize; to look over, examine, inspect, investigate; to certify, authorize
recol·lĭgō -ligĕre -lēgī -lectum *vt* to gather again, gather up, collect; **te recollige** get hold of yourself, pluck up your courage
re·cŏlō -colĕre -colŭī -cultum *vt* to till again; to honor again; to recall to mind, think over, consider; to cultivate once more, practice again, resume
recomminisc·or -ī *vt* to call to mind again, recall
recomposĭt·us -a -um *adj* rearranged
reconciliātĭ·ō -ōnis *f* winning back again, reestablishment, restoration; reconciling, reconciliation
reconcilĭ·ō -āre *vt* to bring back, regain, recover; to restore, reestablish; to win over again, conciliate; to bring together again, reconcile
reconcinn·ō -āre *vt* to set right again, repair
recondĭt·us -a -um *adj* hidden, concealed; recondite, abstruse, profound; reserved (*person*)
recon·dō -dĕre -dĭdī -dĭtum *vt* to put back again, put away, hoard; to hide, conceal; to plunge (*sword*); to

close (*eyes*) again; to store up (*in the mind*)

reconfl•ō -āre *vt* to blow up again, rekindle

re•cŏquō -coquĕre -coxī -coctum *vt* to cook, boil, or bake again; to recast, remold

recordātī•ō -ōnis *f* recollection, remembrance

record•or -ārī -ātus sum *vt* to recall, recollect, remember

recrĕ•ō -āre *vt* to recreate, restore, renew; (fig) to revive, refresh

recrĕp•ō -ĕre *vt & vi* to reecho

re•crescō -crescĕre -crēvī *vi* to grow again; to be renewed

recrūd•escō -escĕre -ŭī *vi* to become raw again; (of a wound) to open up again; (of a revolt) to break out again

rectā *adv* by a direct route, right on, directly

rectē *adv* in a straight line; rightly, correctly, suitably, properly, well; quite; (in answers) well, right, quite well, fine

rectī•ō -ōnis *f* direction, controlling

rect•or -ōris *m* guide, controller, leader, ruler, master, pilot

rect•us -a -um *pp* of **rego;** *adj* in a straight line, straight, direct; correct, right, proper, appropriate; just, upright, conscientious, virtuous; *n* right; uprightness, rectitude, virtue

recŭb•ō -āre *vi* to lie on one's back, lie down, rest

rēcŭl•a -ae *f* little thing

recultus *pp* of **recolo**

re•cumbō -cumbĕre -cubŭī *vi* to lie down again, lie down; to recline (*esp. at table*); to sink down (*e.g., in a swamp*); to fall; (of fog) to settle down

recuperātī•ō -ōnis *f* recovery

recuperāt•or or **reciperāt•or -ōris** *m* recoverer, regainer; (law) arbiter (*member of a bench of from three to five men who expedited cases needing speedy decisions*)

recuperātōrī•us or **reciperātōrī•us -a -um** *adj* of the special court for summary civil suits

recupĕr•ō or **recipĕr•ō -āre** *vt* to regain, recover, get back; to win over again

recūr•ō -āre *vt* to restore, refresh, restore to health

re•currō -currĕre -currī *vi* to run back, hurry back; to return, recur, come back

recurs•ō -āre *vi* to keep running back; to keep recurring

recurs•us -ūs *m* return; retreat

recurv•ō -āre *vt* to curve, bend back

recurv•us -a -um *adj* curving, curved, bent, crooked

recusātī•ō -ōnis *f* refusal; (law) objection, protest; counterplea

recūs•ō -āre *vt* to raise objections to, reject, refuse; (with *inf*) to be reluctant to, refuse to; *vi* to raise an objection, object; to make a rebuttal

recuss•us -a -um *adj* reverberating

recutīt•us -a -um *adj* with the foreskin cut back, circumcised; Jewish

redactus *pp* of **redigo**

redambŭl•ō -āre *vi* to walk back

redăm•ō -āre *vt* to love in return

redargu•ō -ĕre -ī *vt* to disprove, contradict, refute

redauspĭc•ō -āre *vi* to take the return auspices; (coll) to return

red•dō -dĕre -dĭdī -dĭtum *vt* to give back, return, restore, replace; to repay; to repeat, recite (*words*); to translate; to render, make; to give as due, pay, deliver; to reflect, reproduce, imitate; **se reddere** to return, come back

redemptī•ō -ōnis *f* ransoming; bribing; revenue collection

redempt•ō -āre *vt* to ransom, repeatedly

redempt•or -ōris *m* contractor; revenue agent

redemptūr•a -ae *f* revenue collection

redemptus *pp* of **redimo**

red•ĕō -īre -ĭī -ĭtum *vi* to go or come back, return; (of a speaker) to return (*to the main theme*); (with **ad** + *acc*) **a** to return to, revert to; **b** to fall back on, have recourse to, be reduced to; **c** (of power, inheritances, etc.) to revert to, devolve upon; **ad se redire** to come to again, regain consciousness; to control oneself

redhāl•ō -āre *vt* to exhale

redhib•ĕō -ēre — -ĭtum *vt* to take back

red•ĭgō -igĕre -ēgī -actum *vt* to drive back, lead back, bring back; to call in, collect, raise (*money, revenues*); to reduce, diminish (*numbers*); to force, compel, subdue, reduce; (with double *acc*) to render, make; (with **in** or **sub** + *acc*) to bring under the power of; **ad vanum et irritum redigere** to make meaningless; **in memoriam redigere** to remember, recall; **in provinciam redigere** to reduce to the rank of a province

redimīcŭl•um -ī *n* band, chaplet, fillet; chain, fetter

redim•ĭō -īre -ĭī -ītum *vt* to crown, wreathe

red•ĭmō -imĕre -ēmī -emptum *vt* to buy back; to ransom, redeem; to buy off, rescue by payment, rescue, release, set free; to buy up; to buy off, ward off, avert; to pay for, compensate for, atone for; to get by contract, collect under contract

redintĕgr•ō -āre *vt* to make whole again, restore, refresh; (mil) to bring to full strength

redipisc•or -ī *vt* to get back

reditī•ō -ōnis *f* return

redĭt·us -ūs *m* return; revenue, proceeds, returns; (of heavenly bodies) revolution, orbit; (fig) restoration

redivĭa see **reduvia**

redivīv·us -a -um *adj* second-hand (*building materials*)

redol·ĕō -ēre -ŭī *vt* to smell of; *vi* to smell, be redolent

redomĭt·us -a -um *adj* retamed, broken in again

redōn·ō -āre *vt* to restore, give back again; to give up, abandon

redorm·ĭō -īre *vi* to go to sleep again

re·dūcō -dūcĕre -duxī -ductum *vt* to draw back; to lead back, bring back; to escort (*official as mark of honor to his home*); to remarry (*after a separation*); to restore to normal; to withdraw (*troops*); **in gratiam reducere** to restore to favor

reductĭ·ō -ōnis *f* restoration

reduct·or -ōris *m* restorer

reduct·us -a -um *pp* of **reduco;** remote, secluded, aloof, removed

redunc·us -a -um *adj* bent backwards, curved backwards

redundantĭ·a -ae *f* excess; redundancy

redund·ō -āre *vi* to overflow; to be too numerous, be too large; to be soaked (*e.g., with blood*); (with *abl*) to abound in; (with **de** or **ex** + *abl*) to stream from, overflow with

reduvĭ·a or **redivĭ·a -ae** *f* hangnail, loose fingernail

red·ux -ūcis *adj* guiding back, rescuing; brought back, restored

refectus *pp* of **reficio**

refell·ō -ĕre -ī *vt* to refute, disprove

re·fercĭō -fercīre -fersī -fertum *vt* to stuff, cram, choke, crowd

refer·ĭō -īre *vt* to strike back, hit back

refĕrō referre rettŭlī relātum *vt* to bring back, carry back; to give back, return, restore, pay back, repay; to bring back, return, echo (*a sound*); to renew, revive, repeat; to bring back, direct, focus, turn (*mind, attention*); to present again, represent; to say in turn, answer, reply; to announce, report, relate, tell; to note down, enter, register, record; to reckon, consider, regard; to refer, attribute, ascribe; to bring up, spit out, vomit; **gradum referre** to go back, retreat; **gratiam** or **gratias referre** to return thanks, show gratitude; **in rationibus referendis** in accounting; **pedem referre** to go back, retreat, withdraw, retire; **pedes fertque refertque** he walks up and down; **rationes referre ad aerarium** to make an accounting to the treasury; **se referre** to go back, return; **vestigia referre** to retrace footsteps, return; *vi* to make a motion, make a proposal; **ad senatum referre** (with **de** + *abl*) to bring before the senate the matter of, make a proposal to the senate about; *v impers* it is of importance, it is of consequence; **meā (tuā, nostrā) refert** it is of importance, of consequence, of advantage to me (*you, us*); **non refert utrum** it makes no difference whether; **parvi refert** (with *inf*) it is of little importance, of little advantage to; **quid refert?** what's the difference?

refert·us -a -um *pp* of **refercio;** *adj* stuffed, packed, crammed; crowded

referv·ĕō -ēre *vi* to boil over, bubble over

refervesc·ō -ĕre *vi* to begin to boil or bubble

re·ficĭō -ficĕre -fēcī -fectum *vt* to rebuild, repair, restore; to revive (*hope, etc.*); to refresh, invigorate; to get (*e.g., money*) back again; to reappoint, reelect

re·fīgō -fīgĕre -fixī -fixum *vt* to unfasten, undo; to take down (*pictures, posters, etc.*); to annul (*laws*)

refing·ō -ĕre *vt* to refashion

refixus *pp* of **refigo**

reflāgĭt·ō -āre *vt* to demand again, ask back

reflāt·us -ūs *m* head wind

re·flectō -flectĕre -flexī -flexum *vt* to bend back or backwards, turn around, turn away; (fig) to turn back, bring back, change

refl·ō -āre *vt* to breathe out again; *vi* to blow in the wrong direction

reflŭ·ō -ĕre *vi* to flow back, run back; to overflow

reflŭ·us -a -um *adj* ebbing, receding

refocill·ō -āre *vt* to rewarm; to revive

reformāt·or -ōris *m* reformer

reformīdātĭ·ō -ōnis *f* dread

reformīd·ō -āre *vt* to dread, stand in awe of; to shrink from, shun

reform·ō -āre *vt* to reshape, remold, transform

re·fovĕō -fovēre -fōvī -fōtum *vt* to warm again; to restore, revive, refresh

refractārĭŏl·us -a -um *adj* a bit refractory, somewhat stubborn

refractus *pp* of **refringo**

refrāg·or -ārī -ātus sum *vi* (with *dat*) to oppose, resist, thwart

refrēn·ō -āre *vt* to curb, restrain, keep down, control

refrĭc·ō -āre -ŭī -ātum *vt* to rub open, scratch open; to irritate, reopen, inflame (*a wound*); (fig) to irritate, exasperate; (fig) to renew; *vi* to break out again

refrīgerātĭ·ō -ōnis *f* coolness

refrīgĕr·ō -āre *vt* to cool off, cool, chill; to refresh; to weary, exhaust; **refrigerari** to grow cool, grow weary

re·frīgescō -frīgescĕre -frixī *vi* to grow cool, become cool; (fig) to lose force, flag, abate, fail, grow dull, grow stale, fall flat

re·fringō -fringĕre -frēgī -fractum *vt* to break open, break down; to tear off (*clothes*); (fig) to break, check, destroy, put an end to

re·fugiō -fugĕre -fūgī *vt* to run away from; to avoid; *vi* to run away, escape; to disappear

refug·ium -iī or **-ī** *n* place of refuge; recourse

refŭg·us -a -um *adj* receding, vanishing; *m* fugitive

re·fulgĕō -fulgēre -fulsī *vi* to gleam, reflect, reflect light, glitter

re·fundō -fundĕre -fūdī -fūsum *vt* to pour back, pour out; **refundi** to flow back, overflow

refūtāti·ō -ōnis *f* refutation

refūtāt·us -ūs *m* refutation

refūt·ō -āre *vt* to repress, suppress; to refute, disprove

rēgāl·is -e *adj* kingly, regal; king's, of a king, royal

rēgālĭter *adv* royally, in royal style, splendidly; despotically

regĕl·ō -āre *vt* to cool off; to thaw

re·gĕrō -gerĕre -gessī -gestum *vt* to carry back, throw back; (fig) to throw back (*remarks*)

rēgĭ·a -ae *f* palace, castle, court; fortress, residence; (in camp) king's tent; royal family, king and courtiers, court; regia (*originally the palace of King Numa on the Sacred Way in the Roman Forum and later the residence of the Pontifex Maximus*)

rēgiē *adv* royally; despotically

Rēgiens·is -e or **Rēgīn·us -a -um** *adj* of Regium; *m pl* inhabitants of Regium

rēgific·us -a -um *adj* royal, kingly, magnificent

regign·ō -ĕre *vt* to reproduce

Rēgillān·us -a -um or **Rēgillens·is -e** *adj* of or at Lake Regillus

rēgill·us -a -um *adj* royal, magnificent

Rēgill·us -ī *m* lake in Latium famous for the victory over the Latins won by the Romans under the dictator Postumius (496 B.C.)

regĭm·en -ĭnis *n* steering, controlling; rudder; government, rule, command, guidance; director, ruler, governor

rēgīn·a -ae *f* queen; princess; noble woman, lady

regi·ō -ōnis *f* straight line, line, direction; boundary, boundary line; region, area, quarter, neighborhood; ward (*of Rome*); district, province (*of a country*); department, sphere; **ab recta regione** in a straight line; **de recta regione deflectere** to veer off from a straight path; **e regione** in a straight line, directly; **e regione** (with *genit*) in the opposite direction to, exactly opposite; **rectā regione** by a direct route

regiōnātim *adv* by wards, by districts

Rēg·ium or **Rhēg·ium -iī** or **-ī** *n* city on the toe of Italy; town in Cisalpine Gaul

rēgi·us -a -um *adj* king's, kingly, royal, regal; like a king, worthy of a king, magnificent; *m pl* the king's troops; *f* see **regia**

reglūtin·ō -āre *vt* to unglue

regnāt·or -ōris *m* ruler, sovereign

regnātr·ix -īcis *adj fem* imperial

regn·ō -āre *vi* to be king, reign; to be supreme, hold sway; to domineer; (with *genit*) to be king of; (with **in** + *acc*) to rule over; **regnari** to be ruled by a king, be under a king

regn·um -ī *n* monarchy, royal power, kingship; absolute power, despotism, power; supremacy, control, direction, sovereignty; realm, kingdom; domain, estate

regō regĕre rexī rectum *vt* to keep in a straight line; keep in a proper course; to guide, conduct; to govern, rule, command; to manage, direct; **regere finis** (law) to mark out the limits

re·gredior -grĕdī -gressus sum *vi* to step or go back; to come back, return; to march back, retreat

regress·us -ūs *m* return; retreat

rēgŭl·a -ae *f* ruler (*for measuring*); straight stick; straight board; rule, standard, example, model, principle

rēgŭl·us -ī *m* petty king, prince, chieftain; prince

Rēgŭl·us -ī *m* M. Atilius Regulus (*Roman general who was taken prisoner by the Carthaginians in the First Punic War, refused to let himself be ransomed, and was killed in* 250 B.C.)

regust·ō -āre *vt* to taste again; (fig) to delve again into (*e.g., literature*)

rē·iciō -icĕre -jēcī -jectum *vt* to throw back, fling back; to throw over one's shoulders or behind one; to beat back, repel, repulse; to reject, refuse, disdain, scorn; (of judges) to challenge, overrule; to refer, direct, assign; to postpone; **rem reicere** (with **ad** + *acc*) to turn over or refer the matter to (*someone for consideration or decision*); **potestas reiciendi** (law) right to challenge

rējectānĕ·us -a -um *adj* to be rejected

rējecti·ō -ōnis *f* rejection; (law) challenging; **rejectio judicum** challenging of the members of the jury

rēject·ō -āre *vt* to throw back

rējectus *pp* of **reicio**

re·lābor -lābī -lapsus sum *vi* to slide or glide back; to sink down (*upon a couch*); (of rivers) to flow back; to sail back; (fig) to return

relangu·escō -escĕre -ī *vi* to faint; to be relaxed, relax; to weaken

relāti·ō -ōnis *f* report (*made by a*

magistrate to the senate or emperor); repetition, reiteration; **relatio criminis** (law) answering to a charge
relāt·or -ōris *m* proposer of a motion
relātus *pp* of **refero**
relāt·us -ūs *m* official report; narration, recital, listing; **relatus carminum** recital of poems
relaxātĭ·ō -ōnis *f* relaxation, easing; mitigation
relax·ō -āre *vt* to stretch out, widen, open; to loosen, open; to release, set free; to ease, ease the tensions of, relieve, cheer up; to alleviate, mitigate
relectus *pp* of **relego**
relēgātĭ·ō -ōnis *f* banishment, sending into retirement
relēg·ō -āre *vt* to send away, remove, send into retirement, retire; to banish; to put aside, reject; to refer
re·lĕgō -legĕre -lēgī -lectum *vt* to collect again, gather up, gather together, to travel over, sail over again; to go over, review (*in thought, in a speech*); to reread
relentesc·ō -ĕre *vi* to slack off, cool off
relĕv·ō -āre *vt* to lighten; to lift up or raise again; (fig) to relieve, free, lighten, soothe, alleviate
relictĭ·ō -ōnis *f* abandonment
relictus *pp* of **relinquo**
relicŭus see **reliquus**
religātĭ·ō -ōnis *f* tying back, tying up
religĭ·ō -ōnis *f* religious scruple, conscientiousness, sense of right; misgivings; reverence, awe; religion; superstition; sanctity, holiness; religion, sect, cult, mode of worship; object of veneration, sacred object, sacred place; divine service, worship, religious observation
religiōsē *adv* scrupulously, conscientiously, carefully, exactly; reverently, piously, religiously
religiōs·us -a -um *adj* scrupulous, conscientious, exact, precise, accurate; religious, reverent, pious, devout; superstitious; sacred, holy, consecrated; subject to religious claims, under religious liability
relĭg·ō -āre *vt* to bind back, tie up; to moor (*a ship*); to unbind, untie, loosen; (fig) to bind
re·lĭnō -linĕre -lēvī — *vt* to unseal, open
re·linquō -linquĕre -līquī -lictum *vt* to leave behind, not take along; to leave behind, bequeath; to permit to remain, let remain; to leave alive; to forsake, abandon, desert, leave in a lurch; to give up, abandon, relinquish, resign; to leave unmentioned; **locum integrum relinquere** to leave the place untouched
reliquĭ·ae -ārum *f pl* remains, remnants
relĭqu·us or **relicŭ·us -a -um** *adj* remaining, left over, left; remaining, subsequent, future (*time*); outstanding (*debt*); *m pl* the others; *n* remainder, rest, residue; **in reliquum** in the future, for the future; **nihil reliqui facere** to leave nothing undone, omit nothing, leave no stone unturned; **reliqui omnes** all the rest; **reliquum est** (with *inf* or **ut**) it only remains to; **reliquum aliquem facere** to leave someone behind; to spare someone; **reliquum aliquid facere** or **aliquid reliqui facere** to leave something remaining, leave something behind, neglect something
rellig- = **relig-**
relliq- = **reliq-**
re·lūcĕō -lūcēre -luxī *vi* to reflect light, gleam, shine out, blaze
re·lūcescō -lūcescĕre -luxī *vi* to grow bright again, clear
reluct·or -ārī -ātus sum *vi* to fight back, put up a struggle, resist; to be reluctant
re·manĕō -manēre -mansī *vi* to stay behind; to remain, continue (*in a certain state*)
remān·ō -āre *vi* to flow back
remansĭ·ō -ōnis *f* staying behind, stay
remed·ĭum -ĭī or **-ī** *n* remedy, cure, antidote, medicine
remensus *pp* of **remetior**
remĕ·ō -āre *vt* to retrace, relive; *vi* to go or come back, return
re·mētĭor -mētīrī -mensus sum *vt* to remeasure; to retrace, go back over
rēm·ex -ĭgis *m* rower, crew member, oarsman
Rēm·ī -ōrum *m pl* a people of Gaul (*near modern Rheims*)
rēmigātĭ·ō -ōnis *f* rowing
rēmig·ĭum -ĭī or **-ī** *n* rowing; oars; oarsmen, rowers
rēmĭg·ō -āre *vi* to row
remĭgr·ō -āre *vi* to move back, go back, return
reminisc·or -ī *vt* to call to mind, remember; *vi* to remember; (with *genit*) to be mindful of, conscious of, remember
re·miscĕō -miscēre — -mixtum *vt* to mix up, intermingle; **veris falsa remiscere** to intermingle lies with truth
remissē *adv* mildly, gently
remissĭ·ō -ōnis *f* release; easing, letting down, lowering; relaxing (*of muscles*); relaxation, recreation; mildness, gentleness; submissiveness; abatement, diminishing; remission (*of debts*)
remiss·us -a -um *adj* relaxed, loose, slack; mild, gentle; negligent, remiss; easy-going, indulgent, yielding; gay, merry, light; low, cheap (*price*)
re·mittō -mittĕre -mīsī -missum *vt* to send back; to release; to slacken, loosen; to emit, produce, let out,

yield, send forth, give off; to send back, return, restore; to give up, reject, resign, concede; to relax, relieve (*the mind*); to pardon; to remit, remove (*penalty*); (with *inf*) to stop (*doing something*); *vi* (of wind, rain, etc.) to slack off, abate

remixtus *pp* of **remisceo**

remōl·ior -īrī -ītus sum *vt* to push or move back or away, heave back

remollesc·ō -ĕre *vi* to get soft again, soften; to weaken

remŏr·a -ae *f* hindrance, delay

remorāmĭn·a -um *n pl* hindrances, delays

re·mordĕō -mordēre — -morsum *vt* to bite back; to attack in return; to disturb, annoy, worry, torture

remŏr·or -ārī -ātus sum *vt* to delay, hinder, hold back, detain; *vi* to loiter, delay, linger, stay behind

remōtē *adv* at a distance, far away

remōtĭ·ō -ōnis *f* removal

remōt·us -a -um *adj* removed, out of the way, far off, remote, distant; (fig) remote, apart, separate, clear, free; dead; (with **ab** + *abl*) removed from, separate from, apart from, clear of, free from

re·movĕō -movēre -mōvī -mōtum *vt* to move back, withdraw, put away, remove; to shroud, veil; (fig) put out of sight, set aside, abolish; to subtract

remūg·iō -īre *vi* to bellow back; to resound, reecho

re·mulcĕō -mulcēre -mulsī *vt* to stroke, smooth back; **caudam remulcere** to put the tail between the legs (*in fear*)

remulc·um -ī *n* tow rope, tow line

remūnerātĭ·ō -ōnis *f* remuneration, reward, recompense, repayment

remūnĕr·or -ārī -ātus sum *vt* to repay, reward

remurmŭr·ō -āre *vi* to murmur back in reply

rēm·us -ī *m* oar; (fig) wing; **remi corporis** hands and feet (*of a swimmer*)

Rem·us -ī *m* brother of Romulus

renarr·ō -āre *vt* to tell over again, recount

re·nascor -nascī -nātus sum *vi* to be born again; to rise again, spring up again, be restored; to reappear; to recur

renāvĭg·ō -āre *vi* to sail back

ren·ĕō -ēre *vt* to unravel, undo

rēn·ēs -um *m pl* kidneys

renīd·ens -entis *adj* beaming, glad

renīd·ĕō -ēre *vi* to reflect, reflect light, glitter, shine; to smile, grin all over; to beam with joy

renīdesc·ō -ĕre *vi* to begin to reflect light, begin to glitter

renīt·or -ī *vi* to put up a struggle, fight back, resist

ren·ō -āre *vi* to swim back, float back

rēn·ō or **rhēn·ō -ōnis** *m* fur

renōd·ō -āre *vt* to tie back in a knot; to untie

renovām·en -inis *n* renewal, new condition

renovātĭ·ō -ōnis *f* renovation, renewal; revision; compound interest

renŏv·ō -āre *vt* to make new again; to renovate, repair, restore; to plow up (*a fallow field*); to reopen (*wounds*); to revive (*old customs, etc.*); to start (*battles*) all over again; to refresh (*the memory*); to repeat, keep repeating, reaffirm; **faenus renovare in singulos annos** to compound the interest on a yearly basis

renumĕr·ō -āre *vt* to count over again, recount; to pay back, repay

renuntiātĭ·ō -ōnis *f* formal or official report, announcement

renuntĭ·ō -āre *vt* to report; to announce; to retract (*promise, etc.*); to renounce, call off, reject; (with double *acc*) to announce or declare elected as; (with *acc & inf*) to bring back word that

renunt·ius -iī or **-ī** *m* bringer of news, reporter

re·nŭō -nuĕre -nŭī *vt* to nod refusal to, deny, refuse, turn down, decline, say not to, reject; *vi* to shake the head in refusal, refuse, say no; (with *dat*) to say no to, deny (*a charge*)

renūt·ō -āre *vt* to refuse emphatically

reor rērī ratus sum *vt* to think, deem; (with *acc & inf*) to think that; (with *acc & adj* as objective complement) to regard (*something*) as; *vi* to think, suppose

repāgŭl·a -ōrum *n pl* bolts, bars; (fig) restraints, regulations, rules, limits

repand·us -a -um *adj* curved backwards, concave; (*shoes*) with turned-up toes

reparābĭl·is -e *adj* capable of being repaired, reparable, retrievable

reparc·ō -ĕre *vi* (with *dat*) to be sparing with, take it easy with

repăr·ō -āre *vt* to get again, acquire again; to recover, retrieve, make good; to restore, renew, repair; to recruit (*a new army*); **vina merce reparare** to get wine in exchange for wares, barter for wine

repastinātĭ·ō -ōnis *f* digging up again

re·pectō -pectĕre — -pexum *vt* to comb back; to comb again, recomb

repellō repellĕre reppŭlī repulsum *vt* to drive back, push back, repel, repulse; to reject; to remove; to refute

re·pendō -pendĕre -pendī -pensum *vt* to repay, pay back; to ransom, redeem; (fig) to repay in kind, requite, recompense, reward; to compensate for; to balance, balance out; **magna rependere** to pay back in full

rep·ens -entis *adj* sudden, unexpected, unlooked-for, hasty

repensus *pp* of **rependo**

repentē *adv* suddenly, unexpectedly, all of a sudden
repentīnō *adv* suddenly, unexpectedly
repentīn·us -a -um *adj* sudden, unpected, unlooked-for; hasty, impetuous
reperc·ō -ĕre *vi* (with *dat*) **a** to be sparing with; **b** to refrain from
repercussus *pp* of **repercutio;** *adj* rebounding; reflected, reflecting; echoed, echoing
repercuss·us -ūs *m* rebounding, reverberation, echo, repercussion
reper·cutĭō -cutĕre -cussī -cussum *vt* to make (*something*) rebound, reverberate, or reflect
reperĭō reperīre reppĕrī repertum *vt* to find, find again, discover; to get, procure, obtain, win; to find out, ascertain, learn, realize; to invent, devise
repert·or -ōris *m* discoverer, inventor, author
repert·us -a -um *pp* of **reperio;** *n pl* discoveries, inventions
repetītĭ·ō -ōnis *f* repetition; (rhet) anaphora, repetition
repetīt·or -ōris *m* claimant
repĕt·ō -ĕre -īvī or **-ĭī -ītum** *vt* to head back to, try to reach again, return to; to aim at again; to fetch back; to attack again; to prosecute again; to demand anew; to demand back, claim, demand in compensation, retake; to trace back, retrace; to trace in thought, think over, recall, recollect; to trace back (*in speech*); to repeat, undertake again, resume, renew; **lex de pecuniis** (or **rebus**) **repetundis** law on extortion, extortion law; **pecuniam repetere** to sue for the recovery of money; **res repetere** to sue for the recovery of property; **reus pecuniarum repetundarum** guilty of extortion
repetund·ae -ārum *f pl* extortion; money extorted; **repetundarum argui** to be charged with extortion; **repetundarum teneri** to be held on an extortion charge
repexus *pp* of **repecto**
replĕō -plēre -plēvī -plētum *vt* to refill, fill up, replenish; to fill to overflowing; to make up for, replace, compensate for; to recruit, bring (*an army*) to full strength
replēt·us -a -um *adj* filled, full; well provided
replicātĭ·ō -ōnis *f* folding back, rolling back, rolling up; reflex action
replĭc·ō -āre *vt* to fold back, unfold, turn back
rēp·ō -ĕre -sī *vi* to creep, crawl
re·pōnō -pōnĕre -posŭī -posĭtum or **repostum** *vt* to put back, set back, lay (*e.g., the head*) back; to replace; to restore; to substitute; to lay out, stretch out (*the body*); to lay aside, store, keep, preserve; to lay aside, put away; to renew, repeat; to place, class; to replay, requite; **in sceptra reponere** to reinstate in power; **membra reponere** (with *abl* or **in** + *abl*) to stretch out on (*e.g., a bed*); **se in cubitum reponere** to rest on one's elbow, prop oneself up on one's elbow; **spem reponere** (with **in** + *abl*) to put one's hope in or on, count on
report·ō -āre *vt* to bring back; to report; to carry off, gain, obtain; **victoriam reportare** to win a victory
reposc·ō -ĕre *vt* to demand back; to ask for, claim, require, demand
reposĭt·us -a -um *pp* of **repono;** *adj* distant, remote
repost·or -ōris *m* restorer
repostus *pp* of **repono**
repōtĭ·a -ōrum *n pl* second round of drinks
repraesentātĭ·ō -ōnis *f* vivid presentation; cash payment
repraesent·ō -āre *vt* to present again, show, exhibit, display, depict; to pay in cash; to do immediately, accomplish instantly, do on the spot; to rush, speed up (*e.g., plans*); to anticipate; to apply (*medicines*) immediately
repreh·endō or **repr·endō -endĕre -endī -ensum** *vt* to hold back; to restrain, check; to blame, find fault with, rebuke, criticize; (law) to prosecute, convict, condemn; to refute
reprehensĭ·ō -ōnis *f* checking, check; interruption (*of a speech*); blame, rebuke, criticism; refutation
reprehens·ō -āre *vt* to hold back continually; to detain from time to time
reprehens·or -ōris *m* critic
repress·or -ōris *m* restrainer
re·prĭmō -primĕre -pressī -pressum *vt* to hold back, keep back; to restrain, limit, confine, curb, repress, suppress; **se reprimere** to control oneself; **se reprimere** (with **ab** + *abl*) to refrain from
reprōmissĭ·ō -ōnis *f* return promise
reprō·mittō -mittĕre -mīsī -missum *vt* to promise in return
rept·ō -āre *vi* to creep or crawl around
repudiātĭ·ō -ōnis *f* repudiation; refusal, rejection
repudĭ·ō -āre *vt* to repudiate, scorn; to refuse, reject; to jilt; to divorce
repudiōs·us -a -um *adj* objectionable, offensive
repud·ĭum -ĭī or **-ī** *n* repudiation, separation, divorce; **repudium renuntiare** or **repudium remittere** (with *dat*) to send a letter of divorce to, divorce
repuerasc·ō -ĕre *vi* to become a child again; to behave childishly
repugn·ans -antis *n* contradiction
repugnanter *adv* reluctantly
repugnantĭ·a -ae *f* incompatibility
repugn·ō -āre *vi* to fight back; (with *dat*) **a** to oppose, offer opposition to, fight against, be against; **b** to

disagree with, be inconsistent with, be incompatible with; (with **contra** + *acc*) to fight against
repuls·a -ae *f* defeat at the polls; rebuff, cold shoulder; **repulsa consulatūs** defeat in running for the consulship; **repulsam ferre** to lose an election
repuls·ans -antis *adj* throbbing; reechoing
repulsus *pp* of **repello**
repuls·us -ūs *m* reverberation, echo
repung·ō -ĕre *vt* to goad again
repurg·ō -āre *vt* to clean or clear again; to purge away, remove
reputāti·ō -ōnis *f* reconsideration, review
repŭt·ō -āre *vt* to count back, calculate; to think over, reflect upon, reconsider
requĭ·ēs -ētis *f* rest, relief; relaxation, recreation
requi·escō -escĕre -ēvī -ētum *vt* to put to rest, quiet down, calm down; *vi* to rest, take a rest, come to rest, stop, end; to rest, relax; to find rest, be consoled, find relief; to rest, lie quietly, sleep; (of the dead) to rest, sleep
requiēt·us -a -um *adj* rested up, refreshed
requīrĭt·ō -āre *vt* to keep asking for, be on a constant lookout for
re·quīrō -quīrĕre -quīsīvī or **-quīsiī -quīsītum** *vt* to look for, search for, hunt for; to look around for, miss; to ask; to ask for, demand, require; (with **ab** or **de** + *abl*) to ask or demand (*something*) from or of
rēs reī or **rĕī** *f* thing, matter, affair, object, business, circumstance, event, occurrence, deed, condition, case; reality, truth, fact; property, possessions, estate, effects; benefit, advantage, interest, profit; business affair, transaction; cause, reason, motive, ground; (law) case, suit; (mil) operation, campaign, battle; state, government, politics; historical event; theme, topic, subject matter; **ab re** contrary to interests, disadvantageous, useless; **contra rem publicam** unconstitutional(ly), contrary to public interests; **eā re** therefore, for that reason; **ex re** according to the circumstances, according to the situation; **ex re istius** for his good; **ex re publicā** constitutionally, for the common good, in the public interest; **ex tuā re** to your advantage; **in re** in fact, in reality; **in rem** for the good; useful, advantageous; **ob eam rem** for that reason; **ob rem** to the purpose; **pro re** according to circumstances; **re** in fact, in practice, in reality, in truth, actually, really; **rem gerere** to conduct a military operation; **rerum potiri** to get control of the government; **rerum scriptor** historian, annalist; **res est mihi tecum** I have some business with you; **res sit mihi cum his** let me handle them; **res frumentaria** foraging; grain situation, grain supply; **res gestae** exploits, achievements, military achievements; **res judiciaria** administration of justice, department of justice; **res novae** revolution; **res pecuaria et rustica** livestock; **res Persicae** Persian history, Parthian history; **res rustica** agriculture; **res publica** state, government, politics, public life, commonwealth, country; **res secundae** prosperous times, prosperity; **res uxoria** marriage; dowry; **summa rerum** world, universe
resăcr·ō -āre *vt* to ask again for; to free from a curse
resaev·ĭō -īre *vi* to go wild again
resalūt·ō -āre *vt* to greet in return
resān·escō -escĕre -ŭī *vi* to heal up again
re·sarcĭō -sarcīre — -sartum *vt* to patch up, repair; to make good (*a loss*)
re·scindō -scindĕre -scĭdī -scissum *vt* to tear off; to cut down; to tear open; to rescind, repeal, abrogate; (fig) to tear open, expose
re·sciscō -sciscĕre -scīvī or **-scĭī -scītum** *vt* to find out, learn, ascertain
re·scrībō -scrībĕre -scripsī -scriptum *vt* to write back in reply; to rewrite, revise; to enlist, enroll; to repay, pay back; *vi* to write a reply
rescript·um -ī *n* imperial rescript
resĕc·ō -āre -ŭī -tum *vt* to cut back, cut short; to reap; (fig) to trim, curtail; **ad vivum resecare** to cut to the quick
resĕcr·ō or **resăcr·ō -āre** *vt* to ask again for; to free from a curse
resectus *pp* of **reseco**
resecūtus *pp* of **resequor**
resēmĭn·ō -āre *vt* to reproduce
re·sĕquor -sĕquī -secūtus sum *vt* to reply to, answer
resĕr·ō -āre *vt* to unlock, unbar, open; to disclose; to open, begin (*a year*)
reserv·ō - āre *vt* to reserve, hold back; to spare; to hold on to
res·es -ĭdis *adj* remaining, left; lazy, idle, inactive; slow, sluggish; calm
re·sidĕō -sidēre -sēdī *vi* to remain seated; to stay behind, be left, remain; to tarry, linger; to stay, reside
re·sīdō -sīdĕre -sēdī *vi* to sit down, settle back; to sink down, sink, settle, subside; to calm down
residŭ·us -a -um *adj* remaining, left; in arrears, outstanding (*money*); *n* the remainder, rest
resign·ō -āre *vt* to unseal, open; to disclose, reveal; to give up, resign; to annul, cancel; to destroy (*confidence*)
resil·ĭō -īre -ŭī *vi* to spring back,

jump back; to recoil; to contract; to shrink back
resīm•us -a -um *adj* turned up, snub
rēsīn•a -ae *f* resin
resīnāt•us -a -um *adj* resined, rubbed with resin
resip•iō -ĕre *vt* to taste of, have the flavor of
resip•iscō -iscĕre -īvī or **-iī** or **-ŭī** *vi* to come to one's senses
resist•ens -entis *adj* firm, tough
re•sistō -sistĕre -stĭtī *vi* to stand still, stop, pause; to stay, stay behind, remain, continue; to resist, put up resistance; to rise again; (with *dat*) **a** to be opposed to, resist; **b** to reply to
re•solvō -solvĕre -solvī -solūtum *vt* to untie, unfasten, undo; to open; to dissolve, melt, thaw; to relax (*the body*); stretch out (*the limbs*); to unravel; to cancel; to dispel; to unnerve, enervate; to release, set free
resonābĭl•is -e *adj* resounding, answering (*echo*)
resŏn•ō -āre *vt* to repeat, reecho, resound with, make ring; *vi* to resound, ring, reecho; (with *dat* or **ad** + *acc*) to resound in answer to
resŏn•us -a -um *adj* resounding, reechoing
resorb•ĕō -ēre *vt* to suck in, swallow again
respect•ō -āre *vt* to look back on; to keep an eye on, care for; to have regard for; to gaze at, look at; *vi* to look back; to look around
respectus *pp* of **respicio**
respect•us -ūs *m* backward glance, looking back; looking around; refuge, asylum; regard, respect, consideration; **respectum habere** (with *dat* or **ad** + *acc*) to have respect for
re•spergō -spergĕre -spersī spersum *vt* to sprinkle, splash, spray; to defile
respersī•ō -ōnis *f* sprinkling, splashing
respersus *pp* of **respergo**
re•spicīō -spicĕre -spexī -spectum *vt* to look back at, see behind oneself; to look back for, look around for; to look back upon (*the past, etc.*); to look at, gaze at, look upon, regard, contemplate, consider; to notice; to look after, take care of, see to; to respect; *vi* to look back; to look around; (with **ad** + *acc*) to look at, gaze at
respīrām•en -ĭnis *n* windpipe
respīrātī•ō -ōnis *f* respiration, breathing; exhalation; letup, rest, pause (*to catch one's breath*), breathing space
respīrāt•us -ūs *m* respiration
respīr•ō -āre *vt* to breathe, breathe out, exhale; *vi* to breathe, take a breath; to catch one's breath, breathe again, recover (*from fright, etc.*); (of combat, passions, etc.) to slack off, die down, subside; **a continuis cladibus respirare** to catch one's breathe again after continuous fighting; **ab metu respirare** to breathe again after a shock
resplend•ĕō -ēre *vi* to glitter
re•spondĕō -spondēre -spondī -sponsum *vt* to answer; to say in reply; **ficta respondere** to make up answers; **multa respondere** to give a lengthly reply; **par pari respondere** to answer tit for tat; **verbum verbo respondere** to answer word for word; *vi* to answer, respond, reply; to echo; (law) to answer (*to bail*), appeal (*in court*); (of lawyers) to give an opinion, give legal advice; (of priests, oracles) to give a response; (with *dat*) **a** to answer, reply to; **b** to match, balance, correspond to, be equal to, resemble, measure up to; **amori amore respondere** to return love for love
responsī•ō -ōnis *f* response, answer, reply; refutation; **sibi ipsi responsio** a reply to one's own arguments
responsĭt•ō -āre *vi* to give professional advice
respons•ō -āre *vi* to answer, reply; to reecho; (with *dat*) **a** to answer to, agree with; **b** to resist, defy; **c** to answer back to (*in disobedience or defiance*)
respons•or -ōris *m* answerer
respons•us -a -um *pp* of **respondeo;** *n* answer, response, reply; professional advice, oracular response; **responsum auferre** or **ferre** (with **ab** + *abl*) to receive an answer from; **responsum referre** to deliver an answer
rēspūblĭca reīpūblĭcae *f* state, government, politics, public life, commonwealth, country
respŭ•ō -ĕre -ī *vt* to spit out, cast out, eject, expel; to reject, refuse, dislike, spurn
restagn•ō -āre *vi* to form pools; to run over, overflow; to be inundated
restaur•ō -āre *vt* to restore, rebuild
resticŭl•a -ae *f* thin rope, cord
restinctī•ō -ōnis *f* quenching
re•stinguō -stinguĕre -stinxī -stinctum *vt* to quench, extinguish, put out; to snuff out, extinguish, exterminate, destroy
restī•ō -ōnis *m* rope maker; (coll) roper (*person who whipped with ropes*)
restipulātī•ō -ōnis *f* counterclaim
restipŭl•or -ārī -ātus sum *vt* to stipulate in return
rest•is -is *f* rope
restĭt•ō -āre *vi* to stay behind, lag behind, hold back, hang back
restĭtr•ix -īcis *f* stay-behind (*female*)
re•stitŭō -stituĕre -stitŭī -stitūtum *vt* to set up again; to restore, rebuild, reconstruct; to renew, reestablish, revive; to bring back, re-

store, reinstate; to give back, return, replace; to restore, repair, remedy; to reenact (*a law*); to reverse, revoke, make void, undo, cancel; to make good, compensate for, repair

restitūtī·ō -ōnis *f* restoration; reinstatement, pardon; recall (*from exile*)

restitūt·or -ōris *m* restorer, rebuilder

restitūtus *pp* of **restituo**

re·stō -stāre -stitī *vi* to stand firm, stand one's ground, resist; to stay behind, stay in reserve; to be left, be left over; *v impers* (with *inf* or **ut**) it remains to (*do something*)

restrictē *adv* sparingly; exactly, precisely

restrict·us -a -um *adj* tied back, tight; stingy; moderate; strict, stern

re·stringō -stringĕre -strinxī -strictum *vt* to draw back tightly, tie back, tighten; (of dogs) to show (*the teeth*); (fig) to restrain

resūd·ō -āre *vt & vi* to sweat

result·ō -āre *vi* to rebound; to reverberate, resound

re·sūmō -sūmĕre -sumpsī -sumptum *vt* to take up again, resume; to recover (*strength*)

resupīn·ō -āre *vt* to throw (*someone*) on his back, throw over, throw down; (coll) to knock for a loop; to break down (*doors*)

resupīn·us -a -um *adj* bent back, thrown back; supine, lying on the back; leaning backward; proud, haughty (*gait*)

re·surgō -surgĕre -surrexī -surrectum *vi* to rise again, appear again

resuscĭt·ō -āre *vt* to resuscitate, revive, renew

retardātī·ō -ōnis *f* retarding, delaying

retard·ō -āre *vt* to slow down, retard, hold back, delay, keep back, check, hinder

rēt·e -is *n* net; (fig) trap

re·tĕgō -tegĕre -texī -tectum *vt* to uncover; to open

retempt·ō -are *vt* to attempt again, try again, test again

re·tendō -tendĕre -tendī -tentum or **-tensum** *vt* to release from tension, unbend, relax

retentī·ō -ōnis *f* holding back, slowing down; withholding (*of assent*)

retent·ō -āre *vt* to hold back, hold tight; to attempt again, try again, test again

retentus *pp of* **retendo** and **retineo**

re·texō -texĕre -texŭī -textum *vt* to unravel; to cancel, annul, reverse, undo; to weave anew; to renew, repeat; to correct, revise; to take back, retract (*words*)

rētiār·ĭus -ĭī or **-ī** *m* gladiator who tried to entangle his opponent in a net

reticentĭ·a -ae *f* reticence, silence; (rhet) abrupt pause; **poena reticentiae** punishment for suppressing the truth

retic·ĕō -ēre *vt* to be silent about, suppress, keep secret; *vi* to be silent, keep silence; (with *dat*) to make no answer to

rētĭcŭl·um -ī *n* small net; hair net; network bag, reticule (*for protecting bottles*); racket (*for playing ball*)

retinācŭl·a -ōrum *n pl* cable, rope, hawser, tether

retĭn·ens -entis *adj* (with *genit*) clinging to

retinentĭ·a -ae *f* recollection, retention

re·tinĕō -tinēre -tinŭī -tentum *vt* to hold back, keep back; to restrain; to keep, retain; to hold in reserve; to keep, preserve, maintain, uphold; to hold, engross (*attention*); to detain, delay

retinn·iō -īre *vi* to ring again, ring out

retŏn·ō -āre *vi* to resound

re·torquĕō -torquēre -torsī -tortum *vt* to twist or bend back; to hurl back (*weapons*); **mentem retorquere** to change the mind; **oculos retorquere** (with **ad** + *acc*) to look back wistfully at

retorrĭd·us -a -um *adj* parched, dried out, withered; wily, old, shrewd

retortus *pp* of **retorqueo**

retractātĭ·ō -ōnis *f* rehandling, retreatment; hesitation

retract·ō or **retrect·ō -āre** *vt* to rehandle, take in hand again, undertake once more, take up once more; to reexamine, review; to revise; *vi* to refuse, decline; to be reluctant

retract·us -a -um *adj* withdrawn, distant, remote

re·trăhō -trahĕre -traxī -tractum *vt* to draw back, withdraw, drag back; to bring to light again, make known again; (fig) to drag away, divert, remove, turn

retrectō see **retracto**

retrib·ŭō -uĕre -ŭī -ūtum *vt* to give back, restore, repay

retrō *adv* backwards, back, to the rear; behind, on the rear; in the past, formerly, back, past; in return, on the contrary, on the other hand

retrorsum or **retrorsus** *adv* back, backwards, behind; in reversed order

re·trūdō -trūdĕre — -trūsum *vt* to push back; to hide, conceal

retundō retundĕre retŭdī (or **rettŭdī**) **retunsum** (or **retūsum**) *vt* to pound back; to dull, blunt; (fig) to deaden, weaken, repress, restrain

retuns·us or **retūs·us -a -um** *adj* blunt, dull; (fig) dull

re·us -ī *m* defendant, plaintiff, the accused; convict, criminal, culprit

reval·escō -escĕre -ŭī *vi* to regain one's strength, recover; to become valid again
re·vĕhō -vehĕre -vexī -vectum *vt* to carry back, bring back; **revehi** to ride or drive back, sail back; (fig) to go back (*e.g., to an earlier period*)
re·vellō -vellĕre -vellī -vulsum *vt* to pull out, pull back, tear off, tear out; to tear up (*the ground*), dig up; (fig) to abolish, remove
revēl·ō -āre *vt* to unveil, uncover
re·veniō -venīre -vēnī -ventum *vi* to come again, come back, return
rēvērā *adv* in fact, actually
rēverbĕr·ō -āre *vt* to beat back, repel
reverend·us -a -um *adj* venerable, awe-inspiring
revĕr·ens -entis *adj* reverent, respectful
reverenter *adv* respectfully
reverentĭ·a -ae *f* awe, respect, reverence
rever·ĕor -ērī -ĭtus sum *vt* to revere, respect, stand in awe of
reversĭ·ō or **revorsĭ·ō -ōnis** *f* turning back (*before reaching one's destination*); recurrence (*of fever, etc.*)
revert·ō -ĕre -ī or **re·vertor** (or **re·vortor**) **-vertī -versus sum** *vi* to turn back, turn around, come back, return; (in speaking) to return, revert, recur
revictus *pp* of **revinco**
revid·ĕō -ēre *vt* to go back to see, revisit
re·vinciō -vincīre -vinxī -vinctum *vt* to tie back, tie behind, tie up
re·vincō -vincĕre -vīcī -victum *vt* to conquer, crush, repress; to refute, disprove, convict
revinctus *pp* of **revincio**
revir·escō -escĕre -ŭī *vi* to grow green again, become green again; to grow young again; to grow again, grow strong again, revive
revīs·ō -ĕre *vt* to go to see again, revisit; to look back to see; *vi* to come or go back; (with **ad** + *acc*) **a** to look at again, look back at; **b** to return to, revisit
re·vīviscō or **re·vīvescō -vīvescĕre -vixī** *vi* to come back to life, be restored to life, revive; (fig) to revive, recover, gain strength
revocābĭl·is -e *adj* revocable, capable of being recalled
revocām·en -ĭnis *n* recall
revocātĭ·ō -ōnis *f* calling back, calling away, recall; revoking, retracting (*of a word*)
revŏc·ō -āre *vt* to call back, recall; to recall, call off, withdraw (*troops*); to call back (*an actor, singer*) for an encore; to bring back to life, revive; (law) to arraign again; to recover, regain (*strength, etc.*); to resume (*career, studies*); to revoke, retract; to check, control; to cancel; (with **ad** + *acc*) to refer, apply, subject, submit (*someone or something*) to
revŏl·ō -āre *vi* to fly back
revolsus see **revulsus**
revolūbĭl·is -e *adj* able to be rolled back; **non revolubilis** irrevocable (*fate*)
re·volvō -volvĕre -volvī -volūtum *vt* to roll back, unroll, unwind; to retravel (*a road*); to unroll, read over, read again (*a book*); to reexperience; to go over, think over; **revolvi** to revolve, come around again, recur, return
revŏm·ō -ĕre -ŭī *vt* to vomit forth again, disgorge
revor- = **rever-**
revorr·ō -ĕre *vt* to sweep back, scatter again
revulsus *pp* of **revello**
rex rēgis *m* king; (with bad connotations during the republican period) tyrant, dictator; patron; rich man; leader, king (*in children's game*); queen bee
Rhadamanth·us -ī *m* son of Jupiter, brother of Minos, and one of the three judges in the lower world
Rhaet·ī -ōrum *m pl* people of Raetia
Rhaetĭ·a -ae *f* Alpine country between Germany and Italy
rhapsōdĭ·a -ae *f* Homeric lay, selection from Homer
Rhe·a -ae *f* Cybele
Rhe·a Silvĭ·a -ae *f* daughter of Numitor and mother of Romulus and Remus
rhēd- = **raed-**
Rhēg·ium -iī or **-ī** *n* town on the toe of Italy
rhēn·ō -ōnis *m* fur
Rhēnān·us -a -um *adj* Rhenish
Rhēn·us -ī *m* Rhine
Rhēs·us -ī *m* Thracian king who fought as an ally of Troy
rhēt·or -ŏris *m* rhetorician, teacher of rhetoric; orator
rhētorĭc·a -ae or **rhētorĭc·ē -ēs** *f* rhetoric
rhētorĭc·a -ōrum *n pl* treatise on rhetoric
rhētoricē *adv* rhetorically, in an oratorical manner
rhētorĭc·us -a -um *adj* rhetorician's, rhetorical; **doctores rhetorici** rhetoric professors; **libri rhetorici** rhetoric textbooks
rhīnocĕr·ōs -ōtis *m* rhinoceros; vessel made of a rhinoceros's tusk
rhō (indecl) *n* seventeenth letter of the Greek alphabet
Rhodăn·us -ī *m* Rhone
Rhodiens·is -e or **Rhodĭ·us -a -um** *adj* Rhodian, of Rhodes; *m pl* Rhodians
Rhodŏp·ē -ēs *f* mountain range in Thrace
Rhodopēĭ·us -a -um *adj* Thracian
Rhod·os or **Rhod·us -ī** *f* Rhodes (*island off the coast of Asia Minor*)
Rhoetē·us -a -um *adj* Trojan;

Rhoeteus ductor Aeneas; *m* promontory on the Dardanelles near Troy; sea near the promontory of Rhoeteum

rhomb·us -ī *m* magic wheel; turbot (*fish*)

rhomphae·a -ae *f* long javelin

rhythmĭc·us -a -um *adj* rhythmical; *m* teacher of prose rhythm

rhythm·os or **rhythm·us -ī** *m* rhythm, symmetry

rīc·a -ae *f* veil (*worn by Roman women at sacrifices*)

rīcīn·ĭum -ĭī or **-ī** *n* short mantle with a cowl

rict·um -ī *n* snout; wide-open mouth

rict·us -ūs *m* snout; wide-open mouth; **risū rictum diducere** to break into a grin; *m pl* jaws, gaping jaws

rīdĕō rīdēre rīsī rīsum *vt* to laugh at, ridicule; to smile upon; *vi* to smile, laugh; (with *dat* or **ad** + *acc*) to smile to

rīdibund·us -a -um *adj* laughing

rīdiculārĭ·us -a -um *adj* laughable, funny; *n pl* jokes

rīdicŭlē *adv* jokingly, humorously; ridiculously, absurdly

rīdiculōs·us -a -um *adj* funny, amusing; ridiculous

rīdicŭl·us -a -um *adj* funny, amusing, laughable; ridiculous, silly; *m* joker, clown; *n* joke

rig·ens -entis *adj* stiff, rigid, unbending

rig·ĕō -ēre *vi* to be still, be numb, stiffen; to be rigid, stand on end, stand erect; to stand stiff, rise

rig·escō -escĕre -ŭī *vi* to grow stiff, become numbed, stiffen, harden; to stand on end

rigĭdē *adv* rigorously, severely

rigĭd·us -a -um *adj* rigid, stiff, hard, inflexible; stern, rigid, severe; rough, rude

rig·ō -āre *vt* to wet, moisten, water; to conduct, convey (*water*)

rig·or -ōris *m* stiffness; numbness, cold; hardness; sternness, severity

rigŭ·us -a -um *adj* irrigating, watering; irrigated, watered

rīm·a -ae *f* crack; **rimas agere** to be cracked

rīm·or -ārī -ātus sum *vt* to lay open, tear open; to pry into, search, tear at, examine; to ransack; **naribus rimari** to sniff at

rīmōs·us -a -um *adj* full of cracks, leaky

ringor ringī rictus sum *vi* to open the mouth wide, to show the teeth; to snarl; (fig) to be snappy, snarl

rīp·a -ae *f* bank, shore

rīpŭl·a -ae *f* river bank

risc·us -ī *m* chest, trunk

rīsiōn·ēs -um *f pl* laughs

rīs·or -ōris *m* scoffer, teaser

rīs·us -ūs *m* laugh, smile, laughter; laughingstock; **risum continere** to keep back a laugh, keep from laughing; **risum movere** (with *dat* of person) to make (*someone*) laugh; **risūs captare** to try to make people laugh, try to get laughs

rīte *adv* according to religious usage; duly, justly, rightly, fitly; in the usual way, customarily

rīt·us -ūs *m* ceremony, rite; custom, habit, way, manner, style; **ritū** (with *genit*) in the manner of, like; **pecudum ritū** like cattle

rīvāl·is -is *m* one who uses the same stream, neighbor; one who uses the same mistress, rival

rīvālĭt·ās -ātis *f* rivalry in love

rīvŭl·us or **rīvŏl·us -ī** *m* brook, rivulet

rīv·us -ī *m* brook, stream

rix·a -ae *f* brawl, fight; quarrel, squabble

rix·or -ārī -ātus sum *vi* to brawl, come to blows, fight; to quarrel, squabble

rōbīginōs·us or **rūbīginōs·us -a -um** *adj* rusty; envious

rōbīg·ō -ĭnis *f* rust; blight, mildew; film (*on teeth*), tartar

rōborĕ·us -a -um *adj* oak, of oak

rōbŏr·ō -āre *vt* to make strong, strengthen

rōb·ur or **rōb·us -ŏris** *n* hard wood; oak; prison (*at Rome, also called Tullianum*); objects made of hard wood: lance, club, bench; physical strength, power, vigor, toughness; vigor, strength, power, quality (*of mind*); best part, flower, choice, cream, élite; stronghold

rōbust·us -a -um *adj* hardwood; oak; robust, strong, firm, tough (*body*); firm, vigorous, solid (*character*)

rōdō rōdĕre rōsī rōsum *vt* to gnaw, gnaw at; to rust, corrode; to say nasty things about, slander, run down

rogāl·is -e *adj* of a pyre

rogātĭ·ō -ōnis *f* proposal, referendum, bill, resolution; request; (rhet) question; **rogationem ferre** to introduce a bill; **rogationem perferre** to pass a bill; **rogationem suadere** to back, push, speak in favor of a bill; **rogationi intercedere** to veto a bill

rogātiuncŭl·a -ae *f* inconsequential bill; little question

rogāt·or -ōris *m* proposer (*of a bill to the people*); poll clerk (*who collected and counted votes*); beggar

rogāt·us -ūs *m* request

rogitātĭ·ō -ōnis *f* proposal

rogĭt·ō -āre *vt* to keep asking, keep asking for

rog·ō -āre *vt* to ask, ask for, beg, request, solicit, question; to invite; to nominate for election; to bring forward for approval, introduce, propose (*bill or resolution*); (with double *acc*) to ask (*someone for something*), ask (*someone something*); **legem rogare** to introduce a bill; **milites sacramento rogare** to swear in soldiers; **senatorem sententiam rogare** to ask a senator for his opinion, ask a senator how he votes; **sententias rogare** to call the roll (*in the senate*); **populum rogare** to ask the people about a bill, to propose or introduce a bill; **primus sententiam rogari** to have the honor of being the first (*senator*) to be asked his view, be the first to vote

rog·us -ī *m* funeral pile, pyre; (fig) grave, destruction

Rōm·a -ae *f* Rome

Rōmān·us -a -um *adj* Roman; *m pl* Romans

Rōmulē·us -a -um *adj* of Romulus

Rōmulĭd·ae -ārum *m pl* descendants of Romulus, Romans

Rōmŭl·us -a -um *adj* of Romulus; *m* Romulus (*son of Rhea Silvia and Mars, twin brother of Remus, and founder as well as first king of Rome*)

rōrārĭ·ī -ōrum *m pl* skirmishers (*light-armed Roman troops who usually initiated an attack and then withdrew*)

rōrĭd·us -a -um *adj* dewy

rōrĭf·er -ĕra -ĕrum *adj* dew-bringing, dewy

rōr·ō -āre *vt* to drip, trickle, pour drop by drop; to moisten; *vi* to drop dew, scatter dew

rōs rōris *m* dew; moisture; water; teardrop; **ros Arabus** perfume; **ros marinus** or **ros maris** rosemary; **rores pluvii** rain drops; **rores sanguinei** drops of blood

ros·a -ae *f* rose; rose bush; rose bed; wreath of roses

rosār·ĭum -ĭī or **-ī** *n* rose garden

roscĭd·us -a -um *adj* dewy; moistened, sprayed

Rosc·ĭus -ĭī or **-ī** *m* L. Roscius Otho (*friend of Cicero, whose law in* 67 B.C. *reserved fourteen rows of seats in the theater for members of equestrian order*); Q. Roscius (*famous Roman actor and friend of Cicero, d.* 62 B.C.); Sextus Roscius (*of Ameria, defended by Cicero in a patricide trial in* 80 B.C.)

rosēt·um -ī *n* rose bed, rose garden

rosĕ·us -a -um *adj* rosy, rose-colored; of roses

rosmarīn·um -ī *n* rosemary (*spice*)

rostrāt·us -a -um *adj* beaked; (ship) having a pointed bow; **columna rostrata** column adorned with the beaks of conquered vessels to commemorate a naval victory; **corona rostrata** navy medal (*awarded to the first man to board the enemy's ship*)

rostr·um -ī *n* bill, beak; snout, muzzle; curved bow (*of a ship*); *n pl* speaker's stand in the Roman Forum (*so called because it was adorned with the beaks of ships taken from the battle of Antium,* 338 B.C.)

rōsus *pp* of **rodo**

rot·a -ae *f* wheel; potter's wheel; torture wheel; disk; chariot, car

rot·ō -āre *vt* to turn, whirl about; **rotari** to roll around; to revolve

rotŭl·a -ae *f* little wheel

rotundē *adv* smoothly, elegantly

rotund·ō -āre *vt* to make round, round off; to round out, complete

rotund·us -a -um *adj* rolling, revolving; round, circular, spherical; rounded, perfect; well-turned, smooth, polished, balanced (*style*)

rube·faciō -facĕre -fēcī -factum *vt* to make red, redden

rubell·us -a -um *adj* reddish

rub·ens -entis *adj* red; blushing

rub·ĕō -ēre *vi* to be red, be ruddy; to be bloody; to blush

rub·er -ra -rum *adj* red; ruddy

rub·escō -escĕre -ŭī *vi* to grow red, redden; to blush

rubēt·a -ae *f* toad

rubēt·a -ōrum *n pl* bramble bush

rubĕ·us -a -um *adj* bramble, of brambles

Rubĭc·ō -ōnis *m* small stream marking the boundary between Italy and Cisalpine Gaul

rubicundŭl·us -a -um *adj* reddish

rubicund·us -a -um *adj* red; ruddy

rubĭd·us -a -um *adj* reddish, red

rūbĭg- = robig-

rub·or -ōris *m* redness; blush; bashfulness, sense of shame; shame, disgrace

rubrĭc·a -ae *f* red clay; red ochre; red chalk; rubric, law

rub·us -ī *m* bramble bush; blackberry bush; blackberry

ruct·ō -āre or **ruct·or -ārī -ātus sum** *vt & vi* to belch

ruct·us -ūs *m* belch, belching

rud·ens -entis *m* rope; *m pl* rigging

Rudĭ·ae -ārum *f pl* town in Calabria in S. Italy (*birthplace of Ennius*)

rudiār·ĭus -ĭī or **-ī** *m* retired gladiator

rudīment·um -ī *n* first attempt, beginning, commencement; **rudimentum adulescentiae ponere** to pass the novitiate; **rudimentum militare** basic training

Rudīn·us -a -um *adj* of Rudiae

rud·is -e *adj* in the natural state; raw, undeveloped, rough, wild, unformed; inexperienced, unskilled, ignorant, awkward, uncultured, uncivilized; (with *genit* or *abl*, with **ad** + *acc*, or with **in** + *abl*) inexperienced in, ignorant of, awkward at

rud·is -is *f* stick, rod; practice sword

rud·ō -ĕre -īvī -ītum *vi* to roar, bellow, bray; to creak

rūd·us -ĕris *n* crushed stone; rubble; rubbish; piece of brass or copper

rūfŭl·us -a -um *adj* reddish

Rūfŭl·ī -ōrum *m pl* military tribunes appointed by a general (*as opposed to military tribunes elected by the people*)

rūf·us -a -um *adj* red, reddish
rūg·a -ae *f* wrinkle
rūg·ō -āre *vi* to become wrinkled, become creased
rūgōs·us -a -um *adj* wrinkled, shriveled; corrugated
ruīn·a -ae *f* tumbling down, falling down, fall; collapse; debris, ruins; crash; catastrophe, disaster, destruction, defeat; wrecker, destroyer; **ruinam dare** or **trahere** to fall with a crash
ruīnōs·us -a -um *adj* going to ruin, ruinous, ruined, tumbling, fallen
rum·ex -icis *f* sorrel
rūmific·ō -āre *vt* to report
Rūmīn·a -ae *f* Roman goddess who was worshiped near the fig tree under which the she-wolf had suckled Romulus and Remus
Rūmīnāl·is -e *adj* **ficus Ruminalis** fig tree of Romulus and Remus
rūminātī·ō -ōnis *f* chewing of the cud; (fig) rumination
rūmin·ō -āre *vt* to chew again; *vi* to chew the cud
rūm·or -ōris *m* shouting, cheering, noise; rumor, hearsay; popular opinion, current opinion; reputation, fame; notoriety; calumny; **adverso rumore esse** to be in bad repute, be unpopular
rumpi·a -ae *f* long javelin
rumpō rumpĕre rūpī ruptum *vt* to break, break down, break open; to burst, burst through; to tear, split; to force, make (*e.g., a path*) by force; to break in on, interrupt, cut short; to break (*a law, treaty*); to break out in, utter (*complaints, etc.*)
rūmuscŭl·ī -ōrum *m pl* gossip
rūn·a -ae *f* dart
runc·ō -āre *vt* to weed, weed out
ru·ō -ĕre -ī -tum *vt* to throw down, hurl to the ground; to level (*e.g., sand dunes*); to destroy, overthrow, lay waste; to throw up, upturn, churn up; *vi* to fall hard, fall in ruins, totter; to run, dash, rush on, hurry; (of rain) to come pouring down; (of the sun) to set rapidly
rūp·ēs -is *f* cliff
rupt·or -ōris *m* breaker, violator
ruptus *pp* of **rumpo**
rūricŏl·a -ae *m* or *f* rustic, peasant, farmer; *m* ox
rūrigĕn·a -ae *m* rustic, peasant, farmer
rūr·ō -āre *vi* to live in the country
rursus or **rursum** or **rūsum** *adv* back, backwards; on the contrary, on the other hand, in turn; again, back again, once more; **rursus rursusque** again and again
rūs rūris *n* the country, countryside, lands, fields; farm, estate; **rure redire** to return from the country; **ruri** or **rure vitam agere** to live in the country; **rus ire** to go into the country; *n pl* countryside
rusc·um -ī *n* or **rusc·us -ī** *f* broom (*of twigs*)
russ·us -a -um *adj* red, russet
rusticān·us -a -um *adj* rustic, country, rural
rusticātī·ō -ōnis *f* country life
rusticē *adv* like a farmer; plainly, simply; unsophisticatedly, boorishly
rusticit·ās -ātis *f* simple country ways, rusticity; boorishness, coarseness
rustic·or -ārī -ātus sum *vi* to live in the country
rusticŭl·us -a -um *adj* somewhat coarse; *m* peasant
rustic·us -a -um *adj* of or in the country, country, rural; plain, simple, unspoiled, unsophisticated; coarse, boorish, rude; *m* farmer, peasant; *f* country girl
rūsum see **rursus**
rūt·a -ae *f* rue (*bitter herb*); bitterness, unpleasantness
rūt·a -ōrum *n pl* minerals; **ruta caesa** or **ruta et caesa** (law) everything mined or cut down on an estate, timber and minerals
rutil·ō -āre *vt* to make red, color red, dye red; *vi* to glow red
rutil·us -a -um *adj* red, reddish yellow; strawberry-blond
rutr·um -ī *n* spade
rūtŭl·a -ae *f* a bit of rue
Rutŭl·ī -ōrum *m pl* ancient people of Latium whose capital was Ardea
rutus *pp* of **ruo**

S

Sab·a -ae *f* town in Arabia Felix, famous for its incense
Sabae·us -a -um *adj* Sabaean
Sabāz·ius -iī or **-ī** *m* Bacchus; *n pl* festival in honor of Bacchus
sabbăt·a -ōrum *n pl* Sabbath
sabbatāri·ī -ōrum *m pl* Sabbath-keepers, Jews
Sabell·us -a -um *adj* Sabellian, Sabine; *m* Sabine (*i.e., Horace*)
Sabīn·us -a -um *adj & mf* Sabine; *n* Sabine wine; Horace's Sabine estate
Sabrīn·a -ae *f* Severn River
saburr·a -ae *f* sand, ballast
saburr·ō -āre *vt* to ballast; (coll) to gorge with food
Sac·ae -ārum *m pl* Scythian tribe
saccipĕr·ium -iī or **-ī** *n* purse pocket
sacc·ō -āre *vt* to filter, strain

saccŭl·us -ī *m* little bag; purse
sacc·us -ī *m* sack, bag; wallet; filter, strainer
sacell·um -ī *n* chapel
sac·er -ra -rum *adj* sacred, holy, consecrated; devoted to a deity for destruction, accursed; detestable; criminal, infamous; *n* see **sacrum**
sacerd·ōs -ōtis *m* priest; *f* priestess
sacerdōtāl·is -e *adj* sacerdotal
sacerdōt·ium -iī or **-ī** *n* priesthood
sacrāment·um -ī *n* guarantee, deposit (*sum of money which each of the parties to a law suit deposited and which was forfeited by the loser*); civil law suit; dispute; oath; voluntary oath of recruits; military oath; **eum obligare militiae sacramento** to swear him in; **justis sacramentis contendere** to argue on equal terms; **omnes sacramento adigere** or **rogare** to swear in everyone; **sacramentum dicere** to sign up, swear in; **sacramentum dicere** (with *dat*) to swear allegiance to (*a general or emperor*)
sacrār·ium -iī or **-ī** *n* sacristy; shrine, chapel
sacrāt·us -a -um *adj* hallowed, consecrated, holy, sacred
sacrif·er -ĕra -ĕrum *adj* carrying sacred objects
sacrificāl·is -e *adj* sacrificial
sacrificāti·ō -ōnis *f* sacrifice, sacrificing
sacrific·ium -iī or **-ī** *n* sacrifice
sacrific·ō or **sacrufic·ō -āre** *vt & vi* to sacrifice
sacrificŭl·us -ī *m* sacrificing priest
sacrific·us -a -um *adj* sacrificial
sacrileg·ium -iī or **-ī** *n* sacrilege; temple robbing
sacrilĕg·us -a -um *adj* sacrilegious; profane, impious, wicked; *m* temple robber; wicked person; *f* impious woman
sacr·ō -āre *vt* to consecrate; to dedicate; to set apart, devote, give; to doom, curse; to hallow, declare inviolable; to hold sacred, worship; to immortalize
sacrōsanct·us -a -um *adj* sacred, inviolable, sacrosanct
sacruficō see **sacrifico**
sacr·um -ī *n* holy object, sacred vessel; holy place, temple, sanctuary; religious rite, act of worship, religious service, sacrifice; victim; *n pl* worship, religion; secret, mystery; **sacra facere** to sacrifice
saeclum see **saeculum**
saeculār·is or **sēculār·is -e** *adj* centennial
saecŭl·um or **sēcŭl·um** or **saecl·um -ī** *n* generation, lifetime; century; spirit of the age, fashion
saepe *adv* often
saepenumĕrō or **saepe numĕrō** *adv* very often, again and again, oftentimes
saep·ēs or **sēp·ēs -is** *f* hedge, fence, enclosure
saepīment·um or **sēpīment·um -ī** *n* hedge, fence, enclosure
saep·iō or **sēp·iō -īre -sī -tum** *vt* to fence in, hedge in, enclose; to surround, encircle; to guard, fortify, protect, strengthen
saept·um or **sept·um -ī** *n* fence, wall, enclosure; stake; sheepfold; voting booth; *n pl* enclosure; voting booths, polls
saet·a -ae or **sēt·a -ae** *f* stiff hair, bristle
saetig·er -ĕra -ĕrum *adj* bristly; *m* boar
saetōs·us -a -um *adj* bristly, hairy
saevē *adv* fiercely, savagely
saevidic·us -a -um *adj* spoken in anger, savage
saev·iō -īre -iī -ītum *vi* to be fierce, be savage, be furious; (of persons) to be brutal, be violent
saeviter *adv* savagely, ferociously, cruelly
saeviti·a -ae *f* rage, fierceness; brutality, savageness, barbarity (*of persons*)
saev·us -a -um *adj* raging, fierce, furious, cruel; brutal, savage, barbarous (*persons*)
sāg·a -ae *f* fortune-teller (*female*)
sagācit·ās -ātis *f* keenness; sagacity, keenness of perception, shrewdness
sagāciter *adv* keenly; shrewdly, accurately, acutely, sagaciously
sagāt·us -a -um *adj* wearing a military coat
sag·ax -ācis *adj* keen, sharp, acute; intellectually quick, sharp, shrewd; prophetic
sagīn·a -ae *f* stuffing, cramming, fattening up; food, rations; rich food; fattened animal; fatness (*from overeating*)
sagīn·ō -āre *vt* to fatten
sāg·iō -īre *vi* to perceive quickly, catch on quickly
sagitt·a -ae *f* arrow
Sagitt·a -ae *f* Sagitta (*constellation*)
sagittāri·us -a -um *adj* of or for an arrow; *m* archer, bowman
Sagittār·ius -iī or **-ī** *m* Sagittarius (*constellation*)
sagittif·er -ĕra -ĕrum *adj* arrow-bearing
Sagittipŏt·ens -entis *m* Sagittarius (*constellation*)
sagitt·ō -āre *vt* to shoot (*arrows*); *vi* to shoot arrows
sagm·en -inis *n* tuft of sacred herbs (*plucked in the Capitol by the consul or praetor and worn by the fetiales as a sign of inviolability*)
sagŭl·um -ī *n* short military coat (*esp. that of general officers*)
sag·um -ī *n* coarse mantle; military uniform; **ad sagum ire** or **sagum sumere** to get into uniform; **in sagis esse** to be in uniform, be in the armed forces

Saguntīn·us -a -um *adj & m* Saguntine
Sagunt·um -ī *m* Saguntum (*city on the E. coast of Spain which Hannibal attacked and which thereby brought on the First Punic War*)
sāl salis *m* salt; salt water, sea water, sea; seasoning, flavor; good taste, elegance; pungency (*of words*), wit, humor; sarcasm; *m pl* witticisms, jokes, sarcastic remarks
salăc·ō -ōnis *m* braggart, show-off
salamandr·a -ae *f* salamander
Salamīnĭ·us -a -um *adj* of Salamis; *m pl* people of Salamis
Salăm·is -īnis *f* island in the Saronic gulf near Athens; city in Cyprus founded by Teucer
salapūt·ium -ĭī or **-ī** *n* midget
Salārĭ·a -ae *f* Via Salaria (*from the Porta Collina to the Sabine district*)
salārĭ·us -a -um *adj* salt, of salt; **annona salaria** revenue from salt mines; *m* salt-fish dealer; *n* salary; allowance; a meal
sal·ax -ācis *adj* lustful; salacious, provocative
salĕbr·a -ae *f* jolting; rut; harshness, roughness (*of speech*)
Saliār·is -e *adj* Salian, of the Salii; sumptuous
Saliāt·us -ūs *m* office of Salius, Salian priesthood
salict·um -ī *n* willow grove
salient·ēs -ĭum *f pl* springs, fountains
salign·us -a -um *adj* willow, of willow
Salĭ·ī -ōrum *m pl* college of twelve priests dedicated to Mars who went in solemn procession through Rome on the Kalends of March
salill·um -ī *n* small salt cellar
salīn·ae -ārum *f pl* salt pits, salt works; **salinae Romanae** salt works at Ostia (*a state monopoly*)
salīn·um -ī *n* salt cellar
sal·ĭō -īre -ŭī or **-ĭī -tum** *vi* to jump, leap, bound, hop
Salisubsŭl·ī -ōrum *m pl* dancing priests of Mars
saliunc·a -ae *f* wild nard (*aromatic plant*)
salīv·a -ae *f* saliva; taste, flavor
sal·ix -ĭcis *f* willow tree
Sallust·ius -ĭī or **-ī** *m* Sallust (*C. Sallustius Crispus, a Roman historian,* 86-35 B.C.)
Salmăc·is -ĭdis *f* fountain in Caria which made all who drank from it soft and effeminate
Salmōn·eus -ĕos *m* son of Aeolus and brother of Sisyphus who imitated lightning and was thrown by Jupiter into Tartarus
Salmōn·is -ĭdis *f* Tyro (*daughter of Salmoneus*)
salsāment·um -ī *n* salted or pickled fish; brine
salsē *adv* facetiously, humorously
Salsipŏt·ens -entis *adj* ruling the sea
sals·us -a -um *adj* salted; briny, salty; facetious, humorous, sharp, witty; *n pl* salty food; witty remarks, satirical writings
saltātĭ·ō -ōnis *f* dancing, dance
saltāt·or -ōris *m* dancer
saltātōrĭ·us -a -um *adj* dance, for dancing
saltātr·ix -īcis *f* dancing girl, dancer
saltāt·us -ūs *m* dance, religious dance
saltem *adv* at least, in any event, anyhow; **non saltem** not even
salt·ō -āre *vt & vi* to dance
saltuōs·us -a -um *adj* wooded, covered with forest
salt·us -ūs *m* wooded pasture, forest; upland; jungle; ravine; valley, glen; (coll) female organ; leap, leaping; **saltum dare** to leap
salūb·er (or **salūb·ris**) **-re** *adj* healthful, healthy, wholesome; (with *dat* or with **ad** + *acc*) healthful for, good for, beneficial to
salūbrĭt·ās -ātis *f* healthiness, wholesomeness; health, soundness
salūbrĭter *adv* healthfully; healthily; beneficially
sal·um -ī *n* seas, high seas
sal·ūs -ūtis *f* health; welfare; prosperity, safety; greeting, good wish, best regards; **salutem dicere** (abbreviated **s. d.**) to say hello, send greetings; (at the end of a letter) to say good-bye; **salutem magnam dicere** to send warm greetings; (at the end of a letter) to say good-bye; **salutem plurimam dicere** (abbreviated **s.p.d.**) to send warmest greetings; (at the end of a letter) to give best regards
salūtār·is -e *adj* salutary, healthful, wholesome; beneficial, advantageous, useful; **ars salutaris** art of healing; **salutaris littera** vote of acquittal
salūtārĭter *adv* beneficially, profitably, advantageously
salūtātĭ·ō -ōnis *f* greeting, salutation; formal morning reception or morning call at the house of an important person; callers; **ubi salutatio defluxit** when the morning callers have dispersed
salūtāt·or -ōris *m* or **salūtātr·ix -īcis** *f* morning caller
salūtĭf·er -ĕra -ĕrum *adj* health-giving
salūtigerŭl·us -a -um *adj* bringing greetings
salūt·ō -āre *vt* to greet, wish well, salute; to send greetings to; to visit, pay respects to, pay a morning call on; to pay reverence to (*gods*); to greet, welcome; (with double *acc*) to salute as, hail as, e.g., **aliquem imperatorem salutare** to hail someone as a victorious general
salvē *adv* well; in good health; **satine salve?** (coll) everything O.K.?
salv·ĕō -ēre *vi* to be well, be in good

health; to be getting along well; **salve, salvete,** or **salveto!** hello!, good morning!, good day!; goodbye!; **te salvere jubeo** I bid you good day

salv·us or **salv·os -a -um** or **-om** *adj* well, sound, safe, unharmed, unscathed; living, alive; (with substantive in an *abl* absolute) without violation of, without breaking, e.g., **salvā lege** without breaking the law; **salvos sum** (coll) I'm all right, I'm O.K.

sambūc·a -ae *f* triangular stringed instrument, harp

sambūcīn·a -ae *f* harpist (*female*)

sambūcistrĭ·a -ae *f* harpist (*female*)

Sam·ē -ēs *f* ancient name of the island of Cephallenia

Samĭ·us -a -um *adj* of Samos; **Juno Samia** Juno worshiped at Samos; **vir Samius** Pythagoras

Samn·īs -ītis *adj* Samnite; *m* Samnite gladiator; *m pl* Samnites

Samn·ĭum -ĭī or **-ī** *n* district of central Italy

Sam·os or **Sam·us -ī** *f* island off the W. coast of Asia Minor, famous for temple to Juno and as the birthplace of Pythagoras

Samothrāc·ēs -um *m pl* Samothracians

Samothrācĭ·us -a -um *adj* Samothracian; *f* Samothrace (*island in the N. Aegean*)

sānābĭl·is -e *adj* curable

sānātĭ·ō -ōnis *f* healing, curing

sancĭō sancīre sanxī sanctum *vt* to consecrate, hallow, make inviolable; to ratify; to condemn; (with *abl*) to forbid under penalty of

sanctē *adv* solemnly, reverently, religiously, conscientiously, purely

sanctimōnĭ·a -ae *f* sanctity, sacredness; chastity

sanctĭ·ō -ōnis *f* consecration, confirmation, sanctioning; penalty clause (*that part of the law that provided for penalties against those breaking that law*), sanction

sanctĭt·ās -ātis *f* sanctity, sacredness, inviolability; integrity, purity, chastity, holiness

sanctitūd·ō -ĭnis *f* sanctity, sacredness

sanct·or -ōris *m* enactor (*of laws*)

sanct·us -a -um *adj* consecrated, hallowed, sacred, inviolable; venerable, august, divine; pure, holy, chaste, virtuous

sandaligerŭl·ae -ārum *f pl* maids who brought their mistress's slippers

sandal·ĭum -ĭī or **-ī** *n* slipper, sandal

sandapĭl·a -ae *f* cheap coffin (*for people of the lower classes*)

sand·yx -ȳcis *f* vermilion

sānē *adv* reasonably, sanely, sensibly; certainly, doubtless, truly, very; (ironically) of course, naturally; (with negatives) really, at all; (in concessions) to be sure, however; (in answers) yes, of course, to be sure; (with imperatives) then; (with **quam**) how very

sanguen see **sanguis**

sanguĭn·ans -antis *adj* bleeding; (fig) bloodthirsty, savage

sanguinārĭ·us -a -um *adj* bloodthirsty, savage

sanguinĕ·us -a -um *adj* bloody, bloodstained; bloodred

sanguinolent·us -a -um *adj* bloody, bloodstained; bloodred; sanguinary

sangu·is or **sangu·īs -ĭnis** *m* or **sangu·en -ĭnis** *n* blood; blood, consanguinity, descent, family; descendant, offspring; slaughter, murder, bloodshed; forcefulness, life, vigor (*of a speech*); life, strength; **pugnatum plurimo sanguine** fought out in a real massacre; **sanguinem dare** to bleed; **sanguinem effundere** or **profundere** to bleed heavily; **sanguinem haurire** to shed (*someone else's*) blood; **sanguinem mittere** (of a physician) to let blood, bleed

sanĭēs (*genit* not found) *f* blood (*from a wound*); gore; foam, froth, slaver; venom

sānĭt·ās -ātis *f* health; sanity; common sense, discretion; solidity, healthy foundation (*for victory, etc.*); soundness, propriety (*of style*)

sann·a -ae *f* mocking grimace, face

sannĭ·ō -ōnis *m* one who makes faces, clown

sān·ō -āre *vt* to cure, heal; to correct, repair; to allay, quiet, relieve

Sanquāl·is -e *adj* of Sangus (*Sabine deity*); **Sanqualis avis** osprey (*bird*)

sān·us -a -um *adj* sound, hale, healthy; sane, rational, sensible; sober; (with **ab** + *abl*) free from (*faults, vices*)

sap·a -ae *f* new wine

sāperd·a -ae *m* a fish (*from the Black Sea*)

sapĭ·ens -entis *adj* wise, sensible, judicious, discreet; *m* sensible person; sage, philosopher; man of discriminating taste, connoisseur

sapienter *adv* wisely, sensibly, prudently

sapientĭ·a -ae *f* good taste, common sense, prudence, wisdom; science; philosophy

sap·ĭō -ĕre -īvī or **-ĭī** *vt* to have the flavor of, taste of; to have the smell of, smell like; to have knowledge of, understand; *vi* to have a sense of taste; to have sense, be sensible, be discreet, be wise; **sero sapiunt** they are wise too late

sāp·ō -ōnis *m* soap

sap·or -ōris *m* taste, flavor; delicacy, dainty; elegance, refinement, sense of taste

Sapph·ō -ūs *f* celebrated Greek lyric poetess of Lesbos

sarcīn·a -ae *f* package, bundle, pack; burden (*of the womb*); sorrow, trouble; *f pl* luggage, gear
sarcinārĭ·us -a -um *adj* pack, of luggage; **jumenta sarcinaria** pack animals
sarcināt·or -ōris *m* patcher, botcher
sarcināt·us -a -um *adj* loaded down, burdened
sarcinŭl·ae -ārum *f pl* small bundles, little trousseau
sarciō sarcīre sarsī sartum *vt* to patch, fix, repair
sarcophăg·us -ī *m* sarcophagus, tomb
sarcŭl·um -ī *n* light hoe, garden hoe
Sard·ēs or **Sard·ĭs -ĭum** *f pl* Sardis (*capital of Lydia*)
Sardiān·us -a -um *adj* Sardian
Sardinĭ·a -ae *f* Sardinia
Sardiniens·is -e *adj* Sardinian
Sardīs see **Sardes**
sardŏn·yx -ўchis *m* sardonyx (*precious stone*)
Sardŏ·us or **Sard·us -a -um** *adj & m* Sardianian
sarg·us -ī *m* bream (*fish*)
sar·iō or **sarr·io -īre -īvī** or **-ŭī** *vt* to hoe, weed
sarīs·a -ae *f* long Macedonian lance
sarīsophŏr·os -ī *m* Macedonian lancer
sarīt·or or **sart·or -ōris** *m* hoer, weeder
Sarmăt·ae -ārum *m pl* Sarmatians (*barbarous people of S.E. Russia*)
Sarmatĭ·a -ae *f* Sarmatia
Sarmatĭc·us -a -um *adj* Sarmatian
sarm·en -ĭnis or **sarment·um -ī** *n* brushwood; *n pl* twigs, fagots
Sarpēd·ōn -ŏnis *m* king of Lycia who was killed by Patroclus at Troy
Sarr·a -ae *f* Tyre
sarrāc·um or **serrāc·um -ī** *n* cart
Sarrān·us -a -um *adj* Tyrian
sarrĭō see **sario**
sartāg·ō -ĭnis *f* frying pan
sartor see **saritor**
sart·us -a -um *pp* of **sarcio;** *adj* (occurring only with **tectus**) in good repair; **aedem Castoris sartam tectam tradere** to hand over the temple of Castor in good repair; *n pl* repairs; **sarta tecta exigere** to complete the repairs
sat (indecl) *adj* enough, sufficient, adequate; *n* enough; **sat agere** (with *genit*) to have enough of, have the hands full with
sat *adv* sufficiently, quite; **sat scio** I am quite sure
sat·a -ae *f* daughter
sat·a -ōrum *n pl* crops
satăg·ō -ĕre *vi* to have trouble enough, have one's hands full
satell·es -ĭtis *m* or *f* attendant, follower; partisan; accomplice
satĭ·ās -ātis *f* sufficiency; overabundance, satiety, satisfied desire
satiĕt·ās -atis *f* sufficiency, adequacy; satiety, weariness, disgust
satin' or **satine** *adv* quite, really
satĭ·ō -āre *vt* to satisfy, appease; to fill, glut; to saturate; to cloy
satĭ·ō -ōnis *f* sowing, planting; *f pl* sown fields
satis (indecl) *adj* enough, sufficient, adequate; *n* enough; (law) satisfaction, security, guarantee; **satis accipere** to accept a guarantee; **satis dare** (with *dat*) to give a guarantee to; **satis facere** (with *dat*) to satisfy; to pay (*a creditor*); to make amends to (*by word or deed*), apologize to; **satis facere** (with *dat* of person and *acc & inf*) to satisfy (*someone*) with proof that, demonstrate sufficiently to (*someone*) that; **satis superque dictum est** more than enough has been said
satis *adv* enough, sufficiently, adequately, fully; **satis bene** pretty well
satisdatĭ·ō -ōnis *f* putting up bail, giving a guarantee
satisfactĭ·ō -ōnis *f* amends, satisfaction, apology
satĭus (*comp* of **satis**) *adj* **satius est** (with *inf*) it is better or preferable to
sat·or -ōris *m* sower, planter; father; promoter, author
satrapē·a or **satrapī·a -ae** *f* satrapy (*office or province of a satrap*)
satrăp·ēs -is *m* satrap (*governor of a province of the Persian empire*)
sat·ur -ŭra -ŭrum *adj* full, well fed, stuffed; plump; rich, fertile; rich, deep (*colors*); *f* mixture, hotchpotch; medley; satire, satirical poem; **per saturam** at random, pell-mell
saturei·a -ōrum *n pl* savory (*aromatic herb used as seasoning*)
saturĭt·ās -ātis *f* satiety; plenty, overabundance
Sāturnālĭ·a -ōrum *n pl* festival in honor of Saturn, beginning on the 17th of December and lasting several days
Sāturnĭ·a -ae *f* Juno (*daughter of Saturn*)
Sāturnīn·us -ī *m* L. Appuleius Saturninus (*demagogic tribune in* 103 B.C. *and* 100 B.C.)
Sāturnĭ·us -a -um *adj* Saturnian; **Saturnius numerus** Saturnian meter (*archaic Latin meter based on stress accent*); *m* Jupiter; Pluto
Sāturn·us -ī *m* Saturn (*Italic god of agriculture, equated with the Greek god Cronos, ruler of the Golden Age, and father of Jupiter, Neptune, Juno, and Pluto*)
satŭr·ō -āre *vt* to fill, satisfy, glut, cloy, saturate; to satisfy, content
sat·us -a -um *pp* of **sero;** *m* son; *f* see **sata;** *n pl* see **sata**
sat·us -ūs *m* sowing, planting; begetting; race, stock; seed (*of knowledge*)
satyrisc·us -ī *m* little satyr

satȳr·us -ī *m* satyr; satyr play (*Greek drama in which satyrs often formed the chorus*)
sauciātĭ·ō -ōnis *f* wounding
saucĭ·ō -āre *vt* to wound
saucĭ·us -a -um *adj* wounded; (fig) smitten, offended, hurt; melted (*snow*)
Sauromăt·ae -ārum *m pl* Sarmatians (*barbaric tribe of S. Russia*)
sāviātĭ·ō or **suāviātĭ·ō -ōnis** *f* kissing
sāviŏl·um or **suāviŏl·um -ī** *n* little kiss
sāvĭ·or -ārī -ātus sum *vt* to kiss
sāv·ĭum or **suāv·ĭum -ĭī** or **-ī** *n* puckered lips; kiss
saxātĭl·is -e *adj* rock, living among rocks; *m* saxatile (*fish*)
saxēt·um -ī *n* rocky place
saxĕ·us -a -um *adj* rocky, stony; **umbra saxea** shade of the rocks
saxifĭc·us -a -um *adj* petrifying, changing objects into stone
saxōs·us -a -um *adj* rocky, stony
saxŭl·um -ī *n* small rock, little crag
sax·um -ī *n* bolder, rock; Tarpeian Cliff (*W. side of the Capitoline Hill*)
scabellum see **scabillum**
scab·er -ra -rum *adj* itchy; rough, scurfy
scab·ĭēs (*genit* not found) *f* itch; roughness, scurf; (fig) itch
scabill·um or **scabell·um -ī** *n* stool, footstool; castanet tied to the foot
scabiōs·us -a -um *adj* itchy, mangy; moldy
scab·ō -ĕre -ī *vt* to scratch
Scae·a port·a -ae *f* Scaean gate (*W. gate of Troy*)
scaen·a or **scēn·a -ae** *f* stage setting, stage; scene; (fig) public view, publicity; pretense, pretext; **tibi scenae serviendum est** you must keep yourself in the limelight
scaenāl·is or **scēnāl·is -e** *adj* theatrical, scenic
scaenĭc·us or **scēnĭc·us -a -um** *adj* of the stage, theatrical, scenic; *m* actor
Scaevŏl·a -ae *m* C. Mucius Scaevola (*Roman hero who infiltrated into Porsenna's camp to kill Porsenna, and, on being discovered, burned off his own right hand*)
scaev·us -a -um *adj* left, on the left; perverse; *f* sign or omen appearing on the left
scāl·ae -ārum *f pl* ladder, flight of steps, stairs
scalm·us -ī *m* oarlock; oar; boat
scalpell·um -ī *n* scalpel
scalp·ō -ĕre -sī -tum *vt* to carve; to scratch; to tickle
scalpr·um -ī *n* chisel; knife; penknife
scalpurr·iō -īre *vi* to scratch
Scamand·er -rī *m* river at Troy, also called Xanthus
scammōnĕ·a -ae *f* scammony (*plant*)
scamn·um -ī *n* bench, stool; throne
scandō scandĕre scandī scansum *vt & vi* to climb, mount, ascend
scandŭl·a -ae *f* shingle (*for roof*)
scaph·a -ae *f* light boat, skiff
scaph·ĭum -ĭī or **-ī** *n* boat-shaped drinking cup; chamber pot
scapŭl·ae -ārum *f pl* shoulder blades; shoulders, back
scāp·us -ī *m* shaft; yarn beam (*of a loom*)
scarīf·ō -āre *vt* to scratch open
scar·us -ī *m* scar (*fish*)
scatĕbr·a -ae *f* bubbling, gushing, jet
scat·ĕō -ēre or **scat·ō -ĕre** *vi* to bubble up, gush out, jet; to teem
scatūrīgĭn·ēs or **scaturrīgĭn·ēs -um** *f pl* springs
scaturr·iō -īre *vi* to bubble, gush; to bubble over with enthusiasm
scaur·us -a -um *adj* clubfooted
scaz·ōn -ŏntis *m* scazon (*iambic trimeter with a spondee or trochee in the last foot*)
scelerātē *adv* criminally, wickedly
scelerāt·us -a -um *adj* profaned, desecrated; outlawed; criminal, wicked, infamous; *m* villain, criminal
scelĕr·ō -āre *vt* to pollute, desecrate
scelerōs·us -a -um *adj* full of wickedness, vicious
scel·us -ĕris *n* wicked deed, crime, wickedness; calamity; scoundrel, criminal
scēn- = scaen-
sceptrīf·er -ĕra -ĕrum *adj* sceptered
sceptr·um -ī *n* scepter; kingship, dominion, authority; kingdom
sceptūch·us -ī *m* scepter-bearer (*high officer of state in the East*)
sched·a or **scid·a -ae** *f* sheet, page
schēm·a -ae *f* figure, form, style; figure of speech
Schoenē·is -ĭdis *f* Atalanta
Schoenei·us -a -um *adj* of Schoeneus; *f* Atalanta
Schoen·eus -ĕī *m* king of Boeotia and father of Atalanta
schoenobăt·ēs -ae *m* ropewalker
schol·a -ae *f* learned debate, dissertation, lecture; school; sect, followers
scholastĭc·us -a -um *adj* school, scholastic; *m* rhetoric teacher, rhetorician
scida see **scheda**
sci·ens -entis *adj* having knowledge; having full knowledge, with one's eyes open; (with *genit*) having knowledge of, familiar or acquainted with, expert in; (with *inf*) knowing how to
scienter *adv* wisely, expertly
scientĭ·a -ae *f* knowledge, skill
scīlĭcet *adv* of course, evidently, certainly; (ironically) naturally, of course, to be sure; (as an explanatory particle) namely, that is to say, in other words

scill·a or **squill·a -ae** *f* shrimp
scīn = **scisne,** i.e., **scis** + **ne**
scindō scindĕre scidī scissum *vt* to cut, split, tear apart or open; to divide, separate; to interrupt
scindŭla see **scandula**
scintill·a -ae *f* spark
scintill·ō -āre *vi* to sparkle, flash
scintillŭl·a -ae *f* little spark
sciō scīre scīvī or **sciī scītum** *vt* to know; to realize, understand; to have skill in; (with *inf*) to know how to
Scīpiăd·ēs -ae *m* a Scipio, one of the Scipio family
Scīpĭ·ō -ōnis *m* famous family in the gens Cornelia; P. Cornelius Scipio Africanus Major (*conqueror of the Carthaginians in the Second Punic War,* 236-184 B.C.); P. Cornelius Scipio Aemilianus Africanus Minor (*conqueror of the Carthaginians in the Third Punic War, c.* 185-132 B.C.)
scirpĕ·us or **sirpĕ·us -a -um** *adj* wicker, of wicker; *f* wickerwork
scirpicŭl·a -ae *f* wicker basket
scirpicŭl·us -ī *m* wicker basket
scirp·us or **sirp·us -ī** *m* bulrush
sciscĭt·ō -āre or **sciscĭt·or -ārī -ātus sum** *vt* to ask, question, interrogate; to consult; (with *acc* of thing asked about and **ex** or **ab** + *abl* of person) to ask (*something*) of (*someone*), check on (*something*) with (*someone*); *vi* (with **de** + *abl*) to ask about
sciscō sciscĕre scīvī scītum *vt* (pol) to approve, adopt, enact, decree; to learn, ascertain
sciss·us -a -um *pp* of **scindo;** *adj* split, rent; furrowed (*cheeks*); shrill, harsh (*voice*)
scītāment·a -ōrum *n pl* dainties, delicacies
scītē *adv* expertly
scīt·or -ārī -ātus sum *vt* to ask; to consult (*oracle*); (with *acc* of thing and **ab** or **ex** + *abl*) to ask (*something*) of (*someone*); *vi* (with **de** + *abl*) to ask or inquire about
scītŭl·us -a -um *adj* neat, trim, smart
scīt·um -ī *n* statute, decree
scīt·us -a -um *adj* experienced, skillful; suitable, proper; judicious, sensible, witty (*words*); smart, sharp (*appearance*); (with *genit*) skilled in, expert at
scīt·us -ūs *m* decree, enactment
sciūr·us -ī *m* squirrel
scob·is -is *f* sawdust, scrapings, filings
scomb·er -rī *m* mackerel
scōp·ae -ārum *f pl* twigs, shoots; broom
Scop·ās -ae *m* famous Greek sculptor of Paros (*4th cent.* B.C.)
scopulōs·us -a -um *adj* rocky, craggy
scopŭl·us -ī *m* rock, cliff, crag; promontory
scorpĭ·ō -ōnis or **scorp·ĭus** or **scorp·ĭos -ĭī** or **-ī** *m* scorpion; (mil) artillery piece, catapult
Scorpĭ·ō -ōnis *m* Scorpion (*sign of the zodiac*)
scortāt·or -ōris *m* fornicator, lecher
scortĕ·us -a -um *adj* leather, of leather
scort·or -ārī -ātus sum *vi* to associate with prostitutes
scort·um -ī *n* prostitute; sex fiend
screāt·or -ōris *m* one who clears his throat noisily, hawker
screāt·us -ūs *m* clearing the throat, hawking
scre·ō -āre *vi* to clear the throat, hawk, hem
scrīb·a -ae *m* clerk, secretary
scriblīt·a -ae *f* tart
scrībō scrībĕre scripsī scriptum *vt* to write, draw; to write down; to write out, compose, produce; to enlist (*soldiers*); (with double *acc*) to appoint (*someone*) as
scrīn·ium -ĭī or **-ī** *n* bookcase, letter case, portfolio
scriptĭ·ō -ōnis *f* writing, composition, authorship; wording, text
scriptĭt·ō -āre *vt* to keep writing, write regularly
script·or -ōris *m* writer; scribe, secretary; composer, author; **rerum scriptor** historian
scriptŭl·a -ōrum *n pl* lines on a game board
scriptūr·a -ae *f* writing; composing; a writing, written work; tax paid on public pastures; testamentary provision
script·us -a -um *pp* of **scribo;** *n* written composition, treatise, work, book; literal meaning, letter; **orationem de scripto dicere** to read off a speech; **scriptum legis** or **scriptum** written ordinance, law
scrīpŭl·um or **scrūpŭl·um -ī** *n* small weight, smallest measure of weight, scruple (*one twenty fourth of an uncia*)
scrob·is -is *m* ditch, trench; grave
scrōf·a -ae *f* breeding sow
scrōfipasc·us -ī *m* swine keeper, pig breeder
scrūpĕ·us -a -um *adj* stony, rugged, jagged, rough
scrūpōs·us -a -um *adj* full of sharp stones, rugged, jagged, rough
scrūpŭlōsē *adv* precisely, carefully
scrūpulōs·us -a -um *adj* rough, rugged, jagged; precise, careful
scrūpŭlum see **scripulum**
scrūpŭl·us -ī *m* small sharp pebble; uneasy feeling, scruple
scrūp·us -ī *m* rough or sharp stone; uneasiness
scrūt·a -ōrum *n pl* trash, junk
scrūtāt·or -ōris *m* examiner
scrūt·or -ārī -ātus sum *vt* to scrutinize, examine
sculp·ō -ĕre -sī -tum *vt* to carve, chisel, engrave

sculpōnĕ·ae -ārum *f pl* clogs
sculptĭl·is -e *adj* carved, engraved
sculpt·or -ōris *m* sculptor
sculptūr·a -ae *f* carving; sculpture
sculptus *pp* of **sculpo**
scurr·a -ae *m* jester, comedian; man-about-town
scurrīl·is -e *adj* scurrilous
scurrīlĭt·ās -ātis *f* scurrility
scurrīlĭter *adv* jeeringly
scurr·or -ārī -ātus sum *vi* to clown around
scūtāl·e -is *n* thong of a sling
scūtār·ĭus -ĭī or **-ī** *m* shield maker
scūtāt·us -a -um *adj* carrying a shield; *m pl* troops armed with shields
scutell·a -ae *f* saucer, shallow bowl
scutĭc·a -ae *f* whip
scūtigerŭl·us -ī *m* shield bearer
scutr·a -ae *f* pan, flat dish
scutŭl·a or **scytăl·a** or **scytăl·ē -ae** *f* platter; eye patch; wooden cylinder; secret letter
scutulāt·us -a -um *adj* diamond-shaped; *n pl* checkered clothing
scūtŭl·um -ī *n* small shield
scūt·um -ī *n* oblong shield; (fig) shield, defense, protection
Scyll·a -ae *f* dangerous rock on the Italian side of Straits of Messina, said to have been the daughter of Phorcus and transformed by Circe into a sea monster with howling dogs about her midriff; daughter of Nisus who betrayed her father by cutting off his purple lock of hair
Scyllae·us -a -um *adj* Scyllan
scymn·us -ī *m* cub, whelp
scyph·us -ī *m* goblet, cup
Scyr·os or **Scyr·us -ī** *f* island off Euboea
scytăla see **scutula**
scytălē see **scutula**
Scyth·a or **Scyth·ēs -ae** *m* Scythian; *m pl* Scythians (*general name for the nomadic tribes of the section of Europe and Asia beyond the Black Sea*)
Scythĭ·a -ae *f* Scythia
Scythĭc·us -a -um *adj* Scythian
Scyth·is -ĭdis *f* Scythian woman
sē or **sēsē** (*genit:* **suī;** *dat:* **sibī** or **sibi;** *abl* **sē** or **sēsē**) *pron acc* (reflex) himself, herself, itself, themselves; one another; **ad se** or **apud se** at home; **apud se** in one's senses; **inter se** one another, mutually
sēb·um -ī *n* tallow, grease
sē·cēdō -cēdĕre -cessī -cessum *vi* to go apart, go aside, withdraw; to rebel
sē·cernō -cernĕre -crēvī -crētum *vt* to separate; to dissociate; to distinguish; to reject, set aside
sēcessĭ·ō -ōnis *f* withdrawal; secession
sēcess·us -ūs *m* retirement, retreat; isolated spot
sē·clūdō -clūdĕre -clūsī -clūsum *vt* to shut off, shut up; to seclude, bar; to hide
sec·ō -āre -ŭī -tum *vt* to cut, cut off, reap, carve; (in surgery) to cut out, excise, cut off, amputate; to scratch, tear, wound, injure; to cut through, traverse; to cut short, settle, decide; to follow, chase
sēcordĭa see **socordia**
sēcrētĭ·ō -ōnis *f* dividing, separating
sēcrētō *adv* separately, apart; secretly; in private
sēcrēt·us -a -um *pp* of **secerno;** separate; isolated, solitary; secret; (with *genit* or *abl*) deprived of, in need of; *n* secret, mystery; private conversation or interview; isolated place, solitude
sect·a -ae *f* path; way, method, course; school of thought; political party
sectārĭ·us -a -um *adj* gelded; leading
sectāt·or -ōris *m* follower, adherent
sectĭl·is -e *adj* cut, divided
sectĭ·ō -ōnis *f* cutting; auctioning off of confiscated property; right to confiscated property; confiscated property
sect·or -ōris *m* cutter; buyer at a sale of confiscated property, speculator in confiscated estates
sect·or -ārī -ātus sum *vt* to keep following, follow eagerly, run after, keep trailing after; to chase, hunt
sectūr·a -ae *f* digging, excavation; *f pl* diggings, mines
sectus *pp* of **seco**
sēcubĭt·us -ūs *m* sleeping alone
sēcŭb·ō -āre -ŭī *vi* to lie alone, sleep by oneself; to live alone
sēcul- = saecul-
secund·a -ōrum *n pl* success, good fortune
secund·ae -ārum *f pl* secondary role (*in a play*); second fiddle
secundān·ī -ōrum *m pl* soldiers of the second legion
secundārĭ·us -a -um *adj* secondary, second-rate, inferior
secundō *adv* secondly
secund·ō -āre *vt* to favor, further, back, support
secundum *adv* after, behind; *prep* (with *acc*) (of space) beside, by, along; (of time) immediately after, after; (in rank) next to, after; (of agreement) according to, in compliance with; in favor of, to the advantage of
secund·us -a -um *adj* following; next, second (*in time*); backing, favorable, supporting; next, second (*in rank*); secondary, subordinate, inferior, second-string; **anno secundo** the next year; **a mensis fine secunda dies** the second-last day of the month; **in secundam aquam** with the current; **secunda mensa** dessert; **secundo flumine** downstream, with the current; **se-**

cundo lumine on the following day; **secundo mari** with the tide; **secundo populo** with the backing of the people; **secundus panis** inferior bread, stale bread; **secundus ventus** tail wind, fair wind; *f pl* see **secundae;** *n pl* see **secunda**
sēcūrē *adv* securely, safely
secūricŭl·a -ae *f* hatchet
secūrĭf·er -ĕra -ĕrum *adj* carrying an ax, ax-carrying
secūrĭg·er -ĕra -ĕrum *adj* ax-carrying
secūr·is -is *f* ax, hatchet; blow, mortal blow; power of life and death; supreme authority, sovereignty
sēcūrĭt·ās -ātis *f* freedom from care, unconcern, composure; freedom from danger, security, safety; false sense of security; carelessness
sēcūr·us -a -um *adj* carefree; secure, safe; cheerful; careless; offhand
secus (indecl) *n* sex; **secus muliebre** females; **secus viriles** males
secus *adv* otherwise, differently; **non secus ac** or **non secus quam** not otherwise than, just as, exactly as; **si secus accidet** if it turns out otherwise (*than expected*), if it turns out badly
secūt·or -ōris *m* gladiator (*who fought against an opponent who had a net*)
secūtus *pp* of **sequor**
sed or **set** *conj* but; but also; but in fact
sēdātē *adv* sedately, calmly
sēdātĭ·ō -ōnis *f* calming
sēdāt·us -a -um *adj* calm, composed
sēdĕcim (indecl) *adj* sixteen
sēdēcŭl·a -ae *f* little seat, low stool
sedentārĭ·us -a -um *adj* sedentary
sedĕō sedēre sēdī sessum *vi* to sit, remain sitting; (of magistrates, esp. judges) to sit, preside, hold court, be a judge; (of an army) to remain encamped; to keep the field; to settle down in blockade; to be idle, be inactive; (of clothes) to fit; (of places) to be low-lying; to sink, settle; to be firm, be fixed, be established; to stick fast, be stuck; to be determined, be firmly resolved
sēd·ēs -is *f* seat, chair, throne; residence, home; last home, burial place; base, foundation, bottom
sedīl·e -is *n* seat, chair, bench, stool; *n pl* seats in the theater; rowers' benches
sēditĭ·ō -ōnis *f* sedition, insurrection, mutiny; dissension, quarrel, disagreement; warring (*of elements, etc.*)
sēditiōsē *adv* seditiously
sēditiōs·us -a -um *adj* seditious, mutinous; quarrelsome; troubled, disturbed
sēd·ō -āre *vt* to calm, settle, still, allay
sē·dūcō -dūcĕre -duxī -ductum *vt* to lead aside, draw aside, lead away, carry off; to put aside; to separate, divide
sēductĭ·ō -ōnis *f* taking sides, siding
sēduct·us -a -um *pp* of **seduco;** distant, remote
sēdulĭt·ās -ātis *f* application, earnestness; officiousness
sēdŭlō *adv* diligently; intentionally, on purpose
sēdŭl·us -a -um *adj* diligent, busy; officious
seg·es -ĕtis *f* grain field; crop
Segest·a -ae *f* town in N.W. Sicily
Segestān·us -a -um *adj* of Segesta; *m pl* people of Segesta; *n* territory of Segesta
segmentāt·us -a -um *adj* trimmed with a flounce
segment·um -ī *n* trimming, flounce; brocade
segnĭp·ēs -ĕdis *adj* slow-footed
segn·is -e *adj* slow, inactive; sluggish, lazy
segnĭter *adv* slowly, lazily
segnitĭ·a -ae or **segnitĭ·ēs** (*genit* not found) *f* slowness, inactivity, laziness
sēgrĕg·ō -āre *vt* to segregate, separate
sējugāt·us -a -um *adj* separated
sējŭg·is -is *m* six-horse chariot
sējunctim *adv* separately
sējunctĭ·ō -ōnis *f* separation, division
sē·jungō -jungĕre -junxī -junctum *vt* to separate, disunite, part, sever; (fig) to sever, part, disconnect; to distinguish
sēlectĭ·ō -ōnis *f* selection
sēlectus *pp* of **seligo**
Seleuc·us -ī *m* name of a line of kings of Syria
sēlībr·a -ae *f* half pound
sē·lĭgō -ligĕre -lēgī -lectum *vt* to pick out, select, choose
sell·a -ae *f* chair, stool; sedan; magistrate's chair
sellāriŏl·us -a -um *adj* (place) for sitting or lounging
sellār·ĭus -ĭī or **-ī** *m* lecherer
sellisternĭ·a -ōrum *n pl* sacred banquets in honor of goddesses
sellŭl·a -ae *f* stool; sedan
sellulār·ĭus -ĭī or **-ī** *m* mechanic
sēmanĭmis see **semianimis**
semel *adv* once, one time; but once, once for all; first, the first time; once, ever, at some time, at any time
Semĕl·ē -ēs or **Semĕl·a -ae** *f* daughter of Cadmus and mother of Bacchus by Jupiter
Semelei·us -a -um *adj* of Semele
sēm·en -ĭnis *n* seed, germ; seedling, young plant, shoot; offspring; race, stock; (in physics) particle; instigator, cause
sēmenstris see **semestris**
sēmentĭf·er -ĕra -ĕrum *adj* seed-bearing, fruitful
sēmentīn·us -a -um *adj* of the sowing season

sēment·is -is *f* sowing, planting; young crops
sēmentīv·us -a -um *adj* at seed time, of the sowing season
sēmerm·is -e *adj* half-armed
sēmestr·is or **sēmenstr·is -e** *adj* for six months, half-yearly, semiannual
sēmēs·us -a -um *adj* half-eaten
sēmet = emphatic form of **se**
sēmiadapert·us -a -um *adj* half-open
sēmianīm·is -e or **sēmianīm·us** or **sēmanīm·us -a -um** *adj* half-dead
sēmiapert·us -a -um *adj* half-open
sēmīb·ōs -ōvis *adj masc* half-ox; **semibos vir** Minotaur
sēmicăp·er -rī *adj masc* half-goat
sēmicremāt·us or **sēmicrĕm·us -a -um** *adj* half-burned
sēmicubitāl·is -e *adj* half-cubit long
sēmidĕ·us -a -um *adj* semidivine; *m* demigod
sēmidoct·us -a -um *adj* half-educated
sēmierm·is -e or **sēmierm·us -a -um** *adj* half-armed
sēmiēs·us -a -um *adj* half-eaten
sēmifact·us -a -um *adj* half-finished
sēmĭf·er -ĕra -ĕrum *adj* half-beast; half-savage; *m* centaur
sēmifult·us -a -um *adj* half-propped
sēmigermān·us -a -um *adj* half-German
sēmigrăv·is -e *adj* half-drunk
sēmĭgr·ō -āre *vi* to go away, depart
sēmihĭ·ans -antis *adj* half-open
sēmihŏm·ō -ĭnis *m* half man, half beast; subhuman
sēmihōr·a -ae *f* half hour
sēmilăc·er -ĕra -ĕrum *adj* half-mangled
sēmilaut·us -a -um *adj* half-washed
sēmilīb·er -ĕra -ĕrum *adj* half-free
sēmilix·a -ae *m* (term of reproach) sad sack
sēmimarīn·us -a -um *adj* semisubmerged (*in the sea*)
sēmĭm·ās -ăris *adj* gelded, castrated; *m* hermaphrodite
sēmimortŭ·us -a -um *adj* half-dead
sēmināř·ium -ĭī or **-ī** *n* nursery garden; (fig) breeding ground
sēmināt·or -ōris *m* originator, cause, source
sēminĕcis (*genit; nom* does not occur) *adj* half-killed, half-dead
sēmin·ium -ĭī or **-ī** *n* breeding; stock
sēmĭn·ō -āre *vt* to sow; to beget, procreate; to produce
sēminūd·us -a -um *adj* half-stripped; half-unarmed
sēmipāgān·us -ī *m* little clown
sēmiplēn·us -a -um *adj* (garrison) at half strength
sēmiputāt·us -a -um *adj* half-pruned

Semīrăm·is -is or **-ĭdis** *f* famous queen of Assyria, the consort and successor of Ninus
Semīramĭ·us -a -um *adj* of Semiramis
sēmirās·us -a -um *adj* half-shaven
sēmireduct·us -a -um *adj* bent back halfway
sēmirefect·us -a -um *adj* half-repaired
sēmirŭt·us -a -um *adj* half-ruined, half-demolished
sēm·is -issis *m* half; half an ace (*coin*); one half percent a month or six-percent per annum; **non semissis homo** man not worth a penny, worthless fellow
sēmisĕn·ex -is *m* elderly gent
sēmisepult·us -a -um *adj* half-buried
sēmisomn·is -e or **sēmisomn·us -a -um** *adj* half-asleep
sēmisupīn·us -a -um *adj* half-prone
sēmĭt·a -ae *f* path, lane
sēmitāl·is -a -um *adj* of byways
sēmitārĭ·us -a -um *adj* back-alley
sēmiustilāt·us or **sēmiustulāt·us -a -um** *adj* half-burned
sēmĭv·ir -īrī *adj* half-man, half-beast; unmanned; unmanly, effeminate; *m* half-man; eunuch
sēmivīv·us -a -um *adj* half-alive, half-dead
sēmod·ius -ĭī or **-ī** *m* half a peck
sēmōt·us -a -um *adj* remote, distant; *n pl* faraway places
sē·movĕō -movēre -mōvī -mōtum *vt* to move apart, separate, remove, put aside
semper *adv* always, ever; regularly, on each occasion
sempitern·us -a -um *adj* everlasting
Semprōnĭus see **Gracchus**
sēmuncĭ·a -ae *f* half ounce (*one twenty-fourth of a Roman pound*); trifle
sēmunciārĭ·us -a -um *adj* half-ounce; **faenus semunciarium** interest at the rate of one twenty-fourth of the capital (*i.e., about five percent per annum*)
sēmust·us -a -um *adj* half-burned
senăcŭl·um -ī *n* open-air meeting place of the senate in the Forum
sēnāriŏl·us -ī *m* trifling trimeter
sēnārĭ·us -a -um *adj* six-foot (*verse*); *m* iambic trimeter
senāt·or -ōris *m* senator
senātōrĭ·us -a -um *adj* senatorial; in the senate; of a senator
senāt·us -ūs *m* senate; senate session; **senatūs consultum** decree of the senate
Senĕc·a -ae *m* L. Annaeus Seneca (*Stoic philosopher and instructor of Nero*, 4 B.C.-65 A.D.)
senect·us -a -um *adj* aged, old; *f* old age, senility
senect·ūs -ūtis *f* old age; old people

sen·ĕō -ēre *vi* to be old

sen·escō -escĕre -ŭī *vi* to grow old; to decline, become feeble, lose strength; to wane, draw to a close

sen·ex -is *adj* aged, old; *m* old man; *f* old woman

sēn·ī -ae -a *adj* six each, six in a group, six at a time; **seni deni** sixteen each

senīl·is -e *adj* of old people, of an old man; aged; senile

sēnĭ·ō -ōnis *m* a six (*on dice*)

senĭ·or -us (*comp* of **senex**) *adj* older, elder; more mature (*years*); *m* elderly person, an elder (*over forty-five years of age*)

sen·ĭum -ĭī or **-ī** *n* feebleness of age, decline, senility; decay; grief, trouble; gloom; crabbiness; old man

sens·a -ōrum *n pl* thoughts, sentiments, ideas

sensicŭl·us -ī *m* short sentence

sensĭf·er -ĕra -ĕrum *adj* producing sensation

sensĭl·is -e *adj* capable of sensation, sentient

sensim *adv* gropingly; tentatively; carefully, gradually, gently

sens·us -a -um *pp* of **sentio;** *n pl* see **sensa**

sens·us -ūs *m* sense faculty, capacity for feeling, sensation; feeling, emotion, sentiment; attitude, frame of mind, view; understanding, judgment, intelligence; meaning, intent, sense; sentence; **communes sensūs** commonplaces; universal human feelings

sententĭ·a -ae *f* opinion, view, judgment; purpose, intention; (law) sentence, verdict; (in the senate) motion, proposal, view; meaning, sense; sentence; maxim; **de sententia** (with *genit*) in accordance with the wishes of; **ex animi (mei) sententia** (in an oath) to the best of (*my*) knowledge and belief; **ex mea sententia** in my opinion, to my liking; **in sententiam alicujus pedibus ire** to vote in favor of someone's proposal; **sententia est** (with *inf*) I intend to; **sententiam dicere** (in the senate) to express a view; **sententiam pronuntiare** or **dicere** to pronounce or give the verdict

sententiŏl·a -ae *f* phrase; maxim

sententiōsē *adv* sententiously

sententiōs·us -a -um sententious, full of meaning

senticēt·um -ī *n* thorny bush

sentīn·a -ae *f* bilge water; cesspool; bilge; (fig) dregs, scum, rabble

sentĭō sentīre sensī sensum *vt* to perceive with the senses, feel, hear, see, smell; to realize; to feel, observe, notice; to experience; to think, judge; *vi* (law) to vote, decide

sent·is -is *m* thorny bush, bramble, brier

sentisc·ō -ĕre *vt* to begin to realize; to begin to observe, perceive

sent·us -a -um *adj* thorny; untidy (*person*)

seorsum or **seorsus** *adv* apart, separately; (with *abl* or **ab** + *abl*) apart from

sēparābĭl·is -e *adj* separable

sēparātim *adv* apart, separately

sēparātĭ·ō -ōnis *f* severing, separation

sēparātĭus *adv* less closely, more widely

sēparāt·us -a -um *adj* separate, distinct, different

sēpăr·ō -āre *vt* to separate, divide, part; to distinguish

sepelībĭl·is -e *adj* that may be buried

sepelĭō sepelīre sepelīvī or **sepelĭī sepultum** *vt* to bury; (fig) to bury, overwhelm, ruin, destroy, suppress

sēpēs see **saepes**

sēpĭ·a -ae *f* cuttlefish

sēpīmentum see **saepīmentum**

sēpĭō see **saepio**

sēpiŏl·a -ae *f* little cuttlefish

sē·pōnō -pōnĕre -posŭī -posĭtum *vt* to put aside; to separate, pick out, select; to assign, reserve; to remove, take away, exclude; to distinguish

sēposĭt·us -a -um *adj* remote, distant; select; distinct, private

seps sēpis *m* or *f* snake

sepse = emphatic **sē**

septem (indecl) *adj* seven

Septemb·er -ris *adj & m* September

septemdĕcim (indecl) *adj* seventeen

septemflŭ·us -a -um *adj* seven-mouthed (*Nile*)

septemgemĭn·us -a -um *adj* sevenfold

septempedāl·is -e *adj* seven-foot, seven-feet-high

septempl·ex -icis *adj* sevenfold

septemtriōnāl·ia -ium *n pl* northern regions, northern part

septemtriōnāl·is -e *adj* northern

septemtriōn·ēs or **septentriōn·ēs -um** *m pl* seven stars near the North Pole belonging to the Great Bear; the seven stars of the Little Bear; northern regions, the North; north wind

septemvirāl·is -e *adj* of the septemvirs, septemviral; *m pl* septemvirs

septemvirāt·us -ūs *m* septemvirate, office of the septemvirs

septemvĭr·ī -ōrum *m pl* septemvirs (*board of seven officials*)

septēnār·ĭus -ĭī or **-ī** *m* heptameter (*verse of seven feet*)

septendĕcim or **septemdĕcim** (indecl) *adj* seventeen

septēn·ī -ae -a *adj* seven each, seven in a group; **septeni deni** seventeen each, seventeen in a group

septentr- = **septemtr-**

septĭens or **septĭēs** *adv* seven times

septimān·us -a -um *adj* of or on the seventh; *n pl* soldiers of the seventh legion
septĭmum *adv* for the seventh time
septĭm·us or **septŭm·us -a -um** *adj* seventh
septĭm·us decĭm·us -a -um *adj* seventeenth
septingentēsĭm·us -a -um *adj* seven hundredth
septingent·ī -ae -a *adj* seven hundred
septuāgēsĭm·us -a -um *adj* seventieth
septuāgintā (indecl) *adj* seventy
septuenn·is -e *adj* seven-year-old
septum see **saeptum**
septun·x -cis *m* seven ounces; seven twelfths
septus *pp* of **saepio**
sepulcrāl·is -e *adj* of a tomb, sepulchral, funeral
sepulcrēt·um -ī *n* grave, tomb
sepulcr·um -ī *n* grave, tomb
sepultūr·a -ae *f* burial
sepultus *pp* of **sepelio**
Sēquăn·a -ae *m* Seine
sequ·ax -ācis *adj* following, pursuing; penetrating (*fumes*); eager
sequ·ens -entis *adj* next, following
sequest·er -ris (or **-ra**) **-re** *adj* intermediate; negotiating, mediating; **pace sequestrā** under the protection of a truce; *m* trustee; agent, mediator, go-between
sequĭus or **sētĭus** (*comp* of **secus**) *adv* less; worse, more unfavorably; **nihilo setius** or **nilo setius** nevertheless
sequor sequī secūtus sum *vt* to follow, escort, accompany, go with; to chase, pursue; to come after (*in time*); to go after, aim at; to head for (*a place*); *vi* to go after, follow, come next; (of words) to come naturally
ser·a -ae *f* bolt, bar (*of door*)
Serāp·is -is or **-ĭdis** *m* Egyptian god of healing
serēnĭt·ās -ātis *f* fair weather; serenity; favorableness
serēn·ō -āre *vt* to make fair, clear up, brighten
serēn·us -a -um *adj* clear, bright, fair, cloudless; cheerful, serene; *n* clear sky, fair weather
Sēr·es -um *m pl* Chinese
seresc·ō -ĕre *vi* to dry off
sērĭ·a -ae *f* large jar
sērĭ·a -ōrum *n pl* serious matters, serious business
Sērĭc·us -a -um *adj* Chinese; *n pl* silks
serĭ·ēs (*genit* not found) series, row, succession; train, sequence, order, connection; lineage
sērĭō *adv* seriously, in all sincerity
sērĭ·us -a -um *adj* serious, earnest; *n* serious matter; seriousness, earnestness; *n pl* see **seria**
serm·ō -ōnis *m* conversation, talk; discussion, discourse; common talk, rumor, gossip; language, diction; prose, everyday language
sermōcĭn·or -ārī -ātus sum *vi* to talk, converse
sermuncŭl·us -ī *m* small talk, chitchat
serō serĕre serŭī sertum *vt* to join, connect; to entwine, wreathe; to compose, combine, contrive
serō serĕre -sēvī satum *vt* to sow, plant; (fig) to sow the seeds of
sērō *adv* late
serp·ens -entis *m* or *f* creeping thing, snake, serpent, dragon
Serp·ens -entis *m* Serpent, Draco (*constellation*)
serpentigĕn·a -ae *m* dragon offspring
serpentĭp·ēs -ĕdis *adj* dragon-footed
serperastr·a -ōrum *n pl* splints (*for straightening the crooked legs of children*); officer who keeps his soldiers in check
serpillum see **serpyllum**
serpō serpĕre serpsī serptum *vi* to creep, crawl; to move along slowly, spread slowly
serpyll·um or **serpill·um** or **serpull·um -ī** *n* wild thyme
serr·a -ae *f* saw
serrāt·us -a -um *adj* serrated, notched
serrŭl·a -ae *f* small saw
sert·a -ae *f* wreath
sert·a -ōrum *n pl* wreaths, festoons
Sertōr·ĭus -ĭī or **-ī** *m* general of Marius who held out in Spain against the partisans of Sulla until he was assassinated by Perperna (*c.* 122-72 B.C.)
sert·us -a -um *pp* of **sero** (to join); *f* see **serta;** *n pl* see **serta**
ser·um -ī *n* whey; serum
sēr·us -a -um *adj* late; too late; **anni seri** ripe years; **ulmus sera** slow-growing elm; *n* late hour; **in serum rem trahere** to drag out the matter until late
serv·a -ae *f* slave (*female*)
servābĭl·is -e *adj* retrievable
serv·ans -antis *adj* keeping; (with *genit*) observant of
servāt·or -ōris *m* or **servātr·ix -īcis** *f* savior, preserver, deliverer
servīl·is -e *adj* slave, servile
servīlĭter *adv* slavishly
serv·ĭō -īre -īvī or **-ĭī -ītum** *vi* to be a servant or slave; to be obedient; (of buildings, land) to be mortgaged; (with *dat*) **a** to be a slave to, be subservient to; **b** to serve; **c** to comply with, conform to, humor; **d** to be devoted to, work at; **e** to serve, be of use to
servit·ĭum -ĭī or **-ī** *n* slavery, servitude; slaves
servitūd·ō -ĭnis *f* servitude, slavery
servit·ūs -ūtis *f* slavery; serfdom; slaves; property liability, easement
Serv·ĭus Tull·ĭus -ĭī or **-ī** *m* sixth king of Rome

serv·ō -āre *vt* to watch over, preserve, protect; to store, reserve; to keep, retain; to observe; to keep to, continue to dwell in
servŏl·a -ae *f* young slave girl
servolicŏl·a -ae *f* slave of a slave (*female*)
servŏl·us -ī *m* young slave
serv·us or **serv·os -a -um** *adj* slave, servant; *mf* slave, servant
sescēnār·is -e *adj* a year and a half old
sescēnārĭ·us -a -um *adj* six-hundred-man (*cohort*)
sescēn·ī -ae -a *adj* six hundred each, six hundred in a group
sescentēsĭm·us -a -um *adj* six hundredth
sescent·ī -ae -a *adj* six hundred
sescentĭens or **sescentĭēs** *adv* six hundred times
sēsē see **se**
sescuncĭ·us -a -um *adj* inch and a half thick
sesĕl·is -is *f* seseli (*plant*)
sesqui *adv* more by a half, one and a half times
sesquialt·er -ĕra -ĕrum *adj* one and a half
sesquihōr·a -ae *f* an hour and a half
sesquimod·ĭus -ĭī or **-ī** *m* peck and a half
sesquioctāv·us -a -um *adj* having a ratio of nine to eight
sesquiŏp·us -ĕris *n* day and a half's work
sesquipedāl·is -e *adj* foot and a half long or wide
sesquiplāg·a -ae *f* blow and a half
sesquipl·ex -ĭcis *adj* one and a half times as much
sesquitertĭ·us -a -um *adj* containing one and a third; having a ratio of four to three
sessibŭl·um -ī *n* chair, seat, easy chair
sessĭl·is -e *adj* for sitting on; (plants) growing close to the ground, low-growing
sessĭ·ō -ōnis *f* sitting; session; loafing
sessĭt·ō -āre *vi* to sit much, keep sitting, rest
sessiuncŭl·a -ae *f* small group, small circle
sess·or -ōris *m* spectator; resident
sestert·ĭum -ĭī or **-ī** *n* sesterce
sestert·ĭus -ĭī or **-ī** (*genit pl:* **sestertĭum**) (abbreviated HS) *m* sesterce (*small silver coin, equal to one fourth of a denarius, i.e., about 8¢, and used as the ordinary Roman unit in accounting*); **centena milia sestertium** 100,000 sesterces; **deciens** (i.e., **deciens centena milia**) **sestertium** 1,000,000 sesterces
Sest·os or **Sest·us -ī** *f* city on the Hellespont
sēt- = saet-
Sētĭ·a -ae *f* town in Latium famous for its wine
Sētīn·us -a -um *adj* Setine; *n* Setine wine
sētĭus see **sequius**
seu *conj* or if; or; **seu . . . seu** whether . . . or
sevērē *adv* seriously; severely, austerely
sevērĭt·ās -ātis *f* severity, sternness, strictness
sevērĭtūd·ō -ĭnis *f* austerity
sevēr·us -a -um *adj* serious, grave; severe, strict, austere; ruthless, grim
sēvŏc·ō -āre *vt* to call aside, call away; to remove, withdraw, separate
sēv·um -ī *n* tallow, grease
sex (indecl) *adj* six
sexāgēnārĭ·us -a -um *adj* sixty-year-old
sexāgēn·ī -ae -a *adj* sixty each, sixty in a group
sexāgēsĭm·us -a -um *adj* sixtieth
sexāgĭens or **sexāgĭēs** *adv* sixty times
sexāgintā (indecl) *adj* sixty
sexangŭl·us -a -um *adj* hexagonal
sexcēnārĭ·us -a -um *adj* six-hundred-man (*cohort*)
sexcen- = sescen-
sexenn·is -e *adj* six-year-old, of six years; **sexenni die** in a six-year period
sexenn·ĭum -ĭī or **-ī** *n* six-year period, six years
sexĭens or **sexĭēs** *adv* six times
sexprīm·ī or **sex prīm·ī -ōrum** *m pl* six-member council (*in provincial towns*)
sextadecimān·ī -ōrum *m pl* soldiers of the sixteenth legion
sext·ans -antis *m* one sixth; small coin (*one sixth of an ace*); one sixth of a pint
sextār·ĭus -ĭī or **-ī** *m* pint
Sextīl·is -e *adj* of or belonging to the sixth month of the old Roman year which was afterwards called August in honor of Augustus
sextŭl·a -ae *f* sixth of an ounce
sextum *adv* for the sixth time
sext·us -a -um *adj* sixth
sext·us decĭm·us -a -um *adj* sixteenth
sexungŭl·a -ae *f* six-clawed woman, rapacious woman
sex·us -ūs *m* sex
sī *conj* if, if only; **quod si** but if; **si forte** if perchance, in the hope that; **si minus** if not
sibī see **se**
sībĭl·a -ōrum *n pl* hisses, hissing
sībĭl·ō -āre *vt* to hiss at; *vi* to hiss
sībĭl·us -a -um *adj & m* hissing
Sibyll·a or **Sibull·a -ae** *f* sibyl, prophetess
Sibyllīn·us -a -um *adj* sibylline
sīc *adv* thus, so, in this way; thus, as follows; in these circumstances; in such a way, to such a degree; (in assent) yes

Sicān·ī -ōrum *m pl* ancient people of Italy who migrated to Sicily
Sicānĭ·a -ae *f* Sicily
Sicān·is -ĭdis *adj* Sicilian
Sicānĭ·us -a -um *adj* Sicilian; *f* see **Sicania**
Sicān·us -a -um *adj* Sicilian; *m pl* see **Sicani**
sīcār·ius -iī or **-ī** *m* murderer, assassin; **inter sicarios accusare (defendere)** to prosecute (defend) on a murder charge
siccē *adv* firmly, solidly
siccĭt·ās -ātis *f* dryness; drought; firmness, solidity; dullness (*of style*)
sicc·ō -āre *vt* to dry, dry up, drain; to stanch, heal
siccocŭl·us -a -um *adj* dry-eyed
sicc·us -a -um *adj* dry; thirsty; sober; firm, solid (*body*); solid (*argument*); dry, insipid (*style*)
Sicilĭ·a -ae *f* Sicily
sicilicissĭt·ō -āre *vi* to act like a Sicilian
sīcīlicŭl·a -ae *f* sickle
Siciliens·is -e *adj* Sicilian
sīcĭne *adv* is this how . . . ?
sīcŭbi *adv* if anywhere, wheresoever
sīcŭl·a -ae *f* little dagger
Sicŭl·ī -ōrum *m pl* ancient Italian people who migrated to Sicily
sīcunde *conj* if from some place, if from anywhere
sīcut or **sīcŭtī** *conj* as, just as; (in elliptical clauses) just as, like; (introducing a comparison) as it were, so to speak; (introducing an example) as, as for instance; (of condition) as, in the same condition as; as if, just as if; **sicut . . . ita** although . . . yet
Sicy̆·ōn -ōnis *f* town in the N. Peloponnesus
Sicyōnĭ·us -a -um *adj* of Sicyon; *m pl* inhabitants of Sicyon
sīderĕ·us -a -um *adj* starry; star-spangled· heavenly, divine
sīdō sīdĕre sīdī or **sēdī sessum** *vi* to sit down; to settle; (of birds) to alight, land; to sink; to settle down, subside; (of ships) to be grounded
Sīd·ōn -ōnis *f* city of Phoenicia
Sīdōn·is -ĭdis *adj* Phoenician; *f* Dido; Europa
Sīdōnĭ·us -a -um *adj* Sidonian, Phoenician; Theban; *m pl* Sidonians
sīd·us -ĕris *n* constellation; star, heavenly body; sky, heaven; light, glory, beauty, pride; season; climate, weather; (in astrology) star, destiny
Sigambr·ī -ōrum *m pl* powerful German tribe
Sīgē·um -ī *n* promontory near Troy where Achilles was said to have been buried
Sīgē·us -a -um *adj* Sigean
sigill·a -ōrum *n pl* figurines; seal (*on a seal ring*)
sigillāt·us -a -um *adj* adorned with little figures
signāt·or -ōris *m* sealer, signer; witness
signāt·us -a -um *adj* sealed, secured
signĭf·er -ĕra -ĕrum *adj* bearing the constellations, starry; *m* standard-bearer; chief, leader
signifĭc·ans -antis *adj* clear, distinct, expressive
significanter *adv* clearly, graphically
significātĭ·ō -ōnis *f* signal, indication, sign, mark; expression of approval, applause; meaning, sense, signification; emphasis
signifĭc·ō -āre *vt* to show, indicate, point out, express; to intimate; to notify, publish, make known; to portend; to mean, signify
sign·ō -āre *vt* to mark, stamp, impress, imprint; to seal, seal up; to coin; to point out, signify, indicate, express; to adorn, decorate; to distinguish, mark, note
sign·um -ī *n* sign, indication, proof; military standard, banner; password; cohort, maniple; omen, symptom; statue, picture; device on a seal, seal, signet; heavenly sign, constellation; **ab signis discedere** to break ranks, disband; **signa conferre** to engage in close combat; to concentrate troops; **signa constituere** to halt; **signa conversa ferre** to wheel around and attack; **signa ferre** to break camp; **signa movere** to advance; **signa movere in hostem** to advance against the enemy, attack the enemy; **signa proferre** to march forward, advance; **signa servare** to keep the order of battle; **signa sequi** to march in rank; **signa subsequi** to keep the order of battle; **signa transferre** to desert, join the other side; **signis collatis** in regular battle
sīlān·us -ī *m* jet of water
Silăr·us -ī *m* river forming the boundary between Lucania and Campania
sil·ens -entis *adj* silent, calm, quiet; *mf pl* the dead
silent·ium -iī or **-ī** *n* silence; inactivity; **silentium facere** to obtain silence; to keep silence; **silentium significare** to call for silence
Sīlēn·us -ī *m* teacher and constant companion of Bacchus, usually drunk
sil·ĕō -ēre -ŭī *vt* to leave unmentioned, say nothing about; *vi* to be silent, be still; to keep silence; to be hushed; to rest, cease
sil·er -ĕris *n* willow
silesc·ō -ĕre *vi* to become silent, fall silent, become hushed
sil·ex -ĭcis *m* flint, flint stone; cliff, crag; hardheartedness
silicern·ium -iī or **-ī** *n* funeral feast; (coll) old fossil
silīg·ō -ĭnis *f* winter wheat; wheat flour

silīqu·a -ae *f* pod, husk; *f pl* pulse
sillyb·us -ī *m* label giving book's title
sīl·ō -ōnis *m* (man) button nose, snub nose
silūr·us -ī *m* sheatfish
sīl·us -a -um *adj* having a turned-up nose, snub-nosed
silv·a or **silŭ·a -ae** *f* woods, forest; shrubbery, bush, foliage, crop, growth; mass, abundance, quantity, material, supply
Silvān·us -ī *m* god of woods; *m pl* woodland gods
silvesc·ō -ĕre *vi* (of a vine) to run wild
silvestr·is -e *adj* wooded, overgrown with woods; woodland, living in woods; wild, growing wild; rural, pastoral; *n pl* woodlands
silvicŏl·a -ae *m* or *f* denizen of the forest
silvicultr·ix -īcis *adj fem* living in the woods
silvifrăg·us -a -um *adj* forest-smashing (*wind*)
silvōs·us -a -um *adj* wooded, woody
sīmĭ·a -ae *f* ape
simĭl·is -e *adj* similar; (with *genit* or *dat*) resembling, like, similar to; **homines inter se similes** men resembling one another; **veri similis** probable; realistic; *n* comparison, parallel
similĭter *adv* similarly; **similiter atque** or **ac** just as; **similiter ut si** just as if
similitūd·ō -ĭnis *f* likeness, resemblance; imitation; analogy; comparison, simile; monotony; (with *genit*) similarity to; **est homini cum deo similitudo** there is a resemblance between a god and man
sīmiŏl·us -ī *m* monkey
simītū *adv* at the same time; (with **cum** + *abl*) together with
sīm·ĭus -ĭī or **-ī** *m* ape
Simŏ·īs -entis *m* river at Troy
Simōnĭd·ēs -is *m* famous lyric poet of Ceos (*fl* 500 B.C.); celebrated iambic poet of Amorgos (*7th cent.* B.C.)
simpl·ex -ĭcis *adj* single, simple, unmixed; plain, natural; frank; naive; in single file
simplicĭt·ās -ātis *f* simplicity; candor, frankness
simplicĭter *adv* simply, plainly; candidly, frankly
simpl·us -a -um *adj* simple; *n* simple sum
simpŭl·um -ī *n* small ladle
simpuv·ĭum -ĭī or **-ī** *n* libation bowl
simul *adv* together, at the same time; likewise, also; (with *abl* or **cum** + *abl*) with, together with; **simul atque** or **ac** or **et** as soon as; **simul . . . simul** both . . . and; *conj* as soon as
simulācr·um -ī *n* image, likeness, representation; form, shape, phantom, ghost; conception; sign, emblem; mere shadow; portraiture, characterization
simulām·en -ĭnis *n* imitation, copy
simŭl·ans -antis *adj* imitating; (with *genit*) imitative of
simulātē *adv* insincerely, deceitfully
simulātĭ·ō -ōnis *f* faking, bluffing, bluff, pretense; **simulatione** (with *genit*) under the pretense of, under the guise of
simulāt·or -ōris *m* imitator; pretender, phoney
simŭl·ō -āre *vt* to imitate, copy, represent; to put on the appearance of, simulate
simult·ās -ātis *f* enmity, rivalry, feud, jealousy, grudge
sīmŭl·us -a -um *adj* rather snub-nosed
sīm·us -a -um *adj* snub-nosed, pug-nosed
sīn *conj* if however, if on the other hand, but if
sināp·i -is *n* or **sināp·is -is** *f* mustard
sincērē *adv* sincerely, honestly, frankly
sincērĭt·ās -ātis *f* soundness, integrity
sincēr·us -a -um *adj* sound, whole, clean, untainted; real, genuine
sincĭp·ut -ĭtis or **sincipitāment·um -ī** *n* half a head; cheek, jowl (*of a hog*); brain
sind·ōn -ŏnis *f* fine cotton or linen fabric, muslin
sine *prep* (with *abl*) without; **flammā sine** flameless
singillātim *adv* one by one, singly
singlārĭter see **singulariter**
singulār·is -e *adj* single, alone, one at a time; unique, unparalleled; *m pl* crack troops
singulārĭter or **singlārĭter** *adv* singly; particularly
singulārĭ·us -a -um *adj* single, separate
singulātim *adv* singly, individually
singŭl·ī -ae -a *adj* single, one at a time, individual; one each, one apiece; **in singulos dies** on each successive day; every day, daily; *m pl* individuals
singultim *adv* sobbingly, gaspingly; falteringly
singult·ĭō -īre *vi* to hiccup; to throb
singult·ō -āre *vt* to gasp out, spurt out; *vi* to sob, gasp; to gurgle
singult·us -ūs *m* sob, gasp; squirt (*of water, etc.*); death rattle
singŭl·us -a -um *adj* one by one, single; each one, one apiece
sinist·er -ra -rum *adj* left, on the left; (because in Roman augury the augur faced south, having the East on the left) favorable, auspicious, lucky; (because in Greek augury the augur faced north, having the East on his right) unfavorable, inauspicious, unlucky; wrong, perverse, improper; *m pl* soldiers on the left

flank; *f* left, left hand; left side; *n* left side; **a sinistra** on the left
sinisterĭt·ās -ātis *f* awkwardness
sinistrē *adv* badly, wrongly, perversely
sinistrorsum or **sinistrorsus** *adv* to the left
sinō sinĕre sīvī or **siī situm** *vt* to allow; **sine modo** only let, if only
Sin·ōn -ōnis *m* Greek soldier through whose treachery the Greeks were able to get the horse into Troy
Sinōp·a -ae or **Sinīp·ē -ēs** *f* Greek colony on the S. coast of the Euxine Sea
Sinuess·a -ae *f* city on the border between Latium and Campania
sīn·um -ī *n* large drinking cup
sinŭ·ō -āre *vt* to wind, curve, arch
sinuōs·us -a -um *adj* winding, sinuous, serpentine
sin·us -ūs *m* curved or bent surface, indentation, curve, fold, hollow; fold of the toga about the breast; pocket, purse; breast, bosom, lap; bay, gulf, lagoon; winding coast; valley, hollow; heart (*e.g., of a city*), interior; intimacy; **in sinu meo est** he is dear to me
sīn·us -ī *m* large drinking cup
sīpar·ĭum -ĭī or **-ī** *n* theater curtain; **post siparium** behind the scenes
sīph·ō -ōnis *m* siphon; fire engine
sīphuncŭl·us -ī *m* small pipe
Sipȳl·us -ī *m* mountain in Lydia
sīquandō or **sī quandō** *conj* if ever
sīquĭdem *conj* if in fact
siremps or **sirempse** = **si rem ipsam** *adj* the same, e.g., **sirempse legem** the same law
Sīr·ēn -ēnis *f* Siren (*sea nymph who had the power of charming with her song*)
Sīrĭ·us -a -um *adj* of Sirius, of the Dog Star; *m* Sirius, Dog Star
sirp·e -is *n* silphium (*plant*)
sīr·us -ī *m* underground granary
sīs = **sī vīs** please, if you please
sistō sistĕre stitī statum *vt* to cause to stand, make stand, put, place, set; to set up (*monument*); to establish; to stop, check, arrest; to put an end to; to produce in court; **pedem sistere** or **gradum sistere** to halt, stop; **se sistere** to present oneself, appear, come; **sisti non potest** the crisis cannot be met, the case is hopeless; **vadimonium sistere** to answer bail, show up in court; *vi* to stand, rest; to stop, stay; to stand firm, last, endure; to show up in court; (with *dat* or **contra** + *acc*) to stand firm against
sistrāt·us -a -um *adj* with a tambourine
sistr·um -ī *n* rattle, tambourine
Sīsyphĭd·ēs -ae *m* descendant of Sisyphus, i.e., Ulysses
Sīsȳph·us -ī *m* son of Aeolus, king of Corinth, whose punishment in Hades was to roll a rock repeatedly up a hill
sitell·a -ae *f* lottery urn
Sīth·ōn -ŏnis *adj* Thracian
Sīthŏn·is -ĭdis or **Sīthonĭ·us -a -um** *adj* Thracian; *m pl* Thracians
sitīculōs·us -a -um *adj* thirsty, dry
sitĭ·ens -entis *adj* thirsting, thirsty; arid, parched; parching; (with *genit*) eager for
sitienter *adv* thirstily, eagerly
sit·ĭō -īre -īvī -iī *vt* to thirst for; *vi* to be thirsty
sit·is -is *f* thirst; (with *genit*) thirst for
sitīt·or -ōris *m* thirsty person; **sititor aquae** thirster for water
sittȳbus see **sillybus**
sitŭl·a -ae *f* bucket
sit·us -a -um *pp* of **sino**; *adj* lying, situated; founded; (with **in** + *abl*) resting on, dependent on
sit·us -ūs *m* position, situation, site; structure; neglect; mustiness; dust, dirt; idleness, inactivity, lack of use
sīve *conj* or if; or; **sive . . . sive** whether . . . or
smaragd·us -ī *m* or *f* emerald
smar·is -ĭdis *f* a small sea fish
smīl·ax -ăcis *f* smilax, bindweed (*plant*)
Sminth·eus -ĕī *m* epithet of Apollo
Smyrn·a -ae *f* town in Asia Minor
sobol- = **subol-**
sōbrĭē *adv* soberly, moderately; sensibly
sōbriĕt·ās -ātis *f* temperance (*in drinking*)
sōbrīn·a -ae *f* cousin (*female, on the mother's side*)
sōbrīn·us -ī *m* cousin (*on the mother's side*)
sōbrĭ·us -a -um *adj* sober; temperate, continent; sensible, reasonable
soccŭl·us -ī *m* small or short sock
socc·us -ī *m* sock; slipper; low shoe worn by actors in comedies; comedy
soc·er or **soc·ĕrus -ĕrī** *m* father-in-law
socĭ·a -ae *f* associate, companion, ally, partner (*female*)
sociābĭl·is -e *adj* compatible, intimate
sociāl·is -e *adj* allied, confederate; nuptial, conjugal; companionable, sociable
sociālĭter *adv* sociably, in comradeship
sociennus -ī *m* comrade
sociĕt·ās -ātis *f* companionship, fellowship; association, society, partnership, alliance, confederacy
socĭ·ō -āre *vt* to unite, associate; to share
sociofraud·us -ī *m* heel, double crosser
socĭ·us -a -um *adj* joint, allied, confederate; held in common, common; *m* associate, companion, ally, partner; *f* see **socia**
sōcordĭ·a or **sēcordĭ·a -ae** *f* silliness, stupidity; apathy, laziness

sōcordĭus *adv* too apathetically
sōc·ors -ordis *adj* silly, stupid; apathetic, lazy, inactive
Sōcrăt·ēs -is *m* famous Athenian philosopher (469-399 B.C.)
Sōcratĭc·ī -ōrum *m pl* Socratics, disciples of Socrates
socr·us -ūs *f* mother-in-law
sodālicĭ·us -a -um *adj* of companionship; *n* companionship, intimacy; society, secret society
sodāl·is -is *m* or *f* comrade, companion, fellow; member (*of a society, priestly college, etc.*); accomplice, conspirator; gallant
sodālĭt·ās -ātis *f* companionship, fellowship; society, club, association; secret society
sodālit- = **sodalic-**
sōdēs = **si audes** if you will, please
sōl sōlis *m* sun; sunlight, sunshine; day
sōlāciŏl·um -ī *n* bit of comfort
sōlāc·ĭum -ĭī or **-ī** *n* comfort, relief
sōlām·en -ĭnis *n* comfort
sōlār·is -e *adj* sun; **lumen solare** sunlight, sunshine
sōlār·ĭum -ĭī or **-ī** *n* sundial; clock; sunny spot, balcony
sōlāt- = **solac-**
sōlāt·or -ōris *m* comforter
soldūrĭ·ī -ōrum *m pl* retainers (*of a chieftain*)
soldus see **solidus**
solĕ·a -ae *f* sole; sandal; fetter; sole (*flat fish*)
soleār·ĭus -ĭī or **-ī** *m* sandal maker
soleāt·us -a -um *adj* wearing sandals
solĕō solēre solĭtus sum *vi* (with *inf*) to be in the habit of, usually, e.g., **solet cenare sero** he usually eats late; (with **cum** + *abl*) to have intercourse with
solĭdē *adv* for certain; fully, wholly
solidĭt·ās -ātis *f* solidity
solĭd·ō -āre *vt* to make firm, make dense; to strengthen
solĭd·us or **sold·us -a -um** *adj* solid, firm, dense; whole, entire; genuine, real; trustworthy; firm, resolute; *n* entire sum, total; solid, solid body, mass, substance; solid earth
sōliferrĕ·um -ī *n* all-iron spear
sōlistĭm·us -a -um *adj* perfect; **tripudium solistimum** perfectly auspicious omen
sōlitārĭ·us -a -um *adj* solitary, lonely
sōlitūd·ō -ĭnis *f* loneliness; deprivation; wilderness
solĭt·us -a -um *adj* usual, customary, characteristic; *n* the usual, the customary; **formosior solito** more handsome than usual, unusually handsome; **magis solito** or **plus solito** more than usual
sol·ĭum -ĭī or **-ī** *n* seat, chair; throne; dominion, sway; bathtub; stone coffin, sarcophagus
sōlivăg·us -a -um *adj* roaming alone; single, solitary
sollemn·is -e *adj* annual, periodic; religious, solemn; usual; *n* usage, practice; solemn rite, solemnity, ceremony, feast, sacrifice; festival, games (*in observance of Roman holy days*)
sollemnĭter *adv* solemnly, religiously
soll·ers -ertis *adj* skilled, skillful, expert, clever
sollerter *adv* skillfully, expertly, cleverly
sollertĭ·a -ae *f* skill, ingenuity, shrewdness; clever plan; (with *genit*) skill in
sollicitātĭ·ō -ōnis *f* vexation, anxiety; incitement, instigation
sollicĭtē *adv* anxiously, with solicitude; diligently
sollicĭt·ō -āre *vt* to shake, disturb; to disquiet, annoy, molest; to worry, make anxious; to provoke, tempt; to stir up, incite, incite to revolt
sollicitūd·ō -ĭnis *f* anxiety, uneasiness
sollicĭt·us -a -um *adj* stirred up, stormy (*sea*); tossed (*by the waves*); troubled, disturbed, disquieted, restless; anxious, solicitous, apprehensive, worried
sollif- = **solif-**
sollist- = **solist-**
soloecism·us -ī *m* grammatical mistake, solecism
Sol·ōn -ōnis *m* famous Athenian legislator (*c.* 640-*c.* 560 B.C.)
sōl·or -ārī -ātus sum *vt* to console, comfort; to relieve, mitigate (*fear, worry*)
sōlstitiāl·is -e *adj* of the summer solstice; midsummer's; solar
sōlstit·ĭum -ĭī or **-ī** *n* summer solstice; midsummer, summer heat
sol·um -ī *n* bottom, ground, floor; soil, land, country; sole (*of foot or shoe*)
sōlum *adv* only, merely, barely; **non solum . . . sed etiam** not only . . . but also
sōl·us -a -um *adj* only, single, sole, alone; lonely, solitary
solūtē *adv* loosely, freely, without hindrance; negligently; without vigor
solūt·us -a -um *adj* loose, untied, unbandaged; negligent; free; fluent; unrhythmical; uncontrolled; exempt, free; unbiased; unbridled, loose
solūtĭ·ō -ōnis *f* loosening; payment
solvō solvĕre solvī or **solŭī solūtum** *vt* to loosen, untie; to free, release; to dissolve, break up; detach, disengage; to unlock, open; to melt, turn, change; to relax, smooth, soothe; to impair, weaken, destroy; to acquit, absolve; to accomplish, fulfill; to pay, pay off; to solve, explain; to suffer, undergo (*punishment*); to remove, get rid of (*feelings*); *vi* to weigh anchor, set sail
Solȳm·a -ōrum *n pl* Jerusalem

somniculōsē *adv* sleepily, drowsily
somniculōs·us -a -um *adj* sleepy, drowsy
somnĭf·er -ĕra -ĕrum *adj* sleep-inducing, soporific; deadly (*poison*)
somnĭ·ō -āre *vt* to dream of; to day-dream about, imagine; **somnium somniare** to have a dream
somn·ĭum -ĭī or **-ī** *n* dream; day-dreaming; nightmare
somn·us -ī *m* sleep; night; sleep of death; indolence
sonābĭl·is -e *adj* noisy
sonĭp·ēs -ĕdis *adj* loud-hoofed; *m* steed
sonĭt·us -ūs *m* sound, noise
sonivĭ·us -a -um *adj* noisy
son·ō -āre -ŭī -ĭtum *vt* to speak, sound, express; to mean; to sound like; *vi* to sound, ring, resound, make a noise
son·or -ōris *m* sound, noise, clang
sonōr·us -a -um *adj* sonorous, loud, noisy, clanging
sons sontis *adj* guilty, criminal
sontĭc·us -a -um *adj* important
son·us -ī *m* sound, noise; tone (*of style*)
sophĭ·a -ae *f* wisdom
sophist·ēs -ae *m* sophist
Sophŏcl·ēs -is *m* famous Greek writer of tragedies (*c.* 495-406 B.C.)
Sophoclē·us -a -um *adj* Sophoclean, of Sophocles
soph·us -a -um *adj* wise; *m* wise man, sage
sōp·ĭō -īre -īvī or **-ĭī -ītum** *vt* to put to sleep; to stun, knock unconscious: (fig) to calm, still, settle, lull
sop·or -ōris *m* deep sleep; stupor; apathy, indifference; sleeping potion
sopōrāt·us -a -um *adj* stupefied; unconscious; buried in sleep; allayed (*grief*); soporific
sopōrĭf·er -ĕra -ĕrum *adj* sleep-inducing
sopōr·us -a -um *adj* drowsy
Sōract·e -is *n* mountain in Etruria about twenty-six miles from Rome
sōrăc·um -ī *n* hamper
sorb·ĕō -ēre -ŭī *vt* to suck in, gulp down; to absorb; (fig) to swallow (*e.g., hatred*)
sorbill·ō -āre *vt* to sip
sorbĭlō *adv* drop by drop, bit by bit
sorbiti·ō -ōnis *f* drink, pleasant drink
sorb·um -ī *n* Juneberry, serviceberry
sorb·us -ī *f* Juneberry tree, serviceberry tree
sord·ĕō -ēre *vi* to be dirty, be shabby; to appear worthless
sord·ēs -is *f* dirt, filth; shabbiness, squalor; *f pl* shabby clothes, rags (*often worn as a sign of mourning*); mourning; meanness (*of behavior*); low rank, low condition, vileness; dregs, rabble; vulgarity
sord·escō -escĕre -ŭī *vi* to become dirty, become soiled
sordidāt·us -a -um *adj* in dirty or shabby clothes (*esp. as a sign of mourning*)
sordĭdē *adv* vilely, meanly, vulgarly
sordidŭl·us -a -um *adj* rather soiled, rather shabby; (fig) low, mean
sordĭd·us -a -um *adj* dirty, filthy, shabby; soiled, stained; dressed in mourning clothes; low (*rank*); vile, vulgar (*behavior*)
sorditūd·ō -ĭnis *f* dirt, filth
sōr·ex -ĭcis *m* shrewmouse
sōricīn·us -a -um *adj* squealing like mice
sōrīt·ēs -ae *m* sorites (*logical conclusion drawn from cumulative arguments*)
sor·or -ōris *f* sister; cousin; companion, playmate; **sorores doctae** Muses; **sorores tres** three Fates; **sorores tristes** gloomy Fates
sorōricīd·a -ae *f* murderer of a sister
sorōrĭ·us -a -um *adj* sister's, of a sister; sisterly; **stuprum sororium** incest with a sister
sors sortis *f* lot; casting of lots, decision by lot; prophecy; fate, destiny, lot in life; portion, share; sort, kind, class
sorsum see **seorsum**
sortilĕg·us -a -um *adj* prophetic; *m* soothsayer, fortune-teller
sortĭ·ō -īre or **sort·ĭor -īrī -ītus sum** *vt* to cast or draw lots for; to allot, assign by lot, appoint by lot; to obtain by lot; to choose, select; to share, divide; to receive, get by chance; *vi* to cast or draw lots
sortītĭ·ō -ōnis *f* drawing lots, determining by lots
sortītō *adv* by lot; by fate
sortīt·us -ūs *m* lottery
Sosĭ·ī -ōrum *m pl* the Sosii (*two brothers famous as booksellers in Rome at the time of Horace*)
sosp·es -ĭtis *adj* safe and sound; auspicious, lucky
sospĭt·a -ae *f* preserver (*epithet of Juno*)
sospitāl·is -e *adj* beneficial
sospĭt·ō -āre *vt* to preserve, protect
sōt·ēr -ēris *m* savior, deliverer, protector
sōtērĭ·a -ōrum *n pl* party thrown for a person recovering from an illness
spād·ix -īcis *adj* chestnut-brown
spad·ō -ōnis *m* eunuch
spargō spargĕre sparsī sparsum *vt* to scatter, sprinkle, strew; to scatter, disperse; to disseminate, broadcast; to spot, dapple
sparsĭ·ō -ōnis *f* sprinkling
spars·us -a -um *pp* of **spargo;** *adj* freckled, spotty
Spart·a -ae or **Spart·ē -ēs** *f* Sparta (*capital of Laconia, also called Lacedaemon*)
Spartăc·us -ī *m* Thracian gladiator who led a revolt of gladiators against Rome in 73-71 B.C.

Spartān·us -a -um *adj* Spartan
Spartiāt·ēs -ae *m* Spartan
Spartiātic·us or **Spartic·us -a -um** *adj* Spartan
spart·um -ī *n* Spanish broom (*plant, used in making ropes, nets, etc.*)
sparŭl·us -ī *m* bream (*fish*)
spar·us -ī *m* hunting spear
spath·a -ae *f* broad two-edged sword
spati·or -ārī -ātus sum *vi* to walk, stroll, take a walk; to walk solemnly; to spread out
spatiōsē *adv* extensively; long, for a long time
spatiōs·us -a -um *adj* spacious; broad, large; prolonged
spat·ium -iī or **-ī** *n* room, space, extent; open space, public square; distance (*between two points*); walk, promenade (*place*); interval, period; time, opportunity; measure, quantity (*in metrics*); lap; race track
speci·ēs -ēī *f* sight, view; outward appearance, outline, shape; fine appearance, beauty; deceptive appearance, show, semblance, pretense, pretext; resemblance, likeness; display, splendor; vision, apparition; image, statue; idea, notion; reputation; species, sort; **in speciem** or **per speciem** as a pretext, for the sake of appearances
specill·um -ī *n* probe (*surgical instrument*)
specim·en -inis *n* mark, sign, proof, example; model, ideal
speciō specĕre spexī *vt* to look at, behold
speciōsē *adv* splendidly
speciōs·us -a -um *adj* handsome, good-looking, beautiful; plausible; specious
spectābil·is -e *adj* visible; remarkable
spectācŭl·um or **spectācl·um -ī** *n* sight, spectacle; public performance; stage play; theater
spectām·en -inis *n* sign, proof
spectāti·ō -ōnis *f* observation, view; examining, testing
spectāt·or -ōris *m* observer; spectator; critic, judge
spectātr·ix -icis *f* on-looker, observer; spectator
spectāt·us -a -um *adj* tried, tested, proved; esteemed
specti·ō -ōnis *f* observing the auspices; right to take the auspices
spect·ō -āre *vt* to observe, watch; to face in the direction of; to consider; to bear in mind; to aim at, tend towards; to examine, test
spectr·um -ī *n* specter, apparition
specŭl·a -ae *f* look-out, watch tower; summit
spēcŭl·a -ae *f* bit of hope
speculābund·us -a -um *adj* on the look-out
speculār·is -e *adj* transparent; *n pl* windowpane, window
speculāt·or -ōris *m* spy; explorer
speculātōri·us -a -um *adj* for spying, for reconnaissance; *f* reconnaissance ship
speculātr·ix -icis *f* spy (*female*)
specŭl·or -ārī -ātus sum *vt* to reconnoiter, observe, watch for
specŭl·um -ī *n* mirror (*made of polished metal*)
spec·us -ūs *m* or *n* cave, cavern; artificial excavation, ditch, canal, channel, pit; hole, cavity (*of a wound, etc.*)
spēlae·um -ī *n* den, cave
spēlunc·a -ae *f* cave
spērābil·is -e *adj* possible (*able to be hoped for*)
spērāt·us -a -um *adj* hoped for, longed for, desired; *f* fiancee, bride-to-be
Sperchē·is -idis *adj* of the Spercheos
Sperchē·os or **Sperchī·us -ī** *m* large river in S. Thessaly
spernō spernĕre sprēvī sprētum *vt* to remove; to scorn, reject
spēr·ō -āre *vt* to hope for, expect, look forward to; to trust, trust in; to anticipate, await with fear
spēs speī *f* hope, expectation; anticipation, apprehension (*of evil*); **praeter spem** beyond all expectation; unexpectedly
Speusipp·us -ī *m* nephew of Plato and his successor as head of the Academy (347-339 B.C.)
sphaer·a -ae *f* sphere, globe, ball
sphaeristēr·ium -iī or **-ī** *n* tennis court
Sphin·x -gis *f* sphinx
spīc·a -ae *f* point; ear (*of grain*); tuft, top, head (*of plants*)
spīcĕ·us -a -um *adj* made of ears of grain
spīcŭl·um -ī *n* point; sting; dart, arrow
spīc·um -ī *n* ear (*of grain*)
spīn·a -ae *f* thorn; thorn bush; prickle (*of animals*); backbone, spine; back; *f pl* subtleties
spīnēt·um -ī *n* thorn hedge, thorny thicket
spīnĕ·us -a -um *adj* made of thorns, thorn
spīnif·er -ĕra -ĕrum *adj* prickly
spīnōs·us -a -um *adj* thorny, prickly; (fig) stinging, irritating (*worries*); confused, obscure (*style*)
spint·ēr -ēris *m* elastic bracelet
spintri·a -ae *m* male prostitute
spinturnīc·ium -iī or **-ī** *n* bird of ill omen
spīn·us -ī *f* blackthorn, sloe tree
spīr·a -ae *f* coil (*of a serpent*); chin strap
spīrābil·is -e *adj* good to breathe, life-giving (*air*)
spīrācŭl·um -ī *n* pore, vent; breathing space
spīrāment·um -ī *n* pore, vent; breathing space, pause, instant
spīrit·us -ūs *m* breathing, breath; breeze; air; breath of life, life; in-

spiration; spirit, character, courage; pride, arrogance; morale; **spiritum ducere** to take a breath, breathe

spīr·ō -āre *vt* to exhale, breathe out; to aspire to, aim at; *vi* to breathe; to be alive; to be favorable; to have poetic inspiration

spissāt·us -a -um *adj* condensed, concentrated

spissē *adv* thickly, closely, tightly; slowly

spissesc·ō -ĕre *vi* to condense, become thick

spissigrăd·us -a -um *adj* slow-paced

spiss·ō -āre *vt* to condense, concentrate

spiss·us -a -um *adj* thick, tight, dense; slow, late; difficult

splēn splēnis *m* spleen

splend·ĕō -ēre *vi* to be clear and bright, shine, gleam; to be illustrious, be glorious

splendesc·ō -ĕre *vi* to become clear and bright

splendĭd·us -a -um *adj* clear and bright, gleaming, glistening, sparkling; spotless, noble (*character*); splendid, magnificent; sumptuous; showy; illustrious

splend·or -ōris *m* brightness, brilliance; clearness; splendor, magnificence; noble

splēniāt·us -a -um *adj* wearing a patch

splēn·ĭum -ĭī or **-ī** *n* patch (*for the face*)

spoliātĭ·ō -ōnis *f* stripping, plundering; unjust deprivation (*of honor or dignity*); ousting (*from public office*)

spoliāt·or -ōris *m* or **spoliātr·ix -īcis** *f* despoiler, robber

spoliāt·us -a -um *adj* stripped, robbed

spolĭ·ō -āre *vt* to strip of clothes; to pillage, plunder, rob

spol·ĭum -ĭī or **-ī** *n* hide, skin; spoils, booty, loot

spond·a -ae *f* bed frame, sofa frame; bed, sofa

spondāl·ĭum or **spondaul·ĭum -ĭī** or **-ī** *n* ritual hymn accompanied by a flute

spondĕō spondēre spopondī sponsum *vt* to promise solemnly, pledge, vow; to promise in marriage; *vi* (law) to give a guarantee, put up bail; (with **pro** + *abl*) to vouch for

spondē·us -ī *m* spondee

spondȳl·us -ī *m* mussel

spongĭ·a -ae *f* sponge; coat of mail

spons·a -ae *f* fiancée

sponsāl·ĭa -ĭum *n pl* engagement; engagement party

sponsĭ·ō -ōnis *f* solemn promise, guarantee; bet; (law) agreement between two parties that the loser pay a certain sum to the other

spons·or -ōris *m* guarantor, surety

spons·us -a -um *pp* of **spondeo;** *m* fiancé, bridegroom; *f* see **sponsa;** *n* agreement, engagement

spons·us -ūs *m* contract

sponte (only *abl*) *f* (of persons, mostly with possessive *adj*) of one's own accord, voluntarily; by oneself, unaided; (of things) of itself, spontaneously; on its own account, for its own sake

sport·a -ae *f* plaited basket; sieve

sportell·a -ae *f* little basket, lunch basket

sportŭl·a -ae *f* little basket (*in which gifts of food were given by the patron to his clients*); dole, present (*of food or money*); gift

sprētĭ·ō -ōnis *f* scorn, contempt

sprēt·or -ōris *m* despiser

sprētus *pp* of **sperno**

spūm·a -ae *f* foam, froth; lather; scum

spūmāt·us -a -um *adj* covered with foam

spūmesc·ō -ĕre *vi* to grow foamy

spūmĕ·us -a -um *adj* foaming, frothing

spūmĭf·er -ĕra -ĕrum *adj* foaming

spūmĭg·er -ĕra -ĕrum *adj* foaming

spūm·ō -āre *vi* to foam, froth

spūmōs·us -a -um *adj* full of foam, foaming; bombastic (*poem*)

spuō spuĕre spuī spūtum *vt* to spit, spit out; *vi* to spit

spurcāt·us -a -um *adj* foul, filthy

spurcē *adv* filthily; in filthy language

spurcidĭc·us -a -um *adj* foul-mouthed, filthy, smutty, obscene

spurcifĭc·us -a -um *adj* smutty, obscene

spurcitĭ·a -ae or **spurcitĭ·ēs -ēī** *f* filth, smut

spurc·ō -āre *vt* to make filthy, foul up; to defile

spurc·us -a -um *adj* (morally) filthy, dirty

spūtātilĭc·us -a -um *adj* deserving to be spit at, contemptible, disgusting

spūtāt·or -ōris *m* spitter

spūt·ō -āre *vt* to spit, spit out; to avert by spitting

spūt·um -ī *n* spit

squāl·ĕō -ēre -ŭī *vi* to be rough, be scaly, be parched, be wrankled; to be coated, be clotted, be stiff; to be covered with filth; to be covered with weeds, be overgrown; to wear mourning clothes, go in mourning

squālĭdē *adv* coarsely

squālĭd·us -a -um *adj* rough, scaly; stiff, coated with dirt, squalid; in mourning; rough, coarse (*speech*); cracked, parched (*land*)

squāl·or -ōris *m* squalor, dirtiness; desolation; filthy garments (*neglected as a sign of mourning*)

squal·us -ī *m* shark

squām·a -ae *f* scale; scale armor; fish

squāmĕ·us -a -um *adj* scaly

squāmĭf·er -ĕra -ĕrum *adj* scaly

squāmĭg·er -ĕra -ĕrum *adj* scaly; *m pl* fish
squāmōs·us -a -um *adj* covered with scales, scaly
squill·a or **scill·a -ae** *f* shrimp
st *interj* sh!
stabilīment·um -ī *n* support
stabil·iō -īre -īvī -ītum *vt* to stabilize; to establish
stabĭl·is -ē *adj* stable, firm, steady; steadfast, unwavering, immutable
stabilĭt·ās -ātis *f* stability, firmness, steadiness, durability
stabilĭter *adv* firmly
stabŭl·ō -āre *vt* to stable or house (*animals*); *vi* to have a stall
stabŭl·um -ī *n* stable, stall; lair; hut; brothel
stact·a -ae or **stact·ē -ēs** *f* myrrh oil
stad·ium -iī or **-ī** *n* furlong; race track
Stagīr·a -ōrum *n pl* town in Macedonia, the birthplace of Aristotle
Stagīrīt·es -ae *m* Aristotle
stagn·ō -āre *vt* to overflow, inundate; *vi* to form a pool; to be inundated
stagn·um -ī *n* pool, swamp, lake, lagoon; straits; waters
stalagm·ium -iī or **-ī** *n* eardrop, earring (*with pendant*)
stām·en -ĭnis *n* warp (*of a loom*); thread; string (*of an instrument*); fillet (*worn by priests*)
stāminĕ·us -a -um *adj* full of threads, consisting of threads, wrapped in threads
Stat·a -ae *f* surname of Vesta
statārĭ·us -a -um *adj* standing, stationary; steady, calm; *m pl* actors in a type of comedy; *f* quiet or refined comedy
statēr·a -ae *f* scales; **statera aurificis** goldsmith's scales
staticŭl·us -ī *m* a dance
statim *adv* at once, immediately, on the spot
statĭ·ō -ōnis *f* standing still; station, post; position; residence; anchorage; *f pl* sentries
Stāt·ius -iī or **-ī** *m* P. Papinius Statius (*poet of the Silver Age of Latin literature, c.* 40-96 A.D.)
statīv·us -a -um *adj* stationary; *n pl* bivouac
stat·or -ōris *m* magistrate's attendant
Stat·or -ōris *m* Stayer (*epithet of Jupiter, who kept the Roman soldiers from retreating*)
statŭ·a -ae *f* statue
statūm·en -ĭnis *n* rib (*of a hull*)
stat·ŭō -uĕre -ŭī -ūtum *vt* to cause to stand, bring to a stop; to set up, erect; to establish (*precedent, etc.*); to set, fix, determine; to decide, settle; to decree; to strengthen, support; to appoint, create; to inflict, pass (*sentence, punishment*); to hold, think, consider; to fix (*a price*); to draw up, arrange (*a battle line*)
stat·us -a -um *pp* of **sisto;** *adj* fixed, set, appointed
stat·us -ūs *m* position, posture; position, situation, condition; social status, rank; form of government; (mil) position; **status rei publicae** type of government
statūt·us -a -um *adj* tall
steg·a -ae *f* deck
stell·a -ae *f* star; constellation; **stella comans** comet; **stella diurna** Lucifer; **stella errans** planet
stell·ans -antis *adj* starry
stellāt·us -a -um *adj* set with stars, starry; made into a star
stellĭf·er -ĕra -ĕrum *adj* star-bearing, starry
stellĭg·er -ĕra -ĕrum *adj* star-bearing, starry
stellĭ·ō -ōnis *m* newt, lizard with spotted back
stemm·a -ătis *n* genealogical tree, pedigree; *n pl* antiquity, history
stercorĕ·us -a -um *adj* full of dung
stercŏr·ō -āre *vt* to manure, fertilize
sterc·us -ŏris *n* manure, dung
sterĭl·is -e *adj* sterile, barren; causing barrenness, blighting; empty, bare; unprofitable; unrequited (*love*); wild (*trees*)
sterilĭt·ās -ātis *f* sterility, barrenness
stern·ax -ācis *adj* bucking (*horse*)
sternō sternĕre strāvī strātum *vt* to strew, spread; to pave (*roads, etc.*); to knock down, bring low, slay; to raze, level; to flatten, smooth; to calm, calm down; **sterni** to stretch out (*on the ground*)
sternūment·um -ī *n* sneezing, sneeze
sternŭ·ō -ĕre -ī *vt* to give (*e.g., an omen*) by sneezing; *vi* to sneeze; to sputter
Sterŏp·ē -ēs *f* one of the Pleiades
sterquilīnĭ·um -iī or **-ī** or **sterquilīn·um -ī** *n* dung heap; (term of abuse) heap of dung
stert·ō -ĕre *vi* to snore
Stēsichŏr·us -ī *m* Greek lyric poet of Himera in Sicily (*c.* 640-*c.* 555 B.C.)
Sthenĕl·us -ī *m* king of Mycenae, son of Perseus, and father of Eurystheus; king of the Ligurians and father of Cycnus who was changed into a swan
stibad·ium -iī or **-ī** *n* semicircular seat
stigm·a -ătis *n* mark, brand; stigma (*of disgrace*)
stigmatĭ·ās -ae *m* branded slave
stigmōs·us -a -um *adj* branded
still·a -ae *f* drop; mere drop
still·ō -āre *vt & vi* to drip
stil·us -ī *m* stylus (*pointed instrument for writing*); writing, composition; style (*of writing or speaking*)
stimulātĭ·ō -ōnis *f* stimulation, incitement

stimulātr·ix -īcis *f* inciter (*female*)
stimulĕ·us -a -um *adj* of goads
stimŭlō -āre *vt* to goad, torment; to spur on, incite, excite
stimŭl·us -ī *m* or **stimŭl·um -ī** *n* goad, prick; (mil) pointed stake concealed below the ground; (fig) stimulus, incentive, spur
stingu·ō -ĕre *vt* to quench, extinguish
stīpāti·ō -ōnis *f* crowd, throng
stīpāt·or -ōris *m* attendant; *m pl* retinue
stīpendārĭ·us -a -um *adj* liable to tax, tributary; *m pl* tributary peoples; mercenary troops
stīpend·ĭum -ĭī or **-ī** *n* tax, tribute, tariff; (mil) pay; military service; year's service, campaign; **emereri stipendia** to have served out one's term; **emeritis stipendiis** at the end of one's military service, at discharge; **merere stipendia** or **mereri stipendia** to serve, serve in the army
stīp·es -ĭtis *m* log, trunk; branch, tree; blockhead
stīp·ō -āre *vt* to crowd, cram, pack; to crowd around, accompany in a group
stips stipis *f* gift, donation, alms
stipŭl·a -ae *f* stalk, blade; stubble; reed pipe
stipulāti·ō -ōnis *f* agreement, bargain; (law) formal promise
stipulātiuncŭl·a -ae *f* insignificant promise, slight stipulation
stipulāt·us -a -um *adj* promised
stipŭl·or -ārī -ātus sum *vt* to stipulate; *vi* to bargain; (law) to make a formal promise
stīrĭ·a -ae *f* icicle
stirpĭtus *adv* by the roots
stirp·s or **stirp·ēs** or **stirp·is -is** *f* stock, stem, stalk, root; plant, shrub; race, lineage; offspring, descendant; character, nature; root, source, foundation, beginning, origin
stīv·a -ae *f* plow handle
stlattārĭ·us or **stlātārĭ·us -a -um** *adj* imported, costly
stlopp·us -ī *m* slap (*sound produced by slapping an inflated cheek*)
stō stāre stetī statum *vi* to stand, stand still, remain standing; to stand firm, hold one's ground; to stand upright; (of hair) to stand up straight, stand on end; (of eyes) to remain fixed; (of battle) to continue; (of a ship) to be moored, ride at anchor; to be motionless; to be stuck; to depend, rest; to take sides, take part; (with *abl* of price) to come to, cost; (with *abl* or **in** + *abl*) to depend on, rest with; (with **per** + *acc* of person) to depend on, be due to, be the fault of, thanks to
Stōĭc·a -ōrum *n pl* Stoic philosophy
Stōĭcē *adv* like a Stoic
Stōĭc·us -a -um *adj* Stoic; *m* Stoic, Stoic philosopher; *n pl* see **Stoica**
stol·a -ae *f* dress (*long outer garment worn by Roman women and reaching from the neck to the ankles*); ceremonial gown (*worn by musicians*)
stolāt·us -a -um *adj* wearing a stola; (fig) proper for a lady, lady-like
stolĭdē *adv* stupidly
stolĭd·us -a -um *adj* dull, stupid, stolid, slow
stomăch·or -ārī -ātus sum *vi* to be annoyed, fret, fume, glower
stomachōsĭus *adv* rather angrily
stomachōs·us -a -um *adj* irritable, resentful
stomăch·us -ī *m* stomach; taste, appetite; irritation, anger, resentment; **stomachus bonus** good appetite; good humor, patience
storĕ·a or **storĭ·a -ae** *f* straw mat, rope mat
strab·ō -ōnis *m* squinter
străg·ēs -is *f* heap, confused mass, pile of debris; havoc, massacre
strāgŭl·us -a -um *adj* covering, serving as a covering; *n* rug, carpet; bedspread; horse blanket
strām·en -ĭnis *n* straw
strāment·um -ī *n* straw; covering, saddle cloth; **stramentum agreste** straw bed
strāminĕ·us -a -um *adj* straw, made of straw
strangŭl·ō -āre *vt* to choke, stifle
strangūrĭ·a -ae *f* strangury
stratēgēm·a -ătis *n* stratagem; trick
stratēg·us -ī *m* commander, general; master of ceremonies
stratiōtĭc·us -a -um *adj* soldierlike, soldierly, military
strāt·us -a -um *pp* of **sterno;** *n* quilt, blanket; bed, couch; horse blanket, pack saddle; pavement
strēn·a -ae *f* good-luck omen
strēnŭē *adv* briskly, quickly, actively, strenuously
strēnuĭt·ās -ātis *f* briskness, vigor, liveliness
strēnŭ·ō -āre *vi* to be brisk
strēnŭ·us -a -um *adj* brisk, vigorous, active; fast (*ship*); restless
strepĭt·ō -āre *vi* to be noisy, clatter, rustle
strepĭt·us -ūs *m* noise, din, racket; crash, bang, clank, rumble, rustle, creak, squeak; sound (*of musical instruments*)
strep·ō -ĕre -ŭī -ĭtum *vt* to shout; *vi* to make a noise (*of any kind*); to rattle, clatter, clang, rumble, rustle, creak, squeak; to roar; to hum, murmur; (of musical instruments) to sound, blare; (of places) to ring, resound, be filled
striāt·a -ae *f* scallop
strictim *adv* superficially, cursorily
strictūr·a -ae *f* mass of molten iron
strict·us -a -um *pp* of **stringo;** *adj* close, tight, narrow
strīd·ĕō -ēre -ī or **strīd·ō -ĕre -ī** *vi* to make a high-pitched noise; to hiss, whistle, whizz, shriek, scream; to grate, buzz, rattle

strīd·or -ōris *m* shrill sound, hiss, shriek, scream, whine; harsh noise, grating, rattle, buzz
strīdŭl·us -a -um *adj* shrill, strident, hissing, whistling, creaking
strigĭl·is -is *f* scraper
strig·ō -āre *vi* to stop, halt; to lose strength, give out
strigōs·us -a -um *adj* lean, thin; bald (*style*)
stringō stringĕre strinxī strictum *vt* to strip, clip; to draw (*sword*); to draw tight, tie tight; to press together, compress; to touch lightly, graze; to border on, touch (*places*); to affect, touch, move, pain, wound (*mind, good name, etc.*); to waste, consume
string·or -ōris *m* twinge, shock
strix strigis *f* owl, screech owl
stroph·a -ae *f* trick
Strophăd·es -um *f pl* island home of the Harpies
strophiār·ĭus -ĭī or **-ī** *m* brassiere maker
stroph·ĭum -ĭī or **-ī** *n* brassiere; head band, chaplet
Stroph·ĭus -ĭī or **-ī** *m* king of Phocis and father of Pylades
structĭl·is -e *adj* building, for building
struct·or -ōris *m* builder, mason, carpenter; carver (*at table*)
structūr·a -ae *f* construction; structure
structus *pp* of **struo**
stru·ēs -is *f* pile, heap
stru·ix -īcis *f* pile, heap
strūm·a -ae *f* tumor, swollen gland
strūmōs·us -a -um *adj* scrofulous
struō struĕre struxī structum *vt* to build, build up, erect; to arrange, deploy (*troops*); to arrange, regulate; to occasion, contrive, plot
strūthĕ·us -a -um *adj* sparrow's
strūthiocamēl·us -ī *m* ostrich
Strȳm·ōn -ŏnis *m* river forming the border between Macedonia and Thrace
Strȳmonĭ·us -a -um *adj* Strymonian, Thracian
stud·eō -ēre -ŭī *vt* to desire, be eager for; *vi* to be eager; (with *dat*) **a** to be eager for, be keen on, be enthusiastic about, take pains with, busy oneself with, apply oneself to; **b** to study; **c** to be a partisan of
studiōsē *adv* eagerly, enthusiastically, diligently
studiōs·us -a -um *adj* eager, keen, enthusiastic; studious; (with *genit*) partial to (*a person or cause*); (with *genit* or *dat*) eager for, keen on, enthusiastic about, devoted to, fond of, desirous of; **litterarum studiosus** studious
stud·ĭum -ĭī or **-ī** *n* eagerness, keenness, enthusiasm; devotion (*to a person*); party spirit; study; (with *genit*) eagerness for, enthusiasm for
stultē *adv* foolishly
stutiloquentĭ·a -ae *f* or **stultiloqu·ĭum -ĭī** or **-ī** *n* silly talk
stultilŏqu·us -a -um *adj* talking foolishly
stultitĭ·a -ae *f* foolishness, silliness
stultivĭd·us -a -um *adj* foolish-looking
stult·us -a -um *adj* foolish, silly, stupid
stūp·a -ae *f* tow, coarse flax, hemp
stupe·faciō -facĕre -fēcī -factum (passive: **stupe·fīō -fiĕrī -factus sum**) *vt* to stupefy, stun, astonish, knock senseless
stup·ĕō -ēre -ŭī *vt* to be amazed at; *vi* to be knocked senseless, be stunned, be stupefied, be astounded, be amazed; to be stopped in one's tracks
stup·escō -escĕre -ŭī *vi* to become amazed, become bewildered
stūpĕ·us -a -um *adj* of tow, hempen
stupidĭt·ās -ātis *f* stupidity
stupĭd·us -a -um *adj* amazed, astounded; dull, stupid
stup·or -ōris *m* numbness, bewilderment, confusion; dullness, stupidity
stupp·a -ae *f* tow, coarse flax, hemp
stuppĕ·us -a -um *adj* of tow, hempen
stupr·ō -āre *vt* to ravish, rape; to defile
stupr·um -ī *n* immorality; rape; disgrace (*esp. from a sex crime*)
sturn·us -ī *m* starling
Stygiāl·is -e *adj* Stygian
Stygĭ·us -a -um *adj* Stygian, infernal; deadly
Stymphalĭc·us or **Stymphalĭ·us -a -um** *adj* Stymphalian
Stymphăl·um -ī *n* or **Stymphăl·us -ī** *m* district in Arcadia famous for its vicious birds of prey which were killed by Hercules as one of his twelve labors
Sty·x -gis or **-gos** *f* chief river in the lower world; river in Arcadia
suādēl·a -ae *f* persuasion
suādĕō suādēre suāsī suāsum *vt* to recommend, propose, suggest; to urge, impel, induce; *vi* (with *dat*) to advise, urge, suggest to, propose to; **sibi suadere** (with *acc & inf*) to satisfy oneself that
suās·ĭō -ōnis *f* recommendation; support, backing (*a proposal*); persuasive eloquence
suās·or -ōris *m* adviser; advocate, supporter
suās·um -ī *n* dye
suāsus *pp* of **suadeo**
suās·us -ūs *m* advice
suāveŏl·ens -entis *adj* fragrant
suāviātiō see **saviatio**
suāvidĭc·us -a -um *adj* charming
suāvilŏqu·ens -entis *adj* charming
suāviloquentĭ·a -ae *f* charming manner of speech
suāviŏlum see **saviolum**
suāvĭor see **savior**
suāv·is -e *adj* charming, pleasant, agreeable, attractive

suāvĭt·ās -ātis *f* charm, pleasantness, sweetness, attractiveness

suāvĭter *adv* pleasantly, sweetly, charmingly, attractively

suāvitūd·ō -ĭnis *f* (term of endearment) honey

suāvĭum see **savium**

sub *prep* (with *abl*) under, beneath, underneath, behind; at the foot of, close to, near (*mountain, wall*); during, in, within, at, by, in the time of, just before; during the reign of; (with *acc*) under, along under; up to (*walls*); approaching, about, just before, just after

subabsurdē *adv* a bit absurdly

subabsurd·us -a -um *adj* rather absurd

subaccūs·ō -āre *vt* to blame, find fault with

subactĭ·ō -ōnis *f* working (*of the soil*); development (*of the mind*)

subactus *pp* of **subigo**

subaerāt·us -a -um *adj* (gold) having an inner layer of bronze

subagrest·is -e *adj* rather uncouth

subālār·is -e *adj* carried under the arms

subalb·us -a -um *adj* whitish

subamār·us -a -um *adj* somewhat bitter

subaquĭl·us -a -um *adj* somewhat dark, brownish

subarroganter *adv* rather arrogantly

subauscult·ō -āre *vt* to eavesdrop on; *vi* to eavesdrop

subbasilicān·us -ī *m* loafer (*person who hangs around the basilicas*)

subbĭb·ō -ĕre -ī *vt* to drink a little

subbland·ĭor -īrī -ītus sum *vi* (with *dat*) to flirt with

subc- = succ-

subdifficĭl·is -e *adj* rather difficult

subdiffīd·ō -ĕre *vi* to be a little distrustful

subditīcĭ·us -a -um *adj* substituted, phoney

subditīv·us -a -um *adj* substituted, phoney

subdĭtus *pp* of **subdo**

subdiū *adv* by day

sub·dō -dĕre -dĭdī -dĭtum *vt* to put under; to subdue; to substitute; to forge, make up; to spread (*a rumor*) falsely; (with *dat*) **a** to put or apply (*something*) to, add (*something*) to; **b** to subject (*someone*) to; **se aquis subdere** to plunge into the water

subdoc·ĕō -ēre *vt* to instruct (*as an assistant teacher*)

subdŏlē *adv* rather cunningly

subdŏl·us -a -um *adj* underhand, sly, cunning

subdŏm·ō -āre *vt* to tame somewhat

subdubĭt·ō -āre *vi* to be rather undecided

sub·dūcō -dūcĕre -duxī -ductum *vt* to draw up from below; to pull up, raise, to remove, take away, steal; to haul up, beach (*a ship*); to withdraw (*troops*); to balance (*accounts*)

subductĭ·ō -ōnis *f* drydocking, beaching; calculation, computation

sub·ĕdō -esse -ēdī *vt* to eat away or wear away at the bottom; **scopulum unda subedit** water wears away the bottom of the cliff

sub·ĕō -īre -īvī or **-iī -ĭtum** *vt* to enter (*a place*), enter (*the mind*); to approach, attack; to undergo (*dangers, punishment, etc.*); to help, support; to climb; to slip under; to dodge (*a blow*); *vi* to come or go up, climb; to follow; to advance, press forward; (with **ad** or **in** + *acc*) **a** to come up against, attack; **b** to climb (*a mountain*); **c** to approach, enter

sūb·er -ĕris *n* cork tree; cork

subf- = suff-

subg- = sugg-

subhorrĭd·us -a -um *adj* rather coarse, rather uncouth

sub·icĭō -icĕre -jēcī -jectum *vt* to throw up, fling up; to bring up; to bring up close, expose; to suggest; to add, append; to suborn; to substitute; to forge; (with *dat* or **sub** + *acc*) **a** to put, place (*something*) under; **b** to subject (*someone*) to (*authority, danger, risk*); **c** to classify (*something*) under; **d** to submit (*something*) to (*one's judgment*)

subigitātĭ·ō -ōnis *f* lewdness; intercourse

subigitātr·ix -īcis *f* loose woman

subigĭt·ō -āre *vt* to lie with

sub·igō -igĕre -ēgī -actum *vt* to turn up, till, plow; to knead; to whet, sharpen; to rub down; to tame; to train, discipline (*the mind*); to conquer, subdue, subjugate, reduce; to force, impel, constrain; to incite; to row, propel (*a boat*)

subimpŭd·ens -entis *adj* rather shameless

subinān·is -e *adj* rather empty, rather pointless

subinde *adv* immediately afterwards; from time to time

subinsuls·us -a -um *adj* rather insipid

subinvid·ĕō -ēre *vi* (with *dat*) to envy (*someone*) a little

subinvīs·us -a -um *adj* rather disliked, rather unpopular

subinvīt·ō -āre *vt* to invite unenthusiastically

subīr·ascor -ascī -ātus sum *vi* to be annoyed; (with *dat*) to be peeved at

subitārĭ·us -a -um *adj* (mil) suddenly called up (*to meet an emergency*); built in a hurry

subĭtō *adv* suddenly, unexpectedly, at once; **subito dicere** to speak ex-tempore

subĭt·us -a -um *adj* coming on suddenly, sudden, unexpected; rash

(*man*); emergency (*troops*); *n* emergency
subjac·ĕō -ēre -ŭī *vi* to lie nearby; (with *dat*) to lie under or close to; **monti subjacere** to lie at the foot of the mountain
subjectī·ō -ōnis *f* subjection; substitution; forgery
subjectissĭmē *adv* most humbly
subject·ō -āre *vt* to toss up
subject·or -ōris *m* forger
subject·us -a -um *pp* of **subicio;** *adj* (with *dat*) **a** located near, bordering on; **b** subject to; *m* subject (*conquered person*)
sub·jungō -jungĕre -junxī -junctum *vt* (with *dat*) **a** to yoke or harness to; **b** to join to, connect with, add to; **c** to make subject to
sub·lābor -lābī -lapsus sum *vi* to sink, fall down, collapse; to glide imperceptibly; to fall back, fail
sublātē *adv* loftily, in lofty tones
sublātī·ō -ōnis *f* elevation, raising
sublāt·us -a -um *pp* of **suffero** and of **tollo;** *adj* elated
sublect·ō -āre *vt* to coax, cajole
sub·lĕgō -legĕre -lēgī -lectum *vt* to gather up, pick up; to pick up stealthily, steal, kidnap; to substitute; to overhear, pick up
sublest·us -a -um *adj* weak, trifling
sublevātī·ō -ōnis *f* alleviation, lightening
sublĕv·ō -āre *vt* to lift up, raise, support
sublĭc·a -ae *f* stake, pile (*esp. for a bridge*)
sublicĭ·us -a -um *adj* resting upon piles; **pons sublicious** wooden bridge across the Tiber, built by Ancus Marcius
subligăcŭl·um -ī *n* short apron
sublĭg·ar -āris *n* apron
sublĭg·ō -āre *vt* (with *dat*) to tie or fasten (*e.g., a sword*) to or below
sublīmē *adv* aloft, on high
sublīmen *adv* upwards, on high
sublīm·is -e *adj* high, raised up, lifted high; lofty, elevated, exalted; raised high, borne aloft, through the sky; aspiring; eminent, distinguished
sublīm·us -a -um *adj* high, lofty
sublīmĭt·ās -ātis *f* loftiness, sublimity
sublingĭ·ō -ōnis *m* scullion
sub·lĭnō -linĕre -lēvī -lĭtum *vt* to smear secretly; **os sublinere** (with *dat*) to cheat (*someone*)
sublūc·ĕō -ēre *vi* to shine faintly, glimmer
sub·lŭō -luĕre — -lūtum *vt* to wash underneath; to flow at the foot of (*a mountain*)
sublustr·is -e *adj* dimly lighted, throwing some light, glimmering, flickering
subm- = summ-
sub·nascor -nascī -nātus sum *vi* (with *dat*) to grow up underneath
sub·nectō -nectĕre -nexŭī -nexum *vt* to fasten, tie (*something*) underneath; to confine; (with *dat*) to fasten or tie (*something*) below (*something else*)
subnĕg·ō -āre *vt* to halfway refuse; (with *dat*) to halfway refuse (*something*) to (*someone*)
subnĭg·er -ra -rum *adj* blackish
subnimĭ·a -ae *f* robe
subnīs·us or **subnix·us -a -um** *adj* propped up, resting, leaning; (with *dat*) **a** propped up on, resting on, leaning on; **b** relying on, depending on, confiding in
subnŏt·ō -āre *vt* to note down, record, register; to observe secretly
subnŭb·a -ae *f* rival (*female*)
subnūbĭl·us -a -um *adj* somewhat cloudy, overcast
sub·ō -āre *vi* to be in heat
subobscēn·us -a -um *adj* somewhat obscene, shady
subobscūr·us -a -um *adj* rather obscure
subodiōs·us -a -um *adj* annoying
suboffend·ō -ĕre *vi* to give some offense
subŏl·et -ēre *v impers* there is a faint smell; **mihi subolet** I have an inkling, I have a sneaking suspicion, I have a faint idea
subŏl·ēs -is *f* offspring
subolesc·ō -ĕre *vi* to grow up instead
subor·ĭor -īrī *vi* to rise up in succession, arise, proceed
suborn·ō -āre *vt* to equip, supply, provide; to employ as a secret agent, incite secretly, suborn
subp- = supp-
subr- = surr-
sub·scrībō -scrībĕre -scripsī -scriptum *vt* to write underneath; to sign; to write down, record, register; *vi* to sign an accusation, act as prosecutor; (with *dat*) **a** to add (*something*) to, attach (*something*) in writing to; **b** to assent to, agree to; (with **in** + *acc*) to sign an accusation against, indict, accuse, prosecute
subscriptĭ·ō -ōnis *f* inscription underneath; signature; (law) subscription; recording (*of an offense by the censor*); record, register
subscript·or -ōris *m* signer or joint-signer (*of an accusation*)
subscriptus *pp* of **subscribo**
subsc·ūs -ūdis *f* tenon of a dovetail
subsecīvus see **subsicivus**
subsĕc·ō -āre -ŭī -tum *vt* to clip, trim, cut off
subsecūtus *pp* of **subsĕquor**
subsell·ĭum -ĭī or **-ī** *n* low seat or bench; seat or bench on a lower level; judge's seat, the bench; tribunal, court; seat in the senate, senator's seat; bleachers (*where the poor people sat*); **versatus in utrisque subsellis** experienced as judge and lawyer

sub·sentiō -sentīre -sensī *vt* to have some inkling of
sub·sĕquor -sĕquī -secūtus sum *vt* to follow close after, chase, pursue; to back up, support; to imitate; to adhere to, conform to; to come after, succeed (*in time or order*); *vi* to ensue
subserv·iō -īre *vi* (with *dat*) **a** to be subject to; **b** to accommodate oneself to, humor; **c** to support, aid
subsicīv·us -a -um *adj* left over; extra, spare (*time*); extra, overtime (*work*)
subsidiārī·us -a -um *adj* (mil) reserve; *m pl* reserves
subsid·ium -iī or **-ī** *n* aid, support; place of refuge, asylum; protection; (mil) reserves, triarii; military support, relief, aid; **subsidio esse** (with *dat*) to act as support to; **subsidio mittere** to send in support
sub·sīdō -sīdĕre -sēdī -sessum *vt* to lie in wait for; *vi* to sit down, crouch down, settle down; to sink, subside, settle; to establish oneself, settle down, establish residence, stay
subsignān·us -a -um *adj* special reserve (*troops*)
subsign·ō -āre *vt* to endorse, subscribe to (*an opinion*); to register, enter, record; to guarantee
subsil·iō -īre -iī *vi* to jump up
sub·sistō -sistĕre -stitī *vt* to hold out against; *vi* to stand up; to make a stand, take a firm stand; to come to a standstill, stop; to stay behind; (with *dat*) **a** to take a stand against, oppose, fight; **b** to meet (*an expense*)
subsort·ior -īrī -ītus sum *vt* to choose as a substitute by lot; *vi* to choose a substitute by lot; (in a passive sense) to be chosen as a substitute
subsortīti·ō -ōnis *f* substitution by lot
substantī·a -ae *f* substance, essence; means, wealth, property
sub·sternō -sternĕre -strāvī -strātum *vt* to spread underneath; to cover; (with *dat*) to put at the disposal of, make subservient to; **rem publicam libidini suae substernere** to misuse high office to serve one's lust
substit·ŭō -uĕre -ŭī -ūtum *vt* to submit, present; to substitute; (with *dat* or **in locum** with *genit*) to substitute for or in place of; **animo** or **oculis substituere** to imagine
subst·ō -āre *vi* to stand firm, hold out; (with *dat*) to stand up to
substrātus *pp* of **substerno**
substrict·us -a -um *adj* tight, narrow, small
sub·stringō -stringĕre -strinxī -strictum *vt* to tie up, draw up; to restrain, control; (with *dat*) to press (*something*) close to
substructi·ō -ōnis *f* substructure, foundation
sub·strŭō -struĕre -struxī -structum *vt* to lay (*foundation*); **vias glareā substruere** to lay a foundation of gravel on the roads
subsult·ō -āre *vi* to jump up, jump up and down
sub·sum -esse *vi* to be near, be at hand; (with *dat*) **a** to be below or beneath, be under; **b** to be concealed in; **c** to be subject to, subservient to
subsūt·us -a -um *adj* trimmed at the bottom
subtēm·en -inis *n* woof; thread, yarn
subter *adv* below, underneath; *prep* (with *abl*) beneath, below, underneath, under; (with *acc*) underneath, beneath; up to, close to, close beneath
subter·dūcō -dūcĕre -duxī -ductum *vt* to withdraw secretly, lead away secretly
subter·fugiō -fugĕre -fūgī *vt* to evade, avoid; *vi* to run away secretly, get off
subter·lābor -lābī *vt* to glide or flow under; *vi* to slip away, escape
sub·tĕrō -terĕre -trīvī -trītum *vt* to wear away underneath
subterrānĕ·us -ā -um *adj* subterranean, underground
subtex·ō -ĕre -ŭī -tum *vt* to sew on; to veil, cover; (fig) to work up, compose; (with *dat*) **a** to sew onto; **b** to throw (*a covering*) over; **c** to work (*something*) into (*a story or plot*)
subtīl·is -e *adj* woven fine, of fine texture; delicate; subtle; discriminating, precise; plain, direct (*style*)
subtīlit·ās -ātis *f* fineness, minuteness; slenderness; exactness, precision; simplicity (*of style*)
subtīliter *adv* finely, delicately; accurately; plainly, simply
subtim·ĕō -ēre *vt* to be a bit afraid of
sub·trăhō -trahĕre -traxī -tractum *vt* to drag up from beneath, drag out, draw off, withdraw, remove; to avert (*the eyes*); (with *dat*) to drag or draw (*something*) away from
subtrist·is -e *adj* rather sad
subtrītus *pp* of **subtero**
subturpicŭl·us -a -um *adj* somewhat disgraceful
subturp·is -e *adj* rather disgraceful
subtus *adv* below, underneath
subtūs·us -a -um *adj* somewhat bruised
subūcŭl·a -ae *f* man's undershirt
sūbŭl·a -ae *f* awl
subulc·us -ī *m* swineherd
Subūr·a -ae *f* rough, noisy district in Rome, N.E. of the Forum between the Esquiline and Quirinal
Subūrān·us -a -um *adj* of the Subura
suburbānit·ās -ātis *f* nearness to Rome

suburbān·us -a -um *adj* suburban, near Rome; *m* suburbanite; *n* suburban home

suburb·ium -iī or **-ī** *n* suburb

suburg·ĕō -ēre *vt* (with **ad** + *acc*) to keep or turn (*a ship*) close to

subvectī·ō -ōnis *f* transportation

subvect·ō -āre *vt* to bring up regularly

subvectus *pp of* **suveho**

subvect·us -ūs *m* bringing up, transportation

sub·vĕhō -vehĕre -vexī -vectum *vt* to carry or bring up, transport

sub·veniō -venīre -vēnī -ventum *vi* (with *dat*) to come up to aid, reinforce, relieve

subvent·ō -āre *vi* (with *dat*) to rush to the aid of

subver·ĕor -ērī *vi* to be a bit apprehensive

subvers·ō or **subvors·ō -āre** *vt* to ruin completely

subvers·or -ōris *m* subverter, repealer

sub·vertō or **sub·vortō -vertĕre -vertī -versum** *vt* to turn upside down, upset, overthrow, throw over, subvert

subvex·us -a -um *adj* sloping upward

subvŏl·ō -āre *vi* to fly up

subvolv·ō -ĕre *vt* to roll up

subvor- = **subver-**

subvulturi·us -a -um *adj* vulture-like

succăv·us -a -um *adj* hollow underneath

succēdānĕ·us or **succīdānĕ·us -a -um** *adj* substitute

suc·cēdō -cēdĕre -cessī -cessum *vt* to climb; to march on or against, advance to or as far as; *vi* to come up, climb; to come next, follow in succession; to turn out (*successfully*); (with **ad, in,** or **sub** + *acc*) to climb, climb up; (with *dat*) **a** to come next to, follow; **b** to succeed in (*an undertaking*); **c** to yield to, submit to; **d** to relieve, take the place of (*e.g., tired troops*); **e** to enter, go below to (*e.g., a shelter; grave*); (with **in** or **ad** + *acc*) (fig) to reach, attain (*e.g., high honors*), receive by succession, enter upon (*an inheritance*)

suc·cendō -cendĕre -cendī -censum *vt* to set on fire, set fire to; to light (*a fire*); (fig) to inflame

succens·ĕō or **suscens·ĕō -ēre -ī** *vi* to be angry, be enraged; (*with dat*) to be enraged at

succensus *pp of* **succendo**

succenturiāt·us -a -um *adj* in reserve

succenturi·ō -āre *vt* to receive (*someone*) as a substitute into a century or company

succenturi·ō -ōnis *m* assistant centurion, substitute for a centurion

successi·ō -ōnis *f* succession

success·or -ōris *m* successor

success·us -ūs *m* approach, advance uphill; outcome, success

succīdānĕus see **succedaneus**

succīdi·a -ae *f* leg or side of meat; (fig) extra income

suc·cīdō -cīdĕre -cīdī -cīsum *vt* to cut down, cut off, mow down

suc·cĭdō -cidĕre -cĭdī *vi* to sink, give way; to collapse, fail

succĭd·us or **sūcĭd·us -a -um** *adj* juicy; (coll) fresh, plump (*girl*)

succidŭ·us -a -um *adj* sinking, falling

suc·cingō -cingĕre -cinxī -cinctum *vt* to tuck up; to put on (*e.g., a sword*); to equip, arm, fit out

succingŭl·um -ī *n* belt

succĭn·ō -ĕre *vi* to chime in (*in conversation*)

succīsus *pp of* **succīdo**

succlāmāti·ō -ōnis *f* shouting in reply

succlām·ō -āre *vt* to shout out after, interrupt with shouts; (with *dat*) to shout out (*words*) at

succontumēliōsē *adv* rather insolently

suc·crescō -crescĕre -crēvī *vi* to grow up; to be replenished; (with *dat*) to attain to

succrisp·us -a -um *adj* rather curled

suc·cumbō -cumbĕre -cubŭī -cubitum *vi* to fall or sink back; to yield, succumb, submit

suc·currō -currĕre -currī -cursum *vi* (with *dat*) **a** to run up to; **b** to run to help; **c** to occur to, enter the mind of

succ·us or **sūc·us -ī** *m* sap, juice; taste, flavor

succuss·us -ūs *m* shaking, jolt

succust·ōs -ōdis *m* assistant guard

suc·cutiō -cutĕre -cussī -cussum *vt* to toss up

sūcĭdus see **succidus**

sūcĭn·us -a -um *adj & n* amber

suctus *pp of* **sūgō**

sucŭl·a -ae *f* little pig; winch, windlass

sūcus see **succus**

sūdār·ium -iī or **-ī** *n* handkerchief, towel

sūdātōri·us -a -um *adj* sweat, for sweating; *n* sweat room

sūdātr·ix -īcis *adj* causing sweat

sud·is -is *f* stake, pile; pike (*weapon*); dorsal fin

sūd·ō -āre *vt* to sweat, exude; to soak with sweat; (fig) to sweat over; *vi* to sweat; to drip

sūd·or -ōris *m* sweat; moisture; hard work

sūducŭl·um -ī *n* sweat-maker (*i.e., whip*)

sūd·us -a -um *adj* dry; clear, cloudless (*weather*); *n* clear weather, bright sky

su·ĕō -ēre *vi* to be accustomed; (with *inf*) be accustomed or used to

su·escō -escĕre -ēvī -ētum *vt* to

accustom, familiarize; *vi* to become used; (with *dat*) to get used to

Suess·a -ae *f* town in Latium

suēt·us *pp* of **suesco;** *adj* usual, familiar

Suēv·ī -ōrum *m pl* a people of N.E. Germany

sūf·es -ĕtis *m* chief magistrate at Carthage

suffarcināt·us -a -um *adj* stuffed full

suffarcĭn·ō -āre *vt* to stuff full, cram

suffectus *pp* of **sufficio**

suffĕrō sufferre sustŭlī sublātum *vt* to suffer, bear, endure

suf·fĭcĭō -ficĕre -fēcī -fectum *vt* to lay the foundation for; to dip, tinge, dye; to appoint to a vacancy; to yield, supply, afford; **consul suffectus** substitute cousul (*consul appointed to complete an unexpired term of another consul*); *vi* to suffice, be sufficient; (with *dat* or with **ad** or **in** + *acc*) to suffice for, be adequate to

suf·fīgō -fīgĕre -fixī -fixum *vt* to nail up, fasten

suffīm·en -ĭnis *n* incense

suffīment·um -ī *n* incense

suffixus *pp* of **suffigo**

sufflām·en -ĭnis *n* brake (*on a vehicle*)

sufflāt·us -a -um *adj* puffed up, bloated; (fig) fuming (*with anger*)

suffl·ō -āre *vt* to blow up, inflate; *vi* to blow, puff

suffōc·ō -āre *vt* to choke, strangle

suf·fodĭō -fodĕre -fōdī -fossum *vt* to stab, pierce; to dig under (*walls*)

suffrāgātĭ·ō -ōnis *f* voting (*in someone's favor*), support

suffrāgāt·or -ōris *m* supporter (*at the polls*), partisan

suffrāgātōrĭ·us -a -um *adj* partisan

suffrāg·ĭum -ĭī or **-ī** *n* ballot, vote; right to vote, franchise; decision, judgment; applause, approbation; **suffragium ferre** to cast a ballot; **suffragium ferre** (with **de** or **in** + *abl*) to vote on

suffrāg·or -ārī -ātus sum *vi* to cast a favorable vote; (with *dat*) to vote in favor of, support, vote for; **fortunā suffragante** with luck on our side

suffring·ō -ĕre *vt* to break, smash

suf·fugĭō -fugĕre -fūgī *vt* to escape, avoid; *vi* (with **in** + *acc*) to run to for cover

suffug·ĭum -ĭī or **-ī** *n* shelter, cover

suf·fulcĭō -fulcīre -fulsī -fultum *vt* to prop up, underpin, support

suf·fundō -fundĕre -fūdī -fūsum *vt* to pour in, fill; to suffuse, spread; to tinge, color; to infuse; **virgineum ore ruborem suffundere** (with *dat*) to cause (*someone*) to blush

suffūr·or -ārī *vt* to filch

suffusc·us -a -um *adj* darkish, brownish

suffūsus *pp* of **suffundo**

sug·gĕrō -gerĕre -gessī -gestum *vt* to supply, add; to prompt, suggest

suggest·um -ī *m* platform; stage

suggestus *pp* of **suggero**

suggest·us -ūs *m* platform; stage

suggrand·is -e *adj* rather huge

sug·gredĭor -grĕdī -gressus sum *vt & vi* to approach

sūgillātĭ·ō -ōnis *f* bruise; affront

sūgill·ō -āre *vt* to beat black and blue; to affront, insult

sūgō sūgĕre suxī suctum *vt* to suck

suī see **se**

suill·us -a -um *adj* of swine; **grex suillus** herd of swine

sulc·ō -āre *vt* to furrow, plow; to make a line in (*sand*)

sulc·us -ī *m* furrow; ditch, trench (*for plants*); track (*of a wheel or meteor*); wrinkle; plowing; wake (*of ship*)

sulf·ur -ŭris *m* sulfur

Sull·a -ae *m* Sulla (*Cornelius Sulla Felix, Roman general, dictator, champion of the aristocratic party, and political reformer,* 138-78 B.C.)

Sullān·ī -ōrum *m pl* partisans of Sulla

sullātur·ĭō -īre *vi* to wish to be a Sulla

Sulm·ō -ōnis *m* town about ninety miles east of Rome and birthplace of Ovid

Sulmōnens·is -e *adj* of Sulmo

sulp·ur or **sulf·ur -ŭris** *m* sulfur

sulpurāt·us -a -um *adj* saturated with sulfur; *n pl* matches

sulpurĕ·us -a -um *adj* sulfurous

sultis = **si vultis** if you please, please

sum esse fuī *vi* to be, exist; (with *genit* of possession) to belong to, pertain to, be characteristic of, be the duty of; (with *genit* or *abl* of quality) to be of, be possessed of, have; (with *genit* or *abl* of value) to be valued at, cost; (with *dat*) to belong to; (with **ab** + *abl*) to belong to; (with **ad** + *acc*) to be designed for; (with **ex** + *abl*) to consist of; **est** (with *inf*) it is possible to, it is permissible to; **est** (with **ut**) it is possible that; **sunt qui** there are those who, there are people who, they are of the type that

sūm·en -ĭnis *n* breast, teat, udder; breeding sow

summ·a -ae *f* main thing; chief point, gist, summary; sum, amount, contents, substance; sum of money; **ad summam** generally, on the whole; in short; **summa rerum** the world; supreme power; **summa summarum** the whole universe

summān·ō -āre *vi* to drip a bit

Summān·us -ī *m* Roman god of night lightning

summ·ās -ātis *adj* high-born, aristocratic, noble
summātim *adv* on the surface; generally, summarily
summāt·us -ūs *m* supremacy, supreme power
summē *adv* very, extremely
sum·mergō -mergĕre -mersī -mersum *vt* to sink, submerge, drown
summĕr·us -a -um *adj* pure, straight (*wine*)
sumministr·ō -āre *vt* to supply, furnish
summissē or **summissim** *adv* in a low voice, softly; modestly, humbly
summissī·ō -ōnis *f* lowering, dropping
summiss·us -a -um *adj* lowered, stooping; lowered, soft (*voice*); humble, unassuming; submissive; too submissive, abject
sum·mittō -mittĕre -mīsī -missum *vt* to let down, lower, sink, drop; to let (*hair*) grow long; to lower, reduce, moderate, relax, lessen; to bring down, humble; to rear, put forth, produce; to send secretly; to send as a reinforcement; to send as a substitute; **animum summittere** (with *dat*) to yield to; **se summittere** to bend down, stoop over; to condescend; **se summittere** (with *dat*) to yield to, give in to
summolestē *adv* with some annoyance
summolest·us -a -um *adj* rather annoying
summon·ĕō -ēre -ŭī *vt* to give (*someone*) a gentle reminder, remind privately
summopĕre *adv* with the greatest diligence, completely
summōrōs·us -a -um *adj* rather crabby
sum·movĕō -movēre -mōvī -mōtum *vt* to move up, advance; to clear (*e.g., the court*); to remove; to expel, banish; (mil) to dislodge; (fig) to drive away, forget about (*e.g., worries*)
summ·us -a -um *adj* uppermost, highest; the top of, the surface of; last, latest, the end of; greatest, best, top, consummate; most distinguished; most important; *m* head of the table; *f* see **summa;** *n* top, surface, highest place, head of the table
summum *adv* at most; at latest; **uno aut summum altero proelio** in one or at most in two battles
sūmō sūmĕre sumpsī sumptum *vt* to take up; to put on, dress oneself in, wear; to exact, inflect (*penalty*); to take up, begin, enter upon; to eat, consume; to assume, suppose, take for granted; to cite, adduce, mention; to assume, appropriate; to select; to purchase, buy
sumptī·ō -ōnis *f* assumption
sumptuārĭ·us -a -um *adj* expense, relating to expenses, sumptuary, against extravagance
sumptuōsē *adv* sumptuously, expensively
sumptuōs·us -a -um *adj* costly, expensive; lavish, wasteful
sumptus *pp* of **sumo**
sumpt·us -ūs *m* cost, expense, charge; **sumptui esse** (with *dat*) to be costly to, be expensive to; **sumptum suum exercere** to earn one's keep; **sumptu tuo** at your expense, out of your pocket
Sūn·ĭum -ĭī or **-ī** *n* S.E. promontory of Attica
suō suĕre suī sūtum *vt* to sew, stitch, tack together
suōmet = emphatic form of **suo**
suopte = emphatic form of **suo**
suovetaurīl·ĭa -ĭum *n pl* sacrifice of a pig, sheep, and bull
supell·ex -ectĭlis *f* furniture, household utensils; (fig) outfit, qualification
super *adv* on the top, above; besides, moreover; **super esse** to be left over; *prep* (with *abl*) above, over, upon, on; concerning, about; besides, in addition to; at, on (*time*); (with *acc*) over, above, upon; (with numbers) over, more than; besides, over and above
supĕr·a -ōrum *n pl* upper world, sky, Heaven; heavenly bodies
supĕrā *adv* above
superābĭl·is -e *adj* surmountable, climbable; conquerable
super·addō -addĕre — -addĭtum *vt* to add besides, add to boot
supĕr·ans -antis *adj* predominant
superast·ō -āre *vi* (with *dat*) to stand on
superāt·or -ōris *m* conqueror
superbē *adv* arrogantly, haughtily, snobbishly
superbĭ·a -ae *f* arrogance, haughtiness, snobbishness; (justifiable) pride
superbiloquentĭ·a -ae *f* haughty tone, arrogant speech
superb·ĭō -īre *vi* to be haughty; to be superb, be magnificent; (with *abl*) to take pride in
superb·us -a -um *adj* arrogant, haughty, snobbish; overbearing, tyrannical, despotic; fastidious, disdainful; superb, magnificent
supercil·ĭum -ĭī or **-ī** *n* eyebrow; frown, will (*of Jupiter*); summit, brow (*of a hill, etc.*); arrogance, superciliousness
superēmin·ĕō -ēre -ŭī *vt* to tower over, top
superficĭ·ēs -ēī *f* top, surface; (law) fixtures, improvements, buildings (*i.e., anything upon the property, but not the land itself*)
super·fīō -fĭĕrī *vi* to be over and above; to be left over

superfix·us -a -um *adj* attached above
superflŭ·ens -entis *adj* superabundant, running over; (with *abl*) abounding in
superflŭ·ō -ĕre *vi* to overflow
super·fundō -fundĕre -fūdī -fūsum *vt* (with *abl*) to shower (*something*) with; (with *dat*) to pour (*something*) upon; **superfundi** or **se superfundere** to spread, spread out, extend; **fama superfudit se in Asiam** the report spread to Asia
super·gredĭor -grĕdī -gressus sum *vt* to walk or step over; to surpass
supĕr·ī -ōrum *m pl* the gods above; men on earth; mortals; upper world
superimmin·ĕō -ēre *vt* to tower above
superimpend·ens -entis *adj* overhanging, towering overhead
superim·pōnō -pōnĕre -posŭī -posĭtum *vt* to place on top, place overhead
superimposĭt·us -a -um *adj* superimposed
superincĭd·ens -entis *adj* falling from above
superincŭb·ans -antis *adj* lying above or on top
superin·cumbō -cumbĕre -cubŭī *vi* (with *dat*) to lay oneself down upon
superingĕr·ō -ĕre *vt* to pour down
superin·icĭō -icĕre — -jectum *vt* to throw on top
superin·sternō -sternĕre -strāvī *vt* to cover
superĭ·or -us (*comp* of **supĕrus**) *adj* higher, upper; the upper part of; past, previous, preceding; older, elder, more advanced; victorious, conquering; superior, stronger; superior, greater; **de loco superiore dicere** to speak from the tribunal, handle a case in court; to speak from the rostra, deliver a formal address; **ex loco superiore pugnare** to fight from a vantage point
superin·jacĭō -jacĕre -jēcī -jectum or **-jactum** *vt* to overspread, overwhelm; to overdo, exaggerate
superinjectus *pp* of **superinicio**
superlātĭ·ō -ōnis *f* exaggeration
superlāt·us -a -um *adj* exaggerated
supernē *adv* above, from above
supern·us -a -um *adj* upper; situated high up; supernal, celestial
supĕr·ō -āre *vt* to go over, pass over, rise above; to pass or go past, go beyond; to sail past, double; to outdo, surpass; to overcome, vanquish; *vi* to mount, ascend; to be superior, have the advantage; to be left over, survive; to be superfluous; to be abundant; (with *dat*) to pass over, pass above
superobrŭ·ō -ĕre *vt* to cover completely, smother
superpend·ens -entis *adj* towering overhead
super·pōnō -pōnĕre -posŭī -posĭtum *vt* (with *dat*) to put or place (*something*) upon; (with **in** + *acc*) to put (*someone*) in charge of
superscand·ō -ĕre *vt* to step over, climb over
super·sedĕō -sedēre -sēdī -sessum *vi* (with *abl*) to refrain from, give up
superstagn·ō -āre *vi* (of a river) to overflow and form swamps
superst·es -ĭtis *adj* standing by as a witness; surviving; posthumous; (with *genit* or *dat*) outliving, surviving; **superstes esse** to live on; **superstes esse** (with *genit* or *dat*) to outlive (*someone or something*)
superstitĭ·ō -ōnis *f* excessive fear; superstition
superstitĭōsē *adv* superstitiously
superstitiōs·us -a -um *adj* superstitious; having magical powers
superstĭt·ō -āre *vi* to be remaining, be left
superst·ō -āre *vt* to stand over; *vi* (with *dat*) to stand on, stand over
superstrāt·us -a -um *adj* spread over (*as a covering*)
super·strŭō -struĕre -struxī -structum *vt* to build on top
super·sum -esse -fŭī *vi* to be left over, still exist, survive; to abound; to be in excess, be superfluous; to be adequate, suffice; (with *dat*) to outlive, survive (*someone*)
supertĕg·ō -ĕre *vt* to cover, cover over
superurg·ens -entis *adj* putting on pressure, adding pressure
supĕr·us -a -um *adj* upper; of this world, of this life; northern; **ad auras superas redire** to return to the upper air, come back to life; **mare superum** Adriatic Sea; *m pl* see **superi**; *n pl* see **supera**
supervacānĕ·us -a -um *adj* superfluous
supervacŭ·us -a -um *adj* superfluous, needless
supervād·ō -ĕre *vt* to go over, climb over
super·vĕhor -vĕhī -vectus sum *vt* to sail, ride, or drive by or past
super·venĭō -venīre -vēnī -ventum *vt* to come upon, come on top of; to overtake; to come over, close over, cover; to surprise; *vi* to arrive suddenly; (with *dat*) to come upon by surprise
supervent·us -ūs *m* sudden arrival, unexpected arrival
supervolĭt·ō -āre *vt* to hover over
supervŏl·ō -āre *vt* to fly over; *vi* to fly across
supīn·ō -āre *vt* to turn up, lay on its back; to turn over (*by plowing*)
supīn·us -a -um *adj* face-up; lying

upwards, turned upwards; sloping, sloping upwards; (streams) flowing upwards (*to their source*); on one's back; lazy, careless, indifferent

suppactus *pp* of **suppingo**

suppaenit·et -ēre *v impers* (with *acc* of person and *genit* of thing regretted), e.g., **illum furoris suppaenitet** he somewhat regrets the outburst

suppalp·or -ārī *vi* (with *dat*) to coax (*someone*) a little

supp·ār -ăris *adj* nearly equal

supparasīt·or -ārī -ātus sum *vi* (with *dat*) to flatter (*someone*) a little like a parasite

suppăr·um -ī *n* or **suppăr·us -ī** *m* linen dress; small sail

suppeditātī·ō -ōnis *f* good supply, abundance

suppedĭt·ō -āre *vt* to supply, furnish; *vi* to stand by; to be at hand, be in stock, be available; (with *dat*) to be at hand for; (with **ad** or **in** + *acc*) to be adequate for, suffice for

suppēd·ō -ĕre *vi* to break wind quietly

suppetī·ae -ārum *f pl* help, assistance

suppetī·or -ārī -ātus sum *vi* (with *dat*) to help, assist

suppĕt·ō -ĕre -īvī or **-ĭī -ītum** *vi* to be at hand, be in stock, be available; (with *dat*) **a** to be at hand for, be available to; **b** to be equal to, suffice for, be sufficient for; **c** to correspond to

suppīl·ō -āre *vt* to filch

sup·pingō -pingĕre — -pactum *vt* to fasten underneath

supplant·ō -āre *vt* to trip up

supplēment·um -ī *n* full complement; reinforcements

suppl·ĕō -ēre -ēvī -ētum *vt* to fill up; to make good (*losses, damage, etc.*); (mil) to bring to full strength

suppl·ex -ĭcis *adj* kneeling, on one's knees, in entreaty; humble, submissive; *m* suppliant

supplicātī·ō -ōnis *f* public thanksgiving, day of prayer; thanksgiving for victory; day of humiliation

supplicĭter *adv* suppliantly, humbly, submissively

supplic·ĭum -ĭī or **-ī** *n* kneeling down, bowing down, humble entreaty; public prayer, supplication; (because criminals were beheaded kneeling) execution, death penalty; punishment, torture; suffering, distress, pain

supplĭc·ō -āre *vi* (with *dat*) to go on one's knees to, entreat, beg

sup·plōdō -plōdĕre -plōsī *vt* to stamp (*the foot*)

supplōsĭ·ō -ōnis *f* stamping; **supplosio pedis** stamping of the foot

sup·pōnō -pōnĕre -posŭī -posĭtum *vt* (with *dat*) **a** to put, place, set (*something*) under; **b** to put (*something*) next to, add (*something*) to; **c** to substitute (*something*) for; **potentiam in gratiae locum supponere** to put power in place of influence, substitute power for influence

support·ō -āre *vt* to bring or carry up, transport

supposītīcĭ·us -a -um *adj* spurious

supposītĭ·ō -ōnis *f* substitution

suppositus *pp* of **suppono**

suppostr·ix -īcis *f* unfair substituter (*female*)

suppressī·ō -ōnis *f* holding back (*of money*), embezzlement

sup·prĭmō -primĕre -pressī -ressum *vt* to press down or under; to sink; to repress, stop; to suppress, keep secret

supprōm·us -ī *m* assistant butler

suppŭd·et -ēre *v impers* to cause (*someone*) a slight feeling of shame; (with *acc* of person and *genit* of cause), e.g., **eorum me suppudet** I am a bit ashamed of them

suppūr·ō -āre *vi* to fester

supp·us -a -um *adj* (animals) facing the ground

suppŭt·ō -āre *vt* to trim up; to count, compute

suprā *adv* on top, above; up above; earlier; beyond, more; **supra quam** more than; *prep* (with *acc*) over, above; beyond; (of time) before; (of amount) over, beyond; in charge of

suprascand·ō -ĕre *vt* to climb over

suprēmum *adv* for the last time

suprēm·us -a -um (*superl* of **superus**) *adj* highest, topmost; the top of; last, latest, final; greatest, supreme, extreme; closing, dying, final; **suprema manus** the finishing touches; **supremus mons** summit of the mountain, mountain top; *n* last moment; *n pl* moment of death; funeral rites, obsequies; testament

sūr·a -ae *f* calf of the leg

surcŭl·us -ī *m* shoot, sprout, twig; slip, graft

surdast·er -ra -rum *adj* somewhat deaf

surdĭt·ās -ātis *f* deafness

surd·us -a -um *adj* deaf; silent, noiseless; unheeding; dull, faint, indistinct

surēn·a -ae *f* grand vizier (*in the Parthian empire*)

surgō surgĕre surrexī surrectum *vi* to get up, rise, stand up; to get up (*from sleep*); to grow up, spring up

surp·ō -ĕre -ŭī *vt* to snatch, wrest; to pilfer

surrancĭd·us or **subrancĭd·us -a -um** *adj* somewhat rancid

surrauc·us or **subrauc·us -a -um** *adj* somewhat hoarse

surrectus *pp* of **surgo**

surrēmĭg·ō or **subrēmĭg·ō -āre** *vi* to row along

sur·rēpō or **sub·rēpō -rēpĕre -repsī -reptum** *vt* to creep under, crawl under; *vi* to creep up; (with *dat*) to creep up on, steal upon

surreptīcĭ·us or **subreptīcĭ·us -a -um** *adj* surreptitious; stolen
surreptus *pp* of **surrepo** and of **surripio**
sur·rīdĕō or **sub·rīdĕō -rīdēre -rīsī** *vi* to smile
surrīdicŭlē or **subrīdicŭlē** *adv* rather humorously
sur·rĭgō or **sub·rĭgō -rigĕre -rexī -rectum** *vt* to raise, lift up, erect
surring·or or **subring·or -ī** *vi* to grimace, make a face; to be somewhat annoyed
sur·ripĭō or **sub·ripĭō -ripĕre -ripŭī -reptum** *vt* to snatch secretly, pilfer; (with *dat*) to pilfer (*something*) from
surrŏg·ō -āre *vt* to propose as a substitute
surrostrān·ī or **subrostrān·ī -ōrum** *m pl* loafers around the rostra
surrub·ĕō or **subrub·ĕō -ēre** *vi* to blush slightly
surrūf·us or **subrūf·us -a -um** *adj* reddish
sur·rŭō or **sub·rŭō -ruĕre -rŭī -rŭtum** *vt* to undermine, dig under; to tear down, demolish; (fig) to wreck, stamp out, destroy
surrustĭc·us or **subrustĭc·us -a -um** *adj* rather unsophisticated
surrŭtus *pp* of **surruo**
sursum or **sursus** *adv* upwards, high up; **sursum deorsum** up and down, to and fro
sūs suis *m* pig, hog, boar; *f* sow
Sūs·a -ōrum *n pl* capital of Persia
suscensĕō see **succenseo**
susceptĭ·ō -ōnis *f* undertaking
sus·cipĭō -cipĕre -cēpī -ceptum *vt* to catch (*something before it falls*); to support; to pick up, resume (*conversation*); to bear (*children*); to accept, receive (*under one's protection*); to take up, undertake; to acknowledge, recognize (*a child*) as one's own
suscĭt·ō -āre *vt* to stir up; to erect, build; to awaken; to encourage; (fig) to stir up (*rebellion, love, etc.*)
suspect·ō -āre *vt* to gaze up at; to distrust, suspect
suspect·us -a -um *pp* of **suspicio;** *adj* suspected, mistrusted
suspect·us -ūs *m* respect, esteem
suspend·ĭum -ĭī or **-ī** *n* hanging; hanging oneself
sus·pendō -pendĕre -pendī -pensum *vt* to hang up, hang; to prop up, support; to keep in suspense; to check (*temporarily*); to interrupt; **suspendi** (with **ex** + *abl*) to depend on
suspens·us -a -um *adj* hanging, balanced; raised, poised; in suspense, uncertain, hesitant; (with **ex** + *abl*) dependent upon
suspĭc·ax -ācis *adj* suspicious; mistrusted, causing mistrust, suspicious
su·spicĭō -spicĕre -spexī -spectum *vt* to look up at; to look up to, admire; to mistrust, suspect; *vi* to look up; (with **in** + *acc*) to look up at or into
suspīciōsē *adv* suspiciously
suspīciōs·us -a -um *adj* mistrustful, suspicious; suspicious-looking, suspicious; (with **in** + *acc*) suspicious of
suspĭc·ō -āre or **suspĭc·or -ārī -ātus sum** *vt* to mistrust, suspect; to suppose, believe, surmise
suspīrāt·us -ūs *m* deep breath, sigh
suspīr·ĭum -ĭī or **-ī** *n* deep breath, sigh; **suspirium ducere, repetere,** or **trahere** to draw a deep breath, sigh
suspīr·ō -āre *vt* to sigh for; *vi* to sigh, heave a sigh
susque deque *adv* up and down; **de Octavio susque deque est** it's all one (*i.e., of no consequence*) as far as Octavian is concerned
sustentācŭl·um -ī *n* prop, support
sustentātĭ·ō -ōnis *f* forbearance, patience
sustent·ō -āre *vt* to hold up, hold upright, support; to sustain (*with food*); to hold (*enemy*); to uphold (*law*); to delay; to postpone
sus·tinĕō -tinēre -tinŭī -tentum *vt* to hold up, support; to hold back, hold in, check; to uphold (*law*); to sustain, support (*with food*); to bear (*trouble*); to hold up, delay, put off
sustoll·ō -ĕre *vt* to lift up, raise; to destroy
susurrāt·or -ōris *m* mutterer, whisperer
susurr·ō -āre *vt & vi* to mutter, murmur, whisper
susurr·us -ī *m* low, gentle noise; murmur, whisper, buzz, hum
sūtēl·ae -ārum *f pl* patches; tricks
sūtĭl·is -e *adj* sewn together, fastened together
sūt·or -ōris *m* shoemaker
sūtōrĭ·us -a -um *adj* shoemaker's; *m* ex-shoemaker
sūtrīn·us -a -um *adj* shoemaker's; *f* shoemaker's shop; shoemaker's trade
sūtūr·a -ae *f* seam; suture
sūt·us -a -um *pp* of **suo;** *n pl* joints
su·us -a -um *adj* his, her, its, their, one's own; due, proper, peculiar; *pron masc pl* one's own people, one's own friends, one's own family; *pron neut pl* one's own property
Sybăr·is -is *f* town in S. Italy noted for its luxurious living
Sybarīt·a -ae *m* Sybarite
Sȳchae·us -ī *m* husband of Dido
sȳcophant·a -ae *m* sycophant; blackmailer; cheat; slanderer
sȳcophantĭ·a -ae *f* cunning, deceit
sȳcophantiōsē *adv* deceitfully
sȳcophant·or -ārī -ātus sum *vi* to cheat; (with *dat*) to play a trick on
Syēn·ē -ēs *f* town in S. Egypt
syllăb·a -ae *f* syllable
syllabātim *adv* syllable by syllable

symbŏl·a -ae *f* contribution (*of money to a feast*); (coll) blows
symbŏl·us -ī *m* symbol, mark, token
symphōnĭ·a -ae *f* agreement of sound, symphony, harmony
symphōniăc·us -a -um *adj* concert, musical; **pueri symphoniaci** choristers; *m pl* musicians
Symplēgăd·es -um *f pl* two islands in the Euxine which floated about and dashed against each other until they were fixed in place as the Argo sailed by them
symplegm·a -ătis *m* group (*of persons embracing or wrestling*)
synĕdr·us -ī *m* senator (*in Macedonia*)
syngrăph·a -ae *f* promissory note
syngrăph·us -ī *m* written contract; pass, passport
synŏd·ūs -ontis *m* bream (*fish*)
synthĕs·is -is *f* dinner service; suit of clothes; dinner clothes
Syph·ax -ācis *m* king of Numidia at the time of the Second Punic War, siding with Carthage (*d.* 203 B.C.)
Syrācosĭ·us -a -um *adj* Syracusan; *m pl* Syracusans
Syrācūs·ae -ārum *f pl* Syracuse (*chief city in Sicily*)
Syrācūsān·us or **Syrācūsĭ·us -a -um** *adj* Syracusan
Syrĭ·us -a -um *adj* Syrian; *m pl* Syrians; *f* Syria
Syr·us -a -um *adj* Syrian; *m pl* Syrians
Sȳr·inx -ingis *f* nymph who was pursued by Pan and changed into a reed
syrm·a -ae *f* robe with a train (*worn esp. by actors in tragedies*); tragedy
syrt·is -is *f* sand dune; quicksand
Syrt·is -is *f* Gulf of Sidra in N. Africa; Gulf of Cabes; *f pl* the Syrtes (*lakes and sand dunes of that area as representative of a wild, forbidding place*)

T

tabell·a -ae *f* small board; door sill; game board; writing tablet; ballot; picture, painting; votive tablet
tabellārĭ·us -a -um *adj* (law) regulating voting; *m* mailman, courier
tāb·ĕō -ēre *vi* to waste away; to melt away; to stream, run
tabern·a -ae *f* hut, hovel, cottage; booth, stall, shop; inn
tabernācŭl·um -ī *n* tent; **tabernaculum capere** to choose a place for a tent outside the city in which to take the auspices
tabernārĭ·ī -ōrum *m pl* shopkeepers
tāb·ēs -is *f* melting, wasting, decay, dwindling, shrinking; decaying matter, rot; disease, pestilence
tāb·escō -escĕre -ŭī to begin to decay, begin to melt, melt gradually
tābidŭl·us -a -um *adj* wasting, consuming
tābĭd·us -a -um *adj* wasting, decaying, melting; corrupting, infectious
tābifĭc·us -a -um *adj* melting, wasting; (fig) gnawing
tabŭl·a -ae *f* plank, board; writing tablet; advertisement; auction; picture, painting; map; votive tablet; *f pl* account books, records, register, lists
tabulār·ĭum -ĭī or **-ī** *n* archives, archives building
tabulātĭ·ō -ōnis *f* flooring, floor, story
tabulāt·us -a -um *adj* boarded; *n* floor, story; layer; row (*of trees*)
tāb·um -ī *n* putrid matter, decay, rot; disease, plague, pestilence
tac·ĕō -ēre -ŭī -ĭtum *vt* to be silent about, pass over in silence; *vi* to be silent, hold one's tongue; to be still, be noiseless
tacĭtē *adv* silently, secretly
taciturnĭt·ās -ātis *f* silence, taciturnity
taciturn·us -a -um *adj* silent, taciturn; noiseless, hushed, quiet
tacĭt·us -a -um *adj* silent, mute; unmentioned, secret; (law) assumed, implied, tacit; **per tacitum** in silence
Tacĭt·us -ī *m* C. Cornelius Tacitus (*Roman historian, c.* 55-*c.* 115 A.D.)
tactĭl·is -e *adj* tangible
tactĭ·ō -ōnis *f* touch, touching; feeling, sense of touch
tactus *pp* of **tango**
tact·us -ūs *m* touch; handling; influence, effect
taed·a -ae *f* pine wood, pitch pine; torch; wedding torch; wedding; pine board
taedet taedēre taedŭit or **taesum est** *v impers* it irks; (with *acc* of person and *genit* of the cause), e.g., **me taedet stultitiae meae** my foolishness irks me, I am annoyed at my foolishness
taedĭf·er -ĕra -ĕrum *adj* torch-bearing
taed·ĭum -ĭī or **-ī** *n* irksomeness, tediousness, weariness, boredom
taenĭ·a -ae *f* band, ribbon
Taenarĭd·ēs -ae *m* Spartan (*esp. Hyacinthus*)
Taenăr·is -ĭdis *adj* Spartan
Taenăr·um or **Taenăr·on -ī** *n* or **Taenăr·us** or **Taenăr·os -ī** *m* or *f* most southerly point of the Pelo-

ponnesus (*thought to be the entrance to the lower world*); lower world, Hades

taet·er -ra -rum *adj* foul, revolting, offensive, shocking, loathsome; ugly, hideous; disgraceful; *n* offensiveness, repulsiveness

taetrē *adv* foully, hideously, shockingly

taetrĭcus see **tetricus**

tag·ax -ācis *adj* light-fingered

tālār·is -e *adj* ankle-length; *n pl* angle-length clothes; sandals

tālār·ius -a -um *adj* of dice; **ludus talarius** game of dice

talāsiō or **talassiō** *interj* wedding cry

tālĕ·a -ae *f* rod, bar, stake

talent·um -ī *n* talent (*Greek weight, varying from state to state, but equal to about fifty pounds*); sum of money (*consisting of sixty minae*)

tālĭ·ō -ōnis *f* (law) punishment in kind

tāl·is -e *adj* such, of such kind, of that kind; so great, so excellent, so distinguished

talp·a -ae *m* or *f* mole (*animal*)

Talthyb·ius -iī or **-ī** *m* herald of Agamemnon

tāl·us -ī *m* ankle, anklebone; heel, foot; die (*used in playing dice*)

tam *adv* to such an extent, to such a degree, so, so much; **tam . . . quam** the . . . the; **tam magis . . . quam magis** the more . . . the more

tamăr·ix -īcis *f* tamarisk

tamdiū *adv* so long, how long; **tuamdiu quam** or **tuamdiu dum** as long as

tamen *adv* yet, nevertheless, still, all the same; in the same way

Tāmĕs·is -is or **Tāmĕs·a -ae** *m* Thames

tametsī *conj* even if, although

tamquam or **tanquam** *conj* as, just as, as much as; just as if; **tamquam si** just as if

Tanăgr·a -ae *f* town in Boeotia

Tană·is -is *m* river of Sarmatia (*modern Don*)

Tanăqu·il -īlis *f* wife of the elder Tarquin

tandem *adv* at last, in the end, finally; (expressing urgency or impatience) now, tell me, please

tangō tangĕre tetĭgī tactum *vt* to touch; to handle, meddle with; to taste; to come to, reach; to border on; to hit, beat; to wash, anoint; to affect, gall, move to pity; to dupe; to touch upon, mention; to touch, be related to; to undertake

Tantalĕ·us -a -um *adj* of Tantalus

Tantalĭd·ēs -ae *m* descendant of Tantalus

Tantăl·is -ĭdis *f* descendant of Tantalus (*female*)

Tantăl·us -ī *m* son of Jupiter and father of Pelops who was punished in the lower world with constant hunger and thirst

tantill·us -a -um *adj* so small, so little; *n* a bit

tantisper *adv* just so long (*and no longer*); just for the moment

tantopĕre or **tantō opĕre** *adv* so much, so greatly, to such a degree, so earnestly, so hard

tantŭlum *adv* so little, in the least

tantŭl·us -a -um *adj* so little, so small; *n* so little, such a trifle; **tantulo vendere** to sell for such a trifling amount

tantum *adv* so much, so greatly, to such a degree, so far, so long, so; only, just, but just, hardly, scarcely; **tantum modo** only

tantummŏdo *adv* only

tantundem *adv* just so much, just as far, to the same extent

tant·us -a -um *adj* of such size, so great; so much; so little; so important; *pron neut* so much; so little; so small an amount, so small a number; **tanti** of such value, worth so much, at so high a price; of little account, of such small importance; **tanto** (with comparatives) by so much, so much the; **tanto melior!** so much the better!, bravo!, excellent!; **tanto nequior!** so much the worse!

tant·usdem -ădem -undem *adj* so great, just as great, just as large

tapēt·a -ae *m* or **tapēt·a -ōrum** or **tapēt·ia -ium** *n pl* carpet; tapestry; coverlet

tardē *adv* slowly

tardesc·ō -ĕre *vi* to become slow; to falter

tardĭp·ēs -ĕdis *adj* limping

tardĭt·ās -ātis *f* tardiness, slowness; dullness, stupidity

tarditūd·ō -ĭnis *f* tardiness, slowness

tardiuscŭl·us -a -um *adj* rather slow, slowish, dragging

tard·ō -āre *vt* to slow down, delay, hinder; *vi* to go slow, take it easy

tard·us -a -um *adj* tardy, slow; lingering; mentally slow, mentally retarded; deliberate; crippling

Tarentīn·us -a -um *adj* Tarentine; *m pl* Tarentines

Tarent·um -ī *n* town on S. coast of Italy, founded by the Spartans around 700 B.C.

tarm·es -ĭtis *m* wood worm, borer

Tarpēĭ·us -a -um *adj* Tarpeian; **mons Tarpeius** Tarpeian cliff on the Capitoline Hill from which criminals were thrown; *f* Roman girl who treacherously opened the citadel to the Sabine attackers

tarpezīt·a or **trapezīt·a -ae** *m* banker

Tarquiniens·is -e *adj* of the town of Tarquinii

Tarquinĭ·us -a -um *adj* Tarquinian; *m* Tarquinius Priscus (*fifth king of Rome and husband of Tanaquil*); Tarquinius Superbus (*seventh*

and last king of Rome); *m pl* important Etrurian town
Tarracīn·a -ae *f* or **Terracīn·ae -ārum** *f pl* town in Latium
Tartăr·a -ōrum *n pl* or **Tartăr·us** or **Tartăr·os -ī** *m* Tartarus (*lower level of Hades reserved for criminals*)
Tartarĕ·us -a -um *adj* of Tartarus, infernal
tat or **tatae** *interj* exclamation of surprise
tat·a -ae *m* (coll) daddy
Tat·ius -iī or **-ī** *m* Titus Tatius (*king of the Sabines who later ruled jointly with Romulus until the latter had him killed*)
taurĕ·us -a -um *adj* bull's, of a bull; **terga taurea** bulls' hides; drums; *f* rawhide, whip
Taur·ī -ōrum *m pl* barbarous people living in the peninsula now called the Crimea
Tauric·us -a -um *adj* Tauric
taurif·er -ĕra -ĕrum *adj* bull-producing (*regions*)
tauriform·is -e *adj* bull-shaped
taurīn·us -a -um *adj* bull's; made of bull's hide; bull-like
taur·us -ī *m* bull
Taur·us -ī *m* Taurus (*constellation*)
taxāti·ō -ōnis *f* rating, appraisal
taxill·us -ī *m* small die (*for playing dice*)
tax·ō -āre *vt* to appraise
tax·us -ī *f* yew, yew tree
Tāÿgĕt·ē -ēs *f* one of the Pleiades, the daughter of Atlas and Pleione
Tāÿgĕt·us -ī *m* mountain range in Laconia
tē *acc & abl* of **tu**
-te = suffix for **tu** and **te**
Teān·um -ī *n* town in Campania; town in Apulia
techn·a or **techĭn·a -ae** *f* trick
Tecmess·a -ae *f* wife of Ajax the son of Telamon
tectē *adv* cautiously, guardedly
tect·or -ōris *m* plasterer
tectōriŏl·um -ī *n* bit of plaster work
tectōri·us -a -um *adj* roofing; plasterer's; painter's; *n* plaster, stucco; fresco painting; beauty preparation
tect·us -a -um *pp* of **tego;** *adj* concealed; secret; guarded (*words*); reserved, secretive (*person*); *n* roof; ceiling; canopy; cover, shelter; house
tēcum = **cum te**
Tegĕ·a -ae *f* town in Arcadia
Tegeae·us -a -um *adj* Tegean, Arcadian; *m* Pan; *f* Arcadian maiden (*i.e., Atalanta*)
Tegeāt·ae -ārum *m pl* Tegeans
teg·es -ĕtis *f* mat
tegill·um -ī *n* hood, cowl
tegĭm·en or **tegm·en** or **tegŭm·en -ĭnis** *n* cover, covering; vault (*of heaven*)
tegiment·um or **tegment·um** or **tegument·um -ī** *n* cover, covering
tegō tegĕre texī tectum *vt* to cover; to protect, shelter, defend; to hide; to bury; **tegere latus** (with *genit*) to escort (*someone*)
tēgŭl·a -ae *f* tile; *f pl* roof tiles, tiled roof
tegŭmen see **tegimen**
tegumentum see **tegimentum**
tēl·a -ae *f* web; warp (*threads that run lengthwise in the loom*); yarn beam; loom; design, plan
Telăm·ōn -ōnis *m* son of Aeacus, brother of Peleus, king of Salamis, and father of Ajax and Teucer
Telamōniăd·ēs -ae *m* son of Telamon (*i.e., Ajax*)
Telamōn·ius -iī or **-ī** *m* Ajax
Tēlegŏn·us -ī *m* son of Ulysses and Circe
Tēlemăch·us -ī *m* son of Ulysses and Penelope
Tēlĕph·us -ī *m* king of Mysia, wounded by the spear of Achilles and later cured by its rust
tell·ūs -ūris *f* the earth; ground, earth; land, country
tēl·um -ī *n* missile, weapon; spear, javelin, dart; sword, dagger, ax; shaft
temerāri·us -a -um *adj* casual, accidental; rash, thoughtless
temĕre *adv* by chance, without cause; at random; rashly, thoughtlessly; **non temere** not lightly; not easily; hardly ever; **nullus dies temere intercessit quo non scriberet** hardly a day ever passed without his writing
temerit·ās -ātis *f* chance, accident; rashness, thoughtlessness; *f pl* foolhardy acts
temĕr·ō -āre *vt* to darken, blacken; to violate, disgrace, defile
tēmēt·um -ī *n* alcohol, wine
temnō temnĕre tempsī temptum *vt* to slight, offend
tēm·ō -ōnis *m* pole, tongue (*of a carriage or plow*); wagon
Tempē (indecl) *n pl* scenic valley between Olympus and Ossa in Thessaly
temperāment·um -ī *n* moderation
tempĕr·ans -antis *adj* moderate, temperate
temperanter *adv* moderately
temperanti·a -ae *f* self-control, moderation
temperātē *adv* moderately, with due moderation
temperāti·ō -ōnis *f* blending, proportion, symmetry; temperament; organization, constitution; control
temperāt·or -ōris *m* controller
temperāt·us -a -um *adj* tempered; self-controlled, temperate
tempĕrī *adv* in time, on time; in due time, at the right time
temperi·ēs -ēī *f* blending, tempering; temperature, mild temperature
tempĕr·ō -āre *vt* to compound, combine, blend, temper; to regulate, moderate; to tune; to govern, con-

trol, rule; *vi* to be moderate, exercise restraint; (with *abl* or **ab** + *abl*) to abstain from

tempest·ās -ātis *f* time, period, season; stormy weather, storm, tempest

tempestīvē *adv* at the right time, seasonably

tempestīvit·ās -ātis *f* right time, timeliness

tempestīv·us -a -um *adv* timely, seasonable, fit; ripe, mature; in good time, early

templ·um -ī *n* space marked off in the sky or on the earth for observation of omens; open space, quarter; temple, shrine, sanctuary

temporāl·is -e *adj* temporary, transitory

temporārĭ·us -a -um *adj* temporary; changeable (*character*)

tempŏre or **tempŏrī** *adv* in time, on time; in due time, at the right time

temptābund·us -a -um *adj* making constant attempts, trying

temptāment·um -ī *n* attempt, effort; temptation, trial

temptāmĭn·a -um *n pl* attempts, trials

temptātĭ·ō -ōnis *f* trial; attack (*of sickness*)

temptāt·or -ōris *m* assailant

tempt·ō or **tent·ō -āre** *vt* to test, feel, probe; to try, attempt; to attack; to try to influence, tamper with, tempt, try to induce; to urge, incite, sound out; to worry, distress, disquiet

temptus *pp* of **temno**

temp·us -ŏris *n* temple (*of the head*); time, period, season; occasion, opportunity; right time, good time, proper period; times, condition, state, position; need, emergency; measure, quantity, cadence (*in metrics*); **ad tempus** punctually; at the right time, at the appointed time; for the time being, for the moment; for the occasion; **ante tempus** before time, too soon, prematurely; **ex tempore** on the spur of the moment; **id temporis** at that time; **in ipso tempore** in the nick of time; **in tempore** at the right moment, just in time; **in tempus** temporarily, for a time; **per tempus** just in time; **pro tempore** as time permits, according to circumstances; **tempori cedere** to yield to circumstances; **tempus in ultimum** to the last extremity

tēmulent·us -a -um *adj* intoxicated

tenācĭt·ās -ātis *f* tenacity; miserliness

tenācĭter *adv* tightly, firmly

ten·ax -ācis *adj* holding tight, gripping, clinging; sticky; firm; obstinate; stingy; (with *genit*) clinging to, holding on to

tendicŭl·ae -ārum *f pl* little snare, little noose, little trap

tendō tendĕre tetendī tentum or **tensum** *vt* to stretch, stretch out, hold out, spread, strain; to head for (*a place*); to aim, shoot (*an arrow*); to bend (*a bow*); to tune (*an instrument*); to pitch (*a tent*); *vi* to pitch tents, be encamped; to travel, sail, move, march; to endeavor; to contend, fight; to exert oneself; (with *inf*) to try to, endeavor to; (with **ad** + *acc*) **a** to tend toward, be inclined toward; **b** to move toward, travel to, aim for; (with **contra** + *acc*) to fight against

tenĕbr·ae -ārum *f pl* darkness; night; blindness; dark place, haunts; lower world; unconsciousness; death; obscurity, low station; ignorance

tenebricōs·us -a -um *adj* gloomy; darkened (*senses*); blind (*lust*)

tenebrĭc·us -a -um *adj* dark, gloomy

tenebrōs·us -a -um *adj* dark, gloomy

Tenĕd·os or **Tenĕd·us -ī** *f* island off the coast of Troy

tenellŭl·us -a -um *adj* tender little, dainty little

tenell·us -a -um *adj* dainty

ten·ĕō -ēre -ŭī -tum *vt* to hold, hold tight, keep; to grasp, comprehend; to comprise; to possess, occupy, be master of; to hold back, restrain, repress; to hold, charm, amuse; to have control of, get the better of; to keep, detain; *vi* to hold out, last, keep on

ten·er -ĕra -ĕrum *adj* tender, soft, delicate; young, youthful; impressionable; weak; effeminate; voluptuous

tenerasc·ō -ĕre *vi* to grow weak

tenĕrē *adv* softly

tenerĭt·ās -ātis *f* weakness

tēnesm·os -ī *m* straining at stool

ten·or -ōris *m* uninterrupted course; **uno tenore** uninterruptedly

tens·a -ae *f* car carrying images of the gods in procession

tens·us -a -um *pp* of **tendo;** *adj* stretched, drawn tight, stretched out

tentīg·ō -ĭnis *f* lust

tentō see **tempto**

tentōr·ĭum -ĭī or **-ī** *n* tent

tent·us -a -um *pp* of **tendo** and of **teneo;** *adj* stretched, drawn tight, stretched out

tenuicŭl·us -a -um *adj* poor, paltry

tenŭ·is -e *adj* thin, fine; delicate; precise; shallow (*groove, etc.*); slight, puny, poor, insignificant; plain, simple; small, narrow

tenuĭt·ās -ātis *f* thinness, fineness; leanness; simplicity; precision; poverty

tenuĭter *adv* thinly; slightly; poorly, indifferently; exactly, minutely; superficially

tenŭ·ō -āre *vt* to make thin; to con-

tract; to dissolve; to lessen, diminish, weaken
ten·us -ŏris *n* trap, snare
tenus *prep* (with *abl*, always placed after the noun) as far as, up to, down to; **nomine tenus** or **verbo tenus** as far as the name goes, nominally, in name
Te·os or **Te·us -ī** *f* town on the coast of Asia Minor, the birthplace of Anacreon
tepe·faciō -facĕre -fēcī -factum *vt* to make warm, warm up
tep·ĕō -ēre -ŭī *vi* to be warm, be lukewarm; to glow with love; to be lukewarm, indifferent
tep·escō -escĕre -ŭī *vi* to grow warm; to grow lukewarm, grow indifferent
tepidius *adv* rather tepidly
tepid·us -a -um *adj* warm, lukewarm, tepid
tep·or -ōris *m* warmth; coolness, lack of heat (*in the bath*); lack of fire (*in a speech*)
ter *adv* three times, thrice
terdeciens or **terdeciēs** *adv* thirteen times
terebinth·us -ī *f* terebinth, turpentine tree
terĕbr·a -ae *f* borer, drill
terĕbr·ō -āre *vt* to bore, drill, bore out
terēd·ō -ĭnis *f* grub worm
Tēreïd·ēs -ae *m* Itys (*son of Tereus*)
Terent·ius -iī or **-ī** *m* Terence (*M. Terentius Afer, Roman comic poet, c.* 190-159 B.C.)
ter·es -ĕtis *adj* smooth, well-rounded; smooth and round, polished, shapely; round, cylindrical; (fig) smooth, elegant, fine
Tēr·eus -ĕī or **-ĕos** *m* king of Thrace, husband of Procne, and father of Itys
tergemin·us -a -um *adj* triple, threefold
tergĕō tergēre tersī tersum or **terg·ō -ĕre** *vt* to scour, wipe off, wipe dry, clean, cleanse
tergin·um -ī *n* rawhide; scourge
tergiversāti·ō -ōnis *f* refusal; evasion, subterfuge
tergivers·or -ārī -ātus sum *vi* to keep turning one's back; to be shifty, be evasive
tergō see **tergeo**
terg·um -ī or **terg·us -ŏris** *n* back; ridge; hide, leather; leather objects: bag, shield, drum; (mil) rear; **a tergo** in the rear, from behind; **in tergum** backward
term·es -ĭtis *m* branch
Terminăl·ia -ium or **-iōrum** *n pl* festival of Terminus (*the god of boundaries, celebrated on the 23rd of February*)
terminăt·iō -ōnis *f* decision, determining; arrangement, ending (*of a sentence*)
termin·ō -āre *vt* to mark off with boundaries, bound, limit; to fix, determine, define; (rhet) to end, round out (*a sentence*)
termin·us -ī *m* boundary, limit
Termin·us -ī *m* god of boundaries
tern·ī -ae -a *adj* three in a group, three apiece, three each
terō terĕre trīvī trītum *vt* to wear, rub, wear out, crush; to spend, waste; to smooth, grind, sharpen
Terpsichŏr·ē -ēs *f* Muse of dancing; poetry
terr·a -ae *f* the earth; land; earth, ground, soil; country, region, territory
terrāneŏl·a -ae *f* crested lark
terrēn·us -a -um *adj* earthly, terrestrial; earthen, made of earth; *n* land, ground
terr·ĕō -ēre -ŭī -ĭtum *vt* to frighten, scare, terrify; to deter
terrestr·is -e *adj* of the earth, on the earth; land, earth; **proelium terrestre** land battle
terrĕ·us -a -um *adj* sprung from the earth, earth-born
terribĭl·is -e *adj* terrible, frightful
terricŭl·a -ōrum *n pl* scarecrow
terrific·ō -āre *vt* to terrify
terrific·us -a -um *adj* terrifying, awe-inspiring, alarming
terrigĕn·a -ae *m* or *f* earth-born creature
terrilŏqu·us -a -um *adj* ominous, alarming
territ·ō -āre *vt* to keep frightening; to intimidate
territōr·ium -iī or **-ī** *n* land around a town, territory, suburbs
terr·or -ōris *m* terror, alarm, dread, fright
ters·us -a -um *pp* of **tergeo;** *adj* clean, neat; neat, terse
tertiadecimān·ī -ōrum *m pl* soldiers of the thirteenth legion
tertiān·us -a -um *adj* recurring every second day, tertian; *m pl* soldiers of the third legion; *f* tertian fever
tertiō *adv* in the third place, thirdly; the third time
tertium *adv* for the third time
terti·us -a -um *adj* third
terti·us decim·us -a -um *adj* thirteenth
terunc·ius -iī or **-ī** *m* three twelfths of an ace, quarter ace; **heres ex teruncio** heir to one fourth of the estate
tervenēfic·us -ī *m* (term of abuse) three-time killer
tesqu·a -ōrum *n pl* wilderness, wilds
tessell·a -ae *f* cubed mosaic stone
tessellāt·us -a -um *adj* tesselated
tessĕr·a -ae *f* cube; die; watchword, countersign; tally, token; ticket
tesserār·ius -iī or **-ī** *m* officer of the day
tesserŭl·a -ae *f* small cube; ticket
test·a -ae *f* brick, tile; jug, crock; potsherd; shell fish; shell
testāmentāri·us -a -um *adj* per-

taining to a will or testament; *m* forger of a will
testāment·um -ī *n* will, testament
testātĭ·ō -ōnis *f* invoking as witness
testāt·us -a -um *adj* attested, public
testicŭl·us -ī *m* testicle
testificātĭ·ō -ōnis *f* giving evidence, testifying; proof, evidence
testifĭc·or -ārī -ātus sum *vt* to give as evidence, attest; to vouch for; to bring to light; to call to witness
testimōn·ĭum -ĭī or **-ī** *n* testimony, deposition
test·is -is *m* or *f* witness; *m* testicle
test·or -ārī -ātus sum *vt* to give as evidence; to show, prove, vouch for; to call to witness, appeal to; *vi* to be a witness, testify; to make a will
testūdinĕ·us -a -um *adj* of a tortoise; made of tortoise shell
testūd·ō -ĭnis *f* tortoise; tortoise shell; lyre, lute; arch, vault; (mil) protective shed (*for besiegers*)
test·um -ī *n* earthenware lid; pot with a lid
tēte = emphatic form of **te**
Tēth·ys -ȳos *f* wife of Oceanus and mother of the sea nymphs; sea
tetradrachm·um or **tetrachm·um -ī** *n* Greek silver coin (*worth four drachmas*)
tetrarch·ēs -ae *m* tetrarch (*ruler of one fourth of a country*); petty prince
tetrarchĭ·a -ae *f* tetrarchy
tetrĭc·us -a -um *adj* gloomy, sour, crabby
Teuc·er or **Teuc·rus -rī** *m* son of Telamon and brother of Ajax; son of Scamander of Crete, son-in-law of Dardanus, and later king of Troy
Teucrĭ·a -ae *f* Troy
Teucr·us -a -um *adj* Teucrian, Trojan; *m pl* Trojans
Teutŏn·ēs -um or **Teutŏn·ī -ōrum** *m pl* Teutons
texō texĕre texŭī textum *vt* to weave; to plait; to build; to compose
textīl·is -e *adj* woven; brocaded; *n* fabric
text·or -ōris *m* weaver
textrīn·um -ī *n* weaving
textr·ix -īcis *f* weaver (*female*)
textūr·a -ae *f* texture; web; fabric
text·us -a -um *pp* of **texo;** *n* woven cloth, fabric; web
text·us -ūs *m* texture
Thā·is -ĭdis *f* Athenian courtesan
thalăm·us -ī *m* woman's room; bedroom; marriage bed; marriage
thalassĭc·us -a -um *adj* sea-green
thalassĭn·us -a -um *adj* sea-green
Thal·ēs -is or **-ētis** *m* early Ionian philosopher of Miletus, regarded as one of the Seven Sages (*fl* 575 B.C.)
Thalī·a -ae *f* Muse of comedy; sea nymph
thall·us -ī *m* green bough, green stalk
Thaps·os or **Thaps·us -ī** *f* city in Africa where Caesar defeated the Pompeians (46 B.C.)
Thas·os or **Thas·us -ī** *f* island in the Aegean Sea, off the coast of Thrace
Thaumantĭ·as -ădis or **Thaumant·is -ĭdis** *f* Iris (*daughter of Thaumas*)
theātrāl·is -e *adj* theatrical
theātr·um -ī *n* theater
Thēb·ae -ārum *f pl* Thebes (*capital of Boeotia, founded by Cadmus*); Thebes (*city of Upper Egypt*)
Thēbae·us -a -um *adj* & *mf* Theban (*of Egypt*)
Thēbān·us -a -um *adj* & *mf* Theban (*of Boeotia*)
thēc·a -ae *f* case; envelope
Them·is -ĭdis *f* goddess of justice and of prophecy
Themistŏcl·ēs -is or **-ī** *m* Themistocles (*Athenian general and statesman, c.* 528-459 B.C.)
thensaurārĭ·us -a -um *adj* treasure, of treasure
thensaurus see **thesaurus**
Theocrĭt·us -ī *m* founder of Greek pastoral poetry, born at Syracuse (*3rd cent.* B.C.)
theolŏg·us -ī *m* theologian
therm·ae -ārum *f pl* hot springs, hot baths
thermopōl·ĭum -ĭī or **-ī** *n* hot-drink shop
thermopŏt·ō -āre *vt* to warm with a drink
Thermopȳl·ae -ārum *f pl* famous pass in Thessaly between Mt. Oeta and the sea, defended by Leonidas and his four hundred Spartans (490 B.C.)
thermŭl·ae -ārum *f pl* little hot bath
Thersīt·ēs -ae *m* Greek soldier at Troy notorious for his ugliness
thēsaur·us or **thensaur·us -ī** m storehouse; store, treasure, hoard
Thēs·eus -ĕī or **-ĕos** *m* king of Athens, son of Aegeus and Aethra, and husband first of Ariadne and later of Phaedra
Thēsē·us -a -um *adj* of Theseus
Thēsīd·ae -ārum *m pl* Athenians
Thēsīd·ēs -ae *m* Hippolytus (*son of Theseus*)
Thespiăd·es -um *f pl* Muses
Thesp·is -is *m* traditional founder of Greek tragedy
Thespĭ·us -a -um *adj* Thespian; *f pl* town in Boeotia near Mt. Helicon
Thessalĭ·a -ae *f* Thessaly (*most northerly district of Greece*)
Thessalĭc·us -a -um *adj* Thessalian
Thessăl·us -a -um *adj* Thessalian; *m pl* people of Thessaly, Thessalians
Thestorĭd·ēs -ae *m* Calchas (*famous Greek seer who joined the expedition to Troy*)
Thet·is -ĭdis or **-ĭdos** *f* sea nymph, daughter of Nereus and Doris, wife of Peleus, and mother of Achilles

thiăs·us -ī *m* Bacchic dance; Bacchic troop of dancers
Thisb·ē -ēs *f* girl in Babylon, loved by Pyramus
Tho·ās -antis *m* king of Tauris, slain by Orestes; king of Lemnos and father of Hypsipyle
thol·us -ī *m* rotunda
thōr·ax -ācis *m* breastplate
Thrāc·a -ae or **Thrāc·ē -ēs** *f* Thrace (*wild country to the N. of the Aegean*)
Thrācĭ·us -a -um *adj* Thracian; *f* Thrace
Thress·a or **Threiss·a -ae** *f* Thracian woman
Thr·ex -ēcis or **Thr·ax -ācis** *m* Thracian gladiator
thron·us -ī *m* throne
Thūcydĭd·ēs -is *m* Thucydides (*famous Greek historian of the Peloponnesian War, c.* 456-*c.* 400 B.C.)
thunn·us -ī *m* tuna fish
thūr- = tur-
Thūrĭ·ī -ōrum *m pl* city on the Tarentine Gulf in S. Italy
Thūrīn·us -a -um *adj & m* Thurian
thūs thūris *n* incense, frankincense
Thybris see **Tiberis**
Thyēn·ē -ēs *f* nymph who nursed Bacchus
Thyest·ēs -ae *m* son of Pelops, brother of Atreus, and father of Aegisthus
thymbr·a -ae *f* savory (*plant*)
thym·um -ī *n* thyme
Thȳnĭ·a -ae *f* Bithynia (*country in Asia Minor*)
Thȳniăc·us -a -um *adj* Bithynian
Thȳn·us -a -um *adj & m* Bithynian
thynn·us -ī *m* tuna fish
Thyōn·eus -ĕī *m* Bacchus
thyrs·us -ī *m* Bacchic wand twined with vine tendrils and ivy, and crowned with a fir cone
tiār·a -ae *f* or **tiār·ās -ae** *m* tiara
Tiberīn·is -ĭdis *adj* of the Tiber
Tiberīn·us -a -um *adj* of the Tiber; *m* river god of the Tiber
Tibĕr·is or **Tibr·is** or **Thybr·is -is** *m* Tiber River
Tiber·ĭus -ĭī or **-ī** *m* Tiberius (*Tiberius Claudius Nero Caesar, successor of Augustus,* 42 B.C.-37 A.D., *ruling from* 14 A.D. *to* 37 A.D.)
tībĭ·a -ae *f* shinbone, tibia; flute
tībĭc·en -ĭnis *m* flutist; prop; pillar
tībīcĭn·a -ae *f* flutist (*female*)
Tibull·us -ī *m* Albius Tibullus (*Roman elegiac poet, c.* 54-*c.* 19 B.C.)
Tīb·ur -ŭris *n* town of Latium on the Anio (*modern Tivoli*)
Tīburt·ēs -um *m pl* Tiburtines
Tīburtīn·us or **Tīburn·us -a -um** *adj* Tiburtine
Tīcīn·us -ī *m* tributary of the Po
Tigellīn·us -ī *m* notorious favorite of the emperor Nero
tigill·um -ī *n* beam, log
tignārĭ·us -a -um *adj* **faber tignarius** carpenter
tign·um -ī *n* trunk, log, beam, board
tigr·is -is or **-ĭdis** *f* tigress
Tigr·is -is or **-ĭdis** *m* large river of W. Asia which joins with the Euphrates
tīlĭ·a -ae *f* lime tree
Tīmae·us -ī *m* Greek historian of Sicily (*c.* 346-*c.* 250 B.C.); Pythagorean philosopher of Locri in S. Italy after whom Plato named one of his dialogues (5*th cent.* B.C.)
Timāgĕn·ēs -is *m* brilliant rhetorician in the time of Augustus
timefact·us -a -um *adj* alarmed, frightened
tim·ĕō -ēre -ŭī *vt* to fear, be afraid of; *vi* to fear, be afraid
timĭdē *adv* timidly, fearfully
timidĭt·ās -ātis *f* timidity, fearfulness, cowardice
timĭd·us -a -um *adj* timid, fearful, cowardly; (with *genit*) fearful of, afraid of
tim·or -ōris *m* fear, alarm; dread; a terror
tinctĭl·is -e *adj* used for dipping
tinct·us -a -um *pp* of **tingo**
tinĕ·a -ae *f* moth; bookworm
tingō tingĕre tinxī tinctum *vt* to dip, soak; to dye, color; to tinge, imbue
tinnīment·um -ī *n* ringing
tinn·ĭō -īre -īvī -ĭī -ītum *vt & vi* to ring
tinnīt·us -ūs *m* ring, ringing, tinkling, jingling
tinnŭl·us -a -um *adj* ringing, tinkling; shrill
tintinnābŭl·um -ī *n* bell, door bell, cattle bell
tintinnācŭl·us -a -um *adj* jingling; *m pl* chain gang
tintĭn·ō -āre *vi* to ring
tīn·us -ī *m* laurustinus (*shrub*)
Tīph·ys -ȳos *m* pilot of the Argo
tippŭl·a -ae *f* water spider
Tīresĭ·ās -ae *m* famous seer at Thebes at the time of Oedipus
Tīridāt·ēs -ae *m* king of Armenia
tīr·ō -ōnis *m* recruit; beginner
tīrōcin·ĭum -ĭī or **-ī** *n* first campaign; inexperience in military life; body of raw recruits; beginning, first try
tīruncŭl·us -ī *m* young beginner
Tīryn·s -this or **-thos** *f* town in Argolis where Hercules was raised
Tīrynthĭ·us -a -um *adj* Tirynthian
Tīsamĕn·us -ī *m* son of Orestes and king of Argos
Tīsiphŏn·ē -ēs *f* one of the three Furies who haunted murderers
Tīsiphonē·us -a -um *adj* guilty
Tīt·ān -ānis of **Tītān·us -ī** *m* Titan; sun; *m pl* giant sons of Uranus and Ge who rebelled against Uranus and put Cronus on the throne
Tītānĭ·us -a -um *adj* of the Titans, Titanic; *f* Latona (*the mother of Apollo and Diana*); Pyrrha (*as descendant of Prometheus*); Circe (*as daughter of Sol*)

Tīthōnĭ·us -a -um *adj* Tithonian; *f* Aurora
Tīthōn·us -ī *m* son of Laomedon and husband of Aurora from whom he received the gift of immortality without eternal youth
Tit·iēs -ĭum *m pl* one of the three original tribes of Rome
tītillātĭ·ō -ōnis *f* tickling
tītill·ō -āre *vt* to tickle
titivillīt·ĭum -ĭī or **-ī** *n* trifle
titubanter *adv* falteringly
titubātĭ·ō -ōnis *f* staggering
titŭb·ō -āre *vi* to stagger, reel, totter; to falter, waver (*in speech*)
titŭl·us -ī *m* inscription; label; notice, advertisement; title of honor; renown; pretext
Titȳ·os -ī *m* giant slain by Apollo for insulting Latona and thrown into Tartarus
Tītȳr·us -ī *m* shepherd in Vergil's pastorals, sometimes identified with Virgil himself
Tlēpolĕm·us -ī *m* son of Hercules
Tmōl·us or **Timōl·us -ī** *m* mountain in Lydia famous for its wines
toculĭ·ō -ōnis *m* banker
tōf·us or **tōph·us -ī** *m* tufa (*volcanic rock*)
tog·a -ae *f* outer garment of a Roman citizen; **toga candida** white toga (*worn by candidates for office*); **toga picta** brocaded toga (*worn by triumphant generals*); **toga praetexta** crimson-bordered toga (*worn by magistrates and freeborn children*); **toga pulla** dark-grey toga (*worn by mourners*); **toga pura** or **virilis** or **libera** toga of manhood (*worn by young men from about the age of sixteen*)
togāt·us -a -um *adj* wearing a toga; *m* Roman citizen; civilian; humble client; *f* Roman drama (*treating of Roman themes*); prostitute
togŭl·a -ae *f* little toga
tolerābĭl·is -e *adj* tolerable; patient
tolerābilĭus *adv* more patiently, fairly patiently
tolĕr·ans -antis *adj* tolerant; (with *genit*) tolerant of, enduring
toleranter *adv* patiently
tolerantĭ·a -ae *f* toleration, endurance
tolerātĭ·ō -ōnis *f* toleration, endurance
tolerāt·us -a -um *adj* tolerable, endurable
tolĕr·ō -āre *vt* to tolerate, bear, endure; to support, maintain, sustain
tollēn·ō -ōnis *m* crane, lift, derrick
tollō tollĕre sustŭlī sublātum *vt* to lift, raise; to have (*a child*); to acknowledge (*a child*); to raise, educate; to weigh (*anchor*); to take on, take on board; to remove; to do away with, destroy; to cancel, abolish, abrogate; to lift, steal; to uplift, cheer up, excite; to erect, build up; to waste (*time*); **amicum tollere** to cheer up a friend; **animos tollere** to boost the morale; **deos tollere** to deny the existence of the gods; **hominem de medio tollere** to make away with or kill a man; **pecunias ex fano tollere** to steal money from a shrine; **signa tollere** to break camp
tolūtim *adv* at a trot
tomācŭl·um or **tomācl·um -ī** *n* sausage
tōment·um -ī *n* stuffing (*for pillows*)
Tom·ī -ōrum *m pl* or **Tom·is -is** *f* town in Moesia on the Black Sea to which Ovid was exiled
Tomīt·ae -ārum *m pl* people of Tomi
Tomītān·us -a -um *adj* of Tomi
Ton·ans -antis *m* Thunderer (*epithet of several gods, esp. Jupiter*)
tondĕō tondēre totondī tonsum *vt* to clip, shear, shave; to prune; to reap, mow; to crop, browse on; (fig) to fleece, rob; **usque ad cutem tondere** to swindle, fleece
tonitrāl·is -e *adj* thunderous
tonĭtr·us -ūs *m* or **tonitrŭ·um -ī** *n* thunder; *m pl* or *n pl* claps of thunder
ton·ō -āre -ŭī -ĭtum *vt* to thunder out (*words*); *vi* to thunder
tons·a -ae *f* oar blade
tonsĭl·is -e *adj* clipped
tonsill·ae -ārum *f pl* tonsils
tonsĭt·ō -āre *vt* to shear regularly
tons·or -ōris *m* shearer, barber
tonsōrĭ·us -a -um *adj* shaving; barber's
tonstrīcŭl·a -ae *f* little hairdresser, little barber (*female*)
tonstrīn·a -ae *f* barber shop
tonstr·ix -īcis *f* hairdresser, barber (*female*)
tonsūr·a -ae *f* clipping, shearing; **capillorum tonsura** haircut
tons·us -a -um *pp* of **tondeo;** *f* see **tonsa**
tons·us -ūs *m* haircut; hairdo
tōph·us -ī *m* tufa (*volcanic rock*)
topiārĭ·us -a -um *adj* garden, landscape; *m* gardener, landscaper; *f* landscaping
topĭc·e -ēs *f* resourcefulness in finding topics for speeches
tor·al -ālis *n* valance
torcŭl·ar -āris or **torcŭl·um -ī** *n* wine press, oil press
toreum·a -ătis *n* embossing, relief
torment·um -ī *n* windlass; catapult, artillery piece; shot; torture rack, torture; (fig) torture; *n pl* artillery
tormĭn·a -um *n pl* colic
torminōs·us -a -um *adj* prone to colic
torn·ō -āre *vt* to form with a lathe, turn on a lathe
torn·us -ī *m* lathe; burin
torōs·us -a -um *adj* brawny, muscular
torpēd·ō -ĭnis *f* numbness, lethargy, listnessness; crampfish, torpedo (*fish*)

torp·ĕō -ēre -ŭī *vi* to be numb; to be stiff; to be stupefied; to be groggy
torp·escō -escĕre -ŭī *vi* to grow numb, grow listless
torpĭd·us -a -um *adj* groggy
torp·or -ōris *m* torpor, numbness; grogginess
torquāt·us -a -um *adj* wearing a necklace
Torquāt·us -ī *m* T. Manlius Torquatus (*legendary Roman hero who is said to have slain a gigantic Gaul in single combat and to have worn the Gaul's necklace*)
torquĕō torquēre torsī tortum *vt* to twist, turn, wind, wrench; to whirl, hurl, wind up and hurl; to rack; (fig) to torment
torqu·ēs or **torqu·is -is** *m* or *f* necklace; collar; festoon
torr·ens -entis *adj* burning, seething; rushing, roaring (*stream*); fiery (*speech*); *m* roaring stream, torrent
torrĕō torrēre torrŭī tostum *vt* to roast, bake, burn, scorch; to parch, dry up
torr·escō -escĕre -ŭī *vi* to become burned or parched
torrĭd·us -a -um *adj* baked, parched, dried up; frostbitten
torr·is -is *m* firebrand
tortē *adv* crookedly
tortĭl·is -e *adj* twisted, winding, spiral
tort·ō -āre *vt* to twist; **tortari** to writhe
tort·or -ōris *m* torturer, executioner
tortuōs·us -a -um *adj* full of turns, winding; (fig) tortuous, complicated
tort·us -a -um *pp* of **torqueo;** *adj* twisted, crooked; gnarled (*oak*); complicated
tort·us -ūs *m* twisting, twist, spiral; **tortūs dare** (of a serpent) to form loops
torŭl·us -ī *m* tuft (*of hair*)
tor·us -ī *m* knot; bulge; muscle, brawn; bed, couch; mattress; mound; boss; flowery expression
torvĭt·ās -ātis *f* grimness, wildness
torv·us -a -um *adj* grim, fierce, stern, savage
tostus *pp* of **torreo**
tot (indecl) *adj* so many, as many
totĭdem (indecl) *adj* just so many, just as many
totĭens or **totĭēs** *adv* so often, so many times
tōt·us -a -um *adj* the whole, all, entire; **totus in illis** wholly absorbed in those matters; *n* the whole matter, all; **ex toto** wholly, totally; **in toto** on the whole, in general; **in totum** wholly, totally
toxĭc·um -ī *n* poison
trabāl·is -e *adj* of or for beams; **clavus trabalis** spike; **telum trabale** beam-like shaft
trabĕ·a -ae *f* ceremonial robe (*woven in stripes and worn by magistrates, augurs, etc.*)
trabeāt·us -a -um *adj* wearing a ceremonial robe
trab·s -is *f* beam, plank; timber; tree; object made of beams: roof, shaft, table, battering ram
tractābĭl·is -e *adj* manageable; (weather) fit for navigation
tractātĭ·ō -ōnis *f* handling, management, treatment; discussion, treatment (*of a subject*)
tractāt·us -ūs *m* touching, handling, management
tractim *adv* little by little, slowly; at length, in a drawn-out manner
tract·ō -āre *vt* to drag around, haul, pull; to touch, handle; to manage, control, wield; to conduct, carry on, transact, practice; to discuss; **se tractare** to behave oneself, conduct oneself
tract·us -a -um *pp* of **traho;** *adj* flowing, fluent, continuous (*discourse*)
tract·us -ūs *m* dragging; drawing out, dragging out, extension (*e.g., of a war*); track, trail; tract, extent, distance; region, district
trādĭtĭ·ō -ōnis *f* handing over, surrender; transmission
trādĭt·or -ōris *m* betrayer, traitor
trādō trādĕre trādĭdī trādĭtum *vt* to hand over, surrender, deliver; to betray; to hand down, bequeath, transmit, pass on; to relate, recount; to teach; **se tradere** (with *dat*) **a** to surrender to; **b** to devote oneself to
trā·dūcō -dūcĕre -duxī -ductum *vt* to lead across, bring over, transfer, to lead in parade, make a show of; to disgrace, degrade; to broadcast, proclaim; to pass, spend
trāductĭ·ō -ōnis *f* transfer, transference; course, passage (*of time*); metonymy
trāduct·or -ōris *m* conveyor
trāductus *pp* of **traduco**
trād·ux -ŭcis *m* vine branch
tragĭcē *adv* as in tragedy
tragicocōmoedĭ·a -ae *f* melodrama
tragĭc·us -a -um *adj* of tragedy, tragic; in the tragic style, grand, solemn; of a tragic nature, tragic, moving, terrible; **actor tragicus** tragedian; *m* tragic playwright
tragoedĭ·a -ae *f* tragedy
tragoed·us -ī *m* tragic actor, tragedian
trāgŭl·a -ae *f* javelin
trag·us -ī *m* body odor of the armpits; a fish (*of unknown type*)
trah·ax -ācis *adj* greedy
trahĕ·a -ae *f* sledge, drag
trahō trahĕre traxī tractum *vt* to draw, drag, trail; to draw out, pull out, extract; to lead, take along, be followed by; to contract, wrinkle; to inhale; to quaff; to take on, assume, acquire, get; to squander, dissipate; to spin, manufacture; to attract, allure, influence; to win over (*to the other side*); to refer,

ascribe; to distract; to consider, ponder; to spin out, prolong, protract

Trājān·us -ī *m* Trajan (*M. Ulpius Trajanus, Roman emperor,* 97-117 A.D.)

trājectĭ·ō -ōnis *f* crossing, passage; transposition (*of words*); shift of meaning; exaggeration

trājectus *pp* of **trajicio**

trāject·us -ūs *m* crossing over, passage

trā·jicĭō or **trans·icĭō** or **trans·jicĭō -jicĕre -jēcī -jectum** *vt* to have go across, cause to go across, transfer; to ship across, transport; to pass through, break through; to stab through, pierce; (with double *acc*) to bring (*e.g., troops*) across (*river, mountain*); (with **trans** + *acc*) to lead across; (with **in** + *acc*) to lead over into

trālāt- = **translat-**

Trall·ēs -ĭum *f pl* town in Lydia

trālŏqu·or -ī *vt* to talk over, enumerate, recount

trālūcĕō see **transluceo**

trām·a -ae *f* woof, web

trāmĕō = **transmeo**

trām·es -ĭtis *m* path, track, trail

trāmi- = **transmi-**

trānătō = **transnato**

trān·ō or **transn·ō -āre** *vt* to swim across; to pass through, permeate; *vi* to swim across; to pass through

tranquillē *adv* quietly, calmly

tranquillĭt·ās -ātis *f* tranquillity, stillness, calmness

tranquill·ō -āre *vt* to calm, quiet, tranquillize

tranquill·us -a -um *adj* calm, quiet, tranquil; *n* calm, calmness, peace, quiet, tranquillity; quiet sea

trans *prep* (with *acc*) across, over, beyond

transab·ĕō -īre -ĭī *vt* to go through, pierce

transact·or -ōris *m* manager

transactus *pp* of **transigo**

transad·ĭgō -igĕre -ēgī -actum *vt* to pierce; to run (*someone*) through; (with double *acc*) to run (*e.g., a sword*) through (*someone*)

Transalpīn·us -a -um *adj* Transalpine, lying beyond the Alps

tran·scendō or **trans·scendō -scendĕre -scendī -scensum** *vt* to climb or step over, surmount; to overstep, transgress; *vi* to climb or step across

trans·cīdō -cīdĕre -cīdī *vt* to flog soundly

tran·scrībō or **trans·scrībō -scrībĕre -scripsī -scriptum** *vt* to transcribe, copy off; (law) to transfer, convey; to transfer, remove

trans·currō -currĕre -currī or **-cucurrī -cursum** *vt & vi* to run or dash over; to run or dash through; to run or dash by or past

transcurs·us -ūs *m* running through, passage; cursory mention

transd- = **trad-**

transenn·a -ae *f* grating; lattice work, trellis work; lattice window; fowler's net

trans·ĕō -īre -ĭī -ĭtum *vt* to pass over, cross; to desert; to pass (*in a race*); to pass over, make no mention of; to treat cursorily; to overstep, pass beyond; to surpass; *vi* to go over, go across, pass over; to pass by, go by; to shift (*to another opinion, topic, etc.*); (of time) to pass, go by; to pass away; (with **ad** + *acc*) **a** to cross over to (*a place*); **b** to cross over to, desert to; (with **in** + *acc*) to change into, be transformed into; (with **per** + *acc*) to penetrate, permeate, pervade

trans·fĕrō -ferre -tŭlī -lātum (or **trālātum**) *vt* to carry or bring across; to transfer by writing, to copy; to shift, transfer; to transform; to postpone; to translate; to use (*words*) figuratively

trans·fīgō -fīgĕre -fixī -fixum *vt* to pierce, transfix; to run (*someone*) through

transfigūr·ō -āre *vt* to transform

transfixus *pp* of **transfigo**

trans·fodĭō -fodĕre -fōdī -fossum *vt* to run through, stab, pierce

transform·is -e *adj* transformed, changed in shape

transform·ō -āre *vt* to change in shape, transform

transfossus *pp* of **transfodio**

transfŭg·a -ae *m* or *f* deserter, turncoat

trans·fugĭō -fugĕre -fūgī *vi* to desert

transfug·ĭum -ĭī or **-ī** *n* desertion

trans·fundō -fundĕre -fūdī -fūsum *vt* to transfuse; to pour; (with **in** + *acc*) to pour (*a liquid*) into; (with **ad** + *acc*) (fig) to shift (*affection, allegiance*) to (*another person*)

transfūsĭ·ō -ōnis *f* transmigration

transfūsus *pp* of **transfundo**

trans·gredĭor -grĕdī -gressus sum *vt* to cross, pass over; to exceed; *vi* to go across; to cross over (*to another party*)

transgressĭ·ō -ōnis *f* crossing, passage; transposition (*of words*)

transgressus *pp* of **transgredior**

transgress·us -ūs *m* crossing

transicĭō see **trajicio**

transiect- = **traject-**

trans·ĭgō -igĕre -ēgī -actum *vt* to pierce, run through; to finish, settle, transact, accomplish, perform, conclude; to pass, spend (*time*); *vi* to come to an agreement, reach an understanding

transil·ĭō or **transsil·ĭō -īre -ŭī** *vt* to jump over, jump across; to overstep, exceed; to skip, omit; *vi* to jump across

transĭt·ans -antis *adj* passing through

transitĭ·ō -ōnis *f* crossing, passage;

switching (*to another party*); contagion, infection; passageway
transitus *pp* of **transeo**
transit·us -ūs *m* crossing, passage; passing; traffic; crossing over, desertion; change, period of change, transition; fading (*of colors*); **in transitu** in passing
translātīcī·us or **trālātīcī·us -a -um** *adj* transmitted, traditional, customary; usual, common
translātī·ō or **trālātī·ō -ōnis** *f* transfer, shift; transporting; translation; metaphor, figure
translātīv·us -a -um *adj* transferable
translāt·or -ōris *m* middleman (*in a transfer*)
translātus *pp* of **transfero**
translĕg·ō -ĕre *vt* to read through
translūc·ĕō or **trālūc·ĕō -ēre** *vi* to be reflected; to shine through
transmarīn·us -a -um *adj* from beyond the seas, foreign, overseas
transmĕ·ō or **trāmĕ·ō -āre** *vi* to cross, pass
transmīgr·ō -āre *vi* to move, migrate, emigrate
transmissī·ō -ōnis *f* crossing, passage
transmissus *pp* of **transmitto**
transmiss·us -ūs *m* passing over, crossing, passage
trans·mittō or **trā·mittō -mittĕre mīsī -missum** *vt* to send across; to transmit; to let pass; to hand over, entrust, commit; to pass over, leave unmentioned; to pass through, endure; (with **in** + *acc*) to send (*someone*) across to or into; (with **per** + *acc*) to let (*someone*) pass through; *vi* to cross over, cross, pass (*from one place to another*)
transmontān·ī -ōrum *m pl* people across the mountains
trans·movĕō -movēre -mōvī -mōtum *vt* to move, transfer
transmūt·ō -āre *vt* to change, shift
transnăt·ō or **trānăt·ō -āre** *vt* to swim; *vi* to swim across
transnō see **trano**
Transpadān·us -a -um *adj* Transpadane, beyond or N. of the Po River
transpect·us -ūs *m* view, prospect
transpic·iō or **transspic·iō -ĕre** *vt* to look through
trans·pōnō -pōnĕre -posuī -positum *vt* to transfer
transport·ō -āre *vt* to transport
transpositus *pp* of **transpono**
Transrhēnān·us -a -um *adj* beyond the Rhine, E. of the Rhine
transs- = **trans-**
Transtiberīn·us -a -um *adj* across the Tiber
transtin·ĕō -ēre *vi* to pass through
transtr·um -ī *n* thwart
transult·ō -āre *vi* to jump across
transūt·us -a -um *adj* pierced through
transvectī·ō or **trāvectī·ō -ōnis** *f* transportation, crossing
trans·vĕhō or **trā·vĕhō -vehĕre vexī -vectum** *vt* to transport; to carry, lead (*in a parade*); **transvehi** to ride by (*in a parade*); (of time) to elapse
transverbĕr·ō -āre *vt* to pierce through and through, transfix
transversa *adv* sideways; across one's course
transversāri·us -a -um *adj* transverse, lying crosswise
transvers·us or **trāvers·us** or **transvors·us -a -um** *adj* lying across, lying crosswise; inopportune; astray; in the wrong direction; *n* wrong direction, opposite direction; **de transverso** unexpectedly; **ex transverso** unexpectedly; sideways
transvolit·ō -āre *vt* to flit through, fly through
transvŏl·ō or **trāvŏl·ō -āre** *vt & vi* to fly over, fly across, fly by, zip by
transvorsus see **transversus**
trapēt·us -ī *m* oil press
trapezīt·a -ae *m* banker
Trapĕz·ūs -untis *f* city in Pontus on the Black Sea
Trasimenn·us or **Trasumenn·us -ī** *m* lake in Etruria where Hannibal defeated the Romans (217 B.C.)
trāv- = **transv-**
trecēn·ī -ae -a *adj* three hundred each
trecentēsim·us -a -um *adj* three hundredth
trecentiēs *adv* three hundred times
trechedipn·um -ī *n* light garment worn to dinner
tredĕcim (indecl) *adj* thirteen
tremebund·us -a -um *adj* trembling, shivering
treme·faciō -facĕre -fēcī -factum *vt* to shake, cause to shake
tremend·us -a -um *adj* terrible, frightful
trem·escō or **trem·iscō -escĕre -uī** *vt* to tremble at; *vi* to tremble
trem·ō -ĕre -uī *vt* to tremble at; *vi* to tremble, shiver, quake
trem·or -ōris *adj* trembling, shaking, shivering; dread
tremŭl·us -a -um *adj* trembling, quivering, tremulous, shivering
trepidanter *adv* tremblingly, nervously
trepidātī·ō -ōnis *f* nervousness, alarm
trepidē *adv* nervously, in alarm
trepid·ō -āre *vt* to start at, be jumpy or nervous at; *vi* to be nervous, be jumpy, be alarmed; (of a flame) to flicker; (of streams) to rush along
trepid·us -a -um *adj* nervous, jumpy, agitated, hurried, restless; bubbling; perilous, critical, alarming; **in re trepida** in a ticklish situation
trēs (or **trīs**) **tria** *adj* three; (denoting a small number) a couple of

tress·is -is *m* small coin: mere trifle
tresvĭrī (*genit*: **triumvirōrum**) *m pl* three-man board, triumvirs
Trēvĕr·ī -ōrum *m pl* people of E. Gaul
triangŭl·us -a -um *adj* triangular; *n* triangle
triārĭ·ī -ōrum *m pl* soldiers of the third rank in a battle line, reserves
tribuārĭ·us -a -um *adj* tribal
tribūl·is -is *m* fellow tribesman
trībŭl·um -ī *n* threshing sledge (*wooden platform with iron teeth underneath*)
tribŭl·us -ī *m* caltrop (*thistle*)
tribūn·al -ālis *n* raised platform; tribunal, judgment seat; (in camp) general's platform; cenotaph
tribūnāt·us -ūs *m* tribuneship, rank of tribune
tribūnicĭ·us -a -um *adj* tribunician, tribune's; *m* ex-tribune
tribūn·us -ī *m* tribune; **tribunus aerarius** paymaster; **tribunus militaris** or **tribunus militum** military tribune (*six in each legion, serving under the legatus, and elected by the people or at times appointed by a commander*); **tribunus plebis** tribune of the people (*ten in number, serving the interests of the plebeians*)
trib·ŭō -uĕre -ŭī -ūtum *vt* to divide; to distribute, bestow, confer, assign; to give, present; to concede, grant, allow; to ascribe, impute; to devote, spend
trib·us -ūs *m* tribe (*originally three in number and eventually increased to thirty-five*)
tribūtārĭ·us -a -um *adj* subject to tribute; **tributariae tabellae** letters of credit
tribūtim *adv* by tribes
tribūtĭ·ō -ōnis *f* distribution
tribūt·us -a -um *pp* of **tribuo;** *adj* arranged by tribes; *n* tribute, tax, contribution
trīc·ae -ārum *f pl* tricks; nonsense
trīcēn·ī -ae -a *adj* thirty each
tric·eps -ipĭtis *adj* three-headed
trīcēsĭm·us -a -um *adj* thirtieth
trichĭl·a -ae *f* bower, arbor; summer home
trīcĭens or **trīcĭēs** *adv* thirty times
trīclīn·ĭum -ĭī or **-ī** *n* dining couch (*running around three sides of a table*); dining room
trīc·ō -ōnis *m* practical joker, trickster
trīc·or -ārī -ātus sum *vi* to cause trouble; to pull tricks
tricorp·or -ŏris *adj* three-bodied
tricusp·is -ĭdis *adj* three-pronged
trid·ens -entis *adj* three-pronged; *m* trident
Tridentĭf·er or **Tridentĭg·er -ĕrī** *m* Trident Bearer (*epithet of Neptune*)
tridŭ·um -ī *n* three-day period, three days
trienn·ĭa -ĭum *n pl* triennial festival, festival celebrated every three years
trienn·ĭum -ĭī or **-ī** *n* three-year period, three years
tri·ens -entis *m* one third; coin (*one third of an ace*); third of a pint
trientābŭl·um -ī *n* land given by the state as an equivalent for one third of the sum which the state owed
trientĭ·us -a -um *adj* sold for a third
triērarch·us -ī *m* captain of a trireme
triēr·is -is *f* trireme
trietērĭc·us -a -um *adj* triennial, recurring every three years; *n pl* festival of Bacchus
trietēr·is -ĭdis *f* three-year period; triennial festival
trifārĭam *adv* in three places, on three sides
trifau·x -cis *adj* triple-throated
trifĭd·us -a -um *adj* three-forked; split into three parts
triform·is -e *adj* triple
trifĭl·is -e *adj* having three threads or hairs
tri·fūr -fūris *m* archthief
trifurcĭf·er -ĕrī *m* archvillain, hardened criminal
trigemĭn·us or **tergemĭn·us -a -um** *adj* threefold, triple; *m pl* triplets
trīgintā (indecl) *adj* thirty
trig·ōn -ōnis *m* ball game
trilībr·is -e *adj* three-pound
trilingu·is -e *adj* triple-tongued
tril·ix -īcis *adj* three-ply, triple-stranded
trimestr·is -e *adj* of three months
trimĕtr·us -ī *m* trimeter
trīm·us -a -um *adj* three-year-old
Trīnăcr·is -ĭdis *adj* Sicilian
Trīnacrĭ·us -a -um *adj* Sicilian; *f* Sicily
trīn·ī -ae -a *adj* threefold, triple; three each
trinōd·is -e *adj* having three knots, triple-knotted
triōbŏl·us -ī *m* three-obol coin, half-drachma piece
Triōn·ēs -um *m pl* Great Bear and Little Bear (*constellation*)
tripartītō *adv* in three parts, into three parts
tripartīt·us or **tripertīt·us -a -um** *adj* divided into three parts, threefold
tripectŏr·us -a -um *adj* triple-bodied, triple-breasted
tripedāl·is -e *adj* three-foot
tripertītus see **tripartitus**
trip·ēs -ĕdis *adj* three-legged
tripl·ex -ĭcis *adj* threefold, triple; *n* three times as much, threefold portion
tripl·us -a -um *adj* triple, threefold
Triptolĕm·us -a -um *m* son of Celeus the king of Eleusis, favorite of Ceres, inventor of agriculture, and one of the judges in the lower world

tripudĭ·ō -āre *vi* to dance (*as a religious act*); to do a war dance; to leap, dance, hop about
tripudĭum -ĭī or **-ī** *n* solemn religious dance; war dance; dance (*in general*); favorable omen (*when the sacred chickens ate hungrily*)
trip·us -ŏdis *f* tripod (*three-footed vessel*); oracle, Delphic oracle
triquĕtr·us -a -um *adj* triangular; Sicilian
trirēm·is -e *adj* having three banks of oars; *f* trireme
trīs see **tres**
triscurrĭ·a -ōrum *n pl* broad humor, fantastic nonsense
tristicŭl·us -a -um *adj* somewhat sad
tristifĭc·us -a -um *adj* ominous; saddening
tristimōnĭ·a -ae *f* sadness
trist·is -e *adj* sad, sorrowful, melancholy, glum, dispirited; bringing sorrow, saddening, dismal; gloomy, sullen; stern, harsh; disagreeable, offensive (*odor*); bitter (*taste*)
tristitĭ·a -ae *f* sadness, gloom, gloominess, melancholy; severity, sternness
tristitĭ·ēs -ēī *f* sadness, sorrow, melancholy
trisulc·us -a -um *adj* three-forked
trităv·us -ī *m* great-great-great-grandfather
trīticĕ·us -a -um *adj* wheat, of wheat
trītĭc·um -ī *n* wheat
Trīt·ōn -ōnis *m* son of Neptune who blows through a shell to calm the seas; lake in Africa where Minerva was said to be born
Trītōniăc·us -a -um *adj* Tritonian
Trītōn·is -ĭdis or **-ĭdos** *f* Minerva
Trītōnĭ·us -a -um *adj* Tritonian; *f* Minerva
trīt·or -ōris *m* grinder
trītūr·a -ae *f* threshing
trīt·us -a -um *pp* of **tero;** *adj* worn, well-worn; beaten (*path*); experienced, expert; common, trite (*language*)
trīt·us -ūs *m* rubbing, friction
triumphāl·is -e *adj* triumphal; having had a triumph; *n pl* triumphal insignia (*without the actual triumph*)
triumph·ō -āre *vt* to triumph over, conquer completely, vanquish; *vi* to make a triumphal procession, celebrate a triumph, triumph
triumph·us or **triump·us -ī** *m* victory parade, triumph; victory, triumph; **triumphum agere** (with **de** or **ex** + *abl*) to celebrate a triumph over
triumv·ir -ĭrī *m* triumvir, commissioner; mayor (*of a provincial town*)
triumvirāl·is -e *adj* triumviral, of the triumvirs
triumvirāt·us -ūs *m* triumvirate, office of triumvir
triumvĭr·ī -ōrum *m pl* triumvirs, three commissioners, three-man commission (*appointed at various times to serve various purposes*); **triumviri capitales** police commissioners, superintendents of prisons and executions
trivenēfĭc·a -ae *f* nasty old witch
Trivĭ·a -ae *f* Diana
triviāl·is *adj* of the crossroads; found everywhere, common, ordinary
triv·ĭum -ĭī or **-ī** *n* crossroads, intersection; public street, highway
trivĭ·us -a -um *adj* of or at the crossroads
Trō·as -ădis *adj* Trojan; *f* Troad, district of Troy; Trojan woman
trochae·us -ī *m* trochee; tribrach (*metrical foot of three short syllables*)
trochlĕ·a -ae *f* block and tackle
troch·us -ī *m* hoop
Trōĭ·a or **Trōj·a -ae** *f* Troy
Trōiăd·es -um *f pl* Trojan women
Trōĭc·us -a -um *adj* Trojan
Trōĭl·us -ī *m* son of Priam, killed by Achilles
Trōĭ·us -a -um *adj* Trojan; *f* see **Troia**
Trōjān·us -a -um *adj* Trojan; *m pl* Trojans
Trōjugĕn·a *masc & fem adj* Trojan-born, born at Troy, of Trojan descent, Trojan; *m* Trojan
tropae·um -ī *n* trophy, victory memorial; victory; mark, token, memorial, monument
Trōs Trōis *m* Tros (*king of Phrygia after whom Troy was named*)
trucīdātĭ·ō -ōnis *f* slaughter, massacre, butchery
trucīd·ō -āre *vt* to slaughter, massacre, cut down
truculentē or **truculenter** *adv* grimly, fiercely
truculentĭ·a -ae *f* savagery, ferocity; harshness; inclemency
truculent·us -a -um *adj* savage, grim, fierce, cruel
trud·is -is *f* pointed pole, pike
trūdō trūdĕre trūsī trūsum *vt* to push, thrust, drive, shove; to put forth (*buds*)
trull·a -ae *f* dipper, ladle, scoop; brazier; wash basin
trunc·ō -āre *vt* to lop off, mutilate, maim
trunc·us -a -um *adj* lopped; stripped (*of branches and leaves*), trimmed; maimed, mutilated; imperfect, undeveloped; *m* trunk, tree trunk; trunk, body (*of human being*); chunk of meat; blockhead
trūsĭt·ō -āre *vt* to keep pushing, keep shoving
trūsus *pp* of **trudo**
trutĭn·a -ae *f* balance, pair of scales; criterion
trutĭn·or -ārī -ātus sum *vt* to weigh, balance

trux trucis *adj* savage, grim, fierce, wild
trȳgōn·us -ī *m* stingray
tu *pron* you (*singular*)
tuātim *adv* in your manner, as is typical of you
tub·a -ae *f* bugle, war trumpet
tūb·er -ĕris *n* lump, bump, swelling; truffle (*food*)
tub·er -ĕris *f* apple tree; *m* apple
tubĭc·en -ĭnis *m* bugler, trumpeter
tubilustr·ium -iī or **-ī** *n* festival of bugles or trumpets (*celebrated on March 23rd and May 23rd and including a ritual cleaning of the bugles or trumpets*)
tuburcĭn·or -ārī -ātus sum *vt* to devour, gobble up
tub·us -ī *m* tube, pipe
tuccēt·um or **tūcēt·um -ī** *n* sausage
tudĭt·ō -āre *vt* to keep hitting, keep beating
tuĕor *or* **tu·or tuērī tuĭtus sum** or **tūtus sum** *vt* to see, look at, gaze at, watch, observe; to look after, take care of, guard, defend, protect
tugur·ium -iī or **-ī** *n* hut, hovel, cottage
tuitĭ·ō -ōnis *f* guarding, defense; **tuitio sui** self-defense
Tulliān·um -ī *n* state prison in Rome, reputedly built by Servius Tullius
Tulliŏl·a -ae *f* little Tullia (*Cicero's daughter*)
Tull·ius -iī or **-ī** *m* Servius Tullius (*sixth king of Rome*)
tum *adv* then, at that time; next; moreover, besides; **cum . . . tum** both . . . and especially, not only . . . but also, if . . . then surely; **tum cum** at the point when, at the time when, just then when; **tum . . . tum** first . . . then, at one time . . . at another, now . . . now, both . . . and, partly . . . partly
tume·faciō -facĕre -fēcī -factum *vt* to make swell; (fig) to inflate
tum·ĕō -ēre -ŭī *vi* to be swollen, swell up, be inflated; (of business) to be in ferment, be cooking; (of language) to be bombastic; (of a person) to be excited, be in a dither, be in a rage; to be proud
tum·escō -escĕre -ŭī *vi* to begin to swell, begin to swell up; (of wars) to brew; to grow excited, become enraged, become inflated
tumĭd·us -a -um *adj* swollen, swelling; bloated; rising high; proud, inflated, puffed up; arrogant; incensed, enraged, exasperated; bombastic
tum·or -ōris *m* tumor, swelling; protuberance, bulging; elevation (*of the ground*); commotion, excitement, anger, rage; vanity, pride, arrogance
tumŭl·ō -āre *vt* to bury
tumulōs·us -a -um *adj* full of hills, hilly, rolling
tumultuārĭ·us -a -um *adj* hurried, confused, disorderly; (mil) emergency, drafted hurriedly to meet an emergency; **exercitus tumultuarius** emergency army; **pugna tumultuaria** irregular fight or battle (*i.e., not fought in regular battle formation*)
tumultuātĭ·ō -ōnis *f* confusion, hustle and bustle, panic
tumultŭ·ō -āre or **tumultŭ·or -ārī -ātus sum** *vi* to make a disturbance; to be in uproar, be topsyturvy
tumultuōsē *adv* disorderly, in confusion
tumultuōs·us -a -um *adj* boisterous, uproarious, turbulent, panicky
tumult·us -ūs *m* commotion, uproar; insurrection, rebellion, civil war; confusion, agitation (*of the mind*); outbreak (*of crime*)
tumŭl·us -ī *m* mound; rising; ground swell; burial mound; **tumulus inanis** cenotaph
tūn = tūne (tū & ne)
tunc *adv* (of time past) then, at that time, on that occasion, just then; (of future time) then, at that time, in that event; (of succession in time) thereupon; (in conclusion) accordingly, consequently, in that case; **tunc . . . cum** then . . . when, just when, just at the time when; only when, whenever; **tunc demum** not until, then only, not till then; **tunc primum** then for the first time; **tunc quando** whenever; **tunc quoque** then too; **tunc vero** then to be sure, exactly then
tundō tundĕre tutŭdī tunsum or **tūsum** *vt* to beat, pound, hammer, thump; to buffet; to thresh; (fig) to harp on, keep at, importune
tunĭc·a -ae *f* tunic (*ordinary sleeved garment worn by both sexes*); skin, peel, husk, coating
tunicāt·us -a -um *adj* wearing a tunic; in shirt sleeves; coated, covered with skin
tunicŭl·a -ae *f* short tunic; thin skin or coating
tunsus *pp* of **tundo**
tuor see **tueor**
turb·a -ae *f* turmoil, disorder, uproar, commotion; brawl; crowd, disorderly crowd, mob, gang; multitude; common crowd, the masses; a large number
turbāment·a -ōrum *n pl* means of disturbance
turbātē *adv* in confusion, confusedly
turbātĭ·ō -ōnis *f* confusion, disorder
turbāt·or -ōris *m* ringleader, troublemaker, disturber
turbāt·us -a -um *adj* confused, disorderly; disturbed, annoyed
turbell·ae -ārum *f pl* stir, row; **turbellas facere** to cause a row
turben see **turbo** *m*
turbĭdē *adv* confusedly, in disorder
turbĭd·us -a -um *adj* wild, confused, boisterous; muddy, turbid;

troubled, perplexed; vehement; disheveled (*hair*); stormy (*sky, weather*)

turbinĕ·us -a -um *adj* cone-shaped

turb·ō -ĭnis *m* or **turb·en -ĭnis** *n* whirl, twirl, eddy; spinning, revolution; coil; spinning top; reel; spindle; wheel; tornado, whirlwind; wheel of fortune; (fig) whirlwind, storm

turb·ō -āre *vt* to throw into confusion, disturb, agitate; to break, disorganize (*in battle*), cause to break ranks; to confuse, confound; to muddy

turbulentē or **turbulenter** *adv* boisterously, tumultuously, confusedly

turbulent·us -a -um *adj* turbulent, wild, stormy; disturbed, confused; seditious, trouble-making

turd·a -ae *f* or **turd·us -ī** *m* thrush

tūrĕ·us -a -um *adj* of frankincense

turgĕō turgēre tursī *vi* to be swollen, be puffed up; to be bombastic

turgesc·ō -ĕre *vi* to begin to swell, begin to swell up; to begin to blow up (*in anger*)

turgidŭl·us -a -um *adj* poor swollen, swollen little (*eyes*)

turgĭd·us -a -um *adj* swollen, puffed up, inflated; turgid, bombastic

tūribŭl·um -ī *n* censer

tūricrĕm·us -a -um *adj* incense-burning

tūrĭf·er -ĕra -ĕrum *adj* incense-producing

tūrilĕg·us -a -um *adj* incense-gathering

turm·a -ae *f* troop, squadron (*of cavalry*); crowd, group

turmāl·is -e *adj* of a squadron; equestrian; *m pl* troopers

turmātim *adv* by troops, by squadrons, squadron by squadron

Turn·us -ī *m* king of the Rutuli, killed by Aeneas

turpicŭl·us -a -um *adj* ugly little; somewhat indecent

turpificāt·us -a -um *adj* corrupted, debased, degenerate

turpilucricupĭd·us -a -um *adj* (coll) eager to make a fast buck

turp·is -e *adj* ugly, deformed; foul, filthy, nasty; disgraceful, shameless; dirty, obscene, indecent

turpĭter *adv* repulsively; disgracefully, scandalously, shamelessly

turpitūd·ō -ĭnis *f* ugliness, deformity; foulness; disgrace; moral turpitude

turp·ō -āre *vt* to make ugly, disfigure; to soil, dirty, defile, pollute

turrĭg·er -ĕra -ĕrum *adj* turreted; (Cybele) wearing a turreted crown (*representing the earth with its cities*)

turr·is -is *f* turret, tower; howdah (*on an elephant*); (fig) castle, mansion

turrīt·us -a -um *adj* turreted; fortified with turrets; crowned with turrets, adorned with a turret crown

turt·ur -ŭris *m* turtledove

tūs tūris *m* incense, frankincense

Tusculān·us -a -um or **Tusculens·is -e** *adj* Tusculan, of Tusculum; *m pl* Tusculans

Tuscŭl·us -a -um *adj* Tusculan; *n* Tusculum (*town in Latium near Alba Longa, about twelve miles from Rome*)

Tusc·us -a -um *adj* Etruscan

tussicŭl·a -ae *f* slight cough

tuss·iō -īre *vi* to cough, have a cough

tuss·is -is *f* cough

tūsus *pp* of **tundo**

tūtām·en -ĭnis or **tūtāment·um -ī** *n* means of defense, defense, protection

tūte = tū & te emphatic form of **tū**

tūtē *adv* safely

tūtēl·a or **tūtell·a -ae** *f* care, charge, patronage, protection, defense; guardianship; charge, thing protected; guardian, keeper, watcher

tūtĕmet = tū & te & met emphatic form of **tū**

tūt·ō -āre or **tūt·or -ārī -ātus sum** *vt* to guard, protect, defend; to keep safe, watch, preserve; to ward off, avert; (with **ab** + *abl* or with **ad** or **adversus** + *acc*) to protect (*someone*) from, guard (*someone*) against

tūt·or -ōris *m* protector; guardian (*of minors, women, etc.*)

tūt·us -a -um *pp* of **tueor**; *adj* safe, secure; cautious, prudent; *n* safe place, safety, shelter, security; **ex tuto** from a safe place, in safety, safely

tūtō *adv* safely, in safety

tu·us -a -um *adj* your; right for you, proper for you; *pron* yours; **tuā interest** it is of importance to you; **tui** your friends, your people, your family; **tuum est** (with *inf*) it is your duty to, it is up to you to

tuxtax *adv* (word meant to imitate the sound of blows) whack, wham; **tuxtax meo tergo erit** (coll) it's going to go whack, wham, bang over my back

Tȳd·eus -ĕī or **-ĕos** *m* Tydeus (*son of Oeneus, one of the Seven against Thebes, and father of Diomedes*)

Tȳdīd·ēs -ae *m* Diomedes (*son of Tydeus*)

tympanotrīb·a -ae *m* timbrel player, drummer

tympăn·um or **typăn·um -ī** *n* timbrel, drum

Tyndar·ĕus -ĕī or **Tyndăr·us -ī** *m* king of Sparta, husband of Leda, father of Castor and Clytemnestra, and reputed father of Pollux and Helen

Tyndarid·ēs -ae *m* descendant of Tyndareus
Tyndăr·is -ĭdis *f* descendant of Tyndareus (*female*)
Typhō·ĕus -ĕī or **ĕos** or **Typh·ōn -ōnis** *m* giant who was struck with lightning by Jupiter and buried under Mount Etna
typ·us -ī *m* figure, image (*on the wall*)
tyrannactŏn·us -ī *m* tyrannicide, assassin of a tyrant
tyrannĭcē *adv* tyrannically; arbitrarily, cruelly
tyrannicīd·a -ae *m* tyrannicide, assassin of a tyrant
tyrannĭc·us -a -um *adj* tyrannical; arbitrary, cruel
tyrann·is -ĭdis *f* tyranny, despotism
tyrianthĭn·a -ōrum *n pl* violet-colored clothes
Tyrĭ·us -a -um *adj* Tyrian, Phoenician; Carthaginian; Theban; crimson (*because of the famous dye produced at Tyre*); *m pl* Tyrians, Carthaginians
Tyr·ō -ūs *f* daughter of Salmoneus and mother of Pelias and Neleus by Poseidon
Tyr·os or **Tyr·us -ī** *f* Tyre (*famous commercial city of Phoenicia*)
tȳrotarīch·os -ī *m* dish of salted fish and cheese
Tyrrhēnĭ·a -ae *f* Etruria
Tyrrhēnĭc·us -a -um *adj* Etrurian, Etruscan
Tyrrhēn·us -a -um *adj* Etrurian, Etruscan; *m pl* Etruscans (*Pelasgian people who migrated to Italy perhaps from Lydia in Asia Minor and settled to the N. of the Tiber*)
Tyrtae·us -ī *m* Spartan poet (*7th cent.* B.C.)

U

ūb·er -ĕris *adj* rich, fruitful, fertile, plentiful, productive; rich, imaginative (*style*); (fig) fruitful, productive; *n* richness, fruitfulness, fertility; fertile soil, fruitful field; breast, teat; udder, dug
ūberĭus *adv* more fully, more copiously, more fruitfully
ūbert·ās -ātis *f* richness, fertility, productiveness
ūbertim *adv* abundantly, copiously
ubī *adv* (interrog) where; **ubi gentium** (coll) where in the world; *conj* where, in which, whereby, with whom, by whom; when, whenever
ubīcumque *adv* wherever, wheresoever; anywhere, everywhere
Ubĭ·ī -ōrum *m pl* German tribe on the lower Rhine
ubīnam *adv* where; **ubinam gentium** (coll) where in the world
ubīquāque *adv* everywhere
ubīque *adv* anywhere, everywhere
ubiŭbī *adv* wherever
ubīvīs *adv* anywhere, everywhere, wherever you please; **ubivis gentium** (coll) anywhere in the world
ūd·us -a -um *adj* wet, moist, damp, humid
ulcĕr·ō -āre *vt* to make sore; (fig) to wound
ulcerōs·us -a -um *adj* full of sores, ulcerous
ulciscor ulciscī ultus sum *vt* to avenge oneself on, take vengeance on, punish; to avenge, requite, repay
ulc·us -ĕris *n* sore, ulcer
ūlīg·ō -ĭnis *f* moisture, dampness
Ulix·ēs -is or **-ĕī** or **-ei** *m* Ulysses (*king of Ithaca, son of Laertes, husband of Penelope, and father of Telemachus and Telegonus*)
ull·us -a -um *adj* any
ulmĕ·us -a -um *adj* elm, made of elm
ulmitrĭb·a -ae *m* (coll) slaphappy (*from being flogged with elm whips*)
ulm·us -ī *f* elm tree; *f pl* elm rods
uln·a -ae *f* elbow; arm; (as measure of length) ell
ulpĭc·um -ī *n* leek
ulterĭ·or -ūs *adj* farther, on the farther side, more remote; further, more, longer, in a higher degree; worse; *m pl* more remote people, those beyond; *n pl* things beyond
ultĭmum *adv* finally, for the last time
ultĭm·us -a -um *adj* farthest, most distant, extreme; earliest; latest, final, last; greatest; lowest; meanest; *n* last thing; end; **ad ultimum** to the end, to the extreme, in the highest degree, to the last degree, utterly; *n pl* extremes; the worst
ultĭ·ō -ōnis *f* vengeance, revenge
ult·or -ōris *m* avenger, punisher, revenger
ultrā *adv* beyond, farther, besides; *prep* (with *acc*) beyond, past; (of number, measure, degree) over, beyond, more than, over and above
ultr·ix īcis *adj* avenging
ultrō *adv* to the farther side, beyond; on the other side; besides, moreover, too; of one's own accord, without being asked; without being spoken to; **ultro tributa** expenditure incurred by the government for public works
ultus *pp* of **ulciscor**

ulŭl·a -ae *f* screech owl
ululāt·us -ūs *m* crying, wailing (*esp. of mourners*); war cry
ulŭl·ō -āre *vt* to cry out to; *vi* to shriek, yell; (of places) to ring, resound
ulv·a -ae *f* sedge
umbell·a -ae *f* umbrella, parasol
umbilīc·us -ī *m* navel, belly button; midriff; middle, center; projecting end of dowels on which books were rolled; cockle, sea snail
umb·ō -ōnis *m* boss (*of a shield*); shield; elbow
umbr·a -ae *f* shade, shadow; phantom, shade, ghost; mere shadow (*of one's former self, etc.*); shelter, cover; constant companion; grayling, umber (*fish*); **rhetorica umbra** rhetorician's school
umbrācŭl·um -ī *n* bower, arbor; school; umbrella, parasol
umbrāticŏl·a -ae *m* lounger, loafer (*in the shade*)
umbrātĭc·us -a -um *adj* too fond of the shade, lazy
umbrātĭl·is -e *adj* remaining in the shade, private, retired; academic
Umbrĭ·a -ae *f* Umbria (*district in central Italy*)
umbrĭf·er -ĕra -ĕrum *adj* shady
umbr·ō -āre *vt* to shade, cover
umbrōs·us -a -um *adj* shady
ūmect·ō -āre *vt* to wet, moisten
ūmect·us -a -um *adj* moist, damp
ūm·ĕō -ēre *vi* to be moist, be damp, be wet
umĕr·us -ī *m* shoulder
ūmesc·ō -ĕre *vi* to become moist or wet
ūmidŭl·us -a -um *adj* dampish
ūmĭd·us -a -um *adj* moist, damp, wet; green (*lumber*); *n* wet place
ūm·or -ōris *m* moisture; liquid, fluid
umquam or **unquam** *adv* ever, at any time
ūnā *adv* together; **ūnā venire** to come along
ūnanĭm·ans -antis *adj* of one mind, of one accord
ūnanimĭt·ās -ātis *f* unanimity
ūnanĭmus -a -um *adj* unanimous; of one mind, of one heart, harmonious
ūncĭ·a -ae *f* a twelfth; ounce (*one twelfth of a pound or libra*)
ūnciārĭ·us -a -um *adj* containing a twelfth; **faenus unciarium** eight and one third percent interest per annum
ūnciātim *adv* little by little
uncīnāt·us -a -um *adj* hooked, barbed
ūnciŏl·a -ae *f* a mere twelfth
unctĭ·ō -ōnis *f* rubdown; (fig) wrestling
unctĭt·ō -āre *vt* to keep rubbing with oil, keep oiling
unctiuscŭl·us -a -um *adj* somewhat too unctuous
unct·or -ōris *m* anointer, rubdown man
unct·um -ī *n* sumptuous dinner; ointment
unctūr·a -ae *f* anointing
unct·us -a -um *pp* of **ungo;** *adj* greasy; resinous; sumptuous; *n* sumptuous dinner; ointment
unc·us -a -um *adj* hooked, crooked, barbed; *m* hook, clamp; grappling iron
und·a -ae *f* water; liquid; wave, billow; (fig) stream, tide, agitated mass
unde *adv* from where, whence; from whom; **unde unde** or **undeunde** from some place or other, somehow or other, by hook or by crook
undecĭens or **undecĭēs** *adv* eleven times
undĕcim (indecl) *adj* eleven
undecĭm·us -a -um *adj* eleventh
undecumque or **undecunque** *adv* from whatever place, from whatever source
undēn·ō -ae -a *adj* eleven in a group, eleven each, eleven
undēnōnāgintā (indecl) *adj* eighty-nine
undeoctōgintā (indecl) *adj* seventy-nine
undēquadrāgintā (indecl) *adj* thirty-nine
undēquinquāgensĭm·us or **undēquinquāgēsĭm·us -a -um** *adj* forty-ninth
undēquinquāgintā (indecl) *adj* forty-nine
undēsexāgintā (indecl) *adj* fifty-nine
undētrīcensĭm·us or **undētrīcēsĭm·us -a -um** *adj* twenty-ninth
undēvīcēsimān·ī -ōrum *m pl* soldiers of the nineteenth legion
undēvīcēsĭm·us -a -um *adj* nineteenth
undēvīgintī (indecl) *adj* nineteen
undĭque *adv* from all directions, on all sides, everywhere; in all respects, completely
undisŏn·us -a -um *adj* sea-roaring; **undisoni dei** gods of the roaring waves
und·ō -āre *vi* to move in waves, undulate; to billow; to overflow
undōs·us -a -um *adj* full of waves, billowy
ūnetvīcensĭm·us or **ūnetvīcēsĭm·us -a -um** *adj* twenty-first
ūnetvīcēsimān·ī -ōrum *m pl* soldiers of the twenty-first legion
ungō or **unguō ungĕre unxī unctum** *vt* to oil, grease, anoint
ungu·en -ĭnis *n* fat, grease, ointment
unguentār·ĭus -ĭī or **-ī** *m* perfumer
unguentāt·us -a -um *adj* anointed; perfumed, wearing perfume
unguent·um -ī *n* ointment; perfume
unguicŭl·us -ī *m* fingernail; toenail; **a teneris unguiculis** from earliest childhood
ungu·is -is *m* fingernail; toenail; claw, talon, hoof; **ad unguen** to a

tee, complete, perfect; **de tenero ungui** from earliest childhood; **transversum unguem** a hair's breadth

ungŭl·a -ae *f* hoof, claw, talon; (fig) horse

unguō see **ungo**

ūnicē *adv* singularly, solely

ūnicŏl·or -ōris *adj* of one and the same color

ūnicorn·is -e *adj* one-horned

ūnĭ·cus -a -um *adj* sole, only, single, singular, unique; uncommon, unparalleled, outstanding, unique

ūniform·is -e *adj* uniform

ūnigĕn·a -ae *masc & fem adj* only-begotten, only; of the same parentage

ūnimăn·us -a -um *adj* with one hand, one-handed

ūnĭ·ō -ōnis *m* single large pearl

ūnĭter *adv* jointly, conjointly

ūniversāl·is -e *adj* universal

ūniversē *adv* generally, in general

ūniversĭt·ās -ātis *f* aggregate, entirety, whole; whole world, universe

ūnivers·us -a -um *adj* all together, all taken collectively, whole, entire; *n* the whole; whole world, universe; **in universum** on the whole, in general

ūnocŭl·us -ī *m* one-eyed person

ūnomammĭ·a -ae *f* (coll) single-breasted land (*country of the Amazons*)

unquam or **umquam** *adv* ever, at any time

ūn·us -a -um *adj* one; single, only, sole; one and the same; (indef) a, an, one, some; *pron* some one, a mere individual; **ad unum** to a man; **unus et alter** one or two; **unus quisque** every one individually, every single one

ūpilĭ·ō or **ōpilĭ·ō -ōnis** *m* shepherd

upŭp·a -ae *f* hoopoe; hoe, mattock

Ūranĭ·a -ae or **Ūranĭ·ē -ēs** *f* Muse of astronomy

urbānē *adv* politely, courteously; with sophistication; wittily, elegantly

urbānĭt·ās -ātis *f* living in the city, city life; refinement, politeness; sophistication; wit; raillery

urbān·us -a -um *adj* of the city, of the town, city, town; courteous; sophisticated; witty, facetious, humorous; forward, brash; *m* city man; city slicker

urbicăp·us -ī *m* conqueror of cities

urbs urbis *f* city; the city of Rome, the capital

urceŏl·us -ī *m* little pitcher, little pot

urcĕ·us -ī *m* pitcher, water pot

ūrēd·ō -ĭnis *f* blight (*of plants*)

urgĕō urgēre ursī *vt* to prod on, urge, urge forward; to pressure, put pressure on (*someone*); to crowd, hem in; to follow up, keep at, stick by; *vi* to be pressing, be urgent; to be insistent

ūrīn·a -ae *f* urine

ūrīnāt·or -ōris *m* diver

ūrīn·ō -āre or **ūrīn·or -ārī -ātus sum** *vi* to dive

urn·a -ae *f* pot, jar; water pot; voting urn; urn of fate; cinerary urn; money jar

ūrō ūrĕre ussī ustum *vt* to burn; to burn up, reduce to ashes, consume; to scorch, parch, dry up; to sting, pain; to nip, frostbite; to rub sore; to corrode; to annoy, gall, burn up, make angry; to inflame (*with love*), kindle, set on fire

urnŭl·a -ae *f* small urn

urs·a -ae *f* she-bear

Urs·a Major (*genit:* **Urs·ae Major·is**) *f* Great Bear (*constellation*)

Urs·a Minor (*genit:* **Urs·ae Minor·is**) *f* Little Bear (*constellation*)

ursīn·us -a -um *adj* bear, bear's

urs·us -ī *m* bear

urtīc·a -ae *f* nettle; desire, itch

ūr·us -ī *m* wild ox

Usipĕt·ēs -um *m pl* German tribe on the Rhine

ūsitātē *adv* in the usual way, as usual

ūsitāt·us -a -um *adj* usual, customary, familiar; **usitatum est** (with *inf*) it is customary to

uspiam *adv* anywhere, somewhere; in any matter

usquam *adv* anywhere, in any place; anywhere, to any place

usque *adv* all the way, right on, straight on; all the time, continuously; even, as much as; **usque** (with **ab** + *abl*) all the way from; **usque** (with **ad** + *acc*) all the way to; **usque quaque** every moment, continually; on all occasions, in everything

ust·or -ōris *m* cremator

ustŭl·ō -āre *vt* to burn a little, scorch, singe; to burn up

ustus *pp* of **uro**

ūsū·capiō -capĕre -cēpī -captum *vt* (law) to acquire possession of, acquire ownership of (*by long use, by prescription*)

ūsūcapĭ·ō -ōnis *f* (law) acquisition of ownership through long use or long possession

ūsūr·a -ae *f* use, enjoyment; interest (*on capital*)

ūsūrārĭ·us -a -um *adj* for use and enjoyment; paying interest

ūsurpātĭ·ō -ōnis *f* use; (with *genit*) making use of, use of

ūsurp·ō -āre *vt* to make use of, use, employ, adopt, practice, exercise; (law) to take possession of, acquire; to seize wrongfully, usurp; to name, call, speak of; to adopt, assume; to perceive (*with the senses*), observe, experience

ūsus *pp* of **utor**

ūs·us -ūs *m* use, enjoyment; practice, employment; experience, skill; usage, custom; familiarity; usefulness, advantage, benefit; occasion, need, necessity; **ex usu esse** or **usui esse** (with *dat*) to be useful to, be beneficial to, be a good thing for; **si usus veniat** if the need should arise, if the opportunity should present itself; **usus adest a** good opportunity comes along; **usus est** (with *abl*) there is need of; **usus et fructus** use and enjoyment; **usu venit** it happens, it occurs

ūsusfructus (*genit*: **ūsūsfructūs**) *m* use and enjoyment

ut or **utī** *adv* how, in what way; *conj* (comparative) as; (adversative) although; (temporal) when, while; (purpose) in order that; (result) that; (concessive) granted that; (introducing examples) as, as for example; (after verbs of fearing) lest, that not; (introducing an explanation or reason) as, as being, inasmuch as; (introducing indirect commands) that

utcumque or **utcunque** *adv* however; whenever; one way or another

ūtensĭl·is -e *adj* useful; *n pl* utensils, materials

ūt·er -ris *m* bag, skin, bottle

ut·er -ra -rum *adj* which (*of the two*); *pron* which one (*of the two*); one or the other

ut·ercumque -racumque -rumcumque *adj* whichever (*of the two*); *pron* whichever one (*of the two*)

ut·erlĭbet -ralĭbet -rumlĭbet *adj* whichever (*of the two*) you please; *pron* whichever one (*of the two*) you please, either one (*of the two*)

ut·erque -răque -rumque *adj* each (*of the two*), both; **sermones utriusque linguae** conversations in both languages; *pron* each one (*of the two*), both; **uterque insaniunt** both are insane

utĕr·us -ī *m* or **utĕr·um -ī** *n* womb; belly, paunch (*of a man*)

ut·ĕrvīs -răvīs -rumvīs *adj* whichever (*of the two*) you please, either; *pron* whichever one (*of the two*) you please, either one

utī see **ut**

ūtibĭl·is -e *adj* useful, practical

Utĭc·a -ae *f* city in Africa, N.W. of Carthage, where the younger Cato committed suicide

Uticens·is -is *adj* of Utica, Utican

ūtĭl·is -e *adj* useful, profitable, expedient, practical; (with *dat* or **ad** + *acc*) fit for, useful for, practical in

ūtilĭt·ās -ātis *f* usefulness, advantage

ūtilĭter *adv* usefully, profitably

utĭnam *conj* (introducing a wish) if only ,would that

utĭque *adv* anyhow, at least, at any rate

ūtor ūtī ūsus sum *vi* (with *abl*) **a** to use, make use of; **b** to enjoy; **c** to practice, experience; **d** to enjoy the friendship or companionship of

utpŏte *conj* as, inasmuch as; **utpote qui** inasmuch as (*he is one*) who, inasmuch as he, because he

ūtrār·ius -iī or **-ī** *m* water carrier, water boy

utrimque or **utrinque** *adv* from or on both sides, on either side; **utrimque constitit fides** on both sides the word of honor held good, both parties kept their word

utrō *adv* to which of the two sides, in which direction

utrobīque *adv* on both sides, on either hand

utrōlĭbet *adv* to either side

utrōque *adv* to both places, in both directions

utrŭbi or **utrŭbī** *adv* at or on which of two sides

utrubīque *adv* on both sides, on either hand

utrum *conj* either; whether

utut or **ut ut** *adv* however, in whatever way

ūv·a -ae *f* grape; bunch or cluster of grapes; vine; cluster of bees

ūvesc·ō -ĕre *vi* to become moist; (fig) to get drunk

ūvidŭl·us -a -um *adj* moist

ūvĭd·us -a -um *adj* wet, moist, damp, humid; drunken

ux·or -ōris *f* wife; mate (*of animals*)

uxorcŭl·a -ae *f* dear little wife

uxōrĭ·us -a -um *adj* of a wife, wifely; very fond of a wife; henpecked

V

vac·ans -antis *adj* vacant, unoccupied; at leisure, unemployed; unengaged, single; (with *abl*) lacking, without; *n pl* unoccupied estates

vacātĭ·ō -ōnis *f* freedom, exemption (*from duty, service, etc.*); exemption from military service; payment for exemption from military service

vacc·a -ae *f* cow

vaccīn·ium -iī or **-ī** *n* hyacinth

vaccŭl·a -ae *f* heifer

vacē·fīō -fĭerī -factus sum *vi* to become empty, be emptied

vacill·ō -āre *vi* to stagger, reel; to vacillate, waver; to be untrustworthy

vacīvē *adv* at leisure

vacīvĭt·ās -ātis *f* want, lack

vacīv·us or **vocīv·us -a -um** *adj* empty; free; (with *genit*) free of, void of, free from

vac·ō -āre *vi* to be empty, be vacant,

be unoccupied; to be free, be carefree; to be at leisure, have free time; (with *abl* or **ab** + *abl*) to be free from; (with *dat* or with **ad** or **in** + *acc*) to be free for, have time for; *v impers* there is time, room, leisure; (with *inf*) there is time to or for

vacuāt·us -a -um *adj* empty

vacuē·faciō -facĕre -fēcī -factum *vt* to empty, clear, free

vacuĭt·ās -ātis *f* freedom, exemption; vacancy (*in an office*)

vacŭ·ō -āre *vt* to empty, clear, free

vacŭ·us -a -um *adj* empty, clear, free; vacant; worthless, useless; single, unmarried; widowed; at leisure; carefree; (with *genit* or *abl* or with **ab** + *abl*) free from, devoid of, without; (with *dat*) free for

vadimōn·ĭum -ĭī or **-ī** *n* (law) promise (*to appear in court*), bail (*given as a guarantee of one's appearance in court*); **vadimonium deserere** to default, fail to show up in court; **vadimonium differre** to postpone appearance in court, grant a continuance; **vadimonium facere** to put up bail; **vadimonium sistere** to appear in court

vād·ō -ĕre *vi* to go, make one's way, advance

vad·or -ārī -ātus sum *vt* to put (*someone*) under bail

vadōs·us -a -um *adj* shallow

vad·um -ī *n* shallow place, shallow, shoal, ford; body of water, stream, sea; bottom, depths

vae *interj* woe! (with *acc* or *dat*) woe to

vaf·er -ra -rum *adj* sly, cunning; subtle

vafrē *adv* slyly, cunningly

vagē *adv* far and wide

vāgīn·a -ae *f* sheath, scabbard; sheath (*of ear of grain*), hull, husk; vagina

vāg·iō -īre -īvī -iī *vi* (esp. of an infant) to cry; (of swine) to squeal

vāgīt·us -ūs *m* cry; bleating

vāg·or -ōris *m* cry, wail (*of an infant*)

vag·or -ārī -ātus sum or **vag·ō -āre** *vi* to wander, range, roam

vag·us -a -um *adj* wandering, ranging, roaming; unsteady, inconstant; vague, uncertain

vah *interj* ah!, oh!

valdē *adv* greatly, intensely; (with *adj* or *adv*) very; (as affirmative reply) yes, certainly; to be sure

valē *interj* good-bye

val·ens -entis *adj* strong, powerful; healthy, hale, well

valenter *adv* strongly; energetically

valentŭl·us -a -um *adj* a strong little

val·ĕō -ēre -ŭī *vi* to be strong, be vigorous; to be powerful, be effective; to avail, prevail, succeed; to be influential; to be valid; to be strong enough, be adequate, be capable, be able; to be of value, be of worth; to mean, signify; **te valere jubeo** I bid you farewell, good-by to you; **vale!** or **valete!** good-bye!; **vale dicere** to say good-bye, take leave

valesc·ō -ĕre *vi* to grow strong, acquire strength, thrive

valētūdinār·ĭum -ĭī or **-ī** *n* hospital

valētūd·ō -ĭnis *f* state of health; good health; ill health, illness

valg·us -a -um *adj* bowlegged

valĭdē *adv* strongly, vehemently; (in replies) of course, certainly, definitely

valĭd·us -a -um *adj* strong, powerful, able; healthy, robust; fortified; influential; efficacious

vallār·is -e *adj* (decoration) awarded for scaling a rampart

vall·ēs or **vall·is -is** *f* valley

vall·ō -āre *vt* to fortify with a rampart, wall in; to protect, defend

vall·um -ī *n* rampart, palisade, entrenchment; protection

vall·us -ī *m* stake, pale; rampart with palisades, stockade; tooth (*of a comb*)

valv·ae -ārum *f pl* folding doors, double doors

vanesc·ō -ĕre *vi* to vanish, fade, disappear

vānidĭc·us -a -um *adj* lying, boasting; *m* liar, boaster

vāniloquentĭ·a -ae *f* empty talk

vāniloquidōr·us -ī *m* liar

vānilŏqu·us -a -um *adj* talking nonsense; lying, boasting, bragging

vānĭt·ās -ātis *f* falsity, unreality, deception, untruth; boasting, lying; vanity, conceit; worthlessness, frivolity, fickleness

vānitūd·ō -ĭnis *f* falsehood

vann·us -ī *f* fan, winnowing fan

vān·us -a -um *adj* empty, vacant; groundless, pointless; hollow, unreal; lying, false; boastful, conceited, vain; *n* emptiness, uselessness, deceptive appearance

vapĭdē *adv* poorly, badly

vapĭd·us -a -um *adj* flat, vapid, spoiled, bad; morally corrupt

vap·or -ōris *m* vapor, steam, smoke; exhalation, warmth, heat

vapōrār·ĭum -ĭī or **-ī** *n* steam pipe

vapōr·ō -āre *vt* to steam, steam up; to warm, heat; *vi* to steam, smoke

vapp·a -ae *f* sour wine; spoiled lad, good-for-nothing

vāpulār·is -e *adj* in for a flogging

vāpŭl·ō -āre *vi* to get a beating; (of savings, etc.) (fig) to take a beating

variantĭ·a -ae *f* diversity, variations

variātĭ·ō -ōnis *f* variation, difference

vārĭc·ō -āre *vt* to straddle

varicōs·us -a -um *adj* varicose

vārĭc·us -a -um *adj* with legs wide apart

varĭē *adv* variously, in various ways, differently

variĕt·ās -ātis *f* variety, difference, diversity; vicissitudes; inconstancy
varĭ·ō -āre *vt* to diversify, vary, change, make different; to variegate; *vi* to change color; to vary, differ, change; to differ in opinion; to waver
varĭ·us -a -um *adj* colored, variegated, spotted, striped; different, varying, various, changeable; versatile; inconstant, unsteady, untrustworthy
Var·ĭus -ĭī or **-ī** *m* epic and tragic poet and friend of Virgil and Horace (*d. c.* 12 B.C.)
var·ix -ĭcis *f* varicose vein
Varr·ō -ōnis *m* M. Terentius Varro (*Roman antiquarian and philologist whose wide erudition earned him the title of the most learned of the Romans,* 116-27 B.C.)
vār·us -a -um *adj* knock-kneed; bent, crooked; opposed, contrary
vas vadis *m* bail, surety
vās vāsis or **vās·um -ī** (*pl:* **vās·a -ōrum**) *n* vessel, dish; utensil, implement; *n pl* equipment, gear; **vasa conclamare** (mil) to give the signal to pack the gear
vāsār·ĭum -ĭī or **-ī** *n* allowance for furnishings (*given to a provincial governor*)
vasculār·ĭus -ĭī or **-ī** *m* metal worker; goldsmith
vascŭl·um -ī *n* small vessel
vastātĭ·ō -ōnis *f* devastation, ravaging
vastāt·or -ōris *m* devastator, ravager
vastē *adv* vastly, widely; coarsely, harshly; violently
vastific·us -a -um *adj* devastating
vastĭt·ās -ātis *f* wasteland, desert; state of desolation, emptiness; devastation, destruction; vastness, immensity; (fig) destroyer
vastitĭ·ēs -ēī *f* ruin, destruction
vast·ō -āre *vt* to make empty, make desolate, vacate, empty; (mil) to lay waste, ravage, devastate, destroy
vast·us -a -um *adj* empty, deserted, desolate; ravaged, devastated; vast, enormous; uncouth, rude, uncultivated, clumsy
vāt·ēs -is *m* soothsayer, prophet; bard, poet; *f* prophetess; poetess
Vāticān·us -a -um *adj* Vatican; **mons** or **collis Vaticanus** hill in Rome on the right bank of the Tiber
vāticinātĭ·ō -ōnis *f* prophesying, prediction, soothsaying
vāticināt·or -ōris *m* prophet, soothsayer
vāticin·ĭum -ĭī or **-ī** *n* prediction, prophecy
vāticinĭ·us -a -um *adj* prophetic
vāticĭn·or -ārī -ātus sum *vt* to foretell, prophesy; to keep harping on; *vi* to prophesy; to rant and rave, talk wildly
vatill·um -ī *n* brazier
-ve *conj* (enclitic) or; **-ve . . . -ve** either . . . or
vēcordĭ·a -ae *f* senselessness; insanity, madness
vēc·ors -ordis *adj* senseless; foolish; mad
vectīg·al -ālis *n* tax, toll, tariff; revenue, income (*of an individual*); honorarium (*given to a magistrate*)
vectīgāl·is -e *adj* tax, toll, tariff; paying tribute, subject to taxes, taxable, taxed; **pecunia vectigalis** tax money, tribute
vectĭ·ō -ōnis *f* conveyance, transporting
vect·is -is *m* crowbar, lever; bar, bolt (*on a door or gate*)
vect·ō -āre *vt* to carry around; **vectari** to keep riding around
vect·or -ōris *m* bearer, carrier; rider, passenger
vectōrĭ·us -a -um *adj* transportation, of transportation; **navigia vectoria** transport ships, transports
vectūr·a -ae *f* transport, transportation, conveyance; freight costs; fare
vectus *pp* of **veho**
Vēdiŏv·is or **Vējŏv·is -is** *m* Anti-Jove (*Etruscan divinity of the lower world, identified with Apollo and with the Jupiter of the lower world*); Little Jove (*identified with the infant Jupiter*)
vegĕt·us -a -um *adj* lively, vigorous, vivacious
vēgrand·is -e *adj* not huge, small
vehĕm·ens -entis *adj* vehement, violent, impetuous, ardent; great, tremendous; vigorous, active
vehementer or **vēmenter** *adv* vehemently, impetuously, violently, eagerly
vehementĭ·a -ae *f* vehemence
vehicŭl·um -ī *n* vehicle, carriage, cart; vessel, ship
vehō vehĕre vexī vectum *vt* to carry, convey, transport; **vehi** to ride, sail, be borne along
Vei·ens -entis or **Veientān·us -a -um** *adj* of Veii
Vei·ī -ōrum *m pl* old Etrurian city about twelve miles from Rome, captured by Camillus (396 B.C.)
vel *adv* even, actually; perhaps; for instance; *conj* or, or perhaps; or rather; **vel . . . vel** either . . . or
Vēlābr·um -ī *n* low ground between the Capitoline and Palatine
vēlām·en -ĭnis *n* drape, covering, veil; clothing, robe
vēlāment·um -ī *n* curtain, veil; *n pl* olive branches draped with woolen fillets
vēlār·ĭum -ĭī or **-ī** *n* awning (*over the open-air theater*)
vēlāt·ī -ōrum *m pl* (mil) reserves
vēl·es -ĭtis *m* light-armed soldier, skirmisher
vēlĭf·er -ĕra -ĕrum *adj* sail, sailing;

carina velifera sail boat, sailing ship
vēlificāti·ō -ōnis *f* sailing
vēlific·ō -āre or **vēlific·or -ārī -ātus sum** *vt* to sail through; *vi* to sail; (with *dat*) (fig) to be under full sail toward, be hell-bent for (*e.g., high office*)
Velīn·us -ī *m* river and lake in the Sabine territory
vēlitār·is -e *adj* of the light-armed troops
vēlitāti·ō -ōnis *f* skirmishing
vēlitēs = *pl* of **veles**
vēlit·or -ōris *m* skirmisher
vēlivŏl·us -a -um *adj* sail-flying (*ship*); sail-covered (*sea*)
vellic·ō -āre *vt* to pluck, pinch, nip; to carp at, rail at
vellō vellĕre vellī (or **vulsī**) **vulsum** (or **volsum**) *vt* to pluck, pull, tear at, tear away, tear out; to tear up, tear down, destroy
vell·us -ĕris *n* fleece; skin, pelt; wool; *n pl* fleecy clouds
vēl·ō -āre *vt* to veil, wrap, envelop, cover, cover up; to encircle, crown; to cover up, hide, conceal
vēlōcit·ās -ātis *f* speed, velocity
vēlōciter *adv* speedily, swiftly
vēl·ox -ōcis *adj* speedy, swift
vēl·um -ī *n* sail; veil, curtain, awning, covering; **vela dare** or **vela facere** to set sail; **remis velisque** with might and main
velut or **velŭtī** *conj* as, just as, even as; as for example; (to introduce a simile) as, as it were; (in elliptical clauses) like; **velut** or **velut si** just as if, just as though, as if, as though
vēmens see **vehemens**
vēn·a -ae *f* vein, artery; vein of metal; water course; vein (*in wood, stone, etc.*); natural bent or disposition, genius; penis; strength; *f pl* (fig) heart, core
vēnābŭl·um -ī *n* hunting spear
Venāfrān·us -a -um *adj* of Venafrum
Venāfr·um -ī *n* town in S. central Italy
vēnālici·us -a -um *adj* for sale; *m* slave dealer; *n pl* merchandise, imports and exports
vēnāl·is -e *adj* for sale; open to bribes; *mf* slave offered for sale
vēnātic·us -a -um *adj* hunting
vēnāti·ō -ōnis *f* hunt, hunting; wild-beast show; game
vēnāt·or -ōris *m* hunter
vēnātōri·us -a -um *adj* hunter's
vēnātr·ix -īcis *f* huntress
vēnātūr·a -ae *f* hunting
vēnāt·us -ūs *m* hunting
vendibil·is -e *adj* salable; attractive, popular, acceptable, on sale
venditāti·ō -ōnis *f* boasting, showing off
venditi·ō -ōnis *f* sale
vendit·ō -āre *vt* to try to sell; to advertise; to give as a bribe; **se venditare** (with *dat*) to ingratiate oneself with
vendit·or -ōris *m* vendor, seller; recipient of a bribe
vend·ō -ĕre -idī -itum *vt* to put up for sale; to sell, vend; to sell (*someone*) out, betray; to advertise; to praise, recommend
venēfic·a -ae *f* poisoner; sorceress, witch; (term of abuse) hag, witch
venēfic·ium -iī or **-ī** *n* poisoning witchcraft, magic
venēfic·us -a -um *adj* poisoning, poisonous; magic; *m* poisoner; sorcerer, magician
venēnāt·us -a -um *adj* poisonous, venomous; filled with poison; magic; bewitched, enchanted; (fig) venomous, bitter
venēnif·er -ĕra -ĕrum *adj* poisonous, venemous
venēn·ō -āre *vt* to poison; (fig) to poison, injure by slander
venēn·um -ī *n* poison; drug, potion; magic charm; sorcery; ruin, destruction
vēn·eō -īre -iī -itum *vi* to go up for sale, be sold
venerābil·is -e *adj* venerable
venerābund·us -a -um *adj* reverent, reverential
venerand·us -a -um *adj* venerable
venerāti·ō -ōnis *f* veneration, reverence, great respect
venerāt·or -ōris *m* respecter, adorer; admirer
Venerĕ·us or **Veneri·us -a -um** *adj* of Venus; of sexual love, venereal; *m* Venus-throw (*best throw in playing dice*); *m pl* attendants in Venus's temple
venĕr·or -ārī -ātus sum *vt* to venerate, revere, worship, pray to; to implore, beg; to pray for
Venĕt·ī -ōrum *m pl* a people in N.E. Italy in the region around modern Venice
Veneti·a -ae *f* district of the Veneti
Venetic·us -a -um *adj* Venetian
Venĕt·us -a -um *adj* Venetian; bluish; *m* Venetian; a Blue (*i.e., a member of one of the racing factions in Rome which were called Blues, Greens, etc.*)
veni·a -ae *f* kindness, favor, goodwill; permission; pardon, forgiveness; **veniam dare** (with *dat*) to grant forgiveness to, do a favor to, grant permission to; **veniam petere** to ask for permission; **veniā vestrā** with your leave
veniō venīre vēnī ventum *vi* to come; (with **in** + *acc*) **a** to come into, enter into (*e.g., agreement, friendship*); **b** to fall into (*e.g., trouble, disgrace*)
vēn·or -ārī -ātus sum *vt & vi* to hunt
vent·er -ris *m* stomach, belly; womb; embryo, unborn child: belly, protuberance; appetite, gluttony

ventĭl·ō -āre *vt* to fan, wave; to display, show off
ventĭ·ō -ōnis *f* coming
ventĭt·ō -āre *vi* to keep coming, come regularly
ventōs·us -a -um *adj* windy, full of wind; of the wind; wind-like, swift as the wind; conceited; fickle
ventricŭl·us -ī *m* belly; ventricle (*of the heart*)
ventriōs·us -a -um *adj* pot-bellied
ventŭl·us -ī *m* breeze
vent·us -ī *m* wind
vēnūcŭl·a -ae *f* grape (*of the type well suited for preserving*)
vēnum (*genit* not in use; *dat:* **vēnō**) *n* sale, that which is for sale; **venum** or **veno dare** to sell, sell as a slave; **venum** or **veno dari** to be sold; **venum** or **veno ire** to go up for sale, be sold
vēnum·dō or **vēnun·dō -dare -dĕdī -dătum** *vt* to put up for sale, sell
ven·us -ĕris *f* beauty, charm; pleasure of love, sexual indulgence, mating; beloved, love
Ven·us -ĕris *f* Venus (*goddess of love and beauty; planet*); Venus-throw (*highest throw of the dice*)
Venusī·a -ae *f* town in Apulia, the birthplace of Horace
Venusīn·us -a -um *adj* of Venusia
venust·ās -ātis *f* beauty, charm, attraction
venustē *adv* prettily, charmingly
venustŭl·us -a -um *adj* cute, pretty, charming little
venust·us -a -um *adj* beautiful, charming, attractive
vēpallĭd·us -a -um *adj* very pale
veprēcŭl·a -ae *f* little brier bush
vepr·ēs -is *m* thorn bush, bramble bush
vēr vēris *n* spring, springtime; youth
vērātr·um -ī *n* hellebore
vēr·ax -ācis *adj* truthful
verbēn·a -ae *f* vervain; *f pl* sacred branches worn by heralds and priests
verb·er -ĕris *n* scourge, rod, whip; flogging, scourging; thong (*of a sling and similar weapons*); *n pl* strokes, flogging.
verberābilissŭm·us -a -um *adj* altogether deserving of a flogging
verberātī·ō -ōnis *f* flogging
verberĕ·us -a -um *adj* deserving of a flogging
verbĕr·ō -āre *vt* to scourge, flog, whip; to batter, beat
verbĕr·ō -ōnis *m* rascal
verbōsē *adv* verbosely
verbōs·us -a -um *adj* verbose, wordy
verb·um -ī *n* word; saying, expression; verb; proverb; mere talk, mere words; formula; **ad verbum** word for word, verbatim; **verba dare** (with *dat*) to cheat (*someone*); **verba facere** to speak, make a speech; **verbi causā** or **verbi gratiā** for instance; **verbo** orally; in a word, briefly; nominally, in name only; in theory; **verbum de verbo, verbum pro verbo, verbum verbo** word for word
Vercingetŏr·ix -ĭgis *m* famous leader of the Arverni in the Gallic War
vercŭl·um -ī *n* (term of endearment) sweet springtime
vērē *adv* really, truly
verēcundē *adv* bashfully, shyly, modestly
verēcundĭ·a -ae *f* bashfulness, shyness, modesty; respect, awe, reverence; sense of shame, feeling of disgrace, disgrace, shame
verēcund·or -ārī *vi* to be bashful, be shy, feel ashamed
verēcund·us -a -um *adj* bashful, shy, modest, reserved
verēd·us -ī *m* fast hunting horse
verend·us -a -um *adj* venerable; *n pl* the private parts
ver·ĕor -ērī -ĭtus sum *vt* to revere, have respect for, respect; to fear; *vi* to feel uneasy, be apprehensive, be afraid, be anxious; (with *genit*) to stand in awe of, be afraid of; (with *dat*) to be afraid for; (with **de** + *abl*) to be apprehensive about; (with **ut**) to be afraid that not; (with **ne**) to be afraid that
verētr·um -ī *n* the private parts
Vergilĭ·ae -ārum *f pl* Pleiads
Vergil·ĭus or **Virgil·ĭus -ĭī** or **-ī** *m* Virgil (*P. Vergilius Maro, famous epic poet of the Augustan Age,* 70-19 B.C.)
verg·ō -ĕre *vt* to turn, incline; *vi* to turn, incline; to decline; to lie, be situated; (with **ad** + *acc*) **a** to verge toward; **b** to face, face toward
vēridĭc·us -a -um *adj* truthful, speaking the truth; truly spoken
vērīsimĭl·is -e *adj* probable, likely; realistic
vērīsimilitūd·ō -ĭnis *f* probability, likelihood
vērĭt·ās -ātis *f* truth, truthfulness; the truth, the real facts; real life, reality; honesty, integrity; correctness (*in etymology or grammar*); **ex veritate** in accordance with the truth
vēriverb·ĭum -ĭī or **-ī** *n* truthfulness
vermiculāt·us -a -um *adj* inlaid with wavy lines, vermiculated
vermicŭl·us -ī *m* grub worm
vermĭn·a -um *n pl* stomach pains
verm·is -is *m* worm
vern·a -ae *m* or *f* slave (*born in the master's house*), home-born slave; native
vernācŭl·us -a -um *adj* of home-born slaves; native, domestic; *m pl* jesters
vernīl·is -e *adj* slavish, servile; pert, smart
vernīlĭt·ās -ātis *f* slavishness, subservience; pertness

vernīlĭter *adv* slavishly
vern·ō -āre *vi* to show signs of spring; to burgeon, break into bloom; to be young
vernŭl·a -ae *m* or *f* little home-born slave, young home-born slave; native
vern·us -a -um *adj* spring; **tempus vernum** springtime
vērō *adv* in truth, in fact; certainly, to be sure; even; however
Verōn·a -ae *f* city in N. Italy, the birthplace of Catullus and of Pliny the Elder
Vērōnens·is -e *adj* Veronese
verp·a -ae *f* penis
verp·us -ī *m* circumcised man
verr·ēs -is *m* boar, pig
Verr·ēs -is *m* C. Cornelius Verres (*notorious for outrageous conduct in governing Sicily in* 73-70 B.C.)
verrīn·us -a -um *adj* of a boar, boar, hog, pork
verrō verrĕre verrī versum *vt* to pull, drag, drag away, carry off; to sweep, scour, brush; (of the wind) to whip across, sweep (*the land*)
verrūc·a -ae *f* wart (*on the body*); small failing, minor blemish
verrūcōs·us -a -um *adj* full of warts; (fig) faulty, full of blemishes
verrunc·ō -āre *vi* to turn out well
versābĭl·is -e *adj* shifting, movable
versābund·us -a -um *adj* revolving
versātĭl·is -e *adj* capable of turning, revolving, movable; versatile
versicŏl·or -ōris *adj* changing color, of various colors
versicŭl·us -ī *m* short line, single line (*of verse or prose*), versicle; *m pl* poor little verses
versificāt·or -ōris *m* versifier
versipell·is -e *adj* changing appearance, of changed appearance; sly; *m* werwolf
vers·ō or **vors·ō -āre** *vt* to keep turning, twist, wind; to roll; to bend, shift; to move about, agitate; to disturb, harass; to handle; to consider
vers·or or **vors·or -ārī -ātus sum** *vi* to live, stay; (with **in** + *abl*) to be involved in, be engaged in, be busy with
versum or **vorsum** *adv* (usually after another *adv* of direction) back; **rusum vorsum** backward; **sursum versum** up and down
versūr·a or **vorsūr·a -ae** *f* rotation; loan (*of money to pay another debt*); **versuram facere** (with **ab** + *abl*) to get a loan from (*someone to pay another*); **versurā solvere** to pay off (*another debt*) with borrowed money
versus *pp* of **verro** and of **verto**
vers·us or **vors·us -ūs** *m* turning; furrow; line, row; line, verse; line (*in writing*); turn, step (*in a dance*)
versus or **vorsus** *adv* (with **ad** + *acc*) towards, in the direction of; (with **in** + *acc*) into, in towards; **si in urbem versus venturi erunt** if they intend to come into the city; **sursum versus** upwards
versūtē *adv* cunningly
versūtĭ·ae -ārum *f pl* cunning
versūtilŏqu·us -a -um *adj* smooth-speaking, sly
versūt·us or **vorsūt·us -a -um** *adj* clever, shrewd, ingenious; sly, crafty, cunning, deceitful
vert·ex or **vort·ex -ĭcis** *m* whirlpool, eddy, strong current; whirlwind, tornado; crown or top of the head; head; top, summit (*of mountain*); pole (*of the heavens*); **ex vertice** from above
verticōs·us or **vorticōs·us -a -um** *adj* swirling, full of whirlpools
vertīg·ō -ĭnis *f* turning, whirling; dizziness
vert·ō or **vort·ō vertĕre vertī versum** *vt* to turn, turn around; to invert, tilt; to change, alter, transform; to overturn, overthrow, destroy; to ascribe, impute; to translate; **se vertere** or **verti** (with **in** + *acc*) to change into, change oneself into; **verti** (with **in** + *abl*) **a** to be in (*a place or condition*); **b** to be engaged in, be involved in; *vi* to turn; to change; to turn out; (with **in** + abl) to center upon, depend upon
Vertumn·us -ī *m* god of the changing seasons
ver·ū -ūs *n* spit (*for roasting*); javelin, dart
veruīn·a -ae *f* small javelin
vērum *adv* truly, yes; true but; but in fact; but yet, but even; yet, still; **verum tamen** or **verumtamen** nevertheless, but yet
vēr·us -a -um *adj* true, actual, genuine, real; fair, reasonable; *n* truth, the truth, reality; honor, duty, right; **veri similis** probable; realistic; **veri similitudo** probability
verūt·um -ī *n* dart, javelin
verūt·us -a -um *adj* armed with a dart or a javelin
verv·ex -ēcis *m* wether, castrated hog; (term of abuse) muttonhead
vēsānĭ·a -ae *f* insanity, madness
vēsānĭ·ens -entis *adj* furious
vēsān·us -a -um *adj* insane, mad; furious, savage, raging
vesc·or -ī *vi* (with *abl*) to feed on, eat, feast on, enjoy
vesc·us -a -um *adj* nibbled off; little, feeble; corroding, consuming
vēsīc·a or **vensīc·a -ae** *f* bladder; bombast; objects made of bladder: purse, cap, football, lantern
vēsīcŭl·a -ae *f* little bladder; little bag
vesp·a -ae *f* wasp
Vespasiān·us -ī *m* Vespasian (*T. Flavius Vespasianus Sabinus, Roman emperor,* 70-79 A.D., *and father of Domitian and Titus*)
vesp·er -ĕris or **-ĕrī** *m* evening; supper; the West; **ad vesperum**

towards evening; **primo vespere** early in the evening; **sub vesperum** towards evening; **tam vesperi** so late in the evening; **vespere** or **vesperi** in the evening
vespĕr·a -ae *f* evening
vesperasc·ō -āre *vi* to become evening, grow towards evening; to get late
vespertīlĭ·ō -ōnis *m* bat
vespertīn·us -a -um *adj* evening, in the evening; eastern
vesperūg·ō -ĭnis *f* evening star
vespill·ō -ōnis *m* undertaker
Vest·a -ae *f* Roman goddess of the hearth
Vestāl·is -e *adj* Vestal, of Vesta, Vesta's; *f* Vestal, Vestal virgin
vest·er or **vost·er -ra -rum** *adj* (in addressing more than one person) your; *pron* yours; **voster** your master; your own stock or lineage
vestibŭl·um -ī *n* entrance, forecourt; beginning
vestīg·ĭum -ĭī or **-ī** *n* footstep, step; footprint, track; trace, vestige; moment, instant
vestīg·ō -āre *vt* to track, trace; to check, find out
vestīment·um -ī *n* garment, clothes
vest·ĭō -īre -īvī or **-ĭī -ītum** *vt* to dress, clothe; to adorn, deck, array, attire; (fig) to dress, clothe
vestiplĭc·a -ae *f* laundress
vest·is -is *f* garment, clothing; coverlet, tapestry; blanket; slough, skin (*of a snake*); **mutare vestem** to change one's clothes; to put on mourning clothes
vestispĭc·a -ae *f* wardrobe woman
vestīt·us -ūs *m* clothes, clothing, dress, apparel, attire; ornament (*of speech*); **mutare vestitum** to put on mourning clothes; **redire ad suum vestitum** to end the mourning period
vetĕr·a -um *n pl* tradition, antiquity
veterān·us -a -um *adj & m* veteran
veter·ascō -ascĕre -āvī *vi* to grow old
veterāt·or -ōris *m* old hand, expert; sly old fox
veterātōrĭē *adv* cunningly, slyly
veterātōrĭ·us -a -um *adj* cunning, sly
vetĕr·ēs -um *m pl* the ancients; ancient authors
veterīn·us -a -um *adj* of burden; *f pl & n pl* beasts of burden
veternōs·us -a -um *adj* lethargic; sleepy, drowsy
vetern·us -ī *m* lethargy; old age; drowsiness; listlessness
vetĭt·um -ī *n* prohibition
vet·ō or **vot·ō -āre -ŭī** or **-āvī -ĭtum** *vt* to forbid, prohibit, oppose
vetŭl·us -a -um *adj* poor old
vet·us -ĕris *adj* old, aged; long-standing; *m pl* see **veteres;** *n pl* see **vetera**
vetust·ās -ātis *f* age; ancient times, antiquity; long duration, great age
vetust·us -a -um *adj* old, ancient; old-time, old-fashioned, good old (*days, etc.*); antiquated
vexām·en -ĭnis *n* shaking, quaking
vexātĭ·ō -ōnis *f* shaking, jolting, tossing; distress
vexāt·or -ōris *m* jostler; harasser; troublemaker
vexillār·ĭus -ĭī or **-ī** *m* standard-bearer, ensign; *m pl* special reserves
vexill·um -ī *n* standard, ensign, flag (*esp. the red flag hoisted above the general's tent as a signal for battle*); troops; **vexillum praeponere** to hoist the red flag (*as a signal for battle*)
vex·ō -āre *vt* to shake, toss; to vex, annoy; to harass (*troops*), attack
vi·a -ae *f* way, road, street, highway; march, journey; method; right way, right method; **inter vias** on the road
viāl·is -e *adj* highway
viārĭ·us -a -um *adj* for highway maintenance
viāticāt·us -a -um *adj* provided with traveling money
viātĭc·us -a -um *adj* for a trip, for traveling, travel; *n* travel allowance, provisions for the journey; (mil) soldiers' saving fund
viāt·or -ōris *m* traveler; passenger; (law) summoner
vīb·ix -īcis *f* weal, welt (*from a blow*)
vibr·ō -āre *vt* to brandish, shake, wave around; to hurl, fling; *vi* to vibrate, quiver; (of the tongue) to flick
vīburn·um -ī *n* wayfaring tree, guelder rose
vīcān·us -a -um *adj* village; *m pl* villagers
Vic·a Pot·a (*genit:* **Vic·ae Pot·ae**) *f* goddess of victory
vicārĭ·us -a -um *adj* substituted; *m* substitute, deputy, proxy; under-slave (*kept by another slave*)
vīcātim *adv* from street to street; from village to village; in hamlets
vice *prep* (with *genit*) on account of; like, after the manner of
vicem *adv* in turn; *prep* (with *genit*) instead of, in place of; on account of; like, after the manner of
vīcēnārĭ·us -a -um *adj* of the number twenty
vīcēn·ī -ae -a *adj* twenty each, twenty in a group
vīcēsimān·ī -ōrum *m pl* soldiers of the twentieth legion
vīcēsimārĭ·us -a -um *adj* derived from the five-percent tax
vīcēsĭm·us -a -um *adj* twentieth; *f* five-percent tax
vicĭ·a -ae *f* vetch
vīciens or **vīcĭēs** *adv* twenty times
vīcīnāl·is -e *adj* neighboring, nearby
vīcīnĭ·a -ae *f* neighborhood, nearness, proximity
vīcīnĭt·ās -ātis *f* neighborhood, proximity; the neighborhood (*i.e., the neighbors*)

vīcīn·us -a -um *adj* neighboring, nearby, near; *mf* neighbor; *n* neighborhood
vicis (*genit;* the *nom* does not occur; *acc:* **vicem;** *abl:* **vice**) *f* change, interchange, alteration, succession; return, recompense, retaliation; fortune, misfortune, condition, fate, changes of fate; duty, office, position; function, office; **in vicem** or **invicem** by turns, alternately, mutually; **in vicem** or **invicem** (with *genit*) instead of, in place of; **in vicis** by turns, alternately, mutually
vicissim or **vicissātim** *adv* in turn, again
vicissitūd·ō -inis *f* change, interchange, alternation
victim·a -ae *f* victim; sacrifice
victimār·ius -iī or **-ī** *m* assistant at sacrifices
victit·ō -āre *vi* to live, subsist; (with *abl*) to live on, subsist on
vict·or -ōris *m* conqueror; (in apposition) **victor exercitus** victorious army
victōriāt·us -ī *m* silver coin stamped with the image of victory
Victōriōl·a -ae *f* small statue of Victory
victr·ix -īcis *f* or *n* conqueror, victor
victus *pp* of **vinco**
vict·us -ūs *m* living, means of livelihood; way of life
vīcŭl·us -ī *m* hamlet
vīc·us -ī *m* village, hamlet; ward, quarter (*in a town or city*); street, alley (*running through the quarter*)
vidēlĭcet *adv* clearly, evidently; (in irony) of course, naturally; (in explanations) namely
viden = videsne? do you see?, do you get it?
vidĕō vidēre vīdī vīsum *vt* to see, look at; to know; to consider; to understand, realize; (with **ut**) to see to it that, take care that; **vidērī** to seem, appear, seem right, seem good
vidŭ·a -ae *f* widow; spinster
viduit·ās -ātis *f* bereavement; want, lack; widowhood
vīdŭl·us -ī *m* leather travel bag, suitcase, knapsack
vidŭ·ō -āre *vt* to deprive, bereave; (with *genit* or *abl*) to deprive of, bereave of; **viduata** left a widow
vidŭ·us -a -um *adj* bereft, destitute; unmarried; (with *abl* or **ab** + *abl*) bereft of, destitute of, without; *f* see **vidua**
viēt·or -ōris *m* cooper
viēt·us -a -um *adj* shriveled
vig·ĕō -ēre -ŭī *vi* to thrive, be vigorous, flourish
vig·escō -escĕre -ŭī *vi* to become vigorous, gain strength, become lively
vīgēsim·us -a -um *adj* twentieth
vig·il -ilis *adj* awake, wakeful; alert, on one's toes; *m* watchman, guard, sentinel
vigĭl·ans -antis *adj* watchful, alert; disquieting (*worries*)
vigilanter *adv* vigilantly, alertly
vigilantĭ·a -ae *f* wakefulness; alertness
vigĭl·ax -ācis *adj* alert; sleep-disturbing, disquieting (*worries*)
vigilĭ·a -ae *f* wakefulness, sleeplessness, insomnia; standing guard; guards, sentinels; vigil; vigilance, alertness
vigĭl·ō -āre *vt* to spend (*the night*) awake; to make, do, perform, write (*something*) while awake at night; *vi* to remain awake, stay awake; to be alert; (with *dat*) to be attentive to
vīgintī (indecl) *adj* twenty
vīgintīvirāt·us -ūs *m* membership on a board of twenty
vīgintīvir·ī -ōrum *m pl* twenty-man board or commission
vig·or -ōris *m* vigor, liveliness, energy
vīlĭc·a -ae *f* foreman's wife, manager's wife
vīlĭc·ō -āre *vi* to be a foreman, be a manager
vīlĭc·us -ī *m* foreman, manager (*of an estate*)
vīl·is -e *adj* cheap, inexpensive; cheap, mean, common, worthless
vīlĭt·ās -ātis *f* lowness of price, cheapness, low price; worthlessness
vīlĭter *adv* cheaply
vill·a -ae *f* villa, country home, farm
villic- = vilic-
villōs·us -a -um *adj* hairy, shaggy
villŭl·a -ae *f* small villa
vill·um -ī *n* drop of wine
vill·us -ī *m* hair, fleece; nap (*of cloth*)
vīm·en -inis *n* osier; basket
vīment·um -ī *n* osier
Vīminăl·is coll·is (*genit:* **Vīmināl·is coll·is**) *m* one of the seven hills of Rome
vīminĕ·us -a -um *adj* made of osiers
vīn or **vīn' = visne?** do you wish
vīnācĕ·us -a -um *adj* grape, of a grape; *m* a grape seed
Vīnāl·ia -ium *n pl* wine festival (*celebrated on the 23rd of April and on the 19th of August*)
vīnārĭ·us -a -um *adj* wine; *m* wine dealer, vintner; *n pl* wine flasks
vincibĭl·is -e *adj* easily won
vinciō vincīre vinxī vinctum *vt* to bind; to encircle, surround; to restrain; (rhet) to bind together, link together, arrange rhythmically
vincō vincĕre vīcī victum *vt* to conquer, vanquish; to get the better of, beat, defeat, outdo; to surpass, excel; to convince, refute, persuade; to prove, demonstrate; to outlast, outlive; *vi* to be victorious; to prevail, succeed
vinctus *pp* of **vincio**
vincŭl·um or **vincl·um -ī** *n* chain, fetter, cord, band; *n pl* prison
vindēmĭ·a -ae *f* vintage

vindēmiāt·or -ōris *m* vintager, grape gatherer
vindēmiŏl·a -ae *f* small vintage; minor sources of income
vind·ex -icis *adj* avenging; *m* (law) claimant; defender, protector, champion; deliverer, liberator; avenger, punisher
vindicāti·ō -ōnis *f* (law) claim; avenging, punishment
vindici·ae -ārum *f pl* legal claim; things or persons claimed; championship, protection; **vindicias dare, dicere,** or **decernere** to hand over the things or persons claimed
vindic·ō -āre *vt* to lay a legal claim to; to protect, defend; to appropriate; to demand; to demand unfairly; to claim as one's own; to avenge, punish; **in libertatem vindicare** to claim for freedom, set free, free, liberate, emancipate
vindict·a -ae *f* rod used in the ceremony of setting slaves free; defense, protection; vengeance, revenge, satisfaction
vīnĕ·a -ae *f* vineyard; vine; (mil) shed (*used to defend besiegers against the missiles of the enemy*)
vīnēt·um -ī *n* vineyard
vīnit·or -ōris *m* vinedresser
vinnŭl·us -a -um *adj* charming, pleasant
vīnolenti·a -ae *f* wine drinking, intoxication
vīnolent·us -a -um *adj* intoxicated, drunk
vīnōs·us -a -um *adj* fond of wine
vīn·um -ī *n* wine
viŏl·a -ae *f* violet; violet color
violābil·is -e *adj* vulnerable
violār·ium -iī or **-ī** *n* bed of violets
violār·ius -iī or **-ī** *m* dyer of violet color
violāti·ō -ōnis *f* violation, profanation
violāt·or -ōris *m* violator, profaner, desecrator
viŏl·ens -entis *adj* violent, raging, impetuous
violenter *adv* violently, vehemently, impetuously
violenti·a -ae *f* violence, vehemence, impetuosity
violent·us -a -um *adj* violent, vehement, impetuous, boisterous
viŏl·ō -āre *vt* to do violence to, outrage, harm or injure by violence; to violate, break
vīpĕr·a -ae *f* viper; adder, snake
vīperĕ·us -a -um *adj* viper's, adder's, snake's
vīperīn·us -a -um *adj* of a viper or snake
vir virī *m* male person, man; real man; hero; husband; manhood, virility; (mil) infantryman
virāg·ō -inis *f* female warrior; heroine
virect·a -ōrum *n pl* green places; lawn
vir·ĕō -ēre -ŭī *vi* to be green; to be fresh, be vigorous, flourish
vīrēs = *pl* of **vis**
vir·escō -escĕre -ŭī *vt* to grow green
virg·a -ae *f* twig, sprout; graft; rod, switch (*for flogging*); walking stick, cane, staff; magic wand; wand; colored stripe in a garment; branch of a family tree
virgāt·or -ōris *m* flogger
virgāt·us -a -um *adj* made of twigs or osiers; striped
virgēt·um -ī *n* osier thicket
virgĕ·us -a -um *adj* of twigs, of kindling wood
virgidēmi·a -ae *f* (coll) harvest of birch rods (*i.e., sound flogging*)
virgināl·is -e *adj* maiden's, girl's, girlish; *n* female organ
virginār·ius -a -um *adj* maiden's, girl's
virginĕ·us -a -um *adj* maidenly, virgin, of virgins
virginit·ās -ātis *f* virginity, girlhood
virg·ō -inis *f* virgin, maiden, girl, young woman; young married woman
Virg·ō -inis *f* Virgo (*constellation; aqueduct constructed by M. Vipsanius Agrippa*)
virgŭl·a -ae *f* little twig; wand; **virgula divina** divining rod
virgult·a -ōrum *n pl* thickets, brushwood; slips (*of trees*)
virguncŭl·a -ae *f* lass, young girl
virid·ans -antis *adj* growing green, green
viridār·ium -iī or **-ī** *n* garden; plantation
virid·is -e *adj* green; fresh, young; *n pl* greenery
viridit·ās -ātis *f* greenness; freshness
virid·or -ārī *vi* to become green
virīl·is -e *adj* male, masculine; adult; manly; **pro virili parte** or **partione** to the best of one's ability; *n pl* manly or heroic deeds
virīlit·ās -ātis *f* manhood, virility
virīliter *adv* manfully
vīripŏt·ens -entis *adj* almighty
virītim *adv* individually, separately
vīrōs·us -a -um *adj* slimy; strong-smelling, fetid, stinking
virt·ūs -ūtis *f* manliness, manhood, virility; strength; valor, bravery, gallantry; gallant deeds; excellence, worth; virtue, moral perfection, good quality; *f pl* achievements
vīr·us -ī *n* slime; poison; pungency; saltiness
vīs (*genit* not in use) *f* power, strength, force; energy; hostile force, violence, attack, assault; amount, quantity; meaning (*of words*); **vires** *f pl* strength, resources; (mil) troops; **per vim** forcibly, violently; **pro viribus** with all one's might
viscāt·us -a -um *adj* limed

viscĕr·a -um *n pl* viscera, internal organs; womb; heart, vitals, bowels; (fig) innermost part, bowels, heart, center; bosom friend, favorite

viscerātĭ·ō -ōnis *f* public distribution of meat

visc·ō -āre *vt* to make sticky

visc·um -ī *n* mistletoe; birdlime

visc·us -ĕris *n* organ (*of the body*); entrails

vīsĭ·ō -ōnis *f* appearance, apparition; notion, idea

vīsĭt·ō -āre *vt* to keep seeing; to visit, go to visit

vīs·ō -ĕre -ī -um *vt* to look at with attention, view; to come or go to look at; to find out; to visit

vīs·um -ī *n* sight, appearance

vīs·us -ūs *m* faculty of sight, sight; thing seen, sight, vision

vīt·a -ae *f* life, way of life; livelihood; course of life, career; biography

vītābĭl·is -e *adj* undesirable, deserving to be shunned

vītābund·us -a -um *adj* avoiding, evading

vītāl·is -e *adj* of life, vital; likely to live, staying alive; *n* means of life; *n pl* vital parts

vītālĭter *adv* vitally

vītātĭ·ō -ōnis *f* avoidance

Vitell·ĭus -ĭī or **-ī** *m* A. Vitellius (*Roman emperor*, 69 A.D.)

vitell·us -ī *m* little calf; yolk (*of egg*)

vītĕ·us -a -um *adj* of the vine

vītĭcŭl·a -ae *f* little vine

vītĭf·er -ĕra -ĕrum *adj* vine-producing

vītigĕn·us -a -um *adj* produced from the vine

vitilēn·a -ae *f* procuress

vitĭ·ō -āre *vt* to corrupt, spoil, violate, mar; to falsify

vitiōsē *adv* faultily, badly, corruptly

vitiōsĭt·ās -ātis *f* corrupt or bad condition

vitiōs·us -a -um *adj* faulty, defective, corrupt, bad; vicious

vīt·is -is *f* vine; vine branch; centurion's staff; centurionship

vītisāt·or -ōris *m* vine planter

vit·ĭum -ĭī or **-ī** *n* fault, defect, flaw; sin, offense, vice; flaw in the auspices

vīt·ō -āre *vt* to avoid, evade

vīt·or -ōris *m* basket maker

vitrĕ·us -a -um *adj* glass, of glass; glassy; *n pl* glassware

vītrĭc·us -ī *m* stepfather

vitr·um -ī *n* glass

vitt·a -ae *f* headband, fillet

vittāt·us -a -um *adj* wearing a fillet

vitŭl·a -ae *f* heifer

vitulīn·us -a -um *adj* & *f* veal

vītŭl·or -ārī *vi* to celebrate, hold a celebration

vitŭl·us -ī *m* calf, young bull; foal; seal

vituperābĭl·is -e *adj* blameworthy

vituperātĭ·ō -ōnis *f* blaming, censuring; blame; scandalous conduct, blameworthiness

vituperāt·or -ōris *m* censurer

vitupĕr·ō -āre *vt* to spoil (*omen*), render void; to blame

vīvācĭt·ās -ātis *f* will to live

vivār·ĭum -ĭī or **-ī** *n* game preserve; fish pond

vīvāt·us -a -um *adj* animated, lively

vīv·ax -ācis *adj* long-lived; long-lasting, enduring; quick to learn

vīvescō or **vīviscō vīvescĕre vixī** *vi* to become alive, come to life; to grow lively, get full of life

vīvĭd·us -a -um *adj* teeming with life, full of life; true to life, vivid, realistic; quick, lively (*mind*)

vīvirād·ix -īcis *f* development of roots

vīviscō see **vivesco**

vīvō vīvĕre vixī victum *vi* to be alive, live; to be still alive, survive; to reside; (with *abl* or **de** + *abl*) to live on, subsist on

vīv·us -a -um *adj* alive, living; lively; fresh; natural (*rock*); speaking (*voice*); *n* (com) capital; **ad vivum resecare** to cut to the quick

vix *adv* with difficulty, hardly; scarcely

vixdum *adv* hardly then, scarcely yet

vocābŭl·um -ī *n* designation, name; noun

vōcāl·is -ē *adj* having a voice, gifted with speech or song, singing, speaking; tuneful; *f* vowel

vocām·en -ĭnis *f* designation, name

vocātĭ·ō -ōnis *f* summons (*to court*); invitation (*to dinner*)

vocāt·or -ōris *m* inviter, host

vocāt·us -ūs *m* summons, call

vōciferātĭ·ō -ōnis *f* loud cry, yell

vōcifĕr·ō -āre or **vōcifĕr·or -ārī -ātus sum** *vt* & *vi* to shout, yell

vocĭt·ō -āre *vt* to usually call, name; to shout out again and again

voc·ō -āre *vt* to summon; to call, name; to call upon (*the gods*); to invite; (mil) to challenge; **in dubium vocare** to call in question; **in odium vocare** to bring into disfavor; **in periculum vocare** to lead into danger

vōcŭl·a -ae *f* small or weak voice; soft note, soft tone; whisper, gossip

volaem·um -ī *n* large pear

Volaterr·ae -ārum *f pl* old Etruscan town

Volaterrān·us -a -um *adj* of Volaterrae

volātĭc·us -a -um *adj* flying, winged; transitory, passing; inconstant

volātĭl·is -e *adj* flying, winged; rapid, swift; fleeting, transitory

volāt·us -ūs *m* flight

Volcānāl·ĭa -ĭum *n pl* festival of Vulcan (*celebrated on the 23rd of August*)

Volcān·us or **Vulcān·us -ī** *m* Vulcan (*god of fire and son of Juno and Jupiter*)

vol·ens -entis *adj* willing, permitting; willing, ready; favorable; *m* well-wisher
volg- = **vulg-**
volĭt·ans -antis *m* winged insect
volĭt·ō -āre *vi* to flit about, fly about, flutter; to move quickly; to hover, soar
volō velle voluī *vt* to wish, want; to propose, determine; to hold, maintain; to mean; to prefer; *vi* to be willing
volōn·ēs -um *m pl* volunteers (*slaves who enlisted after the battle of Cannae,* 216 B.C.)
volpēs see **vulpes**
Volsc·us -a -um *adj* Vulscan; *m pl* an ancient people in S. Latium
volsell·a -ae *f* tweezers
volsus *pp* of **vello**
volt = older form of **vult** he, she, it wishes
voltis = older form of **vultis** you wish
Voltumn·a -ae *f* Etruscan goddess in whose temple the Etruscan states met
voltus see **vultus**
volūbĭl·is -e *adj* turning, spinning, revolving, swirling; voluble, rapid, fluent; changeable
volūbilĭt·ās -ātis *f* whirling motion; roundness; volubility, fluency; mutability
volūbilĭter *adv* volubly, rapidly, fluently
volŭc·er -ris -re *adj* flying, winged; rapid, speedy; *mf* bird; *f* insect
volūm·en -ĭnis *n* roll, book; chapter, book; whirl, eddy; coil; fold
voluntārĭ·us -a -um *adj* voluntary; *m pl* volunteers
volunt·ās -ātis *f* will, wish, desire, purpose, aim; goodwill; last will, testament; attitude (*good or bad*); **ad voluntatem** (with *genit*) according to the wishes of; **de** or **ex voluntate** (with *genit*) at the desire of
volup *adv* to one's satisfaction, agreeably
voluptābĭl·is -e *adj* agreeable, pleasant
voluptārĭ·us -a -um *adj* pleasant, agreeable; voluptuous; *m* voluptary
volupt·ās -atis *f* pleasure, enjoyment, delight; *f pl* sensual pleasures; games, sports, public performances
voluptuōs·us -a -um *adj* pleasant, agreeable
volūtābr·um -ī *n* wallow (*for swine*)
volūtābund·us -a -um *adj* wallowing about
volūtātĭ·ō -ōnis *f* rolling about, tossing about; wallowing; restlessness
volūt·ō -āre *vt* to roll about, turn over; to engross; to think over; **volutari** to wallow, luxuriate
volūtus *pp* of **volvo**
volv·a or **vulv·a -ae** *f* wrapper, cover; womb; sow's womb (*as a favorite dish*)
volvō volvĕre volvī volūtum *vt* to roll, turn about, wind; (e.g., of a river) to roll (*rocks, etc.*) along; to breathe; to unroll, read (*books*); to pour out, utter fluently; to consider, weigh; (of time) to bring on, bring around; to form (*a circle*); to undergo (*troubles*); **volvi** to roll, tumble, revolve; *vi* to revolve; to roll on, elapse
vōm·er or **vōm·is -ĕris** *m* plowshare; penis
vomĭc·a -ae *f* sore, boil, abscess, ulcer; annoyance
vōmis see **vomer**
vomĭtĭ·ō -ōnis *f* vomiting
vom·ō -ĕre -ŭī -ĭtum *vt & vi* to vomit, throw up
vorāg·ō -ĭnis *f* deep hole, abyss, chasm, depth
vor·ax -ācis *adj* swallowing, devouring; greedy, ravenous
vor·ō -āre *vt* to swallow, devour; (fig) to devour (*by reading*)
vors- = **vers-**
vort- = **vert-**
vōs *pron* you; (reflex) yourselves
vosmet *pron* (emphatic form of **vōs**) you yourselves
voster see **vester**
vōtīv·us -a -um *adj* votive, promised in a vow
votō see **veto**
vōt·um -ī *n* solemn vow (*made to a deity*), vow; votive offering; wish, prayer
vovĕō vovēre vōvī vōtum *vt* to vow, promise solemnly, pledge, devote (*to a deity*); to wish, wish for, desire
vox vōcis *f* voice; sound, tone, cry, call; word, utterance, saying, expression; proverb; language; accent
Vulcānus see **Volcanus**
vulgār·is or **volgār·is -e** *adj* common, general, usual
vulgārĭter or **volgarĭter** *adv* in the common or usual way
vulgāt·or or **volgāt·or -ōris** *m* divulger
vulgāt·us or **volgāt·us -a -um** *adj* common, general; well known; notorious
vulgivăg·us or **volgivăg·us -a -um** *adj* roving; inconstant
vulg·ō or **volg·ō -āre** *vt* to spread, publish, broadcast; to divulge; to prostitute; to level, make common
vulgō or **volgō** *adv* generally, publicly, everywhere
vulg·us or **volg·us -ī** *n* masses, people, public; crowd, herd; rabble, populace
vulnerātĭ·ō or **volnerātĭ·ō -ōnis** *f* wounding, wound
vulnĕr·ō or **volnĕr·ō -āre** *vt* to wound; to damage

vulnific·us -a -um *adj* inflicting wounds

vuln·us or **voln·us -ĕris** *n* wound; blow, stroke; blow, disaster

vulpēcŭl·a or **volpēcŭl·a -ae** *f* little fox, sly little fox

vulp·ēs or **volp·ēs -is** *f* fox; craftiness, cunning

vuls·us or **vols·us -a -um** *pp* of **vello;** *adj* plucked, beardless, effeminate

vulticŭl·us or **volticŭl·us -ī** *m* mere look

vult·um -ī *n* face; looks, expression, features; look, appearance

vultuōs·us or **voltuōs·us -a -um** *adj* full of airs, affected

vult·ur or **volt·ur -ŭris** *m* vulture

Vult·ur or **Volt·ur -ŭris** *m* mountain in Apulia near Venusia

vulturīn·us or **volturnīn·us -a -um** *adj* of a vulture, vulture-like

vultur·ius or **voltur·ius -iī** or **-ī** *m* vulture

Vulturn·us or **Volturn·us -ī** *m* principal river of Campania (*modern Volturno*)

vult·us or **volt·us -ūs** *m* face; looks, expression, features; look, appearance

vulv·a or **volv·a -ae** *f* wrapper, cover; womb; sow's womb (*as a delicacy*)

X

Xanthipp·ē -ēs *f* wife of Socrates

Xanth·us -ī *m* river at Troy, identified with Scamander River

xen·ium -iī or **-ī** *n* gift, present

Xenophăn·ēs -is *m* early Greek philosopher (*c.* 565-470 B.C.)

Xenŏph·ōn -ontis *m* Greek historian and pupil of Socrates (*c.* 430-*c.* 354 B.C.)

xērampelīn·ae -ārum *f pl* dark-colored clothes

Xerx·ēs -is *m* Persian king, defeated at Salamis (*c.* 519-465 B.C.)

xiphi·ās -ae *m* swordfish

xyst·us -ī *m* or **xyst·um -ī** *n* open colonnade or portico, walk, avenue

Z

Zacynth·us or **Zacynth·os -ī** *f* island off W. Greece

Zam·a -ae *f* town in Numidia where Scipio defeated Hannibal and brought the Second Punic War to an end

zāmi·a -ae *f* harm, damage, loss

Zancl·ē -ēs *f* old name of Messana in Sicily

Zēn·ō or **Zēn·ōn -ōnis** *m* founder of Stoic philosophy and a native of Citium in Cyprus (335-263 B.C.); Epicurean philosopher, the teacher of Cicero and Atticus

Zephўr·us -ī *m* zephyr; west wind; wind

Zēth·us -ī *m* son of Jupiter and Antiope and brother of Amphion

zmaragd·us -ī *f* emerald

zōdiăc·us -ī *m* zodiac

Zōïl·us -ī *m* proverbially stern Alexandrine critic of Homer

zōn·a -ae *f* belt, sash, girdle (*worn by women*); money belt; zone

zōnāri·us -a -um *adj* of a belt or girdle; *m* belt maker, girdle maker

zōnŭl·a -ae *f* little girdle

zōthēc·a -ae *f* small room

zōthēcŭl·a -ae *f* small bedroom

ENGLISH-LATIN

A

a *indefinite article, unexpressed in Latin;* **twice — year** bis in anno
aback *adv* **taken —** stupefactus, attonitus, consternatus
abandon *vt* (de)relinquĕre, destituĕre, deserĕre, abjicĕre, omittĕre
abandoned *adj* derelictus, desertus; (*fig*) nefarius, perditus, flagitiosus
abandonment *s* derelictio, destitutio *f*
abase *vt* deprimĕre, comprimĕre, frangĕre, (de)minuĕre
abash *vt* perturbare, confundĕre, pudefacere, percellĕre
abashed *adj* pudendus, erubescens
abate *vt* (*to lower*) imminuĕre; (*to slacken*) laxare; (*the price*) remittĕre, detrahĕre; *vi* (*to lessen*) imminuĕre, decrescĕre; (*to decline*) cadĕre, decedĕre; (*of passion*) defervescĕre
abbess *s* abbatissa *f*
abbey *s* abbatia *f*
abbot *s* abbas *m*
abbreviate *vt* abbreviare, contrahĕre, imminuĕre
abbreviation *s* abbreviatio, contractio, *f* compendium *n*
abdicate *vt* abdicare; *vi* se abdicare
abdication *s* abdicatio *f*
abdomen *s* abdomen *n*
abduct *vt* abducĕre, rapĕre
abduction *s* raptio *f*, rapt·us -ūs *m*
aberration *s* error *m*; declinatio *f*
abet *vt* adjuvare, instigare; favēre (*with dat*)
abeyance *s* **to be in —** jacēre, intermitti
abhor *vt* abhorrēre ab (*with abl*), detestari, odio habēre
abhorrence *s* detestatio *f*, odium *n*
abhorrent *adj* perosus; alienus, repugnans, abhorrens
abide *vt* tolerare, subire; *vi* (*to dwell*) habitare, manēre; **to — by** stare in (*with abl*)
abiding *adj* diuturnus, mansurus; constans, fidus
ability *s* facultas, potestas *f*; ingenium *n*; **to the best of one's —** summa ope; pro sua parte
abject *adj* abjectus, vilis; humilis; **—ly** abjecte; humiliter
abjure *vt* abjurare, ejurare
ablative *s* ablativus *m*
able *adj* potens; valens, capax, peritus; ingeniosus; **to be — to** posse, valēre, quire, sufficĕre
ablution *s* ablutio, lavatio *f*
ably *adv* experte; ingeniose
aboard *adv* in *or* super nave; **to go — a ship** navem conscendĕre
abode *s* domicilium *n*; sedes *f*; commoratio, mansio *f*
abolish *vt* abolēre; exstinguĕre, tollĕre, rescindĕre
abolition *s* abolitio, dissolutio *f*
abominable *adj* detestabilis, infandus, execrabilis; odiosus
abominably *adv* execrabiliter; odiose
abominate *vt* abominari, detestari
abomination *s* destestatio *f*
aborigines *s* aborigines, indigenae *m pl*
abortion *s* abortio *f*; abort·us -ūs *m*
abortive *adj* abortivus; (*fig*) irritus, frustratus
abound *vi* abundare, redundare, superesse; **to — in** abundare (*with abl*)
abounding *adj* abundans; copiosus, largus; creber
about *adv* circa, circiter; fere, ferme
about *prep* (*of place*) circa, circum (*with acc*); (*of number*) circa, ad (*with acc*); (*of time*) circa, sub (*with acc*); (*of respect*) de (*with abl*)
above *adv* supra; insuper; **from —** desuper, superne
above *prep* supra, super (*with acc*)
abrasion *s* attrit·us -ūs *m*
abreast *adv* pariter; ex adverso
abridge *vt* contrahĕre; abbreviare; (*fig*) privare
abridgment *s* compendium *n*, epitome *f*
abroad *adv* (*in a foreign land*) peregre; (*of motion, out of doors*) foras; (*of rest, out of doors*) foris; **from —** extrinsecus; peregre; **to be** *or* **live abroad** peregrinari; patriā carēre; **to get —** (*fig*) divulgari
abrogate *vt* rescindere, abrogare, dissolvĕre
abrupt *adj* praeruptus; (*fig*) subitus, repentinus; (*of style*) abruptus; **—ly** abrupte; raptim
abruptness *s* declivitas, rapiditas, festinatio *f*
abscess *s* abscess·us -ūs *m*; suppuratio *f*; vomica *f*
absence *s* absentia *f*; **in my —** me absente
absent *adj* absens; **to be —** abesse
absent *vt* **to — oneself** se removēre, non comparēre
absentee *s* qui abest *m*; peregrinator *m*
absolute *adj* absolutus, summus, perfectus; (*unlimited*) infinitus; **—ly** absolute; prorsus; penitus, omnino
absolution *s* absolutio *f*; venia, indulgentia *f*
absolve *vt* veniam dare (*with dat*), absolvĕre; dimittĕre; (*from punishment*) condonare

absorb *vt* absorbēre, combibĕre; (*fig*) distringĕre, tenēre
absorbent *adj* bibulus; absorbens
abstain *vi* abstinēre, se abstinēre
abstinence *s* abstinentia *f*; continentia *f*; jejunium *n*
abstract *vt* abstrahĕre; separare, sejungĕre, excludĕre
abstract *adj* abstractus; mente perceptus
abstract *s* compendium *n*; epitome *f*; **in the —** in abstracto
abstracted *adj* abstractus; separatus; contractus; (*in mind*) parum attentus; **—ly** separatim; in abstracto
abstraction *s* separatio *f*; (*idea*) notio *f*
abstruse *adj* abstrusus; reconditus; obscurus, occultus; **—ly** abdite, occulte
absurd *adj* absurdus, insulsus; ridiculus; **—ly** inepte, absurde
absurdity *s* ineptia, insulsitas *f*
abundance *s* abundantia, copia *f*
abundant *adj* abundans; amplus; copiosus, plenus; uber; **to be —** abundare; **—ly** abundanter, copiose; cumulate; (*fruitfully*) feliciter
abuse *s* (*wrong use*) abus·us -ūs *m*; (*insult*) injuria *f*, convicium *n*; contumelia *f*; probra *n pl*, maledicta *n pl*
abuse *vt* (*misuse*) abuti (*with abl*); (*a woman*) stuprare; (*with words*) maledicĕre (*with dat*); lacerare
abusive *adj* contumeliosus; dicax, maledicus; injuriosus; **—ly** contumeliose; maledice, injuriose
abyss *s* profundum *n*, vorago *f*, gurges *m*; (*fig*) barathrum *n*
academic *adj* scholasticus; academicus
academy *s* Academia *f*; schola *f*, collegium *n*; societas *f*
accede *vi* accedĕre, assentire *or* assentiri
accelerate *vt* accelerare, festinare, maturare
acceleration *s* acceleratio *f*
accent *s* accent·us -ūs *m*; sonus *m*; vox *f*; (*mark*) apex *m*
accent *vt* (*in speaking*) acuĕre; (*in writing*) fastigare
accentuation *s* accent·us -ūs *m*
accept *vt* accipĕre; recipĕre
acceptable *adj* acceptus, aptus, gratus; probabilis; **to be —** placēre
acceptably *adv* apte; grate
acceptance *s* acceptio *f*; approbatio *f*
access *s* adit·us -ūs, access·us -ūs *m*; **to have —** admitti
accessible *adj* (*of places*) patens; (*fig*) facilis, affabilis
accession *s* (*addition*) accessio *f*, cumulus *m*; (*to the throne*) regni principium *n*
accessory *adj* adjunctus; (*of crimes*) conscius
accessory *s* affinis, conscius *m*, particeps *m & f*
accident *s* cas·us -ūs *m*; calamitas *f*
accidental *adj* fortuitus; adventicius; **—ly** casu, forte, fortuito
acclaim *s* acclamatio *f*; clamor *m*
acclaim *vt* acclamare
acclamation *s* acclamatio *f*, clamor, consens·us -ūs, plaus·us -ūs *m*
accommodate *vt* accommodare, aptare; (*with lodgings*) hospitium parare (*with dat*)
accommodation *s* accommodatio *f*; (*convenience*) commoditas *f*; (*lodgings*) hospitium, deversorium *n*
accompaniment *s* concinentia *f*
accompany *vt* comitari; deducĕre; (*mus*) concinĕre (*with dat*)
accomplice *s* particeps, socius, conscius *m*; satelles *m*
accomplish *vt* efficĕre, perficĕre; peragere, implēre
accomplished *adj* completus; (*fig*) doctus, eruditus; (*eloquent*) disertus
accomplishment *s* exsecutio, peractio *f*; eruditio *f*
accord *s* consens·us, -ūs *m*, concordia *f*; **of one's own —** sua sponte; ultro; **with one —** unanimiter
accord *vt* concedĕre, dare, praebēre, praestare; *vi* convenire; inter se congruĕre; inter se consentire
accordance *s* **in — with** ex, de (*with abl*); secundum (*with acc*); pro (*with abl*)
accordingly *adv* itaque; ita; pariter; sic
according to *prep* de, ex, pro (*with abl*); secundum (*with acc*)
accost *vt* appellare; compellare; alloqui, affari
account *s* (*financial*) ratio *f*; (*statement*) memoria *f*; (*esteem*) reputatio *f*; (*story*) narratio *f*; **of little —** parvi pretii; vilis; **of no —** nullius pretii; **on — of** ob, propter (*with acc*); causā (*with genit*); **on that —** propterea; ideo; **to call to —** rationem poscĕre; **to give an —** rationem reddĕre; **to take — of** rationem habēre (*with genit*)
account *vt* numerare; (*esteem*) aestimare, habēre, pendĕre; **to — for** rationem reddĕre (*with genit*)
accountable *adj* reus
accountant *s* calculator *m*; a rationibus (procurator) *m*
accredited *adj* aestimatus, honoratus
accretion *s* accessio *f*
accrue *vi* accrescĕre; advenire; cedĕre; (*advantage*) redundare
accumulate *vt* accumulare, coacervare; *vi* crescĕre, augēri
accumulation *s* cumulus, acervus, congest·us -ūs *m*; collectio *f*
accuracy *s* cura *f*; subtilitas *f*
accurate *adj* exactus; subtilis; diligens; **—ly** accurate, exacte; subtiliter; diligenter
accursed *adj* exsecratus; scelestus
accusation *s* accusatio *f*; (*charge*) crimen *n*; **to bring an — against** accusare

accusative *s* accusativus *m*
accuse *vt* accusare; criminari; (*to blame*) reprehendĕre; **to — falsely** calumniari, insimulare
accuser *s* accusator, delator *m*; (*in civil suit*) petitor *m*
accustom *vt* assuefacĕre; **to — oneself** assuefieri, consuescĕre; **to be accustomed to** solēre (*with inf*)
acerbity *s* acerbitas *f*; (*fig*) severitas *f*; rigor *m*
ache *s* dolor *m*
ache *vi* dolēre; **my head —s** caput mihi dolet
achieve *vt* patrare, conficĕre, perficĕre; (*to win*) consequi
achievement *s* res gesta *f*; facinus *n*
acid *adj* acidus; vinosus
acid *s* acidum *n*
acknowledge *vt* agnoscĕre, recognoscĕre; confitēri; (*a child*) tollĕre
acknowledgment *s* recognito *f*, confessio *f*; (*receipt for money*) apocha *f*
acme *s* fastigium *n*
acorn *s* glans *f*; balanus *f*
acoustics *s* acustica *n pl*; res auditoria *f*
acquaint *vt* certiorem facĕre; **to — oneself with** noscĕre, cognoscĕre
acquaintance *s* familiaritas, notitia *f*; (*person*) familiaris *m & f*
acquainted *adj* notus; **— with** gnarus (*with genit*); peritus (*with genit or abl*); **to become — with** noscĕre, cognoscĕre, pernoscĕre
acquiesce *vi* acquiescĕre, assentire
acquiescence *s* assens·us -ūs *m*
acquire *vt* acquirĕre; adipisci, nancisci
acquisition *s* (*act of acquiring*) conciliatio *f*; quaest·us -ūs *m*; (*thing acquired*) quaesitum *n*
acquisitive *adj* quaestuosus
acquit *vt* absolvĕre, liberare; **to — oneself** se gerĕre
acquittal *s* absolutio *f*
acre *s* jugerum *n*; **— by —** jugeratim
acrid *adj* acer, asper
acrimonious *adj* acerbus; asper, truculentus
acrimony *s* acrimonia *f*; acerbitas, amaritudo *f*; acor *m*
acrobat *s* funambulus *m*
across *adv* transversus
across *prep* trans (*with acc*)
act *s* (*deed, action*) factum, gestum *n*; (*decree*) decretum *n*; (*in a play*) act·us -ūs *m*; **caught in the —** deprehensus; **in the very —** in flagranti
act *vt* (*role, part*) agĕre; *vi* agĕre, facĕre, gerĕre
acting *s* actio, gesticulatio *f*
action *s* actio *f*, act·us -ūs *m*; (*deed*) factum, facinus *n*; (*law*) actio *f*; (*mil*) pugna *f*, proelium *n*; (*of speaker*) gest·us -ūs *m*; **to bring an — against** actionem intendĕre (*with dat*)
active *adj* actuosus; activus; agilis; impiger, vegetus, strenuus, sedulus, navus; **—ly** impigre; strenue; (*gram*) active
activity *s* agilitas, mobilitas *f*; (*motion*) mot·us -ūs *m*; (*energy*) industria, sedulitas, gnavitas *f*
actor *s* histrio *m*; mimus *m*; (*in comedy*) comoedus *m*; (*in tragedy*) tragoedus *m*
actress *s* mima, scenica *f*
actual *adj* verus, ipse; **—ly** re vera
actuality *s* veritas *f*
acumen *s* acumen *n*; sagacitas *f*; ingenii acies *f*
acute *adj* acutus; acer; (*fig*) sagax, subtilis; **—ly** acute, acriter
acuteness *s* acies *f*; (*of the mind*) acumen *n*, subtilitas *f*
adage *s* proverbium *n*
adamant *adj* obstinatus
adamant *s* adamas *m*
adapt *vt* accommodare, aptare
adaptation *s* accommodatio *f*
adapted *adj* aptus
add *vt* addĕre, apponĕre, adjungĕre; (*in speaking*) superdicĕre; (*in writing*) subjungĕre; (*to reckon*) adscribĕre; **to — up** computare, supputare; **to be added** accedĕre
adder *s* coluber *m*, vipera *f*
addict *vt* **to be addicted** se addicĕre, se tradĕre, se dare
addition *s* additamentum *n*; adjectio, accessio *f*; appendix *f*; incrementum *n*; **in —** praeterea, insuper; **in — to** praeter (*with acc*)
additional *adj* novus, addititius, adjunctus
address *s* alloquium *n*; allocutio, compellatio *f*; (*on letter*) forma directionis, inscriptio *f*; (*speech*) contio, oratio *f*; (*adroitness*) dexteritas, comitas *f*
address *vt* (*to speak to*) alloqui, aggredi, compellare; (*letter*) inscribĕre
adduce *vt* (*witnesses*) producĕre; (*arguments*) afferre
adept *adj* peritus
adequacy *s* sufficientia *f*
adequate *adj* adaequatus, sufficiens, par; **to be —** sufficĕre; **—ly** satis, apte
adhere *vi* adhaerēre, cohaerēre; **to — to** inhaerēre (*with dat*); (*fig*) stare in (*with abl*)
adherence *s* adhaesio *f*
adherent *s* assectator, fautor, cliens *m*
adhesion *s* adhaesio *f*
adhesive *adj* tenax
adieu *interj* vale, valete; **to bid —** valedicĕre; valēre jubēre
adjacent *adj* confinis, conterminus; vicinus
adjective *s* adjectivum (nomen) *n*
adjectively *adv* adjective; ut appositum; pro apposito
adjoin *vt* adjungĕre; adjacēre (*with dat*); *vi* adjacēre
adjoining *adj* adjacens, confinis
adjourn *vt* comperendinare, differre, prorogare; *vi* deferri
adjournment *s* dilatio *f*

adjudge *vt* addicĕre, adjudicare
adjudicate *vt* addicĕre, decernĕre
adjudication *s* addictio, adjudicatio *f*; sententia *f*; arbitrium *n*
adjunct *s* adjunctum *n*, accessio, appendix *f*
adjuration *s* obtestatio *f*; obsecratio *f*
adjure *vt* adjurare; obtestari
adjust *vt* aptare, accommodare; (*put in order*) componĕre
adjustment *s* accommodatio, compositio *f*; (*of a robe*) structura *f*
adjutant *s* optio *m*
administer *vt* (*to manage*) administrare; (*medicine, etc.*) adhibēre; (*oath*) adigĕre; (*justice*) dispensare, reddĕre
administration *s* administratio, cura, procuratio *f*; jurisdictio *f*; magistrat·us -ūs *m*
administrative *adj* ad administrationem pertinens
administrator *s* administrator, procurator *m*
admirable *adj* admirabilis, mirabilis, admirandus; insignis, egregius
admiral *s* classis praefectus *m*
admiration *s* admiratio *f*
admire *vt* admirari; amare
admirer *s* admirator, mirator, laudator *m*; amator *m*
admiringly *adv* admirans
admissible *adj* accipiendus, aptus, aequus
admission *s* admissio, confessio *f*; adit·us -ūs, access·us -ūs *m*
admit *vt* admittĕre; recipĕre; (*to recognize*) asciscĕre; noscĕre; **it is admitted** constat
admittedly *adv* sane
admonish *vt* monēre, admonēre, commonēre; hortari
admonition *s* monitio, admonitio *f*; monitum *n*
adolescence *s* prima adulescentia *f*
adolescent *adj* adolescens, adulescens
adolescent *s* adulescentulus, adulescens *m*
adopt *vt* (*a minor*) adoptare; (*an adult*) arrogare; (*a custom*) asciscĕre; (*a plan*) capĕre, inire
adoption *s* adoptio, adoptatio *f*; (*of an adult*) arrogatio *f*; (*of a custom*) assumptio *f*; **by —** adoptivus
adoptive *adj* adoptivus
adorable *adj* adorandus, venerandus
adoration *s* adoratio *f*; cult·us -ūs *m*; (*of kings*) veneratio *f*
adore *vt* adorare, venerari; (*fig*) admirari, amare
adorn *vt* ornare, decorare, distinguĕre, illustrare; excolĕre, comare
adornment *s* exornatio *f*; ornat·us -ūs *m*; ornamentum *n*
Adriatic Sea *s* Hadria *m or* Adria *m*
adrift *adv* fluctuans; **to be —** fluctuare
adroit *adj* callidus, dexter, sollers, peritus; **—ly** callide, scite
adroitness *s* dexteritias, sollertia, calliditas *f*
adulation *s* adulatio, assentatio *f*
adult *adj* adultus
adult *s* adultus homo, puber *m*
adulterate *vt* adulterare, vitiare, commiscēre
adulteration *s* adulteratio, commixtio *f*
adulterer *s* adulter *m*; moechus *m*
adulteress *s* adultera *f*; moecha *f*
adulterous *adj* stuprosus, adulterinus, incestus
adultery *s* adulterium, stuprum *n*; **to commit —** moechari; adulterare
advance *vt* promovēre; admovēre; (*money*) praerogare; (*a cause*) fovēre; (*an opinion*) exhibēre, praeferre; (*to honors*) provehere; *vi* procedĕre, progredi, incedĕre; (*mil*) gradum *or* pedem inferre; signa proferre; (*to progress*) proficĕre
advance *s* progress·us -ūs *m*; (*step*) pass·us -ūs *m*; (*attack*) incursio *f*; impet·us -ūs *m*; (*money*) mutuae pecuniae *f pl*; **in —** maturius
advanced *adj* provectus; (*of age*) grandis
advance guard *s* primum agmen *n*
advancement *s* dignitatis accessio, promotio *f*; honos *m*
advantage *s* (*benefit*) commodum *n*, us·us -ūs *m*, bonum *n*; (*profit*) lucrum, emolumentum *n*; utilitas *f*, fruct·us -ūs *m*; **to be of —** prodesse; **to have an — over** praestare (*with dat*); superior esse (*with dat*); **to take — of** uti (*with abl*); (*to deceive*) decipĕre, fallĕre; **with —** faenerato
advantageous *adj* fructuosus, utilis; **—ly** utiliter; bene
advent *s* advent·us -ūs *m*
adventure *s* cas·us -ūs *m*; fors *f*; facinus *n*
adventurer *s* periclitator *m*; latro *m*; pirata *m*
adventurous *adj* audax
adverb *s* adverbium *n*
adverbial *adj* adverbialis; **—ly** adverbialiter
adversary *s* adversarius *m*, hostis *m*; adversatrix *f*
adverse *adj* adversus, infestus; asper; **—ly** male, contrarie, infeliciter
adversity *s* res adversae *f pl*; calamitas *f*
advertise *vt* communefacĕre; proscribĕre
advertisement *s* proscriptio *f*; libellus *m*; indicium *n*
advice *s* consilium *n*; **to ask — of** consulĕre; **to give —** suadēre (*with dat*)
advisable *adj* commodus, utilis
advise *vt* suadēre (*with dat*), censēre (*with dat*), monēre; **to — to the contrary** dissuadēre (*with dat*)
adviser *s* consultor *m*
advocate *s* (*law*) actor, causidicus *m*; (*fig*) patronus *m*; suasor *m*; auctor *m*
aedile *s* aedilis *m*

aegis *s* aegis *f*
aerial *adj* aërius, aethereus
affability *s* comitas, affabilitas, facilitas *f*
affable *adj* affabilis, comis, facilis
affably *adv* comiter
affair *s* negotium *n*; res *f*; (*love*) amores *m pl*
affect *vt* afficĕre; commovēre; jactare; ostentare; attingĕre
affectation *s* simulatio, affectatio *f*
affected *adj* simulatus, fictus; (*in style*) putidus; **—ly** putide
affection *s* amor *m*; benevolentia *f*; studium *n*
affectionate *adj* amans, benevolus; **—ly** amanter
affidavit *s* testimonium *n*
affiliate *vt* adoptare; attribuĕre
affinity *s* affinitas *f*; cognatio *f*
affirm *vt* affirmare, asseverare, testificari
affirmation *s* affirmatio *f*
affirmative *adj* affirmans; **I reply in the —** aio; **—ly** affirmative
affix *vt* affigĕre, annectĕre
afflict *vt* affligĕre, afflictare
affliction *s* afflictio, miseria *f*; res adversae *f pl*
affluence *s* abundantia, copia *f*; divitiae *f pl*
affluent *adj* affluens, abundans; dives; **—ly** abundanter
afford *vt* praebēre; (*to yield*) reddĕre, ferre; **I cannot —** res mihi non suppetit ad (*with acc*)
affront *vt* irritare; contumeliā afficĕre; offendĕre
affront *s* contumelia, injuria *f*
afield *adv* foris
afloat *adj* natans; fluctuans; **to be —** natare, fluctuare
afoot *adv* pedestris, pedibus; **to be —** geri
afraid *adj* timidus, pavidus; **to be —** timēre; **to make —** terrefacĕre
afresh *adv* de integro, iterum, de novo
after *prep* post (*with acc*); a, de, e, ex (*with abl*); (*following immediately upon*) sub (*with acc*); (*in rank or degree*) secundum (*with acc*); (*in imitation of*) ad (*with acc*); **— all** tamen; saltem; **a little —** paulo post; **the day —** postridie
after *conj* postquam
afternoon *adj* postmeridianus, pomeridianus
afternoon *s* pomeridianum *n*; **in the —** post meridiem
afterthought *s* posterior cogitatio *f*
afterwards *adv* post, postea; deinde, deinceps, dehinc
again *adv* iterum, rursus, denuo, rursum; deinde; (*hereafter*) posthac; (*likewise, in turn*) invicem, mutuo, vicissim; contra; **— and —** etiam atque etiam; identidem; **once —** denuo; **over —** de novo
against *prep* contra (*with acc*); adversus (*with acc*); (*in a hostile manner*) in (*with acc*); **— the current** adverso flumine; **to be —** adversari
age *s* (*life*) aetas *f*; (*era*) saeculum *n*, aetas *f*; **of the same —** aequaevus, aequalis; **old —** senectus *f*; **to be of —** sui juris esse; **twelve years of —** duodecim annos natus; **under —** impubis
age *vi* senescĕre; maturescĕre
aged *adj* aetate provectus; senilis; (*things*) antiquus
agency *s* actio *f*; (*medium*) opera *f*; (*office*) procuratio *f*; **through the — of** per (*with acc*)
agent *s* actor, auctor *m*; (*in crime*) minister *m*
aggravate *vt* aggravare; (*pain*) augēre; provocare; (*a wound*) ulcerare; **to become aggravated** ingravescĕre
aggravating *adj* molestus
aggravation *s* exaggeratio *f*
aggregate *adj* aggregatus, totus
aggregate *s* summa *f*
aggregation *s* collatio *f*; aggregatum *n*
aggression *s* incursio *f*
aggressive *adj* hostilis, infensus; ferox
aggressor *s* qui bellum infert *m*; qui alterum prior lacessit *m*
aggrieve *vt* dolore afficĕre
aggrieved *adj* iratus
aghast *adj* attonitus, consternatus, stupefactus; **to stand —** obstupescĕre
agile *adj* agilis; pernix
agility *s* agilitas *f*; pernicitas *f*
agitate *vt* agitare; commovēre; pertubare
agitated *adj* tumultuosus; turbulentus; (*fig*) sollicitus
agitation *s* agitatio, commotio *f*; (*of the sea*) jactatio *f*; trepidatio *f*
agitator *s* concitator, turbator *m*
ago *adv* abhinc; **a short time —** haud ita pridem; dudum; **long —** iamdudum, iampridem, antiquitus; **some time —** pridem
agonize *vt* cruciare, excruciare; *vi* discruciari
agonizing *adj* crucians; horribilis
agony *s* dolor *m*; agonia *f*; cruciat·us -ūs *m*
agrarian *adj* agrarius
agree *vi* assentire, assentiri; convenire; (*to make a bargain*) pacisci; (*of facts*) constare, convenire; **to — with** assentiri (*with dat*), sentire cum (*with abl*)
agreeable *adj* gratus, acceptus; amabilis; congruens, conveniens; **very —** pergratus
agreeably *adv* grate, jucunde; suaviter
agreement *s* consens·us -ūs *m*; concordia *f*; (*pact*) pactio *f*, pactum *n*; (*bargain*) conditio *f*; (*proportion*) symmetria *f*; reconciliatio *f*
agricultural *adj* rusticus, agrestis
agriculture *s* agricultura *f*; res rustica *f*
agriculturist *s* agricola *m*
ah *interj* ah!, eja!, vah!, vae!

ahead *adv use verb with prefix* prae- *or* pro-
aid *s* auxilium, subsidium *n*
aid *vt* succurrĕre (*with dat*), subvenire (*with dat*), adjuvare
aide-de-camp *s* optio *m*
ail *vt* dolēre; *vi* aegrotare
ailing *adj* aegrotus, aeger
ailment *s* aegrotatio *f*; malum *n*; morbus *m*
aim *s* (*mark*) scopus *m*; (*fig*) finis *m*, propositum *n*
aim *vt* intendĕre, tendĕre; *vi* **to — at** affectare, spectare, petĕre, quaerĕre
aimless *adj* vanus, inanis; **—ly** sine ratione
air *s* aër *m*; caelum *n*; (*breeze*) aura *f*; (*attitude*) habit·us -ūs, gest·us -ūs *m*; (*tune*) modus *m*; **in the open —** sub divo *or* sub caelo; **to take the —** deambulare
air *vt* ventilare
airily *adv* hilare
airy *adj* aërius; apertus, patens; ventosus; (*fig*) hilaris
aisle *s* ala *f*
ajar *adj* semiapertus
akin *adj* cognatus, agnatus, consanguineus, propinquus
alabaster *s* alabaster *m*
alacrity *s* alacritas *f*
alarm *s* (*signal*) classicum *n*; (*sudden fright*) trepidatio *f*, pavor *m*; tumult·us -ūs *m*; **to give the —** increpare
alarm *vt* perterrefacĕre, consternĕre, perturbare
alarming *adj* formidolosus
alas *interj* eheu!, heu!
alchemist *s* alchemista *m*
alchemy *s* alchemistica *f*
alcohol *s* spirit·us -ūs vini *m*
alcoholic *adj* alcoolicus
alcove *s* zotheca *f*, cubiculum *n*
ale *s* cerevisia *f*
alert *adj* alacer, promptus, vegetus
alertness *s* alacritas *f*
alias *adv* aliter
alias *s* falsum nomen *n*
alibi *s* (law) absentia rei *f*; (*excuse*) species *f*
alien *adj* peregrinus
alien *s* peregrinus *m*; alienigena, advena *m*
alienate *vt* alienare, abalienare, avertĕre, avocare
alienation *s* abalienatio, alienatio *f*
alight *vi* descendĕre; (*from a horse*) desilire; (*of birds*) subsidĕre
alike *adj* aequus, par, similis
alike *adv* pariter, similiter, aeque
alimony *s* alimentum, alimonium *n*
alive *adj* vivus; (*fig*) alacer; **to be —** vivĕre; superesse
all *adj* omnis, cunctus, totus; integer; universus; **— over** undique, passim; **— the better** tanto melius; **— the more** eo plus
all *s* omnia *n pl*; **at —** omnino; **in —** in summa; **not at —** haudquaquam; **one's all** proprium *n*
allay *vt* sedare, lenire, mitigare; **to be allayed** defervescĕre, temperari
allegation *s* affirmatio *f*; insimulatio *f*
allege *vt* affirmare, arguĕre; citare, allegare
allegiance *s* fides, fidelitas *f*; **to swear —** sacramentum dicĕre
allegorical *adj* allegoricus; **—ly** allegorice
allegorize *vi* allegorice scribĕre; allegorice explicare
allegory *s* allegoria *f*
alleviate *vt* levare, allevare, sublevare
alleviation *s* allevamentum *n*, levatio *f*
alley *s* angiport·us -ūs *m*
alliance *s* (*by blood*) consanguinitas *f*; (*by marriage*) affinitas *f*; (*of states*) foedus *n*; societas *f*
allied *adj* foederatus, socius; junctus, propinquus
alligator *s* crocodilus *m*
alliteration *s* alliteratio *f*
allocate *vt* impertire, assignare
allot *vt* distribuere, assignare
allotment *s* assignatio, portio *f*; assignatum *n*
allow *vt* concedĕre (*with dat*), permittĕre (*with dat*), sinĕre, pati; **it is allowed** licet; **to — for** indulgēre (*with dat*); **to — of** admittĕre
allowable *adj* licitus
allowance *s* (*permission*) licentia, permissio *f*; (*concession*) venia, indulgentia *f*; (*portion*) portio *f*; salarium *n*; diaria *n pl*; cibaria *n pl*; demensum *n*; **to make — for** ignoscĕre (*with dat*), condonare
alloy *s* mixtura *f*
alloy *vt* miscēre, adulterare, diluĕre
allude *vi* **to — to** attingĕre, designare, denotare, spectare
allure *vt* allicĕre, allectare, pellicĕre
allurement *s* illecebra, blanditia *f*; blandimentum *n*
alluring *adj* blandus; **—ly** blande
allusion *s* parodia *f*; indicium *n*, mentio *f*
allusive *adj* obliquus; **—ly** oblique
alluvial *adj* alluvius
ally *s* socius *m*, socia *f*
ally *vt* sociare
almanac *s* fasti *m pl*
almighty *adj* omnipotens
almond *s* amygdala *f*
almond tree *s* amygdalus *f*
almost *adv* fere, paene, prope, ferme
alms *s* stips *f*
aloft *adv* sublime
alone *adj* solus, unus, solitarius, unicus; **all —** persolus; **to leave —** deserĕre; **to let —** omittere, mittĕre
alone *adv* solum
along *adv* porro, protinus; **all —** jamdudum; **— with** una cum (*with abl*)
along *prep* per (*with acc*), praeter (*with acc*), secundum (*with acc*)
aloof *adv* procul; **to stand —** discedere, abstare
aloud *adv* magna voce; clare

alphabet *s* alphabetum *n*; prima elementa *n pl*
alphabetical *adj* litterarum ordine
Alpine *adj* alpinus
already *adv* jam
also *adv* etiam, quoque, et, idem, necnon
altar *s* ara *f*; altaria *n pl*
alter *vt* mutare, commutare; variare; vertĕre
alterable *adj* mutabilis
alteration *s* mutatio, commutatio *f*
altercation *s* altercatio *f*, jurgium *n*
alternate *adj* alternus; **—ly** invicem, per vices; alternis
alternate *vt & vi* alternare, variare
alternation *s* vicissitudo *f*
alternative *adj* alter
alternative *s* discrimen *n*, optio *f*; alternata conditio *f*
although *conj* etsi, etiamsi, tametsi, quamquam, licet, cum
altitude *s* altitudo *f*
altogether *adv* omnino; prorsus, plane
altruism *s* beneficentia *f*
always *adv* semper
amalgamate *vt* miscēre, conjungĕre
amalgamation *s* mixtio *f*
amass *vt* coacervare, cumulare
amateur *s* artium amator *m*; tiro *m*
amaze *vt* obstupefacĕre
amazed *adj* attonitus, stupefactus; **to be —** stupēre; obstupescĕre
amazement *s* stupor *m*; **in —** attonitus, stupefactus
amazing *adj* mirus, mirandus, mirabilis; **—ly** mirabiliter
Amazon *s* Amazon *f*
Amazonian *adj* amazonius, amazonicus
ambassador *s* legatus *m*
amber *s* sucinum *n*; electrum *n*
ambiguity *s* ambiguitas *f*, ambages *f pl*
ambiguous *adj* ambiguus, dubius, anceps; **—ly** ambigue
ambition *s* ambitio *f*; studium *n*
ambitious *adj* laudis *or* gloriae cupidus; studiosus; ambitiosus
amble *vi* ambulare
ambrosia *s* ambrosia *f*
ambush *s* insidiae *f pl*
ambush *vt* insidiari (*with dat*)
ameliorate *vt* meliorem *or* melius facĕre, corrigĕre
amenable *adj* docilis, obediens
amend *vt* emendare, corrigĕre; *vi* proficĕre
amendment *s* emendatio, correctio *f*
amends *s* compensatio, satisfactio *f*; **to make —** expiare, satisfacĕre, compensare
amenity *s* amoenitas *f*; (*comfort*) commodum *n*
amethyst *s* amethystus *f*
amiable *adj* amabilis, suavis
amiably *adv* amabiliter, suaviter
amicable *adj* amicus; pacatus; benevolus
amicably *adv* amice; pacate; benevole
amid *prep* inter (*with acc*)
amity *s* amicitia *f*
ammonia *s* ammoniaca *f*
ammunition *s* belli apparat·us -ūs *m*; missilium copia *f*
amnesty *s* venia, abolitio *f*
among *prep* inter (*with acc*); apud (*with acc*); ad (*with acc*); **from —** e, ex (*with abl*)
amorous *adj* amatorius; libidinosus, mulierosus; **—ly** amatorie; cum amore
amount *s* summa *f*, totum *n*
amount *vi* **to — to** crescĕre, exsurgĕre; (*fig*) esse
amour *s* amores *m pl*
amphitheater *s* amphitheatrum *n*
ample *adj* amplus; copiosus; satis
amplification *s* amplificatio, auctio, dilatatio *f*
amplify *vt* amplificare, dilatare
amply *adv* ample, abunde
amputate *vt* amputare, secare
amputation *s* amputatio, sectio *f*
amuck *adv* furiose; **to run —** delirare
amulet *s* amuletum *n*
amuse *vt* oblectare, delectare; **to — oneself** ludĕre
amusement *s* delectatio, oblectatio *f*; delectamentum *n*; ludibrium *n*
amusing *adj* ridiculus; festivus; facetus
an *indefinite article, unexpressed in Latin*
anachronism *s* temporum inversio *f*
analogous *adj* analogus
analogy *s* analogia, comparatio *f*
analysis *s* analysis *f*; explicatio *f*; separatio *f*
analytical *adj* analyticus; **—ly** per analysin
analyze *vt* in principia resolvĕre; (*words*) subtiliter enodare
anapest *s* anapaestus *m*
anapestic *adj* anapaesticus
anarchist *s* civis sediotiosus *m*
anarchy *s* anarchia *f*; rei publicae perturbatio *f*; licentia *f*
anathema *s* anathema *n*; exsecratio *f*
anatomical *adj* anatomicus
anatomy *s* anatomia, dissectio *f*
ancestor *s* proavus *m*; auctor *m*; **—s** majores, priores *m pl*
ancestral *adj* avitus; proavitus; patrius
ancestry *s* genus *n*; stirps *f*; origo *f*
anchor *s* ancora *f*; **to lie at —** in ancoris stare; **to weigh —** ancoram tollĕre *or* solvĕre
anchor *vt* in ancoris tenēre; *vi* ancoram jacĕre
anchorage *s* statio *f*
ancient *adj* antiquus, vetustus; priscus; pristinus; **in — times** antiquitus; **the —s** veteres *m pl*; barbati *m pl*
and *conj* et, ac, atque, -que
anecdote *s* fabella *f*
anemic *adj* exsanguis
anew *adv* denuo; ab integro
angel *s* angelus *m*

angelic *adj* angelicus; (*fig*) egregius, excellens
anger *s* ira *f*; bilis *f*
anger *vt* irritare, exacerbare
angle *s* angulus *m*
angle *vi* hamo piscari
angler *s* piscator *m*
angrily *adv* irate, iracunde
angry *adj* iratus, iracundus, indignans; **to be —** irasci, succensēre, stomachari; **to make —** irritare, exacerbare
anguish *s* angor *m*; dolor *m*; cruciat·us -ūs *m*
anguished *adj* animo fractus
angular *adj* angularis; angulosus
animal *s* animal *n*; (*wild beast*) bestia, fera *f*; (*domestic*) pecus *n*
animal *adj* animalis
animate *vt* animare; (*fig*) excitare
animated *adj* excitatus, vegetus
animation *s* animatio *f*; vigor, ardor, spirit·us -ūs *m*
animosity *s* acerbitas *f*; invidia *f*; odium *n*; inimicitia *f*
ankle *s* talus *m*
annalist *s* annalium scriptor *m*
annals *s* annales, fasti *m pl*
annex *s* appendix *f*
annex *vt* annectěre, adjungěre, adděre, supponěre
annexation *s* adjectio *f*
annihilate *vt* delēre, exstinguěre
annihilation *s* exstinctio *f*; internecio *f*
anniversary *adj* anniversarius; annuus
anniversary *s* festus dies anniversarius *m*
annotate *vt* annotare, commentari
annotation *s* annotatio, nota *f*
announce *vt* nuntiare; (*to report*) renuntiare; (*officially*) denuntiare, pronuntiare; (*laws, etc.*) proscriběre
announcement *s* denuntiatio, pronuntiatio *f*; (*news*) nuntius *m*
announcer *s* nuntius *m*
annoy *vt* incommodare, vexare, male habēre; **to be annoyed** stomachari, offensus esse
annoyance *s* vexatio, molestia *f*; dolor *m*
annoying *adj* molestus, odiosus
annual *adj* anniversarius, annuus; **—ly** quotannis
annuity *s* annua pecunia *f*; annuus redit·us -ūs *m*; (*law*) annuum *n*
annul *vt* rescinděre, tolěre, dissolvěre, abrogare
annulment *s* abolitio *f*; abrogatio *f*
anoint *vt* ung(u)ěre
anointing *s* unctio *f*
anomalous *adj* anomalus; enormis
anomaly *s* anomalia *f*; enormitas *f*
anonymous *adj* sine nomine; **—ly** sine nomine
another *adj* alius; **—'s** alienus; **one after —** alius ex alio; **one —** inter se; alius alium; **to — place** alio
answer *vt* responděre (*with dat*); (*by letter*) rescriběre (*with dat*); (*to correspond to*) congruěre cum (*with abl*); *vi* **to — for** rationem redděre (*with genit*); **to — to the name of** vocari
answer *s* responsio *f*, responsum *n*; (*solution*) explicatio *f*
answerable *adj* reus; **to be — for** praestare
ant *s* formica *f*
antagonism *s* adversitas, inimicitia *f*
antagonist *s* adversarius *m*; adversatrix *f*; hostis *m*
antarctic *adj* antarcticus
antecedent *adj* antecedens; prior
antecedent *s* antecedens *n*
antechamber *s* atriolum *n*; antithalamus *m*
antedate *vt* diem vero antiquiorem ascriběre (*with dat*)
antelope *s* antilope *f*; dorcas *f*
antepenult *s* syllaba antepenultima *f*
anterior *adj* anterior, prior
anteroom *s* antithalamus *m*; vestibulum *n*
anthem *s* canticum sacrum *n*; hymnus elatior *m*
anthology *s* anthologia *f*; excerpta *n pl*
anticipate *vt* anticipare; (*to expect*) spectare; (*to forestall*) praevenire, praeoccupare; (*mentally*) praesuměre
anticipation *s* anticipatio, praesumptio, anteoccupatio *f*
anticlimax *s* climax inversa *f*
antics *s* joca *n pl*; ineptiae *f pl*
antidote *s* antidotum *n*
antipathy *s* repugnantia, antipathia *f*; fastidium, odium *n*
antiquarian *adj* historicus
antiquarian *s* antiquitatis peritus *m*; antiquarius *m*
antiquated *adj* antiquatus, obsoletus
antique *adj* antiquus, vetus, priscus
antique *s* antiqui artificis opus *n*
antiquity *s* antiquitas, vetustas *f*
antithesis *s* contrarium *n*, contentio *f*
antler *s* cornu *n*
anvil *s* incus *f*
anxiety *s* anxietas, sollicitudo *f*
anxious *adj* anxius, sollicitus; trepidus; avidus; **—ly** anxie, sollicite; trepide; avide
any *adj* ullus; quivis, quilibet; aliquis; **— longer** diutius; **— more** amplius
anybody *pron* aliquis; quivis; quilibet; (*after* si, nisi, num, ne) quis; (*interrog*) ecquis, numquis; (*after negative*) quisquam
anyhow *adv* quoquomodo
anyone *see* **anybody**
anything *pron* aliquid, quicquam, quidpiam, quodvis; (*after* si, nisi, num, ne) quid; (*interrog*) ecquid, numquid; (*after negative*) quicquam; **hardly —** nihil fere
anywhere *adv* ubilibet, alicubi, ubivis
apart *adv* seorsum, separatim; **to be —** distare; **to set —** seponěre; **to stand —** distare
apart from *prep* praeter (*with acc*)
apartment *s* conclave *n*; insula *f*

apathetic *adj* lentus, languidus
apathy *s* apathia, lentitudo *f*, languor *m*
ape *s* simius *m*, simia *f*
ape *vt* imitari
aperture *s* apertura *f*; foramen *n*
apex *s* cacumen *n*; fastigium *n*
aphorism *s* sententia *f*
apiary *s* alvearium *n*
apiece *adv* singuli
aplomb *s* confidentia *f*
apocalypse *s* apocalypsis *f*
apocryphal *adj* apocryphus, commenticius
apogee *s* apogaeum *n*
apologetic *adj* apologeticus; confitens
apologist *s* defensor *m*
apologize *vi* se excusare; veniam petĕre
apology *s* excusatio, defensio *f*; (*written treatise*) apologia *f*, liber apologeticus *m*; **to make an — for** excusare
apoplectic *adj* apoplecticus
apoplexy *s* apoplexia *f*; apoplexis *f*
apostasy *s* apostasia *f*
apostate *s* apostata *m*
apostle *s* apostolus *m*
apostolic *adj* apostolicus
apostrophe *s* apostrophe *f*; (*gram*) apostrophus *f*
apostrophize *vt* abrupte compellare
apothecary *s* (*druggist*) medicamentarius *m*; (*drugstore*) medicina taberna *f*, pharmacopolium *n*
apotheosis *s* apotheosis *f*
appall *vt* exterrēre, percellĕre
apparatus *s* apparat·us -ūs *m*
apparel *s* vestis *f*, vestit·us -ūs *m*; vestimenta *n pl*
apparel *vt* vestire; adornare
apparent *adj* manifestus, apertus, conspicuus; **to be —** apparēre; **—ly** manifeste, aperte, specie, per speciem
apparition *s* spectrum *n*; visum *n*; species *f*
appeal *vi* appellare; provocare; **to — to** (*a magistrate*) appellare; (*the people*) provocare ad (*with acc*); (*the gods*) obsecrare, invocare, testari
appeal *s* (*law*) appellatio *f*; (*entreaty*) obsecratio, testatio *f*; (*to the people*) provocatio *f*
appear *vi* apparēre, comparēre; se ostendĕre; (*to seem*) vidēri; (*to arise*) exoriri, surgĕre; **to begin to —** patescĕre
appearance *s* (*becoming visible*) aspect·us -ūs *m*; (*outward show*) species *f*; (*likelihood*) similitudo *f*; (*vision*) visum *n*; **first —** exort·us -ūs *m*; **to all —s** probabilissime; **to make an —** prodire
appease *vt* placare, sedare; mitigare; (*fig*) expiare
appeasement *s* placatio *f*; (*of an enemy*) pacificatio *f*
appellation *s* nomen *n*
appendage *s* appendix, accessio, appendicula *f*
appendix *s* appendix *f*
appetite *s* appetit·us -ūs *m*, cupiditas *f*; **to have an —** esurire
applaud *vt* applaudĕre; laudare
applause *s* plaus·us -ūs, applaus·us ūs *m*; laus f
apple *s* malum, pomum *n*; **— of my eye** ocellus meus *m*
apple tree *s* malus *f*
appliance *s* instrumentum *n*, apparat·us -ūs *m*
applicable *adj* commodus, conveniens
applicant *s* petitor *m*
application *s* petito *f*; adhibitio, appositio *f*; studium *n*, sedulitas, industria, diligentia *f*; (*med*) fomentum *n*
apply *vt* adhibēre, admovēre, apponere; aptare, accommodare; (*fig*) applicare; *vi* **to — to** pertinēre ad (*with acc*); **to — for** petĕre
appoint *vt* creare; facĕre; designare; destinare; constituĕre
appointment *s* creatio *f*; (*rendezvous*) constitutum *n*; (*order*) mandatum *n*; (*office*) magistrat·us -ūs *m*
apportion *vt* dividĕre, distribuĕre
apportionment *s* divisio, distributio *f*
apposition *s* appositio *f*
appraisal *s* aestimatio *f*
appraise *vt* aestimare
appraiser *s* aestimator *m*
appreciable *adj* aestimabilis, haud exiguus
appreciate *vt* aestimare
appreciation *s* aestimatio *f*
apprehend *vt* apprehendĕre, comprehendĕre, percipĕre; (*to seize*) capĕre; (*to take by surprise*) intercipĕre; (*to fear*) timēre, metuĕre
apprehension *s* comprehensio *f*; facultas, intelligentia *f*; suspicio *f*; (*seizing*) captura *f*; (*fear*) timor, met·us -ūs *m*
apprehensive *adj* timidus, sollicitus
apprentice *s* discipulus *m*; tiro *m*
apprenticeship *s* identura *f*; tirocinium *n*
apprize *vt* docēre
approach *vt* appropinquare (*with dat*), accedĕre ad (*with acc*), adire; *vi* appropinquare, appetere
approach *s* access·us -ūs, adit·us -ūs *m*; appropinquatio *f*; (*by sea*) appuls·us -ūs *m*
approachable *adj* (*person*) facilis, affabilis; (*place*) patens
approbation *s* approbatio, laus *f*
appropriate *adj* proprius, aptus, idoneus; **—ly** apte, congruenter
appropriate *vt* asciscĕre, asserĕre, vindicare; assumĕre
appropriation *s* vindicatio *f*
approval *s* approbatio *f*
approve *vt* approbare, probare; (*law*) sciscĕre; *vi* **to — of** probare
approved *adj* probatus, spectatus
approximate *adj* propinquus, proximus; **—ly** prope, propemodum; (*with numbers*) ad (*with acc*)
approximate *vt* appropinquare (*with dat*); accedĕre ad (*with acc*)

approximation *s* appropinquatio *f*
apricot *s* malum armeniacum *n*
April *s* (mensis) Aprilis *m*
apron *s* praecinctorium *n*; operimentum *n*
apt *adj* aptus, idoneus; (*inclined, prone*) pronus, propensus; **—ly** apte
aptitude *s* habilitas *f*, ingenium *n*
aptness *s* convenientia, congruentia *f*; (*tendency*) proclivitas *f*
aquatic *adj* aquatilis, aquaticus
aqueduct *s* aquaeduct·us -ūs, aquarum duct·us -ūs *m*
aquiline *adj* (*of the nose*) aduncus
arable *adj* arabilis, culturae idoneus; **— land** arvum *n*
arbiter *s* arbiter *m*
arbitrament *s* arbitrat·us -ūs *m*, arbitrium *n*
arbitrarily *adv* ad arbitrium; ad libdinem; libidinoso
arbitrary *adj* libidinosus; imperiosus, superbus
arbitrate *vt & vi* disceptare
arbitration *s* arbitrium *n*, dijudicatio *f*
arbitrator *s* arbiter *m*; disceptator *m*
arbor *s* umbraculum *n*, pergula *f*
arc *s* arc·us -ūs *m*
arcade *s* portic·us -ūs *f*
arch *s* arc·us -ūs, fornix *m*
arch *adj* astutus, callidus, vafer; nimius
arch *vt* arcuare, fornicare
archaeological *adj* archaeologiae (*genit*)
archaeologist *s* antiquitatis investigator *m*
archaeology *s* rerum antiquarum scientia *f*
archaism *s* locutio obsoleta *f*
archbishop *s* archiepiscopus *m*
archer *s* sagittarius *m*; (*constellation*) Arcitenens *m*
archery *s* ars sagittandi *f*
archetype *s* archetypum *n*
archipelago *s* insulis crebrum mare *n*
architect *s* architectus *m*
architectural *adj* architectonicus
architecture *s* architectura *f*
archives *s* tabulae *f pl*; tabularium *n*
arctic *adj* arcticus
ardent *adj* ardens, fervidus; **—ly** ardenter
ardor *s* ardor, fervor *m*
arduous *adj* arduus
area *s* regio *f*; area *f*; superficies *f*
arena *s* (h)arena *f*
argonaut *s* argonauta *m*
argue *vt* arguĕre, probare; *vi* argumentari, disputare, disserĕre
argument *s* (*discussion*) disputatio *f*; controversia *f*; (*theme*) argumentum, thema *n*, ratio *f*
argumentation *s* argumentatio *f*
argumentative *adj* ratiocinativus, litigiosus
aria *s* canticum *n*
arid *adj* aridus, siccus
aright *adv* recte
arise *vi* surgĕre, exoriri, exsistĕre; **to — from** nasci ex (*with abl*)
aristocracy *s* (*class*) optimates, nobiles *m pl*; (*government*) optimatum dominat·us -ūs *m*
aristocrat *s* optimas *m*
aristocratic *adj* patricius, generosus
arithmetic *s* arithmetica *n pl*
ark *s* arca *f*
arm *s* bracchium *n*; (*of the sea*) sin·us -ūs *m*; fretum *n*; **—s** arma *n pl*; **by force of —s** vi et armis; **to be under —s** in armis esse; **to lay down —s** ab armis discedĕre; arma dedĕre; **to take up —s** armare; arma sumĕre
arm *vt* armare; *vi* armari; bellum parare
armada *s* classis magna *f*
armament *s* belli apparat·us -ūs *m*; copiae *f pl*
armchair *s* anconibus fabrefacta sella *f*
armistice *s* indutiae *f pl*
armlet *s* bracchiolum *n*; (*bracelet*) bracchiale *n*
armor *s* armatura *f*, armat·us -ūs *m*; arma *n pl*
armorbearer *s* armiger *m*
armory *s* armamentarium *n*
armpit *s* ala *f*
army *s* exercit·us -ūs *m*; (*in battle*) acies *f*; (*on the march*) agmen *n*
aroma *s* aroma *n*; (*of wine*) flos *m*
aromatic *adj* armomaticus
around *adv* circum, circa; **all —** undique, passim
around *prep* circum (*with acc*)
arouse *vt* suscitare; (*fig*) erigĕre; **to — oneself** expergisci
arraign *vt* accusare
arraignment *s* accusatio, actio *f*
arrange *vt* instruĕre, struĕre, ordinare, disponĕre, componĕre; (*to agree*) pacisci
arrangement *s* ordo *m*, collocatio *f*; dispositio *f*; pactum n
array *s* vestis f, vestit·us -ūs *m*; habit·us -ūs *m*; (*mil*) acies *f*
array *vt* vestire; adornare; instruĕre
arrears *s* reliqua *n pl*; residuum *n*, residuae pecuniae *f pl*; **to be in —** relinqui
arrest *s* prehensio *f*
arrest *vt* (*to seize*) prehendĕre, deprehendĕre, arripĕre; (*movement*) tardare, morari; (*attention*) in se convertĕre
arrival *s* advent·us -ūs *m*; (*by sea*) appuls·us -ūs *m*
arrive *vi* pervenire, advenire; (*of a ship*) advehi, appelli
arrogance *s* arrogantia, superbia *f*
arrogant *adj* arrogans, superbus; **—ly** arroganter, insolenter, superbe
arrogate *vt* arrogare, assumĕre
arrow *s* sagitta, arundo *f*
arsenal *s* armamentarium *n*; navalia *n pl*
arsenic *s* arsenicum *n*
arson *s* incendium dolo malo *n*
art *s* ars *f*; artificium *n*
artery *s* arteria *f*

artful *adj* artificialis; callidus, subtilis; **—ly** callide, eleganter
article *s* (*object*) res *f*; (*ware*) merx *f*; (*term*) condicio *f*; (*clause*) caput *n*; (*gram*) articulus *m*
articulate *adj* distinctus, dilucidus; **—ly** articulatim, distincte
articulate *vt* explanare, exprimĕre; articulatim dicĕre
articulation *s* commissura *f*; (*fig*) explanatio *f*
artifice *s* artificium *n*; ars *f*; dolum *n*
artificial *adj* artificiosus; factitius; **—ly** arte
artillery *s* tormenta *n pl*
artisan *s* faber *m*; artifex, opifex *m*
artist *s* artifex *m*
artistic *adj* artificiosus, elegans; **—ally** artificiose; affabre
as *conj & adv* ut; quam; (*of time*) dum, cum; ita ut; sicut, velut; **— far —** quoad, usque ad, quantum; **— if** quasi, perinde ac si; ita ut si; **— it were** seu, tamquam; **— long —** tamdiu, tantisper dum; **— many —** tot, totidem; quotquot, quodcumque; **— much** tantum; **— often —** toties quoties; **— soon —** cum primum, simul, simul ac, simul atque; **— well —** ut, tamquam; **— yet** adhuc; **not — yet** nondum, necdum
ascend *vt & vi* ascendĕre
ascendency *s* auctoritas *f*
ascent *s* ascensio *f*; ascens·us -ūs *m*; acclivitas *f*
ascertain *vt* confirmare, comperire
ascetic *adj* asceticus
ascetic *s* asceta *m*
asceticism *s* duritia *f*
ascribe *vt* imputare, tribuĕre, ascribĕre
ash *s* cinis *m*; (*tree*) fraxinus *f*
ashamed *adj* pudibundus; **I am — of** pudet me (*with genit*)
ashen *adj* pallidus
ashore *adv* (*motion*) in litus; (*rest*) in litore
Asiatic *adj* Asiaticus
aside *adv* seorsum, oblique; **to call —** sevocare; **to lay** *or* **set —** ponĕre, seponĕre
aside from *prep* praeter (*with acc*)
asinine *adj* asininus
ask *vt* rogare, poscĕre; interrogare; requirĕre; *vi* **to — for** petĕre
askance *adv* oblique
askew *adv* traverse
asleep *adj* dormiens; **to be —** dormire; **to fall —** obdormire, obdormiscĕre
asp *s* aspis *f*
asparagus *s* asparagus *m*
aspect *s* aspect·us -ūs, prospect·us -ūs *m*; facies *f*
aspen *s* populus tremula *f*
asperity *s* acerbitas *f*
aspersion *s* opprobrium *n*, calumniatio *f*
asphalt *s* bitumen *n*
asphyxia *s* asphyxia *f*
aspirant *s* petitor *m*
aspiration *s* affectatio, spes *f*; (*pol*) ambitio *f*
aspire *vi* **to — to** affectare, spectare, petere, anniti
aspiring *adj* appetens; **aspiring to** appetens (*with genit*)
ass *s* asinus *m*; asina *f*; onager *m*; (*fig*) stultus *m*
assail *vt* appetĕre; oppugnare, invehi
assailable *adj* expugnabilis
assailant *s* oppugnator *m*
assassin *s* sicarius *m*; percussor *m*
assassinate *vt* insidiis interficĕre, occidere
assassination *s* caedes *f*
assault *s* impet·us -ūs *m*; oppugnatio, vis *f*; **aggravated —** (*law*) vis *f*; **sexual —** stupratio *f*; **to take by —** expugnare
assault *vt* adoriri, oppugnare; manus inferre (*with dat*); aggredi; (*in speech*) invehi in (*with acc*)
assay *vt* (*metals*) spectare; tentare, conari
assay *s* (*of metals*) obrussa *f*; spectatio *f*
assemblage *s* congregatio *f*; coacervatio *f*
assemble *vt* congregare, convocare; contrahĕre; *vi* convenire
assembly *s* coet·us -ūs *m*; convent·us -ūs *m*; (*pol*) comitia *n pl*; concilium *n*; (*of troops*) contio *f*; synodus *f*
assent *s* assens·us -ūs *m*
assent *vi* assentiri, adnuĕre
assert *vt* asserĕre, affirmare, asseverare; (*to vindicate*) defendĕre
assertion *s* affirmatio, asseveratio *f*; postulatio *f*
assess *vt* (*to tax*) censēre; (*to value*) aestimare
assessment *s* cens·us -ūs *m*; aestimatio *f*; vectigal, tributum *n*
assessor *s* (*judge*) consessor *m*; (*of taxes*) censor *m*
assets *s* bona *n pl*
assiduous *adj* assiduus; **—ly** assidue
assign *vt* attribuĕre, tribuĕre; (*land*) assignare; (*place*) indicare; (*time*) praestituĕre; (*task*) delegare; (*to allege*) suggerĕre, afferre
assignment *s* assignatio, attributio *f*; delegatio *f*
assimilate *vt* assimulare; (*food*) concoquĕre; (*knowledge*) concipĕre
assimilation *s* assimulatio, appropriatio *f*
assist *vt* adesse (*with dat*), succurrĕre (*with dat*), juvare, adjuvare
assistance *s* auxilium *n*; opem (*no nominative*) *f*; **to be of — to** auxilio esse (*with dat*)
assistant *s* adjutor *m*, adjutrix *f*, administer *m*
associate *adj* socius; collegialis
associate *s* socius, sodalis, consors *m*
associate *vt* consociare, adsciscĕre, conjungĕre; *vi* **to — with** familiariter uti (*with abl*); se adjungĕre (*with dat*)

association *s* societas *f*; communitas *f*; consociatio *f*; congregatio *f*
assort *vt* digerĕre, disponĕre; *vi* congruere
assortment *s* digestio, dispositio *f*; variae res *f pl*
assuage *vt* allevare, placare, lenire, mitigare
assume *vt* assumĕre, arrogare; induĕre; (*office*) inire
assuming *adj* arrogans
assumption *s* assumptio *f*; arrogantio *f*; (*hypothesis*) sumptio *f*
assurance *s* fiducia *f*; (*guarantee*) fides *f*; (*boldness*) confidentia, audacia *f*
assure *vt* confirmare, affirmare; promittĕre (*with dat*); adhortari; **to be assured** confidĕre
assuredly *adv* certo, profecto
asterisk *s* asteriscus *m*
asthmatic *adj* asthmaticus; **to be —** suspirio laborare
astonish *vt* obstupefacĕre; **to be astonished at** mirari
astonishingly *adv* admirabiliter
astonishment *s* admiratio *f*; stupor *m*
astound *vt* (ob)stupefacĕre
astray *adj* vagus; **to go —** errare; **to lead —** seducĕre
astride *adj* varicus
astrologer *s* astrologus *m*; Chaldaeus *m*; mathematicus *m*
astrological *adj* astrologicus
astrology *s* astrologia *f*; Chaldaeorum divinatio *f*
astronomer *s* astrologus *m*; astronomus *m*
astronomical *adj* astronomicus
astronomy *s* astrologia, astronomia *f*
astute *adj* callidus
asunder *adv* seorsum, separatim; *use verb with prefix* dis- *or* se-
asylum *s* asylum, perfugium *n*
at *prep* (*of place*) ad (*with acc*), apud (*with acc*), in (*with abl*), *or locative case*; (*of time*) in (*with abl*), ad (*with acc*), *or abl case*
atheism *s* deos esse negare (*used as neuter noun*)
atheist *s* atheos *m*
athlete *s* athleta *m*
athletic *adj* athleticus; lacertosus
atlas *s* orbis terrarum descriptio *f*
atmosphere *s* aër *m*; caelum *n*; inane *n*
atmospheric *adj* aëris (*genit*)
atom *s* atomus *f*; corpus individuum *n*; (*fig*) mica, particula *f*
atomic *adj* atomicus; **— theory** atomorum doctrina *f*
atone *vi* **to — for** piare, expiare
atonement *s* piaculum *n*; expiatio, compensatio *f*
atrocious *adj* atrox, dirus; nefarius, nefandus; immanis; **—ly** nefarie
atrocity *s* atrocitas *f*; atrox facinus *n*
atrophy *s* tabes, atrophia *f*
atrophy *s* tabescĕre, macrescĕre
attach *vt* annectĕre, adjungĕre; applicare; affigĕre; **to be attached to** adhaerēre (*with dat*)
attachment *s* adhaesio *f*; (*emotional*) amor *m*; vinculum *n*; studium *n*
attack *s* impet·us -ūs *m*; oppugnatio *f*; (*of cavalry*) incurs·us -ūs *m*; (*of disease, etc.*) tentatio *f*
attack *vt* adoriri, aggredi, oppugnare; (*with words*) invehi in (*with acc*), insequi; (*of diseases*) corripĕre, invadĕre, tentare
attacker *s* oppugnator, provocator *m*
attain *vt* adipisci, consequi; **to — to** pervenire ad (*with acc*)
attainable *adj* impetrabilis, obtinendus
attempt *s* conat·us -ūs *m*, inceptum *n*; (*risk*) ausum, periculum *n*; **first —** tirocinium *n*
attempt *vt* conari, niti, temptare, moliri
attend *vt* (*to accompany*) comitari; (*to escort*) deducĕre; (*to be present at*) adesse (*with dat*), interesse (*with dat*); *vi* **to — on** apparēre (*with dat*); frequentare, assectari; adesse (*with dat*); **to — to** animadvertĕre, procurare; (*to comply with*) obtemperare (*with dat*); invigilare
attendance *s* frequentia *f*; expectatio, adsectatio, cura, diligentia *f*; obsequium *n*; (*retinue*) comitat·us -ūs *m*
attendant *adj* adjunctus
attendant *s* comes *m*; assecla, apparitor *m*; famulus *m*, famula *f*
attention *s* animadversio *f*; animi attentio *f*; (*to duty*) cura, diligentia *f*; **to call — to** indicare; **to pay — to** operam dare (*with dat*), studēre (*with dat*)
attentive *adj* attentus; sedulus; officiosus; **—ly** attente, intento animo; sedulo; officiose
attenuate *vt* attenuare, extenuare
attenuation *s* extenuatio *f*
attest *vt* testari, testificari
attestation *s* testificatio *f*
attic *s* cenaculum *n*
Attic *adj* Atticus; (*fig*) subtilis, elegans
attire *s* ornat·us -ūs *m*; vestis *f*; habit·us -ūs m; vestit·us -ūs *m*
attire *vt* vestire; adornare
attitude *s* habit·us -ūs, stat·us -ūs *m*; (*mental*) ratio *f*
attorney *s* cognitor, procurator, advocatus, actor *m*
attorney general *s* advocatus fisci, procurator publicus *m*
attract *vt* trahĕre, attrahĕre; (*fig*) allicĕre
attraction *s* vis attractionis *f*; (*fig*) illecebra *f*, invitamentum *n*
attractive *adj* blandus, suavis, lepidus, venustus; **—ly** blande, suaviter, venuste, lepide
attractiveness *s* lepos *m*, venustas *f*
attribute *s* proprium, attributum *n*
attribute *vt* tribuĕre, attribuĕre; assignare, delegare
attrition *s* attrit·us -ūs *m*

attune *vt* modulari
auburn *adj* fulvus; aureus
auction *s* auctio *f*; (*public*) hasta *f*; **to hold an —** auctionem facĕre; **to sell by —** sub hasta vendĕre
auctioneer *s* praeco *m*
audacious *adj* audax; **—ly** audacter
audacity *s* audacia *f*
audible *adj* quod audiri potest
audibly *adv* clara voce
audience *s* auditores *m pl*; (*bystanders*) corona *f*
audit *s* rationum inspectio *f*
audit *vt* inspicĕre
auditory *adj* auditorius
Augean *adj* Augiae (*genit*)
auger *s* terebra *f*
augment *vt* augēre, ampliare; *vi* augēri, accrescĕre
augur *s* augur *m*
augur *vi* augurari
augury *s* augurium, auspicium *n*; auguratio *f*
august *adj* augustus; magnificus
August *s* (mensis) Sextilis, (mensis) Augustus *m*
Augustan *adj* Augustalis
aunt *s* (*on father's side*) amita *f*; (*on mother's side*) matertera *f*
auspices *s* auspicium *n*; **to take —** auspicari; **without taking —** inauspicato
auspicious *adj* auspicatus; faustus, felix; **—ly** auspicato; feliciter
austere *adj* austerus, severus; **—ly** austere, severe
austerity *s* austeritas, severitas *f*
authentic *adj* certus; verus; ratus; (*law*) authenticus; fide dignus; genuinus
authenticate *vt* recognoscĕre
authentication *s* auctoritas *f*; legibus confirmatio *f*
authenticity *s* auctoritas, fides *f*
author *s* auctor, scriptor *m*; (*inventor*) conditor *m*; (*of a crime*) caput *n*
authoress *s* auctor *f*
authoritative *adj* imperiosus; fidus; **—ly** praecise
authority *s* auctoritas, potestas *f*; (*leave*) licentia *f*; jus *n*; imperium *n*; magistrat·us -ūs *m*; **to have it on good —** bono auctore habēre
authorization *s* auctoritate confirmatio *f*; licentia *f*
authorize *vt* potestatem *or* auctoritatem dare (*with dat*), mandare; (*law*) sancire
authorship *s* scriptoris munus *n*; auctoritas *f*
autobiography *s* de vita sua scriptus liber *m*
autocrat *s* dominus *m*
autograph *s* chirographum *n*
autograph *vt* manu propria scribĕre
automatic *adj* necessarius
automaton *s* automaton *n*
autumn *s* autumnus *m*
autumnal *adj* autumnalis
auxiliaries *s* (*mil*) auxilia *n pl*; auxiliarii *m pl*
auxiliary *adj* auxiliaris, auxiliarius
auxiliary *s* adjutor *m*
avail *vt* prodesse (*with dat*); **to — oneself of** uti (*with abl*); *vi* valēre
avail *s* **to be of no —** usui non esse
availability *s* utilitas *f*
available *adj* in promptu; utilis
avalanche *s* montis ruina *f*
avarice *s* avaritia *f*; sordes *f*
avaricious *adj* avarus, avidus; **—ly** avare
avenge *vt* vindicare, ulcisci
avenger *s* ultor *m*, vindex *m & f*
avenging *adj* ultrix, vindex
avenue *s* xystus *m*, xystum *n*
average *s* medium *n*; **on the —** fere
average *vi* fere esse
averse *adj* aversus; **to be — to** abhorrēre ab (*with abl*); **—ly** averse
aversion *s* odium, fastidium *n*; **to have an — for** fastidire
avert *vt* avertĕre, amovēre, abducĕre
aviary *s* aviarium *n*
avid *adj* avidus
avocation *s* officium *n*, negotia *n pl*
avoid *vt* vitare, fugĕre; (*a blow*) declinare
avoidable *adj* evitabilis
avoidance *s* vitatio *f*; declinatio *f*
avow *vt* asserĕre, profitēri
avowal *s* confessio *f*
avowedly *adv* palam, aperte, ex confesso
await *vt* exspectare
awake *adj* vigil, vigilans; **to be —** vigilare
awaken *vt* excitare, suscitare, expergefacĕre; *vi* expergisci
award *s* praemium *n*; (*decision*) arbitrium, judicium *n*
award *vt* tribuĕre; (*law*) adjudicare, addicĕre
aware *adj* gnarus, sciens; **to be — of** scire
away *adv use verbs with prefix* a- *or* ab-; **far —** procul, longe; **to be —** abesse; **to go —** abire
awe *s* reverentia *f*; formido f, met·us -ūs, terror *m*; **to stand in — of** verēri; venerari
awful *adj* formidulosus, dirus, terribilis; **—ly** terribiliter, formidulose
awhile *adv* paulisper, aliquamdiu, parumper
awkward *adj* ineptus; rusticus, rudis; inhabilis; (*fig*) molestus; **—ly** inepte; rustice; dure; inscite
awkwardness *s* ineptia *f*; imperitia, rusticitas *f*
awl *s* subula *f*
awning *s* velarium *n*; inductio *f*
awry *adj* obliquus; pravus
awry *adv* oblique; prave
ax *s* securis *f*
axiom *s* axioma, pronuntiatum *n*, sententia *f*
axis *s* axis *m*
axle *s* axis *m*
azure *adj* caeruleus

B

baa *s* balat·us -ūs *m*
baa *vi* balare
babble *s* garrulitas *f*
babble *vi* blaterare, garrire
babbler *s* blatero, garrulus *m*
babbling *adj* garrulus, loquax
babe *s* infans *m & f*
baboon *s* cynocephalus *m*
baby *s* infans *m & f*
babyish *adj* infantilis
bacchanal *s* bacchans *m*, baccha *f*
bacchanalian *adj* bacchanalis
Bacchic *adj* bacchicus
bachelor *s* caelebs *m*; (*degree*) baccalaureus *m*
back *s* tergum, dorsum *n*; aversum *n*; **at one's —** a tergo
back *adv* retro, retrorsum; *or use verbs with prefix* re- *or* retro-
back *vt* adjuvare; favēre (*with dat*), obsecundare (*with dat*), adesse (*with dat*); *vi* **to — away from** defugĕre; **to — up** retrogradi
backboard *s* pluteus *m*
backbone *s* spina *f*
backdoor *s* posticum *n*
backer *s* adjutor, fautor *m*
background *s* recess·us -ūs *m*
backstairs *s* scalae posticae *f pl*
backward *adv* retro; retrorsum; rursus
backward *adj* (*reversed*) supinus; (*slow*) piger, tardus; (*late*) serus; **to be —** cunctari
backwardness *s* tarditas *f*; pigritia *f*
bacon *s* lardum *n*
bad *adj* malus, parvus, nequam; improbus; aegrotus; (*of weather*) adversus; **to go —** corrumpi; **—ly** male, prave; improbe
badge *s* insigne, signum *n*
badger *s* meles *f*
badger *vt* vexare, inquietare, sollicitare
badness *s* malitia, pravitas, nequitia, improbitas *f*
baffle *vt* decipĕre, fallĕre, eludĕre
bag *s* saccus *m*; (*of leather*) uter *m*; (*of network*) reticulum *n*
baggage *s* sarcinae *f pl*; impedimenta *n pl*; scruta *n pl*
bail *s* vadimonium *n*; vas *m*; (*for debt*) praes *m*; **to accept — for** vadari; **to put up — for** spondēre pro (*with abl*), fidepromittĕre
bailiff *s* (*sergeant of court of justice*) apparitor *m*; (*manager of estate*) villicus *m*
bailiwick *s* jurisdictio *f*
bait *s* esca *f*; (*fig*) incitamentum *n*, illecebra *f*
bait *vt* inescare; (*to tease*) lacessĕre
bake *vt* torrēre, coquĕre
baker *s* pistor *m*
bakery *s* pistrina *f*, pistrinum *n*
balance *s* libra, trutina, statera *f*; (*equipoise*) aequipondium *n*; (*in bookkeeping*) reliquum *n*; (*fig*) compensatio *f*
balance *vt* librare; compensare; (*accounts*) consolidare, dispungĕre; *vi* constare; **the account balances** ratio constat
balance sheet *s* ratio accepti et expensi *f*
balcony *s* maenianum *n*; podium *n*
bald *adj* calvus, glaber; (*fig*) aridus; **—ly** (*in style*) jejune
baldness *s* calvitium *n*; (*of style*) ariditas, jejunitas *f*
bale *s* sarcina *f*, fascis *m*
bale *vt* (*e.g., hay*) involvĕre; **to — out** exhaurire
baleful *adj* funestus; perniciosus, noxius
balk *s* (*of wood*) tignum *n*; (*fig*) frustratio *f*
balk *vt* frustrari, eludĕre, decipĕre
ball *s* globulus *m*; (*for playing*) pila *f*; **to play —** pilā ludĕre
ballad *s* carmen *n*
ballast *s* saburra *f*
ballast *vt* saburrare
ballet *s* pantomimus *m*
ballet dancer *s* pantomimus *m*, pantomima *f*
ballot *s* tabella *f*; suffragium *n*
ballot box *s* cista, cistula *f*
balm *s* balsamum *n*; unguentum *n*; (*fig*) solatium *n*
balmy *adj* balsaminus; suavis, lenis
balsam *s* balsamum *n*
bamboo *s* arundo indica *f*
ban *s* edictum *n*; proscriptio *f*; interdictum *n*
ban *vt* interdicĕre (*with dat*), vetare
banana *s* ariena *f*
band *s* vinculum, ligamentum *n*; (*for the head*) redimiculum *n*, infula *f*; (*troop*) caterva *f*, chorus *m*; grex *f*; man·us -ūs *f*; **in —s** turmatim
band *vi* **to — together** conjungi, consociari
bandage *s* fascia, ligatura *f*
bandage *vt* ligare, obligare
bandit *s* latro *m*
banditry *s* latrocinium *n*
bandy *vt* jactare; **to — words** altercari
bane *s* venenum *n*; virus *n*; (*fig*) pestis, pernicies *f*
baneful *adj* pestiferus, perniciosus, exitiosus
bang *s* crepit·us -ūs, sonit·us -ūs *m*
bang *vt* verberare; *vi* sonare, crepare
banish *vt* expellĕre, pellĕre, relegare, deportare; aquā et igni interdicĕre (*with dat*)
banishment *s* (*act*) ejectio, relegatio *f*; interdictio aquae et ignis *f*; (*state*) exilium *n*
banister *s* epimedion *n*
bank *s* (*of a river*) ripa *f*; (*of earth*) agger *m*; (*com*) argentaria *f*, mensa publica *f*

banker *s* argentarius, mensarius *m*
banking *s* argentaria negotiatio *f*
bank note *s* tessera mensae publicae *f*
bankrupt *s* conturbator, decoctor *m*; **to be** *or* **become —** rationes conturbare; decoquĕre; **to go —** foro cedere
bankruptcy *s* rationum conturbatio *f*; (*fig*) naufragium patrimonii *n*
banner *s* vexillum *n*
banquet *s* convivium *n*, epulae *f pl*
banter *s* cavillatio *f*; jocus *m*
banter *vi* cavillari
bantering *s* cavillatio *f*
baptism *s* baptisma *n*, baptismus *m*
baptize *vt* baptizare
bar *s* vectis *f*; (*of door*) obex *m*; repagulum *n*; (*fig*) impedimentum *n*; (*ingot*) later *m*; (*in court of justice*) cancelli *m pl*, claustra *n pl*; (*legal profession*) forum *n*; (*counter*) abacus *m*; **of the —** forensis; **to practice at the —** causas agĕre
bar *vt* (*door*) obserare; (*to keep away*) obstare (*with dat*), prohibēre, intercludĕre
barb *s* hamus *m*; aculeus *m*
barbarian *adj* barbarus
barbarian *s* barbarus *m*
barbaric *adj* barbaricus
barbarism *s* barbaria, barbaries *f*; feritas *f*; (*of language*) barbarismus *m*
barbarity *s* ferocia, saevitia, immanitas *f*
barbarous *adj* barbarus; ferus, immanis; **—ly** barbare; saeve
barbed *adj* hamatus
barber *s* tonsor *m*, tonstrix *f*
bard *s* vates *m*
bare *adj* nudus; merus; (*of style*) pressus; **to lay —** nudare, detegĕre
bare *vt* nudare, denudare; detegĕre, aperire
barefaced *adj* impudens; **—ly** impudenter
barefoot *adj* nudis pedibus; discalceatus
bareheaded *adj* nudo capite
barely *adv* vix, aegre
bargain *s* pactio *f*, pactum *n*; **to strike a —** pacisci
bargain *vi* pacisci
barge *s* linter *f*
bark *s* (*of tree*) cortex *m & f*, liber *m*; (*of dog*) latrat·us -ūs *m*; (*ship*) navis, ratis *f*
bark *vi* latrare; **to — at** allatrare
barking *s* latrat·us -ūs *m*
barley *s* hordeum *n*
barley *adj* hordeacus
barmaid *s* ministra cauponae *f*
barn *s* granarium, horreum *n*
barometer *s* barometrum *n*
barometric *adj* barometricus
baron *s* baro *m*
barracks *s* castra (stativa) *n pl*
barrel *s* cadus *m*, dolium *n*, cupa *f*
barren *adj* sterilis; macer; jejunus; (*fig*) angustus
barrenness *s* sterilitas *f*
barricade *s* munimentum *n*; claustrum *n*
barricade *vt* obsaepire, obstruĕre, oppilare
barrier *s* limes *m*; cancelli *m pl*; (*fig*) claustra *n pl*
barrister *s* advocatus *m*
barter *s* permutatio *f*; merx *f*
barter *vt* mutare, commutare; *vi* merces mutare, merces pacisci
base *adj* humilis, ignobilis, obscurus; inferior; servilis; infamis, vilis, turpis; **—ly** abjecte; turpiter
base *s* basis *f*; (*mus*) sonus gravis *m*; (*fig*) fundamentum *n*; (*mil*) castra *n pl*
baseless *adj* inanis, vanus, falsus
basement *s* fundamentum *n*, basis *f*; imum tabulatum *n*
baseness *s* humilitas *f*; turpitudo *f*
bashful *adj* erubescens; pudens; modestus; verecundus; **—ly** timide, verecunde; modeste
bashfulness *s* pudor *m*; rubor *m*; verecundia *f*
basic *adj* primus, principalis
basilica *s* basilica *f*
basin *s* (*for washing*) trulleum *n*, trulla *f*; (*reservoir*) labrum *n*
basis *s* fundamentum *n*
bask *vi* apricari
basket *s* corbis *f*, canistrum *n*; (*for wool*) quasillum *n*; cophinus *m*
bas-relief *s* caelamen *n*; toreuma *n*
bass *s* sonus gravissimus *m*
bast *s* tilia *f*
bastard *adj* spurius
bastard *s* nothus, spurius *m*
baste *vt* lardo perfundĕre
bastion *s* propugnaculum, castellum *n*
bat *s* (*bird*) vespertilio *m*; (*club*) clava *f*
batch *s* massa *n*; numerus *m*
bath *s* balneum *n*; (*public*) balnea *n pl*; (*tub*) alveus *m*, labrum *n*; lavatio *f*; **cold —** frigidarium *n*; **hot —** cal(i)darium *n*
bathe *vt* lavare; *vi* balneo uti, lavari, perlui
bathing *s* lavatio *f*; natatio *f*
bathtub *s* alveus *m*
batman *s* calo *m*
baton *s* virga *f*
battalion *s* cohors *f*
batter *vt* percutĕre, obtundĕre, diruĕre, verberare, quassare
battering ram *s* aries *m*
battle *s* proelium *n*, pugna *f*; acies *f*
battle *vi* pugnare, proeliari
battle array *s* acies *f*
battle-ax *s* bipennis *f*
battlement *s* pinna *f*
bauble *s* tricae *f pl*
bawd *s* lena *f*
bawdry *s* lenocinium *n*
bawl *vi* vociferari, clamitare
bawling *s* vociferatio *f*; indecorus clamor *m*
bay *s* (*sea*) sin·us -ūs *m*; (*tree*) laurea, laurus *f*; **at —** interclusus
bay *adj* (*light-colored*) helvus; (*dark-colored*) spadix; (*of bay*) laureus

bay *vi* latrare
bayonet *s* pugio *f*
bayonet *vt* pugione foděre
bazaar *s* forum rerum venalium *n*
be *vi* esse; exsistěre; (*condition*) se habēre; **to — absent** abesse; **to — against** adversari; **to — amongst** interesse (*with dat*); **to — for** (*to side with*) favēre (*with dat*), stare cum (*with abl*); **to — present** adesse
beach *s* litus *n*, acta *f*
beach *vt* subducěre; *vi* vadis impingěre
beacon *s* ignis in specula *m*; (*lighthouse*) pharus *m*
bead *s* pilula, sphaerula *f*
beagle *s* parvus canis venaticus *m*
beak *s* rostrum *n*
beaked *adj* rostratus
beaker *s* poculum *n*, cantharus *m*
beam *s* (*of wood*) tignum *n*, trabs *f*; (*of light*) radius *m*, jubar *n*; nitor *m*
beam *vi* radiare, refulgēre; (*of a person*) arridēre
beaming *adj* nitens, lucidus
bean *s* faba *f*; phaselus *m & f*
bear *vt* (*to carry*) portare, ferre; (*to endure*) ferre, pati, tolerare; (*to produce*) ferre; (*to beget*) parěre; **to — away** auferre; **to — out** (*to confirm*) arguěre; **to — witness to** testari; *vi* **to — down on** appropinquare; **to — upon** (*to refer to*) pertinēre ad (*with acc*); **to — up under** obsistěre (*with dat*), sustinēre; **to — with** indulgēre (*with dat*)
bear *s* ursus *m*, ursa *f*
bearable *adj* tolerandus, tolerabilis
beard *s* barba *f*; (*of grain*) arista *f*
bearded *adj* barbatus; intonsus
beardless *adj* inberbis
bearer *s* (*porter*) bajulus *m*; (*of litter*) lecticarius *m*; (*of letter*) tabellarius *m*; (*of news*) nuntius *m*
bearing *s* (*posture*) gest·us -ūs, vult·us -ūs *m*; (*direction*) regio *f*; **to have a — on** pertinēre ad (*with acc*)
beast *s* belua *f*; bestia *f*; (*wild*) fera *f*; (*domestic*) pecus *f*
beast of burden *s* jumentum *n*
beastly *adj* obscenus, foedus, spurcus
beat *vt* (*to punish*) verberare; (*to knock*) pulsare; (*to conquer*) superare, vincere; (*the body in grief*) plangěre; **to — back** repellěre; **to — down** demoliri; **to — in** perfringere; *vi* palpitare; **to — upon** (*of rain*) impluěre; (*of waves*) illiděre
beat *s* (*blow*) plaga *f*, ict·us -ūs *m*; (*of the heart*) palpitatio *f*; (*mus*) percussio *f*; (*patrol*) vigiles nocte ambulantes *m pl*
beaten *adj* victus; (*worn*) tritus
beating *s* verberatio *f*; ict·us -ūs *m*; verbera *n pl*; (*defeat*) repulsa *f*; clades *f*; (*of the heart*) palpitatio *f*
beautiful *adj* pulcher; (*shapely*) formosus; **—ly** pulchre, belle
beautify *vt* ornare, decorare
beauty *s* pulchritudo *f*; forma *f*; (*of places*) amoenitas *f*
beaver *s* castor, fiber *m*; (*of helmet*) buccula *f*
because *conj* quod, quia, quoniam; quippe qui
because of *prep* ob (*with acc*), propter (*with acc*), gratiā (*with genit*)
beck *s* nut·us -ūs *m*; **at the — and call** ad arbitrium
beckon *vt* nutare, annuěre
become *vt* decēre; *vi* fieri
becoming *adj* decens; decorus; conveniens; **—ly** decenter; digne; honeste
bed *s* lectus *m*, cubile *n*; (*in a garden*) areola *f*; (*of a river*) alveus *m*; **to go to —** cubitum ire; **to make the —** lectum sterněre
bedding *s* stragulum *n*
bedeck *vt* decorare, ornare
bedevil *vt* (*to enchant*) fascinare
bedfellow *s* tori socius *m*, tori socia *f*
bedlam *s* tumult·us -ūs *m*
bedpost *s* fulcrum *n*
bedraggled *adj* sordidus
bedridden *adj* **to be —** lecto tenēri
bedroom *s* cubiculum *n*
bedtime *s* hora somni *f*
bee *s* apis *f*
beef *s* bubula caro *f*
beehive *s* alveus *m*; alvearium *n*
beekeeper *s* apiarius *m*
beer *s* cerevisia *f*
beet *s* beta *f*
beetle *s* scarabaeus *m*
befall *vt* acciděre (*with dat*); contingěre (*with dat*); *vi* acciděre, contingěre, evenire
befit *vt* decēre, convenire in (*with acc*)
befitting *adj* decens; conveniens, idoneus; **it is —** decet
before *prep* ante (*with acc*); prae (*with abl*); pro (*with abl*); coram (*with abl*); apud (*with acc*); **— all things** imprimis; **— long** jamdudum; **— now** antehac
before *conj* antequam, priusquam
beforehand *adv* antea
befriend *vt* favēre (*with dat*), sublevare, adjuvare
beg *vt* petěre, poscěre, orare, obsecrare; *vi* mendicare
beget *vt* gigněre, procreare, generare
beggar *s* mendicus *m*
begging *s* mendicitas *f*; **to go —** mendicare
begin *vt & vi* incipěre, incohare, exordiri; **to — with** incipěre ab (*with abl*)
beginner *s* auctor *m*; inceptor *m*; tiro *m*
beginning *s* inceptio *f*; initium *n*; exordium *n*; origo *f*; principium *n*; **at the — of winter** ineunte hieme
begone *interj* apage!
beguile *vt* fallěre, fraudare
behalf *s* **on — of** pro (*with abl*)
behave *vi* se gerěre; **to — towards**

uti (*with abl*); **well behaved** bene moratus
behavior *s* mores *m pl*
behead *vt* detruncare, obtruncare
beheading *s* decollatio *f*
behest *s* jussum *n*
behind *adv* pone, a tergo, post; **to be left —** relinqui
behind *prep* pone (*with acc*); post (*with acc*)
behold *vt* conspicĕre; obtuēri
behold *interj* ecce!, en!
being *s* ens *n*; natura *f*; essentia *f*; homo *m*
bejewelled *adj* gemmatus, gemmeus
belabor *vt* mulcare, verberare
belch *s* ruct·us -ūs *m*
belch *vi* ructare, eructare
belfry *s* campanile *n*
belie *vt* repugnare; (*to refute*) refutare, refellĕre
belief *s* fides *f*; opinio, persuasio *f*
believe *vt* (*thing*) credĕre; (*person*) credere (*with dat*); (*to suppose*) existimare, opinari, putare, credĕre, arbitrari; **to make —** simulare
believer *s* credens *m & f*; Christianus *m*
bell *s* (*large*) campana *f*; (*small*) tintinnabulum *n*
belle *s* formosa puella *f*
belles lettres *s* litterae *f pl*
belligerent *adj* belliger, belligerans, bellans
bellow *vi* rugire, mugire
bellowing *s* mugit·us -ūs *m*
bellows *s* follis *m*
belly *s* venter *m*; abdomen *n*
bellyache *s* tormina *n pl*
belong *vi* **to — to** esse (*with genit*); inesse (*with dat*); pertinēre ad (*with acc*)
beloved *adj* dilectus, carus; **dearly —** carissimus
below *adj* inferus
below *adv* infra; subter
below *prep* infra (*with acc*); sub (*with abl or acc*)
belt *s* cingulum *n*; (*swordbelt*) balteus *m*; zona *f*
bemoan *vt* deplorare, lamentari
bemused *adj* attonitus
bench *s* scamnum, sedile, subsellium *n*; (*for rowers*) transtrum *n*
bend *vt* flectĕre, curvare; inclinare; (*bow*) intendĕre; (*to persuade*) intendĕre; *vi* se inflectĕre; **to — back** reflectĕre; **to — down** *or* **over** se demittĕre
bend *s* plica *f*; flex·us -ūs *m*; curvamen *n*; (*fig*) inclinatio *f*
bending *s* flexura, curvatura, inclinatio *f*
bending *adj* flexus; inclinans; acclivis; declivis; (*concave*) concavus
beneath *adv* subter
beneath *prep* sub (*with acc or abl*)
benediction *s* benedictio *f*
benefaction *s* beneficium *n*
benefactor *s* largitor *m*; patronus *m*
benefactress *s* patrona *f*
beneficence *s* beneficentia *f*
beneficent *adj* beneficus, benignus, liberalis; **—ly** benefice
beneficial *adj* utilis, commodus; salutaris; **—ly** utiliter
benefit *s* beneficium *n*, gratia *f*; fruct·us -ūs *m*; **to have the — of** frui (*with abl*)
benefit *vt* juvare; prodesse (*with dat*); *vi* proficĕre; lucrari
benevolence *s* benevolentia *f*
benevolent *s* benevolus, beneficus; benignus, liberalis; **—ly** benevole
benign *adj* benignus; **—ly** benigne
bent *adj* curvus, flexus; (*of the mind*) attentus; **— backwards** recurvus; **— forwards** pronus; **— inwards** camur; sinuosus
bent *s* flex·us -ūs *m*, plica *f*; curvatura *f*; (*inclination*) ingenium *n*, inclinatio f
benumb *vt* torpore afficĕre
bequeath *vt* legare
bequest *s* legatum *n*
bereave *vt* orbare; privare; spoliare
bereavement *s* orbitas *f*; damnum *n*
bereft *adj* orbus, orbatus, privatus
berry *s* bacca *f*; acinus *m*
berth *s* statio *f*; (*cabin*) diaeta *f*; **to give wide — to** devitare
beseech *vt* obsecrare, implorare, supplicare
beset *vt* circumdare, obsidēre, circumsedēre; urgēre
beside *prep* ad (*with acc*), apud (*with acc*), juxta (*with acc*); **— the point** nihil ad rem; **to be — oneself** delirare
besides *adv* praeterea, ultro, insuper
besides *prep* praeter (*with acc*)
besiege *vt* circumsedēre, obsidēre
besieging *s* obsessio, circumsessio *f*
besmirch *vt* maculare
best *adj* optimus, praestantissimus; **the — part** major pars *f*
best *s* flos *m*; **to do one's —** pro virili parte agĕre; **to have the — of it** praevalēre, valēre; **to make the — of** aequo animo ferre; **to the — of one's ability** pro viribus
bestial *adj* bestialis; immanis
bestir *vt* **to — oneself** expergisci
bestow *vt* tribuĕre, conferre; donare, largiri
bestower *s* largitor, dator *m*
bet *s* pignus, depositum *n*
bet *vt* deponĕre; *vi* pignore contendĕre
betide *vi* evenire, accidĕre
betoken *vt* indicare, portendĕre
betray *vt* tradĕre, prodĕre; (*feelings*) arguĕre
betrayer *s* proditor, traditor *m*
betroth *vt* spondĕre, despondēre
betrothal *s* sponsalia *n pl*; pactio nuptialis *f*
betrothed *adj* sponsus, pactus
better *adj* melior; potior, praestantior; superior; **it is —** praestat; **to get —** convalescĕre; **to get the — of** superare, vincĕre
better *adv* melius, potius; praestantius; rectius; satius

better *vt* meliorem facĕre; corrigĕre; **to — oneself** proficĕre
betters *s* superiores *m pl*
between *prep* inter (*with acc*); **— whiles** interim
betwixt *prep* inter (*with acc*)
bevel *vt* obliquare
beverage *s* potio *f*, pot·us -ūs *m*
bevy *s* grex *f*
bewail *vt* deplorare, ingemĕre, queri, lamentari
beware *vi* cavēre; **to — of** cavēre
bewilder *vt* perturbare, confundĕre
bewilderment *s* perturbatio *f*
bewitch *vt* fascinare; (*to charm*) demulcēre
beyond *adv* supra, ultra; ulterius
beyond *prep* ultra (*with acc*); (*motion*) trans (*with acc*); supra (*with acc*), extra (*with acc*); **to go —** excedĕre
bias *s* inclinatio *f*; praeponderatio *f*
bias *vt* inclinare
Bible *s* divina scriptura *f*, biblia *n pl*
Biblical *adj* biblicus
bibliography *s* bibliographia *f*
bicker *vi* jurgare, altercari
bickering *s* altercatio *f*
bid *vt* jubēre, mandare, rogare; (*to invite*) invitare; (*at auction*) licitari, licēri; **to — farewell** valedicĕre
bid *s* licitatio *f*; **to make a —** licēri
bidder *s* licitator *m*
bidding *s* jussum *n*; (*auction*) licitatio *f*
bide *vt* exspectare, manēre
biennial *adj* biennalis, bimus
bier *s* feretrum *n*, sandapila *f*
big *adj* ingens, vastus; grandis, amplus; **— with child** gravida; **— with young** praegnans; **very —** permagnus
bigamist *s* bimaritus *m*
bigamy *s* bigamia *f*
bigot *s* nimis obstinatus fautor *m*
bigoted *adj* nimis obstinatus
bigotry *s* contumacia *f*; nimia obstinatio *f*
bile *s* bilis *f*
bilge water *s* sentina *f*
bilious *adj* biliosus
bilk *vt* fraudare: frustrari
bill *s* (*of a bird*) rostrum *n*; (*proposed law*) rogatio *f*; lex *f*; plebiscitum *n*; (*com*) ratio debiti *f*; syngrapha *f*; (*notice*) libellus *m*; **to introduce a —** ferre, legem ferre; populum rogare; **to pass a —** legem perferre; **to turn down a —** antiquare
billet *s* hospitium *n*
billet *vt* per hospitia dispargĕre
billion *s* billio *m*
billow *s* fluct·us -ūs *m*
billowy *adj* fluctuosus, undabundus
bin *s* (*in wine cellar*) loculus *m*; (*for grain*) cista *f*, panarium *n*
bind *vt* ligare, nectĕre, stringĕre, vincire; (*by obligation*) obligare; (*books*) conglutinare; (*wounds*) obligare; **to — fast** devincire; **to — together** colligare; **to — up** alligare; (*med*) astringĕre
binding *adj* obligatorius; (*law*) ratus
binding *s* religatio *f*; compages *f*
biographer *s* vitae scriptor *m*
biography *s* vita *f*
biped *s* bipes *m*
birch *adj* betulinus
birch tree *s* betula *f*
bird *s* avis, volucris *f*
birdcage *s* cavea *f*
birdcall *s* fistula aucupatoria *f*
birdlime *s* viscum *n*
bird's nest *s* nidus *m*
birth *s* part·us -ūs *m*; ort·us -ūs *m*; (*race*) genus *n*
birthday *s* dies natalis *m*
birthday cake *s* libum *n*
birthplace *s* patria *f*
birthright *s* patrimonium *n*
biscuit *s* crustulum *n*
bisect *vt* dividĕre
bishop *s* episcopus *m*
bison *s* bison *m*; urus *m*
bit *s* (*for a horse*) frenum *n*; (*small amount*) pars *f*, fragmentum *n*; (*of food*) frustum *n*; **— by —** minutatim
bitch *s* canis *f*
bite *s* mors·us -ūs *m*; (*fig*) sarcasmus *m*
bite *vt* mordēre; (*as pepper, frost, etc.*) urĕre
biting *adj* mordax; (*fig*) asper; mordens
bitter *adj* amarus; (*fig*) acerbus; asper; gravis; **—ly** acerbe; aspere
bitterness *s* amaritas *f*; (*fig*) acerbitas *f*; asperitas *f*
bitters *s* absinthium *n*
bivouac *s* excubiae *f pl*
blab *s* garrulus *m*
blab *vi* garrire, deblaterare
black *adj* niger; ater; (*in looks*) trux; (*of character*) scelestus
black *s* nigrum *n*; (*negro*) Aethiops *m*; **in —** pullatus
black-and-blue *adj* lividus
blackberry *s* morum *n*
blackbird *s* merula *f*
black death *s* pestis *f*
blacken *vt* nigrare; denigrare
blackguard *s* nebulo *m*
blacklist *s* proscriptio *f*
black magic *s* magicae artes *f pl*
blackness *s* nigritia, nigrities *f*
blacksmith *s* ferrarius faber *m*
bladder *s* vesica *f*
blade *s* (*edge*) lamina *f*; (*of grass*) caulis *m*, herba *f*; (*of oar*) palma *f*
blamable *adj* culpabilis; reus
blame *vt* reprehendĕre, culpare, vituperare
blame *s* culpa *f*; reprehensio *f*
blameless *adj* integer, innoxius; irreprehensus; **—ly** integre, innocenter
blanch *vt* candefacĕre; *vi* exalbescĕre, pallescĕre
bland *adj* blandus
blandishment *s* blanditia *f*, blandimentum *n*; (*charm*) lenocinium *n*
blank *adj* vacuus, albus, purus; (*expression*) stolidus

blanket *s* lodix *f*; stragulum *n*
blare *s* strepit·us -ūs, clangor, stridor *m*
blare *vi* stridēre, canĕre
blaspheme *vi* maledicĕre, execrari; blasphemare
blasphemous *adj* maledicus, impius; blasphemus
blasphemy *s* maledicta *n pl,* impietas *f*; blasphemia, blasphematio *f*
blast *s* flat·us -ūs *m,* flamen *n*
blast *vt* discutĕre, disjicĕre; (*crops*) urĕre, robigine afficĕre
blaze *s* flamma *f*; fulgor *m*
blaze *vi* flagrare, ardēre; **to — up** exardescĕre
bleach *vt* dealbare, candefacĕre
bleak *adj* desertus; immitis
blear-eyed *adj* lippus; **to be —** lippire
bleat *vi* balare
bleating *s* balat·us -ūs *m*
bleed *vi* sanguinem fundĕre
bleeding *adj* crudus, sanguineus
bleeding *s* (*bloodletting*) sanguinis missio *f*; (*flowing of blood*) sanguinis profusio *f*
blemish *s* macula *f,* vitium *n*; labes *f*
blemish *vt* maculare, foedare
blend *vt* commiscēre, immiscēre
bless *vt* beare; (*eccl*) benedicĕre; (*consecrate*) consecrare; (*with success*) secundare
blessed *adj* beatus; pius; fortunatus; (*of emperors*) divus
blessing *s* (*thing*) bonum, commodum *n*; (*eccl*) benedictio *f*
blight *s* robigo, uredo *f*
blight *vt* urĕre; robigine afficĕre; (*fig*) nocēre (*with dat*)
blind *adj* caecus; obscurus; (*fig*) ignarus; **—ly** (*rashly*) temere
blind *vt* caecare, occaecare; (*fig*) occaecare, fallĕre
blindfold *vt* oculos obligare (*with dat*)
blindfolded *adj* obligatis oculis
blindness *s* caecitas *f*; (*fig*) temeritas *f*; stultitia *f*
blink *vi* connivēre
bliss *s* beatitudo *f*
blissful *adj* beatus; **—ly** beate
blister *s* pustula *f*
blister *vt & vi* pustulare
blithe *adj* hilaris, hilarus
bloated *adj* tumidus, turgidus
block *s* truncus, stipes *m*; (*of stone*) massa *f*; (*of houses*) insula *f*
block *vt* claudĕre; (*to impede*) obstare (*with dat*); **to — up** obstruĕre
blockade *s* obsidio *f*; **to raise a —** obsidionem solvĕre
blockade *vt* obsidēre, claudĕre
blockhead *s* caudex *m*
blood *s* sanguis *m*; (*gore*) cruor *m,* sanies *f*; (*fig*) (*slaughter*) caedes *f*; (*lineage*) genus *n*; **bad —** simultas *f*; **to staunch —** sanguinem supprimĕre
bloodless *adj* exsanguis; (*without bloodshed*) incruentus
blood-red *adj* cruentus; sanguineus, sanguinolentus
bloodshed *s* caedes *f*
bloodshot *adj* cruore suffusus
bloodstained *adj* cruentus, cruentatus, sanguinolentus
bloodsucker *s* sanguisuga *f*; hirudo *f*
bloodthirsty *adj* sanguinarius; sanguinolentus
blood vessel *s* vena *f*
bloody *adj* cruentus
bloom *s* flos *m*
bloom *vi* florēre, florescĕre; vigēre
blooming *adj* florens; floridus; nitidus
blossom *s* flos *m*
blot *s* macula, litura *f*; (*fig*) labes *f,* dedecus *n*
blot *vt* maculare; conspurcare; **to — out** delēre; (*to erase*) oblitterare
blotch *s* macula *f*; pustula *f*
blotched *adj* maculosus
blow *s* (*stroke*) plaga *f,* ict·us -ūs *m*; (*with the fist*) colaphus *m*; (*fig*) plaga *f*; calamitas *f*
blow *vt* (*instrument*) canĕre; (*breath*) anhelare; **to — out** extinguĕre; **to — the nose** emungĕre; **to — up** inflare; *vi* flare; (*of a flower*) efflorescĕre; **to — over** (*of a storm*) cadĕre; (*fig*) abire
blowing *s* sufflatio *f*; flat·us -ūs *m*; (*of the nose*) emunctio *f*
blowup *s* scandalum *n*; (*scolding*) objurgatio *f*
blubber *s* adeps balaenarum *m*
blubber *vi* lacrimas effundĕre
blue *adj* caeruleus
blueness *s* caeruleum *n*
blues *s* melancholia *f*
bluff *s* rupes *f*; promunturium *n*
bluff *adj* rusticus; declivis; ventosus
bluff *vt* fallĕre, decipĕre; *vi* ampullari, gloriari
blunder *s* (*in writing*) mendum *n*; error *m,* erratum *n*
blunder *vi* offendĕre, errare
blunderer *s* homo ineptus *m*
blunt *adj* hebes; obtusus; (*fig*) inurbanus, rusticus; **—ly** plane, liberius
blunt *vt* hebetare, obtundĕre, retundĕre
bluntness *s* hebetudo *f*; (*fig*) candor *m*
blur *s* macula *f*
blur *vt* obscurare
blurt *vt* **to — out** inconsultum projicĕre
blush *s* rubor *m*
blush *vi* erubescĕre
bluster *vi* declamitare; fremĕre, strepĕre
bluster *s* jactatio, declamatio *f*; fremit·us -ūs, strepit·us -ūs *m*
boar *s* aper *m*; verres *m*
board *s* (*plank*) tabula *f*; (*table*) mensa *f*; (*food*) vict·us -ūs *m*; (*council, etc.*) collegium *n*; consilium *n*; concilium *n*; (*judicial*) quaestio *f*; (*for games*) abacus, alveus *m*
board *vt* **to — a ship** navem conscendĕre; **to — up** contabulare; *vi* **to — with** devertĕre ad (*with acc*)
boarder *s* convictor, hospes *m*

boardinghouse *s* contubernium *n*
boast *vi* se jactare, gloriari
boast *s* jactantia, jactatio, gloriatio, vanitas *f*
boastful *adj* gloriosus; **—ly** gloriose
boasting *s* gloriatio *f*
boat *s* linter *f*; cymba *f*; scapha *f*; navicula *f*
boatman *s* nauta, lintrarius *m*
bode *vt* portendĕre, praesagire
bodiless *adj* incorporalis
bodily *adj* corporeus; corporalis; in persona
bodily *adv* corporaliter
body *s* corpus *n*; (*corpse*) cadaver *n*; truncus *m*; (*person*) homo *m*; (*of troops*) man·us -ūs, caterva *f*; (*of cavalry*) turma *f*; (*of people*) numerus *m*, multitudo *f*; (*heavenly*) astrum *n*
bodyguard *s* stipatores, satellites *m pl*; cohors praetoria *f*
bog *s* palus *f*
boil *vt* fervefacĕre, coquĕre; **to — down** decoquĕre; *vi* fervēre, effervescere; (*fig*) aestuare
boil *s* furunculus *m*, ulcus *n*
boiler *s* (*vessel*) ahenum, caldarium *n*; (*kettle*) lebes *m*
boisterous *adj* procellosus; violentus, turbidus; **—ly** turbide, turbulente
bold *adj* audax; impavidus; (*rash*) temerarius; (*saucy*) insolens, protervus, impudens; (*language*) liber; (*stout*) intrepidus; **—ly** audacter; temere; fortiter; insolenter
boldness *s* audacia, fidentia *f*; (*in speech*) libertas, impudentia *f*
bolster *s* pulvinar *n*; (*of a bed*) cervical *n*
bolster *vt* supportare, adjuvare; **to — up** suffulcire
bolt *s* (*of a door*) pessulus *m*; (*of thunder*) fulmen *n*; (*pin*) clavus *m*; (*missile*) sagitta *f*, telum *n*
bolt *vt* obserare, oppessulare, claudĕre, occludĕre
bomb *s* pyrobolus *m*
bombard *vt* tormentis verberare; (*fig*) lacessĕre
bombardment *s* tormentis verberatio *f*
bombast *s* ampulla *f pl*
bombastic *adj* inflatus, tumidus; **to be —** ampullari
bond *s* vinculum *n*; nodus *m*; copula, catena *f*, jugum *n*; (*document*) syngrapha *f*
bondage *s* servitus *f*, servitium *n*; captivitas *f*
bondsman *s* servus *m*; verna *m*; addictus *m*
bone *s* os *n*; (*of fish*) spina *f*
boneless *adj* exos
bonfire *s* ignes festi *m pl*
bonnet *s* redimiculum *n*
bony *adj* osseus
book *s* liber *m*; volumen *n*; codex *m*;
bookcase *s* foruli *m pl*; librarium *n*; pegma *n*
bookish *adj* libris deditus
bookkeeper *s* calculator *m*; actuarius *m*
bookshelf *s* pluteus *m*
bookstore *s* bibliopolum *n*, libraria taberna *f*
bookworm *s* tinea *f*; (*fig*) librorum helluo *m*
boom *s* (*of a ship*) longurius *m*; (*of a harbor*) obex *m* & *f*, repagulum *n*
boom *vi* resonare
boon *s* bonum, donum *n*
boor *s* rusticus *m*
boorish *adj* agrestis, rusticus; **—ly** rustice
boost *vt* efferre
boot *s* calceus *m*; caliga *f*; (*peasant's*) pero *m*; (*tragic*) cothurnus *m*; **to —** insuper
boot *vi* prodesse; **what boots it?** cui bono?
booth *s* taberna *f*, tabernaculum *n*
booty *s* praeda *f*; spolia *n pl*
border *s* (*edge*) margo *m* & *f*; (*seam*) limbus *m*, fimbria *f*; (*boundary*) finis, terminus *m*
border *vt* tangĕre, attingĕre; circumjacēre; *vi* **to — on** adjacēre (*with dat*), attingĕre; imminēre (*with dat*)
bordering *adj* affinis, finitimus
bore *vt* terebrare, perforare; excavare; (*fig*) (*to weary*) obtundĕre, fatigare
bore *s* (*tool*) terebra *f*; (*hole*) foramen *n*; (*fig*) importunus, molestus *m*
borer *s* terebra *f*
born *adj* natus; genitus; **to be —** nasci; (*fig*) oriri
borough *s* municipium *n*
borrow *vt* mutuari; (*fig*) imitari
borrowed *adj* mutuatus, mutuus; alienus
borrowing *s* mutuatio *f*
bosom *s* (*breast*) pectus *n*; sin·us -ūs *m*; (*of female*) mammillae *f pl*; (*fig*) gremium *n*
Bosphorus *s* Bosporus *m*
boss *s* bulla *f*; (*of a shield*) umbo *m*; (*of a book*) umbilicus *m*
boss *vt* (*to order about*) dominari in (*with acc*)
botanical *adj* botanicus
botanist *s* herbarius *m*
botany *s* herbaria *f*
botch *s* bubo, carbunculus *m*; (*bungling work*) scruta *n pl*
botch *vt* male sarcire; male gerĕre
both *adj* ambo; uterque
both *pron* ambo; uterque
both *conj* **— . . . and** et . . . et; cum . . . tum; vel . . . vel
bother *vt* vexare, sollicitare; molestus esse (*with dat*); *vi* **to — about** operam dare (*with dat*)
bother *s* negotium *n*; vexatio *f*; sollicitudo *f*
bottle *s* ampulla *f*; lagoena *f*
bottle *vt* in ampullas infundĕre
bottom *s* fundus *m*; (*of a ship*) carina *f*; (*dregs*) faex *f*, sedimentum *n*; (*of a mountain*) radix *f*; **the — of** imus; **the — of the sea** imum mare *n*
bottom *adj* imus, infimus

bottomless *adj* fundo carens, immensus; profundus
bough *s* ramus *m*
boulder *s* saxum *n*
bounce *vi* resilire, resultare
bound *adj* alligatus, obligatus, obstrictus; **it is — to happen** necesse est accidat; **to be — for** tendĕre ad (*with acc*)
bound *s* salt·us -us *m*; (*limit*) modus, terminus *m*; **to set —s** modum facĕre
bound *vt* finire, definire, terminare; *vi* (*to leap*) salire
boundary *s* finis, terminus *m*; (*fortified*) limes *m*
boundless *adj* infinitus, immensus; profundus
bountiful *adj* largus, benignus; **—ly** benigne, large
bounty *s* largitas, benignitas, liberalitas *f*; copia *f*
bouquet *s* corollarium *n*; (*of wine*) flos m
bow *s* arc·us -ūs *m*
bow *s* (*of a ship*) prora *f*; (*greeting*) summissio capitis *f*
bow *vt* flectĕre, inclinare; (*one's head*) demittĕre; *vi* flecti; (*fig*) **to — to** (*to accede to*) obtemperare (*with dat*), obsequi
bowels *s* intestina, viscera *n pl*
bower *s* trichlia *f*, umbraculum *n*
bowl *s* cratera, patera *f*; (*for cooking*) catina *f*
bowlegged *adj* valgus
bowman *s* sagittarius *m*
bowstring *s* nervus *m*
box *s* arca, cista *f*; scrinium *n*; (*for medicine*) pyxis *f*; (*tree*) buxus *f*
box *vt* includĕre; pugnis certare cum (*with abl*); **to — the ears of** alapam adhibēre (*with dat*)
boxer *s* pugil *m*
boxing glove *s* caest·us -ūs *m*
boxing match *s* pugilatio *f*
boy *s* puer, puerulus *m*
boyhood *s* pueritia *f*; aetas puerilis *f*
boyish *adj* puerilis; **—ly** pueriliter
brace *s* (*strap*) fascia *f*; (*couple*) par *n*; copula *f*; (*in architecture*) fibula *f*
brace *vt* ligare, alligare; (*to strengthen*) firmare
bracelet *s* armilla *f*
bracket *s* mutulus *m*; **—s** (*in writing*) unci *m pl*
brag *vi* se jactare, gloriari
braggart *s* jactator, salaco *m*
bragging *s* jactantia *f*
braid *s* limbus *m*; (*of hair*) cincinnus *m*
braid *vt* plectĕre, plicare
brain *s* cerebrum *n*; ingenium *n*
brainless *adj* stolidus, inconsultus, socors
brake *s* (*fern*) filix *f*; (*thicket*) dumetum *n*; (*on wheel*) sufflamen *n*
bramble *s* rubus *m*; (*thicket*) rubetum *n*; (*thorny bush*) sentis, vepris *m*
branch *s* (*of tree*) ramus *m*; (*of pedigree*) stemma *n*; (*division*) pars *f*
branch *vi* (*of trees*) germinare; **to — out** ramos porrigĕre; (*fig*) dividi, scindi, diffundi
brand *s* (*mark*) stigma *n*, nota *f*; (*of fire*) fax *f*, torris *m*; (*type*) genus *n*
brand *vt* inurĕre, notare
branding iron *s* cauter *m*
brandish *vt* vibrare
brandy *s* aqua vitae *f*; vini spirit·us -ūs *m*; spirit·us -ūs gallicus *m*
brass *s* orichalcum, aes *n*
brat *s* infans *m & f*
brave *adj* fortis, animosus, strenuus; **—ly** fortiter, strenue
brave *vt* sustinēre
bravery *s* fortitudo *f*; virtus *f*
bravo *interj* eu!, euge!, bene!, macte!
brawl *s* rixa *f*, jurgium *n*
brawl *vi* rixari, jurgare
brawler *s* rixator, rabula *m*
brawling *adj* contentiosus, jurgans
brawn *s* callum aprugnum *n*; (*muscle*) lacertus, torus *m*
brawny *adj* lacertosus, robustus
bray *vi* (*of asses*) rudĕre; (*of elephants*) barrire; (*to cry out*) emugire
braying *s* tritura *f*; barrit·us -ūs *m*; rugit·us -ūs *m*
brazen *adj* aënus; (*fig*) impudens
brazier *s* foculus *m*
breach *s* ruptura, ruina *f*; (*of treaty*) violatio *f*; dissidium *n*
bread *s* panis *m*; (*fig*) vict·us -ūs *m*
breadth *s* latitudo *f*
break *vt* frangĕre; rumpĕre; **to — apart** diffringĕre; **to — down** demoliri, destruĕre; **to — in** (*to tame*) domare, subigĕre; **to — in pieces** dirumpĕre; **to — off** abrumpĕre; (*friendship or action*) dirumpĕre; (*a meeting*) interrumpĕre; **to — open** effringĕre; **to — up** interrumpĕre, dissolvĕre; *vi* frangi; rumpi; (*of day*) illucescĕre; (*of strength*) deficĕre; **to — forth** erumpĕre; **to — into** irrumpĕre; invadĕre; **to — off** desinĕre; **to — out** erumpĕre; (*of trouble*) exardescĕre; (*of war*) exoriri; (*of fire*) grassari; **to — through** perrumpĕre; **to — up** dissolvi, dilabi; (*of a meeting*) dimitti; **to — with** dissidēre ab (*with abl*)
break *s* interruptio *f*, intervallum *n*; interstitium *n*
breakage *s* fractura *f*
breakdown *s* calamitas *f*; frustratio *f*; (*of health*) debilitas *f*; (*of a machine*) defect·us -ūs *m*
breaker *s* fluct·us -ūs *m*
breakfast *s* prandium *n*
breakfast *vi* prandēre
breakup *s* dissolutio *f*
breast *s* pectus *n*; (*of a woman*) mamma *f*; (*fig*) praecordia *n pl*; **to make a clean — of** confitēri
breastbone *s* sternum *n*; os pectorale *n*
breastplate *s* lorica *f*; thorax *m*
breath *s* spirit·us -ūs *m*, anima *f*; halit·us -ūs *m*; **— of air** aura *f*; **deep —** anhelit·us -ūs *m*; **to catch one's —** obstipescĕre; **to hold**

one's breath animam continēre; **to take one's — away** exanimare; **to waste one's —** operam perdĕre
breathe *vt* ducĕre; spirare; (*to whisper*) susurrare; **to — out** exspirare; *vi* spirare, respirare; **to — upon** inspirare (*with dat*)
breathing *s* respiratio *f*; halit·us -ūs *m*; (*gram*) spirit·us -ūs *m*
breathless *adj* exanimis, exanimus; exanimatus
breeches *s* bracae *f pl*
breed *s* genus *n*
breed *vt* parĕre, gignĕre; (*to cause*) producĕre; (*to engender*) procreare, educare; (*to raise*) alĕre; (*horses*) pascĕre
breeder *s* (*man*) generator *m*; (*stallion*) admissarius *m*; (*animal*) matrix; (*fig*) nutrix *f*
breeding *s* fetura *f*; educatio *f*; **good —** urbanitas, humanitas *f*
breeze *s* aura *f*
breezy *adj* ventosus
brethren *s* fratres *m pl*
brevity *s* brevitas, breviloquentia *f*
brew *vt* coquĕre; *vi* excitari, concitari
bribe *s* pretium *n*, merces *f*
bribe *vt* corrumpĕre, largiri
briber *s* corruptor, largitor *m*
bribery *s* corruptio, corruptela, largitio *f*; ambit·us -ūs *m*
brick *s* later *m*
brick *adj* latericius
bricklayer *s* laterum structor *m*
bridal *adj* nuptialis
bride *s* nupta *f*
bridegroom *s* maritus *m*
bridesmaid *s* pronuba *f*
bridge *s* pons *m*
bridge *vt* pontem imponĕre (*with dat*)
bridle *s* frenum *n*
brief *adj* brevis, concisus; **—ly** breviter, paucis verbis
brief *s* diploma *n*; sententiola *f*; summarium *n*
brigade *s* (*infantry*) legio *f*; (*cavalry*) turma *f*
brigadier *s* tribunus militum *m*
brigand *s* latro, latrunculus *m*
bright *adj* clarus; lucidus, splendidus; nitidus, candidus; (*flashing*) fulgidus; (*smart*) argutus; **—ly** lucide, clare, splendide
brighten *vt* illustrare, illuminare; *vi* lucescĕre; splendescĕre; clarescĕre; (*of a person*) in hilaritatem solvi
brightness *s* nitor, splendor, fulgor, candor *m*; (*of the sky*) serenitas *f*
brilliance *s* splendor *m*; fulgor *m*; (*of style*) nitor *m*, lumen *n*
brilliant *adj* splendidus; nitens; (*fig*) praeclarus, insignis, luculentus; **—ly** splendide, praeclare, luculenter
brim *s* ora, margo *f*, labrum *n*; **to fill to the —** explēre
brimful *adj* ad summum plenus
brimstone *s* sulfur *n*
brine *s* muria *f*, salsamentum *n*; (*sea*) salum *n*
bring *vt* ferre, afferre, inferre; (*by carriage, etc.*) advehĕre; **to — about** efficĕre, perducĕre; **to — back** referre, reducĕre; reportare; (*fig*) revocare; (*by force*) redigĕre; dejicĕre; **to — forth** prodĕre, depromĕre; parĕre; (*to yield*) ferre, efferre; **to — forward** proferre, efferre, agĕre; **to — in** inferre; invehĕre; inducĕre; (*as a farm, etc.*) reddĕre; **to — off** dissuadēre; **to — on** afferre; adducĕre; (*fig*) objicĕre; **to — out** efferre; producĕre; excire; **to — over** perducĕre, traducĕre; (*fig*) perducĕre, trahĕre; conciliare; **to — to** adducĕre; appellĕre; (*fig*) persuadēre; **to — together** conferre; (*to assemble*) contrahĕre; (*fig*) conciliare; **to — to pass** efficĕre; **to — under** subigĕre; **to — up** subducĕre; (*children*) educare; (*to vomit*) evomĕre
brink *s* margo *f*; ora *f*; (*fig*) extremitas *f*
brisk *adj* alacer, agilis, vividus; laetus; **to be —** vigēre; **—ly** alacriter, agiliter·
briskness *s* alacritas *f*, vigor *m*
bristle *s* seta *f*
bristle *vi* horrēre
bristly *adj* setiger, setosus; hirsutus; horridus
Britain *s* Britannia *f*
British *adj* Britannicus
brittle *adj* fragilis
broach *vt* in medium proferre
broad *adj* latus, largus, amplus; (*fig*) manifestus, apertus; **—ly** late
broadcast *vt* divulgare, disseminare
broaden *vt* dilatare
broadsword *s* gladius *m*
brocade *s* Attalica *n pl*
broccoli *s* brassica oleracea Botrytis *f*
brochure *s* libellus *m*
broil *s* rixa, turba *f*
broil *vt* torrēre
broken *adj* fractus; intermissus; dirutus; (*fig*) confectus; (*of speech*) refractus, infractus, corrupte pronuntiatus
brokenhearted *adj* abjectus, dejectus
broker *s* transactor, institor *m*
bronze *s* aes *n*
bronze *adj* aeneus, a(h)enus, aeratus
brooch *s* fibula *f*
brood *s* proles *f*; (*chicks*) pullities *f*
brood *vi* (*as a hen*) incubare; (*fig*) **to — over** agitare, meditari
brook *vt* ferre, tolerare
broom *s* genista *f*; scopae *f pl*
broth *s* jus *n*
brothel *s* lupanar *n*, ganea *f*
brother *s* frater *m*
brotherhood *s* germanitas, fraternitas *f*; (*fig*) sodalitium *n*
brother-in-law *s* levir *m*; sororis maritus *m*
brotherly *adj* fraternus
brow *s* supercilium *n*; frons *f*; (*of a hill*) dorsum *n*
browbeat *vt* terrēre, deprimĕre, exagitare, objurgare

brown *adj* fulvus, fuscus, spadix; (*of skin*) adustus
browse *vi* depasci
bruise *vt* contundĕre, sugillare; infringĕre
bruise *s* contusio *f*, contusum *n*, sugillatio *f*
brunette *s* puella subfusca *f*
brunt *s* impet·us -ūs *m*; vehementia *f*
brush *s* scopula *f*; (*painter's*) penicillus *m*; (*bushy tail*) muscarium *n*; (*skirmish*) aggressio *f*
brush *vt* verrĕre, purgare; **to — aside** neglegĕre, spernĕre; **to — away** amovēre
brutal *adj* atrox, immanis, inhumanus; **—ly** atrociter, immaniter, inhumane
brutality *s* atrocitas, ferocitas, saevitia, immanitas *f*
brute *adj* brutus; stupidus
brute *s* belua, bestia *f*
brutish *adj* ferinus; stupidus
bubble *s* bulla *f*
bubble *vi* bullire; (*to gush up*) scatēre
bubbling *s* bullit·us -ūs *m*; scatebra *f*
buccaneer *s* pirata *m*
buck *s* cervus *m*; (*he-goat*) hircus *m*; (*male rabbit*) cuniculus *m*
bucket *s* hama, situla, fidelia *f*
buckle *vt* fibulā nectĕre; *vi* flectĕre
buckle *s* fibula *f*, spinther *m*
buckler *s* parma *f*
bucolic *adj* bucolicus, agrestis
bud *s* gemma *f*, germen *n*; (*of a flower*) flosculus *m*
bud *vi* gemmare, germinare
budding *s* germinatio *f*; emplastratio *f*
budge *vt* ciēre, movēre; *vi* movēri, cedĕre
budget *s* saccus *m*; publicae pecuniae ratio *f*
buffalo *s* urus *m*
buffet *s* (*sideboard*) abacus *m*; (*slap*) alapa *f*; (*fig*) plaga *f*
buffet *vt* jactare
buffoon *s* scurra *m*; sannio, balatro *m*; **to play the —** scurrari
bug *s* cimex *m* & *f*
bugle *s* buccina *f*
build *vt* aedificare; struĕre, condĕre; (*road*) munire; (*hopes*) ponĕre; **to — up** exstruĕre
builder *s* aedificator, structor *m*
building *s* (*act*) aedificatio *f*; exstructio *f*; (*structure*) aedificium *n*
bulb *s* bulbus *m*
bulge *vi* tumēre, tumescĕre; prominēre
bulk *s* amplitudo, magnitudo *f*; (*mass*) moles *f*; (*greater part*) major pars *f*
bulkiness *s* magnitudo *f*
bulky *adj* crassus; ingens; corpulentus; onerosus
bull *s* taurus *m*
bulldog *s* canis Molossus *m*
bullet *s* glans *f*
bulletin *s* libellus *m*
bullfrog *s* rana ocellata *f*
bullion *s* aurum infectum *n*; argentum infectum *n*; massa *f*
bully *s* salaco, thraso *m*
bully *vt* procaciter lacessĕre
bulwark *s* agger *m*; propugnaculum *n*; moenia *n pl*
bump *s* (*swelling*) tuber *n*; (*thump*) plaga *f*
bump *vt* pulsare, pellĕre; *vi* **to — against** offendĕre
bun *s* libum *n*, placenta *f*
bunch *s* fasciculus *m*; (*of grapes*) racemus *m*
bundle *s* fascis, fasciculus *m*; vesiculus *m*
bundle *vt* consarcinare
bungle *vt* inscite gerĕre; inscite agĕre; *vi* errare
bungler *s* homo rudis *m*
buoy *s* cortex *m*
buoy *vt* **to — up** attollĕre, sublevare
buoyancy *s* levitas *f*; (*fig*) hilaritas *f*
buoyant *adj* levis; (*fig*) hilaris
burden *s* onus *n*; (*fig*) scrupulus *m*
burden *vt* onerare; opprimĕre
burdensome *adj* onerosus, gravis, molestus
bureau *s* armarium, scrinium *n*
burglar *s* fur *m*
burglary *s* (domūs) effractura *f*
burial *s* (*act*) sepultura *f*; (*ceremony*) funus *n*
burial place *s* sepulturae locus *m*; sepulcrum *n*
burlesque *s* ridicula imitatio *f*
burly *adj* corpulentus
burn *vt* urĕre, cremare; (*to set on fire*) incendĕre; **to — down** deurĕre; **to — out** exurĕre; **to — up** amburĕre, comburĕre; *vi* flagrare; ardēre; **to — out** extingui; **to — up** conflagrare
burn *s* adustio *f*; combustum *n*
burning *s* ustio, adustio *f*; deflagratio *f*
burning *adj* ardens; fervens
burrow *s* cuniculus *m*
burrow *vi* defodĕre
bursar *s* dispensator *m*
burst *s* impet·us -ūs *m*; eruptio *f*; (*noise*) fragor *m*
burst *vt* rumpĕre, dirumpĕre; **to — open** effrangĕre; *vi* dirumpi; **to — forth** prorumpĕre; (*of tears*) prosilire; **to — in** irrumpĕre; **to — out** erumpĕre; **to — out laughing** cachinnum tollĕre
bury *vt* sepelire; (*to hide*) abdĕre, condĕre
bush *s* dumetum *n*, frutex *m*; (*of hair*) caesaries *f*
bushel *s* medimnus, modius *m*
bushy *adj* (*full of bushes*) dumosus; (*bush-like*) fruticosus
busily *adv* industrie, sedulo, impigre
business *s* negotium *n*; (*trade, calling*) ars *f*; (*employment*) occupatio *f*; (*matter*) res *f*; **to mind one's own —** negotium suum agĕre
businessman *s* negotiator *m*
buskin *s* cothurnus *m*
bust *s* imago *f*; effigies *f*
bustle *s* festinatio *f*; trepidatio *f*

bustle *vi* festinare; trepidare; **to — about** discurrĕre
busy *adj* occupatus; negotiosus; operosus, impiger; (*meddling*) molestus
busybody *s* ardelio *m*
but *prep* praeter (*with acc*)
but *adv* modo, tantum
but *conj* sed; ast, at; atqui; ceterum; vero, verum; autem; **— if** quodsi; sin, sin autem; **— if not** sin aliter, sin minus
butcher *s* lanius *m*; (*fig*) carnifex *m*
butcher *vt* (*animals*) caedĕre; (*people*) trucidare
butcher shop *s* macellum *n*
butchery *s* caedes, trucidatio *f*
butler *s* promus *m*
butt *s* (*mark*) meta *f*; (*cask*) dolium *n*; (*mound*) agger *m*; **— of ridicule** ludibrium *n*
butt *vt* arietare; *vi* **to — in** interpellare
butter *s* butyrum *n*
butter *vt* butyro inducĕre
buttercup *s* ranunculus tuberosus *m*
butterfly *s* papilio *m*
buttermilk *s* lactis serum *n*
buttock *s* clunis *m & f*
button *s* bulla *f*
button *vt* nectĕre, confibulare
buttress *s* anterides *f pl*; fulcrum *n*
buttress *vt* suffulcire
buxom *adj* alacer, hilaris, laetus
buy *vt* emĕre, mercari; **to — back** *or* **off** redimĕre; **to — up** coemĕre
buyer *s* emptor *m*
buying *s* emptio *f*
buzz *s* bombus *m*; murmur *n*
buzz *vi* bombilare; (*in the ear*) insusurrare
buzzard *s* buteo *m*
by *prep* (*agency*) a, ab (*with abl*); (*of place*) ad (*with acc*), apud (*with acc*), juxta (*with acc*), prope (*with acc*); (*along*) secundum (*with acc*); (*past*) praeter (*with acc*); (*of time*) ante (*with acc*); (*in oaths*) per (*with acc*); **— and —** mox; **— means of** per (*with acc*); **— oneself** solus
bygone *adj* praeteritus; priscus
bylaw *s* praescriptum *n*; regula *f*
bystander *s* arbiter *m*
byway *s* trames *m*, semita *f*, deverticulum *n*
byword *s* adagium *n*

C

cabal *s* factio *f*; societas clandestina *f*
cabbage *s* brassica *f*, caulis *m*
cabin *s* (*cottage*) tugurium *n*; (*on a ship*) stega *f*
cabinet *s* armarium *n*; scrinium *n*; cistula *f*; (*in government*) principis consilium *n*
cable *s* funis, rudens *m*; (*anchor*) ancorale *n*
cackle *vi* gracillare; (*fig*) deblaterare
cackle *s* glocitatio *f*; (*fig*) gerrae *f pl*; clangor *m*
cacophony *s* dissonae voces *f pl*
cactus *s* cactus *f*
cadaver *s* cadaver *n*
cadence *s* numerus *m*
cadet *s* tiro *m*; discipulus militaris *m*
cage *s* cavea *f*, aviarium *n*; septum *n*
cage *vt* includĕre
cajole *vt* inescare, lactare, blandiri
cake *s* libum *n*, placenta *f*
calamitous *adj* calamitosus; funestus; exitiosus
calamity *s* calamitas *f*; clades *f*; malum *n*; res adversae *f pl*
calculate *vt* computare; (*fig*) aestimare, existimare
calculated *adj* aptus, accommodatus
calculation *s* computatio, ratio *f*; (*fig*) ratiocinatio *f*
calculator *s* computator *m*; ratiocinator *m*
caldron *s* ahenum *n*, lebes *m*
calendar *s* fasti *m pl*; calendarium *n*
calends *s* Kalendae *f pl*
calf *s* vitulus *m*; (*of the leg*) sura *f*
caliber *s* (*fig*) ingenium *n*, indoles *f*
call *vt* vocare; (*to name*) appellare; **to — aside** sevocare; **to — away** avocare; (*fig*) devocare; **to — back** revocare; **to — down** devocare; **to — forth** evocare, provocare; (*fig*) exciēre, elicĕre; **to — in** advocare; (*money*) cogĕre; **to — off** avocare, revocare; **to — together** convocare; **to — to mind** recordari; **to — to witness** testari; **to — up** excitare, suscitare, elicĕre; *vi* **to — on** *or* **upon** (*for help*) implorare; (*to visit*) visĕre
call *s* vocatio *f*; clamor *m*; (*visit*) salutatio *f*; (*requisition*) postulatio *f*; (*whistle*) fistula *f*
calling *s* (*profession*) ars *f*, artificium *n*
callous *adj* callosus; (*fig*) durus; expers sensūs; **to become —** occallescĕre; obdurescĕre
calm *adj* tranquillus, placidus, sedatus, quietus; (*mentally*) aequus; **—ly** tranquille, aequo animo, placide
calm *s* tranquillitas *f*, tranquillum *n*
calm *vt* pacare, placare, sedare, mulcēre; *vi* **to — down** defervescĕre
calmness *s* tranquillitas *f*; serenitas *f*
calumny *s* maledictum *n*, obtrectatio *f*, opprobria *n pl*
camel *s* camelus *m*
cameo *s* imago ectypa *f*
camouflage *s* dissimulatio *f*
camouflage *vt* dissimulare

camp *s* castra *n pl*; **summer —** aestiva *n pl*; **to strike —** castra movēre; **winter —** hiberna *n pl*
camp *adj* castrensis
camp *vi* castra poněre
campaign *s* aestiva *n pl*; stipendium *n*; expeditio *f*
campaign *vi* stipendium merēre; expeditioni interesse
campaigner *s* veteranus *m*
camphor *s* camphora *f*
can *s* hirnea *f*
can *vi* posse; scire; **I — not** nequeo; nescio
canal *s* fossa navigabilis *f*
canary *s* fringilla Canaria *f*
cancel *vt* delēre, expungěre; abrogare, tollere
cancellation *s* deletio, abolitio *f*
cancer *s* cancer *m*
cancerous *adj* cancerosus, canceraticus
candid *adj* candidus, apertus, liber, simplex; **—ly** candide
candidacy *s* petitio *f*
candidate *s* petitor *m*; candidatus *m*
candied *adj* saccharo conditus
candle *s* candela *f*; (*taper*) cera *f*
candlelight *s* lucerna *f*; **to study by —** lucubrare
candlestick *s* candelabrum *n*
candor *s* candor *m*, simplicitas, ingenuitas *f*
candy *s* saccharum crystallinum *n*
cane *s* baculus *m*; virga *f*; (*reed*) harundo *f*
cane *vt* baculo *or* virgā ferire; verberare
canine *adj* caninus
canister *s* canistrum *n*, pyxis *f*
canker *s* (*of plants*) rubigo, robigo *f*; (*fig*) aerugo *f*
cannibal *s* anthropophagus *m*
cannon *s* tormentum *n*
cannon shot *s* tormenti ict·us -ūs *m*
canoe *s* linter *m*
canon *s* regula, norma *f*; canon *m*
canonical *adj* canonicus
canopy *s* canopeum *n*; aulaea *n pl*
cant *s* fucus *m*
cantata *s* carmen *n*
canteen *s* caupona castrensis *f*
canter *s* lenis atque quadrupedans grad·us -ūs *m*
canter *vi* leniter quadrupedare
canticle *s* canticum *n*
canto *s* liber *m*
canton *s* pagus *m*
canvas *s* linteum crassum *n*, carbasus *f*, carbasa *n pl*
canvass *s* (*legal*) ambitio *f*; (*illegal*) ambit·us -ūs *m*
canvass *vt* circumire, prensare; *vi* ambire
cap *s* pileus *m*; calyptra *f*; (*in rituals*) galerus *m*
capability *s* facultas, habilitas *f*
capable *adj* capax; idoneus, potens, doctus
capably *adv* bene, docte
capacity *s* capacitas, mensura *f*; modus *m*; ingenium *n*
cape *s* promontorium *n*; (*garment*) humerale *n*, chlamys *f*
caper *vi* saltare, tripudire, assilire; (*of animals*) lascivire
caper *s* salt·us -ūs *m*, exsultatio *f*
capital *adj* praecipuus, princeps; (*law*) capitalis; (*of letters*) uncialis; (*outstanding*) insignis, eximius
capital *s* (*architecture*) capitulum *n*; (*chief city*) caput *n*; (*com*) sors *f*, caput *n*; faenus *n*
capitalist *s* faenerator *m*
capitol *s* capitolium *n*
capitulate *vi* ex pacto urbem traděre; se deděre
capitulation *s* deditio *f*
capon *s* capus, capo *m*
caprice *s* libido, inconstantia *f*
capricious *adj* levis, inconstans; ventosus, mobilis; **—ly** leviter, inconstanter, ex libidine
capricorn *s* capricornus *m*
capsize *vt* evertere; *vi* everti
capsule *s* capsula *f*
captain *s* (*in infantry*) centurio *m*; (*in cavalry*) praefectus *m*; (*in navy*) navarchus *m*, (*in merchant marine*) magister *m*
caption *s* caput *n*
captious *adj* argutus; morosus; fallax; **—ly** captiose, morose
captivate *vt* captare, delenire, mulcēre
captive *adj* captivus
captive *s* captivus *m*
captivity *s* captivitas *f*
captor *s* captor *m*; expugnator *m*; victor *m*
capture *s* captura, comprehensio *f*
capture *vt* capěre, excipěre
car *s* carrus *m*
carat *s* unciae triens *m*
caravan *s* commeat·us -ūs, comitat·us -ūs *m*
carbon *s* carbonium *n*
carbuncle *s* carbunculus, furunculus *m*
carcass *s* cadaver *n*
card *s* charta *f*; (*ticket*) tessera *f*; (*for combing wool*) pecten *n*
card *vt* pectere
cardboard *s* charta crassior *f*
cardinal *adj* principalis, praecipuus
cardinal *s* (*eccl*) cardinalis *m*
care *s* cura, sollicitudo *f*; (*diligence*) diligentia *f*; (*charge*) tutela, curatio, custodia *f*; **to take — of** curare
care *vi* curare; **to — for** (*to look after*) curare; (*to be fond of*) amare
career *s* curriculum *n*; decurs·us -ūs *m*; (*pol*) curs·us -ūs honorum *m*
carefree *adj* securus
careful *adj* (*attentive*) attentus, diligens; (*cautious*) cautus; (*of work*) accuratus; **—ly** diligenter; caute; accurate, exquisite
careless *adj* neglegens, incautus; (*loose*) dissolutus; **—ly** neglegenter; incuriose; (*loosely*) solute
carelessness *s* incuria, neglegentia *f*
caress *s* blanditiae *f pl*; complex·us -ūs *m*
caress *vt* blandiri, fovēre

cargo *s* onus *n*
caricature *s* imago in pejus detorta *f*
caricature *vt* in pejus fingĕre
carnage *s* caedes, strages *f*
carnal *adj* sensualis, carnalis
carnival *s* feriae *f pl*
carnivorous *adj* carnivorus
carol *s* cant·us -ūs *m*; carmen *n*; **Christmas —** hymnus de Christi natu *m*
carol *vi* cantare, cantillare
carouse *vi* comissari, perpotare, perbacchari
carp *s* cyprinus *m*
carp *vi* **to — at** carpĕre, mordēre, vellicare
carpenter *s* faber tignarius *m*
carpentry *s* ars fabrilis *f*
carpet *s* tapes *m*, tapeta *f*
carriage *s* (*act*) vectura *f*; (*vehicle*) vehiculum *n*; raeda *f*, petorritum *n*; (*bearing, posture*) habit·us -ūs, gest·us -ūs, incess·us -ūs *m*
carrier *s* portitor, vector, bajulus *m*; (*of letters*) tabularius *m*
carrion *s* caro morticina *f*
carrot *s* carota *f*; pastinaca *f*
carry *vt* portare, ferre; (*by vehicle*) vehĕre; gerĕre; (*law*) perferre; **to — away** auferre; evehĕre; (*fig*) rapĕre; **to — back** referre; revehĕre; **to — in** importare; invehĕre; **to — off** auferre; rapĕre; **to — on** promovēre; perducĕre; (*fig*) exercēre; gerĕre; **to — out** efferre, exportare; evehĕre; (*fig*) exsequi; **to — over** transferre; **to — round** circumferre; **to — through** perferre; *vi* (*of sound*) audiri; **to — on** pergĕre; se gerĕre
cart *s* plaustrum *n*; curr·us -ūs *m*; curriculus *m*; **to put the — before the horse** praeposteris consiliis uti
cart *vt* plaustro vehĕre; **to — away** auferre
carve *vt* sculpĕre; caelare, incidĕre; (*at table*) secare
carver *s* caelator *m*; (*at table*) carptor *m*; (*knife*) cultellus *m*
carving *s* caelatura *f*
cascade *s* praeceps aquae laps·us -ūs *m*
case *s* (*law*) causa, actio *f*; (*matter*) res *f*; (*instance*) exemplum *n*; (*container*) involucrum *n*; theca *f*; capsula *f*; (*state*) stat·us -ūs *m*; conditio *f*; (*gram*) cas·us -ūs *m*; **in —** si; **in that —** ergo; **since that is the —** quae cum ita sint
cash *s* pecunia numerata *f*; nummi *m pl*; praesens pecunia *f*
cashier *s* dispensator *m*
cash payment *s* repraesentatio *f*
cask *s* cadus *m*, dolium *n*
casket *s* arcula *f*; pyxis *f*
cast *s* (*throw*) jact·us -ūs *m*; (*mold*) typus *m*; forma *f*
cast *vt* jacĕre; (*metal*) fundĕre; **to — about** circumjacĕre; **to — away** abjicĕre; dejicĕre; **to — down** dejicĕre; (*fig*) affligĕre; **to — in** injicĕre; **to — in one's teeth** reprobrare; **to — off** (*the skin*) exuĕre; (*fig*) amovēre, ponĕre; repudiare; **to — out** ejicĕre, expellĕre; **to — over** trajicĕre; **to — upon** superinjicĕre; (*fig*) aspergĕre; conferre; *vi* **to — off** ancoram tollĕre
castaway *s* perditus *m*; ejectus *m*
caste *s* ordo *m*; **to lose —** degenerare
castigate *vt* castigare
castigation *s* castigatio *f*
castle *s* castellum *n*; arx *f*
castor oil *s* cicinum oleum *n*
castrate *vt* castrare
castration *s* castratio, castratura *f*
casual *adj* fortuitus; (*person*) neglegens; **—ly** fortuito, forte, casu
casualty *s* cas·us -ūs *m*; occisus *m*
cat *s* feles *f*
cataclysm *s* cataclysmos *m*
catacombs *s* puticuli *m pl*; catacumbae *f pl*
catalogue *s* catalogus *m*; index *m*
cataract *s* cataracta *f*, cataractes *m*; (*of the eye*) glaucoma *n*
catastrophe *s* calamitas *f*; ruina *f*; exit·us -ūs *n*
catch *vt* capĕre, captare; (*by surprise*) comprehendĕre; (*falling object*) suscipĕre; (*in a net*) illaquēre; (*with bait*) inescare; (*fire*) concipĕre; (*disease*) contrahĕre; *vi* **to — at** arripĕre; (*fig*) captare; **to — up with** consequi
catching *adj* contagiosus; (*fig*) gratus
categorical *adj* categoricus; **—ly** categorice, sine exceptione
category *s* categoria *f*; numerus *m*
cater *vi* obsonari; cibos suppeditare
caterer *s* obsonator *m*
caterpillar *s* eruca *f*
cathedral *s* ecclesia cathedralis *f*
catholic *adj* catholicus, generalis
cattle *s* pecus *n*
cauliflower *s* brassica oleracea botryitis *f*
cause *s* causa, res, materia *f*; (*pol*) partes *f pl*
cause *vt* facĕre, efficĕre; (*feelings*) exciēre, movēre
causeless *adj* sine causa; vanus
causeway *s* agger *m*
caustic *adj* causticus; (*fig*) mordax, acerbus
caution *s* cautio *f*; cura *f*; prudentia *f*; monitio *f*, monitum *n*
caution *vt* (ad)monēre
cautious *adj* cautus, consideratus; circumspectus; providus; **—ly** caute, prudenter; depetentim
cavalcade *s* pompa *f*
cavalier *s* eques *m*
cavalry *s* equitat·us -ūs *m*; equites *m pl*; copiae equestres *f pl*
cave *s* spec·us -ūs *m*; spelunca *f*; caverna *f*; antrum *n*
cavern *s* caverna *f*
cavernous *adj* cavernosus
caviar *s* ova acipenseris *n pl*
cavity *s* cavum *n*; caverna *f*
caw *vi* crocire, crocitare

cease *vi* desiněre, desistěre
ceaseless *adj* assiduus, perpetuus; **—ly** continenter, assidue, perpetuo
ceasing *s* cessatio, intermissio *f*
cedar *s* cedrus *f*
cedar *adj* cedreus, cedrinus
cede *vt* ceděre, conceděre
ceiling *s* laquear, lacunar *n*
celebrate *vt* celebrare; laudare, dicere
celebrated *adj* celeber; nobilis, notus, praeclarus
celebration *s* celebratio *f*; (*of rites*) sollemne *n*
celebrity *s* celebritas *f*; fama *f*; (*person*) vir illustris *m*
celery *s* heleoselinum *n*
celestial *adj* caelestis, divinus
celibacy *s* caelibat·us -ūs *m*, caelebs vita *f*
celibate *s* caelebs *m*
cell *s* cella *f*
cellar *s* cella *f*, cellarium *n*
cement *s* ferrumen *n*; caementum *n*; (*glue*) gluten *n*
cement *vt* conglutinare; ferruminare; *vi* coalescěre
cemetery *s* sepulcretum *n*
censer *s* turibulum *n*
censor *s* censor *m*
censorship *s* censura *f*; magisterium morum *n*
censurable *adj* reprehensione dignus; culpandus
censure *s* vituperatio *f*
censure *vt* animadvertěre, vituperare
census *s* cens·us -ūs *m*; civium enumeratio *f*
centaur *s* centaurus *m*
centenary *adj* centenarius
centenary *s* centesimus annus *m*
center *s* medium *n*; **in the — of the plain** in medio campo
center *vt* in centrum ponere; *vi* **to — on** niti (*with abl*)
central *adj* medius, centralis
centralize *vt* (*authority*) ad unum deferre
centurion *s* centurio *m*
century *s* (*pol*) centuria *f*; saeculum *f*
cereal *s* frumentum *n*
ceremonial *adj* caerimonialis, sollemnis; **—ly** sollemniter, rite
ceremonial *s* rit·us -ūs *m*
ceremonious *adj* sollemnis; (*person*) officiosus; **—ly** sollemniter; officiose
ceremony *s* caerimonia *f*, rit·us -ūs *m*; (*pomp*) apparat·us -ūs *m*
certain *adj* (*sure*) certus; (*indefinite*) quidam, nonnulus; **for —** certe, pro certo; **it is —** constat; **—ly** certe; profecto
certainty *s* certum *n*; (*belief*) fides *f*
certificate *s* testimonium *n*
certify *vt* recognoscěre, confirmare
cessation *s* cessatio, intermissio *f*; **— of hostilities** indutiae *f pl*
chafe *vt* urěre; (*with the hand*) fricare; (*to excoriate*) atterere; (*to vex*) irritare, succensěre; *vi* stomachari
chaff *s* palea *f*; (*fig*) quisquiliae *f pl*
chagrin *s* dolor *m*; stomachus *m*
chain *s* catena *f*; (*necklace*) troques *m & f*; (*fig*) series *f*
chain *vt* catenis constringěre; catenas injicěre (*with dat*)
chair *s* sella, cathedra *f*
chairman *s* praeses *m*
chalice *s* calix *m*
chalk *s* creta *f*; calx *f*
chalk *vt* cretā notare; cretā illiněre; **to — out** designare
chalky *adj* (*chalk-like*) cretaceus; (*full of chalk*) cretosus
challenge *s* provocatio *f*; (*law*) recusatio *f*
challenge *vt* provocare, lacessěre; (*law*) rejicěre; (*to reclaim*) arrogare
challenger *s* provocator *m*
chamber *s* cubiculum *n*, camera *f*, thalamus *m*; pars interior *f*
champ *vt & vi* mandere, morděre
champion *s* propugnator, defensor *m*; (*of a party*) antesignanus *m*
chance *s* (*accident*) cas·us -ūs, event·us -ūs *m*; fortuna *f*; (*fig*) alea *f*; (*probability*) spes *f*; **by —** casu, forte, fortuito
chance *vt* periclitari; *vi* acciděre, contingěre
chance *adj* fortuitus; inexpectatus
chancel *s* cancellus *m*
chancellor *s* cancellarius *m*
change *s* mutatio, commutatio, permutatio *f*; (*variety*) varietas *f*; (*pol*) res novae *f pl*; **small —** nummi *m pl*
change *vt* mutare, commutare, permutare; *vi* mutari, variare; (*of the moon*) renovari
changeable *adj* mutabilis; inconstans; (*of color*) versicolor
changeless *adj* immutabilis
changeling *s* subditus, suppositus *m*
channel *s* canalis *m*; (*of rivers*) alveus *m*; (*arm of the sea*) fretum *n*; (*in architecture*) stria *f*; (*fig*) curs·us -ūs *m*
channel *vt* sulcare, excavare; (*to guide*) ducěre
chant *s* cant·us -ūs *m*
chant *vt* cantare
chaos *s* chaos *n*; (*fig*) confusio *f*
chaotic *adj* confusus; indigestus
chap *s* fissura *f*; (*person*) homo *m*
chap *vt* scinděre, diffinděre; *vi* scindi
chapel *s* aedicula *f*, sacellum *n*
chapter *s* caput *n*
char *vt* amburěre
character *s* character *m*; mores *m pl*; (*inborn*) indoles, natura *f*; ingenium *n*; (*repute*) existimatio *f*; (*type*) genus *n*; (*letter*) littera *f*; (*in drama*) persona *f*
characteristic *adj* proprius; **—ally** proprie
characteristic *s* proprium *n*, proprietas *f*
characterize *vt* describěre, notare, designare
charade *s* aenigma syllabicum *n*
charcoal *s* carbo *m*

charge *s* (*law*) crimen *n*; accusatio *f*; (*mil*) impet·us -ūs, incurs·us -ūs *m*; (*command*) mandatum *n*; (*trust*) cura, custodia *f*; (*office*) munus *n*; (*cost*) impensa *f*, sumpt·us -ūs *m*; **to be in — of** praeesse (*with dat*); **to bring a — against** litem intendĕre (*with dat*); **to put in — of** praeficere (*with dat*)
charger *s* equus bellator *m*
chariot *s* curr·us -ūs *m*; curriculum *n*; (*mil*) essedarium *n*
charioteer *s* auriga *m*
charitable *adj* benignus, beneficus; (*fig*) mitis
charitably *adv* benigne; miti animo
charity *s* caritas *f*; liberalitas *f*
charlatan *s* pharmacopola *m*; ostentator, jactator *m*
charm *s* incantamentum *n*; (*fig*) illecebra, gratia *f*; (*amulet*) amuletum *n*
charm *vt* incantare; (*to delight*) capĕre, captare, delectare; **to — away** recantare
charmer *s* fascinator *m*; (*thing*) deliciae *f pl*
charming *adj* suavis, lepidus, venustus; **—ly** lepide, suaviter, blande, venuste
chart *s* tabula *f*
charter *s* charta *f*, diploma *n*
charter *vt* conducĕre
chase *s* venatio *f*, venat·us -ūs *m*
chase *vt* (*to hunt*) persequi, venari; (*to engrave*) caelare; **to — away** abigere, pellĕre
chasing *s* caelatura *f*
chasm *s* chasma *n*, hiat·us -ūs *m*
chaste *adj* castus, pudicus; (*of language*) purus; **—ly** caste, pudice; pure
chasten *vt* purificare, castigare
chastise *vt* castigare
chastisement *s* castigatio, animadversio *f*
chastiser *s* castigator *m*
chastity *s* pudicitia, castitas *f*, pudor *m*
chat *s* familiaris sermo *m*; **to have a —** fabulari, garrire
chat *vi* fabulari, garrire, colloqui
chattel *s* bona *n pl*
chatter *s* clangor *m*; (*idle talk*) garrulitas *f*, loquacitas *f*; (*of the teeth*) crepit·us -ūs *m*
chatter *vi* balbutire; (*to talk nonsense*) garrire, effutire; (*of teeth*) crepitare
cheap *adj* vilis; **— as dirt** pervilis; **—ly** bene, vili; viliter
cheapen *vt* pretium minuĕre (*with genit*)
cheapness *s* vilitas *f*
cheat *vt* decipere, fraudare
cheat *s* fraus *f*; dolus *m*; (*cheater*) fraudator *m*
check *vt* (*to restrain*) cohibēre, inhibēre; (*to stop*) retardare; (*to bridle*) refrenare; (*accounts*) dispungĕre; (*to verify*) comprobare
check *s* (*hindrance*) coercitio, suppressio *f*; impedimentum *n*; (*reprimand*) reprehensio *f*; (*bridle*) frenum *n*; (*disadvantage*) detrimentum *n*; (*admission ticket*) tessera *f*
checkered *adj* varius
cheek *s* gena *f*
cheekbone *s* maxilla *f*
cheer *s* (*shout*) clamor, plaus·us -ūs *m*; hilaritas *f*
cheer *vt* hortari, hilarare, exhilarare; (*to console*) solari
cheerful *adj* hilaris, alacer, laetus; **—ly** hilare, laete; libenter
cheerfulness *s* hilaritas *f*
cheering *s* acclamatio *f*; plaus·us -ūs *m*
cheerless *adj* maestus, tristis, illaetabilis
cheese *s* caseus *m*
chemical *adj* chemicus
chemical *s* chemicum *n*
chemise *s* indusium *n*
chemist *s* chemicus, chemiae peritus *m*
chemistry *s* chemia, chymia *f*
cherish *vt* (*to nourish*) alĕre; (*to treat tenderly*) fovēre; (*fig*) colere
cherry *s* cerasum *n*
cherry tree *s* cerasus *f*
chest *s* (*of the body*) pectus *n*; (*box*) cista, arca *f*; (*for clothes*) vestiarium *n*; scrinium *n*
chestnut *s* castanea *f*
chew *vt* mandĕre, manducare; **to — the cud** ruminare; (*fig*) meditari
chewing *s* manducatio, ruminatio *f*
chicanery *s* calumnia, praevaricatio *f*
chick *s* pullus *m*; (*term of endearment*) pulla *f*
chicken *s* gallina *f*
chicken-hearted *adj* timidus, ignavus
chicory *s* cichoreum *n*
chide *vt* objurgare; corripĕre
chief *adj* primus; praecipuus, summus; supremus; **—ly** praecipue, imprimis
chief *s* princeps, procer, dux, auctor *m*; caput *n*
chieftain *s* dux *m*
child *s* infans *m & f*; puer, filius *m*, puella, filia *f*; (*in the womb*) embryo *m*; **to bear a —** parturire; **with —** gravida
childbearing *s* part·us -ūs *m*
childbirth *s* part·us -ūs *m*; Lucinae labores *m pl*
childhood *s* infantia *f*; pueritia *f*; **from —** a puero *or* pueris; a primo tempore aetatis, a parvo
childish *adj* puerilis; **—ly** pueriliter
childless *adj* orbus
childlike *adj* puerilis
chill *s* frigusculum, frigus *n*
chill *adj* frigidulus
chill *vt* refrigerare
chilling *adj* algificus; frigidus, gelidus
chilly *adj* alsiosus; frigidulus
chime *s* sonus *m*
chime *vi* canĕre, sonare; **to — in** interpellare
chimera *s* chimaera *f*; figmentum *n*
chimney *s* caminus *m*
chin *s* mentum *n*

china *s* fictilia *n pl*
chink *s* rima *f*; (*sound*) tinnit·us -ūs *m*
chink *vi* tinnire
chip *s* segmen *n*, assula *f*; (*for lighting fire*) fomes *m*
chip *vt* ascio dedolare
chirp *s* (*of birds*) pipat·us -ūs *m*; (*of crickets*) stridor *m*
chirp *vi* (*of birds*) minurire, pipilare; (*of crickets*) stridēre
chisel *s* scalprum, caelum *n*
chisel *vt* scalpro caedĕre, sculpĕre; (*fig*) decipĕre, fraudare
chivalrous *adj* magnanimus, nobilis
chivalry *s* equestris dignitas *f*; (*class*) equites *m pl*
chocolate *s* chocolatum *n*
choice *s* electio *f*, delect·us -ūs *m*; (*power of choosing*) optio *f*; (*diversity*) varietas *f*
choice *adj* electus, exquisitus
choir *s* chorus *m*
choke *vt* suffocare; strangulare; *vi* suffocari; strangulari
choking *s* suffocatio *f*; strangulatio *f*
choose *vt* eligĕre, optare; **to — to** (*to prefer to*) malle (*with inf*)
choosing *s* electio *f*
chop *s* frustum *n*; (*of meat*) ofella *f*
chop *vt* concidĕre; truncare; **to — off** detruncare; abscidĕre; **to — up** minutatim concidĕre
choral *adj* symphoniacus
chord *s* chorda *f*, nervus *m*
chorus *s* chorus *m*; symphonia *f*
Christ *s* Christus *m*
christen *vt* baptizare
Christendom *s* cuncti Christiani *m pl*
Christian *adj* Christianus
Christianity *s* Christianismus *m*
Christian name *s* praenomen in baptismo inditum *n*
Christmas *s* festum nativitatis Christi *n*
chronic *adj* diuturnus, perpetuus; inveteratus
chronicle *s* annales *m pl*; acta publica *n pl*
chronological *adj* **in — order** ordinem temporum respiciens
chronology *s* temporum ordo *m*, temporum ratio *f*
chubby *adj* crassus, pinguis
chuckle *vi* cachinnare
church *s* ecclesia *f*; templum *n*
churl *s* homo rusticus *m*
churlish *adj* agrestis, importunus; **—ly** rustice
cider *s* hydromelum *n*
cinder *s* cinis *m*, favilla *f*
cinnamon *s* cinnamomum *n*
cipher *s* (*code*) nota *f*; (*a nobody*) numerus *m*; (*zero*) nihil *n*
circle *s* circulus, orbis, gyrus *m*; (*around the moon*) halo *m*; **vicious —** circulus vitiosus *m*
circle *vt* circumdare, cingĕre; *vi* circumire
circuit *s* circuit·us -ūs, circulus *m*; **to make a —** circumire
circuitous *adj* devius
circular *adj* orbicus, rotundus
circulate *vt* spargĕre; (*news*) disseminare, divulgare; *vi* circulari
circulation *s* ambit·us -ūs *m*; (*of blood*) circulatio *f*
circumcise *vt* circumcidĕre
circumcision *s* circumcisio *f*
circumference *s* peripheria *f*, ambit·us -ūs, circulus *m*
circumflex *s* circumflex·us -ūs *m*
circumlocution *s* circumlocutio, periphrasis *f*; ambages *f pl*
circumscribe *vt* finire, terminare, circumscribĕre
circumspect *adj* prudens, cautus, providus
circumspection *s* cautio, prudentia *f*
circumstance *s* res, conditio *f*; tempus *n*; sit·us -ūs *m*; **under the —s** quae cum ita sint
circumstantial *adj* adventicius, fortuitus; enumeratus; (*of evidence*) conjecturalis; **—ly** subtiliter
circumvent *vt* circumvenire, fallĕre, circumscribĕre
circumvention *s* circumscriptio, fraus *f*
circus *s* circus *m*
cistern *s* cisterna *f*, lac·us -ūs *m*; puteus *m*
citadel *s* arx *f*
citation *s* citatio, prolatio *f*; (*law*) vocatio *f*
cite *vt* (*law*) citare, evocare; (*to quote*) proferre, memorare
citizen *s* civis *m & f*; (*of a municipality*) municeps *m*
citizen *adj* civicus
citizenship *s* civitas *f*
city *adj* urbanus; urbicus
city *s* urbs *f*
civic *adj* civilis, civicus
civil *adj* civilis; (*polite*) comis, urbanus; (*of war*) civilis, intestinus, domesticus
civilian *s* togatus *m*; privatus *m*
civility *s* urbanitas, comitas *f*
civilization *s* cult·us -ūs *m*; humanitas *f*
civilize *vt* excolĕre; expolire
clad *adj* indutus, vestitus, amictus
claim *s* postulatio, vindicatio *f*, postulatum *n*
claim *vt* postulare, poscĕre, vindicare, arrogare
claimant *s* petitor, vindicator *m*
clam *s* chama *f*
clamber *vi* scandĕre, conscendĕre
clammy *adj* umidus, viscidus, lentus
clamor *s* clamor *m*, vociferatio *f*
clamor *vi* exclamare, vociferari; **— for** flagitare
clamp *s* confibula *f*; uncus *m*
clamp *vt* constringĕre
clan *s* gens *f*
clandestine *adj* clandestinus, furtivus; **—ly** clam, furtim
clang *s* clangor *m*
clang *vi* clangĕre, strepĕre
clank *s* strepit·us -ūs *m*
clank *vi* crepare

clap *s* (*of hand*) plaus·us -ūs *m*; (*of thunder*) fragor *m*
clap *vi* plauděre, applauděre
claptrap *s* apparat·us -ūs *m*
clarification *s* explicatio *f*, explanatio *f*
clarify *vt* deliquare, explanare, explicare
clarion *s* lituus *m*
clarity *s* claritas *f*; perspicuitas *f*
clash *s* concurs·us -ūs *m*; (*sound*) crepit·us -ūs *m*; (*fig*) dissonantia *f*
clash *vi* concurrěre; increpare, increpitare; (*fig*) dissidēre, discrepare
clasp *s* fibula *f*; (*embrace*) amplex·us -ūs *m*
clasp *vt* (*to embrace*) amplecti, complecti; (*to grasp*) comprehenděre
class *s* (*pol*) classis *f*, ordo *m*; (*kind*) genus *n*
class *vt* in classes distribuěre; **to — as** in numero habēre
classical *adj* classicus
classics *s* scriptores classici *m pl*
classification *s* in classes distributio, in genera distributio *f*
classify *vt* describěre, in classes distribuere, in genera distribuěre
clatter *s* strepit·us -ūs, crepit·us -ūs *m*
clatter *vi* crepare, crepitare, strepěre
clause *s* (*gram*) membrum, incisum *n*, articulus *m*, clausula *f*; (*law*) caput *n*
claw *s* unguis *m*
claw *vt* lacerare
clay *s* argilla, creta *f*; **made of —** fictilis
clean *adj* mundus, purus; (*fig*) purus, castus; **—ly** munde, pure
clean *vt* mundare, purgare
cleanliness *s* munditia *f*
cleanly *adj* mundus, nitidus
cleanse *vt* purgare, depurgare, abluěre, detergēre
clear *adj* clarus; (*of weather*) serenus; (*bright*) lucidus; (*of liquids*) limpidus; (*transparent*) liquidus; (*of voice*) candidus, acutus, argutus; (*manifest*) conspicuus, manifestus; (*of space*) apertus, patens; (*of language*) dilucidus; (*of conscience*) rectus; (*of the mind*) sagax; **— of** expers (*with genit*); **it is —** apparet, liquet; **to keep — of** evitare; **—ly** clare; plane, aperte, haud dubie
clear *vt* purgare; (*to acquit*) absolvěre; (*a doubt*) explanare; (*land, forests*) extricare; (*profit*) lucrari; **to — away** detergēre, amovēre, tollěre; **to — out** emundare; **to — up** enodare, explanare, explicare; *vi* **to — up** (*of weather*) disserenascěre, disserenare
clearance *s* purgatio *f*; (*space*) intervallum *n*
clearness *s* claritas *f*; (*of sky*) serenitas *f*; (*of style*) perspicuitas *f*
cleavage *s* discidium *n*
cleave *vt* findere; *vi* **to — to** adhaerēre (*with dat*)
cleaver *s* dolabra *f*
cleft *s* rima, fissura *f*, hiat·us -ūs *m*
clemency *s* clementia *f*
clement *adj* clemens, mitis
clench *vt* compriměre
clerk *s* scriba *m*
clever *adj* sollers, ingeniosus, callidus, astutus, versutus; **—ly** sollerter, callide, ingeniose, astute
cleverness *s* dexteritas, sollertia, astutia *f*
click *s* crepit·us -ūs *m*
click *vi* crepitare
client *s* cliens *m & f*; consultor *m*
cliff *s* cautes *f*, scopulus *m*, rupes *f*
climate *s* caelum *n*
climax *s* gradatio *f*
climb *vt & vi* ascenděre, conscenděre, scanděre
climb *s* ascens·us -ūs *m*
clinch *vt* confirmare
cling *vi* adhaerēre; **to — together** cohaerēre
clink *s* tinnit·us -ūs *m*
clink *vi* tinnire
clip *s* fibula *f*
clip *vt* tondēre, praeciděre; (*words*) mutilare
clipping *s* tonsura *f*; **—s** resegmina *n pl*
cloak *s* pallium *n*; (*for travel*) paenula *f*; (*in rain*) lacerna *f*; (*mil*) sagum, paludamentum *n*
cloak *vt* dissimulare, praetenděre, tegěre
clock *s* horologium *n*; (*sundial*) solarium *n*
clod *s* glaeba *f*
clog *s* (*shoe*) sculponea *f*; (*fig*) impedimentum *n*
clog *vt* impedire
cloister *s* portic·us -ūs *f*; monasterium *n*
close *adj* (*dense*) densus, spissus; (*tight*) artus, angustus; (*shut*) occlusus, clausus; (*fast*) firmus; (*near*) propinquus; (*secret*) arcanus, obscurus; (*niggardly*) avarus, tenax, parcus; **at — quarters** comminus; **— together** confertus, refertus, densus, continuus; **to be — at hand** adesse, instare; **to keep — to** adhaerēre (*with dat*); **—ly** prope; (*attentively*) attente, exacte
close *vt* clauděre, operire; (*to end*) finire, terminare; **to — a bargain** pacisci; *vi* coire; claudi, concludi, terminari; (*in a speech*) perorare
close *s* finis, terminus *m*, terminatio, conclusio *f*; **to bring to a —** finire; **to draw to a —** terminari
close *adv* prope, promime, juxta; **— to** prope (*with acc*), juxta (*with acc*)
closet *s* conclave *n*, cella *f*; (*for clothes*) vestiarium *n*
closing *adj* ultimus
closing *s* conclusio *f*, finis *m*
clot *s* (*of blood*) cruor, concretus sanguis *m*
clot *vi* concrescěre
cloth *s* pannus *m*; (*linen*) linteum *n*
clothe *vt* vestire, induěre; velare

clothes *s* vestit·us -ūs *m*, vestimenta *n pl*, vestis *f*
clothing *s* vestit·us -ūs *m*, vestimenta *n pl*, vestis *f*
cloud *s* nubes *f*
cloud *vt* nubibus velare; (*fig*) obscurare; *vi* nubilare
cloudiness *s* nubilum *n*
cloudless *adj* serenus, purus
cloudy *adj* nubilus; **to grow —** nubilare
clout *s* ict·us -ūs *m*; alapa *f*
cloven *adj* bisulcus, bifidus
clown *s* (*boor*) rusticus *m*; (*buffoon, jester*) scurra *m*
clown *vi* scurrari
clownish *adj* rusticus; scurrilis
cloy *vt* satiare, exsaturare
cloying *adj* putidus
club *s* (*cudgel*) clava *f*, fustis *m*; (*society*) sodalitas *f*, collegium *n*
club *vt* fuste dolare
cluck *vi* glocire; singultire
clue *s* indicium *n*
clump *s* massa *f*; (*of trees*) arbustum *n*, globus *m*
clumsily *adv* rustice, inscite, ineleganter, male, inepte
clumsiness *s* rusticitas, inscitia *f*
clumsy *adj* ineptus, inscitus, rusticus, agrestis; (*of things*) inhabilis
cluster *s* (*of grapes, etc.*) racemus *m*; (*of flowers*) corymbus *m*; (*of people*) corona *f*
cluster *vi* congregari; **to — around** stipare
clutch *s* unguis *m*; comprehensio *f*; **from one's —es** e manibus; **in one's —es** in sua potestate
clutch *vt* arripĕre, prehendĕre
coach *s* curr·us -ūs *m*, raeda *f*; (*trainer*) magister *m*
coagulate *vt* coagulare; *vi* concrescĕre
coagulation *s* coagulatio, concretio *f*
coal *s* carbo *m*
coalesce *vi* coalescĕre, coire
coalition *s* conjunctio, coitio, conspiratio *f*
coal mine *s* fodina carbonaria *f*
coarse *s* (*of material*) crassus, rudis; (*of manners*) incultus, inurbanus, rusticus; **—ly** crasse; inurbane
coarseness *s* crassitudo *f*; rusticitas *f*
coast *s* ora *f*, litus *n*
coast *vi* praetervehi
coastal *adj* maritimus, litoralis
coat *s* tunica, toga *f*; (*of fur*) pellis *f*
coat *vt* illinere, inducĕre, obducĕre
coating *s* corium *n*
coat of arms *s* insignia *n pl*
coat of mail *s* lorica *f*; (*skin*) pellis *f*
coax *vt* cogĕre, mulcēre, blandiri
coaxing *s* blandimenta *n pl*, blanditiae *f pl*
coaxingly *adv* blande
cobbler *s* sutor *m*
cobweb *s* aranea *f*, araneum *n*
cock *s* gallus *m*
cockroach *s* blatta *f*
cocoa *s* faba Cacao *f*
cocoanut *s* nux palmae indicae *f*
cocoon *s* globulus *m*
coddle *vt* indulgēre (*with dat*)
code *s* notae *f pl*
codify *vt* digerĕre
coerce *vt* coercēre, refrenare, cogĕre
coercion *s* coercitio, vis *f*
coeval *adj* coaevus, aequalis
coexist *vi* simul existĕre
coffee *s* coffea Arabica *f*
coffer *s* arca, cista *f*
coffin *s* arca *f*, sarcophagus *m*
cog *s* dens *m*
cogency *s* vis *f*
cogent *adj* cogens, efficax, gravis
cognate *adj* cognatus
cognizance *s* cognitio *f*
cognizant *adj* conscius, gnarus
cohabit *vi* coire, consuescĕre
cohabitation *s* consuetudo *f*, convict·us -ūs *m*
coheir *s* coheres *m & f*
cohere *vi* cohaerēre; (*fig*) congruĕre
coherence *s* context·us -ūs *m*, convenientia *f*
coherent *adj* cohaerens, congruens; **—ly** constanter
cohesion *s* cohaerentia *f*
cohesive *adj* tenax
cohort *s* cohors *f*
coil *s* spira *f*
coil *vt* glomerare; *vi* glomerari
coin *s* nummus *m*
coin *vt* cudĕre, signare; (*fig*) fingĕre
coinage *s* res nummaria, moneta *f*
coincide *vi* congruere, convenire, concurrĕre; eodem tempore fieri
coincidence *s* concursatio *f*, concurs·us -ūs *m*; (*fig*) consens·us -ūs *m*; **by —** casu
coincidental *adj* fortuitus
cold *adj* frigidus, gelidus; **to be —** algēre, frigēre; **to become —** frigescĕre, algescĕre; **—ly** (*fig*) frigide, gelide, lente
cold *s* frigus *n*, algor *m*, gelu *n*; (*sickness*) gravedo *f*; **to catch a —** gravedinem contrahĕre; **to have a —** gravedine dolēre
coldness *s* frigus *n*, algor *m*
colic *s* tormina *n pl*
collapse *s* labes, ruina *f*
collapse *vi* collabi, concidĕre, in se corruĕre
collar *s* (*of garment*) collare *n*; (*for dogs*) millus *m*; jugum *n*
collar *vt* collo comprehendĕre
collarbone *s* jugulum *n*
collate *vt* conferre
collateral *adj* transversus; adjunctus, consentaneus
colleague *s* collega, consors *m*
collect *vt* conferre, colligere; (*to assemble*) convocare; (*money*) exigĕre; **to — oneself** mentem colligĕre, animum colligere; *vi* colligi, aggregari
collected *adj* praesens
collection *s* collectio, conquisitio, collecta, congeries *f*; (*out of authors*) collectanea *n pl*

collective *adj* communis, collectivus; **—ly** una, simul, communiter
college *s* collegium *n*
collegiate *adj* collegialis, collegiarius
collide *vi* confligĕre, concurrĕre
collision *s* concursio, conflictio *f*, concurs·us -ūs *m*
colloquial *adj* quotidianus
collusion *s* collusio, praevaricatio *f*, dolus *m*
colon *s* colon *n*
colonel *s* legatus *m*
colonial *adj* colonicus
colonist *s* colonus *m*
colonize *vt* coloniam constituĕre in (*with abl*)
colonnade *s* portic·us -ūs *f*
colony *s* colonia *f*
color *s* color *m*, pigmentum *n*; **—s** vexillum *n*
color *vt* colorare; (*to dye*) tingĕre, inficĕre; (*fig*) obtegere; *vi* erubescĕre
colossal *adj* ingens, immanis
colossus *s* colossus *m*
colt *s* equulus, pullus equinus *m*
column *s* columna *f*; (*mil*) agmen *n*
comb *s* pecten *m*
comb *vt* pectĕre, comĕre
combat *s* pugna *f*, proelium, certamen *n*
combat *vt* pugnare cum (*with abl*); *vi* pugnare, proeliari
combination *s* conjunctio, junctura *f*; (*of persons*) conspiratio, conjuratio *f*
combine *vt* conjungĕre, miscēre; temperare; *vi* coire; conspirare
combustible *adj* igni obnoxius
combustion *s* concrematio, ustio *f*
come *vi* venire; (*to arrive*) pervenire; (*to happen*) fieri; **to — about** evenire; **to — after** sequi; **to — again** revenire; **to — along** procedere; **to — away** abscedĕre; **to — back** revenire, redire; **to — before** praevenire; **to — by** praeterire; (*to get*) acquirĕre; **to — down** descendĕre; (*to fall down*) decidere; **to — forth** exire; (*fig*) exoriri; **to — forward** procedĕre; **to — in** introire; **to — near** approprinquare, accedĕre; **to — off** recedere, discedĕre; **to — on** pergĕre; **to — out** (*to be published*) edi, emitti; **to — over** supervenire; (*the face*) obire; **to — round** (*fig*) transgredi; **to — to** advenire; (*to come to one's senses*) ad se redire; **to — to pass** evenire, fieri; **to — together** convenire, coire; **to — up** subvenire; (*to occur*) accidĕre, provenire; **to — upon** (*to find*) invenire; (*to attack*) ingruĕre
comedian *s* comoedus *m*; (*playwright*) comicus *m*
comedy *s* comoedia *f*
comely *adj* decens, venustus
comet *s* cometes *m*, stella crinita *f*
comfort *s* consolatio *f*, solatium *n*
comfort *vt* consolari, solari
comfortable *adj* commodus, amoenus
comfortably *adv* commode
comforter *s* consolator *m*
comfortless *adj* solatii expers, incommodus
comic *adj* comicus, facetus
comic *s* scurra *m*
comical *adj* comicus, ridiculus; **—ly** comice, ridicule
coming *adj* venturus
coming *s* advent·us -ūs *m*
comma *s* comma *n*
command *vt* imperare (*with dat*), jubēre; (*view*) prospectare, despectare
command *s* (*order*) jussum, mandatum, praeceptum *n*, juss·us -ūs *m*; (*mil*) imperium *n*; (*jurisdiction*) provincia *f*; **— of language** copia dicendi *f*; **to be in — of** praeesse (*with dat*); **to put someone in — of** aliquem praeficĕre (*with dat*)
commander *s* dux, praefectus *m*
commander in chief *s* imperator *m*
commandment *s* mandatum *n*
commemorate *vt* celebrare
commemoration *s* celebratio *f*
commence *vt* incipere, inchoare
commencement *s* initium, exordium, principium *n*
commend *vt* approbare, laudare; (*to recommend*) commendare; (*to entrust*) committĕre, mandare
commendable *adj* commendabilis, probabilis, laudabilis
commendation *s* commendatio *f*
commensurate *adj* adaequans, conveniens
comment *vi* commentari; **to — on** explicare, enarrare, interpretari
comment *s* sententia *f*, dictum *n*
commentary *s* commentarius *m*, commentarium *n*
commentator *s* interpres *m*
commerce *s* commercium *n*, mercat·us -ūs *m*, mercatura *f*; **to engage in —** negotiari
commercial *adj* negotialis
commiserate *vi* **to — with** miserēri
commiseration *s* misericordia *f*
commissariat *s* commeat·us -ūs *m*, res frumentaria *f*
commissary *s* procurator, curator *m*
commission *s* mandatum *n*; (*mil*) legatio *f*
commission *vt* delegare, mandare
commissioner *s* delegatus *m*
commit *vt* (*crime*) admittĕre, patrare, perpetrare; (*to entrust*) committĕre; **to — to memory** ediscĕre
commitment *s* (*obligation*) munus, officium *n*; (*to jail*) incarceratio *f*
committee *s* consilium *n*
commodity *s* res venalis, merx *f*
common *adj* communis, publicus; (*ordinary*) vulgaris, quotidianus; (*well known*) pervulgatus; (*repeated*) creber; (*inferior*) mediocris; (*gram*) promiscuus; **—ly** vulgo, fere, plerumque
commoner *s* plebeius *m*; **—s** plebs *f*
commonplace *adj* vulgaris, pervulgatus, tritus
commonwealth *s* respublica *f*

commotion *s* commotio, agitatio *f*, tumult·us -ūs *m*
commune *vi* confabulari
communicate *vt* communicare; (*information*) impertire, nuntiare; *vi* **to — with** communicare (*with dat*), agere cum (*with abl*)
communication *s* communicatio *f*; commercium *n*; (*information*) nuntius *m*
communicative *adj* affabilis, facilis
communion *s* communio, societas *f*
community *s* civitas *f*
commutation *s* mutatio, permutatio *f*
commute *vt* commutare
compact *adj* densus, spissus; (*of style*) pressus; **—ly** dense, spisse, confertim
compact *s* pactum, foedus *n*, pactio *f*
compact *vt* densare
companion *s* comes, socius, sodalis; (*mil*) contubernalis, commilito *m*
companionable *adj* affabilis, facilis
companionship *s* societas, sodalitas, consuetudo *f*; (*mil*) contubernium *n*
company *s* societas, consuetudo *f*; (*gathering*) convent·us -ūs *m*; (*guests*) convivium *n*; (*com*) societas *f*; (*mil*) manipulus *m*; (*theatrical*) grex *f*
comparable *adj* comparabilis
comparative *adj* comparatus, relativus; **—ly** comparate
comparative *s* grad·us -ūs comparativus *m*
compare *vt* comparare, conferre; **compared with** ad (*with acc*), adversus (*with acc*)
comparison *s* comparatio, collatio *f*; **in — with** prae (*with abl*), adversus (*with acc*)
compartment *s* loculus *m*, cella, pars *f*
compass *s* ambit·us -ūs *m*; (*limits*) fines *m pl*; (*instrument*) circinus *m*; (*magnetic*) ac·us -ūs magnetica *f*
compass *vt* circumvallare, cingĕre, circumdare; (*to attain*) consequi, patrare
compassion *s* misericordia *f*
compassionate *adj* misericors; **—ly** misericorditer
compatibility *s* congruentia, convenientia *f*
compatible *adj* congruus, conveniens
compatriot *s* civis, popularis *m*
compeer *s* par, aequalis *m*
compel *vt* cogere, compellĕre
compendium *s* summarium *n*
compensate *vt* compensare, renumerare; satisfacĕre (*with dat*)
compensation *s* compensatio *f*; poena *f*
compete *vi* contendĕre, petĕre, certare
competence *s* facultas *f*; (*legal capacity*) jus *n*
competent *adj* congruens, idoneus, peritus, capax; (*of authorities*) locuples; **—ly** satis, idonee
competition *s* contentio, aemulatio *f*, certamen *n*
competitor *s* petitor, rivalis, aemulus *m*
compilation *s* collectio *f*, collectanea *n pl*
compile *vt* colligĕre, componĕre
compiler *s* collector, scriptor *m*
complacency *s* amor sui *m*
complacent *adj* qui sibi placet
complain *vi* queri
complaint *s* querela, querimonia *f*; (*law*) crimen *n*; (*med*) morbus *m*
complaisance *s* comitas, accommodatio *f*, obsequium *n*
complaisant *adj* comis, officiosus; **—ly** comiter
complement *s* complementum, supplementum *n*
complete *adj* perfectus, integer, absolutus, plenus; **—ly** plane, prorsus, omnino, abolute, funditus
complete *vt* complēre; (*to accomplish*) perficĕre, conficere, peragĕre
completion *s* completio *f*; (*accomplishment*) perfectio *f*; (*end*) finis *m*
complex *adj* multiplex, implicatus, complicatus
complexion *s* color *m*
complexity *s* implicatio, multiplex natura *f*
compliance *s* obtemperatio *f*, obsequium *n*
compliant *adj* obsequens
complicate *vt* impedire
complicated *adj* impeditus, implicatus, complicatus, nodosus
complication *s* implicatio *f*
complicity *s* conscientia *f*
compliment *s* blandimentum *n*, verba honorifica *n pl*; **to pay one's —s to** salutare
compliment *vt* gratulari (*with dat*); laudare, blandiri
complimentary *adj* blandus, honorificus
comply *vi* **to — with** concedĕre (*with dat*), cedĕre (*with dat*), parēre (*with dat*), obsequi (*with dat*), morigerari (*with dat*)
component *s* pars *f*, elementum *n*
compose *vt* componĕre; (*verses*) condere, pangĕre; (*to calm*) sedare; (*quarrel*) componĕre; **to — oneself** tranquillari
composed *adj* tranquillus, quietus, placidus
composer *s* scriptor, auctor *m*
composite *adj* compositus, multiplex
composition *s* compositio, scriptura *f*; opus *n*
composure *s* tranquillitas *f*, animus aequus *m*
compound *vt* componĕre, miscēre; (*words*) jungĕre
compound *adj* compositus
compound *s* compositio *f*; (*word*) junctum verbum *n*
compound interest *s* anatocismus *m*
comprehend *vt* continēre, amplectari; (*to understand*) capĕre, percipĕre, comprehendĕre, intellegĕre
comprehensible *adj* perspicuus
comprehension *s* intellect·us -ūs *m*, intellegentia *f*

comprehensive *adj* plenus, capax; **—ly** funditus, omnino
compress *vt* comprimĕre
compression *s* compressio *f*, compress·us -ūs *m*
comprise *vt* continēre
compromise *s* (*unilateral*) accommodatio *f*; (*bilateral*) compromissum *n*
compromise *vt* compromittĕre, implicare; *vi* pacisci
compulsion *s* compulsio, vis, necessitas *f*
compulsory *adj* necessarius, debitus
compunction *s* paenitentia, compunctio *f*
computation *s* ratio, computatio *f*
compute *vt* computare
comrade *s* socius, sodalis *m*; (*mil*) contubernalis *m*
conceal *vt* celare, occultare, abdĕre, dissimulare
concealment *s* occultatio, dissimulatio *f*; (*place*) latebrae *f pl*; **to be in —** latēre
concede *vt* concedĕre
conceit *s* (*haughtiness*) arrogantia, superbia *f*; (*idea*) notio *f*
conceited *adj* arrogans, superbiā tumens
conceive *vt* concipĕre, percipĕre, intellegĕre
concentrate *vt* in unum locum contrahĕre; *vi* **to — on** animum intendere in (*with acc*)
concentration *s* in unum locum contractio *f*; (*fig*) animi intentio *f*
conception *s* (*in womb*) concept·us -ūs *m*; (*idea*) imago, notio *f*
concern *s* (*affair*) res *f*, negotium *n*; (*importance*) momentum *n*; (*worry*) sollicitudo, cura *f*
concern *vt* pertinēre ad (*with acc*), attinēre ad (*with acc*); (*to worry*) sollicitare; **it —s me** meā interest, meā refert
concerned *adj* sollictus, anxius
concerning *prep* de (*with abl*)
concert *s* (*music*) concent·us -ūs *m*, symphonia *f*; **in —** uno animo, ex composito
concert *vt* (*plan*) inire
concession *s* concessio *f*; (*thing*) concessum *n*; **to make —s** concedĕre
conch *s* concha *f*
conciliate *vt* conciliare
conciliation *s* conciliatio *f*
concise *adj* brevis, concisus; (*style*) densus; **—ly** breviter, concise
conciseness *s* brevitas *f*
conclave *s* conclave, consilium *n*
conclude *vt* (*to end*) conficĕre, perficere, terminare, finire; (*to infer*) concludĕre, colligĕre
conclusion *s* (*end*) conclusio *f*; (*decision*) determinatio, sententia *f*; (*of speech*) peroratio *f*; (*of action*) exit·us -ūs *m*; (*inference*) conjectura *f*
conclusive *adj* certus, gravis
concoct *vt* concoquĕre; (*to contrive*) excogitare, conflare
concoction *s* pot·us -ūs *m*; (*fig*) machinatio *f*
concomitant *adj* adjunctus, conjunctus
concord *s* concordia, harmonia *f*; (*mus*) concent·us -ūs *m*
concordat *s* pactum *n*
concourse *s* concurs·us -ūs *m*, concursio *f*
concrete *adj* concretus
concrete *s* concretum *n*, concret·us -ūs *m*
concubinage *s* concubinat·us -ūs *m*
concubine *s* concubina *f*
concupiscence *s* libido *f*
concur *vi* congruĕre, consentire
concurrence *s* consens·us -ūs *m*, consensio *f*
concussion *s* concussio *f*
condemn *vt* damnare, condemnare; **to — to death** capitis damnare
condemnation *s* damnatio, condemnatio *f*
condensation *s* densatio, spissatio *f*
condense *vt* (con)densare, spissare; (*words*) premĕre
condescend *vi* dignari, descendĕre, concedĕre, se submittĕre
condescending *adj* comis; **—ly** comiter
condescension *s* comitas *f*
condition *s* (*state*) stat·us -ūs *m*, condicio, res *f*; (*stipulation*) condicio, lex *f*; **on — that** ea lege ut
condition *vt* formare, informare
conditional *adj* conditionalis; **—ly** (*law*) conditionaliter; sub condicione
condole *vi* **to — with** dolēre cum (*with abl*)
condone *vt* veniam dare (*with dat*), condonare
conducive *adj* utilis, accommodatus
conduct *s* mores *m pl*, vita *f*; (*management*) administratio *f*
conduct *vt* (*to lead*) adducĕre, deducere, perducĕre; (*to manage*) gerĕre, administrare
conductor *s* dux, ductor *m*
conduit *s* canalis, aquaeduct·us -ūs *m*
cone *s* conus *m*
confection *s* conditura, cuppedo *f*
confectionery *s* cuppedia *n pl*, conditura *f*
confederacy *s* (*alliance*) foedus *n*, societas *f*
confederate *adj* foederatus
confederate *s* socius, conjuratus *m*
confederate *vi* foedus facĕre
confederation *s* societas *f*
confer *vt* conferre, tribuĕre; *vi* colloqui
conference *s* colloquium *n*
confess *vt* fatēri, confitēri; agnoscĕre, concedĕre
confessedly *adv* ex confesso; manifesto, aperte
confession *s* confessio *f*
confidant *s* familiaris *m & f*, conscius *m*, conscia *f*
confide *vt* committĕre, credĕre, mandare; *vi* **to — in** (con)fidĕre (*with dat*)
confidence *s* fides, confidentia, fiducia *f*; **to have — in** confidĕre (*with

dat); **to inspire — in** fidem facĕre (*with dat*)
confident *adj* confidens, fidens; **—ly** confidenter
confidential *adj* fidus; (*secret*) arcanus
configuration *s* forma, figura *f*
confine *s* finis *m*
confine *vt* includĕre; (*to restrain*) coercēre, cohibēre; (*to limit*) circumscribĕre; **to be confined to bed** lecto tenēri
confinement *s* inclusio *f*; (*imprisonment*) incarceratio, custodia *f*; (*of women*) puerperium *n*
confirm *vt* confirmare; (*to prove*) comprobare; (*to ratify*) sancire
confirmation *s* confirmatio, affirmatio *f*
confiscate *vt* proscribĕre, publicare
confiscation *s* proscriptio, publicatio *f*
conflagration *s* incendium *n*
conflict *s* conflict·us -ūs *m*, contentio, pugna *f*, certamen *n*
conflict *vi* contendĕre; (*differ*) dissentire, discrepare
conflicting *adj* contrarius, adversus
confluence *s* confluens *m*
conform *vt* accommodare; *vi* obsequi, obtemperare
conformation *s* conformatio, figura, forma *f*
conformity *s* convenientia, congruentia *f*; **in — with** secundum (*with acc*)
confound *vt* confundĕre, permiscēre, perturbare; (*to frustrate*) frustrari
confounded *adj* miser, nefandus
confront *vt* obviam ire (*with dat*), se opponere (*with dat*)
confrontation *s* comparatio *f*
confuse *vt* confundĕre, perturbare, permiscēre
confused *adj* confusus, perplexus; **—ly** confuse, perplexe
confusion *s* confusio, perturbatio *f*; (*shame*) pudor *m*
congeal *vt* congelare, glaciare; *vi* consistĕre, concrescĕre
congenial *adj* consentaneus, concors
congenital *adj* nativus
congested *adj* refertus, densus; frequentissimus
congestion *s* congeries, frequentia *f*
congratulate *vt* gratulari (*with dat*)
congratulation *s* gratulatio *f*
congratulatory *adj* gratulans, gratulabundus
congregate *vt* congregare, colligĕre; *vi* congregari, convenire
congregation *s* coet·us -ūs *m*, auditores *m pl*
conical *adj* conicus
conjectural *adj* conjecturalis, opinabilis; **—ly** ex conjectura
conjecture *s* conjectura *f*
conjecture *vt* conjectare, conjicĕre
conjugal *adj* conjugalis
conjugate *vt* declinare
conjugation *s* conjugatio *f*
conjunction *s* unio *f*, concurs·us -ūs *m*; (*gram*) conjunctio *f*
conjure *vt* obtestari, incantare, fascinare; *vi* praestigiis uti
conjurer *s* magus, praestigiator *m*
conjuring *s* praestigiae *f pl*
connect *vt* connectĕre, jungĕre, copulare; (*in a series*) serĕre
connected *adj* conjunctus; continuus, continens; (*by marriage*) affinis; **to be closely connected with** inhaerēre (*with dat*); **to be connected with** contingere
connection *s* conjunctio, colligatio *f*, nex·us -ūs, context·us -ūs *m*; (*kin*) necessitudo *f*; (*by marriage*) affinitas *f*
connivance *s* indulgentia, dissimulatio *f*
connive *vi* connivēre
connoisseur *s* doctus, peritus, intellegens *m*
conquer *vt* vincĕre, superare; domare
conqueror *s* victor *m*, victrix *f*; domitor *m*
conquest *s* victoria *f*
consanguinity *s* consanguinitas *f*
conscience *s* conscientia *f*; **guilty —** mala conscientia; **to have no —** nullam religionem habēre
conscientious *adj* integer, pius, religiosus, diligens; **—ly** diligenter
conscious *adj* conscius, gnarus; **—ly** scienter
consciousness *s* conscientia *f*
conscript *s* tiro *m*
conscript *vt* conscribĕre
conscription *s* delect·us -ūs *m*
consecrate *vt* sacrare, consecrare, dedicare, devovēre
consecration *s* consecratio, dedicatio *f*
consecutive *adj* continuus; **—ly** deinceps, continenter
consent *vi* assentire, consentire
consent *s* consens·us -ūs *m*, consensio *f*; **without my —** me invito
consequence *s* consequentia, consecutio *f*, event·us -ūs, exit·us -ūs *m*; (*logical*) conclusio *f*; (*importance*) momentum *n*
consequent *adj* consequens, consectarius; **—ly** ergo, igitur, itaque
consequential *adj* consentaneus
conservation *s* conservatio *f*
conservative *adj* reipublicae statūs conservandi studiosus; **— party** optimates *m pl*
conserve *vt* conservare, servare
consider *vt* considerare, animo agitare, revolvĕre; (*to deem*) aestimare, ducĕre, habēre; (*to respect*) respicĕre
considerable *adj* aliquantus; (*of persons*) eximius, illustris; (*of size*) amplus
considerably *adv* aliquantum; multum; (*with comp*) multo, aliquanto
considerate *adj* prudens, humanus, benignus
consideration *s* consideratio, contemplatio, deliberatio *f*; (*regard*) respect·us -ūs *m*; (*ground, motive*)

ratio *f*; (*importance*) momentum *n*; **without —** inconsulte, temere
considering *prep* pro (*with abl*)
consign *vt* committĕre, mandare, consignare, tradĕre
consignment *s* consignatio *f*
consist *vi* consistĕre; **to — of** constare ex (*with abl*)
consistency *s* congruentia, constantia *f*
consistent *adj* constans; consentaneus; **—ly** constanter, congruenter
consolable *adj* consolabilis
consolation *s* consolatio *f*; (*thing*) solacium *n*
console *vt* consolari
consolidate *vt* corroborare, firmare, consolidare, stabilire; *vi* solidescĕre
consonant *adj* consonus, consentaneus
consonant *s* consonans littera *f*
consort *s* consors *m & f*; (*married*) conjux *or* conjunx *m & f*
consort *vi* **to — with** familiariter uti (*with abl*), se associare cum (*with abl*)
conspicuous *adj* conspicuus; insignis, manifestus; **—ly** manifeste, palam
conspiracy *s* conjuratio, conspiratio *f*
conspirator *s* conjuratus *m*
conspire *vi* conjurare, conspirare
constable *s* lictor *m*
constancy *s* constantia, firmitas, perseverantia *f*
constant *adj* constans, firmus; perpetuus; fidelis; **—ly** constanter, crebro
constellation *s* sidus, astrum *n*
consternation *s* consternatio, trepidatio *f*, pavor *m*; **to throw into —** perterrēre
constituent *s* elector, suffragator *m*; (*part*) elementum *n*
constitute *vt* constituĕre, creare
constitution *s* (*of body*) habit·us -ūs *m*, constitutio *f*; (*pol*) civitatis stat·us -ūs *m*, reipublicae leges *f pl*
constitutional *adj* legitimus; (*natural*) naturā insitus; **—ly** legitime
constrain *vt* cogere, compellĕre, detinēre
constraint *s* vis, coercitio, necessitas *f*
construct *vt* construĕre
construction *s* constructio, aedificatio *f*; figura, forma *f*; (*meaning*) sens·us -ūs *m*, interpretatio *f*
constructor *s* structor, fabricator *m*
construe *vt* interpretari; (*gram*) construĕre
consul *s* consul *m*; **— elect** consul designatus *m*
consular *adj* consularis
consulship *s* consulat·us -ūs *m*; **to run for the —** consulatum petĕre; **during my —** me consule
consult *vt* consulĕre, consultare; *vi* deliberare
consultation *s* consultatio, deliberatio *f*
consume *vt* consumĕre, absumĕre; (*food*) edĕre
consumer *s* consumptor *m*
consummate *adj* summus, perfectus
consummate *vt* consummare
consummation *s* consummatio *f*; (*end*) finis *m*
consumption *s* consumptio *f*; (*disease*) tabes *f*
consumptive *adj* pulmonarius
contact *s* contact·us -ūs *m*, contagio *f*; **to come in — with** contingĕre
contagion *s* contagium *n*, contagio *f*
contagious *adj* contagiosus, tabificus
contain *vt* continēre; (*to restrain*) cohibēre
container *s* vas *n*
contaminate *vt* contaminare
contamination *s* contaminatio, labes *f*
contemplate *vt* contemplari, intuēri
contemplation *s* contemplatio, meditatio *f*
contemporaneous *adj* aequalis; **—ly** simul
contemporary *s* aequalis, aequaevus *m*
contempt *s* contemptio *f*, contempt·us -ūs *m*
contemptible *adj* contemnendus, abjectus, vilis
contemptibly *adv* contemptim, abjecte
contemptuous *adj* fastidiosus, superbus; **—ly** fastidiose
contend *vt* (*to aver*) affirmare, asseverare; *vi* contendĕre, certare; (*to struggle*) luctari; (*to dispute*) verbis certare; **to — against** repugnare, adversari
contending *adj* aversus, contrarius
content *adj* contentus
content *vt* satisfacĕre (*with dat*), placēre (*with dat*), mulcēre
contented *adj* contentus; **—ly** aequo animo, leniter
contention *s* contentio *f*; certamen *n*; controversia *f*
contentious *adj* litigiosus; pugnax
contentment *s* aequus animus *m*
contents *s* quod inest, quae insunt; (*of book*) argumentum *n*
contest *s* certamen *n*, contentio, certatio *f*
contest *vt* (*to dispute*) resistĕre (*with dat*), repugnare (*with dat*); (*law*) lege agere de (*with abl*)
contestant *s* petitor, aemulus *m*
context *s* context·us -ūs, sens·us -ūs *m*
contiguous *adj* contiguus, conterminus, adjunctus
continence *s* continentia, abstinentia *f*
continent *adj* abstinens, continens; **—ly** abstinenter, continenter
continent *s* continens *f*
continental *adj* in continenti positus; ad continentem pertinens
contingent *s* (*of troops*) numerus *m*, man·us -ūs *f*
continual *adj* continuus; perpetuus, assiduus; **—ly** assidue, semper

continuance *s* continuatio, perpetuitas, assiduitas *f*
continuation *s* continuatio *f*
continue *vt* continuare, producĕre; *vi* pergĕre; (*to last*) durare, persistere, perstare, (re)manēre
continuity *s* continuitas *f*; (*of speech*) perpetuitas *f*
continuous *adj* continuus, continens, perpetuus; **—ly** continenter
contortion *s* contortio, distortio *f*
contour *s* forma, figura *f*; lineamenta *n pl*
contraband *adj* interdictus, vetitus, illicitus
contract *vt* contrahĕre, astringĕre; (*to shorten*) deminuere; (*sickness*) contrahĕre; (*to undertake*) redimĕre; *vi* pacisci; (*to shrink*) contrahi
contract *s* pactum, conventum *n*; (*pol*) foedus *n*
contraction *s* contractio *f*; (*of word*) compendium *n*
contractor *s* redemptor, susceptor *m*
contradict *vt* contradicĕre (*with dat*), obloqui (*with dat*)
contradiction *s* contradictio *f*; (*of things*) repugnantia *f*
contradictory *adj* contrarius, repugnans
contrary *adj* (*opposite*) contrarius, diversus; (*fig*) aversus, repugnans; **— to** contra (*with acc*)
contrary *s* contrarium *n*, contraria pars *f*; **on the —** contra, e contrario
contrast *s* diversitas, dissimilitudo *f*
contrast *vt* comparare, opponĕre; *vi* discrepare
contribute *vt* contribuĕre, conferre; *vi* **to — towards** conferre ad (*with acc*)
contribution *s* contributio, collatio *f*; (*money*) stips *f*
contributory *adj* contribuens, adjunctus
contrite *adj* paenitens
contrition *s* paenitentia *f*
contrivance *s* inventio, machinatio *f*; (*thing contrived*) inventum, artificium *n*, machina *f*
contrive *vt* (*to invent*) fingĕre; excogitare, machinari, efficĕre
control *s* (*restraint*) continentia *f*; (*power*) potestas, moderatio, dictio *f*, imperium *n*; **to have — over** praeesse (*with dat*)
control *vt* moderari (*with dat*), continēre, regĕre, coercēre
controller *s* moderator *m*
controversial *adj* concertatorius
controversy *s* controversia, disceptatio, concertatio *f*
contusion *s* contusio *f*, contusum *n*
conundrum *s* aenigma *n*; (*quibble*) cavillum *n*
convalesce *vi* convalescĕre
convalescence *s* conditio convalescendi *f*
convalescent *adj* convalescens
convene *vt* convocare
convenience *s* commoditas, opportunitas, convenientia *f*; (*thing*) commodum *n*
convenient *adj* commodus, idoneus, opportunus; **—ly** commode, apte, opportune
convention *s* convent·us -ūs *m*; (*custom*) mos *m*
conventional *adj* usitatus, tralaticius, solitus
converge *vi* vergĕre, coire
conversant *adj* peritus, exercitatus; **to be — with** versari in (*with abl*)
conversation *s* colloquium *n*, sermo *m*
conversational *adj* in colloquio usitatus
converse *vi* colloqui
converse *s* contrarium *n*, convers·us -ūs *m*
conversely *adv* e contrario, e converso
conversion *s* conversio *f*
convert *vt* convertĕre, commutare; deducĕre
convert *s* neophytus, discipulus *m*
convertible *adj* commutabilis
convex *adj* convexus
convey *vt* portare, vehĕre, convehĕre; (*property*) abalienare; (*fig*) significare
conveyance *s* (*act*) advectio, vectura *f*; (*vehicle*) vehiculum *n*; (*law*) abalienatio, transcriptio *f*
convict *s* convictus, evictus, reus *m*
convict *vt* convincĕre
conviction *s* (*law*) damnatio *f*; (*certainty*) persuasio, fides *f*
convince *vt* persuadēre (*with dat*)
convivial *adj* hilaris, laetus
convocation *s* convocatio *f*
convoke *vt* convocare
convoy *s* praesidium *n*, deductor *m*
convoy *vt* deducĕre
convulse *vt* concutĕre, convellĕre
convulsion *s* convulsio *f*, spasmus *m*
convulsive *adj* spasticus
cook *s* coquus *m*, coqua *f*
cook *vt & vi* coquĕre
cool *adj* frigidulus; (*fearless*) sedatus, immotus, impavidus; (*indifferent*) lentus, frigidus; **—ly** frigide; sedate; lente
cool *vt* refrigerare; *vi* refrigerari; (*fig*) defervescĕre
coolness *s* frigus *n*; (*fig*) lentitudo, cautela *f;* animus aequus *m*
coop *s* (*for chickens*) cavea *f*
coop *vt* **to — up** includĕre
cooperate *vi* unā agĕre; **to — with** adjuvare
cooperation *s* adjumentum *n*, consociatio, opera *f*
cope *vi* **to — with** certare cum (*with abl*); **able to — with** par (*with dat*)
copious *adj* copiosus, abundans; **—ly** copiose, abundanter
copper *s* aes, cuprum *n*
copper *adj* aëneus, cuprinus
copse *s* dumetum, fruticetum *n*
copy *s* exemplar *n*, imitatio, imago *f*
copy *vt* imitari; (*writing*) transcribĕre, exscribĕre

coquette *s* lupa, lasciva *f*
coquettish *adj* lascivus
coral *adj* coralinus
coral *s* coralium *n*
cord *s* funis, restis *m*
cordial *adj* benignus, comis; **—ly** benigne, comiter, ex animo
cordiality *s* comitas *f*
cordon *s* corona *f*
core *s* (*of fruit*) volva *f*; (*fig*) nucleus *m*
Corinthian *adj* Corinthiacus, Corinthius
cork *s* cortex *m*; (*stopper*) obturamentum *n*
corn *s* (*grain*) frumentum *n*; (*on toes*) callus *m*
corner *s* angulus *m*; (*of house*) versura *f*; (*of street*) compitum *n*
cornice *s* corona *f*
corollary *s* corollarium *n*
coronation *s* coronae impositio *f*
coronet *s* diadema *n*
corporal *adj* corporeus, corporalis
corporal *s* decurio *m*
corporate *adj* corporatus
corporation *s* collegium *n*; municipium *n*
corporeal *adj* corporeus
corps *s* legio *f*
corpse *s* cadaver *n*
corpulent *adj* corpulentus
corpuscle *s* corpusculum *n*
correct *adj* correctus, rectus, accuratus; **—ly** recte, bene
correct *vt* corrigĕre, emendare; (*to punish*) animadvertĕre, castigare
correction *s* correctio, emendatio *f*; (*punishment*) animadversio, castigatio *f*
correctness *s* puritas, accuratio *f*
correlation *s* reciprocitas, mutua ratio *f*
correspond *vi* congruĕre; (*by letter*) litteras mutuas scribĕre
correspondence *s* congruentia, convenientia *f*; epistolae *f pl*
correspondent *s* epistolarum scriptor *m*
corridor *s* portic·us -ūs *f*, andron, xystus *m*
corroborate *vt* confirmare
corrode *vt* erodĕre, edĕre
corrosion *s* rosio *f*
corrosive *adj* corrosivus; (*fig*) mordax
corrupt *vt* corrumpĕre, depravare; (*a girl*) stuprare
corrupt *adj* corruptus, putridus; (*fig*) pravus, impurus; venalis; **—ly** corrupte; inceste, turpiter
corrupter *s* corruptor *m*, corruptrix *f*, perditor *m*, perditrix *f*
corruption *s* corruptio, putredo *f*; (*fig*) depravatio, pravitas *f*
corselet *s* lorica *f*
corvette *s* celox *f*
cosily *adv* commode
cosmetic *s* medicamen *n*
cost *s* pretium *n*, impensa *f*; **— of living** anona *f*
cost *vi* (con)stare, venire
costliness *s* caritas *f*
costly *adj* carus; (*extravagant*) sumptuosus, lautus
costume *s* habit·us -ūs, vestit·us -ūs *m*
cosy *adj* commodus, gratus
cot *s* lectulus *m*; (*mil*) grabatus *m*
cottage *s* casa *f*, tugurium *n*
cotton *s* xylinum *n*
cotton *adj* gossipinus
couch *s* cubile, pulvinar *n*; lectus *m*
cough *s* tussis *f*; **to have a bad —** male tussire
cough *vi* tussire
council *s* concilium *n*
councilor *s* consiliarius *m*
counsel *s* (*advice*) consilium *n*; (*person*) advocatus *m*
counsel *vt* consulĕre, monēre
counselor *s* consiliarius, consiliator *m*
count *s* computatio, ratio *f*; (*of indictment*) caput *n*
count *vt* numerare, computare; (*to regard as*) ducĕre, habēre; **to — up** enumerare; *vi* aestimari, habēri; **to — upon** confidĕre (*with dat*)
countenance *s* facies *f*, vult·us -ūs, aspect·us -ūs *m*; **to put out of —** confundĕre, perturbare
countenance *vt* favēre (*with dat*), indulgēre (*with dat*), adjuvare
counter *s* (*of shop*) abacus *m*; (*in games*) calculus *m*
counteract *vt* obsistĕre (*with dat*); (*a sickness*) medēri (*with dat*)
counteraction *s* oppositio *f*
counterfeit *vt* imitari, simulare, fingĕre, adulterare
counterfeit *adj* simulatus, spurius, ficticius, adulterinus
counterfeit *s* (*money*) nummus adulterinus *m*; simulatio, imitatio *f*
counterfeiter *s* imitator, falsarius *m*
countermand *vt* renuntiare
counterpart *s* res gemella *f*; par *m*, *f & n*
countersign *vt* contrascribĕre
countless *adj* innumerabilis, innumerus
country *s* terra, regio *f*; (*territory*) fines *m pl*; (*not city*) rus *n*; (*native*) patria *f*
country house *s* villa *f*
countryman *s* civis, popularis *m*
countryside *s* rus *n*, agri *m pl*
couple *s* par *n*; mariti *m pl*; **a — of** duo
couple *vt* copulare, unire; *vi* (*of animals*) coire
courage *s* virtus *f*, animus *m*, fortitudo *f*; **to lose —** animos dimittĕre; **to take —** bono animo esse
courageous *adj* fortis, animosus, acer; **—ly** fortiter, acriter
courier *s* cursor, nuntius, tabellarius *m*
course *s* (*movement*) curs·us -ūs *m*; (*of life*) ratio *f*; (*of water*) duct·us -ūs *m*; (*route*) iter *n*; (*at table*) ferculum *n*; (*order*) series *f*; (*for racing*) circus *m*, stadium *n*; **in due —** mox; **in the — of** inter (*with acc*); **of —** certe, scilicet
court *s* (*law*) forum, tribunal, judi-

cium *n*, judices *m pl*; (*open area*) area *f*; (*of house*) atrium *n*; (*palace*) aula *f*; (*retinue*) comitat·us -ūs *m*
court *vt* colĕre, ambire; (*woman*) petĕre; (*danger*) se offerre (*with dat*)
courteous *adj* comis, urbanus; **—ly** comiter, urbane
courtesan *s* meretrix *f*
courtesy *s* comitas, urbanitas *f*; (*act*) officium *n*
courtier *s* aulicus *m*
courtly *adj* aulicus; officiosus
court-martial *s* judicium castrense *n*
courtship *s* amor *m*, ambitio *f*
courtyard *s* aula *f*
cousin *s* consobrinus *m*, consobrina *f*, patruelis *m & f*
cove *s* sin·us -ūs *m*
covenant *s* pactum *n*, pactio *f*
covenant *vi* pacisci, stipulari
cover *s* tegmen, integumentum *n*; (*lid*) operculum *n*; (*shelter*) tectum *n*, (*mil*) praesidium *n*; (*pretense*) species *f*; **under — of** sub (*with abl*), sub specie (*with genit*)
cover *vt* tegĕre, operire; (*to hide*) celare, velare; **to — up** obtegĕre
coverlet *s* lodix *f*
covet *vt* concupiscĕre, cupĕre, appetĕre
covetous *adj* avidus, appetens, cupidus; **—ly** avide, avare, appetenter
covey *s* grex *m*
cow *vt* domare
coward *s* homo *or* miles ignavus *m*
cowardice *s* ignavia *f*
cowardly *adj* ignavus
cower *vi* sudsidĕre
cowherd *s* bubulcus *m*
cowl *s* cucullus *m*
coy *adj* verecundus, pudens; **—ly** verecunde, pudenter
coyness *s* verecundia *f*, pudor *m*
cozily *adv* commode, jucunde
cozy *adj* commodus, jucundus
crab *s* cancer *m*
crabbed *adj* morosus, difficilis
crack *s* fissura, rima *f*; (*noise*) crepit·us -ūs *m*; **at — of dawn** prima luce
cracked *adj* rimosus; (*fig*) cerritus, delirus
cracker *s* crustulum *n*
crackle *vi* crepitare
crackling *s* crepit·us -ūs *m*
cradle *s* cunae *f pl*, cunabula *n pl*
craft *s* (*cunning*) astutia *f*, artes *f pl*, dolus *m*; (*skill*) ars *f*; (*trade*) ars *f*; (*boat*) scapha, cymba *f*, navigium *n*
craftily *adv* callide, astute; dolose
crafty *adj* astutus, callidus, subdolus
craftsman *s* artifex, faber *m*
craftsmanship *s* artificium *n*, man·us -ūs *f*
cram *vt* farcire; **to — together** constipare
cramp *s* spasmus *m*
cramp *vt* comprimĕre, coartare
crane *s* (*bird*) grus *m & f*; (*machine*) tolleno *f*; machina *f*
crank *s* (*machine*) uncus *m*; (*person*) morosus *m*
crash *s* fragor, strepit·us -ūs *m*, ruina *f*
crash *vi* strepĕre, frangorem dare
crater *s* crater *m*
crave *vt* efflagitare, appetĕre, concupiscĕre, desiderare
craven *adj* ignavus atque abjectus
craving *s* desiderium *n*, appetitio *f*
crawl *vi* repĕre, serpĕre
crayfish *s* commarus *m*
crayon *s* creta *f*
craze *s* libido *f*
craziness *s* imbecillitas, mens alienata *f*, furor *m*
crazy *adj* imbecillus, demens, cerritus; **to drive —** mentem alienare (*with genit*)
creak *vi* stridēre, crepitare
creaking *s* stridor, crepit·us -ūs *m*
creaking *adj* stridulus
cream *s* flos lactis *m*; (*fig*) flos *m*
crease *s* plica, ruga *f*
crease *vt* corrugare, rugare
create *vt* creare; (*fig*) fingĕre
creation *s* (*act*) creatio *f*; (*world*) summa rerum *f*, mundus *m*; (*fig*) opus *n*
creative *adj* creatrix, effectrix
creator *s* creator, opifex, auctor *m*
creature *s* animal *n*; homo *m*; (*lackey*) minister *m*
credence *s* fides *f*; **to give — to** credĕre (*with dat*)
credentials *s* litterae commendaticiae *f pl*; testimonia *n pl*
credibility *s* fides, auctoritas *f*
credible *adj* credibilis; (*of persons*) locuples
credit *s* (*authority*) auctoritas *f*; (*faith*) fides *f*; (*reputation*) existimatio, fama *f*; (*com*) fides *f*; (*recognition*) laus *f*
credit *vt* credĕre (*with dat*); (*com*) acceptum referre (*with dat*)
creditable *adj* honorificus, honestus, laudabilis
creditor *s* creditor *m*
credulity *s* credulitas *f*
credulous *adj* credulus; **—ly** credens
creed *s* fides, religio *f*, dogma *n*
creek *s* aestuarium *n*; fluvius *m*
creep *vi* repĕre, serpĕre; (*of flesh*) horrēre
crescent *s* luna crescens *f*
crescent-shaped *adj* lunatus
crest *s* crista *f*
crested *adj* cristatus
crestfallen *adj* dejectus, demissus
crevice *s* rima, rimula *f*
crew *s* grex *m*; (*of ship*) remiges, nautae *m pl*
crib *s* (*manger*) praesepe *n*; (*small bed*) lectulus *m*
cricket *s* gryllus *m*, cicada *f*
crier *s* praeco *m*
crime *s* scelus, delictum, maleficium, flagitium *n*
Crimea *s* Tauris *f*
criminal *adj* criminosus, scelestus, flagitiosus; **—ly** nefarie, improbe; (*law*) criminaliter
criminal *s* reus, sceleratus *m*
crimp *vt* crispare

crimson *adj* coccineus
crimson *s* coccum *n*
cringe *vi* adulari, assentari
cringing *s* adulatio abjecta *f*
cripple *s* claudus *m*
cripple *vt* claudum facĕre, mutilare, debilitare; (*fig*) frangĕre
crippled *adj* mancus, claudus
crisis *s* discrimen *n*
crisp *adj* crispus, fragilis; (*fig*) alacer
criterion *s* norma *f*, indicium *n*, index *m*
critic *s* judex, censor, existimator *m*; (*literary*) criticus, grammaticus *m*
critical *adj* criticus, intellegens; (*careful*) accuratus; (*blaming*) fastidiosus, censorius; (*crucial*) anceps, periculosus; **—ly** accurate; periculose
criticism *s* ars critica *f*; censura, reprehensio *f*, judicium *n*
criticize *vt* judicare; carpĕre, reprehendĕre, agitare, castigare
croak *vi* coaxare; (*of raven*) crocitare, crocire; (*fig*) queritari
croaking *s* crocitatio *f*; (*fig*) querimonia *f*
croaking *adj* raucus
crock *s* olla *f*
crocodile *s* crocodilus *m*
crook *s* pedum *n*
crook *vt* curvare, flectĕre
crooked *adj* curvatus, flexus; (*fig*) pravus, dolosus; **—ly** prave
crop *s* (*of grain*) messis, seges *f*; (*of bird*) ingluvies *f*
crop *vt* abscidĕre, tondēre; (*to harvest*) metĕre; (*to browse*) carpĕre
cross *s* crux *f*; (*figure*) quincunx *m*, decussis *f*; (*fig*) molestia *f*, cruciat·us -ūs *m*
cross *adj* transversus; (*contrary*) adversus; (*peevish*) acerbus, morosus
cross *vt* transire, transgredi; (*river*) trajicĕre; (*mountain*) transcendĕre; (*to thwart*) frustrari, adversari; **to — out** expungĕre, delēre
cross-examination *s* percontatio, interrogatio *f*
cross-examine *vt* percontari, interrogare
crossing *s* transit·us -ūs, traject·us -ūs *m*; (*of roads*) bivium *n*; (*of three roads*) trivium *n*; (*of four roads*) quadrivium *n*
cross-roads *s* quadrivium *n*
crouch *vi* se submittĕre, subsidĕre
crow *s* (*bird*) cornix *f*; (*of cock*) cant·us -ūs *m*, gallicinium *n*
crow *vi* (*of cocks*) canĕre, cucurire; (*to boast*) jactare, gestire
crowbar *s* vectis *f*
crowd *s* turba, frequentia *f*, concurs·us -ūs *m*; **in —s** gregatim
crowd *vt* arctare, stipare, premĕre; *vi* frequentare; **to — around** stipare, circumfundi
crowded *adj* confertus, frequens, spissus
crowing *s* gallicinium *n*, cant·us -ūs *m*
crown *s* corona *f*, diadema *n*; (*top*) vertex *m*; (*fig*) apex *m*
crown *vt* coronare; (*with garlands, etc.*) cingĕre; (*fig*) cumulare
crucifix *s* imago Christi cruci affixi *f*
crucifixion *s* crucis supplicium *n*
crucify *vt* in cruce suffigĕre
crude *adj* crudus; rudis, incultus, informis; **—ly** imperfecte; inculte
cruel *adj* crudelis, atrox, saevus; **—ly** crudeliter, saeve, dure
cruelty *s* crudelitas, atrocitas, saevitia *f*
cruet *s* guttus *m*, acetabulum *n*
cruise *vi* circumvectari, navigare
cruise *s* navigatio *f*
crumb *s* mica *f*
crumble *vt* friare, putrefacĕre, comminuĕre, conterĕre; *vi* collabi, friari, corruĕre
crumbling *adj* puter, friabilis
crumple *vt* corrugare, duplicare
crunch *vt* dentibus frangĕre
crush *vt* contundĕre, conterĕre; (*fig*) opprimĕre, affligĕre
crush *s* contusio *f*; (*crowd*) turba, frequentia *f*
crust *s* crusta *f*, crustum *n*
crusty *adj* crustosus; (*fig*) cerebrosus, stomachosus
crutch *s* fulcrum *n*
cry *vt* clamare, clamitare; **to — out** exclamare, vociferari; *vi* (*to shout*) clamare, clamitare; (*to weep*) lacrimare, flēre; (*of infant*) vagire; **to — out** exclamare; **to — out against** objurgare
cry *s* clamor *m*; (*of infant*) vagit·us -ūs *m*; (*weeping*) plorat·us -ūs *m*
crying *s* flet·us -ūs, plorat·us -ūs *m*
crypt *s* crypta *f*
crystal *adj* crystallinus, vitreus
crystal *s* crystallum *n*
crystal-clear *adj* pellucidus
cub *s* catulus *m*
cube *s* cubus *m*
cubic *adj* cubicus
cubit *s* cubitum *n*, ulna *f*
cuckoo *s* coccyx, cuculus *m*
cucumber *s* cucumis *m*
cud *s* ruma *f*, rumen *n*; **to chew the —** ruminare
cudgel *s* fustis *m*
cue *s* (*hint*) nut·us -ūs *m*, signum, indicium *n*
cuff *s* (*blow*) colaphus *m*; (*of sleeves*) extrema manica *f*
cull *vt* carpĕre, legĕre, decerpĕre
culminate *vi* ad summum fastigium venire
culpable *adj* culpandus, nocens
culprit *s* reus *m*, rea *f*
cultivate *vt* colĕre; (*the mind*) excolĕre; (*friends*) fovēre
cultivation *s* cultura *f*, cult·us -ūs *m*
cultivator *s* cultor, colonus *m*
culture *s* cultura *f*, cult·us -ūs *m*
cumbersome *adj* onerosus, impediens
cunning *adj* sollers, callidus, doctus, peritus; (*in bad sense*) astutus
cunning *s* calliditas, peritia; astutia *f*
cup *s* poculum *n*, calix *m*; (*of flower*) calyx *m*

cupbearer *s* pocillator *m*
cupboard *s* armarium *n*
Cupid *s* Cupido, Amor *m*
cupidity *s* cupiditas *f*
cupola *s* tholus *m*; turricula rotunda *f*
cur *s* canis *m*; (*fig*) scelestus *m*
curable *adj* medicabilis, sanabilis
curative *adj* medicabilis
curator *s* curator *m*
curb *s* frenum *n*; (*fig*) coercitio *f*, frenum *n*
curb *vt* frenare, infrenare; (*fig*) coercēre, cohibēre
curdle *vt* coagulare; *vi* coagulare, concrescĕre
cure *s* (*remedy*) remedium *n*; (*process*) sanatio *f*
cure *vt* medēri (*with dat*), sanare; (*to pickle*) salire
curiosity *s* curiositas *f*; (*thing*) miraculum *n*
curious *adj* curiosus; (*strange*) mirus, novus, insolitus; **—ly** curiose; mirabiliter, mirum in modum
curl *vt* (*hair*) crispare; torquēre; *vi* crispari; (*of smoke*) volvi
curl *s* (*natural*) cirrus *m*; (*artificial*) cincinnus *m*
curly *adj* crispus
currency *s* (*money*) moneta *f*; (*use*) us·us -ūs *m*
current *adj* vulgaris, usitatus; **—ly** vulgo
current *s* flumen *n*; (*of air*) afflat·us -ūs *m*, aura *f*; **against the —** adverso flumine; **with the —** secundo flumine
curse *s* exsecratio, maledictio *f*, maledictum *n*; (*fig*) pestis *f*
curse *vt* maledicĕre (*with dat*), exsecrari; *vi* exsecratione uti
cursed *adj* exsecrabilis
corsorily *adv* breviter, summatim
cursory *adj* levis, brevis
curt *adj* abruptus; **—ly** breviter
curtail *vt* minuĕre, coartare; decurtare
curtain *s* velum, aulaeum *n*
curvature *s* curvatura *f*
curve *s* curvamen *n*, flex·us -ūs *m*, curvatura *f*
curve *vt* incurvare, flectĕre, inflectĕre, arcuare
curved *adj* curvatus, curvus; (*as a sickle*) falcatus
cushion *s* pulvinar *n*; (*on a seat*) sedularia *n pl*
custard *s* artolaganus *m*
custody *s* custodia, tutela *f*; (*imprisonment*) carcer *m*; **to keep in —** custodire
custom *s* mos, us·us -ūs *m*, consuetudo *f*, institutum, praescriptum *n*; (*duty*) portorium, vectigal *n*
customary *adj* usitatus, consuetus, tralaticius
customer *s* emptor *m*
customs officer *s* portitor *m*
cut *vt* secare; (*to fell*) caedĕre; (*to mow*) succidĕre; **to — apart** intercidĕre, dissecare; **to — away** recidĕre, abscindĕre; (*to amputate*) amputare; **to — down** caedĕre; (*to kill*) occidĕre; **to — in pieces** concidĕre; **to — off** praecidĕre, abscindĕre; (*the head*) detruncare; (*to intercept*) intercludĕre, prohibēre; (*to destroy*) exstinguĕre; **to — open** incidĕre; **to — out** exsecare; (*out of rock, etc.*) excidĕre; **to — short** intercidĕre; (*to abridge*) praecidĕre; (*fig*) (*to interrupt*) interpellare; **to — up** minutatim concidere; (*enemy*) trucidare
cutlass *s* ensis, gladius *m*
cutlery *s* cultri *m pl*
cutlet *s* offa *f*, frustum *n*
cutthroat *s* sicarius *m*
cutting *adj* (*sharp*) acutus; (*fig*) mordax
cutting *s* (*act*) sectio, consectio, exsectio *f*; (*thing*) segmen *n*
cuttlefish *s* loligo, sepia *f*
cycle *s* orbis *m*
cylinder *s* cylindrus *m*
cylindrical *adj* cylindratus
cymbal *s* cymbalum *n*
cynic *adj* cynicus
cynic *s* cynicus *m*
cynical *adj* mordax, difficilis; **—ly** mordaciter
cynicism *s* acerbitas *f*
cypress *s* cupressus *f*

D

dab *vt* illidĕre
dab *s* massula *f*
dabble *vi* **to — in** gustare
dactyl *s* dactylus *m*
dactylic *adj* dactylicus
daffodil *s* asphodelus, narcissus *m*
dagger *s* pugio *m*, sica *f*
daily *adj* diurnus, quotidianus *or* cottidianus
daily *adv* quotidie *or* cottidie, in dies
dainty *adj* (*of persons*) fastidiosus, mollis, elegans; (*of things*) delicatus, exquisitus
dairy *s* cella lactaria *f*
daisy *s* bellis *f*
dale *s* vallis *f*
dalliance *s* lus·us -ūs *m*, lascivia *f*
dally *vi* morari; (*to trifle*) nugari, ludificari
dam *s* moles *f*, agger *m*; (*of animals*) mater *f*
damage *s* damnum, incommodum, detrimentum *n*; (*injury*) injuria, noxa *f*
damage *vt* nocēre (*with dat*), laedĕre; (*reputation*) violare

dame *s* domina, hera, matrona *f*
damn *vt* damnare, exsecrari
damnable *adj* damnabilis, destestabilis
damnably *adv* damnabiliter, improbe
damnation *s* damnatio *f*
damp *adj* (h)umidus
dampen *vt* humectare; (*fig*) infringere, restinguĕre
dampness *s* uligo *f*
damsel *s* puella, virgo *f*
dance *s* saltat·us -ūs *m*, saltatio *f*
dance *vi* saltare
dancer *s* saltator *m*
dancing *s* saltatio *f*, saltat·us -ūs *m*
dandelion *s* taraxacum *n*
dandruff *s* porrigo *f*
dandy *s* homo bellus et lepidus *m*
danger *s* periculum *n*
dangerous *adj* periculosus; **—ly** periculose, graviter
dangle *vi* pendēre, dependēre
dangling *adj* pendulus
dank *adj* (h)umidus, uvidus, udus
dappled *adj* variatus, variegatus
dare *vt* provocare; *vi* audēre
daring *adj* audax; **—ly** audacter
daring *s* audacia, audentia *f*
dark *adj* obscurus, opacus; (*in color*) ater, fuscus; (*fig*) obscurus, ambiguus; atrox; **—ly** obscure
dark *s* tenebrae *f pl*; obscurum *n*; **to keep in the —** celare
darken *vt* obscurare, occaecare; (*of colors*) infuscare
darkness *s* obscuritas, opacitas *f*, tenebrae *f pl*
darling *adj* suavis, mellitus, carus, dilectus
darling *s* deliciae *f pl*, corculum *n*
darn *vt* resarcire
dart *s* jaculum, spiculum *n*
dart *vt* jaculari, jacĕre; *vi* provolare, emicare, se conjicĕre
dash *vt* (*to splash*) aspergĕre; (*hopes*) frustrari, frangĕre; **to — against** illidĕre, incutere, offendĕre; **to — off** (*to write hurriedly*) scriptitare; **to — to pieces** discutĕre; **to — to the ground** prosternĕre; *vi* (*to rush*) ruĕre, ferri
dash *s* impet·us -ūs *m*; curs·us -ūs *m*; (*animation*) alacritas *f*; (*small amount*) admixtio *f*
dashing *adj* acer, alacer, fulgidus, splendidus
data *s* facta *n pl*
date *s* (*time*) dies *m & f*, tempus *n*; (*fruit*) palmula *f*; **to become out of —** exolescĕre; **to —** adhuc; **out of —** obsoletus
date *vt* diem ascribĕre (*with dat*); *vi* **to — from** oriri ab (*with abl*), originem trahĕre ab (*with abl*)
date palm *s* phoenix, palma *f*
dative *s* dativus *m*
daub *vt* oblinĕre, illinĕre
daughter *s* filia *f*
daughter-in-law *s* nurus *f*
daunt *vt* pavefacĕre, perterrēre
dauntless *adj* impavidus, intrepidus; **—ly** impavide, intrepide
dawdle *vi* morari, cessare, cunctari
dawn *s* aurora, prima lux *f*, diluculum *n*; **at —** prima luce
dawn *vi* illucescere, dilucescĕre; (*fig*) **to — on** occurrĕre (*with dat*)
day *s* dies *m & f*; lux *f*, sol *m*; **by —** interdiu; **— by —** in dies; **every —** quotidie, cottidie; **from — to —** in dies; **next —** postridie; **some —** olim; **the — after tomorrow** perendie; **the — before** pridie
day *adj* diurnus, dialis
daybreak *s* lux prima *f*; **before —** antelucio
daylight *s* lux *f*, dies *m & f*
daystar *s* Lucifer, Phosphorus *m*
daytime *s* dies *m*, tempus diurnum *n*; **in the —** interdiu
daze *s* stupor *m*
daze *vt* obstupefacĕre
dazzle *vt* obcaecare, praestringĕre
dazzling *adj* fulgidus, splendidus
deacon *s* diaconus *m*
dead *adj* mortuus; defunctus; (*fig*) torpidus, segnis, iners
dead *s* manes *m pl*; **— of night** media nox *f*; **— of winter** summa hiems *f*
dead *adv* omnino, totaliter, prorsus
deaden *vt* hebetare, obtundĕre; *vi* hebetari, obtundi
deadly *adj* mortifer, letalis; (*fig*) capitalis, implacabilis
deaf *adj* surdus; **to be — to** non audire
deafen *vt* exsurdare, obtundĕre
deaf-mute *adj* surdus idemque mutus
deafness *s* surditas *f*
deal *s* (*quantity*) numerus *m*, copia *f*; (*com*) negotium *n*; **a good — longer** multo diutius; **a good — of** aliquantus
deal *vt* partiri, dividĕre, distribuĕre; *vi* (*com*) mercari, negotiari; **to — with** (*to treat of*) agĕre de (*with abl*), tractare
dealer *s* mercator, negotiator, distributor *m*
dealing *s* negotiatio, mercatura *f*; (*doing*) facta *n pl*
dean *s* decanus *m*
dear *adj* carus, dulcis, gratus; (*costly*) carus, preciosus; **—ly** valde, ardenter; (*at high cost*) magni, magno
dear *interj* (*dismay*) hei!; (*surprise*) ahem!
dearness *s* caritas *f*
dearth *s* inopia, penuria, fames *f*
death *s* mors *f*, obit·us -ūs, interit·us -ūs *m*; (*in violent form*) nex *f*
deathbed *s* **on the —** moriens, moribundus
deathless *adj* immortalis
deathlike *adj* cadaverosus, luridus
deathly *adj* pallidus
debase *vt* depravare, corrumpĕre; (*coinage*) adulterare; **to — oneself** se demittĕre, se prosternĕre
debasement *s* adulteratio *f*; ignominia *f*, dedecus *n*
debatable *adj* disputabilis, controversiosus, ambiguus

debate *vt* disputare, disceptare; *vi* argumentari, disserĕre
debate *s* disceptatio, controversia, altercatio *f*; (*law*) actio *f*
debater *s* disputator *m*
debauch *vt* stuprare, corrumpĕre, vitiare; *vi* (*to revel*) debacchari
debauchery *s* ganea *f*, stuprum *n*
debilitate *vt* debilitare
debit *s* expensum *n*
debit *vt* in expensum referre
debt *s* aes alienum *n*; (*fig*) debitum *n*; **to pay off a —** aes alienum persolvĕre; **to run up a —** aes alienum contrahĕre
debtor *s* debitor *m*
decade *s* decem anni *m pl*
decadence *s* occas·us -ūs *m*
decadent *adj* degener
decalogue *s* decalogus *m*
decamp *vi* (*mil*) castra movēre; (*fig*) aufugĕre, discedĕre
decant *vt* diffundĕre
decanter *s* lagoena *f*
decapitate *vt* detruncare
decay *s* tabes, ruina *f*, laps·us -ūs *m*; (*fig*) defectio *f*
decay *vi* putrescĕre, tabescĕre, senescĕre
decease *s* mors *f*, obit·us -ūs *m*, decess·us -ūs *m*
deceased *adj* mortuus, defunctus
deceit *s* fraus *f*, dolus *m*
deceitful *adj* fallax, dolosus, fraudulentus; **—ly** fallaciter, dolose
deceive *vt* decipĕre, fallĕre, fraudare
December *s* (mensis) December *m*
decency *s* decorum *n*, honestas *f*
decent *adj* honestus, pudicus; **—ly** honeste, pudenter
deception *s* deceptio, fallacia, fraus *f*
deceptive *adj* fallax, fraudulentus, vanus, falsus
decide *vt & vi* (*dispute*) disceptare, dijudicare, decernĕre; **to — to** constituĕre (*with inf*), statuĕre (*with inf*); **the senate decided** placuit senatui; visum est senatui
decided *adj* firmus, constans; (*of things*) certus; **—ly** certe, plane
deciduous *adj* caducus
decimate *vt* decimare; (*fig*) depopulari
decipher *vt* explicare, expedire, enodare
decision *s* sententia *f*; judicium, arbitrium, decretum *n*; (*of senate*) auctoritas *f*
decisive *adj* certus, firmus; **—ly** praecise
deck *vt* exornare, ornare; (*table*) sternĕre
deck *s* pons *m*
declamatory *adj* declamatorius; (*fig*) inflatus
declaration *s* declaratio, professio, affirmatio *f*; (*of war*) denuntiatio *f*
declare *vt* declarare, affirmare, aperire, profitēri; (*war*) denuntiare, indicĕre; (*proclamation*) edicĕre; *vi* **to — for** favēre (*with dat*)
declension *s* declinatio *f*
declinable *adj* declinabilis, casualis
declination *s* declinatio *f*; (*decay*) defectio *f*
decline *s* (*slope*) declive *n*; (*of strength*) defectio, diminutio *f*
decline *vt* (*to refuse*) recusare, renuĕre, abnuĕre; (*gram*) declinare, flectĕre; (*battle*) detrectare; *vi* vergĕre, inclinare; (*to decay, fail*) deficĕre, minui, decrescĕre; (*of prices*) laxare
decode *vt* enodare
decompose *vt* dissolvĕre, resolvĕre; *vi* tabescĕre, putescĕre, dissolvi
decomposition *s* dissolutio *f*
decorate *vt* ornare, decorare
decoration *s* ornatio *f*; (*ornament*) ornamentum *n*; (*distinction*) decus *n*
decorator *s* exornator *m*
decorous *adj* decorus, modestus, pudens; **—ly** decore, modeste, pudenter
decorum *s* decorum, honestum *n*, pudor *m*
decoy *s* illecebra *f*, illicium *n*
decoy *vt* allicĕre, inescare; (*fig*) illicĕre
decrease *s* deminutio, imminutio *f*
decrease *vt* (de)minuere, imminuĕre, extenuare; *vi* decrescĕre, (de)minui
decree *s* decretum, edictum *n*; (*of senate*) consultum *n*, auctoritas *f*; (*of assembly*) scitum *n*
decree *vt* decernĕre, edicĕre; (*of assembly*) jubēre, sciscĕre; **the senate —s** senatui placet, senatui videtur
decrepit *adj* decrepitus, debilis
decry *vt* detrectare, obtrectare, vituperare
dedicate *vt* dedicare, consecrare, devovēre
dedication *s* dedicatio, devotio *f*; (*of a book*) nuncupatio *f*
deduce *vt* deducĕre, concludĕre
deducible *adj* consectarius
deduct *vt* detrahĕre, subtrahĕre, demĕre
deduction *s* deductio, deminutio *f*; (*inference*) conclusio *f*, consequens *n*
deed *s* factum, facinus *n*; (*law*) syngrapha *f*, instrumentum *n*
deem *vt* judicare, existimare, ducĕre, habēre
deep *adj* altus, profundus; (*of sounds*) gravis; (*of color*) satur; (*fig*) abstrusus, gravis; **—ly** alte, profunde; (*inwardly*) penitus; (*fig*) valde, graviter, vehementer
deep *s* profundum, altum *n*
deepen *vt* defodĕre; (*fig*) augēre; *vi* altior fieri; (*fig*) crescĕre, densare
deer *s* cervus *m*, cerva *f*; (*fallow deer*) dama *f*
deface *vt* deformare, turpare, foedare
defaced *adj* deformis
defacement *s* deformitas *f*
defamation *s* calumnia *f*, opprobrium *n*
defamatory *adj* probrosus, contumeliosus
defame *vt* diffamare, infamare, calumniari

default *s* culpa *f*, delictum *n*, defect·us -ūs *m*
defeat *s* clades *f*; (*at polls*) repulsa *f*
defeat *vt* vincĕre, superare; (*to baffle*) frustrari
defect *s* vitium, mendum *n*; (*lack*) defect·us -ūs *m*
defect *vi* (*to desert*) deficĕre
defection *s* defectio *f*
defective *adj* vitiosus, imperfectus, mancus; (*gram*) defectivus
defend *vt* defendere, custodire, tuēri; (*in court*) patrocinari
defendant *s* reus *m*, rea *f*
defender *s* defensor, propugnator *m*; (*law*) patronus *m*
defense *s* (*act*) defensio *f*; praesidium, munimentum *n*, tutela *f*; (*law*) patrocinium *n*; (*speech*) defensio *f*
defenseless *adj* inermis, infensus; defensoribus nudatus
defensible *adj* excusabilis, justus; inexpugnabilis
defensive *adj* defendens; **— weapons** arma *n pl*
defer *vt* differre; *vi* obsequi
deference *s* observantia, reverentia *f*, obsequium *n*; **out of —** reverenter
defiance *s* provocatio, ferocia *f*
defiant *adj* minax, insolens; **—ly** insolenter
deficiency *s* defectio, inopia, penuria *f*, defect·us -ūs *m*
deficient *adj* inops, mancus; **to be —** deficĕre, deesse
deficit *s* lacuna *f*
defile *s* fauces *f pl*
defile *vt* contaminare, inquinare; (*fig*) foedare
define *vt* (*meaning*) explicare; (*limits*) (de)finire, circumscribĕre, terminare
definite *adj* definitus, certus; **—ly** certe, certo, prorsus; definite
definition *s* definitio *f*
definitive *adj* definitivus; **—ly** definite, distincte
deflect *vt* deflectĕre, declinare; *vi* deflectĕre, errare
deflection *s* deflexio, declinatio *f*, flex·us -ūs *m*
deflower *vt* stuprare
deform *vt* deformare
deformed *adj* deformatus, deformis, distortus, pravus
deformity *s* deformitas, pravitas *f*
defraud *vt* fraudare, defraudare
defray *vt* praebēre, suppeditare
defunct *adj* defunctus, mortuus
defy *vt* provocare, contemnĕre, spernĕre
degeneracy *s* mores corrupti *m pl*
degenerate *adj* degener
degenerate *vi* degenerare
degradation *s* dedecus *n*, ignominia, infamia *f*
degrade *vt* dejicĕre, abdicare; ex loco movēre
degrading *adj* indignus
degree *s* grad·us -ūs, ordo *m*
deification *s* apotheosis *f*
deify *vt* divum habēre, inter deos referre, consecrare
deign *vt* dignari, curare
deism *s* deismus *m*
deity *s* numen *n*; deus *m*, dea *f*
dejected *adj* afflictus, demissus; **—ly** maeste
dejection *s* animi abjectio, maestitia *f*
delay *s* mora, cunctatio *f*
delay *vt* detinēre, tardare, remorari; *vi* morari, cunctari
delectable *adj* amoenus, jucundus
delegate *s* legatus *m*
delegate *vt* delegare, mandare, committĕre
delegation *s* delegatio, legatio *f*
delete *vt* delēre
deletion *s* litura *f*
deliberate *adj* deliberatus, consideratus, cautus, prudens; (*speech*) lentus; **—ly** deliberate, de industria; lente
deliberate *vi* deliberare, considerare, consulere
deliberation *s* deliberatio, consultatio *f*
delicacy *s* subtilitas, tenuitas *f*; elegantia *f*; (*manner*) lux·us -ūs *m*; (*health*) suavitas *f*; (*food*) cuppedia *f*
delicate *adj* (*tender*) delicatus, tener, mollis, exquisitus; (*of texture*) subtilis; (*in taste*) elegans, fastidiosus; (*in health*) infirmus; **—ly** delicate; eleganter; subtiliter
delicious *adj* suavis, dulcis
delight *s* delectatio *f*, gaudium *n*, voluptas *f*
delight *vt* delectare, oblectare; *vi* **to — in** delectari (*with abl*)
delightful *adj* suavis, jucundus; **—ly** suaviter, jucunde
delineate *vt* delineare, describĕre, adumbrare
delineation *s* designatio, descriptio *f*
delinquency *s* delictum *n*
delinquent *s* nocens *m & f*, noxius *m*
delirious *adj* delirus, phreneticus
delirium *s* delirium *n*, phrenesis *f*
deliver *vt* (*to hand over*) tradĕre, dare; (*to free*) liberare, eripĕre; (*to surrender*) prodĕre; (*speech*) habēre; (*sentence*) dicĕre; (*message*) referre; (*blow*) intendĕre; (*child*) obstetricari
deliverance *s* liberatio *f*
deliverer *s* liberator *m*; nuntius *m*
delivery *s* liberatio *f*; (*of goods*) traditio *f*; (*of speech*) actio, pronuntiatio *f*; (*of child*) part·us -ūs *m*
delude *vt* decipĕre, deludĕre
deluge *s* diluvium *n*, inundatio *f*
deluge *vt* inundare, obruĕre
delusion *s* delusio *f*, error *m*
demagogue *s* plebicola *m*
demand *s* postulatio, petitio *f*, postulatum *n*
demand *vt* postulare, flagitare, poscĕre; exigĕre
demarcation *s* confinium *n*
demean *vt* **to — oneself** se demittĕre
demeanor *s* gest·us -ūs *m*, mores *m pl*

demerit *s* culpa *f*, delictum *n*
demigod *s* heros *m*
demise *s* decess·us -ūs, obit·us -ūs *m*
democracy *s* civitas popularis *f*, liber populus *m*
democrat *s* homo popularis *m*
democratic *adj* popularis; **—ally** populi voluntate
demolish *vt* demoliri, disjicĕre, diruĕre, destruĕre
demolition *s* demolitio, destructio *f*
demon *s* daemon *m*
demonstrable *adj* demonstrabilis
demonstrably *adv* clare, manifeste
demonstrate *vt* (*to show*) monstrare, ostendĕre; (*to prove*) demonstrare
demonstration *s* demonstratio *f*
demonstrative *adj* demonstrativus; **—ly** demonstrative
demoralization *s* depravatio *f*
demoralize *vt* depravare, labefactare
demote *vt* loco movēre
demure *adj* taciturnus, modestus; **—ly** modeste, pudice
den *s* latibulum *n*
deniable *adj* infitiandus
denial *s* negatio, repudiatio *f*
denomination *s* nominatio *f*, nomen *n*; secta *f*
denote *vt* significare
denounce *vt* denuntiare, deferre
dense *adj* densus, spissus, confertus; **—ly** dense, crebro
density *s* densitas, crassitudo *f*; (*crowd*) frequentia *f*
dent *s* nota *f*
dentist *s* dentium medicus *m*
denude *vt* nudare, denudare
denunciation *s* denuntiatio, accusatio *f*
deny *vt* negare, abnegare; (*to renounce*) renuntiare
depart *vi* abire, discedĕre, proficisci; (*to die*) obire
departed *adj* mortuus, defunctus
department *s* pars, provincia *f*
departure *s* abit·us -ūs, discess·us -ūs, digress·us -ūs *m*; (*deviation*) digressio *f*; (*death*) obit·us -ūs *m*
depend *vi* **to — on** pendēre ex (*with abl*), niti (*with abl*); (*to rely on*) fidĕre (*with dat or abl*)
dependable *adj* fidus
dependence *s* clientela *f*; (*reliance*) fiducia *f*
dependency *s* provincia *f*
dependent *adj* subjectus, obediens, obnoxius
depict *vt* (de)pingĕre; describĕre, exprimĕre
deplete *vt* deminuĕre
depletion *s* deminutio *f*
deplorable *adj* miserabilis, flebilis, plorabilis
deplorably *adv* misere, pessime
deplore *vt* deplorare, deflēre
deploy *vt* (*mil*) explicare, expedire
deponent *adj* (*gram*) deponens
deportment *s* gest·us -ūs, habit·us -ūs *m*
depose *vt* (de)movēre
deposit *vt* deponĕre
deposit *s* depositum *n*, fiducia *f*
deposition *s* depositio *f*, testimonium *n*
depositor *s* depositor *m*
depot *s* (*com*) emporium *n*; (*for military supplies*) armamentarium *n*
deprave *vt* depravare
depravity *s* depravatio, turpitudo, pravitas *f*
deprecate *vt* deprecari
deprecation *s* deprecatio *f*
depreciate *vt* detrectare, obtrectare
depreciation *s* detrectatio, obrectatio *f*; (*of price*) vilitas *f*
depredation *s* spoliatio, direptio *f*
depress *vt* deprimĕre; (*fig*) infringĕre, affligĕre
depressed *adj* depressus, afflictus; (*flat*) planus; (*hollow*) cavus
depression *s* depressio, imminutio *f*; (*fig*) tristitia *f*
depressive *adj* tristis, affligens
deprivation *s* privatio, orbatio *f*; (*state*) inopia *f*
deprive *vt* privare, spoliare
depth *s* altitudo, profunditas *f*, profundum *n*; (*bottom*) fundus *m*
deputation *s* legatio *f*, legati *m pl*
deputy *s* legatus, vicarius *m*
derange *vt* (per)turbare, conturbare
deranged *adj* mente captus
derangement *s* perturbatio, confusio *f*; (*of mind*) mentis alienatio *f*
dereliction *s* derelictio, destitutio *f*
deride *vt* deridēre, irridēre
derision *s* ris·us -ūs *m*, irrisio *f*
derisive *adj* irridens
derivation *s* derivatio, origo *f*
derivative *adj* derivativus, derivatus
derive *vt* derivare, deducĕre; *vi* procedĕre, oriri
derogatory *adj* inhonestus, indignus
descend *vi* descendĕre, delabi; **to — upon** (*to attack*) irrumpĕre in (*with acc*)
descendant *s* progenies *f*; **—s** posteri *m pl*
descent *s* descens·us -ūs *m*; (*slope*) declivitas *f*, clivus *m*; (*lineage*) genus *n*
describe *vt* describĕre, perscribĕre; depingĕre; narrare
description *s* descriptio *f*; narratio *f*
desecrate *vt* profanare, polluĕre
desecration *s* profanatio, violatio *f*
desert *s* (*wilderness*) loca deserta *n pl*, solitudo *f*
desert *s* (*merit*) meritum *n*, dignitas *f*
desert *vt* deserĕre, relinquĕre; *vi* transfugĕre, deficĕre
deserter *s* desertor *m*; (*mil*) transfuga *m*
desertion *s* desertio, defectio *f*; transfugium *n*
deserve *vt* merēre, merēri
deserving *adj* meritus, dignus
design *s* (*drawing*) adumbratio *f*; (*plan*) consilium, propositum *n*
design *vt* designare; (*to sketch*) adumbrare; (*fig*) machinari

designate *vt* designare, nominare, appellare
designation *s* designatio *f*; vocabulum, nomen *n*, titulus *m*
designer *s* inventor, auctor, fabricator, machinator *m*
designing *adj* callidus
desirable *adj* optabilis, desiderabilis
desire *s* appetitio, cupiditas, cupido *f*; (*request*) rogat·us -ūs *m*
desire *vt* cupĕre, optare, expetĕre; (*to request*) orare, petĕre
desirous *adj* cupidus, appetens
desist *vi* desistĕre; (*to cease*) desinĕre
desk *s* scrinium, pulpitum *n*, mensa scriptoria *f*
desolate *adj* desolatus, solitarius; (*of persons*) afflictus
desolate *vt* devastare
desolation *s* vastatio *f*; (*state*) solitudo, vastitas *f*
despair *s* desperatio *f*
despair *vi* desperare
desperado *s* sicarius *m*
desperate *adj* desperatus; (*dangerous*) periculosus; **—ly** desperanter; **to be —ly in love** perdite amare
desperation *s* desperatio *f*
despicable *adj* abjectus, vilis, turpis
despise *vt* despicĕre, spernĕre, contemnĕre
despite *prep* contra (*with acc*)
despite *s* malevolentia *f*, odium *n*
despoil *vt* nudare, spoliare
despondency *s* animi abjectio *f*
despondent *adj* abjectus, demissus; **—ly** animo demisso
despot *s* dominus, tyrannus *m*
despotic *adj* tyrannicus; **—ally** tyrannice
despotism *s* dominatio *f*
dessert *s* secunda mensa *f*, bellaria *n pl*
destination *s* destinatio *f*, propositum *n*
destine *vt* destinare, designare
destiny *s* fatum *n*, sors *f*
destitute *adj* egens, inops, destitutus; **— of** expers (*with genit*)
destitution *s* inopia, mendicitas *f*
destroy *vt* destruĕre, subvertĕre, abolēre, delēre, vastare; **to be destroyed** interire
destroyer *s* deletor, vastator *m*
destruction *s* eversio, clades *f*, exitium *n*
destructive *adj* exitialis, perniciosus; **—ly** perniciose
desultory *adj* inconstans
detach *vt* sejungĕre, separare, amovēre
detached *adj* sejunctus; (*of houses*) solus
detachment *s* separatio *f*; (*mil*) man·us -ūs *f*; (*aloofness*) secess·us -ūs *m*
detail *s* singula *n pl*, singulae res *f pl*
detail *vt* enumerare
detain *vt* detinēre, retinēre, retardare
detect *vt* detegĕre, comperire, patefacere
detection *s* patefacio *f*, indicium *n*
detective *s* inquisitor *m*
detention *s* retentio *f*; (*law*) mora *f*
deter *vt* deterrēre, avertĕre
detergent *s* smegma *n*
deterioration *s* depravatio, corruptio *f*
determination *s* constantia, obstinatio *f*; (*intention*) propositum *n*
determine *vt* (*to decide*) statuĕre, constituĕre, discernĕre; (*to fix*) determinare, definire
determined *adj* certus; (*resolute*) firmus, obstinatus
detest *vt* abominari, detestari
detestable *adj* detestabilis, foedus
dethrone *vt* regno depellĕre
detonate *vi* crepare
detonation *s* fragor *m*
detour *s* circuit·us -ūs *m*
detour *vi* iter flectĕre, circumagi
detract *vt* detrahĕre; *vi* **to — from** detrectare, obtrectare
detraction *s* obtrectatio *f*
detractor *s* obtrectator *m*
detriment *s* detrimentum, damnum *n*
detrimental *adj* injuriosus, damnosus; **to be — to** detrimento esse (*with dat*)
devastate *vt* vastare, depopulari
devastation *s* (*act*) vastatio, populatio *f*; (*state*) vastitas *f*
develop *vt* evolvĕre, explicare; (*person*) alĕre; *vi* crescĕre; **to — into** evadĕre in (*with acc*)
development *s* explicatio *f*, progress·us -ūs *m*
deviate *vi* aberrare, degredi, decedĕre
deviation *s* aberratio, declinatio, digressio *f*
device *s* (*contrivance*) artificium *n*, machina *f*; (*plan*) consilium *n*; (*emblem*) insigne *n*
devil *s* diabolus, daemon *m*; **go to the —!** abi in malam crucem!
devilish *adj* diabolicus, daemonicus; (*fig*) nefandus
devious *adj* devius; vagus, erraticus
devise *vt* fingĕre, excogitare, concoquĕre
devoid *adj* inanis, vacuus, expers; **to be — of** carēre (*with abl*)
devolve *vi* **to — upon** obtingĕre, pervenire ad (*with acc*)
devote *vt* devovēre, consecrare; **to — oneself to** studĕre (*with dat*), se dedĕre (*with dat*)
devoted *adj* deditus, studiosus; **— to** studiosus (*with genit*)
devotee *s* cultor *m*
devotion *s* devotio, addictio *f*, studium *n*
devour *vt* devorare; (*fig*) haurire
devout *adj* pius, religiosus; **—ly** pie, religiose
dew *s* ros *m*
dewdrop *s* gutta roscida *f*
dewy *adj* roscidus, roridus
dexterity *s* sollertia, calliditas *f*
dexterous *adj* sollers, callidus, habilis; **—ly** sollerter, callide, habiliter
diabolical *adj* nefarius, nefandus
diagnose *vt* dijudicare, discernĕre

diagnosis *s* judicium *n*
diagonal *adj* diagonalis; **—ly** in transversum
diagram *s* forma, descriptio *f*
dial *s* solarium *n*
dialect *s* dialectus *f*, sermo *m*
dialectic *adj* dialecticus
dialogue *s* sermo *m*, colloquium *n*; (*written discussion*) dialogus *m*
diameter *s* diametros *f*
diamond *s* adamas *m*
diaper *s* striatura *f*
diaphragm *s* praecordia *n pl*
diarrhea *s* alvi profluvium *n*
diary *s* diarium *n*, commentarii diurni *m pl*
diatribe *s* convicium *n*
dice *s* tali *m pl*; (*game*) alea *f*
dictate *vt* dictare, praescribĕre
dictate *s* praescriptum, praeceptum, jussum *n*
dictation *s* dictatio *f*; dictatum *n*
dictator *s* dictator *m*
dictatorial *adj* imperiosus, dictatorius
dictatorship *s* dictatura *f*
diction *s* dictio, elocutio *f*
dictionary *s* lexicon *n*, thesaurus linguae *m*
didactic *adj* didascalicus
die *s* alea *f*
die *vi* mori, obire, perire; **to — off** demori; **to — out** emori
diet *s* (*food*) vict·us -ūs *m*; (*med*) diaeta *f*
diet *vi* secundum diaetam vivĕre
dietary *adj* diaeteticus
differ *vi* differre, discrepare, distare; (*in opinion*) dissentire
difference *s* differentia, diversitas, dissimilitudo *f*; (*of opinion*) discrepantia, dissensio *f*
different *adj* diversus, dissimilis, dispar; alius; **—ly** diverse, aliter
difficult *adj* difficilis, arduus
difficulty *s* difficultas *f*, labor *m*, negotium *n*; **with —** aegre
diffidence *s* diffidentia, verecundia *f*
diffident *adj* diffidens, verecundus, modestus; **—ly** diffidenter
diffuse *adj* diffusus; (*fig*) verbosus; **—ly** effuse, latius
diffuse *vt* diffundĕre
diffusion *s* diffusio *f*
dig *vt* fodĕre
digest *s* summarium *n*
digest *vt* (*to arrange*) digerĕre; (*food*) concoquĕre
digestion *s* concoctio *f*
digestive *adj* pepticus
digging *s* fossio, fossura *f*
digit *s* numerus *m*
dignified *adj* gravis, augustus
dignify *vt* honestare, honorare
dignitary *s* vir amplissimus *m*
dignity *s* dignitas *f*, honor *m*
digress *vi* digredi, aberrare, abire
digression *s* digressio *f*, digress·us -ūs *m*
dike *s* agger *m*
dilapidated *adj* ruinosus, obsoletus
dilate *vt* dilatare; *vi* dilatari
dilatory *adj* cunctabundus, lentus, segnis
dilemma *s* dilemma *n*; nodus *m*, angustiae *f pl*
diligence *s* diligentia *f*
diligent *adj* diligens, sedulus; **—ly** diligenter, sedulo
dilute *vt* diluĕre, miscēre
dilution *s* temperatio, mixtura *f*
dim *adj* hebes, obscurus; **to become —** hebescĕre; **—ly** obscure, obtuse
dim *vt* hebetare, obscurare; *vi* hebescĕre
dimension *s* dimensio, mensura *f*
diminish *vt* minuĕre, deminuĕre, extenuare; *vi* decrescĕre, minui
diminutive *adj* exiguus, parvulus; (*gram*) deminutivus
diminutive *s* (nomen) deminutivum *n*
dimness *s* hebetudo, obscuritas, caligo *f*
dimple *s* lacuna *f*, gelasinus *m*
din *s* strepit·us -ūs, sonit·us -ūs, fragor *m*; **to make a —** strepare
dine *vi* cenare
diner *s* conviva *m*
dingy *adj* fuscus, squalidus
dining room *s* cenatio *f*, triclinium *n*
dinner *s* cena *f*
dinner party *s* convivium *n*
dint *s* ict·us -ūs *m*; **by — of** per (*with acc*)
dip *vt* immergĕre, ting(u)ĕre; *vi* mergi, tingi; (*to sink*) premi, declinare
dip *s* devexitas, declinatio *f*
diploma *s* diploma *n*
diplomacy *s* (*function*) officium legationis *m*; (*tact*) dexteritas *f*
diplomat *s* legatus *m*
diplomatic *adj* sagax, callidus, astutus
dire *adj* dirus
direct *adj* rectus, directus; **—ly** directe, rectā; (*immediately*) statim
direct *vt* dirigĕre; (*to administer*) administrare; (*to rule*) gubernare; (*to order*) jubēre; imperare (*with dat*); (*weapon*) intendĕre; (*letter*) inscribĕre; (*attention*) admovēre
direction *s* (*act*) directio *f*; (*quarter*) pars, regio *f*; (*management*) administratio *f*; (*instruction*) mandatum *n*; (*order*) praeceptum *n*
director *s* rector, magister, gubernator, curator *m*
directory *s* (*office of director*) curatio *f*, magisterium *n*; (*body of directors*) magistri, curatores *m pl*
dirge *s* nenia *f*
dirt *s* sordes *f*; (*mud*) lutum *n*, limus *m*
dirtiness *s* spurcitia *f*; (*fig*) obscenitas *f*
dirty *adj* spurcus, sordidus; (*fig*) obscenus
dirty *vt* foedare, spurcare
disability *s* impotentia *f*
disable *vt* debilitare, enervare
disabled *adj* inhabilis, debilis, mancus

disabuse *vt* errorem eripĕre (*with dat*)
disadvantage *s* incommodum, detrimentum *n*
disadvantageous *adj* incommodus, iniquus
disagree *vi* discrepare, dissidēre, dissentire
disagreeable *adj* injucundus, molestus, insuavis, gravis; (*of smells*) graveolens; (*of persons*) difficilis, morosus
disagreeably *adv* moleste, graviter, ingrate
disagreement *s* dissensio, discordia *f*, dissidium *n*
disappear *vi* vanescĕre, fugĕre, diffugĕre, abire, perire
disappearance *s* fuga *f*, exit·us -ūs *m*
disappoint *vt* fallĕre, frustrari
disappointment *s* frustratio *f*; incommodum, malum *n*
disapproval *s* reprehensio, improbatio *f*
disapprove *vt* reprehendĕre, improbare
disarm *vt* exarmare
disarrange *vt* (per)turbare, confundĕre
disarray *s* perturbatio *f*
disaster *s* calamitas *f*, incommodum *n*
disastrous *adj* calamitosus, funestus, exitiosus; **—ly** calamitose
disavow *vt* diffitēri, infitiari
disavowal *s* infitiatio *f*
disband *vt* dimittĕre; *vi* dimitti
disbelief *s* diffidentia, incredulitas *f*
disbeliever *s* incredulus *m*
disburse *vt* erogare, expendĕre
disbursement *s* erogatio, solutio *f*
disc *s* orbis *m*
discard *vt* ponĕre, mittĕre; repudiare
discern *vt* discernĕre, distinguĕre
discernible *adj* dignoscendus
discerning *adj* perspicax, sagax, prudens
discernment *s* (*act*) perspicientia *f*; (*faculty*) discrimen, judicium *n*
discharge *vt* (*to unload*) exonerare; (*to dismiss*) dimittere; (*to perform*) perfungi (*with abl*); (*debt*) exsolvĕre; (*weapon*) immittĕre, jacere, jaculari; (*defendant*) absolvĕre
discharge *s* (*unloading*) exoneratio *f*; (*shooting*) emissio, conjectio *f*; (*dismissal*) missio *f*; (*payment*) solutio *f*; (*bodily*) defluxio *f*
disciple *s* discipulus *m*; (*fig*) sectator *m*
discipline *s* disciplina *f*
discipline *vt* assuefacĕre, coercēre
disclaim *vt* infitiari, diffitēri, negare
disclaimer *s* infitiatio *f*
disclose *vt* aperire, detegĕre, enuntiare
disclosure *s* patefactio *f*
discomfit *vt* fundĕre
discomfort *s* incommoda *n pl*, molestiae *f pl*
disconcerting *adj* molestus
disconnect *vt* sejungĕre, disjungĕre
disconsolate *adj* tristis, afflictus; **—ly** insolabiliter, triste
discontent *s* taedium *n*, molestia, offensio *f*
discontented *adj* parum contentus; **—ly** animo iniquo
discontinue *vt* intermittĕre; *vi* desinĕre, desistere
discord *s* discordia, dissensio *f*; (*mus*) dissonantia *f*
discordant *adj* discors, discrepans; (*mus*) dissonus
discount *vt* deducĕre; (*to disregard*) praetermittere
discount *s* (*com*) decessio *f*
discourage *vt* deterrēre, examinare; **to be discouraged** animum demittĕre
discouragement *s* animi abjectio *or* infractio *f*
discouraging *adj* adversus, incommodus
discourse *s* sermo *m*, colloquium *n*; (*written*) libellus *m*
discourse *vi* disserĕre, colloqui, verba facere
discourteous *adj* inurbanus; **—ly** inurbane
discourtesy *s* inurbanitas *f*
discover *vt* invenire, reperire; (*to find out*) explorare; (*to disclose*) patefacĕre
discoverable *adj* indagabilis, visibilis
discoverer *s* inventor, repertor *m*
discovery *s* inventio *f*; (*things discovered*) inventum *n*
discredit *s* dedecus *n*, ignominia *f*
discredit *vt* notare, infamare
discreet *adj* cautus, prudens; **—ly** consulto, prudenter
discrepancy *s* discrepantia *f*
discretion *s* pudentia, circumspectio *f*; (*tact*) judicium *n*
discretionary *adj* interminatus, liber
discriminate *vt* distinguĕre, dijudicare, discernĕre
discriminating *adj* sagax, discernens
discrimination *s* distinctio *f*; judicium, discrimen *n*
discuss *vt* agĕre, disputare, disserĕre
discussion *s* disputatio, disceptatio *f*
disdain *vt* fastidire, despicĕre, aspernari
disdain *s* fastidium *n*, despect·us -ūs, contempt·us -ūs *m*
disdainful *adj* fastidiosus, superciliosus; **—ly** fastidiose, contemptim
disease *s* morbus *m*, malum *n*
diseased *adj* aegrotus
disembark *vt* e navi exponĕre; *vi* e navi conscendĕre
disenchant *vt* errorem demĕre (*with dat*)
disengage *vt* expedire, eximĕre, avocare
disentangle *vt* expedire, extricare, explicare
disfavor *s* invidia *f*

disfigure *vt* deformare, turpare, mutilare
disfranchise *vt* civitatem adimĕre (*with dat*)
disgorge *vt* revomĕre, evomĕre
disgrace *s* dedecus *n*, infamia *f*; (*thing*) flagitium *n*
disgrace *vt* dedecorare
disgraceful *adj* dedecorus, turpis, flagitiosus; **—ly** turpiter, flagitiose
disguise *s* (*mask*) persona *f*; simulatio *f*; (*pretense*) praetext·us -ūs *m*
disguise *vt* obtegĕre; (*fig*) celare, dissimulare
disgust *s* (*loathing*) fastidium, taedium *n*, nausea *f*
disgust *vt* fastidium movēre (*with dat*); **I am disgusted with** me taedet (*with genit*), me piget (*with genit*)
disgusting *adj* taeter, foedus; **—ly** foede
dish *s* (*flat*) patina *f*; (*large*) lanx *f*; (*course*) ferculum *n*, dapes *f pl*
dishearten *vt* exanimare, percellĕre; **to be disheartened** animum demittĕre
disheveled *adj* passus, effusus
dishonest *adj* improbus, perfidus; **—ly** improbe, dolo malo
dishonesty *s* improbitas *f*, dolus malus *m*, fraus, perfidia *f*
dishonor *s* dedecus *n*, infamia, ignominia *f*
dishonor *vt* dedecorare
dishonorable *adj* inhonestus, turpis
disillusion *vt* errorem adimĕre (*with dat*)
disinfect *vt* purgare
disinherit *vt* exheredare
disintegrate *vi* dilabi
disinter *vt* effodĕre
disinterested *adj* integer; (*of judge*) severus; **—ly** integre, gratuito
disjoin *vt* segregare, disjungĕre
disjointed *adj* incompositus; **—ly** incomposite
disk *s* orbis *m*
dislike *s* odium, fastidium *n*, aversatio *f*
dislike *vt* aversari, odisse, fastidire
dislocate *vt* extorquēre, luxare
dislocation *s* luxatura *f*
dislodge *vt* movēre, depellĕre
disloyal *adj* perfidus; **—ly** perfide
disloyalty *s* infidelitas, perfidia *f*
dismal *adj* maestus, funestus, miser; **—ly** maeste, misere
dismantle *vt* diruĕre, spoliare, nudare
dismay *s* pavor *m*, consternatio *f*
dismay *vt* terrēre, perterrefacĕre, territare
dismember *vt* membratim dividĕre, lacerare, discerpĕre
dismemberment *s* mutilatio *f*
dismiss *vt* dimittere; (*fear*) mittĕre; (*to discharge, to cashier*) exauctorare
dismissal *s* missio, dimissio *f*
dismount *vi* ex equo desilire
disobedience *s* inobedientia, contumacia *f*
disobedient *adj* contumax
disobey *vt* non obedire (*with dat*), non parēre (*with dat*)
disorder *s* confusio *f*; (*med*) aegrotatio *f*; (*of mind*) perturbatio *f*; (*pol*) tumult·us -ūs *m*
disordered *adj* turbatus; (*fig*) dissolutus
disorderly *adj* inordinatus, incompositus, (per)turbatus; (*insubordinate*) turbulentus
disorganization *s* dissolutio *f*
disorganize *vt* conturbare, confundĕre; **to be disorganized** dilabi
disown *vt* (*statement*) diffiteri, infitiari; (*heir*) abdicare; (*thing*) repudiare
disparage *vt* obtrectare, detrectare
disparagement *s* obtrectatio *f*
disparaging *adj* obtrectans
disparate *adj* dispar
disparity *s* inaequalitas, discrepantia *f*
dispassionate *adj* sedatus, tranquillus, frigidus; **—ly** sedate, frigide
dispatch *vt* mittĕre, dimittĕre, legare; (*to finish*) absolvĕre, perficĕre; (*to kill*) interficĕre
dispel *vt* dispellĕre; (*worries*) ponĕre
dispensary *s* medicamentaria taberna *f*
dispensation *s* distributio, partitio *f*; (*exemption*) immunitas, exemptio *f*
dispense *vt* distribuĕre, dispertiri; (*to release*) solvĕre; *vi* **to — with** indulgēre (*with dat*), omittĕre, praetermittere
dispenser *s* dispensator *m*
disperse *vt* spargĕre, dispergĕre, dissipare; *vi* dilabi, diffugere
dispersion *s* dispersio, dissipatio *f*
dispirited *adj* abjectus, demissus, animo fractus
displace *vt* summovēre; exauctorare
displacement *s* amotio *f*
display *s* (*exhibit*) ostent·us -ūs *m*; (*ostentation*) ostentatio, jactatio *f*
display *vt* ostendĕre, ostentare, exhibēre
displease *vt* displicēre (*with dat*)
displeased *adj* offensus; **to be — at** aegre ferre
displeasing *adj* odiosus, ingratus
displeasure *s* offensa, offensio *f*
disposable *adj* in promptu
disposal *s* dispositio *f*; arbitrium *n*; **at the — of** penes (*with acc*)
dispose *vt* disponere, ordinare; (*to incline*) parare, praeparare; *vi* **to — of** abalienare, vendĕre; (*to get rid of*) tollĕre
disposed *adj* inclinatus; (*in bad sense*) pronus
disposition *s* (*arrangement*) dispositio *f*; (*character*) natura, mens *f*, ingenium *n*, animus *m*
dispossess *vt* ejicĕre, detrudĕre, pellĕre
disproportion *s* inaequalitas, inconcinnitas *f*
disproportionate *adj* inaequalis, im-

par, inconcinnus; **—ly** impariter, inaequaliter
disprove *vt* refutare, confutare, redarguĕre
disputable *adj* disputabilis, ambiguus
dispute *s* (*debate*) disputatio *f*; (*quarreling*) altercatio, controversia *f*; **beyond —** indisputabilis
dispute *vt & vi* disputare, contendĕre
disqualification *s* impedimentum *n*
disqualify *vt* inhabilem reddĕre, impedire
disquiet *vt* inquietare, vexare
disregard *s* incuria, negligentia *f*
disregard *vt* negligĕre, omittĕre
disreputable *adj* infamis
disrepute *s* infamia *f*
disrespect *s* negligentia, insolentia *f*
disrespectful *adj* irreverens, insolens; **—ly** insolenter, irreverenter
disrupt *vt* dirumpĕre
disruption *s* dirumptio *f*; (*fig*) discidium *n*
dissatisfaction *s* molestia, offensio *f*
dissatisfied *adj* parum contentus
dissatisfy *vt* parum satisfacĕre
dissect *vt* dissecare
dissection *s* incisio *f*
dissemble *vt & vi* dissimulare
disseminate *vt* disseminare, divulgare
dissension *s* dissensio *f*, dissidium *n*
dissent *vi* dissentire, dissidēre
dissent *s* dissensio *f*
dissertation *s* disputatio, dissertatio *f*
dissimilar *adj* dissimilis, dispar
dissimilarity *s* dissimilitudo *f*
dissipate *vt* dissipare, diffundĕre; *vi* dissipari, diffundi
dissipation *s* dissipatio *f*
dissolute *adj* dissolutus, corruptus, perditus; **—ly** immoderate, prodige
dissolution *s* dissolutio *f*
dissolve *vt* dissolvĕre; (*to melt*) liquefacĕre; (*meeting*) dimittĕre; *vi* liquescĕre; (*to break up*) dissolvi
dissonance *s* dissonantia *f*
dissonant *adj* dissonus
dissuade *vt* dissuadēre (*with dat*), dehortari
dissuasion *s* dissuasio *f*
distaff *s* colus *f*
distance *s* distantia *f*, intervallum *n*; (*fig*) frigus *n*; (*long way*) longinquitas *f*; **at a —** procul, longe
distant *adj* distans, disjunctus, longinquus; (*fig*) parum familiaris; **to be —** abesse
distaste *s* fastidium *n*
distasteful *adj* (*of taste*) teter; (*fig*) molestus, odiosus
distemper *s* morbus *m*
distend *vt* distendĕre
distil *vt & vi* stillare, destillare
distillation *s* destillatio *f*
distinct *adj* (*different*) diversus, alius; (*clear*) distinctus; **—ly** clare, distincte, certe
distinction *s* distinctio, discrepantia *f*, discrimen *n*; (*status*) amplitudo *f*; (*honor*) honos *m*; **there is no —** nil interest
distinctive *adj* proprius; **—ly** proprie
distinguish *vt* distinguĕre, discernĕre; **to — oneself** enitēre
distinguished *adj* insignis, clarus, notus, eximius
distort *vt* distorquēre; (*fig*) depravare
distortion *s* distortio *f*; (*fig*) depravatio *f*
distract *vt* distrahĕre, avocare; (*to madden*) furiare
distracted *adj* amens, insanus; **—ly** amens, mente alienatus
distraction *s* (*cause*) invitamentum *n*; (state) negligentia *f*; **to —** efflictim
distress *s* afflictio, aegrimonia, aerumna *f*, dolor, labor *m*
distress *vt* afflictare, angĕre
distressed *adj* anxius, afflictus, sollicitus
distressing *adj* tristis, gravis, acerbus
distribute *vt* distribuĕre
distributer *s* distributor *m*
distribution *s* distributio *f*
district *s* regio *f*
distrust *s* diffidentia *f*
distrust *vt* diffidĕre (*with dat*)
distrustful *adj* diffidens; **—ly** diffidenter
disturb *vt* perturbare; sollicitare, inquietare
disturbance *s* perturbatio *f*; confusio *f*; (*pol*) mot·us -ūs, tumult·us -ūs *m*
disturber *s* turbator, concitator *m*
disuse *s* desuetudo *f*
ditch *s* fossa *f*
ditty *s* cantilena *f*, canticum *n*
divan *s* lectulus *m*
dive *vi* mergi
diver *s* urinator *m*
diverge *vi* deflectĕre, declinare, devertĕre; (*of views*) discrepare
diverse *adj* alius, varius, diversus
diversification *s* variatio *f*
diversify *vt* variare
diversion *s* (*recreation*) oblectamentum *n*; (*of thought*) avocatio *f*; (*of river, etc.*) derivatio *f*
diversity *s* diversitas, varietas *f*
divert *vt* avertĕre, divertĕre; (*attention*) avocare; (*to amuse*) oblectare
divest *vt* exuĕre, nudare, privare; **to — oneself of** exuĕre, ponĕre
divide *vt* dividĕre, partiri, distribuĕre; *vi* discedĕre, se scindĕre
divination *s* divinatio, vaticinatio *f*
divine *adj* divinus; **—ly** divine
divine *s* theologus *m*
divine *vt* divinare, augurari, vaticinari; (*to guess*) conjicĕre
diviner *s* augur, haruspex *m*
divinity *s* divinitas *f*; (*god*) numen *n*; divus *m*, diva *f*
divisible *adj* dividuus, divisibilis
division *s* divisio, partitio *f*; (*part*) pars *f*; (*mil*) legio *f*; **— of opinion** dissensio *f*

divorce *s* divortium *n*
divorce *vt* repudiare, dimittĕre
divulge *vt* vulgare, palam facĕre, aperire, patefacĕre
dizziness *s* vertigo *f*
dizzy *adj* vertiginosus
do *vt* agĕre, facĕre, efficĕre; *vi* agĕre; **how do you —?** quid agis?; **to — away with** tollĕre, perdĕre
docile *adj* docilis, tractabilis
dock *s* navale *n*; (*law*) cancelli *m pl*
dock *vt* subducĕre
docket *s* lemniscus *m*
dockyard *s* navalia *n pl*
doctor *s* medicus *m*; (*teacher*) doctor *m*
doctor *vt* medicari, curare
doctorate *s* doctoris grad·us -ūs *m*
doctrine *s* doctrina *f*, dogma *n*
document *s* documentum, instrumentum *n*
dodge *s* dolus *m*
dodge *vt* eludĕre; *vi* tergiversari
doe *s* cerva *f*
dog *s* canis *m & f*
dogged *adj* pervicax, pertinax; **—ly** pertinaciter
doggedness *s* pervicacia *f*
doggerel *s* versus inepti *m pl*
dog kennel *s* canis cubile *n*
dogma *s* dogma, placitum, praeceptum *n*
dogmatic *adj* dogmaticus; arrogans; **—ally** arroganter
dogmatism *s* arrogantia doctrinae *f*
dog star *s* canicula *f*, Sirius *m*
doing *s* factum, facinus *n*
dole *s* sportula *f*; donatio *f*
dole *vt* **to — out** parce dare
doleful *adj* lugubris, maestus, flebilis; **—ly** maeste, flebiliter
doll *s* pupa *f*
dollar *s* thalerus *m*
dolphin *s* delphinus, delphin *m*
dolt *s* caudex, stipes *m*
domain *s* (*estate*) possessio *f*; (*kingdom*) regnum *n*
dome *s* tholus *m*
domestic *adj* domesticus, familiaris; intestinus
domestic *s* famulus, servus, verna *m*, famula, serva *f*
domesticate *vt* domare, assuefacĕre
domicile *s* domicilium *n*, dom·us -ūs *f*
dominant *adj* praevalens
domination *s* dominium *n*
domineer *vi* dominari
domineering *adj* imperiosus
dominion *s* imperium, regnum *n*
don *vt* induĕre
donation *s* donum *n*, stips *f*
donkey *s* asinus, asellus *m*
donor *s* donator *m*, donatrix *f*
doom *s* fatum, exitium *n*
doom *vt* damnare, condemnare
door *s* janua *f*, ostium *n*, fores *f pl*
doorkeeper *s* janitor *m*, janitrix *f*
doorpost *s* postis *f*
doorway *s* ostium *n*
Doric *adj* Doricus
dormant *adj* sopitus; (*hidden*) latens; **to lie —** jacēre
dormitory *s* cubiculum, dormitorium *n*
dorsal *adj* dorsualis
dose *s* potio *f*
dot *s* punctum *n*
dot *vt* punctum imponĕre (*with dat*)
dotage *s* senium *n*
dotard *s* senex delirus *m*
dote *vi* **to — upon** deamare, deperire
doting *adj* deamans, desipiens; **—ly** perdite amans
double *adj* duplex; (*of pairs*) geminus; (*as much again*) duplus; (*meaning*) ambiguus
double *s* duplum *n*; **to march on the —** currĕre
double *vt* duplicare; (*cape*) praetervehi; *vi* duplicari; (*to run*) currĕre
doubly *adv* bis, dupliciter
doubt *s* dubitatio *f*, dubium *n*; (*distrust*) suspicio *f*
doubt *vt* dubitare; suspicari
doubtful *adj* (*of persons*) dubius; (*of things*) incertus, ambiguus, anceps; **—ly** dubie; (*hesitatingly*) dubitanter
doubtless *adv* scilicet, haud dubie, sine dubio
dough *s* farina *f*
doughty *adj* strenuus, fortis
douse *vt* (*to put out*) exstinguĕre; (*to drench*) madefacĕre
dove *s* columba *f*
dowdy *adj* inconcinnus
down *s* pluma *f*; (*of hair*) lanugo *f*; (*of plants*) pappus *m*
down *adv* deorsum; **— from** de (*with abl*); **— to** usque ad (*with acc*)
down *prep* de (*with abl*)
down *adj* declivis; tristis; ad inopiam redactus
downcast *adj* (*of eyes or head*) dejectus, demissus; (*fig*) afflictus, maestus
downfall *s* occas·us -ūs *m*, ruina *f*
downhill *adj* declivis
downright *adj* directus, sincerus
downright *adv* prorsus, plane
downstream *adv* secundo flumine
downward *adj* declivis; pronus
downwards *adv* deorsum
downy *adj* plumeus; lanuginosus
dowry *s* dos *f*
doze *vi* dormitare
dozen *s* duodecim
drab *adj* cinereus
draft *s* (*act of drawing*) lineatio *f*; (*drink*) haust·us -ūs *m*; (*of ship*) immersio *f*; (*first copy*) exemplar *n*; (*of air*) aura *f*; (*mil*) dilect·us -ūs *m*; (*money*) syngrapha *f*; (*of net*) jact·us -ūs *m*
draft *vt* conscribĕre
draft horse *s* equus rhedarius *m*
drag *vt* trahĕre, rapĕre; *vi* trahi
drag *s* (*fig*) impedimentum *n*
dragnet *s* tragula *f*
dragon *s* draco, anguis *m*
drain *s* cloaca *f*
drain *vt* siccare; derivare; (*to drink*)

exhaurire, ebibĕre; (*strength*) exhaurire
drainage *s* derivatio, exsiccatio *f*; colluvies cloacarum *f*
draining *s* exsiccatio *f*
drake *s* anas *m*
drama *s* drama *n*, fabula *f*
dramatic *adj* dramaticus, scaenicus
dramatist *s* poeta scaenicus, scriptor fabularum *m*
dramatize *vt* ad scaenam componĕre
drape *vt* induĕre, amicire, velare
drapery *s* aulaeum *n*
drastic *adj* vehemens
draw *vt* (*to pull*) trahĕre, ducĕre; (*picture*) scribĕre, delineare; (*sword*) destringĕre; (*bow*) adducĕre; (*inference*) colligĕre; **to — aside** abducĕre, seducĕre; **to — away** avertĕre, distrahĕre; **to — back** retrahĕre; **to — off** detrahĕre, abducĕre; (*wine*) depromĕre; **to — out** extrahĕre; (*sword, etc.*) educĕre; (*fig*) elicĕre; **to — together** contrahĕre; **to — up** subducĕre; scribĕre; (*troops*) instruĕre, constituĕre; *vi* **to — back** pedem referre, cedĕre; (*fig*) recedĕre; **to — near** appropinquare; **to — off** cedĕre; **to — up to** (*of ships*) appetĕre
drawback *s* impedimentum, incommodum *n*, retardatio *f*
drawbridge *s* pons *m*
drawer *s* (*sliding compartment*) loculus *m*; (*chest*) armarium *n*
drawing *s* descriptio *f*; (*art*) graphice *f*
drawing room *s* exedra *f*
drawl *vi* lentius loqui
dray *s* plaustrum *n*
dread *s* terror, pavor *m*, formido *f*
dread *adj* terribilis, dirus
dread *vt* expavescĕre, formidare
dreadful *adj* terribilis, horribilis, atrox; **—ly** horrendum in modum, atrociter
dream *s* somnium *n*; **in a —** in somno
dream *vt & vi* somniare; (*fig*) dormitare
dreamer *s* (*fig*) nugator *m*
dreamy *adj* somniculosus
drearily *adv* triste, misere
dreariness *s* (*place*) solitudo, vastitas *f*; (*mind*) tristitia *f*
dreary *adj* (*place*) vastus, solus, incultus; (*person*) tristis, miser
dredge *s* everriculum *n*
dregs *s* faex *f*; (*fig*) sentina *f*
drench *vt* madefacĕre, perfundĕre
dress *s* habit·us -ūs, vestit·us -ūs *m*, vestis *f*, vestimenta *n pl*
dress *vt* vestire, induĕre; (*to deck out*) (ex)ornare; (*wounds*) curare; (*to bind up*) obligare; *vi* se induĕre
dressing *s* ornatio *f*; (*of foods*) coctio, coctura *f*; (*med*) fomentum *n*
dressing room *s* procoeton *m*
dribble *vi* stillare
drift *s* propositum *n*; (*purpose*) scopus *m*; (*of sand*) cumulus *m*; (*of snow*) vis *f*
drift *vi* ferri, fluitare
drill *s* (*tool*) terebra *f*; (*mil*) exercitatio *f*
drill *vt* (*to bore*) terebrare; (*mil*) exercēre; (*pupil*) instituĕre
drink *vt* bibĕre, potare; **to — in** absorbēre, haurire; **to — up** epotare; *vi* bibĕre, potare; **to — to** propinare (*with dat*)
drink *s* pot·us -ūs *m*, potio *f*
drinkable *adj* potabilis
drinker *s* potor, potator *m*; (*drunkard*) bibax *m*
drinking *adj* (*given to drink*) bibosus
drinking cup *s* poculum *n*
drip *s* stillicidium *n*
drip *vi* stillare
drive *vt* agĕre, pellĕre, impellĕre; (*to force*) compellĕre, cogĕre; (*a nail, etc.*) infigĕre; **to — away** abigĕre; (*fig*) depellĕre; (*to dislodge*) dejicĕre; **to — back** repellĕre; **to — in** (*sheep, etc.*) cogĕre; (*fig*) compellĕre; **to — off** abigĕre; **to — on** impellĕre; **to — out** expellĕre; **to — out of one's senses** infuriare; **to — up** subigĕre; *vi* (*in carriage*) vehi; **to — off** avehi; **to — on** praetervehi; **to — past** praetervehi
drive *s* (*in carriage*) vectio *f*; (*energy*) impigritas *f*
drivel *s* saliva *f*, sputum *n*; (*nonsense*) ineptiae, nugae *f pl*
drivel *vi* (*fig*) delirare
driver *s* agitator *m*; (*of carriage*) auriga *m*
drizzle *vi* leniter pluĕre
drizzle *s* lenis pluvia *f*
dromedary *s* dromas *m*
drone *s* (*bee*) fucus *m*; (*person*) nebulo *m*; (*buzz*) bombus *m*
drone *vi* fremĕre
droop *vt* demittĕre; *vi* languēre; (*of flowers*) languescĕre, tabescĕre
drooping *adj* languidus
drop *s* gutta, stilla *f*; (*a little bit*) paululum *n*; **— by —** guttatim
drop *vt* stillare; (*to let slip*) omittĕre; (*to lay low*) sternĕre; (*hint*) emittĕre; (*anchor*) jacĕre; (*work*) desistĕre ab (*with abl*); *vi* destillare; (*to fall*) cadĕre; **to — behind** cessare; **to — off to sleep** obdormire; **to — out** excidĕre
drought *s* siccitas, ariditas *f*
drove *s* grex *m*
drown *vt* immergĕre, demergĕre; (*fig*) opprimĕre; **to — out** obscurare; *vi* in aqua perire
drowsily *adv* somniculose
drowsy *adj* somniculosus, somnolentus; (*fig*) ignavus
drudge *s* (*slave*) mediastinus *m*; (*fig*) plagiger *m*
drudgery *s* opera servilis *f*
drug *s* medicamentum *n*
drug *vt* medicare
druggist *s* medicamentarius *m*
drugstore *s* taberna medicina, apotheca *f*

Druids *s* Druidae *m pl*
drum *s* typanum *n*
drum *vi* tympanum pulsare
drummer *s* tympanista *m*
drunk *adj* ebrius
drunkard *s* ebriosus, temulentus *m*
drunken *adj* ebrius, ebriosus
drunkenness *s* ebrietas, temulentia *f*
dry *adj* aridus, siccus; (*thirsty*) siticulosus; (*fig*) jejunus; insulsus
dry *vt* siccare, desiccare, arefacĕre; (*in the sun*) insolare; *vi* arescĕre
dryad *s* dryas *f*
dryly *adv* (*fig*) insulse; (*of jokes*) facete
dryness *s* ariditas, siccitas *f*; (*fig*) aridum sermonis genus *n*
dual *adj* duplex
dub *vt* supernominare
dubious *adj* dubius; **—ly** dubie
duck *s* anas *f*
duck *vt* submergĕre, demergĕre; (*an issue*) evitare; *vi* (*under water*) urinari
duckling *s* anaticula *f*
due *adj* debitus, justus, meritus; **to be — to** fieri (*with abl*)
due *adv* rectā; **due east** rectā ad orientem
due *s* debitum *n*
duel *s* certamen *n*
duet *s* bicinium *n*
duke *s* dux *m*
dull *adj* hebes; (*of mind*) tardus, segnes, insulsus; (*of style*) frigidus
dull *vt* hebetare, obtundĕre; stupefacĕre
dullness *s* stupiditas, tarditas *f*
duly *adv* rite; recte
dumb *adj* mutus; **to be —** obmutescĕre
dumbfound *vt* obstupefacĕre
dumb show *s* mimus *m*
dumpling *s* farinae subactae globulus *m*
dumpy *adj* brevis atque obesus
dun *adj* fuscus, furvus
dun *vt* flagitare, exposcĕre
dunce *s* homo stupidus *m*
dung *s* stercus *n*, fimus *m*; (*of birds*) merda *f*
dungeon *s* carcer *m*, ergastulum *n*
dupe *s* homo credulus, homo stolidus *m*
dupe *vt* decipĕre
duplicate *adj* duplex
duplicate *s* duplicitas, fallacia *f*
duplicate *vt* duplicare
duplicity *s* duplicitas *f*
durability *s* firmitudo, stabilitas *f*
durable *adj* firmus, durabilis, stabilis
duration *s* spatium temporis *n*, diuturnitas, perpetuitas *f*
during *prep* per (*with acc*), inter (*with acc*)
dusk *s* crepusculum, obscurum *n*
dusky *adj* obscurus, tenebrosus; fuscus
dust *s* pulvis *m*
dust *vt* detergēre
dusty *adj* pulverulentus, pulvereus
dutiful *adj* pius, officiosus; **—ly** pie, officiose
duty *s* (*social or moral*) officium *n*; (*task*) munus *n*; (*tax*) vectigal *n*; to **be on —** (*mil*) stationem agĕre
dwarf *s* nanus, pumilio *m*
dwarfish *adj* pumilus
dwell *vi* habitare, inhabitare; **to — upon** commorari in (*with abl*)
dweller *s* incola *m & f*, habitator *m*
dwelling place *s* domicilium *n*, sedes, habitatio *f*
dwindle *vi* decrescĕre, imminui
dye *vt* ting(u)ĕre, colorare, inficĕre, fucare
dye *s* tinctura *f*, color *m*
dying *adj* moriens, moribundus; (*last*) ultimus, extremus
dynamics *s* dynamica *f*
dynasty *s* dynastia, dom·us -ūs *f*
dysentery *s* dysenteria *f*

E

each *adj & pron* quisque; (*of two*) uterque; **— other** inter se, invicem
eager *adj* cupidus, avidus, acer, vehemens; **—ly** cupide, avide, acriter, vehementer
eagerness *s* aviditas, cupiditas, alacritas *f*, studium *n*
eagle *s* aquila *f*
ear *s* auris *f*; (*of corn*) spica *f*; **to give —** aurem praebēre
earache *s* aurium dolor *m*
earl *s* comes *m*
early *adj* (*in morning*) matutinus; (*in season*) maturus; (*of early date*) antiquus; (*beginning*) primus, novus
early *adv* (*in morning*) mane; (*too soon*) praemature; (*quickly, soon*) cito
earn *vt* lucrari, merēre *or* merēri, consequi
earnest *adj* intentus, serius, impensus, vehemens; **in —** serio, sedulo, bona fide; **—ly** intente, impense, acriter, graviter
earnestness *s* assiduitas, gravitas *f*, ardor *m*
earnings *s* quaest·us -ūs *m*, lucrum *n*
earring *s* elenchus *m*
earth *s* terra, tellus *f*; (*soil*) solum *n*; (*globe*) orbis (terrarum) *m*
earthen *adj* terrenus; fictilis
earthenware *s* fictilia *n pl*
earthly *adj* terrenus; terrestris; humanus
earthquake *s* terrae mot·us -ūs *m*
earthwork *s* opus terrenum *n*, agger *m*
earthy *adj* terrenus

ease *s* (*leisure*) otium *n*, quies *f*; (*grace*) lepor *m*, facilitas *f*; (*pleasure*) voluptas *f*; **at —** otiosus, vacuus; securus
ease *vt* levare, exonerare, expedire; (*fig*) lenire, mitigare
east *adj* orientalis
east *s* oriens *m*
Easter *s* pascha *f*, sollemnia paschalia *n pl*
eastern *adj* orientalis
eastward *adv* ad orientem
east wind *s* Eurus *m*
easy *adj* facilis; expeditus; (*manner*) facilis, affabilis; (*graceful*) lepidus
eat *vi* vesci (*with abl*), esse; (*fig*) roděre; **to — away** peređěre; (*fig*) corroděre; **to — up** comesse, devorare, exesse
eating *s* es·us -ūs *m*
eaves *s* suggrundia *n pl*
eavesdropper *s* auceps, auricularius *m*
ebb *s* recess·us -ūs *m*; **to be at a low —** jacēre
ebb *vi* recedĕre; (*fig*) decrescĕre
eccentric *adj* insolens, inusitatus, abnormis
ecclesiastic *adj* ecclesiasticus
echo *s* echo, imago *f*
echo *vt* repercutĕre, resonare; (*fig*) subsequi; *vi* resonare, resultare
eclipse *s* (*of sun or moon*) obscuratio solis *or* lunae *f*, defect·us -ūs *m*
eclipse *vt* obscurare, obumbrare
eclogue *s* ecloga *f*
economic *adj* economicus
economical *adj* frugi (*indecl*), parcus; **—ly** parce
economics *s* publicarum opum scientia *f*
economize *vi* parcĕre
economy *s* parsimonia, frugalitas *f*; rei familiaris administratio *f*
ecstasy *s* ecstasis, insania *f*, furor *m*
eddy *s* vortex *m*
eddy *vi* volutari
edge *s* (*brink*) margo *m & f*; (*of knife, etc.*) acies *f*; (*of forest*) ora *f*
edge *vt* (*garment*) praetexĕre; (*to sharpen*) acuĕre; *vi* **to — closer** appropinquare
edged *adj* acutus
edging *s* limbus *m*
edible *adj* esculentus, edulis
edict *s* edictum, decretum *n*
edification *s* eruditio *f*
edify *vt* docēre
edit *vt* edĕre, recensēre
edition *s* editio *f*
editor *s* editor *m*
educate *vt* educare, erudire
education *s* educatio, eruditio *f*
educator *s* praeceptor, magister *m*
eel *s* anguilla *f*
efface *vt* delēre, oblitterare, tollĕre
effect *s* effectum *n*, effect·us -ūs; (*show*) jactatio *f*; **—s** bona *n pl*; **in —** re vera; **without —** irritus
effect *vt* efficĕre, exsequi, facĕre
effective *adj* efficiens, efficax, valens; **—ly** valide, graviter
effectual *adj* efficax, valens, potens, **—ly** efficaciter, potenter
effeminancy *s* mollities *f*
effeminate *adj* effeminatus, mollis, muliebris; **—ly** effeminate, muliebriter
effete *adj* effetus
efficacious *adj* efficax; **—ly** efficaciter
efficacy *s* efficacia, vis *f*
efficiency *s* virtus, peritia *f*
efficient *adj* efficiens, aptus, idoneus; efficax; **—ly** perite, bene
effigy *s* effigies *f*
effort *s* labor, conat·us -ūs, nis·us -ūs *m*, opera *f*; **to make an —** eniti
effrontery *s* audacia, impudentia *f*
effusion *s* effusio *f*
effusive *adj* officiosus
egg *s* ovum *n*; **to lay —s** ova parĕre
egotism *s* amor sui *m*
egotist *s* sui amator *m*
egotistical *adj* sibi soli consulens
egress *s* egress·us -ūs, exit·us -ūs *m*
eight *adj* octo; **— times** octies
eighteen *adj* duodeviginti, decem et octo
eighteenth *adj* decimus octavus, duodevicesimus
eighth *adj* octavus
eighth *s* octava pars *f*
eightieth *adj* octogesimus
eighty *adj* octoginta
either *pron* alteruter; uter; alter
either *conj* **— . . . or** aut . . . aut; vel . . . vel
ejaculate *vt* emittĕre
ejaculation *s* clamor *m*
eject *vt* ejicĕre
ejection *s* dejectio *f*
eke *vt* **to eke out a livelihood** victum aegre parare
elaborate *adj* elaboratus; **—ly** elaborate
elaborate *vt* elaborare
elaboration *s* nimia diligentia *f*
elapse *vi* praeterire, abire, labi
elastic *adj* resiliens; (*fig*) mobilis
elate *vt* inflare, superbum reddĕre; **to be elated** efferri
elation *s* gaudium *n*, laetitia *f*, animus elatus *m*
elbow *s* ulna *f*, cubitus *m*
elbow *vt* cubitis depulsare, cubitis trudĕre
elder *adj* major natu
elderly *adj* aetate provectior
eldest *adj* maximus natu
elect *vt* eligĕre, deligĕre, creare
elect *adj* designatus; (*elite*) lectus
election *s* electio *f*, delect·us -ūs *m*; (*pol*) comitia *n pl*
electioneering *s* ambitio *f*
elective *adj* suffragatorius
elector *s* suffragator *m*
electrical *adj* electricus
electricity *s* vis electrica *f*
electrify *vt* electricā *vi* afficĕre; (*fig*) percellĕre
elegance *s* elegantia *f*
elegant *adj* elegans, concinnus; **—ly** eleganter, cum elegantia

elegiac *adj* elegiacus; **— verse** elegi *m pl*
elegy *s* elegia *f*
element *s* elementum *n*; **—s** principia, initia *n pl*; (*fig*) rudimenta *n pl*
elementary *adj* elementarius
elephant *s* elephantus, elephas *m*
elevate *vt* levare, attollere; (*fig*) efferre, inflare
elevated *adj* editus
elevation *s* elatio *f*; (*height*) altitudo *f*; (*hill*) locus superior *m*
eleven *adj* undecim; **— times** undecies
eleventh *adj* undecimus
elf *s* larva *f*, numen pumilum *n*
elicit *vt* elicĕre
eligible *adj* eligibilis, idoneus
eliminate *vt* amovēre, tollĕre
elision *s* elisio *f*
elite *adj* lectus
elite *s* flos *m*, lecti *m pl*
elk *s* alces *f*
ellipsis *s* ellipsis *f*
elliptical *adj* ellipticus; **—ly** per defectionem
elm *s* ulmus *f*
elocution *s* pronuntiatio *f*
elongate *vt* producĕre
elope *vi* clam fugĕre, aufugĕre
elopement *s* fuga clandestina *f*
eloquence *s* eloquentia *f*; (*natural*) facundia *f*
eloquent *adj* eloquens, disertus; **—ly** diserte, eloquenter, graviter
else *adj* alius; **no one —** nemo alius; **who —** quis alius
else *adv* (*besides*) praeterea; (*otherwise*) aliter
elsewhere *adv* alibi; (*motion*) alio
elucidate *vt* illustrare, explicare
elucidation *s* explicatio *f*
elude *vt* eludĕre, frustrari, evitare
Elysian *adj* Elysius
Elysian fields *s* Elysii campi *m pl*
emaciate *vt* emaciare, macerare
emaciated *adj* macer, macilentus
emaciation *s* macies, tabes *f*
emanate *vi* emanare, oriri
emanation *s* emanatio, exhalatio *f*
emancipate *vt* emancipare, manumittĕre; (*fig*) liberare
emancipation *s* (*of slave*) manumissio *f*; (*of son*) emancipatio *f*; (*fig*) liberatio *f*
emasculate *vt* castrare, emasculare; (*fig*) enervare
embalm *vt* condire, pollingĕre
embalming *s* pollinctura *f*
embankment *s* agger *m*, moles *f*
embargo *s* retentio navium *f*, interdictum *n*; **to lay an — upon a ship** navem retinēre
embark *vt* imponĕre; *vi* conscendĕre; **to — upon** (*fig*) ingredi
embarkation *s* conscensio *f*
embarrass *vt* perturbare, confundĕre, impedire
embarrassing *adj* incommodus, difficilis
embarrassment *s* conturbatio, implicatio *f*; (*financial*) angustiae *f pl*
embassy *s* legatio *f*, legati *m pl*
embellish *vt* ornare, exornare
embellishment *s* ornamentum, decus *n*, exornatio *f*
embers *s* cinis *m*, favilla *f*
embezzle *vt* peculari
embezzlement *s* peculat·us -ūs *m*
embezzler *s* peculator *m*
embitter *vt* exacerbare
emblazon *vt* insignire
emblem *s* emblema, insigne, signum *n*
emblematic *adj* symbolicus
embody *vt* includĕre, repraesentare
emboss *vt* caelare
embrace *s* amplex·us -ūs, complex·us -ūs *m*
embrace *vt* amplecti, complecti; comprehendĕre
embroider *vt* acu pingĕre
embroidery *s* vestis picta *f*
embroil *vt* permiscēre, implicare
embroilment *s* implicatio *f*
embryo *s* immaturus part·us -ūs *m*
emend *vt* emendare, corrigĕre
emendation *s* correctio, emendatio *f*
emerald *s* smaragdus *m*
emerge *vi* emergĕre; (*to arise*) exsistĕre
emergency *s* tempus, discrimen *n*, cas·us -ūs *m*
emigrant *s* emigrans *m*
emigrate *vi* emigrare
emigration *s* migratio *f*
eminence *s* praestantia, amplitudo *f*; (*rise of ground*) locus editus *m*
eminent *adj* eminens, egregius, praestans; **—ly** eximie, insigniter
emissary *s* emissarius, legatus *m*
emit *vt* emittĕre; exhalare
emotion *s* animi mot·us -ūs *m*, commotio *f*
emotional *adj* mobilis
emperor *s* imperator, princeps *m*
emphasis *s* energia, vis *f*, pondus *n*; impressio *f*
emphasize *vt* exprimĕre
emphatic *adj* emphaticus, gravis; **—ally** emphatice, graviter
empire *s* imperium, regnum *n*
empirical *adj* empiricus; **—ly** ex experimentis
empiricism *s* empirice *f*
employ *vt* uti (*with abl*), adhibēre, exercēre, occupare
employer *s* conductor, dominus *m*
employment *s* (*act*) us·us -ūs *m*; (*occupation*) quaest·us -ūs *m*; (*business*) negotium *n*
empower *vt* potestatem facĕre (*with dat*)
empress *s* imperatrix *f*
emptiness *s* inanitas *f*; (*fig*) vanitas *f*
empty *adj* vacuus, inanis; (*of street*) desertus; (*fig*) vanus
empty *vt* evacuare; exhaurire; *vi* (*of river*) influĕre
empyrean *s* aether *m*
emulate *vt* aemulari, imitari
emulation *s* aemulatio *f*
enable *vt* facultatem facĕre (*with dat*)
enact *vt* decernĕre, sancire

enactment *s* lex, sanctio *f*, decretum *n*
enamel *s* smaltum, vitrum metallicum *n*
enamel *adj* smaltinus
enamoured *adj* amans; **to be — of** amare, deamare
encamp *vi* castra poněre
encampment *s* castra *n pl*
encase *vt* includěre
enchant *vt* fascinare; (*fig*) capěre, captare, delectare
enchanter *s* incantator *m*
enchanting *adj* (*fig*) venustus, suavissimus
enchantment *s* incantamentum *n*; (*fig*) illecebrae *f pl*
enchantress *s* maga, cantatrix *f*; venefica *f*
encircle *vt* cingěre, circumdare, circumplecti
enclose *vt* includěre, saepire
enclosure *s* saeptum *n*
encompass *vt* complecti
encounter *s* (*meeting*) congress·us -ūs *m*; (*fight*) certamen *n*, pugna *f*
encounter *vt* congredi cum (*with abl*), obviam ire (*with dat*), occurrěre (*with dat*); (*in battle*) concurrěre cum (*with abl*)
encourage *vt* cohortari, confirmare; favēre (*with dat*)
encouragement *s* hortat·us -ūs *m*, confirmatio *f*, favor *m*
encroach *vi* invaděre; **to — upon** usurpare, occupare, invaděre
encroachment *s* usurpatio *f*
encumber *vt* impedire, onerare, praegravare
encumbrance *s* impedimentum, onus *n*
encyclopedia *s* encyclopaedia *f*
end *s* finis, terminus, exit·us -ūs *m*; (*aim*) propositum *n*; (*of a speech*) peroratio *f*; **in the —** denique; **to put an — to** finem imponěre (*with dat*); **to what —?** quo?, quorsum?
end *vt* finire, terminare, conficěre; *vi* desiněre; (*of time*) exire; (*of events*) evaděre
endanger *vt* periclitari
endear *vt* carum redděre, devincire
endearing *adj* carus, blandus
endearment *s* blanditiae *f pl*, blandimenta *n pl*
endeavor *s* conat·us -ūs, nis·us -ūs *m*
endeavor *vi* conari, eniti, laborare, contenděre
ending *s* finis, exit·us -ūs *m*
endless *adj* infinitus; perpetuus; **—ly** sine fine, perpetuo
endorse *vt* ratum facěre
endow *vt* dotare, donare, instruěre
endowed *adj* praeditus
endowment *s* dotatio, dos *f*, donum *n*
endurable *adj* tolerabilis
endurance *s* tolerantia, patientia *f*; (*duration*) duratio *f*
endure *vt* tolerare, pati; *vi* durare; permanēre
enduring *adj* tolerans; durabilis
enemy *s* (*public*) hostis *m*; (*private*) inimicus, adversarius *m*
energetic *adj* impiger, acer, strenuus, navus; **—ally** acriter, impigre, strenuo
energy *s* vis, vehementia, efficacia *f*, impet·us -ūs *m*
enervate *vt* enervare, debilitare
enforce *vt* exsequi, cogěre; (*arguments*) confirmare
enforcement *s* coactio, sanctio *f*
enfranchise *vt* (*slave*) manumittěre; civitate donare
enfranchisement *s* (*of slave*) manumissio *f*; civitatis donatio *f*
engage *vt* (*to employ*) adhibēre; (*to reserve*) conducěre; (*attention*) occupare; (*to involve*) implicare; (*enemy*) proelium facěre cum (*with abl*); *vi* **to — in** suscipěre, ingredi; **to engage in battle** proeliari, manum *or* manus conserěre
engaged *adj* (*to marry*) sponsus; **to be — in** versari in (*with abl*)
engagement *s* (*to marry*) pactio nuptialis *f*; (*business*) negotium *n*, occupatio *f*; (*mil*) proelium *n*, pugna *f*; (*promise*) pactum *n*, pactio *f*, promissum *n*
engaging *adj* suavis, blandus, amabilis
engender *vt* ingenerare, gigněre
engine *s* machina, machinatio *f*
engineer *s* machinator, faber *m*
engineering *s* machinalis scientia *f*; **civil —** architectura *f*
England *s* Anglia, Britannia *f*
English *adj* Anglicus, Britannicus
Englishman *s* Anglus, Britannus, Britannicus *m*
engrave *vt* inciděre, caelare, insculpěre, scalpěre
engraver *s* sculptor, caelator *m*
engraving *s* sculptura, caelatura *f*
engross *vt* occupare; **to be engrossed in** totus esse in (*with abl*)
enhance *vt* augēre, amplificare, ornare
enigma *s* aenigma *n*, ambages *f pl*
enigmatic *adj* ambiguus, obscurus; **—ally** ambigue
enjoin *vt* jubēre, injungěre
enjoy *vt* frui (*with abl*); uti (*with abl*)
enjoyment *s* fruct·us -ūs *m*, voluptas *f*, gaudium *n*; possessio *f*
enlarge *vt* amplificare, augēre, dilatare; *vi* **to — upon** amplificare, prosequi
enlargement *s* amplificatio, dilatio *f*, auct·us -ūs *m*
enlighten *vt* illustrare, illuminare; erudire
enlightenment *s* eruditio, humanitas *f*
enlist *vt* (*support*) conciliare; (*mil*) conscriběre; *vi* sacramentum dicěre
enlistment *s* conscriptio *f*
enliven *vt* animare, incitare; exhilarare
enmity *s* inimicitia *f*, odium *n*
ennoble *vt* honestare
ennui *s* taedium *n*
enormity *s* immanitas *f*; atrocitas *f*

enormous *adj* ingens, enormis, immanis; **—ly** immensum, praeter modum
enough *adj* satis; **— trouble** satis laboris
enough *adv* satis; **more than —** satis superque
enrage *vt* infuriare, exasperare, incenděre
enrapture *vt* rapěre, captare
enrich *vt* locupletare, ditare
enroll *vt* adscriběre, inscriběre; *vi* nomen dare
enshrine *vt* consecrare, dedicare
enshroud *vt* involvěre, amicire
ensign *s* (*flag*) vexillum *n*; (*officer*) signifer *m*
enslave *vt* in servitutem redigěre
enslavement *s* servitus *f*
ensnare *vt* illaquēre, irretire; (*fig*) illicere
ensue *vi* sequi, insequi
ensuing *adj* insequens, posterus, proximus
entail *vt* afferre, inferre
entangle *vt* illaquēre, irretire, impedire, implicare
entanglement *s* implicatio *f*
enter *vt* intrare, inire, ingredi; introire in *or* ad (*with acc*); **to — politics** ad rem publicam accedĕre; *vi* intrare, inire, ingredi, introire; **to — upon** (*to undertake*) suscipěre, ingredi
enterprise *s* (*undertaking*) inceptum, ausum *n*; (*in bad sense*) facinus *n*; (*quality*) animus alacer, animus promptus *m*
enterprising *adj* acer, promptus
entertain *vt* (*guest*) excipere, invitare, adhibēre; (*idea*) admittěre, habēre; (*to amuse*) oblectare, delectare
entertainer *s* hospes *m*
entertainment *s* (*amusement*) oblectatio *f*, oblectamentum *n*; (*cultural*) acroama *n*; (*by guest*) hospitium *n*
enthrall *vt* captare
enthusiasm *s* studium *n*, fervor, furor, ardor *m*
enthusiastic *adj* fanaticus, ardens, fervidus; **—ally** fanatice, ardenter
entice *vt* allicěre, elicěre
enticement *s* illecebra *f*
enticing *adj* blandus
entire *adj* totus, integer, solidus; **—ly** omnino, plane, penitus
entirety *s* integritas, universitas *f*
entitle *vt* (*to name*) appellare, nominare; inscriběre; (*to give title to*) potestatem dare (*with dat*)
entity *s* ens *n*, res *f*
entomologist *s* entomologicus *m*
entomology *s* entomologia *f*
entrails *s* viscera, exta, intestina *n pl*
entrance *s* adit·us -ūs, introit·us -ūs *m*; ostium *n*; (*act*) introit·us -ūs *m*, ingressio *f*
entrance *vt* rapěre, consopire, capěre
entrance hall *s* vestibulum *n*
entrap *vt* illaquēre, inescare; capěre
entreat *vt* obsecrare, orare, deprecari
entreaty *s* rogatio, obsecratio *f*, preces *f pl*
entrust *vt* creděre, mandare, committěre
entry *s* (*act*) introit·us -ūs *m*, ingressio *f*; (*of house*) vestibulum *n*; adit·us -ūs *m*; (*in accounts*) nomen *n*
entwine *vt* implicare, nectěre
enumerate *vt* enumerare
enumeration *s* enumeratio, recensio *f*
enunciate *vt* enuntiare, pronuntiare, exprimere
enunciation *s* enuntiatio *f*
envelop *vt* involvěre, amicire, implicare
envelope *s* involucrum *n*
enviable *adj* invidiosus
envious *adj* invidus, lividus
envoy *s* nuntius, legatus, orator *m*
envy *s* invidia *f*
envy *vt* invidēre (*with dat*)
ephemeral *adj* brevis; caducus
epic *adj* epicus, heroicus
epic *s* epos *n*
epicure *s* helluo, homo voluptarius *m*
Epicurean *adj* Epicureus
Epicurean *s* Epicureus *m*; (*hedonist*) voluptarius *m*
epidemic *adj* epidemus, contagiosus
epidemic *s* pestilentia *f*
epidermis *s* summa cutis, epidermis *f*
epigram *s* epigramma *n*
epilepsy *s* morbus comitialis *m*, epilepsia *f*
epilogue *s* epilogus *m*
epiphany *s* epiphania *f*
episode *s* embolium, eventum *n*, excurs·us -ūs *m*
epistle *s* epistola *f*
epistolary *adj* epistolaris
epitaph *s* epitaphium *n*, titulus *m*
epithet *s* epitheton *n*
epitome *s* epitome, epitoma *f*
epoch *s* epocha *f*, saeculum *n*
equal *adj* aequalis, aequus, par; **—ly** aeque, aequaliter, pariter
equal *s* par *m, f & n*
equal *vt* aequare, adaequare
equality *s* aequalitas *f*, aequum *n*
equalization *s* (act) aequatio, exaequatio *f*; (*state*) aequalitas *f*
equalize *vt* adaequare, exaequare
equanimity *s* aequus animus *m*
equation *s* aequatio *f*
equator *s* aequinoctialis circulus *m*
equatorial *adj* aequinoctialis
equestrian *adj* equestris
equestrian *s* eques *m*
equidistant *adj* **to be —** aequo intervallo inter se distare
equilibrium *s* aequilibrium *n*
equinox *s* aequinoctium *n*
equip *vt* armare, ornare, instruěre
equipment *s* arma, instrumenta, armamenta *n pl*, armatura *f*, apparat·us -ūs *m*
equitable *adj* aequus, justus
equitably *adv* aeque, juste
equity *s* aequitas *f*, aequum *n*

equivalent *adj* aequus, par
equivocal *adj* ambiguus, anceps; **—ly** ambigue
equivocate *vi* tergiversari
era *s* tempus, saeculum *n*
eradicate *vt* eruere, exstirpare, eradicare
eradication *s* exstirpatio *f*
erase *vt* delēre, eradĕre
erasure *s* litura *f*
ere *conj* priusquam
ere *prep* ante (*with acc*); **— long** brevi, mox; **— now** ante hoc tempus
erect *adj* erectus, arrectus
erect *vt* (*to raise*) erigĕre; (*to build*) exstruere; (*statue*) ponĕre
erection *s* erectio, aedificatio, exstructio *f*
erotic *adj* amatorius, eroticus
err *vi* (ab)errare, peccare
errand *s* mandatum *n*
erratic *adj* inconstans
erroneous *adj* falsus, errore implicitus; **—ly** falso, perperam
error *s* error *m*; vitium *n*; delictum, peccatum *n*; (*in writing*) mendum *n*
erudite *adj* eruditus, doctus
erudition *s* eruditio *f*
erupt *vi* erumpĕre
eruption *s* eruptio *f*
escape *s* fuga *f*, effugium *n*
escape *vt* fugĕre, evitare; **to — the notice of** fallĕre; *vi* effugĕre, evadĕre, elabi; (*secretly*) subterfugĕre
escort *s* comitat·us -ūs *m*; (*protection*) praesidium *n*
escort *vt* comitari, deducĕre
especially *adv* praecipue, praesertim, maxime, in primis
essay *s* experimentum *n*, conat·us -ūs *m*; (*treatise*) libellus *m*
essay *vt* conari, tentare
essence *s* essentia, natura *f*
essential *adj* necessarius, propius; **—ly** naturā, necessario
establish *vt* constituĕre, statuĕre; (*firmly*) stabilire, confirmare; (*to prove*) probare, arguĕre
establishment *s* (*act*) constitutio *f*; (*com*) negotium *n*
estate *s* (*state*) stat·us -ūs *m*, conditio *f*; (*property*) fundus *m*, praedium *n*; (*pol*) ordo *m*, dignitas *f*
esteem *s* aestimatio *f*, honor *m*
esteem *vt* aestimare, putare; (*to respect*) magni facĕre
estimable *adj* aestimandus
estimate *vt* aestimare, censēre
estimate *s* aestimatio *f*, judicium *n*
estimation *s* aestimatio, opinio, sententia *f*, judicium *n*
estimator *s* aestimator, calculator *m*
estrange *vt* abalienare
estrangement *s* alienatio *f*, discidium *n*
estuary *s* aestuarium *n*
eternal *adj* aeternus, sempiternus; **—ly** in aeternum, semper
eternity *s* aeternitas *f*
ether *s* aether *m*
ethereal *adj* aethereus
ethical *adj* moralis
ethics *s* mores *m pl*, ethice *f*; philosophia moralis *f*
etymology *s* etymologia, verborum notatio *f*
eulogize *vt* collaudare
eulogy *s* laudatio *f*, panegyricus *m*
eunuch *s* eunuchus *m*; (*in contempt*) spado *m*
euphony *s* euphonia *f*, sonus dulcis *m*
European *adj* Europaeus
Euxine *s* Euxinus pontus *m*
evacuate *vt* vacuare, vacuefacĕre; (*people*) deducĕre
evacuation *s* discessio *f*; (*of bowels*) egestio *f*
evade *vt* subterfugĕre, eludĕre, devitare
evaporate *vt* exhalare, evaporare; *vi* exhalari
evaporation *s* exhalatio *f*
evasion *s* effugium *n*, tergiversatio *f*
evasive *adj* ambiguus; **—ly** ambigue
eve *s* vesper *m*; (*of feast*) vigiliae *f pl*; **on the — of** sub (*with acc*)
even *adj* aequalis, aequus; (*level*) planus; (*of numbers*) par; **—ly** aequaliter
even *adv* et, etiam, vel; **— if** etsi, etiamsi; **not —** ne . . . quidem
evening *s* vesper *m*; **in the —** vespere, vesperi
evening *adj* vespertinus
evening star *s* Hesperus, Vesper *m*
evenness *s* aequalitas, aequabilitas *f*
event *s* cas·us -ūs *m*, factum *n*; (*outcome*) event·us -ūs, exit·us -ūs *m*; **in any —** saltem
eventful *adj* memorabilis
eventual *adj* ultimus; **—ly** aliquando, olim, denique
ever *adv* (*always*) semper; (*at any time*) umquam; (*after* si, nisi, num, ne) quando; **for —** in aeternum
evergreen *adj* sempervivus
everlasting *adj* sempiternus; **—ly** in aeternum
evermore *adv* semper, in aeternum
every *adj* quisque, omnis; **— now and then** interdum; **— other day** alternis diebus
everybody *pron* quisque, nemo non; omnes *m pl*
everyday *adj* quotidianus *or* cottidianus; usitatus
everything *pron* omnia *n pl*
everywhere *adv* ubique, ubivis
evict *vt* expellĕre, dejicĕre, detrudĕre
evidence *s* testimonium, indicium, argumentum *n*; (*witness*) testis *m & f*
evidence *vt* testari
evident *adj* apertus, manifestus; **it is —** apparet; **—ly** aperte, manifesto
evil *adj* malus, pravus, improbus
evil *s* malum *n*, improbitas *f*
evildoer *s* maleficus, malefactor *m*
evil-minded *adj* malevolus, malignus
evoke *vt* evocare, excitare, elicĕre
evolution *s* progress·us -ūs *m*, progressio *f*
evolve *vt* evolvĕre, explicare
exact *adj* exactus, subtilis, diligens;

—ly accurate, subtiliter, diligenter; **—ly as** sic ut
exact *vt* exigĕre
exaction *s* exactio *f*
exactitude *s* diligentia *f*
exaggerate *vt* exaggerare, augēre, in majus extollĕre
exaggeration *s* trajectio, superlatio *f*
exalt *vt* extollĕre, amplificare, evehĕre
exaltation *s* elatio *f*
examination *s* investigatio *f*; (*in school*) probatio *f*; (*of witnesses*) interrogatio *f*
examine *vt* investigare, inquirĕre, scrutari; (*witnesses*) interrogare
examiner *s* scrutator, investigator *m*
example *s* exemplum, exemplar, documentum *n*; **for —** exempli gratiā, verbi gratiā
exasperate *vt* exasperare, exacerbare, irritare
exasperation *s* ira *f*
excavate *vt* excavare, effodĕre
excavation *s* fossio, excavatio *f*, cavum *n*
exceed *vt* superare, excedĕre
exceedingly *adv* valde, magnopere
excel *vt* superare, praestare (*with dat*); *vi* excellĕre
excellence *s* excellentia, praestantia *f*
Excellency *s* illustrissimus *m*
excellent *adj* praestans, egregius, optimus; **—ly** egregie, optime
except *vt* excipĕre
except *prep* praeter (*with acc*); nisi (*followed by appropriate case*); **— that** nisi quod
exception *s* exceptio *f*; **with the — of** praeter (*with acc*)
exceptional *adj* egregius, praestans, singularis; **—ly** praeter modum
excess *s* excess·us -ūs *m*, intemperantia *f*
excessive *adj* immodicus, nimius; **—ly** immodice, nimis
exchange *s* (*barter*) commutatio *f*; (*of money*) collybus *m*
exchange *vt* mutare, permutare
excise *vt* excidere
excision *s* excisio *f*
excitable *adj* irritabilis, fervidus
excite *vt* excitare, stimulare; (*to inflame*) incendĕre
excitement *s* commotio *f*; perturbatio *f*; incitamentum *n*
exclaim *vt* exclamare; (*as a group*) conclamare; *vi* **to — against** acclamare (*with dat*); declamitare in (*with acc*)
exclamation *s* exclamatio *f*, clamor *m*
exclude *vt* excludĕre, prohibēre
exclusion *s* exclusio *f*
exclusive *adj* proprius; **— of** praeter (*with acc*); **—ly** solum
excommunicate *vt* excommunicare
excommunication *s* excommunicatio *f*
excrement *s* excrementum, stercus *n*
excretion *s* excrementum *n*, excretio *f*
excruciating *adj* acerbissimus
exculpate *vt* (ex)purgare, excusare, absolvere
excursion *s* excursio *f*, iter *n*
excusable *adj* excusabilis
excuse *vt* excusare; ignoscĕre (*with dat*), veniam dare (*with dat*)
excuse *s* excusatio *f*; (*pretense*) pretext·us -ūs *m*, species *f*
execute *vt* (*to perform*) exsequi, efficĕre; (*to punish*) necare, securi ferire
execution *s* effect·us -ūs *m*, effectio *f*; (*capital punishment*) supplicium *n*
executioner *s* carnifex *m*
executive *adj* ad administrationem pertinens
executive *s* administrator *m*
executor *s* curator testamenti *m*
exemplary *adj* egregius, eximius
exemplification *s* expositio *f*
exemplify *vt* explicare
exempt *vt* eximĕre, liberare
exempt *adj* exemptus, immunis, liber
exemption *s* exemptio, immunitas, liberatio *f*
exercise *s* exercitatio *f*, us·us -ūs *m*; (*mil*) exercitium *n*; (*literary*) thema *n*
exercise *vt* exercēre; uti (*with abl*)
exert *vt* adhibēre; **to — oneself** viribus eniti
exertion *s* contentio *f*, nis·us -ūs *m*
exhalation *s* exhalatio *f*, vapor *m*
exhale *vt* exhalare, spargĕre; *vi* exspirare
exhaust *vt* exhaurire; (*to tire*) defatigare, conficĕre, debilitare
exhaustion *s* defatigatio, defectio virium *f*
exhibit *vt* exhibēre, exponĕre, ostendĕre
exhibition *s* exhibitio, propositio *f*; spectaculum *n*
exhilarate *vt* exhilarare
exhilaration *s* hilaritas *f*
exhort *vt* hortari
exhortation *s* hortatio *f*, hortamen *n*
exhume *vt* exhumare, eruĕre
exigency *s* necessitas *f*, angustiae *f pl*
exile *s* (*banishment*) ex(s)ilium *n*; (*person*) exsul, profugus *m*
exile *vt* relegare, in exilium pellĕre, deportare
exist *vi* esse, exsistĕre; vivĕre
existence *s* existentia *f*; vita *f*
exit *s* exit·us -ūs *m*; ostium *n*
exonerate *vt* absolvĕre
exorbitant *adj* nimius, immodicus
exotic *adj* externus, peregrinus
expand *vt* expandĕre, extendĕre, dilatare; *vi* expandi, extendi, dilatari
expanse *s* spatium, expansum *n*
expansion *s* expansio *f*, spatium *n*
expatriate *vt* expellĕre
expect *vt* exspectare, sperare
expectancy *s* spes *f*
expectation *s* exspectatio, spes *f*
expectorate *vt* exspuĕre, exscreare
expediency *s* utilitas *f*
expedient *adj* utilis, commodus; **—ly** apte, commode

expedient *s* modus *m*, ratio *f*
expedite *vt* expedire, maturare
expedition *s* (*mil*) expeditio *f*; (*speed*) celeritas *f*
expeditious *adj* celer, promptus; **—ly** celeriter, mature
expel *vt* expellĕre, ejicĕre
expend *vt* expendĕre, impendĕre
expenditure *s* sumpt·us -ūs *m*, impensa *f*
expense *s* impensa *f*, sumpt·us -ūs *m*
expensive *adj* carus, pretiosus; sumptuosus, lautus; **—ly** sumptuose
experience *s* experientia, peritia *f*, us·us -ūs *m*
experience *vt* experiri, cognoscĕre, pati
experienced *adj* peritus, expertus
experiment *s* experimentum *n*
experiment *vi* **to — with** experiri
experimental *adj* usu comparatus
expert *adj* sciens, peritus, callidus; **—ly** callide, scienter
expertness *s* calliditas, sollertia *f*
expiate *vt* expiare, luĕre
expiation *s* expiatio *f*; piaculum *n*
expiration *s* exspiratio *f*, finis, exit·us -ūs *m*
expire *vi* exspirare; (*of time*) exire
explain *vt* explanare, explicare, exponĕre
explanation *s* explanatio, explicatio, enodatio, interpretatio *f*
explicit *adj* apertus, expressus; **—ly** aperte, plane
explode *vt* displodĕre, discutĕre; *vi* displodi, dirumpi
exploit *s* res gesta *f*, factum, facinus *n*
exploit *vt* uti (*with abl*), abuti (*with abl*)
exploration *s* indagatio, investigatio *f*
explore *vt* explorare, scrutari, perscrutari
explorer *s* explorator *m*
explosion *s* fragor *m*
exponent *s* interpres *m*
export *vt* exportare, evehĕre
exporter *s* exportator *m*
exports *s* merces quae exportantur *f pl*
expose *vt* exponĕre; nudare, detegĕre, patefacĕre; (*to danger*) objicĕre, offerre
exposition *s* explicatio, expositio, interpretatio *f*; (*show*) spectaculum *n*
expostulation *s* expostulatio, querela *f*
exposure *s* (*of guilt*) deprehensio *f*; (*to cold*) expositio *f*
expound *vt* exponĕre, interpretari
express *adj* clarus, expressus; **—ly** plane
express *vt* exprimĕre, eloqui, dicĕre; significare
expression *s* vox *f*, verbum *n*; (*of face*) vult·us -ūs *m*
expressive *adj* significans; (*fig*) loquax; **— of** index (*with genit*)
expulsion *s* exactio, ejectio, expulsio *f*
expunge *vt* delēre, oblitterare
expurgate *vt* expurgare
exquisite *adj* exquisitus, elegans; **—ly** eleganter, exquisite
extant *adj* superstes, exsistens; **to be —** exstare
extempore *adv* ex tempore, subito
extemporize *vi* subito dicĕre, subita dicere
extend *vt* extendĕre, producĕre, propagare; *vi* extendere, porrigi
extension *s* extensio *f*; (*space*) spatium *n*; (*of boundaries*) prolatio *f*
extensive *adj* amplus, latus; **—ly** late
extent *s* spatium *n*; (*of a country*) tract·us -ūs *m*, fines *m pl*; **to a great —** magna ex parte; **to some —** aliqua ex parte; **to this —** hactenus
extenuate *vt* mitigare, minuĕre
extenuation *s* imminutio *f*
exterior *adj* externus, exterior
exterior *s* species *f*
exterminate *vt* exstirpare, exterminare, eradicare
extermination *s* exstirpatio *f*; internecio, occidio *f*
external *adj* externus, extraneus; **—ly** extrinsecus
extinct *adj* exstinctus, obsoletus; **to become —** obsolescĕre
extinction *s* exstinctio *f*, interit·us -ūs *m*
extinguish *vt* exstinguĕre, restinguĕre
extol *vt* laudibus efferre
extort *vt* extorquēre, diripĕre, exprimere
extortion *s* res repetundae *f pl*
extortioner *s* exactor, extortor *m*
extra *adj* additus
extra *adv* insuper, praeterea
extract *vt* extrahĕre, excerpĕre; (*teeth, etc.*) evellĕre
extract *s* (*chemical*) expressio *f*; (*literary*) excerptum *n*; (*synopsis*) compendium *n*
extraction *s* (*act*) evulsio *f*; (*birth, origin*) stirps, origo *f*, genus *n*
extraneous *adj* extraneus, alienus, adventicius
extraordinarily *adv* mire, praeter solitum, extra modum
extraordinary *adj* extraordinarius, insolitus; (*outstanding*) eximius, mirus
extravagance *s* intemperantia *f*; sumpt·us -ūs *m*
extravagant *adj* immodicus, nimius; profusus, luxuriosus; (*spending*) prodigus; **—ly** immodice, absurde; prodige
extreme *adj* extremus, ultimus; **—ly** valde, summe
extreme *s* extremum, summum *n*
extremity *s* extremitas *f*, extremum *n*, finis *m*; (*distress*) miseria *f*
extricate *vt* expedire, extrahĕre, liberare

exuberance *s* ubertas, luxuria, redundantia *f*
exuberant *adj* uber, luxuriosus; **—ly** ubertim
exude *vt* exudare; *vi* emanare
exult *vi* exsultare, gestire
exultant *adj* laetabundus, laetus; **—ly** laete
exultation *s* laetitia *f*
eye *s* oculus *m*; (*of needle*) foramen *n*; (*of plant*) gemma *f*; **to keep one's —s on** oculos defigĕre in (*with abl*)
eye *vt* aspicĕre, intuēri
eyebrow *s* supercilium *n*
eyelash *s* palebrarum pilus *m*
eyelid *s* palpebra *f*
eyesight *s* acies, acies oculi *f*
eyewitness *s* arbiter *m*

F

fable *s* fabula, narratio commenticia *f*
fabric *s* fabrica *f*; (*piece of cloth*) textile *n*
fabricate *vt* fabricare, struĕre; (*fig*) fingĕre
fabrication *s* fabricatio *f*; (*fig*) mendacium *n*
fabulous *adj* fictus, commenticius; **—ly** ficte
face *s* facies *f*, os *n*, vult·us -ūs *m*; **— to —** coram
face *vt* aspicere, intuēre; se opponĕre (*with dat*), obviam ire (*with dat*); obire; *vi* spectare, vergĕre; **to — about** (*mil*) signa convertĕre
facet *s* pars *f*
facetious *adj* facetus; **—ly** facete
facilitate *vt* facilius reddere
facility *s* facilitas *f*; opportunitas *f*
facing *adj* adversus, spectans
facsimile *s* imago *f*, exemplar *n*
fact *s* factum, verum *n*, res *f*; **as a matter of —** enimvero; **in —** vero, re ipsa; enim, etenim; **the — that** quod
faction *s* factio *f*
factory *s* officina, fabrica *f*
faculty *s* facultas, vis *f*; (*of university*) ordo *m*
fade *vi* marcescĕre, deflorescĕre, pallescĕre
fail *vt* (*to disappoint*) relinquĕre, deserĕre, deficĕre; *vi* succumbĕre, concidĕre, cadĕre; (*com*) decoquere, foro cedĕre
fail *s* **without —** certo, plane, omnino
failing *s* (*deficiency*) defect·us ūs *m*; (*fault*) culpa *f*, delictum, vitium *n*; (*disappointment*) frustratio *f*; (*ceasing*) remissio *f*
failure *s* defectio *f*, defect·us -ūs *m*; (*fault*) culpa *f*, delictum *n*
faint *adj* (*weary*) defessus; (*drooping*) languidus; (*of sight, smell, etc.*) hebes; (*of sound*) surdus; (*of color*) pallidus; (*of courage*) timidus; **—ly** languide; timide
faint *vi* collabi, intermori, (animo) linqui
fainthearted *adj* timidus, imbellis, ignavus
faintness *s* (*of impression*) levitas *f*; (*of body*) languor *m*
fair *adj* (*in appearance*) formosus, pulcher; (*of complexion*) candidus; (*of hair*) flavus; (*of weather*) serenus; (*of wind*) secundus; (*impartial*) aequus; (*of ability*) mediocris; **— and square** sine fuco ac fallaciis; **—ly** aeque, juste; (*moderately*) mediocriter
fair *s* nundinae *f pl*
fairness *s* (*of complexion*) candor *m*; (*justice*) aequitas *f*
fairy *s* nympha *f*
faith *s* (*trust*) fides *f*; religio *f*; **to have — in** credere (*with dat*), confidĕre (*with dat*)
faithful *adj* fidelis, fidus; **—ly** fideliter
faithfulness *s* fidelitas, integritas *f*
faithless *adj* infidus, infidelis, perfidus; **—ly** perfide
falcon *s* falco *m*
fall *s* cas·us -ūs, laps·us -ūs *m*; (*season*) autumnus *m*
fall *vi* cadĕre, concidĕre, labi; (*to die*) occidĕre; (*to abate*) decrescĕre; (*violently*) corruĕre; **to — apart** dilabi; **to — at** accidere ad (*with acc*); **to — back** recidĕre; (*to retreat*) pedem referre; **to — down** decidĕre; concidere; **to — forwards** procidĕre, prolabi; **to — foul of** incurrere; **to — in(to)** incidĕre; **to — in with** (*to meet*) incidĕre; (*to agree*) congruere; **to — in love with** amare, adamare; **to — off** (*fig*) in deterius mutari; **to — out with** (*to have a disagreement with*) dissedēre; dissentire ab (*with abl*); **to — short of** non contingĕre; **to — sick** in morbum incidere; **to — to** (*of inheritances, etc.*) obvenire (*with dat*); **to — under** succumbĕre; (*to be reckoned*) pertinēre; (*to become subjected to*) pati; **to — upon** incidĕre ad (*with acc*); (*to assail*) incidere in (*with acc*), ingruĕre in (*with acc*)
fallacious *adj* fallax, captiosus; **—ly** fallaciter
fallacy *s* captio *f*
fallible *adj* errori obnoxius
fallow *adj* (*of land*) novalis; **to lie —** cessare
false *adj* falsus, fictus; **—ly** falso
falsehood *s* mendacium *n*
falsify *vt* supponĕre, corrumpĕre; (*documents*) vitiare, interlinĕre

falter *vi* (*to stammer*) haesitare; (*to totter*) titubare
fame *s* fama *f*, nomen *n*
famed *adj* clarus, illustris
familiar *adj* familiaris, notus; intimus; **—ly** familiariter
familiarity *s* familiaritas, consuetudo *f*, us·us -ūs *m*
familiarize *vt* assuefacĕre
family *s* familia, dom·us -ūs, gens *f*, genus *n*
family *adj* familiaris; (*of home*) domesticus; (*relating to race*) gentilicus
famine *s* fames *f*
famished *adj* famelicus; fame confectus
famous *adj* clarus, celeber, inclitus; **—ly** praeclare, insigniter
fan *s* flabellum *n*; (*admirer*) fautor *m*; (*winnowing*) vannus *f*
fan *vt* ventilare; (*fire*) accendĕre; (*fig*) excitare, inflammare
fanatic *adj* fanaticus; **—ly** fanatice
fanaticism *s* furor religiosus *m*
fancied *adj* opinatus
fanciful *adj* (*capricious*) inconstans, levis; (*imagined*) commenticius
fancy *s* opinio, imaginatio *f*; (*caprice*) libido *f*; (*liking*) prolubium *n*; (*faculty*) phantasia *f*
fancy *vt* imaginari
fang *s* dens *m*
fantastic *adj* vanus; monstruosus
far *adj* longinquus, remotus
far *adv* procul, longe; **as — as** quantum, quatenus; tenus (*with abl*); **by —** longe, multo; **— and near** longe lateque; **— be it from me to say** equidem dicĕre nolim; **— off** procul; **so —** hactenus; **thus —** hactenus
farce *s* mimus *m*
farcical *adj* mimicus; **—ly** mimice
fare *s* (*food*) cibus, vict·us -ūs *m*; (*money*) vectura *f*, portorium *n*
fare *vi* agĕre, se habēre
farewell *interj* vale!; salve!
farm *s* fundus *m*, praedium *n*
farm *vt* (*to till*) arare, colĕre; (*taxes*) redimĕre; **to — out** locare
farmer *s* agricola, colonus *m*; (*of revenues*) publicanus *m*
farming *s* agricultura *f*; res rustica *f*
farsighted *adj* providus
farther *adj* ulterior
farther *adv* longius, ulterius, ultra
farthermost *adj* remotissimus, ultimus
farthest *adj* ultimus, extremus
fasces *n* fasces *m pl*
fascinate *vt* fascinare
fascination *s* fascinatio *f*, fascinum *n*
fashion *s* (*form*) forma, figura *f*; (*manner*) mos, modus, rit·us -ūs *m*; (*custom*) consuetudo *f*, us·us -ūs *m*
fashion *vt* formare, fabricare, effingĕre
fashionable *adj* elegans, concinnus; **it is —** in usu est
fashionably *adv* ad morem; eleganter
fast *adj* (*swift*) celer; (*firm*) firmus, stabilis; (*tight*) astrictus; (*shut*) occlusus
fast *adv* celeriter; firmiter
fast *s* jejunium *n*
fast *vi* jejunare, cibo abstinēre
fasten *vt* affigĕre, astringere; **to — down** defigĕre; **to — to** annectĕre, impingĕre; **to — together** configĕre, colligare; *vi* **to — upon** arripĕre
fastening *s* colligatio *f*, vinculum *n*
fastidious *adj* fastidiosus, delicatus, elegans, morosus; **—ly** fastidiose, morose
fasting *s* jejunium *n*, abstinentia *f*
fat *adj* pinguis, obsesus; (*productive*) fertilis
fat *s* adeps *m & f*, lardum *n*
fatal *adj* fatalis; exitialis, funebris; **—ly** fataliter; funeste
fatality *s* fatum *n*; (*misfortune*) infortunium *n*
fate *s* fatum *n*, sors *f*
fated *adj* fatalis
Fates *s* Parcae *f pl*
father *s* pater *m*; **— of the family** paterfamilias *m*
fatherhood *s* paternitas *f*
father-in-law *s* socer *m*
fatherless *adj* orbus
fatherly *adj* paternus, patrius
fathom *s* ulna *f*
fathom *vt* exputare
fathomless *adj* profundissimus
fatigue *s* (de)fatigatio, lassitudo *f*
fatigue *vt* (de)fatigare, delassare
fatigued *adj* (de)fatigatus, (de)fessus
fatten *vt* saginare, farcire; *vi* pinguescĕre
fattening *s* saginatio *f*
fatty *adj* pinguis
fatuous *adj* fatuus, insulsus
fault *s* culpa *f*, delictum, vitium *n*, error *m*; (*in writing*) mendum *n*; **to find — with** vituperare, carpĕre, incusare
faultless *adj* integer, perfectus; (*corrected*) emendatus
faulty *adj* vitiosus; mendosus
faun *s* faunus *m*
favor *s* favor *m*, gratia *f*; (*goodwill*) benevolentia *f*; (*good turn*) beneficium *n*; (*present*) munus *n*
favor *vt* favēre (*with dat*), secundare
favorable *adj* prosperus, secundus; commodus, idoneus; benignus, propitius
favorably *adv* fauste, felicter, benigne; opportune
favorite *adj* dilectus, gratus
favorite *s* deliciae *f pl*
favoritism *s* indulgentia *f*; iniquitas *f*
fawn *s* hinnuleus *m*
fawn *vi* **to — on** *or* **upon** adulari
fawning *adj* blandus, adulatorius; **—ly** blande, adulatorie
fawning *s* adulatio *f*
fear *s* timor, met·us -ūs *m*, formido *f*
fear *vt & vi* timēre, metuĕre, verēri

fearful *adj* timidus, pavidus; (*terrible*) dirus, terribilis; **—ly** timide
fearless *adj* impavidus, intrepidus; **—ly** impavide, intrepide
feasibility *s* possibilitas *f*
feasible *adj* efficiendus, possibilis
feast *s* (*banquet*) convivium *n*, epulae *f pl*; (*holy day*) dies festus *m*
feast *vt* pascĕre; *vi* epulari, convivari
feat *s* facinus, factum *n*
feather *s* penna *f*; (*downy*) pluma *f*
feather *vt* **to — one's nest** opes accumulare
feathered *adj* pennatus; plumosus
feathery *adj* plumeus, plumosus
feature *s* lineamentum *n*; (*fig*) proprietas *f*, proprium *n*
February *s* (mensis) Februarius *m*
federal *adj* foederatus; rei publicae (*genit*)
federalize *vt* confoederare
federation *s* confoederatio *f*
fee *s* merces *f*
feeble *adj* infirmus, debilis; **to grow —** languescere
feebly *adv* infirme, languide
feed *vt* (*animals*) pascĕre; (*to nourish*) alĕre; (*fig*) (*of streams, etc.*) servire (*with dat*); *vi* pasci; **to — on** vesci (*with abl*)
feed *s* pabulum *n*
feel *vt* sentire; (*with hand*) tangĕre, tractare; **to — pain** dolore affici; **to — pity for** misereri (*with genit*); *vi* **to — happy** gaudēre; **to — sad** maestus esse
feel *s* tact·us -ūs *m*
feeling *s* (*touch*) tact·us -ūs *m*; (*sensibility*) sens·us -ūs *m*; (*emotion*) affect·us -ūs *m*; (*taste*) judicium *n*; (*pity*) miseratio *f*
feign *vt* fingĕre, dissimulare, mentiri
feint *s* simulatio *f*
felicitation *s* congratulatio *f*
felicitous *adj* felix; **—ly** feliciter
felicity *s* felicitas *f*
feline *adj* felin(e)us
fell *adj* atrox, saevus, crudelis
fell *vt* (*trees*) caedĕre; (*person*) sternĕre
fellow *s* socius, aequalis *m*
felon *s* scelestus, sceleratus *m*
felonious *adj* scelestus, sceleratus
felony *s* scelus *n*
felt *s* coacta *n pl*
female *adj* muliebris
female *s* femina *f*
feminine *adj* muliebris, femineus; (*gram*) femininus
fence *s* saepes *f*, saepimentum *n*
fence *vt* saepire; **to — off** intersaepire; *vi* batuĕre
fencing *s* ludus gladiatorius *m*
fend *vt* **to — off** arcēre; *vi* **to — for oneself** sibi providēre, sibi consulĕre
ferment *s* fermentum *n*; (*fig*) aest·us -ūs *m*
ferment *vt* fermentare; excitare; *vi* fermentari; (*fig*) fervēre
fermentation *s* fermentatio *f*
fern *s* filix *f*
ferocious *adj* ferox, truculentus, saevus, atrox; **—ly** truculente
ferocity *s* ferocitas, saevitia *f*
ferret *vt* **to — out** eruĕre
ferry *s* traject·us -ūs *m*
ferry *vt* trajicĕre, transvehĕre
ferryboat *s* scapha, cymba *f*
ferryman *s* portitor *m*
fertile *adj* fertilis, fecundus
fertility *s* fertilitas, ubertas *f*
fertilize *vt* fecundare
fervent *adj* fervidus, ardens; **—ly** ardenter, vehementer
fervid *adj* fervidus; **—ly** fervide
fervor *s* fervor, ardor *m*
fester *vi* suppurare, ulcerari
festival *s* dies festus *m*, sollemne *n*
festive *adj* festus
festivity *s* sollemnia *n pl*; (*gaiety*) festivitas *f*
fetch *vt* adducĕre, afferre, arcessĕre
fetid *adj* foetidus, graveolens
feud *s* simultas, inimicitia, lis *f*
fever *s* febris *f*; **to have a —** febrire
feverish *adj* febriculosus
few *adj* pauci; **a —** aliquot; **in a — words** paucis, breviter
fiasco *s* calamitas *f*
fiber *s* fibra *f*
fibrous *adj* fibratus
fickle *adj* inconstans, mobilis, instabilis
fiction *s* fictio *f*, commentum *n*; fabula *f*
fictitious *adj* fictus, commenticius; **—ly** ficte
fiddle *s* fides *f*
fiddle *vi* fide ludĕre
fiddler *s* fidicen *m*
fidelity *s* fidelitas, constantia *f*
fidget *vi* trepidare
fidgety *adj* inquietus
field *s* ager *m*; (*plowed*) arvum *n*; (*mil*) acies *f*, campus *m*; (*grassy*) pratum *n*; (*of grain*) seges *f*; (*sphere*) area *f*, locus, campus *m*
fieldpiece *s* tormentum *n*
fiend *s* inimicus *m*; diabolus *m*
fiendish *adj* diabolicus
fierce *adj* atrox, saevus, vehemens; **—ly** atrociter, saeve, vehementer
fierceness *s* atrocitas, saevitia, ferocitas *f*
fiery *adj* igneus; (*fig*) ardens, fervidus
fife *s* tibia *f*
fifteen *adj* quindecim; **— times** quindecies
fifteenth *adj* quintus decimus
fifth *adj* quintus; **for the — time** quintum, quinto
fifth *s* quinta pars *f*
fiftieth *adj* quinquagesimus
fifty *adj* quinquaginta
fig *s* ficus *f*
fight *s* pugna *f*, proelium *n*; (*struggle*) contentio, luctatio *f*
fight *vt* pugnare cum (*with abl*); **to — it out** decernĕre, depugnare; *vi* pugnare, dimicare; (*in battle*) proeliari; (*with sword*) digladiari; **to — hand to hand** cominus pugnare

figment *s* commentum *n*
figurative *adj* translatus, assumptus; **—ly** per translationem, tropice
figure *s* figura, forma, imago *f*; (*of speech*) tropus *m*, translatio *f*; (*in art*) signum *n*
figure *vt* figurare, formare; putare, opinari
figured *adj* sigillatus
filament *s* filum *n*, fibra *f*
filbert *s* nux avellana *f*
file *s* (*tool*) lima *f*; (*for papers*) scapus *m*; (*row*) ordo *m*, agmen *n*
file *vt* limare; (*papers*) in scapo condĕre; *vi* **to — off** (*mil*) decurrĕre
filial *adj* pius
filigree *s* diatreta *n pl*
filings *s* scobis *f*
fill *vt* complēre, implēre; (*office*) fungi (*with abl*); **to — out** implēre; **to — up** explēre, complēre, supplēre
fill *s* satietas *f*
fillip *s* talitrum *n*
filly *s* equula *f*
film *s* membranula *f*
filmy *adj* membranaceus; (*fig*) caliginosus
filter *s* colum *n*
filter *vt* percolare; *vi* percolari
filtering *s* percolatio *f*
filth *s* sordes, colluvies *f*, squalor *m*
filthiness *s* foeditas *f*, squalor *m*; (*fig*) obscenitas *f*
filthy *adj* sordidus, spurcus; (*fig*) obscenus
filtration *s* percolatio *f*
fin *s* pinna *f*
final *adj* ultimus, postremus, extremus; **—ly** denique, tandem; postremo
finance *s* (*private*) res familiaris *f*; (*public*) aerarium *n*, ratio aeraria *f*, vectigalia *n pl*
financial *adj* aerarius
find *vt* invenire, reperire; (*to hit upon*) offendĕre; **to — out** comperire, cognoscĕre
fine *adj* (*thin*) subtilis, tenuis; (*of gold*) purus; (*handsome*) bellus, elegans; (*of weather*) serenus; **—ly** subtiliter
fine *s* mul(c)ta *f*, damnum *n*
fine *vt* mul(c)tare
finery *s* ornat·us -ūs *m*
finesse *s* astutia *f*, argutiae *f pl*
finger *s* digitus *m*; (*of glove*) digitale *n*
finger *vt* tractare
finish *vt* conficĕre, perficĕre; (*to put an end to*) terminare; **to — off** conficĕre; peragĕre; *vi* desinĕre
finish *s* finis *m*; (*in art*) perfectio *f*
finite *adj* finitus, circumscriptus
fire *s* ignis *m*; (*conflagration*) incendium *n*; (*of artillery*) conject·us -ūs *m*; (*fig*) fervor, ardor, impet·us -ūs *m*; **by — and sword** ferro ignique; **to be on —** flagrare; **to catch —** flammam concipĕre; **to set on —** incendĕre
fire *vt* accendĕre, incendĕre; (*fig*) inflammare; (*missile*) jaculari; (*to dismiss*) dimittĕre
firefly *s* elater noctilucus *m*
fireplace *s* focus, caminus *m*
fireproof *adj* ignibus impervius
fireside *s* focus *m*
firewood *s* lignum *n*
firm *adj* firmus, solidus; constans; **to be —** perseverare; **to stand —** perstare; **—ly** firme, firmiter; solide; constanter
firm *s* societas *f*
firmament *s* firmamentum *n*
firmness *s* firmitas, constantia *f*
first *adj* primus; (*of two*) prior
first *adv* primum; **at —** primo; **— of all** imprimis
firstborn *adj* primogenitus
firstfruits *s* primitiae *f pl*
fiscal *adj* aerarius, fiscalis
fish *s* piscis *m*
fish *vi* piscari; (*fig*) expiscari
fisherman *s* piscator *m*
fishing *s* piscat·us -ūs *m*, piscatio *f*
fish market *s* forum piscarium *n*
fish pond *s* piscina *f*
fishy *adj* piscosus
fissure *s* fissura, rima *f*
fist *s* pugnus *m*
fit *s* (*of anger, etc.*) impet·us -ūs *m*; (*med*) access·us -ūs *m*; convulsio *f*; (*whim*) libido *f*; **by —s and starts** carptim
fit *adj* aptus, idoneus; habilis; (*becoming*) decens; (*ready*) paratus
fit *vt* accommodare; (*to apply*) applicare; (*to furnish*) instruĕre; *vi* (*fig*) convenire
fitful *adj* mutabilis, inconstans
fitness *s* convenientia *f*; (*of persons*) habilitas *f*
fitting *adj* decens, idoneus; **it is —** convenit, decet
five *adj* quinque; **— times** quinquies
fix *vt* (*to repair*) reficĕre; resarcire; (*to fasten*) figĕre, firmare; (*the eyes*) intendĕre; (*time*) dicĕre; *vi* **to — upon** inhaerēre (*with dat*)
fixed *adj* firmus, fixus; certus; **— on** (*intent upon*) intentus (*with dat*)
fixture *s* affixum *n*
fizz *vi* sibilare
flabbiness *s* mollitia *f*
flabby *adj* flaccidus, flaccus; (*drooping*) marcidus
flaccid *adj* flaccidus
flag *s* vexillum *n*
flagrant *adj* impudens, apparens, nefarius
flail *s* pertica, tribula *f*
flake *s* squama *f*; (*of snow*) nix *f*
flaky *adj* squameus
flame *s* flamma *f*
flame *vi* flammare, flagrare; **to — up** scintillare; (*fig*) exardescĕre
flank *s* (*of animal*) ilia *n pl*; (*mil*) latus *n*; **on the —** a latere
flank *vt* tegĕre latus (*with genit*)
flap *s* (*of dress*) lacinia *f*
flap *vt* plaudĕre (*with abl*); *vi* (*to hang loosely*) fluitare
flare *s* flamma *f*, fulgor *m*
flare *vi* flagrare, exardescĕre

flash *s* fulgor *m*; (*of fire*) coruscatio *f*; (*of lightning*) fulmen *n*; **— of wit** sales *m pl*
flash *vi* fulgēre, coruscare, micare
flask *s* ampulla, laguncula *f*
flat *adj* (*level*) planus, aequus; (*not mountainous*) campester; (*on back*) supinus; (*on face*) pronus; (*insipid*) vapidus; (*fig*) frigidus, insulsus; **to fall —** (*fig*) frigēre
flatness *s* planities *f*
flatten *vt* complanare, planum reddĕre
flatter *vt* adulari (*with dat*), blandiri (*with dat*), assentari (*with dat*)
flatterer *s* adulator, assentator *m*
flattering *adj* adulans, blandus, adulatorius
flattery *s* adulatio *f*, blanditiae *f pl*
flaunt *vt* jactare; *vi* tumēre, gloriari
flaunting *adj* lautus, gloriosus
flaunting *s* jactatio *f*
flavor *s* sapor, gustat·us -ūs *m*
flavor *vt* imbuĕre, condire
flaw *s* (*defect*) vitium *n*; (*chink*) rimula *f*
flawless *adj* emendatus
flax *s* linum *n*
flaxen *adj* lineus
flay *vt* deglubare
flea *s* pulex *m*
fleck *s* macula *f*
fledged *adj* plumatus
flee *vi* fugĕre; **to — away** aufugĕre; **to — back** refugĕre; **to — to** confugĕre ad *or* in (*with acc*)
fleece *s* vellus *n*
fleece *vt* tondēre; (*fig*) spoliare
fleecy *adj* laniger
fleet *s* classis *f*
fleet *adj* celer; (*winged*) volucer; (*fig*) fugax
fleeting *adj* fugax; (*flowing*) fluxus
flesh *s* caro *f*; **in the —** vivus
fleshy *adj* carnosus
flexibility *s* flexibilitas *f*; (*fig*) mollitia *f*
flexible *adj* flexibilis, lentus; (*fig*) exorabilis
flicker *vi* coruscare
flickering *adj* tremulus
flight *s* (*flying*) volat·us -ūs *m*; (*escape*) fuga *f*, effugium *n*; (*covey*) grex *m*; (*of stairs*) scala *f*; **to put to —** fugare; **to take to —** aufugĕre, terga vertĕre
flighty *adj* levis
flimsy *adj* nimis subtilis, praetenuis; (*fig*) frivolus
flinch *vi* retrocedĕre, tergiversari; (*to start*) absilire
fling *vt* jacĕre, conjicĕre; **to — away** abjicĕre; **to — down** dejicĕre; **to — off** rejicĕre; **to — open** vehementer aperire
fling *s* jact·us -ūs *m*
flint *s* silex *m & f*
flinty *adj* siliceus
flippancy *s* petulantia *f*
flippant *adj* petulans; temere loquens; **—ly** temere ac leviter
flirt *s* lupus *m*, lupa *f*
flirt *vi* ludĕre, lascivire
flirtation *s* amores *m pl*
flit *vi* volitare
float *s* (*raft*) rates *f*; (*on fishing line*) cortex *m*
float *vt* (*to launch*) demittĕre; *vi* fluitare, (in)natare; (*in air*) volitare
flock *s* grex *m*; **in —s** gregatim
flock *vi* concurrĕre, convenire, coire
floe *s* fragmentum glaciei *n*
flog *vt* verberare
flogging *s* verberatio *f*, verbera *n pl*
flood *s* (*deluge*) diluvies *f*; (*of river*) torrens *m*; (*tide*) access·us -ūs *m*; (*fig*) flumen *n*
floor *s* (*story of building*) tabulatum *n*; (*on the ground*) solum; (*paved*) pavimentum *n*
floor *vt* (*to throw down*) sternĕre
flooring *s* contabulatio *f*
floral *adj* floreus
florid *adj* floridus
flotilla *s* classicula *f*
flounce *s* fimbria *f*
flounder *vi* volutari; (*in speech*) haesitare
flour *s* farina *f*; (*finest*) pollen *m*
flourish *vt* vibrare; (*to sound*) canĕre; *vi* florēre, virēre; (*mus*) praeludĕre
flourish *s* ornamentum *n*; (*of style*) calamistri *m pl*; (*mus*) praelusio *f*; (*of trumpet*) cant·us -ūs *m*
flout *vt* deridēre, contumeliis afficĕre, aspernari
flow *vi* fluĕre; (*of tide*) affluĕre, accedĕre
flow *s* fluxio *f*, laps·us -ūs *m*; (*of* tide) access·us -ūs *m*
flower *s* flos *m*; (*fig*) (*the best*) flos *m*; (*of army*) robur *n*; (*of age*) adulescentia *f*
flower *vi* florescĕre
flowery *adj* floreus; floridus
fluctuate *vi* fluctuari; (*fig*) jactare
fluctuation *s* fluctuatio *f*; (*fig*) mutatio *f*
flue *s* cuniculus fornacis *m*
fluency *s* copia verborum, volubilitas linguae *f*
fluent *adj* volubilis; (*eloquent*) disertus; **—ly** volubiliter
fluid *adj* fluidus, liquidus
fluid *s* fluidum *n*, fluor *m*
fluke *s* (*of anchor*) dens *m*; (*luck*) fortuitum *n*
flurry *s* commotio *f*, tumult·us -ūs *m*
flurry *vt* perturbare, inquietare
flush *s* rubor *m*
flush *vi* erubescĕre
fluster *vt* turbare, inquietare
flute *s* tibia *f*; (*in architecture*) stria *f*
flutist *s* tibicen *m*
flutter *s* volitatio *f*, tremor *m*; (*fig*) trepidatio *f*
flutter *vi* (*of the heart*) palpitare; (*of bird*) volitare; (*with alarm*) trepidare
flux *s* flux·us -ūs *m*; **to be in a state of —** fluĕre
fly *s* musca *f*
fly *vi* volare; (*to flee*) fugĕre; **to — apart** dissilire; **to — off** avolare;

to — open dissilire; **to — out** provolare; **to — up** subvolare
flying *adj* volatilis, volucer
foal *s* pullus *m*; (*of asses*) asellus *m*; (*of horses*) equulus *m*
foal *vi* parĕre
foam *s* spuma *f*
foam *vi* spumare; (*to boil*) exaestuare
foamy *adj* spumans; spumeus, spumosus
focus *vt* (*the mind*) intendĕre
fodder *s* pabulum *n*
fodder *vt* pabulum praebēre (*with dat*)
foe *s* (*public*) hostis *m*; (*private*) inimicus *m*
fog *s* caligo, nebula *f*
foggy *adj* caliginosus, nebulosus
foible *s* vitium *n*, error *m*
foil *s* (*for fencing*) rudis *f*; (*leaf of metal*) lamina *f*; (*very thin*) bractea *f*; (*contrast*) repulsa *f*
foil *vt* eludĕre; repellĕre
fold *s* sin·us -ūs *m*, plica *f*; (*wrinkle*) ruga *f*; (*for sheep*) ovile *n*; (*for cattle*) stabulum *n*
fold *vt* plicare, complicare
foliage *s* frons *f*, folia *n pl*
folio *s* liber maximae formae *m*
folk *s* homines *m pl*
follow *vt* sequi; (*close*) instare (*with dat*), assectari; (*a calling*) facĕre; (*instructions*) parēre (*with dat*); (*road*) pergĕre; (*to understand*) intellegĕre; **to — out** exsequi, prosequi; **to — up** subsequi
follower *s* sectator *m*; (*of teacher*) auditor *m*
following *adj* sequens; posterus, proximus
folly *s* stultitia, insipientia *f*
foment *vt* fovēre
fond *adj* amans, studiosus; ineptus; **to be — of** amare; **—ly** amanter; (*foolishly*) inepte
fondle *vt* mulcēre, fovēre
fondness *s* caritas *f*, studium *n*
food *s* cibus *m*
fool *s* stultus, fatuus *m*; **to make a — of** ludificare; **to play the —** ineptire
fool *vt* ludificari
foolhardy *adj* temerarius
foolish *adj* stultus, fatuus, ineptus, stolidus; **—ly** stulte, inepte
foot *s* pes *m*; (*of mountain*) radix *f*; (*of pillar*) basis *f*; **on —** pedester
football *s* pila pedalis *f*
footing *s* locus *m*; (*condition*) stat·us -ūs *m*
footprint *s* vestigium *n*
foot soldier *s* pedes *m*
footstool *s* scabellum, scamnum *n*
fop *s* bellus homo *m*
foppish *adj* nitidus, delicatus
for *prep* (*extent of time or space*) *render by acc*; (*price*) *render by genit or abl*; (*on behalf of*) pro (*with abl*); (*cause*) causā (*with genit*), ob (*with acc*), propter (*with acc*); (*after negatives*) prae (*with abl*); (*toward*) erga (*with acc*)
for *conj* nam; enim
forage *s* pabulum *n*
forage *vi* pabulari, frumentari
foray *s* incursio *f*
forbear *vi* parcĕre (*with dat*), desistĕre
forbearance *s* patientia, indulgentia *f*
forbid *vt* vetare, prohibēre, interdicĕre
forbidding *adj* insuavis, odiosus
force *s* vis *f*; (*law*) man·us -ūs *f*; (*mil*) copiae *f pl*, impet·us -ūs *m*; **in —** validus
force *vt* cogĕre, impellĕre; (*door, etc.*) rumpĕre; **to — down** detrudĕre; **to — out** extrudĕre, extorquēre
forced *adj* (*unnatural*) arcessitus, quaesitus
forced march *s* magnum *or* maximum iter *n*
forceps *s* forceps *m & f*
forcible *adj* per vim factus; (*of force*) validus; (*violent*) vehemens; (*weighty*) gravis
forcibly *adv* per vim, vi; violenter; graviter
ford *s* vadum *n*
ford *vt* vado transire
fore *adj* anterior, prior
forearm *s* bracchium *n*
forearm *vt* praemunire; **to be forearmed** praecavēre
forebode *vt* (*to foretell*) portendĕre; (*to be prescient of*) praesagire
foreboding *s* portentum, praesagium *n*; (*feeling*) praesensio *f*
foreboding *adj* praesagus
forecast *vt* providēre, prospicĕre; praedicĕre
forecast *s* praedictio *f*
forecastle *s* prora *f*
foredoom *vt* praedestinare
forefather *s* atavus *m*; **—s** majores *m pl*
forefinger *s* digitus index *m*
forego *vt* abdicare, dimittĕre
foregoing *adj* prior, proximus
forehead *s* frons *f*
foreign *adj* externus, alienus, peregrinus
foreigner *s* peregrinus, advena *m*
foreknowledge *s* providentia *f*
foreman *s* procurator, villicus *m*
foremost *adj* primus, princeps
forenoon *s* antemeridianum tempus *n*; **in the —** ante meridiem
forensic *adj* forensis
fore part *s* prior pars *f*
forerunner *s* praenuntius, antecursor *m*
foresee *vt* providēre, praevidēre, prospicĕre
foreseeing *adj* providus
foresight *s* providentia, prudentia *f*; (*precaution*) provisio *f*
forest *adj* silvestris
forest *s* silva *f*
forestall *vt* occupare, anticipare
foretell *vt* praedicĕre, vaticinari
forethought *s* providentia *f*
forewarn *vt* praemonēre
forewarning *s* praemonit·us -ūs *m*
forfeit *s* multa, poena *f*, damnum *n*

forfeit *vt* mul(c)tari (*with abl*), amittĕre, perdĕre
forfeiture *s* damnum *n*, amissio *f*
forge *vt* fabricari, excudĕre; (*document*) subjicĕre; (*signature*) imitari; **to — money** adulterinos nummos cudĕre
forge *s* furnus fabrilis *m*
forged *adj* falsus, adulterinus
forger *s* fabricator *m*; (*of writings*) falsarius *m*; (*of money*) qui adulterinos nummos cudit
forgery *s* falsum *n*
forget *vt* oblivisci (*with genit*)
forgetful *adj* immemor, obliviosus
forgetfulness *s* oblivio *f*
forgive *vt* ignoscĕre (*with dat*), veniam dare (*with dat*); condonare
forgiveness *s* venia *f*
forgiving *adj* clemens
fork *s* furca *f*; (*of roads*) bivium *n*
forked *adj* bifurcus, bicornis
forlorn *adj* destitutus, derelictus
form *s* forma, figura *f*; **in due —** rite
form *vt* formare, fingĕre; (*to produce*) efficĕre
formal *adj* justus; nimis accuratus; **—ly** frigide ac nimis accurate
formality *s* rit·us -ūs *m*; **with due —** rite
formation *s* conformatio, forma, figura *f*; **in —** (*mil*) instructus
former *adj* prior; (*immediately preceding*) superior; antiquus, priscus; **the —** ille; **—ly** antehac, olim, quondam
formidable *adj* formidabilis
formidably *adv* formidolose
formless *adj* informis, rudis
formula *s* formula *f*, exemplar *n*
forsake *vt* deserĕre, derelinquĕre
forswear *vt* abjurare, repudiare
fort *s* castellum *n*
forth *adv* foras; (*of time*) inde; **and so —** et cetera
forthwith *adv* protinus, statim, extemplo
fortieth *adj* quadragesimus
fortification *s* munitio *f*, munimentum *n*
fortify *vt* munire
fortitude *s* fortitudo *f*
fortress *s* arx *f*, castellum *n*
fortuitous *adj* fortuitus; **—ly** fortuito
fortunate *adj* fortunatus, felix, prosperus; **—ly** feliciter
fortune *s* fortuna, felicitas *f*; (*estate*) opes *f pl*, res *f*, divitiae *f pl*; **to tell —s** hariolari
fortune-teller *s* fatidicus, sortilegus, astrologus *m*
forty *adj* quadraginta
forum *s* forum *n*
forward *adv* porro, prorsus, prorsum
forward *adj* (*person*) audax, protervus; anterior
forward *vt* (*letter*) perferre; (*cause*) adjuvare, promovēre
foster *vt* alĕre, fovēre, nutrire
foster brother *s* collacteus *m*
foster child *s* alumnus *m*, alumna *f*
foster father *s* altor, nutritor, educator *m*
foster mother *s* altrix, nutrix, educatrix *f*
foul *adj* (*dirty*) foedus, lutulentus, squalidus; (*ugly*) deformis; (*of language*) obscenus; (*of weather*) turbidus; **to fall — of** incurrĕre in (*with acc*), inruĕre in (*with acc*); **—ly** foede
foul *vt* foedare, inquinare
found *vt* condĕre, fundare, constituere, instituĕre
foundation *s* fundamentum *n*, substructio *f*
founder *s* conditor, fundator, auctor *m*
founder *vi* titubare, submergi
foundling *s* expositītius *m*, expositītia *f*
fountain *s* fons *m*
fountainhead *s* caput fontis *n*
four *adj* quattuor; **— each** quaterni; **— times** quater; **— years** quadriennium *n*; **on all —s** repens
fourfold *adj* quadruplex, quadruplus
fourscore *adj* octoginta
fourteen *adj* quattuordecim
fourteenth *adj* quartus decimus
fourth *adj* quartus; **—ly** quarto
fourth *s* quadrans *n*, quarta pars *f*; **three —s** tres partes *f pl*
fowl *s* avis, volucris *f*; (*domestic*) gallina *f*
fox *s* vulpes *f*; **an old —** (*fig*) veterator *m*
fraction *s* pars exigua *f*
fracture *s* fractura *f*
fracture *vt* frangĕre
fragile *adj* fragilis; (*fig*) caducus
fragility *s* fragilitas *f*
fragment *s* fragmentum *n*
fragrance *s* odor *m*
fragrant *adj* suaveolens, odorus; **—ly** suavi odore
frail *adj* fragilis; caducus, infirmus
frailty *s* fragilitas, debilitas *f*; (*moral*) error *m*
frame *s* (*of buildings, etc.*) compages *f*; (*of body*) figura *f*; (*of bed*) sponda *f*; (*of mind*) habit·us -ūs *m*
frame *vt* fabricari; (*to contrive*) moliri; (*a picture*) in forma includĕre; (*a document*) componĕre
France *s* Gallia *f*
franchise *s* civitas *f*, suffragium *n*
frank *adj* candidus, sincerus, simplex; **—ly** candide, aperte
frankness *s* libertas, simplicitas, ingenuitas *f*
frantic *adj* amens, furiosus, furens; **—ally** furenter
fraternal *adj* fraternus; **—ly** fraterne
fraternity *s* fraternitas *f*; (*association*) sodalitas *f*
fratricide *s* (*doer*) fratricida *m*; (*deed*) fratris parricidium *n*
fraud *s* fraus *f*, dolus *m*; (*person*) dolus malus *m*
fraudulence *s* fraus *f*

fraudulent *adj* fraudulentus, dolosus; **—ly** fraudulenter, dolo malo
fraught *adj* plenus
fray *s* pugna *f*; (*brawl*) rixa *f*
freak *s* (*whim*) libido *f*; monstrum *n*
freckle *s* lentigo *f*
freckled *adj* lentiginosus
free *adj* liber; (*disengaged*) vacuus, otiosus; (*generous*) liberalis; (*from duty*) immunis; (*unencumbered*) expeditus; (*in speech*) liber, candidus; **—ly** libere; (*of one's own accord*) sponte, ultro; (*frankly*) aperte; (*generously*) large, copiose
free *vt* liberare; (*slave*) manumittĕre; (*son*) emancipare
freeborn *adj* ingenuus
freedman *s* libertus *m*
freedom *s* libertas *f*; (*from duty*) immunitas *f*
freehold *s* praedium liberum *n*
freeholder *s* dominus *m*
freeman *s* liber *m*
free will *s* voluntas *f*, liberum arbitrium *n*; **of one's own —** suā sponte, ultro, arbitrio suo
freeze *vt* congelare, glaciare; *vi* consistĕre, rigescĕre; **it is freezing** gelat
freezing *adj* gelidus
freight *s* onus *n*, vectura *f*
freight *vt* onerare
French *adj* Gallicus; **in —** Gallice; **the —** Galli *m pl*
Frenchman *s* Gallus *m*
frenzied *adj* furens, lymphatus
frenzy *s* furor *m*, insania *f*
frequency *s* crebritas, assiduitas *f*
frequent *adj* creber, frequens; **—ly** crebro, frequenter, saepe
frequent *vt* frequentare
frequenter *s* frequentator *m*
fresco *s* opus tectorium *n*
fresh *adj* (*new*) recens, novus; (*cool*) frigidulus; (*not tired*) integer; (*forward*) protervus; (*green*) viridis; **—ly** recenter
freshen *vt* recreare, renovare; *vi* (*of wind*) increbrescĕre
freshman *s* tiro *m*
freshman *adj* novicius
freshness *s* novitas, viriditas *f*
fret *vi* dolēre, angi
fretful *adj* morosus, stomachosus; **—ly** morose, stomachose
fretted *adj* laqueatus
friction *s* frictio *f*, attrit·us -ūs *m*
friend *s* amicus *m*, amica *f*, familiaris *m & f*; (*of a thing*) amator *m*
friendless *adj* amicorum inops, desertus
friendliness *s* benevolentia, comitas, affabilitas *f*
friendly *adj* amicus, benevolus, comis; **in a — manner** amice
friendship *s* amicitia *f*
frieze *s* zoophorus *m*
fright *s* pavor, terror *m*
frighten *vt* (per)terrēre; **to — away** absterrēre
frightful *adj* terribilis, terrificus; **—ly** foede
frigid *adj* frigidus; **—ly** frigide
frigidity *s* frigiditas *f*
frills *s* segmenta *n pl*; (*rhet*) calamistri *m pl*
fringe *s* fimbria *f*, cirrus *m*; (*fig*) limbus *m*
frisk *vt* scrutari; *vi* lascivire, exsilire
fritter *vt* **to — away** conterĕre, comminuĕre, dissipare
frivolity *s* levitas *f*, nugae *f pl*
frivolous *adj* levis, frivolus, inanis; **—ly** inaniter
fro *adv* **to and —** huc illuc, ultro citroque
frock *s* palla, stola *f*
frog *s* rana *f*
frolic *s* lascivia *f*, ludus *m*
frolic *vi* exsultare, hilarescĕre
from *prep* a *or* ab (*with abl*); de (*with abl*); e *or* ex (*with abl*); (*cause*) ob (*with acc*); **— above** desuper; **— abroad** peregre; **— day to day** de die in diem; **— time to time** interdum, passim; **— within** intus; **— without** extrinsecus
front *s* frons *f*; (*mil*) acies *f*, primum agmen *n*; (*fig*) impudentia *f*; **in —** a fronte, adversus; **in — of** pro (*with abl*)
front *adj* prior
frontier *s* limes *m*, confinia *n pl*
frost *s* gelu *n*, pruina *f*
frostbitten *adj* praeustus, adustus
frosty *adj* gelidus, glacialis
froth *s* spuma *f*
froth *vi* spumare, spumas agĕre
frothy *adj* spumeus, spumosus
frown *s* contractio frontis *f*
frown *vi* frontem contrahĕre *or* adducĕre
frozen *adj* conglaciatus, gelatus, gelu rigens
frugal *adj* parcus, frugi (*indecl*); **—ly** frugaliter, parce
frugality *s* parsimonia, frugalitas *f*
fruit *s* fruct·us -ūs *m*, frux *f*; (*of tree*) mala *n pl*; **—s of the earth** fruges *f pl*
fruitful *adj* fructuosus, fecundus, fertilis; **—ly** fecunde, feraciter
fruitfulness *s* fecunditas, fertilitas, ubertas *f*
fruitless *adj* sterilis; (*fig*) irritus; **—ly** frustra
fruit tree *s* pomus *f*
frustrate *vt* frustrari; (*to baffle*) decipĕre
frustration *s* frustratio *f*
fry *s* (*dish of things fried*) frixa *f*
fry *vt* frigĕre
frying pan *s* sartago *f*
fuel *s* fomes *m*, materia *f*
fugitive *adj* fugitivus
fugitive *s* profugus, transfuga, fugitivus *m*; (*from abroad*) extorris *m*
fulcrum *s* (*of a lever*) pressio *f*
fulfil *vt* explēre, exsequi, perficĕre
fulfilment *s* exsecutio, peractio, perfectio *f*
full *adj* plenus; (*filled up*) expletus; (*entire*) integer, solidus; (*satiated*) satur; (*of dress*) fusus; **—ly** plene, funditus, penitus
full moon *s* plenilunium *n*

fumble *vi* haesitare
fume *s* fumus, vapor, halit·us -ūs *m*
fume *vi* irasci
fumigate *vt* fumigare, suffire
fumigation *s* suffit·us -ūs *m*
fun *s* jocus *m*, ludibrium *n*
function *s* munus, officium *n*
function *vi* munus implēre
functionary *s* magistrat·us -ūs *m*
fund *s* copia *f*, pecuniae *f pl*
fundamental *adj* fundamentalis, primus; **—ly** penitus, funditus
funeral *s* funus *n*, exsequiae *f pl*
funeral *adj* funebris
funereal *adj* funereus, lugubris
fungus *s* fungus *m*
funnel *s* infundibulum *n*
funny *adj* ridiculus, jocularis
fur *s* villi *m pl*, pellis *m*
furious *adj* furiosus, furens; **—ly** furiose, furenter
furl *vt* complicare; (*sail*) legĕre
furlough *s* commeat·us -ūs *m*; **on —** in commeatu
furnace *s* fornax *f*
furnish *vt* suppeditare, ministrare; ornare, exornare, instruĕre
furniture *s* supellex *f*
furrow *s* sulcus *m*
furry *adj* pelle insutus
further *adj* ulterior
further *adv* ultra, longius, ulterius
further *vt* promovēre, provehĕre; (*to aid*) adjuvare
furtherance *s* progress·us -ūs *m*
furthermore *adv* insuper, porro, praeterea
furthest *adj* ultimus, extremus
furthest *adv* longissime
furtive *adj* furtivus; **—ly** furtim, furtive
fury *s* furor *m*
fuse *vt* fundĕre; *vi* coalescĕre
fusion *s* fusura *f*
fuss *s* strepit·us -ūs, tumult·us -ūs *m*
fuss *vi* sollicitari
fussy *adj* fastidiosus, importunus
futile *adj* futilis, inanis
futility *s* futilitas *f*
future *adj* futurus, posterus
future *s* futura *n pl*, posterum tempus *n*; **in the —** posthac
futurity *s* posteritas *f*

G

gab *s* garrulitas *f*
gab *vi* garrire
gable *s* fastigium *n*
gadfly *s* tabanus, oestrus *m*
gag *s* jocus *m*
gag *vt* os obstruĕre (*with dat*)
gaiety *s* hilaritas *f*; nitor, splendor *m*
gaily *adv* hilare, festive
gain *s* quaest·us -ūs *m*, lucrum *n*
gain *vt* consequi, acquirĕre, capĕre; (*profit*) lucrari; (*victory*) reportare; (*case*) vincere; **to — possession of** potiri (*with abl*)
gainful *adj* quaestuosus, lucrosus
gainsay *vt* contradicĕre (*with dat*)
gait *s* incess·us -ūs *m*
gala *s* dies festus *m*
galaxy *s* orbis lacteus *m*
gale *s* ventus *m*
gall *s* fel *n*, bilis *f*
gall *vt* urĕre
gallant *adj* fortis, animosus; (*to ladies*) officiosus; **—ly** fortiter
gallant *s* amator *m*
gallantry *s* virtus, fortitudo *f*; (*to ladies*) urbanitas *f*
galleon *s* navis oneraria *f*
gallery *s* portic·us -ūs *f*; (*open*) peristylium *n*; (*for pictures*) pinacotheca *f*
galley *s* navis longa, triremis *f*; (*kitchen*) culina *f*
Gallic *adj* Gallicus, Gallicanus
galling *adj* mordax
gallon *s* congius *m*
gallop *s* citatissimus curs·us -ūs *m*; **at a —** citato equo, admisso equo
gallop *vi* quadrupedare
gallows *s* patibulum *n*
gamble *vt* **to — away** ludĕre, amittĕre; *vi* aleā ludĕre
gambler *s* aleator, lusor *m*
gambling *s* alea *f*
gambol *s* salt·us -ūs *m*
gambol *vi* lascivire, ludĕre
game *s* ludus *m*; (*with dice*) alea *f*; (*quarry*) praeda *f*, ferae *f pl*; **to make — of** ludificari
gander *s* anser *m*
gang *s* grex *m*, caterva *f*
gangster *s* grassator *m*
gangway *s* forus *m*
gap *s* apertura, fissura, lacuna *f*, hiat·us -ūs *m*
gape *vi* hiare, dehiscĕre
gaping *adj* hians, hiulcus, oscitans; (*fig*) stupidus
garb *s* vestit·us -ūs, habit·us -ūs *m*
garbage *s* quisquiliae *f pl*
garble *vt* vitiare, corrumpĕre
garden *s* hortus *m*
gardener *s* hortulanus, olitor *m*
gardening *s* hortorum cult·us -ūs *m*
gargle *vi* gargarizare
gargling *s* gargarizatio *f*
garland *s* sertum *n*, corona *f*
garlic *s* alium *n*
garment *s* vestimentum *n*, vestit·us -ūs *m*
garner *s* horreum *n*
garnish *vt* decorare, ornare
garret *s* cenaculum *n*
garrison *s* praesidium *n*
garrison *vt* praesidio munire, praesidium collocare in (*with abl*), praesidium imponĕre (*with dat*)

garrulity *s* garrulitas *f*
garrulous *adj* garrulus, loquax
garter *s* periscelis *f*
gas *s* spiritūs naturales *m pl*
gash *s* patens plaga *f*
gash *vt* caesim ferire
gasp *s* anhelit·us -ūs, singult·us -ūs *m*
gasp *vi* anhelare, singultare
gastric *adj* ad stomachum pertinens
gastronomy *s* gula *f*
gate *s* janua *f*, ostium *n*; (*of town*) porta *f*
gatekeeper *s* janitor *m*
gateway *s* porta *f*, postis *m*
gather *vt* (*to assemble*) congregare, colligĕre; (*fruit, etc.*) legĕre; (*to pluck*) decerpĕre, carpĕre; (*in logic*) concludĕre; (*to suspect*) suspicare; *vi* convenire, concurrĕre
gathering *s* convent·us -ūs *m*, congregatio *f*; collectio *f*
gaudily *adv* laute
gaudiness *s* lautitia *f*, ornat·us -ūs, nitor *m*
gaudy *adj* lautus, speciosus, splendidus
gauge *s* modulus *m*
gauge *vt* metiri
gaunt *adj* macer
gauntlet *s* manica *f*
gauze *s* coa *n pl*
gawky *adj* ineptus, stolidus
gay *adj* laetus, hilaris, festivus
gaze *s* conspect·us -ūs *m*; (*fixed look*) obtut·us -ūs *m*
gaze *vi* intuēri; **to — at** intuēri, adspectare, contemplari
gazelle *s* dorcas *f*
gazette *s* acta diurna *n pl*
gazetteer *s* itinerarium *n*
gear *s* instrumenta *n pl*, apparat·us -ūs *m*
gelatin *s* glutinum *n*
gelding *s* (*horse*) canterius *m*
gem *s* gemma *f*
gender *s* genus *n*
genealogical *adj* genealogicus
genealogy *s* genealogia *f*
general *adj* generalis; vulgaris, publicus, universus; **in —** omnino; **—ly** plerumque, fere; generatim
general *s* dux, imperator *m*
generalize *vi* in summam loqui
generalship *s* duct·us -ūs *m*; (*skill*) consilium *n*
generate *vt* generare, gignĕre
generation *s* generatio *f*; (*age*) aetas *f*, saeculum *n*
generic *adj* generalis
generosity *s* liberalitas, largitas *f*
generous *adj* liberalis, largus; **—ly** large, liberaliter
genesis *s* origo *f*
genial *adj* comis, benignus; **—ly** comiter, benigne
geniality *s* comitas, benignitas *f*
genitals *s* genitalia *n pl*, veretrum *n*
genitive *s* genitivus *m*
genius *s* ingenium *n*, indoles *f*; vir ingeniosus *m*; **of —** ingeniosus
genteel *adj* elegans, urbanus; **—ly** eleganter
gentile *adj* gentilicus, gentilis
gentile *s* gentilis *m*
gentility *s* nobilitas, elegantia *f*
gentle *adj* lenis, mitis, clemens; (*gradual*) mollis; (*thing*) lenis
gentleman *s* vir honestus, homo liberalis *m*
gentleness *s* lenitas, clementia *f*; (*tameness*) mansuetudo *f*
gently *adv* leniter, clementer, placide; (*gradually*) sensim
gentry *s* optimates *m pl*
genuine *adj* sincerus, purus, verus; **—ly** sincere, vere
genus *s* genus *n*
geographer *s* geographus *m*
geographical *adj* geographicus
geography *s* geographia *f*
geological *adj* geologicus
geologist *s* geologus *m*
geology *s* geologia *f*
geometrical *adj* geometricus
geometry *s* geometria *f*
germ *s* germen *n*
German *adj* Germanus
germane *adj* affinis
Germanic *adj* Germanicus
Germany *s* Germania *f*
germinate *vi* germinare
germination *s* germinat·us -ūs *m*
gesticulate *vi* gestus agĕre, gestu uti
gesture *s* gest·us -ūs, mot·us -ūs *m*
get *vt* nancisci, adipisci, consequi, acquirĕre; (*by entreaty*) impetrare; **to — back** recuperare; **to — down** depromĕre; **to — hold of** prehendĕre, occupare; **to — out** delēre, oblitterare; **to — rid of** amovēre, tollĕre; **to — the better of** superare; **to — together** colligĕre, cogĕre; congregare; *vi* (*to become*) fieri; (*to arrive at*) pervenire; **to — abroad** (*to spread*) palam fieri, emanare; **to — along** procedĕre; **to — away** aufugĕre; **to — back** revertĕre *or* reverti; **to — down** descendĕre; **to — in** pervenire; **to — off** aufugĕre, dimitti; **to — on** procedĕre, proficisci; (*to succeed*) bene succedĕre; **to — out** exire; (e curru) descendĕre; **to — over** transgredi; **to — together** congregari; **to — up** surgĕre; (*from sleep*) expergisci
ghastly *adj* luridus; (*shocking*) foedus
ghost *s* larva *f*, phantasma *n*; umbra *f*
ghostly *adj* spiritualis
giant *s* gigas *m*
gibberish *s* barbaricus sermo *m*
gibbet *s* furca *f*, patibulum *n*
gibe *s* sanna *f*
gibe *vt* illudĕre, subsannare
giblets *s* gigeria *n pl*, anseris trunculi *m pl*
giddiness *s* vertigo *f*
giddy *adj* vertiginosus; (*fig*) levis, inconsultus
gift *s* donum *n*; (*talent*) ingenium *n*
gifted *adj* (*endowed*) praeditus; ingeniosus
gig *s* (*carriage*) cisium *n*

gigantic *adj* ingens, immanis, praegrandis
giggle *vi* summissim cachinnare
gild *vt* inaurare
gilding *s* (*art*) auratura *f*; (*gilded work*) aurum inductum *n*
gill *s* branchia *f*
gilt *adj* auratus
gin *s* junipero infectus spirit·us -ūs *m*
ginger *s* zinziberi *n* (*indecl*)
gingerly *adv* pedetemptim
giraffe *s* camelopardalis *f*
gird *vt* cingĕre; **to — oneself** cingi
girder *s* tignum *n*
girdle *s* cingulum *n*, zona *f*
girdle *vt* cingĕre
girl *s* puella, virgo *f*
girlhood *s* puellaris aetas *f*
girlish *adj* puellaris, virginalis
girth *s* (*of horse*) cingula *f*; amplitudo *f*, ambit·us -ūs *m*
gist *s* cardo *m*
give *vt* dare, donare; (*to deliver*) tradĕre; **to — away** donare; **to — back** reddĕre; **to — forth** emittĕre; **to — oneself up to** se addicĕre (*with dat*); **to — out** edĕre, emittĕre; nuntiare, proclamare; distribuĕre; **to — over** transferre; relinquere; **to — up** tradĕre; (*to betray*) prodĕre; (*to abandon*) dimittĕre; *vi* **to — in** (*to yield*) cedĕre; **to — way** (*mil*) pedem referre; (*to yield*) cedĕre; (*to comply*) obsequi
giver *s* donator *m*
giving *s* datio, largitio *f*
glacial *adj* glacialis
glacier *s* moles conglaciata *f*
glad *adj* laetus, contentus; **to be —** gaudēre; **—ly** libenter
gladden *vt* laetificare
glade *s* salt·us -ūs *m*
gladiator *s* gladiator *m*
gladness *s* gaudium *n*, laetitia *f*
glamorous *adj* venustus, nitidus; **to be —** nitēre
glamour *s* venustas *f*, nitor *m*
glance *s* aspect·us -ūs *m*
glance *vi* aspicĕre; **to — at** aspicĕre; **to — off** stringĕre
gland *s* glandula *f*
glare *s* fulgor *m*
glare *vi* fulgēre; torvis oculis aspicĕre; **to — at** torvis oculis aspicĕre *or* intuēri
glaring *adj* fulgens; manifestus
glass *s* vitrum *n*; (*for drinking*) calix vitreus *m*
glass *adj* vitreus
glassmaker *s* vitrarius *m*
glassware *s* vitrea *n pl*
glaze *vt* vitrum illinĕre (*with dat*), polire
gleam *s* fulgor *m*, jubar *n*; (*fig*) aura *f*
gleam *vi* coruscare, micare, fulgēre
gleaming *adj* coruscus, renidens
glean *vt* colligĕre, legĕre
gleaning *s* spicilegium *n*
glee *s* laetitia, hilaritas *f*
gleeful *adj* laetus, hilaris; **—ly** laete, hilare
glen *s* vallis *f*
glib *adj* lubricus, volubilis; **—ly** volubiliter
glide *vi* labi
glimmer *s* lux dubia *f*; **— of hope** specula *f*
glimmer *vi* sublucēre
glimpse *s* aspect·us -ūs *m*; **to have a — of** despicĕre
glisten *vi* nitēre
glitter *s* fulgor *m*
glitter *vi* fulgēre, micare, coruscare
gloat *vi* oculos pascĕre; **to — over** inhiare (*with abl*), oculos pascĕre (*with abl*)
globe *s* globus *m*; orbis terrarum *m*
globular *adj* globosus
globule *s* globulus *m*, pilula *f*
gloom *s* tenebrae *f pl*; (*fig*) tristitia *f*
gloomily *adv* maeste
gloomy *adj* tenebrosus, furvus; (*fig*) maestus, tristis
glorification *s* laudatio, glorificatio *f*
glorify *vt* celebrare, glorificare, extollere
glorious *adj* gloriosus, illustris; **—ly** gloriose
glory *s* gloria, laus *f*
glory *vi* gloriari, se jactare
gloss *s* interpretatio *f*; (*sheen*) nitor *m*
gloss *vt* annotare; **to — over** extenuare, dissimulare
glossary *s* glossarium *n*
glossy *adj* nitidus, expolitus
glove *s* chirotheca *f*
glow *s* ardor, fervor, calor *m*
glow *vi* candēre, ardēre, calēre
glowing *adj* candens, fervens; (*fig*) fervidus
glue *s* gluten, glutinum *n*
glue *vt* glutinare
glum *adj* maestus, tristis
glut *s* satietas *f*
glut *vt* satiare, saturare
glutton *s* helluo, homo gulosus, ganeo *m*
gluttonous *adj* gulosus, edax; **—ly** gulose
gnarled *adj* nodosus
gnash *vt* **to — one's teeth** dentibus frendĕre
gnat *s* culex *m*
gnaw *vt & vi* rodĕre
gnawing *adj* mordax
go *vi* ire, incedĕre, proficisci; **to — about** circumire, perambulari; (*fig*) aggredi; **to — abroad** peregrinari; **to — after** sequi, petĕre; **to — aside** discedĕre; **to — astray** aberrare, vagari; **to — away** abire; **to — back** reverti; **to — before** praeire, antecedĕre; **to — between** intervenire; **to — beyond** egredi; (*fig*) excedĕre; **to — by** praeterire; (*fig*) (*to follow*) sequi; **to — down** descendĕre; (*of sun*) occidĕre; **to — for** petĕre; **to — forth** exire; **to — in** introire; **to — into** inire; **to — off** abire; (*as gun*) displodi; **to — on** (*to continue*) pergĕre; (*to happen*)

fieri; (*to succeed, thrive*) succedĕre; **to — out** exire; (*of fire*) extingui; **to — over** transgredi; (*fig*) (*a subject*) percurrĕre; **to — round** circumire; **to — through** obire, pertendĕre; **to — to** adire, accedĕre; **to — towards** petĕre; **to — under** subire; submergi; **to — up** ascendĕre; **to let —** dimittĕre; (*to let fall*) omittĕre
goad *s* pertica *f*, stimulus *m*
goad *vt* instigare; (*fig*) stimulare; (*to exasperate*) exasperare
goal *s* finis *m*; (*at racetrack*) calx *f*
goat *s* caper *m*, capra *f*
gobble *vt* devorare, deglutire
gobbler *s* helluo *m*
goblet *s* poculum *n*, scyphus *m*
goblin *s* larva *f*
god *s* deus, divus *m*
God *s* Deus *m*
goddess *s* dea, diva *f*
godhead *s* deitas *f*, numen *n*
godless *adj* atheus; improbus
godlike *adj* divinus
godliness *s* pietas *f*
gold *adj* aureus
gold *s* aurum *n*
golden *adj* aureus
goldfish *s* hippurus *m*
gold leaf *s* auri breactea *f*
gold mine *s* aurifodina *f*
goldsmith *s* aurifex *m*
good *adj* bonus, probus; (*beneficial*) salutaris; (*kindhearted*) benevolus; (*fit*) aptus, idoneus; **— for nothing** nequam (*indecl*); **to do —** prodesse; **to make —** compensare, restituĕre; **to seem —** vidēri
good *s* bonum *n*; (*profit*) commodum, lucrum *n*, utilitas *f*; **to be — for** prodesse (*with dat*); **—s** bona *n pl*, res *f*; (*for sale*) merx *f*
good *interj* bene!; euge!
good-by *interj* vale!; (*to more than one*) valete!; **to say —** valēre jubēre
goodly *adj* pulcher; (*quantity*) amplus; **a — number of** nonnulli
good-natured *adj* comis, benignus, facilis
goodness *s* bonitas *f*; (*moral*) probitas, virtus *f*; (*generosity*) benignitas *f*
goose *s* anser *m*
gooseberry *s* acinus grossulae *m*
gore *s* cruor *m*
gore *vt* cornu perforare, cornu ferire
gorge *s* fauces *f pl*; (*defile*) angustiae *f pl*
gorge *vt* **to — oneself** se ingurgitare
gorgeous *adj* splendidus, lautus; **—ly** splendide, laute
gory *adj* cruentus, cruentatus
gospel *s* evangelium *n*
gossamer *s* aranea *f*
gossip *s* (*talk*) nugae, gerrae *f pl*; (*person*) garrulus *m*, garrula *f*, loquax *m & f*, lingulaca *f*
gossip *vi* garrire
gouge *vt* evellĕre, eruĕre
gourd *s* cucurbita *f*
gourmand *s* helluo, popino *m*
gout *s* morbus articularis *m*, arthritis *f*; (*in the legs*) podagra *f*; (*in hands*) chiragra *f*
govern *vt* imperare (*with dat*), regĕre, administrare, gubernare
governable *adj* tractabilis
governess *s* magistra, educatrix *f*
government *s* gubernatio, administratio, res publica *f*
governor *s* gubernator, moderator, praefectus *m*; (*of province*) proconsul, legatus *m*; procurator *m*
governorship *s* praefectura *f*
gown *s* (*of Roman citizen*) toga *f*; (*of women*) stola *f*
grace *s* gratia *f*; (*elegance, etc.*) venustas *f*, lepos *m*; (*pardon*) venia *f*; **to say —** gratias agĕre
grace *vt* exornare; honestare
graceful *adj* gratiosus, venustus, lepidus; **—ly** venuste, lepide
gracefulness *s* venustas *f*
graceless *adj* deformis, illepidus
Graces *s* Gratiae *f pl*
gracious *adj* benignus, misericors; **—ly** benigne, humane
gradation *s* grad·us -ūs *m*; (*in speech*) gradatio *f*
grade *s* grad·us -ūs *m*
gradient *s* proclivitas *f*
gradual *adj* lenis, mollis; per gradus; **—ly** gradatim, pedetentim
graduate *vt* gradibus distinguĕre; *vi* gradum suscipĕre
graduate *s* qui gradum academicum adeptus est
graft *s* surculus *m*; (*pol*) ambit·us -ūs *m*
graft *vt* inserĕre
grain *s* granum *n*; (*fig*) particula *f*; **against the —** (*fig*) Minervā invitā
grammar *s* grammatica *f*
grammarian *s* grammaticus *m*
grammatical *adj* grammaticus
granary *s* horreum *n*, granaria *n pl*
grand *adj* grandis
grandchild *s* nepos *m*, neptis *m & f*
granddaughter *s* neptis *f*
grandeur *s* magnificentia, majestas *f*
grandfather *s* avus *m*
grandiloquent *adj* magniloquus
grandmother *s* avia *f*
grandson *s* nepos *m*
granite *s* granites lapis *m*
grant *vt* concedĕre, permittĕre; (*to acknowledge*) fatēri; dare, praebēre
grant *s* concessio *f*
grape *s* uva *f*, acinus *m*
grapevine *s* vitis *f*
graphic *adj* expressus, significans, manifestus; **—ally** expresse
grapple *vt* compleci; *vi* luctari
grasp *s* complex·us -ūs *m*, comprehensio *f*; pugillum *n*; (*power*) potestas *f*; (*of the hand*) man·us -ūs *f*
grasp *vt* prehendĕre, tenēre, arripĕre; (*fig*) appetĕre, percipĕre, intellegĕre; *vi* **to — at** captare, appetĕre
grasping *adj* avidus, cupidus
grass *s* gramen *n*, herba *f*

grasshopper *s* grillus *m*
grassy *adj* graminosus, herbosus, herbidus
grate *s* clathri *m pl*; (*hearth*) caminus *m*
grate *vt* raděre, conterěre; *vi* stridēre; **to — upon** offenděre
grateful *adj* gratus, juncundus; **—ly** grate
gratification *s* gratificatio *f*; (*pleasure, delight*) voluptas, oblectatio *f*
gratify *vt* gratificari (*with dat*), morigerari (*with dat*)
gratifying *adj* gratus
grating *s* clathri, cancelli *m pl*; (*sound*) stridor *m*
gratis *adv* gratuito, gratis
gratitude *s* gratitudo *f*, gratus animus *m*
gratuitous *adj* gratuitus; **—ly** gratuito
gratuity *s* stips *f*, munus, praemium *n*
grave *adj* gravis, serius; (*stern*) severus; **—ly** graviter; severe
grave *s* sepulcrum *n*, tumulus *m*
gravedigger *s* tumulorum fossor *m*
gravel *s* glarea *f*
gravelly *adj* glareosus
gravestone *s* monumentum *n*
gravitate *vi* vergěre
gravitation *s* ponderatio *f*
gravity *s* gravitas *f*, pondus *n*; (*personal*) severitas, dignitas *f*; momentum *n*
gravy *s* (*broth*) jus *n*; (*juice*) sucus *m*
gray *adj* canus; **to become —** canescěre
gray-eyed *adj* caesius
gray-headed *adj* canus
grayish *adj* canescens
grayness *s* canities *f*
graze *vt* (*cattle*) pascěre; (*to touch lightly*) perstringěre, raděre; *vi* pasci
grease *s* adeps *m*, pinguitudo, arvina *f*
grease *vt* ung(u)ěre
greasy *adj* pinguis; unctus; (*dirty*) squalidus
great *adj* magnus; ingens, amplus, grandis; **as — as** tantus quantus; **—ly** magnopere, valde
great-grandfather *s* proavus *m*
greatness *s* magnitudo *f*
greaves *s* ocreae *f pl*
Grecian *adj* Graecus
greed *s* aviditas, avaritia *f*; voracitas *f*
greedily *adv* avide, cupide
greedy *adj* avarus, cupidus; vorax
Greek *adj* Graecus
Greek *s* Graecus *m*
green *adj* viridis; (*fig*) recens; (*unripe*) crudus, immaturus; **to become —** virescěre
green *s* color viridis *m*; (*lawn*) locus herbidus *m*; **—s** olera *n pl*
greenhouse *s* viridarium hibernum *n*
greenish *adj* subviridis
greenness *s* viriditas *f*; (*fig*) cruditas, immaturitas *f*
greet *vt* salutem dicěre (*with dat*), salutare
greeting *s* salutatio *f*
gregarious *adj* gregalis
grenade *s* pyrobolus *m*
greyhound *s* vertagus *m*
gridiron *s* craticula *f*
grief *s* maeror, dolor, luct·us -ūs *m*; **to come to —** perire
grievance *s* injuria, querimonia, querela *f*
grieve *vt* dolore afficěre; *vi* maerēre, dolēre, lugēre
grievous *adj* gravis, durus, atrox; **—ly** graviter, aegre
griffin *s* gryps *m*
grill *vt* torrēre
grim *adj* torvus, atrox, truculentus; **—ly** torve, truculente, atrociter
grimace *s* distortus vult·us -ūs *m*, oris depravatio *f*
grimace *vi* os ducěre
grimy *adj* niger, squalidus
grin *vi* distorto vultu ridēre
grin *s* ris·us -ūs *m*
grind *vt* (*grain*) molěre; (*in mortar*) contunděre; (*on whetstone*) exacuěre; **to — the teeth** dentibus frenděre
grindstone *s* cos *f*
grip *s* pugillum *n*, comprehensio *f*
grip *vt* arripěre, comprehenděre
grisly *adj* horrendus, horridus
grist *s* farina *f*
gristle *s* cartilago *f*
gristly *adj* cartilagineus, cartilaginosus
grit *s* harena *f*
gritty *adj* harenosus, sabulosus
grizzly *adj* canus
groan *s* gemit·us -ūs *m*
groan *vi* geměre
groin *s* inguen *n*
groom *s* agaso, equiso *m*
groom *vt* curare
groove *s* canalis *m*, stria *f*
groove *vt* striare
grope *vi* praetentare
gropingly *adv* pedetentim
gross *adj* crassus, pinguis; turpis, foedus; nimius; **—ly** nimium, valde
grotesque *adj* distortus
grotto *s* antrum *n*
ground *s* solum *n*, terra, humus *f*; (*reason*) causa, ratio *f*; (*place*) locus *m*; **on the —** humi; **to give —** ceděre
ground *vt* fundare; (*to teach*) instruěre; (*a ship*) subducěre
groundless *adj* vanus, falsus, fictus; **—ly** temere, de nihilo
group *s* corona, turba *f*, globus *m*
group *vt* disponěre; *vi* **to — around** circulari, stipari
grouse *s* (*bird*) tetrao *m*
grove *s* lucus *m*, nemus *n*
grovel *vi* serpěre, se prosterněre
grow *vt* colěre, serěre; *vi* crescěre, augēri; (*to become*) fieri; **to — out of** (*fig*) oriri ex (*with abl*); **to — up** adolescěre, pubescěre
grower *s* cultor *m*
growl *s* fremit·us -ūs *m*
growl *vi* freměre

grown-up *adj* adultus; puber
growth *s* incrementum *n*, auct·us -ūs *m*
grub *s* vermiculus, lombricus *m*
grub *vi* effodĕre
grudge *s* odium *n*, invidia *f*; **to hold a — against** succensēre (*with dat*)
grudgingly *adv* invitus, aegre
gruesome *adj* taeter
gruff *adj* torvus, asper; **—ly** torve, aspere
gruffness *s* asperitas *f*
grumble *vi* murmurare, mussitare
grunt *s* grunnit·us -ūs *m*
grunt *vi* grunnire; (*fig*) fremĕre
guarantee *s* fides *f*; (*money*) sponsio *f*; (*person*) praes, vas, sponsor *m*; (*bail money*) vadimonium *n*
guarantee *vt* praestare, spondēre
guarantor *s* sponsor *m*
guard *s* custodia, tutela *f*; (*mil*) praesidium *n*; (*person*) custos *m* & *f*; **to be on one's —** cavēre
guard *vt* custodire, defendĕre; *vi* **to — against** cavēre
guarded *adj* cautus, circumspectus; **—ly** caute
guardian *s* custos, praeses *m* & *f*, defensor *m*; (*of minor or orphan*) tutor *m*
guardianship *s* custodia, tutela, curatio *f*
guerdon *s* merces *f*
guess *s* conjectura *f*
guess *vt* & *vi* conjicĕre, divinare, opinari
guest *s* hospes *m*; advena *m*; (*at dinner*) conviva *m*
guidance *s* duct·us -ūs *m*, curatio, moderatio *f*
guide *s* dux, ductor *m*
guide *vt* ducĕre, regĕre; (*to control*) moderari
guidebook *s* itinerarium *n*
guild *s* collegium, corpus *n*, sodalitas *f*
guile *s* dolus *m*
guileful *adj* dolosus
guileless *adj* simplex, sincerus
guilt *s* culpa *f*, crimen, vitium *n*
guiltless *adj* innocens, insons
guilty *adj* sons, noxius, nocens, sceleratus
guinea hen *s* meleagris *f*
guise *s* species *f*
guitar *s* cithara Hispanica *f*; fides *f pl*; **to play the —** fidibus canĕre
gulf *s* sin·us -ūs *m*; (*abyss*) abyssus *f*, gurges *m*
gull *s* larus marinus, mergus *m*
gullet *s* gula *f*, guttur *n*
gullible *adj* credulus
gulp *vt* absorbēre, glutire, haurire; *vi* singultare
gulp *s* haust·us -ūs, singult·us -ūs *m*
gum *s* (*of mouth*) gingiva *f*; gummi *n* (*indecl*)
gumption *s* alacritas *f*
gun *s* sclopetum *n*; tormentum *n*
gunner *s* tormentarius *m*
gurgle *vi* singultare; (*of stream*) murmurare
gurgling *s* singult·us -ūs *m*; (*of stream*) murmur *n*, murmuratio *f*
gush *vi* micare, scaturire
gush *s* scaturigines *f pl*
gust *s* impet·us -ūs *m*, flamen *n*
gusty *adj* ventosus, procellosus
gut *s* intestinum *n*
gut *vt* exenterare; (*fig*) diripĕre, amburĕre
gutted *adj* (*by fire*) ambustus
gutter *s* canalis *m*; (*rain gutter*) compluvium *n*; (*in fields or upon roofs*) colliciae *f pl*
guttural *adj* gutturalis
guzzle *vi* potare
guzzler *s* potor *m*
gymnasium *s* gymnasium *n*, palaestra *f*
gymnastic *adj* gymnicus
gymnastics *s* palaestra, palaestrica *f*

H

haberdasher *s* linteo *m*
habit *s* consuetudo *f*, mos *m*; (*dress*) habit·us -ūs, vestit·us -ūs *m*
habitation *s* habitatio, dom·us -ūs *f*
habitual *adj* usitatus, inveteratus; **—ly** de more, ex more
habituate *vt* insuescĕre, assuefacĕre
hack *vt* caedĕre; **to — to pieces** concidĕre
hack *s* (*horse*) caballus *m*
hackneyed *adj* tritus, pervulgatus
haddock *s* gadus morhua *m*
hag *f* an·us -ūs *f*
haggard *adj* macer; ferus
haggle *vi* cavillari, licitare
haggler *s* licitator *m*
hail *s* grando *f*
hail *vt* salutare, appellare
hail *vi* **it is hailing** grandinat
hail *interj* salve!; (*to several*) salvete!
hailstone *s* saxea grando *f*
hair *s* capillus, crinis *m*; (*single*) pilus *m*; (*of animals*) saeta *f*, villus *m*
haircloth *s* cilicium *n*
hairdresser *s* concinnator, tonsor *m*
hairless *adj* (*of head*) calvus; (*of body*) glaber, depilis
hairpin *s* crinale *n*
hairy *adj* pilosus, crinitus; (*shaggy*) hirsutus
halberd *s* bipennis *f*
halcyon *s* alcedo, alcyon *f*
halcyon days *s* alcedonia *n pl*
hale *adj* robustus, validus
hale *vt* rapĕre, trahĕre
half *s* dimidia pars *f*, dimidium *n*

half *adj* dimidius, dimidiatus
half-hour *s* semihora *f*
half-moon *s* luna dimidiata *f;* (*shape*) lunula *f*
half-open *adj* semiapertus
half year *s* semestrium *n*
hall *s* atrium *n;* (*entrance*) vestibulum *n*
hallo *interj* heus!, ohe!
hallow *vt* consecrare
hallucination *s* error *m,* somnium *n,* alucinatio *f*
halo *s* corona *f*
halt *vt* sistĕre; *vi* consistĕre; (*fig*) haesitare; (*to limp*) claudicare
halt *s* pausa, mora *f*; **to come to a —** consistĕre
halter *s* capistrum *n*
halting *adj* claudus
halve *vt* ex aequo dividĕre
ham *s* poples *m*; (*smoked, etc.*) perna *f*
hamlet *s* vicus, viculus *m*
hammer *s* malleus *m*
hammer *vt* tundĕre, cudĕre
hamper *s* corbis *f*
hamper *vt* impedire, implicare
hamstring *s* poplitis nervus *m*
hamstring *vt* poplitem succidĕre (*with dat*)
hand *s* man·us -ūs *f*; (*handwriting*) chirographum *n*; (*of dial*) gnomon *m*; **at —** ad manum, praesto, prae manibus, prope; **by —** manu; **— in —** junctis manibus; **— to —** cominus; **on the other —** altera parte; **on the right —** a dextra; **to have a — in** interesse (*with dat*); **to take in —** suscipĕre
hand *vt* tradĕre, porrigĕre; **to — down** tradĕre; **to — over** referre; (*to betray*) prodĕre; **to — round** circumferre
handbill *s* libellus *m*
handbook *s* enchiridion *n*
handcuffs *s* manicae *f pl*
handful *s* manipulus *m*
handicraft *s* artificium *n*
handiwork *s* opus, opificium *n*
handkerchief *s* sudarium *n*
handle *s* manubrium *n;* (*of cup*) ansa, ansula *f*
handle *vt* tractare
handling *s* tractatio *f*
handsome *adj* pulcher, formosus; **—ly** pulchre; (*liberally*) liberaliter
handsomeness *s* pulchritudo, forma, venustas *f*
handwriting *s* man·us -ūs *f*, chirographum *n*
handy *adj* (*of things*) habilis; (*of person*) sollers; (*at hand*) praesto
hang *vt* suspendĕre; (*by a line*) appendĕre; (*head*) demittĕre; *vi* pendēre; **hanging down** demissus; **hanging loose** fluens; **to — down** dependēre; **to — on to** haerēre (*with dat*); **to — over** imminēre (*with dat*)
hanging *adj* pensilis
hanging *s* (*execution*) suspendium, *n*; **—s** aulaea *n pl*
hangman *s* carnifex *m*
haphazard *adj* fortuitus
happen *vi* accidĕre, fieri, evenire, contingĕre; **to — upon** incidĕre in (*with acc*)
happily *adv* beate, feliciter
happiness *s* felicitas *f*
happy *adj* beatus, felix, fortunatus, faustus
harangue *s* contio *f*
harangue *vt & vi* contionari
harass *vt* vexare, inquietare, exagitare, fatigare
harassing *adj* molestus
harassment *s* vexatio *f*
harbinger *s* praenuntius, antecursor *m*
harbor *s* port·us -ūs *m*
harbor *vt* excipĕre
hard *adj* durus; (*difficult*) difficilis, arduus; (*severe*) acer, rigidus, asper; **to become —** durescĕre
hard *adv* valde, sedulo, summa vi
harden *vt* durare; (*fig*) indurare; *vi* durescĕre; (*fig*) obdurescĕre
hardhearted *adj* durus, crudelis, inhumanus
hardihood *s* audacia *f*
hardiness *s* robur *n*
hardly *adv* vix, aegre; **— any** nullus fere
hardness *s* duritia *f; (fig)* iniquitas, acerbitas *f*; (*difficulty*) difficultas *f*
hardship *s* labor *m,* difficultas, aerumna *f*
hardware *s* ferramenta *n pl*
hardy *adj* robustus, durus
hare *s* lepus *m*
harem *s* gynaeceum *n*
hark *interj* heus!
harken *vi* audire; **to — to** auscultare (*with dat*)
harlot *s* meretrix *f*
harm *s* injuria *f,* damnum *n*; **to come to —** detrimentum accipĕre
harm *vt* nocēre (*with dat*), laedĕre
harmful *adj* noxius, nocivus, damnosus
harmless *adj* (*person*) innocens; (*thing*) innocuus; **—ly** innocenter, incolumis
harmonious *adj* canorus, consonus; (*fig*) concors, consentiens; **—ly** consonanter; (*fig*) concorditer, convenienter
harmonize *vt* componĕre; *vi* concinĕre; (*fig*) consentire
harmony *s* harmonia *f,* concent·us -ūs *m*; (*fig*) concordia *f*
harness *s* equi ornamenta *n pl*
harness *vt* ornare, insternĕre
harp *s* lyra *f*
harpist *s* psaltes *m*
harpoon *s* jaculum hamatum *n*
harpoon *vt* jaculo hamato transfigĕre
harpy *s* harpyia *f*
harrow *s* rastrum *n*, irpex *m*
harrow *vt* occare
harsh *adj* asper, raucus, discors, stridulus; (*in taste*) acer; (*fig*) durus, severus, inclemens; **—ly** aspere, acerbe, severe
harshness *s* asperitas, acerbitas, severitas *f*

harvest *s* messis, seges *f*
harvest *vt* metĕre
hash *vt* comminuĕre
hash *s* minutal *n*
haste *s* festinatio, celeritas *f*; **in —** propere; **to make —** properare
hasten *vt* accelerare, properare, praecipitare; *vi* properare, festinare
hastily *adv* propere, raptim; (*without reflection*) temere, inconsulte
hastiness *s* celeritas, temeritas *f*
hasty *adj* properus, praeceps, temerarius, inconsultus
hat *s* pileus, galerus, petasus *m*
hatch *vt* (*fig*) coquĕre, machinari; (*of chickens*) ex ovis excludĕre
hatchet *s* ascia, securis, dolabra *f*
hate *s* odium *n*, invidia *f*
hate *vt* odisse
hateful *adj* odiosus, invisus; **to be — to** odio esse (*with dat*); **—ly** odiose
hatred *s* odium *n*, invidia *f*
haughtily *adv* superbe, arroganter, insolenter
haughtiness *s* superbia, arrogantia *f*, fastidium *n*
haughty *adj* superbus, arrogans, insolens
haul *s* bolus *m*
haul *vt* trahĕre; **to — up** subducĕre
haunch *s* clunis, coxa *f*
haunt *vt* frequentare; (*fig*) agitare, inquietare
haunt *s* locus *m*; (*of animals*) lustra *n pl*, latebrae *f pl*
have *vt* habēre, possidēre, tenēre
haven *s* port·us -ūs *m*
havoc *s* strages *f*
hawk *s* accipiter *m & f*
hawk *vt* venditare
hawser *s* retinaculum *n*
hawthorn *s* crataegus oxyacantha *f*
hay *s* faenum *n*
hayloft *s* faenilia *n pl*
haystack *s* faeni meta *f*
hazard *s* periculum *n*
hazard *vt* periclitari
hazardous *adj* periculosus, anceps; **—ly** periculose
haze *s* nebula *f*
hazy *adj* caliginosus, nebulosus
he *pron* hic, is, ille; (*male*) mas *m*
head *s* caput *s*; (*mental faculty*) ingenium *n*; (*fig*) princeps; **— first** praeceps
head *adj* primus, principalis, capitalis
head *vt* praeesse (*with dat*), ducĕre; *vi* **to — for** petĕre
headache *s* capitis dolor *m*
heading *s* caput *n*, titulus *m*
headland *s* promuntorium *n*
headless *adj* truncus
headlong *adv* praeceps
headquarters *s* praetorium *n*
headstrong *adj* pervicax, contumax
headway *s* profect·us -ūs *m*; **to make —** proficĕre
headwind *s* ventus adversus *m*
heady *adj* (*of drinks*) fervidus, vehemens
heal *vt* medēri (*with dat*), sanare; *vi* sanescĕre; (*of wounds*) coalescĕre
healer *s* medicus *m*
healing *adj* salubris, salutaris
health *s* valetudo, salus *f*; **to be in good —** valēre; **to drink to the — of** propinare (*with dat*)
healthful *adj* salutaris, salubris
healthily *adv* salubriter
healthy *adj* sanus, integer; (*places*) salubris
heap *s* acervus, cumulus *m*, congeries *f*
heap *vt* acervare; **to — up** accumulare, exstruĕre
hear *vt* audire, exaudire; (*to learn*) certior fieri, accipĕre, cognoscĕre
hearing *s* (*act*) auditio *f*; (*sense*) audit·us -ūs *m*; (*law*) cognitio *f*; **hard of —** surdaster
hearken *vi* auscultare
hearsay *s* fama *f*, rumor *m*
heart *s* cor *n*; (*fig*) pectus *n*; (*courage*) animus *m*; **to learn by —** ediscĕre
heartache *s* cura *f*, angor *m*
heartbreak *s* angor *m*
heartbroken *adj* aeger
hearth *s* focus *m*
heartily *adv* sincere, vehementer, valde
heartiness *s* studium *n*, alacritas *f*
heartless *adj* crudelis, inhumanus; **—ly** crudeliter, inhumane
heartlessness *s* inhumanitas *f*
hearty *adj* sincerus, vehemens, alacer
heat *s* calor, ardor *m*; (*fig*) fervor *m*
heat *vt* calefacĕre; *vi* calescĕre
heath *s* (*plant*) erice *f*; (*place*) loca inculta *n pl*
heathen *adj* paganus
heathen *s* paganus *m*
heather *s* erice *f*
heating *s* calefactio *f*
heave *vt* attollĕre, levare; **to — a sigh** gemitum ducĕre; *vi* tumēre, aestuare, fluctuare
heaven *s* caelum *n*; (*fig*) dii, superi *m pl*
heavenly *adj* caelestis, divinus
heavily *adv* graviter; (*slowly*) tarde
heaviness *s* gravitas *f*; (*slowness*) tarditas *f*
heavy *adj* gravis, ponderosus; (*fig*) tardus, segnis, iners; (*sad*) maestus
Hebraic *adj* Hebraicus
Hebrew *s* Hebraeus *m*; (*language*) Hebraea lingua *f*
hecatomb *s* hecatombe *f*
hectic *adj* fervidus, febriculosus
hedge *s* saepes *f*
hedge *vt* **to — in** saepire; **to — off** intersaepire; *vi* tergiversari
hedgehog *s* ericius *m*
heed *s* cura, opera *f*; **to take —** cavēre, curare
heed *vt* curare, observare, respicĕre; (*to obey*) parēre (*with dat*)
heedless *adj* incautus, temerarius; **— of** immemor (*with genit*)
heedlessness *s* neglegentia *f*
heel *s* calx *m & f*
heifer *s* bucula, juvenca *f*
height *s* altitudo *f*; (*of person*) pro-

ceritas *f*; (*top*) culmen *n*; (*fig*) fastigium *n*
heighten *vt* amplificare, exaggerare, augēre
heinous *adj* atrox, nefarius, foedus; **—ly** atrociter
heir *s* heres *m*; **sole** *or* **universal —** heres ex asse
heiress *s* heres *f*
heirloom *s* res hereditaria *f*
hell *s* Tartarus *m*, inferi *m pl*
Hellenic *adj* Hellenicus, Graecus
Hellenism *s* Hellenismus *m*
hellish *adj* infernus, diabolicus, nefarius
helm *s* gubernaculum *n*
helmet *s* cassis, galea *f*
helmsman *s* gubernator, rector *m*
help *s* auxilium, subsidium *n*
help *vt* adjuvare (*with acc*), auxiliari (*with dat*), succurrĕre (*with dat*), opem ferre (*with dat*)
helper *s* adjutor *m*, adjutrix *f*
helpful *adj* utilis
helpless *adj* inops
helplessness *s* inopia *f*
hem *s* ora *f*, limbus *m*
hem *vt* (*to sew*) suĕre; **to — in** circumsidēre, obsidēre
hem *interj* hem!, ehem!
hemisphere *s* hemisphaerium *n*
hemlock *s* cicuta *f*
hemp *s* cannabis *f*
hempen *adj* cannabinus
hen *s* gallina *f*
hence *adv* hinc; (*consequently*) igitur, ideo
henceforth *adv* posthac, dehinc
henpecked *adj* uxorius
her *pron* eam, illam, hanc
her *adj* ejus, illius, hujus; **— own** suus, proprius
herald *s* fetialis *m*; (*crier*) praeco *m*
herald *vt* nuntiare, praenuntiare
herb *s* herba *f*; **—s** herbae *f pl*, olus *n*
herd *s* grex *m*; armentum *n*; (*in contempt*) vulgus *n*
herd *vt* **to — together** congregare, cogĕre; *vi* congregari
herdsman *s* pastor, armentarius *m*
here *adv* hic; **— and there** passim
hereafter *adv* posthac, in reliquum tempus
hereby *adv* ex hoc, ex hac re, hinc
hereditary *adj* hereditarius, patrius
heredity *s* genus *n*; **by —** jure hereditario, per successiones
herein *adv* in hoc, in hac re, hic
heresy *s* haeresis *f*
heretical *adj* haereticus; falsus, pravus
hereupon *adv* hic
herewith *adv* una cum hac re
heritage *s* hereditas *f*
hermaphrodite *s* androgynus, Hermaphroditus *m*
hermit *s* eremita *m*
hermitage *s* eremitae cella *f*
hernia *s* hernia *f*
hero *s* vir *m*; (*demigod*) heros *m*
heroic *adj* fortissimus, magnanimus, heroicus; **—ally** fortissime
heroine *s* virago *f*
heroism *s* virtus, fortitudo *f*
heron *s* ardea *f*
herring *s* harenga *f*
hers *pron* ejus, illius
herself *pron* (*refl*) se; (*intensive*) ipsa; **to —** sibi; **with —** secum
hesitant *adj* dubius, incertus; **—ly** cunctanter, dubitanter
hesitate *vi* dubitare, haesitare
hesitation *s* dubitatio, haesitatio, cunctatio *f*
Hesperian *adj* Hesperius
heterogeneous *adj* diversus
hew *vt* dolare, caedĕre
hey *interj* ohe!
hiatus *s* hiat·us -ūs *m*
hiccup *s* singult·us -ūs *m*
hiccup *vi* singultare
hide *s* pellis *f*, corium *n*
hide *vt* abdĕre, abscondĕre, celare, occultare; (*to flog*) verberare; *vi* latēre, se abdĕre
hideous *adj* foedus, perhorridus, turpis; **—ly** foede, turpiter
hideousness *s* foeditas *f*, horror *m*
hiding *s* occultatio *f*; (*whipping*) verberatio *f*
hiding place *s* latebra *f*
hierarchy *s* hierarchia *f*
high *adj* altus, excelsus, sublimis; (*tall*) procerus; (*of price*) pretiosus, carus; (*of ground*) editus; (*of rank*) amplus; **—ly** (*value*) magni; (*intensity*) vehementer, valde
high *adv* alte, sublimiter; **to aim —** magnas res appetĕre
highborn *adj* generosus, ingenuus, nobilis
high-flown *adj* inflatus, tumidus
highhanded *adj* insolens, superbus; **—ly** insolenter, superbe
highland *s* regio montuosa *f*
highlander *s* montanus *m*
high-minded *adj* (*noble*) magnanimus; (*arrogant*) arrogans, insolens
high priest *s* pontifex maximus *m*
highway *s* via *f*
highwayman *s* latro, grassator *m*
hilarity *s* hilaritas *f*
hill *s* collis, tumulus *m*; (*slope*) clivus *m*
hillock *s* tumulus *m*
hilly *adj* montuosus, clivosus
hilt *s* capulus *m*
him *pron* eum, hunc, illum; **of —** ejus, hujus, illius; de eo, de hoc, de illo
himself *pron* (*refl*) se; (*intensive*) ipse; **to —** sibi; **with —** secum
hind *s* cerva *f*
hind *adj* posterior
hinder *vt* obstare (*with dat*); impedire, morari
hindmost *adj* postremus, ultimus, novissimus
hindrance *s* impedimentum *n*
hinge *s* cardo *m*
hinge *vi* **to — on** (*fig*) niti (*with abl*)
hint *s* indicium *n*, significatio *f*
hint *vt & vi* significare, innuĕre, suggerĕre
hip *s* coxendix *f*

hippodrome *s* hippodromos *m*
hire *s* conductio, locatio *f*; (*wages*) merces *f*
hire *vt* conducĕre; **to — out** locare; *vi* **to — out** operam suam locare
hired *adj* conductus, conducticius, mercenarius
hireling *s* mercenarius *m*
his *adj* ejus, illius, hujus; **— own** suus, proprius
his *pron* ejus, illius, hujus
hiss *vt & vi* sibilare
hissing *s* sibilus *m*
historian *s* historicus, rerum gestarum scriptor *m*
historical *adj* historicus
history *s* historia, memoria rerum gestarum *f*; **ancient —** antiquitas *f*; **modern —** memoria recentioris aetatis *f*
histrionic *adj* histrionalis
hit *s* ict·us -ūs *m*, plaga *f*; **to be a —** bene succedĕre
hit *vt* icĕre, ferire, percutĕre; *vi* **to — upon** invenire
hitch *s* impedimentum *n*, mora *f*
hitch *vt* (ad)jungĕre
hither *adv* huc
hither *adj* citerior
hitherto *adv* (*of time*) adhuc; (*of place*) huc usque
hive *s* alvus *m*, alvearium *n*
hoard *s* acervus *m*
hoard *vt* coacervare, recondĕre
hoarder *s* accumulator *m*
hoarse *adj* raucus; **to get —** irraucescĕre; **—ly** raucā voce
hoary *adj* canus
hoax *s* fraus, ludificatio *f*
hoax *vt* fallĕre, decipĕre, ludificari
hobble *vi* claudicare
hobby *s* avocamentum *n*
hock *s* poples *m*
hoe *s* sarculum *n*
hoe *vt* sarculare; (*weeds*) pectĕre
hog *s* porcus, sus *m*
hoist *vt* sublevare, tollĕre
hold *vt* tenēre, possidēre, habēre; (*to* (*contain*) capĕre; (*to think*) habēre, existimare, censēre; **to — back** retinēre; **to — forth** porrigĕre, extendĕre; (*to offer*) praebēre; **to — in** inhibēre, cohibēre; **to — off** abstinēre, arcēre; **to — up** (*to lift up*) attollĕre, sustinēre; *vi* **to — back** cunctari; **to — out** (*to last*) durare, permanēre
holder *s* possessor *m*; (*handle*) manubrium *n*
holding *s* possessio *f*
hole *s* foramen *n*; (*fig*) latebra *f*; (*of mice*) cavum *n*
holiday *s* dies festus *m*; **—s** feriae *f pl*
holiness *s* sanctitas *f*
hollow *adj* cavus; (*fig*) vanus, inanis
hollow *s* caverna *f*, cavum *n*; (*depression*) lacuna *f*
hollow *vt* **to — out** cavare, excavare
holly *s* ilex aquifolium *n*
holocaust *s* holocaustum *n*
holy *adj* sanctus
homage *s* obsequium *n*, cult·us -ūs *m*; **to pay — to** colere
home *s* domicilium *n*, dom·us -ūs *f*; **at —** domi; **from —** domo
home *adv* (*motion*) domum; (*place where*) domi
home *adj* domesticus
homeless *adj* tecto carens, profugus
homeliness *s* rusticitas *f*
homely *adj* rusticus, simplex
homemade *adj* domesticus, vernaculus, domi factus
homesickness *s* tecti sui desiderium *n*, nostalgia *f*
homestead *s* sedes *f*, fundus *m*
homeward *adv* domum
homicidal *adj* cruentus, sanguinolentus
homicide *s* (*person*) homicida *m*; (*deed*) homicidium *n*
homily *s* sermo, tractat·us -ūs *m*
homogeneous *adj* pari naturā praeditus
hone *vt* acuĕre
honest *adj* probus, sincerus; **—ly** probe, sincere
honesty *s* probitas, sinceritas *f*
honey *s* mel *n*
honeybee *s* apis mellifera *or* mellifica *f*
honeycomb *s* favus *m*
honeysuckle *s* clymenus *m*
honor *s* honos *m*; (*repute*) fama *f*; (*trust*) fides *f*; (*award*) decus *n*; (*official distinction*) dignitas *f*; **sense of —** pudor *m*
honor *vt* honorare; (*to respect*) colĕre
honorable *adj* honestus
honorably *adv* honeste
honorary *adj* honorarius
hood *s* cucullus *m*
hoof *s* ungula *f*
hook *s* hamus, uncus *m*; **by — or by crook** quocumque modo
hook *vt* inuncare; confibulare; (*fig*) capĕre
hooked *adj* hamatus; (*crooked*) curvatus, aduncus
hoop *s* circulus *m*; (*toy*) trochus *m*; (*shout*) clamor *m*
hoop *vi* exclamare
hoot *vt* explodĕre; *vi* obstrepĕre; (*of owls*) canĕre
hop *s* salt·us -ūs *m*
hop *vi* salire, subsultare
hope *s* spes *f*
hope *vt* sperare; **to — for** exspectare
hopeful *adj* bonae spei; **—ly** magna cum spe
hopeless *adj* exspes, desperatus; **—ly** desperanter
hopelessness *s* desperatio *f*
horde *s* turba, caterva *f*, grex *m*
horizon *s* orbis finiens *m*
horizontal *adj* libratus; **—ly** ad libram
horn *s* cornu *n*; (*as trumpet*) buccina *f*
horned *adj* cornutus, corniger
hornet *s* crabo *m*
horoscope *s* horoscopus *m*

horrible *adj* horribilis, foedus; (*excessive*) immoderatus
horribly *adv* horribili modo, foede
horrid *adj* horridus, horrens; **—ly** horride
horrify *vt* horrificare, perterrēre
horror *s* horror *m*; (*deep hatred*) odium *n*
horse *s* equus *m*, equa *f*
horseback *s* **on —** in equo; ex equo; **to fight on —** ex equo pugnare; **to ride on —** in equo vehi
horsehair *s* pilus equinus *m*
horseman *s* eques *m*
horse race *s* curriculum equorum *n*, certatio equestris *f*
horseradish *s* armoracia *f*
horseshoe *s* solea *f*
horsewhip *s* flagellum *n*, scutica *f*
horsewhip *vt* verberare
horticultural *adj* ad hortorum cultum pertinens
horticulture *s* hortorum cult·us -ūs *m*
hose *s* (*stocking*) tibiale *n*; (*tube*) tubulus *m*
hosiery *s* feminalia *n pl*
hospitable *adj* hospitalis
hospitably *adv* hospitaliter
hospital *s* valetudinarium *n*
hospitality *s* hospitalitas *f*
host *s* (*entertainer*) hospes *m*; (*army*) copiae *f pl*, exercit·us -ūs *m*; (*crowd*) multitudo *f*; (*wafer*) hostia *f*
hostage *s* obses *m & f*
hostess *s* hospita *f*; (*at inn*) caupona *f*
hostile *adj* hostilis, infensus, inimicus; **in a — manner** hostiliter, infense
hot *adj* calidus *or* caldus; fervidus; (*boiling*) fervens; (*seething*) aestuosus; (*of spices*) acer; (*fig*) ardens; **to be —** calēre; **to become —** calescĕre; **—ly** acriter, ardenter
hotel *s* hospitium *n*, caupona *f*
hound *s* catulus *m*
hound *vt* instare (*with dat*)
hour *s* hora *f*
hourglass *s* horarium *n*
hourly *adv* in horas
house *s* dom·us -ūs *f*, aedes *f pl*, tectum *n*; (*family*) dom·us -ūs, gens *f*; (*in country*) villa *f*; **at the — of** apud (*with acc*)
house *vt* domo excipĕre; (*things*) condĕre
housebreaker *s* fur, effractarius *m*
housebreaking *s* domūs effractura *f*
household *adj* familiaris, domesticus
household *s* familia, dom·us -ūs *f*
householder *s* paterfamilias *m*
household gods *s* Lares *m pl*; Penates *m pl*
housekeeper *s* promus *m*
housekeeping *s* rei familiaris cura *f*
housemaid *s* ancilla, vernacula *f*
housewife *s* materfamilias *f*
hovel *s* tugurium, gurgustium *n*
hover *vi* pendēre, volitare; **to — over** impendēre (*with dat*)
how *adv* quomodo, quo pacto, qui; (*to what degree*) quam; **— many** quot; **— much** quantum; **— often** quotiens
however *adv* tamen, nihilominus, autem; quamvis, quamlibet; **— great** quantuscunque; **— many** quotquot; **— often** quotiescunque
howl *s* ululat·us -ūs *m*
howl *vi* ululare, fremĕre
hub *s* axis *m*
huckster *s* propola, institor *m*
huddle *vi* congregari
huddle *s* corona *f*
huddled *adj* confertus
hue *s* color *m*
hue and cry *s* conclamatio *f*
huff *s* offensio *f*; **in a —** offensus
huff *vi* stomachari
hug *s* complex·us -ūs *m*
hug *vt* complecti, amplecti
huge *adj* ingens, immensus, vastus, immanis
hulk *s* alveus *m*; navis oneraria *f*
hull *s* alveus *m*
hum *s* murmur *n*, murmuratio *f*; (*of bees*) bombus *m*
hum *vi* murmurare; (*of bees*) bombilare
human *adj* humanus; **— feelings** humanitas *f*; **—ly** humane, humaniter, humanitus
human being *s* homo *m & f*
humane *adj* humanus, misericors; **—ly** humaniter, misericorditer, humanitus
humanity *s* humanitas *f*; homines *m pl*
humanize *vt* excolĕre
humble *adj* (*obscure*) humilis, obscurus; (*modest*) summissus, modestus; **—ly** summisse
humble *vt* deprimĕre, infringĕre; **to — oneself** se summittĕre
humid *adj* humidus
humidity *s* humor *m*
humiliate *vt* humiliare, deprimĕre
humiliation *s* humiliatio *f*, dedecus *n*
humility *s* animus summissus *m*, modestia, humilitas *f*
humor *s* (*disposition*) ingenium *n*, natura *f*; (*whim*) libido *f*; **sense of —** facetiae *f pl*, festivitas *f*
humor *vt* obsequi (*with dat*), morigerari (*with dat*), indulgēre (*with dat*)
humorous *adj* facetus, ridiculus, jocularis; **—ly** facete
hump *s* gibber, gibbus *m*
humpbacked *adj* gibber
hunch *s* opinio *f*; **to have a —** opinari
hundred *adj* centum; **— times** centie(n)s
hundredfold *adj* centuplex
hundredfold *s* centuplum *n*
hundredth *adj* centesimus
hunger *s* fames *f*
hunger *vi* esurire
hungrily *adv* avide, voraciter, rabide; jejune
hungry *s* esuriens, jejunus; (*fig*) avide; **to be —** esurire
hunt *s* venatio *f*, venat·us -ūs *m*

hunt *vt* venari, indagare; *vi* **to — for** quaerĕre, exquirĕre
hunter *s* venator *m*; (*horse*) equus venaticus *m*
hunting *s* venatio *f*, venat·us -ūs *m*
hunting *adj* venaticus
huntress *s* venatrix *f*
huntsman *s* venator *m*
hurdle *s* crates *f*; (*obstacle*) obex *m* & *f*
hurl *vt* jacĕre, conjicĕre, jaculari
hurray *interj* io!, evax!
hurricane *s* procella *f*
hurriedly *adv* raptim, festinanter; (*carelessly*) negligenter
hurry *vt* rapĕre, accelerare, maturare; *vi* festinare, properare, maturare
hurry *s* festinatio *f*; **in a —** festinanter
hurt *vt* nocēre (*with dat*), laedĕre; (*fig*) offendĕre; *vi* dolēre
hurt *s* vulnus *n*; damnum *n*, injuria *f*
hurt *adj* saucius; (*emotionally*) saucius, offensus
husband *s* maritus, vir *m*
husbandry *s* agricultura, res rustica *f*
hush *s* silentium *n*
hush *vt* comprimĕre, pacare; (*a secret*) celare; *vi* tacēre
hush *interj* st!, tace!; (*to several*) tacete!
husk *s* folliculus *m*; (*of beans, etc.*) siliqua *f*; (*of grain*) gluma *f*
husky *adj* robustus; (*of voice*) raucus
hustle *vt* trudĕre, pulsare; *vi* festinare
hut *s* tugurium *n*, casa *f*
hyacinth *s* hyacinthus *m*
hydra *s* hydra *f*
hyena *s* hyaena *f*
hymen *s* Hymenaeus *m*
hymn *s* carmen *n*, hymnus *m*
hyperbole *s* superlatio *f*
hypercritical *adj* nimis severus
hyphen *s* hyphen *n* (*indecl*)
hypochondriac *s* melancholicus *m*
hypocrisy *s* simulatio, dissimulatio *f*
hypocrite *s* simulator, dissimulator *m*
hypocritical *adj* simulatus, fictus
hypothesis *s* hypothesis, sumptio, conjectura *f*
hypothetical *adj* hypotheticus, sumptus
hysteria *s* deliratio *f*
hysterical *adj* hystericus

I

I *pron* ego; **— myself** egomet, ego ipse
iambic *adj* iambeus
ice *s* glacies *f*
icicle *s* stiria *f*
icy *adj* glacialis
idea *s* notio, notitia, imago, conceptio *f*
ideal *adj* perfectus, summus, optimus; (*as mere mental image*) mente conceptus, idealis
ideal *s* exemplar *n*
identical *adj* idem
identify *vt* agnoscĕre
idiocy *s* fatuitas, animi imbecillitas *f*
idiom *s* proprietas linguae, consuetudo *f*
idiomatic *adj* proprius linguae
idiosyncrasy *s* proprium *n*
idiot *s* fatuus, excors *m*
idiotic *adj* fatuus, stultus, ineptus
idle *adj* otiosus, vacuus; (*pointless*) vanus, inanis; (*lazy*) ignavus, iners, deses; **to be —** cessare
idle *vt* **to — away** terĕre; *vi* cessare
idleness *s* otium *n*; ignavia, inertia, desidia *f*
idler *s* cessator, homo ignavus *m*
idle talk *s* nugae *f pl*
idly *adv* otiose; ignave, segniter; (*in vain*) vane, frustra
idol *s* simulacrum *n*; (*eccl*) idolum *n*; (*person*) deliciae *f pl*
idolater *s* simulacrorum cultor *m*
idolatrous *adj* idololatricus
idolatry *s* simulacrorum cult·us -ūs *m*
idolize *vt* venerari
idyl *s* idyllium *n*
if *conj* si; **as —** quasi, tamquam; **and —** quodsi; **but —** sin; quodsi; **even —** etiamsi; **— not** ni, nisi, si non; **— only** si modo, dummodo
igneous *adj* igneus
ignite *vt* accendĕre, incendĕre; *vi* exardescĕre, flammam concipĕre
ignoble *adj* ignobilis, obscurus; (*base*) turpis
ignobly *adv* turpiter
ignominious *adj* ignominiosus, turpis; **—ly** ignominiose, turpiter
ignominy *s* ignominia *f*
ignoramus *s* idiota *m*
ignorance *s* ignoratio, ignorantia *f*
ignorant *adj* ignarus, nescius; (*unlearned*) indoctus; **to be — of** ignorare, nescire; **—ly** inscienter, inscite, indocte
ignore *vt* praetermittĕre, neglegĕre
Iliad *s* Ilias *f*
ill *adj* aegrotus, aeger; (*evil*) malus; **to be —** aegrotare; **to fall —** in morbum incidĕre
ill *adv* male, prave
ill *s* malum *n*
ill-bred *adj* inurbanus, agrestis
illegal *adj* vetitus, illicitus; **—ly** contra leges, illicite
illegitimate *adj* haud legitimus; (*of birth*) spurius, nothus
illiberal *adj* illiberalis; **—ly** illiberaliter
illicit *adj* illicitus; **—ly** illicite

illiterate *adj* illitteratus, indoctus, ineruditus
illness *s* morbus *m*, aegritudo, aegrotatio, valetudo *f*
illogical *adj* absurdus; **—ly** absurde
ill-starred *adj* infelix
ill-tempered *adj* iracundus, stomachosus, difficilis
illuminate *vt* illustrare, illuminare
illumination *s* illuminatio *f*, lumina *n pl*
illusion *s* error *m*
illusive *adj* falsus, vanus
illusory *adj* fallax
illustrate *vt* illustrare; (*fig*) explanare
illustration *s* illustratio *f*; (*fig*) exemplum *n*
illustrative *adj* exemplaris
illustrious *adj* illustris, insignis, praeclarus; **—ly** praeclare
image *s* signum, simulacrum *n*; (*likeness*) effigies, imago *f*
imagery *s* figurae *f pl*
imaginary *adj* fictus, commenticius
imagination *s* cogitatio *f*
imaginative *adj* ingeniosus
imagine *vt* imaginari, fingĕre; (*to suppose*) opinari
imbecile *adj* (*weak*) imbecillus; (*of mind*) animo imbecillus, fatuus
imbecile *s* fatuus *m*
imbibe *vt* imbibĕre
imbue *vt* imbuĕre, tingĕre
imitate *vt* imitari
imitation *s* imitatio *f*; (*copy*) imago *f*
imitative *adj* ad imitandum aptus
imitator *s* imitator *m*, imitatrix *f*, aemulator *m*
immaculate *adj* integer, castus
immaterial *adj* incorporalis; (*unimportant*) nullius momenti
immeasurable *adj* immensus, infinitus
immeasurably *adv* infinito
immediate *adj* praesens, proximus; **—ly** statim, confestim, extemplo; **—ly after** sub (*with acc*)
immemorial *adj* antiquissimus; **from time —** ex omni memoria aetatum
immense *adj* immensus; **—ly** vehementer
immensity *s* immensitas *f*
immerge *vt* mergĕre, immergĕre
immersion *s* immersio *f*
imminent *adj* imminens, impendens
immobility *s* immobilitas *f*
immoderate *adj* immodicus; **—ly** immoderate, nimie
immodest *adj* immodestus, impudicus; **—ly** immodeste, inverecunde
immodesty *s* immodestia *f*
immolate *vt* immolare
immolation *s* immolatio *f*
immoral *adj* pravus, improbus, corruptus; **—ly** prave
immorality *s* mores mali *m pl*, turpitudo, improbitas *f*
immortal *adj* immortalis
immortality *s* immortalitas *f*
immortalize *vt* aeternare, ad deos evehĕre
immovable *adj* immobilis, immotus
immunity *s* immunitas, vacatio *f*
immure *vt* includĕre
immutability *s* immutabilitas *f*
immutable *adj* immutabilis
imp *s* larva *f*; (*child*) puer lascivus *m*
impair *vt* imminuĕre, atterĕre, debilitare
impale *vt* infigĕre
impart *vt* impertire, communicare
impartial *adj* aequus, aequabilis, severus; **—ly** severe
impartiality *s* aequitas, aequabilitas *f*
impassable *adj* insuperabilis, impervius
impassive *adj* impassibilis, frigidus, lentus
impatient *adj* impatiens, trepidus; **—ly** impatienter, aegre
impeach *vt* accusare
impeachment *s* accusatio *f*
impede *vt* obstare (*with dat*), impedire, retardare
impediment *s* impedimentum *n*; (*in speech*) haesitatio *f*
impel *vt* impellĕre
impenetrable *adj* impenetrabilis; (*fig*) occultus
impenitence *s* impaenitentia *f*
imperative *adj* necessarius; (*gram*) imperativus
imperceptible *adj* tenuissimus, obscurus
imperceptibly *adv* sensim
imperfect *adj* imperfectus, mancus, vitiosus; **—ly** imperfecte, vitiose
imperfection *s* vitium *n*, defect·us -ūs *m*
imperial *adj* imperatorius, regius; **—ly** regie
imperil *vt* in periculum adducĕre
imperishable *adj* perennis, aeternus, immortalis
impermeable *adj* impervius
impersonal *adj* impersonalis; **—ly** impersonaliter
impersonate *vt* sustinēre partes (*with genit*), imitari
impertinence *s* insolentia, protervitas *f*
impertinent *adj* (*rude*) insolens, protervus; (*not to the point*) ineptus, nihil ad rem; **—ly** insolenter, proterve; inepte
impervious *adj* impervius, impenetrabilis
impetuosity *s* impet·us -ūs *m*, vehementia, violentia *f*
impetuous *adj* vehemens, fervidus, violentus; **—ly** vehementer, fervide, violenter
impetus *s* impet·us -ūs *m*, vis *f*
impiety *s* impietas *f*
impinge *vi* incidĕre
impious *adj* impius, nefarius; **—ly** impie, nefarie
implacable *adj* implacabilis, inexorabilis, durus
implacably *adv* implacabiliter, dure
implant *vt* ingignĕre, inserĕre, ingenerare
implement *s* instrumentum *n*

implement *vt* exsequi
implicate *vt* implicare, impedire
implication *s* indicium *n*; **by —** tacite
implicit *adj* tacitus, totus; **—ly** tacite, omnino
implore *vt* implorare, obsecrare
imply *vt* significare; **to be implied in** inesse in (*with abl*)
impolite *adj* inurbanus; **—ly** inurbane
impoliteness *s* inurbanitas *f*
impolitic *adj* inconsultus
imponderable *adj* ponderis expers
import *vt* importare, invehĕre; (*to mean*) significare, velle
import *s* significatio *f*; **—s** importaticia *n pl*
importance *s* momentum *n*, gravitas *f*
important *adj* magnus, magni momenti, gravis
importunate *adj* importunus; **—ly** importune
importune *vt* fatigare, efflagitare, sollicitare
impose *vt* imponĕre; (*to enjoin*) injungĕre; **to — upon** abuti (*with abl*)
imposition *s* (*tax*) vectigal, tributum *n*; (*excessive burden*) importunitas *f*
impossibility *s* impossibilitas *f*
impossible *adj* impossibilis
imposter *s* fraudator *m*
imposture *s* fraus *f*
impotence *s* imbecillitas, infirmitas *f*
impotent *adj* imbecillus, infirmus
impound *vt* publicare; (*animals*) includĕre
impoverish *vt* in egestatem redigĕre
impractical *adj* inutilis
imprecate *vt* imprecari, exsecrari
imprecation *s* exsecratio *f*, dirae *f pl*
impregnable *adj* inexpugnabilis
impregnate *vt* imbuĕre, gravidam facĕre
impregnation *s* fecundatio *f*
impress *vt* imprimĕre; (*person*) movēre; **to — something on** inculcare aliquid (*with dat*); (*e.g., someone's mind*) infigĕre aliquid (*with dat*)
impression *s* impressio *f*; (*copy*) exemplar *n*; (*mark*) vestigium *n*; (*idea*) opinio, opinatio *f*; **to make an — on** commovēre
impressive *adj* gravis; **—ly** graviter
imprint *s* impressio *f*
imprint *vt* imprimĕre, infigĕre
imprison *vt* in vincula conjicĕre
imprisonment *s* custodia *f*
improbable *adj* haud credibilis, parum verisimilis
impromptu *adv* ex tempore
improper *adj* indecorus; **—ly** indecore, perperam
impropriety *s* indecorum *n*
improve *vt* emendare, corrigĕre, excolĕre; *vi* melior fieri, proficĕre
improvement *s* emendatio, correctio *f*, profect·us -ūs *m*
improvident *adj* improvidus, imprudens; **—ly** improvide
improvise *vt* ex tempore dicĕre *or* componĕre
imprudence *s* imprudentia *f*
imprudent *adj* imprudens, inconsultus, temerarius; **—ly** imprudenter, inconsulte, temere
impugn *vt* impugnare, in dubium vocare
impulse *s* impuls·us -ūs *m*
impulsive *adj* vehemens, violentus; **—ly** impulsu
impunity *s* impunitas *f*; **with —** impune
impure *adj* impurus, obscenus, incestus; contaminatus; **—ly** impure, obscene, inceste
impurity *s* impuritas, obscenitas, impudicitia *f*
in *prep* in (*with abl*); (*in the writings of*) apud (*with acc*); (*of time*) *render by abl*
in *adv* (*motion*) intro; (*rest*) intra, intus
inability *s* impotentia *f*
inaccessible *adj* inaccessus
inaccuracy *s* neglegentia *f*
inaccurate *adj* neglegens, parum accuratus, minime exactus; **—ly** parum accurate
inactive *adj* iners, quietus, ignavus
inactivity *s* inertia, socordia, cessatio *f*
inadequate *adj* impar; **—ly** parum
inadmissible *adj* illicitus
inadvertence *s* imprudentia *f*
inadvertent *adj* imprudens; **—ly** imprudenter
inalienable *adj* proprius
inane *adj* inanis
inanimate *adj* inanimus, inanimatus
inapplicable *adj* **to be —** non valēre
inappropriate *adj* haud idoneus, parum aptus; **—ly** parum apte
inarticulate *adj* indistinctus
inartistic *adj* durus
inasmuch as *conj* quandoquidem
inattentive *adj* haud attentus, neglegens; **—ly** neglegenter
inaudible *adj* **to be —** audiri non posse
inaugurate *vt* inaugurare, consecrare
inauguration *s* inauguratio, consecratio *f*
inauspicious *adj* infaustus; **—ly** malo omine
inborn *adj* ingenitus, innatus
incalculable *adj* inaestimabilis; (*fig*) immensus, incredibilis
incantation *s* carmen, incantamentum *n*
incapable *adj* incapax, inhabilis; **to be — of** non posse (*with inf*)
incapacitate *vt* debilitare
incarcerate *vt* in vincula conjicĕre
incarnate *adj* incarnatus
incarnation *s* incarnatio *f*
incautious *adj* incautus; —ly incaute
incendiary *adj* incendiarius

incense *s* tus *n*
incense *vt* ture fumigare; (*to anger*) irritare, exasperare
incentive *s* incitamentum *n*
incessant *adj* continuus, assiduus; **—ly** assidue
incest *s* incest·us -ūs *m*
incestuous *adj* incestus
inch *s* uncia *f*; **— by —** unciatim
incident *s* cas·us -ūs, event·us -ūs *m*
incidental *adj* fortuitus; **—ly** fortuito, casu, forte
incipient *adj* nascens, primus
incision *s* incis·us -ūs *m*, incisura *f*
incisive *adj* acer
incite *vt* incitare, stimulare
incitement *s* incitamentum *n*, incitatio *f*
incivility *s* rusticitas *f*
inclemency *s* inclementia *f*; (*of weather*) asperitas *f*
inclination *s* (*act*) inclinatio *f*; (*slope*) proclivitas *f*; (*propensity*) libido, inclinatio *f*
incline *vt* inclinare; *vi* propendēre
incline *s* acclivitas *f*
inclined *adj* inclinatus, propensus, pronus
include *vt* includĕre, comprehendĕre
inclusive *adj* comprehendens
incognito *adv* clam
incoherent *adj* interruptus; **—ly** interrupte
income *s* redit·us -ūs, fruct·us -ūs *m*, merces *f*
incomparable *adj* incomparabilis, singularis, unicus, eximius
incomparably *adv* eximie, unice
incompatibility *s* repugnantia, diversitas *f*
incompatible *adj* repugnans, discors
incompetence *s* jurisdictionis defect·us -ūs *m*; inscitia *f*
incompetent *adj* inscitus, inhabilis
incomplete *adj* imperfectus
incomprehensible *adj* haud comprehensibilis
inconceivable *adj* incredibilis
inconclusive *adj* anceps
incongruous *adj* inconveniens, male congruens; **—ly** parum apte
inconsiderable *adj* levis, exiguus
inconsiderate *adj* inconsultus
inconsistency *s* inconstantia, discrepantia *f*
inconsistent *adj* inconstans, absonus, contrarius; **to be — with** abhorrēre ab (*with abl*); **—ly** inconstanter
inconsolable *adj* inconsolabilis
inconstancy *s* inconstantia, levitas *f*
inconstant *adj* inconstans, levis
incontestable *adj* non contentendus
incontinence *s* incontinentia, impudicitia *f*
incontinent *adj* incontinens, intemperans, impudicus; **—ly** incontinenter
incontrovertible *adj* quod refutari non potest
inconvenience *s* incommodum *n*
inconvenience *vt* incommodare
inconvenient *adj* incommodus; **—ly** incommode
incorporate *vt* concorporare, inserĕre
incorporation *s* coagmentatio, cooptatio *f*
incorporeal *adj* incorporalis
incorrect *adj* mendosus, vitiosus, falsus; **—ly** mendose, falso, perperam
incorrigible *adj* incorrigibilis; (*fig*) perditus
incorrupt *adj* incorruptus, integer
incorruptibility *s* incorruptibilitas *f*, incorrupti mores *m pl*
incorruptible *adj* incorruptibilis, integer
increase *s* (*act*) accretio *f*; incrementum, additamentum *n*
increase *vt* augēre, ampliare; *vi* augēri, crescĕre
incredible *adj* incredibilis
incredibly *adv* incredibiliter, ultra fidem
incredulity *s* incredulitas *f*
incredulous *adj* incredulus
increment *s* incrementum *n*
incriminate *vt* criminari
incubation *s* incubatio *f*
inculcate *vt* inculcare
inculcation *s* inculcatio *f*
incumbent *adj* **it is — on** oportet (*with acc*)
incur *vt* contrahĕre, subire; (*guilt*) admittĕre
incurable *adj* insanabilis
incursion *s* incursio *f*
indebted *adj* obaeratus; (*obliged*) obligatus, devinctus, obnoxius
indecency *s* indecorum *n*, obscenitas *f*
indecent *adj* indecorus, obscenus; **—ly** indecore, obscene
indecision *s* haesitatio, dubitatio *f*
indecisive *adj* anceps, dubius, incertus
indeclinable *adj* indeclinabilis
indeed *adv* vere, profecto, sane; (*concessive*) quidem; (*reply*) certe, vero; (*interr*) itane?, verone?
indefatigable *adj* indefatigabilis, indefessus
indefensible *adj* non excusandus; **to be —** defendi non posse; (*mil*) tenēri non posse
indefinite *adj* infinitus, incertus, anceps, obscurus; **—ly** indefinite
indelible *adj* indelebilis
indelicacy *s* indecorum *n*
indelicate *adj* putidus, indecorus
indemnify *vt* compensare; damnum restitutĕre (*with dat*)
indemnity *s* indemnitas *f*
independence *s* libertas *f*
independent *adj* sui potens, sui juris, liber; **—ly** libere, suo arbitrio
indescribable *adj* inenarrabilis; **—ly** inenarrabiliter
indestructible *adj* perennis, perpetuus
indeterminate *adj* indefinitus
index *s* index, elenchus *m*; (*of dial*) gnomon *m*
Indian *adj* Indicus
Indian *s* Indus *m*

indicate *vt* indicare, significare
indication *s* indicatio *f*, signum, indicium *n*
indicative *adj* indicativus
indict *vt* accusare; diem dicĕre (*with dat*)
indictment *s* libellus *m*, accusatio *f*
indifference *s* neglegentia, incuria, lentitudo *f*
indifferent *adj* (*apathetic*) remissus, neglegens, lentus; (*mediocre*) mediocris; **—ly** neglegenter, lente; (*without discrimination*) promiscue
indigenous *adj* indigena
indigent *adj* egens, inops
indigestible *adj* crudus
indigestion *s* cruditas *f*
indignant *adj* indignans, indignabundus, iratus; **to be —** indignari; **—ly** indignanter
indignation *s* indignatio *f*, dolor *m*
indignity *s* indignitas, contumelia *f*
indirect *adj* indirectus, obliquus; **—ly** indirecte, oblique
indiscreet *adj* inconsultus; **—ly** inconsulte, temere
indiscretion *s* immodestia *f*; (*act*) culpa *f*
indiscriminate *adj* promiscuus; **—ly** promiscue, sine discrimine
indispensable *adj* omnino necessarius
indisposed *adj* aversus; (*in health*) aegrotus; **to be —** aegrotare
indisputable *adj* manifestus, certus
indissoluble *adj* indissolubilis
indistinct *adj* indistinctus, parum clarus, obscurus; **—ly** indistincte
individual *adj* proprius, singularis, singuli; **—ly** singulatim
individual *s* homo *m & f*; **—s** singuli *m pl*
individuality *s* proprium ingenium *n*
indivisible *adj* indivisibilis, individuus
indolence *s* inertia, desidia *f*
indolent *adj* iners, ignavus; **—ly** ignave, segniter
indomitable *adj* indomitus
indorse *vt* ratum facĕre
indubitable *adj* indubitabilis
indubitably *adv* sine dubio
induce *vt* persuadēre (*with dat*), inducĕre
inducement *s* incitamentum *n*, illecebra *f*
indulge *vt* indulgēre (*with dat*), servire (*with dat*)
indulgence *s* indulgentia, venia *f*
indulgent *adj* indulgens, benignus; **—ly** indulgenter, benigne
industrious *adj* industrius, sedulus, strenuus; **—ly** industrie
industry *s* industria, assiduitas *f*
inebriated *adj* ebrius, madidus
ineffable *adj* ineffabilis
ineffective *adj* irritus, inutilis; **to be —** effectu carēre
ineffectual *adj* inefficax; **—ly** frustra, nequiquam
inefficiency *s* inutilitas *f*
inefficient *adj* inscitus, inhabilis
ineligible *adj* non eligibilis
inept *adj* ineptus
inequality *s* inaequalitas *f*
inert *adj* iners, segnis, socors
inertia *s* inertia *f*
inevitable *adj* necessarius
inexact *adj* haud accuratus; (*of persons*) indiligens
inexcusable *adj* inexcusabilis
inexhaustible *adj* inexhaustus
inexorable *adj* inexorabilis, durus
inexperience *s* imperitia, inscitia *f*
inexperienced *adj* imperitus, inexpertus
inexplicable *adj* inexplicabilis, inenodabilis
inexpressible *adj* inenarrabilis
inextricable *adj* inexplicabilis, inextricabilis
infallible *adj* certus, erroris expers
infamous *adj* infamis, turpis, flagitiosus; **—ly** flagitiose
infamy *s* infamia *f*, probrum *n*
infancy *s* infantia *f*
infant *adj* infans; puerilis
infant *s* infans *m & f*
infanticide *s* (*person*) infanticida *m*; (*deed*) infanticidium *n*
infantile *adj* infantilis
infantry *s* peditat·us -ūs *m*, pedites *m pl*
infatuate *vt* infatuare
infatuation *s* amentia, dementia *f*
infect *vt* inficĕre; (*fig*) contaminare
infection *s* contagium *n*, contagio *f*
infectious *adj* contagiosus
infer *vt* inferre, conjicĕre
inference *s* conjectura, conclusio *f*
inferior *adj* inferior, deterior, minor
infernal *adj* infernus
infertility *s* sterilitas *f*
infest *vt* infestare, frequentare
infidel *s* infidelis *m & f*
infidelity *s* infidelitas, perfidia *f*
infiltrate *vi* se insinuare
infinite *adj* infinitus, immensus; **—ly** infinite; (*very greatly*) infinito
infinitive *s* infinitivus modus *m*
infinity *s* infinitas, infinitio *f*
infirm *adj* infirmus, debilis
infirmary *s* valetudinarium *n*
infirmity *s* infirmitas, imbecillitas *f*
inflame *vt* inflammare, incendĕre, accendĕre
inflammable *adj* ad exardescendum facilis
inflammation *s* inflammatio *f*
inflammatory *adj* turbulentus, ardens
inflate *vt* inflare; **to be inflated** tumēre
inflation *s* inflatio *f*
inflect *vt* inflectĕre, curvare
inflection *s* flex·us -ūs *m*, declinatio *f*
inflexible *adj* rigidus; (*fig*) obstinatus, pertinax
inflexibly *adv* obstinate
inflict *vt* infligĕre, imponĕre
infliction *s* malum *n*, poena *f*
influence *s* gratia, auctoritas *f*, momentum *n*; **to have — on** valēre apud (*with acc*)
influence *vt* movēre, impellĕre
influential *adj* gravis, potens

influenza *s* catarrh·us -ūs *m*, gravedo *f*
influx *s* influxio *f*
inform *vt* (*to teach*) instruĕre; certiorem facĕre; *vi* **to — against** deferre de (*with abl*)
informant *s* index, delator *m*
information *s* informatio *f*, indicium *n*, nuntius *m*
informer *s* delator *m*
infraction *s* infractio *f*
infrequency *s* raritas *f*
infrequent *adj* rarus
infringe *vt* infringĕre, violare; *vi* **to — upon** occupare, usurpare
infringement *s* violatio, usurpatio *f*
infuriate *vt* efferare
infuse *vt* infundere; (*fig*) injicĕre
infusion *s* infusio *f*
ingenious *adj* sollers, callidus, ingeniosus; (*of thing*) artificiosus; **—ly** callide, artificiose
ingenuity *s* ars, sollertia *f*
ingenuous *adj* simplex
inglorious *adj* inglorius, inhonestus; **—ly** sine gloria, in honeste
ingrained *adj* insitus, inveteratus
ingratiate *vt* **to — oneself with** gratiam inire ab (*with abl*)
ingratitude *s* ingratus animus *m*
ingredient *s* pars *f*
inhabit *vt* incolĕre, habitare
inhabitable *adj* habitabilis
inhabitant *s* incola *m & f*
inhale *vt* haurire; *vi* spiritum ducĕre
inharmonious *adj* dissonus, absonus
inherent *adj* inhaerens, insitus; **to be — in** inesse (*with dat*)
inherit *vt* excipĕre
inheritance *s* hereditas, successio *f*, patrimonium *n*; **to come into an —** hereditatem adire
inheritor *s* heres *m & f*
inhospitable *adj* inhospitalis
inhospitably *adv* minime hospitaliter
inhospitality *s* inhospitalitas *f*
inhuman *adj* inhumanus; **—ly** inhumane
inhumanity *s* inhumanitas *f*
inimical *adj* inimicus
inimitable *adj* inimitabilis
iniquitous *adj* iniquus, improbus
iniquity *s* iniquitas, injustitia *f*
initial *adj* primus
initiate *vt* initiare, instituĕre
initiation *s* initiatio *f*
initiative *s* initium *n*
inject *vt* injicĕre, infundĕre, immittĕre
injection *s* injectio *f*
injudicious *adj* inconsultus; **—ly** inconsulte, temere
injunction *s* mandatum, imperatum *n*
injure *vt* nocēre (*with dat*), laedĕre
injurious *adj* noxius, damnosus, gravis; **—ly** male
injury *s* injuria f, damnum, detrimentum, malum *n*
injustice *s* injustitia *f*; (*act*) injuria *f*
ink *s* atramentum *n*
inkling *s* (*hint*) rumusculus *m*, obscura significatio *f*
inland *adj* mediterraneus
inlay *vt* inserĕre; (*with mosaic*) tessellare
inlet *s* sin·us -ūs *m*, aestuarium *n*
inmate *s* incola, inquilinus *m*
inmost *adj* intimus, imus
inn *s* caupona *f*, deversorium *n*
innate *adj* innatus, insitus
inner *adj* interior
innermost *adj* intimus, imus
innkeeper *s* caupo *m*
innocence *s* innocentia *f*; castitas *f*
innocent *adj* insons, innocens, integer, castus; **—ly** innocenter, integre, caste
innocuous *adj* innocuus; **—ly** innocue
innovation *s* novum *n*, res nova *f*
innovator *s* rerum novarum auctor *m*
innumerable *adj* innumerabilis
inoffensive *adj* innocens, innoxius
inopportune *adj* inopportunus; **—ly** parum in tempore
inordinate *adj* immoderatus; **—ly** immoderate
inquest *s* inquisitio *f*; (*law*) quaestio *f*; **to hold an —** quaerĕre
inquire *vi* inquirĕre, rogare; **to — into** investigare
inquiry *s* quaestio, investigatio *f*
inquisition *s* inquisitio *f*
inquisitive *adj* curiosus; **—ly** curiose
inquisitor *s* quaesitor *m*
inroad *s* incursio, irruptio *f*
insane *adj* insanus, vecors; **—ly** insane
insanity *s* insania, dementia *f*
insatiable *adj* insatiabilis, inexplebilis
inscribe *vt* inscribĕre, insculpĕre, incidĕre
inscription *s* inscriptio *f*, titulus *m*
inscrutable *adj* occultus, obscurus
insect *s* insectum *n*, bestiola *f*
insecure *adj* incertus, intutus, instabilis
insecurity *s* periculum *n*
insensible *adj* insensilis; (*fig*) durus
inseparable *adj* inseparabilis
insert *vt* inserĕre; (*in writing*) ascribĕre
insertion *s* insertio, interpositio *f*
inside *adj* interior
inside *adv* intrinsecus
inside *s* interior pars *f*, interiora *n pl*
inside *prep* intro (*with acc*)
insidious *adj* insidiosus, subdolus; **—ly** insidiose, subdole
insight *s* (*knowledge*) cognitio, intellegentia *f*; (*intelligence*) consilium, judicium *n*
insignia *s* insignia *n pl*
insignificance *s* exiguitas, levitas *f*
insignificant *adj* exiguus, levis, nullius momenti; (*rank*) humilis
insincere *adj* insincerus, simulatus, fucosus; **—ly** haud sincere, simulate
insincerity *s* simulatio, fallacia *f*

insinuate *vt* insinuare; (*to hint*) significare
insinuation *s* significatio *f*
insipid *adj* insulsus, hebes, frigidus; **—ly** insulse
insist *vt* flagitare, exposcĕre; *vi* instare; **to — on** urgĕre, postulare
insistence *s* pertinacia *f*
insolence *s* insolentia, arrogantia *f*
insolent *adj* insolens, arrogans; **—ly** insolenter
insoluble *adj* insolubilis; (*fig*) inexplicabilis
insolvent *adj* **to be —** solvendo non esse
inspect *vt* inspicĕre, introspicĕre, intuēri; (*mil*) recensēre
inspection *s* inspectio, cura *f*; (*mil*) recensio *f*
inspector *s* curator *m*
inspiration *s* (*divine*) afflat·us -ūs *m*; instinct·us -ūs *m*; (*prophetic*) furor *m*
inspire *vt* inspirare, incendĕre, injicĕre
instability *s* instabilitas *f*
install *vt* inaugurare, constituĕre
installation *s* inauguratio *f*
instalment *s* pensio, portio *f*
instance *s* exemplum *n*; **at my —** me auctore; **for —** exampli gratiā
instance *vt* memorare
instant *adj* instans, praesens; **—ly** extemplo, statim
instant *s* momentum *n*; **this —** statim, actutum
instantaneous *adj* praesens; **—ly** continuo
instead *adv* potius, magis
instead of *prep* pro (*with abl*), loco (*with genit*)
instigate *vt* instigare
instigation *s* incitatio *f*, stimulus *m*
instigator *s* instigator *m*, instigatrix *f*
instill *vt* instillare, imbuĕre, injicĕre
instinct *s* instinct·us -ūs *m*, natura *f*
instinctive *adj* naturalis; **—ly** instinctu
institute *vt* instituĕre, constituĕre, condĕre
institute *s* institutum *n*
institution *s* (*act*) institutio *f*; (*thing instituted*) institutum *n*
instruct *vt* (*to teach*) docēre, instituĕre; (*to order*) praecipĕre (*with dat*), mandare
instruction *s* institutio, eruditio, doctrina *f*; **—s** mandata *n pl*
instructive *adj* ad docendum aptus
instructor *s* praeceptor, magister, doctor *m*, magistra *f*
instrument *s* instrumentum *n*; (*mus*) organum *n*; (*law*) tabula, syngrapha *f*
instrumental *adj* aptus, utilis
insubordinate *adj* seditiosus, male parens
insubordination *s* inobedientia, intemperantia *f*
insufferable *adj* intolerandus, intolerabilis
insufficiency *s* defect·us -ūs *m*, inopia *f*
insufficient *adj* impar, parum sufficiens; **—ly** haud satis
insular *adj* insulanus
insulate *vt* segregare
insult *s* probrum *n*, injuria, contumelia *f*
insult *vt* insultare; contumeliam imponĕre (*with dat*), contumeliā afficĕre
insultingly *adv* contumeliose
insure *vt* tutum praestare
insurgent *adj* rebellis
insurgent *s* rebellis *m*
insurmountable *adj* inexsuperabilis
insurrection *s* rebellio, seditio *f*
intact *adj* integer, intactus, incolumis
intangible *adj* intactilis
integral *adj* necessarius
integrity *s* integritas, innocentia, fides *f*
intellect *s* intellect·us -ūs, animus *m*, mens *f*, ingenium *n*
intellectual *adj* ingeniosus
intelligence *s* ingenium *n*, intellegentia *f*; (*information*) nuntius *m*
intelligent *adj* sapiens, argutus, prudens; **—ly** intellegenter, sapienter, prudenter
intelligible *adj* intellegibilis, perspicuus
intelligibly *adv* intellegibiliter, perspicue
intemperance *s* intemperantia *f*
intemperate *adj* immodicus, intemperatus; **—ly** intemperanter
intend *vt* (*with inf*) intendĕre, in animo habēre; (*with object*) destinare
intended *adj* destinatus; (*of future spouse*) sponsus
intense *adj* acer, fervidus; (*of heat*) rapidus; (*excessive*) nimius; **—ly** vehementer, valde, nimium
intensify *vt* augēre
intensity *s* vehmentia, vis *f*; (*of winter, etc.*) rigor *m*
intent *adj* intentus, attentus; **to be — on** animum intendĕre in (*with acc*); **—ly** intente
intention *s* propositum, consilium *n*; (*meaning*) significatio *f*
intentionally *adv* de industria
inter *vt* inhumare, sepelire
intercede *vi* intercedĕre, deprecari, se interponĕre
intercept *vt* excipĕre, intercipĕre, intercludĕre
intercession *s* deprecatio *f*; (*of tribune*) intercessio *f*
intercessor *s* deprecator *m*
interchange *vt* permutare, commutare
interchange *s* permutatio, vicissitudo *f*
intercourse *s* commercium *n*; (*social*) consuetudo *f*; (*sexual*) congress·us -ūs, coit·us -ūs *m*
interdict *vt* interdicĕre, prohibēre
interdiction *s* interdictio *f*, interdictum *n*
interest *s* (*attention*) studium *n*; (*advantage*) utilitas *f*, us·us -ūs *m*,

commodum *n*; (*money*) faenus *n*, usura *f*; **it is of — to me** meā interest, meā refert
interested *adj* **— in** studiosus (*with genit*), attentus (*with dat*)
interfere *vi* intercedére, intervenire, interpellare
interference *s* intercessio *f*, dissidium *n*, intervent·us -ūs *m*
interim *s* intervallum *n*; **in the —** interim, interea
interior *adj* interior
interior *s* interior pars *f*
interjection *s* interjectio *f*
interlinear *adj* interscriptus
interlude *s* embolium *n*
intermarriage *s* connubium *n*
intermarry *vi* matrimonio inter se conjungi
intermediary *s* internuntius *m*
intermediate *adj* medius
interment *s* sepultura, humatio *f*
interminable *adj* infinitus
intermission *s* intermissio, intercapedo *f*
intermittent *adj* intermittens, interruptus; **—ly** interdum, aliquando
internal *adj* intestinus, domesticus; **—ly** intus, interne; domi
international *adj* inter gentes
interpolate *vt* interpolare
interpolation *s* interpolatio *f*
interpret *vt* interpretari
interpretation *s* interpretatio *f*
interpreter *s* interpres *m*
interrogate *vt* interrogare, percontari
interrogation *s* interrogatio, percontatio *f*
interrogative *adj* interrogativus
interrupt *vt* interrumpĕre, interpellare
interruption *s* interruptio, interpellatio *f*
intersect *vt* intersecare
intersection *s* quadrivium *n*
intersperse *vt* inmiscēre
intertwine *vt* intertexĕre
interval *s* intervallum, spatium *n*
intervene *vi* (*to be between*) interjacēre; (*to come between*) intercedére, intervenire
intervening *adj* medius
intervention *s* intercessio *f*, intervent·us -ūs *m*
interview *s* colloquium *n*, congress·us -ūs *m*
interview *vt* percontari
interweave *vt* intertexĕre, intexĕre
intestinal *adj* ad intestina pertinens
intestine *adj* intestinus; (*pol*) domesticus, civicus
intestines *s* intestina *n pl*; (*of victim*) exta *n pl*
intimacy *s* familiaritas, consuetudo *f*
intimate *adj* familiaris; intimus; **—ly** familiariter; intime
intimate *vt* indicare, innuĕre, denuntiare
intimation *s* indicium *n*, denuntiatio *f*
intimidate *vt* minari (*with dat*), metum injicĕre (*with dat*), terrēre
intimidation *s* minae *f pl*
into *prep* in (*with acc*)
intolerable *adj* intolerabilis, intolerandus
intolerably *adv* intoleranter
intolerance *s* intolerantia *f*; superbia *f*
intolerant *adj* intolerans, impatiens
intonation *s* accent·us -ūs *m*
intone *vt* cantare
intoxicate *vt* ebrium reddĕre
intoxicated *adj* ebrius
intoxication *s* ebrietas *f*
intractable *adj* intractabilis, indocilis
intrepid *adj* intrepidus, impavidus; **—ly** intrepide
intricacy *s* perplexitas, implicatio *f*
intricate *adj* contortus, implicatus, perplexus; **—ly** contorte, perplexe
intrigue *s* conspiratio *f*, dolus *m*, artificia *n pl*
intrigue *vt* fascinare; *vi* machinari, dolis contendere
intrinsic *adj* innatus, verus; **—ally** vere, per se
introduce *vt* introducĕre, inducĕre
introduction *s* (*preface*) praefatio *f*, exordium, prooemium *n*; (*to person*) introductio *f*, adit·us -ūs *m*
intrude *vi* se interponĕre, se inculcare, intervenire
intruder *s* interpellator, advena *m*; homo molestus *m*
intrusion *s* interpellatio, usurpatio *f*
intuition *s* intuit·us -ūs *m*, cognitio *f*, acumen *n*
intuitive *adj* intuitivus; **—ly** mentis propriā vi ac naturā
inundate *vt* inundare
inundation *s* inundatio *f*, diluvium *n*
invade *vt* incurrĕre in (*with acc*), invadĕre
invader *s* invasor *m*
invalid *adj* infirmus, vitiosus; (*sick*) aeger, aegrotus
invalid *s* aegrotus *m*
invalidate *vt* irritum facĕre, rescindĕre
invaluable *adj* inaestimabilis
invariable *adj* constans, immutabilis
invariably *adv* semper
invasion *s* incursio, irruptio *f*
invective *s* convicium, probrum *n*
inveigh *vi* **to — against** invehi in (*with acc*), insectari
invent *vt* invenire, reperire; (*to contrive*) excogitare, fingere
invention *s* (*act*) inventio *f*; (*thing invented*) inventum *n*
inventive *adj* sollers, ingeniosus
inventor *s* inventor, auctor *m*
inventory *s* bonorum index *m*
inverse *adj* inversus, conversus; **—ly** inverso ordine
inversion *s* inversio, conversio *f*
invert *vt* invertĕre
invest *vt* (*money*) collocare, ponĕre; (*to besiege*) obsidēre
investigate *vt* investigare, indagare; (*law*) quaerĕre, cognoscĕre
investigation *s* investigatio *f*; (*law*) cognitio *f*

investigator *s* investigator, indagator *m*; (*law*) quaesitor *m*
investment *s* (*of money*) collocatio *f*; (*money invested*) locata pecunia *f*; (*mil*) obsessio *f*
inveterate *adj* inveteratus
invigorate *vt* corroborare, recreare
invincible *adj* invictus, insuperabilis
inviolable *adj* inviolatus, sacrosanctus
inviolate *adj* inviolatus, intactus
invisible *adj* invisibilis, caecus
invitation *s* invitatio *f*
invite *vt* invitare, adhibēre
inviting *adj* suavis, gratus, blandus; **—ly** blande
invocation *s* invocatio, testatio *f*
invoice *s* libellus *m*
invoke *vt* vocare, invocare, obtestari
involuntarily *adv* invite, coacte
involuntary *adj* non voluntarius, coactus
involve *vt* implicare, involvĕre; (*to comprise*) continēre
involved *adj* **to be —** illigari; **to be — in debt** aere alieno laborare
invulnerable *adj* invulnerabilis
inward *adj* interior; **—ly** intus, intrinsecus
inwards *adv* introrsus
Ionian *adj* Ionicus
irascible *adj* iracundus
ire *s* ira *f*
Ireland *s* Hibernia *f*
iris *s* iris *f*
Irish *adj* Hibernicus
irk *vt* incommodare; **I am irked** taedet me, piget me
irksome *adj* molestus, odiosus
iron *s* ferrum *n*
iron *adj* ferreus
ironical *adj* ironicus, deridens; **—ly** per ironiam
irony *s* ironia, dissimulatio *f*
irradiate *vt* illustrare; *vi* effulgēre
irrational *adj* rationis expers, irrationalis, absurdus; **—ly** absurde
irreconcilable *adj* implacabilis; (*incompatible*) repugnans, insociabilis
irrecoverable *adj* irreparabilis
irrefutable *adj* certus, invictus
irregular *adj* irregularis, abnormis; (*disorderly*) tumultuarius; (*gram*) anomalus; **—ly** irregulariter
irregularity *s* irregularitas *f*; (*of conduct*) luxuries, pravitas *f*; (*gram*) anomalia *f*
irrelevant *adj* non pertinens, alienus; **it is —** nil ad rem pertinet
irreligious *adj* impius
irremediable *adj* insanabilis
irreparable *adj* irreparabilis, irrevocabilis
irreproachable *adj* irreprehensus, integer
irresistible *adj* inexsuperabilis, invictus
irresolute *adj* dubius, incertus animi; (*permanent characteristic*) parum firmus; **—ly** dubitanter
irresolution *s* dubitatio *f*; animus parum firmus *m*
irresponsibility *s* incuria *f*
irresponsible *adj* incuriosus
irretrievable *adj* irreparabilis, irrevocabilis
irreverence *s* impietas *f*
irreverent *adj* impius, inverecundus; **—ly** impie
irrevocable *adj* irrevocabilis
irrigate *vt* irrigare
irrigation *s* irrigatio, inductio aquae *f*
irritability *s* iracundia *f*
irritable *adj* irritabilis, iracundus, difficilis
irritate *vt* irritare; (*wound*) inflammare
irritation *s* irritatio, iracundia *f*, stomachus *m*
island *s* insula *f*
islander *s* insulanus *m*
islet *s* parva insula *f*
isolate *vt* sejungĕre, secernĕre
issue *s* (*result*) event·us -ūs, exit·us -ūs *m*; (*question*) res *f*; (*offspring*) proles *f*; (*of book*) editio *f*; (*of money*) emissio *f*
issue *vt* (*to distribute*) distribuĕre; (*orders, etc.*) edĕre, proponĕre, promulgare; (*money*) erogare; (*book*) edĕre; *vi* emanare, egredi; (*to turn out, result*) evenire, evadĕre
isthmus *s* isthmus *m*
it *pron* id, hoc
itch *s* prurigo *f*, prurit·us -ūs *m*; (*disease*) scabies *f*
itch *vi* prurire; (*fig*) gestire
item *s* res *f*
itinerant *adj* circumforaneus, vagus
itinerary *s* itinerarium *n*
its *pron* ejus; **— own** suus
itself *pron* (*refl*) se, sese; (*intensive*) ipsum
ivory *s* ebur *n*
ivory *adj* eburneus
ivy *s* hedera *f*

J

jabber *vi* blaterare
jackass *s* asinus *m*; (*fig*) stultus *m*
jacket *s* tunica *f*
jaded *adj* defessus
jagged *adj* serratus; (*of rocks*) praeruptus
jail *s* carcer *m*
jailer *s* carcerarius *m*
jam *s* baccarum conditura *f*
jam *vt* frequentare, stipare; (*to obstruct*) impedire, obstruĕre
jamb *s* postis *m*
jangle *vi* crepitare
January *s* (mensis) Januarius *m*

jar *s* olla, amphora *f*, urceus, cadus *m*
jar *vt* vibrare; offenděre; *vi* discrepare
jargon *s* confusae voces *f pl*
jarring *adj* dissonus, discors
jaundice *s* morbus regius *m*
jaundiced *adj* ictericus, felle suffusus; (*fig*) lividus, morosus
jaunt *s* excursio *f*; **to take a —** excurrěre
javelin *s* pilum, jaculum *n*; **to hurl a —** jaculari
jaw *s* mala, maxilla *f*; **—s** (*fig*) fauces *f pl*
jawbone *s* maxilla *f*
jay *s* graculus *m*
jealous *adj* invidus, lividus; **to be — of** invidēre (*with dat*)
jealousy *s* invidia, aemulatio *f*
jeer *s* irrisio *f*, irris·us -ūs *m*
jeer *vt* deridēre, exploděre; *vi* **to — at** irridēre, alluděre
jelly *s* cylon, quilon *n*
jellyfish *s* pulmo, halipleumon *m*
jeopardize *vt* periclitari, in periculum adducěre
jeopardy *s* periculum *n*
jerk *s* verber, ict·us -ūs, impet·us -ūs *m*
jerk *vt* calcitrare, icěre
jerky *adj* (*of style*) salebrosus
jest *s* jocus *m*; **in —** joco, jocose
jest *vi* jocari, luděre
jester *s* joculator *m*; (*buffoon*) scurra *m*
jestingly *adv* per jocum
Jesus *s* Jesus *m*
jet *s* scatebra *f*
jetty *s* moles *f*
Jew *s* Judaeus *m*
jewel *s* gemma *f*
jeweled *adj* gemmeus, gemmifer
jeweler *s* gemmarius *m*
jewelry *s* gemmae *f pl*
Jewish *adj* Judaicus
jig *s* tripudium *n*
jilt *vt* repudiare
jingle *vi* tinnire
jingle *s* tinnit·us -ūs *m*
job *s* negotiolum, opus *n*
jockey *s* agaso *m*
jocose *adj* jocosus; **—ly** jocose
jocular *adj* jocularis, facetus
jog *vi* **to — along** lente progredi
join *vt* (*to connect*) jungěre, conjungěre; (*to come into the company of*) se jungěre (*with dat*), se jungěre cum (*with abl*); *vi* conjungi, adjungi, cohaerēre; **to — in** particeps esse (*with genit*), interesse (*with dat*); **to — together** inter se conjungi
joint *adj* communis; **—ly** una, conjunctim, communiter
joint *s* (*of body*) articulus *m*, commissura *f*; (*of plant*) geniculum *n*; (*of any structure*) compages *f*
jointed *adj* geniculatus
joist *s* tignum *n*
joke *s* jocus *m*
joke *vi* jocari, luděre
joker *s* joculator *m*
joking *s* jocus *m*; **all — aside** joco remoto; **—ly** per jocum
jolly *adj* hilaris, festivus
jolt *vt* jactare, concutěre; (*fig*) percellěre; *vi* jactari
jolting *s* jactatio *f*
jostle *vt* pulsare, agitare, fodicare
jot *s* hilum *n*; **not a —** minime; **to care not a —** non flocci facěre
jot *vt* **to — down** notare, subscriběre
journal *s* ephemeris *f*, acta diurna *n pl*
journey *s* iter *n*
journey *vi* iter facěre; **to — abroad** peregrinari
journeyman *s* opifex *m*
Jove *s* Jupiter *m*
jovial *adj* hilaris
jowl *s* bucca *f*
joy *s* gaudium *n*, laetitia *f*
joyful *adj* laetus; **—ly** laete, libenter
joyless *adj* illaetabilis
joyous *adj* hilaris, festivus
jubilant *adj* laetus, gaudio exsultans, gaudio triumphans
jubilation *s* exsultatio *f*
jubilee *s* dies anniversarius *m*, solemne *n*
Judaic *adj* Judaicus
Judaism *s* Judaismus *m*
judge *s* judex, quaesitor, arbiter *m*
judge *vt* judicare; (*to think*) existimare, censēre; (*to value*) aestimare; (*to decide between*) dijudicare
judgment *s* judicium, arbitrium *n*; (*opinion*) sententia *f*, judicium *n*; **to pass — on** statuěre de (*with abl*); **to pronounce —** jus dicěre
judgment seat *s* tribunal *n*
judicial *adj* judicialis, judicarius; **—ly** jure, lege
judicious *adj* sapiens, sagax, prudens; **—ly** sapienter, sagaciter, prudenter
jug *s* urceus *m*
juggle *vi* praestigias agěre
juggler *s* praestigiator *m*
juice *s* sucus, liquor *m*
juicy *adj* sucidus
July *s* (mensis) Quintilis *or* Julius *m*
jumble *s* congeries, confusio *f*
jumble *vt* confunděre, permiscēre
jump *s* salt·us -ūs *m*
jump *vt* transilire; *vi* salire; **to — at** (*opportunity*) captare; **to — for joy** exsultare
junction *s* conjunctio *f*
juncture *s* tempus *n*; **at this —** hic
June *s* (mensis) Junius *m*
jungle *s* salt·us -ūs *m*
junior *adj* junior, minor natu
juniper *s* juniperus *m*
jurisdiction *s* jurisdictio *f*
jurisprudence *s* jurisprudentia *f*
jurist *s* jurisconsultus *m*
juror *s* judex *m*
jury *s* judices *m pl*
just *adj* justus, aequus; (*deserved*) meritus; **—ly** juste; jure, merito
just *adv* (*only*) modo; (*exactly*) prorsus; (*with adv*) demum, denique; **— after** sub (*with acc*); **— as** aeque ac, perinde ac, sic ut, haud secus

ac; — **before** sub (*with acc*); — **now** modo; — **so** ita prorsus
justice *s* justitia, aequitas *f*; (*just treatment*) jus *n*; (*person*) praetor *m*
justifiable *adj* justus, legitimus, excusatus
justifiably *adv* jure
justification *s* purgatio, excusatio *f*
justify *vt* purgare, excusare, approbare
jut *vi* prominēre; **to — out** prominēre, eminēre, procurrĕre
juvenile *adj* juvenilis, puerilis

K

kale *s* crambe *f*
keel *s* carina *f*
keen *adj* acer, sagax; **—ly** acute, acriter; sagaciter
keenness *s* (*of scent*) sagacitas *f*; (*of sight*) acies *f*; (*of pain*) acerbitas *f*; (*enthusiasm*) studium *n*
keep *vt* tenēre, habēre; (*to preserve*) servare; (*to celebrate*) agĕre, celebrare; (*to guard*) custodire; (*to obey*) observare; (*to support*) alĕre; (*animals*) pascĕre; (*to store*) condĕre; **to — apart** distinēre; **to — away** arcēre; **to — back** retinēre, cohibēre; (*to conceal*) celare; **to — company** comitari; **to — from** prohibēre; **to — in** cohibēre, claudĕre; **to — off** arcēre, defendĕre; **to — secret** celare; **to — together** continēre; **to — under** compescĕre, supprimĕre; **to — up** sustinēre; *vi* remanēre, durare; **to — away** abstinēre; **to — up with** subsequi
keep *s* custodia, cura *f*
keeper *s* custos *m*
keeping *s* tutela, custodia, cura *f*; **in — with** pro (*with abl*)
keepsake *s* monumentum, pignus *n*
keg *s* cadus *m*, testa *f*
ken *s* conspect·us -ūs *m*
kennel *s* stabulum *n*
kernel *s* nucleus *m*; (*fig*) medulla *f*
kettle *s* lebes *f*
kettledrum *s* tympanum aeneum *n*
key *s* clavis *f*; (*of a position*) claustra *n pl*
keyhole *s* foramen *n*
kick *vt* calce ferire; *vi* calcitrare
kid *s* haedus *m*
kidnap *vt* surripĕre
kidnapper *s* plagiarius *m*
kidney *s* ren *m*
kill *vt* interficĕre, caedĕre, occidĕre, necare; (*time*) perdĕre
killer *s* interfector, necator *m*
kiln *s* fornax *f*
kin *s* cognati, consanguinei, necessarii *m pl*
kind *adj* amicus, benignus, benevolus; **—ly** benigne, clementer
kind *s* genus *n*; **what — of** qualis
kindhearted *adj* benignus
kindle *vt* incendĕre, accendĕre, inflammare
kindly *adj* benignus
kindness *s* benignitas, benevolentia *f*; (*deed*) beneficium, officium *n*
kindred *adj* consanguineus, cognatus
kindred *s* consanguinitas, cognatio *f*; cognati, propinqui *m pl*
king *s* rex *m*
kingdom *s* regnum *n*
kingfisher *s* alcedo *f*
kingly *adj* regius, regalis
kinsman *s* necessarius, cognatus, propinquus *m*
kinswoman *s* necessaria, cognata, propinqua *f*
kiss *s* osculum, basium *n*
kiss *vt* osculari
kissing *s* osculatio *f*
kitchen *s* culina *f*
kite *s* (*bird*) milvus *m*
kitten *s* catulus felinus *m*
knack *s* sollertia, calliditas *f*
knapsack *s* sarcina *f*
knave *s* nebulo, veterator *m*
knavish *adj* nefarius, improbus; (*mischievous*) malitiosus
knead *vt* subigĕre
knee *s* genu *n*
kneel *vi* genibus niti
knell *s* campana funebris *f*
knife *s* culter *m*; (*for surgery*) scalprum *n*
knight *s* eques *m*
knighthood *s* equestris dignitas *f*
knightly *adj* equester
knit *vt* texĕre; **to — the brow** frontem contrahĕre
knob *s* tuber *n*, nodus *m*; (*of door*) bulla *f*
knock *vt* **to — down** dejicĕre, sternĕre; (*fig*) (*at auction*) addicĕre; **to — in** impellĕre, infigĕre; **to — off** excutĕre, decidĕre; **to — out** excutĕre; *vi* **to — about** (*to ramble*) vagari; **to — at** pulsare
knock *s* pulsatio *f*, puls·us -ūs *m*
knoll *s* tumulus *m*
knot *s* nodus *m*, geniculum *n*; (*of people*) corona *f*
knot *vt* nodare, nectĕre
knotty *adj* nodosus; (*fig*) spinosus
know *vt* scire; (*person*) novisse; **not to —** ignorare, nescire; **to — how to** scire (*with inf*)
knowing *adj* callidus, prudens; **—ly** sciens, de industria, consulto
knowledge *s* scientia, doctrina *f*; (*of something*) cognitio *f*; (*skill*) peritia *f*; (*learning*) eruditio *f*
known *adj* notus; (*common*) tritus; **to become —** enotescĕre; **to make —** divulgare, declarare
knuckle *s* articulus, condylus *m*
kowtow *vi* adulari

L

label *s* titulus *m*
labor *s* labor *m*; (*manual*) opera *f*; (*work done*) opus *n*; **to be in —** laborare utero; **woman in —** puerpera *f*
labor *vi* laborare, eniti; **to — under** laborare (*with abl*)
laboratory *s* officina *f*
labored *adj* affectatus
laborer *s* operarius *m*
labyrinth *s* labyrinthus *m*
labyrinthine *adj* labyrinthicus; (*fig*) inextricabilis
lace *s* opus reticulatum *n*
lace *vt* (*to tie*) nectĕre, astringĕre; (*to beat*) verberare
lacerate *vt* lacerare, laniare
laceration *s* laceratio *f*
lack *s* inopia *f*, defect·us -ūs *m*, defectio *f*
lack *vt* carēre (*with abl*), egēre (*with abl*)
lackey *s* pedisequus, servus a pedibus *m*
laconic *adj* brevis, astrictus; **—ally** breviter, paucis
lad *s* puer, adulescens *m*
ladder *s* scala *f*
ladle *s* ligula, spatha *f*, cochlear *n*
lady *s* domina, matrona *f*
lag *vi* cessare, morari, cunctari
lagoon *s* lacuna *f*, stagnum *n*
lair *s* cubile, latibulum *n*
laity *s* laici *m pl*
lake *s* lac·us -ūs *m*
lamb *s* agnus *m*, agna *f*; (*meat*) agnina *f*
lame *adj* claudus; **to walk —** claudicare; **—ly** (*fig*) inconcinne
lameness *s* clauditas *f*
lament *s* lamentum *n*, lamentatio *f*
lament *vt* lamentari, deplorare; *vi* flēre
lamentable *adj* lamentabilis, miserabilis
lamentably *adv* miserabiliter
lamentation *s* lamentatio *f*
lamp *s* lucerna *f*, lynchnus *m*
lampoon *s* satira *f*, libellus *m*
lampoon *vt* famosis carminibus lacessĕre
lance *s* lancea, hasta *f*
lance *vt* incidĕre
land *s* (*soil*) terra, tellus *f*; (*country*) regio *f*; (*estate*) fundus *m*, praedium *n*
land *vt* in terram exponĕre; *vi* egredi, appellĕre
landing place *s* egress·us -ūs *m*
landlord *s* (*of inn*) caupo *m*; (*of land*) dominus *m*
landmark *s* lapis, terminus *m*
landscape *s* regionis sit·us -ūs *m*
landslide *s* terrae laps·us -ūs *m*
land tax *s* vectigal *n*
lane *s* semita *f*
language *s* lingua *f*; (*style or manner of verbal expression*) oratio *f*, sermo *m*, verba *n pl*
languid *adj* languidus; **—ly** languide
languish *vi* languēre, languescĕre
languishing *adj* languidus, tabescens
languor *s* languor *m*
lanky *adj* prolixus, exilis
lantern *s* la(n)terna *f*
lap *s* sin·us -ūs *m*; (*fig*) gremium *n*; (*in racing*) spatium *n*
lap *vt* lambĕre
lapse *s* laps·us -ūs *m*; (*error*) erratum, peccatum *n*, error *m*
lapse *vi* labi; (*of agreement*) irritus fieri; (*to err*) peccare
larceny *s* furtum *n*
lard *s* laridum, lardum *n*, adeps *m & f*
large *adj* magnus, amplus, grandis; **to a — extent** magna ex parte; **—ly** plerumque
largess *s* donativum *n*, largitio *f*; **to give a —** largiri
lark *s* alauda *f*
larynx *s* guttur *n*
lascivious *adj* lascivus, salax, libidinosus; **—ly** lascive, libidinose
lash *s* verber, flagellum *n*, scutica *f*; (*mark*) vibex *m*
lash *vt* (*to whip*) flagellare; (*to fasten*) alligare; (*fig*) castigare
lashing *s* verberatio *f*
lass *s* puella, virgo *f*
lassitude *s* lassitudo *f*
last *adj* postremus, ultimus; (*in line*) novissimus; (*preceding*) proximus; **at —** demum, tandem; **for the — time** postremo
last *vi* durare, perdurare
lasting *adj* diuturnus, perennis
lastly *adv* denique, postremo
latch *s* obex *m & f*
latch *vt* oppessulare
late *adj* serus, tardus; (*new*) recens; (*deceased*) demortuus; (*said of deceased emperor*) divus
late *adv* sero; **too —** sero, serius
lately *adv* modo, recens, nuper
latent *adj* latens, latitans, occultus
lateral *adj* lateralis
lather *s* spuma *f*
Latin *adj* Latinus; **to speak — Latine** loqui; **to translate into —** Latine reddere; **to understand —** Latine scire
Latinity *s* Latinitas *f*
latitude *s* latitudo *f*; (*liberty*) licentia *f*
latter *adj* posterior; **the —** hic
lattice *s* cancelli *m pl*
laudable *adj* laudabilis
laudably *adv* laudabiliter
laudatory *adj* laudativus, honorificus
laugh *s* ris·us -ūs *m*
laugh *vi* ridēre; **to — at** deridēre; **to — with** arridēre (*with dat*)
laughingstock *s* ludibrium *n*

laughter *s* ris·us -ūs *m*; (*loud*) cachinnus *m*, cachinnatio *f*
launch *vt* deducĕre; (*to hurl*) jaculari, contorquēre; *vi* **to — forth** *or* **out** proficisci
laundress *s* lotrix *f*
laundry *s* lavatorium *n*
laureate *adj* laureatus
laurel *adj* laureus
laurel tree *s* laurus *f*
lava *s* liquefacta massa *f*
lavish *adj* prodigus; **—ly** prodige
lavish *vt* prodigĕre, profundĕre
lavishness *s* prodigalitas, profusio *f*
law *s* lex *f*; (*right*) jus *n*; (*rule*) norma *f*; (*divine*) fas *n*; **to break the —** leges violare; **to pass a —** legem perferre
law-abiding *adj* bene moratus
law court *s* judicium *n*; (*building*) basilica *f*
lawful *adj* legitimus, licitus, fas; **—ly** legitime, lege
lawless *adj* exlex, illegitimus; **—ly** illegitime, licenter
lawlessness *s* licentia *f*
lawn *s* pratulum *n*
lawsuit *s* lis, causa *f*
lawyer *s* jurisconsultus, causidicus *m*
lax *adj* remissus; (*fig*) neglegens; **—ly** remisse; neglegens
laxity *s* remissio *f*
lay *vt* ponĕre; (*eggs*) parĕre; (*foundations*) jacĕre; (*hands*) injicĕre; (*plans*) capĕre, inire; **to — an ambush** insidiari; **to — aside** ponĕre, amovēre; **to — before** proponĕre; **to — claim to** arrogare, vindicare; **to — down** (*office*) resignare; (*rules*) statuĕre; **to — down arms** ab armis discedĕre; **to — hold of** prehendĕre, arripĕre; **to — open** patefacĕre; **to — out** (*money*) expendĕre; (*plans*) designare; **to — up** condĕre, reponĕre; **to — waste** vastare
lay *s* cantilena *f*
layer *s* (*stratum*) corium *n*; (*of a plant*) propago *f*
lazily *adv* ignave, pigre
laziness *s* segnities, pigritia *f*
lazy *adv* ignavus, piger, iners
lead *s* plumbum *n*
lead *vt* ducĕre; (*life*) agĕre; **to — about** circumducĕre; **to — away** abducĕre; **to — off** divertĕre; **to — on** conducĕre; *vi* **to — up to** tendĕre ad (*with acc*)
leaden *adj* plumbeus
leader *s* dux, ductor *m*; (*fig*) auctor *m*
leadership *s* duct·us -ūs *m*
leading *adj* princeps, primus, praecipuus
leaf *s* folium *n*; (*of vine*) pampinus *m*; (*of paper*) pagina, scheda *f*; (*of metal*) bractea *f*
leafless *adj* fronde nudatus
leafy *adj* frondosus, frondeus
league *s* foedus *n*, societas *f*
leak *s* rima *f*, hiat·us -ūs *m*
leak *vi* perfluĕre, rimas agĕre
leaky *adj* rimosus
lean *adj* macer, macilentus
lean *vt* inclinare; *vi* inclinare, niti; **to — back** se reclinare; **to — on** inniti in (*with abl*), incumbĕre (*with dat*)
leap *s* salt·us -ūs *m*
leap *vi* salire; **to — for joy** exsultare
leap year *s* bisextilis annus *m*
learn *vt* discĕre, cognoscĕre; (*news*) accipĕre, audire; **to — by heart** ediscĕre
learned *adj* eruditus, doctus; **—ly** docte
learning *s* (*act*) discĕre; (*knowledge*) eruditio *f*
lease *s* conductio, locatio *f*
lease *vt* conducĕre; **to — out** locare
leash *s* lorum *n*
least *adj* minimus
least *adv* minime; **at —** saltem; **not in the —** ne minimum quidem
leather *s* corium *n*; (*tanned*) aluta *f*
leather *adj* scorteus
leathery *adj* lentus
leave *vt* relinquĕre, deserĕre, destituĕre; (*to entrust*) mandare, tradĕre; (*legacy*) legare; **to — behind** relinquĕre; **to — out** omittĕre, praetermittĕre; *vi* (*to depart*) discedĕre, proficisci, abire; **to — off** desinĕre, desistĕre
leave *s* permissio *f*; **— of absence** commeat·us -ūs *m*; **to ask —** veniam petĕre; **to obtain —** impetrare; **to take — of** valēre jubēre; **with your —** pace tua
leaven *s* fermentum *n*
leaven *vt* fermentare
lecherous *adj* libidinosus, salax
lecture *s* lectio, praelectio, acroasis *f*
lecture *vi* (*to reprove*) objurgare; *vi* praelegĕre
lecturer *s* lector, praelector *m*
ledge *s* projectura *f*, limen, dorsum *n*
ledger *s* codex (accepti et expensi) *m*
leech *s* sanguisuga, hirudo *f*
leer *vi* limis oculis spectare
leering *adj* limus, lascivus
left *adj* laevus, sinister; **on the —** a sinistra; **to the —** ad sinistram, sinistrorsum
leftover *adj* reliquus
leftovers *s* reliquiae *f pl*
leg *s* crus *n*; (*of table, etc.*) pes *m*
legacy *s* legatum *n*
legal *adj* legalis, legitimus; judicialis; **—ly** legitime, lege
legalize *vt* sancire
legate *s* legatus *m*
legation *s* legatio *f*
legend *s* fabula *f*; (*inscription*) titulus *m*
legendary *adj* commenticius, fabulosus
legging *s* ocrea *f*
legible *adj* clarus
legion *s* legio *f*
legislate *vi* leges facĕre

legislation *s* leges *f pl*
legislator *s* legum lator *m*
legitimate *adj* legitimus; **—ly** legitime
leisure *s* otium *n*; **at —** otiosus, vacuus
leisure *adj* otiosus, vacuus; **—ly** otiose
leisurely *adj* lentus
lemon *s* pomum citreum *n*
lemonade *s* aqua limonata *f*
lend *vt* commodare; **to — money** pecuniam mutuam dare; (*at interest*) pecuniam faenerare *or* faenerari; **to — one's ear** aures praebēre
length *s* longitudo *f*; (*of time*) longinquitas, diuturnitas *f*; **at —** tandem
lengthen *vt* extendĕre, protrahĕre, producĕre
lengthwise *adv* in longitudinem
lengthy *adj* longus, prolixus
leniency *s* lenitas, clementia, mansuetudo *f*
lenient *adj* lenis, mitis, clemens; **—ly** leniter, clementer
lentil *s* lens *f*
leopard *s* leopardus, pardus *m*
leper *s* leprosus *m*
leprosy *s* leprae *f pl*
less *adj* minor
less *adv* minus
lessee *s* conductor *m*
lessen *vt* minuĕre; *vi* decrescĕre, minui
lesson *s* documentum *n*; **to give —s in** docēre
lessor *s* locator *m*
lest *conj* ne
let *vt* (*to allow*) sinĕre, pati, permittĕre; (*to lease*) locare; **to — alone** omittĕre; **to — down** (*to disappoint*) deesse (*with dat*), destituĕre; **to — fall** a manibus mittĕre; **to — fly** emittĕre, contorquēre; **to — go** (di)mittĕre; **to — in** admittĕre; **to — off** absolvĕre; **to — out** emittĕre; **to — pass** omittĕre; **to — slip** omittĕre
lethargic *adj* lethargicus
lethargy *s* lethargus *m*; (*fig*) veternus *m*
letter *s* (*of alphabet*) littera *f*; (*epistle*) litterae *f pl*, epistula *f*; **by —** per litteras; **to the —** ad verbum
letter carrier *s* tabellarius *m*
lettered *adj* litteratus
lettering *s* titulus *m*
lettuce *s* lactuca *f*
level *adj* planus, aequus
level *s* planities *f*; (*tool*) libra, libella *f*
level *vt* aequare, adaequare; (*to the ground*) solo aequare, sternĕre
lever *s* vectis *m*
levity *s* levitas *f*
levy *s* delect·us -ūs *m*
levy *vt* (*troops*) conscribĕre; (*tax*) exigĕre
lewd *adj* impudicus, incestus
lewdness *s* impudicitia *f*
liable *adj* obnoxius
liar *s* mendax *m & f*
libation *s* libatio *f*; **to pour a —** libare
libel *s* calumnia *f*
libel *vt* calumniari
libelous *adj* famosus, probrosus
liberal *adj* liberalis, munificus; (*fig*) ingenuus; **—ly** liberaliter
liberality *s* liberalitas, munificentia *f*
liberate *vt* liberare; (*slave*) manumittĕre
liberation *s* liberatio *f*
liberator *s* liberator *m*
libertine *s* homo dissolutus *m*
liberty *s* libertas *f*; licentia *f*; **at —** liber
librarian *s* librarius *m*
library *s* bibliotheca *f*
license *s* (*permission*) copia, potestas *f*; (*freedom*) licentia *f*
license *vt* potestatem dare (*with dat*)
licentious *adj* dissolutus, impudicus; **—ly** dissolute, impudice
lick *vt* lambĕre; (*daintily*) liqurrire
lictor *s* lictor *m*
lid *s* operculum, operimentum *n*
lie *s* mendacium *n*; **to give the — to** redarguĕre; **to tell a —** mentiri
lie *vi* (*to tell a lie or lies*) mentiri; (*to be lying down*) jacēre, cubare; (*to be situated*) situs esse; **to — down** jacēre; **to — in wait** insidiari; **to — on** *or* **upon** incubare (*with dat*), incumbĕre (*with dat*)
lieu *s* **in — of** loco (*with genit*), pro (*with abl*)
lieutenant *s* legatus, praefectus *m*
life *s* vita, anima *f*; (*fig*) vigor *m*, alacritas *f*
lifeblood *s* sanguis *m*
life history *s* vita *f*
lifeless *adj* inanimus, exanimis; (*fig*) exsanguis, frigidus; **—ly** (*fig*) frigide
lifetime *s* aetas *f*
lift *vt* tollĕre, attollĕre, sublevare; **to — up** attollĕre, efferre
ligament *s* ligamentum, ligamen *n*
ligature *s* ligatura *f*
light *s* lux *f*, lumen *n*; (*lamp*) lucerna *f*; **to bring to —** in lucem proferre; **to throw — on** lumen adhibēre (*with dat*)
light *adj* (*bright*) lucidus, fulgens; (*in weight*) levis; (*of colors*) candidus, dilutus; (*easy*) facilis; (*nimble*) agilis; **—ly** leviter
light *vt* accendĕre, incendĕre; (*to illuminate*) illuminare; *vi* flammam concipĕre; **to — on** *or* **upon** incidĕre (*with dat*), offendĕre; **to — up** (*fig*) hilaris fieri
lighten *vt* (*to illumine*) illustrare; (*weight*) allevare, exonerare; *vi* (*in sky*) fulgurare
lighthouse *s* pharus *f*
lightness *s* levitas, agilitas *f*
lightning *s* fulmen, fulgur *n*; **struck by —** fulmine ictus, de caelo tactus

like *adj* similis (*with dat*); (*equal*) par (*with dat*), aequus (*with dat*)
like *prep* instar (*with genit*); tamquam, ut, velut
like *vt* amare, diligĕre; **I — this** hoc mihi placet; **I — to do this** me juvat hoc facĕre
likelihood *s* verisimilitudo *f*
likely *adj* verisimilis, probabilis
likely *adv* probabiliter
liken *vt* comparare
likeness *s* similitudo *f*; (*portrait*) imago, effigies *f*
likewise *adv* pariter, similiter, item
liking *s* amor *m*; (*fancy*) libido *f*
lilac *s* syringa vulgaris *f*
lily *s* lilium *n*
lily of the valley *s* convallaria majalis *f*
limb *s* art·us -ūs *m*, membrum *n*
limber *adj* flexilis
lime *s* calx *f*
limestone *s* calx *f*
lime tree *s* tilia *f*
limit *s* finis, terminus, modus *m*
limit *vt* terminare, finire, definire; (*to restrict*) circumscribĕre
limitation *s* determinatio *f*; (*exception*) exceptio *f*
limp *s* claudicatio *f*
limp *vi* claudicare
limp *adj* flaccidus, languidus
limpid *adj* limpidus
linden tree *s* tilia *f*
line *s* (*drawn*) linea *f*; (*row*) series *f*, ordo *m*; (*lineage*) stirps *f*, genus *n*; (*mil*) acies *f*; (*of poetry*) vers·us -ūs *m*; (*cord*) funis *m*
line *vt* (*streets*) saepire
lineage *s* stirps *f*, genus *n*
lineal *adj* linearis; **—ly** rectā lineā
lineament *s* lineamentum *n*
linear *adj* linearis
linen *adj* linteus, lineus
linen *s* linteum, linum *n*
linger *vi* morari, cunctari, cessare
lingering *adj* cunctabundus, tardus; **—ly** cunctanter
lingering *s* cunctatio *f*
linguist *s* linguarum peritus *m*
liniment *s* unguentum *n*, linit·us -ūs *m*
link *s* (*of chain*) anulus *m*; (*bond*) vinculum *n*, nex·us -ūs *m*
link *vt* connectĕre, conjungĕre
linseed *s* lini semen *n*
lint *s* linamentum *n*
lintel *s* limen superum *n*
lion *s* leo *m*
lioness *s* lea, leaena *f*
lip *s* labrum *n*; (*edge*) ora *f*
liquefy *vt* liquefacĕre
liquid *adj* liquidus
liquid *s* liquidum *n*, liquor *m*; **to become —** liquescĕre
liquidate *vt* solvĕre, persolvĕre
liquor *s* liquor *m*
lisp *vi* balbutire
lisping *adj* blaesus
list *s* index *m*, tabula *f*; (*of ship*) inclinatio *f*
list *vt* enumerare; *vi* inclinare
listen *vi* auscultare, audire; **to — to** auscultare, audire
listless *adj* remissus, languidus; **—ly** languide
litany *s* litania *f*
literal *adj* litteralis; **—ly** ad litteram, ad verbum
literary *adj* (*person*) litteratus; **— style** scribendi genus *n*
literature *s* litterae *f pl*
litigant *s* litigator *m*
litigate *vi* litigare
litigation *s* lis *f*
litter *s* (*vehicle*) lectica *f*; (*of straw, etc.*) stramentum *n*; (*brood*) fet·us -ūs, part·us -ūs *m*
litter *vt* sternĕre
little *adj* parvus, exiguus
little *adv* parum, paulum; **a —** paulum, aliquantulum; **— by —** paulatim
little *s* paulum, aliquantulum *n*
live *vi* vivĕre, vitam agĕre; (*to reside*) habitare; **to — on** vesci (*with abl*)
live *adj* vivus; (*of colors*) vegetus
livelihood *s* vict·us -ūs *m*
lively *adj* vivus, vividus, alacer; (*of colors*) vegetus
liver *s* jecur *n*
livid *adj* lividus; **to be —** livēre
living *adj* vivus, vivens
living *s* (*livelihood, food*) vict·us -ūs *m*
lizard *s* lacerta *f*
load *s* onus *n*
load *vt* onerare
loaf *s* panis *m*
loaf *vi* grassari
loafer *s* grassator *m*
loam *s* lutum *n*
loan *s* mutuum *n*, pecunia mutua *f*
loathe *vt* fastidire
loathing *s* fastidium *n*
loathsome *adj* foedus, taeter
lobby *s* vestibulum *n*
lobe *s* lobus *m*
lobster *s* astacus *m*
local *adj* indigena; loci (*genit*), regionis (*genit*)
locality *s* locus *m*, natura loci *f*
lock *s* (*of hair*) cinnus, floccus *m*; (*of door*) sera *f*
lock *vt* obserare, oppessulare; **to — in** includĕre; **to — out** exludĕre; **to — up** concludĕre
locker *s* loculamentum, armarium *n*
lockjaw *s* tetanus *m*
locust *s* locusta *f*
lodge *s* casa *f*
lodge *vt* (*complaint*) deferre; *vi* (*to stay*) deversari; (*to stick*) inhaerēre
lodger *s* inquilinus *m*
lodging *s* hospitium, deversorium *n*
loft *s* tabulatum, cenaculum *n*
lofty *adj* (ex)celsus, sublimis; (*fig*) sublimis, superbus
log *s* tignum *n*, stipes *m*
logic *s* dialectica *n pl*
logical *adj* logicus, dialecticus; **—ly** dialectice, ex ratione
loin *s* lumbus *m*
loiter *vi* cessare, cunctari, grassari
loiterer *s* cessator, grassator *m*

loll *vi* recumbĕre
lone *adj* solus
loneliness *s* solitudo *f*
lonely *adj* solitarius; desolatus
long *adj* longus; (*of time*) diuturnus; (*lengthened*) productus
long *adv* diu; **— after** multo post; **— ago** jamdudum, jampridem; **— before** multo ante
long *vi* avēre; **to — for** desiderare
longevity *s* longaevitas *f*
longing *s* desiderium *n*
longing *adj* avidus; **—ly** avide
longitude *s* longitudo *f*
long-lived *adj* vivax
long-suffering *adj* patiens
long-winded *adj* longus
look *s* aspect·us -ūs, vult·us -ūs *m*; (*appearance*) facies, species *f*
look *vi* vidēre; (*to seem*) vidēri; **to — about** circumspicĕre; **to — after** curare; **to — around** circumspicĕre, respicĕre; **to — at** intuēri, aspicĕre; **to — back** respicĕre; **to — for** quaerĕre; **to — forward to** exspectare; **to — into** inspicĕre, introspicĕre; (*to examine*) perscrutari; **to — on** intuēri; **to — out** prospicĕre; **to — out for** quaerĕre; **to — towards** spectare; **to — up** suspicĕre; **to — upon** habēre, aestimare
loom *s* tela *f*
loom *vi* in conspectum prodire
loop *s* sin·us -ūs *m*
loophole *s* fenestra *f*; (*fig*) effugium *n*
loose *adj* laxus, solutus, remissus; (*morally*) dissolutus; **—ly** laxe; dissolute
loosen *vt* solvĕre, laxare; *vi* solvi
loquacious *adj* loquax, garrulus
lord *s* dominus *m*
Lord *s* Dominus *m*
lord *vi* **to — it over** dominari in (*with acc*)
lordly *adj* imperiosus
lordship *s* dominatio *f*, imperium *n*
lore *s* doctrina *f*
lose *vt* amittĕre, perdĕre; **to — one's way** aberrare
loss *s* (*act*) amissio *f*; damnum, detrimentum *n*; (*mil*) repulsa *f*
lost *adj* perditus; **to be —** perire
lot *s* pars, portio, sors *f*; **casting of —s** sortitio *f*, sortit·us -ūs *m*; **to draw —s for** sortiri
lotion *s* lotio *f*
lottery *s* sortitio *f*
loud *adj* magnus; **—ly** magnā voce
lounge *vi* cessare, otiari
lounge s lectulus *m*
louse *s* pediculus *m*
lousy *adj* pediculosus; (*fig*) vilis
lout *s* rusticus *m*
loutish *adj* agrestis, rusticus
love *s* amor *m*; **to fall in —** amare, adamare
love *vt* amare, diligĕre
love affair *s* amores *m pl*
lovely *adj* venustus, amabilis
love potion *s* philtrum *n*
lover *s* amator, amans *m*
lovesick *adj* amore aeger
loving *adj* amans; **—ly** amanter
low *adj* humilis; (*of price*) vilis; (*of birth*) obscurus; (*of voice*) summissus; (*vile*) turpis; (*downcast*) abjectus
low *adv* humiliter; summissā voce
low *vi* mugire
lowborn *adj* obscurus, degener
lower *vt* demittĕre, deprimĕre; (*price*) imminuĕre; *vi* (*of sky*) obscurari
lower *adj* inferior; **of the — world** infernus; **the — world** inferi *m pl*
lowermost *adj* infimus
lowing *s* mugit·us -ūs *m*
lowlands *s* loca plana, campestria *n pl*, campi *m pl*
lowly *adj* humilis, obscurus
loyal *adj* fidelis, fidus; **—ly** fideliter
loyalty *s* fidelitas, fides *f*
lubricate *vt* unguĕre
lucid *adj* lucidus, clarus, perspicuus; (*transparent*) pellucidus
Lucifer *s* Lucifer *m*
luck *s* fortuna *f*; **bad —** fortuna *f*, infortunium *n*; **good —** fortuna *f*, felicitas *f*
luckily *adv* feliciter, fauste
luckless *adj* infelix
lucky *adj* felix, faustus
lucrative *adj* quaestuosus
lucre *s* lucrum *n*, quaest·us -ūs *m*
ludicrous *adj* ridiculus; **—ly** ridicule
luggage *s* sarcinae *f pl*, impedimenta *n pl*
lukewarm *adj* tepidus; (*fig*) segnis, frigidus; **—ly** (*fig*) segniter
lull *s* quies, intermissio *f*
lull *vt* sopire; (*to calm, as a storm*) sedare; (*fig*) demulcēre
lumber *s* scruta *n pl*
luminary *s* lumen *n*
luminous *adj* lucidus, illustris; (*fig*) dilucidus
lump *s* glaeba, massa, congeries *f*; (*on body*) tuber *n*
lump *vt* **to — together** coacervare
lumpy *adj* glaebosus, crassus
lunacy *s* alienatio mentis *f*
lunar *adj* lunaris
lunatic *s* insanus *m*
lunch *s* merenda *f*, prandium *n*
lunch *vi* prandēre
luncheon *s* prandium *n*
lung *s* pulmo *m*
lunge *s* ict·us -ūs *m*, plaga *f*
lunge *vi* prosilire
lurch *s* impedimentum *n*; **to leave in the —** deserĕre, destituĕre
lurch *vi* titubare
lure *s* illecebra, esca *f*
lure *vt* illicĕre, inescare
lurk *vi* latēre, latitare
luscious *adj* suavis, praedulcis
lush *adj* luxuriosus
lust *s* libido *f*
lust *vi* concupiscĕre
luster *s* splendor, nitor *m*
lustful *adj* libidinosus, salax; **—ly** libidinose, lascive

lustily *adv* valide, strenue
lusty *adj* validus, robustus
lute *s* cithara *f*, fides *f pl*
luxuriance *s* luxuries, ubertas *f*
luxuriant *adj* luxuriosus; (*fig*) luxurians
luxuriate *vi* luxuriare, luxuriari
luxurious *adj* sumptuosus, lautus; **—ly** sumptuose, laute
luxury *s* luxuria *f*, lux·us -ūs *m*
lye *s* lixivia *f*
lying *adj* mendax, fallax
lying *s* mendacium *n*
lymph *s* lympha *f*
lynx *s* lynx *m* & *f*
lyre *s* lyra *f*, fides *f pl*, barbitos *m*
lyric *adj* lyricus
lyric *s* carmen *n*

M

macaroni *s* collyra *f*
mace *s* fasces *m pl*
mace bearer *s* lictor *m*
macerate *vt* macerare
machination *s* dolus *m*
machine *s* machina *f*
machinery *s* machinamentum *n*, machinatio *f*
mackerel *s* scomber *m*
mad *adj* insanus, vesanus, demens, furiosus; **to be —** furĕre, insanire; **—ly** insane, dementer
madam *s* domina *f*
madden *vt* mentem alienare (*with dat*); (*fig*) furiare
maddening *adj* furiosus
madman *s* homo furiosus *m*, demens *m*
madness *s* insania, dementia *f*, furor *m*
magazine *s* (*journal*) ephemeris *f*; (*storehouse*) horreum, armamentarium *n*
maggot *s* vermis, vermiculus *m*
magic *adj* magicus
magic *s* ars magica *f*
magically *adv* velut magica quadam arte
magician *s* magus *m*
magisterial *adj* ad magistratum pertinens
magistracy *s* magistrat·us -ūs *m*
magistrate *s* magistrat·us -ūs *m*
magnanimity *s* magnanimitas *f*
magnanimous *adj* magnanimus
magnet *s* magnes *m*
magnetic *adj* magneticus
magnetism *s* vis magnetica *f*
magnetize *vt* magnetica vi afficĕre
magnificence *s* magnificentia *f*, splendor *m*
magnificent *adj* magnificus, splendidus; **—ly** magnifice, splendide
magnify *vt* amplificare, exaggerare
magnitude *s* magnitudo *f*
maid *s* ancilla *f*
maiden *s* virgo, puella *f*
maidenhood *s* virginitas *f*
maidenly *adj* puellaris, virginalis
mail *s* (*letters*) epistulae *f pl*; (*armor*) lorica *f*
maim *vt* mutilare
maimed *adj* mancus
main *adj* primus, praecipuus, princeps; **— point** caput *n*; **—ly** praecipue, maxime
main *s* (*sea*) altum *n*, pelagus *m*
mainland *s* continens *f*
maintain *vt* (*to keep*) tenēre; (*to keep alive*) nutrire, alĕre, sustentare; (*to defend*) tuēri, sustinēre; (*to argue*) affirmare
maintenance *s* (*support*) defensio, sustentatio *f*; (*means of living*) vict·us -ūs *m*, alimentum *n*
majestic *adj* augustus, imperatorius; **—ally** auguste
majesty *s* majestas, dignitas *f*
major *adj* major
major *s* (*mil*) tribunus militum *m*; (*in logic*) major praemissa *f*
majority *s* major pars *f*
make *vt* facĕre; (*to form*) fingĕre; (*to render*) reddere, facĕre; (*to appoint*) creare, facĕre, instituĕre; **to — amends** corrigĕre; **to — good** resarcire, reparare; **to — haste** accelerare, festinare; **to — much of** magni facĕre; **to — over** transferre; **to — ready** praeparare; **to — up** (*story*) fingĕre; (*to compensate*) resarcire; (*one's mind*) decernĕre; **to — way** cedĕre; *vi* **to — away with** tollĕre, amovēre; **to — for** petĕre
make *s* forma, figura, formatio *f*
maker *s* fabricator *m*; auctor *m*
maladministration *s* administratio mala *f*
malady *s* morbus *m*
male *adj* mas, masculinus
male *s* mas, masculus *m*
malediction *s* dirae *f pl*, exsecratio *f*
malefactor *s* homo maleficus, reus *m*
malevolence *s* malevolentia *f*
malevolent *adj* malevolus
malice *s* malevolentia, invidia *f*
malicious *adj* malevolus, invidiosus, malignus; **—ly** malevolo animo
malign *vt* obtrectare, vexare
malign *adj* malignus, invidiosus
malignant *adj* malevolus
malleable *adj* ductilis
mallet *s* malleus *m*
malpractice *s* delicta *n pl*
maltreat *vt* vexare, mulcare
man *s* (*human being*) homo *m*; (*male human being*) vir *m*
man *vt* (*ship*) complēre; (*walls*) praesidio firmare
manacle *s* manica *f*, compes *m*
manacle *vt* manicas injicĕre (*with dat*)
manage *vt* administrare, curare

manageable *adj* tractabilis
management *s* administratio, cura *f*
manager *s* curator *m*; (*steward*) procurator *m*; (*of estate*) villicus *m*
mandate *s* mandatum *n*
mandrake *s* mandragora *f*
mane *s* juba *f*
maneuver *s* (*mil*) decurs·us -ūs *m*, decursio *f*; (*trick*) dolus *m*, artificium *n*
maneuver *vi* (*mil*) decurrĕre; (*fig*) machinari
mange *s* scabies *f*
manger *s* praesepe *n*
mangle *vt* lacerare, laniare
mangy *adj* scaber
manhood *s* pubertas *f*; virilitas, fortitudo *f*
mania *s* insania *f*
maniac *s* furiosus *m*
manifest *adj* manifestus, apertus; **—ly** manifeste, aperte
manifest *vt* declarare, ostendĕre, aperire
manifestation *s* patefactio *f*
manifesto *s* edictum *n*
manifold *adj* multiplex, varius
manipulate *vt* tractare
manipulation *s* tractatio *f*
mankind *s* genus humanum *n*
manliness *s* virtus, fortitudo *f*
manly *adj* virilis
manner *s* modus *m*, ratio *f*; (*custom*) consuetudo *f*, mos *m*; **after the — of** ritu (*with genit*), more (*with genit*); **bad —s** rusticitas *f*; **good —s** urbanitas *f*
mannerism *s* affectatio *f*
mannerly *adj* urbanus
mannikin *s* homunculus, homuncio *m*
man-of-war *s* navis longa *f*
manor *s* praedium *n*, fundus *m*
man servant *s* servus, famulus *m*
mansion *s* dom·us -ūs, sedes *f*
manslaughter *s* homicidium *n*
mantle *s* penula, palla *f*
mantle *vt* celare, tegĕre, dissimulare
manual *adj* manualis
manual *s* enchiridion *n*
manufacture *s* fabrica *f*
manufacture *vt* fabricari, fabrefacĕre
manufacturer *s* fabricator, opifex *m*
manure *s* stercus *n*, fimus *m*
manure *vt* stercorare
manuscript *s* codex, liber *m*
many *adj* multi, plerique, complures; **a good —** nonnulli; **as — . . . as** quot . . . tot; **how —** quot; **— ways** multifariam; **so —** tot
many-colored *adj* multicolor
map *s* tabula geographica *f*
map *vt* **to — out** designare, describĕre
maple *adj* acernus
maple tree *s* acer *n*
mar *vt* foedare, vitiare, corrumpĕre
marauder *s* praedator, latro *m*
marauding *s* praedatio *f*, latrocinium *n*
marble *adj* marmoreus
marble *s* marmor *n*
March *s* (mensis) Martius *m*
march *s* iter *n*
march *vt* ducĕre; *vi* iter facĕre, incedĕre, gradi; **to — on** signa proferre; **to — on a town** oppidum aggredi
mare *s* equa *f*
margin *s* margo *m & f*
marginal *adj* margini ascriptus
marigold *s* caltha *f*
marine *adj* marinus
marine *s* miles classicus, miles classiarius *m*
mariner *s* nauta *m*
maritime *adj* maritimus
mark *s* nota *f*, signum *n*; (*brand*) stigma *n*; (*impression*) vestigium *n*; (*target*) scopus *m*; (*of wound*) cicatrix *f*; (*fig*) indicium *n*
mark *vt* notare, signare; (*to observe*) animadvertĕre; (*with pencil, etc.*) designare; **to — out** metari
marker *s* index *m*
market *s* macellum *n*, mercat·us -ūs *m*
marketable *adj* venalis
market day *s* nundinae *f pl*
marketing *s* emptio *f*
market place *s* forum *n*
market town *s* emporium *n*
marksman *s* jaculandi peritus *m*
marmalade *s* quilon ex aurantiis confectum *n*
marquee *s* tabernaculum *n*
marriage *s* matrimonium *n*, nuptiae *f pl*
marriageable *adj* nubilis
marriage contract *s* pactio nuptialis *f*
married *adj* (*of woman*) nupta; (*of man*) maritus
marrow *s* medulla *f*
marry *vt* (*said of man*) in matrimonium ducĕre, uxorem ducĕre (*with acc*); (*said of woman*) nubĕre (*with dat*); **to get married** matrimonio *or* nuptiis conjungi
marsh *s* palus *f*
marshal *s* dux, imperator *m*
marshal *vt* disponĕre
marshy *adj* paluster
mart *s* forum, emporium *n*
martial *adj* bellicosus, ferox, militaris
martyr *s* martyr *m & f*
martyrdom *s* martyrium *n*
marvel *s* res mira *f*, mirum *n*
marvel *vi* **to — at** mirari, admirari
marvelous *adj* mirus, mirabilis; **—ly** mire
masculine *adj* masculus, virilis; (*gram*) masculinus
mash *s* mixtura *f*; (*for cattle*) farrago *f*
mash *vt* commiscēre; (*to bruise*) contundĕre
mask *s* persona, larva *f*; (*fig*) praetext·us -ūs *m*
mask *vt* (*fig*) dissimulare
mason *s* lapicida, caementarius *m*
masonry *s* opus caementicium *n*

mass *s* moles *f*; (*of people*) turba *f*; (*eccl*) missa *f*; **the —es** vulgus *n*
mass *vt* congerĕre, coacervare
massacre *s* caedes, trucidatio *f*
massacre *vt* trucidare
massive *adj* solidus, ingens
mast *s* (*of ship*) malus *m*; (*for cattle*) glans *f*, balanus *m*
master *s* dominus, herus *m*; (*teacher*) magister, praeceptor *m*; (*controller*) arbiter *m*; **to be — of** potens esse (*with genit*), compos esse (*with genit*); **not to be — of** impotens esse (*with genit*)
master *vt* superare, vincĕre; (*to learn*) perdiscĕre; (*passion*) continēre
masterly *adj* (*artist*) artificiosus; imperiosus
masterpiece *s* magnum opus *n*
mastery *s* dominatio *f*, imperium, arbitrium *n*
masticate *vt* mandĕre
mastiff *s* Moiossus *m*
mat *s* teges, storea, matta *f*
match *s* (*marriage*) nuptiae *f pl*; (*contest*) certamen *n*; (*an equal*) par, compar *m & f*; **a — for** par (*with dat*); **not a — for** impar (*with dat*)
match *vt* adaequare, exaequare; *vi* quadrare
matchless *adj* incomparabilis
mate *s* socius, collega *m*; conju(n)x *m & f*
mate *vi* conjungi
material *adj* corporeus; (*significant*) haud levis, magni momenti; **—ly** magnopere
material *s* materia, materies *f*
maternal *adj* maternus
maternity *s* conditio matris *f*
mathematical *adj* mathematicus
mathematician *s* mathematicus *m*
mathematics *s* mathematica *f*, numeri *m pl*
matricide *s* (*murder*) matricidium *n*; (*murderer*) matricida *m & f*
matrimony *s* matrimonium *n*
matrix *s* forma *f*
matron *s* matrona *f*
matronly *adj* matronalis
matter *s* (*substance*) materia *f*; (*affair*) res *f*, negotium *n*; pus *n*; **no —** nihil interest
matter *v impers* **it does not —** nihil interest, nihil refert
matting *s* tegetes *f pl*
mattress *s* culcita *f*
mature *adj* maturus, adultus; **—ly** mature
mature *vi* maturescĕre
maturity *s* maturitas, aetas matura *f*
maudlin *adj* flebilis
maul *vt* mulcare, delaniare
mausoleum *s* mausoleum *n*
maw *s* ingluvies *f*
mawkish *adj* putidus; **—ly** putide
maxim *s* axioma, praeceptum *n*, sententia *f*
maximum *adj* quam maximus, quam plurimus
May *s* (mensis) Maius *m*
may *vi* posse; **I —** licet mihi
maybe *adv* forsitan
mayor *s* praefectus urbi *m*
maze *s* labyrinthus *m*
me *pron* me; **by —** a me; **to —** mihi; **with —** mecum
mead *s* (*drink*) mulsum *n*
meadow *s* pratum *n*
meager *adj* macer, exilis, jejunus; **—ly** exiliter, jejune
meagerness *s* macies *f*; (*of soil*) exilitas *f*; exigua copia *f*
meal *s* farina *f*; (*food*) cibus *m*; (*dinner*) epulae *f pl*
mean *adj* (*middle*) medius; (*low*) humilis; (*cruel*) crudelis, vilis
mean *s* medium *n*, mediocritas *f*
mean *vt* dicĕre, significare; (*to intend*) velle, cogitare, in animo habēre; (*to refer to*) significare, intellegere
meander *vi* sinuoso cursu labi
meaning *s* significatio, vis *f*, sens·us -ūs *m*
meanness *s* humilitas *f*; (*cruelty*) crudelitas *f*
means *s* (*way, method*) ratio, via *f*, consilium *n*; (*wealth*) opes *f pl*; **by all —** maxime, omnino; **by — of** *render by abl or* per (*with acc*); **by no —** nullo modo, haudquaquam
meanwhile *adv* interea, interim
measles *s* morbilli *m pl*
measurable *adj* mensurabilis
measure *s* mensura *f*, modus *m*; (*course of action*) ratio *f*, consilium *n*; (*law*) rogatio, lex *f*; **in some —** aliqua ex parte
measure *vt* metiri; (*land*) metari; **to — out** admetiri, dimetiri
measurement *s* mensura *f*
meat *s* caro *f*; (*food*) cibus *m*
mechanic *s* opifex, faber *m*
mechanical *adj* mechanicus, machinalis; **—ly** mechanica quadam arte
mechanics *s* mechanica ars, machinalis scientia *f*
mechanism *s* machinatio *f*
medal *s* insigne *n*
medallion *s* numisma sollemne *n*
meddle *vi* se interponĕre
meddler *s* ardelio *m*
mediate *vi* intercedĕre
mediation *s* intercessio *f*
mediator *s* intercessor, conciliator *m*
medical *adj* medicus, medicinalis
medicate *vt* medicare
medicinal *adj* medicus, salutaris
medicine *s* (*science*) medicina *f*; (*remedy*) medicamentum *n*
medieval *adj* medii aevi (*genit, used as adj*)
mediocre *adj* mediocris
mediocrity *s* mediocritas *f*
meditate *vi* meditari, cogitare
meditation *s* meditatio, cogitatio *f*
meditative *adj* cogitabundus
Mediterranean *s* mare internum *or* medium, mare nostrum *n*
medium *s* (*middle*) medium *n*; (*expedient*) modus *m*, ratio *f*; (*agency*) conciliator *m*

medium *adj* mediocris
medley *s* farrago *f*
meek *adj* mitis, demissus; **—ly** summisse
meekness *s* animus demissus *m*
meet *adj* aptus, idoneus; **it is —** convenit
meet *vt* obviam ire (*with dat*), occurrĕre (*with dat*); (*fig*) obire; *vi* convenire; **to — with** offendĕre, excipĕre
meeting *s* congressio *f*; (*assembly*) convent·us -ūs *m*
melancholy *s* tristitia, maestitia *f*
melancholy *adj* tristis, maestus
mellow *adj* maturus, mitis; (*from drinking*) temulentus
mellow *vt* maturare, coquĕre; *vi* maturescĕre
melodious *adj* canorus; **—ly** canore, modulate
melody *s* melos *n*, modus *m*
melt *vt* liquefacĕre, dissolvĕre; *vi* liquescĕre, tabescĕre
member *s* membrum *n*; (*fig*) sodalis *m*
membrane *s* membrana *f*
memento *s* monumentum *n*
memoirs *s* commentarii *m pl*
memorable *adj* memorabilis, memoriā dignus
memorandum *s* nota *f*
memorial *s* monumentum *n*
memory *s* memoria *f*; **from —** ex memoria, memoriter; **in the — of man** post hominum memoriam; **to commit to —** ediscĕre, memoriae mandare
menace *s* minae *f pl*
menace *vt* minari, minitari; (*of things*) imminēre (*with dat*)
menacing *adj* minax; (*only of persons*) minitabundus
mend *vt* emendare, corrigĕre, restaurare, reparare; (*clothes*) sarcire; *vi* melior fieri
mendicant *s* mendicus *m*, mendica *f*
menial *adj* servilis, sordidus
menial *s* servus, famulus *m*
mental *adj* mente conceptus; **—ly** mente
mention *s* mentio, commemoratio *f*; **to make — of** mentionem facĕre (*with genit*)
mention *vt* commemorare, nominare; **to not —** silentio praeterire
mercantile *adj* mercatorius
mercenary *adj* mercenarius, venalis
mercenary *s* miles mercenarius *m*
merchandise *s* merces *f pl*
merchant *s* mercator, negotiator *m*
merciful *adj* misericors, clemens; **—ly** misericorditer, clementer
merciless *adj* immisericors, inclemens; **—ly** duriter, inhumane
mercurial *adj* vividus, acer, levis
Mercury *s* Mercurius *m*
mercury *s* argentum vivum *n*
mercy *s* misericordia *f*
mere *adj* merus; **—ly** tantummodo, solum, modo
meretricious *adj* meretricius, fucatus
merge *vt* confundĕre; *vi* confundi
meridian *s* meridianus circulus *m*; meridies *m*
merit *s* meritum *n*
merit *vt* merēre, merēri
meritorious *adj* laudabilis
mermaid *s* nympha *f*
merrily *adv* hilare, festive
merry *adj* hilaris, festivus
mesh *s* (*of net*) macula *f*
mess *s* (*dirt*) squalor *m*; (*confusion*) turba, rerum perturbatio *f*
messenger *s* nuntius *m*
metal *adj* metallicus, ferreus, aereus
metal *s* metallum *n*
metallurgy *s* metallurgia, scientia metallorum *f*
metamorphosis *s* transfiguratio *f*
metaphor *s* translatio *f*
metaphorical *adj* translatus; **—ly** per translationem
mete *vt* metiri
meteor *s* fax caelestis *f*
meteorology *s* prognostica *n pl*
meter *s* metrum *n*, numerus *m*
method *s* ratio *f*, modus *m*
methodical *adj* dispositus; (*person*) diligens; **—ly** ratione et viā
meticulous *adj* accuratus; **—ly** accurate
metonymy *s* immutatio *f*
metrical *adj* metricus, numerosus
metropolis *s* caput *n*
mettle *s* animus *m*, virtus, magnanimitas *f*
miasma *s* halit·us -ūs *m*
microscope *s* microscopium *n*
mid *adj* medius
midday *adj* meridianus
midday *s* meridies *m*, meridianum tempus *n*
middle *adj* medius
middle *s* medium *n*; **in the — of the road** in media via
midget *s* pumilio *m & f*
midnight *s* media nox *f*
midriff *s* diaphragma *n*, praecordia *n pl*
midst *s* medium *n*; **in the — of** inter (*with acc*)
midsummer *s* summa aestas *f*
midway *adv* medius; **he stood — between the lines** stabat medius inter acies
midwife *s* obstetrix *f*
midwinter *s* bruma *f*
midwinter *adj* brumalis
mien *s* vult·us -ūs *m*
might *s* vis, potestas, potentia *f*; **with all one's —** summa ope
might *vi render by imperfect subjunctive*
mightily *adv* valde, magnopere
mighty *adj* potens, validus
migrate *vi* migrare, abire
migration *s* peregrinatio *f*
migratory *adj* advena, migrans
mild *adj* mitis, lenis; (*person*) placidus, clemens; **—ly** leniter, clementer
mildew *s* robigo *f*, mucor, sit·us -ūs *m*
mildness *s* clementia, lenitas, mansuetudo *f*

mile *s* mille passuum, milliare *n*
milestone *s* milliarium *n*
militant *adj* ferox
military *adj* militaris
militia *s* milites *m pl*
milk *s* lac *n*
milk *vt* mulgēre
milky *adj* lacteus
Milky Way *s* orbis lacteus *m*, via lactea *f*
mill *s* mola *f*, pistrinum *n*
millennium *s* mille anni *m pl*
miller *s* molitor, pistor *m*
million *adj* decies centena milia (*with genit*)
millionaire *s* homo praedives *m*
millionth *s* pars una ex decies centenis milibus partium *f*
millstone *s* mola *f*
mime *s* mimus *m*
mimic *s* mimus *m*
mimic *vt* imitari
mimicry *s* imitatio *f*
mince *vt* concidĕre; **not to — words** plane aperteque loqui
mind *s* mens *f*, animus *m*, ingenium *n*; (*opinion*) sens·us -ūs *m*, sententia *f*; **to call to —** recordari; **to make up one's —** animum inducĕre, statuĕre, constituĕre; **to show presence of —** praesenti animo uti
mind *vt* (*to look after*) curare; (*to regard*) respicĕre; (*to object to*) aegre ferre; **to — one's own business** suum negotium agĕre
mindful *adj* attentus, diligens; memor
mine *s* fodina *f*, metallum *n*; (*mil*) cuniculus *m*; (*fig*) thesaurus *m*
mine *vt* effodĕre
mine *pron* meus
miner *s* (*of metals*) metallicus *m*; fossor *m*
mineral *s* metallum *n*
mineral *adj* metallicus, fossilis
mineralogist *s* metallorum peritus *m*
mineralogy *s* metallorum scientia *f*
mingle *vt* commiscēre, confundĕre; *vi* commiscēri, se immiscēre
miniature *s* pictura minuta *f*
minimum *adj* quam minimus
minimum *s* minimum *n*
minion *s* cliens *m & f*
minister *s* minister, administer *m*
minister *vi* ministrare, servire
ministry *s* ministratio *f*, munus, officium *n*
minor *s* pupillus *m*, pupilla *f*
minor *adj* minor
minority *s* minor pars *f*
minstrel *s* fidicen *m*
mint *s* (*plant*) mentha *f*; (*for making money*) moneta *f*
mint *vt* cudĕre
minute *s* temporis momentum *n*
minute *adj* (*small*) minutus, exiguus, pusillus; (*exact*) accuratus, subtilis; **—ly** accurate, subtiliter
minx *s* puella procax *f*
miracle *s* miraculum, monstrum *n*
miraculous *adj* miraculosus; **—ly** divinitus
mirage *s* falsa species *f*
mire *s* lutum *n*
mirror *s* speculum *n*
mirth *s* hilaritas, laetitia *f*
mirthful *adj* hilaris
misadventure *s* infortunium *n*
misalliance *s* matrimonium impar *n*
misapply *vt* abuti (*with abl*)
misapprehend *vt* male intellegĕre
misapprehension *s* falsa conceptio *f*
misbehave *vi* indecore se gerĕre
misbehavior *s* morum pravitas *f*
misbelief *s* fides prava *f*
miscalculate *vi* errare
miscalculation *s* error *m*
miscarriage *s* abort·us -ūs *m*; (*fig*) malus success·us -ūs *m*
miscarry *vi* abortum facĕre; (*fig*) male succedĕre
miscellaneous *adj* promiscuus
miscellany *s* conjectanea, miscellanea *n pl*
mischance *s* infortunium *n*
mischief *s* incommodum, maleficium *n*; (*of children*) lascivia *f*
mischievous *adj* maleficus, noxius; (*playful*) lascivus
misconceive *vt* male intellegĕre
misconception *s* falsa conceptio, falsa opinio *f*
misconduct *s* delictum, peccatum *n*
misconstruction *s* sinistra interpretatio *f*
misconstrue *vt* male interpretari; perverse interpretari
misdeed *s* delictum, peccatum *n*
misdemeanor *s* levius delictum *n*
misdirect *vt* fallĕre
miser *s* avarus, sordidus *m*
miserable *adj* miser, infelix, aerumnosus
miserably *adv* misere
miserly *adj* avarus, sordidus
misery *s* miseria, aerumna *f*
misfortune *s* infortunium, incommodum *n*
misgiving *s* sollicitudo *f*
misgovern *vt* male regĕre
misguide *vt* seducĕre, fallĕre
misguided *adj* (*fig*) demens
mishap *s* incommodum *n*
misinform *vt* falsa docēre (*with acc*)
misinterpret *vt* male interpretari
misinterpretation *s* prava interpretatio *f*
misjudge *vt* male judicare
mislay *vt* amittĕre
mislead *vt* seducĕre, decipĕre
mismanage *vt* male gerĕre
mismanagement *s* mala administratio *f*
misnomer *s* falsum nomen *n*
misplace *vt* alieno loco ponĕre
misprint *s* erratum typographicum, mendum *n*
misquote *vt* falso citare, falso proferre
misquotation *s* falsa prolatio *f*
misrepresent *vt* calumniari
misrepresentation *s* calumnia *f*; falsa descriptio *f*

misrule *s* prava administratio *f*
miss *s* adulescentula, virgo *f*; error *m*
miss *vt* (*to overlook*) omittere, praetermittĕre; (*one's aim*) non ferire, non attingĕre; (*to feel the want of*) desiderare; (*to fail to find*) requirĕre; *vi* (*to fall short*) errare
misshapen *adj* pravus, deformis
missile *s* telum, missile, tormentum *n*
missing *adj* absens; **to be —** deesse
mission *s* legatio, missio *f*
misspell *vt* perperam scribĕre
misspend *vt* prodigĕre, perdĕre, dissipare
misstate *vt* parum accurate memorare
misstatement *s* falsum, mendacium *n*
mist *s* nebula, caligo *f*
mistake *s* error *m*, erratum *n*; (*written*) mendum *n*; **to make a —** errare, peccare
mistake *vt* habēre pro (*with abl*)
mistaken *adj* falsus; **to be —** falli; **unless I am —** ni fallor
mistletoe *s* viscum *n*
mistress *s* domina, hera *f*; (*sweetheart*) amica *f*; (*paramour*) concubina *f*; (*teacher*) magistra *f*
mistrust *s* diffidentia, suspicio *f*
mistrust *vt* diffidĕre (*with dat*)
mistrustful *adj* diffidens; **—ly** diffidenter
misty *adj* nebulosus, caliginosus; (*fig*) obscurus
misunderstand *vt* perperam intellegĕre
misunderstanding *s* error *m*; (*disagreement*) offensio *f*, dissidium *n*
misuse *vt* abuti (*with abl*); (*to revile*) conviciari
misuse *s* abus·us -ūs *m*; (*ill treatment*) injuria *f*
mite *s* (*bit*) parvulus *m*; (*coin*) sextans *m*
miter *s* mitra *f*
mitigate *vt* mitigare, lenire
mitigation *s* mitigatio *f*
mix *vt* miscēre; **to — in** admiscēre; **to — up** commiscēre; (*fig*) confundĕre
mixed *adj* promiscuus, confusus
mixture *s* mixtura, farrago *f*
moan *vi* gemĕre, ingemiscĕre
moan *s* gemit·us -ūs *m*
moat *s* fossa *f*
mob *s* turba *f*, vulgus *n*
mob *vt* conviciis insectari, stipare
mobile *adj* mobilis
mobility *s* mobilitas *f*
mock *s* irrisio, derisio *f*
mock *vt* ludĕre, ludificari, irridēre
mock *adj* fictus, fucatus
mockery *s* irrisio *f*, irris·us -ūs *m*
mode *s* modus *m*, ratio *f*; (*fashion*) us·us -ūs *m*
model *s* exemplar, exemplum *n*
model *vt* formare, delineare, fingĕre
moderate *adj* moderatus, mediocris, modicus; **—ly** moderate, mediocriter, modice
moderate *vt* moderari, temperare, coercēre
moderation *s* moderatio, temperantia *f*, modus *m*
moderator *s* praeses *m*
modern *adj* recens, hodiernus, novus
modest *adj* (*restrained*) modestus, pudens, verecundus; (*sight*) modicus, mediocris; **—ly** pudenter, verecunde
modesty *s* modestia, pudicitia, verecundia *f*
modification *s* modificatio, mutatio *f*
modify *vt* (im)mutare
modulate *vt* (*voice*) flectĕre; modulari
modulation *s* flexio *f*, flex·us -ūs *m*
moist *adj* humidus, uvidus, madidus
moisten *vt* (h)umectare, rigare
moisture *s* humor *m*
molar *s* dens genuinus *m*
molasses *s* sacchari faex *f*
mold *s* (*form*) forma, matrix *f*; (*mustiness*) mucor *m*
mold *vt* formare, fingĕre; (*to knead*) subigĕre; *vi* mucescĕre
molder *vi* putrescĕre, dilabi
moldiness *s* mucor, sit·us -ūs *m*
moldy *adj* mucidus, situ corruptus
mole *s* (*animal*) talpa *f*; (*sea wall*) moles *f*, agger *m*; (*on skin*) naevus *m*
molecule *s* particula *f*
molehill *s* **to make a mountain out of a —** e rivo flumina magna facĕre
molest *vt* vexare, sollicitare
molt *vi* plumas ponĕre
molten *adj* liquefactus
moment *s* (*of time*) punctum temporis *n*; (*importance*) momentum *n*; **in a —** statim; **of great —** magni ponderis; **this —** ad tempus
momentarily *adv* statim, confestim
momentary *adj* brevis
momentous *adj* gravis, magni momenti (*genit, used adjectively*)
monarch *s* rex, princeps, dominus *m*
monarchical *adj* regius
monarchy *s* regnum *n*
monastery *s* monasterium *n*
monetary *adj* pecuniarius, argentarius, nummarius
money *s* pecunia *f*, nummi *m pl*; **for —** mercede
moneychanger *s* nummularius *m*
moneylender *s* faenerator *m*
mongrel *s* hybrida *m*
monitor *s* admonitor *m*
monk *s* monachus *m*
monkey *s* simia *f*
monogram *s* monogramma *n*
monologue *s* oratio *f*
monopolize *vt* monopolium exercēre in (*with acc*)
monopoly *s* monopolium *n*
monosyllabic *adj* monosyllabus
monosyllable *s* monosyllabum *n*
monotonous *adj* semper idem; (*singsong*) canorus
monotony *s* taedium *n*
monster *s* monstrum, portentum *n*, belua *f*
monstrosity *s* monstrum *n*
monstrous *adj* monstrosus, portentosus, prodigiosus; **—ly** monstrose

month *s* mensis *m*
monthly *adj* menstruus
monthly *adv* singulis mensibus
monument *s* monumentum *n*
monumental *adj* (*important*) gravis, magnus; (*huge*) ingens
mood *s* animi affect·us -ūs, habit·us -ūs *m*; (*gram*) modus *m*
moodiness *s* morositas *f*
moody *adj* morosus, maestus
moon *s* luna *f*
moonlight *s* lunae lumen *n*; **by —** per lunam
moonstruck *adj* lunaticus
Moor *s* Maurus *m*
moor *vt* religare, anchoris retinēre
moor *s* tesca *n pl*
mop *s* peniculus *m*
mop *vt* detergēre
mope *vi* maerēre
moral *adj* (*relating to morals*) moralis, ethicus; (*morally proper*) honestus; **—ly** moraliter; honeste
moral *s* (*of story*) documentum *n*
morale *s* animus *m*, animi *m pl*; **— is low** animus jacet, animi deficiunt
morality *s* boni mores *m pl*
moralize *vi* de moribus disserěre
morals *s* mores *m pl*
morass *s* palus *f*
morbid *adj* morbidus, morbosus
more *adj* plus (*with genit*); plures
more *adv* plus, magis, amplius; ultra; **— and —** magis magisque; **— than** plus quam; **— than enough** plus satis; **no —** non diutius
moreover *adv* praeterea, ultro, etenim vero
morning *s* mane *n* (*indecl*); tempus matutinum *n*; **early in the —** multo mane, bene mane, prima luce; **in the —** mane, matutino tempore; **this —** hodie mane
morning *adj* matutinus
morning star *s* Lucifer, phosphorus *m*
morose *adj* morosus; **—ly** morose
moroseness *s* morositas *f*
morsel *s* offa *f*, frustulum *n*
mortal *adj* mortalis; (*deadly*) mortifer, letalis; **—ly** letaliter
mortal *s* mortalis *m & f*, homo *m & f*
mortality *s* mortalitas *f*
mortar *s* mortarium *n*
mortgage *s* hypotheca *f*, pignus *n*
mortgage *vt* obligare
mortification *s* dolor *m*
mortify *vt* mortificare, coercēre; (*to vex*) offenděre
mosaic *s* tessellatum opus *n*
mosaic *adj* tesselatus
mosquito *s* culex *m*
moss *s* muscus *m*
mossy *adj* muscosus
most *adj* plurimus, maximus, plerusque; **for the — part** maximam partem
most *adv* maxime, plurimum
mostly *adv* plerumque, fere
mote *s* corpusculum *n*
moth *s* blatta *f*
mother *s* mater *f*
motherhood *s* matris conditio *f*
mother-in-law *s* socr·us -ūs *f*
motherless *adj* matre orbus
motherly *adj* maternus
motion *s* motio *f*, mot·us -ūs *m*; (*proposal of bill*) rogatio *f*; **to make a —** ferre; **to set in —** ciēre
motion *vi* significare, innuěre
motionless *adj* immotus, immobilis
motive *s* causa, ratio *f*, incitamentum *n*
motive *adj* movens, agens
motley *adj* varius, versicolor
mottled *adj* maculosus
motto *s* sententia *f*, praeceptum *n*
mound *s* tumulus, agger *m*, moles *f*
mount *s* mons *m*; (*horse*) equus *m*
mount *vt* scanděre, ascenděre, conscenděre; *vi* ascenděre, conscenděre, sublime ferri; subvolare
mountain *s* mons *m*
mountaineer *s* montanus *m*
mountainous *adj* montuosus, montanus
mounted *adj* (*on horseback*) inscensus
mourn *vt* lugēre, deflēre; *vi* lugēre, maerēre
mourner *s* plorator *m*
mournful *adj* lugubris, luctuosus, tristis, flebilis, maestus; **—ly** maeste, flebiliter
mourning *s* luct·us -ūs, maeror *m*; (*dress*) vestis lugubris *f*; **in —** pullatus, sorditatus; **to go into —** vestitum mutare
mouse *s* mus *m*
mousetrap *s* muscipulum *n*
mouth *s* os *n*; (*of beast*) faux *f*; (*of river*) ostium *n*; (*of bottle*) lura *f*
mouthful *s* buccella *f*
mouth piece *s* interpres *m*
movable *adj* mobilis
movables *s* res *f pl*, supellex *f*
move *vt* movēre; (*emotionally*) commovēre; (*to propose*) ferre; *vi* movēri, se movēre; (*to change residence*) migrare; **to — on** progredi
movement *s* mot·us -ūs *m*
moving *adj* flebilis, miserabilis
mow *vt* demetěre, secare
mower *s* faenisex *m & f*
mowing *s* faenisicium *n*
much *adj* multus; **as — . . . as** tantus . . . quantus; **how —** quantus; **so —** tantus; **too —** nimius; **very —** plurimus
much *adv* multum, valde; (*with comparatives*) multo; **too —** nimium; nimis; **very —** plurimum
muck *s* stercus *n*
mucous *adj* mucosus
mud *s* lutum *n*, limus *m*
muddle *vt* turbare; (*fig*) perturbare
muddle *s* confusio, turba *f*
muddy *adj* lutosus, lutulentus; (*troubled*) turbidus
muffle *vt* involvěre; **to — up** obvolvěre
muffled *adj* surdus
mug *s* poculum *n*
muggy *adj* humidus
mulberry *s* morum *n*

mulberry tree *s* morus *f*
mule *s* mulus *m*
muleteer *s* mulio *m*
mulish *adj* obstinatus
multifarious *adj* varius, multiplex
multiplication *s* multiplicatio *f*
multiply *vt* multiplicare; *vi* augēri, crescĕre
multitude *s* multitudo, turba *f*
multitudinous *adj* creberrimus
mumble *vt* opprimĕre; *vi* murmurare
munch *vt* manducare, mandĕre
mundane *adj* mundanus
municipal *adj* municipalis
municipality *s* municipium *n*
munificence *s* munificentia, largitas *f*
munificent *adj* munificus, liberalis; **—ly** munifice
munitions *s* belli apparat·us -ūs *m*
mural *adj* muralis
murder *s* caedes, nex *f*, homicidium *n*
murder *vt* necare, trucidare, obtruncare
murderer *s* homicida *m & f*, sicarius *m*
murderous *adj* (*fig*) sanguinarius, cruentus
murky *adj* caliginosus, tenebrosus
murmur *s* murmur *n*, fremit·us -ūs *m*
murmuring *s* admurmuratio *f*
muscle *s* musculus, lacertus, torus *m*
muscular *adj* lacertosus, robustus
Muse *s* Musa *f*
muse *vi* meditari, secum agitare
mushroom *s* fungus, boletus *m*
music *s* musica *f*; (*of instruments and voices*) cant·us -ūs, concent·us -ūs *m*
musical *adj* (*of person*) musicus; (*of sound*) canorus
musician *s* musicus *m*; (*of stringed instrument*) fidicen *m*; (*of wind instrument*) tibicen *m*
muslin *s* sidon *f*
must *s* mustum *n*
must *vi* **I — go** mihi eundum est, me oportet ire, debeo ire, necesse est (ut) eam
mustard *s* sinapi *n*
muster *vt* lustrare; (*fig*) cogĕre, convocare; **to — up courage** animum sumĕre; *vi* convenire, coire
muster *s* copiarum lustratio *f*, recens·us -ūs *m*
musty *adj* mucidus
mutable *adj* mutabilis
mute *adj* mutus
mutilate *vt* mutilare, truncare
mutilated *adj* mutilus, truncus
mutilation *s* mutilatio, laceratio *f*
mutineer *s* seditiosus *m*
mutinous *adj* seditiosus
mutiny *s* seditio *f*, mot·us -ūs *m*
mutiny *vi* tumultuari, seditionem facĕre
mutter *vi* murmurare, mussitare
mutter *s* murmuratio *f*
mutton *s* ovilla *f*
mutual *adj* mutuus; **—ly** mutuo, inter se
muzzle *s* capistrum *n*
muzzle *vt* capistrare
my *adj* meus; **— own** proprius
myriad *adj* decem milia (*with genit*); (*innumerable*) sescenti
myrrh *s* myrrha, murrha *f*
myrtle *s* myrtus *f*
myself *pron* (*reflexive*) me; **to —** mihi; (*intensive*) ipse, egomet
mysterious *adj* arcanus, occultus; **—ly** arcane, occulte
mystery *s* mysterium, arcanum *n*; (*fig*) res occultissima *f*
mystical *adj* mysticus; **—ly** mystice
mystification *s* ambages *f pl*
mystify *vt* confundĕre, fallĕre
myth *s* mythos *m*, fabula *f*
mythical *adj* fabulosus
mythology *s* fabulae *f pl*, mythologia *f*

N

nab *vt* prehendĕre
nadir *s* fundus *m*
nag *s* caballus *m*
nag *vt* objurgitare
naiad *s* naias *f*
nail *s* clavus *m*; (*of finger*) unguis *m*
nail *vt* defigĕre
naive *adj* simplex; **—ly** simpliciter
naked *adj* nudus, apertus; **—ly** aperte
name *s* nomen *n*, appellatio *f*; (*reputation*) fama, celebritas *f*; (*term*) vocabulum *n*; **by —** nominatim
name *vt* nominare, appellare; (*to appoint*) dicĕre
nameless *adj* nominis expers
namely *adv* scilicet, videlicet
nap *s* brevis somnus *m*; (*of cloth*) villus *m*; **to take a —** meridiari, jacēre
nape *s* **— of the neck** cervix *f*
napkin *s* mappa *f*, mantele *n*
narcotic *adj* somnificus
narcotic *s* medicamentum somnificum *n*
nard *s* nardus *f*, nardum *n*
narrate *vt* narrare
narration *s* narratio, expositio *f*
narrative *s* fabula *f*
narrator *s* narrator *m*
narrow *adj* angustus; (*fig*) arctus; **—ly** vix, aegre
narrow *vt* coarctare; *vi* coarctari
narrow-minded *adj* animi angusti *or* parvi (*genit, used adjectively*)
narrowness *s* angustiae *f pl*
nasty *adj* (*foul*) foedus; (*mean*) amarus

natal *adj* natalis
nation *s* gens, natio *f*; (*as political body*) populus *m*; (*state*) res publica *f*
national *adj* publicus, civilis; rei publicae (*genit, used adjectively*)
nationality *s* civitas *f*
native *adj* indigena
native *s* indigena *m & f*
native land *s* patria *f*
native tongue *s* patrius sermo *m*
nativity *s* ort·us -ūs *m*
natural *adj* naturalis; (*innate*) nativus, innatus, insitus; (*fig*) sincerus, simplex; **—ly** naturā; (*unaffectedly*) simpliciter; (*of its own accord*) sponte
naturalization *s* civitatis donatio *f*
naturalize *vt* civitate donare
nature *s* natura, rerum natura *f*; (*character*) ingenium *n*, indoles *f*
naught *pron* nihil; **to set at —** parvi facĕre
naughty *adj* improbus, malus
nausea *s* nausea *f*; (*fig*) fastidium *n*
nauseate *vt* fastidium movēre (*with dat*); **to be nauseated** nauseare, fastidire
nautical *adj* nauticus
naval *adj* navalis, maritimus
nave *s* (*of church*) navis *f*
navel *s* umbilicus *m*
navigable *adj* navigabilis, navium patiens
navigate *vt* gubernare; *vi* navigare
navigation *s* navigatio *f*, res nauticae *f pl*
navigator *s* nauta, gubernator *m*
navy *s* classis *f*, copiae navales *f pl*
nay *adv* non ita
near *prep* prope (*with acc*), ad (*with acc*)
near *adj* propinquus, vicinus; (*of relation*) proximus; **— at hand** propinquus, in promptu
near *adv* prope, juxta
near *vt* appropinquare (*with dat*)
nearly *adv* prope, paene, fere, ferme
nearness *s* propinquitas *f*
nearsighted *adj* myops
neat *adj* mundus, nitidus, concinnus; **—ly** munde, concinne
neatness *s* munditia, concinnitas *f*
nebulous *adj* nebulosus
necessarily *adv* necessario
necessary *adj* necessarius; **it is —** opus est
necessitate *vt* cogĕre
necessity *s* necessitas *f*; (*want*) egestas, necessitudo *f*; (*thing*) res necessaria *f*
neck *s* collum *n*, cervis *f*
necklace *s* monile *n*, torques *m*
necktie *s* collare *n*
nectar *s* nectar *n*
need *s* (*necessity*) opus *n*, necessitas *f*; (*want*) inopia, egestas, penuria *f*; **there is — of** opus est (*with abl*)
need *vt* egēre (*with abl*), indigēre (*with abl*); (*to require*) requirĕre
needle *s* ac·us -ūs *f*
needless inutilis, minime necessarius, vanus; **—ly** sine causa
needy *adj* egens, indigens, inops
nefarious *adj* nefarius
negation *s* negatio *f*
negative *adj* negans, negativus; **—ly** negando
negative *s* negatio *f*; **to answer in the —** negare
neglect *vt* neglegĕre, omittĕre; deserĕre
neglect *s* neglegentia, incuria *f*, neglect·us -ūs *m*
neglectful *adj* neglegens
negligence *s* neglegentia, incuria *f*
negligent *adj* neglegens; **—ly** neglegenter
negligible *adj* levis, tenuis
negotiable *adj* mercabilis
negotiate *vt* (*a deal*) agĕre; agĕre de (*with abl*); *vi* negotiari
negotiation *s* transactio, actio *f*, pactum *n*
negotiator *s* conciliator, orator *m*
Negro *s* Aethiops *m*
neigh *vi* hinnire
neigh *s* hinnit·us -ūs *m*
neighbor *s* vicinus, finitimus *m*
neighborhood *s* vicinia, vicinitas *f*; proximitas *f*
neighboring *adj* vicinus, finitimus
neighborly *adj* familiaris, comis, benignus
neither *pron* neuter
neither *conj* nec, neque, neve, neu; **neither . . . nor** neque . . . neque
neophyte *s* tiro *m*
nephew *s* fratris filius, sororis filius *m*
Nereid *s* Nereis *f*
nerve *s* nervus *m*; (*fig*) temeritas, audacia *f*
nervous *adj* trepidus; **—ly** trepide
nervousness *s* diffidentia, sollicitudo *f*
nest *s* nidus *m*
nest *vi* nidificare
nestle *vi* recubare
net *s* rete *n*
net *vt* irretire
netting *s* reticulum *n*
nettle *s* urtica *f*
nettle *vt* (*fig*) vexare
network *s* reticulum, opus reticulatum *n*
neuter *adj* neuter, neutralis
neutral *adj* medius, neuter
neutrality *s* nullam in partem propensio *f*
neutralize *vt* aequare
never *adv* nunquam
nevermore *adv* nunquam posthac
nevertheless *adv* nihilominus, attamen
new *s* novus, recens, integer; **—ly** nuper, modo
newcomer *s* advena *m & f*
news *s* fama *f*, rumor, nuntius *m*
newspaper *s* acta diurna *n pl*
next *adj* proximus; (*of time*) insequens; **— day** postridie
next *adv* dein, deinde, deinceps
nibble *vt* arrodĕre; (*fig*) carpĕre; *vi* rodĕre
nice *adj* (*dainty*) delicatus; (*choice*)

exquisitus; (*exact*) accuratus; (*fine*) bellus; (*effeminate*) mollis; (*amiable*) suavis; (*of weather*) serenus; **—ly** delicate, exquisite, belle; accurate

nicety *s* accuratio, subtilitas, elegantia *f*

niche *s* aedicula *f*

nick *s* incisura *f*; **in the very — of time** in ipso articulo temporis

nick *vt* incidĕre

nickname *s* agnomen *n*

niece *s* fratris filia, sororis filia *f*

niggardly *adj* parcus, avarus

nigh *adj* propinquus

night *s* nox *f*; **by —** nocte, noctu; **to spend the —** pernoctare

nightfall *s* primae tenebrae *f pl*; **at —** sub noctem

nightingale *s* luscinia *f*

nightly *adj* nocturnus

nightly *adv* noctu, de nocte

nightmare *s* incubus *m*

night watch *s* vigilia *f*; (*guard*) vigil *m*

nimble *adj* pernix, agilis

nine *adj* novem; **— times** noviens

nineteen *adj* undeviginti, decem et novem

nineteenth *adj* undevicesimus

ninetieth *adj* nonagesimus

ninety *adj* nonaginta

ninth *adj* nonus

nip *vt* vellicare; (*of frost*) urĕre; **to — off** desecare

nippers *s* forceps *m*

nipple *s* papilla *f*

no *adj* nullus; **— one** nemo *m*

no *adv* non, minime; **to say —** negare

nobility *s* nobilitas *f*; nobiles, optimates *m pl*; (*moral excellence*) honestas *f*

noble *adj* nobilis, generosus; (*morally*) ingenuus, honestus, liberalis

noble *s* optimas *m*

nobleman *s* vir nobilis *m*

nobly *adv* nobiliter, praeclare, generose

nobody *pron* nemo *m*

nocturnal *adj* nocturnus

nod *s* nut·us -ūs *m*

nod *vi* nutare; (*to doze*) dormitare; (*in assent*) annuĕre

noise *s* strepit·us -ūs *m*; (*high-pitched*) stridor *m*; (*loud*) fragor *m*; **to make —** strepĕre, strepitare, increpare

noise *vt* **to — abroad** promulgare, divulgare

noiseless *adj* tacitus; **—ly** tacite

noisily *adv* cum strepitu

noisome *adj* noxius, foedus, taeter

noisy *adj* clamosus

nomad *s* nomas *m & f*

nomadic *adj* vagus, vagabundus

nominal *adj* nominalis; **—ly** nomine, verbo

nominate *vt* nominare, designare

nomination *s* nominatio, designatio *f*; (*of heir*) nuncupatio *f*

nominative *adj* nominativus

nominee *s* nominatus, designatus *m*

none *pron* nemo *m*

nonentity *s* nihilum *n*

nones *s* Nonae *f pl*

nonplus *vt* (*to puzzle*) ad incitas redigĕre

nonsense *s* ineptiae, nugae *f pl*; **to talk —** absurde loqui, garrire

nonsense *interj* gerrae!

nonsensical *adj* ineptus, absurdus

nook *s* angulus *m*

noon *s* meridies *m*; **before —** ante meridiem

noonday *adj* meridianus

no one *pron* nemo *m*

noose *s* laqueus *m*

nor *conj* nec, neque, neve, neu

norm *s* norma *f*

normal *adj* solitus; **—ly** plerumque

north *s* septentriones *m pl*

north *adj* septentrionalis

northern *adj* septentrionalis

northern lights *s* aurora Borealis *f*

north pole *s* arctos *f*

northwards *adv* septentriones versus

north wind *s* aquilo *m*

nose *s* nas·us -ūs *m*, nares *f pl*; **to blow the —** emungĕre

nostril *s* naris *f*

not *adv* non, haud; **— at all** nullo modo, haudquaquam; **— even** ne . . . quidem

notable *adj* notabilis, insignis, insignitus

notably *adv* insignite

notary *s* scriba *m*

notation *s* notatio *f*, signum *n*

notch *s* incisura *f*

notch *vt* incidĕre

note *s* (*mark*) nota *f*; (*comment*) adnotatio *f*; (*mus*) sonus *m*, vox *f*; (*com*) chirographum *n*; (*letter*) litterulae *f pl*

note *vt* notare; (*to notice*) animadvertĕre

notebook *s* commentarius *m*, tabulae *f pl*, pugillares *m pl*

noted *adj* insignis, insignitus, notus, praeclarus

noteworthy *adj* notabilis, memorabilis

nothing *pron* nihil, nil, nihilum; **for —** (*free*) gratis, gratuito; (*in vain*) frustra; **good for —** nequam; **— but** nihil nisi; **to think — of** nihili facĕre

notice *s* (*act of noticing*) notatio, animadversio *f*; (*announcement*) denuntiatio *f*; (*sign*) proscriptio *f*, titulus, libellus *m*; **to escape —** latēre; **to escape the — of** fallĕre; **to give — of** denuntiare

notice *vt* animadvertĕre, observare

noticeable *adj* insignis, conspicuus

noticeably *adv* insigniter

notification *s* denuntiatio, declaratio *f*

notify *vt* certiorem facĕre

notion *s* notio, suspicio *f*

notoriety *s* infamia *f*

notorious *adj* famosus, infamis, notus, manifestus; **—ly** manifeste

notwithstanding *adv* nihilominus

nought *pron* nihil; **to set at —** parvi facĕre
noun *s* nomen *n*
nourish *vt* alĕre, nutrire
nourishment *s* (*act*) alimentum *n*, cibus *m*
novel *adj* novus, inauditus
novel *s* fabula *f*
novelty *s* res nova *f*; novitas *f*
November *s* (mensis) November *m*
novice *s* tiro *m*
now *adv* nunc; (*past*) jam; **— and then** interdum, nonnunquam; **— . . . —** modo . . . modo
nowhere *adv* nusquam
noxious *adj* noxius
nozzle *s* ansa *f*
nude *adj* nudus
nudge *vt* fodicare
nudity *s* nudatio *f*
nugget *s* massa *f*
nuisance *s* incommodum *n*, molestia *f*
null *adj* irritus
nullify *vt* irritum facĕre
numb *adj* torpidus, torpens; **to become —** torpescĕre; **to be —** torpēre
numb *vt* torpefacĕre; (*fig*) obstupefacĕre
number *s* numerus *m*; **a — of** aliquot; **without —** innumerabilis
number *vt* numerare, enumerare, dinumerare
numberless *adj* innumerus, innumerabilis
numbness *s* torpor *m*; (*fig*) stupor *m*
numerical *adj* numeralis; **—ly** numero, ad numerum
numerous *adj* frequens, creber, multus
numismatics *s* doctrina nummorum *f*
nuptial *adj* nuptialis, conjugalis
nuptials *s* nuptiae *f pl*
nurse *s* nutrix *f*
nurse *vt* (*a baby*) nutrire; (*fig*) fovēre; (*the sick*) ancillari (*with dat*), curare
nursery *s* (*for children*) infantium cubiculum *n*; (*for plants*) plantarium, seminarium *n*
nurture *vt* nutrire, educare
nut *s* nux *f*; **a hard — to crack** (*fig*) quaestio nodosa *f*
nutriment *s* nutrimentum, alimentum *n*
nutrition *s* nutritio *f*, nutrimentum *n*
nutritious *adj* alibilis, salubris
nutshell *s* putamen *n*; **in a —** (*fig*) paucis verbis
nymph *s* nympha *f*

O

oaf *s* stultus, hebes *m*
oak *adj* querceus, quernus
oak *s* querc·us -ūs *f*; (*evergreen*) ilex *f*; (*timber*) robur *n*
oakum *s* stuppa *f*
oar *s* remus *m*; **to pull the —s** remos ducĕre
oarsman *s* remex *m*
oath *s* jusjurandum *n*; (*mil*) sacramentum *n*; **false —** perjurium *n*; **to take an —** jurare; (*mil*) sacramentum dicĕre
oats *s* avena *f*
obdurate *adj* obstinatus, pertinax; **—ly** obstinate, pertinaciter
obedience *s* obedientia *f*, obsequium *n*
obedient *adj* obediens, obsequens; **—ly** obedienter
obeisance *s* obsequium *n*, capitis summissio *f*; **to make — to** flectĕre ante (*with acc*); (*fig*) obsequi (*with dat*)
obelisk *s* obeliscus *m*
obese *adj* obesus
obesity *s* obesitas *f*
obey *vt* parēre (*with dat*), obedire (*with dat*), obtemperare (*with dat*), obsequi (*with dat*)
obituary *s* Libitinae index *m*
object *s* objectum *n*, res *f*; (*aim*) finis *m*, propositum *n*
object *vi* (*to feel annoyance*) gravari; (*to make objections*) recusare; **to — to** aegre ferre
objection *s* objectio *f*; impedimentum *n*, mora *f*
objectionable *adj* injucundus, improbabilis
objective *s* finis *m*, propositum *n*
objective *adj* externus, objectivus, verus
oblation *s* donum *n*
obligation *s* debitum, officium *n*; **under —** noxius
obligatory *adj* necessarius, debitus
oblige *vt* (*to force*) cogĕre, impellĕre; (*to put under obligation*) obligare, obstringĕre; (*to do a favor for*) morigerari (*with dat*); **to be obliged to** debēre (*with inf*); (*to feel gratitude toward*) gratiam habēre (*with dat*)
obliging *adj* officiosus, comis, blandus; **—ly** officiose, comiter
oblique *adj* obliquus; **—ly** oblique
obliterate *vt* delēre, oblitterare
oblivion *s* oblivio *f*
oblivious *adj* obliviosus, immemor
oblong *adj* oblongus
obloquy *s* vituperatio *f*, maledictum *n*
obnoxious *adj* invisus, noxius
obscene *adj* obscenus; **—ly** obscene
obscenity *s* obscenitas *f*
obscure *adj* obscurus; **—ly** obscure

obscure *vt* obscurare
obscurity *s* obscuritas *f*, tenebrae *f pl*; (*of birth*) humilitas *f*
obsequies *s* exsequiae *f pl*
obsequious *adj* officiosus, morigerus, nimis obsequens
obsequiousness *s* obsequium *n*, assentatio *f*
observable *adj* notabilis
observance *s* observantia *f*; (*rite*) rit·us -ūs *m*
observant *adj* attentus; — **of** diligens (*with genit*)
observation *s* observatio, animadversio *f*; (*remark*) notatio *f*, dictum *n*
observe *vt* (*to watch*) observare, contemplari, animadvertĕre; (*to keep*) conservare, observare; (*to remark*) dicĕre
observer *s* spectator *m*
obsess *vt* occupare
obsession *s* studium *n*
obsolescent *adj* **to be —** obsolescĕre
obsolete *adj* obsoletus, antiquatus; **to become —** exolescĕre
obstacle *s* impedimentum *n*; (*barrier*) obex *m*
obstinacy *s* obstinatio *f*, animus obstinatus *m*
obstinate *adj* obstinatus, pertinax; **—ly** obstinate
obstreperous *adj* tumultuosus, clamosus
obstruct *vt* obstare (*with dat*), obstruĕre, impedire
obstruction *s* obstructio *f*, impedimentum *n*; (*pol*) intercessio *f*
obtain *vt* nancisci, adipisci, consequi; (*by entreaty*) impetrare; *vi* valēre
obtainable *adj* impetrabilis
obtrusive *adj* molestus, importunus
obtuse *adj* obtusus, hebes, stolidus
obviate *vt* praevertĕre
obvious *adj* apertus, manifestus, perspicuus; **—ly** aperte, manifesto
occasion *s* occasio *f*, locus *m*; (*reason*) causa *f*; (*time*) tempus *n*
occasion *vt* locum dare (*with dat*), movēre
occasionally *adv* interdum
occidental *adj* occidentalis
occult *adj* occultus, arcanus
occupant *s* possessor *m*
occupation *s* possessio *f*; (*engagement*) occupatio *f*; (*employment*) negotium *n*, quaest·us -ūs *m*
occupy *vt* occupare, tenēre; (*to possess*) possidēre; (*space*) complēre
occur *vi* accidĕre, evenire; (*to the mind*) occurrĕre, in mentem venire
occurrence *s* cas·us -ūs, event·us -ūs *m*
ocean *s* oceanus *m*, mare oceanum *n*
oceanic *adj* oceanus, oceanensis
October *s* (mensis) October *m*
ocular *adj* ocularis
oculist *s* ocularius medicus *m*
odd *adj* (*of number*) impar; (*quaint*) insolitus, novus; **—ly** mirum in modum
oddity *s* raritas *f*, ridiculum *n*
odds *s* **the — are against us** impares summus; **to be at — with** dissidēre ab (*with abl*)
odious *adj* odiosus, invisus
odium *s* invidia *f*
odor *s* odor *m*
odorous *adj* odoratus
Odyssey *s* Odyssea *f*
of *prep* (*possession*) *rendered by genit;* (*origin*) de (*with abl*), ex (*with abl*)
off *adv* procul; **far —** longe, procul; **well —** bene nummatus
off *prep* de (*with abl*)
offend *vt* offendĕre, laedĕre; *vi* **to — against** violare
offender *s* peccator, reus *m*
offense *s* (*fault*) offensa, culpa *f*; (*insult*) injuria *f*; (*displeasure*) offensio *f*
offensive *adj* injuriosus; (*odors, etc.*) odiosus, foedus, gravis; (*language*) malignus, contumeliosus; (*aggressive*) bellum inferens; **—ly** injuriose; odiose
offer *vt* offerre, donare, praebēre; (*violence*) adferre; (*help*) ferre
offer *s* conditio *f*
offhand *adj* incuriosus
offhand *adv* confestim, illico
office *s* (*place of work*) officina *f*; (*pol*) honos, magistrat·us -ūs *m*; (*duty*) munus, officium *n*
officer *s* magistrat·us -ūs *m*; (*mil*) praefectus *m*
official *adj* publicus
official *s* minister, magistrat·us -ūs *m*
officiate *vi* officio *or* munere fungi, interesse; (*of clergyman*) rem divinam facĕre
officious *adj* officiosus, molestus; **—ly** officiose, moleste
offing *s* **in the —** procul
offset *vt* compensare
offspring *s* proles, progenies *f*
often *adv* saepe; **very —** persaepe
ogre *s* larva *f*, monstrum *n*
oh *interj* oh!, ohe!
oil *s* oleum *n*
oil *vt* ung(u)ĕre
oily *adj* oleosus; (*like oil*) oleaceus
ointment *s* unguentum *n*
old *adj* (*aged*) senex; (*out of use*) obsoletus; (*worn*) exesus, tritus; (*ancient*) antiquus, priscus; **of —** olim, quondam; **to grow —** senescĕre
old age *s* senectus *f*
old-fashioned *adj* priscus, antiquus
old man *s* senex *m*
old woman *s* an·us -ūs *f*
oligarchy *s* optimates *m pl*
olive *s* olea *f*
olive grove *s* olivetum *n*
Olympiad *s* Olympias *f*
Olympic *adj* Olympicus
omelet *s* laganum de ovis confectum *n*
omen *s* omen, auspicium *n*
ominous *adj* infaustus; **—ly** malis ominibus
omission *s* praetermissio, neglegentia *f*

omit *vt* omittĕre, mittĕre, praetermittĕre
omnipotence *s* omnipotentia, infinita potentia *f*
omnipotent *adj* omnipotens
omnivorous *adj* omnivorus
on *prep* (*place*) in (*with abl*); (*time*) *render by abl*; (*about, concerning*) de (*with abl*); (*ranged with*) a(b) (*with abl*); (*depending, hanging on*) de (*with abl*); (*near*) ad (*with acc*)
on *adv* porro; (*continually*) usque; **and so —** et cetera, ac deinceps; **to go —** pergĕre
once *adv* (*one time*) semel; (*formerly*) olim, quondam; **at —** statim, illico, ex templo; **for —** aliquando; **— and for all** semel in perpetuum; **— more** iterum; **— upon a time** olim
one *adj* unus
one *pron* unus; unicus; (*a certain person or thing*) quidam; **it is all —** perinde est; **— after another** alternus; **— another** inter se, alius alium; **— by —** singulatim; **— or the other** alteruter; **— or two** unus et alter
one-eyed *adj* luscus
onerous *adj* onerosus, gravis
oneself *pron* (*refl*) se; **to —** sibi; **with —** secum; (*intensive*) ipse
one-sided *adj* inaequalis, iniquus, impar
onion *s* caepa *f*
only *adj* unicus, unus, solus
only *adv* solum, tantum, modo; **not — . . . but also** non solum . . . sed etiam
only-begotten *adj* unigenitus
onset *s* impet·us -ūs *m*
onslaught *s* incurs·us -ūs *m*
onward *adv* porro
ooze *vi* manare, (de)stillare
opaque *adj* densus, opacus
open *adj* (*not shut*) apertus, patens; (*evident*) manifestus; (*sincere*) candidus, ingenuus; (*public*) publicus, communis; (*of space*) apertus; (*of question, undecided*) integer; **in the — air** sub divo; **to lie —** patēre; **—ly** aperte, palam
open *vt* aperire, patefacĕre; (*to uncover*) retegĕre; (*letter*) resignare; (*book*) evolvére; (*to begin*) exordiri; (*with ceremony*) inaugurare; *vi* patescĕre, se pandĕre; (*to gape*) dehiscĕre; (*of wound*) recrudescĕre
open-handed *adj* liberalis, largus
open-hearted *adj* simplex, ingenuus
opening *s* (*act*) apertio *f*; (*aperture*) foramen *n*, hiat·us -ūs *m*; (*opportunity*) locus *m*, occasio *f*
open-minded *adj* docilis
operate *vt* agĕre, gerĕre; *vi* operari
operation *s* effectio *f*; (*business*) negotium *n*; (*med*) sectio *f*
operative *adj* efficax, activus
operator *s* opifex *m*
opiate *s* mendicamentum somnificum *n*
opinion *s* opinio, sententia, mens *f*; (*esteem*) existimatio *f*; **public —** fama *f*
opium *s* opion *n*
opponent *s* adversarius *m*
opportune *adj* opportunus, idoneus, commodus; **—ly** opportune, in tempore
opportunity *s* copia, occasio, opportunitas *f*
oppose *vt* opponĕre, objicĕre; *vi* repugnare, resistĕre, adversari
opposite *adj* adversus, contrarius, diversus
opposite *prep* contra (*with acc*)
opposite *adv* contra, ex adverso
opposition *s* oppositio, repugnantia, discrepantia *f*; (*obstacle*) impedimentum *n*; (*party*) adversa factio *f*
oppress *vt* opprimĕre, vexare, gravare, onerare
oppression *s* gravatio, injuria *f*
oppressive *adj* praegravis, acerbus, molestus; **to become —** ingravescĕre
oppressor *s* tyrannus *m*
opprobrious *adj* turpis, probrosus
opprobrium *s* dedecus, probrum *n*
optical *adj* opticus
option *s* optio *f*
opulence *s* opulentia *f*
opulent *adj* opulens, opulentus
or *conj* vel, aut, —ve; (*in questions*) an; **— else** aut, alioquin; **— not** annon; (*in indirect questions*) necne
oracle *s* oraculum *n*
oracular *adj* fatidicus
oral *adj* verbalis, verbo traditus; **—ly** voce, verbis
orange *s* malum aurantium *n*
oration *s* oratio *f*
orator *s* orator *m*
oratorical *adj* oratorius
oratory *s* ars oratoria, eloquentia, rhetorice *f*
orb *s* orbis, gyrus *m*
orbit *s* orbis *m*; (*in astronomy*) ambit·us -ūs *m*
orchard *s* pomarium *n*
orchestra *s* symphoniaci *m pl*
ordain *vt* (*to appoint*) edicĕre
ordeal *s* discrimen *n*, labor *m*
order *s* (*class, arrangement*) ordo *m*; (*command*) mandatum, jussum, imperatum *n*; (*fraternity*) collegium *n*; **by — of** jussu (*with genit*); **in —** dispositus; **in — that** ut; **in — that not** ne; **out of —** incompositus; **to put in —** ordinare, disponĕre
order *vt* (*to command*) imperare (*with dat*), jubēre; (*to demand*) imperare (*with acc*); (*to put in order*) ordinare, disponĕre, digerĕre
orderly *adj* compositus, ordinatus; (*well-behaved*) modestus
orderly *s* accensus *m*; (*mil*) tesserarius *m*
ordinal *adj* ordinalis
ordinance *s* edictum, rescriptum *n*
ordinarily *adv* fere, plerumque
ordinary *adj* usitatus, vulgaris, solitus, quottidianus
ordnance *s* tormenta *n pl*
ore *s* aes *n*

organ *s* (*of body*) membrum *n*; (*musical*) organum *n*
organic *adj* organicus
organism *s* compages *f*
organization *s* ordinatio *f*, structura *f*
organize *vt* ordinare, instituĕre
orgy *s* comissatio *f*
Orient *s* oriens *m*
oriental *adj* Asiaticus
orifice *s* foramen, os *n*
origin *s* origo *f*, principium *n*; (*birth*) genus *n*; (*source*) fons *m*
original *adj* pristinus, primitivus, primus; (*one's own*) proprius; (*new*) novus, inauditus; **—ly** primum, principio, initio
original *s* archetypum, exemplar *n*; (*writing*) autographum *n*
originality *s* proprietas ingenii *f*
originate *vt* instituĕre; *vi* oriri
originator *s* auctor *m*
ornament *s* ornamentum *n*, ornat·us -ūs *m*
ornament *vt* ornare, decorare
ornamental *adj* decorus
ornate *adj* ornatus; **—ly** ornate
orphan *s* orbus *m*, orba *f*
orphaned *adj* orbatus
orphanage *s* orphanotrophium *n*
oscillate *vi* agitari; (*fig*) dubitare
oscillation *s* agitatio *f*; (*fig*) dubitatio *f*
ostensible *adj* simulatus, fictus
ostensibly *adv* specie, per speciem
ostentation *s* ostentatio, jactatio *f*
ostentatious *adj* ambitiosus, gloriosus, jactans; **—ly** ambitiose, jactanter
ostracism *s* ostracismus *m*
ostrich *s* struthiocamelus *m*
other *adj* (*different*) alius, diversus; (*remaining*) ceterus; **every — day** tertio quoque die; **on the — hand** contra, autem; **the —** alter
otherwise *adv* aliter
otter *s* lutra *f*
ought *vi* **I —** debeo, oportet me
ounce *s* uncia *f*
our *adj* noster
ours *pron* noster
ourselves *pron* (*reflex*) nos, nosmet; **to —** nobis; (*intensive*) nosmet ipsi
oust *vt* ejicĕre
out *adv* (*outside*) foris; (*motion*) foras; **— of** de (*with abl*), e(x) (*with abl*); (*on account of*) propter (*with acc*); **— of the way** devius
outbreak *s* eruptio *f*; (*fig*) seditio *f*
outburst *s* eruptio *f*
outcast *s* exsul, extorris, profugus *m*
outcome *s* event·us -ūs *m*
outcry *s* clamor *m*, acclamatio *f*, convicium *n*
outdo *vt* superare
outdoors *adv* foris, sub divo
outer *adj* exterior
outermost *adj* extremus
outfit *s* apparat·us -ūs *m*; (*costume*) vestimenta *n pl*
outflank *vt* circumire, circumvenire
outgrow *vt* excedĕre ex (*with abl*), staturā superare
outing *s* excursio *f*
outlandish *adj* externus, barbarus
outlast *vt* diutius durare (*with abl*)
outlaw *s* proscriptus *m*
outlaw *vt* aquā et igni interdicĕre (*with dat*), proscribĕre
outlay *s* sumpt·us -ūs *m*, impensa *f*
outlet *s* exit·us -ūs *m*
outline *vt* describĕre, adumbrare
outline *s* adumbratio *f*
outlive *vt* supervivĕre (*with dat*), superesse (*with dat*)
outlook *s* prospect·us -ūs *m*
outlying *adj* externus; (*distant*) remotus
outnumber *vt* multitudine superare
outpost *s* statio *f*
outpouring *s* effusio *f*
output *s* fruct·us -ūs *m*
outrage *s* injuria *f*, flagitium *n*
outrage *vt* flagitio afficĕre, violare
outrageous *adj* flagitiosus, atrox; (*excessive*) immodicus; **—ly** flagitiose; immodice
outright *adv* (*at once*) statim; (*completely*) prorsus, penitus
outrun *vt* praevertĕre, linquĕre
outset *s* initium, inceptum *n*
outshine *vt* praelucēre (*with dat*)
outside *s* pars exterior, superficies *f*; (*appearance*) species *f*; **on the —** extrinsecus
outside *adj* externus
outside *adv* foris, extra; (*motion*) foras; **from —** extrinsecus
outside *prep* extra (*with acc*)
outskirts *s* suburbium *n*, ager suburbanus *m*
outspoken *adj* candidus, liber
outspread *adj* patulus
outstanding *adj* praestans; (*of debts*) residuus
outstretched *adj* extentus, porrectus, passus
outstrip *vt* praevertĕre, cursu superare
outward *adj* externus
outward *adv* extra, extrinsecus
outweigh *vt* praevertĕre (*with dat*), praeponderare
outwit *vt* deludĕre, decipĕre
oval *adj* ovatus
ovation *s* plaus·us -ūs *m*; (*triumph*) ovatio *f*
oven *s* furnus *m*, fornax *f*
over *prep* (*across*) super (*with acc*), trans (*with acc*), per (*with acc*); (*above*) super (*with abl*), supra (*with acc*); (*with numbers*) plus quam
over *adv* supra; (*excess*) nimis; **all —** ubique, passim; **— and above** insuper; **— and — again** iterum ac saepius, identidem
overall *adj* totus
overawe *vt* (de)terrēre
overbalance *vt* praeponderare
overbearing *adj* superbus, insolens
overboard *adv* ex nave; **to jump —** ex nave desilire
overburden *vt* nimis onerare
overcast *adj* obnubilus

overcharge *vt* plus aequo exigĕre ab (*with abl*)
overcoat *s* paenula, lacerna *f*
overdo *vt* exaggerare, in majus extollĕre
overdue *adj* (*money*) residuus
overestimate *vt* majoris aestimare
overflow *s* inundatio *f*
overflow *vt* inundare; *vi* abundare, redundare
overgrown *adj* obductus, obsitus; (*too big*) praegrandis
overhang *vt* impendēre
overhaul *vt* reficĕre
overhead *adv* desuper, insuper
overhear *vt* excipĕre, auscultare
overjoyed *adj* **to be —** nimio gaudio exsultare
overladen *adj* praegravatus
overland *adj* per terram
overlay *vt* inducĕre, illinĕre
overload *vt* nimis onerare
overlook *vt* (*not to notice*) praetermittĕre; (*to pardon*) ignoscĕre (*with dat*); (*a view*) despectare
overlord *s* dominus *m*
overpower *vt* exsuperare, opprimĕre
overrate *vt* nimis aestimare
overreach *vt* circumvenire
overriding *adj* praecipuus
overripe *adj* praematurus
overrun *vt* (per)vagari; (*fig*) obsidēre
overseas *adj* transmarinus
oversee *vt* praeesse (*with dat*)
overseer *s* curator, praeses, custos *m*
overshadow *vt* obumbrare; (*fig*) obscurare
overshoot *vt* excedĕre, transgredi
oversight *s* incuria, neglegentia *f*, error *m*
oversleep *vi* diutius dormire
overspread *vt* obducĕre
overstate *vt* in majus extollĕre
overstep *vt* excedĕre, transgredi
overt *adj* apertus; **—ly** palam
overtake *vt* consequi
overtax *vt* (*fig*) abuti (*with abl*)
overthrow *s* eversio, ruina *f*, excidium *n*
overthrow *vt* subvertĕre, evertĕre, dejicĕre
overture *s* (*mus*) exordium *n*; (*proposal*) conditio *f*; **to make —s to** agĕre cum (*with abl*)
overturn *vt* evertĕre, subvertĕre
overweening *adj* superbus, insolens, arrogans
overwhelm *vt* obruĕre, opprimĕre
overwork *vt* **to — oneself** plus aequo laborare
owe *vt* debēre
owing to *prep* propter (*with acc*)
owl *s* bubo *m*, strix *f*
own *adj* proprius; **one's —** suus, proprius
own *vt* possidēre, tenēre; (*to acknowledge*) fatēri, confitēri
owner *s* dominus, possessor *m*
ownership *s* possessio *f*, mancipium, dominium *n*
ox *s* bos *m*
oyster *s* ostrea *f*
oyster shell *s* ostreae testa *f*

P

pace *s* (*step*) pass·us -ūs, grad·us -ūs *m*; (*measure*) pass·us -ūs *m*; (*speed*) velocitas *f*, grad·us -ūs *m*
pace *vi* incedĕre, gradi; **to — up and down** spatiari
pacific *adj* pacificus, tranquillus
pacification *s* pacificatio *f*
pacify *vt* pacare, placare, sedare
pack *s* (*bundle*) sarcina *f*, fasciculus *m*; (*of animals*) grex *m*; (*of people*) turba *f*, grex *m*
pack *vt* (*items of luggage*) colligĕre, componĕre; (*to fill completely*) frequentare, complēre; (*to compress*) stipare; *vi* vasa colligĕre
package *s* sarcina *f*, fasciculus *m*
packet *s* fasciculus *m*
pack horse *s* equus clitellarius *m*
packsaddle *s* clitellae *f pl*
pact *s* pactum *n*, pactio *f*; **to make a —** pacisci
pad *s* pulvinus, pulvillus *m*
pad *vt* suffarcinare
padding *s* fartura *f*
paddle *s* remus *m*
paddle *vi* remigare
paddock *s* saeptum *n*
pagan *s* paganus *m*
page *s* (*of book*) pagina, scheda *f*; puer *m*
pageant *s* pompa *f*, spectaculum *n*
pail *s* hama, situla *f*
pain *s* dolor *m*; (*fig*) angor *m*; **to be in —** dolēre; **to take —s** operam dare
pain *vt* dolore afficĕre, excruciare; *vi* dolēre
painful *adj* gravis, acerbus, molestus; **—ly** graviter, magno cum dolore
painless *adj* doloris expers
painstaking *adj* operosus
paint *s* pigmentum *n*; (*for face*) fucus *m*
paint *vt* pingĕre, depingĕre
paintbrush *s* penicillus *m*
painter *s* pictor *m*
painting *s* pictura *f*
pair *s* par *n*; (*of oxen*) jugum *n*
pair *vt* conjungĕre, componĕre
palace *s* regia *f*, palatium *n*
palatable *adj* jucundus, suavis, sapidus
palate *s* palatum *n*
palatial *adj* regius

pale *adj* pallidus; **to be —** pallēre; **to grow —** pallescĕre
pale *s* palus *m*
paling *s* saepes *f*
palisade *s* vallum *n*
pall *s* pallium *n*
pall *vt* satiare; *vi* vapescĕre
pallet *s* grabat·us -ūs *m*
palliative *s* lenimentum *n*
pallid *adj* pallidus
pallor *s* pallor *m*
palm *s* (*of hand*) palma *f*; (*tree*) palma *f*
palpable *adj* tractabilis; (*fig*) apertus, manifestus
palpitate *vi* palpitare
palsied *adj* paralyticus
palsy *s* paralysis *f*
paltry *adj* vilis, minutus
pamper *vt* indulgēre (*with dat*)
pamphlet *s* libellus *m*
pan *s* patina, patella *f*; (*for frying*) sartago *f*
pancake *s* laganum *n*
pander *s* leno *m*
pander *vi* lenocinari
panegyric *s* laudatio *f*
panel *s* (*of wall*) abacus *m*; (*of ceiling*) lacunar *n*; (*of jury*) decurio *m*; (*of door*) tympanum *n*
paneled *adj* laqueatus
pang *s* dolor *m*
panic *s* pavor *m*
panic-stricken *adj* pavidus
panoply *s* arma *n pl*
panorama *s* conspect·us -ūs *m*
pant *vi* palpitare, anhelare; **to — after** (*fig*) gestire
pantheism *s* pantheismus *m*
pantheist *s* pantheista *m*
pantheon *s* Pantheon *n*
panther *s* pantera *f*
panting *adj* anhelus
panting *s* anhelit·us -ūs *m*
pantomime *s* (*play and actor*) mimus *m*
pantry *s* cella penaria *f*
pap *s* papilla, mamilla *f*
paper *s* (*stationery*) charta *f*; (*newspaper*) acta diurna *n pl*; **—s** scripta *n pl*
paper *adj* chartaceus, charteus
papyrus *s* papyrus *f*
par *s* **to be on a — with** par esse (*with dat*)
parable *s* parabole *f*
parade *s* (*mil*) decurs·us -ūs *m*; pompa *f*; (*display*) apparat·us -ūs *m*, pompa *f*
parade *vt* (*fig*) ostentare, jactare; *vi* (*mil*) decurrĕre
paradise *s* paradisus *m*
paradox *s* oxymora verba *n pl*
paragon *s* specimen, exemplar *n*
paragraph *s* caput *n*
parallel *adj* parallelus; (*fig*) consimilis
parallel *vt* exaequare
paralysis *s* paralysis *f*; (*fig*) torpedo *f*
paralytic *adj* paralyticus
paralyze *vt* debilitare, enervare, percellĕre
paramount *adj* supremus
paramour *s* (*man*) moechus, adulter *m*; (*woman*) meretrix, pellex *f*
parapet *s* pluteus *m*
paraphernalia *s* apparat·us -ūs *m*
paraphrase *s* paraphrasis *f*
paraphrase *vt* vertĕre, interpretari
parasite *s* parasitus *m*
parasol *s* umbella *f*, umbraculum *n*
parcel *s* fasciculus *m*; (*plot of land*) agellus *m*
parcel *vt* **to — out** partire, dispertire
parch *vt* torrēre
parched *adj* torridus, aridus; **to be —** arēre
parchment *s* membrana *f*
pardon *s* venia *f*
pardon *vt* ignoscĕre (*with dat*); (*an offense*) condonare
pardonable *adj* ignoscendus, condonandus
pare *vt* (*vegetables*) deglubĕre; (*the nails*) resecare
parent *s* parens *m & f*
parentage *s* genus *n*, stirps *f*
parental *adj* patrius
parenthesis *s* interpositio, interclusio *f*
parity *s* paritas, aequalitas *f*
park *s* horti *m pl*
parlance *s* sermo *m*
parley *s* colloquium *n*
parley *vi* colloqui
parliament *s* senat·us -ūs *m*
parliamentary *adj* senatorius
parlor *s* exedrium *n*
parody *s* ridicula imitatio *f*
parole *s* fides *f*
paroxysm *s* access·us -ūs *m*
parricide *s* (*murder*) parricidium *n*; (*murderer*) parricida *m & f*
parrot *s* psittacus *m*
parry *vt* avertĕre, defendĕre
parse *vt* flectĕre
parsimonious *adj* parcus; **—ly** parce
parsing *s* partium orationis flexio *f*
parsley *s* apium *n*
part *s* pars *f*; (*in play*) partes *f pl*; (*duty*) officium *n*; **for the most —** maximam partem; **in —** partim; **on the — of** ab (*with abl*); **to act the — of** sustinēre partes (*with genit*); **to take — in** interesse (*with dat*), particeps esse (*with genit*)
part *vt* separare, dividĕre; **to — company** discedĕre; *vi* discedĕre, abire; (*to go open*) dehiscĕre; **to — with** dimittĕre
partial *adj* iniquus; (*incomplete*) mancus; **to be —** favēre (*with dat*); **—ly** aliqua ex parte
partiality *s* iniquitas *f*
participant *s* particeps *m & f*
participate *vi* interesse; **to — in** interesse (*with dat*), particeps esse (*with genit*)
participation *s* participatio, societas *f*
participle *s* participium *n*
particle *s* particula *f*

particular *adj* (*own*) proprius; (*special*) peculiaris, singularis, praecipuus; (*fussy*) fastidiosus; **—ly** praecipue, praesertim
particularize *vt* exsequi
particulars *s* singula *n pl*
parting *s* discess·us -ūs, digress·us -ūs *m*
partisan *s* fautor *m*
partition *s* partitio *f*; (*between rooms*) paries *m*; (*enclosure*) saeptum *n*
partly *adv* partim, ex parte
partner *s* socius *m*, socia *f*, particeps *m & f*; (*in office*) collega *m*; (*in marriage*) conju(n)x, consors *m & f*
partnership *s* consociatio, societas, consortio *f*
partridge *s* perdix *m & f*
party *s* (*entertainment*) convivium *n*; (*pol*) factio *f*, partes *f pl*; (*detachment*) man·us -ūs *f*; **to join a —** partes sequi
pass *s* angustiae *f pl*
pass *vt* (*to go by*) praeterire, transire, transgredi; (*to exceed*) excedĕre; (*to approve*) probare; (*time*) agĕre, degĕre; (*a law*) perferre; **to — around** circumferre, tradĕre; **to — down** tradĕre; **to — sentence** jus dicĕre; **to — the test** approbari; *vi* (*of time*) transire, abire, praeterire; **to come to —** evenire, fieri; **to let —** praetermittĕre, dimittĕre; **to — away** (*to die*) perire, abire; **to — for** habēri, vidēri; **to — on** (*to go forward*) pergĕre; (*to die*) perire; **to — out** collabi, intermori; **to — over** transire
passable *adj* (*of road*) pervius; (*fig*) mediocris, tolerabilis
passably *adv* mediocriter, tolerabiliter
passage *s* (*act*) transit·us -ūs *m*; (*by water*) transmissio, trajectio *f*; (*of book*) locus *m*
passenger *s* viator *m*; (*on ship*) vector *m*
passer-by *s* praeteriens *m*
passing *s* obit·us -ūs *m*
passion *s* cupiditas, permotio *f*, fervor *m*; (*anger*) ira *f*; (*lust*) libido *f*
passionate *adj* fervidus, ardens; iracundus; **—ly** ardenter; iracunde
passive *adj* passivus; **—ly** passive
passport *s* diploma *n*
password *s* tessera *f*
past *adj* praeteritus; (*immediately preceding*) proximus, superior
past *s* tempus praeteritum *n*
past *prep* praeter (*with acc*), post (*with acc*)
paste *s* gluten *n*
paste *vt* agglutinare, conglutinare
pasteboard *s* charta crassa *f*
pastime *s* oblectamentum *n*, ludus *m*
pastoral *adj* pastoralis, bucolicus
pastoral *s* poema bucolicum *n*
pastry *s* crustum *n*
pasture *s* past·us -ūs *m*, pascuum *n*, pastio *f*
pasture *vt* pascĕre; *vi* (*to graze*) pasci
pat *adj* idoneus
pat *vt* permulcēre, demulcēre
patch *s* assumentum *n*, pannus *m*
patch *vt* resarcire, assuĕre
patchwork *s* cento *m*
patent *adj* apertus, manifestus; **—ly** manifesto
patent *s* privilegium *n*
paternal *adj* paternus
paternity *s* paternitas *f*
path *s* semita *f*, trames, callis *m*; (*fig*) via *f*
pathetic *adj* maestus; **—ally** maeste
pathless *adj* invius
pathos *s* pathos *n*, dolor *m*
pathway *s* semita *f*, callis, trames *m*
patience *s* patientia *f*
patient *adj* patiens, tolerans; **—ly** patienter, aequo animo
patient *s* aegrotus *m*, aegrota *f*
patriarch *s* patriarcha *m*
patriarchal *adj* patriarchicus
patrician *adj* patricius
patrician *s* patricius *m*
patrimony *s* patrimonium *n*
patriot *s* amans patriae *m*
patriotic *adj* amans patriae
patriotism *s* amor patriae, amor in patriam *m*
patrol *s* excubiae *f pl*
patrol *vt* circumire; *vi* excubias agĕre
patron *s* patronus *m*
patronage *s* patrocinium, praesidium *n*
patroness *s* patrona *f*
patronize *vt* favēre (*with dat*), fovēre
patronymic *s* patronymicum nomen *n*
pattern *s* exemplar, exemplum, specimen *n*
paucity *s* paucitas *f*
paunch *s* ingluvies *f*
pauper *s* pauper *m*
pause *s* pausa, mora *f*; (*mus*) intermissio *f*, intervallum *n*
pause *vi* insistĕre, intermittĕre
pave *vt* sternĕre
pavement *s* pavimentum *n*, stratura *f*
pavilion *s* tentorium *n*
paving stone *s* saxum quadratum *n*
paw *s* ungula *f*, pes *m*
paw *vt* pedibus pulsare
pawn *s* pignus *n*
pawn *vt* pignerare
pawnbroker *s* pignerator *m*
pay *s* merces *f*; (*mil*) stipendium *n*
pay *vt* solvĕre; (*in full*) persolvĕre, pendĕre; (*mil*) stipendium numerare (*with dat*); **to — a compliment to** laudare; **to — for** solvĕre (*with acc of thing and dat of person*); **to — respects to** salutare; **to — the penalty** poenam dare, poenam luĕre; *vi* **it pays** operae pretium est, prodest, lucro est
payable *adj* solvendus
paymaster *s* dispensator *m*; (*mil*) tribunus aerarius *m*
payment *s* (*act*) solutio *f*; (*sum of money*) pensio *f*

pea *s* pisum, cicer *n*
peace *s* pax *f*; quies *f*, otium *n*
peaceful *adj* tranquillus, placidus, pacatus; **—ly** tranquille, placide, cum bona pace
peacemaker *s* pacificator *m*
peace offering *s* placamen, placamentum, piaculum *n*
peacetime *s* otium *n*
peach *s* malum Persicum *n*
peacock *s* pavo *m*
peak *s* (*of mountain*) cacumen *n*; vertex, apex *m*
peal *s* (*of thunder*) fragor *m*; (*of bells*) concent·us -ūs *m*
peal *vi* resonare
pear *s* pirum *n*
pearl *s* margarita *f*
pearly *adj* gemmeus
peasant *s* agricola, colonus *m*
peasantry *s* agricolae, agrestes *m pl*
pebble *s* lapillus, calculus *m*
peck *s* modius *m*
peck *vt* rostro impetĕre, vellicare
peculation *s* peculat·us -ūs *m*
peculiar *adj* proprius, peculiaris, praecipuus, singularis; **—ly** praecipue
peculiarity *s* proprietas *f*
pecuniary *adj* pecuniarius
pedagogue *s* paedagogus *m*; (*schoolmaster*) magister *m*
pedant *s* scholasticus *m*
pedantic *adj* putidus, nimis diligens; **—ally** nimis diligenter
pedantry *s* eruditio insulsa *f*
peddle *vt* venditare, circumferre
peddler *s* venditor, institor *m*
pedestal *s* basis *f*
pedestrian *adj* pedester
pedestrian *s* pedes *m*
pedigree *s* stemma *n*, stirps *f*
pediment *s* fastigium *n*
peel *s* cortex *m*
peel *vt* decorticare, glubĕre
peep *s* aspect·us -ūs, tuit·us -ūs *m*
peep *vi* inspicĕre
peephole *s* conspicillum *n*
peer *s* par *m*; (*of peerage*) patricius *m*
peer *vi* **to — at** intuēri
peerless *adj* unicus, incomparabilis
peevish *adj* stomachosus, morosus, difficilis; **—ly** stomachose, morose
peg *s* clavus, paxillus *m*
pelican *s* pelicanus, onocrotalus *m*
pellet *s* globulus *m*
pelt *s* pellis *f*
pelt *vt* (*to hurl*) jacĕre; (*to beat*) verberare, petĕre
pen *s* (*to write with*) calamus, stylus *m*; (*enclosure*) saeptum *n*; (*for sheep*) ovile *n*; (*for pigs*) suile *n*
pen *vt* scribĕre, componere; **to — in** includĕre
penal *adj* poenalis
penalize *vt* poenā afficĕre, mul(c)tare
penalty *s* poena, mul(c)ta *f*
penance *s* satisfactio *f*
pencil *s* stilus *m*, graphis *f*
pending *adj* suspensus; (*law*) sub judice
pending *prep* inter (*with acc*)
pendulum *s* libramentum *n*
penetrate *vt* penetrare
penetrating *adj* acer, perspicax
penetration *s* acies mentis *f*, acumen *n*
peninsula *s* paeninsula *f*
penitence *s* paenitentia *f*
penitent *adj* paenitens; **—ly** paenitenter
penitentiary *s* carcer *m*
penknife *s* scalpellum *n*
penmanship *s* man·us -ūs *f*
pennant *s* vexillum *n*
penniless *adj* inops
penny *s* quadrans *m*
pension *s* annua *n pl*
pensive *adj* meditabundus
penultimate *s* paenultima syllaba *f*
penurious *adj* parcus, sordidus
penury *s* egestas, inopia *f*
people *s* (*nation*) populus *m*; homines *m pl*; (*common people*) plebs *f*; **— say** dicunt
people *vt* frequentare
pepper *s* piper *n*
pepper *vt* pipere condire; (*fig*) (*with blows*) verberare
peppermint *s* mentha *f*
perceive *vt* percipĕre, sentire, vidēre, intellegĕre
percentage *s* portio *f*
perceptible *adj* percipiendus, manifestus
perceptibly *adv* sensim
perception *s* perceptio *f*, sens·us -ūs *m*
perch *s* (*for birds*) pertica *f*; (*type of fish*) perca *f*
perch *vi* insidēre
perchance *adv* forte
percolate *vt* percolare; *vi* permanare
percussion *s* ict·us -ūs, concuss·us -ūs *m*
perdition *s* interit·us -ūs *m*; exitium *n*
peremptory *adj* arrogans
perennial *adj* perennis
perfect *adj* perfectus, absolutus; (*gram*) praeteritus; **—ly** perfecte, absolute; (*entirely*) plane
perfect *vt* perficĕre, absolvĕre
perfection *s* perfectio, absolutio *f*
perfidious *adj* perfidus, perfidiosus; **—ly** perfidiose
perfidy *s* perfidia *f*
perforate *vt* perforare, terebrare
perforation *s* foramen *n*
perform *vt* perficĕre, peragĕre; (*duty*) fungi (*with abl*); (*to play*) agĕre
performance *s* perfunctio, executio *f*; (*work*) opus *n*; (*of a play*) actio *f*; (*play, drama*) fabula *f*
performer *s* actor *m*; (*in play*) histrio *m*
perfume *s* odor *m*, unguentum *n*
perfume *vt* odoribus imbuĕre
perhaps *adv* forte, forsitan, fortasse
peril *s* periculum *n*
perilous *adj* periculosus; **—ly** periculose
period *s* (*gram*) periodus *f*; tempus, spatium *n*, aetas *f*; (*rhet*) circuit·us -ūs *m*

periodic *adj* certus; (*style*) periodicus; **—ally** certis temporibus
periphery *s* peripheria *f*, ambit·us -ūs *m*
periphrastic *adj* per periphrasin dictus
perish *vi* perire, interire
perishable *adj* fragilis, caducus, mortalis
peristyle *s* peristyl(i)um *n*
perjure *vt* **to — oneself** pejerare, perjurare
perjured *adj* perjurus
perjury *s* perjurium *n*; **to commit —** pejerare, perjurare
permanence *s* stabilitas, constantia *f*
permanent *adj* diuturnus, perpetuus, mansurus; **—ly** perpetuo
permeable *adj* pervius
permeate *vt* penetrare; *vi* permanare
permission *s* permissio, venia, potestas *f*
permit *vt* permittĕre (*with dat*), sinere
permutation *s* permutatio *f*
pernicious *adj* perniciosus; **—ly** perniciose
peroration *s* peroratio *f*
perpendicular *adj* perpendicularis, directus
perpendicular *s* linea perpendicularis *f*
perpetrate *vt* facĕre, perficĕre
perpetrator *s* auctor, reus *m*
perpetual *adj* perpetuus, perennis, sempiternus; **—ly** perpetuo
perpetuate *vt* perpetuare, continuare
perpetuity *s* perpetuitas *f*
perplex *vt* turbare, confundĕre
perplexing *adj* perplexus, ambiguus
perplexity *s* perturbatio, dubitatio *f*
persecute *vt* persequi, insequi, vexare
persecution *s* insectatio *f*
persecutor *s* insectator *m*
perseverance *s* perseverantia, constantia *f*
persevere *vi* perseverare, perstare, constare
persevering *adj* perseverans, constans, tenax; **—ly** perseverante, constanter
persist *vi* perstare, perseverare
persistence *s* permansio, pertinacia, perseverantia *f*
persistent *adj* pertinax; **—ly** pertinaciter
person *s* homo *m & f*, quidam *m*; (*body*) corpus *n*; **in —** ipse
personage *s* persona *f*
personal *adj* privatus, suus; (*gram*) personalis; **—ly** ipse, per se, coram
personality *s* persona, natura *f*, ingenium *n*
personification *s* prosopopoeia *f*
personify *vt* personā induĕre
personnel *s* membra *n pl*, socii *m pl*
perspective *s* scaenographia *f*
perspicacious *adj* perspicax
perspicacity *s* perspicacitas *f*
perspiration *s* sudatio *f*, sudor *m*
perspire *vi* sudare
persuade *vt* persuadēre (*with dat*)
persuasion *s* persuasio *f*
persuasive *adj* suasorius; **—ly** persuasibiliter
pert *adj* procax; **—ly** procaciter
pertain *vi* pertinēre, attinēre
pertinent *adj* appositus; **to be —** ad rem pertinēre; **—ly** apposite
perturb *vt* turbare, perturbare
perturbation *s* perturbatio *f*
perusal *s* perlectio *f*
peruse *vt* perlegere, evolvĕre
pervade *vt* invadĕre, permanare, perfundĕre
perverse *adj* perversus, pravus; **—ly** perverse
perversion *s* depravatio *f*
perversity *s* perversitas, pravitas *f*
pervert *vt* (*words*) detorquēre; depravare, corrumpĕre
pest *s* pestis *f*
pester *vt* vexare, infestare, sollicitare
pestilence *s* pestilentia *f*
pestle *s* pilum *n*
pet *s* corculum *n*, deliciae *f pl*
pet *vt* fovēre, in deliciis habēre
petal *s* floris folium *n*
petition *s* petitio *f*, preces *f pl*; (*pol*) libellus *m*
petition *vt* supplicare, orare
petitioner *s* supplex *m*
petrify *vt* in lapidem convertĕre; *vi* lapidescĕre
petticoat *s* subucula *f*
pettiness *s* animus angustus *m*
petty *adj* minutus, angustus, levis
petulance *s* petulantia, protervitas *f*
petulant *adj* protervus
phalanx *s* phalanx *f*
phantom *s* simulacrum, phantasma *n*, species *f*
pharmacy *s* ars medicamentaria *f*; (*drugstore*) taberna medicina, apotheca *f*
phase *s* (*of moon*) lunae facies *f*; (*fig*) vices *f pl*
pheasant *s* phasianus *m*, phasiana *f*
phenomenal *adj* singularis
phenomenon *s* res *f*; (*remarkable event*) portentum, prodigium *n*
philanthropic *adj* humanus
philanthropy *s* humanitas *f*
philologist *s* philologus, grammaticus *m*
philology *s* philologia *f*
philosopher *s* philosophus, sapiens *m*
philosophical *adj* philosophicus; **—ly** philosophice, sapienter; (*calmly*) aequo animo
philosophize *vi* philosophari
philosophy *s* philosophia, sapientia *f*; (*theory*) ratio *f*
philter *s* philtrum *n*
phlegm *s* pituita *f*, phelgma *n*
phlegmatic *adj* (*fig*) lentus
phosphorus *s* phosphorus *m*
phrase *s* locutio *f*; (*gram*) incisum *n*
phraseology *s* locutio, loquendi ratio *f*
physical *adj* physicus; (*natural*) corporis (*genit, used adjectively*); **—ly** naturā

physician *s* medicus *m*
physicist *s* physicus *m*
physics *s* physica *n pl*
physiognomy *s* oris habit·us -ūs *m*
physique *s* vires *f pl*
pick *vt* (*to choose*) eligĕre; (*to pluck*) carpĕre; (*to gather*) decerpĕre; **to — off** avellĕre; **to — out** eligĕre; **to — up** tollĕre
pick *s* (*tool*) dolabra *f*; (*best part*) flos *m*, lecti *m pl*
pickax *s* dolabra *f*
picked *adj* electus, delectus
picket *s* (*mil*) statio *f*
pickle *s* muria *f*
pickle *vt* in aceto condire, in muriā condire
pickled *adj* muriā conditus
picture *s* tabula picta, pictura *f*; (*fig*) descriptio *f*
picture *vt* (*to imagine*) fingĕre, ante oculos ponĕre
picture gallery *s* pinacotheca *f*
picturesque *adj* venustus, amoenus
pie *s* crustum *n*
piece *s* pars, portio *f*; (*of food*) frustum *n*; (*of cloth*) pannus *m*; (*broken off*) fragmentum *n*; (*coin*) nummus *m*; (*drama*) fabula *f*; **to fall to —s** dilabi; **to tear to —s** dilaniare, lacerare
piece *vt* resarcire; **to — together** fabricari, consuĕre
piecemeal *adv* frustatim, membratim
pier *s* moles *f*, agger *m*
pierce *vt* perforare; (*with sword, etc.*) transfigĕre, perfodĕre; (*fig*) pungĕre
piercing *adj* acutus, stridulus
piety *s* pietas, religio *f*
pig *s* porcus *m*, sus *m & f*
pigeon *s* columba *f*
pigment *s* pigmentum *n*
pigsty *s* hara *f*, suile *n*
pike *s* (*weapon*) hasta *f*; (*fish*) lupus *m*
pilaster *s* parasta, columella *f*
pile *s* (*heap*) acervus, cumulus *m*; (*for cremation*) rogus *m*; (*for building*) moles *f*; (*nap of cloth*) villus *m*
pile *vt* coacervare, congerĕre; **to — up** exstruĕre
pilgrim *s* peregrinator *m*
pilgrimage *s* peregrinatio *f*
pill *s* pilula *f*
pillage *s* vastatio, direptio, expilatio, rapina *f*
pillage *vt* vastare, diripĕre, depopulari, expilare, praedari
pillar *s* columna, pila *f*, columen *n*
pillow *s* pulvinus *m*, culcita *f*, cervical *n*
pillowcase *s* cervicalis integumentum *n*
pilot *s* gubernator *m*
pilot *vt* gubernare
pimp *s* leno *m*
pimple *s* pustula *f*
pimply *adj* pustulosus
pin *s* ac·us -ūs, acicula *f*; (*peg*) clavus *m*
pin *vt* acu figĕre; affigĕre
pincers *s* forceps *m & f*
pinch *vt* vellicare; (*as cold*) (ad)urĕre; (*to squeeze*) coartare; (*of shoe*) urĕre
pine *s* pinus *f*
pine *vi* **to — away** tabescĕre, languēre; **to — for** desiderare
pineapple *s* (nux) pinea *f*
pink *adj* rosaceus, rubicundus
pinnacle *s* fastigium *n*, summus grad·us -ūs *m*
pint *s* sextarius *m*
pioneer *s* praecursor *m*
pious *adj* pius; (*scrupulous*) religiosus; (*saintly*) sanctus; **—ly** pie, religiose, sancte
pipe *s* (*tube*) tubus *m*; (*mus*) fistula *f*
pipe *vt* fistulā canĕre
piper *s* tibicen *m*
piquant *s* salsus, facetus; **—ly** salse
pique *s* offensio *f*
pique *vt* offendĕre
piracy *s* latrocinium *n*
pirate *s* pirata, praedo *m*
piratical *adj* praedatorius
pit *s* fossa, fovea *f*, puteus *m*; (*in theater*) cavea *f*; (*quarry*) fodina *f*
pitch *s* pix *f*; (*sound*) sonus *m*; (*degree*) grad·us -ūs *m*, fastigium *n*; (*slope*) fastigium *n*; **to such a — of** eo (*with genit*)
pitch *vt* (*to fling*) conjicĕre; (*camp*) ponĕre; (*tent*) tendĕre
pitcher *s* urceus *m*
pitchfork *s* furca *f*
piteous *adj* miserabilis; **—ly** miserabiliter, misere
pitfall *s* fovea *f*
pith *s* medulla *f*
pithy *adj* (*fig*) sententiosus
pitiable *adj* miserandus
pitiful *adj* misericors; (*pitiable*) miserabilis, miserandus; **—ly** misere
pitiless *adj* immisericors, durus; **—ly** immisericorditer
pittance *s* (*allowance for food*) demensum *n*; (*trifling sum*) mercedula *f*
pity *s* misericordia, miseratio *f*
pity *vt* miserēri (*with genit*); **I — him** miseret me ejus
pivot *s* axis, paxillus *m*; (*fig*) cardo *m*
placard *s* titulus, libellus *m*
place *s* locus *m*; **in — of** pro (*with abl*), loco (*with genit*); **in the first —** primum, primo; **out of —** intempestivus; **to take —** fieri, accidĕre
place *vt* ponĕre, locare, collocare
placid *adj* placidus, tranquillus; **—ly** placide, tranquille
plagiarism *s* furtum litterarium *n*
plagiarist *s* fur litterarius *m*
plagiarize *vt* furari
plague *s* pestilentia *f*; (*fig*) pestis *f*
plague *vt* vexare, exagitare
plain *s* campus *m*, planities *f*; **of the —** campester
plain *adj* (*clear*) apertus, manifestus, perspicuus; (*unadorned*) inornatus, simplex; (*of one color*) unicolor; (*frank*) sincerus; (*homely*)

invenustus; **—ly** aperte, manifeste; simpliciter; sincere
plaintiff *s* petitor *m*
plaintive *adj* querulus, flebilis; **—ly** flebiliter
plan *s* consilium, propositum *n*; (*drawing*) descriptio *f*; (*layout*) forma *f*
plan *vt* (*to scheme*) excogitare, meditari; (*to intend to*) in animo habēre (*with inf*); (*to draw*) designare, describĕre
plane *s* (*tool*) runcina *f*; (*level surface*) planities *f*
plane *vt* runcinare
planet *s* planeta, stella errans *or* vaga *f*
plank *s* assis *m*, tabula *f*
plant *s* planta, herba *f*
plant *vt* serĕre, conserĕre; (*feet*) ponĕre
plantation *s* plantarium *n*
planter *s* sator *m*
planting *s* sat·us -ūs *m*, consitura *f*
plaster *s* tectorium, gypsum *n*; (*med*) emplastrum *n*
plaster *vt* gypsare, dealbare
plastic *adj* plasticus, ductilis
plate *s* (*dish*) patella *f*, catillus *m*; (*coating*) lamina *f*; (*silver*) argentum *n*
plated *adj* bracteatus
platform *s* suggest·us -ūs *m*, suggestum *n*
platitude *s* trita sententia *f*
Platonic *adj* Platonis (*genit, used adjectively*)
platter *s* patella, lanx *f*
plausible *adj* verisimilis
play *s* ludus *m*; (*drama*) fabula *f*
play *vt* ludĕre; (*instrument*) canĕre (*with abl*); (*game*) ludĕre (*with abl*) (*role*) agĕre; **to — a trick on** ludificari
player *s* (*in game*) lusor *m*; (*on stage*) histrio, actor *m*; (*on wind instrument*) tibicen *m*; (*on string instrument*) fidicen *m*
playful *adj* lascivus, jocosus, ludibundus; (*words*) facetus; **—ly** per ludum, per jocum
playmate *s* collusor *m*
plaything *s* ludibrium *n*
playwright *s* fabularum scriptor *m*
plea *s* (*law*) petitio, exceptio, defensio *f*; (*excuse*) excusatio *f*
plead *vi* (*in court*) causam agĕre; (*to beg*) obsecrare, implorare, orare; **to — against** causam dicĕre contra (*with acc*); **to — for** defendĕre
pleasant *adj* amoenus, gratus, jucundus, suavis; **—ly** jucunde, suaviter
pleasantry *s* jocosa dicacitas *f*, facetiae *f pl*
please *vt* placēre (*with dat*), delectare; **if you —** si placet; **please!** obsecro!; sis!, amabo! (*colloquial*)
pleasing *adj* gratus, jucundus
pleasurable *adj* jucundus
pleasure *s* voluptas *f*; **it is my —** libet; **to derive —** voluptatem capĕre
plebeian *adj* plebeius
plebeians *s* plebs *f*
pledge *s* pignus *n*; (*proof*) testimonium *n*
pledge *vt* (op)pignerare, obligare; **to — one's word** fidem obligare
Pleiads *s* Pleiades *f pl*
plenary *adj* plenus, perfectus
plenipotentiary *s* legatus *m*
plentiful *adj* largus, affluens, uber; **—ly** large, ubertim
plenty *s* copia, abundantia *f*
plethora *s* pletura *f*
pleurisy *s* pleuritis *f*
pliable *adj* flexibilis, tractabilis, mansuetus
pliant *adj* lentus
plight *s* conditio *f*, stat·us -ūs *m*, discrimen *n*
plod *vi* assidue laborare
plodder *s* sedulus homo *m*
plodding *adj* laboriosus, assiduus, sedulus
plot *s* (*conspiracy*) conjuratio *f*, insidiae *f pl*; (*of drama*) argumentum *n*; (*of ground*) agellus *m*
plot *vi* conjurare, moliri
plow *s* aratrum *n*
plow *vt* arare; **to — up** exarare
plowing *s* aratio *f*
plowman *s* bubulcus, arator *m*
plowshare *s* vomer *m*
pluck *s* animus *m*
pluck *vt* carpĕre; **to — off** avellĕre, decerpĕre; **to — out** evellĕre, eripĕre; **to — up** eruĕre; **to — up courage** animo esse
plug *s* obturamentum *n*
plug *vt* obturare
plum *s* prunum *n*
plumage *s* plumae, pennae *f pl*
plumber *s* plumbarius *m*
plume *s* crista *f*
plummet *s* perpendiculum *n*
plump *adj* pinguis, obesus
plum tree *s* prunus *f*
plunder *s* (*act*) rapina *f*; (*booty*) praeda *f*
plunder *vt* praedari
plunderer *s* praedator *m*
plundering *s* rapina, praedatio *f*
plundering *adj* praedatorius, praedabundus
plunge *vt* mergĕre, submergĕre; (*sword, etc.*) condĕre; *vi* immergi, se mergĕre
pluperfect *s* plus quam perfectum tempus *n*
plural *adj* pluralis
plurality *s* multitudo *f*, numerus major *m*
plush *adj* lautus
ply *vt* exercēre, urgēre
poach *vt* (*eggs*) frigĕre; *vi* illicita venatione uti
poacher *s* fur *m*
pocket *s* sin·us -ūs, sacculus *m*
pocket *vt* in sacculis condĕre
pocket book *s* pugillaria *n pl*
pockmark *s* cicatrix *f*
pod *s* siliqua *f*
poem *s* poema, carmen *n*
poet *s* poeta, vates *m*

poetess *s* poetria, poetris *f*
poetic *adj* poeticus; **—ly** poetice
poetics *s* ars poetica *f*
poetry *s* (*art*) poetice *f*; (*poems*) poemata, carmina *n pl*, poesis *f*
poignancy *s* acerbitas *f*
poignant *adj* acerbus, pungens
point *s* punctum *n*; (*pointed end*) acumen *n*, acies *f*; (*of swords, etc.*) mucro *m*; (*fig*) quaestio, res *f*, stat·us -ūs *m*, argumentum *n*; **beside the —** ab re; **from this — on** posthac, hinc; **— of view** sententia *f*; **to the —** ad rem; **up to this —** adhuc, hactenus
point *vt* (*to sharpen*) acuĕre; **to — out** monstrare, indicare
pointed *adj* acutus; (*fig*) salsus; (*stinging*) aculeatus; **—ly** acute, aperte
pointer *s* index *m & f*
pointless *adj* (*fig*) insulsus, frigidus; **—ly** insulse
poise *s* (*fig*) urbanitas *f*
poise *vt* ponderare, pendĕre, librare
poison *s* venenum, virus *n*
poison *vt* venenare, veneno necare; (*fig*) vitiare
poisoning *s* veneficium *n*
poisonous *adj* venenatus, venenosus
poke *vt* (*to jab*) cubito pulsare, fodicare; (*fire*) fodĕre
polar *adj* arcticus
polarity *s* polaritas *f*
pole *s* asser, contus *m*, pertica *f*; (*of earth*) polus *m*
polemic *s* controversiae *f pl*
pole star *s* stella polaris *f*
police *s* vigiles, custodes *m pl*
policeman *s* vigil *m*
policy *s* ratio *f*, consilium *n*
polish *vt* polire; **to — up** expolire
polish *s* nitor, levor *m*; (*refined manners*) urbanitas *f*; (*literary*) lima *f*
polite *adj* comis, urbanus; **—ly** comiter, urbane
politeness *s* urbanitas, comitas *f*
politic *adj* prudens, astutus
political *adj* civilis, publicus
politician *s* magistrat·us -ūs *m*
politics *s* res publica *f*; **to enter —** ad rem publicam accedĕre
poll *s* caput *n*; **—s** comitia *n pl*
poll *vt* suffragiis petĕre
polling booth *s* saeptum *n*
poll tax *s* capitum exactio *f*
pollute *vt* polluĕre, inquinare, contaminare
pollution *s* (*act*) contaminatio *f*; (*filth*) colluvio, impuritas *f*
polygamy *s* polygamia *f*
polysyllabic *adj* polysyllabus
polytheism *s* multorum deorum cult·us -ūs *m*
pomegranate *s* malum Punicum *n*
pommel *vt* pulsare, verberare
pomp *s* pompa *f*, apparat·us -ūs *m*
pomposity *s* magnificentia *f*
pompous *adj* magnificus, gloriosus; **—ly** magnifice, gloriose
pond *s* stagnum *n*
ponder *vt* in mente agitare, considerare, ponderare
ponderous *adj* ponderosus, praegravis
pontiff *s* pontifex *m*
pontifical *adj* pontificalis
pontificate *s* pontificat·us -ūs *m*
pontoon *s* ponto *m*
pony *s* mannulus, equulus *m*
pool *s* lacuna *f*, stagnum *n*
pool *vt* conferre
poor *adj* (*needy*) pauper, inops, egens; (*inferior*) tenuis, mediocris; (*of soil*) macer; (*pitiable*) miser; (*meager*) exilis; **—ly** parum, mediocriter, misere, tenuiter
pop *s* crepit·us -ūs *m*
pop *vi* crepare; **to — out** exsilire
poplar *s* populus *f*
poppy *s* papaver *n*
populace *s* vulgus *n*, plebs *f*
popular *adj* popularis; **—ly** populariter
popularity *s* populi favor *m*, populi studium *n*
populate *vt* frequentare
population *s* civium numerus, incolarum numerus *m*
populous *adj* frequens
porcelain *s* fictilia *n pl*
porch *s* vestibulum *n*, portic·us -ūs *f*
porcupine *s* hystrix *f*
pore *s* foramen *n*
pore *vi* **to — over** assidue considerare, scrutari
pork *s* porcina *f*
porous *adj* rarus
porpoise *s* porculus marinus *m*
porridge *s* puls *f*
port *s* port·us -ūs *m*
portal *s* porta *f*
portend *vt* praesagire, portendĕre, significare
portent *s* monstrum, portentum, prodigium *n*
portentous *adj* monstruosus, prodigiosus
porter *s* janitor, ostiarius *m*; (*carrier*) bajulus *m*
portfolio *s* scrinium *n*
portico *s* portic·us -ūs *f*
portion *s* portio, pars *f*
portion *vt* partire
portly *adj* amplus, opimus
portrait *s* imago, effigies *f*
portray *vt* depingĕre, exprimĕre
pose *s* stat·us -ūs, habit·us -ūs *m*
pose *vi* habitum *or* statum sumĕre
position *s* positio *f*, sit·us -ūs *m*; (*of body*) gest·us -ūs *m*; (*office*) honos *m*; (*state*) conditio *f*, stat·us -ūs *m*; (*rank*) amplitudo, dignitas *f*
positive *adj* certus; (*gram*) positivus; (*fig*) confidens; **—ly** praecise, certo
possess *vt* possidēre, tenēre
possession *s* possessio *f*; (*estate*) bona *n pl*; **in the — of** penes (*with acc*); **to gain — of** potiri (*with abl*), occupare
possessive *adj* quaestuosus, avarus; (*gram*) possessivus
possessor *s* possessor, dominus *m*
possibility *s* facultas *f*
possible *adj* **as quickly as —** quam celerrime; **it is —** fieri po-

test; **it is — for me to** possum (*with inf*)
possibly *adv* fortasse
post *s* (*stake*) postis, cippus *m*; (*station*) statio, sedes stativa *f*; (*position*) munus *n*
post *vt* collocare, ponĕre, constituĕre; **to — a letter** tabellario litteras dare
postage *s* vectura (epistulae) *f*
postdate *vt* diem seriorem scribĕre (*with dat*)
poster *s* libellus *m*
posterior *adj* posterior
posterity *s* posteri, minores *m pl*, posteritas *f*
posthaste *adv* quam celerrime
posthumous *adj* postumus
postman *s* tabellarius *m*
postpone *vt* differre, prorogare
postscript *s* ascriptio *f*
posture *s* stat·us -ūs, habit·us -ūs, gest·us -ūs *m*
pot *s* olla *f*, ahenum *n*
potato *s* solanum tuberosum *n*
potentate *s* tyrannus *m*
potential *adj* futurus
potion *s* potio *f*
potter *s* figulus *m*
pottery *s* fictilia *n pl*
pouch *s* sacculus *m*, pera *f*
poultry *s* aves cohortales *f pl*
pounce *vi* **to — on** insilire (*with dat or* **in** + *acc*)
pound *s* libra *f*
pound *vt* contundĕre, conterĕre
pour *vt* fundere; **to — in** infundĕre; **to — out** effundĕre; *vi* fundi, fluĕre; **to — down** (*of rain*) ruĕre
pouring *adj* (*of rain*) effusus
pout *vi* stomachari
poverty *s* paupertas, pauperies *f*
powder *s* pulvis *m*
powder *vt* pulvere conspergĕre
power *s* vis, potestas *f*; (*pol*) imperium *n*; (*mil*) copiae *f pl*; (*excessive*) potentia *f*; (*divine*) numen *n*; **to have great —** multum posse, multum valēre
powerful *adj* validus, potens; (*effectual*) efficax; **—ly** valde
powerless *adj* invalidus, impotens; (*vain*) irritus; **to be —** nil valēre
practical *adj* utilis, habilis; **—ly** fere, paene
practice *s* us·us -ūs *m*, experientia, exercitatio *f*; (*custom*) mos *m*, consuetudo *f*
practice *vt* (*to engage in*) exercēre, tractare; (*to rehearse*) meditari
practitioner *s* exercitator *m*; (*medical*) medicus *m*
pragmatic *adj* pragmaticus
prairie *s* campus *m*
praise *s* laus *f*
praise *vt* laudare
praiseworthy *adj* laudabilis, laudandus
prance *vi* exsultare, subsultare; (*of persons*) jactare
prank *s* ludus *m*; (*trick*) jocus, dolus *m*
pray *vt* precari, orare; *vi* precari, orare; **to — for** petĕre, precari; **to — to** adorare, supplicare
prayer *s* preces *f pl*
preach *vt & vi* praedicare
preamble *s* prooemium, exordium *n*
precarious *adj* precarius, periculosus, incertus; **—ly** precario
precaution *s* cautio, provisio *f*; **to take —** cavēre, praecavēre
precede *vt* praeire (*with dat*), antecedĕre
precedence *s* prior locus *m*; **to take — over** antecedĕre
precedent *s* exemplum *n*
preceding *adj* prior, superior
precept *s* praeceptum *n*
preceptor *s* praeceptor, magister *m*
precinct *s* termini, limites *m pl*, templum *n*; (*ward*) regio *f*
precious *adj* pretiosus, carus; **— stone** gemma *f*
precipice *s* praeceps *n*; **down a —** in praeceps
precipitate *vt* praecipitare
precipitous *adj* praeceps, praeruptus, declivis
precise *adj* certus, definitus; (*exact*) accuratus, exactus; **—ly** subtiliter, accurate
precision *s* accuratio, cura *f*
preclude *vt* praecludere, excludĕre
precocious *adj* praecox
preconceive *vt* praecipĕre, praesentire; **preconceived idea** praejudicium *n*
preconception *s* praeceptio, praejudicata opinio *f*
precursor *s* praenuntius *m*
predatory *adj* praedatorius, praedabundus
predecessor *s* antecessor, decessor *m*
predestine *vt* praedestinare
predicament *s* discrimen *n*, angustiae *f pl*
predicate *vt* praedicare
predicate *s* praedicatum *n*
predict *vt* praedicĕre, augurari
prediction *s* praedictio *f*, praedictum, vaticinium *n*
predilection *s* studium *n*
predispose *vt* inclinare
predisposition *s* inclinatio *f*
predominant *adj* praevalens
predominate *vi* praevalēre
preeminence *s* praestantia, excellentia *f*
preeminent *adj* praecipuus, praestans, excellens; **—ly** praecipue, excellenter
preexist *vi* antea exstare *or* esse
preface *s* praefatio *f*
prefatory *adj* **to make a few — remarks** pauca praefari
prefect *s* praefectus *m*
prefecture *s* praefectura *f*
prefer *vt* praeponere, anteponĕre; (*charges*) deferre; **to — to** (*would rather*) malle (*with inf*)
preferable *adj* potior, praestantior
preference *s* favor *m*; **in — to** potius quam; **to give — to** anteponĕre
preferment *s* honos *m*
prefix *s* syllaba praeposita *f*

prefix *vt* praefigĕre, praeponĕre
pregnancy *s* graviditas *f*
pregnant *adj* gravida; (*of language*) pressus
prejudge *vt* praejudicare
prejudice *s* praejudicata opinio *f*, praejudicium *n*
prejudice *vt* **to be prejudiced against** praejudicatam opinionem habēre in (*with acc*), invidēre (*with dat*); **to — the people against** studia hominum inclinare in (*with acc*)
prejudicial *adj* noxius
preliminary *adj* praevius; **to make a few — remarks** pauca praefari
prelude *s* (*mus*) prooemium *n*, praelusio *f*
prelude *vt* praeludĕre
premature *adj* praematurus, immaturus, praeproperus; **—ly** ante tempus
premeditate *vt* praemeditari
premier *s* princeps *m*
premise *s* (*major*) propositio *f*; (*minor*) assumptio *f*; **—s** fundus *m*, praedium *n*
premium *s* praemium *n*; **at a —** carus
premonition *s* monit·us -ūs *m*, monitum *n*
preoccupation *s* praeoccupatio *f*
preoccupy *vt* praeoccupare
preparation *s* comparatio, praeparatio *f*, apparat·us -ūs *m*; (*rehearsal*) meditatio *f*
prepare *vt* parare, comparare, apparare; (*to rehearse*) meditari; **to — to** parare (*with inf*)
preponderance *s* praestantia *f*
preposition *s* praepositio *f*
preposterous *adj* praeposterus; **—ly** praepostere, absurde
prerogative *s* jus *n*
presage *s* praesagium *n*
presage *vt* praesagire, portendĕre, significare
prescience *s* providentia *f*
prescient *adj* providus, sagax
prescribe *vt* praescribĕre, proponĕre
prescription *s* praescriptum *n*; (*of physician*) medicamenti formula *f*
presence *s* praesentia *f*; (*look*) aspect·us -ūs *m*; **in my —** me praesente; **in the — of** coram (*with abl*)
present *adj* praesens, hic; **for the —** in praesens tempus; **to be —** adesse; **—ly** mox, illico, statim
present *s* donum, munus *n*
present *vt* donare, offerre; introducĕre; (*in court*) sistĕre; (*to bring forward*) praebēre, offerre; **to — itself** *or* **oneself** occurrĕre, obvenire
presentation *s* donatio *f*; (*on stage*) fabula *f*
presentiment *s* praesagitio *f*, praesagium *n*
preservation *s* conservatio *f*
preserve *vt* conservare; (*fruits*) condire
preserver *s* conservator *m*
preside *vi* praesidēre, praeesse; **to — over** praesidēre (*with dat*), praeesse (*with dat*)
presidency *s* praefectura *f*
president *s* praeses, praefectus *m*
press *s* (*for wine*) prelum *n*; (*of people*) turba *f*
press *vt* premĕre, comprimĕre; (*fig*) urgēre; **to — down** deprimĕre; *vi* **to — forward** anniti; **to — on** pergĕre, contendĕre
pressing *adj* gravis, urgens
pressure *s* pressio, pressura *f*, press·us -ūs *m*
pressure *vt* urgēre
prestige *s* auctoritas *f*
presumably *adv* sane
presume *vt* sumĕre, credĕre, conjicĕre; (*to take liberties*) sibi arrogare
presumption *s* (*conjecture*) conjectura *f*; (*arrogance*) arrogantia *f*
presumptuous *adj* arrogans, insolens, audax; **—ly** insolenter, arroganter
presuppose *vt* praesumĕre
pretend *vt* simulare, dissimulare, fingĕre
pretender *s* simulator, captator *m*
pretense *s* simulatio, species *f*; **under — of** per speciem (*with genit*); **without —** sine fuco
pretension *s* (*claim*) postulatio *f*; (*display*) ostentatio *f*; **to make —s to** affectare
preterite *s* tempus praeteritum *n*
preternatural *adj* praeter naturam
pretext *s* species *f*, praetextum *n*; **under the — of** specie (*with genit*), sub specie (*with genit*), sub praetextu (*with genit*)
pretor *s* praetor *m*
pretorian *adj* praetorianus
pretorship *s* praetura *f*
prettily *adv* belle, concinne
pretty *adj* bellus, venustus, lepidus
pretty *adv* satis, admodum; **— well** mediocriter
prevail *vi* (*to be prevalent*) esse, obtinēre; (*to win*) vincĕre; **to — upon** persuadēre (*with dat*)
prevalent *adj* (per)vulgatus; **to become —** increbrescĕre
prevaricate *vi* tergiversari
prevarication *s* praevaricatio, tergiversatio *f*
prevaricator *s* praevaricator, mendax *m*
prevent *vt* impedire, prohibēre
prevention *s* anticipatio, impeditio *f*
preventive *adj* prohibens, anticipans
previous *adj* prior, superior; **—ly** antea, antehac
prey *s* praeda *f*
prey *vi* **to — on** praedari, rapĕre; (*fig*) vexare, consumĕre
price *s* pretium *n*; **at a high —** magni; **at a low —** parvi
priceless *adj* inaestimabilis
prick *vt* pungĕre; (*fig*) stimulare; **to — up the ears** aures arrigĕre
prickle *s* aculeus *m*
prickly *adj* spinosus

pride *s* superbia *f*; (*source of pride*) decus *n*
pride *vt* **to — oneself on** jactare
priest *s* sacerdos *m*; (*of particular god*) flamen *m*
priestess *s* sacerdos *f*
priesthood *s* (*office*) sacerdotium *n*; (*collectively*) sacerdotes *m pl*
priestly *adj* sacerdotalis
prig *s* homo fastidiosus *m*
prim *adj* (nimis) diligens
primarily *adv* praecipue
primary *adj* primus, principalis; (*chief*) praecipuus
prime *s* flos *m*; **to be in one's —** florēre, vigēre
prime *adj* primus, egregius, optimus, exquisitus
primeval *adj* pristinus, priscus
primitive *adj* priscus, antiquus, incultus
primordial *adj* priscus
primrose *s* primula vulgaris *f*
prince *s* regulus, regis filius *m*; (*king*) rex, princeps *m*
princely *adj* regius, regalis
princess *s* regia puella, regis filia *f*
principal *adj* principalis, praecipuus; **—ly** praecipue, maxime
principal *s* caput *n*, praeses, praefectus, princeps *m*; (*money*) caput *n*, sors *f*
principality *s* principat·us -ūs *m*
principle *s* principium *n*; (*in philosophy*) axioma *n*; (*maxim*) institutum *n*
print *s* nota impressa *f*; (*of foot*) vestigium *n*
print *vt* imprimĕre
prior *adj* prior, potior
priority *s* primat·us -ūs *m*
prism *s* prisma *n*
prison *s* carcer *m*, vincula *n pl*
prisoner *s* reus *m*, rea *f*; (*for debt*) nex·us -ūs *m*
prisoner of war *s* captivus *m*
pristine *adj* pristinus
privacy *s* solitudo *f*, secretum *n*
private *adj* (*secluded*) secretus; (*person*) privatus; (*home*) domesticus; (*one's own*) proprius; (*mil*) gregarius; **—ly** clam, secreto; (*in a private capacity*) privatim
private *s* miles, miles gregarius *m*
privation *s* egestas, inopia *f*
privilege *s* privilegium *n*, immunitas *f*
privy *adj* privatus, secretus; **— to** conscius (*with genit*)
privy *s* forica, latrina *f*
prize *s* (*reward*) praemium *n*, palma *f*; (*prey*) praeda *f*
prize *vt* magni aestimare, magni facĕre
prize fighter *s* pugil *m*
probability *s* veri similitudo, probabilitas *f*
probable *adj* verisimilis, probabilis
probably *adv* probabiliter
probation *s* probatio *f*
probe *vt* scrutari, inspicĕre
probity *s* probitas, honestas *f*
problem *s* quaestio *f*; **to have —s** laborare
problematical *adj* anceps, incertus
procedure *s* progress·us -ūs, modus *m*, ratio *f*
proceed *vi* (*to go on*) pergĕre, procedĕre, incedĕre; **to — against** persequi; **to — from** oriri ex (*with abl*)
proceedings *s* acta *n pl*; (*law*) lis, actio *f*
proceeds *s* redit·us -ūs *m*
process *s* ratio *f*; (*law*) lis, actio *f*
proclaim *vt* promulgare, edicĕre, pronuntiare, declarare
proclamation *s* pronuntiatio *f*, edictum *n*
proconsul *s* proconsul *m*
proconsular *adj* proconsularis
proconsulship *s* proconsulat·us -ūs *m*
procrastinate *vi* cunctari, procrastinare
procrastination *s* procrastinatio *f*
procreate *vt* procreare, generare
procreation *s* procreatio *f*
proctor *s* procurator *m*
procurable *adj* procurandus
procurator *s* procurator *m*
procure *vt* parare, acquirĕre, nancisci, adipisci
procurement *s* comparatio *f*
procurer *s* leno *m*
prodigal *adj* prodigus
prodigal *s* ganeo *m*
prodigality *s* dissipatio, effusio *f*
prodigious *adj* prodigiosus, immanis, ingens
prodigy *s* prodigium, monstrum, portentum *n*; (*fig*) miraculum *n*
produce *s* fruct·us -ūs *m*; (*of earth*) fruges *f pl*; (*in money*) redit·us -ūs *m*
produce *vt* (*to bring forward*) proferre, producĕre; (*to bring into existence*) parĕre, procreare, gignĕre; (*to cause*) efficĕre, facĕre; (*to put on, as a play*) docēre; (*crops*) ferre
product *s* (*of earth*) fruges *f pl*; opus *n*
production *s* productio *f*
productive *adj* ferax, fecundus, uber
productivity *s* feracitas, ubertas *f*
profanation *s* violatio *f*
profane *adj* profanus, impius; **—ly** impie
profane *vt* vilare, profanare, polluĕre
profanity *s* impietas *f*, nefas *n*
profess *vt* profitēri
professed *adj* apertus, manifestus
profession *s* professio *f*
professional *adj* ad professionem pertinens; (*expert*) peritus
professor *s* doctor *m*
professorship *s* doctoris munus *n*
proffer *vt* offerre, promittĕre, proponĕre
proficiency *s* progress·us -ūs *m*, peritia *f*
proficient *adj* habilis, peritus
profile *s* facies obliqua *f*; (*portrait*) imago obliqua *f*

profit *s* quaest·us -ūs, redit·us -ūs *m*, lucrum *n*
profit *vt* prodesse (*with dat*); *vi* proficĕre; **to — by** uti (*with abl*), frui (*with abl*)
profitable *adj* fructuosus, quaestuosus, utilis; **to be —** prodesse
profitably *adv* utiliter
profitless *adj* inutilis, vanus
profligacy *s* nequitia *f*, perditi mores *m pl*
profligate *adj* perditus, flagitiosus, nequam (*indecl*)
profligate *s* nepos, ganeo *m*
profound *adj* altus, subtilis, abstrusus; **—ly** penitus
profundity *s* altitudo *f*
profuse *adj* profusus, effusus; **—ly** effuse
profusion *s* effusio, profusio, abundantia *f*
progeny *s* progenies, proles *f*
prognosticate *vt* praedicĕre
prognostication *s* praedictio *f*, praedictum *n*
program *s* libellus *m*
progress *s* progress·us -ūs *m*; **to make —** proficĕre
progress *vi* progredi
progression *s* progress·us -ūs *m*
progressive *adj* proficiens; **—ly** gradatim
prohibit *vt* interdicĕre (*with dat*), vetare
prohibition *s* interdictum *n*
project *s* propositum, consilium *n*
project *vt* projicĕre; *vi* prominēre, exstare; (*of land*) excurrĕre
projectile *s* missile *n*
projecting *adj* eminens, prominens
projection *s* projectura, eminentia *f*
proletarian *adj* proletarius
proletariat *s* plebs *f*
prolific *adj* fecundus
prolix *adj* longus, verbosus
prolixity *s* verbositas *f*
prologue *s* prologus *m*
prolong *vt* producĕre, prorogare, extendĕre
prolongation *s* proragatio, dilatio *f*
promenade *s* (*walk*) ambulatio *f*; (*place*) xystus *m*
promenade *vi* spatiari, ambulare
prominence *s* eminentia *f*
prominent *adj* prominens, insignis
promiscuous *adj* promiscuus; **—ly** promiscue, sine ullo discrimine
promise *s* promissio *f*, promissum *n*; **to break a —** fidem fallĕre; **to make a —** fidem dare
promise *vt* promittĕre, pollicēri; (*in marriage*) despondēre
promising *adj* bonā spe (*abl used adjectively*)
promissory note *s* chirographum *n*
promontory *s* promontorium *n*
promote *vt* (*in rank*) producĕre, provehĕre; (*a cause, etc.*) favēre (*with dat*), adjuvare
promoter *s* adjutor, fautor *m*
promotion *s* amplior grad·us -ūs *m*, dignitas *f*
prompt *adj* promptus, paratus; **—ly** statim, extemplo
prompt *vt* subjicĕre, suggerĕre; (*to incite*) impellĕre, commovēre
promulgate *vt* promulgare
promulgation *s* promulgatio *f*
prone *adj* pronus, propensus
prong *s* dens *m*
pronominal *adj* pronominalis
pronoun *s* pronomen *n*
pronounce *vt* (*to declare*) pronuntiare; (*to articulate*) enuntiare, eloqui; (*sentence*) dicĕre, pronuntiare
pronunciation *s* appellatio, elocutio, locutio *f*
proof *s* documentum, argumentum, indicium, signum *n*
proof *adj* tutus, securus; **— against** invictus ab (*with abl*), adversus (*with acc*)
prop *s* tibicen *m*, fulcrum *n*; (*for vines*) adminiculum *n*
prop *vt* fulcire, sustinēre
propaganda *s* divulgatio *f*
propagate *vt* propagare, vulgare, disseminare
propagation *s* propagatio *f*
propel *vt* impellere, propellĕre
propeller *s* impulsor *m*
propensity *s* propensio, inclinatio *f*
proper *adj* (*becoming*) decorus, decens; (*suitable*) aptus, idoneus; **it is —** decet; **—ly** decore; apte
property *s* (*characteristic*) proprium *n*, proprietas *f*; (*things owned*) res *f*, bona *n pl*, fortuna *f*; **private —** res familiaris *f*
prophecy *s* praedictum *n*, praedictio, vaticinatio *f*
prophesy *vt* vaticinari, praedicĕre
prophet *s* vates *m & f*, fatidicus *m*; (*Biblical*) propheta *f*
prophetess *s* vates, fatiloqua *f*
prophetic *adj* fatidicus, divinus, vaticinus; **—ally** divinitus
propitiate *vt* propitiare, placare
propitiation *s* propitiatio *f*, placamentum *n*
propitious *adj* felix, faustus; **—ly** fauste
proportion *s* ratio, proportio *f*; **in —** pro rata parte; **in — to** pro (*with abl*)
proportionately *adv* pro portione
proposal *s* propositio, conditio *f*; (*of senate*) rogatio *f*
propose *vt* ferre, rogare; **to — a toast to** propinare (*with dat*)
proposition *s* (*offer*) condicio *f*; (*logic*) propositio *f*, pronuntiatum *n*
propound *vt* proponĕre, exponĕre
proprietor *s* possessor, dominus *m*
propriety *s* decorum *n*, convenientia *f*
propulsion *s* propulsio *f*
prosaic *adj* aridus, jejunus
proscribe *vt* proscribĕre
proscription *s* proscriptio *f*
prose *s* prosa *f*
prosecute *vt* (*to carry out*) exsequi; (*law*) litem intendĕre (*with dat*), accusare
prosecution *s* exsecutio *f*; (*law*) accusatio *f*
prosecutor *s* accusator, actor *m*

prospect *s* prospect·us -ūs *m*; (*hope*) spes *f*
prospective *adj* futurus
prosper *vt* prosperare, secundare; *vi* prosperā fortunā uti, florēre, vigēre
prosperity *s* res secundae *f pl*
prosperous *adj* prosperus, secundus; **—ly** prospere, bene
prostitute *s* scortum *n*, meretrix *f*
prostitute *vt* prostituěre
prostrate *vt* sterněre, projicěre; (*fig*) affligěre
prostrate *adj* prostratus, projectus; (*fig*) afflictus, fractus; **to fall —** se projicěre
prostration *s* (*act*) prostratio *f*; (*state*) animus fractus *m*
protect *vt* tuēri, protegěre, defenděre, custodire
protection *s* praesidium *n*, tutela *f*
protector *s* defensor, patronus *m*
protest *s* obtestatio, denuntiatio *f*
protest *vt* affirmare; *vi* obtestari, reclamare; (*pol*) interceděre
protestation *s* affirmatio *f*
prototype *s* exemplar *n*
protract *vt* protrahěre, differre
protrude *vt* protruděre; *vi* prominēre
protuberance *s* tuber *n*, tumor, gibbus *m*
proud *adj* superbus, arrogans; **to be —** superbire; **—ly** superbe, arroganter
prove *vt* probare, confirmare, evincěre, arguěre; *vi* (*of person*) se praebēre, se praestare; (*of thing, event, etc.*) evaděre, fieri, exire
proverb *s* proverbium *n*
proverbial *adj* proverbialis, tritus, notus
provide *vt* (*to furnish*) suppeditare, (com)parare, praebēre; *vi* **to — for** providēre (*with dat*), consulěre (*with dat*); (*of laws*) jubēre
provided that *conj* dum, modo, dummodo, eā condicione ut
providence *s* providentia *f*
provident *adj* providus, cautus; **—ly** caute
providential *adj* divinus; **—ly** divinitus
province *s* provincia *f*
provincial *adj* provincialis; (*countrified*) inurbanus, rusticus; (*narrow*) angusti animi (*genit, used adjectively*)
provincialism *s* dialectos *f*
provision *s* (*stipulation*) condicio *f*; **—s** cibus, vict·us -ūs *m*, alimentum *n*; (*mil*) commeat·us -ūs *m*, res frumentaria *f*
provisional *adj* temporarius; **—ly** ad tempus
proviso *s* condicio *f*; **with the — that** eā lege ut
provocation *s* provocatio, offensio *f*
provoke *vt* provocare, irritare, stimulare
provoking *adj* molestus, odiosus
prow *s* prora *f*
prowess *s* virtus *f*
prowl *vi* vagari, grassari
prowler *s* praedator *m*
proximity *s* propinquitas *f*
proxy *s* vicarius *m*
prude *s* fastidiosa *f*
prudence *s* prudentia *f*
prudent *adj* prudens; **—ly** prudenter
prudish *adj* tetricus
prune *s* prunum conditum *n*
prune *vt* (am)putare, resecare, reciděre
pruning *s* putatio *f*
pry *vi* perscrutor; **to — into** investigare, explorare
prying *adj* curiosus
pseudonym *s* falsum nomen *n*
puberty *s* pubertas *f*
public *adj* publicus, communis; (*known*) vulgatus; **—ly** palam, aperte
public *s* homines *m pl*, vulgus *n*
publican *s* publicanus *m*
publication *s* publicatio, promulgatio *f*; (*of book*) editio *f*; (*book*) liber *m*
publicity *s* celebritas, lux *f*
publish *vt* publicare, divulgare, patefacěre; (*book*) eděre
publisher *s* editor *m*
pucker *vt* corrugare
pudding *s* placenta *f*
puddle *s* lacuna *f*, stagnum *n*
puerile *adj* puerilis
puerility *s* puerilitas *f*
puff *s* aura *f*, flamen *n*
puff *vt* inflare, sufflare; *vi* anhelare
puffy *adj* sufflatus, tumens
pugilist *s* pugil *m*
pugnacious *adj* pugnax
pull *vt* (*to drag*) trahěre, tractare; **to — apart** distrahěre; **to — away** avellěre; **to — down** detrahěre; (*buildings*) demoliri, destruěre, evertěre; **to — off** avellěre; **to — out** extrahěre; (*hair, etc.*) evellěre; *vi* **to — at** vellicare; **to — through** pervincěre; (*illness*) convalescěre
pull *s* (*act*) tract·us -ūs *m*; (*effort*) nis·us -ūs *m*; (*influence*) gratia *f*
pulley *s* trochlea *f*
pulmonary *adj* pulmoneus, pulmonaceus, pulmonarius
pulp *s* pulpa, caro *f*
pulpit *s* suggest·us -ūs *m*, rostra *n pl*
pulsate *vi* palpitare
pulse *s* puls·us -ūs *m*; (*plant*) legumen *n*; **to feel the —** venas temptare
pulverization *s* pulveratio *f*
pulverize *vt* pulverare, contunděre
pumice *s* pumex *m*
pump *s* antlia *f*
pump *vt* haurire, exantlare; **to — with questions** percontari
pumpkin *s* pepo, melopepo *m*
pun *s* verborum lus·us -ūs *m*, agnominatio *f*
punch *s* (*tool*) veruculum *n*; (*blow*) pugnus, ict·us -ūs *m*
punch *vt* pugnum ducěre (*with dat*)
punctilious *adj* scrupulosus, religiosus
punctual *adj* promptus, accuratus, diligens; **—ly** ad tempus, ad horam

punctuality *s* diligentia *f*
punctuate *vt* interpungĕre
punctuation *s* interpunctio *f*
punctuation mark *s* interpunctum *n*
puncture *s* punctio *f*, punctum *n*
pungent *adj* pungens, acutus; (*caustic, as speech*) mordax, aculeatus
Punic *adj* Punicus
punish *vt* punire
punishable *adj* puniendus, poenā dignus
punishment *s* (*act*) punitio, castigatio *f*; (*penalty*) poena *f*, supplicium *n*; **without —** impune
punster *s* argutator *m*
puny *adj* pusillus
pup *s* catulus *m*
pupil *s* pupillus, discipulus *m*, pupilla, discipula *f*; (*of eye*) pupilla, pupula *f*
puppet *s* pupa *f*
puppy *s* catulus *m*
purchase *s* (*act*) emptio *f*; (*merchandise*) merx *f*
purchase *vt* emere
purchase price *s* pretium *n*; (*of grain*) annona *f*
purchaser *s* emptor *m*
pure *adj* mundus, purus; (*unmixed*) merus; (*morally*) castus, integer; **—ly** pure, integre; (*quite*) omnino; (*solely*) solum
purgation *s* purgatio *f*
purge *vt* purgare, mundare
purge *s* purgatio *f*; (*pol*) proscriptio *f*
purification *s* purificatio, purgatio *f*
purify *vt* purgare; (*fig*) expiare
purity *s* puritas, munditia *f*; (*moral*) castitas, integritas *f*
purple *s* purpura *f*; **dressed in —** purpuratus
purple *adj* purpureus
purport *s* significatio, sententia, vis *f*
purport *vt* significare, spectare ad (*with acc*)
purpose *s* propositum, consilium *n*, animus *m*; (*end, aim*) finis *m*; (*wish*) mens *f*; **on —** consulto; **to good —** ad rem; **to no —** frustra, nequaquam; **to what —** quo, quorsum
purpose *vt* in animo habēre, velle
purposely *adv* consulto, de industria
purr *s* murmur *n*
purr *vi* mumurare
purring *s* murmuratio *f*
purse *s* crumena *f*, marsupium *n*
purse *vt* corrugare, contrahĕre
pursuance *s* continutatio *f*; **in — of** ex (*with abl*), secundum (*with acc*)
pursuant *adj* **— to** ex (*with abl*), secundum (*with acc*)
pursue *vt* (per)sequi, insequi, insectari; (*plan, course*) insistĕre
pursuit *s* persecutio, insectatio *f*; (*occupation*) studium, artificium *n*, occupatio *f*
pus *s* pus *n*, sanies *f*
push *vt* trudĕre, urgēre, impellĕre; *vi* **to — on** contendĕre, iter facĕre
push *s* ict·us -ūs, puls·us -ūs, impuls·us -ūs *f*; (*fig*) conat·us -ūs *m*
pushing *adj* audax, confidens; (*energetic*) strenuus
pusillanimous *adj* timidus
put *vt* ponĕre, collocare; **to — an end to** finem facĕre (*with dat*); **to — aside** ponĕre; **to — away** seponĕre, abdĕre, amovēre; (*in safety*) recondĕre; **to — back** reponĕre; **to — down** deponĕre; (*to suppress*) supponĕre, sedare; (*in writing*) scribĕre; **to — in** inserĕre; **to — in order** ordinare; **to — off** (*to postpone*) differre; **to — on** imponĕre; (*clothes*) se induĕre (*with abl*); (*to add*) addĕre; **to — out** ejicĕre, extrudĕre; (*fire*) extinguĕre; (*money*) ponĕre; **to — out of the way** demovēre; **to — together** componĕre, conferre; **to — up** erigĕre, statuĕre; **to — up for sale** proponĕre, venum dare; *vi* **to — in** (*of ships*) portum petĕre, appellĕre; **to — out to sea** solvĕre; **to — up with** tolerare
putrefaction *s* putredo *f*
putrefy *vi* putrescĕre, putrefieri
putrid *adj* puter *or* putris, putridus
puzzle *s* quaestio abstrusa *f*, nodus *m*, aenigma *n*
puzzle *vt* confundĕre, perturbare; **to be puzzled** haerēre, dubitare
puzzling *adj* perplexus, ambiguus
pygmy *s* nanus, pumilio, pumilus *m*
pyramid *s* pyramis *f*
pyre *s* rogus *m*
Pythagorean *adj* Pythagoraeus
Pythian *adj* Pythius

Q

quack *s* (*charlatan*) circulator, pharmacopola *m*
quack *vi* tetrinnire
quadrangle *s* area *f*
quadruped *s* quadrupes *m & f*
quadruple *adj* quadruplex, quadruplus
quadruple *vt* quadruplicare
quaestor *s* quaestor *m*
quaestorship *s* quaestura *f*
quaff *vt* ducĕre, haurire
quagmire *s* palus *f*
quail *s* coturnix *f*
quail *vi* pavēre
quaint *adj* rarus, insolitus, novus
quake *vi* tremĕre
qualification *s* (*endowment*) indoles *f*; (*limitation*) exceptio, condicio *f*
qualified *adj* (*suited*) aptus, idoneus, dignus; (*competent*) peritus, doctus

qualify *vt* aptum *or* idoneum redděre, instruěre; (*to limit*) temperare, mitigare, extenuare
quality *s* proprietas, qualitas *f*; **—s** ingenium *n*, indoles *f*
qualm *s* fastidium *n*; **— of conscience** religio *f*, scrupulus *m*
quandry *s* confusio *f*, angustiae *f pl*
quantity *s* numerus *m*, multitudo, vis, copia *f*; (*in scansion*) quantitas, mensura *f*
quarrel *s* jurgium *n*; (*dispute*) altercatio, controversia *f*; (*violent*) rixa *f*
quarrel *vi* altercari, jurgare, rixari
quarrelsome *adj* jurgiosus, rixosus, pugnax
quarry *s* lapicidinae, lautumiae *f pl*; (*prey*) praeda *f*
quart *s* duo sextarii *m pl*
quarter *s* quarta pars *f*, quadrans *m*; (*side, direction*) pars, regio *f*; (*district*) regio *f*; **at close —s** comminus; **—s** (*dwelling*) tectum *n*, habitatio *f*; (*temporary abode*) hospitium *n*; (*mil*) castra, contubernia stativa *n pl*; (*of moon*) lunae phases *f pl*; **to give — to** parcěre (*with dat*)
quarter *vt* in quattuor partes dividěre; (*to receive in one's house*) hospitium praeběre (*with dat*)
quarterly *adj* trimestris
quarterly *adv* quadrifariam, tertio quoque mense
quartermaster *s* castrorum praefectus *m*
quash *vt* (*to subdue*) opprimĕre; (*law*) rescinděre, abolēre
quatrain *s* tetrastichon *n*
queasy *adj* fastidiosus; **to feel —** nauseare
queen *s* regina *f*
queen bee *s* rex *m*
queer *adj* novus, insolitus, rarus, ineptus
quell *vt* opprimĕre, sedare, domare
quench *vt* exstinguěre; **to — the thirst** sitim sedare
querulous *adj* querulus, queribundus
query *s* quaestio, interrogatio *f*
query *vt* dubitare; *vi* quaerěre, quaeritare
quest *s* inquisitio *f*; **to be in — of** quarěre, requirěre; **to go in — of** investigare
question *s* interrogatio *f*; (*doubt*) dubitatio *f*, dubium *n*; (*matter*) res, causa *f*; **there is no — that** non dubium est quin; **to ask a —** quaerěre, rogare; **to call in —** dubitare; **without —** sine dubio, haud dubie
question *vt* interrogare, percontari; (*to doubt*) dubitare, in dubium vocare; (*to examine*) scrutari
questionable *adj* dubius, incertus
questioning *s* interrogatio, inquisitio *f*
questor *s* quaestor *m*
questorship *s* quaestura *f*
quibble *s* captio, argutiola *f*
quibble *vi* cavillari
quibbler *s* cavillator, sophista *m*
quibbling *s* cavillatio, captio *f*
quick *adj* (*swift*) celer, velox; (*nimble*) agilis; (*mentally*) sagax, astutus, acutus; (*with hands*) facilis; (*of wit*) argutus; **—ly** cito, velociter; (*with haste*) propere, festinanter
quicken *vt* accelerare; (*to enliven*) vivificare, animare; (*to rouse*) excitare
quicksand *s* syrtis *f*
quicksilver *s* argentum vivum *n*
quiet *adj* quietus, tranquillus, placidus; (*silent*) tacitus, taciturnus; **to keep —** quiescěre; (*to refrain from talking*) silēre, tacēre; **—ly** quiete, tranquille; tacite, per silentium
quiet *s* quies, tranquillitas *f*; (*leisure*) otium *n*; (*silence*) silentium *n*
quiet *vt* tranquillare, pacare, sedare
quill *s* penna *f*, calamus *m*
quilt *s* culcita *f*
quince *s* cydonium *n*
quince tree *s* cydonia *f*
quintessence *s* vis, medulla *f*, flos *m*
quip *s* dictum *n*, facetiae *f pl*
quirk *s* cavillatio, proprium *n*
quit *vt* relinquěre, deserěre
quite *adv* omnino, penitus, prorsus, magnopere; **not —** minus, parum; (*not yet*) nondum
quiver *s* pharetra *f*; **wearing a —** pharetratus
quiver *vi* treměre, contremiscěre, trepidare
quivering *s* tremor *m*, trepidatio *f*
Quixotic *adj* ridiculus
quoit *s* discus *m*
quota *s* portio, pars, rata pars *f*
quotation *s* (*act*) prolatio *f*; (*passage*) locus *m*
quote *vt* adducěre, proferre, commemorare

R

rabbit *s* cuniculus *m*
rabble *s* plebecula, faex populi *f*; (*crowd*) turba *f*
rabid *adj* rabidus; **—ly** rabide
race *s* (*lineage*) genus *n*, stirps *f*; (*nation*) gens *f*; (*contest*) certamen *n*; curs·us -ūs *m*, curriculum *n*
race *vi* certare, cursu contenděre
race horse *s* equus cursor *m*
racer *s* (*person*) cursor *m*; (*horse*) equus cursor *m*
racetrack *s* circus *m*, curriculum *n*
rack *s* (*shelf*) pluteus *m*; (*for punishment*) equuleus *m*, tormentum *n*
racket *s* (*noise*) strepit·us -ūs *m*

radiance *s* fulgor, splendor *m*
radiant *adj* radians, fulgidus, spendidus
radiate *vt* emittĕre; *vi* radiare, fulgēre, nitēre
radiation *s* radiatio *f*
radical *adj* insitus, innatus; (*thorough*) totus; **—ly** penitus, omnino
radical *s* rerum novarum cupidus *m*
radish *s* raphanus *m*
radius *s* radius *m*
raffle *s* alea *f*
raffle *vt* **to — off** aleā vendĕre
raft *s* ratis *f*
rafter *s* trabs *f*
rag *s* panniculus, pannus *m*
rage *s* furor *m*, rabies *f*
rage *vi* furĕre, saevire
ragged *adj* pannosus
raid *s* incursio, invasio *f*, latrocinium *n*
raider *s* praedator, latro *m*
raid *vt* praedari
rail *s* palus, asser transversus, longurius *m*
rail *vt* **to — off** consaepire; *vi* **to — at** insectari, conviciari
railing *s* (*fence*) saepimentum *n*; (*abuse*) convicium, maledictum *n*
raiment *s* vestis *f*, vestit·us -ūs *m*
rain *s* pluvia *f*, imber *m*
rain *vi* pluere; **it is raining** pluit
rainbow *s* pluvius arc·us -ūs *m*
rain cloud *s* imber *m*
rainy *adj* pluvius, pluvialis; pluviosus
raise *vt* tollĕre, elevare; (*to erect*) erigĕre; (*to build*) exstruĕre; (*money*) cogĕre; (*army*) conscribĕre; (*siege*) solvĕre; (*to stir up*) excitare; (*children*) educare; (*to promote*) provehĕre, producĕre; (*price*) augēre; (*crops*) colĕre; (*beard*) demittĕre; **to — up** sublevare
raisin *s* astaphis *f*
rake *s* rastellus, irpex *m*; (*person*) nebulo, nepos *m*
rake *vt* radére; **to — together** corradĕre
rally *s* convent·us -ūs *m*, contio *f*
rally *vt* in aciem revocare; *vi* ex fuga convenire; (*from sickness*) convalescĕre
ram *s* aries *m*
ram *vt* fistucare, paviare; (*to cram*) infercire
ramble *s* vagatio *f*
ramble *vi* vagari, errare; **to — on** (*in speech*) garrire
rambling *adj* errans; (*fig*) vagus
ramification *s* ramus *m*
rampage *vi* saevire
rampant *adj* ferox
rampart *s* vallum, propugnaculum *n*
rancid *adj* rancidus
rancor *s* simultas *f*, dolor *m*
random *adj* fortuitus; **at —** temere
range *s* series *f*, ordo *m*; (*of mountains*) jugum *n*; (*reach*) jact·us -ūs *m*
range *vt* ordinare, disponĕre; *vi* pervagari
rank *s* series *f*, ordo, grad·us -ūs *m*, dignitas *f*
rank *vt* in numero habēre; *vi* in numero habēri
rank *adj* luxuriosus; (*extreme*) summus, maximus; (*of smell*) foetidus, gravis, graveolens
rankle *vi* suppurare, exulcerare
ransack *vt* diripĕre, spoliare; (*to search thoroughly*) exquirĕre
ransom *s* (*act*) redemptio *f*; pretium *n*
ransom *vt* redimere
rant *vi* ampullari; **to — and rave** debacchari
rap *s* (*slap*) alapa *f*; (*blow*) ict·us -ūs *m*; (*at door*) pulsatio *f*; (*with knuckles*) talitrum *n*
rap *vt* (*to criticize*) exagitare; *vi* **to — at** pulsare, ferire
rapacious *adj* rapax, avidus
rapacity *s* rapacitas, aviditas *f*
rape *s* stuprum *n*; (*act of carrying away*) rapt·us -ūs *m*
rape *vt* violare, per vim stuprare
rapid *adj* rapidus, celer, velox; **—ly** rapide, cito, velociter
rapidity *s* rapiditas, velocitas *f*
rapier *s* verutum *n*
rapine *s* rapina *f*
rapture *s* exsultatio *f*, animus exsultans *m*
rapturous *adj* mirificus
rare *adj* rarus, inusitatus; (*fig*) eximius, singularis; (*thin*) tenuis; **—ly** raro
rarefy *vt* extenuare, rarefacĕre
rarity *s* raritas, paucitas *f*; (*thing*) res rara, res singularis *f*
rascal *s* homo nequam, scelestus *m*
rascally *adj* scelestus, flagitiosus; nequam (*indecl*)
rash *adj* praeceps, temerarius; **—ly** temere, inconsulte
rash *s* eruptio pustulae *f*
rashness *s* temeritas *f*
raspberry *s* morum idaeum *n*
raspberry bush *s* rubus idaeus *m*
rat *s* sorex, mus *m*; (*person*) transfuga *m*
rate *s* proportio *f*; (*price*) pretium *n*; (*scale*) norma *f*; (*tax*) vectigal *n*; **— of interest** faenus *n*, usura *f*
rate *vt* aestimare
rather *adv* potius, prius, libentius; (*somewhat*) aliquantum, paulo, *or render by comparative of adjective*
ratification *s* sanctio *f*
ratify *vt* ratum facĕre, sancire
rating *s* aestimatio *f*
ratio *s* proportio *f*
ration *s* (*portion*) demensum *n*; (*mil*) cibaria *n pl*
ration *vt* demetiri
rational *adj* ratione praeditus, intellegens; **—ly** ratione, sapienter
rationalize *vi* ratiocinari
rattle *s* crepit·us -ūs, strepit·us -ūs *m*; (*toy*) crepitaculum *n*
rattle *vt* crepitare (*with abl*); *vi* increpare, crepitare; **to — on** inepte garrire
raucous *adj* raucus
ravage *vt* vastare, spoliare, populari
ravages *s* vastatio, direptio *f*
rave *vi* furĕre, saevire, bacchari

ravel *vt* involvĕre, implicare
raven *s* corvus *m*, cornix *f*
ravenous *adj* rapax, vorax; **—ly** voraciter
ravine *s* fauces *f pl*
raving *adj* furiosus, furens, insanus
ravish *vt* constuprare
raw *adj* crudus, incoctus; (*of person*) rudis, imperitus; (*of weather*) asper
rawboned *adj* strigosus
ray *s* radius *m*
raze *vt* solo aequare, excidĕre
razor *s* novacula *f*
reach *s* (*grasp, capacity*) capt·us -ūs *m*; (*of weapon*) ict·us -ūs, jact·us -ūs *m*; **out of my —** extra ictum meum
reach *vt* attingĕre; (*of space*) pertinēre ad (*with acc*), extendi ad (*with acc*); (*to come up to*) assequi; (*to arrive at*) pervenire ad (*with acc*); (*to hand*) tradĕre
react *vi* affici; **to — to** ferre
read *vt & vi* legĕre; **to — aloud** recitare
readable *adj* lectu facilis
reader *s* lector *m*; (*lecturer*) praelector *m*
readily *adv* (*willingly*) libenter; (*easily*) facile
readiness *s* facilitas *f*; **in —** in promptu
ready *adj* paratus, promptus, expeditus; (*easy*) facilis; **— money** praesens pecunia *f*; **to be —** praesto esse
real *adj* verus, sincerus; **—ly** re vera; (*surely*) sane, certe
real estate *s* fundus *m*
realistic *adj* verisimilis
reality *s* veritas, res ipsa *f*, verum *n*
realization *s* effectio *f*; (*of ideas*) cognitio, comprehensio *f*
realize *vt* (*to understand*) intellegĕre, vidēre, comprehendĕre; (*to effect*) efficĕre, ad exitum perducĕre; (*to convert into money*) redigĕre
realm *s* regnum *n*
ream *s* (*of paper*) scapus *m*
reap *vt* metĕre, desecare; (*fig*) percipĕre, capĕre
reaper *s* messor *m*
reappear *vi* redire, revenire, resurgĕre
rear *vt* educare, alĕre; *vi* (*of horses*) arrectum se tollĕre
rear *s* tergum *n*; (*mil*) novissimum agmen *n*, novissima acies *f*; **on the —** a tergo; **to bring up the —** agmen cogĕre
rearing *s* educatio *f*
reascend *vt & vi* denuo ascendĕre
reason *s* (*faculty*) mens, ratio, intellegentia *f*; (*cause*) causa *f*; (*moderation*) modus *m*; **by — of** ob (*with acc*), propter (*with acc*), a(b) (*with abl*); **there is no — why** non est cur
reason *vi* ratiocinari; **to — with** disceptare cum (*with abl*)
reasonable *adj* (*fair*) aequus, justus; (*moderate*) modicus; (*judicious*) prudens
reasonably *adv* ratione, juste; modice
reasoning *s* ratiocinatio, ratio *f*; (*discussing*) disceptatio *f*
reassemble *vt* recolligĕre, cogĕre
reassert *vt* iterare
reassume *vt* resumĕre
reassure *vt* confirmare, redintegrare
rebel *s* rebellis *m*
rebel *vi* rebellare, desciscĕre, seditionem commovēre
rebellion *s* rebellio, seditio *f*, rebellium *n*
rebellious *adj* rebellis, seditiosus; (*disobedient*) contumax
rebound *s* result·us -ūs *m*
rebound *vi* resilire, resultare
rebuff *s* repulsa *f*
rebuff *vt* repellĕre, rejicĕre
rebuild *vt* reparare, reficĕre
rebuke *s* reprehensio *f*
rebuke *vt* reprehendĕre, vituperare
rebuttal *s* refutatio *f*
recall *s* revocatio *f*
recall *vt* revocare; **to — to mind** in memoriam redigĕre
recant *vt* retractare, revocare
recantation *s* recept·us -ūs *m*
recapitulate *vt* repetĕre, summatim colligĕre
recapitulation *s* repetitio, enumeratio *f*
recapture *s* recuperatio *f*
recapture *vt* recipĕre, recuperare
recede *vi* recedĕre, refugere
receipt *s* (*act*) acceptio *f*; (*note of acceptance*) apocha *f*; (*money*) acceptum *n*
receive *vt* accipĕre, capĕre, excipĕre
receiver *s* receptor *m*
recent *adj* recens; **—ly** nuper
receptacle *s* receptaculum *n*
reception *s* adit·us -ūs *m*, admissio *f*; (*of guest*) hospitium *n*
recess *s* (*place*) recess·us -ūs *m*; (*in wall*) adytum *n*, angulus *m*; (*intermission*) intermissio *f*; (*vacation*) feriae *f pl*
recipe *s* praescriptum, compositio *f*
recipient *s* acceptor *m*
reciprocal *adj* mutuus; **—ly** mutuo, vicissim, inter se
reciprocate *vt* reddĕre
reciprocity *s* reciprocatio *f*
recital *s* narratio, enumeratio, recitatio *f*
recitation *s* recitatio, lectio *f*
reckless *adj* temerarius; **—ly** temere
reckon *vt* numerare, computare, aestimare; *vi* **to — on** confidĕre (*with dat*)
reckoning *s* numeratio *f*; (*account to be given*) ratio *f*
reclaim *vt* reposcĕre, repetĕre
recline *vi* recubare, recumbĕre; (*at table*) accumbĕre
recluse *s* homo solitarius *m*
recognition *s* cognitio, agnitio *f*
recognize *vt* agnoscĕre, recognoscĕre; (*to acknowledge*) noscĕre; (*to admit*) fatēri
recoil *vi* resilire; **to — from** rece-

dĕre ab (*with abl*), refugĕre ab (*with abl*)
recoil *s* recessio *f*
recollect *vt* recordari
recollection *s* memoria, recordatio *f*
recommence *vt* redintegrare, renovare
recommend *vt* commendare
recommendation *s* commendatio, laudatio *f*; **letter of —** litterae commendaticiae *f pl*
recompense *s* remuneratio *f*
recompense *vt* remunerare; (*to indemnify*) compensare
reconcilable *adj* placabilis; (*of things*) conveniens
reconcile *vt* reconciliare, componĕre; **to be reconciled** in gratiam restitui
reconciliation *s* reconciliatio *f*, in gratiam redit·us -ūs *m*
reconnoiter *vt* explorare
reconquer *vt* revincĕre, recuperare
reconsider *vt* revolvĕre, retractare
reconstruct *vt* restituĕre, renovare
reconstruction *s* renovatio *f*
record *s* monumentum *n*, historia *f*; **—s** annales *m pl*, tabulae *f pl*
recorder *s* procurator ab actis *m*
recount *vt* referre, enarrare, commemorare
recoup *vt* recuperare
recourse *s* refugium *n*; **to have — to** (*for safety*) fugĕre ad (*with acc*); (*to resort to*) descendĕre ad (*with acc*)
recover *vt* recuperare, recipĕre; *vi* (*from illness*) convalescĕre; (*to come to one's senses*) ad se redire
recoverable *adj* reparabilis, recuperandus; (*of persons*) sanabilis
recovery *s* recuperatio, reparatio *f*; (*from illness*) recreatio *f*
recreate *vt* recreare
recreation *s* oblectatio, remissio *f*, lus·us -ūs *m*
recriminate *vi* invicem accusare
recrimination *s* mutua accusatio *f*
recruit *vt* (*mil*) conscribĕre; (*strength*) reficĕre
recruit *s* tiro *m*
recruiting *s* delect·us -ūs *m*
recruiting officer *s* conquisitor *m*
rectification *s* correctio *f*
rectify *vt* corrigĕre, emendare
rectitude *s* probitas *f*
recumbant *adj* resupinus
recur *vi* recurrĕre, redire
recurrence *s* redit·us -ūs *m*
recurrent *adj* assiduus
red *adj* ruber; (*ruddy*) rubicundus; **to be —** rubēre; **to grow —** rubescĕre
redden *vt* rubefacĕre, rutilare; *vi* rubescĕre; (*to blush*) erubescĕre
reddish *adj* subrufus, subruber, rubicundulus
redeem *vt* redimĕre, liberare
redeemer *s* liberator *m*
Redeemer *s* Redemptor *m*
redemption *s* redemptio *f*
redhead *s* rufus *m*
red-hot *adj* candens
redness *s* rubor *m*
redolence *s* fragrantia *f*
redolent *adj* fragrans, redolens; **to be —** redolēre
redouble *vt* ingeminare
redoubt *s* propugnaculum *n*
redoubtable *adj* formidolosus
redound *vi* redundare
redress *vt* restituĕre
redress *s* satisfactio *f*; **to demand —** res repetĕre
reduce *vt* minuĕre, deminuĕre; (*to a condition*) redigĕre; (*mil*) vincĕre, expugnare
reduction *s* deminutio *f*; (*mil*) expugnatio *f*
redundancy *s* redundantia *f*
redundant *adj* redundans, superfluus
reed *s* harundo *f*, calamus *m*
reef *s* scopulus *m*, saxa *n pl*
reek *s* fumus, vapor *m*
reek *vi* fumare; **to — of** olēre
reel *s* fusus *m*
reel *vi* (*to stagger*) titubare
reestablish *vt* restituĕre
reestablishment *s* restitutio *f*
refer *vt* referre, remittĕre; *vi* **to — to** perstringĕre, attingĕre
referee *s* arbiter *m*
reference *s* ratio *f*; (*in book*) locus *m*
refine *vt* purgare, excolĕre, expolire; (*metals*) excoquĕre
refined *adj* politus; (*fig*) elegans, urbanus, humanus
refinement *s* (*of liquids*) purgatio *f*; (*fig*) urbanitas, humanitas, elegantia *f*
reflect *vt* repercutĕre, reverberare; (*fig*) afferre; *vi* **to — on** considerare, revolvĕre
reflection *s* repercussio *f*, repercuss·us -ūs *m*; (*thing reflected*) imago *f*; (*fig*) consideratio, meditatio, cogitatio *f*; **without —** inconsulte
reflective *adj* cogitabundus
reflexive *adj* reciprocus
reform *vt* reficĕre, refingĕre; (*to amend*) corrigĕre, emendare; *vi* se corrigĕre
reform *s* correctio, emendatio *f*
reformation *s* correctio *f*
reformer *s* corrector, emendator *m*
refract *vt* refringĕre
refraction *s* refractio *f*
refractory *adj* contumax, indocilis
refrain *s* vers·us -ūs intercalaris *m*
refrain *vi* **to — from** abstinēre ab (*with abl*), parcĕre (*with dat*); **I — from speaking** abstineo quin dicam
refresh *vt* recreare, reficĕre; (*the memory*) redintegrare
refreshing *adj* jucundus, dulcis
refreshment *s* (*food*) cibus *m*; (*drink*) pot·us -ūs *m*
refuge *s* refugium, perfugium, asylum *n*; **to take — with** confugĕre in (*with acc*)
refugee *s* profugus *m*, ex(s)ul *m & f*
refulgence *s* fulgor *m*
refulgent *adj* fulgidus
refund *vt* refundĕre, rependĕre

refusal *s* recusatio, repulsa *f*
refuse *vt* recusare, negare; (*scornfully*) repudire, renuĕre
refutation *s* refutatio, confutatio *f*
refute *vt* refutare, refellĕre, redarguĕre
regain *vt* recipĕre, recuperare
regal *adj* regalis, regius; **—ly** regaliter
regale *vt* excipĕre
regalia *s* insignia regia *n pl*
regard *s* respect·us -ūs *m*, ratio *f*; (*care*) cura *f*; (*esteem*) gratia *f*
regard *vt* (*to look at*) respicĕre, intuēri; (*to concern*) spectare ad (*with acc*); (*to esteem*) aestimare; (*to consider*) habēre
regarding *prep* de (*with abl*)
regardless *adj* neglegens, incuriosus
regency *s* procuratio regni *f*, interregnum *n*
regenerate *vt* regenerare
regeneration *s* regeneratio *f*
regent *s* interrex *m*
regicide *s* (*murderer*) regis occisor *m*; (*murder*) caedes regis *f*
regime *s* administratio *f*
regimen *f* vict·us -ūs *m*
regiment *s* cohors, caterva *f*
region *s* regio, plaga *f*, tract·us -ūs *m*
register *s* tabulae *f pl*, catalogus *m*, album *n*
register *vt* in tabulas referre; (*emotion*) ostendĕre; *vi* profitēri, nomen dare
registrar *s* tabularius, actuarius *m*
registration *s* perscriptio, in tabulas relatio *f*
registry *s* tabularium *n*
regret *s* indignatio, paenitentia *f*, dolor *m*
regret *vt* dolēre; **I —** paenitet me (*with genit*), piget me (*with genit*)
regretful *adj* paenitens
regular *adj* (*common*) usitatus; (*proper*) justus, rectus; (*consistent*) constans, certus; **—ly** ordine, constanter; juste, recte
regularity *s* symmetria *f*; (*consistency*) constantia *f*
regulate *vt* ordinare, disponĕre, dirigĕre; (*to control*) moderari
regulation *s* ordinatio, temperatio, moderatio *f*; (*rule*) lex *f*, jussum *n*
rehabilitate *vt* restituĕre
rehearsal *s* meditatio *f*
rehearse *vt* meditari
reign *s* regnum *n*
reign *vi* regnare, dominari
reimburse *vt* rependĕre
reimbursement *s* pecuniae restitutio *f*
rein *s* habena *f*; **to give full — to** habenas immittĕre (*with dat*); **to loosen the —s** frenos dare; **to tighten the —s** habenas adducĕre
reindeer *s* reno *m*
reinforce *vt* firmare, supplēre
reinforcement *s* supplementum, subsidium *n*; **—s** (*mil*) novae copiae *f pl*
reinstate *vt* restituĕre
reinstatement *s* restitutio *f*
reinvest *vt* iterum locare
reiterate *vt* iterare
reiteration *s* iteratio *f*
reject *vt* rejicĕre, repudiare, repellére, respuĕre
rejection *s* rejectio, repulsa *f*
rejoice *vi* gaudēre, exsultare
rejoin *vt* redire ad (*with acc*); *vi* respondēre
rejoinder *s* responsum *n*
rekindle *vt* resuscitare
relapse *s* novus laps·us -ūs *m*
relate *vt* referre, memorare, narrare; (*to compare*) conferre; *vi* **to — to** pertinēre ad (*with acc*)
related *adj* propinquus, conjunctus; (*by blood*) consanguineus, cognatus; (*by marriage*) affinis
relation *s* narratio *f*; (*reference*) ratio *f*; (*relationship*) cognatio *f*; (*relative*) cognatus *m*, cognata *f*
relationship *s* (*by blood*) consanguinitas, cognatio *f*; (*by marriage*) affinitas *f*; (*connection*) necessitudo, vicinitas, conjunctio *f*
relative *adj* attinens; cum ceteris comparatus; **—ly** pro ratione, ex comparatione
relative *s* cognatus, propinquus *m*, cognata, propinqua *f*
relax *vt* remittĕre, laxare; *vi* languescĕre
relaxation *s* remissio, relaxatio, requies *f*
relaxing *adj* remissivus
release *s* liberatio, absolutio, missio *f*
release *vt* (*prisoner*) liberare; solvĕre, resolvĕre
relegate *vt* relegare
relent *vi* mitescĕre, mollescĕre, flecti
relentless *adj* immisericors, inexorabilis, atrox; **—ly** atrociter
relevant *adj* **to be —** ad rem attinēre
reliance *s* fiducia, fides *f*
reliant *adj* fretus
relic *s* reliquiae *f pl*
relief *s* (*alleviation*) levatio *f*, levamentum *n*; (*comfort*) solatium, lenimen *n*; (*help*) auxilium *n*; (*in sculpture*) toreuma *n*; (*of sentries*) mutatio *f*
relieve *vt* levare, allevare, mitigare; (*to aid*) succurrĕre (*with dat*); (*a guard*) succedĕre (*with dat*), excipĕre
religion *s* religio *f*, deorum cult·us -ūs *m*
religious *adj* religiosus, pius; **—ly** religiose
relinquish *vt* relinquĕre; (*office*) se abdicare ab (*with abl*)
relish *s* (*flavor*) sapor *m*; (*enthusiasm*) studium *n*; (*seasoning*) condimentum *n*
relish *vt* gustare
reluctance *s* aversatio *f*; **with —** invite
reluctant *adj* invitus; **—ly** invite
rely *vi* **to — on** confidĕre (*with dat*), niti (*with abl*)
remain *vi* manēre, permanēre; (*of things*) restare

remainder *s* reliquum *n*
remains *s* reliquiae *f pl*
remark *vt* dicĕre
remark *s* dictum *n*
remarkable *adj* insignis, memorabilis, mirus, egregius
remarkably *adv* insignite, mire, egregie
remediable *adj* sanabilis
remedial *adj* medicabilis; emendatorius
remedy *s* remedium *n*; (*law*) regress·us -ūs *m*
remedy *vt* medēri (*with dat*), sanare, corrigĕre
remember *vt* meminisse (*with genit*); reminisci (*with genit*); recordari
remembrance *s* memoria, commemoratio *f*
remind *vt* admonēre, commonefacĕre
reminder *s* admonitio *f*, admonitum *n*
reminisce *vi* meditari; **to — about** recordari
reminiscence *s* recordatio *f*
remiss *adj* neglegens
remission *s* venia, remissio *f*
remit *vt* remittĕre, condonare
remittance *s* remissio *f*
remnant *s* reliquum, residuum *n*; **—s** reliquiae *f pl*
remodel *vt* reformare, transfigurare
remonstrance *s* objurgatio *f*
remonstrate *vi* reclamare, reclamitare; **to — with** objurgare
remorse *s* paenitentia *f*
remorseless *adj* immisericors
remote *adj* remotus, longinquus, reconditus; **—ly** procul
remoteness *s* longinquitas, distantia *f*
removable *adj* mobilis
removal *s* amotio *f*; (*banishment*) amandatio *f*; (*change of residence*) migratio *f*
remove *vt* amovēre, tollĕre, auferre; *vi* migrare
remunerate *vt* remunerari
remuneration *s* remuneratio *f*
rend *vt* lacerare, scindĕre; (*to split*) findĕre
render *vt* reddĕre, tradĕre; (*to translate*) vertĕre; (*thanks*) referre
rendering *s* (*translation*) conversio *f*; (*interpretation*) interpretatio *f*
rendezvous *s* constitutum *n*
renegade *s* desertor, transfuga *m*
renew *vt* renovare, instaurare, redintegrare
renewal *s* renovatio, instauratio, repetitio *f*
renounce *vt* renuntiare, repudiare, abdicare; (*an office*) se abdicare (*with abl*)
renovate *vt* renovare, reficĕre
renovation *s* renovatio, reparatio *f*
renown *s* fama, gloria *f*
renowned *adj* praeclarus, insignis, celebris
rent *s* (*of lands*) vectigal *n*; (*of houses*) merces, pensio *f*; (*tear; fissure*) scissura *f*
rent *vt* (*to let out*) locare; (*to hire*) conducĕre
renunciation *s* repudiatio, cessio, abdicatio *f*
reopen *vt* iterum aperire
repair *vt* reparare, reficĕre, restituĕre; (*clothes*) resarcire
repair *s* refectio *f*; **in bad —** ruinosus
reparation *s* satisfactio *f*
repartee *s* sales *m pl*
repast *s* cena *f*
repay *vt* remunerari; (*money*) reponĕre, retribuĕre
repayment *s* solutio, remuneratio *f*
repeal *vt* abrogare, rescindĕre, tollĕre
repeal *s* abrogatio *f*
repeat *vt* iterare, repetĕre; (*ceremony*) instaurare
repeatedly *adv* iterum atque iterum, identidem
repel *vt* repellĕre; (*fig*) aspernari
repent *vi* **I —** paenitet me
repentance *s* paenitentia *f*
repentant *adj* paenitens
repercussion *s* repercuss·us -ūs *m*
repetition *s* iteratio, repetitio *f*
repine *vi* conquēri
replace *vt* reponĕre, restituĕre
replant *vt* reserĕre
replenish *vt* replēre
replete *adj* repletus, plenus
repletion *s* satietas *f*
reply *vi* respondēre
reply *s* responsum *n*
report *vt* referre, narrare, nuntiare; (*officially*) renuntiare
report *s* (*rumor*) fama *f*, rumor *m*; (*official*) renuntiatio *f*; (*noise*) fragor *m*
repose *vt* ponĕre, reponĕre; *vi* quiescĕre
repose *s* quies, requies *f*
repository *s* receptaculum *n*
reprehend *vt* reprehendĕre, vituperare
reprehensible *adj* culpā dignus, improbus
represent *vt* repraesentare, exprimĕre, describĕre, proponĕre; (*a character*) partes agĕre (*with genit*)
representation *s* (*act*) repraesentatio *f*; (*likeness*) imago *f*
representative *s* legatus, vicarius *m*
repress *vt* reprimĕre, coercēre, cohibēre
repression *s* coercitio, cohibitio *f*
reprieve *s* supplicii dilatio, mora, venia *f*; **to grant a —** supplicium differre, veniam dare
reprieve *vt* veniam dare (*with dat*)
reprimand *s* reprehensio *f*
reprimand *vt* reprehendĕre
reprint *vt* denuo imprimĕre
reprisal *s* ultio *f*; **to make —s on** ulcisci
reproach *s* exprobratio, vituperatio *f*, probrum *n*; (*cause for reproach*) opprobrium *n*
reproach *vt* opprobrare, vituperare, increpitare
reproachful *adj* objurgatorius, contumeliosus; **—ly** contumeliose
reprobate *s* perditus *m*

reproduce *vt* regenerare, propagare; (*likeness*) referre
reproduction *s* regeneratio, propagatio *f*; (*likeness*) effigies *f*
reproof *s* reprehensio, vituperatio, objuratio *f*
reprove *vt* reprehenděre, objurgare
reptile *s* serpens, bestia serpens *f*
republic *s* civitas popularis, libera civitas *f*
republican *adj* popularis
repudiate *vt* repudiare
repudiation *s* repudiatio *f*
repugnance *s* fastidium *n*, aversatio *f*
repugnant *adj* aversus, repugnans, alienus
repulse *s* depulsio *f*; (*political defeat*) repulsa *f*
repulse *vt* repellěre
repulsion *s* repulsio *f*
repulsive *adj* odiosus, foedus
reputable *adj* honestus
reputation *s* fama *f*, nomen *n*
repute *s* fama, opinio *f*, nomen *n*
request *s* petitio, rogatio *f*; **to obtain a —** impetrare
request *vt* rogare, petěre
require *vt* postulare, poscěre; (*to need*) egēre (*with abl*); (*to call for*) requirěre
requirement *s* necessarium *n*
requisite *adj* necessarius
requisition *s* postulatio *f*, postulatum *n*
requital *s* retributio, merces *f*; (*return for a service*) gratia *f*
requite *vt* compensare, retribuěre; (*for a favor*) remunerari
rescind *vt* rescinděre, tollěre
rescue *s* liberatio, salus *f*; **to come to the — of** subvenire (*with dat*)
rescue *vt* liberare, servare, eripěre
research *s* investigatio *f*
resemblance *s* similitudo, imago *f*, instar *n* (*indecl*)
resemble *vt* similis esse (*with genit, esp. of persons, or with dat*)
resembling *adj* similis (*with genit, esp. of persons, or with dat*)
resent *vt* aegre ferre
resentful *adj* iracundus, indignans
resentment *s* indignatio *f*, dolor *m*
reservation *s* retentio *f*; (*mental*) exceptio *f*; (*proviso*) condicio *f*
reserve *s* (*restraint*) pudor *m*, taciturnitas *f*; (*stock*) copia *f*; (*mil*) subsidium *n*; **in —** subsidiarius; **without —** aperte
reserve *vt* servare, reservare, reponěre
reserved *adj* (*of seat*) assignatus; (*of disposition*) taciturnus
reservoir *s* cisterna *f*, lac·us -ūs *m*
reset *vt* reponěre
reside *vi* habitare, commorari; **to — in** inhabitare
residence *s* habitatio, sedes *f*, domicilium *n*
resident *s* incola *m & f*
residue *s* residuum *n*
resign *vt* ceděre, remittěre; se abdicare a(b) (*with abl*); **to — oneself** animum summittěre (*with dat*); *vi* se abdicare
resignation *s* (*act*) abdicatio *f*; (*fig*) aequus animus *m*
resigned *adj* summissus; **to be —** aequo animo esse; **to be — to** aequo animo ferre
resilience *s* mollitia *f*
resilient *adj* resultans, mollis
resin *s* resina *f*
resist *vt* resistěre (*with dat*), obstare (*with dat*), repugnare (*with dat*)
resistance *s* repugnantia *f*; **to offer to —** obsistěre (*with dat*), repugnare (*with dat*)
resolute *adj* firmus, constans, fortis; **—ly** constanter, fortiter
resolution *s* (*determination*) constantia *f*; (*decision, decree*) decretum *n*; (*of senate*) consultum *n*
resolve *s* constantia *f*
resolve *vt* decerněre, statuěre, constituěre; (*to reduce, convert*) resolvěre, dissolvěre
resonance *s* resonantia *f*
resonant *adj* resonus
resort *s* locus celeber *m*; (*refuge*) refugium *n*
resort *vi* **to — to** (*to frequent*) frequentare, celebrare; (*to have recourse to*) confugěre ad (*with acc*)
resource *s* subsidium *n*; **—s** facultates, opes, copiae *f pl*
respect *s* (*regard*) respect·us -ūs *m*; (*reference*) ratio *f*; **in every —** ex omni parte
respect *vt* (re)verēri, observare
respectability *s* honestas *f*
respectable *adj* honestus, bonus
respectably *adv* honeste
respectful *adj* observans, reverens; **—ly** reverenter
respecting *prep* de (*with abl*)
respective *adj* proprius, suus; **—ly** mutuo
respiration *s* spirit·us -ūs *m*
respite *s* intermissio, cessatio, requies *f*
resplendence *s* nitor, splendor *m*
resplendent *adj* resplendens, splendidus; **—ly** splendide
respond *vi* responděre
respondent *s* (*law*) reus *m*
response *s* responsum *n*
responsibility *s* cura *f*; **it is my —** est mihi curae
responsible *adj* obnoxius, reus
rest *s* quies, requies *f*; (*support*) fulcrum, statumen *n*; (*remainder*) reliqua pars *f*, reliquum *n*; **the — of the men** ceteri *m pl*
rest *vt* (*to lean*) reclinare; *vi* (re)quiescěre; (*to pause*) cessare; **to — on** inniti in (*with abl*), niti (*with abl*)
restitution *s* restitutio *f*; (*restoration*) refectio *f*
restive *adj* (*balky, unruly*) contumax; (*impatient*) impatiens
restless *adj* inquietus, turbidus, tumultuosus; (*agitated*) sollicitus; **—ly** inquiete, turbulenter
restoration *s* restauratio, refectio, renovatio *f*
restore *vt* restituěre, redděre; (*to re-*

build) restaurare, reficĕre; (*to health*) recurare, recreare; **to — to order** in integrum reducĕre
restrain *vt* cohibēre, coercēre, continēre; (*to prevent*) impedire
restraint *s* temperantia, moderatio *f*
restrict *vt* cohibēre, restringĕre, circumscribĕre, (de)finire
restriction *s* modus, finis *m*, limitatio *f*
result *s* exit·us -ūs, event·us -ūs *m*; eventum *n*; **without —** nequiquam
result *vi* evenire, fieri, evadĕre
resume *vt* resumere, repetĕre
resumption *s* resumptio, continuatio *f*
resurrection *s* resurrectio *f*
resuscitate *vt* resuscitare
retail *vt* divendĕre
retailer *s* caupo, propola *m*
retain *vt* retinēre, obtinēre, conservare
retainer *s* (*adherent*) cliens, asectator, satelles *m*; (*fee*) arrabo *m*
retake *vt* recipĕre, recuperare
retaliate *vi* ulcisci
retaliation *s* ultio *f*
retard *vt* retardare
retch *vi* nauseare
retention *s* retentio, conservatio *f*
retentive *adj* tenax
reticence *s* taciturnitas *f*
reticent *adj* taciturnus
retinue *s* comitat·us -ūs *m*
retire *vi* recedĕre, regredi; (*from office*) abire; (*for the night*) dormitum ire
retired *adj* (*of place*) remotus, solitarius; (*from work*) emeritus
retirement *s* (*act*) recess·us -ūs *m*, abdicatio *f*; (*state*) otium *n*, solitudo *f*
retiring *adj* modestus
retort *s* responsum *n*
retort *vt* respondĕre
retrace *vt* repetĕre, iterare
retract *vt* revocare, recantare, renuntiare
retraction *s* retractatio *f*
retreat *vi* recedĕre, refugĕre, se recipĕre, pedem referre
retreat *s* (*act*) recess·us -ūs *m*, fuga *f*; (*place*) recess·us -ūs *m*, refugium *n*; (mil) recept·us -ūs *m*
retrench *vt* recidĕre
retrenchment *s* recisio *f*
retribution *s* compensatio, poena *f*
retrieve *vt* recuperare, recipĕre
retrogression *s* regress·us -ūs, retrogress·us -ūs *m*
retrospect *s* retrospect·us -ūs *m*; **in —** respicienti
retrospective *adj* respiciens; **—ly** retro
return *s* (*coming back*) redit·us -ūs *m*; (*repayment*) remuneratio *f*; (*income, profit*) fruct·us -ūs *m*
return *vt* (*to give back*) reddĕre, restituĕre, referre; *vi* (*to go back*) redire; (*to come back*) revenire, reverti
reunion *s* readunatio *f*, convivium *n*
reunite *vt* iterum conjungĕre; reconciliare; *vi* reconciliari
reveal *vt* retegĕre, recludĕre, aperire; (*to unveil*) revelare
revel *s* comissatio, bacchatio *f*; **—s** orgia *n pl*
revel *vi* comissari, debacchari, luxuriare *or* luxuriari
revelation *s* patefactio, revelatio *f*
reveler *s* comissator *m*
revelry *s* comissatio *f*, orgia *n pl*
revenge *vt* ulcisci
revenge *s* ultio, vindicta *f*; **to take — on** se vindicare in (*with acc*)
revengeful *adj* ulciscendi cupidus
revenue *s* redit·us -ūs, fruct·us -ūs *m*, vectigal *n*
reverberate *vi* resonare
reverberation *s* repercuss·us -ūs *m*, resonantia *f*
revere *vt* reverēri, venerari
reverence *s* reverentia, veneratio, religio, pietas *f*
reverend *adj* reverendus
reverent *adj* reverens, pius, religiosus; **—ly** reverenter, religiose
reverential *adj* venerabundus
reverie *s* cogitatio, meditatio *f*
reversal *s* infirmatio *f*
reverse *s* contrarium *m*; (*change*) conversio, commutatio *f*; (*defeat*) clades *f*
reverse *vt* invertĕre, (com)mutare; (*decision*) rescindĕre, abrogare
revert *vi* redire, reverti
review *s* recognitio *f*; (*critique*) censura *f*; (*mil*) recensio, lustratio *f*
review *vt* recensēre, inspicĕre; (*mil*) recensēre, lustrare
reviewer *s* censor, editor *m*
revile *vt* maledicĕre (*with dat*), insectari
revise *vt* corrigĕre, recognoscĕre
revision *s* emendatio *f*; (*of literary work*) recensio, lima *f*
revisit *vt* revisĕre, revisitare
revival *s* redanimatio *f*; (*fig*) renovatio *f*
revive *vt* resuscitare; (*to renew*) renovare; (*to encourage*) animare, instigare, excitare; *vi* reviviscĕre
revocation *s* revocatio *f*
revoke *vt* revocare, renuntiare; (*a law*) rescindĕre
revolt *vt* offendĕre; *vi* rebellare, desciscĕre, deficĕre
revolt *s* rebellio, seditio, defectio *f*
revolting *adj* taeter, foedus
revolution *s* conversio *f*; (*change*) commutatio *f*; (*of planets*) ambit·us -ūs *m*; (*pol*) res novae *f pl*, mot·us -ūs *m*
revolutionary *adj* seditiosus, novarum rerum cupidus
revolutionize *vt* novare
revolve *vt* (*in mind*) meditari, volutare; *vi* revolvi, se (re)volvĕre
revulsion *s* taedium, fastidium *n*; **to cause —** fastidium movēre
reward *s* praemium *n*
reward *vt* remunerare, compensare
rewrite *vt* rescribĕre
rhapsody *s* rhapsodia *f*
rhetoric *s* rhetorica *n pl* or *f*

rhetorical *adj* rhetoricus, oratorius; **to practice —** declamare
rhetorician *s* rhetor *m*
rheumatism *s* dolor artuum *m*
rhinoceros *s* rhinoceros *m*
rhubarb *s* radix Pontica *f*
rhyme *s* homoeteleuton *n*
rhythm *s* numerus, rhythmus *m*
rhythmical *adj* numerosus
rib *s* costa *f*
ribald *adj* obscenus, spurcus
ribaldry *s* obscenitas *f*
ribbed *adj* costatus, striatus
ribbon *s* infula *f*
rice *s* oryza *f*
rich *adj* dives, locuples; (*of soil*) fertilis, uber, opimus; (*food*) pinguis; (*costly*) pretiosus, lautus; **—ly** copiose, pretiose, laute
riches *s* divitiae, opes *f pl*
rickety *adj* instabilis
rid *vt* liberare; **to get — of** dimittěre, deponěre, exuěre
riddle *s* aenigma *n*
ride *vt* **to — a horse** equo vehi; *vi* equitare; vehi; **to — away** *or* **off** avehi
ride *s* (*on horseback*) equitatio *f*; (*in carriage*) vectio *f*
rider *s* eques *m*; (*in carriage*) vector *m*; (*attached to documents*) adjectio *f*
ridge *s* jugum, dorsum *n*
ridicule *s* ridiculum, ludibrium *n*, irris·us -ūs *m*
ridicule *vt* irridēre
ridiculous *adj* ridiculus; **—ly** ridicule
riding *s* equitatio *f*
rife *adj* frequens
riffraff *s* plebecula, faex populi *f*
rifle *vt* despoliare, diripěre
rig *vt* adornare; (*ship*) armare, ornare
rigging *s* armamenta *n pl*, rudentes *m pl*
right *adj* rectus; (*just*) aequus, justus; (*opposed to left*) dexter; (*suitable*) idoneus, aptus; (*true*) verus, rectus; **—ly** recte, rite, juste, vere
right *s* (*hand*) dextra *f*; (*law*) jus, fas, aequum *n*; **on the —** a dextra
right *vt* emendare, corrigěre; (*to replace*) restituěre; (*to avenge*) vindicare, ulcisci
righteous *adj* justus, pius; **—ly** juste, pie
righteousness *s* justitia, pietas, probitas *f*
rightful *adj* legitimus, justus; **—ly** juste
rigid *adj* rigidus; **—ly** rigide
rigidity *s* rigiditas *f*
rigor *s* severitas, duritia *f*
rigorous *adj* severus, asper; (*hardy*) durus
rill *s* rivulus *m*
rim *s* ora, margo *f*, labrum *n*
rind *s* crusta *f*
ring *s* anulus *m*; (*of people*) corona *f*; (*for fighting*) arena *f*; (*sound*) sonit·us -ūs *m*; (*of bells*) tinnit·us -ūs *m*
ring *vt* **to — a bell** tintinnabulum tractare; *vi* tinnire, resonare
ringing *s* tinnit·us -ūs *m*
ringleader *s* auctor, dux *m*
rinse *vt* colluěre, eluěre
rinsing *s* colluvies *f*
riot *s* tumult·us -ūs, mot·us -ūs *m*; **to run —** luxuriari
riot *vi* seditionem movēre, tumultuari
rioter *s* seditiosus *m*
riotous *adj* seditiosus, tumultuosus; **— living** luxuria *f*
rip *vt* scinděre; **to — apart** discinděre, diffinděre; (*fig*) discerpěre
ripe *adj* mitis, maturus, tempestivus
ripen *vt* maturare; *vi* maturescěre
ripple *s* flucticulus *m*
ripple *vi* trepidare
rise *vi* oriri, surgěre; (*from sleep*) expergisci; (*to mount*) ascenděre; (*to increase*) crescěre; (*of rioters*) consurgěre; (*of passion*) tumescěre; **to — again** resurgěre, reviviscěre; **to — up** exsurgěre
rise *s* (*ascent*) ascens·us -ūs *m*; (*origin*) origo *f*, ort·us -ūs *m*; (*increase*) incrementum *n*; (*slope*) clivus *m*; **to give — to** parěre
rising *s* (*of sun*) ort·us -ūs *m*; (*insurrection*) mot·us -ūs, tumult·us -ūs *m*
risk *s* periculum *n*; **to run a —** periculum subire, periclitari
risk *vt* in periculum vocare, periclitari
rite *s* rit·us -ūs *m*
ritual *s* rit·us -ūs *m*, caeremonia *f*
rival *s* rivalis, aemulus, competitor *m*
rival *vt* aemulari
rivalry *s* aemulatio *f*, certamen *n*; (*in love*) rivalitas *f*
river *s* flumen *n*, amnis *m*
rivet *s* clavus *m*
rivet *vt* (*eyes, attention*) defigěre
rivulet *s* rivus, rivulus *m*
road *s* via *f*, iter *n*; **on the —** in itinere; **to build a —** viam munire
roam *vi* errare, vagari
roar *s* fremit·us -ūs, rugit·us -ūs, strepit·us -ūs *m*
roar *vi* freměre, ruděre, rugire
roast *vt* torrēre; (*in a pan*) frigěre, assare, coquěre
roast *adj* assus
roast *s* assum *n*
rob *vt* spoliare, compilare, latrocinari
robber *s* latro, fur *m*
robbery *s* latrocinium *n*, spoliatio *f*
robe *s* vestis, palla *f*
robe *vt* vestire
robin *s* sylvia rubecula, rubisca *f*
robust *adj* robustus, validus, lacertosus
rock *s* saxum *n*; (*cliff*) scopulus *m*, rupes *f*
rock *vt* jactare; **to — a cradle** cunas agitare; *vi* vibrare, vacillare
rocket *s* missile *n*
rocky *adj* saxosus, scopulosus
rod *s* virga, ferula *f*
roe *s* caprea *f*; (*of fish*) ova *n pl*
roebuck *s* capreolus *m*
rogue *s* nequam (homo), furcifer *m*
roguish *adj* malus, improbus

roll *vt* volvĕre, versare; *vi* volvi; (*of tears*) labi
roll *s* (*book*) volumen *n*; (*of names*) catalogus *m*, album *n*; (*of bread*) collyra *f*
roller *s* cylindrus *m*
Roman *adj* Romanus
Roman *s* Romanus, Quiris *m*
romance *s* fabula, narratio ficta *f*; (*affair*) amores *m pl*
romantic *adj* fabulosus, commenticius, amatorius
roof *s* tectum, fastigium *n*; (*of mouth*) palatum *n*
roof *vt* contegĕre, integĕre
room *s* (*space*) spatium *n*, locus *m*; (*of house*) conclave *n*
roomy *adj* laxus, spatiosus
roost *s* pertica *f*
roost *vi* cubitare, insidēre
root *s* radix *f*; (*fig*) fons *m*, origo *f*; **to take —** coalescĕre
root *vt* **to become rooted** (*fig*) inveterascĕre; **to be rooted** inhaerēre; **to — out** eradicare, exstirpare; *vi* radices agĕre; (*fig*) inveterascĕre
rope *s* funis *m*, restis *f*
rose *s* rosa *f*
roseate *adj* roseus
rosy *adj* roseus, rosaceus
rot *vi* putrescĕre, tabescĕre
rot *s* putredo, tabes, caries *f*
rotate *vi* volvi, se convertĕre
rotation *s* ambit·us -ūs *m*, conversio *f*; (*succession*) vicissitudo *f*; **in —** ordine
rote *s* **by —** memoriter
rotten *adj* putridus, tabidus, cariosus
rotunda *s* tholus *m*
rouge *s* fucus *m*
rough *adj* asper; (*of character*) agrestis, durus; (*of weather*) inclemens; (*shaggy*) hirsutus; **—ly** aspere, duriter
roughen *vt* asperare
roughness *s* asperitas *f*; (*brutality*) feritas *f*
round *adj* rotundus, globosus; **—ly** aperte, plane, praecise
round *s* orbis, circulus *m*; (*series*) ambit·us -ūs *m*
round *vt* (*a corner*) circumire, flectĕre; (*a cape*) superare; **to — off** concludĕre, complēre
rouse *vt* excitare, animare
rout *s* fuga *f*; (*defeat*) clades *f*; (*crowd*) turba *f*
rout *vt* fugare, fundĕre
route *s* via *f*, iter *n*
routine *s* consuetudo *f*, ordo, us·us -ūs *m*
rove *vi* vagari, errare
rover *s* ambulator *m*
row *s* series *f*, ordo *m*; (*quarrel*) rixa *f*
row *vt* remis propellĕre; *vi* remigare
rower *s* remex *m*
rowing *s* remigatio *f*, remigium *n*
royal *adj* regalis, regius; **—ly** regaliter, regie
royalty *s* regia potestas *f*, regnum *n*
rub *vt* fricare; **to — away** *or* **off** detergēre
rub *s* fricatio *f*; (*fig*) difficultas *f*
rubbing *s* attrit·us -ūs, affrict·us -ūs *m*, fricatio, frictio *f*
rubbish *s* rudus *n*; (*fig*) quisquiliae *f pl*
rubble *s* rudus *n*
rubric *s* rubrica *f*
ruby *s* rubinus, carbunculus *m*
rudder *s* gubernaculum *n*
ruddy *adj* rubicundus, rubens, rutilus
rude *adj* rudis, rusticus, inurbanus; (*impertinent*) impudicus; **—ly** rustice, incondite
rudeness *s* rusticitas, inhumanitas, insolentia *f*
rudiment *s* elementum, initium, rudimentum, principium *n*
rudimentary *adj* inchoatus, elementarius
rue *vt* **I —** me paenitet (*with genit*)
rueful *adj* maestus, luctuosus
ruffian *s* sicarius, grassator *m*
ruffle *vt* agitare, turbare; (*to irritate*) commovēre
ruffle *s* limbus *m*
rug *s* stragulum *n*
rugged *adj* asper, praeruptus
ruin *s* pernicies *f*, exitium *n*; ruina *f*; **—s** ruinae *f pl*
ruin *vt* perdĕre, corrumpĕre; (*morally*) depravare
ruination *s* vastatio *f*
ruinous *adj* damnosus, exitiosus
rule *s* (*regulation*) praeceptum *n*, lex *f*; (*government*) regimen, imperium *n*, dominatio *f*; (*instrument*) regula, norma *f*
rule *vt* regĕre, moderari; *vi* regĕre, dominari
ruler *s* (*person*) rector, dominus, rex *m*; (*instrument*) regula *f*
ruling *s* edictum *n*
rum *s* sicera *f*
rumble *s* murmur *n*
rumble *vi* murmurare, crepitare, mugire
rumbling *s* murmur *n*, mugit·us -ūs *m*
ruminate *vi* ruminare
rumination *s* ruminatio *f*
rummage *vi* **to — through** rimari
rumor *s* rumor *m*, fama *f*
rump *s* clunis *f*
rumple *s* (*in garment*) plica, ruga *f*
rumple *vt* corrugare
run *vt* (*to manage*) gerĕre, administrare; **to — aground** impingĕre; **to — up** (*an account*) augēre; *vi* currĕre; (*to flow*) fluĕre; **to — about** discurrĕre, cursare; **to — after** sequi, petĕre, sectari; **to — aground** offendĕre; **to — away** aufugĕre; **to — away from** defugĕre; **to — down** decurrĕre; (*as water*) defluĕre; **to — for** conquirĕre; **to — foul of** collidi; **to — into** (*to meet*) incidĕre in (*with acc*); **to — off** aufugĕre; (*as water*) defluĕre; **to — on** percurrĕre, continuare; **to — out** excurrĕre; (*of time*) exire; (*of supplies*) deficĕre; **to — over** (*details*) percurrĕre; (*of fluids*) superfluĕre; **to — short** deficĕre; **to — through** (*to dissipate*)

dissipare; **to — together** concurrĕre; **to — up** accurrĕre; **to — up against** incurrĕre in (*with acc*)
runaway *s* transfuga *m*
runner *s* cursor *m*
running *s* curs·us -ūs *m*; (*flowing*) flux·us -ūs *m*
rupture *s* hernia *f*; seditio, dissensio *f*
rupture *vt* rumpĕre, abrumpĕre; *vi* rumpi
rural *adj* agrestis, rusticus
ruse *s* dolus *m*, fraus *f*
rush *s* (*plant*) juncus *m*; (*charge*) impet·us -ūs *m*
rush *vt* rapĕre; *vi* ruĕre, ferri; **to — forward** prorumpĕre, se proripĕre; **to — in** inruĕre, incurrĕre; **to — out** erumpere, evolare
russet *adj* russus, rufus, ravus
rust *s* rubigo, aerugo *f*; (*of iron*) ferrugo *f*
rust *vi* rubiginem contrahĕre
rustic *adj* rusticus, agrestis
rustic *s* rusticus *m*, ruricola *m & f*
rustle *vi* crepitare, increpare
rustle *s* crepit·us -ūs *m*
rusty *adj* rubiginosus, aeruginosus; **to become —** rubigine obduci; (*fig*) desuescĕre
rut *s* (*of wheel*) orbita *f*
ruthless *adj* immisericors, inexorabilis, crudelis; **—ly** incrudeliter
rye *s* secale *n*

S

Sabbath *s* sabbata *n pl*
saber *s* acinaces *m*
sable *adj* pullus, ater, niger
sable *s* (*fur*) pellis zibellina *f*
sack *s* saccus *m*; (*mil*) direptio *f*
sack *vt* (*mil*) vastare, diripĕre
sackcloth *s* cilicium *n*
sacred *adj* sacer, sanctus, sacrosanctus
sacrifice *s* (*act*) sacrificium *n*, immolatio *f*; (*victim*) hostia, victima *f*; (*fig*) jactura *f*
sacrifice *vt* immolare, mactare, sacrificare; (*fig*) devovēre
sacrilege *s* sacrilegium *n*
sacrilegious *adj* sacrilegus
sad *adj* tristis, maestus, miserabilis; **—ly** maeste
sadden *vt* contristare, dolore afficĕre
saddle *s* ephippium *n*
saddle *vt* imponĕre (*with acc of thing and dat of person*); **to — a horse** equum sternĕre
saddlebags *s* clitellae *f pl*
sadness *s* tristitia, maestitia *f*
safe *adj* tutus; (*without hurt*) incolumis; **— and sound** salvus; **—ly** tute
safe-conduct *s* tutela *f* commeat·us -ūs *m*
safeguard *s* praesidium *n*, tutela *f*
safety *s* salus, incolumitas *f*; **in —** tuto
saffron *adj* croceus
sagacious *adj* sagax; **—ly** sagaciter
sagacity *s* sagacitas *f*
sage *s* (*wise man*) sapiens *m*
sage *adj* sapiens, prudens; **—ly** sapienter
sail *s* velum *n*; **to set —** vela dare
sail *vi* nave vehi, vela facĕre, navigare
sailing *s* navigatio *f*
sailor *s* nauta *m*
saint *s* vir sanctus *m*, femina sancta *f*
saintly *adj* sanctus, pius
sake *s* **for the — of** gratiā (*with genit*), causā (*with genit*), pro (*with abl*)
salad *s* acetaria *n pl*, moretum *n*
salamander *s* salamandra *f*
salary *s* salarium *n*, merces *f*
sale *s* venditio *f*; **for —** venalis; **to put up for —** venum dare
salesman *s* venditor *m*
salient *adj* prominens, saliens
saline *adj* salsus
saliva *s* saliva *f*, sputum *n*
sallow *adj* pallidus, luridus
sally *s* eruptio *f*, impet·us -ūs *m*
sally *vi* eruptionem facĕre, erumpĕre
salmon *s* salmo *m*
saloon *s* caupona *f*
salt *s* sal *m*
salt *vt* salire, sale condire
salting *s* salsura *f*
saltless *adj* insulsus
salt mine *s* salifodina *f*
salt shaker *s* salinum *n*
salt water *s* aqua marina *f*
salubrious *adj* salubris
salutary *adj* salutaris, utilis
salutation *s* salutatio, salus *f*
salute *s* salus, salutatio *f*
salute *vt* salutare
salvage *vt* servare, eripĕre
salvation *s* salus *f*
salve *s* unguentum *n*
same *adj* idem; **at the — time** eodem tempore, simul; **the very —** ipsissimus
sameness *s* identitas *f*
sample *s* exemplum, specimen *n*
sample *vt* libare
sanctify *vt* sanctificare, consecrare
sanctimonious *adj* sanctitatem affectans
sanction *s* comprobatio, auctoritas, confirmatio *f*
sanction *vt* ratum facĕre, sancire
sanctity *s* sanctitas, sanctimonia *f*
sanctuary *s* sanctuarium *n*; (*refuge*) asylum *n*
sand *s* (h)arena *f*
sandal *s* solea, crepida *f*
sandstone *s* tofus, tophus *m*
sandy *adj* (h)arenosus, sabulosus, (h)arenaceus; (*in color*) rufus

sane *adj* sanus
sanguinary *adj* sanguinarius, cruentus
sanguine *adj* sanguineus, alacer
sanitary *adj* salubris
sanity *s* sanitas, mens sana *f*
sap *s* sucus *m*
sap *vt* subruĕre, haurire
sapling *s* surculus *m*
Sapphic *adj* Sapphicus
sapphire *s* sapphirus *f*
sarcasm *s* dicacitas *f*
sarcastic *adj* acerbus, mordax; **—ally** acerbe, amare
sarcophagus *s* sarcophagus *m*
sardine *s* sarda *f*
sardonic *adj* amarus
sash *s* cingillum *n*, zona *f*
Satan *s* Satanas, Satan *m*
satchel *s* sacculus *m*, pera *f*
satellite *s* satelles *m & f*
satiate *vt* satiare, saturare
satire *s* satura *f*
satirical *adj* acerbus, satiricus
satirist *s* derisor, saturarum scriptor *m*
satirize *vt* notare, perstringĕre
satisfaction *s* compensatio *f*; (*feeling*) voluptas *f*
satisfactorily *adv* ex sententia (meā, tuā, *etc.*)
satisfactory *adj* idoneus, jucundus, gratus
satisfied *adj* contentus
satisfy *vt* satisfacĕre (*with dat*); (*to indemnify*) compensare; (*desires*) explēre
satrap *s* satrapes *m*
saturate *vt* saturare, imbuĕre
satyr *s* satyrus *m*
sauce *s* condimentum *n*; (*of meat*) eliquamen *n*
saucer *s* patella, scutella *f*
saucily *adv* petulanter
saucy *adj* petulans, procax, protervus
saunter *vi* vagari, ambulari
sausage *s* farcimen *n*
savage *adj* ferus, efferatus; (*cruel*) saevus, atrox, immanis; **—ly** crudeliter, immaniter
save *vt* servare, conservare; (*from danger*) liberare, eripĕre; **to — up** reservare
save *prep* praeter (*with acc*)
saving *s* conservatio *f*; **—s** peculium *n*
savior *s* servator, liberator *m*
Saviour *s* Salvator (mundi) *m*
savor *s* sapor, gust·us -ūs *m*
savor *vi* sapĕre
savory *adj* sapidus
saw *s* (*tool*) serra *f*; (*saying*) proverbium *n*
saw *vt* serrā secare; *vi* serram ducĕre
sawdust *s* scobis *f*
say *vt* dicĕre; **that is to —** scilicet; **to — that . . . not** negare
saying *s* dictum, proverbium *n*
scab *s* crusta *f*
scabbard *s* vagina *f*
scaffold *s* tabulatum *n*, fala *f*
scald *vt* urĕre
scale *s* (*of fish*) squama *f*; (*for weighing*) libra, trutina *f*; (*mus*) diagramma *n*; (*gradation*) grad·us -ūs *m*
scale *vt* (*fish*) desquamare; **to — a wall** murum per scalas ascendĕre
scallop *s* pecten *m*
scalp *s* pericranium *n*
scaly *adj* squamosus, squameus
scamp *s* furcifer *m*
scamper *vi* cursare; **to — about** discurrĕre, cursitare; **to — away** aufugĕre
scan *vt* examinare, explorare; (*verses*) scandĕre
scandal *s* ignominia *f*, opprobrium *n*
scandalize *vt* offendĕre
scandalous *adj* probrosus, flagitiosus
scantily *adv* exigue, anguste
scanty *adj* tenuis, exiguus, exilis
scapegoat *s* piaculum *n*
scar *s* cicatrix *f*
scarce *adj* rarus; **—ly** vix, aegre
scarcity *s* paucitas, inopia *f*
scare *vt* terrēre, territare
scarecrow *s* terriculum *n*
scarf *s* fascia *f*, focale *n*
scarlet *s* coccum *n*
scarlet *adj* coccinus, coccineus
scathing *adj* acerbus, aculeatus
scatter *vt* spargĕre, dispergĕre, dissipare; *vi* dilabi, diffugĕre
scavenger *s* cloacarius *m*
scene *s* prospect·us -ūs *m*, spectaculum *n*; (*on stage*) scaena *f*; (*place*) locus *m*
scenery *s* (*in theater*) scaenae apparat·us -ūs *m*; (*of nature*) species regionis *f*
scent *s* (*sense*) odorat·us -ūs *m*; (*of dogs*) sagacitas *f*; (*fragrance*) odor *m*
scent *vt* odorari
scented *adj* odoratus
scepter *s* sceptrum *n*
sceptic *s* scepticus *m*
sceptical *adj* dubitans, incredulus
schedule *s* ratio *f*
scheme *s* consilium *n*
scheme *vt & vi* moliri, machinari
schism *s* schisma, discidium *n*
scholar *s* litteratus *m*
scholarly *adj* litteratus, doctus
scholarship *s* litterae *f pl*, eruditio *f*
scholastic *adj* scholasticus
scholiast *s* scholiastes, interpres *m*
school *s* ludus *m*, schola *f*; (*group holding like opinions*) secta *f*
schoolboy *s* discipulus *m*
schoolmaster *s* magister *m*
schoolroom *s* schola *f*
science *s* scientia, doctrina, disciplina, ars *f*
scientific *adj* physicus; **—ally** physice; (*systematically*) ratione
scientist *s* physicus *m*
scimitar *s* acinaces *m*
scion *s* edit·us -ūs *m*, progenies *f*
scissors *s* forfex *f*
scoff *s* irrisio, derisio, cavillatio *f*
scoff *vi* cavillari; **to — at** irridēre, deridēre
scoffer *s* derisor, irrisor *m*

scold *vt* objurgare, increpare; *vi* desaevire
scolding *s* objurgatio *f*
scoop *s* trulla *f*
scoop *vt* **to — out** excavare
scope *s* campus *m*, spatium *n*
scorch *vt* adurĕre, torrēre
score *s* nota *f*; (*total*) summa *f*; (*twenty*) viginti; (*reckoning*) ratio *f*
score *vt* notare
scorn *s* contemptio *f*
scorn *vt* contemnĕre, spernĕre, aspernari
scornful *adj* fastidiosus; **—ly** fastidiose, contemptim
scorpion *s* scorpio, scorpius *m*
Scot *adj* Scoticus
Scotchman *s* Scotus *m*
Scotland *s* Scotia *f*
Scottish *adj* Scoticus
scoundrel *s* nebulo, furcifer *m*
scour *vt* (*to rub clean*) (de)tergēre; (*to range over*) pervagari, percurrĕre
scourge *s* flagellum *n*; (*fig*) pestis *f*
scourge *vt* verberare
scourging *s* verberatio *f*, verbera *n pl*
scout *s* explorator, speculator *m*
scout *vt* speculari, explorare
scowl *vi* frontem contrahĕre
scowlingly *adv* fronte contractā
scramble *vi* **to — up** scandĕre, escendĕre
scrap *s* fragmentum, frustum *n*
scrape *vt* radĕre, scabĕre; **to — together** corradĕre
scrape *s* difficultas *f*; (*quarrel*) rixa *f*
scraper *s* radula *f*
scraping *s* rasura *f*; **—s** ramenta *n pl*
scratch *s* levis incisura *f*
scratch *vt* radĕre, scalpĕre
scrawl *s* scriptio mala *f*
scrawl *vt & vi* male scribĕre
scream *s* ululat·us -ūs, clamor *m*; (*of an infant*) vagit·us -ūs *m*
scream *vi* ululare, clamitare
screech *s* stridor *m*
screech *vi* stridēre
screen *s* umbraculum *n*, obex *m*
screen *vt* protegĕre
screw *s* cochlea *f*
screw *vt* torquēre
scribble *vt & vi* scriptitare
scribe *s* scriba *m*
script *s* scriptum *n*; (*hand*) man·us -ūs *f*
scrofulous *adj* strumosus
scroll *s* volumen *n*, schedula *f*
scrub *vt* defricare, detergēre
scruple *s* scrupulus *m*, religio, dubitatio *f*
scrupulous *adj* religiosus, anxius; **—ly** religiose
scrutinize *vt* scrutari, perscrutari
scrutiny *s* scrutatio, perscrutatio *f*
scud *vi* celeriter aufugĕre
scuffle *s* rixa *f*
scuffle *vi* rixari
sculptor *s* sculptor, scalptor *m*
sculpture *s* (*art*) sculptura *f*; (*work*) opus, signum *n*
sculpture *vt* sculpĕre
scum *s* spuma *f*; (*fig*) sentina *f*
scurrilous *adj* scurrilis
scurvy *s* scorbutus *m*
scutcheon *s* scutum *n*
scythe *s* falx *f*
sea *s* mare, aequor *n*, pontus *m*
sea captain *s* navarchus *m*
seacoast *s* ora maritima *f*
seafaring *adj* maritimus, nauticus
sea gull *s* larus *m*
seal *s* sigillum, signum *n*; (*animal*) phoca *f*
seal *vt* signare; (*fig*) sancire; **to — up** obsignare
seam *s* sutura *f*
seaman *s* nauta *m*
seamanship *s* nauticarum rerum us·us -ūs *m*, ars navigandi *f*
sear *vt* adurĕre
search *s* investigatio, scrutatio *f*
search *vt* investigare, explorare; (*a person*) excutĕre; *vi* **to — for** quaerĕre, exquirĕre; **to — out** explorare
seasick *adj* nauseabundus; **to be —** nauseare
season *s* tempestas *f*, anni tempus *n*; (*proper time*) opportunitas *f*, tempus *n*; **in —** tempestive
season *vt* condire; (*fig*) assuefacĕre, durare
seasonable *adj* tempestivus, opportunus
seasoning *s* condimentum *n*
seat *s* sedes, sella *f*; (*dwelling*) sedes *f*, domicilium *n*
seat *vt* sede locare; **to — oneself** considĕre
seaweed *s* alga *f*
secede *vi* secedĕre
secession *s* secessio *f*
seclude *vt* secludĕre, removēre, abdĕre
secluded *adj* remotus, solitarius
seclusion *s* solitudo *f*, locus remotus *m*
second *adj* secundus, alter; **a — time** iterum; **—ly** deinde, tum
second *s* (*person*) adjutor *m*; (*of time*) punctum temporis *n*
second *vt* adesse (*with dat*), favēre (*with dat*), adjuvare
secondary *adj* secundarius, inferior
secondhand *adj* alienus, tritus
second-rate *adj* inferior
secrecy *s* secretum *n*; (*keeping secret*) silentium *n*
secret *adj* secretus, occultus, arcanus; **to keep —** celare; **—ly** clam
secret *s* secretum *n*, res arcana *f*; **in —** clam
secretary *s* scriba, amanuensis *m*
secrete *vt* celare, occultare, abdĕre
secretion *s* secretio *f*
sect *s* secta *f*
section *s* pars, sectio *f*
sector *s* sector *m*, regio *f*
secular *adj* profanus
secure *adj* tutus; **—ly** tuto
secure *vt* confirmare, munire; (*to obtain*) parare, nancisci; (*to fasten*) religare

security *s* salus, incolumitas *f*; (*pledge*) satisdatio *f*, pignus *n*
sedan *s* lectica *f*
sedate *adj* gravis, sedatus; **—ly** graviter, sedate
sedentary *adj* sedentarius
sedge *s* ulva, carex *f*
sediment *s* sedimentum *n*, faex *f*
sedition *s* seditio, rebellio *f*
seditious *adj* seditiosus, turbulentus; **—ly** seditiose
seduce *vt* seducĕre, corrumpĕre, depravare
seducer *s* corruptor *m*
seduction *s* corruptela *f*
seductive *adj* blandus; **—ly** blande
see *vt & vi* vidēre, cernĕre, conspicĕre; (*to understand*) vidēre, intellegĕre, sentire; **to go to —** visĕre; **to — to** curare
seed *s* semen *n*; (*offspring*) progenies *f*; (*of fruit*) acinum *n*
seedling *s* surculus *m*
seek *vt* quaerĕre, petĕre; **to — to** conari (*with inf*), laborare (*with inf*)
seem *vi* vidēri
seeming *adj* speciosus; **—ly** in speciem, ut videtur
seemly *adj* decens, decorus
seep *vi* manare
seer *s* vates *m*
seethe *vi* fervēre, aestuare
segment *s* segmentum *n*
segregate *vt* segregare, secernĕre
segregation *s* separatio *f*
seize *vt* prehendĕre, arripĕre, rapĕre; (*mil*) occupare; (*fig*) afficĕre
seizure *s* comprehensio, occupatio *f*
seldom *adv* raro
select *vt* seligĕre, eligĕre, deligĕre
select *adj* electus, lectus, exquisitus
selection *s* (*act*) selectio *f*; (*things chosen*) electa *n pl*
self-confident *adj* sibi fidens, confidens
self-conscious *adj* pudibundus
self-control *s* continentia, temperantia *f*
self-denial *s* abstinentia *f*
self-evident *adj* manifestus
self-indulgent *adj* intemperans
selfish *adj* avarus
selfishness *s* avaritia *f*
self-respect *s* pudor *m*
sell *vt* vendĕre; *vi* venire
seller *s* venditor *m*
semblance *s* species, similitudo *f*
semicircle *s* hemicyclium *n*
semicircular *adj* semicirculus
senate *s* senat·us -ūs *m*; (*building*) curia *f*
senator *s* senator *m*
senatorial *adj* senatorius
send *vt* mittĕre; (*on public business*) legare; **to — away** dimittĕre; **to — for** arcessĕre; **to — forward** praemittĕre
senile *adj* senilis, aetate provectus
senior *adj* natu major
seniority *s* aetatis praerogativa *f*
sensation *s* sens·us -ūs *m*; (*fig*) mirum *n*
sense *s* (*faculty; meaning*) sens·us -ūs *m*; (*understanding*) prudentia *f*; (*meaning*) vis, significatio *f*
sense *vt* sentire
senseless *adj* absurdus, ineptus; (*unconscious*) omni sensu carens
sensible *adj* sapiens, prudens
sensibly *adv* prudenter, sapienter
sensitive *adj* sensilis, patibilis, (*touchy*) mollis
sensual *adj* voluptarius, libidinosus; **—ly** libidinose
sensualist *s* homo voluptarius *m*
sensuality *s* libido *f*
sentence *s* (*gram*) sententia *f*; (*law*) judicium *n*; **to pass —** judicare
sentence *vt* damnare, condemnare
sententious *adj* sententiosus; **—ly** sententiose
sentiment *s* (*opinion*) sententia, opinio *f*; (*feeling*) sens·us -ūs *m*
sentimental *adj* mollis, effeminatus
sentimentality *s* mollities animi *f*
sentinel *s* custos, vigil *m*
sentry *s* custos, vigil *m*; **sentries** excubiae, stationes, vigiliae *f pl*
separable *adj* separabilis
separate *adj* separatus, disjunctus; **—ly** separatim
separate *vt* separare, disjungĕre, dividĕre; *vi* separari, disjungi
separation *s* separatio, disjunctio *f*
September *s* (mensis) September *m*
sepulcher *s* sepulcrum *n*
sepulchral *adj* sepulcralis
sequel *s* exit·us -ūs *m*
sequence *s* ordo *m*, series *f*
seraph *s* seraphus *m*
serenade *vt* occentare
serene *adj* serenus, tranquillus; **—ly** serene
serenity *s* serenitas, tranquillitas *f*
serf *s* servus *m*
serfdom *s* servitium *n*, servitus *f*
sergeant *s* optio *m*
series *s* series *f*, ordo *m*
serious *adj* serius, gravis; **—ly** serio
seriousness *s* gravitas *f*, serium *n*
sermon *s* oratio sacra *f*
serpent *s* serpens *f*, anguis *m & f*
servant *s* famulus *m*, famula *f*, servus *m*, serva *f*; (*public servant*) minister *m*
serve *vt* servire (*with dat*); (*food*) apponĕre; (*to be useful to*) prodesse (*with dat*); **to — a sentence** poenam subire; *vi* (*mil*) merēre, militare; (*to suffice*) sufficĕre
service *s* (*favor*) officium *n*; (*mil*) militia *f*, stipendia *n pl*; (*work*) ministerium *n*; **to be of — to** prodesse (*with dat*), bene merēri de (*with abl*)
serviceable *adj* utilis
servile *adj* servilis, humilis
servility *s* humilitas *f*, animus abjectus *m*
servitude *s* servitus *f*
session *s* sessio *f*, convent·us -ūs *m*
set *vt* ponĕre, sistĕre, collocare; (*course*) dirigĕre; (*example*) dare; (*limit*) imponĕre; (*sail*) dare; (*table*) instruĕre; **to — apart** secernĕre, seponĕre; **to — aside** ponĕre; (*fig*)

rescindĕre; **to — down** deponĕre; (*in writing*) perscribĕre; **to — forth** exponĕre; **to — free** liberare; **to — in motion** ciēre; **to — in order** componĕre; **to — off** (*to adorn*) adornare; **to — on fire** incendĕre, accendere; **to — someone over** aliquem praeficĕre (*with dat*); **to — up** statuere; *vi* (*of stars, etc.*) occidĕre; **to — in** (*to begin*) incipĕre; **to — out** proficisci
set *adj* (*fixed*) certus, praescriptus
set *s* congeries *f*
setting *s* occas·us -ūs *m*
settle *vt* statuĕre; (*business*) transigĕre; (*colony*) deducĕre; (*argument*) componĕre; (*debts*) solvĕre, expedire; *vi* (*to take up residence*) considĕre; (*to sink*) subsidĕre
settlement *s* constitutio *f*; (*agreement*) pactum *n*; (*colony*) colonia *f*; (*of liquids*) sedimentum *n*
settler *s* colonus *m*
seven *adj* septem; **— times** septies
sevenfold *adj* septemplex
seventeen *adj* septemdecim, decem et septem
seventeenth *adj* septimus decimus
seventh *adj* septimus; **the — time** septimum
seventieth *adj* septuagesimus
seventy *adj* septuaginta
sever *vt* separare; *vi* disjungi
several *adj* aliquot, complures; **—ly** singulatim
severe *adj* severus, gravis, durus; (*of weather*) asper; **—ly** severe, graviter
severity *s* severitas, gravitas *f*
sew *vt* suĕre; **to — up** consuĕre
sewer *s* cloaca *f*
sewing *s* sutura *f*
sex *s* sex·us -ūs *m*
sextant *s* sextans *m*
sexton *s* aedituus *m*
sexual *adj* sexualis
shabbily *adv* sordide, obsolete
shabbiness *s* sordes *f pl*
shabby *adj* sordidus, obsoletus
shackle *vt* compedibus constringĕre
shackles *s* vincula *n pl*, compedes *f pl*
shade *s* umbra *f*; **—s** (*of the dead*) manes *m pl*
shade *vt* opacare, adumbrare
shadow *s* umbra *f*
shadowy *adj* umbrosus, opacus; (*fig*) inanis, vanus
shady *adj* umbrosus, opacus
shaft *s* (*arrow*) sagitta *f*; (*of spear*) hastile *n*; (*of mine*) puteus *m*
shaggy *adj* hirsutus, villosus
shake *vt* quatĕre, concutĕre; (*head*) nutare; *vi* tremĕre; (*to totter*) vacillare
shaking *s* quassatio *f*; (*with cold, fear, etc.*) tremor, horror *m*
shaky *adj* instabilis
shallow *adj* brevis, vadosus; (*fig*) insulsus, levis
sham *s* dolus *m*, simulatio, species *f*
sham *adj* fictus, simulatus
shambles *s* laniena *f*, laniarium *n*
shame *s* pudor *m*; (*disgrace*) dedecus *n*, infamia, ignominia *f*
shame *vt* ruborem incutĕre (*with dat*)
shamefaced *adj* pudens, verecundus
shameful *adj* probrosus, turpis; **—ly** probrose, turpiter
shameless *adj* impudens; **—ly** impudenter
shamrock *s* trifolium *n*
shank *s* crus *n*
shanty *s* tugurium *n*
shape *s* forma, figura, facies *f*
shape *vt* formare, fingĕre
shapeless *adj* informis, deformis
shapely *adj* formosus
share *s* pars, portio *f*; (*of plow*) vomer *m*
share *vt* partire, impertire; particeps esse (*with genit*)
shark *s* p(r)istix *m*
sharp acutus; (*bitter*) acer, acerbus; (*keen*) acutus, acer, sagax; **—ly** acriter, acute; (*bitterly*) acerbe
sharpen *vt* acuĕre
shatter *vt* quassare, confringĕre; (*fig*) frangĕre
shave *vt* radĕre
shavings *s* ramenta *n pl*
shawl *s* amiculum *n*
she *pron* ea, illa, haec
sheaf *s* manipulus, fascis *m*
shear *vt* tondēre
shearing *s* tonsura *f*
shears *s* forfices *f pl*
sheath *s* vagina *f*
sheathe *vt* in vaginam recondĕre
shed *vt* fundĕre, effundĕre
shed *s* tugurium *n*; (*mil*) vinea *f*
sheep *s* ovis *f*
sheepfold *s* ovile *n*
sheephook *s* pedum, baculum pastorale *n*
sheepish *adj* pudibundus; **—ly** pudenter
sheepskin *s* pellis ovilla *f*
sheer *adj* merus
sheet *s* linteum *n*; (*of paper*) plagula, scheda *f*; (*of metal*) lamina *f*
shelf *s* pluteus *m*, tabula *f*, pegma *n*
shell *s* concha, crusta *f*; (*husk*) folliculus *m*; (*of nuts, etc.*) putamen *n*
shell *vt* decorticare
shellfish *s* concha *f*
shelter *s* tegmen *n*; (*refuge*) refugium *n*; (*lodgings*) hospitium *n*
shelter *vt* tegĕre, defendĕre; (*refugee*) excipĕre
shepherd *s* pastor, opilio, pecorum custos *m*
shield *s* scutum *n*, parma *f*
shield *vt* tegĕre, protegĕre
shield bearer *s* scutigerulus, armiger *m*
shift *vt* mutare, amovēre; *vi* (*as the wind*) vertĕre; (*to change position*) se movēre, mutari
shift *s* (*change*) mutatio *f*
shifty *adj* varius, mobilis
shin *s* tibia *f*, crus *n*
shine *s* nitor *m*
shine *vi* lucēre, fulgēre, nitēre; **to — forth** elucēre, enitēre, exsplen-

descĕre; **to — on** *or* **upon** affulgēre (*with dat*)
shiny *adj* lucidus, fulgidus, nitidus
ship *s* navis *f*, navigium *n*
ship *vt* navi invehĕre
shipbuilder *s* naupegus *m*
shipbuilding *s* architectura navalis *f*
shipmaster *s* navicularius *m*
shipwreck *s* naufragium *n*; **to suffer —** naufragium facĕre
shipwrecked *adj* naufragus
shirk *vt* defugĕre, detrectare
shirt *s* subulca, camisia *f*
shiver *vi* contremiscĕre, horrēre
shoal *s* caterva *f*, grex *m*; (*shallow*) brevia *n pl*
shock *vt* percutĕre, percellĕre; (*fig*) offendĕre
shock *s* concussio *f*, impet·us -ūs *m*; (*fig*) offensio *f*
shocking *adj* flagitiosus, atrox
shoe *s* calceus *m*
shoemaker *s* sutor *m*
shoot *vt* (*missile*) conjicĕre, jaculari; (*person*) transfigĕre; *vi* volare
shoot *s* surculus *m*
shooting star *s* fax caelestis *f*
shop *s* taberna, officina *f*
shopkeeper *s* tabernarius *m*
shore *s* litus *n*, ora *f*
short *adj* brevis; **to run —** deficĕre; **—ly** brevi, mox
shortage *s* inopia *f*
shortcoming *s* defect·us -ūs *m*, delictum *n*
shorten *vt* coarctare, contrahĕre; *vi* contrahi, minui
shorthand *s* notae breviores *f pl*
shortness *s* brevitas, exiguitas *f*; **— of breath** asthma *n*
short-sighted *adj* myops; (*fig*) improvidus, imprudens
short-winded *adj* anhelus
shot *s* ict·us -ūs *m*; (*reach, range*) jact·us -ūs *m*
should *vi* debēre; **I — go** mihi eundum est
shoulder *s* (h)umerus *m*; (*of animal*) armus *m*
shoulder *vt* suscipĕre
shout *s* clamor *m*, acclamatio *f*
shout *vt & vi* clamare, acclamare, vociferari
shove *vt* trudĕre, pulsare
shovel *s* pala *f*, rutrum *n*
shovel *vt* palā tollĕre
show *vt* monstrare; (*to display*) exhibēre; (*to teach*) docēre; **to — off** ostendĕre; *vi* **to — off** se jactare
show *s* (*appearance*) species *f*; (*display*) ostentatio *f*; (*pretense*) simulatio *f*; (*entertainment*) spectaculum *n*
shower *s* imber *m*
shower *vt* fundĕre, effundĕre
showy *adj* speciosus
shred *s* segmentum panni *n*; (*scrap*) frustum *n*
shrew *s* mulier jurgiosa *f*
shrewd *adj* acutus, astutus, callidus, sagax; **—ly** acute, callide, sagaciter
shrewdness *s* calliditas, astutia, sagacitas *f*
shriek *s* ululat·us -ūs *m*, ejulatio *f*
shriek *vi* ululare, ejulare
shrill *adj* peracutus, stridulus
shrimp *s* cancer pagurus *m*; (*person*) pumilio, homulus *m*
shrine *s* fanum, delubrum *n*
shrink *vt* contrahĕre; *vi* contrahi; (*to withdraw*) refugĕre; **to — from** abhorrēre ab (*with abl*), refugĕre ab (*with abl*)
shrivel *vt* corrugare, torrefacĕre; *vi* corrugari, torrescĕre
shroud *s* integumentum *n*; (*of ship*) rudentes *m pl*
shroud *vt* involvĕre, obducĕre
shrub *s* frutex *m*
shrubbery *s* fruticetum *n*
shrug *s* (h)umerorum allevatio *f*
shrug *vt* **to — the shoulders** (h)umeros contrahĕre *or* allevare
shudder *vi* horrēre; **to — at** horrēre
shuffle *vt* miscēre; *vi* claudicare
shun *vt* vitare, devitare, fugĕre
shut *vt* claudĕre, occludere; **to — out** excludĕre; **to — up** concludĕre; *vi* **to — up** conticescĕre
shutter *s* claustrum *n*, foricula *f*
shy *adj* timidus, pudibundus; **—ly** timide
shyness *s* timiditas, verecundia *f*
sibyl *s* sibylla *f*
sick *adj* (*mentally or physically*) aeger; (*physically*) aegrotus; **I am — of** me taedet (*with genit*), fastidio; **to be —** aegrotare
sicken *vt* fastidium movēre (*with dat*); *vi* in morbum incidĕre, nauseare
sickle *s* falx *f*
sickly *adj* infirmus
sickness *s* morbus *m*, aegrotatio *f*
side *s* latus *n*; (*direction*) pars *f*; (*district*) regio *f*; (*faction*) partes *f pl*; (*kinship*) genus *n*; **at the — of a** latere (*with genit*); **on all —s** undique; **on both —s** utrimque; **on one —** unā ex parte; **on that —** illinc; **on the mother's —** materno genere; **on this —** hinc; **on this — of** cis (*with acc*), citra (*with acc*); **to be on the — of** stare ab (*with abl*), sentire cum (*with abl*)
side *adj* lateralis, obliquus
side *vi* **to — with** partes sequi (*with genit*), stare ab (*with abl*), sentire cum (*with abl*)
sideboard *s* abacus *m*
sidelong *adj* obliquus, transversus
sideways *adv* in obliquum, oblique
siege *s* obsessio, oppugnatio, obsidio *f*; **to lay — to** obsidēre
siesta *s* meridiatio *f*; **to take a —** meridiare
sieve *s* cribrum *n*; (*little sieve*) cribellum *n*
sift *vt* cribrare; (*fig*) serutari
sigh *s* suspirium *n*
sigh *vi* suspirare; **to — for** desiderare
sight *s* (*sense*) vis·us -ūs *m*; (*act of seeing*) aspect·us -ūs *m*; (*range*) conspect·us -ūs *m*; (*appearance*) species *f*; (*show*) spectaculum *n*; **at**

first — primo aspectu; **to catch — of** conspicĕre; **to lose — of** e conspectu amittĕre
sight *vt* conspicari
sightless *adj* caecus
sightly *adj* decorus, decens
sign *s* signum, indicium *n*; (*mark*) nota *f*; (*distinction*) insigne *n*; omen, portentum *n*
sign *vt* (*e.g., a document*) subscribĕre, signare, consignare
signal *vi* signum dare; (*by a nod*) annuĕre
signal *s* signum *n*; (*mil*) classicum *n*
signal *adj* insignis, egregius
signature *s* signatura *f*, nomen *n*
signer *s* signator *m*
signet *s* sigillum *n*
significance *s* (*meaning*) significatio, vis *f*, sens·us -ūs *m*; (*importance*) momentum *n*
significant *adj* gravis, magnus, magni momenti (*genit*)
signify *vt* significare, portendĕre
silence *s* silentium *n*
silence *interj* tace!; (*to more than one person*) tacete!
silence *vt* comprimĕre; (*by argument*) refutare
silent *adj* tacitus, taciturnus; **to become —** conticescĕre; **to be —** tacēre; **—ly** tacite
silk *s* sericum *n*, bombyx *m & f*
silk *adj* sericus, bombycinus
silkworm *s* bombyx *m & f*
sill *s* limen inferum *n*
silly *adj* stultus, ineptus
silver *s* argentum *n*
silver *adj* argenteus
silversmith *s* faber argentarius *m*
silvery *adj* argenteus; (*of hair*) canus
similar *adj* similis; **—ly** similiter, pariter
similarity *s* similitudo *f*
simile *s* translatio, similitudo *f*
simmer *vi* lente fervēre
simper *vi* inepte ridēre
simple *adj* simplex; (*easy*) facilis; (*frank*) sincerus; (*silly*) stultus
simpleton *s* stultus, ineptus *m*
simplicity *s* simplicitas *f*
simplify *vt* faciliorem reddĕre
simply *adv* simpliciter; solum, tantummodo
simulate *vt* simulare
simulation *s* simulatio *f*
simultaneous *adj* eodem tempore; **—ly** simul, unā, eodem tempore
sin *s* peccatum, delictum *n*
sin *vi* peccare
since *prep* ex (*with abl*), ab (*with abl*), post (*with acc*); **ever —** usque ab (*with abl*)
since *adv* abhinc; **long —** jamdudum, jampridem
since *conj* (*temporal*) ex quo tempore, postquam, cum; (*causal*) quod, quia, quoniam, cum
sincere *adj* sincerus, candidus; **—ly** sincere, vere
sinew *s* nervus, lacertus *m*
sinewy *adj* nervosus, lacertosus
sinful *adj* impius, pravus; **—ly** impie, improbe
sing *vt & vi* canĕre, cantare
singe *vt* adurĕre, amburĕre
singer *s* cantator *m*, cantatrix *f*
singing *s* cant·us -ūs *m*
single *adj* solus, unicus, unus, singularis; (*unmarried*) caelebs; **not a — one** ne unus quidem
single *vt* **to — out** eligĕre
singly *adv* singulatim, viritim
singsong *s* canticum *n*
singsong *adj* canorus
singular *adj* unicus, singularis; (*outstanding*) egregius, eximius; **—ly** singulariter, unice, egregie
sinister *adj* infaustus, malevolus, iniquus
sink *vt* submergĕre, demergĕre, deprimĕre; (*money*) collocare; *vi* considĕre, subsidĕre; (*in water*) mergi; (*of morale, etc.*) cadĕre
sink *s* sentina *f*
sinless *adj* peccati expers
sinner *s* peccator *m*, peccatrix *f*
sinuous *adj* sinuosus
sip *vt* libare, sorbillare, degustare
siphon *s* sipho *m*
sir *s* (*title*) eques *m*
sir *interj* (*to a master*) ere!; (*to an equal*) bone vir!, vir clarissime!
sire *s* genitor *m*
siren *s* siren *f*
sister *s* soror *f*
sister-in-law *s* glos *f*
sisterly *adj* sororius
sit *vi* sedēre; **to — beside** assidēre (*with dat*); **to — down** considēre; **to — on** insidēre (*with dat*); **to — up** (*to be awake at night*) vigilare
site *s* sit·us -ūs *m*
situated *adj* situs, positus
situation *s* sit·us -ūs *m*; (*circumstances*) res, conditio *f*
six *adj* sex; **— times** sexies
sixfold *adj* sextuplus
sixteen *adj* sedecim
sixteenth *adj* sextus decimus
sixth *s* sexta pars *f*
sixtieth *adj* sexagesimus
sixty *adj* sexaginta
size *s* magnitudo, mensura *f*
skein *s* glomus *m*
skeleton *s* sceletos *m*, ossa *n pl*
sketch *s* adumbratio, lineatio *f*
sketch *vt* adumbrare, delineare; (*fig*) describĕre
skiff *s* scapha *f*
skilful *adj* dexter, peritus, scitus; (*with hands*) habilis; **—ly** perite, scite
skill *s* sollertia, calliditas, peritia *f*
skilled *adj* peritus, doctus
skillet *s* cucumella *f*
skim *vt* despumare; (*fig*) percurrĕre, stringĕre
skin *s* (*of men*) cutis *f*; (*of animals*) pellis *f*; (*prepared*) corium *n*
skin *vt* pellem exuĕre (*with abl*)
skinny *adj* macilentus
skip *vt* praeterire; *vi* subsultare; **to — over** transilire
skirmish *s* concursatio, velitatio *f*
skirmish *vi* velitari

skirmisher *s* veles *m*
skirt *s* instita *f*; (*border*) fimbria *f*
skirt *vt* tangĕre, legĕre
skull *s* cranium, caput *n*
sky *s* caelum *n*, aether *m*; **under the open —** sub divo
slab *s* tabula, tessera *f*
slack *adj* remissus, laxus; (*fig*) piger, neglegens
slacken *vt* remittĕre, laxare, minuĕre; *vi* minui, remitti
slag *s* scoria *f*
slain *adj* occisus
slake *vt* exstinguĕre, sedare
slander *s* calumnia, obtrectatio *f*
slander *vt* obtrectare (*with dat*), calumniari
slanderer *s* obtrectator *m*
slanderous *adj* calumniosus, maledicus
slang *s* vulgaria verba *n pl*
slant *vt* acclinare; (*fig*) detorquēre
slanting *adj* obliquus
slap *s* alapa *f*
slap *vt* alapam dare (*with dat*), palmā ferire
slash *s* (*cut*) caesura *f*; (*blow*) ict·us -ūs *m*; (*wound*) vulnus *n*
slash *vt* caedĕre, incidĕre
slaughter *s* caedes, trucidatio *f*
slaughter *vt* mactare, trucidare
slaughterhouse *s* laniena *f*
slave *s* servus *m*, serva *f*
slave dealer *s* venalicius, mancipiorum negotiator *m*
slavery *s* servitus *f*, servitium *n*
slave trade *s* venalicium *n*
slavish *adj* servilis; **—ly** serviliter
slay *vt* interficĕre, occidĕre, necare
slayer *s* necator, homicida *m*
sledge *s* traha, trahea *f*
sleek *adj* levis, politus, nitidus, pinguis
sleep *s* somnus *m*
sleep *vi* dormire
sleepless *adj* insomnis, pervigil
sleepy *adj* somniculosus, semisomnis; (*fig*) iners
sleet *s* nivosa grando *f*
sleeve *s* manica *f*
slender *adj* gracilis, tenuis
slice *s* segmentum, frustum *n*, offula *f*
slice *vt* secare
slide *vi* labi
slight *adj* levis, exiguus, tenuis; **—ly** leviter, paululum
slight *s* neglegentia, contemptio *f*
slight *vt* neglegĕre, contemnĕre
slily *adv* astute, callide, vafre
slim *adj* gracilis
slime *s* limus *m*
slimy *adj* limosus, mucosus, viscosus
sling *s* funda *f*; (*for arm*) fascia *f*
sling *vt* jaculari
slink *vi* **to — away** furtim se subducĕre
slip *s* laps·us -ūs *m*; (*of paper*) scheda *f*; (*in grafting*) surculus *m*; (*error*) peccatum *n*, culpa *f*
slip *vt* (*to give furtively*) furtim dare; *vi* labi; **to let —** omittĕre; **to — away** elabi
slipper *s* solea, crepida *f*
slippery *adj* lubricus; (*deceitful*) subdolus
slit *s* incisura *f*
slit *vt* incidĕre, discidĕre
slop *s* vilis pot·us -ūs *m*
slope *s* declivitas *f*, clivus *m*
slope *vi* proclinari, vergĕre
sloping *adj* declivis, pronus; (*upward*) acclivis
sloppy *adj* lutulentus, sordidus
slot *s* rima *f*
sloth *s* ignavia, pigritia, inertia *f*
slothful *adj* piger, segnis, iners; **—ly** pigre, segniter, ignave
slouch *vi* languide incedĕre
slough *s* (*of snake*) exuviae *f pl*; (*mire*) caenum *n*
slovenly *adj* sordidus, ignavus
slow *adj* tardus, lentus; (*gentle*) lenis; **—ly** tarde, lente, sensim
sluggard *s* homo piger *m*
sluggish *adj* piger, ignavus, segnis; **—ly** pigre, segniter
sluice *s* cataracta *f*
slumber *s* somnus, sopor *m*
slumber *vi* obdormiscĕre, dormitare
slur *s* macula *f*
slur *vt* inquinare; *vi* **to — over** extenuare, leviter attingĕre
slut *s* meretrix *f*
sly *adj* astutus, vafer, callidus; **on the —** clam; **—ly** astute, callide, vafre
smack *s* (*flavor*) sapor *m*; (*blow*) alapa *f*
smack *vt* (*to strike*) ferire; *vi* **to — of** sapĕre
small *adj* parvus, exiguus, tenuis
smart *adj* (*clever*) sollers, callidus; (*elegant*) lautus, nitidus; (*of pace*) velox; **—ly** callide; nitide
smart *s* dolor *m*
smart *vi* dolēre
smash *s* concussio, fractura *f*
smash *vt* confringĕre
smattering *s* cognitio manca, levis scientia *f*
smear *vt* illinĕre, oblinĕre
smell *s* (*sense*) odorat·us -ūs *m*; (*odor*) odor *m*
smell *vt* olfacĕre, odorari; *vi* olēre; **to — of** olēre, redolēre
smelly *adj* olidus, graveolens
smelt *vt* (ex)coquĕre, fundĕre
smile *s* ris·us -ūs *m*; **with a —** subridens
smile *vi* subridēre; **to — at** arridēre (*with dat*)
smirk *vi* subridēre
smite *vt* ferire, percutĕre
smith *s* faber *m*
smithy *s* ferramentorum fabrica *f*
smock *s* tunica *f*
smoke *s* fumus *m*
smoke *vt* (*to cure by smoking*) infumare; *vi* fumare
smoky *adj* fumeus, fumidus, fumosus
smooth *adj* levis; (*of skin*) glaber; (*polished*) teres; (*calm*) placidus; (*of talk*) blandus; **—ly** leviter; blande
smooth *vt* polire, limare
smother *vt* suffocare, opprimĕre
smudge *s* sordes *f*

smudge *vt* inquinare, conspurcare
smug *adj* lautus, nitidus, sui contentus
smuggle *vt* furtim importare, sine portorio importare
smut *s* fuligo *f*
smutty *adj* obscenus; (*blackened*) fumosus
snack *s* portio, morsiuncula *f*
snail *s* cochlea *f*, limax *m & f*
snake *s* anguis *m & f*, serpens *f*
snap *vt* (*to break*) frangĕre; **to — the fingers** digitis concrepare; **to — up** corripĕre; *vi* disilire, frangi; **to — at** mordēre
snap *s* crepit·us -ūs *m*
snare *s* laqueus *m*, pedica *f*; (*fig*) insidiae *f pl*
snare *vt* illaquēre, irretire
snarl *vi* (*as a dog*) ringĕre, hirrire
snatch *vt* rapĕre, corripĕre; **to — away** eripĕre; **to — up** surripĕre
sneak *s* perfidus *m*
sneak *vi* repĕre, serpĕre, latitare
sneer *s* rhonchus *m*, irrisio *f*
sneer *vi* irridēre, deridēre
sneeringly *adv* cum irrisione
sneeze *s* sternutamentum *n*
sneeze *vi* sternuĕre
sniff *vt* odorari, naribus captare
snip *vi* amputare; **to — off** decerpĕre, praecidĕre
snivel *s* mucus *m*
snivel *vi* mucum resorbēre
snob *s* homo arrogans *m*, homo fastidiosus *m*
snobbish *adj* fastidiosus
snore *s* rhonchus *m*
snore *vi* stertĕre
snort *s* fermit·us -ūs *m*
snort *vi* fremĕre
snout *s* rostrum *n*
snow *s* nix *f*
snow *vi* ningĕre; **it is snowing** ningit
snowball *s* glebula nivis *f*
snowdrift *s* niveus agger *m*
snowstorm *s* ningor *m*
snowy *adj* niveus, nivalis; (*full of snow*) nivosus
snub *vt* reprehendĕre, neglegĕre
snub *s* repulsa *f*
snuff *vt* **to — out** exstinguĕre
snug *adj* commodus; **—ly** commode
so *adv* sic, ita, (*before adjectives*) tam; **— far** eatenus, adhuc; **— much** tantum; **— so** mediocriter; **— that** ita ut; **— that not** ne; **— then** quare, quapropter
soak *vt* madefacĕre, macerare; *vi* madēre
soap *s* sapo *m*
soar *vi* in sublime ferri; (*of birds*) subvolare
sob *s* singult·us -ūs *m*
sob *vi* singultare
sober *adj* sobrius; (*fig*) moderatus, modestus; **—ly** sobrie; moderate
sobriety *s* sobrietas *f*; (*fig*) continentia *f*
sociable *adj* sociabilis, facilis, affabilis
social *adj* socialis, civilis, communis
society *s* societas *f*; **high —** optimates *m pl*; **secret —** sodalitas *f*
sock *s* pedale *n*, udo *m*
socket *s* (*in anatomy*) cavum *n*
sod *s* caespes *m*, glaeba *f*
soda *s* (*in natural state*) nitrum *n*; (*prepared*) soda *f*
sofa *s* lectulus, grabatus *m*
soft *adj* mollis, tener; (*fig*) delicatus, effeminatus; **—ly** molliter, leniter
soften *vt* mollire, mitigare; (*fig*) lenire, placare; *vi* mollescĕre; (*of fruits*) mitescĕre; (*fig*) mansuescĕre, mitescĕre
softness *s* mollitia, teneritas, lenitas *f*; (*effeminacy*) mollities *f*
soil *s* solum *n*, terra *f*
soil *vt* inquinare, contaminare
sojourn *s* commoratio, mansio *f*
sojourn *vi* commorari
solace *s* solatium *n*
solace *vt* consolari
solar *adj* solaris; solis (*genit*)
soldier *s* miles *m*
soldierly *adj* militaris
soldiery *s* miles *m*
sole *adj* solitarius; **—ly** solum, modo, tantum
sole *s* (*of foot*) planta *f*; (*of shoe*) solea *f*; (*fish*) solea *f*
solemn *adj* sollemnis; gravis; **—ly** sollemniter; graviter
solemnity *s* sollemne *n*, sollemnitas *f*; gravitas *f*
solemnization *s* celebratio *f*
solemnize *vt* celebrare
solicit *vt* rogare, flagitare
solicitation *s* flagitatio *f*
solicitor *s* flagitator *m*; (*law*) advocatus *m*
solicitous *adj* anxius, trepidus; **—ly** anxie, trepide
solicitude *s* sollicitudo, anxietas *f*
solid *adj* solidus; purus; (*fig*) verus, firmus; **—ly** solide
soliloquize *vi* secum loqui
soliloquy *s* soliloquium *n*
solitary *adj* solitarius; (*of places*) desertus
solitude *s* solitudo *f*
solstice *s* solstitium *n*
soluble *adj* dissolubilis
solution *s* dilutum *n*; (*fig*) solutio, explicatio *f*
solve *vt* solvĕre, explicare
solvency *s* facultas solvendi *f*
some *adj* aliqui; (*a certain*) quidam; nonnulli, aliquot
some *pron* aliqui; nonnulli; (*certain people*) quidam
somebody *pron* aliquis; **— or other** nescio quis
someday *adv* olim
somehow *adv* quodammodo, nescio quomodo, aliquā (viā)
someone *pron* aliquis; **— else** alius
something *pron* aliquid; **— else** aliud; **— or other** nescio quid
sometime *adv* aliquando
sometimes *adv* interdum, nonnumquam; **sometimes . . . sometimes** modo . . . modo

somewhat *adv* aliquantum; (*with comparatives*) aliquanto, paulo
somewhere *adv* alicubi; (*with motion*) aliquo; **— else** alibi; (*with motion*) alio
somnolence *s* somni cupiditas *f*
somnolent *adj* semisomnus
son *s* filius *m*
song *s* cant·us -ūs *m*; (*tune*) melos *n*
son-in-law *s* gener *m*
sonorous *adj* sonorus, canorus; **—ly** sonore, canore
soon *adv* brevi tempore, mox; **as — as** simul, simulac, simulatque; **as — as possible** quamprimum; **— after** paulo post
sooner *adv* prius; (*preference*) potius; **— or later** serius ocius
soot *s* fuligo *f*
soothe *vt* permulcēre, mitigare, delenire
soothsayer *s* hariolus, sortilegus *m*
soothsaying *s* vaticinatio *f*
sooty *adj* fumosus
sop *s* offa, offula *f*
sophism *s* sophisma *n* cavillatio *f*
sophist *s* sophistes *m*
sophisticated *adj* urbanus, lepidus
sophistry *s* cavillatio captiosa *f*
soporific *adj* soporifer
sorcerer *s* magus *m*
sorceress *s* maga, saga *f*
sorcery *s* veneficium *n*
sordid *adj* sordidus, foedus; **—ly** sordide
sore *adj* (*aching*) tener; (*grievous*) atrox, durus; **—ly** graviter, vehementer
sore *s* ulcus *n*
sorrow *s* dolor, maeror, luct·us -ūs *m*
sorrow *vi* dolēre, lugēre
sorrowful *adj* luctuosus, tristis, maestus; **—ly** maeste
sorry *adj* (*pitiable*) miser; **I am — about** me paenitet (*with genit*); **I feel — for** me miseret (*with genit*), misereo (*with genit*)
sort *s* genus *n*, species *f*; **of that —** ejusmodi
sort *vt* digerēre, ordinare
sot *s* fatuus *m*; (*drunkard*) ebrius, potator *m*
sottish *adj* ebriosus
soul *s* (*principle of life*) anima *f*; (*principle of intellection and sensation*) animus *m*; (*person*) caput *n*
sound *adj* (*healthy*) validus, sanus; (*strong*) robustus; (*entire*) integer; (*in mind*) mentis compos; (*true, genuine*) verus; (*of sleep*) artus; (*valid*) ratus; **—ly** (*of beating*) vehementer, egregie; (*of sleeping*) arte
sound *s* sonus *m*; (*noise*) strepit·us -ūs, sonit·us -ūs *m*; (*of trumpet*) clangor *m*; (*strait*) fretum *n*
sound *vt* (*trumpet*) canĕre; *vi* canĕre, sonare; (*to seem*) vidēri
soundness *s* sanitas, integritas *f*
soup *s* jus *n*
sour *adj* acidus, acerbus; (*fig*) amarus, morosus; **to turn —** acescĕre; (*fig*) coacescĕre
source *s* fons *m*; (*of stream*) caput *n*; (*fig*) origo *f*, fons *m*
South *s* meridies, auster *m*
southern *adj* australis, meridionalis
southward *adv* in meridiem, meridiem versus
south wind *s* auster, notus *m*
souvenir *s* monumentum *n*
sovereign *adj* supremus
sovereign *s* princeps, rex, regnator *m*
sovereignty *s* dominatio *f*, principat·us -ūs *m*
sow *s* sus *m & f*
sow *vt* serĕre, seminare; (*a field*) conserĕre
space *s* spatium *n*; (*of time*) intervallum *n*
spacious *adj* spatiosus, amplus
spade *s* ligo *m*, pala *f*
span *s* (*extent*) spatium *n*; (*measure*) palmus *m*
spangle *s* bractea *f*
spangle *vt* bracteis ornare
Spaniard *s* Hispanus *m*
Spanish *adj* Hispanicus, Hispaniensis
spar *s* tignum *n*
spar *vi* dimicare; (*fig*) digladiari
spare *vt* parcĕre (*with dat*), parce uti (*with abl*)
spare *adj* parcus, frugalis, exilis
sparing *adj* parcus; **—ly** parce
spark *s* scintilla *f*; (*fig*) igniculus *m*
sparkle *vi* scintillare; (*as wine*) subsilire
sparkling *adj* coruscans
sparrow *s* passer *m*
Spartan *adj* Laconicus, Spartanus
spasm *s* spasmus *m*, convulsio *f*
spasmodically *adv* interdum
spatter *vt* aspergĕre, inquinare
spatula *s* spatha *f*
spawn *s* ova *f pl*
spawn *vi* ova gignĕre
speak *vt & vi* loqui, fari, dicĕre; **to — of** dicĕre de (*with abl*); **to — to** alloqui (*with acc*); **to — with** colloqui cum (*with abl*)
speaker *s* orator *m*
spear *s* hasta *f*
spear *vt* hastā transfigĕre
special *adj* specialis, praecipuus; **—ly** specialiter, praecipue
specialty *s* proprietas *f*
species *s* species *f*, genus *n*
specific *adj* certus
specify *vt* enumerare, designare
specimen *s* specimen, exemplum *n*
specious *adj* speciosus
speck *s* macula *f*
speckle *vt* maculis variare
spectacle *s* spectaculum *n*
spectator *s* spectator *m*
specter *s* larva *f*, phantasma *n*
spectral *adj* larvalis
spectrum *s* spectrum *n*
speculate *vi* cogitare, conjecturam facĕre; (*com*) foro uti
speculation *s* cogitatio, conjectura *f*; (*com*) alea *f*
speculative *adj* conjecturalis
speculator *s* contemplator *m*; (*com*) aleator *m*

speech *s* oratio *f*, sermo *m*; (*faculty*) lingua *f*
speechless *adj* mutus, elinguis; (*fig*) obstupefactus
speed *s* celeritas, velocitas *f*
speed *vt* accelerare, maturare; *vi* properare, festinare
speedily *adv* cito, celeriter
speedy *adj* citus, velox, celer
spell *s* incantamentum, carmen *n*
spelling *s* orthographia *f*
spelt *s* far *n*
spend *vt* impendĕre, consumĕre; (*to exhaust*) effundĕre; (*time*) agĕre
spendthrift *s* nepos, prodigus *m*
spew *vt* vomĕre
sphere *s* sphaera *f*, globus *m*; (*fig*) provincia *f*
spherical *adj* sphaericus, sphaeralis, globosus
sphinx *s* sphinx *f*
spice *s* condimentum *n*
spice *vt* condire
spicy *adj* conditus, aromaticus
spider *s* aranea *f*
spider web *s* araneum *n*
spigot *s* epistomium *n*
spike *s* clavus *m*
spill *vt* effundĕre, profundĕre
spin *vt* (*thread*) nēre; **to — round** versare, circumagĕre; *vi* versari
spinach *s* spinacea oleracea *f*
spinal *adj* dorsalis
spine *s* spina *f*
spinster *s* innupta *f*
spiral *adj* intortus
spiral *s* spira, involutio *f*
spirit *s* spirit·us -ūs *m*, anima *f*; (*character*) ingenium *n*; (*ghost*) anima *f*; **—s** (*of the dead*) manes *m pl*
spirited *adj* animosus, alacer
spiritless *adj* piger, ignavus
spiritual *adj* animi (*genit*)
spit *s* veru *n*; (*spittle*) sputum *n*
spit *vt & vi* sputare, spuĕre
spite *s* livor *m*, malevolentia *f*, odium *n*
spite *vt* offendĕre
spiteful *adj* lividus, malevolus; **—ly** malevole
spittle *s* sputum *n*
splash *vt* aspergĕre
splash *s* fragor *s*
splendid *adj* splendidus; **—ly** splendide
splendor *s* splendor *m*
splint *s* ferula *f*
splinter *s* assula *f*
splinter *vt* assulatim findĕre
split *s* fissura *f*
split *vt* findĕre; *vi* findi
spoil *vt* spoliare; (*to mar*) corrumpĕre; (*to ruin*) perdĕre, depravare, vitiare
spoils *s* spolia *n pl*, praeda *f*
spoke *s* radius *m*
spokesman *s* orator *m*
spondee *s* spondeus *m*
sponge *s* spongia *f*
spongy *adj* spongiosus
sponsor *s* sponsor *m*
spontaneity *s* impuls·us -ūs *m*
spontaneous *adj* voluntarius; **—ly** sponte, ultro
spool *s* fusus *m*
spoon *s* cochleare *n*
spoonful *s* cochleare *n*
sport *s* ludus, lus·us -ūs *m*; (*mockery*) ludibrium *n*, irrisio *f*
sport *vi* ludĕre, lascivire
sportive *adj* jocosus; **—ly** jocose
sportsman *s* venator *m*
spot *s* macula *f*; (*stain*) macula, labes *f*; (*place*) locus *m*
spot *vt* (*to speckle*) maculis notare; (*to stain*) inquinare, maculare
spotless *adj* integer, purus, castus
spotted *adj* maculosus, maculis distinctus
spouse *s* conju(n)x *m & f*
spout *s* (*pipe*) canalis *m*; (*of jug*) os *n*; (*of water*) torrens *m*
spout *vt* ejaculare; (*speeches*) declamare; *vi* emicare
sprain *vt* intorquēre, convellĕre
sprawl *vi* se fundĕre, prostratus jacēre
spray *s* aspergo *f*
spray *vt* aspergĕre
spread *vt* pandĕre, distendĕre, extendĕre; diffundĕre; (*to make known*) divulgare; *vi* patēre; (*of news*) manare, divulgari; (*of disease*) evagari
sprig *s* ramusculus *m*, virgula *f*
sprightly *adj* alacer, vegetus
spring *s* (*season*) ver *n*; (*leap*) salt·us -ūs *m*; (*of water*) fons *m*, scaturgo *f*
spring *adj* vernus
spring *vi* (*to come from*) oriri, enasci; (*as rivers, etc.*) scatēre, effluĕre; (*to leap*) salire, exsilire
springtime *s* vernum tempus *n*
sprinkle *vt* spargĕre, aspergĕre; *vi* rorare
sprite *s* spectrum *n*
sprout *s* pullus, surculus *m*
sprout *vi* pullulare
spruce *adj* lautus, nitidus, comptus; **—ly** nitide
spur *s* calcar *n*; (*fig*) incitamentum *n*
spur *vt* calcaribus concitare; (*fig*) urgēre
spurious *adj* fictus, fucosus, spurius
spurn *vt* spernĕre, aspernari
spurt *vi* emicare
sputter *vi* balbutire
spy *s* explorator, speculator *m*
spy *vt* conspicĕre; *vi* speculari
squabble *s* jurgium *n*, rixa *f*
squabble *vi* rixari
squad *s* manipulus *m*, decuria *f*
squadron *s* (*of cavalry*) ala, turma *f*; (*of ships*) classis *f*
squalid *adj* squalidus, sordidus
squall *s* procella *f*
squalor *s* squalor *m*, sordes *f*
squander *vt* dissipare, effundĕre
squanderer *s* prodigus *m*
square *adj* quadratus; (*fig*) honestus, probus
square *s* quadratum *n*, quadra *f*; (*tool*) norma *f*
square *vt* quadrare; *vi* convenire, congruĕre
squash *vt* conterĕre, contundĕre

squat *vi* succumběre, recumběre, subsiděre
squat *adj* parvus atque obesus
squeak *vi* stridēre; (*as a mouse*) dintrire
squeak *s* stridor *m*
squeamish *adj* fastidiosus; **to feel —** fastidire
squeeze *vt* comprimĕre, premĕre; **to — out** exprimĕre
squint *vi* strabo esse
squint-eyed *adj* paetus
squire *s* armiger *m*; (*landowner*) dominus *m*
squirrel *s* sciurus *m*
squirt *vt* projicĕre; *vi* emicare
stab *s* ict·us -ūs *m*, puncta *f*
stab *vt* foděre, perforare
stability *s* stabilitas *f*
stabilize *vt* stabilire, firmare
stable *adj* stabilis, solidus
stable *s* stabulum *n*; (*for horses*) equile *n*; (*for cows, oxen*) bubile *n*
stack *s* acervus *m*, strues *f*
stack *vt* coacervare, cumulare
staff *s* baculum *n*, scipio *m*, virga *f*; (*of a magistrate*) consilium *n*; (*mil*) contubernales *m pl*
staff officer *s* contubernalis *m*
stag *s* cervus *m*
stage *s* (*in theater*) scaena *f*; (*degree*) grad·us -ūs *m*; (*on journey*) iter *n*
stagger *vt* obstupefacĕre; *vi* titubare
stagnant *adj* stagnans, torpens; (*fig*) iners
stagnate *vi* stagnare; (*fig*) refrigescĕre
stagnation *s* cessatio *f*, torpor *m*
staid *adj* gravis
stain *s* macula, labes *f*
stain *vt* maculare, contaminare; (*to dye*) tingĕre
stainless *adj* immaculatus, purus, integer
stair *s* scala *f*, grad·us -ūs *m*
staircase *s* scalae *f pl*
stake *s* palus *m*; (*wager*) depositum *n*; **to be at —** agi
stake *vt* deponĕre, appignerare
stale *adj* vetus, obsoletus; (*of bread*) secundus; (*of wine*) vapidus
stalk *s* (*of plant*) caulis, stipes *m*; (*of grain*) calamus *m*
stalk *vt* venari; *vi* incedĕre
stall *s* stabulum *n*
stall *vt* sistĕre; *vi* consistĕre
stallion *s* admissarius *m*
stamina *s* patientia *f*
stammer *vi* balbutire, linguā haestitare
stammering *adj* balbus
stammering *s* balbuties *f*
stamp *s* (*mark*) nota *f*; (*with the foot*) vestigium *n*; (*impression made*) impressio *f*
stamp *vt* imprimĕre, notare; (*money*) cudĕre; (*feet*) supplodĕre
stand *s* locus *m*, statio *f*; (*halt*) mora *f*; (*platform*) suggest·us -ūs *m*
stand *vt* (*to set upright*) statuĕre, constituĕre; (*to tolerate*) tolerare, perferre, sustinēre; *vi* stare; **to — aloof** abstare; **to — by** adesse (*with dat*); **to — fast** consistĕre; **to — for office** petĕre; **to — in awe of** in metu habēre; **to — in need of** indigēre (*with abl*); **to — on end** horrēre; **to — out** exstare, eminēre, prominēre; **to — still** consistere, subsistĕre
standard *adj* solitus
standard *s* (*mil*) vexillum, signum *n*; (*measure*) norma, mensura *f*
standard-bearer *s* vexillarius, signifer *m*
standing *s* stat·us -ūs, ordo *m*, conditio *f*; **of long —** vetus
standing *adj* perpetuus
standstill *s* **to be at a —** haerēre
stanza *s* tetrastichon *n*
staple *adj* praecipuus
star *s* stella *f*, sidus *n*; (*fig*) lumen *n*
starch *s* amylum *n*
starch *vt* amylare
stare *s* obtut·us -ūs *m*, oculorum intentio *f*
stare *vi* stupēre; **to — at** intuēri
stark *adj* rigidus
stark *adv* omnino, penitus
starlight *s* siderum lumen *n*
starling *s* sturnus *m*
starry *adj* sidereus, stellatus
start *s* initium *n*; (*sudden movement*) salt·us -ūs *m*; (*of journey*) profectio *f*
start *vt* incipĕre, instituĕre; (*game*) excitare; *vi* (*to begin*) incipĕre, (ex)ordiri; (*to take fright*) resilire
starting gate *s* carceres *m pl*
startle *vt* terrēre, territare
starvation *s* fames *f*
starve *vt* fame interficĕre; *vi* fame confici
state *s* stat·us -ūs, locus *m*; (*pol*) civitas, respublica *f*; (*pomp*) magnificentia *f*
state *vt* declarare, dicĕre, affirmare
state *adj* publicus
stately *adj* grandis, lautus, splendidus
statement *s* affirmatio *f*, dictum *n*; testimonium *n*
statesman *s* vir reipublicae regendae peritus *m*
statesmanship *s* reipublicae regendae ars *f*
station *s* statio *f*, locus *m*
station *vt* locare, disponĕre
stationary *adj* stabilis, statarius, immotus
stationery *s* res scriptoriae *f pl*
statistics *s* cens·us -ūs *m*
statue *s* statua *f*, signum *n*
stature *s* statura *f*
statute *s* statutum, decretum *n*, lex *f*
staunch *adj* certus, firmus, fidus
staunch *vt* (*blood*) sistĕre
stave *vt* perrumpĕre; **to — off** arcēre
stay *vt* detinēre, sistĕre; (*to curb*) coercēre; *vi* manēre, commorari
stay *s* (*sojourn*) commoratio, mansio *f*; (*delay*) mora *f*; (*prop*) fulcrum *n*
steadfast *adj* constans, firmus, stabilis; **—ly** constanter

steadily *adv* constanter, firme, magis magisque
steadiness *s* stabilitas, constantia *f*
steady *adj* stabilis, firmus; (*fig*) constans, gravis
steak *s* offa, offula *f*
steal *vt* furari; *vi* furari; **to — away** se subducĕre
stealing *s* furtum *n*
stealthily *adv* furtim
steam *s* vapor *m*
steam *vi* fumare
steed *s* equus bellator *m*
steel *s* chalybs *m*
steep *adj* arduus, praeceps, praeruptus
steep *vt* imbuĕre, madefacĕre
steeple *s* turris *f*
steepness *s* acclivitas, declivitas *f*
steer *s* juvencus *m*
steer *vt* gubernare, dirigĕre
steering *s* gubernatio *f*
stem *s* stipes *m*; (*of ship*) prora *f*
stem *vt* obsistĕre (*with dat*), cohibēre, reprimĕre
stench *s* foetor *m*
step *s* pass·us -ūs, grad·us -ūs *m*; (*plan, measure*) ratio *f*; **flight of —s** scalae *f pl*; **— by —** gradatim, pedetentim
step *vi* gradi
stepbrother *s* (*on father's side*) vitrici filius *m*; (*on mother's side*) novercae filius *m*
stepdaughter *s* privigna *f*
stepfather *s* vitricus *m*
stepmother *s* noverca *f*
stepson *s* privignus *m*
sterile *adj* sterilis
sterility *s* sterilitas *f*
sterling *adj* verus, bonus
stern *adj* durus, severus, torvus; **—ly** dure, severe, torve
stern *s* puppis *f*
sternness *s* severitas *f*
stew *s* carnes cum condimentis elixae *f pl*
stew *vt* lento igne coquĕre
steward *s* procurator *m*; (*of estate*) vilicus *m*
stewardship *s* procuratio *f*
stick *s* fustis *m*; (*cane*) baculum *n*
stick *vt* affigĕre; *vi* haerēre, haesitare
sticky *adj* viscosus, viscidus
stiff *adj* rigidus; (*fig*) severus, frigidus; **—ly** rigide
stiffen *vt* rigidum facĕre; (*with starch*) amylare; *vi* obdurescĕre
stifle *vt* suffocare; (*fig*) restinguĕre
stigma *n* stigma *n*, nota *f*
stigmatize *vt* notare
still *adj* quietus, immotus, tranquillus
still *adv* (*adversative*) tamen, nihilominus; (*yet*) adhuc, etiamnum; (*with comparatives*) etiam
still *vt* pacare, sedare
stillborn *adj* abortivus
stillness *s* silentium *n*, taciturnitas *f*
stilts *s* grallae *f pl*
stimulant *s* irritamentum *n*, stimulus *m*
stimulate *vt* stimulare, excitare
stimulus *s* stimulus *m*
sting *s* aculeus *m*; (*fig*) (*of conscience*) angor *m*
sting *vt* pungĕre, mordēre
stinginess *s* avaritia *f*, sordes *f pl*
stingy *adj* avarus, sordidus
stink *s* foetor *m*
stink *vi* foetēre; **to — of** olēre (*with acc*)
stint *s* modus *m*
stint *vt* coercēre
stipend *s* salarium *n*, merces *f*
stipulate *vt* stipulari
stipulation *s* stipulatio, conditio, lex *f*
stir *vt* excitare; *vi* se movēre
stir *s* tumult·us -ūs *m*
stirring *adj* (*of a speech*) ardens
stitch *vt* suĕre
stock *s* (*supply*) copia *f*; (*race*) stirps *f*, genus *n*; (*handle*) lignum *n*
stock *vt* instruĕre; suppeditare
stockade *s* vallum *n*
stockbroker *s* argentarius *m*
stocking *s* tibiale *n*
Stoic *s* Stoicus *m*
stoical *adj* patiens, durus; **—ly** patienter
Stoicism *s* Stoica disciplina *f*
stole *s* stola *f*
stolen *adj* furtivus
stomach *s* stomachus *m*
stomach *vt* tolerare, perferre, pati
stone *s* lapis *m*, saxum *n*
stone *vt* lapidare
stonecutter *s* lapicida, lapidarius *m*
stone quarry *s* lapidicina *f*
stony *adj* (*full of stones*) lapidosus; (*of stone*) saxeus; (*fig*) durus
stool *s* scabellum *n*
stoop *vi* proclinare; (*fig*) se summittĕre
stop *vt* sistĕre, obturare, prohibēre; *vi* subsistĕre; (*to cease*) desistĕre
stop *s* mora, pausa *f*
stopgap *s* tibicen *m*
stoppage *s* obstructio *f*, impedimentum *n*
stopper *s* obturamentum *n*
store *s* (*supply*) copia *f*; (*shop*) taberna *f*
store *vt* condĕre, reponĕre
storehouse *s* promptuarium *n*; (*for grain*) horreum *n*; (*fig*) thesaurus *m*
stork *s* ciconia *f*
storm *s* tempestas, procella *f*
storm *vt* (*mil*) expugnare; *vi* desaevire
stormy *adj* turbidus, procellosus; (*fig*) tumultuosus
story *s* narratio, fabula *f*; (*lie*) mendacium *n*; (*of house*) tabulatum *n*
storyteller *s* narrator *m*; (*liar*) mendax *m*
stout *adj* corpulentus; (*brave*) fortis; (*strong*) firmus, validus; **—ly** fortiter
stove *s* focus, caminus *m*
stow *vt* condĕre, recondĕre; *vi* **to — away** in navi delitescĕre
straddle *vi* varicare
straggle *vi* palari
straggler *s* palans *m*
straight *adj* rectus, directus
straight *adv* directo, rectā

straighten *vt* rectum facĕre; **to — out** corrigĕre
straightforward *adj* apertus, simplex, directus
straightway *adv* statim
strain *vt* contendĕre; (*muscle*) luxare; (*to filter*) percolare; *vi* eniti
strain *s* contentio *f*; (*effort*) labor *m*; (*mus*) modus *m*
strained *adj* (*style*) arcessitus
strainer *s* colum *n*
strait *adj* angustus, artus
strait *s* fretum *n*; **—s** (*fig*) angustiae *f pl*
straiten *vt* contrahĕre, artare
strand *s* litus *n*; (*of hair*) floccus *m*
strand *vt* vadis illidĕre; *vi* impingi
strange *adj* insolitus, novus; mirus; (*foreign*) peregrinus; **— to say** mirabile dictu; **—ly** mirum in modum
strangeness *s* novitas *f*
stranger *s* advena, peregrinus *m*
strangle *vt* strangulare
strap *s* lorum *n*, strupus *m*
strapping *adj* robustus
stratagem *s* stratagema *n*; (*trickery*) dolus *m*
strategic *adj* idoneus
strategy *s* consilium *n*
straw *adj* stramineus
straw *s* stramentum *n*; (*for thatch*) stipula *f*
strawberry *s* fragum *n*
stray *vi* errare, aberrare
streak *s* linea *f*; (*of character*) vena *f*
streak *vt* lineis distinguĕre
stream *s* flumen *n*, amnis *m*
stream *vi* fluĕre, currĕre
streamer *s* vexillum *n*
street *s* via *f*; (*narrow*) vicus *m*
strength *s* robur *n*, vires *f pl*, nervi *m pl*
strengthen *vt* roborare, confirmare; munire
strenuous *adj* strenuus, sedulus; **—ly** strenue
stress *s* (*accent*) ict·us -ūs *m*; (*meaning*) vis *f*, pondus *n*; (*effort*) labor *m*
stress *vt* exprimĕre
stretch *vt* tendĕre, extendĕre, distendĕre; **to — oneself** pandiculari; **to — out** (*hands*) porrigĕre; (*to lengthen*) producĕre; *vi* extendi, distendi; produci; patescĕre
stretch *s* spatium *n*
stretcher *s* lecticula *f*
strew *vt* spargĕre, sternĕre
stricken *adj* saucius, vulneratus
strict *adj* (*severe*) severus, rigidus; (*accurate*) accuratus, exactus, diligens; **—ly** severe, diligenter; **—ly speaking** immo
stricture *s* vituperatio *f*
stride *s* grad·us -ūs, pass·us -ūs *m*
stride *vi* varicare
strife *s* jurgium *n*, lis, pugna, discordia *f*
strike *vt* ferire, pulsare, percutĕre; **to — fear into** incutĕre in (*with acc*)
strike *s* cessatio operis *f*; (*blow*) ict·us -ūs *m*
strikingly *adv* mirum in modum
string *s* filum *n*; (*for bow*) nervus *m*; (*for musical instrument*) chorda *f*; (*fig*) series *f*
string *vt* (*bow*) intendĕre
stringent *adj* severus
stringy *adj* fibratus
strip *vt* spoliare; denudare; (*clothes*) exuĕre
strip *s* (*of cloth*) lacinia *f*; (*of paper*) scheda *f*; (*of land*) spatium *n*
stripe *s* linea *f*; (*blow*) ict·us -ūs *m*; (*mark of blow*) vibex *f*; (*on toga*) clavus *m*
strive *vi* (e)niti, moliri, conari, laborare; **to — for** anniti, sectari
striving *s* contentio *f*, nis·us -ūs *m*
stroke *s* ict·us -ūs *m*, plaga *f*; (*with pen*) pennae duct·us -ūs *f*; (*of oar*) puls·us -ūs *m*
stroke *vt* (per)mulcēre
stroll *s* ambulatio *f*
stroll *vi* perambulare, spatiari
strong *adj* robustus, firmus, validus; (*smell*) gravis; (*powerful*) potens; (*feeling*) acer; (*language*) vehemens; **—ly** valide, graviter, vehementer, acriter
stronghold *s* arx *f*, castellum *n*
structure *s* structura *f*; (*building*) aedificium *n*
struggle *s* certamen *n*, pugna *f*; (*fig*) luctatio *f*
struggle *vi* contendĕre, (ob)niti, luctari
strumpet *s* scortum *n*, meretrix *f*
strut *s* incess·us -ūs *m*
strut *vi* turgēre, tumēre
stubble *s* stipula *f*
stubborn *adj* obstinatus, contumax, pervicax; **—ly** obstinate, pervicaciter
stubbornness *s* obstinatus animus *m*, obstinatio, pertinacia *f*
stud *s* clavus *m*; equus admissarius *m*
student *s* discipulus *m*
studied *adj* meditatus; (*style*) exquisitus
studious *adj* studiosus discendi; (*careful*) attentus
study *s* studium *n*; (*room*) bibliotheca *f*
study *vt* studēre (*with dat*); (*to scrutinize*) perscrutari
stuff *s* materia, materies *f*
stuff *vt* farcire; (*with food*) saginare
stuffing *s* (*in cooking*) fartum *n*; (*in upholstery*) tomentum *n*
stultify *vt* ad irritum redigĕre
stumble *vi* offendĕre; **to — upon** incidĕre in (*with acc*)
stumbling block *s* offensio *f*
stump *s* truncus, caudex *m*
stun *vt* stupefacĕre; (*fig*) confundĕre, obstupefacĕre
stunted *adj* curtus
stupefy *vt* obstupefacĕre, perturbare
stupendous *adj* mirus, admirabilis
stupid *adj* stupidus, fatuus; **—ly** stupide
stupidity *s* stupiditas, fatuitas *f*
stupor *s* stupor, torpor *m*
sturdiness *s* robur *n*, firmitas *f*
sturdy *adj* robustus, validus, firmus

sturgeon *s* acipenser *m*
stutter *vi* balbutire
sty *s* suile *n*, hara *f*
style *s* (*literary*) scribendi genus *n*; (*rhetorical*) dicendi genus *n*; (*architectural*) rit·us -ūs *m*; (*of dress*) habit·us -ūs *m*
style *vt* appellare, nominare
stylish *adj* speciosus, affectatus, elegans
suave *adj* suavis, urbanus
subdivide *vt* iterum dividěre
subdivision *s* pars *f*
subdue *vt* subjicěre, domare, vincěre
subject *adj* — **to** obnoxius (*with dat*), subjectus (*with dat*)
subject *s* homo subditus *m*; civis *m*; (*topic*) materia *f*, argumentum *n*; (*matter*) res *f*; (*gram*) subjectum *n*
subject *vt* subjicěre, subigěre
subjection *s* servitus *f*; patientia *f*
subjective *adj* proprius
subjugate *vt* subigěre, domare
subjunctive *s* subjunctivus modus *m*
sublime *adj* sublimis, excelsus; **—ly** excelse
sublimity *s* elatio, sublimitas *f*
submerge *vt* demergěre, inundare; *vi* se demergěre
submission *s* obsequium, servitium *n*, reverentia *f*
submissive *adj* summissus, obsequiosus; **—ly** summisse
submit *vt* (*e.g., a proposal*) referre; *vi* se deděre; **to — to** obtemperare (*with dat*)
subordinate *vt* subjicěre, supponěre
subordinate *adj* secundus, subjectus, inferior
suborn *vt* subornare
subscribe *vt* (*to contribute*) conferre; *vi* **to — to** assentiri (*with dat*)
subscriber *s* subscriptor *m*
subscription *s* collatio *f*
subsequent *adj* sequens, posterior, serior; **—ly** postea, deinde
subserve *vt* subvenire (*with dat*)
subservient *adj* obsequiosus
subside *vi* desiděre; (*of wind*) caděre; (*of passion*) defervescěre
subsidiary *adj* secundus
subsidy *s* subsidium *n*, collatio *f*, vectigal *n*
subsist *vi* subsistěre
subsistence *s* vict·us -ūs *m*
substance *s* substantia *f*; res *f*; (*gist*) summa *f*; (*wealth*) opes *f pl*
substantial *adj* solidus, firmus; (*real*) verus; (*rich*) opulentus; (*important*) magnus; **—ly** magnā ex parte, re
substantiate *vt* confirmare
substantive *s* nomen, substantivum *n*
substitute *s* vicarius *m*
substitute *vt* supponěre
substitution *s* substitutio *f*
subterfuge *s* effugium *n*, praetext·us -ūs *m*
subterranean *adj* subterraneus
subtle *adj* subtilis, tenuis; (*shrewd*) acutus, vafer
subtlety *s* subtilitas, tenuitas *f*; (*cleverness*) astutia *f*
subtract *vt* subtraherě, detraherě, deducěre
subtraction *s* detractio, deductio *f*
suburb *s* suburbium *n*
suburban *adj* suburbanus
subversion *s* eversio *f*
subversive *adj* seditiosus
subvert *vt* evertěre
succeed *vt* succeděre (*with dat*), insequi, excipěre; *vi* (*of persons*) rem bene gerere; (*of activities*) prospere evenire, succeděre
success *s* success·us -ūs, bonus event·us -ūs *m*, res secundae *f pl*
successful *adj* fortunatus, prosper; **—ly** fortunate, prospere
succession *s* successio *f*; (*series*) series *f*
successive *adj* continuus; **—ly** in ordine, continenter
successor *s* successor *m*
succinct *adj* succinctus, brevis, pressus; **—ly** presse
succor *s* subsidium, auxilium *n*
succor *vt* succurrěre (*with dat*), subvenire (*with dat*)
succulence *s* sucus *m*
succulent *adj* sucosus, suculentus
succumb *vi* succumběre
such *adj* talis; **— . . . as** talis . . . qualis
suck *vt* sugěre; **to — in** sorbēre; **to — up** exsorbēre, ebiběre; *vi* ubera ducěre
suckle *vt* nutricari
suction *s* suct·us -ūs *m*
sudden *adj* subitus, repentinus, inexpectatus; **—ly** subito, repente
sue *vt* litem intenděre (*with dat*); *vi* **to — for** orare, rogare, petěre
suffer *vt* pati, tolerare, sustiněre; *vi* dolēre, affici
sufferable *adj* tolerabilis, tolerandus
suffering *s* dolor *m*
suffice *vi* sufficěre, satis esse
sufficient *adj* satis (*with genit*); **—ly** satis
suffocate *vt* suffocare
suffocation *s* suffocatio *f*
suffrage *s* suffragium *n*
suffuse *vt* suffuncěre
suffusion *s* suffusio *f*
sugar *s* saccharum *n*
sugar *vt* saccharo condire
sugar cane *s* arundo sacchari *f*
suggest *vt* suggerěre, subjicěre, admonēre
suggestion *s* suggestio, admonitio *f*
suicide *s* suicidium *n*; **to commit —** sibi mortem consciscěre
suit *s* lis, causa *f*; (*clothes*) vestit·us -ūs *m*
suit *vt* accommodare; convenire (*with dat*), congruěre (*with dat*)
suitable *adj* aptus, idoneus, congruus
suite *s* comitat·us -ūs *m*; (*apartment*) conclave *n*
suitor *s* procus *m*
sulfur *s* sulfur *n*
sulk *vi* aegre ferre
sulky *adj* morosus

sullen *adj* torvus, tetricus, morosus; **—ly** morose
sully *vt* inquinare, contaminare
sultry *adj* aestuosus, torridus
sum *s* summa *f*
sum *vt* **to — up** computare; (*to summarize*) summatim describĕre, breviter repetĕre
summarily *adj* breviter, summatim
summarize *vt* summatim describĕre
summary *adj* subitus, brevis
summary *s* epitome *f*, summarium *n*
summer *adj* aestivus
summer *s* aestas *f*
summit *s* culmen *n*; (*fig*) fastigium *n*
summon *vt* arcessĕre; (*a meeting*) convocare; **to — up courage** animum erigĕre, animum colligĕre
summons *s* vocatio *f*
sumptuary *adj* sumptuarius
sumptuous *adj* sumptuosus, lautus; **—ly** sumptuose
sun *s* sol *m*
sunbeam *s* radius *m*
sunburnt *adj* adustus
Sunday *s* Dominica *f*
sunder *vt* separare, sejungĕre
sundial *s* solarium *n*
sundry *adj* diversi, varii
sunlight *s* sol *m*
sunny *adj* apricus
sunrise *s* solis ort·us -ūs *m*
sunset *s* solis occas·us -ūs *m*
sunshine *s* sol *m*
sup *vi* cenare
superabundant *adj* nimius; **—ly** satis superque
superannuated *adj* emeritus
superb *adj* magnificus; **—ly** magnifice
supercilious *adj* superbus, arrogans
superficial *adj* levis; **—ly** leviter
superfluity *s* redundantia *f*
superfluous *adj* superfluus, supervacaneus
superhuman *adj* divinus, major quam humanus
superintend *vt* praeesse (*with dat*), administrare
superintendence *s* cura, curatio *f*
superintendent *s* praefectus, curator *m*
superior *adj* superior, melior; **to be — to** praestare (*with dat*)
superior *s* praepositus *m*
superiority *s* praestantia *f*
superlative *adj* eximius; (*gram*) superlativus
supernatural *adj* divinus
supernumerary *adj* ascripticius, accensus
supersede *vt* succedĕre (*with dat*)
superstition *s* superstitio *f*
superstitious *adj* superstitiosus
supervise *vt* procurare
supervision *s* cura, curatio *f*
supine *adj* supinus; **—ly** supine
supper *s* cena *f*; **after —** cenatus
supple *adj* flexibilis, flexilis
supplement *s* supplementum *n*, appendix *f*
supplement *vt* amplificare
suppliant *s* supplex *m & f*
supplicate *vt* supplicare
supplication *s* supplicatio, obsecratio *f*
supply *s* copia *f*; **supplies** (*mil*) commeat·us -ūs *m*
supply *vt* praebēre, suppeditare
support *s* (*prop*) fulcrum *n*; (*help*) subsidium *n*; (*maintenance*) alimentum *n*
support *vt* (*to hold up*) fulcire, sustinēre; (*to help*) adjuvare; (*to maintain*) alĕre
supportable *adj* tolerabilis
supporter *s* adjutor, fautor *m*
suppose *vt* opinari, putare, credĕre
supposition *s* opinio *f*
supremacy *s* dominat·us -ūs, principat·us -ūs *m*, imperium *n*
supreme *adj* supremus, summus; **—ly** unice, maxime
sure *adj* certus; (*faithful*) fidus; (*safe*) tutus; **—ly** certe, scilicet, profecto
surety *s* vas *n*; (*person*) sponsor *m*
surf *s* aest·us -ūs *m*
surface *s* superficies *f*; **the — of the sea** summum mare *n*
surfeit *s* satietas *f*; (*fig*) taedium *n*
surfeit *vt* saturare; (*fig*) satiare
surge *s* fluct·us -ūs, aest·us -ūs *m*
surge *vi* tumescĕre, surgĕre; **to — forward** proruĕre
surgeon *s* chirurgus *m*
surgery *s* chirurgia *f*
surgical *adj* chirurgicus
surly *adj* morosus, difficilis
surmise *s* conjectura *f*
surmise *vt* conjicĕre, suspicari
surmount *vt* superare, vincĕre
surmountable *adj* superabilis
surname *s* cognomen *n*
surpass *vt* superare, excedĕre, antecedĕre
surplus *s* reliquum, residuum *n*
surprise *s* (ad)miratio *f*; **to take by —** deprehendĕre
surprise *vt* admirationem movēre (*with dat*); (*mil*) opprimĕre; **to be surprised at** mirari, admirari
surprising *adj* mirus, mirabilis; inexpectatus; **—ly** mire, mirabiliter
surrender *s* (*mil*) deditio *f*; (*law*) cessio *f*
surrender *vt* dedĕre, tradĕre, cedĕre; *vi* se tradĕre, se dedĕre
surreptitious *adj* furtivus, clandestinus; **—ly** furtim, clam
surround *vt* circumdare, circumvenire, cingĕre
surroundings *s* vicinia *f*
survey *s* inspectio, contemplatio *f*; (*of land*) mensura *f*
survey *vt* inspicĕre, contemplari; (*land*) permetiri
surveyor *s* agrimensor, metator *m*
survival *s* salus *f*
survive *vt* supervivĕre (*with dat*); *vi* superstes esse
survivor *s* superstes *m & f*
susceptible *adj* mollis
suspect *vt* suspicari, suspicĕre; **to be suspected of** in suspicionem

venire quasi (*with verb in subjunctive*)
suspend *vt* suspendĕre, intermittĕre, differre
suspense *s* dubitatio *f*; **in —** suspensus
suspension *s* suspensio, dilatio *f*
suspicion *s* suspicio *f*; **to throw — on** suspicionem adjungĕre ad (*with acc*)
suspicious *adj* suspicax; (*suspected*) suspectus; **—ly** suspiciose
sustain *vt* sustinēre, sustentare; (*hardships, etc.*) ferre
sustenance *s* vict·us -ūs *m*
swab *s* peniculus *m*
swab *vt* detergēre
swaddling clothes *s* fasciae *f pl*, incunabula *n pl*
swagger *vi* se jactare
swaggerer *s* homo gloriosus *m*
swallow *s* (*bird*) hirundo *f*
swallow *vt* vorare, sorbēre; **to — up** devorare, absorbēre
swamp *s* palus *f*
swamp *vt* demergĕre
swampy *adj* paludosus
swan *s* cygnus *m*
swank *adj* lautus
swarm *s* examen *n*
swarm *vi* congregari
swarthy *adj* fuscus
swathe *s* fascia *f*
sway *s* dicio, dominatio *f*, imperium *n*
sway *vt* regĕre, movēre; *vi* vacillare
swear *vt* jurare; **to — in** sacramento adigĕre, sacramento rogare; *vi* jurare
sweat *s* sudor *m*
sweat *vi* sudare
sweep *vt* verrĕre; **to — out** everrĕre; *vi* **to — by** (*to dash by*) praetervolare; **to — over** (*to move quickly over*) percurrĕre
sweet *adj* dulcis, suavis; (*fig*) blandus, jucundus; **—ly** suaviter
sweeten *vt* dulcem facĕre; (*fig*) lenire, mulcēre
sweetheart *s* deliciae *f pl*, amica *f*
sweetness *s* dulcedo, suavitas *f*
sweets *s* cuppedia *n pl*
swell *s* aest·us -ūs *m*, unda *f*
swell *vt* inflare, tumefacĕre; *vi* tumēre
swelling *s* tumor *m*
swelter *vi* aestu laborare
swerve *vi* aberrare, vagari
swift *adj* celer, velox; **—ly** celeriter, velociter
swiftness *s* celeritas, velocitas *f*
swim *vi* natare, nare
swimmer *s* natator *m*
swimming *s* natatio *f*; (*of head*) vertigo *f*
swimming pool *s* piscina *f*
swindle *vt* fraudare, circumvenire
swindle *s* fraus *f*
swindler *s* fraudator *m*
swine *s* sus *m & f*
swineherd *s* suarius *m*
swing *s* oscillatio *f*
swing *vt* librare; *vi* oscillare
switch *s* (*stick*) virga, virgula *f*; (*change*) commutatio *f*
switch *vt* (*to flog*) flagellare; (*to change* (com)mutare
swoon *vi* intermori, collabi
swoop *s* impet·us -ūs *m*
swoop *vi* incurrĕre; **to — down on** involare in (*with acc*)
sword *s* gladius, ensis *m*, ferrum *n*; **with fire and —** ferro ignique
sycamore *s* sycomorus *f*
sycophant *s* sycophanta, assentator *m*
syllable *s* syllaba *f*
syllogism *s* syllogismus *m*, ratiocinatio *f*
symbol *s* signum, symbolum *n*
symbolical *adj* symbolicus; **—ly** symbolice
symmetrical *adj* congruens, concinnus
symmetry *s* symmetria, concinnitas *f*
sympathetic *adj* concors, misericors
sympathize *vi* consentire; **to — with** miserēri (*with genit*)
sympathy *s* consens·us -ūs *m*, misericordia, concordia *f*
symphony *s* symphonia *f*, concent·us -ūs *m*
symptom *s* indicium, signum *n*
synagogue *s* synagoga *f*
syndicate *s* societas *f*
synonym *s* verbum idem declarans *n*
synonymous *adj* idem declarans, idem valens
synopsis *s* breviarium *n*, epitome *f*
syntax *s* syntaxis *f*
system *s* ratio, disciplina *f*
systematic *adj* ordinatus; **—ally** ratione, ordine

T

tab *vt* designare, notare
tabernacle *s* tabernaculum *n*
table *s* mensa *f*; (*list*) index *m*, tabula *f*
tablecloth *s* mantele *n*
table napkin *s* mappa *f*
tablet *s* tabula, tabella *f*, album *n*
tacit *adj* tacitus; **—ly** tacite
taciturn *adj* taciturnus
tack *s* clavulus *m*
tack *vt* **to — on** assuĕre, affigĕre; *vi* (*of ships*) reciprocari
tact *s* judicium *n*, dexteritas *f*
tactful *adj* prudens, dexter; **—ly** prudenter, dextere
tactician *s* rei militaris peritus *m*
tactics *s* res militaris, belli ratio *f*
tadpole *s* ranunculus *m*

tag *s* appendicula *f*
tail *s* cauda *f*
tailor *s* vestitor, textor *m*
taint *s* contagio *f*, vitium *n*
taint *vt* inficere, contaminare; (*fig*) corrumpĕre
take *vt* capĕre, sumĕre, accipĕre; **to — away** demĕre, auferre, adimĕre; **to — down** (*in writing*) exscribĕre; **to — for** habēre pro (*with abl*); **to — hold of** prehendere; **to — in** (*e.g., a guest*) recipĕre; (*through deception*) decipĕre; **to — in hand** suscipere; **to — off** exuĕre; **to — out** eximĕre; (*from storage*) promĕre; **to — up** suscipĕre; **to — upon oneself** sibi sumĕre; *vi* **to — after** similis esse (*with genit or dat*); **to — off** (*to depart*) abire; **to — to** amare, diligĕre
tale *s* fabula, narratio *f*
talent *s* talentum *n*; (*fig*) ingenium *n*
talented *adj* ingeniosus
talk *s* sermo *m*, colloquium *n*; **idle —** nugae *f pl*
talk *vi* loqui; **to — with** colloqui cum (*with abl*)
talkative *adj* loquax, garrulus
talker *s* (*idle*) gerro *m*
tall *adj* altus, celsus, procerus
tallow *s* sebum *n*
tally *s* tessera *f*
tally *vi* convenire
talon *s* unguis *m*
tambourine *s* tympanum *n*
tame *adj* cicur, mansuetus, domitus; **—ly** mansuete, leniter
tame *vt* domare, mansuefacĕre
tamer *s* domitor *m*
tamper *vi* **to — with** (*persons*) sollicitare; (*writings*) depravare
tan *vt* (*by sun*) adurĕre; (*hides*) perficĕre
tangible *adj* tractabilis
tangle *s* implicatio *f*, nodus *m*
tangle *vt* implicare
tank *s* lac·us -ūs *m*
tankard *s* cantharus *m*
tantalize *vt* vexare
tantamount *adj* par
tap *s* levis ict·us -ūs *m*
tap *vt* leviter ferire; (*wine, etc.*) relinĕre
tape *s* taenia *f*
taper *s* cereus *m*
taper *vt* fastigare; *vi* fastigari
tapestry *s* aulaeum, tapete *n*
taproom *s* taberna *f*
tar *s* pix *f*
tardily *adv* tarde, lente
tardiness *s* tarditas, segnitia *f*
tardy *adj* tardus, lentus
target *s* scopus *m*
tariff *s* portorium *n*
tarnish *vt* infuscare; *vi* infuscari
tarry *vi* commorari, cunctari
tart *adj* acerbus, amarus
tart *s* scriblita *f*, crustulum *n*
task *s* pensum, opus *n*; **to take to —** objurgare
taste *s* (*sense*) gustat·us -ūs *m*; (*flavor*) sapor *m*; (*fig*) judicium *n*
taste *vt* (de)gustare; *vi* sapĕre
tasteful *adj* elegans; **—ly** eleganter
tasteless *adj* insipidus; (*fig*) insulsus, inelegans; **—ly** insulse
tasty *adj* sapidus, dulcis
tattered *adj* pannosus
tatters *s* panni *m pl*
taunt *s* convicium *n*
taunt *vt* exprobrare
taut *adj* intentus
tavern *s* taberna, caupona *f*
tavern keeper *s* caupo *m*
tawdry *adj* fucatus, vilis
tawny *adj* fulvus
tax *s* vectigal, tributum *n*
tax *vt* vectigal imponĕre (*with dat*)
taxable *adj* vectigalis, stipendiarius
taxation *s* vectigalia *n pl*
tax collector *s* exactor *m*
teach *vt* docēre, instituĕre, erudire
teachable *adj* docilis
teacher *s* magister, praeceptor *m*; (*of primary school*) litterator *m*; (*of secondary school*) grammaticus *m*; (*of rhetoric*) rhetor *m*
teaching *s* institutio, eruditio *f*
team *s* jugales *m pl*; (*of animals*) jugum *n*
tear *s* lacrima *f*, flet·us -ūs *m*; (*a rent*) scissura *f*
tear *vt* scindĕre; **to — apart** discindĕre; **to — in pieces** dilacerare, dilaniare; **to — off** abscindĕre; **to — open** rescindĕre; **to — out** evellĕre; **to — up** convellĕre
tease *vt* vexare, ludĕre
teat *s* mamma *f*
technical *adj* (*term*) proprius; technicus, artificialis
technique *s* ars *f*
technology *s* officinarum artes *f pl*
tedious *adj* molestus; **—ly** moleste
tedium *s* taedium *n*
teem *vi* scatēre, redundare
teethe *vi* dentire
teething *s* dentitio *f*
tell *vt* narrare, memorare, referre; (*to order*) imperare (*with dat*), jubēre; **— me the truth** dic mihi verum
teller *s* numerator *m*
temerity *s* temeritas *f*
temper *s* temperatio *f*, animus *m*, ingenium *n*; (*bad*) iracundia *f*
temper *vt* temperare; (*fig*) lenire
temperament *s* animus *m*
temperance *s* temperantia *f*
temperate *adj* temperatus, moderatus, sobrius; **—ly** temperanter, sobrie
temperature *s* calor *m*, caloris grad·us -ūs *m*
tempest *s* tempestas *f*
tempestuous *adj* turbulentus, procellosus
temple *s* templum *n*, aedes *f*; (*of forehead*) tempus *n*
temporal *adj* humanus; profanus
temporarily *adv* ad tempus
temporary *adj* brevis
temporize *vi* tergiversari
tempt *vt* temptare, illicĕre
temptation *s* illecebra *f*
ten *adj* decem; **— times** decies

tenable *adj* defensibilis, stabilis
tenacious *adj* tenax, pertinax; **—ly** tenaciter, pertinaciter
tenacity *s* tenacitas, pertinacia *f*
tenancy *s* conductio *f*
tenant *s* conductor, colonus, incola *m*
tend *vt* curare; *vi* tenděre, spectare
tendency *s* inclinatio *f*
tender *adj* tener, mollis; **—ly** tenere, indulgenter
tender *vt* offerre
tenderness *s* mollitia *f*; (*affection*) indulgentia *f*
tendon *s* nervus *m*
tendril *s* (*of vine*) pampinus *m*; (*of plants*) claviculus *m*
tenement *s* conductum *n*
tenement house *s* insula *f*
tenet *s* dogma *n*
tenfold *adj* decemplex, decuplus
tennis *s* **to play —** pilā luděre
tennis court *s* sphaeristerium *n*
tenor *s* tenor, sens·us -ūs *m*
tense *adj* intentus, attentus
tense *s* tempus *n*
tension *s* intentio *f*
tent *s* tentorium, tabernaculum *n*
tentative *adj* tentans
tenth *adj* decimus
tenth *s* decima pars *f*
tenuous *adj* tenuis, rarus
tenure *s* possessio *f*
tepid *adj* tepidus
term *s* (*word*) verbum *n*; (*limit*) terminus *m*; (*condition*) condicio, lex *f*
terminate *vt* terminare, finire; *vi* terminari, desiněre; (*of words*) caděre
termination *s* terminatio *f*, finis, exit·us -ūs *m*
terrace *s* ambulatio *f*
terrestrial *adj* terrestris, terrenus
terrible *adj* terribilis
terribly *adv* horrendum in modum
terrific *adj* terrificus, terrens, formidabilis
terrify *vt* terrēre, perterrēre
territory *s* regio *f*, ager *m*, fines *m pl*
terror *s* terror *m*, formido *f*
terse *adj* brevis, pressus; **—ly** presse
test *s* probatio *f*, experimentum *n*
test *vt* probare, experiri
testament *s* testamentum *n*
testamentary *adj* testamentarius
testator *s* testator *m*
testify *vt* testificari, testari
testimonial *s* laudatio *f*
testimony *s* testimonium *n*
testy *adj* stomachosus, obstinatus, morosus
tether *s* retinaculum *n*
tether *vt* religare
text *s* verba *n pl*
textbook *s* enchiridion *n*
textile *adj* textilis
texture *s* textura *f*
than *adv* quam; atque, ac
thank *vt* gratias agěre (*with dat*)
thankful *adj* gratus; **—ly** grate
thankless *adj* ingratus; **—ly** ingrate
thanks *s* gratiae, grates *f pl*
thanks *interj* gratias!
thanksgiving *s* grates *f pl*, gratulatio *f*; (*public act*) supplicatio *f*
that *adj* ille, is, iste
that *pron demonstrative* ille, is, iste; *pron rel* qui
that *conj* (*purpose, result, command*) ut; (*after verbs of fearing*) ne
thatch *s* stramentum *n*
thatch *vt* stramento tegěre
thaw *vt* (dis)solvěre; *vi* tabescěre
the *article, not expressed in Latin*
the *adv* (*with comparatives*) **the . . . the** quo . . . eo
theater *s* theatrum *n*
theatrical *adj* scenicus, theatralis
thee *pron* te; **of —** de te; **to —** tibi; **with —** tecum
theft *s* furtum *n*
their *adj* illorum, eorum, istorum; **— own** suus
them *pron* eos, illos, istos; **to —** eis, illis, istis
theme *s* thema, argumentum *n*
themselves *pron reflex* se; **to —** sibi; **with —** secum; *pron intensive* ipsi
then *adv* (*at that time*) tum, tunc; (*after that*) deinde, inde; (*therefore*) igitur, ergo; **now and —** interdum, nonnumquam
thence *adv* inde, illinc; (*therefore*) ex eo, exinde
thenceforth *adv* ex eo tempore, dehinc
theologian *s* theologus *m*
theological *adj* theologicus
theology *s* theologia *f*
theoretical *adj* contemplativus
theory *s* ratio *f*
there *adv* ibi, illic; (*thither*) illuc; **— are** sunt; **— is** est
thereabouts *adv* circa, circiter, fere
thereafter *adv* deinde, postea
thereby *adv* eā re, eo
therefore *adv* itaque, igitur, idcirco, ergo
therefrom *adv* exinde, ex eo
therein *adv* in eo, in ea re
thereupon *adv* exinde, subinde
thesis *s* thesis *f*, propositum *n*
they *pron* ii, illi, isti
thick *adj* densus, spissus; **—ly** dense
thicken *vt* densare, spissare; *vi* concrescěre
thicket *s* dumetum, fruticetum *n*
thickness *s* crassitudo *f*
thief *s* fur *m*
thievery *s* furtum *n*
thigh *s* femur *n*
thin *adj* tenuis, exilis, rarus; (*lean*) macer; **—ly** tenuiter, rare
thin *vt* attenuare; **to — out** rarefacěre
thine *adj* tuus
thine *pron* tuus
thing *s* res *f*; **—s** (*possessions*) bona *n pl*; (*clothes*) vestimenta *n pl*
think *vt* cogitare; (*to believe, imagine, etc.*) putare, creděre, opinari; **to — over** in mente agitare; *vi* **to — highly of** magni habēre
thinker *s* philosophus *m*
thinking *s* cogitatio *f*
thinness *s* tenuitas, raritudo *f*; (*of person*) macies *f*

third *adj* tertius; **—ly** tertio
third *s* tertia pars *f*
thirst *s* sitis *f*
thirst *vi* sitire; **to — for** sitire
thirstily *adv* sitienter
thirsty *adj* sitiens
thirteen *adj* tredecim, decem et tres
thirteenth *adj* tertius decimus
thirtieth *adj* tricesimus
thirty *adj* triginta
this *adj* hic
thistle *s* carduus *m*
thither *adv* illuc, istuc, eo
thong *s* lorum *n*
thorn *s* spina *f*, aculeus *m*
thorny *adj* spinosus; (*fig*) nodosus
thorough *adj* germanus, perfectus; **—ly** penitus, funditus
thoroughbred *adj* generosus, genuinus
thoroughfare *s* pervium *n*, via pervia *f*
though *conj* quamquam, quamvis
thought *s* (*act and faculty*) cogitatio *f*; (*product of thinking*) cogitatum *n*
thoughtful *adj* cogitabundus; providus; **—ly** anxie, provide
thoughtless *adj* inconsultus, improvidus; **—ly** temere, inconsulte
thousand *adj* mille; **a — times** millies
thousandth *adj* millesimus
thraldom *s* servitus *f*
thrall *s* servus *m*
thrash *vt* terĕre; (*fig*) verberare
thrashing *s* verbera *n pl*
thread *s* filum *n*
thread *vt* inserĕre
threadbare *adj* tritus, obsoletus
threat *s* minae *f pl*, minatio *f*
threaten *vt* minari (*with dat of person*); *vi* impendēre, imminēre
three *adj* tres; **— times** ter
threefold *adj* triplex, triplus
three-legged *adj* tripes
thresh *vt* terĕre
threshing floor *s* area *f*
threshold *s* limen *n*
thrice *adv* ter
thrift *s* frugalitas, parsimonia *f*
thriftily *adv* frugaliter
thrifty *adj* parcus, frugalis
thrill *s* gaudium *n*, voluptas *f*; (*of fear*) horror *m*
thrill *vt* commovēre, percellĕre
thrilling *adj* mirus, mirabilis
thrive *vi* virēre, vigēre, valēre
thriving *adj* vegetus, prosperus
throat *s* jugulum, guttur *n*, fauces *f pl*
throb *s* palpitatio *f*, puls·us -ūs *m*
throb *vi* palpitare
throes *s* dolor *m*
throne *s* solium *n*; (*fig*) regia dignitas *f*
throng *s* multitudo, turba, frequentia *f*
throng *vi* **to — around** stipare
throttle *vt* strangulare
through *prep* per (*with acc*); (*on account of*) ob (*with acc*), propter (*with acc*)
through *adv render by compound verb with* trans- *or* per-, e.g., **to read —** perlegĕre; **— and —** penitus, omnino
throughout *adv* prorsus, penitus
throughout *prep* per (*with acc*)
throw *vt* jacĕre, conjicĕre; (*esp. weapons*) mittere, jaculari; **to — away** abjicĕre; **to — back** rejicĕre; **to — down** dejicĕre; **to — open** patefacĕre; **to — out** ejicĕre; **to — together** conjicĕre in unum; *vi* **to — up** vomĕre
throw *s* jact·us -ūs *m*
thrush *s* turdus *m*
thrust *s* impet·us -ūs, ict·us -ūs *m*
thrust *vt* trudĕre, impellĕre; (*with sword*) perfodĕre
thumb *s* pollex *m*
thump *s* percussio *f*
thump *vt* tundere
thunder *s* tonitr·us -ūs *m*
thunder *vi* tonare
thunderbolt *s* fulmen *n*
thunderstruck *adj* attonitus, obstupefactus
thus *adv* ita, sic; **and —** itaque
thwart *vt* obstare (*with dat*), frustrari
thy *adj* tuus
tiara *s* diadema *n*
tick *s* (*insect*) ricinus *m*; (*clicking*) levis ict·us -ūs *m*
ticket *s* tessera *f*
tickle *vt & vi* titillare
tickling *s* titillatio *f*
ticklish *adj* periculosus
tide *s* aest·us -ūs *m*
tidings *s* nuntius *m*
tie *s* vinculum *n*; (*relationship*) necessitudo *f*
tie *vt* (al)ligare; (*in a knot*) nodare, nectĕre
tier *s* ordo *m*
tiger *s* tigris *m*
tight *adj* strictus, astrictus, artus; **—ly** arte
tighten *vt* astringĕre, adducĕre, contendĕre
tile *s* tegula, imbrex *f*
till *conj* dum, donec
till *prep* usque ad (*with acc*)
till *vt* colĕre
tillage *s* agricultura *f*
tiller *s* (*person*) agricola *m*; (*helm*) gubernaculum *n*
tilt *vt* proclinare
timber *s* materia *f*, lignum *n*
time *s* tempus *n*, dies *f*; (*age, period*) aetas *f*; (*leisure*) otium *n*; (*opportunity*) occasio *f*; (*interval*) intervallum, spatium *n*; (*of day*) hora *f*; **another —** alias; **at the same —** simul; **for a —** parumper; **for a long —** diu; **for some —** aliquamdiu; **from — to —** interdum; **in a short —** brevi; **in —** ad tempus; **on —** tempestive; **what — is it?** quota hora est?
timely *adj* tempestivus, opportunus
timepiece *s* horarium, horologium *n*
timid *adj* timidus
timidity *s* timiditas *f*
timorous *adj* pavidus
tin *s* stannum, plumbum album *n*
tin *adj* stanneus

tincture *s* color *m*
tinder *s* fomes *m*
tinge *vt* tingĕre, imbuĕre
tingle *vi* formicare, verminare
tinkle *vi* tinnire
tinsel *s* bractea, bracteola *f*
tip *s* cacumen, acumen *n*, apex *m*
tip *vt* praefigĕre; (*to incline*) invertĕre
tipple *vi* potare
tippler *s* potor *m*
tipsy *adj* ebriolus, temulentus
tiptoe *adv* in digitos erectus
tire *vt* fatigare, lassare; *vi* defatigari
tired *adj* fessus, lassus; **I am — of** me taedet (*with genit*); **— out** defessus
tiresome *adj* laboriosus; molestus
tissue *s* text·us -ūs *m*
titanic *adj* ingens
tithe *s* decuma *f*
title *s* titulus *m*; (*of book*) inscriptio *f*; (*of person*) appellatio, dignitas *f*; (*claim*) jus *n*
title page *s* index *m*
titter *s* ris·us -ūs *m*
to *prep commonly rendered by the dative;* (*motion, except with names of towns, small islands and* rus) ad (*with acc*), in (*with acc*); **— and fro** huc illuc
toad *s* bufo *m*
toast *s* (*bread*) panis tosti offula *f*; (*health*) propinatio *f*; **to drink a — to** propinare (*with dat*)
toast *vt* torrēre; (*in drinking*) propinare (*with dat*)
today *adv* hodie
today *s* hodiernus dies *m*
toe *s* digitus *m*
together *adv* simul, unā
toil *s* labor *m*, opera *f*
toil *vi* laborare
toilsome *adj* laboriosus, operosus
token *s* signum, pignus, indicium *n*
tolerable *adj* tolerabilis; mediocris
tolerably *adv* tolerabiliter; mediocriter
tolerance *s* patientia *f*
tolerant *adj* tolerans, indulgens, patiens; **—ly** indulgenter
tolerate *vt* tolerare, ferre
toleration *s* toleratio, indulgentia, patientia *f*
toll *s* vectigal *n*; (*at ports*) portorium *n*
toll collector *s* exactor, portitor *m*
tomb *s* sepulcrum *n*
tombstone *s* lapis, cippus *m*
tomorrow *adv* cras
tomorrow *s* crastinus dies *m*; **the day after —** perendie
tone *s* sonus *m*, vox *f*; (*in painting*) color *m*
tongs *s* forceps *m & f*
tongue *s* lingua *f*; (*of shoe*) ligula *f*; (*pole of carriage*) temo *m*
tonsils *s* tonsillae *f pl*
too *adv* nimis, nimium; (*also*) quoque, insuper
tool *s* instrumentum *n*; (*dupe*) minister *m*
tooth *s* dens *m*; **— and nail** totis viribus
toothache *s* dentium dolor *m*
toothless *adj* edentulus
toothpick *s* dentiscalpium *n*
tooth powder *s* dentifricium *n*
top *adj* summus
top *s* vertex, apex *m*; (*of tree*) cacumen *n*; (*of house*) fastigium *n*; (*toy*) turbo *m*; **the — of the mountain** summus mons *m*
top *vt* superare
topic *s* res *f*, argumentum *n*
topmost *adj* summus
topography *s* regionum descriptio *f*
topple *vt* evertĕre; *vi* titubare
torch *s* fax *f*
torment *s* tormentum *n*, cruciat·us -ūs *m*
torment *vt* (ex)cruciare, torquēre
tormenter *s* tortor *m*
torpid *adj* torpens; **to be —** torpēre
torpor *s* torpor *m*
torrent *s* torrens *m*
torrid *adj* torridus
tortoise *s* testudo *f*
tortoise shell *s* testudo *f*
torture *s* tormentum *n*, cruciat·us -ūs *m*
torture *vt* torquēre, (ex)cruciare
torturer *s* cruciator, tortor *m*
toss *s* jact·us -ūs *m*
toss *vt* jactare; *vi* jactari
total *adj* totus, universus; **—ly** omnino, prorsus
totality *s* summa, universitas *f*
totter *vi* vacillare, titubare
touch *vt* tangĕre, attingĕre; (*to stir emotionally*) movēre, commovēre, afficĕre; *vi* inter se contingĕre; **to — on** attingĕre
touch *s* (con)tact·us -ūs *m*, tactio *f*
touching *adj* mollis, flexanimus
touchstone *s* (*fig*) obrussa *f*
touchy *adj* stomachosus
tough *adj* durus, lentus; (*fig*) strenuus; difficilis
tour *s* (*rounds*) circuit·us -ūs *m*; (*abroad*) peregrinatio *f*
tourist *s* peregrinator *m*
tournament *s* certamen *n*
tow *s* stuppa *f*
tow *vt* remulco trahĕre
toward *prep* versus (*with acc*), ad (*with acc*); (*of feelings*) erga (*with acc*), in (*with acc*); (*of time*) sub (*with acc*)
towel *s* mantele *n*; sudarium *n*
tower *s* turris *f*
tower *vi* **to — over** imminēre (*with dat*)
towering *adj* excelsus, arduus
towline *s* remulcum *n*
town *s* urbs *f*; (*fortified*) oppidum *n*
town hall *s* curia *f*
townsman *s* oppidanus *m*
toy *s* crepundia *n pl*, oblectamentum *n*
trace *s* vestigium *n*; (*for horse*) helcium *n*
trace *vt* delinēre, describĕre; indagare, investigare; **to — back** repetĕre
track *s* vestigium *n*; (*path*) semita *f*, calles *m*
track *vt* investigare
trackless *adj* avius, invius

tract *s* (*of land*) tract·us -ūs *m*, regio *f*; (*treatise*) tract·us -ūs *m*
tractable *adj* tractabilis, docilis, obsequiosus
trade *s* mercatura *f*, commercium *n*; (*calling*) ars *f*, quaest·us -ūs *m*
trade *vt* commutare; *vi* negotiari, mercaturas facĕre
trader *s* mercator *m*
tradesman *s* opifex *m*
tradition *s* traditio, fama, memoria *f*, mos majorum *m*
traditional *adj* patrius, a majoribus traditus
traduce *vt* calumniari, infamare
traffic *s* commercium *n*; (*on street*) vehicula *n pl*
tragedian *s* (*playwright*) tragoedus, tragicus poeta *m*; (*actor*) tragicus actor *m*
tragedy *s* tragoedia *f*
tragic *adj* tragicus; (*fig*) tristis, miserabilis; **—ally** tragice; miserabiliter
trail *vt* investigare; (*to drag*) trahĕre; *vi* trahi, verrĕre
trail *s* vestigium *n*; (*path*) calles *m*
train *s* (*line*) series *f*, ordo *m*; (*of robe*) instita *f*; (*retinue*) comitat·us -ūs *m*; (*of army*) impedimenta *n pl*
train *vt* educare, instruĕre, assuefacĕre
trainer *s* lanista, aliptes *m*
training *s* disciplina, institutio *f*; (*practice*) exercitatio *f*
trait *s* mos *m*
traitor *s* proditor *m*
traitorous *adj* perfidus; **—ly** perfide
trammel *vt* impedire, vincire, irretire
tramp *s* vagabundus, homo vagus *m*; (*of feet*) puls·us -ūs *m*
tramp *vi* gradi
trample *vt* calcare, conculcare; *vi* **to — on** obterĕre, proterĕre, opprimĕre
trance *s* stupor *m*, ecstasis *f*
tranquil *adj* tranquillus; **—ly** tranquille
tranquility *s* tranquillitas *f*, tranquillus animus *m*
tranquilize *vt* tranquillare
transact *vt* transigĕre, gerĕre
transaction *s* negotium *n*, res *f*
transcend *vt* superare, vincĕre
transcendental *adj* sublimis, divinus
transcribe *vt* transcribĕre
transcription *s* transcriptio *f*
transfer *s* translatio *f*; (*of property*) alienatio *f*
transfer *vt* transferre; (*property*) abalienare
transference *s* translatio *f*
transfigure *vt* tranfigurare
transform *vt* vertĕre, commutare
transformation *s* commutatio *f*
transgress *vt* violare, perfringĕre; *vi* peccare, delinquĕre
transgression *s* violatio *f*, delictum *n*
transgressor *s* violator, maleficus *m*
transient *adj* transitorius, brevis, fluxus
transition *s* transitio *f*, transit·us -ūs *m*
transitive *adj* transitivus; **—ly** transitive
transitory *adj* transitorius, brevis, fluxus
translate *vt* vertĕre, transferre
translation *s* translata *n pl*
translator *s* interpres *m*
transmission *s* transmissio *f*
transmit *vt* transmittere
transmutation *s* transmutatio *f*
transparent *adj* pellucidus; (*fig*) perspicuus
transpire *vi* perspirare, emanare; (*to happen*) evenire
transplant *vt* transferre
transport *vt* transportare, transvehĕre
transport *s* vectura *f*; (*ship*) navigium vectorium *n*, navis oneraria *f*; (*rapture*) sublimitas *f*
transportation *s* vectura *f*
transpose *vt* transponĕre
transposition *s* transpositio, trajectio *f*
trap *s* laqueus *m*, pedica *f*; (*fig*) insidiae *f pl*; **to lay a —** insidiari
trap *vt* (*to snare*) irretire; (*fig*) inlaqueare
trappings *s* ornamenta *n pl*, apparat·us -ūs *m*; (*of horse*) phalerae *f pl*
trash *s* scruta *n pl*; (*fig*) nugae *f pl*
trashy *adj* vilis; obscenus
travel *vi* iter facĕre; **to — abroad** peregrinari
traveler *s* viator, peregrinator *m*
traverse *vt* transire, peragrare, lustrare
travesty *s* perversa imitatio *f*
tray *s* ferculum *n*, trulla *f*
treacherous *adj* perfidus, dolosus; **—ly** perfidiose
treachery *s* perfidia *f*
tread *vt* calcare; *vi* incedĕre
tread *s* grad·us -ūs, incess·us -ūs *m*, vestigium *n*
treason *s* perduellio, proditio *f*
treasonable *adj* perfidus, proditorius
treasure *s* thesaurus *m*
treasure *vt* fovēre, magni aestimare
treasurer *s* aerarii praefectus *m*
treasury *s* aerarium *n*, fiscus *m*
treat *vt* uti (*with abl*), tractare; (*patient*) curare; (*topic*) tractare; (*to entertain*) invitare
treatise *s* libellus *m*, dissertatio *f*
treatment *s* tractatio *f*; (*by doctor*) curatio *f*
treaty *s* foedus, pactum *n*; **to make a —** foedus icĕre
treble *adj* triplex, triplus; (*of sound*) acutus
treble *vt* triplicare
tree *s* arbor *f*
trellis *s* clathrus *m*
tremble *vi* tremĕre, tremiscĕre
trembling *adj* tremulus
trembling *s* trepidatio *f*
tremendous *adj* immanis, ingens, vastus; **—ly** valde, maxime
tremulous *adj* tremulus, vacillans
trench *s* fossa *f*

trespass *vt* violare, offenděre; *vi* delinquěre
trespass *s* violatio, culpa *f*
tress *s* crinis, cirrus *m*
trestle *s* fulcimentum *n*
trial *s* tentatio, experientia *f*; (*test*) probatio *f*; (*trouble*) labor *m*; (*law*) judicium *n*, quaestio *f*
triangle *s* triangulum *n*
triangular *adj* triangulus, triquetrus
tribe *s* trib·us -ūs *f*
tribulation *s* tribulatio, afflictio *f*
tribunal *s* (*raised platform*) tribunal *n*; (*court*) judicium *n*
tribune *s* tribunus *m*
tribuneship *s* tribunat·us -ūs *m*
tributary *adj* vectigalis, stipendiarius
tributary *s* amnis in alium influens *m*
tribute *s* tributum, vectigal *n*
trick *s* dolus *m*, artificium *n*, fraus, ars *f*
trick *vt* fallěre, decipěre
trickle *s* guttae *f pl*
trickle *vi* stillare, manare
trickster *s* veterator, fraudator *m*
trident *s* tridens *m*
triennial *adj* triennis
trifle *s* res parvi momenti *f*, nugae *f pl*
trifle *vi* nugari
trifling *adj* levis, exiguus, frivolus
trill *s* sonus modulatus *m*
trill *vt* vibrare
trim *adj* nitidus, comptus, bellus
trim *vt* adornare; (*to prune*) putare, tonděre
trinket *s* tricae *f pl*
trip *s* iter *n*
trip *vt* supplantare; *vi* titubare; (*fig*) errare
tripartite *adj* tripartitus
tripe *s* omasum *n*
triple *adj* triplex
triple *vt* triplicare
tripod *s* tripus *m*
trireme *s* triremis *f*
trite *adj* tritus
triumph *s* (*entry of victorious Roman general*) triumphus *m*; (*victory*) victoria *f*
triumph *vi* triumphare; vincěre; **to — over** devincěre
triumphal *adj* triumphalis
triumphant *adj* victor; elatus, laetus
trivial *adj* levis, tenuis
triviality *s* nugae *f pl*
troop *s* turma, caterva *f*, grex, globus *m*; **—s** (*mil*) copiae *f pl*
trooper *s* eques *m*
trope *s* tropus *m*
trophy *s* tropaeum *n*
tropical *adj* tropicus
tropics *s* loca fervida *n pl*
trot *vi* tolutim ire
trouble *s* labor, dolor *m*, incommodum *n*, aerumna, molestia *f*
trouble *vt* turbare, vexare, angěre
troublesome *adj* molestus, operosus
trough *s* alveus *m*
trounce *vt* (*to punish*) castigare; (*to defeat decisively*) devincěre
troupe *s* grex *m*
trousers *s* bracae *f pl*
trout *s* tru(c)ta *f*
trowel *s* trulla *f*
truant *s* cessator *m*
truce *s* indutiae *f pl*
truck *s* carrus *m*
truculent *adj* truculentus
trudge *vi* repěre
true *adj* verus; (*genuine*) germanus; (*faithful*) fidus; (*exact*) rectus, justus
truism *s* verbum tritum *n*
truly *adv* vere, profecto
trump *vt* **to — up** effingěre, ementiri
trumpet *s* tuba, bucina *f*
trumpeter *s* tubicen, bucinator *m*
truncheon *s* fustis *m*
trundle *vt* volvěre
trunk *s* truncus *m*; (*for luggage*) cista *f*; (*of elephant*) proboscis *f*
trust *s* fiducia, fides *f*
trust *vt* fiděre (*with dat*), creděre (*with dat*); (*to entrust*) committěre
trustee *s* fiduciarius, tutor *m*
trusteeship *s* tutela *f*
trustful *adj* credulus
trusting *adj* fidens; **—ly** fidenter
trustworthiness *s* integritas, fides *f*
trustworthy *adj* fidus; (*of witness*) locuples; (*of an authority*) bonus
trusty *adj* fidus
truth *s* veritas *f*, verum *n*; **in —** vero
truthful *adj* verax; **—ly** veraciter, vere
try *vt* tentare, probare, experiri; (*law*) cognoscěre; (*to endeavor*) laborare; **to — one's patience** patientiā abuti
trying *adj* molestus, incommodus, gravis
tub *s* labrum, dolium *n*
tube *s* fistula *f*
tuck *vt* **to — up** succingěre
tuft *s* floccus, cirrus *m*, crista *f*
tug *s* conat·us -ūs, nis·us -ūs *m*; (*ship*) navis tractoria *f*
tug *vt* trahěre
tuition *s* tutela *f*
tumble *vi* corruěre, collabi, volvi
tumbler *s* poculum vitreum *n*
tumor *s* tumor, tuber *m*
tumult *s* tumult·us -ūs *m*
tumultuous *adj* tumultuosus, turbulentus; **—ly** tumultuose
tune *s* tonus *m*, moduli *m pl*
tuneful *adj* canorus
tunic *s* tunica *f*
tunnel *s* canalis, cuniculus *m*
turban *s* mitra, tiara *f*
turbid *adj* turbidus, turbulentus
turbulence *s* tumult·us -ūs *m*
turbulent *adj* turbulentus; **—ly** turbulente
turf *s* caespes *m*
turgid *adj* turgidus
turkey *s* meleagris gallopavo *f*
turmoil *s* turba, perturbatio *f*, tumult·us -ūs *m*
turn *s* (*circuit*) circuit·us -ūs *m*; (*revolution*) conversio *f*, circumact·us -ūs *m*; (*change, course*) vicissitudo *f*; (*inclination of mind*) inclinatio

f, ingenium *n*; **a good —** officium, beneficium *n*; **in —** invicem
turn *vt* vertĕre, convertĕre; (*to twist*) torquēre; (*to bend*) flectĕre; **to — aside** deflectĕre; **to — away** avertĕre; **to — down** (*refuse*) recusare, denegare, respuere; **to — into** mutare in (*with acc*), vertĕre in (*with acc*); **to — over** (*to hand over*) tradĕre, transferre; (*property*) alienare; (*in mind*) agitare; **to — one's attention to** animadvertĕre; **to — out** ejicĕre, expellĕre; **to — round** volvĕre, circumagĕre, rotare; **to — up** (*with hoe*) invertĕre; **to — up the nose** nares corrugare; *vi* verti, converti, versari; **to — against** disciscĕre ab (*with abl*), alienari ab (*with abl*); **to — aside** devertĕre, se declinare; **to — away** discedĕre, aversari; **to — back** reverti; **to — into** (*to be changed into*) vertĕre in (*with acc*), mutari in (*with acc*); **to — out** cadĕre, evadĕre, contingĕre, evenire; **to — round** converti; **to — up** intervenire, adesse
turnip *s* rapum *n*
turpitude *s* turpitudo *f*
turret *s* turricula *f*
turtle *s* testudo *f*
turtledove *s* turtur *m*
tusk *s* dens *m*
tutelage *s* tutela *f*
tutor *s* praeceptor, magister *m*
tutor *vt* edocēre
tweezers *s* volsella *f*
twelfth *adj* duodecimus
twelve *adj* duodecim; **— times** duodecies
twentieth *adj* vicesimus
twenty *adj* viginti; **— times** vicies
twice *adv* bis
twig *s* surculus, ramulus *m*, virga, virgula *f*
twilight *s* crepusculum *n*; (*dawn*) diluculum *n*
twin *adj* geminus
twin *s* geminus, gemellus *m*
twine *s* filum *n*, resticula *f*
twine *vt* circumplicare, contorquēre; *vi* circumplecti
twinge *s* dolor *m*
twinkle *vi* micare, coruscare
twinkling *s* (*of eye*) nict·us -ūs *m*
twirl *vt* versare, circumagĕre; *vi* versari
twist *vt* torquēre; *vi* flecti
twit *vt* exprobrare, objurgare
twitch *s* vellicatio *f*
twitch *vt* vellicare; *vi* micare
twitter *vi* minurire
two *adj* duo; **— at a time** bini; **— times** bis
twofold *adj* duplex, duplus
type *s* (*model*) exemplum, exemplar *n*; (*class*) genus *n*, forma, figura *f*
typhoon *s* turbo *m*
typical *adj* solitus, proprius
tyrannical *adj* tyrannicus, superbus; **—ly** tyrannice, superbe
tyrannicide *s* (*act*) tyrannicidium *n*; (*person*) tyranni interfector, tyrannicida *m*
tyrannize *vi* dominari
tyranny *s* tyrannis, dominatio *f*
tyrant *s* tyrannus, dominus superbus *m*
tyro *s* tiro *m*

U

udder *s* uber *n*
ugliness *s* deformitas, foeditas *f*
ugly *adj* deformis, turpis, foedus
ulcer *s* ulcus *n*
ulcerous *adj* ulcerosus
ultimate *adj* ultimus, extremus; **—ly** tandem
umbrage *s* offensio *f*; **to take — at** aegre ferre
umbrella *s* umbella *f*
umpire *s* arbiter, disceptator *m*
unabashed *adj* intrepidus
unabated *adj* integer
unable *adj* impotens, invalidus; **to be — to** non posse, nequire
unaccented *adj* accentu carens
unacceptable *adj* ingratus, odiosus
unaccompanied *adj* incomitatus, solus
unaccomplished *adj* infectus, imperfectus
unaccountable *adj* inexplicabilis, inenodabilis
unaccountably *adv* praeter opinionem, sine causa
unaccustomed *adj* insolitus, insuetus, inexpertus
unacquainted *adj* **— with** ignarus (*with genit*), expers (*with genit*)
unadorned *adj* inornatus, incomptus, simplex
unadulterated *adj* merus, integer
unaffected *adj* simplex, candidus
unafraid *adj* impavidus
unaided *adj* non adjutus, sine ope
unalterable *adj* immutabilis
unaltered *adj* immutatus
unanimous *adj* unanimus, concors; **—ly** concorditer, consensu omnium
unanswerable *adj* irrefragabilis
unappeased *adj* implacatus
unapproachable *adj* inaccessus
unarmed *adj* inermis
unasked *adj* injussus, non vocatus
unassailable *adj* inexpugnabilis
unassuming *adj* modestus, moderatus, demissus
unattached *adj* liber, vacuus
unattainable *adj* arduus
unattempted *adj* inexpertus, inausus, intentatus
unattended *adj* incomitatus, sine comitibus

unattractive *adj* invenustus
unauthorized *adj* illicitus
unavailing *adj* inutilis, irritus
unavenged *adj* inultus
unavoidable *adj* inevitabilis
unaware *adj* inscius, nescius, ignarus
unbearable *adj* intolerabilis
unbeaten *adj* invictus
unbecoming *adj* indecorus, indecens; **it is —** dedecet
unbefitting *adj* indecorus
unbend *vi* animum remittěre
unbending *adj* inflexibilis, inexorabilis
unbiased *adj* incorruptus, integer
unbidden *adj* injussus, ultro
unbleached *adj* crudus
unblemished *adj* integer, intactus
unblest *adj* infortunatus
unborn *adj* nondum natus
unbroken *adj* irruptus; integer; (*of horses*) indomitus
unbuckle *vt* refibulare
unburden *vt* exonerare
unbutton *vt* refibulare
unceasing *adj* constans, assiduus; **—ly** assidue
uncertain *adj* incertus, dubius; **—ly** incerte, dubie
uncertainty *s* dubium *n*, dubitatio *f*
unchangeable *adj* immutabilis
unchanged *adj* immutatus
unchanging *adj* integer, idem
uncharitable *adj* immisericors
unchaste *adj* impudicus, obscenus; **—ly** impudice, impure
uncivil *adj* inurbanus
uncivilized *adj* incultus
unclasp *vt* defibulare
uncle *s* (*father's brother*) patruus *m*; (*mother's brother*) avunculus *m*
unclean *adj* immundus
uncomfortable *adj* incommodus, molestus
uncommon *adj* rarus, insolitus, inusitatus; **—ly** raro, praeter solitum
unconcerned *adj* securus, incuriosus
unconditional *adj* absolutus, sine exceptione; **—ly** nullā condicione
unconnected *adj* disjunctus
unconquerable *adj* invictus
unconscionable *adj* iniquus, injustus, absurdus
unconscious *adj* omni sensu carens; **— of** ignarus (*with genit*), inscius (*with genit*)
unconstitutional *adj* illicitus; **—ly** contra leges
uncontrollable *adj* impotens
unconventional *adj* insolitus
unconvinced *adj* non persuasus
unconvincing *adj* non verisimilis
uncooked *adj* rudus
uncorrupted *adj* incorruptus
uncouth *adj* inurbanus, agrestis
uncover *vt* detegěre, recluděre, nudare
uncritical *adj* credulus
uncultivated *adj* incultus; indoctus
uncut *adj* intonsus
undamaged *adj* integer, inviolatus
undaunted *adj* impavidus, intrepidus
undecided *adj* incertus, dubius, anceps
undefended *adj* indefensus, nudus
undefiled *adj* purus, incontaminatus
undefined *adj* infinitus
undeniable *adj* haud dubius
under *adv* subter, infra
under *prep* (*position*) sub (*with abl*); (*motion*) sub (*with acc*); (*less than*) intra (*with acc*), infra (*with acc*)
underage *adj* impubes
underestimate *vt* minoris aestimare
undergarment *s* subucula *f*
undergo *vt* subire, pati
underground *adj* subterraneus
undergrowth *s* virgulta *n pl*
underhanded *adj* clandestinus, furtivus; **—ly** clam, furtive
underline *vt* subnotare
underling *s* minister, assecla *m*
undermine *vt* subruěre, suffoděre; (*fig*) labefacěre, labefactare
underneath *adv* infra, subter
underneath *prep* (*position*) infra (*with acc*), sub (*with abl*); (*motion*) sub (*with acc*)
underrate *vt* minoris aestimare
understand *vt* intellegěre, comprehenděre
understanding *adj* prudens, sapiens
understanding *s* mens *f*, intellectus -ūs *m*; (*agreement*) consens·us -ūs *m*; (*condition*) condicio *f*
undertake *vt* adire ad (*with acc*), suscipěre; (*to begin*) incipěre
undertaker *s* vespillo, libitinarius *m*
undertaking *s* inceptum, coeptum *n*
undervalue *vt* minoris aestimare
underworld *s* inferi *m pl*
undeserved *adj* immeritus, injustus; **—ly** immerito
undeserving *adj* indignus
undiminished *adj* imminutus
undiscernible *adj* imperceptus, invisus
undisciplined *adj* immoderatus; (*mil*) inexercitatus
undisguised *adj* apertus
undismayed *adj* impavidus, intrepidus
undisputed *adj* certus
undistinguished *adj* ignobilis, inglorius
undisturbed *adj* imperturbatus, immotus
undivided *adj* indivisus
undo *vt* (*knot*) expedire; (*fig*) infectum redděre; (*to ruin*) perděre
undone (*adj*) (*not completed*) infectus, imperfectus; (*ruined*) perditus
undoubted *adj* certus, haud dubius; **—ly** haud dubie
undress *vt* exuěre; *vi* vestes exuěre
undressed *adj* nudus; (*fig*) rudis
undue *adj* nimius, iniquus
undulate *vi* undare, fluctuare
undulation *s* undarum agitatio *f*
unduly *adv* nimis, plus aequo
undying *adj* aeternus, sempiternus
unearth *vt* detegěre, efforděre
unearthly *adj* humano major, divinus
uneasiness *s* sollicitudo, anxietas *f*

uneasy *adj* sollicitus, anxius
uneducated *adj* indoctus, illiteratus
unemployed *adj* vacuus, otiosus
unemployment *s* otium *n*, cessatio *f*
unencumbered *adj* expeditus
unending *adj* infinitus, perpetuus
unendurable *adj* intolerandus
unenjoyable *adj* injucundus
unenlightened *adj* ineruditus
unenviable *adj* non invidendus, miser
unequal *adj* inaequalis, dispar, impar; **—ly** inaequaliter, impariter, inique
unequaled *adj* singularis, eximius
unerring *adj* certus; **—ly** certe
uneven *adj* inaequalis, iniquus; (*rough*) asper
unexpected *adj* inopinatus, insperatus, improvisus; **—ly** de improviso
unexplored *adj* inexploratus
unfading *adj* semper recens
unfailing *adj* certus, perpetuus; **—ly** semper
unfair *adj* iniquus; **—ly** inique
unfaithful *adj* infidus, perfidus, infidelis; **—ly** perfide
unfamiliar *adj* ignotus, alienus
unfashionable *adj* obsoletus
unfasten *vt* laxare, resolvĕre
unfavorable *adj* adversus, iniquus, inopportunus
unfavorably *adv* male, inique
unfed *adj* impastus
unfeeling *adj* durus, crudelis; **—ly** dure, crudeliter
unfetter *vt* vincula demĕre (*with dat*)
unfinished *adj* imperfectus; (*crude*) rudis, impolitus
unfit *adj* inhabilis, ineptus, inutilis
unfold *vt* explicare, evolvĕre; (*story*) enarrare; *vi* dehiscĕre, patescĕre
unforeseeing *adj* imprudens, improvidus
unforeseen *adj* improvisus, insperatus
unforgiving *adj* inexorabilis
unfortified *adj* immunitus, nudus
unfortunate *adj* infelix, infortunatus, nefastus; **—ly** infeliciter
unfounded *adj* vanus, fictus
unfriendly *adj* parum amicus, inimicus, alienus
unfruitful *adj* infructuosus, sterilis, infecundus
unfulfilled *adj* infectus
unfurl *vt* pandĕre, solvĕre
unfurnished *adj* imparatus
ungainly *adj* ineptus, inhabilis
ungenerous *adj* illiberalis
ungentlemanly *adj* inurbanus, illepidus
ungird *vt* discingĕre
ungodly *adj* impius
ungovernable *adj* indomabilis, intractabilis
ungracious *adj* iniquus, asper
ungrateful *adj* ingratus; **—ly** ingrate
ungrudging *adj* non invitus; **—ly** sine invidia
unguarded *adj* incustoditus, indefensus; (*of words*) inconsultus
unhandy *adj* inhabilis
unhappily *adv* infeliciter, misere
unhappiness *s* tristitia, miseria, maestitia *f*
unhappy *adj* infelix, infortunatus, miser
unharness *vt* disjungĕre
unhealthiness *s* valetudo, gravitas *f*
unhealthy *adj* infirmus, morbosus; (*unwholesome*) gravis, insalubris
unheard-of *adj* inauditus
unheeded *adj* neglectus
unhelpful *adj* invitus, difficilis
unhesitating *adj* promptus, confidens; **—ly** confidenter
unhinge *vt* de cardine detrahĕre; (*fig*) perturbare
unholy *adj* impius, profanus
unhoped-for *adj* insperatus
unhurt *adj* incolumis, salvus
unicorn *s* monoceros *m*
uniform *adj* constans, aequabilis; **—ly** constanter, aequabiliter
uniform *s* vestit·us -ūs *m*; (*mil*) sagum *n*
uniformity *s* constantia, aequabilitas *f*
unify *vt* conjungĕre
unilateral *adj* unilaterus
unimaginative *adj* hebes
unimpaired *adj* integer, intactus
unimpeachable *adj* probatissimus
unimportant *adj* nullius momenti (*genit*), levis
uninformed *adj* indoctus
uninhabitable *adj* non habitabilis, inhabitabilis
uninhabited *adj* desertus
uninjured *adj* incolumis
uninspired *adj* hebes
unintelligible *adj* obscurus
uninteresting *adj* frigidus, jejunus
uninterrupted *adj* continuus, perpetuus
uninviting *adj* injucundus, non alliciens
union *s* (*act*) conjunctio *f*; (*social*) consociatio, societas *f*; (*agreement*) consens·us -ūs *m*; (*marriage*) conjugium *n*
unique *adj* unicus, singularis
unison *s* concent·us -ūs *m*
unit *s* monas *f*, unio *m*
unite *vt* conjungĕre, consociare; *vi* coalescĕre, coire; conjurare
unity *s* concordia *f*
universal *adj* universus, universalis; **—ly** universe, ubique
universe *s* mundus *m*, summa rerum *f*
university *s* academia, universitas *f*
unjust *adj* injustus, iniquus; **—ly** injuste, inique
unjustifiable *adj* indignus
unkempt *adj* incomptus, neglectus
unkind *adj* inhumanus; **—ly** inhumane
unknowingly *adv* insciens
unknown *adj* ignotus, incognitus
unlawful *adj* illegitimus, illicitus; **—ly** contra legem *or* leges
unless *conj* nisi
unlike *adj* dissimilis, dispar, diversus
unlikely *adj* parum verisimilis
unlimited *adj* infinitus, immensus
unload *vt* exonerare

unluckily *adv* infeliciter
unlucky *adj* infelix, infaustus
unmanageable *adj* intractabilis, contumax
unmanly *adj* mollis
unmannerly *adj* male moratus, inurbanus
unmarried *adj* (*man*) caelebs; (*woman*) innupta
unmask *vt* detegĕre
unmatched *adj* unicus, singularis
unmerciful *adj* immisericors; **—ly** immisericorditer
unmindful *adj* immemor
unmistakable *adj* certissimus
unmistakably *adv* sine dubio
unmoved *adj* immotus
unnatural *adj* (*event*) monstruosus; (*deed*) immanis, crudelis; **—ly** contra naturam
unnecessarily *adv* ex supervacuo, nimis
unnecessary *adj* haud necessarius, supervacaneus
unnerve *vt* debilitare
unnoticed *adj* praetermissus; **to go —** latēre
unobjectionable *adj* culpae expers, honestus
unoccupied *adj* vacuus; otiosus; (*of land*) apertus
unofficial *adj* privatus
unpack *vt* e cistis eximĕre
unpaid *adj* (*of money*) debitus; (*of a service*) gratuitus
unpalatable *adj* amarus, insuavis
unparalleled *adj* unicus, singularis
unpardonable *adj* inexcusabilis
unpatriotic *adj* immemor patriae
unpitying *adj* immisericors, inexorabilis
unpleasant *adj* injucundus, incommodus; **—ly** injucunde, incommode
unpolluted *adj* impollutus; (*fig*) integer, intactus
unpopular *adj* invisus, invidiosus
unpracticed *adj* inexpertus, imperitus
unprecedented *adj* novus, inauditus
unprejudiced *adj* aequus
unpremeditated *adj* subitus, ex tempore
unprepared *adj* imparatus
unprincipled *adj* improbus
unproductive *adj* infecundus, infructuosus, sterilis
unprofitable *adj* vanus, inutilis
unprofitably *adv* inutiliter, frustra
unprotected *adj* indefensus
unprovoked *adj* non lacessitus, ultro
unpunished *adj* inpunitus, inultus
unqualified *adj* haud idoneus, inhabilis
unquenchable *adj* inexstinctus
unquestionable *adj* haud dubius, certissimus
unquestionably *adv* certe
unquestioning *adj* credulus
unravel *vt* retexĕre; (*fig*) enodare, explicare
unreasonable *adj* rationis expers, absurdus; iniquus
unreasonably *adv* absurde, inique
unrefined *adj* rudis, crudus, incultus
unrelenting *adj* implacabilis, inexorabilis
unremitting *adj* assiduus, continuus
unrepentant *adj* impaenitens
unrestrained *adj* effrenatus, indomitus, effusus
unrighteous *adj* injustus, iniquus; **—ly** injuste
unripe *adj* immaturus, crudus
unroll *vt* evolvĕre, explicare
unruliness *s* petulantia *f*
unruly *adj* effrenatus, turbulentus
unsafe *adj* intutus, periculosus
unsatisfactory *adj* non idoneus, malus
unsavory *adj* insipidus, insulsus, insuavis
unseasonable *adj* intempestivus, immaturis; incommodus, importunus
unseemly *adj* indecorus, indecens
unseen *adj* invisus
unselfish *adj* suae utilitatis immemor, liberalis; **—ly** liberaliter
unsettle *vt* turbare, sollicitare
unsettled *adj* incertus, inconstans; (*of mind*) sollicitus
unshaken *adj* immotus
unshaved *adj* intonsus
unsheathe *vt* destringĕre, e vagina educĕre
unsightly *adj* turpis, foedus
unskilful *adj* imperitus, inscitus; **—ly** imperite, inscite
unskilled *adj* imperitus, indoctus
unsophisticated *adj* simplex
unsound *adj* infirmus; (*mentally*) insanus; (*ill-founded*) vanus
unsparing *adj* inclemens; (*lavish*) prodigus, largus; **—ly** inclementer; prodige, large
unspeakable *adj* ineffabilis, inenarrabilis
unstable *adj* instabilis; (*fig*) levis, inconstans
unstained *adj* incontaminatus, purus
unsteadily *adv* inconstanter, instabiliter
unsteady *adj* inconstans, instabilis
unsuccessful *adj* infelix, infaustus; **—ly** infeliciter
unsuitable *adj* inhabilis, incommodus, alienus
unsuited *adj* haud idoneus
unsullied *adj* incorruptus
unsuspected *adj* non suspectus
untamed *adj* indomitus, ferus
untasted *adj* ingustatus
untaught *adj* indoctus, rudis
unteachable *adj* indocilis
untenable *adj* infirmus, inanis
unthankful *adj* ingratus
untie *vt* solvĕre
until *conj* dum, donec, quoad
until *prep* usque ad (*with acc*), in (*with acc*); **— now** adhuc
untimely *adj* intempestivus, importunus, immaturus
untiring *adj* assiduus, indefessus
untold *adj* innumerus
untouched *adj* intactus, integer; (*fig*) immotus
untrained *adj* inexercitatus

untried *adj* inexpertus, intemptatus
untrodden *adj* non tritus, avius
untroubled *adj* placidus, tranquillus; (*of sleep*) levis
untrue *adj* falsus, mendax; (*disloyal*) infidus
untrustworthy *adj* infidus
unusual *adj* inusitatus, insolitus, insuetus; **—ly** praeter solitum, raro
unutterable *adj* infandus, inenarrabilis
unvarnished *adj* (*fig*) nudus, simplex
unveil *vt* detegĕre, patefacĕre
unversed *adj* imperitus
unwarranted *adj* injustus, iniquus
unwary *adj* imprudens, incautus
unwearied *adj* indefessus, impiger
unwelcome *adj* ingratus, injucundus
unwholesome *adj* insalubris
unwieldy *adj* inhabilis
unwilling *adj* invitus; **—ly** invite
unwind *vt* revolvĕre, retexĕre
unwise *adj* imprudens, insipiens; **—ly** imprudenter, insipienter
unworthy *adj* indignus
unwrap *vt* explicare, evolvĕre
unwritten *adj* non scriptus
unyielding *adj* inflexibilis, obstinatus
unyoke *vt* disjungĕre
up *adv* sursum; **— and down** sursum deorsum
upbringing *s* educatio *f*
upheaval *s* eversio *f*
uphold *vt* servare, sustinēre, sustentare
upkeep *s* impensa *f*
uplift *vt* sublevare
upon *prep* (*position*) super (*with abl*), in (*with abl*); (*motion*) super (*with acc*), in (*with acc*); (*directly after*) e(x) (*with abl*); (*dependence*) e(x) (*with abl*)
upper *adj* superus, superior
uppermost *adj* summus, supremus
upright *adj* erectus; (*of character*) honestus, integer; **—ly** recte; integre
uproar *s* tumult·us -ūs *m*, turba *f*
uproot *vt* eradicare, eruĕre
upset *vt* evertĕre, subvertĕre, percellĕre
upset *adj* perculsus
upstream *adv* adverso flumine
up to *prep* usque ad (*with acc*), ad (*with acc*), tenus (*postpositive, with abl or genit*)
upwards *adv* sursum, sublime; **— of** (*of number*) plus quam
urban *adj* urbanus, oppidanus
urge *vt* urgēre, impellĕre, hortari; **to — on** stimulare
urge *s* impuls·us -ūs *m*
urgency *s* gravitas, necessitas *f*
urgent *adj* gravis, instans, vehemens; **to be —** instare; **—ly** vehementer, magnopere, graviter
urn *s* urna *f*
us *pron* nos; **to —** nobis; **with —** nobiscum
usage *s* mos *m*, consuetudo *f*
use *s* us·us -ūs, mos *m*, consuetudo, usura *f*; **no —!** frustra!; **to be of —** usui esse, prodesse; **to make — of** uti (*with abl*)
use *vt* uti (*with abl*); (*to take advantage of*) abuti (*with abl*); **to — something for** aliquid adhibĕre (*with dat*); **to — up** consumĕre, exhaurire; *vi* **I used to** solebam (*with inf*)
used *adj* usitatus; **— to** (*accustomed to*) assuetus (*with dat*)
useful *adj* utilis, commodus, aptus; **—ly** utiliter, commode, apte
useless *adj* inutilis, inhabilis; (*of things*) inanis; **—ly** inutiliter, frustra
usual *adj* usitatus, solitus, consuetus; **—ly** plerumque, fere, ferme; **I — go** soleo ire
usurp *vt* usurpare, occupare
usurper *s* usurpator *m*
usury *s* usura *f*; **to practice —** faenerari
utensils *s* utensilia, vasa *n pl*, supellex *f*
utility *s* utilitas *f*
utilize *vt* uti (*with abl*), adhibēre
utmost *adj* extremus, ultimus, summus; **to do one's —** omnibus viribus contendĕre
utter *adj* totus extremus, summus; **—ly** omnino, funditus
utter *vt* eloqui, proferre, pronuntiare, edĕre
utterance *s* elocutio, pronuntiatio *f*, dictum *n*
uttermost *adj* extremus, ultimus

V

vacant *adj* vacuus, inanis; **to be —** vacare
vacation *s* vacatio *f*, feriae *f pl*
vacillate *vi* vacillare
vacuum *s* inane *n*
vagabond *s* vagabundus, grassator *m*
vagrant *adj* vagabundus, vagus
vague *adj* vagus, dubius, ambiguus; **—ly** incerte, ambigue
vain *adj* vanus, futilis; superbus, arrogans; **in —** frustra; **—ly** frustra
valet *s* cubicularius *m*
valiant *adj* fortis; **—ly** fortiter
valid *adj* validus, legitimus, ratus; (*argument*) gravis
valley *s* vallis *f*
valor *s* fortitudo *f*
valuable *adj* pretiosus
valuation *s* aestimatio *f*
value *s* pretium *n*, aestimatio *f*
value *vt* aestimare, ducĕre; **to — highly** magni aestimare, magni habēre
valueless *adj* vilis, inutilis
vanguard *s* (*mil*) primum agmen *n*

vanish *vi* vanescĕre, diffugĕre
vanity *s* gloria, ostentatio *f*
vanquish *vt* vincĕre, superare
vapor *s* vapor *m*, exhalatio *f*
variable *adj* commutabilis, varius
variation *s* varietas, commutatio, vicissitudo *f*
variety *s* varietas, diversitas, multitudo *f*
various *adj* varii, diversi; **—ly** varie, diverse
vary *vt* variare, mutare; *vi* mutari
vase *s* amphora *f*, vas *n*
vast *adj* vastus, ingens, immensus; **—ly** valde
vastness *s* immensitas *f*
vault *s* fornix, camera *f*; (*leap*) salt·us -ūs *m*
vault *vi* salire
vaunt *vt* jactare; *vi* se jactare
veal *s* caro vitulina *f*
vegetable *s* holus *n*
vegetable *adj* holitarius
vehemence *s* vehementia, vis *f*, impet·us -ūs *m*
vehement *adj* vehemens, violentus, fervidus; **—ly** vehementer, valde
vehicle *s* vehiculum *n*
veil *s* velamen *n*, rica *f*; (*bridal*) flammeum *n*; (*fig*) integumentum *n*
veil *vt* velare, tegĕre
vein *s* vena *f*
velocity *s* velocitas, celeritas *f*
velvet *s* velvetum *n*
vend *vt* vendĕre
veneer *s* ligni bractea *f*; (*fig*) species *f*
venerable *adj* venerabilis
venerate *vt* venerari, colĕre
veneration *s* adoratio *f*, cult·us -ūs *m*
vengeance *s* ultio, poena *f*; **to take — on** vindicare in (*with acc*), ulcisci
venom *s* venenum, virus *n*
vent *s* spiramentum, foramen *n*
vent *vt* aperire; **to — one's wrath on** iram erumpere in (*with acc*)
ventilate *vt* ventilare
venture *s* ausum *n*
venture *vt* periclitari; audēre
veracious *adj* verax
veracity *s* veracitas *f*
verb *s* verbum *n*
verbal *adj* verbalis; **—ly** verbo tenus
verbatim *adv* ad verbum
verbose *adj* verbosus; **—ly** verbose
verdict *s* sententia *f*; **to deliver a —** sententiam pronuntiare
verge *s* margo, ora *f*; **to be on the — of** non procul abesse ut
verge *vi* vergĕre
verification *s* affirmatio *f*
verify *vt* ratum facĕre, confirmare
vermin *s* bestiolae *f pl*
versatile *adj* varius, agilis, versatilis
verse *s* vers·us -ūs *m*
versed *adj* peritus, exercitatus
version *s* forma, translatio *f*
vertex *s* vertex, vortex *m*
vertical *adj* rectus, directus; **—ly** ad lineam, ad perpendiculum
very *adj* ipse
very *adv* valde, admodum
vessel *s* vas *n*; (*ship*) navigium *n*
vest *s* subucula *f*
vestal *s* virgo vestalis *f*
vestige *s* vestigium, indicium *n*
vestment *s* vestimentum *n*
veteran *s* (*mil*) veteranus, vexillarius, emeritus *m*; (*fig*) veterator *m*
veterinarian *s* veterinarius *m*
veto *s* intercessio *f*, interdictum *n*
veto *vt* interdicĕre (*with dat*); (*as tribune*) intercedĕre (*with dat*)
vex *vt* vexare, sollicitare
vexation *s* vexatio, offensio *f*, stomachus *m*
via *prep* per (*with acc*)
vial *s* phiala *f*
vibrate *vi* tremĕre, vibrare
vibration *s* tremor *m*
vicar *s* vicarius *m*
vice *s* vitium *n*, turpitudo *f*
vicinity *s* vicinitas, vicinia *f*
vicious *adj* vitiosus, perditus; (*of temper*) ferox; **—ly** ferociter
vicissitude *s* vicissitudo *f*
victim *s* victima, hostia *f*; (*exploited*) praeda *f*
victimize *vt* circumvenire
victor *s* victor *m*, victrix *f*
victorious *adj* victor; (*of woman*) victrix; **to be —** vincĕre
victory *s* victoria *f*; **to win a —** victoriam reportare
vie *vi* certare, contendĕre; **to — with** aemulari (*with dat*)
view *s* aspect·us -ūs, conspect·us -ūs *m*; (*from above*) despect·us -ūs *m*; (*opinion*) opinio, sententia *f*, judicium *n*; **in my —** me judice; **to have in —** praevidēre
view *vt* visĕre, conspicĕre, intuēri, inspicĕre
vigil *s* pervigilatio *f*, pervigilium *n*
vigilance *s* vigilantia, diligentia *f*
vigilant *adj* vigilans, diligens, intentus; **—ly** vigilanter, diligenter
vigor *s* vigor, impet·us -ūs *m*, robur *n*
vigorous *adj* strenuus, acer, vegetus; **—ly** strenue, acriter
vile *adj* vilis, abjectus, perditus, flagitiosus
vilify *vt* infamare, calumniari
villa *s* villa *f*
village *s* vicus, pagus *m*
villager *s* vicanus, paganus *m*
villain *s* scelestus, nequam (*indecl*) *m*
villany *s* scelus *n*, improbitas, nequitia *f*
vindicate *vt* vindicare; (*to justify*) purgare; (*person*) defendĕre
vindictive *adj* ultionis cupidus
vine *s* vitis *f*
vinegar *s* acetum *n*
vineyard *s* vinea *f*, vinetum *n*
violate *vt* violare
violation *s* violatio *f*
violator *s* violator *m*
violence *s* violentia, vis *f*, impet·us -ūs *m*; (*cruelty*) saevitia *f*
violent *adj* violentus, vehemens; **—ly** violenter, vehementer
virgin *adj* virginalis
virgin *s* virgo *f*
virile *adj* virilis
virility *s* virilitas *f*
virtually *adv* fere

virtue *s* virtus, probitas *f*; (*power*) vis *f*; **by — of** per (*with acc*), ex (*with abl*)
virtuous *adj* probus, honestus; (*chaste*) castus, pudicus; **—ly** honeste, caste
virulence *s* vis *f*, virus *n*; (*fig*) acerbitas *f*
visage *s* facies *f*, os *n*
viscous *adj* viscosus, lentus
visible *adj* aspectabilis, conspicuus, manifestus; **to be —** apparēre
visibly *adv* manifesto
vision *s* (*sense*) vis·us -ūs *m*; (*apparition*) visum *n*, visio *f*
visionary *adj* vanus, fictus, inanis
visit *s* salutatio *f*
visit *vt* visĕre, visitare
visitor *s* salutator *m*, salutatrix *f*; advena, hospes *m*
visor *s* buccula *f*
vista *s* prospect·us -ūs *m*
visual *adj* oculorum (*genit*)
vital *adj* vitalis; (*essential*) necessarius; **—ly** praecipue
vitality *s* vis *f*, animus *m*
vitiate *vt* vitiare, corrumpĕre
vituperate *vt* vituperare, reprehendĕre
vituperative *adj* maledicus
vivacious *adj* vividus, alacer, hilaris; **—ly** acriter
vivacity *s* alacritas *f*
vivid *adj* vividus, acer; **—ly** acriter
vivify *vt* animare, vivificare
vocabulary *s* verborum copia *f*
vocal *adj* vocalis, canorus
vocation *s* officium, munus *n*
vociferous *adj* clamosus
vogue *s* mos *m*; **to be in —** in honore esse
voice *s* vox *f*, sonus *m*; (*vote*) suffragium *n*
void *s* inane, vacuum *n*
volatile *adj* levis, volaticus
volcanic *adj* flammas eructans
volcano *s* mons ignivomus *m*
volition *s* voluntas *f*
volley *s* conject·us -ūs *m*
voluble *adj* volubilis
volume *s* (*book*) volumen *n*; (*quantity*) copia, multitudo *f*; (*size*) amplitudo *f*
voluminous *adj* copiosus, amplus, magnus
voluntary *adj* voluntarius; (*unpaid*) gratuitus
volunteer *s* voluntarius *m*; (*mil*) miles voluntarius, evocatus *m*
volunteer *vi* sponte nomen dare
voluptuous *adj* voluptarius, voluptuosus, delicatus
vomit *vt* vomere, evomĕre
voracious *adj* vorax; **—ly** voraciter
voracity *s* voracitas *f*
vortex *s* vortex *m*
vote *s* suffragium *n*; (*fig*) (*judgment*) sententia *f*
vote *vi* suffragium ferre, suffragium inire; (*of judge*) sententiam ferre; (*of senator*) censēre; **to — against** antiquare; **to — for** suffragari (*with dat*)
votive *adj* votivus
vouch *vi* spondēre; **to — for** testificari, asseverare
voucher *s* (*person*) auctor *m*; (*document*) testimonium *n*
vow *s* votum *n*
vow *vt* (*to promise*) (de)vovēre, spondēre, promittĕre
vowel *s* vocalis littera *f*
voyage *s* navigatio *f*
voyage *vi* navigare
voyager *s* navigator *m*
vulgar *s* vulgaris, communis; (*low*) plebeius, vilis
vulgarity *s* insulsitas *f*
vulnerable *adj* obnoxius
vulture *s* vultur *m*

W

wade *vi* per vada ire; **to — across** vado transire
wag *vt* vibrare, agitare
wage *vt* **to — war** bellum gerĕre
wager *vt* deponĕre; *vi* sponsionem facĕre
wages *s* merces *f*, stipendium *n*
wagon *s* carrus *m*, plaustrum *n*
wail *vi* plorare, plangĕre, ululare
wailing *s* plorat·us -ūs, planct·us -ūs *m*
waist *s* medium corpus *n*
wait *vi* manēre; **to — for** exspectare; **to — on** servire (*with dat*)
wait *s* mora *f*; **to lie in — for** insidiari (*with dat*)
waive *vt* decedĕre de (*with abl*), remittĕre
wake *vt* exsuscitare, excitare; *vi* expergisci
wake *s* vestigia *n pl*; **in the — of** post (*with acc*)
wakeful *adj* insomnis, vigil
waken *vt* exsuscitare, excitare; *vi* expergisci
walk *s* (*act*) ambulatio *f*; (*place*) ambulacrum *n*, xystus *m*; (*covered*) portic·us -ūs *m*; (*gait*) incess·us -ūs *m*
walk *vi* incedĕre, ambulare, gradi
wall *s* (*of house*) paries *f*; (*of town*) moenia *n pl*, murus *m*
wall *vt* muro cingĕre, moenibus munire
wallow *vi* volutari
walnut *s* juglans *f*
wan *adj* pallidus, exsanguis
wander *vi* vagari, errare; **to — about** pervagari; **to — over** pererrare
wanderer *s* erro, vagus *m*
wandering *s* erratio *f*
wane *vi* decrescĕre, minui, tabescĕre

want *s* egestas, inopia, indigentia, defectio *f*
want *vt* (*to wish*) velle; (*to lack*) egēre (*with abl*), indigēre (*with abl*), carēre (*with abl*); (*to miss*) desiderare
wanting *adj* (*defective*) vitiosus; (*missing*) absens; **to be —** deficĕre, deesse
wanton *adj* protervus, lascivus, petulans; **—ly** lascive, petulanter
war *s* bellum *n*; **to declare —** bellum indicĕre; **to declare — on** bellum indicĕre (*with dat*); **to enter —** bellum suscipĕre; **to wage —** bellum gerĕre
war *vi* bellare
war cry *s* ululat·us -ūs *m*
ward *s* (*of town*) regio *f*; (*guard*) custodia *f*; (*minor*) pupillus *m*, pupilla *f*
ward *vt* **to — off** arcēre, avertĕre, defendĕre
warden *s* custos *m*; (*of prison*) carcerarius *m*
warehouse *s* apotheca *f*
wares *s* merx *f*
warfare *s* bellum *n*, res bellica *f*
war horse *s* equus bellator *m*
warlike *adj* militaris, bellicosus
warm *adj* calidus; (*fig*) acer; **to be —** calēre; **—ly** ardenter, acriter
warm *vt* calefacĕre, tepefacĕre
warmth *s* calor, fervor *m*
warn *vt* monēre, praemonēre
warning *s* monitio *f*, monit·us -ūs *m*; (*object lesson*) exemplum *n*
warrant *s* auctoritas *f*, mandatum *n*
warrant *vt* praestare, promittĕre
warranty *s* satisdatio *f*
warrior *s* bellator, miles *m*, bellatrix *f*
wart *s* verruca *f*
wary *adj* cautus, providus, circumspectus
wash *vt* lavare; **to — away** abluĕre, diluĕre; **to — out** eluĕre; *vi* lavari
wash *s* (*clothes*) lintea lavanda *n pl*
washing *s* lavatio, lotura *f*
wasp *s* vespa *f*
waste *s* detrimentum *n*, effusio, dissipatio *f*; (*of time*) jactura *f*
waste *adj* vastus, desertus; **to lay —** vastare, (de)populari
waste *vt* consumĕre, perdĕre, dissipare; (*time*) absumĕre, terĕre; *vi* **to — away** tabescĕre, intabescĕre
wasteful *adj* profusus, prodigus; **—ly** prodige
wasteland *s* solitudo, vastitas *f*
watch *s* (*guard*) vigilia *f*; (*sentry*) excubiae *f pl*; **to keep —** excubare; **to keep — over** invigilare (*with dat*), custodire
watch *vt* (*to observe*) observare, spectare, intuēri; (*to guard*) custodire; *vi* **to — out for** exspectare
watchful *adj* vigilans; **—ly** vigilanter
watchman *s* vigil, excubitor *m*
watchtower *s* specula *f*
watchword *s* tessera *f*, signum *n*
water *s* aqua *f*
water *vt* irrigare; (*animals*) adaquare
waterfall *s* cataracta *f*
watering place *s* aquarium *n*
watery *adj* aquaticus, aquosus
wave *s* unda *f*, fluct·us -ūs *m*
wave *vt* agitare, vibrare, jactare; *vi* undare, fluctuare
waver *vi* fluctuare, labare, dubitare
wavering *adj* dubius, incertus
wavy *adj* undans, undosus; (*of hair*) crispus
wax *s* cera *f*
wax *vt* incerare; *vi* crescĕre, augēri
waxen *adj* cereus
way *s* via *f*, iter *n*; (*manner*) ratio *f*, modus *m*; (*habit*) mos *m*; **all the — from** usque ab (*with abl*); **all the — to** usque ad (*with acc*); **to get in the — of** intervenire (*with dat*); **to give —** (*of a structure*) labare; (*mil*) pedem referre; **to give — to** indulgēre (*with dat*); **to stand in the — of** obstare (*with dat*)
wayfarer *s* viator *m*
waylay *vt* insidiari (*with dat*)
wayward *adj* inconstans, levis, mutabilis
we *pron* nos; **— ourselves** nosmet ipsi
weak *adj* infirmus, debilis, imbecillus; (*argument*) tenuis; (*senses*) hebes; **—ly** infirme
weaken *vt* infirmare, debilitare, enervare; *vi* labare, hebescĕre, infirmus fieri
weakness *s* infirmitas, debilitas *f*; (*of mind*) imbecillitas *f*; (*flaw*) vitium *n*; (*of arguments*) levitas *f*
wealth *s* divitiae, opes *f pl*; copia, abundantia *f*
wealthy *adj* dives, opulentus; abundans
wean *vt* ab ubere depellĕre; (*fig*) desuefacĕre
weapon *s* telum *n*
wear *vt* (*clothes*) gerĕre; **to — out** terĕre, exedere; *vi* durare
weariness *s* lassitudo *f*
wearisome *adj* molestus
weary *adj* lassus, fessus, fatigatus
weather *s* caelum *n*, tempestas *f*
weather *vt* **to — a storm** procellam superare
weave *vt* texĕre
web *s* (*on loom*) tela, textura *f*; (*spider's*) araneum *n*
wed *vt* (*a woman*) ducĕre; (*a man*) nubĕre (*with dat*); *vi* (*of husband*) uxorem ducĕre; (*of bride*) nubĕre
wedge *s* cuneus *m*
wedlock *s* matrimonium *n*
weed *s* herba inutilis *f*
weed *vt* eruncare
week *s* hebdomas *f*
weekly *adj* hebdomadalis
weep *vi* flēre, lacrimare; **to — for** deplorare
weeping *s* plorat·us -ūs *m*, lacrimae *f pl*
weigh *vt* pendĕre, ponderare, trutinari; (*fig*) meditari; **to — down** degravare; (*fig*) opprimĕre; *vi* **to — much** magni ponderis esse

weight *s* pondus *n*, gravitas *f*; (*influence*) (*fig*) auctoritas *f*; (*importance*) momentum *n*
weighty *adj* ponderosus, gravis
welcome *s* gratulatio, salutatio *f*
welcome *vt* salvēre jubēre, excipĕre
welcome *interj* salve!; (*to several*) salvēte!
weld *vt* (con)ferruminare
welfare *s* salus *f*
well *s* puteus, fons *m*
well *adj* sanus, validus, salvus
well *adv* bene, recte, probe; **very —** optime
well *interj* heia!
well-bred *adj* generosus, liberalis
well-known *adj* pervulgatus; notus, nobilis
welter *s* congeries, turba *f*
west *s* occidens, occas·us -ūs *m*
western *adj* occidentalis
westward *adv* in occasum, occasum versus
west wind *s* Zephyrus, Favonius *m*
wet *adj* humidus, uvidus, madidus
wet *vt* madefacĕre, rigare
whale *s* balaena *f*, cetus *m*
wharf *s* navale *n*, crepido *f*
what *pron interrog* quid, quidnam, ecquid
what *adj interrog* qui; **— sort of** qualis
whatever *pron* quisquis
whatever *adj* quicumque
wheat *s* triticum *n*
wheedle *vt* blandiri, delenire
wheedling *adj* blandus
wheel *s* rota *f*
wheelbarrow *s* pabo *m*
whelp *s* catulus *m*
when *adv* quando
when *conj* cum, ubi, ut
whence *adv* unde
whenever *conj* quandocumque, utcumque, quotiens
where *adv* ubi
where *conj* quā, ubi
whereas *conj* quandoquidem
whereby *adv* re, quā viā, quo, per quod
wherefore *adv* quare, quamobrem, quapropter
wherein *adv* in quo, in quibus, ubi
whereof *adv* cujus, quorum; de quo, de quibus
whereto *adv* quo, quorsum
whereupon *adv* quo facto, post quae
wherever *conj* quacumque, ubicumque
whet *vt* acuĕre; (*fig*) exacuĕre
whether *conj* (*in single indirect question*) num, -ne, an; **whether . . . or** (*in multiple indirect questions*) utrum . . . an, -ne . . . an, . . . an; (*in disjunctive conditions*) sive . . . sive, seu . . . seu; **whether . . . or not** utrum . . . necne
whetstone *s* cos *f*
which *pron interrog* quis; (*of two*) uter; *pron rel* qui
which *adj interrog* qui; (*of two*) uter; *adj rel* qui
whichever *pron* quisquis, quicumque; (*of two*) utercumque
while *s* tempus, spatium *n*; **a little —** paulisper; **a long —** diu; **it is worth —** operae pretium est; **once in a —** interdum
while *conj* dum, quoad, donec
whim *s* libido *f*
whimper *vi* vagire
whimper *s* vagit·us -ūs *m*
whimsical *adj* levis, mobilis
whine *vi* miserabiliter vagire
whip *s* flagellum *n*, scutica *f*
whip *vt* flagellare, verberare
whirl *vt* torquēre, rotare; *vi* torquēri, rotari
whirlpool *s* vertex, gurges *m*
whirlwind *s* turbo, typhon *m*
whisper *s* susurrus *m*
whisper *vt & vi* susurrare
whistle *s* (*pipe*) fistula *f*; (*sound*) sibilus *m*; (*of wind*) stridor *m*
whistle *vi* sibilare
white *adj* albus; (*brilliant*) candidus; (*of hair*) canus
whiten *vt* dealbare, candefacĕre; *vi* albescĕre, canescĕre
who *pron interrog* quis; *pron rel* qui
whoever *pron* quicumque, quisquis
whole *adj* totus, cunctus; integer
whole *s* totum *n*, summa *f*; **on the —** plerumque
wholesome *adj* saluber, salutaris
wholly *adv* omnino, prorsus
whose *pron* cujus; quorum
why *adv* cur, quare, quamobrem
wicked *adj* improbus, nefarius, impius; **—ly** improbe, nefarie
wickedness *s* nequitia, improbitas, impietas *f*, scelus *n*
wicker *adj* vimineus
wide *adj* latus, amplus; **—ly** late
widen *vt* dilatare, laxare, extendĕre; *vi* patescĕre, dilatari, laxari
widow *s* vidua *f*
widower *s* viduus *m*
widowhood *s* viduitas *f*
width *s* latitudo, amplitudo *f*
wield *vt* tractare, vibrare
wife *s* uxor, conju(n)x *f*
wifely *adj* uxorius
wig *s* capillamentum *n*
wild *adj* ferus; (*of trees, plants, etc.*) silvestris; (*of land*) vastus, incultus; (*of disposition*) saevus, amens, ferox; **—ly** saeve, ferociter
wilderness *s* vastitas, solitudo *f*, loca deserta *n pl*
wile *s* fraus *f*, dolus *m*
wilful *adj* pervicax, consultus; **—ly** de industria
will *s* voluntas *f*, animus *m*; (*intent*) propositum, consilium *n*; (*document*) testimonium *n*; (*of gods*) nut·us -ūs *m*; **at —** ad libidinem
will *vt* velle; (*legacy*) legare, relinquĕre
willing *adj* libens, promptus; **to be —** velle; **—ly** libenter
willow *s* salix *f*
wily *adj* vafer, astutus
win *vt* adipisci, nancisci, consequi, (*victory*) reportare; (*friends*) sibi

conciliare; **to — over** conciliare; *vi* vincĕre, superare
wind *s* ventus *m*
wind *vt* circumvolvĕre, circumvertĕre, glomerare, torquēre; **to — up** (*to bring to an end*) concludĕre; *vi* sinuare
windfall *s* (*fig*) lucrum insperatum *n*
winding *adj* sinuosus, flexuosus
windmill *s* venti mola *f*
window *s* fenestra *f*
windpipe *s* aspera arteria *f*
windy *adj* ventosus
wine *s* vinum *n*; (*undiluted*) merum *n*; (*sour or cheap*) vappa *f*; (*new*) mustum *n*
wing *s* ala *f*; (*mil*) cornu *n*
winged *adj* alatus, volucer
wink *vi* nictare, connivēre
winner *s* victor *m*
winning *adj* (*fig*) blandus, amoenus
winnings *s* lucrum *n*
winnow *vt* ventilare
winter *s* hiems *f*; **in the dead of —** media hieme; **to spend the —** hiemare
winter *vi* hiemare, hibernare
winter *adj* hibernus
winter quarters *s* hiberna *n pl*
wintry *adj* hiemalis, hibernus
wipe *vt* detergēre; **to — away** abstergēre; **to — out** delēre, abolēre, expungĕre
wire *s* filum aeneum *n*
wisdom *s* sapientia, prudentia *f*
wise *adj* sapiens, prudens; **—ly** sapienter, prudenter
wise *s* modus *m*; **in no —** nequaquam
wish *s* optatum, votum *n*; **best —es** salus *f*
wish *vt* optare, velle, cupĕre; *vi* **to — for** exoptare, expetĕre
wisp *s* manipulus *m*
wistful *adj* desiderii plenus; **—ly** oculis intentis
wit *s* (*intellect*) ingenium *n*, argutiae *f pl*; (*humor*) sales *m pl*, facetiae *f pl*; (*person*) homo facetus *m*; **to be at one's —s' end** delirare; **to —** scilicet
witch *s* venefica, saga *f*
witchcraft *s* ars magica *f*, veneficium *n*
with *prep* cum (*with abl*); apud (*with acc*)
withdraw *vt* seducĕre, avocare; (*words*) revocare; *vi* recedĕre, discedĕre
wither *vt* torrēre, corrumpĕre; *vi* marcēre, arescĕre
withered *adj* marcidus
withhold *vt* retinēre, abstinēre, cohibēre
within *adv* intus, intra; (*motion*) intro
within *prep* intro (*with acc*), in (*with abl*); **— a few days** paucis diebus
without *adv* extra, foris; **from —** extrinsecus
without *prep* sine (*with abl*), absque (*with abl*), expers (*with genit*); **to be —** carēre (*with abl*)
withstand *vt* obsistĕre (*with dat*), resistĕre (*with dat*)
witness *s* testis *m* & *f*; (*to a signature*) obsignator *m*; **to bear —** testificari; **to call to —** testari, antestari
witness *vt* testificari; (*to see*) intuēri, vidēre
witticism *s* sales *m pl*
witty *adj* facetus, salsus, acutus
wizard *s* magus, veneficus *m*
woe *s* dolor, luct·us -ūs *m*; **—s** mala *n pl*
woeful *adj* tristis, luctuosus, miser; **—ly** triste, misere
wolf *s* lupus *m*, lupa *f*
woman *s* mulier, femina *f*
womanhood *s* muliebris stat·us -ūs *m*
womanly *adj* muliebris
womb *s* uterus *m*
wonder *s* admiratio *f*; (*astonishing object*) miraculum, mirum *n*
wonder *vi* (ad)mirari; **to — at** admirari
wonderful *adj* mirabilis, admirandus; **—ly** mirabiliter, mirifice
wont *adj* **to be — to** solēre (*with inf*)
woo *vt* petĕre
wood *s* lignum *n*; (*forest*) silva *f*, nemus *n*
wooded *adj* lignosus, silvestris
wooden *adj* ligneus
woodland *s* silvae *f pl*
woodman *s* lignator *m*
wood nymph *s* Dryas *f*
wooer *s* procus, amator *m*
wool *s* lana *f*
woolen *adj* laneus
word *s* verbum, vocabulum *n*; (*spoken*) vox *f*; (*promise*) fides *f*; (*news*) nuntius *m*; **in a —** denique; **to break one's —** fidem fallĕre; **to give one's —** fidem dare; **to keep one's —** fidem praestare; **— for —** ad verbum
wordy *adj* verbosus
work *s* opera *f*, opus *n*; (*trouble*) labor *m*; (*task*) pensum *n*
work *vt* (*to exercise*) exercēre; (*to till*) colĕre; *vi* laborare, operari
workman *s* (*unskilled*) operarius *m*; (*skilled*) faber, opifex *m*
workmanship *s* opus *n*, ars *f*
workshop *s* officina *f*
world *s* (*universe*) mundus *m*, summa rerum *f*; (*earth*) orbis terrarum *m*; (*nature*) rerum natura *f*; (*mankind*) homines *m pl*
worldly *adj* profanus
worm *s* vermis, vermiculus *m*, tinea *f*
worm-eaten *adj* vermiculosus
worry *s* sollicitudo, cura *f*
worry *vt* vexare, sollicitare; *vi* sollicitari
worse *adj* pejor, deterior; **to grow —** ingravescĕre
worsen *vi* ingravescĕre
worship *s* veneratio *f*, cult·us -ūs *m*
worship *vt* venerari, adorare, colĕre
worshiper *s* cultor, venerator *m*
worst *adj* pessimus, deterrimus
worst *vt* vincĕre

worth *s* (*value*) pretium *n*; (*merit*) dignitas, virtus *f*; **to be —** valēre
worthless *adj* vilis, inutilis; (*of person*) nequam (*indecl*)
worthy *adj* dignus
wound *s* vulnus *n*
wound *vt* vulnerare; (*fig*) offendĕre, laedĕre
wounded *adj* saucius
wrap *vt* involvĕre; **to — up** complicare
wrath *s* ira, iracundia *f*
wrathful *adj* iratus, iracundus; **—ly** iracunde
wreak *vt* **to — vengeance on** ulcisci, vindicare
wreath *s* sertum *n*, corona *f*
wreathe *vt* (*to twist*) torquēre; (*to adorn with wreaths*) coronare, nectĕre
wreck *s* naufragium *n*
wreck *vt* frangĕre; (*fig*) perdĕre
wren *s* regulus *m*
wrench *vt* detorquēre, luxare
wrest *vt* extorquēre, eripĕre
wrestle *vi* luctari
wrestler *s* luctator, athleta *m*
wretch *s* miser, perditus, nequam (*indecl*) *m*
wretched *adj* miser, infelix, abjectus; **—ly** misere, abjecte
wretchedness *s* miseria, aerumna *f*
wring *vt* contorquēre, stringĕre; **to — the neck** gulam frangĕre
wrinkle *s* ruga *f*
wrinkle *vt* corrugare; **to — the forehead** frontem contrahĕre
wrinkled *adj* rugosus
writ *s* (*law*) mandatum *n*
write *vt* scribĕre, perscribĕre; (*poetry*) componĕre; (*history*) perscribĕre
writer *s* scriptor, auctor *m*
writhe *vi* torquēri
writing *s* (*act*) scriptio *f*; (*result*) scriptum *n*, scriptura *f*; (*hand*) man·us -ūs *f*
wrong *adj* pravus, perversus, falsus; (*unjust*) injustus, iniquus; **—ly** falso, male, perperam; **to be —** errare, falli
wrong *s* nefas *n*, injuria *f*, malum *n*; **to do —** peccare
wrong *vt* nocēre (*with dat*), injuriam inferre (*with dat*), laedĕre
wrought *adj* factus, confectus, fabricatus
wry *adj* distortus, obliquus

Y

yard *s* (*court*) area *f*; (*measure*) tres pedes *m pl*; **a — long** tripedalis
yawn *vi* oscitare, hiare; (*to gape open*) dehiscĕre
year *s* annus *m*; **every —** quotannis; **five —s** quinquennium *n*; **four —s** quadriennium *n*; **three —s** triennium *n*; **two —** biennium *n*
yearly *adj* annuus, anniversarius
yearly *adv* quotannis
yearn *vi* **to — for** desiderare
yeast *s* fermentum *n*
yell *s* ululat·us -ūs *m*, ejulatio *f*
yell *vi* ululare, ejulare
yellow *adj* flavus, luteus, gilvus, croceus
yelp *vt* gannire
yes *adv* ita, immo, sane
yesterday *adv* heri
yet *adv* (*contrast, after adversative clause*) tamen, nihilominus; (*time*) adhuc; (*with comparatives*) etiam; **as —** adhuc; **not —** nondum
yield *vt* (*to produce*) ferre, parĕre, praebēre; (*to surrender*) dedĕre, concedĕre; *vi* cedĕre
yoke *s* jugum *n*; (*fig*) servitus *f*
yoke *vt* jugum imponĕre (*with dat*), conjungĕre
yonder *adv* illic
you *pron* (*thou*) tu; (*ye*) vos; **— yourself** tu ipse
young *adj* juvenis, adulescens; (*of child*) parvus; (*fig*) novus
younger *adj* junior, minor natu
youngster *s* adulescentulus *m*
your *adj* tuus; vester
yours *pron* tuus; vester
yourself *pron reflex* te; **to —** tibi; **with —** tecum; *intensive* tu ipse
yourselves *pron reflex* vos; **to —** vobis; **with —** vobiscum; *intensive* vos ipsi, vosmet ipsi
youth *s* (*age*) adulescentia *f*; (*collectively*) juventus *f*; (*young man*) juvenis, adulescens *m*
youthful *adj* juvenalis, puerilis; **—ly** juveniliter, pueriliter

Z

zeal *s* studium *n*, ardor, fervor *m*
zealous *adj* studiosus, ardens; **—ly** studiose, ardenter *m*
zenith *s* vertex *m*
zephyr *s* Zephyrus, Favonius *m*
zero *s* nihil, nihilum *n*
zest *s* (*taste*) sapor, gust·us -ūs *m*; (*fig*) gustat·us -ūs, impet·us -ūs *m*
zigzag *adj* tortuosus
zodiac *s* signifer orbis *m*
zone *s* zona, regio *f*
zoology *s* zoologia, animantium descriptio *f*